ENVIRONMENTAL PROTECTION:

Law and Policy

ENVIRONMENTAL PROTECTION:

Law and Policy

Frederick R. Anderson

Ann Loeb Bronfman Professor of Law
American University

Daniel R. Mandelker

Stamper Professor of Law
Washington University

A. Dan Tarlock

Professor of Law
IIT Chicago-Kent College of Law

Little, Brown and Company
Boston   Toronto   London

Library of Congress Catalog Card No. 89-63642
ISBN 0-316-03960-8

Second Edition

Third Printing

MV PA

Published simultaneously in Canada
by Little, Brown & Company (Canada) Limited

PRINTED IN THE UNITED STATES OF AMERICA

To my father

F.R.A.

To Marlene

D.R.M.

To Vivien, Robert, Katherine, and Marc

A.D.T.

SUMMARY OF CONTENTS

TABLE OF CONTENTS

CHAPTER III.   PROTECTING THE
AIR RESOURCE   145

CHAPTER IV.   PROTECTING THE
WATER RESOURCE   331

CHAPTER V.   CONTROLLING TOXIC AND
HAZARDOUS SUBSTANCES   491

CHAPTER VI.   THE ENVIRONMENT AND THE COMMON LAW   697

PREFACE TO FIRST EDITION

Until the late 1960s, the "environmental perspective" was not often brought to bear in the formulation of natural resources management policy; conservationism was the major philosophy. Progressive conservationism assumed the wisdom of developing and using natural resources, and the key questions were, when and by whom? The great debates centered on issues such as whether there should be private or public ownership and development of particular resources. The idea that the physical integrity of natural systems should be respected, either for their own sake or to benefit man, was mainly represented by advocates of resource preservation. Preservationism was an elite political movement concerned almost exclusively with preserving from development scenic portions of federal public lands. Pollution usually was only a local public health problem. Only in Los Angeles, because of the combination of population and geography, did air pollution emerge in the 1950s as other than a smoke nuisance problem.

Until the late 1960s what we now call environmental law did not exist; the term was first used in 1969. There were air and water cases dealing with the question of when an activity was a nuisance or violated a downstream riparian's rights, and there were a few decisions reviewing public intervention to protect what we would now call environmental quality. But lawyers, legal scholars, and judges did not see the cases as constituting a unified subject matter. Concepts such as that of an ecosystem or environmental values were simply neither part of the popular nor the legal vocabulary. The state of law school curricula circa 1969 is described in Tarlock, Current Trends in the Development of an Environmental Curriculum, in Law and the Environment 297 (M. Baldwin & J. Page, Jr., eds. 1970). See also Dunning, Notes for an Environmental Law Course, 55 Cornell L. Rev. 804 (1970), and Irwin, The Law School and the Environment, 12 Nat. Resources J. 278 (1972). Compare Mintz, Teaching Environmental Law: Some Observations on Curriculum and Materials, 33 J. Legal Educ. 94 (1983).

The first suggestion that a body of law might be built around the duty to consider nondevelopmental values was the Second Circuit's opinion in Scenic Hudson Preservation Conference v. FPC, 354 F.2d 608 (2d Cir. 1965), *cert. denied sub nom.* Consolidated Edison Co. v. Scenic Hudson Preservation Conference, 384 U.S. 941 (1966), which remanded a hydroelectric power license for a pumped storage project because the FPC had failed to consider adequately the project's impact on scenic values and on fish and wildlife. For reasons we explore in Chapter I, environmental quality suddenly became a popular political issue in the late 1960s. Lawyers rushed to create an environmental law out of the modest law of nuisance, the then-anemic pollution control statutes, *Scenic Hudson* and a few related cases, and a mix of older precedents restraining governmental action that were reinterpreted as being environmental. Professor Joseph Sax's pioneering article, The Public Trust Doctrine in Natural Resource Law: Effective Judicial Intervention, 68 Mich. L. Rev. 471 (1970), gave lawyers hope that they would be successful in creating environmental precedent. However, the speculative period of environmental law did not last long. As every teacher and students knows, the Congress and state legislatures responded to public concerns in the 1970s by passing a series of complex statutes regulating a wide range of environmental insults, and like the New Deal-inspired subjects of labor law and securities regulation, environmental law quickly won a place in the law school curriculum.

In many important respects, environmental law grew out of the same grass roots movement that succeeded so well in persuading Congress to enact far-reaching environmental legislation. As a result, the field still retains significant vestiges of the energy, voluntarism, and idealism that characterized it in the early 1970s. Suits by citizens' organizations, whose attorneys often donated their time pro bono publico or who earned low wages under foundation grants, thrust the courts into a new era of judicial supervision of the administrative process, in an attempt to democratize traditional agency decisionmaking practices; European-style technocratic environmental management was forestalled until a later day.

There are more differences than similarities between environmental regulation and previous social legislation. Perhaps this is a function of the accelerated germination time for new political ideas — witness the current debate over industrial policy. Environmental regulation differs from previous regulatory schemes, which were mainly directed toward a specific industry and had well-defined objectives both to restrain and to promote the industry. Environmental regulation is problem- rather than industry-directed, cutting across the entire private sector. When the environmental problem was first discovered, it was widely assumed that the dimensions of the problem were known, that the objectives to be attained were clear, and that command-and-control regulation would do the job. The common law was quickly downgraded to a supporting role. Subsequent experience has taught that all of the original assumptions were either wrong or at least questionable. There is widespread agreement that environmental degradation is an undesirable consequence of industrial and technological progress and that such degradation needs to be curbed, but there is sharp controversy about the level of restraint and the best means to institute restraint. Early legislation was rather indifferent to the cost of achieving environmental objectives, but as the consensus about objectives has disintegrated, cost has emerged as a major factor. Environmental positions range from a grudging acknowledgment that some problem exists to neo-Kantian imperatives and apocalyptic visions.

This casebook tries to explain the logic behind our current regulatory programs and related programs and to force the student to evaluate critically the nature of the perceived problem and the choice of available means. These materials represent three teachers' opinions about the content of an environmental law course. Because most environmental law teachers are independent-minded and may have valid reasons for questioning our emphasis, we have tried to provide the teacher with a set of basic building blocks around which to build his own course. Environmental law can be presented as a series of discrete subject matter areas or regulatory programs (e.g., the National Environmental Policy Act and air and water pollution) or as a set of common themes that permeate each subject matter area (e.g., regulation in the face of scientific uncertainty, technology-forcing, and federalism). We have chosen the first type of organization, for two reasons. First, it stresses the factual, scientific, and technical context; a detailed knowledge of a specific problem informs and colors the whole range of legal issues raised by the resulting regulatory program, and this casebook emphasizes scientific perspectives more than most other casebooks. Second, most teachers are accustomed to this organization.

To accommodate individual tastes, many different chapters and subchapters can be combined to make an effective course. A teacher wishing to stress pollution control may place Chapters III, IV, and V at the core of the syllabus, with attention to NEPA, the common law, and land use, as time allows. Another may prefer to stress resource management issues by focusing first on NEPA and then on private and public land use, with less attention to pollution and the common law. Many teachers will wish to start traditionally with the common law remedies for pollution control and land abuse, taking advantage of the last section of the common law chapter, which we deliberately designed as a bridge to the statutory chapters, and move on to either pollution control or land and resource management. We believe, however, that our placement of the common law chapter later in the book properly reflects the interstitial role left for the common law in an age of statutes.

To fit these and the other topics covered within the allotted page limitations, we have been forced to make many hard choices about coverage. On the basis of complexity of issues and topical importance, air pollution and toxic substances are treated in the greatest detail. Water pollution is treated comprehensively but in less detail because many of the basic issues are settled and because the frontier issues, toxic discharges and groundwater, are treated in the toxic substances chapter. NEPA is also covered in detail, but we have been terse when an issue basically has been settled after extensive litigation. This organization has forced us to omit detailed coverage of some important areas. Noise, nuclear energy, and strip mine reclamation are three topics that are treated only in relation to broader themes. Likewise, important statutes such as the Endangered Species Act, the Marine Protection Research and Sanctuaries Act of 1972, and the National Historic Preservation Act are covered only in the context of other issues. Teachers with a special interest in these topics will have to supplement this casebook.

The volatile nature of our subject matter also forced us to make other hard, somewhat unsatisfactory choices. Environmental law is a young yet rapidly maturing area of the law. Writing in 1981 through 1983, we had the advantage of a well-developed case law in air and water pollution and of the National Environmental Policy Act, but we also had to contend with nascent case law in areas such as toxic substances regulation. We have tried both to reflect what seems settled law and to focus on problems to come. For this reason, we give considerable attention to proposals for a reformed common law to reach injuries not prevented through regulation, to land use and public lands issues, and to toxic substances regulation because these topics seem to be sources of future litigation. The 1980 election produced a president and members of Congress who have substantial doubts about the thrust of much environmental legislation and who have introduced more volatility into the subject matter. From a pedagogical standpoint, we were forced to decide whether to concentrate on changes that were likely to occur in the basic statutes or largely to ignore the debates about legislative changes. In general, we opted to outline the philosophical underpinnings of current environmental policy debates but not to focus too much on either the details of specific current programs or on proposed legislation.

Because it is difficult — if not impossible — to cover our entire casebook in one semester, we offer an explanation of our outline and some suggestions for reorganization and material selection. Chapter I is the perspectives chapter. It aims to introduce the student to the important ideas that make up the environmental perspective and to survey the range of methods for promoting environmental quality. This chapter either can be taught or assigned and folded into the other chapters. We have tried, through a series of problems, to ask what an environmental problem is, so that the student understands the diversity and ambiguity inherent in labeling a conflict "environmental." The readings focus on the fundamental premises of various disciplines that have addressed environmentalism, primarily ecology and welfare economics. The teacher can teach these readings like a case, drawing out the implications of each reading, or can integrate them into the book as a whole. Chapter II also is an introductory chapter. Fundamentally, environmental law is a law of judicial review of agency action. Modern administrative law has been enriched — if not made — by environmental litigation, and therefore the student must understand the fundamental problems of access to the courts and the different approaches to judicial review. However, if the teacher thinks the students are familiar with the material, it can be assigned as a reading.

Chapters III, IV, and V are the heart of regulatory environmental law. More attention is given to air pollution because air quality management raises virtually all of the key legal, economic, and political issues involved in modern regulatory environmental law, and the federal Clean Air Act provides the paradigm of the basic federal approach to controlling pollution. Also, the Act is now an important feature of the national legal landscape, involving hundreds of lawyers in its implementation. Over 200,000 stationary sources and millions of mobile sources are regulated; in the decade prior to 1988 the Act will cost American industry an additional $300 billion — over half the total investment under all federal environmental regulatory statutes combined. Finally, the Act has been much criticized and thus presents the student with the challenge of finding a better way to protect air quality.

The length of the air chapter may require the teacher to omit some sections, e.g., prevention of significant deterioration or enforcement. Most candidates for omission include summary material that can be read in lieu of the entire section. The teacher who intends essentially to skip air pollution but who wants students at least to have a bare bones introduction to the Clean Air Act may assign the summary overview provided in part C.

Hazardous substances control, the subject of Chapter V, presents what may eventually become the central organizing issue for environmental law: What precautionary or preventive measures should society adopt, based on evidence suggesting, but not proving, that substantial harm to human beings and the environment may occur at some time in the future? In the arena of hazardous substances control, the most challenging problems occur when risks are presented through prolonged exposures to trace quantities of substances, usually modern industrial chemicals, the damage from which may occur only after decades-long latency periods. The response to such hazards, which is as heavily federalized as is air and water pollution control, has been marked by the passage of not one but a score of detailed regulatory statutes. Some twenty federal statutes and six major agencies are involved. The course of implementation remains far from settled for such major statutes as the Toxic Substances Control Act of 1976, the Resource Conservation and Recovery Act of 1976, the Safe Drinking Water Act Amendments of 1977, the Hazardous Materials Transportation Control Act Amendments of 1976, and the Comprehensive Environmental Response, the Compensation and Liability Act of 1980 (Superfund) as well as the hazardous pollutant provisions of the Clean Air and Clean Water Acts. These statutes raise problems destined to confront environmental law for many years: the use of "good" versus "bad" science in determining cause; the adoption of the threat of cancer as a proxy for other environmental threats for which controls are politically harder to obtain; the difficulty of quantifying and comparing the health risks and the economic benefits of toxic exposures; whether the burden of proof of safety should shift to a potentially responsible party if an agency or plaintiff can make only a rudimentary evidentiary showing of risk; and how responsibility should be apportioned for the cleaning up of hazardous chemical wastes that were jettisoned in previous decades. To compress this chapter into fewer class days, it may be necessary to omit consideration of one or more individual statutes.

The pollution statutes that provide the nuclei for Chapters III, IV, and V presented us with a special problem. Pre-enforcement litigation challenging the complex regulations adopted under the federal statutes provides almost all the important case law on the pollution control programs. Federal circuit court decisions covering dozens of issues and running one hundred to three hundred pages in length are not uncommon, yet the traditional casebook format calls for numerous case excerpts followed by a few notes and questions. We found this approach undesirable; instead, we provide fewer, heavily edited cases, accompanied by a larger than usual amount of explanatory notes. At times our method casts the appellate case in a secondary role in solving the larger problem of how a statute should be interpreted and implemented. Sometimes we abandon the appellate decision as a teaching tool altogether. In such instances, as with the pesticide, toxic substances, and hazardous waste regulation laws, we invite the teacher and the student to consider the entire statute, with our explanatory notes as a guide, as a "decision," the fundamental "ratio" or controlling principle of which must be gleaned from the wealth of detailed statutory provisions. For some teachers and students our more limited reliance on appellate decisions will be welcome; others, we believe, will overcome initial resistance and become receptive to this approach, at least in this one field of law, in which environmental lawyers fight out issues of policy and procedure largely outside the courtroom, in informal meetings and conversations with federal and state agency officials, in formal agency rather than court proceedings, and in written comments on regulations proposed in the Federal Register.

Chapter IV, water pollution, inevitably duplicates some of the coverage of Chapter III because issues such as technology-forcing and the role of cost-benefit analysis are the same. But we have tried to focus on the distinctive features of water pollution, including the greater continuing attention to land use approaches to the control of non-point sources and the fact that many water pollution issues are use- rather than health-based problems.

The National Environmental Policy Act (NEPA), which is covered in Chapter VII, is the magna carta of environmental law. Just as the pollution statutes pervasively regulate private industry, NEPA requires environmental impact statements from the entire federal establishment. Yet, unlike the pollution legislation, NEPA enacts a process in which agencies must consider environmental values, not environmental standards with which they must comply. The treatment of NEPA is conventional. The chapter first considers the all-important question of when an environmental impact statement must be prepared. It then considers the scope of the impact statement and what must be done to make the discussion of environmental effects in an impact statement adequate. Throughout the chapter, questions about the merits of the environmental impact statement process are raised.

Land use control is perhaps the key to environmental regulation because so many pollution problems are at base land use problems. Land use has been part of environmental law from the beginning, but most materials have focused more attention on NEPA and air and water pollution. Chapter VIII tries to expand this coverage by including an extensive treatment of private and public land use issues. Land use law is well established in the legal curriculum; indeed, two of the authors of this casebook also have their own land use casebooks. This casebook does not attempt a comprehensive treatment of land use law as it applies to environmental issues; instead, it concentrates on environmental resource areas such as floodplains, wetlands, agricultural areas, the coastal zone, and public lands. The first part of Chapter VIII considers federal and state programs, most of them regulatory, that seek to preserve and protect these areas. Two state land use control programs with an environmental orientation, adopted in Vermont and in Florida, also are considered. The second part of the chapter is an overview of federal public lands law, with emphasis on incorporation of environmental values into management decisions.

Chapter VI, dealing with the common law, has been described at various points in this preface. Basically, we adhere to the traditional view that the common law is now quite subordinate to statutes. Various chapters treat the common law as an aid to understanding the origins of a statute or as an aid to construction, so that the course can be taught without assigning Chapter VI. But because there is considerable interest in using the common law to redress toxic injuries, we reopen the debate about the common law's role and speculate about the shape of a "reformed" common law.

A statutory supplement to this casebook is indispensable. We have printed only a few statutory provisions verbatim. To save space and to encourage recourse to the full texts themselves, we have also deleted most statutory passages from the cases. Teachers may want to compile their own supplement, but several published supplements exist, e.g., West's Selected Environmental Law Statutes and the Environmental Law Institute's Statutes and Regulations. We have ordinarily cited to the federal public law sections in our notes, after an initial United States Code citation, and have edited the case excerpts accordingly, but the user should adopt a supplement with parallel textual citations to the original public law section numbers and to the United States Code.

A few words are necessary about the mechanics of the casebook. To keep the text uncluttered, citations to the United States Code, state codifications, the Code of Federal Regulations, and the Federal Register do not carry a year; in addition, in parallel cites, jump cites are given only for the unofficial (West) reporter. Footnotes in quoted material retain their original numbering, and author footnotes are designated with an asterisk or a dagger. Finally, at the risk of seeming out of step with the times, we use the masculine pronoun "he" exclusively in the casebook, but we mean to include the feminine pronoun by implication. We adhere to this convention for purposes of expediency only.

The authors owe numerous debts of gratitude to those who helped in the preparation of these materials. Countless students suffered through mimeographed versions of these materials, and their distress helped us to decide what worked and what did not work in the classroom. We were fortunate to have had the assistance of diligent and committed research assistants. Professor Mandelker would like to acknowledge the patient and always supportive assistance of Kathleen Chovan, J.D., Washington University, 1983. Professor Tarlock would like to thank Marcia Holland, J.D., IIT Chicago-Kent College of Law, 1982; Michael J. Maliciki, J.D., IIT Chicago-Kent College of Law, 1983; and David Goldenberg, J.D., IIT Chicago-Kent College of Law, 1984. Each of us was blessed with secretaries who went beyond the call of duty. Professor Anderson gratefully acknowledges the assistance of DeLys Ostlund; Professor Mandelker acknowledges the invaluable assistance of Virginia C. Autry; and Professor Tarlock thanks Janice Hogan. All three authors are grateful to Virginia Autry, who assumed the responsibility of coordinating the final preparation of the manuscript.

Finally, we would like to thank the Law Division of Little, Brown and Company for the superb professional help it gave us, in keeping with its commitment to high-quality legal education. Richard R. Heuser, Associate Editor, was a constant source of encouragement and sound advice. Our designer, P.J. Collins, used all of her considerable skills to make aesthetic sense out of the many categories we used to present the kaleidoscopic information that is environmental law and policy. Most of all, we would like to thank our editor, Carol McGeehan. With wit, charm, and deft pen, she helped us to produce a better manuscript and to present more clearly to a new generation of law students the evolution of our subject over the past decade and a half.

Frederick R. Anderson
Daniel R. Mandelker
A. Dan Tarlock

Santa Fe, New Mexico
August 1983

PREFACE TO SECOND EDITION

The first edition of Environmental Protection: Law and Policy synthesized the complex of laws and regulations put in place between 1969 and 1980, the years known as the "Environmental Decade." This second edition surveys the state of environmental law after ten years of intense efforts to modify the basic approaches put in place in the 1970s. Over the past decade, environmental law has been characterized by two major and paradoxical developments, which are only partially reflected in the case law. First, the subject has continued to mature. Some no longer find environmental law as interesting because it has grown so technical. But environmental law is becoming a major specialty within the legal profession because environmental considerations have become an integral part of many commercial transactions and activities. Superfund and aggressive state hazardous waste regulatory programs account for much of the growth of the environmental bar, but other federal and state programs have had a wide influence on the practice of law as well. Second, this maturation occurred in the face of considerable opposition to environmental protection by the Reagan administration, especially the first administration. Environmental law continued to develop despite this opposition because the legislative programs of the 1970s were left in place and enforcement efforts increased in the mid-1980s. Since 1980 Congress has considered the reauthorization of almost all major programs and has rejected fundamental revisions in their structure.

The primary environmental legislation that has emerged from Congress in the past few years, such as the Hazardous and Solid Waste Amendments of 1984 and the Superfund Amendments and Reauthorization Act of 1986, has expanded rather than contracted previous programs. When this edition was prepared, Congress was revising the Clean Air Act, the only major environmental statute that was not amended during the 1980s. The expected changes will not affect the structure of the program covered in this book, but new programs for acid rain control and non-attainment areas may be put in place if the sharp regional differences over the costs and benefits of pollutant reduction can be resolved. Future supplements will add coverage of these programs as they are enacted. The legacy of the 1980s would seem to ensure the survival of environmental law as a legitimate restraint on a wide variety of human activities. As the preface to the Fifteenth Annual Report on Environmental Quality concedes, "[p]ossibly no other national goal retains such strong public support from a broad base of the population. In a very real sense, all American are now environmentalists." The issue is now truly a global one. The urgency of action on issues such as marine pollution, acid rain, ozone depletion, and sustainable development, especially in rain forests and other wildlife habitats, has been accepted in varying degrees by all major countries, regardless of political structure. There is even a revival of interest in fundamental questions of environmental ethics and institutions, which have been ignored in recent years because of the focus on toxic pollution.

This second edition integrates the major judicial and statutory developments of the past ten years as well as references to the most notable secondary literature. It includes leading Clean Air and Water Act cases and new toxic tort developments that define the scope of recoverable damages for risk exposure. The most significant class of recent cases for students and lawyers is the district and circuit court Superfund cases that flesh out much of the original Act and begin to address the 1986 amendments. To give adequate coverage to this development, we have added a new unit on Superfund that examines the principal case law on the cleanup process and includes materials on issues such as "how clean is clean" and negotiation policy that are just now working their way into the cases.

To make room for these important new developments, a decision was made to drop Chapter 8. This chapter focused on local, state, and federal land use regulation for environmental objectives. Unfortunately, this required the omission of expanded materials on the public trust and the Endangered Species Act as well as new materials on state and federal land use regulation. These concepts are briefly introduced in Chapter 4, but the teacher may wish to use supplementary materials or make brief presentations to do justice to these increasingly important aspects of environmental law. We continue to believe that land use controls is a crucial dimension of environmental law, and we have tried to integrate land use issues into all chapters. Teachers who want a revised version of Chapter 8 may obtain one from Little, Brown.

With the exception of our deletion of Chapter 8, the structure of the casebook and our pedagogical objectives remain unchanged. These are set forth in detail in the preface to the first edition. We have paid close attention to the many formal and informal comments from students and teachers who have done us the honor of using the book. We have tried to correct errors and to make numerous small improvements in the presentation of the materials. We remain convinced that there is a need for a basic environmental law casebook that can stand on its own or can serve as a set of building blocks for more specialized or localized treatment of certain issues.

Professor Mandelker would like to thank Ms. Lynn Moss for her research assistance and to especially thank Ms. Peggy McDermott, research librarian at Washington University, for her assistance in finding difficult-to-locate but vital materials. Professor Tarlock gratefully acknowledges the assistance of Ms. Laura

Rose. Special thanks go to our editor, Virginia Vitzthum, for her intelligent and helpful editing.

Frederick R. Anderson
Daniel R. Mandelker
A. Dan Tarlock

Taos, New Mexico
January 1990

ACKNOWLEDGMENTS

The authors gratefully acknowledge the permissions granted to reproduce the following materials.

Ackerman & Stewart, Reforming Environmental Law, 37 Stanford Law Review 1333, at 1346, Reprinted material first appeared in 37 Stanford Law Review at page 1333. Copyright © 1985 by the Board of Trustees of Leland Stanford Junior University. Reprinted by permission of the copyright holder, the authors, and Fred B. Rothman Company.

Anderson, Kneese, Reed, Stevenson & Taylor, Environmental Improvement through Economic Incentives 3-4, 22-26 (1977). Reprinted with permission of Resources for the Future, Inc. and The Johns Hopkins University Press. Copyright © 1977 by Resources for the Future, Washington, D.C.

Boulding, The Economics of the Coming Spaceship Earth, in Environmental Quality in a Growing Economy 3 (H. Jarrett ed. 1971). Reprinted with permission of Resources for the Future, Inc. and the Johns Hopkins University Press. Copyright © 1966 by Resources for the Future.

Bureau of National Affairs, Inc., Environment Reporter (BNA) Monograph No. 21, at 2 (July 25, 1975). Copyright © 1975 Environment Reporter, Bureau of National Affairs, Inc., Washington, D.C., 20037. Reprinted with permission.

Calabresi & Melamed, Property Rules, Liability Rules, and Inalienability: One View of the Cathedral, 85 Harv. L. Rev. 1089, 1118-1119 (1972). Copyright © 1972 by the Harvard Law Review Association. Reprinted with permission.

Check, Environmental Law Study Materials, Financial Responsibility Requirements under RCRA: Insurance Coverage for and beyond the Grave (ALI-ABA Committee on Continuing Professional Education 1983). Copyright © by The American Law Institute. Reprinted with the permission of Leslie Check, III, Crum & Forster Insurance Companies, and the American Law Institute-American Bar Association Committee on Continuing Professional Education.

Cohen, The Pathless Way: John Muir and American Wilderness 330-331. Copyright © 1984 The University of Wisconsin Press, Madison.

Cronon, Changes in the Land: Indians, Colonists, and the Ecology of New England. Copyright © 1983 by William Cronon. Reprinted with permission by Hill and Wang, a division of Farrar, Straus & Giroux, Inc.

Dales, Pollution, Property and Prices 81-84, 93 (1968). Reprinted with permission of the University of Toronto Press.

Diamond, The Federalist on Federalism: "Neither a Nation nor a Federal Constitution, but a Composition of Both," 86 Yale L.J. 1273, 1274, 1276 (1977). Reprinted by permission of the Yale Law Journal Company and Fred B. Rothman & Company.

Dorfman, Introduction, in Measuring Benefits of Government Investments 4-7 (R. Dorfman ed. 1965). Reprinted with permission.

Goetzman, Exploration and Empire 356. Copyright © 1966. Reprinted with permission of Alfred A. Knopf, Inc.

Hardin, The Tragedy of the Commons, 162 Science 1243, 1243-1248 (1968). Reprinted with permission of Science and the author.

Heal, Economics and Resources, in Economics of Environmental and Natural Resources Policy 62, 64, 66-68 (J.A. Butlin ed. 1981). Reprinted with permission of the Longman Group Limited.

Hellerich, Imminent Irreparable Injury: A Need for Reform, 45 S. Cal. L. Rev. 1025, 1030-1032 (1972). Reprinted with the permission of the Southern California Law Review.

Hines, A Decade of Nondegradation Policy in Congress and the Courts: The Erratic Pursuit of Clean Air and Clean Water, 62 Iowa Law Review 643 (1977). Copyright © 1977, University of Iowa (Iowa Law Review). Reprinted with permission.

Jaffe, Benefit-Cost Analysis and Multiple-Objective Evaluation of Federal Water Projects, 4 Harv. Envtl. L. Rev. 58, 59-72 (1980). Reprinted with permission. Copyright © 1980 by the President and Fellows of Harvard College.

Kneese, Ayres & D'Arge, Economics and the Environment: A Materials Balance Approach 2-6 (1970). Reprinted with permission of Resources for the Future, Inc. and The Johns Hopkins University Press. Copyright © 1970 by Resources for the Future.

Kneese, Measuring the Benefits of Clean Air and Water 103. Reprinted with permission of Resources for the Future, Inc. and The Johns Hopkins University Press. Copyright © 1984 by Resources for the Future.

Latin, Environmental Deregulation and Consumer Decision-making under Uncertainty, 6 Harv. Envtl. L. Rev. 187, 218 (1982). Copied with the permission of the Harvard Environmental Law Review Copyright © 1982 by the President and Fellows of Harvard University.

Latin, Ideal vs. Real Regulatory Efficiency, 37 Stanford Law Review 1267, at 1271. Reprinted material first appeared in 37 Stanford Law Review at page 1267. Copyright © 1985 by the Board of Trustees of Leland Stanford Junior University. Reprinted by permission of the copyright holder, the authors, and Fred B. Rothman Company.

Stewart, The Reformation of American Administrative Law, 88 Harv. L. Rev. 1667, 1712 (1975). Copyright © 1975 by the Harvard Law Review Association. Reprinted with permission.

Susskind, Environmental Mediation and the Accountability Problem, 6 Vt. L. Rev. 114 (1981). Reprinted with permission.

Tarr, McCurley & Yosie, The Development and Impact of Urban Wastewater Technology: Changing Concepts of Water Quality Control, 1850-1930, in Pollution and Reform in American Cities, 1870-1930, at 63, 64, 68, 70 (M. Melosi ed. 1980). Copyright © 1980 by the University of Texas Press. All rights reserved. Reprinted with permission.

Tribe, Ways Not to Think about Plastic Trees: New Foundations for Environmental Law, 83 Yale L.J. 1315, 1345 (1974). Reprinted by permission of the Yale Law Journal Company and Fred B. Rothman Company.

ENVIRONMENTAL PROTECTION:

Law and Policy

I

WHAT IS ENVIRONMENTALISM, AND WHAT ARE ITS INTELLECTUAL ORIGINS, FOUNDATIONS, AND LEGAL RAMIFICATIONS?

A. INTRODUCTION

Many societies ultimately rise or fall as a result of the choices they make about their stocks of natural resources. Throughout history, resources have been consumed with little thought to the adverse present or, more importantly, future consequences of such consumption. Certain resources were completely destroyed, which is not surprising when one considers that most people were too engrossed in the day-to-day business of survival to have time to think about how resources should best be used. See Calder, Mortgaging the Old Homestead, 48 For. Aff. 207 (1970). China under Mao is a recent example of extreme resource depletion without attention to the environmental consequences. "For example, fragile grasslands in northwestern China were extensively damaged in the 1970s when they were ploughed up in an effort to make each area of the country self-sufficient in grain production." L. Ross and M. Silk, Environmental Law and Policy in the People's Republic of China 2 (1987).

In the United States, the nineteenth century New England transcendentalists were among the first to voice romantic reactions to the social disruption caused by the Industrial Revolution. They blended the Jeffersonian pastoral ideal of self-sufficient yeomen with the claim that nature "enjoyed its own morality which, when understood, could lead the sympathetic and responsive human being to a new spiritual awareness of his own potential, his obligations to others, and his responsibilities to the life-supporting processes of his natural surroundings" (T. O. Riordan, Environmentalism 3 (2d ed. 1980). L. Marx, The Machine in the Garden: Technology and the Pastoral Ideal in America (1964), is a full exploration of the tension between pastoral visions and the realities of an industrialized society. See also R. Tomalin & W. H. Hudson: A Bibliography

1

(1982), and I. K. Thomas, Man and the Natural World: A History of Modern Sensibility (1983). The romantic origins of the environmental movement still surface. A recent German essay grandly characterized the nineteenth century as the one of the bourgeois revolution and the triumph of individual freedom, the twentieth as one of social reform and predicted the twenty-first would be concerned with countering the adverse consequences of industrial development observing "[t]he 'dying forests' will no longer be ridiculed with shakes of the head as the 'hysterical' invention of the German soul unable to choose between Marx and myth." H. Bieber, Es Grünt So Grün, Die Zeit, No. 26, June 30, 1989, p. 1, col. 3.

From the transcendentalists' attempts to develop a theory of the relationship between democracy and nature came the two major resource use philosophies that have greatly influenced the modern environmental movement. The first philosophy loosely can be called preservationism. Initially, the preservation movement was primarily concerned with preserving large areas of wilderness in their natural state as national parks, either to prove that America had scenic beauty comparable to that of Europe or to allow individuals to go to the wilderness to find the spiritual fulfillment that no longer seemed attainable in modern society. See R. Nash, Wilderness and the American Mind (3d ed. 1982), and J. Sax, Mountains with Handrails: Reflections on the National Parks (1980). However, until the late 1960s the preservation movement, based on ambiguous claims about the morality of nature, was merely an influential but minor strain in the second, and dominant, resource use philosophy, conservationism, which has shaped American natural resources policy. The conservation movement was part of a deeper progressive effort to make science compatible with democratic values and thus counter then-prevailing theories of social Darwinism. As historian Edward A. Purcell explains, this led progressives to the notion that all environments can be bettered by human intervention:

> First, they interpreted the struggle for survival in terms of the species against its environment, pointing out that nature revealed mutual aid among all members of the same species. Sympathetic unity of the species implied equality and cooperation. Second, they destroyed fatalistic determinism by insisting that evolution had produced human intelligence, which enabled man to control his environment for the benefit of all members of the species. Intelligence suggested the possibility of the conscious creation of a more just social order. Pragmatism and instrumentalism thus commandeered evolutionary naturalism and argued that it was egalitarian in theory and humanitarian in practice. [E. Purcell, The Crisis of Democratic Theory: Scientific Naturalism and the Problem of Value 10 (1973).]

The intellectual roots of the conservation movement are usually traced to a book written in 1864 by a lawyer, diplomat, and self-trained scientist, George Perkins Marsh, but they can also be traced to the scientific surveys of the West in the middle of the last century:

> The geologists and topographers were members of a newer elite community which was fast replacing that formed by the old army. As such, they often saw the

West in terms of the scientific rather than the military problems involved. And where they were called upon to apply their knowledge, they thought largely in terms of efficiency and waste. This was in sharp contrast to the ideas of Western legislators and the demands of Western citizens, who had always thought of the West as a place to live in and develop and exploit. To them the geologist was not much different from a fur trader's guide, or a wagon master. His job was to lead them to the promised land and show them the way to the riches.

There arose then in the 1860s still another West to be placed beside the passage to India, the imperial domain, the beaver kingdom, the Great American Desert, the paradise of flocks and herds, the empty Algeria, Arcadia, Golconda, and the Creator's mighty firmament. These had been revealed by explorers in the past. The new West was, by implication, the "resource West," to be revealed by the scientific explorer, but also to be guarded when the occasion demanded against reckless exploitation and the rampant, often illicit speculation that came to characterize the Grant administration, both in the East and in the West. Thus it became clear that in an age which depended upon and demanded exploitation and speculation, the explorer was once again ahead of his time and even running counter to it. Out of his Western experience came conservation and the first great national agencies dedicated to that proposition. [W. Goetzman, Exploration and Empire 356 (1966).]

Marsh's Man and Nature, republished ten years later as The Earth Modified by Human Action, was the first popular book to use what we now call the ecological perspective to draw attention to the consequences of overusing resources and to reach the normative conclusion that natural resource use policy should be based on use — rather than abuse — of nature's "spontaneous arrangements."

Man and Nature contributed significantly to the growth of interest in conservation. Conservationism was and is concerned with moderating the rate of present resource use to assure plentiful supplies of needed commodities in the foreseeable future. Preservationism and conservationism, like the Anglican and Roman communions, share certain principles, but the two movements have remained somewhat separate because in the 1880s the founding fathers of the two movements, John Muir of the preservation movement and Gifford Pinchot of the conservation movement, split over forest use and later over water use policy. The conservation movement, which stressed the use of scientific principles to make rational resource use choices, become a powerful political force in the first two decades of this century and helped to shape the structure and thrust of federal and state resource use programs. Powerful government agencies were established to develop resources in the name of reclamation of arid lands, flood control, and public power. In the debate over how best to use natural resources, preservationists became dissenters who lobbied Congress on an ad hoc basis to block certain projects or federal actions. See generally J. Petulla, American Environmental History: The Exploitation and Conservation of Natural Resources (2d ed. 1987); and Hargrove, The Historical Foundations of American Environmental Attitudes, 1 Envtl. Ethics 209 (1979). The standard history of the conservation movement is the superb S. Hays, Conservation and the Gospel of Efficiency: The Progressive Conservation Movement 1890-1920 (1959); see also D. Strong, The Conservationists (1971). Under the leadership of John Muir, the

preservation movement scored a number of important political successes in setting aside national parks and curbing excessive use of public lands, but it lacked
the breadth of vision acceptable to the American mind to displace scientific
conservation as the dominant resource use policy. John Muir's ecological vision
was too advanced for his time:

> Hetch Hetchy was a part of the flow of Nature. It was filled with waterfalls,
> and was the path of the Tuolumne River. It was the path of ancient glaciers, and
> a path new life had taken as it entered the mountains. And damming it was an act
> by men which bespoke their arrogance. Men who built dams believed they could
> control and harness the flow of Nature. Hetch Hetchy was also a consummation,
> as all the inseparable sections of the flow were. It was not an 'exceptional' creation,
> since none of God's gardens were. It was part of a larger whole, and edenic valley.
> Yet when men chose to stop its flowing life, and did so not for the farmers of the
> Central Valley, but for the businessmen of the City of San Francisco, Muir saw in
> this action civilization's willingness to kill Nature for its own convenience. In the-
> ory — for the young Muir certainly — all dams in all valleys were arrogant gestures
> by men.
>   . . . The entire idea behind Yosemite Park, an idea so long in taking shape,
> was to hold inviolate the whole watersheds of the Merced and Tuolumne rivers.
> To violate that precedent was to damage the concept of a national park as more
> than a collection of scenic features. So it was that the principle of a national park
> as an ecological whole was also at stake. [M. Cohen, The Pathless Way: John Muir
> and American Wilderness 330-331 (1984).

S. Fox, John Muir and His Legacy: The American Conservation Movement (1980), is a useful biography of "Saint John of the Mountains" and a history
of the preservation movement prior to the 1960s. F. Turner, Rediscovering
America: John Muir in His Time and Ours (1985) is also a probing effort to trace
the sources of Muir's ideas.

The subordination of preservationism to conservationism continued until
1969-1970, when what is now referred to as the environmental decade began.
Suddenly, environmental quality changed from a national but specific public
lands or reservoir construction issue or a local air or water pollution problem to
become the subject of a broadly based national political movement that triggered
an unprecedented legislative response from Congress. Council on Environmental Quality, Tenth Annual Report 1-15 (1979), offers several reasons for the sudden emergence of environmental quality as a major political priority. The first
of the two most important long-range trends was the post-World War II growth
in affluence, which allowed many people to relocate in suburban communities.
Many people who moved to the suburbs witnessed firsthand the degradation of
the very amenities they had relocated to enjoy. The second major long-range
trend was the growth of the synthetic organic chemical industry. As the synthetic
chemical industry grew, and as more sophisticated monitoring devices were developed, it became increasingly clear that pollution posed a serious threat to
human health. In this connection, an event of signal importance was the publication of Rachel Carson's brief against DDT, Silent Spring, in 1962.

Many have observed that crises trigger political responses, and the crisis that immediately preceded Earth Day in April 1970 (which showed the breadth of the environmental movement's support), was the Santa Barbara oil spill.* It is paradoxical that this spill, which took no human lives, caused no permanent impairment of human health, and seems to have produced no long-range ecological damage, became a national crisis that "brought home to a great many Americans a feeling that protection would not simply happen, but required their active support and involvement." Council on Environmental Quality, Tenth Annual Report, at 12.

Finally, a major catalyst for the birth of the environmental movement was the transfer of political energy from the bitterly controversial and often violent civil rights and anti-Vietnam War movements to a movement that was clean, enjoyed widespread support, and promised to transcend old ideological issues. Individual polluters made better devils than the very soul of America, which was at war with itself over civil rights and the Vietnam War.

The leading historian of the progressive conservation movement, Samuel P. Hays, has written the most thorough history of the environmental movement. Like others, he traces the movement to the public taste for quality fueled by post World War II affluence, but he reaches a somewhat surprising conclusion about the tension between the popular taste for environmental quality and those charged with delivering it:

> The public sought to bring to the fore the notion that natural environments were valuable and should be a central aspect of environmental progress, but those in positions of managerial leadership minimized these goals in favor of their own commitments to more traditional types of commodity development. . . . There was similar reluctance of that leadership to move rapidly toward higher levels of personal health, toward wellness and optimum fitness, with a shift in emphasis from the acute effects of high-level exposures to the chronic effects of low level ones. Managers seemed more concerned with reducing developmental costs than with increasing environmental benefits. . . . By the 1980s the managerial and technical leadership had also tended to assert that the general public would have to accept a permanent level of human and environmental contamination as the price of material progress." [S. Hays (with B. Hays), Beauty, Health and Permanence 540 (1987).]

One can find many instances of ecological disasters in history (see P. Sears, Deserts on the March (1935)), but generally little effort was made to reverse ecological damage; usually there was a new resource to replace the one lost. In the eighteenth century Malthus speculated about the relationship between finite resources and population growth, but according to conventional wisdom it was not until the twentieth century that the full consequences of man's powers over

---

*L. Dye, Blowout at Platform A: A Crisis That Awakened a Nation (1971), contains a useful account of the reactions of the citizens of Santa Barbara to the spill. The mood of the late 1960s is described in Editors of Fortune, The Environment: A National Mission for the Seventies (1970).

nature began to portend disaster. As a result of the factors enumerated above, by 1970 concern over resource use had secured a prominent place on political agendas, and the notion of resource mismanagement had acquired a sense of urgency it had lacked previously. The working assumption of the modern environmental movement was set forth by Barbara Ward and Rene Dubos in their book Only One Earth (1972):

> What *is* certain is that our sudden, vast accelerations — in numbers, in the use of energy and new materials, in urbanization, in consumptive ideals, in consequent pollution — have set technological man on a course which could alter dangerously and perhaps irreversibly, the natural systems of his planet upon which his biological survival depends. [Only One Earth, at 11 (original emphasis).]

The Reagan administration, 1981-1988, tested severely the depth of the public commitment to the protection of environmental quality. Despite many strenuous administration efforts to the contrary, especially between 1981 and 1983, all major programs continued in place and were generally strengthened by Congress. As one of the leading advocates of the substitution of new entitlements for traditional command and control regulation has written:

> The administration showed neither an appreciation of the political importance of environmentalism nor a vision of how to formulate an environmental policy that reflected the president's philosophy. Simply streamlining regulations and procedures seemed to become the goal. In its eight years in office, the Reagan administration presented no alternative to Superfund and even supported amendments designed to strengthen the program. Command-and-control programs, criticized by liberal and conservative analysts alike, escaped serious reform. [Stroup, Environmental Policy, in The Reagan Record and the Task Ahead, Regulation No. 3, 1988 p. 47.]

In this chapter we explore the scientific, philosophical, economic, and political values that underlie the various analyses of the "environmental problem" and how the multitude of existing and proposed legal responses to the problem are shaped by these values.

As you study the myriad possible perspectives on environmentalism and, ultimately, on environmental law, consider the following problems. How would each perspective characterize each problem and why? Are they all "environmental insults"? Are all "insults" of equal significance? Which "insults" are adequately redressed by the common law? Which can only be redressed through new doctrines and legal institutions?

1. A truck carrying toxic wastes is negligently driven and consequently overturns; bystanders are burned as a result of the accident.

2. The toxic wastes from the same truck seep into a farmer's well water and contaminate his water supply, causing crops to die from lack of water.

3. The toxic wastes from the same truck contaminate a city's water supply. Existing water wells must be closed and an alternative supply stream developed.

4. The toxic wastes from the same truck seep into the ground. Five years after the accident, doctors find a modest but significant increase in certain diseases that could be caused by the wastes, but no scientific consensus exists that the accident caused the increase in disease or that genetic mutations will materialize in the future as a result of the accident. But the doctors refuse to rule out the possibility that the accident's effects will be felt far into the future, perhaps over several generations. There is evidence that the most serious health risks will be experienced by a small group of persons with a peculiar susceptibility to certain types of disease.

5. An administrator with control over a scenic forest area is forced to make a choice: Will the forest be used for a wilderness area, for timber production, for mass recreation, or for a surface mine? He chooses the surface mine because it will produce the greatest immediate benefits. There is also evidence that the most productive use of the forest area, using a low discount rate to translate future worth into present value, would be for timber production.

6. Mine wastes are discharged into streams near the forest area, but the streams have long been used for this purpose and are not used for fishing, swimming, or drinking water. However, there is evidence that applicable water pollution regulations will not fully prevent the discharge of mine wastes into nearby streams.

7. The administrator chooses the mass recreation option and allows a large hotel complex, including a ten-story hotel, to be built on a spot where Indian ceremonies were once performed and the first European expedition to the area sighted a spectacular rock formation. In addition, the view of the scenic wonder from a nearby park is partially blocked by the hotel.

8. Before the administrator can approve any decision he must evaluate the environmental impact of proposed projects, complete certain planning studies, and consult with other interested government agencies. Assume that he does none of these things. Assume he does the first. Assume he does the first and second but not the third.

9. Assume that the administrator completes all three steps above but a national environmental citizen's group of hikers and bird-watchers thinks that the environmental evaluation is superficial and narrow and that the planning document produced validated a decision already made.

B.   THE LESSONS OF ECOLOGY

Man will, in the foreseeable future, confront the moral obligation to make himself extinct — to commit racial suicide. He will lie under a duty to preserve nature: that is, the life process and the earth. And the only way in which this obligation can be discharged is by man decreeing his own extinction. [Jenkins, Nature's Rights and Man's Duties, in Law and the Ecological Challenge 91 (E. Dais ed. 1978).]

The extreme position articulated above rests, in Jenkins' words, on the "claim that nature has rights which impose duties on man." Since the 1970s, there has been a lively debate about the meaning of "nature." Is nature a totally artificial construct that is responsive to cultural changes, or is it the product of objective research — unchanging and irrefutable scientific knowledge about the physical environment that supports life on this planet? Our attitudes toward nature changed dramatically in the eighteenth and nineteenth centuries as this description of the chateau of Jacques Necker, Louis XVI's last minister of finance, illustrates:

> The chateau, an imposing, handsome edifice, is hidden from the lake front by the tall trees of its park. Only the upper windows offer a view of the lake and the snow-capped mountains of Savoy; built in an age when beauty was seen in restful greenery and gentle, harmonious lines rather than in the wild majesty of desolate peaks, the house is oriented toward the land and the Jura, not the lake and the Alps. [J. Christopher Herold, Mistress to An Age: The Life of Madame de Staël 103 (1958).]

Whatever the answer, all disciplines that think systematically about environmental problems have been influenced by the science of ecology. The word "ecology," derived from the Greek word "oikos" ("house" or "place to live"), was not coined until 1869, and the science of ecology dates from only 1890. Ecology has to do with the structure and function of nature, considered in a grand perspective. Initially, the science was attractive to policy makers looking for a quick fix because it was thought to offer scientific laws, or a fairly certain promise of them, that would translate directly into moral and thus legal imperatives. In his introduction to a collection of essays, The Subversive Science: Essays toward an Ecology of Man (P. Shepard & D. McKinley eds. 1969), Paul Shepard expressed this idea as follows: "Ecology may testify as often against our uses of the world, even against conservation techniques of control and management for sustained yield, as it does for them. Although ecology may be treated as a science, its greater and overriding wisdom is universal" (Introduction: Ecology and Man — A Viewpoint, The Subversive Science 1, at 4-5).

However, ecology as a science was ill prepared to realize its potential when the environmental decade began. Until the environmental decade, ecology was an unprestigious branch of learning. True, it boasted some brilliant scientists and some gifted, almost poetic, writers, but the state of its knowledge was crude because its path had diverged from that of pure science, which, in the name of elegance and in the name of obtaining directly useful knowledge, gradually had shifted its focus from nineteenth century holistic views of nature to the application of smaller and smaller units of analysis. See Odum, A New Ecology for the Coast, in Coastal Alert: Scientists Speak Out 145 (T. Jackson & D. Reische eds. 1981). Carpenter, The Scientific Basis of NEPA — Is It Adequate?, 6 Envtl. L. Rep. (Envtl. L. Inst.) 50,014 (1976); and Carpenter, Ecology in Court, and Other Disappointments of Environmental Science and Environmental Law, 15 Nat. Resources Lawyer 573 (1983) are useful summaries of the gap between the information demands of regulation and available research. Sagoff, Ethics, Ecology, and the Environment: Integrating Science and Law, 56 Tenn. L. Rev. 77 (1988) is a thorough review of the debates within ecology about its mission.

Before we turn to a detailed analysis of the moral basis that is claimed for ecology, we must start with some core specific scientific concepts. At the risk of over-simplification, we present a brief sketch of ecology drawn from the leading casebook on the subject.

E. ODUM, FUNDAMENTALS OF ECOLOGY
10-11, 27, 88-89 (2d ed. 1959)

Living organisms and their nonliving (abiotic) environment are inseparably interrelated and interact upon each other. Any area of nature that includes living organisms and nonliving substances interacting to produce an exchange of materials between the living and nonliving parts is an ecological system or ecosystem. From a functional standpoint, an ecosystem has two components (which are usually partially separated in space and time), an *autotrophic component* (autotrophic = self-nourishing), in which fixation of light energy, use of simple inorganic substances, and buildup of complex substances predominate; and, secondly, a *heterotrophic component* (heterotrophic = other-nourishing) in which utilization, rearrangement and decomposition of complex materials predominate. It is convenient to recognize four constituents as comprising the ecosystem: (1) *abiotic substances*, basic inorganic and organic compounds of the environment; (2) *producers*, autotrophic organisms, largely green plants, which are able to manufacture food from simple inorganic substances; (3) *consumers* (or macro-consumers), heterotrophic organisms, chiefly animals, which ingest other organisms or particulate organic matter; (4) *decomposers* (micro-consumers, saprobes or saprophytes), heterotrophic organisms, chiefly bacteria and fungi, which break down the complex compounds of dead protoplasms, absorb some of the decomposition products and release simple substances usable by the producers.

The ecosystem is the basic functional unit in ecology, since it includes both organisms (biotic communities) and abiotic environment, each influencing the properties of the other and both necessary for maintenance of life as we have it on the earth. A lake is an example of an ecosystem. . . .

The habitat of an organism is the place where it lives, or the place where one would go to find it. The ecological niche, on the other hand, is the position or status of an organism within its community and ecosystem resulting from the organism's structural adaptations, physiological responses and specific behavior (inherited and/or learned). The ecological niche of an organism depends not only on where it lives but also on what it does. By analogy, it may be said that the habitat is the organism's "address," and the niche is its "profession," biologically speaking. . . .

To occur and thrive in a given situation, an organism must have essential materials which are necessary for growth and reproduction. These basic requirements vary with the species and with the situation. The essential material available in amounts most closely approaching the critical minimum needed will tend to be the limiting one.

The presence and success of an organism depend upon the completeness of a complex of conditions. Absence or failure of an organism can be controlled by the qualitative or quantitative deficiency or excess with respect to any one of several factors which may approach the limits to tolerance for that organism.

Environmentalists generally have drawn normative conclusions from ecology, most of them traceable to the following classic, first published in 1949.

A. LEOPOLD, A SAND COUNTY ALMANAC AND SKETCHES HERE AND THERE
202-204, 214-216, 220, 224-225 (Oxford University Press paperback ed. 1968)

An ethic, philosophically, is a differentiation of social from anti-social conduct. These are two definitions of one thing. The thing has its origin in the tendency of interdependent individuals or groups to evolve modes of co-operation. The ecologist calls these symbioses. Politics and economics are advanced symbioses in which the original free-for-all competition has been replaced, in part, by co-operative mechanisms with an ethical content.

The complexity of co-operative mechanisms has increased with population density, and with the efficiency of tools. It was simpler, for example, to define the anti-social uses of sticks and stones in the days of the mastodons than of bullets and billboards in the age of motors.

The first ethics dealt with the relation between individuals; the Mosaic Decalogue is an example. Later accretions dealt with the relation between the individual and society. The Golden Rule tries to integrate the individual to society; democracy to integrate social organization to the individual.

There is as yet no ethic dealing with man's relation to land and to the animals and plants which grow upon it. Land, like Odysseus' slave-girls, is still property. The land-relation is still strictly economic, entailing privileges but not obligations.

The extension of ethics to this third element in human environment is, if I read the evidence correctly, an evolutionary possibility and an ecological necessity. It is the third step in a sequence. The first two have already been taken. Individual thinkers since the days of Ezekiel and Isaiah have asserted that the despoliation of land is not only inexpedient but wrong. Society, however, has not yet affirmed their belief. I regard the present conservation movement as the embryo of such an affirmation.

An ethic may be regarded as a mode of guidance for meeting ecological situations so new or intricate, or involving such deferred reactions, that the path of social expediency is not discernible to the average individual. Animal instincts are modes of guidance for the individual in meeting such situations. Ethics are possibly a kind of community instinct in-the-making.

All ethics so far evolved rest upon a single premise: that the individual is a member of a community of interdependent parts. His instincts prompt him to compete for his place in that community, but his ethics prompt him also to co-operate (perhaps in order that there be a place to compete for).

The land ethic simply enlarges the boundaries of the community to include soils, waters, plants, and animals, or collectively: the land.

This sounds simple: do we not already sing our love for and obligation to the land of the free and the home of the brave? Yes, but just what and whom do we love? Certainly not the soil, which we are sending helter-skelter downriver. Certainly not the waters, which we assume have no function except to turn turbines, float barges, and carry off sewage. Certainly not the plants, of which we exterminate whole communities without batting an eye. Certainly not the animals, of which we have already extirpated many of the largest and most beautiful species. A land ethic of course cannot prevent the alteration, management, and use of these "resources," but it does affirm their right to continued existence, and, at least in spots, their continued existence in a natural state.

In short, a land ethic changes the role of Homo sapiens from conqueror of the land-community to plain member and citizen of it. It implies respect for his fellow-members, and also respect for the community as such. [pp. 202-204]

The image commonly employed in conservation education is "the balance of nature." For reasons too lengthy to detail here, this figure of speech fails to describe accurately what little we know about the land mechanism. A much truer image is the one employed in ecology: the biotic pyramid. I shall first sketch the pyramid as a symbol of land, and later develop some of its implications in terms of land-use.

Plants absorb energy from the sun. This energy flows through a circuit called the biota, which may be represented by a pyramid consisting of layers. The bottom layer is the soil. A plant layer rests on the soil, an insect layer on the plants, a bird and rodent layer on the insects, and so on up through various animal groups to the apex layer, which consists of the larger carnivores.

The species of a layer are alike not in where they came from, or in what they look like, but rather in what they eat. Each successive layer depends on those below it for food and often for other services, and each in turn furnishes food and services to those above. Proceeding upward, each successive layer decreases in numerical abundance. Thus, for every carnivore there are hundreds of his prey, thousands of their prey, millions of insects, uncountable plants. The pyramidal form of the system reflects this numerical progression from apex to base. Man shares an intermediate layer with the bears, raccoons, and squirrels which eat both meat and vegetables.

The lines of dependency for food and other services are called food chains. Thus soil-oak-deer-Indian is a chain that has now been largely converted to soil-corn-cow-farmer. Each species, including ourselves, is a link in many chains.

The deer eats a hundred plants other than oak, and the cow a hundred plants other than corn. Both, then, are links in a hundred chains. The pyramid is a tangle of chains so complex as to seem disorderly, yet the stability of the system proves it to be a highly organized structure. Its functioning depends on the co-operation and competition of its diverse parts.

In the beginning, the pyramid of life was low and squat; the food chains short and simple. Evolution has added layer after layer, link after link. Man is one of thousands of accretions to the height and complexity of the pyramid. Science has given us many doubts, but it has given us at least one certainty: the trend of evolution is to elaborate and diversify the biota.

Land, then, is not merely soil; it is a fountain of energy flowing through a circuit of soils, plants, and animals. Food chains are the living channels which conduct energy upward; death and decay return it to the soil. The circuit is not closed; some energy is dissipated in decay, some is added by absorption from the air, some is stored in soils, peats, and long-lived forests; but it is a sustained circuit, like a slowly augmented revolving fund of life. There is always a net loss by downhill wash, but this is normally small and offset by the decay of rocks. It is deposited in the ocean and, in the course of geological time, raised to form new lands and new pyramids.

The velocity and character of the upward flow of energy depend on the complex structure of the plant and animal community, much as the upward flow of sap in a tree depends on its complex cellular organization. Without this complexity, normal circulation would presumably not occur. Structure means the characteristic numbers, as well as the characteristic kinds and functions, of the component species. This interdependence between the complex structure of the land and its smooth functioning as an energy unit is one of its basic attributes.

When a change occurs in one part of the circuit, many other parts must adjust themselves to it. [pp. 214-216]

The combined evidence of history and ecology seems to support one general deduction: the less violent the man-made changes, the greater the probability of successful readjustment in the pyramid. Violence, in turn, varies with human population density; a dense population requires a more violent conversion. In this respect, North America has a better chance for permanence than Europe, if she can contrive to limit her density.

This deduction runs counter to our current philosophy, which assumes that because a small increase in density enriched human life, that an indefinite increase will enrich it indefinitely. Ecology knows of no density relationship that holds for indefinitely wide limits. All gains from density are subject to a law of diminishing returns. [p. 220]

A thing is right when it tends to preserve the integrity, stability, and beauty of the biotic community. It is wrong when it tends otherwise. [pp. 224- 225]

NOTES AND QUESTIONS

1. Leopold's call for a new land conservation ethic has had a profound influence on many policymakers and scholars concerned with resource management. Other important early books include F. Osborn, Our Plundered Planet (1948), and H. Brown, The Challenge of Man's Future (1954). In his book The Quiet Crisis (1963), one of the first books about the environmental crisis, Stewart L. Udall, John F. Kennedy's Secretary of the Interior, incorporated Leopold's proposed land ethic into the central policy for the future of what was then called the conservation movement. Similarly, in his lectures on the foundations of environmental thought, published as An Introduction to Environmental Thought: Some Sources and Some Criticisms, 50 Ind. L. J. 426 (1975), Dean Charles J. Meyers called A Sand County Almanac "the epitome of environmental thinking." Two new important books on Leopold and his thinking are Companion to a Sand County Almanac (B. Callicott ed. 1988) and C. Meine, Aldo Leopold: His Life and Work (1988). Although Leopold hoped that individuals would eventually internalize respect toward nature, Leopold's essay contains the basis for new, and potentially radical, forms of social organization. See Hefferman, The Land Ethic: A Critical Appraisal, 4 Envtl. Ethics 235 (1982). Leopold seems to advocate a new approach to social organization when he asserts that the root of our disregard for nature lies in the Judeo-Christian belief that man is apart from and above nature, a belief that forms the foundation of the concept of private property, which to many is the cause of the over-exploitation of natural resources. Blaming the idea that resources are here to be exploited on Judeo-Christian ethics has become quite commonplace in recent years, but this blame may be partially misplaced. See p. 15 *infra*.

2. What are the implications of A Sand County Almanac for lawyers? The most common use has been to bolster assertions of the police power to protect the environment. For example, in Application of Christensen, 417 N.W. 2d 607, 615 (Minn. 1988) the Minnesota supreme court upheld the denial of a wetland drainage permit with this language:

> Over ten years ago this court cited the conservationist Aldo Leopold for his espousal of a "land ethic" which envisions a community of interdependent parts. "The land ethic simply enlarges the boundaries of the community to include soils, waters, plants, and animals, or collectively: the land." County of Freeborn v. Bryson, 243 N.W. 2d at 322, citing Sand County Almanac (1949) p. 203. We reaffirm our statement that the state's environmental legislation had given this land ethic the force of law, and imposed on the courts a duty to support the legislative goal of protecting our state's environmental resources. Vanishing wetlands require, even more today than in 1976 when *Bryson* was decided, the protection and preservation that environmental legislation was intended to provide.

3. Environmental philosophers and others read Leopold much more strongly. The argument is that the rejection of the individualistic, anthropocen-

tric bias in western philosophy leads to specific duties, not just a plea for the evolution of changed attitudes toward nature, although Leopold himself held a dualistic view of the relationship between man and nature. The basic premise is that the prevailing theory of western civilization that man commands nature should be replaced with the radical view that he is just a participant in the biotic community. As Roderick Nash has observed, "If Darwin killed dualism, the ecologists presided over its burial." Nash, The Rights of Nature: A History of Environmental Ethics 70 (1989). The stakes are high in part because ecological triage may be a logical consequence of the theory. The new morality requires that certain species be abandoned to predation "for the sake of the integrity, stability, and beauty of the biotic community." J. Baird, The Conceptual Foundations of the Land Ethic 186, 206 in A Companion to A Sand County Almanac (B. Callicott ed.), *supra* Note 1.

4. The effort to construct a theory of ecological right faces formidable conceptual hurdles. First, rights are generally limited to sentient beings. This affords some hope for animal rights advocates. The best articulation of the possibility of bringing animals within a modified rights framework remains R. Nozick, Anarchy, State and Utopia 35-42 (1975). But, this extension of sentency offers no help for proponents of ecosystem rights. Second, the argument that moral duties flow from ecological awareness flies in the face of the dominant human separation of fact and value. Rolston, Can and Ought We to Follow Nature?, 1 Envtl. Ethics 7 (1979) explores the different meanings of the simple idea that we can derive prescriptive rules from nature. Expanded rights theories have been further criticized because they require the attribution of intrinsic values to things when most justification of environmental ethics turn out to be appeals to human or attributed values. See, Weston, Beyond Intrinsic Value: Pragmatism in Environmental Ethics, 7 Envtl. Ethics 321 (1985). Can one avoid the problem by dissolving the categories and by adopting moral concern for the functioning of the entire ecological system as the value? The leading articles advocating this position are Rolston, Are Values in Nature Objective or Subjective? 4 Envtl. Ethics at 147 (1982); B. Callicott, Hume's *Is/Ought* Dichotomy and the Relation of Ecology to Leopold's Land Ethic, 4 Envtl. Ethics at 163-174 (1982); Non-anthropocentric Value Theory and Environmental Ethics, 21 Am. Philosophical Q. at 229-309 (1984); On the Intrinsic Value of Nonhuman Species, in Bryan G. Norton, ed., The Preservation of Species 138-172 (1986); and Intrinsic Value, Quantum Theory, and Environmental Ethics, 7 Envtl. Ethics 257-275 (1985). Third, all environmental conflicts require resource allocation choices but rights based theories prohibit the necessary weighing of interests necessary to make the required choice. Norton, Environmental Ethics and Nonhuman Rights, 4 Envtl. Ethics 17 (1982). See also Weston, Beyond Intrinsic Value: Pragmatism in Environmental Ethics, 7 Envtl. Ethics 7 (1985); Regan, The Nature and Possibility of an Environmental Ethics, 3 Envtl. Ethics 31 (1981); McDaniel, Physical Matter as Creative and Sentient, 5 Envtl. Ethics 291 (1983); Taylor, The Ethics of Respect for Nature, 3 Envtl. Ethics 197 (1981) and Taylor, In Defense of Biocentrism, 5 Envtl. Ethics 237 (1983); Rolston, Is There an

Ecological Ethic?, in Ethics and the Environment 41 (D. Shere & T. Attig eds. 1983).

5. At the other end of the spectrum, non-anthropocentric theories can be used to argue against environmental rights. The Gaian thesis, named for the Greek goddess of the Earth, that the Earth is a living organism can support the idea that she is more resilient than we think. See Weston, Forms of Gaian Ethics, 9 Envtl. Ethics 217 (1987). The Gaia hypothesis, suggested by the British scientist James Lovelock, originally asserted that the biosphere was regulated comfortably because of the behavior of living organisms. The established scientific community initially dismissed Lovelock's thinking, but in 1988 Lovelock restated the thesis and it has begun to attract serious attention among scientists. His most recent definition of Gaia is:

> So what is Gaia? If the real world we inhabit is self-regulating in the manner of Daisyworld, and if the climate and environment we enjoy and freely exploit is a consequence of an automatic, but not purposeful, goal-seeking system, then Gaia is the largest manifestation of life. The tightly coupled system of life and its environment, Gaia, includes:
>
> 1. Living organisms that grow vigorously, exploiting any environmental opportunities that open.
> 2. Organisms that are subject to the rules of Darwinian natural selection: the species of organisms that leave the most progeny survive.
> 3. Organisms that affect their physical and chemical environment. Thus animals change the atmosphere by breathing: taking in oxygen and letting out carbon dioxide. Plants and algae do the reverse. In numerous other ways, all forms of life incessantly modify the physical and chemical environment.
> 4. The existence of constraints or bounds that establish the limits of life. It can be too hot or too cold; there is a comfortable warmth in between, the preferred state. It can be too acid or too alkaline; neutrality is preferred. Almost all chemicals have a range of concentrations tolerated or needed by life.

J. Lovelock, The Ages of Gaia: A Biography of Our Living Earth 39-40 (1988).

Stone, Earth and Other Ethics (1987) is an ambitious lawyerly attempt to steer a middle ground in the debate through the development of a process of moral considerateness as opposed to rights for nontraditional human and non-human communities. See Symposium, Developing an Environmental Ethos: Christopher Stone and Earth and Other Ethics, 56 Tenn. L. Rev. vii (1988). See also P. Wenz, Environmental Justice (1988).

J. PASSMORE, MAN'S RESPONSIBILITY FOR NATURE
5-6, 10, 12-14 (1974)

We shall begin . . . with the principal accusation — that Western attitudes to nature are infected with "arrogance," an arrogance which has continued into the post-Christian world and makes men think of nature as a "captive to be raped" rather than as a "partner to be cherished." Genesis will be our starting-point, a Genesis so often assailed as the fount and origin of the West's ecological troubles. That it is justly so condemned we shall find reason for questioning.

The Lord God created man, so Genesis certainly tells us, to have "dominion over the fish of the sea, and over the fowl of the air, and over the cattle, and over all the earth and over every creeping thing that creepeth upon the earth" (I: 26). This has been read not only by Jew but by Christian and Muslim as man's charter, granting him the right to subdue the earth and all its inhabitants. And God, according to Genesis, also issued a mandate to mankind: "Be fruitful and multiply and replenish the earth and subdue it" (I: 28). So Genesis tells men not only what they can do, but what they should do — multiply and replenish and subdue the earth. . . .

The view that man in any sense rules over nature inevitably presumes that nature is not itself divine. And the striking peculiarity of the religion of the Hebrews, when we compare it with the middle Eastern religions which surrounded it, is its sharp distinction between God and nature. The Hebrew God, to put the difference technically, is transcendent, not immanent; he creates and rules nature but is not to be identified with it. "The keeping of Jahweh's covenant," Frankfort therefore writes, "meant . . . sacrificing the greatest good ancient Near East religion could bestow — the harmonious integration of man's life with the life of nature." Man's dealings with nature were sharply separated from his dealings with God. And it was his relationship with God which really mattered. "Man," Frankfort sums up, "remained outside nature, exploiting it for a livelihood, offering its first fruits as a sacrifice to Jahweh, using its imagery for the expression of his moods, but never sharing its mysterious life."

We may well cavil at Frankfort's suggestion — so typical of Romanticism — that in nature there is a "mysterious life" from which the Hebrews somehow cut themselves off. But the Hebrew desacralization of nature certainly left man free to exploit it with none of the qualms which, in many other societies, he would have felt when he cut down a tree or killed an animal. There are societies in which the axeman or the slaughterer, before taking up his axe or his knife, would first have begged the tree's or the animal's pardon, explaining the necessity which forced him to destroy it. Indeed, such an attitude to nature lingered on among German foresters as late as the nineteenth century. But this feeling is not compatible with orthodox Hebraic or Christian teaching.

It is certainly a mistake to suggest, as the biologist L. C. Birch has recently suggested, that "the doctrine of creation" — the Hebrew doctrine, that is — "stands for the sacredness of all things." Nothing is sacred, in this tradition, except God and what, like Sinai, is specifically dedicated to God. "The Lord is in his holy temple; the Lord's throne is in heaven." No doubt God owns the earth and all it contains, "every beast of the forest and the cattle upon a thousand hills." But man is at liberty, under a special charter from God, to exploit it as he wills — subject only to restrictions specifically imposed by God. He is not, when he kills "the cattle upon a thousand hills," killing something sacred. . . .

There are, of course, problems in talking about "the Old Testament" as if it were a single book with, in all respects, a single point of view. Running through it there is a conflict between the new man-centred agriculture and the old nature-oriented nomadic pastoral life to which so many of the Jews looked back with nostalgia. (Cain's offer to Yahweh of the fruits of the earth was, it will be remembered, spurned; God accepted Abel's oxen, only.) The nomadic pastoralist is more conscious than is the agriculturalist that he shares the earth with other living things, which go their own way largely indifferent to his presence; the agriculturalist deliberately transforms nature in a sense in which the nomadic pastoralist does not. The conflict of attitudes persists in later Jewish thought, influenced as it also was by Greek humanism. The Egyptian-Jewish Saadia, writing in the tenth century A.D., committed himself very firmly to the view that "the entire universe was created on account of man." The greatest Jewish orthodox philosopher, Maimonides, at first took the same view in his early commentary on the Mishnah. "All things in the sublunary world," he there writes, "exist only for the sake of man." But he later rejected that view as in essence profoundly non-Jewish. Genesis makes it perfectly clear, he then argues, that the world was good *before* man was created: "It should not be believed," he concludes, "that all beings exist for the sake of the existence of man. On the contrary, all the other beings, too, have been intended for their own sakes and not for the sake of something else." And this is the more typically Jewish attitude.

Christianity, on the other hand, with its God who took human shape, is, or tends to be, anthropocentric, at least so far as the things of this world are concerned. For the Jews, as for the Muslims, it is blasphemous to suppose that God could become a man; for many other religions, God was as likely to become a bull, or a monkey, as a man. The peculiarities of Christian attitudes to nature derive in large part from its man-centredness. So Calvin, for example, is quite confident that God "created all things for man's sake." God, Calvin's argument runs, could have created the universe, had he so chosen, in one day. He chose, however, to take six days in order to demonstrate to man that everything had been made ready for him, that he entered the earth like a royal guest whose importance is indicated by the fact that he enters last. "But he willed to commend his providence and fatherly solicitude towards us, in that before he fashioned man, he prepared everything he foresaw would be useful and salutory for him."

Calvin's description of a creation prepared for man was echoed, in an ecological form, by G. P. Marsh in his Man and Nature, published in 1864, and the first work to describe in detail man's destructiveness. Nature, according to Marsh, "has left it within the power of man irreparably to derange the combinations of inorganic matter and of organic life, which through the night of aeons she had been proportioning and balancing, to prepare the earth for his habitation, when, in the fullness of time, his Creator should call him forth to enter into its possession." Although with very different intentions, Calvin and Marsh both emphasize man's ingratitude when, whether by Adam's sin (Calvin) or by man's destructive acts (Marsh), they vandalize the home which God (Calvin) or nature (Marsh) had in six days (Calvin) or over aeons (Marsh) prepared for their residence. The difference between Marsh and Calvin is nevertheless crucial: for Christianity men entered nature as its rightful master, for the ecologist as a potentially dangerous intruder. To that extent the critics of Christianity are right. Christianity has encouraged man to think of himself as nature's absolute master, for whom everything that exists was designed. They are wrong only in supposing that this is also the Hebrew teaching; it originates with the Greeks.

Traditional Greek religion, admittedly, did nothing to encourage the view that man either was, or should seek to become, master of the world. To seek that mastery would be hubris, an attempt on man's part to set himself up as a god; such presumption would undoubtedly bring calamities about his head, as the fate of Prometheus served to illustrate. The situation was very different, however, after the Greek Enlightenment, with its rejection of the concept of hubris. One then finds it explicitly maintained that animal life exists purely and simply for man's sake. Aristotle argues in his Politics that "plants are created for the sake of animals, and the animals for the sake of men; the tame for our use and provision; the wild, at least for the greater part, for our provision also, or for some other advantageous purpose, as furnishing us with clothes, and the like." He takes this conclusion to follow necessarily from the premise that "nature makes nothing either imperfect or in vain" — as indeed it does follow if the test of a thing's "perfection" and "usefulness" is first presumed to be its suitability for man's purposes.

Passmore goes on to discuss the alternative Western tradition of the stewardship of nature, which is rooted in the idea that one must cooperate with nature to perfect it. This idea is traced to the post-Platonists and subsequently to Fichte and other German metaphysicians. The tradition of stewardship is quite different from Eastern traditions because "[t]he ideal of active care for nature forms no part of Eastern religion, whether Hindu or Buddhist. Such religions not infrequently teach . . . that men should take all possible steps not to destroy any living thing. But the Western stewardship tradition goes further than that. It demands from man an active concern for the earth's fertility." Id. at 15.

The terror of the French Revolution provoked a reaction to the rationalism of the Enlightenment, and the early 19th century looked back to nature and to "classical" Greece and Rome for guidance. One can see a somewhat similar interest in non- or post-rational approaches to environmental problems. The new environmental literature contains pleas that one must seek wisdom beyond the scientific and rational. For example proponents of ecosophy, derived in part from Sophia, the feminine Greek word for wisdom, argue that "[t]he Western world, if it is to regain . . . [a] lost androgyne consciousness, must reopen its eyes to an entirely different way of perceiving the environment. To embrace Sophia . . . involves both a renunciation of the primordial bond with nature and the honesty of perception found in primitive or pagan epistemologies . . . as feminine fire within us. . . . To become spiritually whole, the masculine must embrace the feminine in an androgyne act of empathy and love." Davis, Ecosophy: The Seduction of Sophia, 8 Envtl. Ethics 151, 161-162 (1986). Environmental philosophy has blossomed since Passmore's pioneering book. Important recent books include: P. Taylor, Respect for Nature (1986); W. Gravberg-Michaelson, A Worldly Spirituality, The Call to Take Care of the Earth (1984); and J. Hart, The Spirit of the Earth: A Theology of the Law (1984). Newer scholars have also begun to challenge the idea that Christianity, as influenced by Hellenistic thought, is anti-environmental. See R. Attfield, The Ethics of Environmental Concern (1983), but the core idea that Christianity rejected "the discovery of God through attunement to fellow creatures" because "it smacked of pantheism: an idolatrous identification of God with nature" holds true. McDaniel, Christian Spirituality as Openness to Fellow Creatures, 8 Envtl. Ethics 33, 35 (1986). R. Nash, The Rights of Nature (1989) traces the gradual expansion of the circle of rights and speculates on the implication of this expansion for environmentalism. He observes "environmental ethics created entirely new definitions of what liberty and justice mean on planet earth. It recognized that there can be no individual welfare (or liberty) apart from the ecological matrix in which individual life must exist. A biocentric ethical philosophy . . . can be understood . . . as both the end and a new beginning of the American liberal tradition." Id. at 160.

C.   THE LESSONS OF ECONOMICS

1.   *Introduction*

When economists tried to find an explanation for the environmental problem, they looked at the same facts that Leopold did but drew the opposite conclusion. To Leopold, the Abrahamic concept of private property had to give way to a land ethic based on "love, respect, and admiration for land, and a high regard for its value"; by "value" Leopold meant "something far broader than mere economic value; I mean value in the philosophic sense" (A Sand County Almanac at 223). To economists, the problem is not the well-established phenomenon of private property but the lack of clearly assigned property rights in all resources. Economics and ecology, two disciplines that some say are related, have provided us with the most powerful analyses of the environmental problem. Economists largely ignored adverse environmental impacts until the 1960s, but they quickly made up for lost time and greatly influenced the public policy debate in the 1970s. The following article on the problem of overpopulation, written by a biologist, has substantially influenced economic thinking about the relationship between property and environmental problems.

HARDIN, THE TRAGEDY OF THE COMMONS
162 Science 1243, 1243-1248 (1968)

It is fair to say that most people who anguish over the population problem are trying to find a way to avoid the evils of overpopulation without relinquishing any of the privileges they now enjoy. They think that farming the seas or developing new strains of wheat will solve the problem — technologically. I try to show here that the solution they seek cannot be found. The population problem cannot be solved in a technical way, any more than can the problem of winning the game of tick-tack-toe.

What Shall We Maximize?

Population, as Malthus said, naturally tends to grow "geometrically," or, as we would now say, exponentially. In a finite world this means that the per capita share of the world's goods must steadily decrease. Is ours a finite world?

A fair defense can be put forward for the view that the world is infinite: or that we do not know that it is not. But, in terms of the practical problems that we must face in the next few generations with the foreseeable technology, it is clear that we will greatly increase human misery if we do not, during the immediate future, assume that the world available to the terrestrial human population is finite. "Space" is no escape.

A finite world can support only a finite population; therefore, population growth must eventually equal zero. (The case of perpetual wide fluctuations above and below zero is a trivial variant that need not be discussed.) When this condition is met, what will be the situation of mankind? Specifically, can Bentham's goal of "the greatest good for the greatest number" be realized?

No — for two reasons, each sufficient by itself. The first is a theoretical one. It is not mathematically possible to maximize for two (or more) variables at the same time. This was clearly stated by von Neumann and Morgenstern, but the principle is implicit in the theory of partial differential equations, dating back at least to D'Alembert (1717-1783).

The second reason springs directly from biological facts. To live, any organism must have a source of energy (for example, food). This energy is utilized for two purposes: mere maintenance and work. For man, maintenance of life requires about 1600 kilocalories a day ("maintenance calories"). Anything that he does over and above merely staying alive will be defined as work, and is supported by "work calories" which he takes in. Work calories are used not only for what we call work in common speech; they are also required for all forms of enjoyment, from swimming and automobile racing to playing music and writing poetry. If our goal is to maximize population it is obvious what we must do: We must make the work calories per person approach as close to zero as possible. No gourmet meals, no vacations, no sports, no music, no literature, no art. . . .

I think that everyone will grant, without argument or proof, that maximizing population does not maximize goods. Bentham's goal is impossible.

In reaching this conclusion I have made the usual assumption that it is the acquisition of energy that is the problem. The appearance of atomic energy has led some to question this assumption. However, given an infinite source of energy, population growth still produces an inescapable problem. The problem of the acquisition of energy is replaced by the problem of its dissipation, as J. H. Fremlin has so wittily shown. The arithmetic signs in the analysis are, as it were, reversed; but Bentham's goal is still unobtainable.

The optimum population is, then, less than the maximum. The difficulty of defining the optimum is enormous; so far as I know, no one has seriously tackled this problem. Reaching an acceptable and stable solution will surely require more than one generation of hard analytical work — and much persuasion. . . .

We can make little progress in working toward optimum population size until we explicitly exorcize the spirit of Adam Smith in the field of practical demography. In economic affairs, The Wealth of Nations (1776) popularized the "invisible hand," the idea that an individual who "intends only his own gain," is, as it were, "led by an invisible hand to promote . . . the public interest." . . .

The Tragedy of Freedom in a Commons

The rebuttal to the invisible hand in population control is to be found in a scenario first sketched in a little-known pamphlet in 1833 by a mathematical amateur named William Forster Lloyd (1794-1852). We may well call it "the tragedy of the commons," using the word "tragedy" as the philosopher White-head used it: "The essence of dramatic tragedy is not unhappiness. It resides in the solemnity of the remorseless working of things." He then goes on to say, "This inevitableness of destiny can only be illustrated in terms of human life by incidents which in fact involve unhappiness. For it is only by them that the futility of escape can be made evident in the drama."

The tragedy of the commons develops in this way. Picture a pasture open to all. It is to be expected that each herdsman will try to keep as many cattle as possible on the commons. Such an arrangement may work reasonably satisfactorily for centuries because tribal wars, poaching, and disease keep the numbers of both man and beast well below the carrying capacity of the land. Finally, however, comes the day of reckoning, that is, the day when the long-desired goal of social stability becomes a reality. At this point, the inherent logic of the commons remorselessly generates tragedy.

As a rational being, each herdsman seeks to maximize his gain. Explicitly or implicitly, more or less consciously, he asks, "What is the utility to *me* of adding one more animal to my herd?" This utility has one negative and one positive component.

1. The positive component is a function of the increment of one animal. Since the herdsman receives all the proceeds from the sale of the additional animal, the positive utility is nearly + 1.

2. The negative component is a function of the additional overgrazing created by one more animal. Since, however, the effects of overgrazing are shared by all the herdsmen, the negative utility for any particular decision-making herdsman is only a fraction of − 1.

Adding together the component partial utilities, the rational herdsman concludes that the only sensible course for him to pursue is to add another animal to his herd. And another; and another. . . . But this is the conclusion reached by each and every rational herdsman sharing a commons. Therein is the tragedy. Each man is locked into a system that compels him to increase his herd without limit — in a world that is limited. Ruin is the destination toward which all men rush, each pursuing his own best interest in a society that believes in the freedom of the commons. Freedom in a commons brings ruin to all. . . .

What shall we do? We have several options. We might sell them off as private property. We might keep them as public property, but allocate the right to enter them. The allocation might be on the basis of wealth, by the use of an auction system. It might be on the basis of merit, as defined by some agreed-upon standards. It might be by lottery. Or it might be on a first-come, first-served basis, administered to long queues. These, I think, are all the reasonable possibilities. They are all objectionable. But we must choose — or acquiesce in the destruction of the commons that we call our National Parks.

Pollution

In a reverse way, the tragedy of the commons reappears in problems of pollution. Here it is not a question of taking something out of the commons, but of putting something in — sewage, or chemical, radioactive, and heat wastes into water; noxious and dangerous fumes into the air; and distracting and unpleasant advertising signs into the line of sight. The calculations of utility are much the same as before. The rational man finds that his share of the cost of the wastes he discharges into the commons is less than the cost of purifying his wastes before releasing them. Since this is true for everyone, we are locked into a system of "fouling our own nest," so long as we behave only as independent, rational, free-enterprisers.

The tragedy of the commons as a food basket is averted by private property, or something formally like it. But the air and waters surrounding us cannot readily be fenced, and so the tragedy of the commons as a cesspool must be prevented by different means, by coercive laws or taxing devices that make it cheaper for the polluter to treat his pollutants than to discharge them untreated. We have not progressed as far with the solution of this problem as we have with the first. Indeed, our particular concept of private property, which deters us from exhausting the positive resources of the earth, favors pollution. The owner of a factory on the bank of a stream — whose property extends to the middle of the stream — often has difficulty seeing why it is not his natural right to muddy the waters flowing past his door. The law, always behind the times, requires elaborate stitching and fitting to adapt it to this newly perceived aspect of the commons. . . .

How to Legislate Temperance?

Analysis of the pollution problem as a function of population density uncovers a not generally recognized principle of morality, namely: *the morality of an act is a function of the state of the system at the time it is performed.* Using the commons as a cesspool does not harm the general public under frontier conditions, because there is no public; the same behavior in a metropolis is unbearable. A hundred and fifty years ago a plainsman could kill an American bison, cut out only the tongue for his dinner, and discard the rest of the animal. He was not in any important sense being wasteful. Today, with only a few thousand bison left, we would be appalled at such behavior.

Freedom to Breed Is Intolerable . . .

If each human family were dependent only on its own resources; *if* the children of improvident parents starved to death; *if,* thus, overbreeding brought its own "punishment" to the germ line — *then* there would be no public interest in controlling the breeding of families. But our society is deeply committed to the welfare state, and hence is confronted with another aspect of the tragedy of the commons.

In a welfare state, how shall we deal with the family, the religion, the race, or the class (or indeed any distinguishable and cohesive group) that adopts overbreeding as a policy to secure its own aggrandizement? To couple the concept of freedom to breed with the belief that everyone born has an equal right to the commons is to lock the world into a tragic course of action. . . .

Conscience Is Self-eliminating

It is a mistake to think that we can control the breeding of mankind in the long run by an appeal to conscience. Charles Galton Darwin made this point when he spoke on the centennial of the publication of his grandfather's great book. The argument is straightforward and Darwinian.

People vary. Confronted with appeals to limit breeding, some people will undoubtedly respond to the plea more than others. Those who have more children will produce a larger fraction of the next generation than those with more susceptible consciences. The difference will be accentuated, generation by generation.

Pathogenic Effects of Conscience

The long-term disadvantage of an appeal to conscience should be enough to condemn it; but it has serious short-term disadvantages as well. If we ask a man who is exploiting a commons to desist "in the name of conscience," what are we saying to him? What does he hear? — not only at the moment but also in the wee small hours of the night when, half asleep, he remembers not merely the words we used but also the nonverbal communication cues we gave him unawares? Sooner or later, consciously or subconsciously, he senses that he has received two communications, and that they are contradictory: (1, the intended communication) "If you don't do as we ask, we will openly condemn you for not acting like a responsible citizen"; (2, the unintended communication) "If you *do* behave as we ask, we will secretly condemn you for a simpleton who can be shamed into standing aside while the rest of us exploit the commons." . . .

Mutual Coercion Mutually Agreed Upon

The social arrangements that produce responsibility are arrangements that create coercion, of some sort. Consider bank robbing. The man who takes money from a bank acts as if the bank were a commons. How do we prevent such action? Certainly not by trying to control his behavior solely by a verbal appeal to his sense of responsibility. Rather than rely on propaganda we follow Frankel's lead and insist that a bank is not a commons; we seek the definite social arrangements that will keep it from becoming a commons. That we thereby infringe on the freedom of would-be robbers we neither deny nor regret. . . .

Coercion is a dirty word to most liberals now, but it need not forever be so. As with the four-letter words, its dirtiness can be cleansed away by exposure to the light, by saying it over and over without apology or embarrassment. To many, the word coercion implies arbitrary decisions of distant and irresponsible bureaucrats; but this is not a necessary part of its meaning. The only kind of coercion I recommend is mutual coercion, mutually agreed upon by the majority of the people affected.

To say that we mutually agree to coercion is not to say that we are required to enjoy it, or even to pretend we enjoy it. Who enjoys taxes? We all grumble about them. But we accept compulsory taxes because we recognize that voluntary taxes would favor the conscienceless. We institute and (grumblingly) support taxes and other coercive devices to escape the horror of the commons.

An alternative to the commons need not be perfectly just to be preferable. With real estate and other material goods, the alternative we have chosen is the institution of private property coupled with legal inheritance. Is this system perfectly just? As a genetically trained biologist I deny that it is. It seems to me that, if there are to be differences in individual inheritance, legal possession should be perfectly correlated with biological inheritance — that those who are biologically more fit to be the custodians of property and power should legally inherit more. But genetic recombination continually makes a mockery of the doctrine of "like father, like son" implicit in our laws of legal inheritance. An idiot can inherit millions, and a trust fund can keep his estate intact. We must admit that our legal system of private property plus inheritance is unjust — but we put up with it because we are not convinced, at the moment, that anyone has invented a better system. The alternative of the commons is too horrifying to contemplate. Injustice is preferable to total ruin.

Recognition of Necessity

Perhaps the simplest summary of this analysis of man's population problems is this: the commons, if justifiable at all, is justifiable only under conditions of low-population density. As the human population has increased, the commons has had to be abandoned in one aspect after another.

First we abandoned the commons in food gathering, enclosing farm land and restricting pastures and hunting and fishing areas. These restrictions are still not complete throughout the world.

Somewhat later we saw that the commons as a place for waste disposal would also have to be abandoned. Restrictions on the disposal of domestic sewage are widely accepted in the Western world; we are still struggling to close the commons to pollution by automobiles, factories, insecticide sprayers, fertilizing operations, and atomic energy installations. . . .

Every new enclosure of the commons involves the infringement of somebody's personal liberty. . . .

The only way we can preserve and nurture other and more precious freedoms is by relinquishing the freedom to breed, and that very soon. "Freedom is the recognition of necessity" — and it is the role of education to reveal to all the necessity of abandoning the freedom to breed. Only so, can we put an end to this aspect of the tragedy of the commons.

Before we turn to mainstream economic analyses, mention should be made of an apocalyptic strain of writing that was popular in the early 1970s, a strain very different from the radical but gentle writing of Aldo Leopold. Kenneth Boulding's 1966 paper, The Economics of the Coming Spaceship Earth, in Environmental Quality in a Growing Economy (H. Jarrett ed. 1971), constructed two

economic models — the cowboy and the spaceman — and concluded that the
present lay with the former but the future lay with the latter:

> The closed earth of the future requires economic principles which are some-
> what different from those of the open earth of the past. For the sake of picturesque-
> ness, I am tempted to call the open economy the "cowboy economy," the cowboy
> being symbolic of the illimitable plains and also associated with reckless, exploi-
> tative, romantic, and violent behavior, which is characteristic of open societies.
> The closed economy of the future might similarly be called the "spaceman" econ-
> omy, in which the earth has become a single spaceship, without unlimited reser-
> voirs of anything, either for extraction or for pollution, and in which, therefore,
> man must find his place in a cyclical ecological system which is capable of contin-
> uous reproduction of material form even though it cannot escape having inputs of
> energy. The difference between the two types of economy becomes most apparent
> in the attitude towards consumption. In the cowboy economy, consumption is
> regarded as a good thing and production likewise; and the success of the economy
> is measured by the amount of the throughput from the "factors of production," a
> part of which, at any rate, is extracted from the reservoirs of raw materials and
> noneconomic objects, and another part of which is output into the reservoirs of
> pollution. If there are infinite reservoirs from which material can be obtained and
> into which effluvia can be deposited, then the throughput is at least a plausible
> measure of the success of the economy. The gross national product is a rough
> measure of this total throughput. It should be possible, however, to distinguish that
> part of the GNP which is derived from exhaustible and that which is derived from
> reproducible resources, as well as that part of consumption which represents efflu-
> via and that which represents input into the productive system again. Nobody, as
> far as I know, has ever attempted to break down the GNP in this way, although it
> would be an interesting and extremely important exercise, which is unfortunately
> beyond the scope of this paper.
>
> By contrast, in the spaceman economy, throughput is by no means a desi-
> deratum, and is indeed to be regarded as something to be minimized rather than
> maximized. The essential measure of the success of the economy is not production
> and consumption at all, but the nature, extent, quality, and complexity of the total
> capital stock, including in this the state of the human bodies and minds included
> in the system. In the spaceman economy, what we are primarily concerned with
> is stock maintenance, and any technological change which results in the mainte-
> nance of a given total stock with a lessened throughput (that is, less production and
> consumption) is clearly a gain. This idea that both production and consumption
> are bad things rather than good things is very strange to economists, who have been
> obsessed with the income-flow concepts to the exclusion, almost, of capital-stock
> concepts. [Environmental Quality in a Growing Economy, at 3.]

Boulding's sketch of the future was followed by neo-Malthusian eco-dis-
aster scenarios, sponsored by the Club of Rome, a private international group
concerned with population and pollution. D. H. Meadows, D. L. Meadows, J.
Randers & W. Behrens, The Limits to Growth (1972), argued that the exponential growth rates of population and of industrial production (and thus pollution)
would soon press the finite limits of the planet Earth, with catastrophic declines
in the welfare of all. The models used in The Limits to Growth were based on
J. Forrester, World Dynamics (1971). The Limits to Growth produced a spate of
critical responses. See, e.g., Kaysen, The Computer That Printed Out

W＊O＊L＊F, 50 For. Aff. 660 (1972), and P. Passell & L. Ross, The Retreat from Riches (1973). (A similar document, A Blueprint for Survival, appeared in the January 1972 issue of the British Ecologist.) The collapse thesis was thoroughly reevaluated in Thinking about the Future (1973), edited by H. S. D. Cole, C. Freeman, M. Jahoda & K. L. R. Pavitt, an interdisciplinary team from the University of Sussex, in England. Heller, Coming to Terms with Growth and the Environment, in Energy, Economic Growth and the Environment 3 (S. Schurr ed. 1972), is a thoughtful examination of the positive relationship that might exist between economic growth and pollution control.

In 1971-1972 a schism developed among members of the apocalyptic school over the question of whether it would be population growth or technology that would cause the coming eco-crisis. The protagonists were Paul Ehrlich, for Malthus, and Barry Commoner, for technology — the new devil. Ehrlich's work includes The Population Bomb (1970), (with A. Ehrlich) Population, Resources, Environment (1972) and The End of Affluence (1974). Commoner's thesis was stated in The Closing Circle (1971). The Ehrlich-Commoner debate is set forth in Ehrlich & Holdern, Book Review, 14 Environment 24 (April 1972) (reviewing The Closing Circle), and Commoner, Book Review (ibid. at 25, replying to Ehrlich and Holdern). The first chapter of the first major environmental law casebook, E. Hanks, A. Tarlock & J. Hanks, Environmental Law and Policy (1974), largely is devoted to presenting the issues outlined above, and most of the sources listed above, along with questions and comments, can be found there. The most complete impartial review of the issues is T. O. Riordan, Environmentalism 37-84 (1980 ed.). A useful short critical analysis of the Club of Rome model is J. E. Meade, Economic Policy and the Threat of Gloom, in The Economics of Environmental and Natural Resources Policy 9 (J. Bullin ed. 1981). Krier and Gillette, in The Uneasy Case for Technological Optimism, 84 Mich. L. Rev. 405 (1985), present a thoughtful argument for reopening the debate about the ability of technology, as promoted and constrained by markets and government intervention, to solve environmental problems.

Attention to these problems will increase in the next decade because environmental protection has become a global issue and there will be increased attention to the deterioration of global commons. The official assessment of the United States government of world environmental problems can be found in two documents, The Global 2000 Report to the President (1980) and Global Future: Time to Act, Report to the President on Global Resources, Environmental Quality (1981), by the Council on Environmental Quality and the United States Department of State. The Global 2000 Report identified as principal global problems continued global population growth; food shortages; continued reliance on fossil fuels with the adverse results of acid rain and the possibility of elevated CO_2 levels, which would make the earth's climate warmer; and destruction of croplands, grasslands, and rain forests. The United States's interest in solving these problems, which was defined in both altruistic and self-interested terms, included (1) the loss of tropical forest products, (2) "accelerated erosion and situation from deforested watersheds [that] are undercutting development assistance investments in agriculture and water supply projects, many financed by the United States" (Global 2000 Report at xxxvii), and (3) worldwide political disruption caused by the migration of "ecological refugees" from depleted crop forest and rangelands." The report of the World Commission on Environment and Development, Our Common Future (1987) rejects the earlier disaster scenarios and argues that sustainable development ideas will both do economic justice and eliminate the root causes of environmental degradation.

2.   The Classic Model of Environmental Problems

Economists who turned their attention to environmental quality problems unanimously started from the premise that environmental quality was simply another example of a resource that had become scarce because demand exceeded supply. For economists, clean air, clean water, or wilderness was the same as any other resource, be it exercise bicycles or blue corn chips and yogurt: how much clean air, clean water, or wilderness should there be, compared with alternative possibilities such as industrial waste disposal sinks, mines, or ski resorts? Economists also generally agree that in an ideal world these resource allocation choices can be made most efficiently and fairly through the operation of the free market economy. See H. Macaulay & B. Yandle, Environmental Use and the Market (1977). Consumers would vote with their dollars to allocate resources between wilderness and ski resorts or levels of risk exposure just as they decide between Coke and Seven-Up; no one, however, asserts that the market is currently capable of doing this. The reason for the failure of the market to allocate resources efficiently is the tragedy of the commons. Below are two widely accepted analyses that represent the view of the consensus about the lessons of welfare economics for environmental quality. The first sets out the standard explanation of neo-welfare economics that environmental problems are an example of market failure. The second carries forward the market failure analysis but challenges the conventional treatment of pollution in welfare economics, arguing that pollution is not an isolated problem but rather is a pervasive feature of modern industrial production.

F. ANDERSON, A. KNEESE, P. REED, R. STEVENSON & S. TAYLOR, ENVIRONMENTAL IMPROVEMENT THROUGH ECONOMIC INCENTIVES
3-4, 22-26 (1977)

The concepts which must be understood before the connection between environmental problems and the economy is clear are the role of prices in allocating resources, the damaging environmental consequences of the free use of valuable resources that as yet have no prices, and the manner in which these resources can be given prices. In a market economy, which the United States still enjoys in a modified form, prices perform the key function of allocating all types of resources — raw materials, production capacity, goods, services — to their most efficient use. When the markets in the economy are functioning properly, the price each resource can command is equal to the value of other resources that are used in producing it. In an economically efficient market, it is not possible to produce an additional unit of a good without reducing the production of another good. One individual cannot be given more of any good without someone else getting less.

However, many environmental resources are still unpriced and remain outside the market. Because ownership rights have not been assigned to them, and because they are not easily broken up into units that can be bought and sold, such valuable environmental assets as watercourses, the air mantle, landscape features, and even silence are "used up," but their use is not accurately reflected in the price system. Economists describe the harms caused by such as "externalities," because the burden of the resources consumed falls on society at large, not just on the user who actually consumes them.

Usually such resources are consumed on a first-come, first-served basis — industrial air pollution spoils clear, breathable air; upstream polluters preclude downstream uses; noisy transportation and construction crowd out silence; and discarded beverage containers litter a community's open spaces. It is true that joint, non-exclusive uses may sometimes be possible. But such common property resources as clean air, open spaces, and even sunlight are increasingly scarce because of preemptive uses that do not take into account the fairness and overall social desirability of the choices made. . . .

The success of the market system in allocating resources efficiently depends upon the maximization of individual self-interests by producers and consumers. A firm will pick that output or combination of outputs which maximizes its profits. Similarly, consumers allocate their incomes so that they acquire the greatest total satisfaction from the bundle of goods which is consumed.

Externalities frequently lead to a breakdown in the performance of market mechanisms. Externalities have obvious visible effects on that class of nonmarket goods known as environmental amenities — clean air, clean water, peace and quiet, and open space. They affect the allocation of many other goods and services, including the harvest of fish from the oceans, traffic flow on urban highways, and the production of petroleum from jointly owned pools.

In order that the maximization of individual self-interest lead to the efficient allocation of resources, four basic assumptions must be satisfied. First, the individual units of production and consumption must be small compared to the overall size of each market; economists refer to this as a competitive situation. (By way of contrast, when one unit of production controls all output in a market, a monopoly situation exists.) Second, producers and consumers must be fully informed as to present and future prices. Third, there must be no externalities; that is, the activities of an individual economic agent acting alone must not affect the costs or satisfaction experienced by another. Fourth, there must be free entry into a profitable activity and free exit from an unprofitable activity. In reality, none of these assumptions is fully satisfied in a typical market economy. . . .

In a competitive market setting with many producers and consumers, an individual producer or consumer has no control over the key cog in the system, the prices of goods and services. Each individual producer or consumer pays the market price for those things he wishes to purchase and accepts the market price for those things he wishes to sell. It is easy to see that a producer will decide how much of his products to make by comparing the market price for those products with the costs of production. Consider a farmer engaged in the production of wheat. Suppose the principal variable under the control of the farmer is the amount of fertilizer that he will apply to his fixed quantity of land. (Labor, seed, machinery, and other inputs are assumed fixed.) . . .

Let us assume that the cost of applying fertilizer consists of a fixed cost of application of $5 per acre, plus $5 for each ton of fertilizer used. Other costs of operation, such as labor, taxes, seed, and insurance, amount to $65 per acre. Wheat is sold for $3 per bushel.

The profit-maximizing farmer will increase his use of fertilizer until profits reach a maximum. This occurs when 3 tons of fertilizer are used and a profit of $20 per acre is earned. . . . Notice that profits increase as long as the costs associated with the use of each additional ton of fertilizer fall short of the corresponding gain in revenue contributed by the ton of fertilizer. Economists term the incremental cost of the fertilizer its marginal factor cost . . . , and the incremental increase in revenue the marginal revenue product (or equivalently, the value of the marginal product of the fertilizer). . . . Technically then, more of an input is purchased until the marginal cost of the input, which is just the input price in a competitive market setting, equals the marginal revenue product derived from the input. . . .

When all users of fertilizer make similar profit-maximizing calculations, the total available supply of fertilizer is said to be allocated efficiently. For each farmer, or other user of fertilizer, the last units applied bring forth a quantity of additional output just equal to the value of fertilizer which is used. There would be no way to reallocate fertilizer applications to produce outputs which would have a higher value to society.[2]

Now let us turn to the issue of externalities. Suppose that the farmer's fertilizer does not all remain in the soil, that in fact some of it dissolves in runoff

---

2.   This situation is often referred to as a "Pareto optimum," named for Vilfredo Pareto, a prominent Italian economist and social theoretician. Pareto optimality has been demonstrated to result from exchange in theoretical, competitive market models which contain labor markets, markets for raw materials, markets for intermediate goods, and markets for consumer goods; in other words, for a reasonably complete if highly abstract characterization of the functions performed in an actual economy. The basic paper is by K. J. Arrow & G. Debreu, "Existence of an Equilibrium for a Competitive Economy," Econometrica vol. 22, no. 3 (1954). A summary of the literature is printed in Hukukane Nikaido, Convex Structures in Economic Theory (New York, Academic Press, 1968).

from heavy rains and pollutes downstream water supplies. Suppose that the downstream pollution caused by the fertilizer in the runoff costs the users of the water supply approximately $3 for every ton of fertilizer applied to each acre. Because the farmer does not pay this cost, he does not factor the $3 into his profit-maximizing computations. The consequence is that from the viewpoint of society as a whole, too much fertilizer is being used. If the farmer were made to pay the pollution cost of runoff contaminated with fertilizer, for instance, if the stream were private property and he had to pay legal damages, he would use less fertilizer. As shown in Table 1-1, the marginal factor cost of each ton of fertilizer used would be increased from 5 to 8. Since the marginal revenue product from the second ton (9) is greater than the marginal cost, but the marginal revenue from the third ton (6) is less, the farmer's optimal use would be only 2 tons per acre. The third ton yields the farmer a private profit of $1, but when a charge equal to the extra social cost of pollution is added, he would incur a loss of $2 on the third ton.

As we have seen . . . , with fertilizer at $5 a ton, the farmer's profit is maximized at 3 tons of fertilizer per acre. The social damage, or externalities, of using this amount of fertilizer is $9 (3 tons × $3 damages per ton); therefore the net social benefit is $11 ($20 per acre profit − $9 damage). When a pollution tax is added to the fertilizer cost, bringing it up to $8 per ton, the farmer's profit is maximized at 2 tons of fertilizer per acre and the social damage is reduced to $6 (Table 1-1). The tax revenue yielded on 2 tons of fertilizer is $6 and the net social benefit is thus $13 ($13 profit − $6 social damage + $6 tax). Thus a pollution tax of $3 per ton of fertilizer encourages the farmer to reduce his use of fertilizer by 1 ton and produces a social gain of $2, an optimal result. Who enjoys the gain depends on how the tax revenues are distributed.

TABLE 1-1
(Costs and Revenues with External Costs Internalized)

1 Fertilizer Tons Per Acre	2 Fertilizer Cost	3 Total Cost	4 Marginal Factor Cost	5 Bushels of Wheat Per Acre	6 Total Revenue	7 Marginal Revenue Product	8 Profit
0	0	65		25	75		10
1	13	78	13	30	90	15	12
2	21	86	8	33	99	9	13
3	29	94	8	35	105	6	11
4	37	102	8	36	108	3	6

A. KNEESE, R. AYRES & R. D'ARGE, ECONOMICS AND THE ENVIRONMENT: A MATERIALS BALANCE APPROACH
2-6 (1970)

Externalities and Economic Theory

Economic theory has long recognized in a limited way the existence of "common property" problems and resource misallocations associated with them. It was early appreciated that when property rights to a valuable resource could not be parceled out in such a way that one participant's activities in the use of that resource would leave the others unaffected, except through market exchange, unregulated private exchange would lead to inefficiencies. These inefficiencies were of two types: those associated with "externalities" and those associated with "user costs." The former term refers to certain broader costs (or benefits) of individual action which are not taken into account in deciding to take that action. For instance, the individual crude petroleum producer, pumping from a common pool, has no market incentive to take account of the increased cost imposed on others because of reduced gas pressure resulting from his own pumping. Also, because he cannot be sure that a unit of petroleum he does not exploit now will be available for his later use, acting individually he has no reason to conserve petroleum for later and possibly higher value use. Thus he has no incentive to take account of his user cost. The only limit to his current exploitation is current cost — not the opportunity cost of future returns. Consequently the resource will be exploited at an excessively rapid rate in the absence of some sort of collective action. While these problems were recognized with respect to such resources as petroleum, fisheries, and groundwater, and there was rather sophisticated theorizing with respect to them, still private property and exchange have been regarded as the keystones of an efficient allocation of resources.

To quote the famous welfare economist Pigou:

> When it was urged above, that in certain industries a wrong amount of resources is being invested because the value of the marginal social net product there differs from the value of the marginal private net product, it was tacitly assumed that in the main body of industries these two values are equal.[2]

And Scitovsky, another important student of externalities, after having described his cases two and four, which deal with externalities affecting consumers and producers respectively, says: "The second case seems exceptional, because most

----

2.   A. C. Pigou, Economics of Welfare (The Macmillan Co., 1952). Even Baumol who saw externalities as a rather pervasive feature of the economy, tends to discuss external diseconomies like "smoke nuisance" entirely in terms of particular examples. W. J. Baumol, Welfare Economics and the Theory of the State (Harvard University Press, 1967). A perspective more like that of the present book is found in K. W. Kapp, The Social Costs of Private Enterprise (Harvard University Press, 1950).

instances of it can be and usually are eliminated by zoning ordinances and industrial regulations concerned with public health and safety. . . . The fourth case seems unimportant, simply because examples of it seem to be few and exceptional.[3]"

It is the main thesis of this book that at least one class of externalities — those associated with the disposal of residuals resulting from modern consumption and production activities — must be viewed quite differently.[4] In reality they are a normal, indeed inevitable, part of these processes. Their economic significance tends to increase as economic development proceeds, and the ability of the natural environment to receive and assimilate them is an important natural resource of rapidly increasing value.[5] We suggest below that the common failure to recognize these facts in economic theory may result from viewing the production and consumption processes in a manner which is somewhat at variance with the fundamental physical law of conservation of mass.

Modern welfare economics concludes that if (1) preference orderings of consumers and production functions of producers are independent and their shapes appropriately constrained, (2) consumers maximize utility subject to giv-

---

3.   T. Scitovsky, "Two Concepts of External Economies," The Journal of Political Economy, Vol. 62 (Apr. 1954), pp. 143-51.

4.   We by no means wish to imply that this is the only important class of externalities associated with production and consumption. Also, we do not wish to imply that there has been a lack of theoretical attention to the externalities problem. In fact, the past few years have seen the publication of several excellent articles which have gone far toward systematizing definitions and illuminating certain policy issues. Of special note are R. H. Coase, "The Problem of Social Cost," Journal of Law and Economics, Vol. 3 (Oct. 1960) pp. 1-44; O. A. Davis and A. Whinston, "Externalities, Welfare, and the Theory of Games," Journal of Political Economy, Vol. 70 (June 1962), pp. 241-62; J. W. Buchanan and G. Tullock, "Externality," Economica, Vol. 29 (Nov. 1962), pp. 371-84; and R. Turvey, "On Divergencies between Social Cost and Private Cost," Economica, Vol. 30 (Nov. 1963), pp. 309-13. However, all these contributions deal with externality as a comparatively minor aberration from Pareto optimality in competitive markets and focus upon externalities between two parties. Mishan, after a careful review of the literature, has commented on this as follows:

> The form in which external effects have been presented in the literature is that of partial equilibrium analysis; a situation in which a single industry produces an equilibrium output, usually under conditions of perfect competition, some form of intervention being required in order to induce the industry to produce an 'ideal' or 'optimal' output. If the point is not made explicitly, it is tacitly understood that unless the rest of the economy remains organized in conformity with optimum conditions, one runs smack into Second Best problems.

E. J. Mishan, "Reflections on Recent Developments in the Concept of External Effects," The Canadian Journal of Economics and Political Science, Vol. 31 (Feb. 1965), pp. 1-34.

5.   That external diseconomies are integrally related to economic development and increasing congestion has been noted in passing in the literature. Mishan has commented: "The attention given to external effects in the recent literature is, I think, fully justified by the unfortunate, albeit inescapable, fact that as societies grow in material wealth, the incidence of these effects grows rapidly. . . ." Mishan, "Reflections." And Buchanan and Tullock have stated that as economic development proceeds, "congestion" tends to replace "cooperation" as the underlying motive force behind collective action, i.e., controlling external diseconomies tends to become more important than cooperation to realize external economies. J. W. Buchanan and G. Tullock, "Public and Private Interaction under Reciprocal Externality," in J. Margolis, ed., The Public Economy of Urban Communities (Johns Hopkins Press for RFF, 1965), pp. 52-73.

en income and price parameters, and (3) producers maximize profits subject to these price parameters, then a set of prices exists such that no individual can become better off without making some other individual worse off. For a given distribution of income this is an efficient state. Given certain further assumptions concerning the structure of markets, this "Pareto optimum" can be achieved via a pricing mechanism and voluntary decentralized exchange.

If the capacity of the environment to assimilate residuals is scarce, the decentralized voluntary exchange process cannot be free of uncompensated technological external diseconomies unless (1) all inputs are fully converted into outputs, with no unwanted material and energy residuals along the way, and all final outputs are utterly destroyed in the process of consumption, or (2) property rights are so arranged that all relevant environmental attributes are in private ownership and these rights are exchanged in competitive markets. Neither of these conditions can be expected to hold in an actual economy, and they do not.

Nature does not permit the destruction of matter except by annihilation with antimatter, and the means of disposal of unwanted residuals which maximizes the internal return of decentralized decision units is by discharge to the environment, principally watercourses and the atmosphere. Water and air are traditionally examples of free goods in economics. But in reality in developed economies they are common property resources of great and increasing value, which present society with important and difficult allocation problems that exchange in private markets cannot solve. These problems loom larger as increased population and industrial production put more pressure on the environment's ability to dilute, chemically degrade, and simply accumulate residuals from production and consumption processes. Only the crudest estimates of present external costs associated with residuals discharge exist, but it would not be surprising if these costs were already in the tens of billions of dollars annually. Moreover, as we shall emphasize again, technological means for processing or purifying one or another type of residuals do not destroy the residuals but only alter their form. Thus, given the level, patterns, and technology of production and consumption, recycle of materials into productive uses or discharge into an alternative medium are the only general operations for protecting a particular environmental medium such as water. Residual problems must be seen in a broad regional or economy-wide context rather than as separate and isolated problems of disposal of gaseous, liquid, solid, and energy waste products.

Standard economic treatments of environmental quality include W. Baumol & W. Oates, The Theory of Environmental Policy (2d ed. 1988), and A. Freeman, R. Haveman & A. Kneese, The Economics of Environmental Quality (1973). The literature up to 1976 is surveyed in Fisher & Peterson, The Environment in Economics, 14 J. Econ. Literature 1 (1976). A useful summary of the content of an undergraduate environmental economics course is contained in Rooney, Environmental Economics, 1 U.C.L.A.J. Envtl. L. & Poly. 47 (1980).

3. The Application and the Relevance of Economic Analysis

Economic analyses of environmental quality problems are seductively powerful because they not only purport to explain the cause of the problem but they purport to justify legislative and judicial intervention to solve the problem and specify the proper means of intervention. What more could one ask for? Further, because welfare economics accepts the legitimacy of current patterns of production and consumption, neither its explanations nor its prescriptions for change are radical. Yet although the application of economic analysis is increasingly accepted and often legislatively mandated, economic analysis remains controversial, posing two distinct questions. First, how effectively can economic prescriptions be applied? No matter how elegant various explanations and models are, it is not always clear that the data necessary to utilize the models can be collected in order to produce resource allocations superior to those being made by means of messy political and administrative processes. The second and broader question is, how relevant is economic analysis per se? We start by looking at some of the problems of application and then will turn to questions of relevance.

4. The Application of Classic Welfare Economic Models to Environmental Problems

Why is pollution not the sign of an efficient allocation of resources? Residual discharges that cause injury to human health or property are generally called "negative externalities" by economists. Externalities may also be positive, such as a pleasing view over underdeveloped tracts of land or the reduction of a risk. Although conceptually both types of externalities are simply different manifestations of incomplete property rights, practically the classification is important because, generally speaking, in the first instance we want to discourage certain activities and in the second we want to provide incentives that will result in the maintenance or the increase of certain other activities. For the time being, we will explore the legal relevance of negative externalities.

Let us start with two basic situations. First, B's factory emits a residual that damages A's crops and A's health. Second, A opens up a thin-crust pizza restaurant but B opens up a Chicago-style pizza restaurant across the street and attracts all of A's customers, driving A out of business. In recent years, society has deemed that the factory owner should be subjected to sanctions, but, in the second case, except in certain special circumstances, society applauds B and shows little sympathy for A. But could one argue that in both cases A is the victim of a negative externality and hence is entitled to some form of legal redress? Two of the early giants of modern welfare economics, Marshall and Pigou, thought that two such cases were the same, but in 1931 Jacob Viner introduced a distinction that has influenced economists ever since. Viner divided externalities into those that are technological and those that are pecuniary and, more importantly, argued that society need only worry about the former. Technological externalities are potentially undesirable because they may signal a misallocation of resources. In the case of residual technological discharges, the discharger may shift part of the cost of producing a good to third parties, who in effect, subsidize the cost of production by absorbing the negative externality without charge. Thus, the ultimate price charged for the good may be understated because it does not reflect all the relevant externalities (see Buchanan & Stubblebine, Externality, 29 Economica 371 (1962)), because there is a potential divergence between private and social cost. The same has been said not to be true with respect to pecuniary externalities — not to worry because "the implied gains in efficiency are adequately signaled by the input price, and profit maximizing levels by . . . firms are socially efficient." Bator, The Anatomy of Market Failure, 72 Q.J. Econ., 351 (1958). In recent years, some economists have reflected the technological-pecuniary distinction but still conclude that the external effects of price competition are not a cause for social concern, if only because it would be inefficient to run an economic system that guaranteed first entrants into the market the right to retain customers. Demsetz, Some Aspects of Property Rights, 9 J.L. & Econ., 61 (1966). See further Mishan, The Post-War Literature on Externalities: An Interpretive Essay, 9 J. Econ. Literature 1 (1971).

   Must the polluter pay? It is tempting to conclude that if a technological negative externality exists the discharger must assume responsibility for all of the social costs of his activity; in short, the polluter must pay. A few economists and many lawyers have drawn this conclusion from new-welfare economics, but the normative conclusion does not flow from the theory of negative externalities because it rests on two assumptions that may be unwarranted. First, lawyers schooled in the law of torts usually argue that A, the factory owner, has caused injury to B and thus is prima facie liable, especially under modern theories of liability without fault. Second, it is widely assumed that all negative externalities are bad because they are inefficient. In a seminal article, The Problem of Social Cost 3 J.L. & Econ. 1 (1960), Ronald Coase argued that it is wrong to think in terms of one party causing harm to another. According to Coase, the problem is bilateral rather than unilateral because externalities arise when two parties, whose resource uses are incompatible with each other, compete for the right to use the same resource. Coase contended that competing parties are likely to negotiate an efficient allocation of resources, if expensive litigation can be avoided. Coase's argument has not gone unchallenged. Mishan, Pareto, Optimality and the Law, 19 Oxford Econ. Papers (N.S.) 255 (1967), and Mishan, the Economics of Disamenity, 14 Nat. Resources J. 55 (1974), mount a detailed technical argument to show that an optimal allocation depends on the existing assignment of rights ("existing law") and that the costs of reaching an ideal solution also depend on the existing assignment of rights. Jules Coleman has advanced the argument that Coase was wrong in denying the existence of nonreciprocal causal claims, but right in arguing that cause is not a per se justification for state intervention. J. Coleman, Markets, Morals and the Law

76-81 (1988). Thus, one should worry about who is liable. We return to this problem in Chapter 6.

The Natural Resources Journal for 1973-1974 contains a symposium on the Coase thesis. A number of the articles, e.g., Samuels, The Coase Theorem and the Study of Law and Economics, 14 Nat. Resources J. 1 (1974), point out one of the troubling aspects of the Coase thesis. To focus exclusively on efficiency, one must be indifferent to distributional effects on various solutions, and these effects vary according to the preexisting assignment of property rights. But cf. Demsetz, When Does the Rule of Liability Matter? 1 J. Legal Stud. 13 (1972).

Does choosing whether an area should be designated a wilderness area represent the same type of choice as choosing between Coke and Seven-Up? Is willingness to pay the only criterion for allocating resources? Neo-welfare economics assumes that consumers can measure their preferences rationally when confronted with a range of choices. Measurement is possible because properly established market prices will accurately reveal the value a consumer attaches to a product. If this analysis holds true for problems such as wilderness preservation, a wilderness area should be designated by Congress only if people are willing to pay more for this land use compared with all other possible land uses. The lack of a market for wilderness areas is no excuse for failing to use opportunity cost (the value foregone as the result of a resource allocation) as the criterion for choice. In recent years, economists have devoted some effort to constructing shadow prices for various environmental goods. However, if wilderness is different, perhaps need cannot be measured by means of the price system but only can be revealed as a value preference. One of the earliest preservations of natural areas was advanced by the economist John V. Krutilla in an article entitled Conservation Reconsidered, 57 Am. Econ. Rev. 777 (1967). He argued that public intervention to preserve unique natural environments, especially when development would produce irreversible change, was economically justified in order to prevent future shortages caused by a progressive change in taste favoring amenities. It was rational to "purchase" a present option for future use:

> Another reason for questioning the allocative efficiency of the market for the case in hand has been recognized only more recently. This involves the notion of option demand. This demand is characterized as a willingness to pay for retaining an option to use an area or facility that would be difficult or impossible to replace and for which no close substitute is available. Moreover, such a demand may exist even though there is no current intention to use the area or facility in question and the option may never be exercised. If an option value exists for rare or unique occurrences of nature, but there is no means by which a private resource owner can appropriate this value, the resulting resource allocation may be questioned. [57 Am. Econ. Rev. at 780.]

Krutilla subsequently explored the technical problems of developing a dynamic model of valuing option demand and tried to test it by applying it to several case studies. J. Krutilla & A. Fisher, The Economics of Natural Environments; Studies in the Valuation of Commodity and Amenity Resources (1975). Does the concept of option demand provide a complete justification for programs such as endangered species protection? Consult Hanemann, Economics and the Preservation of Biodiversity, in Biodiversity 193 (E. Wilson ed. 1988); Randall, What Mainstream Economists Have to Say about Biodiversity, id. at 217; and Norton, Commodity, Amenity, and Morality, The Limits of Quantification in Valuing Diversity, id. at 200.

Krutilla's article stimulated a rebuttal to his argument, which in turn triggered a number of interesting justifications for preserving natural areas and protecting environmental quality generally. In a provocatively titled piece, What's Wrong with Plastic Trees? 179 Science 446 (1973), Martin Krieger argued that just as people can be educated to prefer wilderness, people could be educated to accept low-cost artificial environments in place of high-cost natural areas. As one might expect, in response to the question "What's wrong with plastic trees?" Krieger answered "very little," because "more can be done with plastic trees to give most people the feeling that they are experiencing nature." This argument is profoundly disturbing to environmentalists. Professor Lawrence Tribe of Harvard University went far beyond Aldo Leopold's sturdy midwestern theory of respect for nature's power to a tentative theory, rooted in pantheism or, more accurately, panpsychism (a theory that accords all objects in the universe an inner or psychological being), of a social order based on equal dignity under the law for all aspects of nature:

> What is crucial to recognize is that the human capacity for empathy and identification is not static; the very process of recognizing *rights* in those higher vertebrates with whom we can already empathize could well pave the way for still further extensions as we move upward along the spiral of moral evolution. It is not only the human liberation movements — involving first blacks, then women, and now children — that advance in waves of increased consciousness. The inner dynamic of every assault on domination is an ever broadening realization of reciprocity and identity. Viewed from a slightly different perspective, new possibilities for respect and new grounds for community elevate both master and slave simultaneously, reaffirming the truth that the oppressor is among the first to be liberated when he lifts the yoke, that freedom can be realized only in fidelity to obligation.
>
> A passage in Faulkner's Absalom, Absalom! may hold the key: "Maybe happen is never once but like ripples maybe on water after the pebble sinks, the ripples moving on, spreading, the pool attached by a narrow umbilical water-cord to the next pool. . . ." But there are some shores too remote for even these concentric circles to reach in the foreseeable future. When it is urged that legal protection be extended to nonliving entities like canyons and cathedrals, not for our sake but for theirs, it may be precisely such distant shores at which we are asked to gaze. Saint Francis of Assisi could embrace Brother Fire and Sister Water, but Western societies in the last third of this century may be unable to entertain seriously the notion that a mountain or a seashore has intrinsic needs and can make independent moral claims upon our designs. [Tribe, Ways Not to Think about Plastic Trees: New Foundations for Environmental Law, 83 Yale L.J. 1315, 1345 (1974).]

Tribe's attempt to refute the Krieger thesis caught the attention of a young philosopher. In On Preserving the Natural Environment, 84 Yale L.J. 205

(1975), Mark Sagoff found that Tribe's attempts to transcend the homocentric perspective of a Western civilization failed because in the end Tribe's proposal was simply a plea for including more votes for environmental quality in any utilitarian-based calculations. Sagoff went on to propose that a constitutional right to the natural environment be recognized based on the "concept of nationhood, the structure created by the Constitution as a single instrument functioning in all its parts" (84 Yale L.J. at 266). Why? Because areas such as a wilderness are symbols of our cultural tradition and the values we respect. Whether this ingenious argument, based both on the history of America's recognition of the value of wilderness and modern theories of aesthetics, is good constitutional law is doubtful. See Tribe, From Environment Foundations to Constitutional Structures: Learning from Nature's Future, 84 Yale L.J. 545 (1975), and pp. 779-780 *infra*. For our purposes, what is directly relevant is that Sagoff, recycled as an environmental policy analyst, built on his earlier work to construct the following argument that willingness to pay is irrelevant in resource allocation choices in which environmental values are at stake.

SAGOFF, ECONOMIC THEORY AND ENVIRONMENTAL LAW
79 Mich. L. Rev. 1393, 1411-1412 (1981)

[According to Sagoff, the willingness-to-pay argument is based on a logical category-mistake:]

This confusion involves what logicians call a category-mistake.[80] One makes a category-mistake by treating facts or concepts as if they belong to one logical type or category, when they actually belong to another. Several examples are illustrative. It is logically correct to predicate whiteness of snow or even of coal. (It may not be true, but it is intelligible.) To say that the square root of four is white, however, makes no sense because it is impossible meaningfully to predicate color of a number. When two concepts are in different categories, one cannot measure the first by methods that are appropriate only to the second. Similarly, although the average American household may consist of 2.75 individuals, this does not mean that such a household exists somewhere in America. A person who inquires about the address of the average American family asks an absurd question, and commits a category-mistake.

Private and public preferences also belong to different logical categories. Public "preferences" do not involve desires or wants, but opinions or beliefs. They state what a person believes is best or right for the community or group as a whole. These opinions or beliefs may be true or false, and we may meaningfully ask the individual for the reasons that he or she holds them. But an economist who asks how much citizens would pay for opinions that they advocate

---

80. For a technical explanation of the concept of a category-mistake, see Ryle, Categories, in Essays on Logic and Language 65 (A. Flew ed. 1953). For a less technical treatment, see G. Ryle, The Concept of Mind 16-18 (1966).

through political association commits a category-mistake. The economist asks of objective beliefs a question that is appropriate only to subjective wants.

When an environmentalist argues that we ought to preserve wilderness areas because of their cultural importance and symbolic meaning, he or she states a *conviction* and not a *desire*.[83] When an economist asserts that we ought to attain efficient levels of pollution, he or she, too, states a belief. Both beliefs are to be supported by arguments, not by money. One cannot establish the validity of these beliefs by pricing them, nor can that mechanism measure their importance to society as a whole. One can judge how strongly people hold their beliefs by asking how much they would pay to see them implemented, but that is not how we make policy decisions. Those who think that Creationism should be taught in the public schools, for example, are able to raise a lot of money. But the amount of money that partisans raise does not demonstrate the merit of their position. A person who wants his or her child taught a particular doctrine is free to pay for that; willingness to pay may correctly measure the strength of that desire. When a person advocates a policy as being right or appropriate for society as a whole, however, the intensity of the desire is no longer relevant. Rather, advocates must present arguments that convince the public or its representatives to adopt a policy.[84] Political decision makers judge ideas on their merits, and make decisions based on what is good for us all. These policymakers may consider economic factors, but they should not use the economic method to evaluate competing beliefs.

The distinction between public and private interests is indispensable to the study of political philosophy. "To abolish the distinction," as one commentator has written, "is to make a shambles of political science by treating things that

---

83.   Society rests on shared convictions, which, like Plato's "good lie," hold it together as a society. See Plato's Republic 42-62 (G. Grube trans. 1974). Convictions about nature — about what is "pure" and what is "dangerous," what counts as "safe" and what as "pollution" — are shared beliefs of this sort. These convictions rest on meaning and symbol systems that constitute our common cultural heritage and distinguish it, say, from the Balinese or Lele cultures. Anthropologists have argued that it is impossible for a society to replace these meaning or symbol systems with a system of objective economic and scientific analysis:

> We should be able to see that we can never ask for a future society in which we can only believe in real, scientifically proved pollution dangers. We *must* talk threateningly about time, money, God and nature if we hope to get anything done. We must believe in the limitations and boundaries of nature which our community projects."

M. Douglas, Implicit Meanings 245-46 (1975). I have argued elsewhere that one reason to preserve wilderness is that the distinction between it and civilization is crucial to our culture: that to destroy our remaining wilderness would be to destroy an important basis for this distinction and, therefore, an important basis of our common culture. See Sagoff, On Preserving the Natural Environment, 84 Yale L.J. 205 (1974).

84.   For example, when Professor Friedman advocated a voucher system in education . . . no one asked him how much he would pay to see that policy implemented. The question would have been inappropriate because he was not expressing a consumer preference; a voucher system would probably not affect his children. Rather, he was proposing what he thought would be good for society. He was presenting an idea, to be judged on its merits, concerning what we should do about public education. It is my thesis that cost-benefit analysis has no plausible way of assessing ideas of this kind or taking them into account.

are different as if they were alike." Markets are the appropriate arena for the competition of private interests. This competition may best be understood and regulated in terms of individual willingness to pay. When one advocates not a special or private interest but what one describes as the public interest or the interest of all, however, the framework of debate completely changes. Public discussion must then be carried on in public terms.

———————————

What obligations, if any, are owed to future generations? A major justification for many environmental policies is that the present consumption of resources should be limited to protect the interests of future generations. Considerable controversy exists among philosophers about whether rights can be possessed by unidentifiable (unborn) individuals and thus whether any duties or moral obligations are owed to those yet to come. See Kavka, The Paradox of Future Individuals, 11 Phil. & Pub. Aff. 93 (1982), and Parfit, Future Generations: Future Problems, 11 Phil. & Pub. Aff. 113 (1982). Norton, Environmental Ethics and the Rights of Future Generations, 4 Envtl. Ethics 319 (1982), speculates about the possibilities for a new theory of rights for future generations outside our tradition of rights limited to the protection of *individual* interests. The result reached in the debate about the rights of future generations is important for the question that constantly confronts policymakers: How should present as opposed to future consumption be valued? Heal, Economics and Resources, in Economics of Environmental and Natural Resources Policy 62 (J. A. Butlin ed. 1981), discusses the two dominant approaches to this question:

> [T]here are two frameworks within which economists have worked when approaching this, the Utilitarian and the Rawlsian — the latter named after John Rawls, the present Professor of Philosophy at Harvard, whose work A Theory of Justice is probably known to many of you. The Utilitarian approach would suggest that a depletion rate ought to be chosen so as to maximize the sum of the benefits from resource use accruing to all generations, present and future. Though sounding rather abstract, this is the kind of approach that can be made operational within the conventional framework of cost-benefit analysis, and indeed has been made operational in this way on many occasions. One of the issues that has to be faced in thus making it operational, is how to weight the various benefits accruing at different dates when adding them up. For example, if we have benefits of 100 units in each of the next thirty years, do we declare their sum to be 30×100? Or do we adopt a more complex approach, giving different weights to benefits in different years? If we were to follow the kind of approach which individuals seem implicitly to follow in making their own economic decisions, then we would give benefits occurring in the future less weight than those occurring at present, the differential in the weights increasing with the degree of futurity. This is a practice economists refer to as *discounting* future beliefs. . . .
>   . . . This utilitarian approach to defining an optimal depletion rate would then have us choose that policy giving the highest sum of appropriately-discounted benefits. The role of discount rates is worth emphasizing, because the Utilitarian approach is the one usually chosen by governments, and whenever they operate it they have, explicitly or implicitly, to choose a discount rate. The UK government does this quite explicitly, and chooses a rate of about 10 percent, sometimes a little

higher. This implies that 10 percent is deducted from the value of a benefit for each year of futurity, and the destructive power of such a rate is remarkable: if one discounts at 10 percent for each year of futurity, £100 in 1984 is worth only £37 today, by 1994 it is worth only £13.50, and by the end of the century it is hardly worth having, at £7.42. Do you really believe that £100 to our children is only worth £7.42 as far as we are concerned?

. . . Rawls, in his unusually ambitious book A Theory of Justice (1972), enunciates, and attempts to justify and spell out the implications of, what he regards as the two principles of justice. These are that: Each person is to have an equal right to the most extensive total system of equal basic liberties compatible with a similar system of liberty for all.

This is a widely-acceptable nostrum, and certainly not one that is at issue here. More relevant is the second principle, which requires that: Social and economic inequalities are to be arranged so that they are both (a) to the greatest benefit of the least advantaged, consistent with the just savings principle, and (b) attached to offices and positions open to all under conditions of fair equality of opportunity. . . .

Pursuing this approach, then, an optimal resource-depletion rate is one so chosen as to maximize the benefits from resource-use that will accrue to that generation who will receive the smallest such benefits: in other words, which maximizes the benefits accruing to that intertemporal group which will receive minimum benefits. Now, fairly obviously, the identity of the group which will receive minimum benefits from a depletion policy will change as that policy changes: under very rapid depletion policies, it will be a far-distant group, but under a very strict conservation ethic it might be the present generation. It follows from this that in identifying an optimum, in this Rawlsian sense, one has to follow a two-stage procedure: firstly, for each possible depletion policy, identify the least-advantaged group, and, secondly, then select that policy whose least-advantaged group is best treated. In case this should sound unpleasantly complex, and indeed so complex as to violate by earlier requirement that our approaches should yield operational criteria, let me reassure you on this point. It can be shown that if we carry out this two-stage search procedure, then what we will eventually identify is in fact beautifully simple: we shall in the end select that depletion rate which gives the highest *sustainable* level of consumption of those outputs for which resources constitute essential inputs. Paraphrasing this, we shall select the highest-possible *steady* consumption rate in those areas dependent on resource-use. Although the precise manner in which this rabbit emerges from the hat may not be clear — reasonably so, as the detailed argument is very complex — it is perhaps not too difficult to grasp the point intuitively: the Rawlsian criterion manifests a strong concern for intergenerational equity, and its implication is that all generations should be treated equally — for this is of course what is involved in choosing a steady, sustainable consumption path. [Economics of Environmental and Natural Resources, at 64, 66-68.]

Weiss, The Planetary Trust: Conservation and Intergenerational Equity, 11 Ecology L.Q. 495 (1984) is an interesting approach to the problem that uses the public trust concept as a basis for intergenerational equity. Professor Weiss has expanded her argument in In Fairness to Future Generations: International Law, Common Patrimony, and Intergenerational Equity (1989).

The validity of option demand for preservation decisions has also been questioned by a group of economists who argue that our public lands have been managed inefficiently and that it would be better to privatize them by auctioning them off to the highest bidder, including environmental groups. See Gardner, The Case for Divestiture, in Rethinking the Federal Lands 156 (S. Brubaker ed. 1983) and Private Rights and Public Lands (P. Truluck ed. 1983).

In recent years economists have worked to develop an accurate method of estimating the shadow price of resource values. The method currently in vogue is contingent valuation. See R. Cummings, D. Brookshire & W. Schulze, Valuing Public Goods: The Contingent Valuation Method (1985) and Knetsch and Sinden, Willingness to Pay and Compensation Demanded: Experimental Evidence of an Unexpected Disparity in Measures of Value, 76 Q. J. Economics 507 (1984). The ethical questions increase when the subject is freedom from risk rather than the value of a resource under different conditions of development or management.

5. *Cost-Benefit Analysis*

Every decision to promote environmental quality at the expense of some other objective is an allocation choice. Thus, every choice to promote environmental quality has an opportunity cost — the value of the foregone alternative. *The* question that has plagued decisionmaking and those affected by decisions is whether such allocation choices can be made rationally. As we have seen, one school denies the possibility of a rational choice because, it is argued, there are no objective criteria by which most environmental choices can be evaluated. See further Rogers, Benefits, Costs and Risks: Oversight of Health and Environmental Decisionmaking, 8 Ecology L.Q. 473 (1980). The opposite argument, of course, is that objective criteria exist. Money is the most obvious candidate, but other proxies have been explored. Proponents of the possibility of rational choice place great reliance on cost-benefit analysis. In the environmental sphere, cost-benefit analysis was originally a tool used to judge the comparative merits of alternative flood control and reclamation project investments. The U.S. Army Corps of Engineers and the Bureau of Reclamation in the Department of Interior gained considerable experience with the use of cost-benefit analysis to evaluate water resource projects. See Liroff, Cost-Benefit Analysis in Federal Environmental Programs, in Cost-Benefit Analysis and Environmental Regulations 35 (D. Schwartzman, R. Liroff & K. Crolce eds. 1982). Two well-written analyses of the use of cost-benefit analysis in the water resources field are R. McKean, Efficiency in Government through System Analysis (1958), and Prest & Turvey, "Cost-Benefit" Analysis: A Survey, 75 Econ. J. 683 (1965). For a recent survey of the status of the technique see J. Kampen, Benefit, Cost, and Beyond (1988).

The application of cost-benefit analysis to resource allocation decisions is straightforward: The analysis produces a ratio of benefits to costs for a proposed project. Investment in a project, such as a flood control project, is considered justified if the cost-benefit ratio is in excess of $1.00. In cost-benefit jargon, the ratio in this case is considered to be in excess of "unity." Decisionmakers also use cost-benefit analysis to make choices among alternative projects. Absent countervailing considerations, the project having the highest cost-benefit ratio should be selected.

Before we consider the major philosophical issues raised by cost-benefit analysis, a brief description of the uses and procedures of the technique is in order.

DORFMAN, INTRODUCTION, IN MEASURING BENEFITS OF GOVERNMENT INVESTMENTS
1, 4-7 (R. Dorfman ed. 1965).

Incentives for Government Enterprise

Governments rush in where businessmen decline to tread. As a general rule, if a good or a service is desirable, it will also be profitable and thus will be provided by private enterprise. But there are important exceptions to this rule. Government initiative is, for example, called for in cases where investments that businessmen would deem unprofitable are socially worthwhile. These exceptions can arise from a number of circumstances: some relate to the conditions under which a product is distributed and consumed; some to the conditions of its production; some have other justifications.

Conditions of consumption. The circumstances that favor government provision cluster around the concept of collectability or, rather, uncollectability. In the usual economic transaction, the user is charged for the good or service he consumes, the amount he is willing to pay measures the value of the commodity to him, and, since his use of the commodity precludes anyone else from benefiting from it, the value of the commodity to the user is also its value to the entire society. This standard analysis of social value is not strictly valid for any transaction (there are always side effects), and for a few types of transactions it is too wide of the mark to be acceptable. The most important of these latter cases are (1) collective goods and (2) goods that are characterized by external economies of consumption: in neither case is the provider of the good able to collect from beneficiaries a charge commensurate with the benefits conferred.

In general, a *collective good* is a facility or service that is made freely available to all comers without user charge, either because to assess a charge on each occasion of use would be excessively cumbersome or because use is not voluntary or even clearly definable. It is, for example, not feasible or desirable to levy a charge on every shipmaster who sees a lighthouse, on every householder whose door the patrolman passes, or on every housewife when a health officer inspects a food market.

With rare exceptions, collective goods cannot be provided by private firms, because they do not induce a flow of income to the provider. Therefore the responsibility for providing them falls frequently — but not invariably — to the government. In addition to the examples cited above, some important collective goods are national defense, civil and criminal justice, streets and most highways, and outdoor recreational facilities. Other significant categories include the findings of scientific research, since even patents usually do not enable the scientist or his employer to collect from beneficiaries more than a portion of the benefits conferred, and aesthetic amenities, such as a fine building or a landscape that confers benefits on passersby for which they cannot be assessed. The important feature of collective goods for our purpose here is that, since they are not sold, there are no market prices to assist in appraising their value.

Collective goods are allied to *external economies of consumption* but the latter come into being in a different way. When a man is treated for a communicable disease the relief afforded him is only part of the social value; every resident of his community benefits from the reduced danger of infection. When a high school student is dissuaded from leaving school, his neighbors receive benefits (among them a reduction in potential delinquency) over and above the direct benefit to the boy and his family. In other words the consumer of a good or service is not the sole beneficiary, and the amount he is willing to pay does not measure the entire value of the good to society. The act of consumption, in effect, creates a collective good. In such instances it may be socially desirable to provide the good, although the amounts collectable from direct users do not suffice to cover production costs. Market prices are not, in those cases, adequate measures of social value.

Conditions of production. The circumstances that conduce to government initiative relate to economies of scale. Some activities can be performed economically only on such a very large scale that for private enterprise to undertake them is infeasible or undesirable. For example, without invoking governmental power, it is not practicable to assemble the large areas of property required for highways, urban redevelopment, or hydroelectric projects. Some natural monopolies, such as water supply, are retained by the government as an alternative to regulating private development. It is probable, however, that whatever the condition of production the government would not undertake a project unless important collective goods or external benefits were involved.

Other incentives. The supposition that private investors may take an unduly short view of the consequences of their investments is an important justification for all investments having to do with the preservation of natural resources and their orderly exploitation. It is pertinent also to investments in urban renewal and improvements. In a way, the justification is related to the collective goods theme: there is little reason to believe that current prices for urban property or rural woodlands reflect adequately the importance of these depletable resources to future generations. Society as a whole may assign quite different values to such resources than do the participants in current markets.

And sometimes government undertakings are stimulated by an incentive of a very different sort: the desire to influence the distribution of income. The desire for a regional redistribution, for example, is one of the explicit motivations for the Appalachia Program, and the desire for socioeconomic redistribution plays a large role in urban renewal programs. Appraising the social value of such redistributions presents peculiarly difficult problems.

Formulas for Comparing Benefits and Costs

As the above discussion of incentives suggests, the government tends to intervene in precisely those markets in which prices are either lacking or are seriously divergent from social values. It is inherent in government enterprises, therefore, that market prices cannot be used in appraising their social contributions. Still, some economic basis is needed for judging which potential government undertakings are worthwhile and which are not. Benefit-cost analysis provides this basis.

Benefit-cost analysis is closely analogous to the methods of investment project appraisal used by businessmen. The only difference is that estimates of social value are used in place of estimates of sales value when appropriate. There are in use a number of slightly different formulas for comparing benefits and costs of government undertakings; two of the most popular ones are sketched below.

The starting point of any of the formulas is a projection of the physical output of the undertaking, either in each year of its life or in some typical year of operation. If the undertaking is a highway, for example, there would have to be estimates of the number of passenger-car miles, truck miles, and bus miles to be traveled on it in each year or in a typical year. Next, there would have to be estimates of the unit social value of each of these physical outputs, be they passenger-car miles, kilowatt hours, or whatever. These two estimates induce at once an estimate of the gross social contribution of the enterprise in a single year.

At this point the different formulas begin to diverge. One approach is to perform the gross benefit calculation for a typical year and to make a parallel computation for social costs in a typical year. The costs consist of two major components: current costs — the typical year expenditures for operating and maintaining the facilities; and capital costs — a charge levied against a year's operations to amortize the initial expenses of construction and installation. The ratio of gross annual benefits to total annual costs is the benefit-cost ratio. This formula amounts to a businessman's calculation of the ratio of sales to cost of goods sold, or of a profit-sales ratio, except, of course, that the value of output used in a benefit-cost computation is the social, rather than the market, value.

An alternative formula subtracts current costs in each year, or in a typical year, from gross benefits to obtain an estimate of current net benefits. The current net benefits for each year are discounted back to the date of inception of the project and added up to obtain an estimate of the present value of discounted net benefits. The ratio of this figure to the estimated capital cost of the project is then the benefit-cost ratio. This formula is therefore analogous to a businessman's calculation of the rate of profit that can be earned by capital invested in the undertaking.

Recent attempts to mandate rationality in government regulation include mandated cost-benefit processes. The current procedure is outlined in Exec. Order 12,291, 46 Fed. Reg. 13,193, reprinted in 5 U.S.C. §601. See Note, Regulatory Analyses and Judicial Review of Informal Rulemaking, 91 Yale L.J. 739 (1982). Agencies are required, to the extent permitted by law, to (1) refrain from adopting regulations unless potential benefits outweigh costs, (2) choose the objective that maximizes net benefits to society, (3) select alternatives that impose the least cost on society, and (4) set regulatory priorities that maximize net benefits to society, taking into account the national economy and the problems of specific industries. Enforcement is delegated to the Office of Management and Budget (OMB), which has the power to force an agency to suspend the publication of a regulation — unless publication is mandated by a statute or a court — until OMB has reviewed the regulation, the agency has made its response, and the OMB's comments and the agency's response have been made part of the rule-making record. In 1982 the Senate passed legislation adopting most of the requirements of executive order. 5 U.S.C. §601. See Rosenberg, Presidential Control of Agency Rulemaking: An Analysis of Constitutional Issues That May Be Raised by Executive Order 12,291, 23 Ariz. L. Rev. 1199 (1981), and Costle, Environmental Regulation and Regulatory Reform, 57 Wash. L. Rev. 409 (1982). But see E. Mishan, Cost-Benefit Analysis 310-311 (1971). See pp. 84 to 85, Chapter 2, for a discussion of the constitutional and administrative law issues by the application of cost-benefit analysis by OMB.

Policy questions about the use of cost-benefit analysis permeate this casebook. We consider the relationship between cost-benefit relationship and environmental impact statements in Chapter 7; we study the feasibility of incorporating "soft" variables such as aesthetic enjoyment into the cost-benefit equation in Chapter 3; the perhaps impossible task of putting a dollar value on human life and health is taken up in Chapters 3 and 4; and finally, the relationship between cost-benefit analysis and agency duties and privileges to consider economic reasonableness in setting regulations and varying their effects is discussed in Chapters 3 and 4.

As you consider the problems of implementing cost-benefit analysis, keep in mind the following important questions. Is cost-benefit analysis a mechanical procedure, or is it a process? For example, if an agency concludes that a proposed action has a ratio in excess of unity, must it implement the regulation or must it only consider the costs and benefits of the proposed action? What is gained by forcing a decisionmaker to analyze a problem in cost-benefit terms even if he is not bound by the formal logic of cost-benefit analysis? It has been suggested that cost-benefit analysis is undemocratic because it delegates the power to make value judgments to an elite rather than to the public. See Green, Cost-Risk-

Benefit Assessment and the Law: An Introduction and Perspective, 45 Geo. Wash. L. Rev. 901 (1977), Lovins, Cost-Risk-Benefits Assessments in Energy Policy, 45 Geo. Wash. L. Rev. 911 (1977), and Tribe, Policy Science: Analysis or Ideology? 2 Phil. & Pub. Aff. 66 (1972).

A NOTE ON ALTERNATIVE ECONOMIC AND PROPERTY RIGHTS THEORIES

Although Western thought has increasingly rejected the theory of human dominance over nature, many environmentalists have looked to Marxism and Eastern philosophy for the basis of a new environmental ethic, one based on stewardship. Those who view the roots of resource misuse in the system of private property have been attracted to formal Marxist theory, which posits that social production will promote environmental values (England & Bluestone, Ecology and Social Conflict, in Toward a Steady-State Economy 198 (H. Daly ed. 1973). However, the mounting evidence of severe environmental degradation in the Soviet Union and in other eastern European countries does not lead one to be optimistic about the idea that state planning is a better way of promoting an environmental ethic. See M. Goldman, The Spoils of Progress (1974). Many have found Eastern religions and philosophy attractive; humanity is seen as a part of nature, not above it, and thus consumption is limited to promote community stability. See Schumacher, Buddhist Economics, in Economics, Ecology, Ethics: Essays toward a Steady-State Economy 138 (H. Daly ed. 1973). But one need not go beyond the United States for an influential theory of the proper relationship between man and nature. The respected architectural historian Vincent Scully, in his book Pueblo: Mountain, Village, Dance (1975), joins many other observers of the American Indian in praising the Indian's deep respect for nature:

> Something true and clear, massively unsentimental, runs through all their works, and this is, at bottom, the relationship between men and nature that they all embody and reveal. In this they occupy a clear position in relation to the fundamental problem of human life: how to get along — which means in the end how to live and die — with the natural world and its laws. [Pueblo: Mountain, Village, Dance, at 4.]

Environmentalists have been attracted to Indian communal traditions, including traditions of land use. In contrast with theories of property that confer on present occupants an exclusive right of enjoyment (the law of waste aside), Indians feel that they hold the property they control in trust for past and future generations and thus use resources conservatively. See, e.g., Large, This Land Is Whose Land?: Changing Concepts of Land as Property, 1973 Wis. L. Rev. 1039. Recent scholarship indicates that Indian attitudes toward nature cannot simply be described in terms of contemporary conservation or ecological perspectives. See, e.g., C. Martin, Keepers of the Game: Indian-Animal Relationships and the Fur Trade (1978), and Regan, Environmental Ethics and the Ambiguity of the Native American's Relationship with Nature, in All That Dwell Therein 206 (T. Regan ed. 1982). Still, it is argued that environmental ethics can be learned from the Indians. See Callicott, Traditional American Indian and Western European Attitudes toward Nature: An Overview, 4 Envtl. Ethics 293 (1982). A Yale University historian has provided support for this thesis in a book that describes the way in which the New England colonists altered the landscape and the ecology of the region. With respect to the Indians' use of resources, W. Cronan, Changes in the Land: Indians, Colonists, and the Ecology of New England 53 (1983), writes:

> The relationships of the New England Indians to their environment, whether in the north or the south, revolved around the wheel of the seasons: throughout New England, Indians held their demands on the ecosystem to a minimum by moving their settlements from habitat to habitat. As one of the earliest European visitors noted, "They move . . . from one place to another according to the richness of the site and the season." By using other species when they were most plentiful, Indians made sure that no single species became overused. It was a way of life to match the patchwork of the landscape. On the coast were fish and shellfish, and in the salt marshes were migratory birds. In the forests and lowland thickets were deer and beaver; in cleared upland fields were corn and beans; and everywhere were the wild plants whose uses were too numerous to catalog. For New England Indians, ecological diversity, whether natural or artificial, meant abundance, stability, and a regular supply of the things that kept them alive.
>
> The ecological relationships which the English sought to reproduce in New England were no less cyclical than those of the Indians; they were only simpler and more concentrated. The English too had their seasons of want and plenty, and rapidly adjusted their false expectations of perpetual natural wealth to match New World realities. But whereas Indian villages moved from habitat to habitat to find maximum abundance through minimal work, and so reduce their impact on the land, the English believed in and required permanent settlements. Once a village was established, its improvements — cleared fields, pastures, buildings, fences, and so on — were regarded as more or less fixed features of the landscape. English fixity sought to replace Indian mobility; here was the central conflict in the ways Indians and colonists interacted with their environments. The struggle was over two ways of living and using the seasons of the year, and it expressed itself in how two peoples conceived of property, wealth, and boundaries on the landscape.

Before one argues for a "trust" theory built upon Indian traditions, one must ponder the Indians' fatalistic view of nature — respect is not so much a choice as fate. See Paul Horgan's masterpiece, Great River: The Rio Grande in American History (1954). Consider Scully's description of the Santo Domingo hunting dance:

> Santo Domingo's hunting dance of late February is this continent's most searching mystery play. As Greek drama grew out of the animal chorus of Dionysus, so here Thespis, in the person of the buffalo, is just on the brink of stepping forward as a tragic hero who will say no to fate and nature's law. . . .

The long plaza was crowned with its long cornices of watchers on the roofs in rich mulberry reds, purples, blues, and greens. The earth color of the abode is thus set off and the architectural frame is finally completed as it is meant to be. Below, in the dance, the mood is Aeschylean. What occurs is truly awful. The proud kings are brought low, but worse than this, they betray each other and try to flee like the poor antelope, and in the end, weapons and all, are butchered like the others and carried as meat away.

So it is the maiden who conquers. She remains queen despite the heroes' challenge, and she is always untouched, gentle, and impassive. Nature personified, tyrant mistress of all, the true, ancient pòthnia thèron [an ancient deity to whom bulls were sacrificed], she gives her orders to her horned consorts with the touch of her feathered evergreen bough, waits for one instant to see that they are carried out, and then goes her way; ordering all, demanding all, reconciling all, healing, commanding, and leading each animal and hunter to his fated rendezvous and to his ending. [Pueblo: Mountain, Village, Dance, at 195, 204-205]

Are the Indians right? Would the student be better advised to drop this course, return the book to the bookstore and devote herself to the study of Gibbon, accompanied by Bach?

D.   INSTITUTIONAL RESPONSES

In the past two decades, governments in this country and throughout the world have responded to the argument that an environmental perspective, however defined, can offer meaningful principles for policy formulation for all questions of physical resource allocation. See, e.g., C. Enloe, The Politics of Pollution in a Comparative Perspective: Ecology and Power in Four Nations (1975). The environmental perspective, it is argued, provides a common denominator that allows decisionmakers to see similar issues in diverse resource allocation problems, and *more importantly*, the perspective offers a generally acceptable hierarchy of values decisionmakers can use when making difficult allocation choices. For an early and influential formulation of this argument, see L. K. Caldwell, Environment: A New Focus for Public Policy, 23 Policy Admin. Rev. 301 (1963), and Caldwell's later book, Environment: A Challenge to Modern Society (1971). Bartlett, Ecological Rationality: Reason and Environmental Policy, 8 Envtl. Ethics 221 (1986) compares and contrasts ecological rationality — the rationality of biogeochemical systems — with other forms of rationality — economic, legal, and political — and argues for the need to fully integrate ecological rationality with other modes of decisionmaking.

Just what the environmental perspective is and what it offers the student of government is, however, not easy to define. From the point of view of government organization, there is some theoretical consensus that one should take a holistic, ecological view of resource problems. If you take a substance out of the environment at point A but put it back in at point B, has any benefit been achieved? From the point of view of public policy, there is now widespread agreement that as a society we should be more careful about using air, land, and watersheds as sinks for the disposal of residuals and more careful about the application of technology, such as nuclear power and inorganic chemicals.

M'Gonigle, The Tribune and the Tribe: Toward a Natural Law of the Market/Legal State, 13 Ecology L.Q. 233 (1986), is an interesting attempt to apply communitarian ideals to environmental issues. See also Farber, From Plastic Trees to Arrow's Theorem, 1986 Ill. L. Rev. 337; and Sagoff, Where Ickes Went Right *or* Reason and Rationality in Environmental Law, 14 Ecology L.Q. 265 (1987).

1.   *Federalism and Individual Freedom*

Federalism is a theme that resonates through the cases in this casebook. The environmental decade occurred near the end of a century in which power became more and more centralized in the federal government. The controversy surrounding the expanding role of the federal government is one of the — if not *the* — major themes of recent U.S. history. Given the geographical and ethnic diversity of this country, the balance among various levels of government in various parts of the country will always be subject to great tension. Thus, it is inevitable that the forces that led to centralization would be met by other forces counterpressing for decentralization. Environmental regulation nicely mirrors this tension. The central feature of most environmental regulations is uniform national quality standards; but Congress has tried to respond to "federalism" concerns by assigning the states major roles in carrying out national mandates. As you encounter different arguments that "federalism" principles are relevant to the outcome of a specific dispute, it is useful to try to define this most overworked term. "Federalism" interests are often advanced by persons whose ox has been gored by national regulation, so in the cases it is not easy to separate valid from spurious constitutional concerns. Some of the most important fundamental questions include:

1. Do we have a federal system at all? Diamond, The Federalist on Federalism: "Neither a National nor a Federal Constitution, But a Composition of Both," 86 Yale L.J. 1273 (1977), argues:

> The Federalist was operating with a typology, so to speak, composed of two fundamental modes of political organization, the federal and the national. The founders thought that they had combined these two fundamental modes or "elements" into a "compound" system. We disagree and think, instead, that they invented a third fundamental mode or element, which we call federal government. In so thinking, we are operating with a typology composed of three elemental forms: confederation, federal government, and national or unitary government. The difference between our thinking and that of the founders evidently turns on the distinction that we make, and they did not, between confederalism and federalism. That familiar distinction will be found in almost all contemporary writing

on federalism. But The Federalist and the whole founding generation saw no more difference between confederalism and federalism than we see, say, between the words inflammable and flammable. . . .

. . . While we have largely rejected his theory of the concurrent majority, we have nonetheless taken over Calhoun's tripartite framework and the elemental status it assigns to federal government. Many scholars have, of course, been perfectly aware that the founding generation conceived their handiwork differently than Calhoun did and we do. But the difference has not been taken seriously. Either there has been a patronizing assumption that our understanding has scientifically superseded theirs, or the difference has been shrugged off as a mere matter of their having their terminology and we ours. But this is surely too serious a matter to be so quickly dismissed; if The Federalist is analytically right in its compound view, then we have lost ground in our understanding of federalism. [86 Yale L.J. at 1274, 1276.]

See also Diamond, The Ends of Federalism, 3 Publicus 133 (Fall 1973)

2. At what geographical level of government should environmental decisions be made? Stewart, Pyramids of Sacrifice? Problems of Federalism in Mandating State Implementation of National Policy, 86 Yale L.J. 1196 (1977), suggests that the vices of centralized regulation are (1) the impairment of self-determination and accountability, and (2) the moral repugnancy generated by making sacrifices on the local level in order to realize elite ideals. The values of decentralized decisionmaking "include the greater sensitivity of local officials to the preferences of citizens and the cost of achieving environmental goals in a given locality; the diffusion of governmental power and the promotion of cultural and societal diversity; and the enhancement of individual participation in an identification with governmental decisionmaking" (86 Yale L.J. at 1231).

3. If responsibility for implementing a program is to be shared, how should it be shared? In a perceptive article, two public policy analysts characterize the national government's vision of federalism as "managerial federalism," which "in practice has increasingly relegated the states to a role of administrative instruments in a national system." Leman & Nelson, The Rise of Managerial Federalism: An Assessment of Benefits and Costs, 12 Envtl. L. 980, 1012 (1982). For an examination of the tensions this sharing of responsibility has caused in environmental programs, see Lyons, Federalism and Resources Development: A New Role for the States? 12 Envtl. L. 931 (1982) (Surface Mining Control and Reclamation Act), and L. Lake, Environmental Regulation, The Political Effects of Implementation (1982). After reading this casebook, can you suggest better ways institutions can share the responsibility of deciding how resources are used?

2.   Beyond Federalism and Individual Freedom

As we have discussed earlier, at its extreme the environmental perspective is said to require a static society, in which population growth and economic growth are sharply curtailed and man evolves to new and higher levels of spiritual awareness, discarding the modern goals of growth and aggressive consumption and replacing them with a preference for a steady state existence; the neoclassical welfare economist's assumption that consumer preferences are fixed and revealed by relative prices is replaced with a theory of preferences based on externally defined needs.

Today the essence of environmentalism, broadly defined, is the subordination of individual choice to community choice. Thus environmentalism goes against the grain of deeply held values. In our society, the core idea of individual dignity has been extended to property held by individuals, and the idea of subordination of individual property to the state has long been associated with arbitrary governmental action. More people have agreed with Blackstone's statement that "[so] great moreover is the regard of the law for private property, that it will not authorize the least violation of it; no, not even for the general good of the whole community" 1 W. Blackstone, Commentaries on the Law of England 139 (Lippincott ed. 1879) than with the qualification he and the great Lord Coke agreed should be placed on exclusive control: All property is limited "by the law of the land." See Whelan, Property as Artifice: Hume and Blackstone, in Property, Nomos XXII 101, 118-120 (J. Pennock & J. Chapman eds. (1980).

As the famous statements of Blackstone and Coke well illustrate, the subordination of the individual to the community has been alien to the Anglo-American political and legal tradition since the seventeenth century. A dominant assumption has been that individual self-interest and community values are not inconsistent; political debate in this country as well as in Europe has, of course, centered on whether this assumption is or should be true. It is not our purpose to teach the history of Western political and intellectual thought, although many of the questions considered in these materials ultimately must be related to larger spheres of thought. Rather, our more modest purpose is to ask why, in the political arena, the subordination of individual choice to community choice is now said to be a necessary and appropriate way to make resource use choices.

The institutional reforms that follow from a modern welfare economics analysis are appealing precisely because they represent no intrusions into the individualistic values around which our industrial society is organized; value is determined exclusively by individual choice. However, many serious students of environmentalism have drawn much darker and chilling imperatives from the consequences of human intervention in ecosystems, population growth projections, and impending critical resource shortages. In fact, much neo-Malthusian writing comes close to asking whether man's abuse of the earth is analogous, under the Christian doctrine, to man's committing original sin, from which there is no earthly redemption. Analyses that stop short of this nihilistic answer nonetheless make fundamental criticism of existing forms of political and economic organization and suggest profound changes that are so costly morally and economically that one can ask if environmental redemption is possible or desirable. Starting from the premise that "the essential message of ecology is *limitation*," political scientist William Ophuls argues that our values and political organization are ill suited to cope with environmental imperatives. Like other environmentalists, he is led to a vision of a steady state society in which ecological aristocrats will lead us to a social organization in which communalism and politics will replace individualism and the market. The market will be replaced by resource "stewardship," and individuals will be asked to adopt cultural norms of modesty, diversity, holism, and "genuine morality, as opposed to a purely instrumental set of ethics." In contrast with this proposed set of ethics is the present destructive hedonism, which Ophuls finds spiritually barren. What are the social costs of this higher and transcendent society? In the following excerpt, Ophuls considers the question of whether such a society is compatible with democratic values as we have evolved them from the Hebrews and the Greeks.

W. OPHULS, ECOLOGY AND THE POLITICS OF SCARCITY
159-163 (1977)

Democracy versus Elite Rule: The Issue of Competence

One of the key philosophical supports of democracy is the assumption that people do not differ greatly in competence; for if they do, effective government may require the sacrifice of political equality and majority rule. Indeed, under certain circumstances democracy *must* give way to elite rule; as the eminent political scientist and democratic theorist Robert Dahl points out, in a political association whose members "differ *crucially* in their competence, such as a hospital or a passenger ship, a reasonable man will want the most competent people to have authority over the matters on which they are most competent."

Ecological scarcity appears to have created precisely such a situation. Critical decisions must be made. Although it is true that most of them are "transscientific" in that they can only be made politically by prudent men, at least the basic scientific elements of the problems must be understood reasonably well before an informed political decision is possible. However, the average man has neither the time to inform himself nor the requisite background for understanding such complex technical problems. Moreover, he may simply not be intelligent enough to grasp the issues, much less the important features of the problems. Indeed, it is apparent that even highly attentive and competent specialists do not always understand the problems fully. Even when they do (or claim to do), they can almost always be found on both sides of any major question of public policy. (The dispute over nuclear-reactor safety is a prime example, with Nobelists lining up both for and against nuclear power.) Thus, even assuming that the politicians and people understand the issue well enough to ask the right questions, which experts should they listen to? Can they understand what the experts are saying? If we grant that the people in their majority probably will not understand and are therefore not competent to decide such issues, is it very likely that the political leaders they select will themselves be competent enough to deal with these issues? And even if they are, how can these leaders make authoritative decisions that impose heavy present costs or that violate popular expectations for the sake of future advantages revealed to them only as special knowledge derived from complicated analysis, perhaps even as the Delphic pronouncements of a computer?

Such questions about the viability of democratic politics in a super-technological age propel us toward the political thought of Plato. In The Republic, the fountainhead of all Western political philosophy, Plato argued that the polity was like a ship sailing dangerous waters. It therefore needed to be commanded by the most competent pilots; to allow the crew, ignorant of the art of navigation, to participate in running the vessel would be to invite shipwreck. Thus the polity would have to be run by an elite class of guardians, who would themselves be guided by the cream of this elite — the philosopher-kings. . . . [F]rom Aristotle on, those who have favored democratic rather than oligarchic politics have concerned themselves with keeping the political community small enough and simple enough so that elite rule would not be necessary for social survival. The emerging large, highly-developed, complex technological civilization operating at or very near the ecological margin appears to fit Plato's premises more and more closely, foreshadowing the necessity of rule by a class of Platonic guardians, the "priesthood of responsible technologists" who alone know how to run the spaceship.

Such a development has always been implicit in technology, as the ideas of Saint-Simon suggest. It is simply that its necessity has become overwhelmingly manifest in a crowded world living close to the ecological limits, for only the most exquisite care will avert the collapse of the technological consequence of ecological scarcity, major ethical, political, economic and social changes are inevitable whatever we do. The choice is between change that happens to us as a "side effect" of ever more stringent technological imperatives and change that is deliberately selected to accord with our values.

. . . During the transition to any form of steady state one can envisage it would be imperative to use physical resources as efficiently as possible, and this probably would mean greater centralization and expert control in the short term, even if the long-term goal is a technologically simple, decentralized society favorable to a democratic politics.

Even beyond the transition period, whether a steady-state society can be democratic (as we understand it) is at least questionable. A society cannot persist as a genuine democracy unless the people in their majority understand technology and ecology well enough to make responsible decisions; and although the technology of a frugal steady state should be more accessible to the common man's understanding than our own current brand is, the same may not be true of the ecological knowledge upon which the steady-state society will have to be based. Intuition and common sense alone are of little help in understanding the counterintuitive complexity of the human ecosystem — and nowhere else can a little knowledge be so dangerous. Thus, although not intrinsically mysterious, ecology is esoteric in the sense that only those whose talents and training have equipped them to be the "specialists in the general" discussed in the Introduction are likely to possess the kind of competence that would satisfy Dahl's "reasonable man." The ecologically complex steady-state society may therefore require, if not a class of ecological guardians, then at least a class of ecological mandarins who possess the esoteric knowledge needed to run it well. Thus, whatever its level of material affluence, the steady-state society will not only be more authoritarian and less democratic than the industrial societies of today — the necessity to cope with the tragedy of the commons would alone ensure that — but it will also in all likelihood be much more oligarchic as well, with only those possessing the ecological and other competencies necessary to make prudent decisions allowed full participation in the political process. . . . . C. S. Lewis observed that "What we call Man's power over Nature turns out to be a power exercised by some men over other men with Nature as its instrument," and it appears that the greater the technological power, the more absolute the political power that must be yielded up to some men by the others. Thus we must ask ourselves if continued technological growth will not merely serve to replace the so-called tyranny of nature with a potentially even more odious tyranny of men. Why indeed should we deliver ourselves over to a "priesthood of responsible technologists" who are merely technical experts and mainly lack the excellence of character and deep philosophical understanding that Plato insists his guardians must possess in order to justify their rule? In fact, why accept the rule of even a genuinely Platonic elite possessed of both wisdom and expertise, when all history teaches us that the abilities, foresight, and goodwill of mortal men are limited and imperfect? The technological response to ecological scarcity thus raises profound political issues, in particular one of the most ancient and difficult political dilemmas — quis custodiet ipsos custodes? or "Who will watch the guardians themselves?"

Technology and the Path to a Brave New World

Modern man has used technology along with energy to try to transcend nature. We have seen that it cannot be done; nature is not to be transcended by a biological organism that depends on it. Worse, the attempt to do so will have momentous political and social consequences. Far from protecting us from painful and disruptive social changes, as the technological optimist is wont to claim, continued technological growth is likely to force such changes on us. We are, in fact, in the process of making the Faustian bargain without ever having consciously decided to do so. As a result, we appear to be traveling down the road to total domination by technique and the machine, to the "Brave New World" that Aldous Huxley (1932) warned was the logical end point of a hedonistic, high-technology civilization.

Technology may not be inherently evil, but it does have side effects and it does exact a social price. Moreover, in the hands of less than perfect human beings, technology can never be neutral, as its proponents too often claim; it can only be used for good or evil. Thus technological fixes are dangerous surrogates for political decisions. There is no escape from politics.

Is this argument just another variation on Plato's philosopher-king? See Hoffert, The Scarcity of Politics: Ophuls and Western Political Thought, 8 Envtl. Ethics 5, 28 (1986). Compare the deep movement which has had a substantial influence on the increasingly powerful Green parties in Europe. Deep ecology seeks to transform social values and thus individual behavior through a "relational, total-field image of life and non-life in which diversity, complexity, autonomy, decentralization, symbiosis, egalitarianism, and classlessness are operative and which is clear and forcefully normative." Naess, The Shallow and the Deep, Long Range Ecology Movement, 16 Inquiry 95, 98 (1973). See Devall, The Deep Ecology Movement, 20 Nat. Resources J. 299 (1980); B. Devall and G. Sessions, Deep Ecology: Living as if Nature Mattered (1985) and Deep Ecology (M. Tobias ed. 1985). The consistency between deep ecology and ecological science is explored in Golley, Deep Ecology from the Perspective of Ecological Science, 9 Envtl. Ethics 45 (1987).

The general relationship between political freedom and a market economy is explored and strongly defended in C. Lindbloom, Politics and Markets (1977). Review Hardin, The Tragedy of the Commons, p. 20 *supra*. In 1974, Hardin wrote an essay, The Ethics of a Lifeboat (American Association for the Advancement of Science, 1974), in which he advocated the practice of triage by wealthy nations against the poor. Otherwise, "[i]f a poor country can always draw on the world bank in time of need, its population can continue to grow, and likewise its 'need.'" id. at 16. Compare Paul Ehrlich, who at one time advocated military action against countries that failed to curb their populations. Might refusing to toss a life preserver be counterproductive? See Revelle, The Ghost at the Feast, 186 Science 500 (1974). Even if they wanted to, could industrialized nations control the destiny of developing nations? Is the Jonah strategy consistent with stewardship of the earth's commons? See also Hardin, Second Thoughts on "The Tragedy of the Commons," in Economics, Ecology, Ethics: Essay toward a Steady-State Economy 115 (H. Daly ed. 1980). See also Potter, The Simple Structure of the Population Debate: The Logic of the Ecology Movement, in Ethics and the Environment 177 (D. Scherer & T. Attig eds. 1983). Sagoff, Can Environmentalists Be Liberals? Jurisprudential Foundations of Environmentalism, 16 Envtl. L. 775 (1986), explores the tension between assertions of environmental rights and theories of liberal democracy. See also Wandesforde-Smith, Learning from Experience, Planning for the Future: Beyond the Parable (and Paradox?) of Environmentalists as Pin-Striped Pantheists, 13 Ecology L.Q. 715 (1986). R. Paehlke, Environmentalism and the Future of Progressive Politics (1989) is a useful survey of political context of environmentalism.

E.   LEGAL RESPONSES TO THE ENVIRONMENTAL PROBLEM

1.   Common Law Actions

Generally, modern environmental law provides for a system of regulation that is command-and-control centralized. This system replaced a decentralized response system — common law tort actions brought by injured plaintiffs. From an economic or resource allocation perspective, a possible function of tort law is to force those who generate external costs to bear those costs as a means of moving toward a more efficient allocation of resources. See G. Calabresi, The Costs of Accidents (1970).

F. GRAD et al., INJURIES AND DAMAGES FROM HAZARDOUS WASTES — ANALYSIS AND IMPROVEMENT OF LEGAL REMEDIES: A REPORT TO CONGRESS IN COMPLIANCE WITH SECTION 301(e) OF THE COMPREHENSIVE ENVIRONMENTAL RESPONSE, COMPENSATION, AND LIABILITY ACT OF 1980 (P.L. 96-510) BY THE SUPERFUND SECTION 301(e) STUDY GROUP, S. REP. NO. 12, 97TH CONG., 2d SESS.
97-98, 101-102, 105-107, 110-112, 114, 116, 117 (1982)

(1) NEGLIGENCE

The cause of action in negligence is clearly available as a remedy for personal injury and property damage arising out of exposure to hazardous wastes. A private action for negligence could arise out of the improper disposal of hazardous wastes, improper transportation of such wastes, the occurrence of spills caused negligently, and the negligent causation of hazardous surface water runoff or the negligent contamination of subsurface water.

Negligence requires a breach of a duty of due care. The Restatement (Second) of Torts defines negligence as "conduct which falls below the standard established by law for the protection of others against unreasonable risk of harm. . . ." Negligence thus deals with *conduct*, rather than conditions — the defendant must be charged with having done some act, or failed to do some act he had a duty to undertake in a manner which violates a standard of care by negligence or recklessness.

Thus, to establish a cause of action in negligence, it must be shown that defendant was under a duty to conform to a standard of conduct; that he breached the established duty; that there was a reasonably close connection between the conduct and the resulting injury — i.e., that the conduct was the proximate cause of the injury; and that plaintiff suffered actual loss or damage.

A duty of care or reasonable standard of conduct may be imposed by legislative enactment or administrative regulation, or may be implied by a court from such law or regulation; this subject has been discussed in another context. Earlier judicial decisions may also establish a standard, and in the absence of more formal standards, the standard of conduct of a reasonable man under the given conditions and circumstances, will be determined by the triers of fact. . . .

(2) TRESPASS

The cause of action for trespass has some significant applications in pollution control, particularly in private actions involving air pollution and runoff of liquid wastes or contamination of percolating groundwater. However, the nature and characteristics of trespass make it less than a fully effective remedy in pollution cases and in cases involving injury or damage from hazardous [substances].

Trespass requires an interference with plaintiff's possessory interest in land — an entry on plaintiff's land, either by defendant, or by some physical or observable object which defendant has caused to enter.

The definition of trespass reflects one reason it is of limited use in hazardous waste cases. A cause of action based on trespass protects only the interest in exclusive possession of the plaintiff's property and would not apply in two situations that might be common in hazardous waste litigation. If the plaintiff is not in possession of the property, he cannot sue in trespass, and because trespass refers to invasion of property, trespass does not provide a remedy for injury unrelated to such an invasion.

As the law of trespass has developed in the United States, it has several other limitations that are obstacles to recovery in a hazardous waste case. A trespass must be intentional, negligent or result from an ultrahazardous activity; the old common law rule of strict liability for trespass based on the fact of invasion alone has been virtually abandoned. Another limitation exists in some jurisdictions that still distinguish invasions by visible or "tangible" matter from pollutants the presence of which can be proved only by scientific evidence. Although the law is changing, some of the older approaches require such visible invasions to find trespass. A limitation on the use of trespass which creates serious problems in hazardous waste cases involving contamination of percolating groundwater, is the American rule followed in most states, that a landowner is not absolutely entitled to pure percolating groundwater. The landowner must show negligence on the part of the defendant; or that the defendant had knowledge that such contamination was likely to result from the defendant's activities, or that the defendant's activity was ultrahazardous. Some courts would treat a cause of action based on negligence or ultrahazardous activity as entirely separate causes of action for negligence and strict liability, rather than for trespass, in which case the considerations raised in the discussion of negligence and strict liability would be relevant. . . .

(3) NUISANCE

(A)   PRIVATE NUISANCE

A private nuisance is an unreasonable interference with plaintiff's use and enjoyment of his land. The action for private nuisance, which may seek injunctive relief as well as damages, grows out of conditions that are disturbing and create harm in using the land. Private nuisance actions are appropriate for the interference with use and enjoyment created by noise, by odors, and other air pollution, by water pollution and the contamination or pollution of subsurface waters. The maintenance of a hazardous waste disposal site easily fits the description of a private nuisance and the threat of personal discomfort or disease interferes with the use and enjoyment of property. Such a threat to health is an appropriate basis for enjoining a private nuisance for the future, and Prosser states that "Once the invasion of the property interest is established . . . consequential damages to the possessor which result from it, such as injuries to his own health . . . may be recovered."

A private nuisance action, however, is primarily a device to obtain injunctive relief for the future, or damages for past interference with the use of property.

In situations of nuisance involving environmental pollution, the cause of action for private nuisance often blends with the cause of action for trespass, because a continuing trespass, such as the continued invasion by particulate or gaseous air pollution, may be regarded as a nuisance.

Liability for a private nuisance is often a form of strict liability, where the person who maintains a nuisance is said to be responsible regardless of fault or negligence. The issue of the responsibility of the present landowner for conditions, or the nuisance, on his land, which he did not create in the first place is likely to recur in hazardous waste nuisances, and has been discussed earlier.

The resolution of nuisance cases requires a balancing of the equities — i.e., a weighing of the plaintiff's interest against the social and economic utility of the defendant's activities that cause the interference. The generation of wastes may or may not be socially desirable, but waste disposal sites, whether or not hazardous, meet a substantial need, and the interference with plaintiff's use and enjoyment of property may not be considered unreasonable, thus adding to the difficulty of a nuisance claim.

In some jurisdictions, available defenses include "coming to the nuisance," where the location of the nuisance preceded the location of the plaintiff in the area. However, it has been held repeatedly that the fact that the waste disposal site has a government permit is not a defense against a private nuisance action.

(B)   PUBLIC NUISANCE

In spite of the similarity in the name of public and private nuisance causes of action, the public nuisance is quite distinct in its historical origin. A public nuisance is generally based on the violation of a law which characterizes certain conditions as nuisance. A public nuisance may also be more broadly defined as an unreasonable interference with a general right of the public. Among tort law experts, there was at one time a lively disagreement on whether there could ever be a public nuisance without a crime or breach of law — a dispute which was resolved by the Restatement (Second) of Torts in favor of the broader, more inclusive definitions.

Because a public nuisance interferes with a public right, it is not tied to interference with enjoyment and use of property. Moreover, because it is an interference with a public right, it gives rise to an action or prosecution by the public prosecutor. . . .

(4) STRICT LIABILITY

Strict liability for injury due to hazardous waste would seem to be a viable theory for plaintiffs because of the dangerous nature of the activity of hazardous waste disposal. However, it is not at all clear that all states would impose strict liability for injuries from exposure to hazardous waste.

It is true, as Dean Prosser states, if one includes cases decided on a nuisance theory, the Rylands v. Fletcher principle of liability regardless of fault for certain dangerous activities is "in reality universally accepted." Widespread acceptance of the principle in theory has not meant uniform application of the principle due to two factors: first, courts rely on different formulations to determine what activities should be covered by the principle, and second, even courts referring to the same formulation apply it differently. This latter factor has resulted in a situation where often two opinions applying different formulations are more easily reconciled, than two opinions applying the same formulation. This makes comparison of cases difficult.

Existing case law suggests that (1) strict liability is not absolute liability; defenses are available, and the application of strict liability for conducting dangerous activities yields to a number of other principles, and (2) strict liability for hazardous waste disposal would be more easily available if the focus of inquiry is on the nature of the activity rather than on the locale in which the activity was conducted.

Before examining alternative formulations of the strict liability doctrine, it is useful to consider the competing interests involved in imposing strict liability in a hazardous waste situation, and to examine these interests by analogizing the hazardous waste area to the product liability area.

Analogy to Strict Product Liability

Product liability law developed to shift the burden of risks and costs of the injuries caused by defectively manufactured products to the industry creating the risks, and to encourage manufacturers to design and manufacture safe products. Similar reasons exist for the imposition of strict liability in hazardous waste cases.

Although product liability cases involve injury or damage caused by a defect in a known product produced by an identifiable manufacturer, other characteristics of product liability are similar to hazardous waste situations and the problems have been analogized by commentators.

Strict liability is imposed in product liability to ease plaintiff's burden of proof, and on the grounds that imposition of liability on the manufacturer most readily and efficiently provides for cost internalization and for equitable distribution of the costs of product-caused injuries. Similar, if not greater difficulties of proof are encountered in the case of injuries caused by hazardous wastes. As in product liability, strict liability for hazardous waste disposal may also encourage the reduction of risks by disposers. So, too, the distribution of costs of injury often may be easily passed on by imposing liability on parties such as the generator of the waste or the owner/operator of disposal sites who can spread the costs most easily, by purchasing liability insurance, or in the case of the disposal site owner/operator, by transferring them to the generator of wastes through disposal charges. The analogy to strict product liability can be most easily drawn in the "toxic tort" cases, where questions of scientific proof, long latency periods of disease, and high risk recur, whether the injury was caused by exposure to a chemical product or to toxic waste. . . .

Rylands v. Fletcher: Strict Liability for a "Non-natural" Use of Land

The doctrine of strict liability based on the theory that a condition or activity is abnormally dangerous because of its "non-natural" character is usually traced to the English case, Rylands v. Fletcher.

Under the principle developed since *Rylands*, the court determines whether an activity is "natural" by considering whether it is appropriate in the context of the place, and by reviewing the manner and relationship of the activity to its surroundings, not simply on whether or not the activity itself is ultrahazardous.

First Restatement — "Ultrahazardous Activity"

The initial Restatement's reliance on the "ultrahazardous" nature of the activity to justify the applications of strict liability was an apparent shift from the *Rylands* doctrine in that greater emphasis was placed on the dangerous nature of the activity itself, rather than on the appropriateness to the place where the activity was carried on.

Adopted in 1934, the first Restatement devotes chapter 21 to a discussion of "ultrahazardous activities" defined in §520 which states: "An activity is ultrahazardous if it (a) necessarily involves a risk of serious harm to the person, land or chattels of others which cannot be eliminated by the exercise of utmost care, and (b) is not a matter of common usage." This definition emphasizes two factors: unavoidable risk and unusual usage. Ultrahazardous activities are distinguishable from nuisances or negligent activities because the ultrahazardous activity has sufficient utility; otherwise, incurring the risk would represent negligence as defined in §282 of the Restatement.

Restatement (Second) — "Abnormally Dangerous"

The Restatement (Second)'s "abnormally dangerous" test adopted by the American Law Institute in 1976 reflected something of a return to the *Rylands* doctrine. Section 520 of the Restatement (Second) outlines factors that are important in determining whether an activity is abnormally dangerous:

> In determining whether an activity is abnormally dangerous, the following factors are to be considered:
>
> (a) existence of a high degree of risk and some harm to the person, land or chattels of others;
> (b) likelihood that the harm that results from it will be great;
> (c) inability to eliminate the risk by the exercise of reasonable care;
> (d) extent to which the activity is not a matter of common usage;
> (e) inappropriateness of the activity to the place where it is carried out; and
> (f) extent to which its value to the community is outweighed by its dangerous attributes.

However, analysis of no one factor is determinative. An activity which ·is abnormally dangerous under one set of circumstances is not necessarily abnormally dangerous on all occasions. In determining whether activities involving hazardous waste are abnormally dangerous, it is not necessary that each of the factors of §520 be present, particularly if others weigh heavily. It is clear, however, that considerations of the appropriateness to the place weigh heavily.

As in the first Restatement formulation, the strict liability of an operator of an abnormally dangerous activity does not extend to those who intentionally or negligently trespass, even though the trespasser has no reason to know that the activity is conducted there.

A NOTE ON THE ADEQUACY OF COMMON
LAW REMEDIES

At the start of the environmental decade, common law actions basically were assigned an interstitial, transitional role in the grand strategy for legal protection of the environment. Individual lawsuits were interim actions pending the enactment of comprehensive regulatory legislation that would make the need for such suits irrelevant or unusual. Today, for reasons discussed in Chapter VI, this strategy is being reevaluated. For the present, let us focus on the reasons for the rejection of decentralized control strategies. The two objections to the common law were its insensitivity to environmental issues and the likelihood that it would not be invoked often enough to promote the level of environmental quality demanded by society.

The narrow focus. In The Spirit of the Common Law 91-92 (1921), the great legal scholar Roscoe Pound described the influence of natural law on American and English jurisprudence. He wrote: "A legal system attains its end by recognizing certain interests, individual, public and social. . . . [I]t does not create these interests . . . it only recognizes them." Natural law took as self-evident the rights recognized in Roman law, which were premised on giving every person, and his private property, his due. Thus, it is not surprising that the common law is primarily concerned with the protection of bodily integrity, personal dignity, and property. Any theory of shared interests in property, other than navigable waters, died with the enclosure movement in England. The common law dealt with obvious environmental insults — those that caused immediate damage to persons or property — but not the more subtle ones, stemming from injuries to aesthetic sensibilities.

In the late 1960s and early 1970s there was a flurry of interest in environmental law on the part of the personal injury bar, which saw damage actions as a replacement for the loss of business it anticipated no-fault legislation would cause. This did not immediately occur, but dissatisfaction with the performance of regulatory institutions and the perceived incompleteness of their statutory mandates initially helped to revive this interest, and in the 1980s toxic torts litigation became a growth industry.

Common law and equity imposed substantial barriers for individual and group environmental plaintiffs. The law did not protect the two plaintiffs who are the beneficiaries of modern environmental regulation: the hypersensitive plaintiff in nuisance law and the plaintiff who suffers aesthetic impairment. The threshold requirement rooted in the human dignity origins of tort law, that a plaintiff must prove cause in fact, was a major barrier that largely had to be overcome by legislation. Claims that the plaintiff has merely been exposed to risk of future injury were dismissed in equity as speculative. Further, the public was not always able to assert a property interest when an individual could not. Finally, the injury had to be physical. Aesthetic injuries, as such, did not count. Modern environmental law may justifiably be said to have orginated in a 1965 Second Circuit Court of Appeals decision written by Judge Paul Hays, a former Columbia University Law School professor, in Scenic Hudson Preservation

Conference v. FPC, 354 F.2d 608 (2d Cir. 1965), *cert. denied*, 384 U.S. 941 (1966). The court remanded, for the first time, a Federal Power Commission (FPC) license because of the FPC's failure to consider adequately its impact on fish and wildlife in the area in question. Judge Hays held that a nonprofit, unincorporated association had standing even though its injury was only aesthetic and then closed his opinion with the observation that opened up the possibility of a law based on interests broader than the calculus protected by common law and equity: "The Commission's renewed proceedings must include a basic concern for the preservation of beauty and national historical shrines, keeping in mind that in our affluent society, the cost of a project is only one of several factors to be considered" (354 F.2d at 624). Judge Henry J. Friendly has described the opinion as "Judge Hays's most influential opinion for the court." Judge Friendly's remarks, along with some insights into the making of Judge Hays's opinion, from his clerk at the time, can be found in In Memoriam, 635 F.2d lxi (1981).

Transactions costs and barriers to bringing private lawsuits. In addition to the problems discussed above, yet another problem with common law actions is that they are unlikely to be brought in sufficient numbers to make a difference in environmental quality. A large number of persons may have suffered some damage, but not enough to warrant individual efforts at redress. In this situation, potential plaintiffs have an incentive to sit back and wait for others to bring a suit from which they would benefit or to partially conceal their preferences when asked to join a coalition. The problem of free riders as a barrier to coalition formation was first explored in M. Olson, The Logic of Collective Action (1965), and was applied to non-exclusive environmental resources in Krier, Environmental Watchdogs: Some Lessons from a "Study" Council, 23 Stan. L. Rev. 623 (1971).

2.   Command and Control Regulation

This country has long relied on what Professor James E. Krier has called "The Great Regulatory Tradition" to solve social problems. Krier, The Pollution Problem and Legal Institutions: A Conceptual Overview, 18 U.C.L.A.L. Rev. 429 (1971). Why this is so is not completely clear. To some, regulation was promoted by the "regulated community" as a means of moderating the rigors of competition. Intellectually, the idea of regulation as a cure for market malfunction is generally traced to Pigou. A. Pigou, Economics of Welfare (4th ed. 1932). Pigou's influence is critically surveyed in S. Cheung, The Myth of Social Costs 13-22 (Cato Paper No. 6, 1980). Pigou proposed a mix of subsidies and taxes to control externalities, but this country has used more centralized commands and control regulations almost exclusively. During the New Deal and in the post-World War II era, the idea that Congress should delegate broad grants of authority to expert administrative agencies was widely but not completely accepted. The theory was that all problems were technical and the agencies would establish their legitimacy by solving them correctly. The classic exposition of this theory is J. Landis, The Administrative Process (1938). For a variety of reasons, agencies never fully established their legitimacy, despite the Supreme Court's refusal to use the nondelegation doctrine to invalidate Congress' acts and the erection of a strong presumption of validity for administrative action. See Freedman, Crisis and Legitimacy in the Administrative Process, 27 Stan. L. Rev. 1041 (1975), for a perceptive exploration of the failure of agencies to convince Congress, the public and ultimately the courts of the legitimacy of their actions. In the 1970s, after agency missions were deemed hostile or indifferent to environmental quality, Congress began to reassert its legislative prerogative to control administrative discretion. The time was ripe for this type of legislation. Concern over health was rising in a public that was becoming accustomed to longer life expectancies and the wealth with which to enjoy the benefits of medicine. Exposés of widespread, low-probability cancer and other risks politicized the issue of risk minimization. The New Deal legacy of the administrative state was accepted as desirable or at least inevitable in a complex society, and the power of groups that traditionally had blocked national intervention in the economy weakened. Congress became balkanized, and individual members seized on ideological issues to advance themselves. The result was environmental legislation whose drafters had precise ideas about how statutes were to be implemented and how agencies had to be reformed to accomplish their objectives:

> When legal activists tried to give their environmental hopes statutory expression in the early 1970s, their concrete experiences gave added weight to the growing suspicion of New Deal models among the American establishment. Before 1970, environmental protection was principally a matter for the states rather than the federal government. And when environmentalists surveyed the state scene, the agencies they observed seemed to parody New Deal hopes. The typical state agency was so understaffed that it could not even pretend to understand the environment it was trying to regulate. Although state agencies frequently took the form of "independent" commissions, their memberships were often dominated by the very interests that had the most to gain from pollution.

The different types of modern environmental regulation are described in the following excerpt.

ANDERSON, HUMAN WELFARE AND THE ADMINISTERED SOCIETY: FEDERAL REGULATION IN THE 1970's TO PROTECT HEALTH, SAFETY AND ENVIRONMENT, IN ENVIRONMENTAL AND OCCUPATIONAL MEDICINE
835, 846-848 (W. Rom ed. 1983)

A Taxonomy of Standards . . .

Standards lie at the heart of virtually all regulatory programs. The following discussion presents a general classification of the standards that protect human health and the environment. This taxonomy also may provide a basis for preferring one type of standard to another, as well as for comparing standards with other possible means of attacking the mischief at hand.

Performance Standards

Performance standards establish an acceptable level of protection or control without specifying the particular method to be used for complying with them. In the case of products or product components, performance standards usually specify results which the product or component must achieve under specified circumstances. . . .

Performance standards are particularly important in pollution control. Effluent (water) and emission (air) standards specify a mean or maximum permissible discharge of a pollutant from a type of source, but air and water pollutants are not the only type of pollution regulated. For example, truck-mounted solid waste compactors must be built so that at the time of sale they will not emit noise in excess of 76 dB measured a specified distance from the compactor. Emission and effluent standards promulgated under the Clean Air Act and Clean Water Act may specify performance in terms of a permissible concentration of a pollutant per quantity of discharge. . . .

Emission and effluent standards should not be confused with emission and effluent limitations. An emission or effluent standard applies to a type of source, such as coal-burning electrical generating facilities, coke ovens, or craft paper mills. An emission or effluent limitation specifies performance levels to be achieved by a single identified source; for example, "Frombridge Corporation Plant No. One shall discharge no more than x pounds of sulfur oxides per day." In general, performance standards are output-oriented. They are intended to force technological improvement and innovation. The critics of regulation prefer performance standards to design standards, because the former leave at least some choice about how they will be attained. Members of Congress and the agency regulators have not always trusted in such latitude.

Ambient Standards

The typical *ambient standard* specifies the minimum conditions that must be met in an indoor or outdoor environment. Unlike emission and effluent standards, which control actual discharges into the environment, ambient standards place quality requirements on the receiving water or air. For example, in the federally approved water quality standards for Arizona, an ambient standard requires that the mean annual total phosphate concentration in the Colorado River from the Utah border to Willow Beach must not exceed 0.04 milligrams of phosphate per liter. . . .

At bottom, ambient standards merely state objectives. Obviously, the larger the ambient zone covered, the more numerous are the sources of environmental contamination, and thus the more difficult is the task of implementing a regulatory program. Ambient standards become meaningful only when used in tandem with performance or design standards applicable to individual sources.

Design Standards

As their name suggests, *design standards* attempt to protect against health and safety hazards by specifying the manner in which equipment, structures, products, and production processes must be constructed or arranged. . . .

Design standards are based on the premise that, if properly chosen, explicit design requirements can prevent the harm that might otherwise occur. Unfortunately, the many alternative designs usually available to achieve a given goal are not equal in cost or efficacy. An agency's favorite design, enshrined in a standard, may not perform as well or cost as little as a design selected by a producer or operator. Widespread discontent with design standards has produced a trend toward performance standards, which, despite their own problems, at least afford some measure of flexibility in implementation.

Behavioral Standards

Behavioral standards prescribe procedures intended to reduce the incidence of injury or illness. They also may proscribe conduct that presents unreasonable health or safety risks. . . .

A dispute has arisen about some agencies' preferences for structural (and costly) regulatory solutions to problems as opposed to behavioral or "soft" solutions that require workers, product users, and users of the ambient environment to assume the primary burden of compliance (for example, elderly persons staying indoors on days of high pollution levels). Supporters of structural solutions deny that they are paternalistic and unnecessarily costly. They argue that serious information deficiencies exist that make behavioral standards unrealistic. Proponents of human behavioral standards argue that information deficiencies can be overcome by providing the proper incentives to workers and product users.

Information Standards

The final family of standards, more closely related to human and behavioral standards than to performance or ambient standards, requires that information be supplied to affected parties or to the governmental agency charged with protecting the public. *Information standards* may be applied in circumstances where it is either difficult or impossible to enforce design and performance standards, but they also may be promulgated where a legislative or administrative judgment has been made that paternalistic protection is unnecessary and that persons suitably warned can adjust their behavior to the risks involved.

In response to this dismal reality, the Clean Air Amendments of 1970 not only massively increased the federal presence but took steps to guard against the repetition of yet another New Deal failure. Instead of permitting a group of "independent" commissioners to run off in different directions, the act placed primary responsibility on a single administrator squarely situated within the executive branch. Moreover, to ensure that the administrator implemented the act fully, Congress permitted "any citizen" to sue to compel the agency to carry out the act's mandatory sections.

Just as the act refused to insulate the EPA in New Deal fashion, so too it challenged the New Deal affirmation of expertise in two very different ways. First, the act not only required the administrator to set quantitative clean air targets that "protect the public health" but it also insisted that the nation actually fulfill these clean air targets by 1977 at the latest. In taking these steps, Congress forced the agency to specify its goals far more clearly than required by the New Deal model. No longer could expertise be used as an excuse for avoiding the inevitably controversial task of defining ultimate environmental objectives; instead the agency had to define its goals in a highly visible way and recognize that Congress would call it to account by a specific date if it found the agency's performance unsatisfactory. B. Ackerman & W. Hassler, Clean Coal/Dirty Air or How the Clean Air Act Became a Multibillion-dollar Bailout for High-Sulfur Coal Producers and What Should Be Done about It 8-9 (1982).

Compare Henderson & Pearson, Implementing Federal Environmental Policies: The Limits of Aspirational Commands, 78 Colum. L. Rev. 1429, 1434 (1978), which argues that regulation based on "aspirational commands" is likely to be unsuccessful because sanctions are not an effective threat when the regulated community does not share the values sought to be furthered by the statute. See also Schoenbrod, Goals Statutes or Rules Statutes: The Case of the Clean Air Act, 30 U.C.L.A.L. Rev. 201 (1983). Sagoff, The Principles of Federal Pollution Control Law, 71 Minn. L. Rev. 19, 79-80, 92, 93 (1986), is a probing exploration of the ethical and economic bases of pollution control law. Much of the non-economics literature discusses the tension, but Sagoff attempts the following resolution:

> The Clean Air and Water Act and other pollution control statutes resemble laws that prohibit child labor and discrimination and those that combat poverty and illiteracy. Environmental statutes, in short, stand squarely in the tradition of legislation that seeks to control and eliminate moral evils. The Clean Air Act, for example, puts an ethical concern with public safety and health ahead of economic and commercial interests. It "does not allow economic growth to be accommodated at the expense of the public health." Courts have concurred that the protection of public health is the "paramount consideration" of the Act. "It is generally accepted that the Clean Air Act mandates a safety-first approach to investment in air quality.". . .

Efforts to achieve a cleaner, safer, more beautiful environment are constrained, of course, by economic costs. "Ought" does not mean "can." What "can" be done, however, depends in part on the importance of the ethical duty at stake. A determination of the environmental quality that "can" be achieved must therefore, at least in part, depend on the significance of underlying ethical principles.

The relationship proposed here between the ethical and the economic is familiar in both individual and societal decisions. For instance, in deciding how much to donate to relieve hunger in Africa, a person must consider economic factors. An initial consideration is how much can be afforded; one may be expected to give only "until it hurts." One might try to assess one's "fair share" given the ability of others to help. It is also useful to know which organizations direct contributions most effectively in providing famine relief. . . .

The difficult question is whether the principles of pollution control law . . . impose perfect or imperfect obligations. Society is horrified to hear reports that a corporation willfully or even negligently vented toxic substances that killed identifiable individuals. The government, equally plainly, has an obligation to prohibit this sort of serious incident, both through statutory and tort law. The EPA, for example, moved swiftly to reduce exposure to vinyl chloride when it discovered that deaths resulted from exposure to that pollutant. When deaths can be attributed to particular exposures, society must honor the right of innocent individuals not to be killed.

With respect to background hazards and risks, however, it is different. No one has a right to be protected from de minimis hazards or to a completely risk-free environment. The highways, for example, can hardly be safe, and although everyone has a perfect obligation not to drive recklessly, no one is bound to drive at ten miles per hour, even if that would reduce traffic fatalities by many thousands. At some point, a duty of obligation shades into a duty of virtue. At that point, safety becomes more a matter of virtue than an ethical requirement. . . .

3.   Mandated Rational Planning

Command and control regulation proceeds from the assumption that any activity that complies with applicable regulations may proceed. However, from an environmental perspective the issue is often whether *any* activity should be allowed at a given location. Suppose that a factory plans to locate on a river; the factory will meet all applicable water quality and effluent reduction standards, but if five factories cluster around the first it will be impossible to meet the standards. If a problem like this is to be avoided, the application of regulations to the first factory, and the issuance of a permit, should be preceded by some kind of planning process. Federal and state environmental statutes attempt to subject a great deal of decisionmaking to the progressive ideal of national planning. Examples include §208 and §303 of the Clean Water Act, which require planning processes for the location of publicly owned sewage treatment plants, the control of non-point sources of pollution, and the implementation of water quality standards. Plans such as those for transportation control are an important element of state implementation plans required by the Clean Air Act, although Congress has cut back the power of state and federal agencies to approach air pollution as a land use planning problem. Federal land managers are subject to rigorous planning requirements when making decisions about a wide variety of matters, such as land sales, coal leases, and land classification.

All of these statutes — whether they mandate single- or multiple-use planning — are distinguished from past statutes that mandate the preparation of plans in that they are much more specific about the planning process and about the content of plans. The goal of these statutes is to produce a rational decision — one that collects available data, presents alternative choices, and assesses the consequences of proposed actions in light of statutory goals. A similar rationalist approach to decisionmaking can be found in federal and state environmental impact assessment statutes and related statutes. Although these statutes focus on specific decisions rather than on a full range of future options, the approach is often the same since many environmental impact statements, especially programmatic ones, require some effort at regional planning.

In recent years, powerful criticisms of rational planning as a method of policy analysis have been mounted. The theoretical criticisms focus on the problem of information overload. Rational decisionmaking processes often either require technical and preference value information that is not available at any reasonable cost or else swamp the decisionmaker with more information than he needs to make the decision at hand. See Simon, Rationality as a Process and as a Product of Thought, 68 Am. Econ. Rev. 1 (1980), and A. Wildavsky, Speaking the Truth to Power: The Art and Craft of Policy Analysis (1979). Observers of the rational planning process in practice have argued that plans and other documents produced by formal rational planning tend to contain too little or too much information; are vague, in that hard choices are not addressed; and cannot be adapted to changed conditions. In short, formal planning processes tend to produce formal documents of limited utility. For an excellent case study of one celebrated effort to introduce rationality into public land decisionmaking, see Leman, Formal v. DeFacto Systems of BLM Planning: Integrating Multiple Use and Focused Approaches, in Developing Strategies for Public Range Land Management: A Report Prepared for the Committee on Developing Strategies for Rangeland Management 1851 (1984). See also the following case studies of the federal coal leasing program: R. Nelson, The Making of Federal Coal Policy (1983), and Tarlock, Western Coal in Context, 53 U. Colo. L. Rev. 315 (1982). As you survey the instances of mandated rational decisionmaking in this casebook, ask yourself what processes might be substituted for existing procedures. A useful starting point for answering this question is Leman & Nelson, Ten Commandments for Policy Economists, J. Poly. Analysis & Mgmt. 1 (Fall 1981).

F.   ALTERNATIVES TO REGULATION

Lawyers are trained to think regulation; economists are trained to think markets. When economists turned their attention to environmental quality issues, they reached conclusions quite different form those reached by lawyers and legislators who were concerned with promoting environmental quality. Recall p. 65 *supra*. Economists start from the premise that if externalities exist, it is because property rights in relation to the use of waste sinks are incomplete; therefore the most efficient solution is to turn a free good into a priced good. Although legislatures have, by and large, stuck with command and control regulation, the argument that much pollution can best be controlled by pricing it has greatly influenced the debate about the goals of environmental regulations. See, e.g., Council on Environmental Quality, Fourth Annual Report ch. 3 (1973). At various times, pricing proposals have secured a place on the agenda of politicians, see generally Instead of Regulation ch. 11 (R. Poole ed. 1982), but they have been vigorously resisted by both industry and environmental groups. There is, however, a growing worldwide appreciation of the limits of command and control regulation and of the need to change the incentive structures for environmentally detrimental activities. One of the earliest influential economic analyses of environmental quality problems follows.

J. H. DALES, POLLUTION, PROPERTY AND PRICES
81-84, 93 (1968)

Three Possible Ways of Implementing a Policy

To an economist, there are only three basically different ways of implementing the [Water Control] Board's policy. The first we shall call "regulation." . . .

The second technique can be called "subsidization." . . .

The third technique we shall call "pollution charges." The Board, under this system, announces that it is going to levy a "disposal fee" on all those who dispose of their wastes into natural water systems. The fee per ton of waste may vary at different outfalls, and the charge may also increase as the number of tons of discharge increases. This technique is based on the principle that if you charge a person for disposing of his wastes he will find ways to reduce the amount of wastes he disposes of, and that the more you charge him the stronger the incentive he will have to find some less damaging method of disposing of his wastes. The Board, however, may have to do quite a bit of "trial-and-error pricing" before it hits on a system of charges that results in the total amount of wastes that are discharged into water systems being equal to, or slightly less than, its target future. . . .

Note, first, that even though we have referred to our three techniques as "basically different" they in fact appear to amount to much the same thing. The WCB's policy can be met by a particular set of regulations, a particular set of subsidies, or a particular set of charges. "But who pays?" you will ask. Actually, we answered that question in the last chapter, when we were discussing the cost of the English system of "property rights in fishing" to the fishermen and the municipal or industrial polluters. If people are divided into groups, different control techniques have different results; under a subsidy scheme the polluter receives money (or equipment) while under a changing scheme he pays out money. However, if we carry the analysis a step further, we see that in a charging scheme producers and municipalities will recoup the money they pay out by charging higher prices and higher taxes for their goods and services; the same will be true of the higher costs industries and municipalities will be forced to bear if the WCB uses regulations rather than charges. If subsidies are used, prices of goods and municipal services will not go up, but provincial taxes will. In the end, the costs will be spread around, and the general population will pay for pollution control. . . . [W]e are dealing with what economists call "general equilibrium" situations, in which we are all simultaneously producers *and* consumers, polluters *and* pollutees. It is then true that, no matter who passes the money to whom in the first place, we all pay in the end. . . .

Does it, then, make no difference which technique the WCB uses to enforce its policy? It certainly *does* make a difference, an enormous difference; even though the costs of getting the benefit are shared, the amount of cost (and also the type of cost) differs greatly from one scheme to another. Consider a simpler case for a moment. Suppose that we wanted to decrease the number of high-school drop-outs by, say, 90 percent. We could do so by paying prospective drop-outs whatever price would lead nine out of ten of them *not* to drop out; or by charging them a fee for the right to drop out that would result in only one out of ten prospects deciding to do so; or by passing a law forbidding drop-out (but allowing kick-outs). The paying scheme would be very costly to the taxpayer in terms of money because every student worth his salt would think of dropping out in order to collect his payment for deciding not to! The law forbidding drop-outs would, I think, be worse; those who wanted to drop out badly enough would have to do enough damage or otherwise make enough of a nuisance of themselves to be kicked out. The taxpayer would have to pay for the damage, or for controlling the nuisance. Much more serious, though, would be the feelings of resentment at being forced to stay in school by those who would otherwise have dropped out, and even by those who would like to think they could drop out if they wanted to; the cost in terms of educational morale might be high. The *charging* scheme would cost practically nothing to administer; those who still decided to drop out would actually be a small source of revenue to taxpayers; and there would probably be a lot less idle talk among students about dropping out than there is now — those who wanted to drop out badly enough would simply pay their exit fee and leave. A rather similar analysis applies to our three techniques of pollution control, though here there are many more things to consider.

Markets in Pollution Rights

Let us try to set up a "market" in "pollution rights." The Board starts the process by creating a certain number of Pollution Rights, each Right giving whoever buys it the right to discharge one equivalent ton of wastes into natural waters during the current year. Suppose that the current level of pollution is roughly satisfactory. On this assumption, if half a million tons of wastes are currently being dumped into the water system, the Board would issue half a million Rights. All waste dischargers would then be required to buy whatever number of Rights they need; if a factory dumps 1000 tons of waste per year it will have to buy 1000 Rights. To put the market into operation, let us say that the Board decides to withhold 5 percent of the Rights in order to allow for the growth of production and population during the first year, and therefore offers 475,000 Rights for sale. Since the demand is for 500,000, the Rights will immediately command some positive price — say, 10 cents each.

NOTES AND QUESTIONS

1. The case for some form of charge system is powerful:

> Charges systems are a cost-effective means of achieving environmental quality goals because, with charges, each source decides how much to control on the basis of its own control costs. Thus, sources whose costs of control are high will control less: those with low costs will control more. The logical net result is that the average cost of control per unit of pollutant would be lower than it would be under regulatory schemes that do not allow this type of private decision making to take place. With charges, the cost of environmental cleanup is less for the overall economy. [F. Anderson, A. Kneese, R. Stevenson & S. Taylor, Environmental Improvement through Economic Incentives 10 (1977).]

2. Pollution-right auctions have been thought to be too controversial politically because they acknowledge a right to pollute, although the necessity of states to establish a floor on pollution rights is acknowledged. The reasons for resistance to economic remedies are explored in Kelman, Economists and the Environmental Muddle, 64 Pub. Interest 106 (1981). Most charge schemes have been more directly tied to the achievement of ambient standards. Taxes on sulfur oxide emissions, automobile exhaust emissions, and effluent charges, to maintain the necessary pollution controls work are among the proposals that have been floated in the past few years. The sources, in addition to Environmental Improvement through Economic Incentives, *supra*, include A. Kneese & B. Bower, Managing Water Quality: Economics, Technology, and Institutions (1968), and Effluent Charges on Air and Water Pollution: A Conference Report of the Council on Law Related Studies (E. Selig ed., Environmental Law Institute 1973). J. Coleman, Markets, Morals and the Law 89 (1988) offers another criticism of pollution auctions. He argues that many people confuse exchanges, as defined by Coase in the Problem of Social Cost, p. 36, *supra*, with auctions:

> There are significant differences between auction and exchange markets. Exchanges (by rational, well-informed persons) are made only when they are to

the advantage of all parties to them. Auctions are not trades; they do not guarantee that all parties to the bidding gain or are at least not disadvantaged by the result. Some auctions — for example, those involving works of art — have the effect of improving the lot of some individuals without worsening the lot of others.

What follows? Might losers in some auctions have a legitimate claim to compensation? See id. at pp. 91-94.

3. In addition to the political unpopularity of the explicit acknowledgement of a right to pollute, charges turn out to be very hard to implement because of information requirements. For example, the charge should be based on the marginal rate of damage done by a source, meaning that what is needed is information about the impacts of each increment on total resource quality — information that is unavailable at any reasonable cost. See Roberts, River Basin Authorities: A National Solution to Water Pollution, 83 Harv. L. Rev. 1527 (1970), and Organizing Water Pollution Control: The Scope and Structure of River Basin Authorities, 19 Pub. Poly. 75 (1971), for a question of the difficulty, if not impossibility, of assembling the information necessary to calculate an economically correct charge.

4. In addition to the administrative problems, there are legal issues. Is a tax an unconstitutional use of the taxing power for regulatory purposes? Would a charge program violate the payor's right to due process? Equal protection problems are presented by schemes that envision different classes of charges and differential rates among classes. See Environmental Improvement through Economic Incentives, *supra*.

5. Even if discharges and other environmental insults are not directly priced, what lessons about the objectives of command and control regulations can one gain from economic policy analysis? Council on Environmental Quality: Fourth Annual Report, draws a widely accepted lesson:

> This and the succeeding section discuss the four categories of costs that must be examined and balanced in environmental decisionmaking. *Damage* costs are those costs which directly result from a polluting activity, for example, illness and property damage stemming from air pollution. *Avoidance* costs are those that people incur in order to avoid or reduce damage costs, for example, the cost of driving farther to find an unpolluted beach. *Transaction* costs represent the resources consumed in making and enforcing policies and regulations, such as the costs of monitoring air pollution. *Abatement* costs are those associated with reducing the amount of environmental degradation, such as the cost of sewage treatment plants. [Fourth Annual Report, at 74.]

6. The debate about the proper objectives and means of regulation continues. Latin, Ideal versus Real Regulatory Efficiency: Implementation of Uniform Standards and "Fine-Tuning" Regulatory Reforms, 37 Stan. L. Rev. 1267, 1271 (1985), vigorously defends reliance on uniform standards in many situations:

> In recognition of severe implementation constraints on environmental regulation, this article identifies numerous advantages of uniform standards in

comparison with more particularized and flexible regulatory strategies. These advantages include decreased information collection and evaluation costs, greater consistency and predictability of results, greater accessibility of decisions to public scrutiny and participation, increased likelihood that regulations will withstand judicial review, reduced opportunities for manipulative behavior by agencies in response to political or bureaucratic pressures, reduced opportunities for obstructive behavior by regulated parties, and decreased likelihood of social dislocation and "forum shopping" resulting from competitive disadvantages between geographical regions or between firms in regulated industries. A realistic implementation analysis indicates that "fine-tuning" would prove infeasible in many important environmental contexts; indeed, the effectiveness of environmental regulation could often be improved by reducing even the degree of "fine-tuning" that is currently attempted.

Professor Latin's analysis is equally vigorously challenged by the two leading environmental law scholars that he criticizes. Ackerman and Stewart, Reforming Environmental Law, 37 Stan. L. Rev. 1333, 1346 (1985), characterize current regulatory programs as extremely wasteful programs kept in place by congressional committees, government bureaucracies, and industrial and environmental groups, and argue that waste discharge permits should be auctioned off by the government:

> A system of marketable permits, then, not only promises to save Americans many billions of dollars a year, to reward innovative improvements in existing clean-up techniques, and to eliminate the BAT system's penalty on new, productive investment. It also offers formidable administrative advantages. It relieves agencies of the enormous information-processing burdens that overwhelm them under the BAT system; it greatly reduces litigation and delay; it offers a rich source of budgetary revenue in a period of general budgetary stringency; and it forces agencies to give new importance to the critical business of enforcing the law in a way that America's polluters will take seriously. Despite his emphasis on administrative realities, Latin has failed to take any of these advantages seriously. Instead, he speaks forebodingly of the dangers of "fine-tuning" that the market reform entails. What precisely *are* these dangers?
>
> The reformed system we have described involves the execution of four bureaucratic tasks. First, the agency must estimate how much pollution presently is permitted by law in each watershed and air quality region. Second, it must run a system of fair and efficient auctions in which polluters can regularly buy rights for limited terms. Third, it must run an efficient title registry in each region that will allow buyers and sellers to transfer rights in a legally effective way. Fourth, it must consistently penalize polluters who discharge more than their permitted amounts.
>
> And that's that. So far as the fourth bureaucratic task is concerned, we have already given reasons to believe that the EPA would enforce the law far more effectively under the new regime than it does at present. So far as the first three management functions are concerned, we think that they are, in the aggregate, far *less* demanding than those they displace under the BAT system.

See also Stewart, Economics, Environment, and the Limits of Legal Control, 9 Harv. Envtl. L. Rev. 1 (1985).

G.   INFORMATION DISCLOSURE

If environmental problems are simply a subset of market failure problems, one standard economic remedy for improving the bargaining process is information disclosure, as opposed to regulation. Would such a strategy be appropriate for solving most environmental problems?

LATIN, ENVIRONMENTAL DEREGULATION AND CONSUMER DECISIONMAKING UNDER UNCERTAINTY
6 Harv. Envtl. L. Rev. 187, 218 (1983)

C.   *Producer Advertising and Market Incentives*

Before decentralized producers could remedy consumer uncertainty directly through advertising, they would have to acquire adequate environmental knowledge themselves and then communicate relevant information to the environmentalists who might be interested in it. In the context of direct environmental consumption, advertisers would generally be resource owners who might sell their property rights either to developers or environmentalists. Property owners might publicize the ecological, recreational, and esthetic qualities of their resources in order to generate environmentalist demand for them. In the context of indirect environmental consumption, advertisers might include the sellers of any commodity manufactured or consumed in a relatively benign manner. The same basic requirements apply in both settings: environmental research, information collection, and public disclosure.

Whether producers obtain and disclose sufficient environmental information is a question of market incentives.[119] It may generally be true that producers are in the best position to know the technical components and economic ramifications of their production processes, but they are seldom equally well-positioned to understand the environmental consequences of their activities. The great majority of economic actions do not contribute to the production of environmental commodities but to the production of other types of goods that entail some measure of ecological damage. Producers have little economic incentive to understand the environmental consequences of pollution, habitat destruction, and many other ecologically harmful activities. When environmental commodities are social goods, such as pollution control or preservationist satisfaction, the lack of market incentives for private production correspondingly reduces the incentive for information collection on the negative consequences of resource

---

119.   Every decisionmaking system must be evaluated in terms of the incentives of its principal actors. See Hurwicz, On Informationally Decentralized Systems, in Studies in Resource Allocation Processes 425, 426 (K. Arrow & L. Hurwicz eds. 1977).

exploitation. Similarly, the absence of distinct property rights to many environmental resources decreases the motivation for market actors to monitor ecological degradation. Our society has had centuries of experience with decentralized decisionmaking in environmental markets, but that experience has not led to an adequate understanding of ecological conditions and the impacts of developmental services.

The costs of obtaining sufficient information are usually high because of the variety and complexity of possible environmental effects. The data and interpretive skills necessary to understand environmental problems are substantially different from the kinds of information and expertise that producers acquired in the past. Moreover, if producers wanted to demonstrate that their commodities are more desirable or less harmful from an environmentalist perspective, they would often need knowledge about their competitors' production outputs and resulting ecological impacts as well as their own. Information on these subjects frequently is concealed for trade secret or other legitimate business reasons. Without the coercive authority available to government regulators, private producers often would be unable to obtain the necessary information on comparative environmental consequences.

Even when producers do understand the consequences of their actions, they often have no incentive to disclose that information to the public. The primary objective of advertising and product promotion is the generation of additional sales, not the provision of unbiased data. Advertisers would be unlikely to disseminate environmental information unless they believed it presented their products in a favorable light. The problem of selective disclosure arises in all advertising contexts, but it is likely to be especially severe in environmental advertising. There are no generally accepted standards for how data on environmental quality should be communicated to the public;[123] disagreements frequently arise over the most effective levels of information content and modes of presentation.[124] Because environmental commodities are highly differentiated

---

123.   See, e.g., Natl. Research Council [Research and Development in the Environmental Production Agency (1975)] at 37; W. Baumol & W. Oates; [The Theory of Environmental Policy (1975)] at 135-36; Sixth CEQ Report [United States Council on Environmental Quality, Environmental Quality — 1975 (1975)], at 338; Timmons, Identification and Achievement of Quality levels in Managing the Use of Natural Resources, in Economics and Decision Making for Environmental Quality 204, 208 (J. Conner & E. Loehman eds. 1974). Environmental complexity and differentiation require diverse and sensitive indices of environmental quality. See e.g., Third CEQ Report [United States Council on Environmental Quality, Environmental Quality — 1972 (1972)], at 3-49; Craik & Zube, The Development of Perceived Environmental Quality Indices, in Perceiving Environmental Quality 3, 3-20 (K. Craik & E. Zube eds. 1976).

124.   See, e.g., Third CEQ Report, at 4:

Information on the environment can be presented to the public in a format which lies anywhere along a continuum ranging from the raw data at one extreme to a single index number for the whole environment at the other. The raw data end of the continuum is the most precise in the sense of providing the details of a particular environmental condition — but the least meaningful to policymakers and the general public. At the other extreme, a single index number representing total environmental quality might seem meaningful to the public but would involve aggregating and summarizing so much diverse data that it would likely be misleading in many important respects.

and very numerous, it would be hard for advertisers to target their promotional efforts at the particular consumers who might be interested in a specific commodity. Yet, the ratio of added sales to advertising expenditures might be unacceptably low if environmentalists were inundated with information on many potential commodities.[125] Environmental phenomena are complex: a large amount of data is required for rational environmental decisionmaking; therefore, it may be considerably more expensive, on the average, for advertisers adequately to inform environmentalists than to notify developers of the comparatively few commodity attributes relevant for their purposes. If environmental advertising is generally more expensive than the promotion of alternative types of goods, that would decrease the net returns to producers of environmental commodities and would consequently reduce their incentive to collect and disclose environmental information.

Given the wide range of potentially useful information, environmental advertisements would rarely if ever include all relevant data. Any exercise of selectivity, however, would increase the appearance and often the reality of biased presentation. . . . In view of the broad range of environmental impacts associated with most commodities, the great majority of producers can argue truthfully that their goods are environmentally superior according to *some* criterion. Inadvertent or intentional deception is also possible because misleading advertising can be profitable from the private perspective of the advertiser.

Environmental advertising in conjunction with the promotion of products such as automobiles presents another serious conceptual problem. A person who is affected by pollution or resource exploitation associated with the automotive manufacturing process, for example, might be willing to pay to avoid the resulting ecological damage. An environmentalist, however, usually would not become aware of the information in the manufacturer's advertisement if he is not currently shopping for a car. Even if product advertisements did disclose the full environmental consequences of those commodities, that information often would not reach the particular environmentalist consumers who may be most interested in it.

It may appear that advertising represents a more realistic information source in the context of direct environmental consumption. Owners of environmental resources could advertise the ecological and esthetic characteristics of their property and the damage that would occur if those resources were used for developmental purposes instead. Yet, environmental degradation resulting from development frequently entails externalized costs. In effect, when owners sell environmental resources to developers, they often sell the opportunity to externalize some of the social costs associated with resource exploitation. People harmed by externalities frequently do not obtain compensation because it would

---

125. See Stigler, The Economics of Information, in Economics of Information and Knowledge 61, 67 (D. Lamberton ed. 1971): "[A]dvertising itself is an expense, and one essentially independent of the value of the item advertised. The advertising of goods which have few potential buyers relative to the circulation of the advertising medium is especially expensive.

be prohibitively expensive for them to identify the extent and causes of the externalized damage. If resource owners collected that information and then disseminated it to potential consumers of environmental protection, they would facilitate compensation actions that might later be brought if their resources were eventually allocated to exploitative uses. The direct consequence of that might be to reduce the value of their property for development. Indeed, advertisers who identify and publicize the environmental degradation likely to result from development would increase the risk that development may be stringently regulated or prohibited by law.

H.   ALTERNATIVE DISPUTE RESOLUTION PROCEDURES: MEDIATION-ARBITRATION

There is widespread dissatisfaction with existing processes for resolving environmental disputes, especially with formal adjudication and lawsuits. Negotiation finally settled the litigation that provided the first theoretical underpinning for environmental law, Scenic Hudson Preservation Conference v. FPC, 354 F.2d 608 (2d Cir. 1965), *cert. denied*, 384 U.S. 941 (1966). *Scenic Hudson* grew out of a campaign started in the early 1960s to preserve the natural beauty of the Hudson River. Ultimately, though, the litigation focused on the preservation of the river's fisheries, which were threatened by Consolidated Edison of New Yorks' plans to build a pumped storage facility at Storm King Mountain. In December 1980, the principal parties in the case signed a settlement agreement; Consolidated Edison agreed to surrender its original federal license to built the power plant in return for a promise from the environmentalists not to oppose the use of once-through cooling systems for several other Hudson River plants that were ultimately involved in the litigation. The utilities also agreed to a program of power outages during crucial spawning seasons; to the installation of state-of-the-art fish screens around intakes; and to other measures to protect fish. Those wishing to study this litigation, once a staple of environmental law courses, should start with the Hudson River Power Plan Settlement: Materials Prepared for a Conference Sponsored by the New York University School of Law and the Natural Defense Council (R. Sandler & D. Schoenbrod eds. 1981). The history of the conflict up until 1971 is told in A. Talbot, Power along the Hudson (1972).

A number of efforts, some of them successful, have been made to use mediation and arbitration to resolve resource allocation controversies. There are three conventional techniques. Negotiation, the oldest, involves direct talks among the interested parties. Arbitration generally involves submitting the dispute to a neutral party who has a contractual or statutory power to render a binding decision; mediation involves the intervention into the dispute of a third party who does not have a direct stake in the outcome, in an effort to achieve a mutually agreeable substantive agreement among interested parties. McCroy, Environmental Mediation — Another Piece for the Puzzle, 6 Vt. L. Rev. 49, 52-53 (1981). Many efforts borrow the concept of interest-based negotiation from the labor movement and seek consensus building among the interested parties through the use of "facilitators" and focus groups. Susskind, Environmental Mediation and the Accountability Problem, 6 Vt. L. Rev. 114 (1981), sets out a nine-step mediation process:

> (1) [A]ll the parties that have a stake in the outcome of a dispute must be identified; (2) the relevant interest groups must be appropriately represented; (3) fundamentally different values and assumptions must be confronted; (4) a sufficient number of possible solutions options must be developed; (5) the boundaries and time horizon for analyzing impacts must be agreed upon; (6) the weighing, scaling, and amalgamation of judgments about cost and benefits must be undertaken jointly; (7) fair compensation and mitigatory actions must be negotiated; (8) the legality and financial feasibility of bargains that are made must be ensured, and (9) all parties must be held to their commitments. Although these steps will ensure a fair and efficient process, the success of a mediation effort must also be judged in terms of the fairness and stability of agreements that are reached. From this standpoint, a mediator should probably refuse to enter a dispute in which the power relationships among the parties are so unequal that a mutually acceptable agreement is unlikely to emerge. In addition, environmental mediators should probably withdraw from negotiations in which any of the parties seek an agreement that would not be just from the standpoint of another participant or from the standpoint of a party not at the bargaining table. [6 Vt. L. Rev. at 14 (footnotes omitted).]

Susskind's mediator is not neutral; in fact, he must be sufficiently connected with the community to be able to use clout to achieve a fair solution. For a different view that argues that a mediator must be neutral because of his bridge-building functions, see Stulberg, The Theory and Practice of Mediation: A Reply to Professor Susskind, 6 Vt. L. Rev. 85 (1981). These articles summarize much of the growing literature on this process (much of it in hard-to-get papers). See L. Lake, Environmental Mediation: The Search for Consensus (1980), and A. Talbot, Settling Things: Six Case Studies in Environmental Mediation (1983). See also Amy, The Politics of Environmental Mediation, 11 Ecology L.Q. 1 (1983), discussing the risks of co-optation and unequal bargaining power faced by environmentalists when they participate in a mediation process. Schoenbrod, Limits and Dangers of Environmental Mediation: A Review Essay, 58 N.Y.U.L. Rev. 1453 (1983), is a "hard look" at the mediation movement. The first comprehensive study of environmental dispute resolution, G. Bingham, Resolving Environmental Disputes: A Decade of Experience (Conservation Foundation, 1986), suggests that the successes of negotiation — broadly defined — are surprisingly large and must soon be given equal weight with administrative regulation and litigation. The Conservation Foundation study examined some 160 disputes. Parties in 132 of the disputes studied agreed to seek a negotiated settlement. Of these 132, 103 (78 percent) settled. Her major conclusion is: [t]here are several factors that mediators generally believe have significant influence on the likelihood of success — among them that the parties have sufficient incentives to reach an agreement, that all the parties are willing to participate in the dispute resolution process, that the parties can agree on the scope of issues to negotiate, and that a reasonable deadline exists. Id. at 93. L. Bacow & M. Wheeler, Environmental Dispute Resolution (1984), draws on decision theory, law and economics and negotiation theory to analyze the problems and processes of environmental dispute resolution.

II

AN INTRODUCTION TO THE ADMINISTRATIVE LAW OF ENVIRONMENTAL PROTECTION

Chapter 1 outlined the nature of environmental interests and values, the case for government intervention, and an array of legal techniques that can protect the social interest in environmental quality. Chapter 1 also sketched the classic model of the expert administrative agency. Because the judicial role is so important in the implementation of federal environmental legislation, this chapter provides a brief introduction to judicial intervention in agency decisionmaking under traditional doctrines of administrative law.

American administrative law was altered root and branch during the 1970s, in large part because of skillful advocacy by environmental and other interests before newly sympathetic judges. Environmentalists were unhappy with the performance of federal administrative agencies and with the opportunities available under standard administrative law doctrines to challenge the actions of agencies. The agencies, they believed, were insensitive to environmental concerns because they doggedly adhered to narrow missions or had been captured by the regulated community. Professor Joseph Sax described what environmentalists perceived to be the lassitude, unresponsiveness, and arrogance of government agencies in his influential book, Defending the Environment (1970).

The Atomic Energy Commission was held up as the classic example of an agency hostile to environmental values because of its adherence to its mission of promoting atomic power and because of what some perceived to be its capture by the nuclear industry. D. Ford, The Cult of the Atom: The Secret Papers of the Atomic Energy Commission (1982), documents the agency's promotion of atomic power at the expense of environmental and safety considerations. By the mid-1970s Congress had stripped the Commission of its promotional role, had renamed it the Nuclear Regulatory Commission, and had placed promotional functions in the Energy Research and Development Administration (and subsequently in the Department of Energy).

Judicial challenges to agency actions alleged to harm the environment faced a number of doctrinal hurdles. Administrative law circa 1970 offered relatively bleak prospects for judicial challenges to administrative action claiming that the agency either had ignored or had given insufficient attention to environmental values. First, the federal courts do not apply the delegation doctrine to hold that Congress was so indefinite in conferring statutory authority that it failed to empower the agency to make the contested decision. Until very recently, only one member of the Court seriously considered reviving the nondelegation doctrine to invalidate agency actions. Industrial Union Department v. American Petroleum Institute, 448 U.S. 607, 687 (1980) (Rehnquist, J., concurring). A revived delegation doctrine for environmental legislation is endorsed in Schoenbrod, Goals Statutes or Rules Statutes: The Case of the Clean Air Act, 30 U.C.L.A.L. Rev. 201, 287 (1983). See also Aranson, Gellhorn & Robinson, A Theory of Legislative Delegation, 68 Cornell L. Rev. 1. (1982).

In the 1980s, the Court returned to separation of powers analysis to delineate more precisely the exclusive functions of Congress and the executive branch, compare Bowsher v. Synar, 478 U.S. 714 (1986) with Morrison v. Olson, 108 S. Ct. 2597 (1988), and to articulate more clearly the role of the courts vis-à-vis other administrative agencies. To date, this return to first principles has not directly altered the structure of environmental law, but the courts are starting to hear more separation of powers arguments, and separation of powers principles influence the whole range of administrative law issues to a greater extent than they have in the past. For example, Stop H-3 Association v. Transportation Department, — F.2d — (9th Cir. 1989), reviewed a congressional statute that ended a long highway location dispute in Hawaii by exempting the segment from review under §4(f) of the Federal Highway Act of 1968, see p. 115 *infra*, and rejected the plaintiffs' argument that the statute was an unconstitutional effort to control the Secretary of Transportation's execution of the law:

> Moreover, even if we were to accept appellants' argument that section 114 represents an attempt by Congress to control the Executive branch's execution of the 4(f) statutes with respect to H-3, we still could not conclude that Congress violated the separation of powers. Simply put, Congress may change its mind, so long as it complies with the Constitution's requirements for action that alters the delegation of authority to the Executive branch. Thus in *Chadha* the Court observed that once the Attorney General had exercised his legislatively delegated authority to determine that an alien should be permitted to remain in the United States, Congress could only achieve the deportation of that alien, if at all, "by legislation requiring deportation." *Id.* at 952-54. Similarly, one House of Congress could not have passed a resolution reversing a determination by the Secretary that the 4(f) requirements had not been satisfied and that construction of H-3 could therefore not proceed; yet Congress could achieve construction of H-3 notwithstanding the 4(f) statutes by legislation ordering the Secretary to approve the project.
>
> The Supreme Court's opinion in Bowsher v. Synar, 478 U.S. 714 (1986), provides further support for our conclusion. In *Bowsher*, the Court invalidated the reporting provisions of the Balanced Budget and Emergency Deficit Control Act (the Act) because the provisions conferred executive functions upon the Comptroller General, an officer removable by Congress. The Court observed that under section 251 of the Act, the Comptroller General was required to exercise judgment concerning facts that affect the application of the Act, to interpret the provisions

of the Act, and to determine precisely what budgetary calculations were required. 478 U.S. at 733. As the Court noted, decisions of this kind "are typically made by officers charged with executing a statute." Id. See also id. (discussing executive nature of Comptroller General's functions under section 252 of the Act). The Court invalidated these provisions, holding that "once Congress makes its choice in enacting legislation its participation ends. *Congress can thereafter control the execution of its enactment only indirectly — by passing new legislation.*" Id. (citing *Chadha*, 462 U.S. at 958) (emphasis added).

One area of environmental law that is ripe for separation of powers analysis is the Office of Management and Budget (OMB). OMB exerts a profound influence over agency policy through its ability to review proposed regulations and other actions. Not only does the agency monitor agency spending to protect the public fisc, it also reviews the substance of agency regulations. The ultimate policy issue is who should control the cabinet and independent regulatory agencies. Congress has objected to OMB oversight because it impedes agencies from swiftly executing congressional mandates. See Senate Committee on Environment and Public Works, Office of Management and Budget Influence on Agency Regulation, 99th Cong., 2d Sess. (1986). Other students of government endorse the theory of executive oversight, Strauss & Sunstein, The Role of the President and OMB Informal Rulemaking, 38 Admin. L. Rev. 181 (1986), while recognizing the potential for abuse. See McGarity, Regulatory Analysis and Regulatory Reform, 65 Tex. L. Rev. 1243 (1987). The principal legal issue is whether OMB oversight violates separation of powers principles because Congress has delegated the rulemaking function to a specific agency rather than to the executive office. Olson, The Quiet Shift of Power: Office of Management and Budget Supervision of Environmental Protection Agency Rulemaking under Executive Order 12,191, 4 Va. J. Nat. Resources L. 1 (1984), argues that Executive Order 12,191, see page 47 *supra*, may violate separation of powers principles and give the OMB unwarranted authority to encroach on discretion delegated to the agency by Congress. Executive Order 12,248, issued January 4, 1985, 46 Fed. Reg. 1,036 (1985), gives OMB even greater discretion to review EPA actions for consistency with administration policies. A federal district court has limited the power of OMB to delay the promulgation of EPA regulations mandated by Congress. The 1984 RCRA Amendments required the promulgation of regulation for leaking underground storage tanks (LUSTs), but EPA failed to meet the deadline because of OMB review. EDF v. Thomas, 627 F. Supp. 566 (D.D.C. 1986), holds that OMB lacks the power to delay compliance with Congressional mandates. "This is incompatible with the will of Congress and cannot be sustained as a valid exercise of the President's Article II powers." See generally Environmental Policy under Reagan's Executive Order: The Role of Benefit-Cost Analysis (V.K. Smith ed. 1984); DeMuth & Ginsburg, White House Review of Agency Rulemaking, 99 Harv. L. Rev. 1075 (1986); and Morrison, OMB Interference with Agency Rulemaking: The Wrong Way to Write a Regulation, 99 Harv. L. Rev. 1059 (1986).

Second, until well into the 1970s the Department of Justice continued to assert that the doctrine of sovereign immunity barred suits against the government. This defense was first overcome through technical rulings by sympathetic judges, such as rulings allowing mandamus against officials to compel the performance of non-discretionary duties, and finally by general statutory waivers in 1976. Third, access to the courts and agencies was difficult because the law regarding standing to sue seemed to require a tangible, even pecuniary, interest in the controversy; for parties with nontraditional interests such as environmental organizations, the right to sue was far less well defined. Around 1970 the first environmental lawyers perceived broadened standing as the most important issue facing their young field, and the issue remains crucial today as many judges articulate vigorous new theories of judicial deference to administrative agencies.

Fourth, in the early 1970s there was very little federal environmental statutory law, and what there was conferred vast discretion on agency officials. In many fields Congress gave the agencies such broad discretion to manage environmental resources that the courts had no law to apply in correcting agency decisions. Many believed that judicial review of these decisions was not available at all because they were "committed to agency discretion." Finally, even if a plaintiff convinced a court to review a decision, judicial review of agency action was limited. All agency decisions came to a court with a presumption of validity, and the opponent of the decision had a difficult time convincing a court that an agency action was "arbitrary and capricious" if it was an informal agency action or, if a formal record had been produced in an agency hearing, that "substantial evidence" did not exist to support the agency's decision. Questions of law could be decided de novo by a court, but even then an agency's construction of its enabling legislation was entitled to deference. Litigants could hope to be successful only if they claimed that an action was beyond the agency's powers or procedurally defective.

Lawsuits brought largely by public interest law firms and environmental organizations challenged each of these doctrines and thus the very foundations of administrative law. The courts, especially the District of Columbia Circuit Court of Appeals, led the movement toward more vigorous judicial supervision of the administrative process. The administrative law of judicial review changed rapidly, and a new model of the administrative process emerged in response to judicial intervention. In his synthesis of these developments, Professor Richard Stewart argued that the "new" administrative law rejected the expertise model, which confined the courts to protecting unconstitutional and illegal agency intrusions on individual rights, and replaced it with a model of the agency as a forum for resolving conflicts between various antagonistic groups. In short, the courts stood on its head a classic corollary of the expertise model — that experts must be shielded from crass political influence:

> Faced with the seemingly intractable problem of agency discretion, courts have changed the focus of judicial review (in the process expanding and transforming traditional procedural devices) so that its dominant purpose is no longer the prevention of unauthorized intrusions on private autonomy, but the assurance of fair

representation for all affected interests in the exercise of the legislative power delegated to agencies.

Implicit in this development is the assumption that there is no ascertainable, transcendent "public interest," but only the distinct interests of various individuals and groups in society. Under this assumption, legislation represents no more than compromises struck between competing interest groups.[206] This analysis suggests that if agencies were to function as a forum for all interests affected by agency decisionmaking, bargaining leading to compromises generally acceptable to all might result, thus replicating the process of legislation. Agency decisions made after adequate consideration of all affected interests would have, in microcosm, legitimacy based on the same principle as legislation and therefore the fact that statutes cannot control agency discretion would become largely irrelevant. [Stewart, The Reformation of American Administrative Law, 88 Harv. L. Rev. 1667, 1712 (1975).]

Because administrative agencies have no constitutional footing, their legal status has always been ambiguous and subject to intense debate. Any debate about the constitutional status of the administrative process must, of necessity, include the role of the courts in reviewing administrative action. In the 1980s the idea of widespread deregulation, the intellectual foundations of which had been laid at least two decades earlier, gained political legitimacy. Deregulation debates sparked a renewed interest in fundamental administrative law questions such as the constitutional legitimacy of agencies and the role of Congress, the executive branch, and the courts in promoting greater agency accountability. One outcome has been the development of theories that stress the need for a strong or unitary executive to counter inefficient congressional decisions. Courts are increasingly receptive to theories of increased executive control and thus diminished judicial control of the administrative process. The reasons for this are well explored in Aman, Administrative Law in a Global Era: Progress, Deregulatory Change, and the Rise of the Administrative Presidency, 73 Cornell L. Rev. 1101 (1988).

There are many reasons for this development. The statutes put in place during the environmental decade delegated vast amounts of discretion and power to the executive. The idea of active judicial review within a republican system of government has never been accepted by all judges and commentators, and in the last decade new theories of judicial deference have been constructed. Scholars and judges influenced by public choice theory stress the need for judges to view legislative delegations as interest group bargains struck by Congress and further argue that courts should generally uphold such bargains by limiting their inquiry into the meaning of the statute. The two leading advocates of this posi-

---

206. See, e.g., A. Bentley, The Process of Government (1908); D. Truman, The Governmental Process (1951). In the extreme form of this view, there is no objective, independent yardstick by which one can measure the content of compromise; compromises are legitimated by the process of their negotiation. For criticism of such analysis, see T. Lowi, [The Poverty of Liberalism (1968)]; R. Wolff, [The End of Liberalism (1969)]. Pluralist political theory may be regarded as a translation into collective terms of the principle of subjectivity of individual values. See . . . R. Unger, [Knowledge and Politics (1975)].

tion are judges Frank Easterbrook and Richard Posner of the Seventh Circuit Court of Appeals. See Easterbrook, The Supreme Court, 1983 Term-Forward: The Court and the Economic System, 98 Harv. L. Rev. 4 (1984) and Posner, Economics, Politics, and the Reading of Statutes and the Constitution, 49 U. Chi. L. Rev. 261 (1982). These theories are based not so much on a respect for the legislative process as a loss of faith in the ability of the Congress as currently structured to be other than a conduit for special interests. Alternative theories also have been influenced by public choice theory but hold that courts should articulate fundamental substantive standards, Sunstein, Constitutionalism after the New Deal, 101 Harv. L. Rev. 421 (1987), or play a more aggressive role in insisting on greater rationality between means and ends of regulatory programs. Rose-Ackerman, Progressive Law and Economics — and the New Administrative Law, 98 Yale L.J. 341 (1988). Many of the leading participants in this debate have restated and refined their positions in A Symposium on Administrative Law: The Uneasy Constitutional Status of Administrative Agencies, 36 American U.L. Rev. 277 (1987). See also Farber & Frickey, The Jurisprudence of Public Choice, 65 Tex. L. Rev. 873 (1987) and Symposium on the Theory of Public Choice, 74 Va. L. Rev. 167 (1988). The net result is that after the burst of judicial creativity of the 1970s, administrative law has once again become formal and thus deferential to agency discretion. This is confusing for the student because environmental and other precedents that created the "new" administrative law now co-exist uneasily with newer precedents that seek to confine judicial review of administrative decisions.

A.   ACCESS TO THE COURTS: STANDING AND RELATED PRECLUSION DOCTRINES

Quite frequently, administrative actions that are claimed to have negative environmental impacts will or may be challenged only by organizations and individuals who did not participate in the agency action. For example, if the Interior Department enters into a lease with a private company for mining on public lands, both parties will probably be satisfied with this decision. Judicial review will be sought, if at all, only by third parties concerned about the adverse environmental consequences of the Department's action.

Third parties who seek judicial review of agency actions must have standing. These third party plaintiffs traditionally have faced difficult standing problems because of the rule that a plaintiff must show injury to a common law or statutory legal interest, a theory of access that left no room for the generally concerned citizen representing a broad public interest, such as a public policy concern that was ecological or even philosophical in nature. In the leading case of Associated Industries, Inc. v. Ickes, 134 F. 2d 694 (2d Cir. 1943), Judge Frank held that Congress could constitutionally authorize "so to speak, private Attorney Generals" to bring suit to prevent an administrative official from acting in violation of this statutory power. Leading administrative law scholar Professor Louis Jaffe has endorsed the idea of a public action as consistent with the fundamental principles of representative government. See Jaffe, The Citizen as Litigant in Public Actions: The Non-Hohfeldian or Ideological Plaintiff, 116 U. Pa. L. Rev. 1033 (1968), and, Standing Again, 84 Harv. L. Rev. 633 (1971). The major constitutional argument against the public action is that it violates the "case or controversy" requirement of article III of the Constitution. See Berger, Standing to Sue in Public Actions: Is It a Constitutional Requirement? 78 Yale L.J. 816 (1969). Constitutional challenges to standing in environmental cases rarely occur and almost never succeed; rather, such challenges ordinarily arise under statutes, principally the U.S. Administrative Procedure Act (APA), as was the case in the following landmark decision. Still, the decisions swing between the theory that administrative standing should be based on private rights, created by common law or statute, and the theory that public actions can legitimately be policed by members of the public, which were intended to be benefited by regulatory programs. See generally Fletcher, The Structure of Standing, 98 Yale L. J. 221, 250-265 (1988).

SIERRA CLUB v. MORTON
405 U.S. 727 (1972)

Mr. Justice STEWART delivered the opinion of the Court.

I

The Mineral King Valley is an area of great natural beauty nestled in the Sierra Nevada Mountains in Tulare County, California, adjacent to Sequoia National Park. It has been part of the Sequoia National Forest since 1926, and is designated as a national game refuge by special Act of Congress. Though once the site of extensive mining activity, Mineral King is now used almost exclusively for recreational purposes. Its relative inaccessibility and lack of development have limited the number of visitors each year, and at the same time have preserved the valley's quality as a quasi-wilderness area largely uncluttered by the products of civilization.

The United States Forest Service, which is entrusted with the maintenance and administration of national forests, began in the late 1940s to give consideration to Mineral King as a potential site for recreational development. Prodded by a rapidly increasing demand for skiing facilities, the Forest Service published a prospectus in 1965, inviting bids from private developers for the construction and operation of a ski resort that would also serve as a summer recreation area. The proposal of Walt Disney Enterprises, Inc., was chosen from those of six bidders, and Disney received a three-year permit to conduct surveys and explorations in the valley in connection with its preparation of a complete master plan for the resort.

The final Disney plan, approved by the Forest Service in January 1969, outlines a $35 million complex of motels, restaurants, swimming pools, parking lots, and other structures designed to accommodate 14,000 visitors daily. This complex is to be constructed on 80 acres of the valley floor under a 30-year use permit from the Forest Service. Other facilities, including ski lifts, ski trails, a cog-assisted railway, and utility installations, are to be constructed on the mountain slopes and in other parts of the valley under a revocable special-use permit. To provide access to the resort, the State of California proposes to construct a highway 20 miles in length. A section of this road would traverse Sequoia National Park, as would a proposed high-voltage power line needed to provide electricity for the resort. Both the highway and the power line require the approval of the Department of the Interior, which is entrusted with the preservation and maintenance of the national parks.

Representatives of the Sierra Club, who favor maintaining Mineral King largely in its present state, followed the progress of recreational planning for the valley with close attention and increasing dismay. They unsuccessfully sought a public hearing on the proposed development in 1965, and in subsequent correspondence with officials of the Forest Service and the Department of the Interior, they expressed the Club's objections to Disney's plan as a whole and to particular features included in it. In June 1969 the Club filed the present suit in the United States District Court for the Northern District of California, seeking a declaratory judgment that various aspects of the proposed development contravene federal laws and regulations governing the preservation of national parks, forests, and game refuges,[2] and also seeking preliminary and permanent injunctions restraining the federal officials involved from granting their approval or issuing permits in connection with the Mineral King project. The petitioner Sierra Club sued as a membership corporation with "a special interest in the conservation and the sound maintenance of the national parks, game refuges and forests of the country," and invoked the judicial-review provisions of the Administrative Procedure Act, 5 U.S.C. §701 et seq.

After two days of hearings, the District Court granted the requested prelim-

---

2.   As analyzed by the District court, the complaint alleged violations of law falling into four categories. First, it claimed that the special-use permit for construction of the resort exceeded the maximum-acreage limitation placed upon such permits by 16 U.S.C. §497, and that issuance of a "revocable" use permit was beyond the authority of the Forest Service. Second, it challenged the proposed permit for the highway through Sequoia National Park on the grounds that the highway would not serve any of the purposes of the park, in alleged violation of 16 U.S.C. §1, and that it would destroy timber and other natural resources protected by 16 U.S.C. §§41 and 43. Third, it claimed that the Forest Service and the Department of the Interior had violated their own regulations by failing to hold adequate public hearings on the proposed project. Finally, the complaint asserted that 16 U.S.C. §45c requires specific congressional authorization of a permit for construction of a power transmission line within the limits of a national park.

inary injunction. It rejected the respondents' challenge to the Sierra Club's standing to sue, and determined that the hearing had raised questions "concerning possible excess of statutory authority, sufficiently substantial and serious to justify a preliminary injunction. . . ." The respondents appealed, and the Court of Appeals for the Ninth Circuit reversed. 433 F.2d 24. With respect to the petitioner's standing, the court noted that there was "no allegation in the complaint that members of the Sierra Club would be affected by the actions of [the respondents] other than the fact that the actions are personally displeasing or distasteful to them," id., at 33, and concluded: "We do not believe such club concern without a showing of more direct interest can constitute standing in the legal sense sufficient to challenge the exercise of responsibilities on behalf of all the citizens by two cabinet level officials of the government acting under Congressional and Constitutional authority." Id., at 30. Alternatively, the Court of Appeals held that the Sierra Club had not made an adequate showing of irreparable injury and likelihood of success on the merits to justify issuance of a preliminary injunction. The court thus vacated the injunction. The Sierra Club filed a petition for a writ of certiorari which we granted, 401 U.S. 907, to review the questions of federal law presented.

II

The first question presented is whether the Sierra Club has alleged facts that entitle it to obtain judicial review of the challenged action. Whether a party has a sufficient stake in an otherwise justiciable controversy to obtain judicial resolution of that controversy is what has traditionally been referred to as the question of standing to sue. Where the party does not rely on any specific statute authorizing invocation of the judicial process, the question of standing depends upon whether the party has alleged such a "personal stake in the outcome of the controversy," Baker v. Carr, 369 U.S. 186, 204, as to ensure that "the dispute sought to be adjudicated will be presented in an adversary context and in a form historically viewed as capable of judicial resolution." Flast v. Cohen, 392 U.S. 83, 101. Where, however, Congress has authorized public officials to perform certain functions according to law, and has provided by statute for judicial review of those actions under certain circumstances, the inquiry as to standing must begin with a determination of whether the statute in question authorizes review at the behest of the plaintiff.[3]

The Sierra Club relies upon §10 of the Administrative Procedure Act

---

3.   Congress may not confer jurisdiction on Art. III federal courts to render advisory opinions, Muskrat v. United States, 219 U.S. 346, or to entertain "friendly" suits, United States v. Johnson, 319 U.S. 302, or to resolve "political questions," Luther v. Borden, 7 How. 1, because suits of this character are inconsistent with the judicial function under Art. III. But where a dispute is otherwise justiciable, the question whether the litigant is a "proper party to request an adjudication of a particular issue," Flast v. Cohen, 392 U.S. 83, 100, is one within the power of Congress to determine. . . .

(APA), 5 U.S.C. §702, which provides: "A person suffering legal wrong because
of agency action, or adversely affected or aggrieved by agency action within the
meaning of a relevant statute, is entitled to judicial review thereof." Early decisions under this statute interpreted the language as adopting the various formulations of "legal interest" and "legal wrong" then prevailing as constitutional
requirements of standing. But, in Data Processing Service v. Camp, 397 U.S.
150, and Barlow v. Collins, 397 U.S. 159, decided the same day, we held more
broadly that persons had standing to obtain judicial review of federal agency
action under §10 of the APA where they had alleged that the challenged action
had caused them "injury in fact," and where the alleged injury was to an interest
"arguably within the zone of interests to be protected or regulated" by the statutes
that the agencies were claimed to have violated.[5]

In *Data Processing*, the injury claimed by the petitioners consisted of harm
to their competitive position in the computer-servicing market through a ruling
by the Comptroller of the Currency that national banks might perform data-
processing services for their customers. In *Barlow*, the petitioners were tenant
farmers who claimed that certain regulations of the Secretary of Agriculture adversely affected their economic position vis-à-vis their landlords. These palpable
economic injuries have long been recognized as sufficient to lay the basis for
standing, with or without a specific statutory provision for judicial review. Thus,
neither *Data Processing* nor *Barlow* addressed itself to the question, which has
arisen with increasing frequency in federal courts in recent years, as to what must
be alleged by persons who claim injury of a noneconomic nature to interests that
are widely shared. That question is presented in this case.

III

The injury alleged by the Sierra Club will be incurred entirely by reason of the
change in the uses to which Mineral King will be put, and the attendant change
in the aesthetics and ecology of the area. Thus, in referring to the road to be
built through Sequoia National Park, the complaint alleged that the development "would destroy or otherwise adversely affect the scenery, natural and historic objects and wildlife of the park and would impair the enjoyment of the park
for future generations." We do not question that this type of harm may amount
to an "injury in fact" sufficient to lay the basis for standing under §10 of the
APA. Aesthetic and environmental well-being, like economic well-being, are
important ingredients of the quality of life in our society, and the fact that particular environmental interests are shared by the many rather than the few does
not make them less deserving of legal protection through the judicial process.
But the "injury in fact" test requires more than an injury to a cognizable interest.
It requires that the party seeking review be himself among the injured.

---

5.   In deciding this case we do not reach any questions concerning the meaning of the
"zone of interests" test or its possible application to the facts here presented.

The impact of the proposed changes in the environment of Mineral King will not fall indiscriminately upon every citizen. The alleged injury will be felt directly only by those who use Mineral King and Sequoia National Park, and for whom the aesthetic and recreational values of the area will be lessened by the highway and ski resort. The Sierra Club failed to allege that it or its members would be affected in any of their activities or pastimes by the Disney development. Nowhere in the pleadings or affidavits did the Club state that its members use Mineral King for any purpose, much less that they use it in any way that would be significantly affected by the proposed actions of the respondents.[8]

The Club apparently regarded any allegations of individualized injury as superfluous, on the theory that this was a "public" action involving questions as to the use of natural resources, and that the Club's longstanding concern with and expertise in such matters were sufficient to give it standing as a "representative of the public."[9] This theory reflects a misunderstanding of our cases involving so-called "public actions" in the area of administrative law.

The origin of the theory advanced by the Sierra Club may be traced to a dictum in Scripps-Howard Radio v. FCC, 316 U.S. 4, in which the licensee of a radio station in Cincinnati, Ohio, sought a stay of an order of the FCC allowing another radio station in a nearby city to change its frequency and increase its range. In discussing its power to grant a stay, the Court noted that "these private litigants have standing only as representatives of the public interest." Id., at 14. But that observation did not describe the basis upon which the appellant

8. The only reference in the pleadings to the Sierra Club's interest in the dispute is contained in paragraph 3 of the complaint, which reads in its entirety as follows:

Plaintiff Sierra Club is a non-profit corporation organized and operating under the laws of the State of California, with its principal place of business in San Francisco, California since 1892. Membership of the club is approximately 78,000 nationally, with approximately 27,000 members residing in the San Francisco Bay Area. For many years the Sierra Club by its activities and conduct has exhibited a special interest in the conservation and the sound maintenance of the national parks, game refuges and forests of the country, regularly serving as a reponsible representative of persons similarly interested. One of the principal purposes of the Sierra Club is to protect and conserve the national resources of the Sierra Nevada Mountains. Its interests would be vitally affected by the acts hereinafter described and would be aggrieved by those acts of the defendants as hereinafter more fully appears.

In an amici curiae brief filed in this Court by the Wilderness Society and others, it is asserted that the Sierra Club has conducted regular camping trips into the Mineral King area, and that various members of the Club have used and continue to use the area for recreational purposes. These allegations were not contained in the pleadings, nor were they brought to the attention of the Court of Appeals. Moreover, the Sierra Club in its reply brief specifically declines to rely on its individualized interest, as a basis for standing. See n.15, *infra*. Our decision does not, of course, bar the Sierra Club from seeking in the District Court to amend its complaint by a motion under Rule 15, Federal Rules of Civil Procedure.

9. This approach to the question of standing was adopted by the Court of Appeals for the Second Circuit in Citizens Committee for the Hudson Valley v. Volpe, 425 F.2d 97, 105:

We hold, therefore, that the public interest in environmental resources — an interest created by statutes affecting the issuance of this permit — is a legally protected interest affording these plaintiffs, as responsible representatives of the public, standing to obtain judicial review of agency action alleged to be in contravention of that public interest.

was allowed to obtain judicial review as a "person aggrieved" within the meaning of the statute involved in that case, since Scripps-Howard was clearly "aggrieved" by reason of the economic injury that it would suffer as a result of the Commission's action. The Court's statement was, rather, directed to the theory upon which Congress had authorized judicial review of the Commission's actions. That theory had been described earlier in FCC v. Sanders Bros. Radio Station, 309 U.S. 470, 477, as follows: "Congress had some purpose in enacting §402(b)(2). It may have been of opinion that one likely to be financially injured by the issue of a license would be the only person having a sufficient interest to bring to the attention of the appellate court errors of law in the action of the Commission in granting the license. It is within the power of Congress to confer such standing to prosecute an appeal."

Taken together, *Sanders* and *Scripps-Howard* thus established a dual proposition: the fact of economic injury is what gives a person standing to seek judicial review under the statute, but once review is properly invoked, that person may argue the public interest in support of his claim that the agency has failed to comply with its statutory mandate. It was in the latter sense that the "standing" of the appellant in *Scripps-Howard* existed only as a "representative of the public interest." It is in a similar sense that we have used the phrase "private attorney general" to describe the function performed by persons upon whom Congress has conferred the right to seek judicial review of agency action. See *Data Processing, supra,* at 154.

The trend of cases arising under the APA and other statutes authorizing judicial review of federal agency action has been toward recognizing that injuries other than economic harm are sufficient to bring a person within the meaning of the statutory language, and toward discarding the notion that an injury that is widely shared is ipso facto not an injury sufficient to provide the basis for judicial review. We noted this development with approval in *Data Processing,* 397 U.S., at 154, in saying that the interest alleged to have been injured "may reflect 'aesthetic, conservational, and recreational' as well as economic values." But broadening the categories of injury that may be alleged in support of standing is a different matter from abandoning the requirement that the party seeking review must himself have suffered an injury.

Some courts have indicated a willingness to take this latter step by conferring standing upon organizations that have demonstrated "an organizational interest in the problem" of environmental or consumer protection. Environmental Defense Fund v. Hardin, 138 U.S. App. D.C. 391, 395, 428 F.2d 1093, 1097. It is clear that an organization whose members are injured may represent those members in a proceeding for judicial review. See, e.g., NAACP v. Button, 371 U.S. 415, 428. But a mere "interest in a problem," no matter how longstanding the interest and no matter how qualified the organization is in evaluating the problem, is not sufficient by itself to render the organization "adversely affected" or "aggrieved" within the meaning of the APA. The Sierra Club is a large and long-established organization, with a historic commitment to the cause of protecting our Nation's natural heritage from man's depredations. But if a "special interest" in this subject were enough to entitle the Sierra Club to commence this litigation, there would appear to be no objective basis upon which to disallow a suit by any other bona fide "special interest" organization, however small or short-lived. And if any group with a bona fide "special interest" could initiate such litigation, it is difficult to perceive why any individual citizen with the same bona fide special interest would not also be entitled to do so.

The requirement that a party seeking review must allege facts showing that he is himself adversely affected does not insulate executive action from judicial review, nor does it prevent any public interests from being protected through the judicial process.[15] It does serve as at least a rough attempt to put the decision as to whether review will be sought in the hands of those who have a direct stake in the outcome. That goal would be undermined were we to construe the APA to authorize judicial review at the behest of organizations or individuals who seek to do no more than vindicate their own value preferences through the judicial process. The principle that the Sierra Club would have us establish in this case would do just that.

As we conclude that the Court of Appeals was correct in its holding that the Sierra Club lacked standing to maintain this action, we do not reach any other questions presented in the petition, and we intimate no view on the merits of the complaint. The judgment is affirmed.

Justice POWELL and Justice REHNQUIST took no part in the consideration or decision of this case.

[The dissenting opinions of Justices BLACKMUN, BRENNAN, and DOUGLAS are not reproduced here.]

NOTES AND QUESTIONS

1. Has the Court's "user standing" rule placed any serious limitations on the standing of plaintiffs with ideological interests? The Sierra Club had no difficulty amending its complaint to allege facts sufficient to confer standing. *Sierra Club v. Morton*, 348 F. Supp. 219 (N.D. Cal. 1972). Note also that the Court did not determine whether the Sierra Club satisfied the "zone of interests" test. Did it in fact meet the test? For a critique of the *Sierra Club* decision, see Sax,

---

15.   In its reply brief, after noting the fact that it might have chosen to assert individualized injury to itself or to its members as a basis for standing, the Sierra Club states:

> The Government seeks to create a "heads I win, tails you lose" situation in which either the courthouse door is barred for lack of assertion of a private, unique injury or a preliminary injunction is denied on the ground that the litigant has advanced private injury which does not warrant an injunction adverse to a competing public interest. Counsel have shaped their case to avoid this trap.

The short answer to this contention is that the "trap" does not exist. The test of injury in fact goes only to the question of standing to obtain judicial review. Once this standing is established, the party may assert the interests of the general public in support of his claims for equitable relief. . . .

Standing to Sue: A Critical Review of the Mineral King Decision, 13 Nat. Resources J. 76 (1973). The subsequent history of the Mineral King development is detailed in Lundmark, Mester, Cordes & Sandals, Mineral King Goes Downhill, 5 Ecology L.Q. 555 (1976). For another view of the *Sierra Club* problem, see Baude, Sierra Club v. Morton: Standing Trees in a Thicket of Justiciability, 48 Ind. L.J. 197 (1973).

2. The relaxed user standard of the *Sierra Club* decision would appear to provide a basis for third party standing in much environmental litigation, especially when a specific project is challenged. Problems arise only when the link between the challenged project and the claimed environmental harm is not clear. This issue arose in United States v. Students Challenging Regulatory Agency Procedures (*SCRAP I*), 412 U.S. 669 (1973). A student group and environmental organization brought suit challenging an interim rate increase by the U.S. Interstate Commerce Commission (ICC). They argued that the rate increase would discourage the use of recycled materials since recycled goods incur higher transportation charges, and they sought to compel the ICC to prepare an environmental impact statement. The Supreme Court held that the plaintiffs had standing:

> Unlike the specific and geographically limited federal action of which the petitioner complained in *Sierra Club*, the challenged agency action in this case is applicable to substantially all of the Nation's railroads, and thus allegedly has an adverse environmental impact on all the natural resources of the country. Rather than a limited group of persons who used a picturesque valley in California, all persons who utilize the scenic resources of the country, and indeed all who breathe its air, could claim harm similar to that alleged by the environmental groups here. But we have already made it clear that standing is not to be denied simply because many people suffer the same injury. Indeed some of the cases on which we relied in *Sierra Club* demonstrated the patent fact that persons across the Nation could be adversely affected by major governmental actions. . . . [To deny standing to persons who are in fact injured simply because many others are also injured, would mean that the most injurious and widespread Government actions could be questioned by nobody.] We cannot accept that conclusion.
>
> But the injury alleged here is also very different from that at issue in *Sierra Club* because here the alleged injury to the environment is far less direct and perceptible. The petitioner there complained about the construction of a specific project that would directly affect the Mineral King Valley. Here, the Court was asked to follow a far more attenuated line of causation to the eventual injury of which the appellees complained — a general rate increase would allegedly cause increased use of nonrecyclable commodities as compared to recyclable goods, thus resulting in the need to use more natural resources to produce such goods, some of which resources might be taken from the Washington area, and resulting in more refuse that might be discarded in national parks in the Washington area. The railroads protest that the appellees could never prove that a general increase in rates would have this effect, and they contend that these allegations were a ploy to avoid the need to show some injury in fact. [412 U.S., at 687-688.]

The Court then noted that the case was at the pleading stage and that the pleading alleged facts sufficient to show standing; if the railroads believed that the allegations in the pleadings were untrue, they should have moved for summary judgment.

3. *SCRAP I* can reduce the injury in fact to a fiction. See No Gwen Alliance of Lane County, Inc. v. Aldridge, 855 F.2d 1380 (9th Cir. 1988). Occasionally the government and other defendants have attempted to disprove plaintiffs' allegations of injury, but such attempts have generally not been successful, e.g., National Wildlife Federation v. Burford, 878 F.2d 422 (D.C. Cir. 1989). See Note 4, *infra*. While the liberalized "environmental" standard is secure under *SCRAP I*, in cases involving other subject matter the Supreme Court has responded sympathetically to the argument that expanded standing rules thrust the Court into the position of having to deal with political questions and has begun to find new constitutional and nonconstitutional standing requirements. The need to limit standing for both constitutional and prudential reasons is summarized in a five-to-four decision involving first amendment standing:

> The judicial power of the United States defined by Art. III is not an unconditioned authority to determine the constitutionality of legislative or executive acts. The power to declare the rights of individuals and to measure the authority of governments, this Court said 90 years ago, "is legitimate only in the last resort, and as a necessity in the determination of real, earnest and vital controversy." Chicago & Grand Trunk R. Co. v. Wellman, 143 U.S. 339, 345 (1892). Otherwise, the power "is not judicial . . . in the sense in which judicial power is granted by the Constitution to the courts of the United States." United States v. Ferreira, 13 How. L.J. 40, 48 (1852).
>
> As an incident to the elaboration of this bedrock requirement, this Court has always required that a litigant have "standing" to challenge the action sought to be adjudicated in the lawsuit. The term "standing" subsumes a blend of constitutional requirements and prudential considerations, and it has not always been clear in the opinions of this Court whether particular features of the "standing" requirement have been required by Art. III ex proprio vigore, or whether they are requirements that the Court itself has erected and which were not compelled by the language of the Constitution. See Flast v. Cohen, 392 U.S., at 97 [1968].
>
> A recent line of decisions, however, has resolved that ambiguity, at least to the following extent: at an irreducible minimum, Art. III requires the party who invokes the court's authority to "show that he personally has suffered some actual or threatened injury as a result of the putatively illegal conduct of the defendant," Gladstone Realtors v. Village of Bellwood, 441 U.S. 91, 99 (1979), and that the injury "fairly can be traced to the challenged action" and "is likely to be redressed by a favorable decision," Simon v. Eastern Kentucky Welfare Rights Org., 426 U.S. 26, 38, 41 (1976). In this manner does Art. III limit the federal judicial power "to those disputes which confine federal courts to a role consistent with a system of separated powers and which are traditionally thought to be capable of resolution through the judicial process." Flast v. Cohen, *supra*, at 97.
>
> The requirement of "actual injury redressable by the court" serves several of the "implicit policies embodied in Article III." It tends to assure that the legal questions presented to the court will be resolved, not in the rarified atmosphere of a debating society, but in a concrete factual context conducive to a realistic appreciation of the consequences of judicial action. The "standing" requirement serves other purposes. Because it assures an actual factual setting in which the litigant asserts a claim of injury in fact, a court may decide the case with some confidence

that its decision will not pave the way for lawsuits which have some, but not all, of the facts of the case actually decided by the court.

The Art. III aspect of standing also reflects a due regard for the autonomy of those persons likely to be most directly affected by a judicial order. The federal courts have abjured appeals to their authority which would convert the judicial process into "no more than a vehicle for the vindication of the value interests of concerned bystanders." United States v. SCRAP, 412 U.S. 669, 687 (1973). Were the federal courts merely publicly funded forums for the ventilation of public grievances or the refinement of jurisprudential understanding, the concept of "standing" would be quite unnecessary. But the "cases and controversies" language of Art. III forecloses the conversion of courts of the United States into judicial versions of college debating forums . . . The exercise of judicial power, which can so profoundly affect the lives, liberty, and property of those to whom it extends, is therefore restricted to litigants who can show "injury in fact" resulting from the action which they seek to have the Court adjudicate.

The exercise of the judicial power also affects relationships between the co-equal arms of the national government. The effect is, of course, most vivid when a federal court declares unconstitutional an act of the Legislative or Executive branch. While the exercise of that "ultimate and supreme function," Chicago & Grand Trunk R. Co. v. Wellman, 143 U.S., at 345, is a formidable means of vindicating individual rights, when employed unwisely or unnecessarily it is also the ultimate threat to the continued effectiveness of the federal courts in performing that role. While the propriety of such action by a federal court has been recognized since Marbury v. Madison, 1 Cranch 137 (1803), it has been recognized as a tool of last resort on the part of the federal judiciary throughout its nearly 200 years of existence. . . .

Beyond the constitutional requirements, the federal judiciary has also adhered to a set of prudential principles that bear on the question of standing. Thus, this Court has held that "the plaintiff generally must assert his own legal rights and interests, and cannot rest his claim to relief on the legal rights or interests of third parties." Warth v. Seldin, 422 U.S., at 499. In addition, even when the plaintiff has alleged redressable injury sufficient to meet the requirements of Art. III, the Court has refrained from adjudicating "abstract questions of wide public significance" which amount to "generalized grievances," pervasively shared and most appropriately addressed in the representative branches. Id., at 499-500. Finally, the court has required that the plaintiff's complaint fall within "the zone of interests to be protected or regulated by the statute or constitutional guarantee in question." Data Processing Service v. Camp, 397 U.S. 150, 153 (1969).

Merely to articulate these principles is to demonstrate their close relationship to the policies reflected in the Art. III requirement of actual or threatened injury amenable to judicial remedy. But neither the counsels of prudence nor the policies implicit in the "case or controversy" requirement should be mistaken for the rigorous Art. III requirements themselves. Satisfaction of the former cannot substitute for a demonstration of "'distinct and palpable injury' . . . that is likely to be redressed if the requested relief is granted." Gladstone Realtors v. Village of Bellwood, supra, 441 U.S., at 100. That requirement states a limitation on judicial power, not merely a factor to be balanced in the weighing of so-called "prudential" considerations.

We need not mince words when we say that the concept of "Art. III standing" has not been defined with complete consistency in all of the various cases decided by this Court which have discussed it, nor when we say that this very fact is probably proof that the concept cannot be reduced to a one-sentence or one-paragraph definition. But of one thing we may be sure: Those who do not possess

Art. III standing may not litigate as suitors in the courts of the United States. Art. III, which is every bit as important in its circumscription of the judicial power of the United States as in its granting of that power, is not merely a troublesome hurdle to be overcome if possible so as to reach the "merits" of a lawsuit which a party desires to have adjudicated; it is a part of the basic charter promulgated by the framers of the Constitution at Philadelphia in 1787, a charter which created a general government, provided for the interaction between that government and the governments of the several States, and was later amended so as to either enhance or limit its authority with respect to both States and individuals. [Valley Forge Christian College v. Americans United for Separation of Church and State, 470 U.S. 464, 471-476 (1982).]

In the 1970s the Justice Department did not vigorously assert lack of standing in environmental cases. Factual affidavits on plaintiffs' injury were seriously but unsuccessfully contested in Sierra Club v. Morton, 514 F.2d 856 (D.C. Cir. 1975), *rev'd on other grounds sub nom.* Kleppe v. Sierra Club, 427 U.S. 390 (1976). However, the specificity of injury continues to be litigated. In a challenge to the enforcement of the Surface Mine Reclamation Act, the coal mining industry challenged the National Wildlife Federation's failure to describe the injury caused by specific mine terraces. The court, however, concluded that the 70 affidavits submitted by the plaintiff were sufficient to establish injury in fact. National Wildlife Federation v. Hodel, 839 F.2d 694 (D.C. Cir. 1988). Does *Valley Forge* suggest that environmental standing is inconsistent with the Court's broader principles? For an ambitious attempt to articulate a limitless theory of the public action based on the ability of judges to articulate new public values, see J. Vining, Legal Identity: The Coming of Age of Public Law (1978), critically reviewed in Stewart, Standing for Solidarity, 88 Yale L. Rev. 1559 (1979).

4. *Valley Forge* and its progeny, for example, Allen v. Wright, 468 U.S. 737 (1984), can raise substantial standing barriers for certain kinds of environmental suits. For sharply contrasting views of the lessons of *Valley Forge* see Center for Auto Safety v. NHTSA, 793 F.2d 1322 (D.C. Cir. 1986) and Center for Auto Safety v. Thomas, 806 F.2d 1071 (D.C. 1986), *vacated per curiam* 810 F.2d 302 (D.C. Cir. 1987) (en banc), *reinstated per curiam by an equally divided court*, 847 F.2d 843 (en banc), *vacated per curiam*, 856 F.2d 1557 (1988) (en banc). Two Seventh Circuit Court of Appeals cases illustrate some of the modern standing barriers. Northside Sanitary Landfill, Inc. v. Thomas, 804 F.2d 371 (7th Cir. 1986), held that a landfill operator did not have standing to challenge the denial of a RCRA (Resource Conservation and Recovery Act) permit. EPA Region V had denied Northside's application for a RCRA Part B permit because it contained insufficient closure information and ordered the facility closed to hazardous waste disposal, although the state of Indiana had been delegated sole RCRA permitting and enforcement authority. The landfill operator did not challenge the denial of the Part B permit. Instead, he argued that EPA's decision, especially remarks made by agency personnel at the Part B hearing, related to an issue that had been delegated to the state and thus denied him due process because he had not received a fair hearing on the administrative determination of

the issue. The court concluded that EPA's action could not have caused the landfill operator injury because EPA lacked the legal authority to conduct an enforcement action. Judge Eshbach was more sympathetic to the argument that EPA's conclusions would nonetheless be rubber-stamped by the state and thus the landfill operator had standing; he concluded, however, that review of EPA's action was not ripe.

Valley Forge may also bar suits to challenge the adverse environmental impacts of agency activities that the Council on Environmental Quality has categorically exempted from compliance with the National Environmental Policy Act. Various city officials of Evanston, Illinois sued to require the preparation of an environmental impact statement (EIS) for a regional bus maintenance facility located at an abandoned steel plant in an area zoned for heavy industry. The Urban Mass Transportation Administration exempted such facilities from the EIS requirement. The Seventh Circuit found that plaintiffs had failed to demonstrate the constitutionally required "distinct and palpable" injury: "Considering the present steel business use in light of nothing but some vague and general allegations of environmental harms, we cannot see why or how the new proposed use will not be in fact an environmental improvement." City of Evanston v. Regional Transportation Authority, 825 F.2d 1121, 1125-1126 (7th Cir. 1987), *cert. denied*, 108 S. Ct. 697 (1988). Two protesting aldermen lacked standing because they failed to allege where they lived and thus demonstrated no personal stake in the proposed change of use. Does *City of Evanston* hold that adverse environmental impact is a pure question of law? If not, what is the basis for the denial of standing? For a critical analysis of the tendency of some recent cases to return to the pre-*Data Processing* legal interests test see Sunstein, Standing and the Privatization of Public Law, 88 Colum. L. Rev. 1432 (1988).

5. Do the post-*SCRAP I* Supreme Court decisions change the law applied in cases brought by plaintiffs with environmental concerns? If *Valley Forge* were vigorously applied in each of the following cases, what would be the result? The following cases suggest some of the problems raised in the scores of standing decisions:

a. State of Alabama v. E.P.A., 871 F.2d 1548 (11th Cir. 1989), *cert. denied*, — U.S. — (1990). The governor and attorney general of Alabama sought a preliminary injunction to prevent the shipment of PCB-contaminated soil from a Superfund site in Texas to a facility in Alabama that had received all the necessary federal and state permits. Initially, Alabama supported the permits and participated fully in the federal proceedings but state officials decided to protest the shipment in 1988 because they had not participated in the Superfund process in Texas that led to the decision to ship the soil out of state. The court held that no plaintiff had alleged sufficient injury in fact. Alabama officials alleged that the shipment would require increased state funds to ensure that it was done safely and that there was a threat to the environment of the state. The state officials lacked standing as taxpayers because they did not allege that the expenditure of additional funds was unconstitutional. Nor did they have standing as citizens.

"In this case there is no necessary causal connection between the injury to Alabama's environment and the lack of notice and opportunity to participate in the selection of the remedial action for the Geneva Industries site." Why?

b. Glover River Organization v. Department of the Interior, 675 F.2d 251 (10th Cir. 1982). The plaintiff, an organization organized to promote flood control, challenged the designation of the leopard darter as an endangered species under the Endangered Species Act because no environmental impact statement had been filed. The plaintiff alleged that its members had suffered and would continue to suffer losses from flooding and that the listing of the leopard darter prevented Congressional funding of flood control projects because the projects would threaten the darter. The court held that the plaintiff had alleged sufficient concrete injury but that it had not shown that the court could grant relief that would redress its injury; further, the plaintiff had not presented sufficient proof indicating that flood control projects would be funded if the darter were not listed. The court said, "Such relief must come from Congress and the President, not the Secretary of the Interior." The court noted that Congress could always repeal or amend the Endangered Species Act to authorize flood control projects that would threaten the leopard darter. Redressability also tripped up a poultry processor who discharged into a new publicly owned sewage treatment facility. After the facility was built, rates were raised to cover a shortfall. At the same time, the Alabama Department of Environmental Management issued a stringent NPDES permit and the discharger tried to protest the higher rates at a hearing but the Board dismissed the complaint for lack of standing. In affirming, the court wrote "[E]ven if this court were to grant the relief requested . . . and the new NPDES permit were to be revoked by the Commission, . . . sewage rates would still not decline because the source of those rate increases, the new sewage treatment facility, has already been built and now must be paid for." Marshall Durbin Co. v. Alabama Dept. of Environmental Management, 537 So. 2d 490, 494 (Ala. Civ. App. 1987).

c. Animal Welfare Institute v. Kreps, 561 F.2d 1002 (D.C. Cir. 1977). Environmental organizations brought suit challenging an action by the federal government waiving a ban on the importation of the skins of South African baby seals. They alleged injury in fact, claiming in part that the waiver of the ban would contribute to the death and injury of marine mammals; they also alleged that the waiver would interfere with their opportunities to observe South African seals alive in their native state. The court held that these allegations alleged injury in fact that satisfied the traditional test and added: "Where an act is expressly motivated by considerations of humaneness toward animals, who are uniquely incapable of defending their own interests in court, it strikes us as eminently logical to allow groups specifically concerned with animal welfare to invoke the aid of the courts in enforcing the statute" (561 F.2d at 1007). Accord Japan Whaling Association v. American Cetacean Society, 478 U.S. 221 (1986). Compare Mountain States Legal Foundation v. Costle, 630 F.2d 754 (10th Cir. 1980). Suit was brought claiming that the Environmental Protection Agency had imposed sanctions under the Clean Air Act that unconstitutionally infringed on the rights of the state of Colorado under the tenth amendment. The court held that only the state, not the foundation, had standing to challenge the EPA action. Compare also Animal Lover's Volunteer Association, Inc. v. Weinberger, 765 F.2d 939 (9th Cir. 1985). The court denied standing to protest the killing of goats on federal property because plaintiffs had not differentiated their concern for animals "from the generalized abhorrence other members of the public may feel at the prospect of cruelty to animals."

Environmental plaintiffs generally avoid these problems by detailed allegations of use of the affected area, but such allegations may not always be sufficient. Wilderness Society v. Griles, 824 F.2d 4 (D.C. Cir. 1987), reversed a grant of summary judgment and dismissal of an action brought by the Wilderness Society to challenge the conveyance of submerged lands in Alaska. Judge Wald noted that plaintiffs could not establish that they had used any of the lands for recreation. She concluded, however, that they had alleged facts sufficient to survive a motion to dismiss and were entitled to discovery to try to meet the higher standards of injury and causation required to survive a motion for summary judgment.

d. Coughlin v. Seattle School District Number 1, 27 Wash. App. 888, 621 P.2d 183 (Wash. Ct. App. 1980). The plaintiff brought suit claiming an environmental impact statement was required under a state counterpart of the National Environmental Policy Act (NEPA) on the closing of five elementary schools in the school district in question. Holding that the plaintiff did not have standing, the court noted that it had followed federal standing rules: "These requirements preclude standing based solely upon the harm claimed by Coughlin in her capacity as a concerned and active citizen, taxpayer and resident of the District. Such harm is too remote to establish standing" (621 P.2d at 186). Might the plaintiff have been able to claim standing under the SCRAP I rationale?

e. Benton County Savings & Loan v. FHLBB, 450 F. Supp. 884 (W.D. Ark. 1978). A group of banks demanded that the Federal Home Loan Bank Board file an environmental impact statement when it approved a branch facility for a rival bank. The court disagreed, holding that NEPA does not "protect persons whose sole motivation is their own economic interest and welfare" (450 F. Supp. at 890).

Compare Lake Erie Alliance for the Protection of the Coastal Corridor v. Corps of Engineers, 486 F. Supp. 707 (W.D. Pa. 1980), on reh'g, 526 F. Supp. 1063 (W.D. Pa. 1981), aff'd mem., 707 F.2d 1392 (3d Cir. 1983). Steelworkers employed locally, among others, brought an action challenging the failure of the Corps to file an environmental impact statement on the construction of a new steel plant by a private company; the Corps had issued a navigable water permit for the project. The plaintiffs claimed that they were threatened with unemployment because the new facility would cause other plants to close. The court held that the steelworkers had standing: "While the 'real' interest of the steelworkers before us undoubtedly is job security, all live in or around the tri-state area which will be affected environmentally by this project, and all have alleged a concern with those adverse environmental effects" (486 F. Supp. at 713).

See also Delaware River Port Authority v. Tiemann, 403 F. Supp. 1117 (D.N.J. 1975). The Authority challenged the Federal Highway Administration's refusal to file an environmental impact statement in connection with its decision to lower tolls on bridges within the Authority's jurisdiction. While the court recognized that the Authority would suffer economic harm because of the decreased revenues resulting from the lower tolls, the court found this harm not within the zone of interests protected by NEPA. The Authority also claimed that the decrease in tolls would lead to an increase in urban congestion and pollution, an assertion that was not sufficient to confer standing, which cannot be based on "generalized grievances" common to all citizens. Neither, the court held, may a plaintiff base standing on an assertion of the rights of third parties.

Hancock County v. EPA, 742 F.2d 1455 (6th Cir. 1984), denied standing to a company to challenge EPA's review of a rival company's application to use part of a county's PSD increments.

6. The Court has recently reiterated the zone of interests test as prudential standard, Clark v. Securities Industry Assn., 479 U.S. 388 (1987), and the District of Columbia Circuit Court of Appeals has interpreted *Clark* to draw a sharp distinction between consumer and competitor standing. This distinction, which had been eroding, can pose problems as more and more waste treatment industries raise environmental issues. Hazardous Waste Treatment Council v. EPA, 861 F.2d 277, 281-284 (D.C. Cir. 1988) is such a case. Plaintiff challenged EPA's use of Resource and Recovery Conservation Act (RCRA) rules as insufficiently strict. Judge Williams had no problem with the allegation that the council's members would suffer consumer injuries if they received contaminated oil; he had more trouble with the argument that the regulations would diminish the demand for high tech services that were "in sync with those sought to be served by RCRA." This was classified as an incidental benefit, and he concluded that despite the court's previous competitor standing cases and those that grant standing to parties who sell to regulated industries, Moneghan, Third Party Standing, 84 Colum. L. Rev. 277 (1984), that a presumption against intent to benefit should be drawn because there is a risk that judicial review will produce perverse results:

II. Standing and Jurisdiction

A. STANDING

The Hazardous Waste Treatment Council is a national trade organization of firms engaged in the treatment of hazardous waste and the manufacture of equipment for that purpose. The gist of its complaint here is that EPA's regulations are not comprehensive and strict enough to comply fully with the controlling statute, RCRA. Concerned with the apparent anomaly of regulated entities demanding stricter regulation, we requested the parties to brief the issue of standing. Besides its brief, the Council has submitted the affidavits of its executive director and also of executives of five member companies.

We conclude that the Council has standing insofar as it represents members on whom regulatory laxity may inflict environmental injury; we reject standing for it as representative of firms that may suffer competitive loss because EPA has not forced on their competitors as demanding (and expensive) techniques as they themselves employ.

1. ALLEGATIONS AS TO STANDING.

The Council's member firms operate facilities in 48 states. They provide treatment or disposal services employing both established and emerging technologies and methods for treatment and management: incineration and other thermal destruction, reclamation, biological and chemical treatment, land disposal after pre-treatment, and hazardous site cleanups. A number of member companies are engaged in the reclamation of used oil, the blending of used oil for use as industrial fuel, and the treatment and disposal of used oil.

The Council's Articles of Incorporation declare that among its purposes is

> To promote the protection of the environment through the adoption of environmentally sound procedures and methods of destroying and treating hazardous wastes and the proper management of residues of those treatment and destruction processes.

The affidavits submitted by the Council and various members reveal the members' varied relations to the substantive issues raised in this case. We can identify three different types:

a. *Competitor claims.* At least three members claim that the asserted laxity of the regulations will diminish the market for their high-tech control services. (CF Systems Corporation, Swatz Affidavit; SYSTECH Corporation, Eifert Affidavit; Ross Environmental Services, Stiff Affidavit.) Firms with contaminated used oil on hand will, they argue, be free to re-use that oil without either using the treatment services of Council members or incurring the expense of themselves providing the high-quality treatment that Council members offer. . . .

e. *Claims of supply diminution.* Affidavits filed by several members assert that the alleged regulatory laxity will cause their *supply* of contaminated used fuels to be diverted elsewhere. (SYSTECH Corporation, Eifert Affidavit; Ross Environmental Services, Stiff Affidavit; ThermalKEM Inc., Zeigler Affidavit.) These affidavits make no effort to explain how regulatory laxity reduces supply in any normal sense of the word. So far as we are able to discern, these claims must fit into one of the two categories discussed above. Either the firms suffer because there is less demand for their services or because the oils they receive are less pure. Accordingly, we drop these allegations from any separate consideration here.

2. APPLICATION OF STANDING PRINCIPLES.

It is a commonplace that standing encompasses two components: constitutional and prudential. . . .

a. *The consumer claims.* We have no difficulty finding that the consumer interests represented by the Council are entitled to standing. According to the affidavit of the affected member company's executive, it suffers direct losses as a recipient of contaminated used oils. That the injury is commercial is no obstacle. "[S]neering at [commercial] gains by adding 'mere' to them does not make them go away." United States Department of the Air Force v. FLRA, 838 F.2d 29, 233 (7th Cir. 1988). Owners of a lake who licensed its use by fishermen and boaters would surely have standing to attack regulatory laxity that led to increased water pollution; there appears no principle by which one could reasonably distinguish the injury alleged here.

We will address below the problem of whether the *Council* is an appropriate representative of the consumer interests of BVER.

b. *The competitor claims.* The Council's competitor claims appear quite similar to those asserted in Calumet Industries, Inc. v. Brock, 807 F.2d 225 (D.C. Cir. 1986). There the petitioners objected to the Occupational Safety and Health Administration's decision to adopt a narrow definition of the class of oils that vendors were required to label as health hazards. Petitioners' oils indisputably required such labelling. We found that "the interest to be protected by the OSH Act is worker safety . . . and *not* business profits" and consequently held that "[a]s petitioners here [did] not come before us as protectors of worker safety, but instead as entrepreneurs seeking to protect their competitive interests, we think it plain they lack standing." Id. at 228 (emphasis in original).

Here, however, the Council asserts that its interests, though pecuniary, are in sync with those sought to be served by RCRA. In essence they suggest that tightening of environmental standards will generally foster not only a cleaner environment but also the member companies' profits, as it will expand the market for their services.[1]

The Supreme Court's decision in *Clarke* leaves the status of this sort of incidental benefit somewhat unclear. *Clarke* explained that the zone of interests "test is not meant to be especially demanding; in particular, there need be no indication of congressional purpose to benefit the would-be plaintiff. *Investment Company Institute, supra* [401 U.S. 617 (1971)]." 107 S. Ct. at 757 (footnotes omitted).[2] On the other hand, it said the test "denies a right of review if the plaintiff's interests are so marginally related to or inconsistent with the purposes implicit in the statute that it cannot reasonably be assumed that Congress intended to permit the suit." Id. We must thus find operational meaning for a test that demands less than a showing of congressional intent to benefit but more than a "marginal[ ] rela[tionship]" to the statutory purposes.

The answer may lie in presumptions revolving around the congressional intent to benefit. Where that intent is plain, we may entertain a presumption of standing — a presumption that can be overcome by, for example, a finding that suit by intended beneficiaries would "severely disrupt [a] complex and delicate administrative scheme." Block v. Community Nutrition Institute, 467 U.S. 340, 348

---

1.   As its executive director notes, the Council

is unique in that it represents firms whose economic interests and future viability depend on the presence, not the absence, of appropriate regulations for the protection of the environment which create the demand for their advanced waste treatment and management services. . . . Thus the linkage between effective implementation and enforcement by EPA of regulatory programs under RCRA, increased protection of human health and the environment, and increased use of the waste treatment services provided by the HWTC member companies is a direct one. HWTC exists to represent the collective interest of its member companies in proper environmental control.

Fortuna Affidavit at 2-3.

2.   It further observed that our decision in Control Data Corp. v. Baldrige, 655 F.2d 283, 293-94 (D.C. Cir.), *cert. denied*, 454 U.S. 881 (1981), to the extent that it "suggests otherwise," is "inconsistent with our understanding of the zone of interest test, as now formulated." Id. at 757 n.15. We followed *Control Data* in Glass Packaging Inst. v. Regan, 737 F.2d 1083 (D.C. Cir), *cert. denied*, 469 U.S. 1035 (1984), and Copper & Brass Fabricators Council, Inc. v. Department of the Treasury, 679 F.2d 951 (D.C. Cir. 1982), which are presumably condemned to the same extent.

(1984), quoted in *Clarke*, 107 S. Ct. at 757. In the absence of apparent congressional intent to benefit, however, there may still be standing if some factor — some indicator that the plaintiff is a peculiarly suitable challenger of administrative neglect — supports an inference that Congress would have intended eligibility. Cf. Haitian Refugee Center v. Gracey, 809 F.2d 794, 812-13 (D.C. Cir. 1987) (pre-*Clarke* case stating that the initial inquiry is whether "from the face of the statute" the interest was arguably intended to be protected or regulated, but that clear evidence in the legislative history of intent to afford or deny standing may rebut the initial answer).

Here the Council points essentially to Congress's indisputable intent to encourage proper disposal and recycling of hazardous wastes. See, e.g., 42 U.S.C. §§6901(a) (4), 6902(a) (6). But that intent, of course, shows neither that Congress intended to benefit recycling and disposal firms nor that such firms' interests are more than "marginally related" to Congress's environmental purposes. Whenever Congress pursues some goal, it is inevitable that firms capable of advancing that goal may benefit. If Congress authorized bank regulators to mandate physical security measures for banks, for example, a shoal of security services firms might enjoy a profit potential — detective and guard agencies, manufacturers of safes, detection devices and small arms, experts on entrance control, etc. But in the absence of either some explicit evidence of an intent to benefit such firms, or some reason to believe that such firms would be unusually suitable champions of Congress's ultimate goals, no one would suppose them to have standing to attack regulatory laxity. And of course a rule that gave any such plaintiff standing merely because it happened to be disadvantaged by a particular agency decision would destroy the requirement of prudential standing; any party with constitutional standing could sue.

It is worth remembering that judicial intervention may defeat statutory goals if it proceeds at the behest of interests that coincide only accidentally with those goals. The companion case, Hazardous Waste Treatment Council v. EPA, No. 86-1658, illustrates the risk that the interests may diverge significantly. There EPA refused to list certain types of used oil as hazardous wastes because it thought this would have the boomerang effect of increasing illegal dumping and thus would result in net harm to the environment. Although the court finds that Congress did not authorize the EPA to consider such an effect, it is a perfectly plausible one. See Martin T. Katzman, From Horse Carts to Minimills, 92 The Public Interest 121, 132 (Summer 1988) (discussing effect of expectation that EPA would list as hazardous waste oil from dismantled cars). When we grant standing to a party with only an oblique relation to the statutory goal, we run the risk that the outcome could, even assuming technical fidelity to law, in fact thwart the congressional goal. Further, of course, technical fidelity to law cannot be assumed; judges err.

The risk is present here as well. A regulatory extension sought by the competitor interests in the Council might benefit recyclers' profits (e.g., by forcing the use of more advanced recycling techniques) but harm the environment (because, for example, its cost might lead to substitution of more environmentally harmful fuels). [Hazardous Waste Treatment Council v. EPA, 861 F.2d 277, 281-284 (D.C. Cir. 1988).]

The Council next tried to obtain standing in Hazardous Waste Treatment Council v. Thomas, 885 F.2d 918 (D.C. Cir. 1989) (HWTC IV) with the argument that the board judicial review provisions of RCRA, *infra*, Chapter 5, pp. 604 to 613, "simply does not admit of any prudential limitation," but Judge

D.H. Ginsburg rejected the argument and further found that none of the Council's members had prudential standing.

7. Although attorneys' fees are not usually available to prevailing parties under the American rule, some federal courts developed a "private attorney general" exception that permitted the recovery of attorneys' fees in public interest litigation, such as environmental litigation. The Supreme Court rejected this exception in Alyeska Pipeline Service Co. v. Wilderness Society, 421 U.S. 240 (1975), but Congress has since authorized the award of attorneys' fees under most environmental statutes, e.g., Clean Air Act, 42 U.S.C. §7604(d).

Congress also has enacted a statute, the Equal Access to Justice Act, 28 U.S.C. §2412(d)(1)(A), authorizing the mandatory award of attorneys' fees and expenses to any party "prevailing" against the United States unless a court finds "that the position of the United States was substantially justified or that special circumstances make an award unjust." This statute authorizes attorneys' fee awards under environmental statutes, such as NEPA, that do not expressly authorize attorneys' fee awards.

A NOTE ON EXHAUSTION OF ADMINISTRATIVE REMEDIES, PRIMARY JURISDICTION, AND RIPENESS

In addition to the doctrines discussed above, a number of other administrative law doctrines can defeat judicial review of administrative agency decisions. Generally, these doctrines require judicial deference to agency decisionmaking when agency action is considered necessary to establish a basis for judicial review. Since these doctrines can defeat a court action or postpone it for a considerable time, an understanding of their function is important to environmental litigants.

Exhaustion of administrative remedies. Exhaustion is a defense to judicial review when the administrative agency has not had an opportunity to consider the claim for relief. The rationale for the exhaustion doctrine was spelled out in West v. Bergland, 611 F.2d 710 (8th Cir. 1979) (action to enjoin hearing on whether Secretary of Agriculture's meat grading and inspection services should be withdrawn for misconduct):

> First among these governmental interests [in the exhaustion of administrative remedies] is that of allowing the agency to "perform functions within its special competence." Parisi v. Davidson, 405 U.S. 34, 37 (1972). These functions include specialized fact-finding, . . . interpretations of disputed technical matter, . . . and resolving disputes concerning the meaning of the agency's regulations. . . .
>
> A second governmental interest in requiring exhaustion is discouraging "frequent and deliberate flouting of the administrative process." . . .
>
> . . . [T]he exhaustion doctrine requires us to consider two other interests. The first is . . . [an interest] in allowing the agency to have the first opportunity to develop the facts and apply the law it was designed to administer. . . . [The court

quoted from McKart v. United States, 395 U.S. 195 (1969), the leading Supreme Court exhaustion decision.] Permitting the agency to perform its "trial court" function not only serves interests in administrative autonomy and efficiency but also generally assists ultimate judicial review. . . .

A second interest in administrative autonomy, which parallels an interest in judicial efficiency, is that of allowing agencies to correct their own errors, and in so doing moot controversies and obviate judicial review. [611 F.2d at 715, 716.]

Courts may invoke the exhaustion doctrine when agency determination of factual issues is necessary to judicial consideration of a litigant's claim. See Izaak Walton League of America v. St. Clair, 497 F.2d 849 (8th Cir. 1974). The court remanded the case to allow the U.S. Forest Service to determine the extent of a challenged mining activity on a wilderness area and whether a permit with protective conditions should be issued.

In other cases, courts have found sufficient flexibility in the exhaustion doctrine to avoid application of the doctrine to the case before it. Courts frequently have made exceptions to the doctrine in NEPA cases. See Jette v. Bergland, 579 F.2d 59 (10th Cir. 1978). In this case, the Forest Service determined not to issue an environmental impact statement on exploratory drilling activities in a forest area. An appeal from the agency decision was pending when an action was brought challenging the failure to prepare the statement, but the court noted that the exhaustion doctrine "has some flexibility depending on the circumstances." It added that "[e]xceptions to the requirement of exhaustion have been made in NEPA cases when the drawbacks of the requirement outweigh the advantages in the circumstances of a particular case" (579 F.2d at 62). The court allowed the plaintiff's action to stand. The requirement of exhaustion of administrative remedies is strongly defended in Gelpe, Exhaustion of Administrative Remedies: Lessons from Environmental Cases, 53 Geo. Wash. L. Rev. 1 (1985).

Primary jurisdiction. The defense of primary jurisdiction is related to the exhaustion doctrine. It arises when a court has original jurisdiction of a claim requiring the resolution of issues also placed within the competence of an administrative agency. In these cases, the judicial process is suspended until the administrative agency can resolve these issues, if the court recognizes the agency's primary jurisdiction. A court action for an injunction to abate a nuisance or to enforce a statutory environmental obligation is an example of a case of this kind.

The competence of the judiciary to decide complex technical issues often underlies an assertion of the primary jurisdiction defense. As one court put it: "[T]he doctrine of primary jurisdiction involves the deferring of jurisdiction by the court to the agency's specialized competence in interpreting policy and factual circumstances in order to avoid inconsistent adjudication and to allow the agency to employ its specialized expertise." Minnesota Public Interest Research Group v. Adams, 482 F. Supp. 170, 181 (D. Minn. 1979) (action to enjoin highway construction for failure to prepare impact statement).

The need for uniformity in the interpretation of regulatory legislation is another basis for the primary jurisdiction rule. See Consolidated Rail Corp. v.

City of Dover, 450 F. Supp. 966 (D. Del. 1978). In dismissing a suit by the city of Dover to enjoin excessive noise from railroad switching yard operations, the court noted that primary jurisdiction lay with EPA, which was then engaged in rule-making regarding noise pollution problems, under authority conferred by the federal Noise Control Act.

Environmental litigants can argue that agency referrals should not be made when the agency is hostile to the environmental claim. See Note, Primary Jurisdiction in Environmental Cases: Suggested Guidelines for Limiting Referral, 48 Ind. L.J. 676 (1973). This note makes this argument and suggests that referral is proper only when the agency is currently and actively involved with the issues under consideration in the court proceeding.

Both the Clean Air and the Clean Water Acts contain provisions authorizing citizen suits to enforce statutory requirements. The congressional decision to make the citizen remedy available argues against a recognition of primary agency jurisdiction. See Friends of the Earth v. Carey, 535 F.2d 165 (2d Cir. 1976). An Illinois court relied on a similar state statute authorizing the state's attorney general to bring court enforcement proceedings to reject the primary jurisdiction claim altogether. Village of Wilsonville v..SCA Services, Inc., 77 Ill. App. 618, 396 N.E.2d 552 (Ill. App. 1979). Note that, in this case, both the village and the attorney general had brought actions seeking injunctive relief against a hazardous waste landfill. The court accepted the case even though it was "painfully aware of the lack of expertise in courts to fully understand the complicated technical matters involved in a case of this nature" (396 N.E.2d at 556). Similarly, Natural Resources Defense Council, Inc. v. Outboard Marine Corp., 692 F. Supp. 801 (N.D. Ill. 1988) refused to apply the doctrine to a citizen suit alleging violations of existing permits even though the discharger was pursuing administrative permits to modify the permits.

Ripeness. The ripeness and finality doctrine is intended to prevent judicial consideration of controversies before the administrative agency has made a final decision that puts the case in a concrete context. Building from the traditional equity doctrine that a court will not issue an injunction without a showing of imminent irreparable harm, statutes and judicial opinions generally condition judicial review on the entry of a final order. This makes sense when agencies issue final decisions affecting individual parties, as courts do, but it creates problems in judicial review of agency regulations and other less informal actions. If the agency has taken a final position on an issue but has not yet begun an enforcement action, is there any reason to deny pre-enforcement judicial review? Abbott Laboratories v. Gardner, 387 U.S. 136 (1967), answered this question no. Characterizing the purpose of the ripeness requirement as the "avoidance of premature adjudication," the Court substituted crystallization of the agency position for the "final order" rule. Once this threshold standard is met, the court balances the harm to the regulated entity from delayed review against the public interest in allowing the regulatory program to proceed without judicial interference. The Court followed this approach in Pacific Gas & Electric Co. v. State Energy Resources Conservation & Development Commission, 461 U.S. 190

(1983). California adopted an initiative that imposed a moratorium on new nuclear plants until the United States demonstrated that a demonstrated technology existed for the disposal of high-level nuclear wastes. The issue was whether the Atomic Energy Act preempted the issue so there was no need to wait until California interpreted and applied its statute. A second statute, which required that the state energy agency make a determination that adequate spent fuel rod storage existed when a plant required such storage, was not found ripe because it was premature to determine whether a plant's storage capacity would ever be found inadequate.

The combination of a clear legal issue and hardship was again present in Thomas v. Union Carbide Agricultural Products Co., 473 U.S. 568 (1985). Justice O'Connor held that an Article III challenge to a provision of Federal Pesticide Act of 1978 which required binding arbitration for the EPA's determination of the compensation due to a pesticide registrant whose data was shared with other applicants was ripe for review. "Doubts about the validity of the FIFRA data-consideration and compensation scheme have plagued the pesticide industry and seriously hampered the effectiveness of FIFRA's reforms of the registration process."

Ripeness problems can arise in environmental litigation when plaintiffs challenge agency policies that provide the basis for agency actions but do not challenge a specific decision by the agency. Plaintiffs may believe that a court challenge to a specific decision may turn on the facts of the case, obscuring the policy basis on which the agency acted.

In National Wildlife Federation v. Benn, 491 F. Supp. 1234 (S.D.N.Y. 1980), the plaintiffs challenged regulatory policies of the U. S. Army Corps of Engineers that governed federal decisions authorizing individual ocean-dumping permits. The plaintiffs claimed, in fact, that the Corps had violated NEPA, arguing that the Corps had failed to draft what is known as a "programmatic" environmental impact statement evaluating the cumulative environmental effect of continuously dumping dredged material at a site off New York and New Jersey coasts. The Corps argued that "plaintiffs are litigating on the basis of hypothetical facts and speculation about future agency action because no specific permit or project has been challenged." The court disagreed:

> The plaintiffs have not simply leveled generalized charges against the Corps; they are challenging specific procedures and policies to which the Corps concededly adheres in issuing permits and approving projects. The issues raised by the plaintiffs concern the construction and intent of the . . . [Corps's policies] and do not turn on the factual circumstances of an individual permit [491 F. Supp. at 1241].

Compare Commonwealth Edison Co. v. Train, 649 F.2d 481 (7th Cir. 1980). Utility companies brought an action challenging the legality of regulations adopted by EPA requiring states to adopt a policy in their water quality control plans preventing the degradation of water quality. The court held that the regulations were not ripe for decision. EPA's regulation was directed to the states, and it was "impossible to determine at this point with any degree of certainty whether the utilities will be injured by future action by the states" (649 F.2d at 484). The District of Columbia Circuit Court of Appeals has held that neither the problem that budget decisions must be made under a cloud of uncertainty nor the need to incur future costs to challenge a regulation are a sufficient hardship, Diamond Shamrock Corp. v. Costle, 580 F.2d 670 (D.C. Cir. 1978), but statutory provision authorizing pre-enforcement review may tip the balance toward review when the agency's position is fully crystallized and the issues are purely ones of law. Compare Eagle-Picher Industries, Inc. v. EPA, 759 F.2d 905 (D.C. Cir. 1985) with Natural Resources Defense Council v. EPA, 859 F.2d 156 (D.C. Cir. 1988).

Ripeness problems also arise when an agency issues an interlocutory decision and the affected party seeks review of this decision rather than await further agency action. In Illinois v. EPA 621 F.2d 259 (7th Cir. 1980), the agency served a Notice of Deficiency on the state of Illinois, indicating that deficiencies existed in its clean air state implementation plan. All states are required to prepare such plans under the national Clean Air Act. Dismissing a court action challenging the Notice of Deficiency, the court said: "The notice only informs and 'requests,' it does not 'order.' The [EPA] Administrator lacks statutory authority to order the state to do anything about the alleged deficiencies" (621 F.2d at 261). Note that the "final action" rule has been codified in §704 of the APA and has also been included or implied in environmental legislation.

B.   JUDICIAL REVIEW OF ADMINISTRATIVE ENVIRONMENTAL DECISIONMAKING

In the early 1970s, at the beginning of the environmental decade, environmentalists relied heavily on the courts to police what were perceived as hostile agencies. Once environmental plaintiffs cleared the standing, ripeness, exhaustion, and primary jurisdiction hurdles, the issue became the scope of judicial review. They were soon joined by business interests seeking review of agency decisions newly hostile to their viewpoint after the "environmental awakening" of 1970, the creation of EPA, and the outpouring of new statutes mandating strict environmental standards. For both sides the basic task was to convince the court to reach the merits of the action or prod the agency to make a different decision on remand. The rub was that the doctrine of separation of powers precluded courts from directly substituting their judgment for that of the agency unless the question was one of law; courts are confined to review of the process of decision, rather than the substance of the decision. Despite separation of powers principles, both sides had some success in convincing courts to adopt new standards of judicial review that indirectly approach the merits; whether these new approaches represent a lasting change in administrative law is an open question.

1.   The Types of Reviewable Administrative Action

An early result of closer judicial scrutiny of environmental issues in the 1970s was a clarification of what types of actions federal agencies undertake. This clarification occurred because standards of judicial review, usually under §706 of the APA, varied depending on the type of agency action. But the clarification also helped agencies decide how much of a hearing to give various contenders for attention and how carefully to document decisions. If an agency had any lingering doubt, the instructions of the court on remand vacating the agency's decision usually clarified the steps required.

Generally speaking, lawmaking by the administrative process oscillates between the two extremes represented by courts and legislatures. If the existing rights of one or a few individuals are challenged, the judicial model usually applies and the agency acts more like a court, conducting a trial-type hearing on the record with cross-examination and other procedural formalities. If noncompetitive governmental permissions or broad policies that will apply prospectively to large numbers of organizations or individuals are in question, the freewheeling informality of the legislative model usually applies. If an agency must dispose of a large amount of money, decide basic individual rights, or explore factual questions in detail, the two models may be mixed.

A threshold issue, fundamental to administrative procedures, involves the requirements of constitutional procedural due process. In addressing this issue, the Supreme Court has adhered to a firm distinction between quasi-judicial agency "adjudication" and quasi-legislative agency "rule-making." In United States v. Florida East Coast Railway, 410 U.S. 224 (1973), the precise issue was whether the ICC had to hold a trial-type hearing for a "rule" on joint-line use of freight cars. The enabling act required that the decision be made "after hearing." The Court refused to construe this statutory language as requiring an on-the-record hearing; one of the reasons it offered for this holding was that the railroads had no constitutional right to a trial-type hearing because the factual basis of the decision was "a basically legislative-type judgment, for prospective application only, rather than in adjudicating a particular set of disputed facts." Relying on two of the Court's seminal administrative law decisions, Justice Rehnquist explained:

> The basic distinction between rulemaking and adjudication is illustrated by this Court's treatment of two related cases under the Due Process Clause of the Fourteenth Amendment. In Londoner v. Denver, cited in oral argument by appellees, 210 U.S. 373 (1908), the Court held that due process had not been accorded a landowner who objected to the amount assessed against his land as its share of the benefit resulting from the paving of a street. Local procedure had

accorded him the right to file a written complaint and objection, but not to be heard orally. This Court held that due process of law required that he "have the right to support his allegations by argument however brief, and if need be, by proof, however informal." But in the later case of Bi-Metallic Investment Co. v. State Board of Equalization, 239 U.S. 441 (1915), the Court held that no hearing at all was constitutionally required prior to a decision by state tax officers in Colorado to increase the valuation of all taxable property in Denver by a substantial percentage. The Court distinguished *Londoner* by stating that there a small number of persons "were exceptionally affected, in each case upon individual grounds." . . . While the line dividing them may not always be a bright one, these decisions represent a recognized distinction in administrative law between proceedings for the purpose of promulgating policy-type rules or standards, on the one hand, and proceedings designed to adjudicate disputed facts in particular cases, on the other. [410 U.S. at 244-245.]

Today, most important administrative actions fall into four categories: (1) formal adjudication, (2) formal rule-making, (3) informal notice-and-comment rule-making, and (4) informal adjudication or other informal action. A fifth category might be said to exist — one consisting of informal actions that require minimal procedural formalities (e.g., nonbinding policy statements).

Although most federal environmental decisionmaking today involves informal rule-making under regulatory statutes (see especially Chapters 3, 4, and 5), many environmental "managerial" decisions that fall into the informal adjudication or other informal action category are also made. For example, such informal decisions include approval of the location and funding of an interstate highway by the Secretary of Transportation or a decision by the Secretary of the Interior to allow the construction of a modern hotel with a disco and a video room in a national park. The following excerpt addresses the administrative procedures required in environmental regulation:

Agency decision making in regulating to protect health, safety, and the environment is overwhelmingly of the legislative sort, with a frequent dash of extra formality. It involves selecting and implementing statute-like policies that will apply prospectively to large classes of manufacturers, employers, and polluters. In developing their policies through standards, guidelines, and regulations — or *rules*, as they are collectively called — agencies follow a more or less standard process that is often called notice-and-comment rule making. First, they provide notice about what they want to require regulatees to do by publishing their proposed rules in the Federal Register. A period for public comment and counterproposal follows, which may include informal public hearings. Oral or written rebuttal and cross-examination between proponents of antagonistic views may be permitted, especially if factual matters remain in dispute. If they are doing their jobs properly, agencies respond in detail to the public commentary in the Federal Register when they issue rules in final form. Sometimes they propose significantly modified rules and reopen the comment period. In some rule making, a more formal trial-type hearing takes place before an administrative law judge, who, in recommending a decision to the agency, applies decisional principles quite similar to those a judge applies in deciding a case in a court of law, although it is still a rule the judge is propounding.
    One of the obvious reasons agencies rely on rule making rather than adju-

dication is that Congress provided them with rule-making powers and indicated informally that it expected them to get the job done through rules, not case-by-case adjudications. . . .

The rule-making style the agencies have evolved allows them to make the best of a difficult situation. . . . Congress charged the agencies to be comprehensive, yet to focus on specific conditions. It expected the agencies to set precise numerical standards, but to base them on scientific data that are sometimes exceedingly tentative. The agencies are to act swiftly, but also systematically and inclusively, and they must open their fact-finding and policy-formulation processes to whoever wants to participate.

Rule making is the fastest, least expensive, and politically most expedient way for agencies to carry out these diverse imperatives. It leaves the agencies maximum freedom to act within minimum procedural, informational, and participational restraints. A far cry from unfettered decision in a closed room with a few trusted advisers armed with a supportive consultant's study, this regulatory style nevertheless goes a long way toward giving the regulatory agency the upper hand.

A massive system of rules seems more compatible with the charge to be comprehensive than does the ad hoc evolution of policy over time. Detailed rules enable the agency not only to forbid the specific conduct that caused legislation to be enacted, but also to anticipate problems, so that the agency can act now to proscribe harms that are only distantly like those that prompted legislation in the first place. Once agency personnel get a feel for the task, writing a profusion of rules to cover events that have not yet occurred is far easier than analyzing facts and adjudicating rights for events that have occurred; thus they rationalize any overregulation as thoroughness, so that none of a wide number of generally similar harms ever occur. [Anderson, Human Welfare and the Administered Society: Federal Regulation in the 1970s to Protect Health, Safety, and the Environment, in Environmental and Occupational Medicine 835, 856-857 (W. Rom ed. 1983).]

2.   *Judicial Review under the* Overton Park *Standard*

How are the environmental decisions of agencies to be reviewed in court, particularly the two large classes of notice-and-comment rule-making and informal adjudication or other informal action? The next case, Citizens to Preserve Overton Park v. Volpe, destined to become a landmark in administrative law, addressed this question. In contrast with formal agency action, for informal agency action the APA neither requires detailed procedures nor provides a specific standard of judicial review. Until *Overton Park* it was widely thought that judicial review was precluded for many informal decisions because the scope of agency discretion was too great to permit effective judicial review consistent with the separation of powers doctrine.

CITIZENS TO PRESERVE OVERTON PARK v. VOLPE
401 U.S. 402 (1971)

Opinion of the Court by Justice MARSHALL, announced by Justice STEWART.
The growing public concern about the quality of our natural environment

has prompted Congress in recent years to enact legislation designed to curb the accelerating destruction of our country's natural beauty. We are concerned in this case with §4(f) of the Department of Transportation Act of 1966, as amend-ed,[2] and §18(a) of the Federal-Aid Highway Act of 1968, 23 U.S.C. §138 (1964 ed., Supp. V) [The text of §138 is almost verbatim the text of §4(f).]. . . .

Petitioners, private citizens as well as local and national conservation or-ganizations, contend that the Secretary [of Transportation] has violated these statutes by authorizing the expenditure of federal funds for the construction of a six-lane interstate highway through a public park in Memphis, Tennessee. Their claim was rejected by the District Court, which granted the Secretary's motion for summary judgment, and the Court of Appeals for the Sixth Circuit affirmed. After oral argument, this Court granted a stay that halted construction and, treat-ing the application for the stay as a petition for certiorari, granted review. 400 U.S. 939. We now reverse the judgment below and remand for further proceed-ings in the District Court.

Overton Park is a 342-acre city park located near the center of Memphis. The park contains a zoo, a nine-hole municipal golf course, an outdoor theater, nature trails, a bridle path, an art academy, picnic areas, and 170 acres of forest. The proposed highway, which is to be a six-lane, high-speed, expressway,[10] will sever the zoo from the rest of the park. Although the roadway will be depressed below ground level except where it crosses a small creek, 26 acres of the park will be destroyed. The highway is to be a segment of Interstate Highway I-40, part of the National System of Interstate and Defense Highways. I-40 will pro-vide Memphis with a major east-west expressway which will allow easier access to downtown Memphis from the residential areas on the eastern edge of the city.

. . . [T]he enactment of §4(f) of the Department of Transportation Act prevented distribution of federal funds for the section of the highway designated to go through Overton Park until the Secretary of Transportation determined

2.

It is hereby declared to be the national policy that special effort should be made to preserve the natural beauty of the countryside and public park and recreation lands, wildlife and waterfowl refuges, and historic sites. The Secretary of Transportation shall cooperate and consult with the Secretaries of the Interior, Housing and Urban Development, and Ag-riculture, and with the States in developing transportation plans and programs that in-clude measures to maintain or enhance the natural beauty of the lands traversed. After August 23, 1968, the Secretary shall not approve any program or project which requires the use of any publicly owned land from a public park, recreation area, or wildlife and waterfowl refuge of national, State, or local significance as determined by the Federal, State, or local officials having jurisdiction thereof, or any land from an historic site of national, State, or local significance as so determined by such officials unless (1) there is no feasible and prudent alternative to the use of such land, and (2) such program includes all possible planning to minimize harm to such park, recreational area, wildlife and wa-terfowl refuge, or historic site resulting from such use.

82 Stat. 824, 49 U.S.C. §1653(f) (1964 ed., Supp. V).

10.   The proposed right-of-way will be 250 to 450 feet wide and will follow the route of a presently existing, nonaccess bus route, which carries occasional bus traffic along a 40- to 50-foot right-of-way.

whether the requirements of §4(f) had been met. Federal funding for the rest of the project was, however, available, and the state acquired a right-of-way on both sides of the park. In April 1968, the Secretary announced that he concurred in the judgment of local officials that I-40 should be built through the park. And in September 1969 the State acquired the right-of-way inside Overton Park from the city. Final approval for the project — the route as well as the design — was not announced until November 1969, after Congress had reiterated in §138 of the Federal-Aid Highway Act that highway construction through public parks was to be restricted. Neither announcement approving the route and design of I-40 was accompanied by a statement of the Secretary's factual findings. He did not indicate why he believed there were no feasible and prudent alternative routes or why design change could not be made to reduce the harm to the park.

Petitioners contend that the Secretary's action is invalid without such formal findings and that the Secretary did not make an independent determination but merely relied on the judgment of the Memphis City Council. They also contend that it would be "feasible and prudent" to route I-40 around Overton Park either to the north or to the south. And they argue that if these alternative routes are not "feasible and prudent," the present plan does not include "all possible" methods for reducing harm to the park. Petitioners claim that I-40 could be built under the park by using either of two possible tunneling methods,[18] and they claim that, at a minimum, by using advanced drainage techniques the expressway could be depressed below ground level along the entire route through the park including the section that crosses the small creek.

Respondents argue that it was unnecessary for the Secretary to make formal findings, and that he did, in fact, exercise his own independent judgment which was supported by the facts. In the District Court, respondents introduced affidavits, prepared specifically for this litigation, which indicated that the Secretary had made the decision and that the decision was supportable. These affidavits were contradicted by affidavits introduced by petitioners. . . .

The District Court and the Court of Appeals found that formal findings by the Secretary were not necessary and refused to order the deposition of the former Federal Highway Administrator because those courts believed that probing of the mental processes of an administrative decisionmaker was prohibited. And, believing that the Secretary's authority was wide and reviewing courts' authority narrow in the approval of highway routes, the lower courts held that the affidavits contained no basis for a determination that the Secretary had exceeded his authority.

We agree that formal findings were not required. But we do not believe that in this case judicial review based solely on litigation affidavits was adequate.

---

18.   Petitioners argue that either a bored tunnel or a cut-and-cover tunnel, which is a fully depressed route covered after construction, could be built. Respondents contend that the construction of a tunnel by either method would greatly increase the cost of the project, would create safety hazards, and because of increases in air pollution would not reduce harm to the park.

A threshold question — whether petitioners are entitled to any judicial review — is easily answered. Section 701 of the Administrative Procedure Act, 5
U.S.C. §701 (1964 ed., Supp. V), provides that the action of "each authority of
the Government of the United States," which includes the Department of Transportation, is subject to judicial review except where there is a statutory prohibition on review or where "agency action is committed to agency discretion by
law." In this case, there is no indication that Congress sought to prohibit judicial
review and there is most certainly no "showing of 'clear and convincing evidence'
of a . . . legislative intent" to restrict access to judicial review. Abbott Laboratories v. Gardner, 387 U.S. 136, 141 (1967). . . .

Similarly, the Secretary's decision here does not fall within the exception
for action "committed to agency discretion." This is a very narrow exception.
Berger, Administrative Arbitrariness and Judicial Review, 65 Colum. L. Rev. 55
(1965). The legislative history of the Administrative Procedure Act indicates that
it is applicable in those rare instances where "statutes are drawn in such broad
terms that in a given case there is no law to apply." S. Rep. No. 752, 79th Cong.,
1st Sess., 26 (1945).

[The Court quoted §4(f), especially the "feasible and prudent" and "all
possible planning" language (see note 2) and continued:] This language is a plain
and explicit bar to the use of federal funds for construction of highways through
parks — only the most unusual situations are exempted.

Despite the clarity of the statutory language, respondents argue that the
Secretary has wide discretion. They recognize that the requirement that there be
no "feasible" alternative route admits of little administrative discretion. For this
exemption to apply the Secretary must find that as a matter of sound engineering
it would not be feasible to build the highway along any other route. Respondents
argue, however, that the requirement that there be no other "prudent" route
requires the Secretary to engage in a wide-ranging balancing of competing interests. They contend that the Secretary should weigh the detriment resulting
from the destruction of parkland against the cost of other routes, safety considerations, and other factors, and determine on the basis of the importance that
he attaches to these other factors whether, on balance, alternative feasible routes
would be "prudent."

But no such wide-ranging endeavor was intended. It is obvious that in most
cases considerations of cost, directness of route, and community disruption will
indicate that parkland should be used for highway construction whenever possible. Although it may be necessary to transfer funds from one jurisdiction to
another, there will always be a smaller outlay required from the public purse
when parkland is used since the public already owns the land and there will be
no need to pay for right-of-way. And since people do not live or work in parks,
if a highway is built on parkland no one will have to leave his home or give up
his business. Such factors are common to substantially all highway construction.
Thus, if Congress intended these factors to be on an equal footing with preservation of parkland there would have been no need for the statutes.

Congress clearly did not intend that cost and disruption of the community were to be ignored by the Secretary.[28] But the very existence of the statutes[29] indicates that protection of parkland was to be given paramount importance. The few green havens that are public parks were not to be lost unless there were truly unusual factors present in a particular case or the cost or community disruption resulting from alternative routes reached extraordinary magnitudes. If the statutes are to have any meaning, the Secretary cannot approve the destruction of parkland unless he finds that alternative routes present unique problems.

Plainly, there is "law to apply" and thus the exemption for action "committed to agency discretion" is inapplicable. But the existence of judicial review is only the start: the standard for review must also be determined. For that we must look to §706 of the Administrative Procedure Act, 5 U.S.C. §706 (1964 ed., Supp. V), which provides that a "reviewing court shall . . . hold unlawful and set aside agency action, findings, and conclusions found" not to meet six separate standards. In all cases agency action must be set aside if the action was "arbitrary, capricious, an abuse of discretion, or otherwise not in accordance with law" or if the action failed to meet statutory, procedural, or constitutional requirements. 5 U.S.C. §§706(2)(A), (B), (C), (D) (1964 ed., Supp. V). In certain narrow, specifically limited situations, the agency action is to be set aside if the action was not supported by "substantial evidence." And in other equally narrow circumstances the reviewing court is to engage in a de novo review of the action and set it aside if it was "unwarranted by the facts." 5 U.S.C. §§706(2)(E), (F)(1964 ed., Supp. V).

Petitioners argue that the Secretary's approval of the construction of I-40 through Overton Park is subject to one or the other of these latter two standards of limited applicability. First, they contend that the "substantial evidence" standard of §706(2)(E) must be applied. In the alternative, they claim that §706(2)(F) applies and that there must be a de novo review to determine if the Secretary's action was "unwarranted by the facts." Neither of these standards is, however, applicable.

Review under the substantial-evidence test is authorized only when the agency action is taken pursuant to a rulemaking provision of the Administrative Procedure Act itself, 5 U.S.C. §553 (1964 ed., Supp. V), or when the agency action is based on a public adjudicatory hearing. See 5 U.S.C. §§556, 557 (1964 ed., Supp. V). The Secretary's decision to allow the expenditure of federal funds

---

28.   The legislative history indicates that the Secretary is not to limit his consideration to information supplied by state and local officials but is to go beyond this information and reach his own independent decision. 114 Cong. Rec. 24036-24037.

29.   The legislative history of both §4(f) . . . and §138 . . . is ambiguous. The legislative committee reports tend to support respondents' view that the statutes are merely general directives to the Secretary requiring him to consider the importance of parkland as well as cost, community disruption, and other factors. See, e.g., S. Rep. No. 1340, 90th Cong., 2d Sess., 19; H. R. Rep. No. 1584, 90th Cong., 2d Sess., 12. Statements by proponents of the statutes as well as the Senate committee report on §4(f) indicate, however, that the Secretary was to have limited authority. See, e.g., 114 Cong. Rec. 24033-24037; S. Rep. No. 1659, 89th Cong., 2d Sess., 22. See also H.R. Conf. Rep. No. 2236, 89th Cong., 2d Sess., 25. Because of this ambiguity it is clear that we must look primarily to the statutes themselves to find the legislative intent.

to build I-40 through Overton Park was plainly not an exercise of a rulemaking function. See 1 K. Davis, Administrative Law Treatise §5.01 (1958). And the only hearing that is required by either the Administrative Procedure Act or the statutes regulating the distribution of federal funds for highway construction is a public hearing conducted by local officials for the purpose of informing the community about the proposed project and eliciting community views on the design and route. 23 U.S.C. §128 (1964 ed., Supp. V). The hearing is nonadjudicatory, quasi-legislative in nature. It is not designed to produce a record that is to be the basis of agency action — the basic requirement for substantial-evidence review. See H.R. Rep. No. 1980, 79th Cong., 2d Sess.

Petitioners' alternative argument also fails. De novo review of whether the Secretary's decision was "unwarranted by the facts" is authorized by §706(2)(F) in only two circumstances. First, such de novo review is authorized when the action is adjudicatory in nature and the agency factfinding procedures are inadequate. And, there may be independent judicial factfinding when issues that were not before the agency are raised in a proceeding to enforce nonadjudicatory agency action. H.R. Rep. No. 1980, 79th Cong., 2d Sess. Neither situation exists here.

Even though there is no de novo review in this case and the Secretary's approval of the route of I-40 does not have ultimately to meet the substantial-evidence test, the generally applicable standards of §706 require the reviewing court to engage in a substantial inquiry. Certainly, the Secretary's decision is entitled to a presumption of regularity. See e.g., Pacific States Box & Basket Co. v. White, 296 U.S. 176, 185 (1935); United States v. Chemical Foundation, 272 U.S. 1, 14-15 (1926). But that presumption is not to shield his action from a thorough, probing, in-depth review.

The Court is first required to decide whether the Secretary acted within the scope of his authority. This determination naturally begins with a delineation of the scope of the Secretary's authority and discretion. L. Jaffe, Judicial Control of Administrative Action 359 (1965). As has been shown, Congress has specified only a small range of choices that the Secretary can make. Also involved in this initial inquiry is a determination of whether on the facts the Secretary's decision can reasonably be said to be within that range. The reviewing court must consider whether the Secretary properly construed his authority to approve the use of parkland as limited to situations where there are no feasible alternative routes or where feasible alternative routes involve uniquely difficult problems. And the reviewing court must be able to find that the Secretary could have reasonably believed that in this case there are no feasible alternatives or that alternatives do involve unique problems.

Scrutiny of the facts does not end, however, with the determination that the Secretary has acted within the scope of his statutory authority. Section 706(2)(A) requires a finding that the actual choice made was not "arbitrary, capricious, an abuse of discretion, or otherwise not in accordance with law." 5 U.S.C. §706(2)(A) (1964 ed., Supp. V). To make this finding the court must consider whether the decision was based on a consideration of the relevant factors and whether there has been a clear error of judgment. Jaffe, *supra*, at 182. . . .

Although this inquiry into the facts is to be searching and careful, the ultimate standard of review is a narrow one. The court is not empowered to substitute its judgment for that of the agency.

[The Court then held that neither the APA, the Department of Transportation Act, nor the Federal-Aid Highway Act required formal findings of fact by the Secretary. It noted that the administrative record in the case was not before it since the lower courts had based their review on litigation affidavits that were post hoc rationalizations. It then remanded the case to the district court for "plenary review of the Secretary's decision" based on the record before the Secretary at the time he made his decision. The district court could require "the administrative officials who participated in the decision to give testimony explaining their action," though "inquiry into the mental processes of administrative decisionmakers is usually to be avoided."]

Reversed and remanded. [Justice Douglas took no part in the consideration or decision of the case; Justice Black filed a separate and concurring opinion, in which Justice Brennan joined.]

NOTES AND QUESTIONS

1. *Overton Park* came as a surprise, even to environmentalists in the U.S. Department of Transportation. For discussion of the background of the "parklands statutes," see Netherton, Transportation Planning and the Environment, 1970 Urb. L. Ann. 65, and Gray, Section 4(f) of the Department of Transportation Act, 32 Md. L. Rev. 327 (1973).

On remand, the government asked for six weeks to prepare for trial. Preparation actually required four months, and even then the Department had great difficulty finding in its files anything resembling the "record before the Secretary" at the time the decision was made. Trial took 35 days; 240 exhibits were prepared. After all this, the district court concluded that Secretary Volpe never actually made the decision to approve the highway and that if he did he misconstrued the parklands statutes. The district court remanded the matter to the Department. 335 F. Supp. 873 (W.D. Tenn. 1972). This time the Secretary said that he could not approve the route, based on the record then before him, and attempts by the state to force Volpe to specify an acceptable route were rebuffed. Citizens to Preserve Overton Park v. Brinegar, 357 F. Supp. 846 (W.D. Tenn. 1973), *reversed*, 494 F.2d 1212 (6th Cir. 1974), *cert. denied*, 421 U.S. 991 (1975). For §4(f) litigation involving former President James E. Carter's presidential library, see Druid Hills Civic Assn. v. Federal Highway Administration, 772 F.2d 700 (11th Cir. 1985).

2. Justice Marshall had no difficulty in holding that §4(f) had enacted law for the Secretary of Transportation to apply and that his decision under that section was not "committed to agency discretion" under the APA. Was he right?

The Secretary claimed that §4(f) had enacted what might be termed a balancing test. Why is this claim relevant to the "committed to agency discretion" problem?

Some commentators have borrowed a phrase from the late Professor Lon Fuller and have argued that the issues posed by legislation like §4(f) are polycentric: "A case is polycentric if a court [or a decisionmaker] must consider a number of variables when making its decision. The variables in a polycentric case are interdependent, and the court's decision requires a trade-off among the conflicting interests they represent. Any number of decisions is possible." D. Mandelker, Environment and Equity 64 (1981). Why is the required decision polycentric? Legislation requiring a polycentric decision can provide a "decision rule" for balancing variables under consideration or can simply leave the balancing process to the decisionmaker, with no legislative direction. Does Justice Marshall's interpretation of §4(f) provide a decision rule? What is it? Environmental legislation often requires polycentric decisionmaking. Why is this so? See generally, Rubin, Law and Legislation in the Administrative State, 89 Colum. L. Rev. 361 (1989). Has *Overton Park* been qualified by Block v. Community Nutrition Institute, 467 U.S. 340 (1984). With no mention of *Overton Park*, the Court held, quoting *Data Processing Service*, p. 92 *supra*, that the presumption of judicial review may be overcome "whenever the congressional intent to preclude judicial review is 'fairly discernible in the statutory scheme.'"

3. Justice Marshall believed that the "arbitrary and capricious" standard of judicial review provided by the APA applied to the Secretary's decision under §4(f). But his views that the court must determine whether there has been a "clear error of judgment" after a "searching and careful" inquiry into the "full administrative record" — "a thorough, probing, indepth review" — considerably raised the level of judicial inquiry under the standard. Prior to *Overton Park*, the "arbitrary and capricious" standard was widely believed to be highly indulgent toward the exercise of administration discretion; it was seen as a congressional afterthought to provide at least some judicial surveillance of all the residual assorted types of informal agency action. There is even some indication that "clear error of judgment" was meant to be equivalent to the standard used by appellate courts when they review findings of fact in trials before a judge rather than a jury. See Casenote, 1 Envtl. L. Rep. (Envtl. L. Inst.) 10,062 (1971).

The two deferential standards encountered most frequently in environmental cases are the substantial evidence and the "arbitrary and capricious" standards, with the *Overton Park* gloss on the latter heavily predominating because the lower federal courts now commonly cite *Overton Park* as providing the applicable judicial review standard for notice-and-comment rule-making. The older substantial evidence standard discussed in *Overton Park* was developed for review of formal adjudications, for which a trial-type hearing record was available to the reviewing court; consequently, despite *Overton Park*, it is still viewed as the more searching of the two standards. The "arbitrary and capricious" standard applies to quasi-legislative or informal decisionmaking, for which a "proper" record and hearing were not required; thus the reviewing court was more permissive and deferential — at least until *Overton Park*.

You may find it helpful to rank the standards of judicial review according to strictness. Professor Schotland has written:

> I have always thought of scope of review as a spectrum, with de novo at one end, with unconstitutionality at the other end, and in between a number of what I will call "mood-points" or degrees of judicial aggressiveness or restraint, such as preponderance of the evidence, clearly erroneous, substantial evidence on the whole record, scintilla of evidence, abuse of discretion and last, right next to or even into unconstitutionality, arbitrary and capricious. And since these are only "mood-points," there is considerable room within each for difference. [Schotland, Scope of Review of Administrative Action — Remarks Before the D.C. Circuit Judicial Conference, 34 Fed. B.J. 54, 59 (1975).]

The strictest standards possible are the various APA §706(2) provisions requiring that courts themselves decide the meaning of the law. On such issues the court can substitute its opinion for that of the agency. Courts have consistently adhered to the theory that they are better than agencies at construing statutes. In general, the APA is deferential; it shields the court from reaching the merits of a decision. Thus, it is not surprising that environmentalists sought to convince courts that most environmental questions were questions of law. A leading environmental litigator wrote an early influential article arguing this position:

> [H]e who seeks to overturn determinations of fact by any trier thereof, however fact and law are distinguished, has a difficult task; and if the position of a class of litigants is such that he generally must assume that burden of proof and persuasion, he is typically David challenging Goliath. [Sive, Some Thoughts of an Environmental Lawyer in the Wilderness of Environmental Law, 70 Colum. L. Rev. 612, 617 (1970).]

Sive argued for an expansion of judicial review in environmental litigation through conversion of factual into legal questions, especially when key terms in newly enacted environmental litigation demand judicial interpretation. He also argued for a "practical" approach to judicial review:

> "[T]he bulk of the important questions in environmental cases call more for the talents and training of the courts and judges than for those of the administrative agencies and administrators. The basic reason is the very breadth of the questions, the requirement of opposing economic and social interests. Such balancing and weighing require more art than science. [70 Colum. L. Rev. at 629.]

How well do you suppose the Sive proposal has fared since 1970?

Note that some important informal agency action, nonbinding on private parties, is subject neither to *Overton Park*'s recordmaking strictures nor to the rule-making procedures required by APA §553 (general policy statements, interpretive statements, internal guidance manuals, etc.). See Morton v. Ruiz, 415 U.S. 199 (1974); Pacific Gas & Electric Co. v. FPC, 506 F.2d 33 (D.C. Cir. 1974). But see the APA §552(a) notice requirements, which may apply.

4. Despite Justice Marshall's decision, does *Overton Park* in effect require agencies to compile records of decision in informal rule-making and adjudication that are just as detailed as they must be in formal proceedings? Consider the impact on the bulk of agency environmental decisionmaking. Examining the legislative history of the APA, Professor Nathanson concluded that "there is not the slightest indication that the purpose of the notice-and-comment proceeding was to develop a record by which a reviewing court could test the validity of the rule which the Administrator finally adopted." Probing the Mind of the Administrator: Hearing Variations and Standards of Judicial Review under the Administrative Procedure Act and Other Federal Statutes, 75 Colum. L. Rev. 721, 754-755 (1975). In Camp v. Pitts, 411 U.S. 138 (1973), the Court tried to redress the district court's overreaction to *Overton Park* by steering it away from a de novo hearing on the agency decision similar to that undertaken by the Tennessee district court after the remand in *Overton Park*. Yet is not the effect of the "substantial inquiry" endorsed in *Overton Park* to cause agencies to develop exhaustive records, a "paper trail" marking the course of decision, in order to avoid judicial invalidation of their decisions? For a recommendation of such an approach, see Pedersen, Formal Records and Informal Rulemaking, 85 Yale L.J. 38, 59-65 (1975). See also Verkuil, Judicial Review of Informal Rulemaking, 60 Va. L. Rev. 185 (1974).

5. The Court in *Overton Park* did not discuss the basis for federal court jurisdiction over the appeal from the Secretary's decision. This case has been qualified by Califano v. Sanders, 430 U.S. 99 (1977), which holds that the APA does not make an independent grant of subject-matter jurisdiction. Jurisdiction must be conferred by the applicable federal statute or by the federal jurisdiction act, 28 U.S.C. §1331.

3.   *In the Wake of* Overton Park: *The "Hard Look" Doctrine*

a.   The Origins of "Hard Look" and Its Application in the District of Columbia Circuit Court of Appeals

Justice Marshall stated in *Overton Park* that courts were to engage in a "substantial inquiry" into the Secretary's §4(f) decision, language that represents the bedrock of Supreme Court support for the "hard look" doctrine of judicial review that has become common in environmental decisions. The phrase originated with the late Judge Harold Leventhal, in the same year *Overton Park* was decided:

Its supervisory function calls on the court to intervene not merely in case of procedural inadequacies, or bypassing of the mandate in the legislative charter, but more broadly if the court becomes aware, especially from a combination of danger signals, that the agency has not really taken a hard look at the salient problems, and has not genuinely engaged in reasoned decision-making. [Greater Boston Television Corp. v. FCC, 444 F.2d 841, 850 (D.C. Cir. 1970), *cert. denied*, 403 U.S. 923 (1971).]

Judge Leventhal's "hard look" gloss on the "arbitrary and capricious" standard thrusts courts into an examination of the methodology and substance of agency decisionmaking to ensure that the decision has adequate factual support. Yet how far should the courts go? When federal environmental agencies must base their determinations on complex scientific and technical evidence, there may be a persuasive argument that under *Overton Park* courts should not second-guess the agency's substantive decisions but should be concerned only that the decision be made through procedures that adequately protect the rights of interested parties.

The issue of judicial review was dramatically highlighted in a decision by the District of Columbia Circuit Court of Appeals, Ethyl Corp. v. EPA, 541 F.2d 1 (D.C. Cir. 1976), *cert. denied*, 426 U.S. 941 (1977). In this case, the court reviewed a decision by EPA under §211(c)(1)(A) of the Clean Air Act to restrict the use of lead in gasoline. This statute required EPA, on the basis of incomplete evidence, to assess the health risk that would result if the use of lead additives in gasoline was not prohibited. The health risk problem considered by *Ethyl* has made it one of the leading decisions in the environmental law of hazardous risk control. See Chapter 5 at pp. 548-549.

In the course of the *Ethyl* decision, which was en banc, the judges of the court engaged in an extended debate on the proper scope of judicial review in environmental litigation. Excerpts from opinions by three of these judges follow. After pointing out that §211(c)(1)(A) required notice-and-comment rule-making and that therefore the "arbitrary and capricious" standard applied, Judge Wright continued:

> This standard of review is a highly deferential one. It presumes agency action to be valid. Moreover, it forbids the court's substituting its judgment for that of the agency and requires affirmance if a rational basis exists for the agency's decision.
>
> This is not to say, however, that we must rubberstamp the agency decision as correct. [Here the court quoted language from *Overton Park*.] . . . This is particularly true in highly technical cases such as this one. "A court does not depart from its proper function when it undertakes a study of the record, hopefully perceptive, even as to the evidence on technical and specialized matters, for this enables the court to penetrate to the underlying decisions of the agency, to satisfy itself that the agency has exercised a reasoned discretion, with reasons that do not deviate from or ignore the ascertainable legislative intent." Greater Boston Television Corp. v. FCC, 444 F.2d 841, 850 (1970), *cert. denied* 403 U.S. 923 (1971).
>
> There is no inconsistency between the deferential standard of review and the requirement that the reviewing court involve itself in even the most complex evidentiary matters; rather, the two indicia of arbitrary and capricious review stand in careful balance. The close scrutiny of the evidence is intended to educate the court. It must understand enough about the problem confronting the agency to comprehend the meaning of the evidence relied upon and the evidence discarded;

the questions addressed by the agency and those bypassed; the choices open to the agency and those made. The more technical the case, the more intensive must be the court's effort to understand the evidence, for without an appropriate understanding of the case before it the court cannot properly perform its appellate function. But that function must be performed with conscientious awareness of its limited nature. The enforced education into the intricacies of the problem before the agency is not designed to enable the court to become a superagency that can supplant the agency's expert decision-maker. To the contrary, the court must give due deference to the agency's ability to rely on its own developed expertise. The immersion in the evidence is designed *solely* to enable the court to determine whether the agency decision was rational and based on consideration of the relevant factors. It is settled that we must affirm decisions with which we disagree so long as this test is met. . . .

Thus, after our careful study of the record, we must take a step back from the agency decision. We must look at the decision not as the chemist, biologist or statistician that we are qualified neither by training nor experience to be, but as a reviewing court exercising our narrowly defined duty of holding agencies to certain minimal standards of rationality. . . . [541 F.2d at 34-36.]

Chief Judge Bazelon, with whom Circuit Judge McGowan joined, concurring, said:

I agree with the court's construction of the statute that the Administrator is called upon to make "essentially legislative policy judgments" in assessing risks to public health. But I cannot agree that this automatically relieves the Administrator's decision from the "procedural . . . rigor proper for questions of fact." Quite the contrary, this case strengthens my view that ". . . in cases of great technological complexity, the best way for courts to guard against unreasonable or erroneous administrative decisions is not for the judges themselves to scrutinize the technical merits of each decision. Rather, it is to establish a decision-making process that assures a reasoned decision that can be held up to the scrutiny of the scientific community and the public."[5] This record provides vivid demonstration of the dangers implicit in the contrary view, ably espoused by Judge Leventhal, which would have judges "steeping" themselves "in technical matters to determine whether the agency 'has exercised a reasoned discretion.'" It is one thing for judges to scrutinize FCC judgments concerning diversification of media ownership to determine if they are rational. But I doubt judges contribute much to improving the quality of the difficult decisions which must be made in highly technical areas when they take it upon themselves to decide, as did the panel in this case, that "in assessing the scientific and medical data the Administrator made clear errors of judgment." The process [of] making a de novo evaluation of the scientific evidence inevitably invites judges of opposing views to make plausible-sounding, but simplistic, judgments of the relative weight to be afforded various pieces of technical data. . . .

Because substantive review of mathematical and scientific evidence by technically illiterate judges is dangerously unreliable, I continue to believe we will do more to improve administrative decision-making by concentrating our efforts on strengthening administrative procedures. [541 F.2d at 66-67.]

---

5.   International Harvester Co. v. Ruckelshaus, 478 F.2d 615, 652 (D.C. Cir. 1973) (Bazelon, C.J., concurring).

Judge Leventhal answered:

> Taking [Chief Judge Bazelon's] opinion in its fair implication, as a signal to judges to abstain from any substantive review, it is my view that while giving up is the easier course, it is not legitimately open to us at present. In the case of legislative enactments, the sole responsibility of the courts is constitutional due process review. In the case of agency decision-making the courts have an additional responsibility set by Congress. Congress has been willing to delegate its legislative powers broadly — and courts have upheld such delegation — because there is court review to assure that the agency exercises the delegated power within statutory limits, and that it fleshes out objectives within those limits by an administration that is not irrational or discriminatory. Nor is that envisioned judicial role ephemeral, as *Overton Park*[6] makes clear. . . .
>
> The aim of the judges is not to exercise expertise or decide technical questions, but simply to gain sufficient background orientation. Our obligation is not to be jettisoned because our initial technical understanding may be meager when compared to our initial grasp of FCC or freedom of speech questions. When called upon to make de novo decisions, individual judges have had to acquire the learning pertinent to complex technical questions in such fields as economics, science, technology and psychology. Our role is not as demanding when we are engaged in review of agency decision, where we exercise restraint, and affirm even if we would have decided otherwise so long as the agency's decisionmaking is not irrational or discriminatory.
>
> The substantive review of administrative action is modest, but it cannot be carried out in a vacuum of understanding. Better no judicial review at all than a charade that gives the imprimatur without the substance of judicial confirmation that the agency is not acting unreasonably. Once the presumption of regularity in agency action is challenged with a factual submission, and even to determine whether such a challenge has been made, the agency's record and reasoning has to be looked at. If there is some factual support for the challenge, there must be either evidence or judicial notice available explicating the agency's result, or a remand to supply the gap. . . .
>
> On issues of substantive review, on conformance to statutory standards and requirements of rationality, the judges must act with restraint. Restraint, yes, abdication, no. [541 F.2d at 68-69.]

NOTES AND QUESTIONS

1. Judge Leventhal's views are further set forth in his article Environmental Decision Making and the Role of the Courts, 122 U. Pa. L. Rev. 509 (1974). In the conclusion to the article, Judge Leventhal appeared to favor substantive review because of the check it could place on agency decisionmaking:

> The common theme one can draw from these observations on the role of the courts in environmental matters is the court's central role of ensuring the principled in-

---

6. [*Overton Park*] requires the reviewing court to scrutinize the facts and consider whether the agency decision was "based on a consideration of the relevant factors" in the context of nonformalized, discretionary executive decisionmaking. A fortiori, at least that rigor of review should apply to more formal decisionmaking processes like informal rulemaking.

tegration and balanced assessment of both environmental and nonenvironmental considerations in federal agency decisionmaking. The rule of administrative law, as applied to the congressional mandates for a clean environment, ensures that mission-oriented agencies . . . will take due cognizance of environmental matters. It ensures at the same time that environmental protection agencies will take into account the congressional mandate that environmental concern be reconciled with other social and economic objectives of our society. [122 U. Pa. L. Rev. at 604.]

On which side does the decision in *Ethyl* fall? What costs might be imposed on the industry and on consumers by a decision to prohibit lead additives in gasoline? Does the Leventhal formulation ignore another problem, the balancing of risk against cost? Is this a judicial function?

Judge Oakes of the Second Circuit Court of Appeals has defended the "hard look" doctrine in The Judicial Role in Environmental Law, 52 N.Y.U.L. Rev. 498 (1977). He argues that in comparison with other fields of public regulation, decisions in the environmental field require consideration of a large number of variables; in short, they are polycentric. He further argues that because of their complex nature environmental decisions also turn on particular facts and require subjective judgments. Finally, Judge Oakes writes that Congress has avoided the resolution of many of the difficult policy problems in environmental legislation. You may want to reconsider Judge Oakes's arguments once you have completed this casebook and the substantive environmental legislation it covers.

2. In the *Ethyl* opinion Judges Wright and Leventhal justified "hard look" judicial review by noting the willingness of the federal courts to uphold broad delegations of legislative power to administrative agencies. Until the New Deal period of the 1930s, the Supreme Court had often invalidated congressional legislation on delegation of power grounds. Professor Rodgers notes:

It is clear that today's hard look doctrine of judicial review and yesterday's delegation doctrine are grounded upon similar insights about the deficiencies of broadly written regulatory legislation — lack of notice to the affected, lack of opportunity to participate in rule formulation, prospects of administrative caprice and discrimination, and legislative cowardice in handing over lawmaking power while retreating to the role of second-guessing opportunist. [Judicial Review of Risk Assessments: The Role of Decision Theory in Unscrambling the Benzene Decision, 11 Envtl. L. 301, 317 (1981).]

For an exploration of the link between procedural rigor and the shift from incrementalism to comprehensive rationality as the ideal administrative policy see Diver, Policy Making Paradigms in Administrative Law, 95 Harv. L. Rev. 393 (1981).

Does intensive judicial procedural review compensate for overbroad congressional delegation? Intensive substantive judicial review? Rodgers adds that "invalidating vague delegations would appear most appealing to courts subscribing to the classic conception of legislation as a stable expression of consensus" (11 Envtl. L. at 301). Is consensus likely in the environmental field?

b.   The Supreme Court Intervenes

Overton Park came at the beginning of the environmental decade when courts seemed the most open forum to raise environmental issues and the New Deal theories of judicial deference seemed devoid of much empirical foundation. But, like all products of a zeitgeist, the doctrine may be historically limited. The next case represents the Court's latest attitude toward judicial review of agency decisions. The Supreme Court never shared the District of Columbia Circuit Court of Appeals' faith in the ability of judicial review to supervise an agency and began to repudiate the approach in the late 1970s. For example, Vermont Yankee Power Corp. v. Natural Resources Defense Council, Inc., 435 U.S. 519 (1978) denied the power of courts to develop hybrid rulemaking procedures to facilitate judicial review and sent a strong warning to courts to confine themselves to the justifications advanced by the agency:

> We have made it abundantly clear before that when there is a contemporaneous explanation of the agency decision, the validity of that action must "stand or fall on the propriety of that finding, judged, of course, by the appropriate standard of review. If that finding is not sustainable on the administrative record made, then the Comptroller's decision must be vacated and the matter remanded to him for further consideration." Camp v. Pitts, 411 U.S. 138, 143 (1973). See also SEC v. Chenery Corp., 318 U.S. 80 (1943). The court should engage in this kind of review and not stray beyond the judicial province to explore the procedural format or to impose upon the agency its own notion of which procedures are "best" or most likely to further some vague, undefined public good.

CHEVRON, USA, INC. v. NATURAL RESOURCES DEFENSE COUNCIL, INC.
467 U.S. 837 (1984)

Justice STEVENS delivered the opinion of the Court. In the Clean Air Act Amendments of 1977, Congress enacted certain requirements applicable to States that had not achieved the national air quality standards established by the Environmental Protection Agency (EPA) pursuant to earlier legislation. The amended Clean Air Act required these "nonattainment" States to establish a permit program regulating "new or modified major stationary sources" of air pollution. Generally, a permit may not be issued for a new or modified major stationary source unless several stringent conditions are met. The EPA regulation promulgated to implement this permit requirement allows a State to adopt a plantwide definition of the term "stationary source." Under this definition, an existing plant that contains several pollution-emitting devices may install or modify one piece of equipment without meeting the permit conditions if the alteration will not increase the total emissions from the plant. The question presented by this case is whether EPA's decision to allow States to treat all of the pollution-emitting devices within the same industrial grouping as though they were encased within a single "bubble" is based on a reasonable construction of the statutory term "stationary source."

I

The EPA regulations containing the plantwide definition of the term stationary source were promulgated on October 14, 1981. 46 Fed. Reg. 50,766. Respondents filed a timely petition for review in the United States Court of Appeals for the District of Columbia Circuit. . . . The Court of Appeals set aside the regulations. . . .

The basic legal error of the Court of Appeals was to adopt a static judicial definition of the term stationary source when it had decided that Congress itself had not commanded that definition. Respondents do not defend the legal reasoning of the Court of Appeals. Nevertheless, since this Court reviews judgments, not opinions, we must determine whether the Court of Appeals' legal error resulted in an erroneous judgment on the validity of the regulations.

II

When a court reviews an agency's construction of the statute which it administers, it is confronted with two questions. First, always, is the question of whether Congress has directly spoken to the precise question at issue. If the intent of Congress is clear, that is the end of the matter; for the court, as well as the agency, must give effect to the unambiguously expressed intent of Congress. If, however, the court determines Congress has not directly addressed the precise question at issue, the court does not simply impose its own construction on the statute, as would be necessary in the absence of an administrative interpretation. Rather, if the statute is silent or ambiguous with respect to the specific issue, the question for the court is whether the agency's answer is based on a permissible construction of the statute.

"The power of an administrative agency to administer a congressionally created . . . program necessarily requires the formulation of policy and the making of rules to fill any gap left, implicitly or explicitly, by Congress." Morton v. Ruiz, 415 U.S. 199, 231 (1974). If Congress has explicitly left a gap for the agency to fill, there is an express delegation of authority to the agency to elucidate a specific provision of the statute by regulation. Such legislative regulations are given controlling weight unless they are arbitrary, capricious, or manifestly contrary to the statue. Sometimes the legislative delegation to an agency on a particular question is implicit rather than explicit. In such a case, a court may not substitute its own construction of a statutory provision for a reasonable interpretation made by the administrator of an agency.

We have long recognized that considerable weight should be accorded to an executive department's construction of a statutory scheme it is entrusted to administer, and the principle of deference to administrative interpretations

> has been consistently followed by this Court whenever decision as to the meaning or reach of a statute has involved reconciling conflicting policies, and a full understanding of the force of the statutory policy in the given situation has depended upon more than ordinary knowledge respecting the matters subjected to agency regulations. . . .

In light of these well-settled principles it is clear that the Court of Appeals misconceived the nature of its role in reviewing the regulations at issue. Once it determined, after its own examination of the legislation, that Congress did not actually have an intent regarding the applicability of the bubble concept to the permit program, the question before it was not whether in its view the concept is "inappropriate" in the general context of a program designed to improve air quality, but whether the Administrator's view that it is appropriate in the context of this particular program is a reasonable one. Based on the examination of the legislation and its history which follows, we agree with the Court of Appeals that Congress did not have a specific intention on the applicability of the bubble concept in these cases, and conclude that the EPA's use of that concept here is a reasonable policy choice for the agency to make.

III

[The Court discussed the Clean Air Act provisions governing the NAAQSs, the SIPs, and the New Source Performance Standards.] Section 111(a) defined the terms that are to be used in setting and enforcing standards of performance for new stationary sources. It provided: "For purposes of this section: . . . (3) The term 'stationary source' means any building, structure, facility, or installation which emits or may emit any air pollutant." 84 Stat. 1683. In the 1970 Amendments that definition was not only applicable to the NSPS program required by §111, but also was made applicable to a requirement of §110 that each state implementation plan contain a procedure for reviewing the location of any proposed new source and preventing its construction if it would preclude the attainment or maintenance of national air quality standards.

In due course, the EPA promulgated NAAQSs, approved SIPs, and adopted detailed regulations governing NSPSs for various categories of equipment. In one of its programs, the EPA used a plantwide definition of the term "stationary source." In 1974, it issued NSPSs for the nonferrous smelting industry that provided that the standards would not apply to the modification of major smelting units if their increased emissions were offset by reductions in other portions of the same plant.[17]

_____

17.   The Court of Appeals ultimately held that this plantwide approach was prohibited by the 1970 Act, see ASARCO, Inc. This decision was rendered after enactment of the 1977 Amendments, and hence the standard was in effect when Congress enacted the 1977 Amendments.

NONATTAINMENT

The 1970 legislation provided for the attainment of primary NAAQSs by 1975. In many areas of the country, particularly the most industrialized States, the statutory goals were not attained. In 1976, the 94th Congress was confronted with this fundamental problem, as well as many others respecting pollution control. As always in this area, the legislative struggle was basically between interests seeking strict schemes to reduce pollution rapidly to eliminate its social costs and interests advancing the economic concern that strict schemes would retard industrial development with attendant social costs. The 94th Congress, confronting these competing interests, was unable to agree on what response was in the public interest: legislative proposals to deal with nonattainment failed to command the necessary consensus.

In light of the situation, the EPA published an Emissions Offset Interpretative Ruling in December 1976, see 41 Fed. Reg. 55,524, to "fill the gap," as respondents put it, until Congress acted. The Ruling stated that it was intended to address "the issue of whether and to what extent national air quality standards established under the Clean Air Act may restrict or prohibit growth of major new or expanded stationary air pollution sources." Id., at 55,524-55,525. In general, the ruling provided "that a major new source may locate in an area with air quality worse than a national standard only if stringent conditions can be met." Id., at 55,525. The Ruling gave primary emphasis to the rapid attainment of the statute's environmental goals. Consistent with that emphasis, the construction of every new source in nonattainment areas had to meet the "lowest achievable emission rate" under the current state of the art for that type of facility. See ibid. The 1976 Ruling did not, however, explicitly adopt or reject the "bubble concept."

IV

The Clean Air Act Amendments of 1977 are a lengthy, detailed, technical, complex, and comprehensive response to a major social issue. A small portion of the statute (Part D of Title I of the amended Act, 42 U.S.C. §7501-7508) expressly deals with nonattainment areas. The focal point of this controversy is one phrase in that portion of the Amendment.[22]

Basically, the statute required each State in a nonattainment area to prepare and obtain approval of a new SIP by July 1, 1979. In the interim those States were required to comply with the EPA's interpretive Ruling of December 21, 1976. 91 Stat. 745. The deadline for attainment of the primary NAAQSs was extended until December 31, 1982, and in some cases until December 31, 1987, but the SIPs were required to contain a number of provisions designed to achieve the goals as expeditiously as possible.

---

22.   Specifically, the controversy in this case involves the meaning of the term "major stationary sources" in §172(b)(6) of the Act, 42, U.S.C. §7502(b)(6). The meaning of the term "proposed source" in §173(2) of the Act, 42 U.S.C. §7503(2), is not at issue.

Most significantly for our purposes, the statute provided that each plan shall: "(6) require permits for the construction and operation of new or modified major stationary sources in accordance with section 173. . . ." 91 Stat. 747. . . .

[The Court then discussed the requirements of §173.] The 1977 Amendments contain no specific reference to the "bubble concept." Nor do they contain a specific definition of the term "stationary source," though they did not disturb the definition of "stationary source" contained in §111(a)(3), applicable by the terms of the Act to the NSPS program. Section 302(j), however, defines the term "major stationary source" as follows:

> (j) Except as otherwise expressly provided, the terms 'major stationary source' and 'major emitting facility' mean any stationary facility or source of air pollutants which directly emits, or has the potential to emit, one hundred tons per year or more of any air pollutant (including any major emitting facility or source of fugitive emissions of any such pollutant, as determined by rule by the Administrator).

91 Stat. 770.

V

The legislative history of the portion of the 1977 Amendments dealing with nonattainment areas does not contain any specific comment on the "bubble concept" or the question whether a plantwide definition of a stationary source is permissible under the permit program. It does, however, plainly disclose that in the permit program Congress sought to accommodate the conflict between the economic interest in permitting capital improvements to continue and the environmental interest in improving air quality. Indeed, the House Committee Report identified the economic interest as one of the "two main purposes" of this section of the bill. It stated:

> Section 117 of the bill, adopted during full committee markup, establishes a new section 127 of the Clean Air Act. The section has two main purposes: (1) to allow reasonable economic growth to continue in an area while making reasonable further progress to assure attainment of the standards by a fixed date; and (2) to allow States greater flexibility for the former purpose than EPA's present interpretative regulations afford.
>
> The new provision allows States with nonattainment areas to pursue one of two options. First, the State may proceed under EPA's present "tradeoff" or "offset" ruling. The Administrator is authorized, moreover, to modify or amend that ruling in accordance with the intent and purposes of this section.
>
> The State's second option would be to revise its implementation plan in accordance with this new provision

H.R. Rep. No. 95-294, 211 (1977), U.S. Code Cong. & Admin. News 1977, pp. 1077, 1290.[25]

25.   During the floor debates Congressman Waxman remarked that the legislation struck

The portion of the Senate Committee Report dealing with nonattainment areas states generally that it was intended to "supersede the EPA administrative approach," and that expansion should be permitted if a State could "demonstrate that these facilities can be accommodated within its overall plan to provide for attainment of air quality standards." S. Rep. 95-127, p. 55 (1977). . . .

VI

As previously noted, prior to the 1977 Amendments, the EPA had adhered to a plantwide definition of the term "source" under a NSPS program. After adoption of the 1977 Amendments, proposals for a plantwide definition were considered in at least three formal proceedings. . . .

[The Court reviewed the history of EPA's rule making for the bubble concept.]

In August 1980, however, the EPA adopted a regulation that, in essence, applied the basic reasoning of the Court of Appeals in this case. The EPA took particular note of the two then-recent Court of Appeals decisions, which had created the bright-line rule that the bubble concept should be employed in a program designed to maintain air quality but not in one designed to enhance air quality. Relying heavily on those cases, EPA adopted a dual definition of "source" for nonattainment areas that required a permit whenever a change in either the entire plant, or one of its components, would result in a significant increase in emissions even if the increase was completely offset by reductions elsewhere in the plant. The EPA expressed the opinion that this interpretation was "more consistent with congressional intent" than the plantwide definition because it "would bring in more sources or modifications for review," 45 Fed. Reg. 52,697 (1980), but its primary legal analysis was predicated on the two Court of Appeals decisions.

In 1981 a new administration took office and initiated a "government-wide reexamination of regulatory burdens and complexities." 46 Fed. Reg. 16,281. In the context of that review, the EPA reevaluated the various arguments that had been advanced in connection with the proper definition of the term "source" and concluded that the term should be given the same definition in both nonattainment areas and PSD areas.

---

a proper balance between environmental controls and economic growth in the dirty air areas of America. . . . There is no other single issue which more clearly poses the conflict between pollution control and new jobs. We have determined that neither need be compromised. . . .

This is a fair and balanced approach, which will not undermine our economic vitality, or impede achievement of our ultimate environmental objectives.

123 Cong. Rec. 27076 (1977).

The second "main purpose" of the provision allowing the States "greater flexibility" than the EPA's interpretative ruling as well as the reference to the EPA's authority to amend its ruling in accordance with the intent of the section, is entirely consistent with the view that Congress did not intend to freeze the definition of source contained in the existing regulation into a rigid statutory requirement.

In explaining its conclusion, the EPA first noted that the definitional issue was not squarely addressed in either the statute or its legislative history and therefore that the issue involved an agency "judgment as how to best carry out the Act." Ibid. It then set forth several reasons for concluding that the plantwide definition was more appropriate. It pointed out that the dual definition "can act as a disincentive to new investment and modernization by discouraging modifications to existing facilities" and "can actually retard progress in air pollution control by discouraging replacement of older, dirtier processes or pieces of equipment with new, cleaner ones." Ibid. Moreover, the new definition "would simplify EPA's rules by using the same definition of 'source' for PSD, nonattainment new source review and the construction moratorium. This reduces confusion and inconsistency." Ibid. Finally, the agency explained that additional requirements that remained in place would accomplish the fundamental purposes of achieving attainment with NAAQSs as expeditiously as possible. These conclusions were expressed in a proposed rulemaking in August 1981 that was formally promulgated in October. See id., at 50,766.

VII

In this Court respondents expressly reject the basic rationale of the Court of Appeals' decision. That court viewed the statutory definition of the term "source" as sufficiently flexible to cover either a plantwide definition, a narrower definition covering each unit within a plant, or a dual definition that could apply to both the entire "bubble" and its components. It interpreted the policies of the statute, however, to mandate the plantwide definition in programs designed to maintain clean air and to forbid it in programs designed to improve air quality. . . .

STATUTORY LANGUAGE

The definition of the term "stationary source" in §111(a)(3) refers to "any building, structure, facility, or installation" which emits air pollution. This definition is applicable only to the NSPS program by the express terms of the statute; the text of the statute does not make this definition applicable to the permit program. Petitioners therefore maintain that there is no statutory language even relevant to ascertaining the meaning of "stationary source" in the permit program aside from §302(j), which defines the term "major stationary source." We disagree with petitioners on this point.

The definition in §302(j) tells us that the word "major" means a source must emit at least 100 tons of pollution to qualify but it sheds virtually no light on the meaning of the term "stationary source." It does equate a source with a facility — a "major emitting facility" and a "major stationary source" are synonymous under §302(j). The ordinary meaning of the term "facility" is some collection of integrated elements which has been designed and constructed to achieve some purpose. Moreover, it is certainly no affront to common English usage to take a reference to a major facility or a major source to connote an entire plant as opposed to its constituent parts. Basically, however, the language of §302(j) simply does not compel any given interpretation of the term source. Respondents recognize that, and hence point to §111(a)(3). Although the definition in that section is not literally applicable to the permit program, it sheds as much light on the meaning of the word "source" as anything in the statute. As respondents point out, use of the words "building, structure, facility, or installation," as the definition of source, could be read to impose the permit conditions on an individual building that is a part of a plant. . . .

We are not persuaded that parsing of general terms in the text of the statute will reveal an actual intent of Congress. We know full well that this language is not dispositive; the terms are overlapping and the language is not precisely directed to the question of the applicability of a given term in the context of a larger operation. To the extent any congressional "intent" can be discerned from this language, it would appear that the listing of overlapping, illustrative terms was intended to enlarge, rather than to confine, the scope of the agency's power to regulate particular sources in order to effectuate the policies of the Act.

LEGISLATIVE HISTORY

In addition, respondents argue that the legislative history and policies of the Act foreclose the plantwide definition, and that the EPA's interpretation is not entitled to deference because it represents a sharp break with prior interpretations of the Act.

Based on our examination of the legislative history, we agree with the Court of Appeals that it is illuminating. . . .

More importantly, that history plainly identifies the policy concerns that motivated the enactment; the plantwide definition is fully consistent with one of those concerns — the allowance of reasonable economic growth — and, whether or not we believe it most effectively implements the other, we must recognize that the EPA has advanced a reasonable explanation for its conclusion that the regulations serve the environmental objectives as well. Indeed, its reasoning is supported by the public record developed in the rulemaking process, as well as by certain private studies.[37]

37.

> Economists have proposed that economic incentives be substituted for the cumbersome administrative-legal framework. The objective is to make the profit and cost incentives that work so well in the marketplace work for pollution control. . . . [The 'bubble' or 'netting' concept] is a first attempt in this direction. By giving a plant manager flexibility to find the places and processes within a plant that control emissions most cheaply, pollution control can be achieved more quickly and cheaply.

L. Lave & G. Omenn, Cleaning the Air: Reforming the Clean Air Act 28 (1981) (footnote omitted).

Our review of the EPA's varying interpretations of the word "source" — both before and after the 1977 Amendments convince us that the agency primarily responsible for administering this important legislation has consistently interpreted it flexibly — not in a sterile textual vacuum, but in the context of implementing policy decisions in a technical and complex arena. The fact that the agency has from time to time changed its interpretation of the term "source" does not, as respondents argue, lead us to conclude that no deference should be accorded the agency's interpretation of the statute. An initial agency interpretation is not instantly carved in stone. On the contrary, the agency, to engage in informed rulemaking, must consider varying interpretations and the wisdom of its policy on a continuing basis. Moreover, the fact that the agency has adopted different definitions in different contexts adds force to the argument that the definition itself is flexible, particularly since Congress has never indicated any disapproval of a flexible reading of the statute.

Significantly, it was not the agency in 1980, but rather the Court of Appeals that read the statute inflexibly to command a plantwide definition for programs designed to maintain clean air and to forbid such a definition for programs designed to improve air quality. The distinction the court drew may well be a sensible one, but our labored review of the problem has surely disclosed that it is not a distinction that Congress ever articulated itself, or one that the EPA found in the statute before the courts began to review the legislative work product. We conclude that it was the Court of Appeals, rather than Congress or any of the decisionmakers who are authorized by Congress to administer this legislation, that was primarily responsible for the 1980 position taken by the agency.

POLICY

The arguments over policy that are advanced in the parties' briefs create the impression that respondents are now waging in a judicial forum a specific policy battle which they ultimately lost in the agency and in the 32 jurisdictions opting for the bubble concept, but one which was never waged in the Congress. Such policy arguments are more properly addressed to legislators or administrators, not to judges.[38]

In this case, the Administrator's interpretation represents a reasonable accommodation of manifestly competing interests and is entitled to deference; the regulatory scheme is technical and complex, the agency considered the matter in a detailed and reasoned fashion, and the decision involves reconciling conflicting policies. Congress intended to accommodate both interests, but did not do so itself on the level of specificity presented by this case. Perhaps that body

---

38.   Respondents point out if a brand new factory that will emit over 100 tons of pollutants is constructed in a nonattainment area, that plant must obtain a permit pursuant to §172(b)(6) and in order to do so, it must satisfy the §173 conditions, including the LAER requirement. Respondents argue if an old plant containing several large emitting units is to be modernized by the replacement of one or more units emitting over 100 tons of pollutant with a new unit emitting less but still more than 100 tons the result should be no different simply because "it happens to be built not at a new site, but within a *pre-existing plant.*"

consciously desired the Administrator to strike the balance at this level, thinking that those with great expertise and charged with responsibility for administering the provision would be in a better position to do so; perhaps it simply did not consider the question at this level; and perhaps Congress was unable to forge a coalition on either side of the question, and those on each side decided to take their chances with the scheme devised by the agency. For judicial purposes, it matters not which of these things occurred.

Judges are not experts in the field, and are not part of either political branch of the Government. Courts must, in some cases, reconcile competing political interests, but not on the basis of the judges' personal policy preferences. In contrast, an agency to which Congress has delegated policymaking responsibilities may, within the limits of that delegation, properly rely upon the incumbent administration's views of wise policy to inform its judgments. While agencies are not directly accountable to the people, the Chief Executive is, and it is entirely appropriate for this political branch of the Government to make such policy choices — resolving the competing interests which Congress itself either inadvertently did not resolve, or intentionally left to be resolved by the agency charged with the administration of the statute in light of everyday realities.

When a challenge to an agency construction of a statutory provision, fairly conceptualized, really centers on the wisdom of the agency's policy, rather than whether it is a reasonable choice within a gap left open by Congress, the challenge must fail. In such a case, federal judges who have no constituency have a duty to respect legitimate policy choices made by those who do. The responsibilities for assessing the wisdom of such policy choices and resolving the struggle between competing views of the public interest are not judicial ones: "Our Constitution vests such responsibilities in the political branches." TVA v. Hill, 437 U.S. 153, 195 (1978).

We hold that the EPA's definition of the term "source" is a permissible construction of the statute which seeks to accommodate progress in reducing air pollution with economic growth. "The Regulations which the Administrator has adopted provide what the agency could allowably view as . . . [an] effective reconciliation of these twofold ends. . . ." United States v. Shimer, 367 U.S., at 383.

The judgment of the Court of Appeals is reversed.

It is so ordered.

Justice MARSHALL and Justice REHNQUIST did not participate in the consideration or decision of these cases.

Justice O'CONNOR did not participate in the decision of these cases.

NOTES

1. How does the Court's standard of review in *Chevron* differ from that in *Overton Park*? See Shapiro & Glicksman, Congress, The Supreme Court, and the Quiet Revolution in Administrative Law, 1988 Duke L.J. 819, 858-863. Do

you agree with the following interpretation of the case? "[I]f . . . the opinion is taken to its full extent to prescribe a rule of agency law-making from Congressional silence, then, I think *Chevron* is simply wrong." Hirshman, Postmodern Jurisprudence and the Problem of Administrative Discretion, 82 Nw. U.L. Rev. 646, 687-688 (1988). Proponents of strong executive control of administrative agencies applaud the decision, Pierce, *Chevron* and Its Aftermath: Judicial Review of Agency Interpretation of Its Statutory Provisions, 41 Vand. L. Rev. 301 (1988). Likewise, scholars influenced by public choice theory advocate a narrow role for courts in policing legislative bargains among interest groups. See Easterbrook, Statutes' Domains, 50 U. Chi. L. Rev. 533 (1983) and The Supreme Court, 1983 Term-Forward: The Court and the Economic System, 98 Harv. L. Rev. 4 (1984). Was *Chevron* correctly decided under this theory because the agency simply ratified the bargain struck in Congress among competing interest groups? Whether this is an accurate reading of the legislative history of the Clean Air Act is explored in Chapter 3, page 160. Is *Chevron* compelled by separation of powers principles? Is *Chevron* at bottom an estoppel case: once Congress authorizes the exercise of such broad discretion, has it authorized the executive to interpret the statute as it chooses? Compare Farina, Statutory Interpretation and the Balance of Power in the Administrative State, 89 Colum. L. Rev. 452 (1989) with Kmiec, Judicial Deference to Executive Agencies and the Decline of the Nondelegation Doctrine, 2 Admin. L.J. 269 (1988).

2. *Vermont Yankee* preceded the deregulation movement in the 1980s, but *Chevron* was decided at the height of it. Does the fact that the agency is relaxing a previous regulatory burden have any influence on the standard of review? The issue raised in Motor Vehicle Manufacturers Assn. of the United States v. State Farm Mutual Automobile Insurance Co., 463 U.S. 49 (1983), was whether the Department of Transportation, responding to the Reagan Administration's push for deregulation, could rescind a previously adopted rule requiring passive restraints (airbags) in new cars. The automobile industry argued that the decision to rescind was within the Agency's discretion since the issue was the same as a decision not to adopt a rule in the first instance, and *Vermont Yankee* made "any agency decision . . . by definition unimpeachable." But the Court unanimously held that the decision to rescind the airbag rule was arbitrary and capricious. Rescision of a previously adopted rule is different from a decision not to adopt a rule in the first place, the Court held, because there is a presumption that congressional policies contained in the enabling statute will be served best by a settled rule. "Accordingly, an agency changing its course by rescinding a rule is obligated to supply a reasoned analysis for change beyond that which may be required when an agency does not act in the first instance." Id. at 42. DOT's deregulation decision was arbitrary and capricious because no reasons were offered for the rejection of airbags in light of their safety benefits.

Of particular interest to environmental law is Justice White's rejection of the automobile industry's reading of *Vermont Yankee*:

Specifically, it is submitted [by the industry] that to require an agency to consider an airbags-only alternative is, in essence, to dictate to the agency the procedures it is to follow. Petitioners both misread *Vermont Yankee* and misconstrue the nature of the remand that is in order. In *Vermont Yankee*, we held that a court may not impose additional procedural requirements upon an agency. We do not require today any specific procedures which NHTSA [National Highway Traffic Safety Administration] must follow. Nor do we broadly require an agency to consider all policy alternatives in reaching [a] decision. . . . But the airbag is more than a policy alternative to the passive restraint standard; it is a technological alternative within the ambit of the existing standard. [Id. at 58-59.]

The District of Columbia Circuit Court of Appeals subsequently held that the Secretary of Transportation's response to *State Farm* was not ripe for review. State Farm Mutual Automobile Insurance Co. v. Dole, 802 F.2d 474 (D.C. Cir. 1986), *cert. denied*, 107 S. Ct. 1616 (1987).

Garland, Deregulation and Judicial Review, 98 Harv. L. Rev. 507, 586-587 (1985), reviews the arguments that deregulation should trigger either a higher or lower standard of judicial review as well as the courts' response to deregulation challenges and speculates about the new standard of judicial review that is emerging:

It is possible to detect in the current judicial critique of interest representation the outlines of a newly emerging model of administrative law. At its core is a return to the traditional model's central tenet that agency action is justifiable only if it remains faithful to the dictates of the legislative process. Interest representation, with its effort to base legitimacy on the provision of a surrogate legislative process within the agency, has lost adherents. In rejecting interest representation, however, the evolving fidelity model is not blind to its predecessor's insights. It does not — as it cannot — return to the traditional model as if nothing had transpired over the last fifty years.

Like interest representation, the emerging model plainly lacks the traditional model's faith that a one-to-one correlation (the "transmission belt" analogy) can be found between congressional intent and agency action. The new model does not ignore the problem of discretion, but rather makes an effort to harness it in the service of fidelity. The exercise of discretion must not only be rational in some abstract sense; it must also be reasonable in light of the legislative purpose. In other words, the agency must act as would a reasonable administrator intent on accomplishing the statutory objective. This approach results in a blurring of the traditional two-stage process of judicial review, in which the court first satisfied itself that the agency had not exceeded the scope of its delegated authority within the meaning of §10(e)(2)(C) of the APA, and then went on to consider whether action within its authority nonetheless constituted an abuse of discretion under §10(e)(2)(A). Under the emerging model, courts ensure not only that fidelity to congressional purpose marks the outer bounds of agency discretion, but also that it animates the exercise of that discretion.

The Court's continuing confusion about the allocation of responsibility between courts and agencies in interpreting acts of Congress, compare ETSI Pipeline Project v. Missouri, 108 S. Ct. 805 (1988) with Young v. Community Nutrition Institute, 106 S. Ct. 2360 (1986) (Stevens, J. dissenting), has given rise to an extensive literature. Among the most important works are Hirshman, Post-Modern Jurisprudence and the Problem of Administrative Discretion, 82 Nw. U.L. Rev. 646 (1988); Macey, Promoting Public-Regarding Legislation through Statutory Interpretation: An Interest Group Model, 84 Colum. L. Rev. 1689 (1984); Pierce, The Role of Constitutional and Political Theory in Administrative Law, 64 Tex. L. Rev. 469 (1985); Posner, Economics, Politics and the Reading of Statutes and the Constitution, 49 U. Chi. L. Rev. 263 (1982); and Sunstein, Deregulation and the Courts, 5 J. Poly. Analysis & Mgmt. 517 (1986).

3. Judicial activism continues to have its defenders. Shapiro & Levy, Heightened Scrutiny of the Fourth Branch: Separation of Powers and the Requirement of Adequate Reasons for Agency Decisions, 1987 Duke L.J. 387, defend the hard look doctrine on the ground that rationalism promotes both liberal and progressive values; Shapiro and Glicksman, The Supreme Court, and the Quiet Revolution in Administrative Law, 1988 Duke L.J. 819 suggest that the judicial deference undermines congressional attempts to limit agency discretion through techniques such as regulatory deadlines and detailed statutory standards. Similarly, Levy & Glicksman, Judicial Activism and Restraint in the Supreme Court's Environmental Law Decisions, 42 Vand. L. Rev. 343 (1989) find Congressional objectives undermined by the pro-development bias of the Court's environmental decisions.

c.   Judicial Reform of Agency Procedures: Softening the "Hard Look"

The APA's basic dichotomy between adjudication and rule-making assumes that agencies act either like courts or like legislatures. In practice, no such facile dichotomy exists. An adjudication is much like a trial, but so is much rule-making if the issues are focused, the class of those directly affected by the rule is reasonably well defined, and the factual predicate for the rule is disputed. Environmentalists and others trying to influence and ultimately challenge notice-and-comment rule-making were dissatisfied with the limited procedures imposed by the APA to build a better record for judicial review. There was little opportunity to challenge disputed factual assertions through cross-examination, and the record that resulted from the proceeding was sparse and untidy, despite *Overton Park*. Thus, it was hard to explain to a court just why a rule was arbitrary or unreasonable. To cure the defects in rule-making, challengers sought to convince courts to require "hybrid" procedures that allow cross-examination at crucial points and impose higher duties on the agency to explain the basis of its decision — in short, to require a more trial-like record.

The District of Columbia Circuit Court of Appeals first recognized a right of cross-examination on an ad hoc basis in a case reviewing the EPA's refusal to grant an extension of the 1975 deadlines for certain automobile emission limitations because of its inadequate response to industry criticisms of its methodologies. International Harvester Co. v. Ruckelshaus, 478 F.2d 615 (D.C. Cir. 1973). Note that his emphasis on "hard look" substantive review did not deter Judge Leventhal, the author of the *International Harvester* opinion, from serving as the chief architect of judge-imposed hybrid procedures. Two important articles that explore agency responses to the District of Columbia Circuit's experiment with hybrid rule-making are Pedersen, Formal Records and Informal Rulemaking, 86 Yale L.J. 38 (1975), and Williams, "Hybrid Rulemaking" under the Administrative Procedure Act: A Legal and Empirical Analysis, 42 U. Chi. L. Rev. 401 (1975). See also Judge J. Skelly Wright's The Rulemaking Process: The Limits of Judicial Review, 59 Cornell L. Rev. 375 (1974). The Supreme Court, however, took a dim view of the District of Columbia's hybrid rule-making. Vermont Yankee Nuclear Power Corp. v. Natural Resources Defense Council, 435 U.S. 519 (1978):

> In 1946, Congress enacted the Administrative Procedure Act, which as we have noted elsewhere was not only "a new, basic and comprehensive regulation of procedures in many agencies," Wong Yang Sung v. McGrath, 339 U.S. 33 (1950), but was also a legislative enactment which settled "long-continued and hard-fought contentions, and enacts a formula upon which opposing social and political forces have come to rest." Id., at 40. Section 4 of the Act, 5 U.S.C. §553 (1976 ed.), dealing with rulemaking, requires in subsection (b) that "notice of proposed rule making shall be published in the Federal Register . . . ," describes the contents of that notice, and goes on to require in subsection (c) that after the notice the agency "shall give interested persons an opportunity to participate in the rule making through submission of written data, views, or arguments with or without opportunity for oral presentation. After consideration of the relevant matter presented, the agency shall incorporate in the rules adopted a concise general statement of their basis and purpose." Interpreting this provision of the Act in United States v. Allegheny-Ludlum Steel Corp., 406 U.S. 742 (1972), and United States v. Florida East Coast R. Co., 410 U.S. 224 (1973), we held that generally speaking this section of the Act established the maximum procedural requirements which Congress was willing to have the courts impose upon agencies in conducting rulemaking procedures. Agencies are free to grant additional procedural rights in the exercise of their discretion, but reviewing courts are generally not free to impose them if the agencies have not chosen to grant them. This is not to say necessarily that there are no circumstances which would ever justify a court in overturning agency action because of a failure to employ procedures beyond those required by the statute. But such circumstances, if they exist, are extremely rare.
>
> Even apart from the Administrative Procedure Act this Court has for more than four decades emphasized that the formulation of procedures was basically to be left within the discretion of the agencies to which Congress had confided the responsibility for substantive judgments. . . . But although the judicial battle has been lost, the war has been won. Congress has imposed hybrid requirements in various statutes, such as the Clean Air Act, and agencies have adopted such procedures on their own initiative. The Senate has passed a regulatory reform bill that would amend §533 of the APA — the notice-and-comment rule-making provision — to require hybrid rule-making for "major" regulations, those with an annual economic impact greater than $100 million. (S. 1080, 97th Cong., 1st Sess. (1981).

NOTES

1. The question of the judiciary's authority to add to the APA's rule-making procedures has been an important one in environmental litigation. This question

arose because of the way in which administrative decisionmaking was structured, the complex and technical nature of agency rules, and the nature of the judicial review provided for agency rule adoptions. The procedure for adopting air quality and emissions standards under the 1970 Clean Air Act illustrates this process. A proposed rule was published and comments were received, and these, together with EPA's own internal file provided the basis for judicial review. EPA rules adopted under this procedure were directly reviewable in the courts of appeals. With no intervening district court trial, there was no opportunity to introduce additional evidence or to make a decision record. Faced with this informal clutter of documentation, it is no wonder the courts of appeals often remanded for additional agency clarification and called for protective procedures in the rulemaking process to supplement those provided by the APA.

The Clean Air Act's §307(b) now provides more formalized rule-making procedures for the adoption of emission standards and for many of the other rules authorized by the Act. Section 307(b) requires the development of a decision record by EPA that includes a summary of the factual data on which the rule is based; the record also is to include "the major legal interpretations and policy considerations underlying the proposed rule" (§307(d)(3)(C)). See Pedersen, Formal Records and Informal Rulemaking, 86 Yale L.J. 38 (1975).

Did the Court in *Overton Park* specify the type of procedure to be followed in compiling a decision record? If not, did that case raise the questions considered by the Court in *Vermont Yankee*? Can you reconcile these two cases? What alternatives are there for bypassing the *Vermont Yankee* holding? Note that the Court left open the possibility of a constitutional challenge to the adequacy of agency procedures. Could a court interpret the statutory requirements for notice-and-comment rule-making to include procedures not specifically mandated by the APA?

2. *Vermont Yankee* has provoked considerable debate. Professor Kenneth Davis has attacked the decision, claiming it is inconsistent with previous Supreme Court rulings and the long-standing tradition of federal courts of supplementing APA procedures when necessary. He claims that the Court's statements on the effect of the APA on judicial power to prescribe additional procedures was "broad dictum . . . [that] was probably intended to be no broader than the problem before the Court. . . . [The problem] was whether to reverse the lower court's holding based on the Bazelon procedural emphasis; in another aspect, the problem was whether what the Court called 'adjudicatory' procedure should be required in whole or in part for informal rulemaking." 1 K. Davis, Administrative Law Treatise 609 (2d ed. 1978); see also ibid. §6.37 (Supp. 1980). Do you agree?

Professor Stewart also disagrees with the *Vermont Yankee* holding:

> Despite residual uncertainties, the evolution of hybrid procedures has been a salutary step. Particularly in the field of environmental controls, where experience with the "paper hearing" form of hybrid procedures has been most fully developed, such procedures have opened the door to effective judicial review of the merits of

agency decisions, which has in turn produced material improvement in the quality of these decisions. Except for an initial "shakedown" period of agency adaptation, these advantages have been secured without debilitating cost, uncertainty, or delay. [Stewart, *Vermont Yankee* and the Evolution of Administrative Procedure, 91 Harv. L. Rev. 1805, 1813-1814 (1978).]

For a reply to Professor Stewart, see Byse, *Vermont Yankee* and the Evolution of Administrative Procedure: A Somewhat Different View, 91 Harv. L. Rev. 1823 (1978). Professor Byse agrees that "paper hearings" may serve a useful purpose but believes that the decision to utilize such hearings rests with the administrative agency or with Congress. See also Stewart, The Development of Administrative and Quasi-Constitutional Law in Judicial Review of Environmental Decisionmaking: Lessons from the Clean Air Act, 62 Iowa L. Rev. 713 (1977).

Well before *Vermont Yankee*, about the time of Judge Leventhal's call for a hard look and reasoned decisionmaking, Judge Bazelon wrote for the court in Environmental Defense Fund Inc. v. Ruckelshaus, 439 F.2d 584 (D.C. Cir. 1971), a case involving review of EPA's refusal to suspend registration of the pesticide DDT or to commence a formal administrative proceeding to cancel the registration. Clearly, Judge Bazelon was destined to agree with the approach in *Vermont Yankee*:

> [J]udicial review alone can correct only the most egregious abuses. Judicial review must operate to ensure that the administrative process itself will confine and control the exercise of discretion. Courts should require administrative officers to articulate the standards and principles that govern their discretionary decisions in as much detail as possible. Rules and regulations should be freely formulated by administrators, and revised when necessary. Discretionary decisions should more often be supported with findings of fact and reasoned opinions. When administrators provide a framework for principled decision-making, the result will be to diminish the importance of judicial review by enhancing the integrity of the administrative process, and to improve the quality of judicial review in those cases where judicial review is sought. [439 F.2d at 598.]

But consider Professor Sax's reaction to this language:

> I cannot imagine a more dubious example of wishful thinking. I know of no solid evidence to support the belief that requiring articulation, detailed findings or reasoned opinions enhances the integrity or propriety of administrative decisions. I think the emphasis on the redemptive quality of procedural reform is about nine parts myth and one part coconut oil. [The (Unhappy) Truth About NEPA, 26 Okla. L. Rev. 239 (1973).]

Do you agree with Professor Sax that the effort in *Overton Park*, *Ethyl*, *International Harvester*, Environmental Defense Fund v. Ruckelshaus, *Vermont Yankee*, and scores of other opinions was wasted? What actions would make the agencies responsive?

In Environmental Defense Fund v. Ruckelshaus Judge Bazelon also remarked:

> As a result of expanding doctrines of standing and reviewability, and new statutory causes of action, courts are increasingly asked to review administrative action that touches on fundamental personal interests in life, health, and liberty. These interests have always had a special claim to judicial protection, in comparison with the economic interests at stake in a ratemaking or licensing proceeding. [439 F.2d at 597-598.]

Should environmental decisions have their own separate standard of review? Would judicially imposed procedures be justified under it? What basis exists for such a standard? Is it "quasi-constitutional"? See Stewart, The Development of Administrative and Quasi-Constitutional Law in Judicial Review of Environmental Decisionmaking: Lessons from the Clean Air Act, 62 U. Iowa L. Rev. 713 (1977). See also Soper, The Constitutional Framework of Environmental Law, in Federal Environmental Law 20, 114 (E. Dolgin & T. Guilbert eds. 1974).

III

PROTECTING THE AIR RESOURCE

The problem of air pollution prompted Congress, after 15 years of study, to enact the most complex, expensive, and pervasive of the federal regulatory environmental statutes, the Clean Air Act of 1970. The Act, the first of the many pollution statutes enacted during the environmental decade and the first major environmental legislation analyzed in this casebook, regulates all new vehicles and some 200,000 stationary sources throughout the nation. Between 1972 and 1984 the United States spent $310 billion dollars on air pollution control (in 1982 dollars). Conservation Foundation, State of the Environment 23 (1987).

Implementation of the Clean Air Act has matured, and a new set of issues, such as acid rain, command public attention. Nor has the Act succeeded in eliminating air pollution in urban centers, although the problem is now limited to a few of the most difficult areas, such as the Los Angeles basin. As you review this chapter, consider whether the Act is still the most effective way to combat the air pollution problem. Is cleaning the air primarily a political problem, a cost problem, or a technology problem? See, e.g., Moore, We Already Have the Technology to Clean up Our Air, Washington Post Natl. Weekly Ed., June 26-July 2, 1989, at 23 (author is former counsel to Senate Environment and Public Works Committee).

The courts have been deeply involved in the implementation of the Act, and have pushed EPA into certain programs and timetables against its will. This trend continues, although judicial activism has declined as the makeup of the federal courts tilts to the right and as courts follow the Supreme Court's lead in paying more deference to EPA decisionmaking. For criticism of an activist judicial role see R. Melnick, Regulation and the Courts: The Case of the Clean Air Act (1983); Melnick, Pollution Deadlines and the Coalition for Failure, 75 Pub. Interest 123 (1984).

A. DEFINING, MEASURING, AND PREDICTING AIR POLLUTION: SCIENTIFIC AND TECHNICAL ASPECTS

Like much other environmental law, air pollution control law rests upon a factual foundation that is scientifically more complex than that underpinning other legal regimes with which you may be familiar. Chemistry, engineering, medicine, and meteorology interact with law to produce modern air quality control policy. Scientific understanding of air pollution is constantly in flux, which challenges air quality management schemes to stand ready for change. See Pedersen, Why the Clean Air Act Works Badly, 129 U. Pa. L. Rev. 1059, 1062 (1981).

1.   Air Pollution: Types, Sources, and Impacts

Air pollution consists of particles and gases in the air that for various reasons are viewed as undesirable. Whether a substance is a pollutant thus necessarily depends on a social judgment, because an air pollutant may be a valuable resource that is simply out of place in the air. Urban air pollutants include carbon monoxide, sulfur and nitrogen oxides, a great variety of hydrocarbon compounds, and trace amounts of industrial materials such as lead, mercury, asbestos, and chlorine.

Nature may cause pollution. For example, hydrocarbons and hydrogen sulfide (later becoming sulfur oxides) form when organic materials decompose; forest fires and volcanoes release tons of carbon monoxide, hydrocarbons, and particulate matter into the air; "background" radiation that occurs naturally adds to radiation caused by human activities; and, as we shall soon see, introduction of lead into the environment by humans adds to levels occurring naturally. Recent research supports President Reagan's assertion that trees cause pollution by contributing to ozone formation. 19 Envt. Rep. (BNA): Current Developments 1086 (1988). Do you anticipate special problems in controlling pollution that also has natural causes?

Major conventional pollutants. Several air pollutants appear in such quantities or cause such serious harm that they have received major regulatory attention over the past several decades. The odorless and colorless gas carbon monoxide (CO) forms when fossil fuels do not burn completely. Vehicles are its major source (over 50 percent), and because of its weight CO tends to collect in city street "canyons." CO bonds strongly with hemoglobin in the blood, impairs mental functions and fetal development, and aggravates cardiovascular diseases. Its formation could be drastically reduced by combustion at higher engine temperatures in the presence of more oxygen, but this would produce more nitrogen oxides. Controls require proper motor vehicle engine tuning and the use of catalytic or thermal exhaust gas conversion to combustible compounds.

Nitrogen oxides form when air (78 percent nitrogen and 21 percent oxygen) is heated to exceptionally high temperatures, principally in motor vehicle engines and high-temperature power plant furnaces. Nitrogen oxide (NO_x) usually forms first but converts to nitrogen dioxide (NO_2), a pungent, brownish-red gas that aggravates respiratory and cardiovascular diseases, causes kidney inflammation, impairs visibility, injures paints and dyes, and retards plant growth. NO_2 emissions abatement techniques, which are less effective than they are for other pollutants, include employing "three-way" catalytic control of motor vehicle emissions, inducing reduced combustion temperatures, and "scrubbing" stack gases with caustic substances or urea.

Like CO, gaseous and particulate hydrocarbon compounds (HC) form when fuels or other carbon-bearing substances are burned. Vehicle engines and fuel evaporation are the major source of these compounds (50 percent nationwide), but volatile HC escapes in the manufacture or handling of asphalt, rubber, and petroleum products such as gasoline, oils, solvents, and plastics. Rotting organic materials, home fireplaces, and forest fires also generate HC. Some HC causes or contributes to cancer. HC contributes to the health and visibility impairment associated with smog because they are major precursors in the formation of photochemical oxidants through atmospheric reactions. HC emissions reductions can be achieved essentially the same way CO emissions are reduced for both mobile and stationary sources. Various procedures for closed handling of petroleum compounds at service stations and refineries have also helped.

Photochemical oxidants are formed when precursor pollutants such as HC and NO_x react with each other and with atmospheric gases in the presence of sunlight. Themselves colorless gases, certain photochemical oxidants in combination appear to produce smog. The principal oxidant component of smog is ozone (O_3), but peroxyacetyl nitrate (PAN), aldehydes, and other compounds are implicated as well. Photochemical oxidants aggravate respiratory and cardiovascular illnesses and irritate the eyes and the respiratory tract; they also contribute to visibility impairment, injure rubber, textiles, and paints, and cause plants to drop their leaves and fruit prematurely. Controls require reductions in NO_x, HC, and possibly sulfur dioxide (SO_2) emissions.

Lead, a ubiquitous, naturally occurring element, appears in the air as an oxide aerosol or dust chiefly through emissions from motor vehicles that burn leaded gasoline. Lead smelting and processing, the manufacture of lead products, the combustion of coal and refuse, and use of pesticides containing lead contribute as well. Lead accumulates in body organs and impairs bone growth and the nervous, circulatory, and renal systems. It can be controlled by eliminating lead additives from gasoline and paint, cleaning stack gases, eliminating lead soldering from tin cans, and imposing dietary controls.

A colorless gas with a pungent odor, sulfur dioxide forms when coal and oil are burned in power plants or space heaters or when sulfur-bearing metal ores such as lead and copper are smelted. Electric utilities produce a major portion of the SO_2 emitted in the United States. Like most other major air pollutants, SO_2 is acrid, corrosive, and toxic. It aggravates respiratory diseases, particularly emphysema, and irritates the eyes and the respiratory tract. A relatively heavy gas, it tends to collect against prominent features of the landscape such as cliffs. SO_2 emissions can be successfully reduced by using low sulfur fuels, removing sulfur before fuel use, scrubbing stack gases with lime, and catalytic conversion to sulfuric acid.

The public has a fairly good understanding of the polluting nature of total suspended particulates (TSP), the collection of solid or liquid particles such as dust, pollen, soot, metals, and chemical compounds dispersed in the atmosphere. Cinders and soot from urban waste incinerators are common sources, but any burning or abrasion of a solid or splashing of a liquid typically contributes to TSP. The particulates from modern power plants contain virtually no cinders and soot. Power plant particulates are small, spherical, glassy particles, usually less than 50 microns in diameter, the diameter of a typical human hair. Soot is a lacy, mostly carbonaceous material, and cinders are generally flaky, like the ashes from a wood fire. Particulates may cause injury or may aggravate the effects of other pollutants. They exacerbate asthma and other respiratory or cardiovascular symptoms, soil and injure building materials, impair visibility, contribute to cloud formation, and interfere with plant growth.

Particle size and weight vary dramatically from visible soot to air particles detectable only under an electron microscope. Hence they may drift to earth immediately after leaving a chimney, or they may be transported on prevailing winds for thousands of miles. In recent years researchers have concluded that settleable particles (50 microns and up) present few health risks compared with aerosols (smaller than 50 microns) and fine particulates (less than 3 microns). TSP are reduced quite successfully (up to 99.75 percent efficiency) by cleaning stack gases with electrostatic precipitators, scrubbers, or fabric filters. "Fugitive" emissions can be controlled by spraying construction and demolition sites with water.

The foregoing discussion suggests a natural distinction between primary pollutants, which are directly emitted as a result of human activities, and secondary pollutants, which form after human emissions combine with naturally occurring atmospheric gases, water vapor, and each other, usually with sunlight powering the chemical reactions. Scientific understanding of the chemical transformation, fate (ultimate resting place), and impacts of pollutants has expanded considerably in the past decade, and ultimately it may be concluded that secondary pollutants are more important than primary ones. Which of the pollutants thus far discussed are primary and which secondary? Although regulators' main concern may be with the harm caused by secondary pollutants such as photochemical oxidants, regulators have to reduce them by controlling primary pollutants such as HC and NO_x. Moreover, because photochemical oxidants are not all directly implicated in smog formation, regulators may have to focus on reduced levels of a single oxidant, e.g., O_3 as an indicator of progress in controlling the more complex photochemical oxidant problem.

Evidence now suggests that sulfates, very small secondary particulates derived from gaseous SO_2, may be primarily responsible for the health effects originally attributed to SO_2 and large primary particulates. Fine particulates may be carcinogenic. They can penetrate deeply into the lungs, but many of the larger particulates now regulated are caught in the nose and pulmonary mucous membranes and eventually excreted. Similar data document the transformation of NO_2 to fine nitrate particles and suggest that nitrates cause many of the health effects formerly attributed to NO_2. Sulfate and nitrate aerosols are formed when chemical reactions occur in the atmosphere, sometimes days after emission from smokestacks or motor vehicles. When they combine with water, the aerosols form sulfuric and nitric acid. These acids may then show up as acid rain, snow, or dew hundreds of miles from the source ultimately responsible for them. For more on the acid deposition problem, see p. 312 *infra*. Hence two of the major primary pollutants (NO_x, SO_2) are transformed into a subset of a third (TSP). The resulting highly mobile sulfates and nitrates take on several lives of their own: fine respirable particulates, mild acids in the presence of water, or (in the absence of water) another type of environmental pollutant entirely — a thinly dispersed dust.

Toxic chemicals and other hazardous air pollutants. The seven pollutant groupings just discussed have been regulated through ambient standards under the federal Clean Air Act. Many additional pollutants have also been regulated that endanger health or the environment only under certain conditions and in particular locales. These pollutants include toxic metals such as arsenic, beryllium, cadmium, and mercury; minerals such as asbestos; gases such as chlorine; radioactive substances; and scores of organic compounds. A chemist's cacophony of hundreds of additional air pollutants awaits an effective policy response. The control of hazardous substances in all media is a key environmental problem facing Congress, the states, and regulatory agencies.

Documenting the health effects of air pollution. Air pollution clearly damages property and natural environmental systems. Egyptian monuments in London and New York have corroded more in the last few decades than in the previous three millenia. See Graedel & McGill, Degradation of Materials in the Atmosphere, 20 Envtl. Sci. & Tech. 1093 (1986). Nylon clothing disintegrates minutes after exposure to sulfuric acid aerosols. Air pollutants enter the root and leaf structure of plants, block light, and destroy cells. Acid rain harms natural ecosystems. But air pollution chiefly threatens human health. Emissions are widely believed to cause significant harm to human beings, but marshaling the medical proof has defied the best efforts of health scientists for decades.

> Describing the direct physiological effects of air pollution on humans can be like describing the shape of an iceberg floating in the sea. A few historical episodes, periods of intense air-pollution concentrations when mortality rates have risen sharply, stand out clearly and are described thoroughly in the literature. Numbers of persons, symptoms, circumstances, and the associated statistics can be clearly linked to air pollution without strong dissension. But we know that the most massive health problem with air pollution is not associated with identifiable episodes but in the gradual erosion of health by frequent and long-term exposures. Hypotheses linking this type of exposure with specific illness require murky assumptions and estimates that are easily attacked piecemeal by dissenters. . . .
>
> [Crisis] circumstances existed in the horseshoe-shaped Monongahela Valley around Donora, Pennsylvania, in October, 1948. Toxic fumes and smoke were

rising from numerous factories along the river, and freight trains operated on both banks with coal-burning, steam locomotives. The air was cold and damp. For more than five days after October 26th, no breezes disturbed the thickening smog that accumulated in the valley basin. About twenty deaths were attributed to the episode, and nearly 6,000 persons representing nearly half of the area's population were stricken with irritation of the eyes, nose, and throat, labored breathing, coughing, chest pains, headaches, nausea, and vomiting. . . .

[But] [m]ost victims of air pollution will not die during an air episode. They will contract a respiratory disease or another symptom associated with air pollution, gradually weaken, and then typically die from pneumonia, a heart attack, or failure of some other vital organ. Or they will bear a child with a birth defect that future medical research will link to an air pollutant. Or perhaps they will develop a disease, such as cancer, caused by a dimly understood set of factors with air pollution as only one possible component. [G. Sewall, Environmental Quality Management 168-170 (1975).]

See also Smith, Air Pollution: Assessing Total Exposure in the United States, Envt. Vol. 30, No. 8, at 11 (1988).

The state of air quality and its improvement. Pollution levels for all of the six major pollutants have declined in recent years. This is how improvement is measured:

The Pollutant Standard Index (PSI), developed in 1976, can be used to analyze trends in urban air quality and to make comparisons among urban areas. This index compares air quality monitoring to the primary ambient air quality standards (excluding those for lead). In theory, the higher the index reading, the more severe the pollution and the greater the threat to human health. The index is an imperfect measure of air quality, not only because it relies on fixed monitoring stations but because it focuses only on the most common pollutants. [Conservation Foundation, State of the Environment 57-58 (1987).]

According to EPA, improvements in pollution levels for the major pollutants between 1978 and 1987 were: ozone, 9 percent; lead, 88 percent; sulfur dioxide, 35 percent; carbon monoxide, 32 percent; nitrogen dioxide, 12 percent; and particulates, 21 percent. EPA, National Air Quality and Emission Trends Report, 1987, at 6-17 (1989). These aggregate changes hide some important trouble spots. Ozone levels remain high in many urban areas, which are designated non-attainment for this pollutant because their ozone levels exceed the national standards. A substantial number of urban areas are non-attainment for this pollutant, but it is a serious problem only in a few areas, such as Los Angeles. Acid rain is a serious problem and one that will be expensive to remedy. Two-thirds of all sulfur dioxide emissions are produced by electric utilities, with most coming from coal-fired power plants.

The subject of the economic costs and benefits of air pollution and its control is a burgeoning subfield of environmental economics. See, e.g., R. Crandall, Controlling Industrial Pollution: The Economics and Politics of Clean Air (1983). While burdens and benefits are almost certainly unevenly distributed among classes of emitters and receptors, it appears that the view that air quality control policies are regressive is unfounded. The poor benefit more than the rich from these policies, see, e.g., Gianessi, Peskin & Wolff, The Distributional Effects of Uniform Air Pollution Policy, 93 Q.J. Econ. 281 (Spring 1979). L. Lave & E. Seskin, Air Pollution and Human Health (1978), found that the initial benefits of the Clean Air Act ($23 billion) exceeded its costs ($15 billion). See generally A. Freeman, The Benefits of Environmental Improvement: Theory and Practice (1979); R. Halversen & M. Ruby, Benefit-Cost Analysis of Air-Pollution Control (1981); A. Kneese, Measuring the Benefits of Clean Air and Water 123 (1984) (suggesting that economic damage from air pollution may be more serious than health effects).

A NOTE ON GLOBAL WARMING AND THE GREENHOUSE EFFECT

The summer drought of 1988 made everyone aware of the greenhouse effect and what it means for global warming. Greenhouse is primarily an air pollution problem, as the following statement indicates:

> The greenhouse effect has been a part of the Earth's history for several million years. Primordial, background concentrations of carbon dioxide (CO_2) and water vapor (H_2O) were transparent to incoming solar radiation but trapped the outbound, long-wave radiation emitted from the earth's surface. This phenomenon, commonly referred to as the greenhouse effect, warmed the lower part of the atmosphere (the troposphere) by about 33 degrees centigrade (70 degrees fahrenheit). The impact of this warming process was to allow water to remain on the planet's surface as a liquid, rather than ice, and to facilitate the complex biochemical processes that led to the evolution . . . [of man]. Without this greenhouse effect, the Earth, like Mars, would be a cold and lifeless place.
>
> The greenhouse effect became the greenhouse problem when the buildup of CO_2 and other trace gases began to exceed natural background levels by substantial amounts, trapping an increasing amount of heat close to the Earth's surface. Five other gases now contribute significantly to the process of global warming. These other greenhouse gases are nitrous oxide (N_2O), methane (CH_4, better known as natural gas), tropospheric ozone (O_3), and the fully-halogenated chlorofluorocarbons (CFCs), especially CFC-11 and CFC-12. . . .
>
> The increasing concentrations of these gases in the atmosphere threaten, within our lifetime, to warm the planet to levels which would alter global climate, disrupt traditional patterns of rainfall, cause sea levels to rise, and disrupt economically important activities in both industrialized and developing countries. . . .
>
> Historically, CO_2 has contributed the most to global warming. Today, the other greenhouse gases add about as much each year to the atmospheric commitment as CO_2 does. . . .
>
> If current warming trends continue, the combined effect of the buildup of these six trace gases is expected to commit the planet to an average surface warming of 1.5-4.5 degrees centigrade (3-9 degrees fahrenheit) by about 2030. This is equal to the warming effect of doubling the pre-industrial concentration of CO_2 alone, holding all other gases at their pre-industrial levels. A warming of this magnitude would be accompanied by a rise in average global sea levels of . . . [one to four

feet]. Such a rise would cause extensive coastal flooding, especially in low-lying areas like New Orleans which are close to the great river deltas. It would also inundate fragile wetland ecosystems and cause salt-water intrusion into aquifers and other fresh-water storage facilities. . . .

[This predicted global warming] . . . is also expected to cause substantial changes in winds, rainfall, and ocean currents . . . [and] could cause hotter and drier conditions in many of the mid-continent, mid-latitude regions which are the bread-baskets of the world food economy. The U.S. Mid-West, for example, could see a rapid return to the Dust Bowl conditions of the 1930s. . . . [Statement of Dr. Irving Mintzer, World Resources Institute, in Hearing Before the House Comm. on Foreign Affairs, 100th Cong., 2d Sess. 96-98 (1988).]

The greenhouse effect and global warming is only in part an American problem as fuel consumption in other countries and deforestation, including the destruction of the rain forests, are major contributors. Greenhouse becomes an American and a Clean Air Act problem to the extent that carbon monoxide production contributes to the global warming trend. Clearly a reduction in the use of fuels, such as coal, which are high CO_2 producers, is a major strategy in reducing global warming. Reducing CO_2 production in this country requires a mix of strategies that include increased energy efficiency and the use of alternative energy sources such as natural gas and nuclear power. See generally Technologies for Remediating Global Warming, Hearing Before the House Comm. on Science, Research & Technology, 100th Cong., 2d Sess. (1988). For a more conservative view on greenhouse see The Greenhouse Effect, Climatic Change, and Ecosystems (B. Bolin, B. Doos, J. Jager & R. Warrick eds. 1986). See also Sen. Comm. on Agriculture, Nutrition, and Forestry, Agriculture, Forestry, and Global Climate Change — A Reader (1989); The Greenhouse Effect: How It Can Change Our Lives, EPA Journal, Vol. 15, No. 1 (Jan.-Feb. 1989).

Congress has not yet acted on how to factor a response to the greenhouse effect into Clean Air Act requirements, but has directed EPA to study and report on the greenhouse issue. Assume you are the Administrator of EPA. What would you recommend? Keep in mind when answering this question that over half of carbon monoxide emissions are produced by motor vehicles.

A NOTE ON RADON AND INDOOR AIR POLLUTION

The problem. Recent research has revealed that the air within homes and other "weatherized" and "energy efficient" structures contains significantly higher concentrations of many pollutants than outdoor air. The sources of these pollutants are items and products very common in the home or office: asbestos (from insulation); formaldehyde and other toxic compounds (from cleaning products and chemical cleaning such as dry cleaning); tobacco smoke (which contains over 2,000 chemicals, many known carcinogens); pesticides; volatile organic compounds from such varied sources as hot water, deodorizers, paints; and plastics and biological contaminants like microorganisms, molds and mildews. A colorless gas, radon, is also present in many homes.

These substances cause human health problems that range from allergies and asthma to cancer. These problems are aggravated because most Americans spend up to 70 percent of their time indoors. People most susceptible to the health problems triggered by indoor air pollutants, such as the very old, the very young and the infirm, often spend more than 90 percent of their time indoors.

The numerous office buildings throughout the country that suffer from "sick building syndrome" are another health concern. These are buildings whose unclean air causes physical illness to those exposed to it regularly. They are usually modern structures which use mostly recirculated air, are tightly constructed for energy efficiency and have no windows that open.

Radon. Radon has been a known cancer causing agent for centuries, ever since it was found in the 16th century to be the cause of the high death rate among Czech silver miners in the Erz mountains. Latin medical texts described a syndrome among these miners that later came to be recognized, through toxicology, microbiology, and epidemiology, as lung cancer. Researchers in the 1940s and 1950s identified radon as the cause of lung cancer among the Czech miners by comparing the medical history of this group with the medical history of a group of Colorado uranium miners.

Radon is a decay product of radium, which is a decay product of uranium. In the natural radioactive decay process, radon is given off as a colorless, odorless, tasteless gas. Although radon in its pure form is not hazardous, it is highly volatile and rapidly breaks down in a series of radioactive processes to the inert element lead. It is the radon products (or radon daughters) that pose a threat to human health. These radioactive decay products are highly magnetic and attach easily to dust particles in the air. These dust particles can then be inhaled, thereby depositing the still radioactive particles in the human lung. It is this radioactivity which, over the years, can cause cancer.

Until 1984 radon was thought to be a threat only to miners of uranium and other substances containing a high uranium content. All this changed when radioactivity in a Pennsylvania engineer was traced to his home, where radon levels were 2,500 times the average. Subsequent testing in the area found that 60 percent of the homes had high levels of radon. EPA now estimates that between 5,000 and 20,000 lung cancer deaths annually are caused by radon exposure, and that as many as one million homes may have dangerous radon levels.

Federal legislation. Congress became concerned enough about the presence of indoor air pollutants to enact legislation specifically dealing with it. After adopting legislation authorizing a research program in 1986, it adopted an Indoor Air Abatement act in 1988 as an amendment to the Toxic Substances Control Act. 15 U.S.C. §§4661-4771. The Act includes authority for the development of model voluntary standards for controlling radon in new buildings and information programs.

For discussion of radon and indoor air quality see Jackowitz, Radon's Radioactive Ramifications: How Federal and State Governments Should Address the Problem, 16 B.C. Envtl. Aff. L. Rev. 329 (1988); Kirsch, Behind Closed Doors: Indoor Air Pollution and Government Policy, 6 Harv. Envtl. L. Rev. 339

(1983); Comment, Radon: An Environmental Problem that is Too Close to Home, 4 J. Contemp. Health, Law and Policy 415 (1988).

2.   Monitoring and Modeling Air Pollution

Attorneys have a tendency to assume that technology can monitor air emissions and predict their impacts far more accurately than it actually can. The expense and imprecision of monitoring and modeling technologies have major consequences for legal control regimes, which set precise numerical standards, assuming that accurate monitoring and modeling can be achieved.

Monitoring. The techniques for monitoring ambient conditions require different samplers for particulates and gases because of their different chemical forms. Several types of particulate measuring devices are in use. The Ringelmann Smoke Chart, devised just before the turn of the century, consists of four progressively more shaded gray spots in a line on a chart. The spots can be compared at the plant site to the plume of smoke under inspection. The chart is not indexed to volume, only to opacity and density, and cannot be used at night, in the rain, or during high winds. Nevertheless, use of such subjective opacity readings for enforcement purposes still survives judicial review today, e.g., Chemithon Corp. v. Puget Sound Air Pollution Control Agency, 18 Envt. Rep. Cas. (BNA) 1647 (Wash. Ct. App. 1983). Obviously, more is required in properly managed emissions control programs, and other simple sampling techniques, for example, particulate filtration devices, do exist.

By contrast, gases must be measured by more complicated absorption, adsorption, and direct physical measurement techniques. Direct physical measurement techniques, such as chemiluminescence (the flash of light that some pollutants release when they react with another gas), are gaining favor, although no direct technique yet developed is cheap and reliable. See G. Sewall, Environmental Quality Management 187 (1975).

Reported conditions vary enormously depending on the distance of the monitoring device from smokestacks, streets, and highways, how high above the ground the device is positioned, winds, the time of day, the weather while readings are taken, the configuration of the terrain, and the placement of buildings and complex sources of pollution such as airports and shopping centers. Yet the concept of a uniform background of ambient air quality persists, perhaps only because regulatory programs must focus upon reasonably ascertainable conditions.

One might expect that it might be easier to monitor emissions at individual sources since the uncertainties just described can be eliminated, but this is not the case. Local agencies still resort extensively to the Ringelmann Chart because it is inexpensive, quick, and simple to use. Engineering inspections provide better data but require experienced inspectors. Accurate measurements are provided by performance tests of control equipment and stack emissions, but such tests take several days and cost several thousands of dollars. Continuous monitors are required at a few sources, but in general their cost is viewed as prohibitive. For discussion of the materials balance method and other alternatives to "in-stack" measurement, see F. Anderson, A. Kneese, P. Reed, R. Stevenson & S. Taylor, Environmental Improvement through Economic Incentives 102-104 (1977).

For EPA's regulations on ambient air quality monitoring see 40 C.F.R. Pt. 58. See also 54 Fed. Reg. 24,213 (1989) (proposed source test for new PM10 standard). In Dow Chemical Co. v. United States, 476 U.S. 227 (1986), the Court held that §114 authorized aerial surveillance and that the use of aerial photography without a warrant did not violate the Fourth Amendment.

Modeling. Today, air pollution control requires much more than a monitoring program. Modeling enables officials to predict the amount by which specific sources will have to cut back on emissions to achieve a predetermined level of ambient air quality or how much a proposed new source will increase ambient concentrations. A computerized model predicting how sources will generate a specific pattern of pollutant flow over time at different emission levels under varying meteorological conditions enables air quality experts to explore rapidly the many implications that flow from small assumed changes in emissions levels or meteorological conditions.

Most models are either rollback or diffusion models. Simple and inexpensive rollback models assume that if all sources in an area reduce emissions by the same percentage in the same time interval, a directly proportional reduction in the ambient level of pollution will occur throughout the area. If all emitters "roll back" emissions by 50 percent, ambient concentrations of pollution will be reduced by 50 percent. Yet rollback models assume that meteorological conditions never change in a way that alters the relative contribution of a source to ambient conditions, and they ignore the fact that chemical reactions among pollutants and atmospheric gases can increase the proportions of pollutants in the ambient air. See generally de Nevers, Enforcing the Clean Air Act of 1970, 228 Sci. Am. 14 (1973). Despite these shortcomings, the first rollback models successfully survived judicial attack. See, e.g., Texas v. EPA, 499 F.2d 289 (5th Cir. 1974).

Diffusion models, by contrast, are more versatile and have a greater potential for accuracy but require detailed monitoring data and are more expensive and difficult to apply. Diffusion models simulate mathematically the physical and chemical processes that affect primary pollutants after their release. If the model works properly, its operators can feed emissions rates and patterns into the model's computer program, run the program to simulate pollution dispersion throughout a day or other time period, and read off a computer printout the predicted concentrations of pollutants at specified points.

The simplest diffusion models are Gaussian, that is, they assume that all of a pollutant stays in the atmosphere and must be accounted for and that such factors as temperature, wind speed and direction, emissions rates, and mixing height (the height above which a spreading plume does not rise) remain constant. The models then produce the "life story" of a smoke plume or puff as it disperses through time over a prescribed area. Such "plume and puff" models are reasonably reliable in predicting the dispersion of SO_2, CO, and TSP.

More advanced diffusion models, which attempt to account for meteorological and terrain variations and complex chemical reactions such as photochemical smog, depend upon massive infusions of data. Estimation is often
relied on to remedy deficiencies in the database, but because modeling results
are extremely sensitive to even small estimated changes in weather, emissions
rates, or terrain, estimation may cause models to mispredict pollutant concentrations by as much as 50 percent. The measurement problem would not be so
important if precise numerical standards were not required by emissions control
laws. See Conn, The Difficulty of Forecasting Ambient Air Quality: A Weak
Link in Pollution Control, 44 Am. Inst. Planners J. 334, 342 (1978). Diffusion
models are used widely in determining compliance with current emissions control standards. See Kramer, Air Quality Modeling: Judicial, Legislative and Administrative Reactions, 5 Colum. J. Envtl. L. 236 (1979).

EPA's most recent guidance on air quality models is contained in Guidelines on Air Quality Models (Revised) and Supplement A (1988). For discussion
of the advanced models considered for inclusion in the supplement see 53 Fed.
Reg. 392 (1988). Models being considered by EPA for inclusion in revised guidelines are discussed in 53 Fed. Reg. 32,081 (1988). For criticism of air quality
models see Hayes & Moore, Air Quality Model Performance: A Comparative
Analysis of 15 Model Evaluation Studies, 20 Atmospheric Envt. 1894 (1986).
As you study this chapter, keep in mind the claim that modeling is both a critical
link and the Achilles Heel in the implementation of the Clean Air Act.

B.   THE HISTORY OF AIR POLLUTION: FROM COMMON LAW NUISANCE TO THE CLEAN AIR ACT

Although air pollution was scarcely acknowledged as a national problem until
World War II and did not move to the top of the public agenda until the end of
the 1960s, the legal foundations of air pollution control were laid centuries earlier in England. The earliest relief from air pollution was provided through private common law nuisance actions; public nuisances broadly affecting the
community were abatable after jury trial. The common law crime of public
nuisance is the earliest example of quasi-statutory intervention by local government to protect environmental quality. For discussion of the modern common
law providing environmental protection, see Chapter 6.

Early beginnings. The first smoke abatement ordinance appears to have
been enacted in 1273, in the reign of Edward I. It forbade the burning of coal
in the city of London and was used to obtain the conviction and execution of a
hapless coal-burner. Smoke ordinances were enacted in the United States in the
late nineteenth century (e.g., Chicago and Cincinnati in 1881), as the colder

northeastern cities grew large enough to experience the ill effects of thousands of separate coal-burning hearths and expanding numbers of industrial sources. The early ordinances levied a fine (from $10 to $100) on offenders, required furnaces to be built to consume their own smoke, or forbade the burning of high-sulfur coal. See generally Laitos, Legal Institutions and Pollution: Some Intersections between Law and History, 15 Nat. Resources J. 423, 434 (1975).

The smoke ordinances attempted to abate the smoke "nuisance" without a showing of harm, which raised an interesting question for the courts: To enforce a smoke ordinance against an emitter, did a municipality have to prove actual harm, or was the much simpler proof that dense smoke had in fact been emitted alone sufficient? The courts eventually held that nuisance law principles did not control the interpretation of local smoke ordinances. Like other police power regulation, smoke controls ultimately became constrained only by an indulgent judicial requirement that they be "reasonably necessary" for the protection of public welfare or that they not be "unduly oppressive." Northwestern Laundry v. City of Des Moines, 239 U.S. 486 (1916). By 1960, in a case upholding a local smoke abatement ordinance, the Supreme Court could declare that "[l]egislation designed to free from pollution the very air people breathe clearly falls within the exercise of even the most traditional concept of what is compendiously known as the police power." Huron Cement Co. v. City of Detroit, 362 U.S. 440, 442 (1960).

Under the smoke ordinances, municipalities did not know how far to re-duce ambient pollutant concentrations or how to link emissions controls to a desired citywide pollutant concentration level. See Pollack, Legal Boundaries of Air Pollution Control — State and Local Legislative Purpose and Techniques, 33 Law & Contemp. Probs. 331 (1968). Yet as unsatisfactory as the half-century epoch of the smoke ordinance was, modern air pollution control law owes it a certain debt. The more sophisticated ordinances empowered municipal health officials and the courts to specify air pollution control equipment performance levels and, occasionally, to specify the equipment itself. The ordinances helped develop technology-based standards, fuels and raw materials specifications, land use controls, and some understanding of the health effects of smoke.

The demise of the common law requirement for proof of actual harm was a legal innovation of great importance. Indicators such as dense smoke or the burning of soft coal became legal surrogates for actual harm. The legislature, freed from establishing a strong factual basis for pollution control, could legis-late out of precaution without having to wait for scientific evidence to accumu-late — an important first step toward plenary legislative proscription of social evils, even if compelling compliance was difficult. Modern pollution control laws make extensive use of devices for foreclosing inquiry into the extent and nature of the injury on which regulatory programs are predicated. Later in this text, we will have many occasions to consider the limitations on legislative or judicial action when cause is difficult to establish.

Early legislation. After World War II, state and city governments expanded their arsenal of pollution control techniques, yet air pollution slowly increased, as did congressional frustration with ineffectual state efforts to combat the problem. In 1955 the federal government entered the field for the first time with a modest program of research and technical assistance, primarily directed at the causes and effects of air pollution, which had not been established. Air Pollution Control Act, Pub. L. No. 84-159, 69 Stat. 322. In the 1950s the smog in Los Angeles was linked with motor vehicle emissions, and after that the motor vehicle played the leading role in the development of air pollution legislation. In 1960 Congress enacted a research and technical assistance program for motor vehicles. Motor Vehicle Act of 1960, Pub. L. No. 86-493, 74 Stat. 162.

Congress expanded the federal role in 1963. Clean Air Act, Pub. L. No. 88-206, 77 Stat. 392. The 1963 statute required the Department of Health, Education, and Welfare (HEW) (now called the Department of Health and Human Services) to provide scientific information, called "criteria documents," to the states on the effects of various air pollutants. The states were not required to base their abatement programs on the criteria documents, but in time these studies were to provide the technical basis for HEW to set mandatory uniform national ambient air quality standards.

The 1963 legislation empowered the Secretary of HEW to investigate interstate pollution "hot spots," but any recommended abatement could only be undertaken by the state and local governments themselves. Further, if pollution "endangered the health or welfare of persons" the Secretary was empowered to launch a lengthy enforcement process that theoretically could result in an action by the U.S. Attorney General to enjoin polluting sources. This endangerment provision provided for the first time for direct federal legal action to abate air pollution, but the series of conferences and procedures prescribed by the provision so thoroughly diffused responsibility that no effective enforcement actions were ever mounted under it. Only 11 conferences ever took place, and only one federal enforcement action was ever filed. Ridicule of the ineffectual conference procedure helped obtain the tight procedural deadlines in the 1970 Clean Air Act. See J. Esposito & R. Nader, Vanishing Air 114-118 (1970).

In 1965, Congress enacted the first direct federal air pollution emissions standards into law. Motor Vehicle Air Pollution Control Act, Pub. L. No. 89-272, 79 Stat. 992. Half of all air pollution nationwide was by then attributed to automobile exhaust, and the Surgeon General had suggested that some components of smog might possibly be carcinogenic. Emissions standards were to be promulgated by HEW, based on "technological feasibility and economic costs." Manufacturers of new vehicles and engines had to be given at least two years' notice and a "reasonable" amount of time to comply with new standards. See J. Krier & E. Ursin, Pollution and Policy pt. 2 (1979). Congress exempted California (but only California) from the uniform federal standards in 1967.

The 1967 act. The 1967 Air Quality Act established a comprehensive federal-state framework for air pollution control. Air Quality Act, Pub. L. No. 90-148, 81 Stat. 485. HEW was to designate national geographic air quality control regions. The states were to adopt numerical ambient air quality standards for each major pollutant; the standards were to define the levels of pollution that would maintain health and welfare in each region. The standards were to be based upon HEW criteria documents and were subject to HEW approval. HEW could establish its own standards if a state's proposed standards did not adequately reflect the findings of the federal criteria documents. Each state was required to adopt an implementation plan, subject to HEW approval, in which the state was to specify the specific numerical emissions limitations that individual sources would have to achieve if the ambient standards were to be met.

Federal enforcement still depended upon the 1963 Act's conference-initiated procedure or upon a new provision authorizing the Attorney General to act if air quality in a state was below the standards and the state had not taken reasonable action to implement and enforce them. For intrastate pollution, enforcement had to be requested by the affected state. A new provision enabled the Attorney General to act immediately if an "imminent and substantial" endangerment to health existed. But federal enforcement still required a balancing of the equities and a showing of harm reminiscent of the common law of public nuisance.

As comprehensive as the 1967 Act appeared at the time, it failed completely in practice. Part of its failure can be attributed to the genuinely difficult scientific and institutional problems the federal and state agencies faced. The task of preparing implementation plans and enforcing standards was enormous. Unfortunately the states lacked adequate resources for the task, and federal subsidies did not make up the difference. The worst zones of air pollution seemed to be concentrated at the very places state and local governments were conjoined and already overworked, such as urban concentrations along navigable rivers that formed political boundaries. See generally D. Currie, Air Pollution §§1.08-1.12 (1981).

One can also overstate the extent to which local air pollution control actually failed before 1970. Cities and states accumulated a considerable body of experience in using technology-limited standards. Other state and local laws regulated the installation, start-up, and operation of industrial equipment, the type of fuels permitted, and the qualifications of emissions control equipment operators. States pioneered the use of permits that enabled regulators to obtain a specific, written agreement in advance that sources would comply with abatement requirements. Currie, State Pollution Statutes, 48 U. Chi. L. Rev. 27 (1981).

Whatever the underlying facts about the intrinsic difficulty of controlling air pollution or the sincerity of state and local efforts, by 1970 these factors carried little weight; Congress prepared to adopt an essentially federal solution. The ground had been well prepared in field hearings across the United States. State pollution control agencies and the federal National Air Pollution Control Agency (NAPCA) were excoriated for ineffectual performances. Proponents of strong federal measures drew upon the rhetoric of the activist civil rights and anti-war movements of the 1960s, calling for "immediate action" to adopt "long overdue" public health protection measures.

The 1970 act. The politics of national air pollution are always controversial, yet Congress overhauled federal air pollution control in 1970 by votes that rivaled those on declarations of war (Senate: 73-0; House of Representatives: 374-1). Democratic Senator Edmund Muskie, a presidential aspirant, and Republican President Richard Nixon vied to take credit for the strict statute.

Yet the appearances of air pollution politics in the spring of 1970 were deceiving. Under the seeming unanimity of the moment, deep conflicts and contradictions lurked:

> [Today the] . . . prevailing wisdom is that the current federal air pollution policy was chosen irrationally. . . . Legal scholars complain that the provisions of the Clean Air Amendments of 1970 lack precision and clarity and that, consequently, needless expense, confusion, and seemingly interminable litigation impede the implementation process. Scientists argue that the legislation is based on misconceptions about biological and physical systems. Atmospheric chemists suggest that the notion of threshold levels of emissions that are damaging to health is not supported by research. Physicists believe that the diffusion of pollutants and their chemical interaction are much more complex than can be appropriately handled by the simple standards in the 1970 act. Engineers claim that the deadlines set by the legislation are not technically realistic. Economists, the most outspoken of critics, condemn federal regulations as inefficient, inequitable, and ineffectual. What must Congress have been thinking?
>
> Many blame "politics," as though politics were senseless and random and without patterns of predictable behavior. Politicians are viewed as souls lost to reason who are pushed about by political "forces" and not as individuals who are as subject to discipline and perspective as lawyers, scientists, physicians, engineers, and economists. . . . From a political perspective, [however,] federal air pollution policy is rational. [Ingram, The Political Rationality of Innovation: The Clean Air Act Amendments of 1970, in Approaches to Controlling Air Pollution 12, 12-13 (A. Friedlander ed. 1978).]

Professor Ingram explains how the Clean Air Act was politically rational. Senator Muskie chaired the Senate subcommittee in charge of air pollution legislation, but the less enthusiastic House committee was disorganized and did not have experience with pollution legislation. President Nixon saw support of environmental causes as politically useful, and his Administration proposed a relatively strong air bill, which Congress promptly rewrote with even stronger requirements. By the time the outlines of the final legislation were known, it was too late for opposition to organize. At the final vote, the widely dispersed costs of air pollution control were not well perceived. You will have to make up your own mind, as you learn more about the Clean Air Act, which type of "rationality" you prefer. See generally C. Jones, Clean Air: The Policies and Politics of Pollution Control (1974).

Conflicting goals. The apparent irrationality of federal air pollution control begins with the failure to agree at the outset about what the term "air pollution" means. Its meaning hinges on which of two major reduction goals is adopted. The conservation goal implies that air pollution is any concentration that degrades air below the "background" levels of substances that natural processes place in the ambient air; pollution is any change produced artificially. The economic goal defines pollution in terms of the costs of degradation. Beyond proof of mere degradation, any proposed reduction in damage from pollution must yield tangible benefits in excess of the tangible costs of cleaner air. These two approaches are the predominant ones in the political battle over clean air. This chapter will use the term "air pollution" to refer to air quality levels allowed by a legislature, agency, or court.

The conflict between the conservation and economic strategy in Congress remains strong. The conservation strategy is based in part on moral and philosophical grounds. Fueled by two centuries of romantic literary arguments asserting the superiority of nature, conservationists argue that natural environments should be preserved or restored for aesthetic or moral reasons. See Ingram, The Political Rationality of Innovation: The Clean Air Act Amendments of 1970, in Approaches to Controlling Air Pollution, *supra*, at 15-22); Wildavsky, Economy and Environment/Rationality and Ritual: A Review of the Uncertain Search for Environmental Quality, 29 Stan. L. Rev. 183 (1976).

The rational imperative of the economic goal also remains strong: in a society of limited resources, the nation should strive to adopt efficient pollution reduction levels and cost-effective reduction strategies. This can only be done by assembling information about air pollution control benefits and reducing these benefits, to the greatest extent possible, to monetary values, after which it becomes possible to compare at the margin the costs of emission reduction with the benefits achieved. Cost-benefit analysis in the air pollution and other regulatory programs was institutionalized in the Reagan Administration.

Despite the strengths of the economic goal, its proponents were singularly ineffectual in 1970 in convincing the public that by requiring costly air pollution controls it was sacrificing other valuable social benefits that the money spent on air pollution control otherwise could have bought. Most members of Congress in 1970 seemed blind to any attempt at calculating the opportunity costs of substantial emission reductions. Further, in 1970 Congress also chose to ignore that the cost of air pollution varies among regions and that an ideal policy would correlate reduction levels in each region with the costs imposed in that region.

The 1977 amendments. By 1977 Congress was more aware of the limits of its original approach. The result was a pragmatic, politically balanced bill, although the 1977 amendments were called a "mid-course correction" that was not supposed to alter fundamentally the national strategy for air pollution control adopted in 1970. By 1977 Congress's pro-environmental ardor had cooled somewhat, the opposition to strong air pollution controls had rallied, the Arab oil embargo had occurred, some components of air pollution programs had foundered on political shoals, and industry and consumers had begun to pay the high costs of pollution control. Industry obtained delays in meeting the 1970 vehicle emissions standards and secured concessions for coal-burning power plants and favored treatment for smelters and, later, for steel plants. Industry also backed the states in obtaining delays in meeting compliance deadlines and relief from burdensome traffic management strategies EPA had imposed to control smog-producing traffic. The amendments also included strong air quality protection measures: detailed controls over new construction in both clean air and dirty air areas of the country, an explicit basis for preventing the erosion of existing high air quality, a visibility protection program, the expanded use of source-specific permits, some new types of technology-limited emissions standards, and stricter federal enforcement provisions.

The political situation in the 1980s. Although the Clean Air Act was to be reviewed and revised in 1982, the year came and went without legislative change. President Reagan had proposed a set of changes generally favorable to industry, but Congress balked and the President then lost interest. The Administration then sought changes in the Act through regulatory amendments, such as amendments that eased compliance by industry with the Act's emission limitations.

As Congress and the Administration stalemated over legislative revision, the basis for controversy changed. Regional interests became dominant as air quality problems sharpened and localized. Acid rain problems in the northeast and ozone problems in cities like Los Angeles and Houston are examples. These regional-specific issues brought regional conflict as the northeast clashed with a midwest dependent on coal-produced electricity and with the coal mining states, and as Detroit automakers fought more stringent controls required to deal with smog problems.

Powerful congressional figures protected regional interests. In the Senate, former Democratic Majority Leader Robert C. Byrd of West Virginia stalled legislation on acid rain that would threaten coal mining jobs. In the House, Democratic Representative John D. Dingell of Michigan, one of its most powerful members and chairman of the Energy and Commerce Committee, blocked action on motor vehicle emissions. Dingell blocked California Democratic Representative Henry A. Waxman, chair of the subcommittee that considers clean air legislation, in a drive for more stringent legislation. How clean air politics will play out in the Bush and later administrations, and whether the Republicans will be able to outflank squabbling Democrats is not yet clear. See Kriz, Politics in the Air, 21 Natl. J. 1098 (1989); Stanfield, Plotting Every Move, 20 Natl. J. 792 (1988) (article on Dingell's congressional influence).

C.   THE CLEAN AIR ACT TODAY

The Clean Air Act, as amended in 1970 and 1977,* provides the basic framework for modern air pollution control. The Clean Air Act is the first major federal pollution control statute you will examine in this book. It occupies 118

---

*Pub. L. No. 95-95, 91 Stat. 685, amended by Pub. L. No. 95-190, 91 Stat. 1401-1402 (technical and conforming amendments). The 1970 Act, codified at 42 U.S.C. §§1857-1858a, has been recodified in 42 U.S.C. §§7401-7642 to incorporate the 1977 amendments.

pages of the United States Code; regulations under it require four volumes in the Code of Federal Regulations. Some environmental statutes, such as the National Environmental Policy Act, contain a brief mandate that can be analyzed word for word, but not the Clean Air Act. Thus the coverage of this chapter is selective, and more textual guidance is provided than you might otherwise encounter in the study of a regulatory statute.**

The summary that follows highlights the key elements of the Act. You may want to consult it later to regain your perspective. You should always feel free to supplement this discussion by reading firsthand the provisions explicated here.

Implementation strategies. The Clean Air Act contains several distinct types of legislation. The regulatory provisions dominate the Act and will receive virtually all of our attention, yet the Act is also laced with a variety of other measures Congress adopted to pursue its goals. Congress provided generous federal subsidies to state and local governments to aid them in implementing their programs. Other provisions direct the EPA to provide technical assistance to states, to aid interstate cooperative projects, and to advise operators of pollution sources about control measures. The Act provides for federal studies and research and development, as well as research grants, fellowships, and training for the academic and the private sectors. Finally, various sections of the Act delimit the powers of the federal bureaucracy created to administer the Act. See §§101-106. During the 1980s, although its regulatory responsibilities increased substantially, EPA's budget actually declined somewhat and the number of employees declined slightly.

The regulatory provisions: a preview. The regulatory program depends on two very different types of regulatory standards (ambient and technology-limited) and two very different types of governmental roles (federal standard setting and state implementation). Standards and implementation procedures vary depending on two additional factors: whether sources are stationary or mobile and whether sources are located in clean air or dirty air areas of the country. When you fully understand the interaction of these four pairs of components (ambient versus technology-limited standards; federal versus state implementation; stationary versus mobile sources; clean air versus dirty air areas), you will have a firm grasp on the regulatory provisions of the Act.

A fundamental contradiction permeates the regulatory framework just sketched. The paramount goals of the Act are to clean up dirty air to acceptable levels and to maintain high air quality where it already exists. The federal ambient standards and state implementation plans are shaped to meet these goals. However, other provisions are keyed to the ability of air pollution control technology to reduce emissions at an acceptable cost. Examples include stringent "technology-forcing" performance standards for new vehicles and industrial

---

**Beginning now, you will need to refer constantly to the text of the Clean Air Act. You will also need to refer to other basic environmental statutes throughout the remainder of the course. Since frequent use of the primary statute books may be awkward, you may want to acquire a handier compilation of basic environmental legislation. Consult the list of compilations in the preface to this casebook and follow your professor's guidance.

plants. Here technology's utmost capability or limit becomes the governing factor.

Ambient air quality standards. Ambient standards specify maximum pollutant concentrations that are deemed by regulation to be safe for exposure over various time periods. Because they do not in themselves specify any limitation that must be placed on an actual source, ambient standards cannot provide a complete basis for air pollution control; they must be coupled with measures that limit individual source emissions. In the Clean Air Act uniform national ambient air quality standards are promulgated by administrative regulation after the agency has gathered the necessary scientific information in the criteria documents first required by the 1963 legislation. Primary ambient air quality standards must be set to protect human health with an adequate margin of safety; secondary standards must also be promulgated that protect additional environmental values such as plant and animal life, property, and aesthetic sensibilities (§§108-109). Standards currently exist for six "criteria pollutants"; see Table 3-1. The TSP standard included in the Table was replaced by the PM-10 standard in 1987.

The primary emphasis of the Clean Air Act is on the "attainment" — a statutory term — of these ambient standards. The Act requires states to select and implement the combination of individual emissions limitations on existing stationary sources, constraints on vehicles in use, and additional siting and emissions limitations applicable to new sources that will ensure that the ambient standards are met and maintained.

Emissions standards. Technology-limited uniform national emissions standards specify the pollution control performance levels expected from particular types of air pollution sources. The Act contains four types of federally uniform emissions standards; three additional emissions standards that have been combined, somewhat untidily, with the ambient standards approach will emerge later in this discussion. First, the Clean Air Act includes the oldest technology-based pollution standard vehicle emissions standards. The 1970 Act set deadlines requiring vehicle manufacturers to reduce emissions of CO, HC, and NO_x by 90 percent from 1970 levels in five years. Through a series of administrative extensions and congressional amendments, the achievement of these standards has been delayed into the 1980s (§201 ff). The 1970 Act preempts the states (except California) from setting standards for new vehicles different from those set by Congress. State inspections and traffic management plans supplement the emissions standards, but the primary strategy for reducing vehicular pollution remains federal specification of performance standards for new vehicles.

Second, the Act requires nationally uniform new source performance standards (NSPS) for the various categories of stationary sources. The NSPS require "the application of the best system of emissions reduction which (taking into account the cost of achieving such reductions) the Administrator determines has been adequately demonstrated" (§111). The NSPS cover all types of emissions that "may be reasonably anticipated to endanger public health or welfare." Congress ordered EPA to accelerate its NSPS program in the 1977 amendments.

TABLE 3-1
National Ambient Air Quality Standards (NAAQS) in Effect in 1987

Pollutant	Primary (Health Related)		Secondary (Welfare Related)	
	Averaging Time	Standard Level Concentration[a]	Averaging Time	Concentration
TSP[b]	Annual Geometric Mean	75 $\mu g/m^3$		
PM$_{10}$[c]	Annual Arithmetic Mean	50 $\mu g/m^3$	Same as Primary	
	24-hour	150 $\mu g/m^3$	Same as Primary	
SO$_2$	Annual Arithmetic Mean	(0.03 ppm) 80 $\mu g/m^3$	3-hour	1300 $\mu g/m^3$ (0.50 ppm)
	24-hour	(0.14 ppm) 365 $\mu g/m^3$		
CO	8-hour	9 ppm (10 $\mu g/m^3$)	No Secondary Standard	
	1-hour	35 ppm (40 $\mu g/m^3$)	No Secondary Standard	
NO$_2$	Annual Arithmetic Mean	0.053 ppm (100 $\mu g/m^3$)	Same as Primary	
O$_3$	Maximum Daily 1-hour Average	0.12 ppm[d] (235 $\mu g/m^3$)	Same as Primary	
Pb	Maximum Quarterly Average	1.5 $\mu g/m^3$	Same as Primary	

[a]Parenthetical value is an approximately equivalent concentration.

[b]TSP was the indicator pollutant for the original particulate matter (PM) standards. This standard has been replaced with the new PM$_{10}$ standard and it is no longer in effect.

[c]New PM standards were promulgated in 1987, using PM$_{10}$ (particles less than 10μ in diameter) as the new indicator pollutant. The 24-hour standard is attained when the expected number of days per calendar year above 150 $\mu g/m^3$ is equal to or less than 1, as determined in accordance with Appendix K of the PM NAAQS.

[d]The standard is attained when the expected number of days per calendar year with maximum hourly average concentrations above 0.12 ppm is equal to or less than 1, as determined in accordance with Appendix H of the Ozone NAAQS.

Source: EPA, National Air Quality and Emission Trends Report, 1987, at 22 (1989)

Third, the Act provides uniform national emissions standards for hazardous air pollutants (NESHAP) that "may cause, or contribute to, an increase in mortality, or an increase in serious, irreversible, or incapacitating reversible illness" (§112). The Act subjects NESHAP promulgation to a strict timetable and requires highly protective measures that eliminate serious risks, apparently without regard to cost. In 1970 Congress believed that §112 would apply only to a limited number of pollutants. Later, hundreds of hazardous substances appeared to fall within the NESHAP definition, but in the 1977 amendments Congress did not change §112, although EPA had listed only four substances for NESHAP preparation (asbestos, beryllium, mercury, and vinyl chloride).

Finally, in 1977 Congress required that existing sources in dirty air areas install, at a minimum, "reasonably available control technology" (RACT).

State implementation plans. Emissions standards are the Clean Air Act's front line of attack against pollution from new stationary sources and vehicles, but achievement of the nationally uniform ambient air quality standards remains the Act's paramount objective. The states have the primary responsibility for designing and implementing plans to achieve the ambient standards (§110). The state implementation plans (SIPs) may use any of a complex array of controls on existing stationary sources, transportation control plans (TCPs), and new source emissions and site locations in especially polluted or clean air areas on a case-by-case basis (§110(a)(2)). SIP components have the force of state and federal law when finally approved and are enforceable by both state and federal governments (§113).

The SIPs are vital components of the Clean Air Act scheme. In the process of designing a SIP, state officials make many costly, controversial decisions detailing the steps industrial plants, businesses, mobile source owners, airports, highway departments, and local traffic control officials must take to bring the state's Air Quality Control Regions (the nation has been divided into over 200 of them) into compliance with the ambient standards.

Because of their complexity, SIPs rarely become finished documents. SIPs attempt to codify (in the voluminous pages of part 52 of the Code of Federal Regulations) the results of never-ending negotiations between EPA, states, industry, and citizen oversight bodies. State and local governments are constantly seeking separate EPA approvals for SIP components. SIPs are made up of scores of various specific actions taken over many months (some 500 a year nationwide). See Pedersen, Why the Clean Air Act Works Badly, 129 U. Pa. L. Rev. 1059, 1082-1088 (1981).

Under the 1970 Act, the first generation of SIPs was supposed to achieve the ambient air quality standards by 1975, with extensions possible until 1977 for CO and photochemical oxidants. These early SIPs served as vehicles for inventorying existing emissions sources, for deciding in a rough-and-ready way how existing stationary sources would reduce emissions to achieve the ambient standards, and for making the first attempt to come to grips with the political implications of controlling mobile sources via TCPs. Private stationary sources did a passably good job of complying with the requirements of the first generation SIPs and reduced total emissions of TSP, SO_2, and HC nationwide. Yet despite these overall improvements, the clean air program was threatening to foreclose growth in the industrial regions of the country by making it extremely difficult for new sources to be built. The 1970 Act itself gave few hints about how new industrial facilities were to be rationally accommodated.

The first-round state effort to comply with the ambient standards for mobile source pollutants met with far less success, for a number of reasons. First, the standards were too optimistic in light of the serious oxidant and CO problem in some urban areas. Second, the emissions standards for new vehicles did not play the central abatement role expected of them because vehicle manufacturers obtained delays in their deadlines for achieving the standards. The manufacturers' failure thrust the states back on such TCP strategies as dispersing traffic, providing incentives not to drive or to take mass transit, inspection and maintenance programs, and setting standards for older vehicles. Therein lies the third reason for failure. These secondary techniques directly affected the driving public, sometimes in ways that drivers viewed as exceedingly restrictive and intrusive. When states and cities balked at secondary controls, EPA tried to force them to put them in their TCPs. Further, EPA officials themselves took over the management of the transportation control portions of a few urban SIPs. The results were a political disaster for clean air programs. A series of lawsuits and congressional amendments to the Act quickly brought the EPA initiatives to a standstill. By 1977 the stage was set for reappraisal of the role of land use and transportation controls in air quality management.

The 1977 amendments and the SIPs. The experience with the SIPs in the six years after 1970 had been chastising. The six years revealed that the Act provided no coherent policy for allocating the cleanup burden between old and new stationary sources in heavily polluted urban areas; that attaining the mobile source pollutant standards would take far longer in some urban areas than anticipated in 1970; and that the Act was ambiguous about whether the clean air that already met the ambient standards was to be maintained at high levels or allowed to deteriorate to the level of the standards. To address these issues, the 1977 amendments had to alter the 1970 approach by implementing more than mere "mid-course corrections." The reform, in retrospect, was root and branch.

To move beyond the 1970 SIP requirements requires contending with the 1977 Clean Air Act's central distinction between "clean air" and "dirty air" areas of the nation. Since 1977 the Clean Air Act has applied different standards and procedural requirements in regions that have yet to attain even the primary or secondary ambient standards and regions that have relatively clean or even pristine air quality. New non-attainment program provisions spelled out SIP requirements for the former (§§171-178), and Congress addressed clean air regions in a lengthy new part entitled "Prevention of Significant Deterioration of Air Quality" (PSD) (§§160-169A). The different SIP requirements for PSD and non-attainment regions apply to each SIP-controlled pollutant individually. In effect, a separate "sub-SIP" applies to each pollutant depending on its PSD or non-attainment status. Understanding how the United States has been divided up — one might say zoned — into PSD and non-attainment areas on a pollutant-by-pollutant basis, with overlapping designations when an area has attained the ambient standards for one pollutant but not for another, will be the task of sections G and H of this chapter.

Non-attainment and stationary sources. The 1977 Act gave the states until 1979 to prepare new SIPs that would achieve the ambient standards by the end of 1982, a seven-year lag in meeting the original 1975 goal. Failure to obtain EPA approval could result in loss of federal aid for highway and sewerage construction and a ban on the construction of major sources. These deadlines were not met, and the issue of how to deal with the ozone non-attainment areas has become one of the most difficult Clean Air Act problems.

After 1977 major new or modified stationary sources had to obtain a permit that requires that each source meet a strict technology-based emissions standard defined by the "lowest achievable emissions rate" (LAER) for the applying facility and that all other plants in the state owned by the applicant are on an approved SIP schedule. If the state SIP does not require existing sources to reduce emissions enough to accommodate new construction without exceeding the ambient standards, the applicant itself must purchase or secure from existing sources a reduction in their emissions more than sufficient to offset new emissions from the proposed facility. The benchmark for measuring whether new construction will be permitted is whether the SIP for the area in which the applicant proposes to locate is progressing satisfactorily toward the overall goal of attaining the ambient standards.

Non-attainment and mobile source pollution. The 1977 amendments further restricted federal authority to mandate indirect transportation control measures. In 1974 and 1975 Congress had already prohibited EPA from imposing parking surcharges and from spending federal funds to tax or regulate parking facilities. The 1977 Act suspended existing TCP provisions for private vehicle emissions control retrofit, gas rationing, parking supply reduction, and bridge tolls. It also prohibited federal controls on indirect sources that attract large numbers of vehicles, for example, shopping centers, sports complexes, and airports.

The 1977 Act permitted the states to request an extension until 1987 to achieve the ambient standards for CO and photochemical oxidants (by now measured almost exclusively by ozone (O_3)), but imposed strict procedures on states requesting the extension. A state had to adopt a vehicle emissions control inspection and maintenance (I & M) program if the extension was granted. As an indication of the status of mobile source pollution cleanup in the late 1970s, consider that 29 states requested the extension for either CO or O_3 and prepared I & M programs for 47 major metropolitan areas. Revised TCP measures also included expanded car pool programs, preferential parking for ride-sharing vehicles, residents-only parking limits, "flex time" work hour schemes, and some provision for bicycle use.

Prevention of significant deterioration. The failure of the 1970 Act to provide a specific program for maintaining air quality in clean air areas could have vitally affected the pristine air quality of the American Southwest, where relatively common 80-mile scenic vistas were threatened by the growing number of coal-fired power plants in the region. However, the 1970 Act did state that its purpose was to "protect and enhance" the nation's air resources, a phrase the courts interpreted as requiring the EPA to produce a plan for maintaining air quality in clean air areas.

The controversy that EPA's non-significant deterioration program consequently spawned ended with the enactment in 1977 of a detailed preconstruction review for 28 types of major new stationary sources that wanted to locate in clean air areas. Such plants were obligated to install the "best available control technology" (BACT), to be determined individually for each facility. Applicants had to show that their plants would not cause ambient air to be "significantly" degraded. What constituted a significant increment in relation to existing pollution was numerically defined in the 1977 Act and depended upon the exact location of the proposed facility. Under a statutory designation process, all clean air areas of the country were placed in one of three zones or classes. The increment allowed within Class I areas, which mainly consisted of major national parks and wildernesses, was quite small (e.g., 2 parts per million (ppm) for SO_2 annual arithmetic mean), necessarily constricting new industrial development near the southwestern parklands. Class III increments were set generously at approximately half the ambient standards, and Class II increments fell roughly in between. Visibility per se was given a separate protection program, with "best available retrofit technology" (BART) to be applied as needed to existing sources that impair visibility.

The 1977 "hybrid" standards. Notice that the three emission standards — LAER, BACT, BART — are not technology-based in the same sense as the mobile source standards, the new source performance standards (NSPS), and reasonably available control technology (RACT) for existing sources. The new standards are not applied uniformly, but on a case-by-case basis. In setting them, the states are supposed to play a larger role than the federal EPA, depending on PSD and non-attainment SIP needs. Perhaps these hybrid standards — part ambient-quality-oriented and part technology-oriented in nature — can best be viewed as technical guidelines to officials as they negotiate with source operators for the abatement necessary to achieve local air quality goals. In this process NSPS have provided a benchmark; ordinarily BACT and even the stricter LAER are set close to the NSPS baseline. This fact and the complexity of the PSD and non-attainment programs have caused some to suggest a uniform technology-limited standard based on the current BACT to substitute for NSPS, BACT, and LAER, to simplify determinations of applicable technology throughout the Act.

Enforcement. Numerous "action-forcing" procedures punctuate the Clean Air Act's substantive provisions. A distrustful and impatient Congress equipped each major substantive provision with a specific deadline for its implementation. Congress intended to allow no escape from a strict standard of compliance for what in 1970 it believed to be indolent federal and state air pollution control bureaucracies.

Congress provided effective federal enforcement procedures for the first time in the 1970 Act. Section 113 provides that after 30 days' notice to the state and to a source that is not in compliance with a SIP emissions limitation or the relevant federal emissions standard, the EPA Administrator may either issue an administrative order requiring the source to comply or bring a civil action in federal district court for injunctive relief and civil penalties of not more than $25,000 per day. Criminal penalties are also provided. Knowing violations expose a source to imprisonment and fines of up to $25,000 per day of violation ($50,000 for a second offense). The Administrator may promulgate the EPA's own SIP or may enforce part or all of an existing SIP on a finding that widespread violations appear to result from the state's failure to enforce the SIP effectively. EPA may order a state to implement some SIP provisions, so long as EPA does not interfere with functions of local government essential to the federal system.

The Administrator must pursue administrative or judicial remedies in the case of a noncomplying source that emits more than 100 tons of a pollutant annually. Additionally, §120 of the Act, added in 1977, empowers the EPA to assess civil noncompliance penalties computed in such a way as to remove the economic benefit a source gains by noncompliance. The penalty equals the sums emitters would ordinarily save and earn by not investing in pollution control equipment. A final note: The conference procedure was quietly dropped from federal air pollution control law not until 1977.

Citizens' suits. Just as §113 allows the EPA to step in when state enforcement is lax, §304 allows the citizen to step in if the Act's provisions are not being implemented by the federal and state agencies and the sources themselves. Provided that adequate statutory notice has been given, §304 allows "any person" to commence a civil action on his own behalf against emitters and governmental entities alleged to be in violation of emissions standards or limitations and state or federal orders or alleged to have not obtained the necessary permits for new facility construction under the Act's non-attainment and PSD provisions. The Administrator may be compelled under §304 to perform only "non-discretionary" duties. Reasonable attorneys' and expert witnesses' fees may be awarded any party within the court's discretion.

Overriding the regulatory scheme. States may impose standards stricter than federal ones, except those for motor vehicles, aircraft, and fuel additives (§116). States can and do elect to impose requirements that go beyond those contemplated by the Act. More importantly, §304 preserves all the rights citizens and local units of government possess under other statutes and under the common law. Damage awards in suits of common law may still be freely sought, as may injunctive relief, unless thwarted by the doctrines of exhaustion of administrative remedies, primary jurisdiction, or preemption.

Health endangerment. On receiving evidence that air pollution is presenting "an imminent and substantial endangerment to the health of persons" and that local government has not acted to remedy the problem, the Administrator may issue administrative orders or sue in federal district court to abate the dangerous condition. When present danger can be shown, the Administrator may act to secure prompt relief from a dangerous condition before the Act's primary but more cumbersome regulatory programs take effect. The Administrator must show the presence of an imminent and substantial danger, but this burden is lighter than the showing of actual or potential harm required in a suit to enjoin dangerous conditions at common law (§303). For a discussion of EPA efforts to enforce the Clean Air Act, see Comment, Marking Time: A Status Report on the Clean Air Act between Deadlines, 15 Envtl. L. Rep. (Envtl. L. Inst.) 10022 (1985).

Judicial review. Since 1977, §307 has detailed a procedural structure and standards for review by the U.S. Courts of Appeals of the myriad of rule-makings necessary under the Act. The section supplants the provisions of the Administrative Procedure Act (APA) and substitutes a process that is in many ways superior to the time-honored APA model. This 1977 addition to the Clean Air Act rationalizes the expansion of participatory rights in notice-and-comment rule-making that took place in the decade prior to the 1977 amendments. It guarantees broad rights of participation at all stages of the regulatory process to virtually "any person" inclined to participate. Through §307, participants are assured access to a plainly identified regulatory docket of relevant studies, comments, and agency memoranda that may affect the agency's final decision.

D. UNIFORM NATIONAL PRIMARY AND SECONDARY AMBIENT AIR QUALITY STANDARDS

Congress conferred a prominent role on ambient standards in the Clean Air Act scheme for improving and maintaining air quality. In developing uniform primary and secondary national ambient air quality standards (NAAQS), EPA faces the formidable task of determining correctly, for each of the major air pollutants, separate numerical time-limited ambient pollutant concentration levels that can be tolerated without endangering health and welfare anywhere in the nation. Yet standard setting must be carefully done, because the necessity for costly, difficult-to-implement SIP components directly depends upon the scientific integrity of the ambient air quality standards.

Keep in mind that once EPA has promulgated ambient standards, responsibility under the Act shifts from the federal government to the states. After promulgation of the standards, each state must submit a state implementation plan that contains emission limitations and other measures necessary to attain the primary standards "as expeditiously as practicable," but no later than three to five years after EPA approval of the plan, and to attain the secondary standards within a reasonable period of time.

Note that ambient standard setting (as well as most other rule-making in the Act) is also governed by §307(d), which imposes standards and procedures for judicial review and an array of rule-making and record-keeping requirements intended to facilitate judicial review and to minimize the opportunity for undue executive influence on EPA decisionmaking. Section 307(d) attempts to answer for the Clean Air Act most of the issues raised above in Chapter 2 regarding the administrative law of environmental management.

The materials in this section are designed to explore the role of the

NAAQS in the overall Clean Air Act scheme, to examine how these provisions may be set in motion by EPA or private groups, and to introduce the problem of setting numerical standards to protect public health under conditions of scientific uncertainty. The vehicle selected for analyzing these issues is the problem of controlling injury to humans from exposure to the element lead.

1.   Lead as a Pervasive Environmental Pollutant

Lead is one of the most useful metals in modern industrial society, but it is also one of its most toxic. A hundred times more abundant in the earth than cadmium or mercury, lead can be easily "roasted" from its ores and put to a variety of uses. Because it is malleable and impervious to corrosion, it has been used since Phoenician times in piping, roofing, pigments, and caulkings. Today its chief uses are in coverings, gasoline antiknock additives, and solder for the joints in metallic cans. Total national consumption is almost 1.2 million metric tons per year.

Despite its utility, lead has long been known to cause serious injury to a variety of human organ systems. When present in sufficient concentrations, lead attacks the blood, the kidneys, and the central nervous system. Some accounts partially attribute the decline of Roman civilization to lead poisoning. In The Uncommercial Traveller, Dickens described the symptoms of disorientation, coma, and death that accompany acute lead poisoning. The Uncommercial Traveller 239, 400-404 (The Temple ed. 1900).

In recent times, injury from low-level exposures to lead has been more serious than the occasional instances of acute poisoning. Chronic exposure to small quantities of lead produces difficult-to-diagnose symptoms of anemia, nervous disorders, fatigue, headache, poor appetite, clumsiness, and diminished mental capacity. Small children are particularly susceptible. As a natural constituent, lead does not usually threaten ecosystems; however, as lead has spread through the environment in the heavy concentrations associated with human activity, it has also injured domestic animals, wildlife, and aquatic life.

We ingest or inhale lead from almost every environmental medium (see Figure 3-1); some lead compounds can even be absorbed through the skin. Lead concentration in the national diet may be 100 times that prevailing for persons living in prehistoric times. Adults consume some 100 to 500 μg of lead a day, although their gastrointestinal and circulatory systems absorb only 6 to 10 percent of this amount. The rest is excreted or sweated away. Children are not so fortunate; their gastrointestinal retention may be 30 to 50 percent. Estimates indicate that 12 million children are exposed to leaded paint in residences, 5.6 million to leaded gasoline and 10.4 million to lead in water and plumbing. For a discussion of lead sources see Ferguson, Lead: Petrol Lead in the Environment and Its Contribution to Human Blood Lead Levels, 50 Sci. Total Envt. 3 (1986). See also Needleman, The Persistent Threat of Lead: Medical and Sociological Issues, 18 Current Prob. Pediatrics 703 (1988).

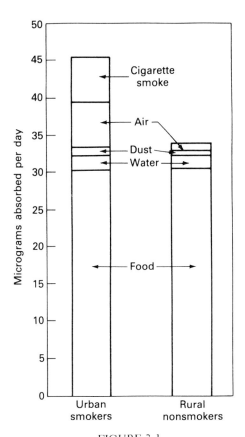

FIGURE 3-1

Sources of Lead Intake in Urban Smokers and Rural Nonsmokers

Source: National Academy of Sciences, Lead in the Human Environment 119 (1980).

Although plant root lead uptake and leaf deposition vary considerably, crops (especially leafy vegetables like spinach) may absorb significant quantities of lead from dustfall onto soil and water and from lead arsenate pesticide sprays. A surprisingly large fraction — perhaps as high as one half — of total ingested lead may come from canned foods. Food absorbs the lead in the solder used in the can seams.

Lead concentrations in the atmosphere may be 100 to 100,000 times those that existed in prehistoric times. Urban residents breathe air containing .5 to 10 μg m^3 (millionths of a gram per cubic meter of air) of lead. Retention in the lungs may be as high as 20 to 40 percent, depending on particle size and the frequency and vigor of respiration. Dietary lead reaches humans via a different route and a different physiological process than inhaled lead. Inhalation is a more direct form of exposure, accounting for the higher retention rate. (Of course, some inhaled lead is actually ingested, after deposition on the linings of the nose, throat, and esophagus.)

The major natural source of lead is volcanic dust, but this source provides less than 1 percent of the emissions resulting from human activity. Vehicle emissions of lead overwhelm all other human sources. Vehicle emissions and the burning of waste oil account for 95 percent of airborne lead, with vehicle emissions alone generating 88 percent of that total. Lead smelters and other industrial sources account for a low 4 percent of total lead emissions. Incineration of solid wastes provides the remaining 1 percent.

Among adults, cigarette smoke is the primary remaining source of body lead. Among children, the primary source is ingestion of paint chips and flakes from leaded paints and of dirt and dust contaminated by the slow lead fallout. These intense exposures, combined with the exceptionally high retention of lead in children's organ systems, mean that those with the longest lives to live and consequently the most to lose are the most susceptible subgroup of the population.

2.   The Choice of Strategies for Control of Human Exposure to Lead

NATURAL RESOURCES DEFENSE COUNCIL, INC. v. TRAIN*
411 F. Supp. 864 (S.D.N.Y. 1976)

STEWART, District Judge:

Natural Resources Defense Council, Inc. ("NRDC") and other named plaintiffs bring this action against the Environmental Protection Agency ("EPA") and its administrator Russell Train for failure to list lead as a pollutant under §108 of the Clean Air Act of 1970. . . . Defendants argue that the listing of pollutants under §108 is a discretionary function and therefore no jurisdiction is vested in this court by virtue of §304 [of the Clean Air Act]. While §304 does not provide jurisdiction over distinctly discretionary functions of the Administrator, it does permit jurisdiction to decide whether a function is mandatory or discretionary. We therefore do not need to consider plaintiffs' other asserted jurisdictional grounds. . . . Plaintiffs contend that the statutory language, legislative history and purpose, as well as current administrative interpretation of the 1970 Clean Air Act, all militate in favor of finding that the Administrator's function to list pollutants under §108 is mandatory, once it is determined by the Administrator that a pollutant "has an adverse effect on public health or welfare" and comes from the requisite numerous or diverse sources. Defendants concede

_____

*In all of the cases reproduced in this chapter the federal statutory citations have been converted to the section number of the bill that became the Clean Air Act of 1970. Citations to the U.S. Code are omitted.

in this action that lead comes from the requisite sources and that the Administrator has found lead to have the required "adverse effect." Defendants argue, however, that the language of §108(a)(1)(C) "for which . . . [the Administrator] plans to issue air quality criteria" is a separate and third criterion to be met before §108 requires placing a pollutant on the list. This construction of §108(a) leaves the initial decision to list a pollutant within the sole discretion of the Administrator. Defendants contend such discretion is required because the Administrator must choose between alternative remedies provided in various sections of the Act and that any decision to utilize the remedies provided by §§108-110 "involves complex considerations.". . .

[W]e do not think that the statutory language supports defendants' construction of the Act. There is no language anywhere in the statute which indicates that the Administrator has discretion to choose among the remedies which the Act provides. Rather, the language of §108 indicates that upon certain enumerated conditions, one factual and one judgmental, the Administrator "shall" list a pollutant which triggers the remedial provisions of §§108-110. The statute does not provide, as defendants would have it, that the Administrator has authority to determine whether the statutory remedies which follow a §108 listing are appropriate for a given pollutant. . . .

With specific reference to the lead pollution at issue here and in support of their position that the Administrator should have discretion under the Act to choose among remedies provided by various sections, defendants point us to the Administrator's decision to regulate lead in gasoline under §211(c)(1). Defendants assert that the EPA considered regulating lead pollution either by setting national ambient air standards under §108 or by establishing standards for the lead content of motor vehicle gasoline under §211. However, as we read the two statutory sections, §108 and §211, they are neither mutually exclusive nor alternative provisions. Defendants' argument is premised upon the misconception, as discussed above, that the statutory scheme provides alternative remedies for pollutants. We think the misconception becomes clear through analysis of the specific case of lead pollution regulation.

Defendants state the reasons for the Administrator's decision to regulate lead under §211.

> It was the Administrator's judgment that (a) uniform standards would make industry compliance simpler than a proliferation of differing state standards, (b) federal controls at the refinery level would be more efficient than state or local controls directed at thousands of distributors and retailers, and (c) the states were hard-pressed to implement the six existing ambient air quality standards and should not be assigned another major regulatory task when equally effective alternatives were available.

These reasons could have no bearing upon a policy decision, if one were permissible under the Act, of whether or not to establish national standards under §108. The benefits of uniform standards, of federal controls and of averting "another major regulatory task" for the states can all accrue from regulations under

§211 when lead is listed under §108. If the Administrator sets standards under §211 which effectively decrease the level of lead in the ambient air by taking lead out of gasoline, then the decrease in pollution brought about by the §211 regulations will be taken into account by each state when it submits its plan to meet the national standard set under §110. . . .

Finally, we turn to an additional argument of defendants that the Administrator needs discretion not to list lead under §108 because the data which would be necessary to support an ambient air standard for lead is arguably lacking. Defendants concede, however, that such a potential lack of data did not enter into the Administrator's decision not to list lead at the time it was made. We do not think that the potential lack of data would have been an appropriate consideration prior to listing a pollutant under §108 in any event. Under the statutory scheme, the listing of a pollutant is no more than a threshold to the remedial provisions. Before a listing, the statute provides for the Administrator to exercise his judgment concerning whether or not a pollutant, here lead, has an adverse effect upon the public health. Once he has made that judgment, however, the Administrator does not have discretion not to list lead as a pollutant because necessary data other than that necessary to make the initial decision as to "adverse effect" is unavailable. The statute appears to assume that, for each pollutant which must be listed, criteria and a national standard can be established. A twelve month period is provided for that purpose. However, Congress cannot require the impossible. It may be that a pollutant exists which meets the listing requirements of §108 but for which no criteria or national standard is possible. That issue is not before this court. The only question here is the threshold one of whether lead must be listed according to §108 and we have determined that it must.

We cannot find support for defendants' position that there is "much to be lost by limiting EPA's ability to select from its sources of authority in the Clean Air Act the control strategy best suited to the pollution problem at hand." We are convinced that the Administrator has considerable, and sufficient, discretion. Not only does he exercise his judgment over the initial determination of whether a pollutant "has an adverse effect upon health," but also he must set the national standard "which in [his] judgment . . . is requisite to protect the public health." (§109(b)(1). Finally, the Administrator must approve the implementation plans of the states. We think that these provisions give the Administrator all the discretion which Congress contemplated that he have.

NOTES AND QUESTIONS

1. Carefully read §§108, 109, and 110(a)(1) of the Clean Air Act. In theory, but not necessarily in practice, attainment of the primary ambient standard is time-limited at a maximum of five years and nine months from the time the pollutant is first listed (unless a state obtains a two-year extension under §110(e)). See also §307(d)(10). The adoption of a new standard for fine particulates may trigger these deadlines for revisions in some state implementation plans.

Are you convinced that the plain meaning of §108(a)(1) required the Administrator to propose ambient air quality standards for lead? The requirement for an "adverse effect" on public health or welfare in §108(a)(1)(A) was changed in 1977 to a requirement that emissions only "endanger" public health or welfare, the same standard as that applicable in §211. Does this change in wording affect the court's decision?

The district court's judgment was affirmed in National Resources Defense Council, Inc. v. Train, 545 F.2d 320 (2d Cir. 1976). The circuit court agreed that Congress did not give EPA the discretion to list only the pollutants for which the Administrator thought ambient standards were the most appropriate strategy. It concluded that Congress intended the ambient standard and state implementation plan strategy to be the linchpin of the Clean Air Act and built safeguards into the Act to prevent delays: "The Congress sought to eliminate, not perpetuate, opportunity for administrative foot-dragging" (545 F.2d at 328). Does it strike you that EPA was dragging its feet in regulating airborne lead? In 1971, EPA indicated that it viewed itself as being obligated to list all pollutants for which it had made the adverse-effects diverse-sources determination (36 Fed. Reg. 1,515). Does this affect your answer?

2. Is EPA put in an awkward situation by this decision? It cannot "determine" that a widely distributed pollutant causes danger without risking a §304 citizens' suit to compel EPA to apply the ambient standard approach. The legislative history of the 1970 amendments mentioned other pollutants that EPA's predecessor, NAPCA, had identified as having adverse health effects and for which Congress expected criteria and standards to be issued: fluorides, polynuclear organic matter, and odors. Senate Comm. on Environment and Public Works, 95th Cong., 2d Sess., S. Rep. No. 16, in 1 Legislative History of the Clean Air Act Amendments of 1977, at 409-410, 430-432, 454 (1978). Moreover, in 1969 NAPCA had studied the adverse effects of some 30 pollutants and had scheduled the preparation of criteria documents for them. Hays, Clean Air: From the 1970 Act to the 1977 Amendments, 17 Duq. L. Rev. 33, 36 (1978). Does this mean that a citizens' suit is all that is needed to add 30 or more pollutants to the 7 currently regulated under the ambient air quality standards approach? Advocates of acid rain control have pushed for EPA designation of sulfates as a pollutant. Has EPA studied the effects of acid rain enough to provide the basis for a citizens' suit to compel this listing? See the Vermont decision, reproduced *infra* p. 295.

EPA is constantly appraising the adverse effects of pollutants. To force premature regulation of a pollutant merely because the Administrator has informally expressed concern about it would force EPA to be extremely cautious in sharing its research results with the public. Section 122 requires the Administrator to determine, after notice and opportunity for a public hearing, whether radioactive pollutants, cadmium, arsenic, and polycyclic organic matter should be listed under §108. Although §122 was not enacted until 1977, could the Administrator now argue that a determination under §108 that a pollutant that endangers public health or welfare requires the type of formality set out in §122?

A NOTE ON CITIZENS' SUITS UNDER THE CLEAN AIR ACT

Natural Resources Defense Council, Inc. v. Train, forced a basic change in EPA's air quality management strategy for lead. Besides the lead case, other important Clean Air Act policy challenges have begun with a §304 citizens' suit. One of these led to enactment of the PSD program of the 1977 amendments. The court held that EPA had a nondiscretionary duty, based on language in the preamble to the 1970 Act and its legislative history, to develop a program for the prevention of significant deterioration of air quality nationwide. Sierra Club v. Ruckelshaus, 344 F. Supp. 253 (D.D.C.), *aff'd per curiam without opinion* (D.C. Cir. 1972), *aff'd by an equally divided Court*, 412 U.S. 541 (1973). When EPA failed to adopt a satisfactory program, Congress acted. See section H below.

How is it that a private environmental organization can obtain such a large say in how the EPA conducts its business? The key lies in §304 and its authority to bring suits to compel EPA to take nondiscretionary actions. Section 304 enlists the assistance of private citizens and organizations in seeing that the Clean Air Act is vigorously implemented. A similar provision appears in 11 other federal environmental statutes.

Although not used extensively at first, §304 has generated a flurry of lawsuits in recent years, some brought to enforce the requirements of state implementation plans as the 1987 deadline was exceeded, and some to take actions required by statute concerning the listing of pollutants and the adoption of emission limitations. Can suit be brought against a corporation that violates the act? See §304(a)(1). But see People v. Celotex Corp., 516 F. Supp. 716 (C.D. Ill. 1981) (corporate executive officer exempted).

Just how far can citizen surveillance of EPA policy functions be carried under §304? Most EPA policy decisions are clearly discretionary, such as its rules setting pollution control standards and approving elements of state implementation plans. For example, the court in Natural Resources Defense Council, Inc. v. Train said that the initial determination of adverse effects in the lead case involved "much discretion." Likewise, the regulation of the lead content of gasoline under §211(c)(1)(A) left to EPA's discretion whether to propose standards at all. In such instances, §304 would not be available.

A leading statement on what is a nondiscretionary deadline is contained in Sierra Club v. Thomas, 828 F.2d 783 (D.C. Cir. 1987), which refused to compel EPA to decide whether to include strip mines as a source of fugitive emissions:

> In order to impose a clear-cut nondiscretionary duty, we believe that a duty of timeliness must "categorically mandat[e]" that *all* specified action be taken by a date-certain deadline. [Id. at 791.]

Accord NRDC v. Thomas, 689 F. Supp. 246 (S.D.N.Y. 1988) (determining which substances are hazardous under §112 is discretionary). Compare NRDC

v. New York State Dept. of Environmental Conservation, 700 F. Supp. 173 (S.D.N.Y. 1988) (EPA has mandatory duty to specify the date for revision of SIP that it finds inadequate); Sierra Club v. Thomas, 658 F. Supp. 165 (N.D. Cal. 1987) (EPA required to adopt regulations to prevent significant deterioration of air quality by nitrogen oxide emissions); Sierra Club v. Ruckelshaus, 602 F. Supp. 892 (N.D. Cal. 1984) (EPA required to adopt emission standards for radionuclides).

Section 304(f)(3) limits suits to violations of "conditions or requirements" of the Act. This has presented problems when citizen plaintiffs have attempted to litigate violations of SIPs that cause nonattainment problems. In Wilder v. Thomas, 854 F.2d 605 (2d Cir. 1988), *cert. denied*, 109 S. Ct. 1314 (1989), the court dismissed a suit to compel EPA to take action to eliminate carbon monoxide "hot spots" created by a downtown Manhattan redevelopment project. The court found no such requirement in the SIP and held that §304 did not confer jurisdiction to compel action to meet the carbon monoxide or other ambient standards. It added that to accept the suit would eliminate the distinction between the ambient standards and measures designed to ensure attainment of the standards. Do you see the distinction? Compare American Lung Association v. Keane, 871 F.2d 319 (3d Cir. 1989) (§304 confers jurisdiction to enforce SIP containing detailed ozone reduction strategies).

Because of the nondiscretionary action problem, many important suits by citizens are not brought under §304 but under §307. Section 307 sets out the types of EPA decisionmaking that may be reviewed, specifies appropriate venues for actions filed, establishes a record-making process for all important Clean Air Act standard setting and other notice-and-comment rule-making, and specifies the scope of judicial review of various agency determinations. Although a minimal Administrative Procedure Act, §307 provides the procedural rules for all key regulatory decisions and their review by courts under the Act. For a "judicial essay" on §307, see Sierra Club v. Costle, 657 F.2d 298, 392-396 (1981). The relationship between §307 and §304 has been extensively litigated. See Sierra Club v. Thomas, *supra*.

Does §304 extend standing beyond constitutional limits? For discussion of the issue and an argument that it does not, see Comment, Citizen Suits under the Clean Air Act: Universal Standing for the Uninjured Private Attorney General?, 16 B.C. Envtl. Aff. L. Rev. 283 (1988). Standing under §307 is governed by §702 of the APA, which functionally seems as generous as the "any person" test of §304.

Section 304(d) authorizes an award of attorneys' and expert witnesses' fees. In Pennsylvania v. Delaware Valley Citizens' Council, 478 U.S. 546 (1986), the Court held that fees could be awarded to a successful plaintiff who monitored state performance under a consent decree requiring the state to adopt a motor vehicle inspection and maintenance program and who participated in EPA proceedings that could have authorized a more restricted program. See also Pennsylvania v. Delaware Valley Citizens' Council, 483 U.S. 711 (1987) (lodestar attorneys' fee cannot be enhanced to take into account risk of not being paid.)

In 1977 Congress extended the provision of attorneys' and expert witnesses' fees, formerly restricted to §304, to §307. In Ruckelshaus v. Sierra Club, 463 U.S. 680 (1983), the Court held that in a §307 suit for attorneys' fees, absent some degree of success on the merits, it is inappropriate to award attorneys' fees. See Note, Awards of Attorneys' Fees to Unsuccessful Environmental Litigants, 96 Harv. L. Rev. 677 (1983). In its attempt to force EPA to adopt an ambient lead standard, standing was assured and the Natural Resources Defense Council did not seek attorneys' fees in this pre-1977 action. So why didn't NRDC bring its case under §307, evading the nondiscretionary duty problem entirely?

NOTES AND QUESTIONS ON OTHER STRATEGIES FOR CONTROLLING EXPOSURE TO LEAD

1. *The basic policy choice.* Natural Resources Defense Council, Inc. v. Train focused on two Clean Air Act strategies for regulating airborne lead. What strategies for controlling airborne lead do the facts suggest? Is lead a serious problem only for children 1 to 5 years old who live near highways and smelters? Should the lead strategy therefore consist of targeted measures designed only to combat airborne lead in specific locations for specific population subgroups? Gasoline combustion accounts for 88 percent of airborne lead; smelters contribute just under 4 percent. The EPA observed that some primary lead and copper smelters may be "severely strained economically" in meeting the ambient standards that ultimately were adopted (43 Fed. Reg. 46,256). Smelters are not very numerous and usually are located in less populous regions. Does this suggest concentrating on mobile source lead pollution and letting the smelters go? Economists and environmental policy analysts argue compellingly that in selecting among pollution control strategies the optimal strategy will minimize the sum of damage, avoidance, transaction, and abatement costs:

> *Damage* costs are those costs which directly result from a polluting activity, for example, illness and property damage stemming from air pollution. *Avoidance* costs are those that people incur in order to avoid or reduce damage costs. . . . *Transaction* costs represent the resources consumed in making and enforcing policies and regulations, such as the costs of monitoring air pollution. *Abatement* costs are those associated with reducing the amount of environmental degradation. [Council on Environmental Quality, Fourth Annual Report 74 (1973).]

Is lead avoidance a least-cost option? Could parents keep children indoors during rush hours and pollution episodes? Relocate during child-rearing years?

2. *Regulatory choices available under the Act.* Consider briefly the full Clean Air Act arsenal that might be leveled at airborne lead. The exercise is very much like that undertaken by lawyers from congressional staffs, agencies, public interest groups, and industry each time they try to match the Act's requirements and imperfections against a real air pollution problem. In examining the available Clean Air Act options, keep in mind the possibility for minimizing the sum of abatement, damage, avoidance, and especially transaction costs.

What differences in approach distinguish §211(c)(1)(A) from §108? Was EPA rightfully impatient with having to establish ambient standards when it has known for years what the health effects and major sources of airborne lead are? Federal and state responsibilities are different under each. What difference does this make? The difference between the two approaches may be the same fundamental difference that exists between ambient standards and technology-limited uniform national emissions standards. Is the court persuasive that the two alternative strategies do not conflict? Under the ambient approach, nothing need be done in the vast regions of the country where lead is not a problem, whereas the §211(c)(1)(A) approach requires costly controls on lead in gasoline throughout the nation. The ambient approach theoretically permits use of selective land use planning to regulate the spacing and timing of lead emissions as needed, whereas fuel controls blanket the nation. Should EPA modify its strategy in view of the substantial reduction in air emissions of lead in recent years?

Despite being forced to promulgate an ambient standard for lead, EPA still places primary reliance on its unleaded (§211(c)(2)(B)) and low-lead (§211(c)(2)(A)) gasoline regulations. EPA attributes 65 percent of airborne lead reductions to its §211 program, and it has asserted that these regulations and the increasing use of unleaded gasoline will result in attainment of the ambient standards in urban areas without the need for SIP controls (43 Fed. Reg. 46,247). Note that the lead phase-down was temporarily halted in 1986 when Congress exempted farm vehicles from the lead-free gasoline requirement.

Is regulation §112 (NESHAP) an alternative? Section 112(a)(1) says that §112 is unavailable if an ambient air quality standard "is applicable" to the pollutant in question. NESHAP are discussed further in Chapter 5. Should EPA regulate new stationary sources of lead with §111 NSPS? Note that the "endanger" standard also triggers regulation under §111. If no ambient standard had been required, as EPA urged, lead emissions from *existing* stationary sources could have been regulated as well. See §111(d).

3.   EPA's Final Ambient Air Quality Standards for Lead

The second step in promulgating an ambient standard is the preparation of a criteria document, which is a scientific study of the pollutant and its effects. The third step, required by §109(a)(2) to occur simultaneously with the publication of the study, is release for public comment of the agency's proposed numerical primary and secondary ambient standards. These standards must be based on the criteria document. Do not be misled by the use of the term "criteria document" to describe the scientific study. The Act §108(a)(2) makes clear that the "criteria" are descriptive rather than prescriptive and refer not to standards or guidelines that sources must meet but rather to the latest scientific knowledge of the injury to public health or welfare that the pollutant may cause — a tall order, but definitely not "criteria" in the usual sense. Similarly, do not be confused by the use of the term "public welfare" in the provision for secondary ambient air quality standards. Consult the description of "welfare effects" provided in

§302(h), a subsection of the definitions section of the statute. Perhaps you see the difficulty in finding a short phrase to describe the plethora of environmental, social, and economic effects that the secondary standard is supposed to address.

After the court decisions requiring EPA to promulgate an ambient air quality standard, the agency listed lead in March 1976 and in December 1977 proposed a standard of a monthly average of 1.5 micrograms of lead per cubic meter of ambient air (1.5 μg Pb/m^3), a quarterly (three-month) average, and released a printed 306-page criteria document providing the scientific foundation for its proposal. The agency also proposed SIP regulations to implement the new standard and held a public hearing on its proposal in mid-February 1978. Eight months later, it promulgated a final standard — the same 1.5 μg Pb/m^3 as proposed. In its statement accompanying the final standards, excerpted below, EPA explained how it developed the standard and responded to comments it had received during the public comment period.

Imagine that you are the Administrator of EPA, an attorney (as many Administrators have been) and a presidential political appointee (as all Administrators must be), and that your staff brings you the following justification for the final lead rule. As you read, ask whether, in the jargon of the federal government, you are prepared to "sign off" on the standard. Pay particular attention to the method used. Is the method defensible?

EPA, NATIONAL PRIMARY AND SECONDARY AMBIENT AIR QUALITY STANDARDS FOR LEAD
43 Fed. Reg. 46,246 (1978)

Sensitive Population

EPA believes that the health of young children is at particular risk from lead exposure. This is because children have a greater physiological sensitivity to the effects of lead than do adults and may have greater exposure to environmental lead from playing in contaminated areas. Other sensitive populations identified by EPA include those occupationally exposed, and pregnant women and their fetuses. Comments received on the proposed standard did not challenge EPA's position that young children are the most sensitive population for determining the standard. A number of comments did point out that within the general population of children there were subgroups with enhanced risk due to genetic factors, dietary deficiencies, or residence in urban areas. EPA acknowledges the higher risk status of such groups but does not have information either in the air quality criteria or in the comments received for estimating a threshold for adverse effects separate from that of all young children. Concern about these high risk subgroups has, however, influenced EPA's determination of the percentage of the population of children (99.5 percent) to be maintained below 30 μg Pb/dl [dl = a tenth of a liter, in this case of blood].

EPA continues to be concerned about the possible health risk of lead exposure for pregnant women and their fetuses. The stress of pregnancy may place pregnant women in a state more susceptible to the effects of lead, and transplacental transfer of lead may affect the prenatal development of the child. There is, however, insufficient scientific information for EPA to either confirm or dismiss this suggestion, or to establish that pregnant women and fetuses are more at risk than young children.

The Maximum Safe Exposure for Children

In determining the maximum safe exposure to lead for children, EPA has taken the measurement of blood lead as the indicator of total lead dose. There are other possible indicators of exposure, for example the level of zinc protoporphyrin (ZPP), but most health studies reported in the criteria document utilize blood lead levels as indications of the mobile body burden of lead. The criteria document reports . . . effect thresholds for children with increasing blood lead levels [set out in the table below].

Summary of Lowest Observed Effect Levels in
Young Children

	μg Pb/dl
δ ALAD inhibition	10
Erythrocyte protoporphyrin elevation	15–20
Increased urinary δ ALA excretion	40
Anemia	40
Coproporphyrin elevation	40
Cognitive (CNB) deficits	50–60
Peripheral neuropathies	50–60
Encephalopathic symptoms	80–100

[After concluding that inhibition of the enzyme δ-ALAD was not harmful, EPA continued:] The criteria document reports that above a threshold of 15-20 μg Pb/dl there is an elevation of protoporphyrin in erythrocytes. Protoporphyrin is an organic chemical compound used by all cells in the production of heme [a deep red, iron-containing component of hemoglobin in blood]. In the final stage of heme synthesis, erythrocyte protoporphyrin (EP) and iron are brought together in the cell mitochondria. In the presence of lead, this step is blocked, possibly by inhibition of the enzyme ferrochelatase or by interference in the transport of iron across the mitochondrial membrane. Without incorporation into heme, the levels of protoporphyrin in the cell become elevated.

From review of the information provided by the air quality criteria document as well as the evidence and arguments offered by medical professionals commenting on the proposed standard, EPA has concluded that the effects of lead on the cellular synthesis of heme, as indicated by elevated erythrocyte protoporphyrin, are potentially adverse to the health of young children. This appears, however, to be a question of the degree to which the effect has progressed.

[Earlier in the document (at 46,249) EPA had stated:

EPA agrees with the comments received that the initial elevation of EP as a result of exposure to lead, while indicating an impairment of heme synthesis, may not be a disease state or be seen as a clinically detectable decline in performance. However, the criteria document points out . . . that this impairment does increase progressively with lead dose. . . .

The fact that other conditions, such as iron deficiency, may also impair heme synthesis does not obviate concern that lead is interfering with an essential biological function. There is the possibility that a nutritional deficiency is an additional stress to the heme synthetic system which may increase the sensitivity of a child to the adverse effects of lead exposure. . . .]

. . . EPA does not believe that there is significant risk to health at the point where the elevation of EP can first be correlated with an increase in blood lead (15 to 20 μg Pb/dl). On the other hand, EPA regards as clearly adverse to health the impairment of heme synthesis, and other effects of lead which result in clinical symptoms of anemia above 40 μg Pb/dl. These effects are followed quickly by the risk of nervous system deficits for some children with blood lead levels of 50 μg Pb/dl.

EPA has concluded that the maximum safe blood lead level for an individual child is 30 μg Pb/dl. This is based on the following factors:

(1) The maximum safe blood lead level should be somewhat lower than the threshold for a decline in hemoglobin levels (40 μg Pb/dl).

(2) The maximum safe blood lead level should be at an even greater distance below the threshold for risks of nervous system deficits (50 μg Pb/dl).

(3) The maximum safe blood lead level should be no higher than the blood lead range characterized as undue exposure by the Center for Disease Control of the Public Health Service, as endorsed by the American Academy of Pediatrics, because of elevation of erythrocyte protoporphyrin (above 30 μg Pb/dl).

(4) The maximum safe blood lead level for an individual need not be as low as the detection point for the initial elevation of EP (15-20 μg Pb/dl). . . .

[EPA then defended its use of a geometric standard deviation that it believed would protect 99.5 percent of inner-city children from blood lead levels above 30 μg Pb/dl. Later (at 46,255) EPA stated that in a population of 5 million children in central urban areas, if air lead was at the standard level, 693,000 children would be over 20 μg Pb/dl, 126,500 over 25 μg Pb/dl, and 20,605 above 30 μg Pb/dl.]

Contribution to Total Lead Exposure from Nonair Sources

In the proposed standard, EPA argued that the air standard should take into account the contribution to blood lead levels from lead sources unrelated to air pollution. No comments were received challenging this argument. EPA continues to base its calculation of the ambient air standard on the assumption that, to an extent, the lead contribution to blood lead from nonair sources should be subtracted from the estimate of safe mean population blood lead. Without this subtraction, the combined exposure to lead from air and nonair sources would result in a blood lead concentration exceeding the safe level.

EPA notes that the level of the standard is strongly influenced by judgments about nonair contribution to total exposure, and that there are difficulties in attempting to estimate exposure from various lead sources. Studies reviewed in the criteria document do not provide detailed or widespread information about the relative contribution of various sources to children's blood lead levels. Estimates can only be made by inference from other empirical or theoretical studies, usually involving adults. Also, it can be expected that the contribution to blood lead levels from nonair sources can vary widely, is probably not in constant proportion to air lead contribution, and in some cases may alone exceed the target mean population blood lead level.

In spite of these difficulties, EPA has attempted to assess available information in order to estimate the general contribution to population blood lead levels from air and nonair sources. This has been done with evaluation of evidence from general epidemiological studies, studies showing decline of blood lead levels with decrease in air lead, studies of blood lead levels in areas with low air lead levels, and isotopic tracing studies.

Studies reviewed by the criteria document show that the geometric mean blood lead levels for populations of children are frequently above 15 μg Pb/dl. In studies reported, the range of mean population blood lead levels for children was from 16.5 μg Pb/dl to 46.4 μg Pb/dl with most studies showing mean levels greater than 25 μg Pb/dl. EPA believes that, for many of these populations, the contribution to blood lead levels from nonair sources may exceed the desired target mean blood lead level.

In a number of studies, reduction in air lead levels resulted in a decline in children's blood lead levels. . . . A study of blood lead levels in children in New York City showed that children's mean blood lead levels declined from 30.5 μg Pb/dl from 1970 to 1976, while during the same period air lead levels at a single monitoring site fell from 2.0 μg Pb/dl to 0.9 μg/Pb (Billick, 1977). Studies at Omaha, Neb. (Angle, 1977) and Kellogg, Idaho (Yankel & von Lindern, 1977) also show a drop in mean blood lead levels with declines in air lead levels. As air lead levels decline there appears to be a rough limit to the drop in blood lead levels.

EPA has also examined epidemiological studies in the criteria document where air lead exposure is low, and can be assumed to be a minor contributor to blood lead. These studies provide an indication of blood lead levels resulting from a situation where nonair sources of lead are predominant. . . . The range of mean blood lead levels in those studies is from 10.2 μg Pb/dl to 14.4 μg Pb/dl, with an average at 12.7 μg Pb/dl.

In addition to epidemiological investigations, EPA has reviewed studies that examine the source of blood lead by detecting characteristic lead isotopes. A study using isotopic tracing (Manton, 1977) suggests that for several adults in Houston, Tex., 7 to 41 percent of blood lead could be attributed to air lead sources. An earlier isotopic study (Rabinowitz, 1974) concluded that for two adult male subjects studied, approximately one-third of total daily intake of lead could be attributed to exposure to air lead levels of 1-2 μg Pb/m^3. While these results cannot be directly related to children, it is reasonable to assume that children may exhibit the same or higher percentages of air lead contribution to blood lead level because of a greater potential for exposure to indirect air sources, soil and dust.

From reviewing these areas of evidence, EPA concludes that:

1. In studies showing mean blood lead levels above 15 μg Pb/dl, it is probable that both air and nonair sources of lead contribute significantly to blood lead with the possibility that contributions from nonair sources exceed 15 μg Pb/dl.

2. Studies showing a sustained drop in air lead levels show a corresponding drop in blood lead levels, down to an apparent limit in the range of 10.2 to 14.4 μg Pb/dl.

3. Isotopic tracing studies show air contribution to blood lead to be 7-41 percent in one study and about 33 percent in another study.

In considering this evidence, EPA notes that if, from the isotopic studies, approximately two-thirds of blood lead is typically derived from nonair sources, a mean blood lead target of 15 μg Pb/dl would attribute 10 μg Pb/dl to nonair sources. On the other hand, the average blood lead level from the limited studies available where air exposure was low is 12.7 μg Pb/dl. In the absence of more precise information, EPA is calculating the lead standard based on the attribution of 12 μg Pb/dl of the blood lead level in children to lead sources unaffected by the lead air quality standard. EPA is aware that actual population blood lead levels, either individually or as a population mean, may exceed this benchmark. However, if EPA were to use a larger estimate of nonair contribution to blood lead, the result would be an exceptionally stringent standard, which would not address the principal source of lead exposure.

The Relationship between Air Lead Exposure and Resulting Blood Lead Level

EPA has reviewed the studies discussed in the criteria document which report changes in blood lead levels with different air lead levels. The Agency believes that one of the strongest epidemiological studies is that by Azar et al., which used personal dosimeters to measure lead intake. This eliminated some of the uncertainty about the extent to which air quality observations accurately reflect actual exposure. From the Azar data, the relationship of lead in the air to lead in the blood, evaluated at 1.5 μg Pb/m^3, was 1:1.8. The Azar study was, however, limited to an adult population.

A clinical study of adults, Griffin et al., gives roughly the same conclusion for a group of adults confined to a chamber with controlled exposure to lead aerosol. This study was conducted over a three month period with control over lead ingestion. As air lead levels in the chamber were increased from 0.15 μg Pb/m³ to 3.2 μg Pb/m³, the air lead to blood lead relationship was 1:1.7.

Because children are known to have greater net absorption and retention of lead than adults, it is reasonable to assume that the air lead to blood lead relationship for this sensitive population, exposed to air lead levels in the range of the proposed standard, is equal to if not greater than for adults. EPA also notes that the air lead to blood lead relationship is nonlinear, which will result in a higher ratio at lower air levels.

In an epidemiological study of children near a smelter, Yankel et al., the response of blood lead to air lead, averaged over the exposure range, was 1.95. . . . EPA believes that these studies as well as others reported in the criteria document support the document's conclusion that:

> Ratios between blood lead levels and air lead exposures were shown to range generally from 1:1 to 2:1. These were not, however, constant over the range of air lead concentrations encountered. There are suggestive data indicating that the ratios for children are in the upper end of the range and may even be slightly above it. There is also some slight suggestion that the ratios for males are higher than those for females. . . .

[Earlier (at 46,252) EPA summarized its derivation of the numerical level of the final standard:

EPA's objective in setting the level of the standard is to estimate the concentration of lead in the air to which all groups within the general population can be exposed for protracted periods without an unacceptable risk to health.

This estimate is based on EPA's judgment in four key areas:

(1) Determining the "sensitive population" as that group within the general population which has the lowest threshold for adverse effects or greatest potential for exposure. EPA concludes that young children, aged 1 to 5, are the sensitive population.

(2) Determining the safe level of total lead exposure for the sensitive population, indicated by the concentration of lead in the blood. EPA concludes that the maximum safe level of blood lead for an individual child is 30 μg Pb/dl and that population blood lead, measured as the geometric mean, must be 15 μg Pb/dl in order to place 99.5 percent of children in the United States below 30 μg Pb/dl.

(3) Attributing the contribution to blood lead from nonair pollution sources. EPA concludes that 12 μg Pb/dl of population blood lead for children should be attributed to nonair exposure.

(4) Determining the air lead level which is consistent with maintaining the mean population blood lead level at 15 μg Pb/dl. Taking into account exposure from other sources (12 μg Pb/dl) EPA has designed the standard to limit air contribution after achieving the standard to 3 μg Pb/dl. On the basis of an estimated relationship of air lead to blood lead of 1 to 2, EPA concludes that the ambient air standard should be 1.5 μg Pb/m³.]

Selection of the Averaging Period for the Standard

Based on comments received and consideration by the Agency, the proposed averaging period of a calendar month is extended to a calendar quarter. EPA believes that this change will significantly improve the validity of lead air quality data which will be gathered to monitor progress toward attainment without placing an undue burden on State and local environmental agencies, or significantly reducing the protectiveness of the standard.

NOTES AND QUESTIONS

1. Does the 1.5 $\mu g/m^3$ standard provide a reliable lead abatement goal? A National Academy of Sciences study stated:

> Three critical variables in the . . . [EPA] calculations are subject to important uncertainties. The assumed 2-to-1 ratio between lead in air and lead in blood is based on very few data on children, and might easily be 50 percent high or low. The estimate of 10 to 12 $\mu g/100$ ml of lead in blood from nonair sources certainly could be in error by at least ± 3 $\mu g/100$ ml. Finally, the calculated target geometric mean blood lead level of 15 $\mu g/100$ ml is extremely sensitive to the assumed geometric standard deviation. If the value chosen had been 1.5, which is equally supported by the meager available data, the mean blood lead level required to keep 99.5 percent of children below 30 $\mu g/100$ ml would be about 10 $\mu g/100$ ml, and the tolerable exposure to lead in air could be calculated as zero. [Lead in the Human Environment 214-215 (1980).]

Thus even a zero microgram standard — which would bankrupt many industries — might be inadequate in some parts of the country to reduce children's blood lead levels below the 15 $\mu g/dl$ mean. Likewise, interpreting these observations in the way least favorable to EPA, a standard of 18 $\mu g/m^3$ — 12 times the standard might be entirely adequate, requiring abatement measures in only a few regions.

When all the uncertainties associated with route of exposure (inhalation, ingestion, absorption), level of exposure (terrain, meteorology, urbanization), and personal factors (age, race, personal susceptibility) are combined, the choice of a single numerical ambient standard presents a challenge of enormous proportions. Would a less quantitative approach have been permissible?

2. Recall that lead reaches the human body through a variety of products, production processes, and environmental media. The most common means of exposure is by ingestion of food, water, dust, and paint flakes, not by inhalation. The release of lead from plumbing in drinking water is another source that has escaped attention until recently. With lead's ubiquity in the human environment, does it make sense to give excessive attention to airborne lead?

The data supporting EPA's determination that 12 $\mu g/dl$ of children's blood lead comes from nonair sources are particularly soft, as the agency admits. Nervous system, renal, and other disorders caused by lead are not directly related to blood lead levels. If the data on the nonair contribution to blood lead provide an uncertain guide, should EPA have fallen back on the more general concept of a total acceptable daily dose for all sources? Even if EPA singles out blood lead levels as the exclusive basis for setting the standard, does §108 require something more than elevated EP levels to qualify as the type of health injury or "danger" that ambient standards are supposed to prevent? Would the EPA be justified in refusing to take the ingested non-air contribution into account at all? To what extent should EPA consider actions taken in other federal programs to regulate lead, which are discussed in the following note?

3. A number of other federal programs are directed at controlling and removing lead, and the tendency has been to transfer regulation of lead-related issues to EPA. One of the most important of these programs, for example, is the program for removing lead-based paint from federally assisted housing. Once the responsibility of the Department of Housing and Urban Development (HUD), Congress has now directed EPA to look at the lead-based paint issue because of serious implementation problems with the HUD program. See the Hearing Before the House Comm. on Banking, Finance & Urban Affairs, 100th Cong., 2d Sess. (1988), on the lead-based paint program.

Other congressional actions added to EPA's responsibilities for lead. A 1986 amendment to the Safe Drinking Water Act prohibited the use of lead in plumbing for drinking water, 42 U.S.C. §1417. A 1984 amendment to RCRA prohibited the land disposal of lead in hazardous waste disposal sites. 42 U.S.C. §6924(d). EPA is also conducting a study of the cleanup of lead in soils under Superfund. Other agencies continue to have important regulatory responsibilities. See, e.g., 29 C.F.R. §1910.1025 (OSHA; lead in workplace). How does all this affect your view of the regulation of airborne lead under the Clean Air Act?

4. For the reasons stated, the nonair blood lead burden varies enormously from area to area. Would it make more sense to monitor children's blood lead levels in different regions and select a strategy for controlling airborne lead that keeps blood lead under a mean 15 μg/dl? In other words, the 15 μg/dl mean would become the "uniform standard," and SIP controls could vary the content of lead in the ambient air as necessary to achieve this blood lead content standard. Depending on the region, ambient lead levels would vary between zero and 7.5 μg/m³. Does §108 authorize such an approach? What legal consequences would flow from a showing by a state that while ambient lead in its cities was consistently over the standard, children's actual monitored blood lead levels were never even near the 15 μg/dl threshold? Would EPA and the state still have to enforce the standard?

5. The FDA criticized EPA for not focusing in on the youngest, most susceptible children as the target population, calling the 15 μg/dl mean "disturbingly narrow" (43 Fed. Reg. 46,257). Under the EPA approach, some 20,605 children may still have blood lead levels above 30 μg/dl. But if the mean blood level sought were relaxed just a bit, to 16.5 μg/dl rather than to 15 μg/dl, approximately 126,500 children would experience blood lead levels of about 30

μg/dl, but the standard could then be 2.25 μg/m³ (.5(16.5 − 12) = 2.25), or over 80 percent laxer. Would the risk be worth the lower standard? Remember that most of children's blood lead comes from ingested substances. See also Agency for Toxic Substances and Disease Registry, The Nature and Extent of Lead Poisoning in Children in the US (US DHHS, 1988).

What if EPA had set the target blood lead level at a relaxed 30 μg/dl? This would still assure that the bulk of the sensitive subgroup would not experience lead's ill effects and that the overall population would be almost totally protected. Even a 30 μg/dl goal would include a margin of safety. Would this approach satisfy §108?

New studies suggest that adults are also at risk from lead poisoning. Silbergeld, Implications of New Data on Lead Toxicity for Managing and Prevention of Exposure, Envtl. Health Perspectives (forthcoming). Silbergeld notes that lead toxicity is a major problem in industry, that EPA estimates 42 million Americans are exposed to lead in drinking water in excess of 20 ppb, and that lead is released in the disposal of consumer products containing lead, especially when incineration is the disposal method. What do these studies suggest for a federal lead strategy? Silbergeld also notes that infants are at risk because lead is excreted into breastmilk during lactation, but the kinetics of lead excretion are not yet well known.

6. Does the example of lead show that the entire notion of safe thresholds, on which the ambient approach is implicitly based, is wrong? Consider also that estimates of threshold danger levels and the risks from lead exposure have changed considerably. The Clean Air Scientific Advisory Committee has concluded that critical health effects from lead apparently start at a blood level one-third less than that used by the EPA to set the lead standard. 16 Envt. Rep. (BNA): Current Developments 197 (1985). Recent studies also indicate that fetal exposure to lead levels previously considered safe is linked to impairment of infant mortality development. Davis & Svendsgaard, Lead and Child Development, 329 Nature 297 (1987). And the effects of lead stored in bone may alter estimations of long-term risk at low exposure levels. Over 95 percent of absorbed lead is retained in bone. What effect should these findings have on a Clean Air Act strategy for controlling lead exposure?

4.   Judicial Review of the Final Lead Standard

LEAD INDUSTRIES ASSOCIATION, INC. v. EPA
647 F.2d 1330 (D.C. Cir.), cert. denied, 449 U.S. 1042 (1980)

[In a lengthy opinion by Chief Judge Skelly Wright, the court upheld the national ambient air quality standards for lead, which were attacked by St. Joe Minerals Corporation and the Lead Industries Association (LIA), among others. After examining the statutory requirements, the criteria document, the proposed and final ambient standards, and the standard of judicial review to be applied in the rule-making, the court addressed the petitioner's key claims in the following manner:]

The petitioners' first claim is that the Administrator exceeded his authority under the statute by promulgating a primary air quality standard for lead which is more stringent than is necessary to protect the public health because it is designed to protect the public against "sub-clinical" effects which are not harmful to health. According to petitioners, Congress only authorized the Administrator to set primary air quality standards that are aimed at protecting the public against health effects which are known to be *clearly harmful*. They argue that Congress so limited the Administrator's authority because it was concerned that excessively stringent air quality standards could cause massive economic dislocation. . . .

Where Congress intended the Administrator to be concerned about economic and technological feasibility, it expressly so provided. For example, Section 111 of the Act directs the Administrator to consider economic and technological feasibility in establishing standards of performance for new stationary sources of air pollution based on the best available control technology. S. Rep. No. 91-1196, 91st Cong., 2d Sess. 416 (1970). In contrast, Section 109(b) speaks only of protecting the public health and welfare. Nothing in its language suggests that the Administrator is to consider economic or technological feasibility in setting ambient air quality standards.

The legislative history of the Act also shows the Administrator may not consider economic and technological feasibility in setting air quality standards; the absence of any provision requiring consideration of these factors was no accident; it was the result of a deliberate decision by Congress to subordinate such concerns to the achievement of health goals. Exasperated by the lack of significant progress toward dealing with the problem of air pollution under the Air Quality Act of 1967, 81 Stat. 485, and prior legislation, Congress abandoned the approach of offering suggestions and setting goals in favor of "taking a stick to the States in the form of the Clean Air Amendments of 1970. . . ." Train v. Natural Resources Defense Council, Inc. [421 U.S. 60 (1975)], *supra*, 421 U.S. at 64; see Union Electric Co. v. EPA, 427 U.S. 246, 256-257 (1976). Congress was well aware that, together with Sections 108 and 110, Section 109 imposes requirements of a "technology-forcing" character. Id. at 257. . . .

It may well be that underlying St. Joe's argument is its feeling that Congress could not or should not have intended this result, and that this court should supply relief by grafting a requirement of economic or technological feasibility onto the statute. The Supreme Court confronted a similar suggestion in the Tellico Dam case. TVA v. Hill, 437 U.S. 153 (1978). There TVA argued that the Endangered Species Act should not be construed to prevent operation of the dam since it had already been completed at a cost of approximately $100 million, Congress had appropriated funds for the dam even after the Act was passed, and the species at risk the snail darter was relatively unimportant and ways might ultimately be found to save it. The Court rejected the invitation to "view the . . . Act 'reasonably,' and hence shape a remedy that 'accords with some modicum of common sense and the public weal.'" Id. at 194. . . .

According to LIA, Congress was mindful of the possibility that air quality standards which are too stringent could cause severe economic dislocation. For this reason it only granted the Administrator authority to adopt air quality standards which are "designed to protect the public from adverse health effects that are clearly harmful[.]" LIA finds support for its interpretation of congressional intent in various portions of the legislative history of the Act. For example, it notes that the Senate Report on the 1970 legislation states that EPA "would be required to set a national *minimum* standard of air quality," S. Rep. No. 91-1196, *supra*, at 10 (emphasis added). . . . LIA then argues that the Administrator based the lead air quality standards on protecting children from "subclinical" effects of lead exposure which have not been shown to be harmful to health, that in so doing the Administrator ignored the clear limitation that Congress imposed on his standard-setting powers, and that the Administrator's action will in fact cause the very result that Congress was so concerned about avoiding.

LIA's argument appears to touch on two issues. The first concerns the type of health effects on which the Administrator may base air quality standards, i.e., the point at which the Administrator's regulatory authority may be exercised. This issue, as LIA suggests, does concern the limits that the Act, and its legislative history, may place on the Administrator's authority. The second issue appears to be more in the nature of an evidentiary question: whether or not the evidence in the record substantiates the Administrator's claim that the health effects on which the standards were based do in fact satisfy the requirements of the Act. Although these two issues are closely related, they are conceptually distinct, and they are best examined separately.

Section 109(b) does not specify precisely what Congress had in mind when it directed the Administrator to prescribe air quality standards that are "requisite to protect the public health." The legislative history of the Act does, however, provide some guidance. The Senate Report explains that the goal of the air quality standards must be to ensure that the public is protected from "adverse health effects." S. Rep. No. 91-1196, *supra*, at 10. And the report is particularly careful to note that especially sensitive persons such as asthmatics and emphysematics are included within the group that must be protected. It is on the interpretation of the phrase "adverse health effects" that the disagreement between LIA and EPA about the limits of the Administrator's statutory authority appears to be based. LIA argues that the legislative history of the Act indicates that Congress only intended to protect the public against effects which are known to be *clearly harmful* to health, maintaining that this limitation on the Administrator's statutory authority is necessary to ensure that the standards are not set at a level which is more stringent than Congress contemplated. The Administrator, on the other hand, agrees that primary air quality standards must be based on protecting the public from "adverse health effects," but argues that the meaning LIA assigns to that phrase is too limited. In particular, the Administrator contends that LIA's interpretation is inconsistent with the precautionary nature of the statute, and will frustrate Congress' intent in requiring promulgation of air quality standards.

The Administrator begins by pointing out that the Act's stated goal is "to protect and enhance the quality of the Nation's air resources so as to promote the public health and welfare and the productive capacity of its population[.]" Section 101(b)(1). This goal was reaffirmed in the 1977 Amendments. For example, the House Report accompanying the Amendments states that one of its purposes is "[t]o emphasize the preventive or precautionary nature of the act, i.e., to assure that regulatory action can effectively prevent harm before it occurs; to emphasize the predominant value of protection of public health[.]" H.R. Rep. No. 95-294, 95th Cong., 1st Sess. 49 (1977). The Administrator notes that protecting the public from harmful effects requires decisions about exactly what these harms are, a task Congress left to his judgment. He notes that the task of making these decisions is complicated by the absence of any clear thresholds above which there are adverse effects and below which there are none. Rather, as scientific knowledge expands and analytical techniques are improved, new information is uncovered which indicates that pollution levels that were once considered harmless are not in fact harmless. Congress, the Administrator argues, was conscious of this problem, and left these decisions to his judgment partly for this reason.[43] In such situations the perspective that is brought to bear on the problem plays a crucial role in determining what decisions are made. Because it realized this, Congress, the Administrator maintains, directed him to err on the side of caution in making these judgments. First, Congress made it abundantly clear that considerations of economic or technological feasibility are

---

43.   Section 109(b), 42 U.S.C. §7409(b), specifically states that the Administrator is to use his judgment in determining what air quality standards are necessary to protect the public health, a task which requires him to make factual determinations as well as policy judgments. The Administrator notes that the issue of the uncertainty that surrounds attempts to set air quality standards which protect the public health featured prominently in the discussion about the 1977 Amendments. For example, noting that the primary standards are based on the assumption that there is a discoverable no-effects threshold, the House Report on the Amendments observed:

> However, in no case is there evidence that the threshold levels have a clear physiological meaning, in the sense that there are genuine adverse health effects at and above some level of pollution, but no effects at all below that level. On the contrary, evidence indicates that the amount of health damage varies with the upward and downward variations in the concentration of the pollutant, with no sharp lower limit.

H.R. Rep. No. 95-294., *supra* at 110 (quoting 1974 National Academy of Sciences Report at 17). See H.R. Rep. No. 95-294, *supra* at 105-127. And during the Senate debate on the Amendments Senator Muskie summarized the problems the Administrator faces in attempting to set air quality standards:

> . . . I wish it were possible for the Administrator to set national primary and secondary standards that fully implement the statutory language. . . . The fact is, as testimony and documents disclose, the standards do not fully protect in accordance with the statutory language which gives the Administrator authority to provide for additional protection. He has had to make a pragmatic judgment in the face of the fact that he found there is no threshold on health effects, which makes it very difficult then to apply absolute health protection, and he has not been able to do that.

123 Cong. Rec. S9426 (daily ed. June 10, 1977).

to be subordinated to the goal of protecting the public health by prohibiting any consideration of such factors. Second, it specified that the air quality standards must also protect individuals who are particularly sensitive to the effects of pollution. Third, it required that the standards be set at a level at which there is "an absence of adverse effect" on these sensitive individuals. Finally, it specifically directed the Administrator to allow an adequate margin of safety in setting primary air quality standards in order to provide some protection against effects that research has not yet uncovered. The Administrator contends that these indicia of congressional intent, the precautionary nature of the statutory mandate to protect the public health, the broad discretion Congress gave him to decide what effects to protect against, and the uncertainty that must be part of any attempt to determine the health effects of air pollution, are all extremely difficult to reconcile with LIA's suggestion that he can only set standards which are designed to protect against effects which are *known to be clearly harmful to health.*

. . . It may be . . . LIA's view that the Administrator must show that there is a "medical consensus that [the effects on which the standards were based] are harmful. . . ." If so, LIA is seriously mistaken. This court has previously noted that some uncertainty about the health effects of air pollution is inevitable. And we pointed out that "[a]waiting certainty will often allow for only reactive, not preventive regulat[ory action]." Ethyl Corp. v. EPA, [541 F.2d 1 (D.C. Cir. 1976)], *supra,* 541 F.2d at 25. Congress apparently shares this view; it specifically directed the Administrator to allow an adequate margin of safety to protect against effects which have not yet been uncovered by research and effects whose medical significance is a matter of disagreement. This court has previously acknowledged the role of the margin of safety requirement. In Environmental Defense Fund v. EPA, 598 F.2d 62, 81 (D.C. Cir. 1978), we pointed out that "[i]f administrative responsibility to protect against unknown dangers presents a difficult task, indeed, a veritable paradox calling as it does for knowledge of that which is unknown then, the term 'margin of safety' is Congress's directive that means be found to carry out the task and to reconcile the paradox." Moreover, it is significant that Congress has recently acknowledged that more often than not the "margins of safety" that are incorporated into air quality standards turn out to be very modest or nonexistent, as new information reveals adverse health effects at pollution levels once thought to be harmless. See H.R. Rep. No. 95-294, *supra,* at 103-117. Congress' directive to the Administrator to allow an "adequate margin of safety" alone plainly refutes any suggestion that the Administrator is only authorized to set primary air quality standards which are designed to protect against health effects that are known to be clearly harmful.

Furthermore, we agree with the Administrator that requiring EPA to wait until it can conclusively demonstrate that a particular effect is adverse to health before it acts is inconsistent with both the Act's precautionary and preventive orientation and the nature of the Administrator's statutory responsibilities. Congress provided that the Administrator is to use his judgment in setting air quality standards precisely to permit him to act in the face of uncertainty. And as we read the statutory provisions and the legislative history, Congress directed the

Administrator to err on the side of caution in making the necessary decisions. We see no reason why this court should put a gloss on Congress' scheme by requiring the Administrator to show that there is a medical consensus that the effects on which the lead standards were based are *"clearly harmful to health."* All that is required by the statutory scheme is evidence in the record which substantiates his conclusions about the health effects on which the standards were based. Accordingly, we reject LIA's claim that the Administrator exceeded his statutory authority and turn to LIA's challenge to the evidentiary basis for the Administrator's decisions. . . .

LIA attacks the Administrator's determination that 30 μg Pb/dl should be considered the maximum safe individual blood lead level for children, maintaining that there is no evidence in the record indicating that children suffer any health effects that can be considered adverse at this blood lead level. As previously noted, the Administrator's selection was based on his finding that EP elevation at 30 μg Pb/dl is the first adverse health effect of lead exposure, and his determination that a maximum safe individual blood lead level of 30 μg Pb/dl will allow an adequate margin of safety in protecting children against the more serious effects of lead exposure anemia, symptoms of which appear at blood lead levels of 40 μg Pb/dl and central nervous system deficits which begin to occur at blood lead levels of 50 μg Pb/dl.

LIA challenges each of these findings. First, it contends that nothing in the record supports the suggestion that EP elevation at 30 μg Pb/dl is harmful to health, arguing that EP elevation is a mere "subclinical effect" a biological response to lead exposure which is without health significance, and noting that a number of its experts brought this matter to EPA's attention in their comments on the proposed standards. In LIA's view, the Administrator did not explain precisely how impairment of heme synthesis at blood lead levels of 30 μg Pb/dl adversely affects the health of children.[54] Second, LIA challenges the Administrator's determination that a maximum safe individual blood lead level of 30 μg Pb/dl is justified by the need to allow an adequate margin of safety in protecting children against anemia and central nervous system deficits. It maintains that the evidence in the record does not support the Administrator's conclusion that the blood lead threshold for the symptoms of anemia in children is 40 μg Pb/dl. LIA claims that this error was brought to the Administrator's attention by comments on the proposed standard, but that he failed to respond to these comments, thereby violating the statutory provision requiring him to respond to "significant comments, criticisms, and new data submitted . . . during the comment period [§307(d)(6)(B)]." Third, LIA contends that the preamble to the final regulations does not state the basis for the Administrator's finding that central nervous system deficits occur in children at blood lead levels of 50 μg Pb/dl, thereby precluding this court from being able to test the soundness of this determination. Finally, LIA argues that even if it were to concede that EPA's conclusions about the

---

54. In LIA's view, the first clearly adverse effect of lead exposure is anemia, which occurs in children at blood lead levels well in excess of 40 μg Pb/dl.

blood lead thresholds for anemia and central nervous system deficits are correct, there is still no explanation of why the Administrator concluded that a maximum individual safe blood level of 30 μg Pb/dl rather than 35 μg Pb/dl, for example is necessary to provide an adequate margin of safety against these effects.

Our review of the record persuades us that there is adequate support for each of the Administrator's conclusions about the health effects of lead exposure and, consequently, that LIA's challenges to the evidentiary support for these findings must be rejected. . . .

[The court then reviewed EPA's development and use of the criteria document and its reliance on medical and scientific opinion in determining that the maximum safe individual blood lead level should be no higher than 30 μg Pb/dl. In the course of considering each of LIA's contentions, the court observed:] LIA's challenge to the Administrator's findings concerning the health significance of EP elevation also stresses that this phenomenon is only a "subclinical" effect. But the clinical/subclinical distinction has little to do with the question whether a particular effect is properly viewed as adverse to health. Rather, the distinction pertains to the means through which the particular effect may be detected: observation or physical examination in the case of clinical effects, and laboratory tests in the case of subclinical effects. Thus describing a particular effect as a "subclinical" effect in no way implies that it is improper to consider it adverse to health. While EP elevation may not be readily identifiable as a sign of disease, the Administrator properly concluded that it indicates a lead-related interference with basic biological functions. Expert medical testimony in the record confirms that the modern trend in preventive medicine is to detect health problems in their "subclinical" stages, and thereupon to take corrective action. Moreover, as we have already noted, the Center for Disease Control uses the same "subclinical" effect as the key indicator of the need for medical intervention in its lead poisoning screening program. The accepted use of this "subclinical" effect to determine the need for medical observation or intervention properly influenced the Administrator's decision. . . .

To be sure, the Administrator's conclusions were not unchallenged; both LIA and the Administrator are able to point to an impressive array of experts supporting each of their respective positions. However, disagreement among the experts is inevitable when the issues involved are at the "very frontiers of scientific knowledge," and such disagreement does not preclude us from finding that the Administrator's decisions are adequately supported by the evidence in the record. It may be that LIA expects this court to conclude that LIA's experts are right, and the experts whose testimony supports the Administrator are wrong. If so, LIA has seriously misconceived our role as a reviewing court. It is not our function to resolve disagreement among the experts or to judge the merits of competing expert views. AFL-CIO v. Marshall, 617 F.2d 636, 651 & n.66 (D.C. Cir. 1979); cf. Hercules Inc. v. EPA, 598 F.2d 91, 115 (D.C. Cir. 1978) ("[c]hoice among scientific test data is precisely the type of judgment that must be made by EPA, not this court"). Our task is the limited one of ascertaining that the choices made by the Administrator were reasonable and supported by the record. Ethyl Corp. v. EPA, *supra*, 541 F.2d at 35-36. . . .

Both LIA and St. Joe argue that the Administrator erred by including multiple allowances for margins of safety in his calculation of the lead standards. Petitioners note that the statute directs the Administrator to allow an "adequate margin of safety" in setting primary air quality standards, and they maintain that as a matter of statutory construction the Administrator may not interpret "margin" of safety to mean "margins" of safety. In petitioners' view, the Administrator in fact did just this insofar as he made allowances for margins of safety at several points in his analysis. They argue that margin of safety allowances were reflected in the choice of the maximum safe individual blood lead level for children, in the decision to place 99.5 percent of the target population group below that blood lead level, in the selection of an air lead/blood lead ratio at 1:2, and in the Administrator's estimate of the contribution to blood lead levels that should be attributed to non-air sources. The net result of these multiple allowances for margins of safety, petitioners contend, was a standard far more stringent than is necessary to protect the public health. St. Joe suggests that EPA should have adopted an approach which required decisions on:

1) The maximum level of lead in air which is protective of health; i.e., a threshold beyond which the public health is not protected; and

2) An adequate margin of safety by which the level which is protective of health must be reduced.

EPA responds by maintaining that allowances for a margin of safety were made only at two points in its analysis: in the selection of a maximum safe individual blood lead level of 30 μg Pb/dl and in the decision to set a standard designed to keep 99.5 percent of the target population below that blood lead level. It argues that the statutory requirement of a margin of safety does not mandate adoption of the method suggested by St. Joe. Rather, EPA suggests, it indicates the precautionary orientation the Administrator is to bring to bear on the task of setting air quality standards. How conservative he must be in making particular judgments must, the Agency maintains, depend on such factors as the amount of uncertainty involved, the size of the population affected, and the severity of the effect. EPA argues that petitioners' claims about multiple allowances for margins of safety indicate that they have failed to recognize the difference between providing for a margin of safety and making a scientific judgment in the face of conflicting evidence.

We agree with the Administrator that nothing in the statutory scheme or the legislative history requires him to adopt the margin of safety approach suggested by St. Joe. Adding the margin of safety at the end of the analysis is one approach, but it is not the only possible method. Indeed, the Administrator considered this approach but decided against it because of complications raised by the multiple sources of lead exposure. The choice between these possible approaches is a policy choice of the type that Congress specifically left to the Administrator's judgment. This court must allow him the discretion to determine which approach will best fulfill the goals of the Act.

NOTES AND QUESTIONS

1. Do you think flexibility should be allowed at some point in the implementation of ambient air quality standards to mitigate the economic hardship on sources that may have to close down in order for their area to meet the standards? See Union Electric v. EPA, 427 U.S. 246 (1976), excerpted at p. 237 *infra*. How could the ambient air quality standards be set through an economic analysis that did take costs into account?

What criterion must the Administrator apply in deciding how strict to make a primary ambient standard? From what sources do Judge Wright and the EPA draw this criterion? Section 109(b) says the standards must be those "requisite to protect public health." What in the law constrains an Administrator whose imagination springs to life after only a whiff of evidence? Does the precautionary approach authorize the Administrator to set a strict standard based on a theory built on speculative inferences projecting a possible course of events in which widespread harm may occur unless a strict standard is promulgated?

Does §307(d)(9), governing the scope of judicial review, offer more meaningful constraints on EPA's discretion than the substantive provisions of §§108 and 109? Fourteen months after sustaining the ambient standards for lead against all challenges, the D.C. Circuit sustained EPA's relaxation of the ambient standards for photochemical oxidants (measured by ozone) from .08 ppm to .12 ppm hourly average. American Petroleum Institute v. Costle, 665 F.2d 1176 (D.C. Cir. 1981), *cert. denied*, 455 U.S. 1034 (1982). Citing, inter alia, §307(d)(9), the court said:

> These provisions of the Act assign this court a restricted role in reviewing air quality standards. Lead Industries Assn., Inc. v. EPA, *supra*. The Administrator's construction of the Act will be upheld if it is reasonable, id., and though it is our duty to undertake a searching and careful inquiry into the facts, our view of the evidence is not designed to enable us to second-guess the agency's expert decision maker. Id. Reversal for procedural defaults under the Act will be rare because the court must first find that the Administrator was arbitrary or capricious, that he overruled a relevant and timely objection on the point in question, and that the errors were so significant that the challenged rule would likely have been different without the error. [665 F.2d at 1441.]

2. The precautionary approach was first fully articulated in two landmark decisions, Reserve Mining Co. v. EPA, 514 F.2d 492 (8th Cir. 1975) (en banc), and Ethyl Corp. v. EPA, 541 F.2d 1 (D.C. Cir. 1976) (en banc), which will be discussed at length in Chapter 5, which deals with the regulation of hazardous substances. These opinions state the now generally accepted judicial view that whenever a statute instructs a regulator to protect the public from exposure to the danger (risk) of possible harm as opposed to harm certain to occur unless exposure is prevented Congress intended for the regulator to weigh subjectively the magnitude of the harm (if it did occur) against the probability that it will occur at all and decide what regulatory action is warranted in the light of the

seriousness of the danger (risk) presented. Since the precautionary standard in §109 gives the Administrator great leeway to set standards despite scientific uncertainty (almost as much as the statutes in *Reserve Mining* and *Ethyl*), why did the EPA apply such an elaborate and superficially precise methodology in selecting the ambient air quality standard for lead? Under the more permissive standard, EPA could have marshalled the existing studies, first to show "danger," so that the statutory standard was met, then to demonstrate that profound uncertainties existed in almost all the data. Having established these imponderables and uncertainties, EPA could then set ambient standards "requisite to protect the public health and welfare." Conceivably, in so doing the economic impact of the standard might influence the Administrator. Under Judge Wright's interpretation of the requirements of §§108 and 109, would this approach survive judicial review?

This approach was adopted by the EPA in promulgating standards under §211(c)(1)(A) for the phase-down of the lead content of gasoline. The statute simply authorized the Administrator to regulate the lead content of gasoline if he determined that emissions "will endanger" public health; it gave no guidance about how strict the standard had to be. Compared with the ambient standard-setting technique reviewed in *Lead Industries*, EPA's methodology for setting the gasoline lead content phase-down standard was free-wheeling and subjective. Yet it was sustained on judicial review in the *Ethyl* case, Judge Wright writing for the en banc majority.

Is it possible that by adopting a quantitative "scientific" approach to setting the ambient standard to lead EPA hoped to avoid political pressure to loosen its final standard? The political pressure on EPA was enormous before its earlier leaded gasoline standards were made final. J. Quarles, Cleaning Up America 117-142 (1977). Or is it likely that EPA felt more confident about using a quantitative approach than it did in the early 1970s? What effect, if any, might §§307(d)(4)(B) and 307(d)(5) and (6) have on the efforts of other agencies and of the White House to influence EPA rules, and on EPA's efforts to resist such influence? See American Petroleum Institute v. Costle, 665 F.2d 1176, 1192 (D.C. Cir. 1981), for an unsuccessful attempt by the Natural Resources Defense Council to raise an objection under §307(d)(4)(B)(ii) of undue White House influence on a revision of the ozone standard.

The EPA Scientific Advisory Board's Subcommittee on Scientific Criteria for Environmental Lead severely criticized the first two drafts of the EPA criteria document, which finally caused EPA to issue a substantially revised third draft. The Environmental Research, Development, and Demonstration Authorization Act of 1978, §8, 42 U.S.C. §4365, provides statutory authorization for the existing EPA Scientific Advisory Board. Is such outside scientific peer review likely to raise significantly the level of EPA analysis? Will peer review make EPA analysis more conservative, because of scientists' typical reluctance to come to firm conclusions in the face of uncertainty? Should such a panel have veto authority over EPA's proposed ambient standards? The D.C. Circuit held that §109(d) did not require approvals by the Clean Air Scientific Advisory Committee (CASAC) in American Petroleum Institute v. Costle, 665 F. 2d at 1188. Established by the 1977 amendments in §109(d), this seven-member independent advisory committee is to review ambient standards and criteria documents every five years. CASAC must publicly review any proposed EPA standard under §§109, 111, or 112. For a stinging accusation by the attorney (now law professor) who handled NRDC's case that the federal government relied only on industry-dominated scientific review throughout the lead standard-setting process, see Schoenbrod, Why the Regulation of Lead Has Failed, in Low Level Lead Exposure 259 (H. Needleman ed. 1980).

This concludes our examination of how the ambient standards for lead were set — just one of dozens of difficult decisions the Administrator of EPA had to make each year in the 1970s under the Clean Air Act. One last question: Would you like to be appointed Administrator of EPA?

A NOTE ON THE STANDARD-SETTING CONTROVERSY: IS EPA DRAGGING ITS FEET?

The Clean Air Act requires EPA to initiate a formal review of criteria documents and standards in 1980 and at least every five years thereafter. §109(d)(1). This review is critical. How stringent the standards are and whether standards are adopted for new pollutants, such as sulfates, has a critical effect on the scope of the clean air program and the demands it makes on polluters. For an argument that factors such as increased costs in urban areas and a reluctance to redesign implementation strategies has led EPA to reaffirm existing standards see Oren, Prevention of Significant Deterioration: Control-Compelling vs. Site-Shifting, 74 Iowa L. Rev. 1, 64-81 (1988). Oren claims EPA has reaffirmed standards even though the studies on which they were based were discredited. See also GAO, EPA's Standard Setting Process Should Be More Timely and Better Planned (1986).

Particulates. The primary total suspended particulates (TSP) standard was criticized because the terms in which it was expressed, weight per volume, unduly emphasized the larger, less dangerous particles. A region may not be in compliance, but for the wrong reason; heavy particulates are usually swallowed rather than breathed deeply into the lungs. Conversely, an area may be in compliance, but its TSP may still pose serious health risks if the particulates are very small. Tiny inhalable particles penetrate deeply into the lungs and remain there longer. Moreover, these particles usually result from fossil fuel combustion or petroleum processing byproducts and include a number of trace metals (for example, lead, vanadium, and manganese), polycyclic organic compounds, and sulfate and nitrate aerosols. Fine particulates may cause cancer and genetic and fetal injury.

A new inhalable particulate standard replaced the existing TSP standard and covers particles less than 10 millionths of a meter in diameter (μm or microns). See 52 Fed. Reg. 24,634 (1987). In response to claims by CASAC that the new standard would not protect visibility, which is particularly affected by fine particles, EPA has solicited comments on a standard for particles of less than 2.5 micrometers. Id. at 24,670. Particulate diesel vehicle emissions are also a growing problem (see section E *infra*).

Sulfur dioxide. The sulfur dioxide standards have been affirmed, although EPA may later adopt a one-hour standard to take account of recent controlled human exposure studies indicating that short-term exposure can be harmful. 18 Envt. Rep. (BNA): Current Developments 2525 (1988). See 53 Fed. Reg. 14,926 (1988). Despite mounting evidence that sulfate and nitrate aerosols resulting from SO_2 and NO_x transformation cause cancer when breathed, contribute to acid rain, and impair visibility EPA has not adopted a sulfate or sulfuric acid NAAQS. In its proposed rule making on the sulfur dioxide standard, EPA stated that a regulatory program for acid rain would be premature because of scientific uncertainty. Id. at 14,936.

The secondary standard for SO_2 was the only first-generation NAAQS to be challenged in court. In Kennecott Copper Corp. v. EPA, 462 F.2d 846 (D.C. Cir. 1972), the court remanded for a fuller justification that would "enlighten" the court about the basis of the proposed 60 $\mu g/m^3$ standard. While the Administrative Procedure Act required only a "concise general statement," the court remarked that "[t]here are contexts, however, contexts of fact, statutory framework and nature of action in which the minimum requirements of the Administrative Procedure Act may not be sufficient" (462 F.2d at 850). Does *Kennecott Copper* help explain why the criteria document for lead and the justification for the lead standard in the Federal Register are so detailed? After *Kennecott Copper*, EPA withdrew the proposed SO_2 secondary standard for lack of evidence and has never reproposed it.

Nitrogen oxide. EPA affirmed its nitrogen oxide standard in 1985. 16 Envt. Rep. (BNA): Current Developments 269 (1985). See 50 Fed. Reg. 25,532 (1985). Although short-term exposure to nitrogen oxide can be harmful, EPA again deferred action on a short-term standard even though the 1977 amendment required action on a short-term standard within one year.

Carbon monoxide. The primary carbon monoxide standard has been retained but EPA dropped the secondary standard because it found there were no known secondary effects on vegetation or materials from carbon monoxide at ambient levels. 16 Envt. Rep. (BNA): Current Developments 859 (1985). EPA also believes the primary standard adequately addresses high-altitude effects of carbon monoxide. The diminished availability of oxygen may aggravate the effects of carbon monoxide at high altitudes.

Ozone. In 1979 EPA abandoned its broader approach to photochemical oxidants and focused exclusively on ozone controls. It relaxed the one-hour primary and secondary ozone standards from .08 ppm to .12 ppm. As noted, the relaxation was upheld on judicial review in *American Petroleum Institute*. EPA revoked the hydrocarbon standard as technically inadequate. 48 Fed. Reg. 628 (1983). Although HC is still considered a primary cause of ozone, the atmospheric transformation process is too complex to ensure that attainment of any single HC standard would also cause the ozone standard to be attained.

The appropriate level for the ozone standard is debatable because of uncertainties about effects, the cost of compliance, and the difficulties in attaining the existing standard. The ozone NAAQS is currently under active review and criteria documents have been prepared. Although the current secondary standard is the same as the primary standard, concern is expressed in the criteria documents that ozone has adverse secondary effects on crops and forests at allowable ambient levels. See EPA, Air Quality Criteria for Ozone and Other Photochemical Oxidants (1986). See also Krupnick, Economics and the Ambient Ozone Standard, Resources, Summer, 1988, at 9.

Note that for some pollutants the secondary standard has been dropped or is the same as the primary standard. What does this indicate about air quality, air pollution, and the basis for the air quality program in the Clean Air Act? Read again the definition of the "welfare" effects protected by secondary standards in §302(h). EPA has also proposed that it will drop its long-standing policy and take costs into account in setting secondary standards. 49 Fed. Reg. 10417 (1984).

E.   EMISSIONS STANDARDS IN THE CLEAN AIR ACT

To complement ambient standards, the Clean Air Act also calls for emissions standards. Emissions standards are direct federal limitations on the emissions that all members of a category of sources can discharge into the atmosphere. In contrast to the health-based ambient air quality approach, most emissions standards are "technology-based" or "technology-limited," because they require EPA to determine the technical and engineering feasibility of pollution control by sources that utilize similar production processes. With its feasibility studies as its guide, EPA must then set performance-oriented standards that specify the quantity of pollutant that may be emitted per unit of product, raw material, or fuel input. Under various statutory formulas, such as "best technical system adequately demonstrated" and "least achievable" emissions rates, the standards pressure the regulated sources to make steady improvements in pollution control by installing emissions control technologies and by changing to fuels, raw materials, and manufacturing processes that emit less pollution.

Although attainment of the ambient standards was enshrined as the overall goal of the 1970 Clean Air Act, Congress subjected all new mobile and stationary sources to uniform federal emissions standards. It tightened the existing controls on mobile sources and added sections for stationary sources. New Source Performance Standards (NSPS) for conventional pollutants were based on technological achievement in controlling emissions and are often viewed as the Clean Air Act's best example of a technology-limited standard (§111). The National Emissions Standards for Hazardous Air Pollutants (NESHAP) were based on protecting health, with little or no regard for cost or technological achievement.

Thus uniform performance-oriented federal emissions standards do not necessarily have to be purely technology-based. Later, in 1977, Congress clarified both the mobile source and the NSPS provisions.

Emissions standards have become an important centerpiece of the air quality program in the 1980s. The acid rain problem, which is traced to sulfur dioxide emissions from stationary sources; the ozone problem, which is largely attributed to motor vehicle pollution; and the global warming problem, which is caused in part by motor vehicle carbon monoxide pollution, have concentrated attention on the emissions standards problem.

1.   Motor Vehicle Emissions Standards

Motor vehicles are heavy contributors to air pollution. EPA estimated in 1985 that they contributed 70 percent of total carbon monoxide emissions, 34 percent of hydrocarbon emissions, and 45 percent of nitrogen oxide emissions nationwide. Despite substantial emission controls, motor vehicles still contribute the same percentage of emissions that they did before emission controls went into effect. A rise in the number of motor vehicle miles travelled and an aging of the motor vehicle rate due to longer vehicle retention rates have offset the reductions achieved through emission standards. This section will not chronicle, battle by battle, the prolonged emission wars that have taken place in Congress, EPA and the courts, but will outline the major issues raised by the motor vehicle emission problem and how they have been resolved.

a.   From the Goals of 1970 to Contemporary Realities

Emission controls for motor vehicles date from the 1965 Motor Vehicle Air Pollution Control Act, as amended by the 1967 Air Quality Act. Standards adopted under this legislation were expressed in grams of pollutant emitted per mile travelled by the vehicle (gpm) for the "big three": hydrocarbons, carbon monoxide, and nitrogen oxides. The standards took effect for the automobile industry's 1968 model year, i.e., in the early fall of 1967. The 1968 standards were short-lived. Evidence that vehicular emissions were likely to cause serious damage to health was accumulating steadily; public concern about air pollution kept pace. The 1970 Clean Air Act established new, stringent motor vehicle emissions control goals. For discussion of the health effects of motor vehicle pollution see Air Pollution, The Automobile, and Public Health (A. Watson, R. Bates & D. Kennedy eds. 1988).

The 90 percent rollback objective. In 1970 Congress stunned automobile manufacturers by ordering them to curtail new vehicle emissions of HC and CO by 90 percent within five years and NO_x within six years. The 90 percent rollback provoked a fierce debate over feasibility, cost, and the automobile industry's capacity for innovation.

Because the 90 percent rollback continues to be the national objective for emissions control, it is worth inquiring into how it was set. Anxious not to allow Democratic senator and presidential hopeful Edmund Muskie to capture all of the political support of the environmental movement, the Nixon Administration moved quickly in 1970 to propose a 90 percent reduction in vehicle emissions by 1980. The proposal was based on the straightforward notion that since ambient levels of CO, HC, and NO_x in Chicago and Los Angeles were roughly five times the "safe" levels identified in studies prepared under the 1967 legislation, an 80 percent rollback (with an additional 10 percent added to take account of growth in vehicle use and for some continued use of older, more polluting vehicles) would make the air safe everywhere in the nation. H.R. Rep. No. 1196, 91st Cong., 2d Sess. 24-27 (1970).

Yet Democratic senator Gaylord Nelson threatened to steal the limelight from both the Republican administration and Senator Muskie. He proposed banning the internal combustion engine by 1975, a symbolic gesture that received much press coverage. Not to be outdone, Muskie used his position as chairman of the pollution subcommittee of the Senate Committee on Public Works to fashion a bill that included the Nixon administration's 90 percent rollback, but with Nelson's 1975 deadline. Congress ultimately enacted Muskie's bill into law. J. Krier & E. Ursin, Pollution and Policy 203 (1977). Did the 90 percent rollback apply to the emissions levels resulting when vehicles had no pollution control equipment installed at all, or did it require a 90 percent reduction in addition to any emissions reductions required under existing standards? For discussion of how the baseline of emissions on which the 90 percent reduction was computed, see W. Rodgers, Environmental Law: Air and Water §3.24 (1986). But see Currie, The Mobile Source Provisions of the Clean Air Act, 46 U. Chi. L. Rev. 811, 816-817 n.36 (1979).

Congress appeared to ignore the automobile manufacturers' contention that there was no emissions control technology in existence that could meet the new standards and that such a technology could not be brought into existence by the statutory deadline. In rejecting their argument, Congress adopted the principle that if protection of the public health and welfare required it, strict standards might be necessary that would give industry an overwhelming incentive to invest in the necessary research and development, literally forcing an acceleration in the pace of technological innovation. The new "technology-forcing" approach departed radically from the prior legislative policies of all levels of government, which ordinarily conceded that technical feasibility and impossibility set limits beyond which pollution control did not have to go. The concept of technology-forcing, which also affects other portions of the Clean Air Act, is discussed at pp. 210-222 *infra*.

To implement technology-forcing, the Act contained sanctions that prohibited the sale of noncomplying vehicles and provided a $10,000 penalty for the sale of each noncomplying vehicle, a measure that critics promptly labeled a "hydrogen bomb" deterrent. Jacoby & Steinbruner, Salvaging the Federal Attempt to Control Auto Pollution, 21 Pub. Poly. 1, 3 (1973). In retrospect, however, it is clear that Congress never intended to allow the automobile industry to shut down if it could not produce the requisite technology. Even Senator Muskie conceded that Congress would act to forestall such a possibility. 116 Cong. Rec. 32,905 (1970). The Act itself provided that the EPA Administrator could extend the 1975 deadline for HC and CO to 1976 and the 1976 deadline for NO$_x$ to 1977.

Retreat from the 1970 goals. For over a decade, the automobile industry has successfully combatted technology-forcing through congressional amendments, lawsuits, and administrative challenges. The chronicle of national vehicle emissions standards fills thousands of pages of congressional testimony, technical studies, rule-makings, and scholarly analyses. This intriguing, sometimes disappointing story lays bare wider issues regarding the role of government in stimulating and channeling technological development. Is Congress capable of using complex technical information to fashion sound public policy? The mobile source emissions problem has spawned a great deal of commentary. See, e.g., R. Crandall, H. Gruenspecht, T. Keeler & L. Lave, Regulating the Automobile (1986), critically reviewed in Book Review, 95 J. Pol. Econ. 438 (1987); L. White, The Regulation of Air Pollution from Mobile Sources (1982).

The internal combustion engine and public policy. The battle over emissions control pitted the manufacturers, who in less than a generation had created an enormous and successful industry, against a loose coalition of environmental and consumer interests that believed that the conventional internal combustion engine was finally producing much-diminished social benefits. The critics urged the manufacturers to show their capacity for innovation once again to design cars and engines not for power, size, and appearance but for emissions control, fuel economy, and safety. That was not all. Many believed that the problem of mobile source air pollution required, as Senator Nelson suggested, a broader national effort to develop alternative power supplies, to improve public transportation, to change traffic patterns and land uses to reduce pollution, and to reduce public dependence on the automobile.

The automobile industry could not have been less prepared to respond. Technically, the internal combustion engine itself was not impervious to change. Emissions are a function of vehicle size, type of fuel, and the design of the vehicle's crankcase, carburetor, combustion chamber, exhaust system, and gear ratio; each component can be substantially reconfigured to reduce emissions. But other factors blinded Detroit to these possibilities. The auto manufacturers comprised an oligopoly that thrived on performance innovation, unlike, for example, the electrical utility industry. Emissions reductions might impair performance. As a concentrated industry of a few huge companies, basic innovations such as scaling down the size of cars or redesigning engines threatened to introduce uncertainty about market share and production lead times that could cost hundreds of millions if the decision to innovate went awry.

Fear of the untoward consequences of innovation drove the industry to adopt extreme measures that rapidly undermined its public image. In the end, a mixture of government and market forces stimulated the industry to embrace smaller, less-polluting, fuel-efficient autos. Yet when Congress acted in 1970, the industry was several years away from change. As a result, it proposed a "technological fix" for air pollution that was entirely consistent with its policy of innovation by the smallest possible increments, its lack of belief that over the long run Congress would actually insist on strict motor vehicle pollution controls, and its plan to fight the 90 percent rollback. Each manufacturer proposed to develop the catalytic converter, an exhaust system add-on that despite its many imperfections continues to be a central element in the technical strategy to reduce emissions. The converter possesses two characteristics that prompted Detroit to adopt it in the first place. It need not affect basic engine design; it can be abandoned at low cost in the event Congress has a belated change of heart. For a discussion of engine options that go far beyond simply retooling the internal combustion engine, see p. 224 *infra*.

A mini-history of delayed federal emissions standards. This chapter will not chronicle, battle by battle, the prolonged emissions wars that have taken place in Congress, EPA, and the courts. The federal tactic of fight and retreat began in 1972 when EPA Administrator Ruckelshaus refused to grant the major automobile manufacturers a one-year extension of the 1975 HC and CO standards. The three major auto companies challenged that decision in International Harvester Co. v. Ruckelshaus, 478 F.2d 615 (D.C. Cir. 1973), a watershed decision in which Judge Harold Leventhal glossed the concept of technology forcing, defined the scope of judicial review of scientifically complex decisions under the Act, and explored the reorientation of the relationships between EPA, the scientific community, and the courts that Congress had wrought in the Clean Air Act. The court remanded for further proceedings because the manufacturers appeared to have established that the technology was not available and because the EPA test data was at variance with data generated by the National Academy of Sciences under a statutory mandate to issue a recommendation on the extension. See D. Currie, Air Pollution §§2.21-2.24 (1981), and Leventhal, Environmental Decision Making and the Role of the Courts, 122 U. Pa. L. Rev. 509 (1974). On remand, the EPA decided to grant the one-year extensions for both the HC and the CO standards but promulgated interim standards for 1975. Perhaps stung by the *International Harvester* decision, the EPA later granted a one-year extension of the 1976 NO_x deadline without a fight.

As Figure 3-2 shows, the original 1975 deadline for a 90 percent reduction of HC emissions to .41 gpm was further delayed until 1980 (recall that this was the Nixon Administration's original proposed deadline), after EPA granted two waivers and Congress two extensions. Similarly, Figure 3-3 illustrates how the original 1975 deadline for a 90 percent reduction of CO emissions to 3.4 gpm fell prey to four EPA waivers and two congressional extensions. The new deadline for a 90 percent rollback of CO emissions for all vehicles was set for 1983.

Recall that the deadline set in 1970 for a 90 percent rollback of NO_x emissions was 1976. After the 1973 EPA waiver and a congressional extension in 1974, Congress voted in 1977 to drop a firm deadline for a 90 percent rollback and decided instead on a less stringent NO_x 1 gpm standard by 1981, subject to various waivers through the 1984 model year (see Figure 3-4).

Trains, planes, vessels, and evaporative hydrocarbons. There are no emission standards for trains, airplanes, seagoing vessels, construction equipment, or

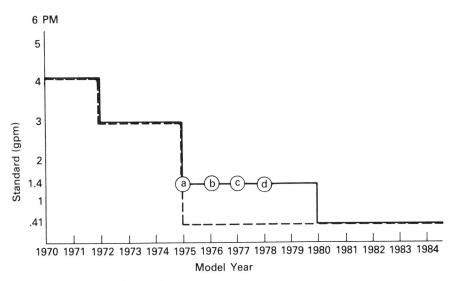

Note: In Figures 3-2, 3-3, and 3-4:

——————— the standard actually enforced after EPA and congressional extensions.
— — — — — the standard contemplated by Congress as of 1970.

a. In 1973 EPA extended the 1975 deadline to 1976, and it adopted an interim standard for 1975.
b. In 1974 Congress extended the 1976 deadline to 1977.
c. In 1975 EPA extended the 1977 deadline to 1978.
d. In 1977 Congress extended the 1978 deadline to 1980.

FIGURE 3-2
Hydrocarbon Emissions Standard

farm machinery, which contribute relatively small amounts of HC, CO, or NO_x to the nation's air pollution problem. The Clean Air Act does empower EPA, however, to regulate aircraft emissions (§§231-234). See D. Currie, Air Pollution §§2.49, 2.50 (1981). Because gasoline is so volatile, non-exhaust emissions that evaporate during fueling need to be minimized. See 40 C.F.R. pt. 87.

Trucks and other large vehicles. So far we have been discussing only automobile emission standards for "light duty vehicles," defined in *International Harvester* to mean passenger cars only, not light trucks. (478 F.2d at 638-640). Light trucks include campers and recreational vehicles; heavy duty vehicles (i.e., in excess of 6,000 pounds) include trucks, buses, and off-highway vehicles (§§202(a)(3)(F), 202(b)(3)(C)). EPA has separate emissions standards for light duty trucks and heavy duty vehicles. See D. Currie, Air Pollution §§2.09, 2.26, 2.29, 2.30 (1981).

As amended in 1977, the Clean Air Act requires heavy duty vehicles to reduce HC and CO emissions 90 percent by 1981 and NO_x emissions 75 percent by 1985. §202(a)(3)(A)(ii). The 90 percent and 75 percent reductions are to be computed using as a basis of comparison emissions from heavy duty vehicles manufactured in 1979, free of emissions controls. See also §§202(a)(3)(B),

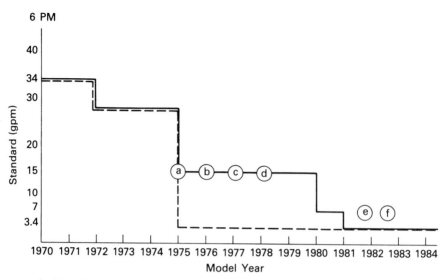

a. In 1973 EPA extended the 1975 deadline to 1976. EPA also adopted an interim standard,
    effective 1975.
b. In 1974 Congress extended the 1976 deadline to 1977.
c. In 1975 EPA extended the 1977 deadline to 1978.
d. In 1977 Congress extended the 1978 deadline to 1981. Congress also adopted an interim
    standard, effective 1980.
e. Pursuant to the terms of the 1977 Clean Air Act Amendments, EPA granted waivers for about
    thirty percent of all 1981 and 1982 automobiles.
f. The automobile industry has lobbied Congress for return to the 1980 interim standard of 7
    gpm.

FIGURE 3-3
Carbon Monoxide Emissions Standard

202(a)(3)(E). Furthermore, EPA has mandated a 90 percent HC and CO reduction for light trucks by 1985.

    California. California occupies a unique status in the field of auto emissions control. Los Angeles was the first major city to face up to massive air pollution caused by the automobile. As a result, California enacted legislation in 1959 mandating motor vehicle emission standards. J. Krier & E. Ursin, Pollution and Policy 103 (1977). California emissions standards have generally led the country by two to five years, and are generally lower than the federal standards. Federal emission standards preempt all state standards, but California may escape preemption by applying to the Administrator. Unless Congress extends the California exemption to other states, it must ultimately make the decision on whether to make auto emission controls more stringent. Compare Currie, Air Pollution, *supra*, at §2.52) (arguments for preemption are at their strongest for mobile sources), with Krier & Ursin, Pollution and Policy, *supra*, at 341-344 (Congress should reconsider its policy of preempting state controls on new motor vehicles).

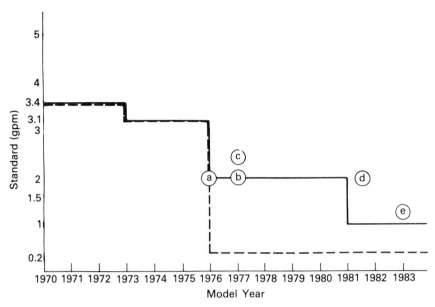

a. In 1973 EPA extended the 1976 deadline to 1977, and it adopted an interim standard, effective 1976.
b. In 1974 Congress extended the 1977 deadline to 1978.
c. In 1977 Congress dropped a firm deadline for 90 percent reduction of NO_x emissions; a new deadline was set for 1981 with a new standard of 1.0 gpm. The 90 percent reduction of NO_x was kept in the Clean Air Act as a "research objective."
d. In the 1977 amendments EPA granted waivers to American Motors Co. (as a small manufacturer) for model years 1981 and 1982, not to exceed 2 gpm. EPA also granted waivers for most diesels for model years 1981-1984, not to exceed 1.5 gpm.
e. The automobile industry has lobbied Congress for return to the 1976 interim standard of 2 gpm.

FIGURE 3-4
Nitrogen Oxides Emissions Standard

The emissions problem today. The stand-off on emission reductions continued through the 1980s as congressional efforts to amend the Clean Air Act stalled, but important technological changes occurred as emission controls tightened. There are two types of catalytic converters. The two-way converter controls only for CO and HC. The three-way converter adds controls for nitrogen oxides. Effective operation of the three-way converter requires more precise control of air-fuel mixtures, so these converters are responsible for improved air-fuel management systems as well as the development of electronic controls.

Today, almost all cars and light duty trucks are equipped with catalytic converters, and the vast majority are equipped with three-way converters. Fuel injection has increased to where it is installed on three-fourths of all new light duty vehicles, and the automobile industry has undergone a revolutionary shift from mechanical to electronic controls. These technological advances have allowed emissions to be lowered while fuel economy has improved. Technology continues to evolve. Fast flames, compact combustion chambers, lean air to fuel ratios and substantially modified powerplants that can accept alternative fuels are on the horizon. See Walsh, Critical Analysis of the Federal Motor Vehicle Control Program 30-34 (Report prepared for Northeast States for Coordinated Air Use Management, 1988). Walsh claims emission control strategy is available to reduce HC standards to 0.25 gpm and 0.4 gpm for nitrogen oxides while retaining the CO standard but improving emissions under cold temperatures. Id. at xii. Industry, of course, disagrees. See Sierra Research, Inc., The Feasibility and Costs of More Stringent Mobile Source Emission Controls (U.S. Office of Technology Assessment, 1988).

b.   Forcing Technology: Setting Emissions Standards for Diesel Engines

Diesel engines are an attractive engine alternative because they provide about 35 percent more miles per gallon. Their superior fuel economy makes them attractive for use in buses and heavy duty trucks. Diesels emit less CO and HC than gasoline engines but more NO_x and many times more small particulates. This is why trucks and buses contribute 80 percent of particulate emissions from motor vehicles. Some of these particulates are coated with carcinogenic compounds. Diesels illustrate the high environmental costs that may accompany modern technological advances and the unrelenting challenge to produce an appropriate regulatory response. See National Academy of Sciences, Diesel Cars: Benefits, Risks, and Public Policy (1982).

Congress did not set emission standards for diesel engines in the Clean Air Act but delegated this function to EPA. This provides EPA and the courts an opportunity to determine how much technology-forcing the Act permits in the setting of emission standards. Despite the importance of heavy duty diesel trucks in the emission of particulate emissions, EPA dragged its feet on this issue for years and finally published emission standards for heavy duty diesel trucks only after a court order. The case that considered the validity of these emission standards follows:

NATURAL RESOURCES DEFENSE COUNCIL v. THOMAS
805 F.2d 410 (D.C. Cir. 1986)

WALD, Chief Judge:

The Clean Air Act Amendments of 1977 mandated for the first time emissions reduction for heavy duty motor vehicles. Congress required the Environmental Protection Agency to set standards for both gaseous and particulate matter emissions. After years of delay, and pursuant to an order of the District Court for the District of Columbia, the agency issued a notice of proposed rulemaking in 1984, and finally promulgated regulations to reduce heavy duty motor vehicle emissions in 1985. Raising a variety of substantive and procedural challenges, the Natural Resources Defense Council and the Engine Manufacturers Association petitioned this court for review of those regulations, the former arguing, essentially, that the standards were too lenient, the latter maintaining, predictably, that the standards were too stringent. We find that the agency has in the main acted reasonably in interpreting the substantive mandate of the law, but find that in two instances the agency failed to follow the appropriate statutory procedure. Therefore, we affirm in part, and reverse and remand in part.

I.   Background

A.   CONGRESSIONAL ACTION

The regulations under attack in this case represent one aspect of a twenty year old quest by Congress for effective motor vehicle emissions reduction. Responding to a national outcry for air pollution control, the Clean Air Act Amendments of 1965 first authorized the Environmental Protection Agency (agency or EPA) to regulate heavy duty vehicle (HDV) emissions. By the mid-1970s little had been done, however, and in 1977 Congress enacted a detailed, mandatory set of standards (Clean Air Act Amendments of 1977 or 1977 amendments) to effect emissions reduction from HDVs.[2]

At issue here are the provisions requiring emissions reduction of oxides of nitrogen (NO_x) and of particulate matter (PM). Along with carbon monoxide and hydrocarbons, oxides of nitrogen are a type of gaseous emission that Congress set out to reduce in three statutory provisions. First, Congress installed interim, less stringent standards; it required the agency [by statute] to prescribe regulations for model years 1979 to 1982 that

> contain standards which reflect the greatest degree of emission reduction achievable through the application of technology which the Administrator determines will be available for the model year to which such standards apply, giving appropriate consideration to the cost of applying such technology within the period of time available to manufacturers and to noise, energy, and safety factors associated with the application of such technology.

§202(a)(3)(A)(i).

Second, Congress established a specific target for later reductions: . . . [The court quoted §202(a)(3)(A)(ii).]

Third, subparagraph (B) of the same section, which authorizes the EPA to promulgate revised standards for gaseous emissions and is the source of much of

---

2. . . . . "Heavy duty vehicle" is defined as a truck, bus, or other vehicle weighing more than 6,000 pounds. §202(b)(3)(C). "Light duty vehicle" (LDV) is defined as any "passenger car or passenger car derivative capable of seating 12 passengers or less." 40 C.F.R. §86.082-2 (1985). The issues in this case relate to HDVs only.

the controversy in this case, provided for periodic revision of the NO_x standards: . . . [The court quoted §202(a)(3)(B).]

Congress also provided in the 1977 amendments for PM reduction: . . . [The court quoted §202(a)(3)(A)(iii), which is similar to the section for initial NO_x standards.]

Finally, the amendments instituted nonconforming penalties (NCPs), whereby a manufacturer can pay a tax on its engines that fail to meet the standards (dirty engines), rather than pull those engines off the market: . . . [The court quoted §202(g)(1).]

B.   AGENCY ACTION

The agency fell behind the statutory timetable, almost from the beginning. . . . [Suit was brought to compel the agency to act. The court ordered publication of proposed NO_x and PM standards by October 15, 1984, and the agency complied with the order.]

Finding that the specified NO_x reduction in §202(a)(3)(A)(ii) could not be met by diesel engines, the agency proposed a revised NO_x standard of 6.0 grams per brake horsepower-hour (g/BHP-hr) for all 1987 and later model year vehicles, and of 4.0 g/BHP-hr for all 1990 and later model year vehicles. 49 Fed. Reg. at 40,267-40,268. Both diesel and gasoline engines were to meet this diesel-based standard. 49 Fed. Reg. at 40,267.

With regard to PM, the agency proposed a 0.60 g/BHP-hr standard to be effective for model years 1987 through 1989. 49 Fed. Reg. at 40,263. For 1990 and later model year vehicles, the agency proposed a 0.25g/BHP-hr PM standard. The EPA explained that the 1990 but not the 1987 standard would probably require the use of trap-oxidizers[10] to reduce PM emissions. The agency also proposed that manufacturers be allowed to demonstrate compliance with the 1990 standard by averaging emissions levels across engine families.[11]

The official public comment period remained open through December 17, 1984. In addition to the heavy volume of written comments received, the agency

---

10. A trap-oxidizer consists of a trap (or filter) that catches particulate matter in the exhaust gas stream, and a mechanism to oxidize (burn) the collected particulate matter in order to regenerate the trap and thereby maintain its collection efficiency. Such devices are (or soon will be) widely used on LDVs, but are only in the developmental stage for HDVs. See part III *infra*.

11. The agency describes emissions averaging as follows:

A participating manufacturer would be required to determine emission limits (subject to ceilings. . . .) for each heavy-duty engine family to be produced in a given model year. This family emission limit would serve as the effective standard by which EPA would determine compliance of all engines within the family.

The participating manufacturer's year end sales and power-weighted average . . . of all engine families' emissions would then be required to comply with the applicable . . . standard.

50 Fed. Reg. 10,606, 10,633 (1985). See part II.B. *infra*.

held two public hearings, in Ann Arbor, Michigan, on November 13 and 14, and in Denver, Colorado, on November 15.[12]

On March 15, 1985, the agency promulgated, inter alia, final NO_x and PM standards. With regard to the revised NO_x standards, the agency agreed with manufacturers' comments that 1987 was too soon for the 6.0 g/BHP-hr standard to be instituted, and that a 1990 4.0 g/BHP-hr standard was both too soon and too stringent. Accordingly, the agency set final NO_x standards at 6.0 g/BHP-hr by 1988, and 5.0 g/BHP-hr by 1991.

With regard to the PM standards, the agency agreed with manufacturers that more time was needed for the 0.60 g/BHP-hr standard, and accordingly delayed the adoption of this target until 1988. Similar concerns led the agency to delay the adoption of the 0.25 g/BHP-hr PM standard until 1991. However, the agency found that a 0.10 g.BHP-hr standard would be feasible by 1994, and promulgated such a standard.

Finally, the agency adopted an emissions averaging program for the 1991 NO_x standard and for both the 1991 and 1994 PM standards.

C. PRESENT LITIGATION

On May 17, 1985, the NRDC and various environmental groups, as well as the Engine Manufacturers Association (EMA) and several individual manufacturers, filed petitions (Nos. 85-1294 and 85-1296, respectively) in this court for review of various provisions of the March 15, 1985, final rule. Specifically, the NRDC argues that the NO_x and PM standards should have been based on the capability of the "technological leader" and that the emissions averaging program usurps the role of the NCPs. Intervenor California, in No. 85-1294, maintains that the NO_x revised standards should have been based on the capability of the lower polluting gasoline engine.

The EMA contends that the PM standards should not have been technology-forcing but rather should have been based upon "adequately demonstrated technology." It also argues that the EPA's methodology with regard to the PM standards was faulty. . . .

We now affirm the challenged regulations except for the effective date of the near-term NO_x standards.

---

12. More than 150 different manufacturers, environmental groups, state and local governmental units, and individual citizens submitted materal to the public docket during the comment period. Not surprisingly, the manufacturers tended to observe that the proposed levels were too high, or that not enough lead time had been granted; the environmental groups and state and local governmental units tended to remark that the standards were not high enough. The comments and the agency's responses to them, with regard to all of the elements of the NPRM, can be found at 50 Fed. Reg. 10,606, 10,609-44 (1985).

II.   *Substantive Challenges*

A.   MUST HDV EMISSIONS STANDARDS BE BASED SOLELY ON THE CAPABILITY OF THE TECHNOLOGICAL LEADER?

1.   NO$_x$ REVISED STANDARDS

The NRDC's main argument is that the EPA failed to set HDV emissions standards at levels based on the capability of the technological leader in the industry, thereby running afoul of congressional intent. In reviewing an administrative agency's construction of its own enabling statute, we must follow the now familiar dictates of Chevron U.S.A. Inc. v. Natural Resources Defense Council, Inc., 467 U.S. 837 (1984). . . . Accordingly, we may reverse the agency's interpretation only if it is either contrary to a clear congressional mandate or if it is an unreasonable construction of that mandate.

The NRDC first maintains that the statutory language for both NO$_x$ and PM emissions reduction mandates that the agency set standards based not on what the engine manufacturing industry as a whole can meet, but rather on what the most advanced engine, i.e., the technological leader, is capable of achieving. The NO$_x$ and PM emissions reduction provisions that the NRDC relies on read, respectively, as follows:

> In revising any [NO$_x$] standard . . . , the Administrator shall determine the maximum degree of emission reduction which can be achieved by means reasonably expected to be available for production of such period and shall prescribe a revised emission standard in accordance with such determination. . . .
>
> [PM] regulations shall contain standards which reflect the greatest degree of emission reduction achievable through the application of technology which the Administrator determines will be available for the model year to which such standards apply, giving appropriate consideration to the cost of applying such technology within the period of time available to manufacturers and to noise, energy, and safety factors associated with the application of such technology.

§§202(a)(3)(B), (a)(3)(A)(iii).

The NRDC contends that by using the words "maximum" and "greatest" before the phrase "degree of emission reduction," in the NO$_x$ revised standards provision and the PM standards provision, respectively, Congress expressly indicated its intention that HDV emissions reduction standards be set at the performance level of the engine capable of achieving the "maximum" or "greatest" emissions reduction, i.e., the technological leader. However, the NRDC's focus on the words "maximum" and "greatest" is too narrow. Both the NO$_x$ revised standards provision and the PM standards provision, as quoted above, demand that the "maximum" or "greatest" "degree of emission reduction" be calculated in the context of other factors. The revised NO$_x$ standards provision does not specify these factors, but does state that the "maximum degree of emission reduction" be one that "can be achieved by means reasonably expected to be available for production for such period." §202(a)(3)(B). A separate provision requiring the agency to make certain findings before issuing a revised NO$_x$ standard does, however, specify two factors to be balanced against emissions reduction capability. It states that before issuing a revised NO$_x$ standard the Administrator

> must find that compliance with the emissions standards otherwise applicable for such model year cannot be achieved by technology, processes, operating methods, or other alternatives reasonably expected to be available for production for such model year without increasing cost or decreasing fuel economy to an excessive and unreasonable degree.

§202(a)(3)(C).

The PM standards provision, likewise, demands that "appropriate consideration" be given "to the cost of applying such technology within the period of time available to manufacturers and to noise, energy, and safety factors associated with the application of such technology." §202(a)(3)(A)(iii). The thrust of both the NO$_x$ revised standards provision and the PM standards provision, as well as the separate findings requirement for NO$_x$ revised standards, is to require a balancing of emissions reduction capability against several other factors, such as cost, noise, energy, and safety.

The NRDC agrees that a balance must take place, but maintains that it must occur within the confines of the technological leader. That is, the NRDC believes that the statute requires the agency to determine which engine can achieve the greatest emissions reduction, ascertain what level of emissions would result from that reduction, and then ratchet the standard back up to account for cost and other factors as they affect that leading engine. We find, however, nothing in the language of the provisions quoted above to indicate that Congress mandated such a leader-specific balancing of all the relevant factors in emissions reduction. Since the law was obviously meant to affect the whole industry, the more natural reading of the provisions as a whole is that Congress intended the balancing of emissions reduction capability versus cost and other factors to be done on an industry-wide basis, taking into account the broad spectrum of technological capabilities as well as cost and other factors. To read these provisions as mandating a standard that balances all the relevant statutory factors within the framework of one engine rather than on an industry-wide basis would be a sufficiently novel interpretation as to require laser-like clarity on the part of Congress. Under basic statutory construction principals of clear statement, we certainly cannot imply such an interpretation from the language cited above.

Perhaps recognizing the insubstantiality of its textual argument, the NRDC maintains that language in the 1977 House Report discussing the authority to revise NO$_x$ standards specifically mandates a technological leader standard. . . . [The Report discussed language from the International Harvester decision indicating the court's concern that standards would be set by the "laggard's" technological capability rather than that of the "technological leader."

NRDC also relied on other language in the Report to support its claim. The court concluded:]

While the NRDC's reading of the House Report may be a plausible one, it is not necessarily the only one. The EPA contends that the thrust of these House Report passages is to eliminate the possibility of laggard-based standards, and that the technological leader concept was introduced mainly as a contrast, to ensure that standards were set at a level geared to what the more progressive manufacturers could achieve. According to the EPA, the sections require only the best balance of emissions reduction, cost, safety, and fuel efficiency that a predominant segment of the industry can meet. This construction is a reasonable one, and if an agency's statutory interpretation is reasonable, then congressional intent cannot be clearly to the contrary. . . .

The NRDC has put together a scenario that may convince sympathetic viewers that if one engine can be considered the leader, all other engines, however they differ in noise, safety, fuel efficiency, or cost, must be required to match that leading engine's performance. We find, however, that the EPA's variant interpretation that its multifactored statutory mandate can be satisfied only if the final standards account for emissions reduction, noise, safety, fuel efficiency, and cost on an industry-wide level is also reasonable. In those circumstances Chevron requires that we defer to the agency.

2.   PM STANDARDS

. . . [The court rejected for the same reasons an argument made by NRDC for leader-based PM standards.]

D.   MUST THE PM STANDARDS BE BASED ON ADEQUATELY
     DEMONSTRATED TECHNOLOGY?

Petitioner EMA argues that the EPA inappropriately adopted technology-forcing PM standards for 1991 and 1994, disregarding Congress' intent that such standards be based on adequately demonstrated technology.[30] The EPA claims that no party raised this argument below. . . . However, in order to pass on the

---

30. Intervenor International Harvester attempts to enlist Sierra Club v. Costle, 657 F.2d 298 (D.C. Cir. 1981), to show that trap-oxidizer technology for HDVs is not adequately demonstrated. Indeed, Sierra Club did conclude, in a detailed footnote, that dry scrubbing could not be considered an adequately demonstrated technology, and some of the concerns of that court would be equally pressing here were we to confront squarely the issue of whether trap-oxidizer technology for HDVs is adequately demonstrated. However, because we hold, *infra*, that the agency properly set technology-forcing PM standards, we need not determine whether the current state of trap-oxidizer technology would suffice to meet a non-technology forcing standard.

This analysis is based on an assumption that all parties appear to share, namely that a standard cannot both require adequately demonstrated technology and also be technology-forcing. The agency describes technology-forcing standards as those that "are to be based upon that technology which the Administrator determines *will* be available, and not necessarily that technology which is *already available*. The adoption of such standards helps to encourage and hasten the development of new technology." 49 Fed. Reg. 40,258 (1984) (emphasis in original).

EMA's methodological challenges to the PM standards, see part III, *infra*, we must first decide on the appropriate interpretation of the statutory authority for those standards. In that context, and for that reason, we examine the EMA's statutory arguments.

The EMA points to what it considers a critical difference between the more liberal NO_x revised standards provision, which looks to the "means reasonably expected to be available for production," and the more stringent PM standards provision, which requires the Administrator to determine the technology that "will be available." §202(a)(3)(B) [and] (a)(3)(A)(iii). The EPA responds, correctly in our opinion, that both guidelines level their sights on the future, permitting the agency to set standards based on projections of technology that is not currently available. The PM standards provision, on its face, does not constrict the agency to technology that is "now" available. Even if there is a theoretical distinction between the agency's expert prediction that something "will be available" and its "reasonable expectation" of availability, it is hardly a bright enough line for courts to enforce. . . . [The court also concluded that the legislative history did not support EMA's contention.]

III.   PM Methodological Challenges

The EMA challenges the methodology that the EPA used to set the PM standards in five areas. It argues that trap-oxidizers have not been shown to be sufficiently durable, that a safe oxidizing agent for trap-oxidizers has yet to be found, that a trap plugging problem remains unsolved, that the level of the PM standards inadequately reflects in-use engine deterioration, and that lab to lab measurement variability was overlooked. . . . [The court rejected all of these objections. The discussion on durability follows:]

A.   DURABILITY

A trap-oxidizer (trap), which catches particulate emissions and then burns them up at a high temperature, must last over the lifetime of a HDV, which is

---

On the other hand, an adequately demonstrated technology "is one which has been *shown* to be reasonably reliable, reasonably efficient, and which can reasonably be expected to serve the interests of pollution control without becoming exorbitantly costly in an economic or environmental way." Essex Chemical Corp. v. Ruckelshaus, 486 F.2d 427, 433 (D.C. Cir. 1973) (emphasis added), *cert. denied*, 416 U.S. 969 (1974). That the provisions at issue in this case seek to promote technological advances while also accounting for cost does not detract from their categorization as technology-forcing standards. As we pointed out in NRDC v. EPA, 655 F.2d 318, 328 (D.C. Cir.), *cert. denied*, 454 U.S. 1017 (1981):

> The legislative history of both the 1970 and the 1977 amendments demonstrates that Congress intended the agency to project future advances in pollution control capability. It was "expected to press for the development and application of improved technology rather than be limited by that which exists today." S. Rep. No. 1196, 91st Cong., 2d Sess. 24 (1970), *reprinted in* 1 Legislative History 424. . . .

projected at 150,000 miles. The question raised by the EMA here is whether various extrapolations by the EPA are an adequate substitute for actual experience of HDVs with trap-oxidizers over the requisite mileage. General Motors (GM) successfully tested a dump truck with a trap over 50,000 miles, see 50 Fed. Reg. 10,606, 10,626 (1985), and Mack Trucks tested a trap on a HDV for 6,000 miles. The EMA contends, however, that neither 50,000 miles on a dump truck nor 6,000 miles on a HDV can be extrapolated to 150,000 miles on a HDV and that GM noted that the driving conditions the dump truck underwent were not representative of a normal driving cycle. The EPA's response is a familiar one, representative of its reaction to all of the EMA's methodological challenges: "[T]rap feasibility in some future year does not require that traps be fully developed today." The statute, as we have discussed, permits technology-forcing for PM standards; therefore, it must permit reasonable extrapolations. An issue, of course, remains as to what constitutes reasonable extrapolations.

The EPA cites, in addition to the 50,000 mile sojourn of the GM dump truck and the 6,000 mile trek of the HDV, a Daimler-Benz (the trap leader) test with a bus over 100,000 miles, see 50 Fed. Reg. 10,606, 10,626 (1985); the EMA objects and the EPA acknowledges that traps will be easier to keep functional for buses than for trucks.

The EPA also cites an independent contractor's assessment that successful LDV trap technology can be extrapolated to HDVs; the EMA argues that this study was based on the fragmentary evidence cited above, not on any independent HDV tests. Finally, the EPA relies on opinions expressed by Daimler-Benz, Volvo White, and the Manufacturers of Emissions Control Associates, that trap-oxidizers will be feasible by 1991.

These five pieces of evidence are understandably not totally reassuring to the industry. But our task stops with an assessment of the reasonableness of the agency's decision given the evidence it had before it.[37] Here we have reasonable extrapolations from some reliable evidence, not wispy hopes based on no evidence at all. Even the independent study does provide evidence supportive of HDV trap feasibility, though it was not based on an actual HDV trap test.

The agency, utilizing discretion based upon its expertise, has reached a plausible conclusion regarding the potential for developing durable trap-oxidizers that we cannot reject as arbitrary. . . .

[The court also held that EPA violated the statute by not giving the industry four years lead time before the revised NO_x standard went into effect.]

---

37. See, e.g., Environmental Defense Fund v. EPA, 598 F.2d 62, 83-84 (D.C. Cir. 1978); Ethyl Corp. v. EPA, 541 F.2d 1, 28 (D.C. Cir.) (footnotes omitted), cert. denied, 426 U.S. 941, (1976): . . . . Where a statute is precautionary in nature, the evidence difficult to come by, uncertain, or conflicting because it is on the frontiers of scientific knowledge, the regulations designed to protect the public health, and the decision that of an expert administrator, we will not demand rigorous step-by-step proof of cause and effect. . . . The Administrator may apply his expertise to draw conclusions from suspected, but not completely substantiated, relationships between facts, from trends among facts, from theoretical projections from imperfect data, from probative preliminary data not yet certifiable as "fact," and the like.

NOTES AND QUESTIONS

1. *The dynamics of technological innovation.* EPA frequently is required to set standards predicated on the agency's assessment of the likely future course of technological development. The path from theoretical concept to marketable device passes through a welter of overlapping phases: concept, design, laboratory prototype construction, laboratory testing, in-service reliability testing, and mass production. By using the lead time concept, Congress can instruct EPA to allow more time when technology has made less progress down the path of development. The inefficiency of crash research and development programs, the uncertainty about how many firms could comply at all, the likelihood that Congress would be asked to relent at the last moment, and the possibility that a hurriedly developed technology would not perform well all support the lead time concept. Where precisely on the continuum of development do you place diesel particulate control technology?

2. *The concept of technology-forcing.* The court in *Thomas* held that EPA could impose a technology-forcing standard. Does the court's emphasis lie on merely projecting and predicting future development or on pressing and motivating the manufacturers to do better? To help to answer this question, consider the following:

> Early federal efforts in the field of air pollution tried to attack the engineering problem through public funding of research and development projects. It was assumed that equipment would be used if it were available. But as it became recognized that the owner of a pollution source did not have a natural incentive to install abatement equipment even when available, federal legislation moved into a second phase, requiring installation by federal enforcement. In this second phase, however, it was still assumed that the responsibility to develop new equipment lay with the Government rather than the polluter. Thus, federal laws requiring installation of available equipment were accompanied by a stepped-up effort to solve the engineering problem through federal research and development.
>
> Eventually it was recognized that government resources alone could not solve the engineering problem, nor was the problem being solved by other means. In fact, there was every incentive for a polluter *not* to solve it, just as there was every incentive not to install pollution control equipment already in existence. This led to the third phase of legislation, which directly confronted the policy problem of who bears the responsibility, and endorsed the concept of "technology-forcing." The polluter, it was decided, has the responsibility not only to install needed equipment, but also to invent it. This makes sense for a number of reasons. The polluter is likely to have far greater knowledge of the cause of the problem, the best ways to abate it, and the most efficient ways of integrating the potential solutions into normal business practices. The competitive system normally discourages any individual polluter from voluntarily undertaking additional expenses for the sake of pollution control. But this new approach can be used to encourage individuals (whether owners of pollution sources or independent entrepreneurs) to search for solutions. If a government-imposed emission limit is scheduled to take effect on a certain date, the one who finds a solution has a ready-made market for his invention. [J. Bonine, The Evolution of Technology-Forcing in the Clean Air Act, 6 Envt. Rep. (BNA) Monograph No. 21, at 2 (July 25, 1975).]

Senator Muskie's Subcommittee on Pollution of the Senate Committee on Public Works rather quickly evolved the concept of technology-forcing over the summer of 1970. The automobile emissions standards, already mildly technology-forcing, were the first to be rewritten. In the summer of 1970, emissions reduction goals first envisioned for 1980 became hard and fast 1975 standards. The final debate on the Senate floor left no doubt that if by the 1975 model year some or all of the auto manufacturers could not meet the standards, they might not be able to market their automobiles.

Other sections of the Muskie bill soon incorporated the logic of technology-forcing as well. Primary ambient air quality standards now had to be achieved within a strict three-year deadline, instead of within a "reasonable time," which would have allowed technological and economic feasibility to be considered in preparing the state implementation plans. The Senate report stated that sources on which emissions limitations had been imposed in order for states to achieve the ambient standards "should either meet the standard of the law or close down." S. Rep. No. 1196, 91st Cong., 2d Sess. 2-3 (1970). Tests of technical and economic feasibility were also removed from the section regulating hazardous pollutants. The only major sections to be included in the law that explicitly allowed technology and costs to be taken into account were the provisions governing standards for new stationary sources (§111) and for diesel vehicles. In explaining the conference committee agreement to the Senate, Senator Muskie said, referring particularly to automobiles, "Predictions of technological impossibility, of infeasibility were not considered sufficient reasons to avoid tough deadlines, and thus to compromise the public health." 116 Cong. Rec. 32,902 (1970). See also S. Rep. No. 1196, 91st Cong., 2d Sess. 24 (1970).

In the intervening years before the 1977 amendments, judicial opinion and scholarly interpretation provided a more considered rationale for the philosophy that hastily had been conceived in the summer of 1970. Consider South Terminal Corp. v. EPA, 504 F.2d 646, 675 (1st Cir. 1974): "Minimum public health requirements are often, perhaps usually, set without consideration of other economic impacts. . . . Congress had already made a judgment . . . , and EPA and the courts are bound." See also D. Currie, Air Pollution §2.51 (1981); La Pierre, Technology-Forcing and Federal Environmental Protection Statutes, 62 Iowa L. Rev. 771 (1977).

In 1977, Congress did not reexamine the technology-forcing concept but instead focused once again on the type of threat or injury that would trigger Clean Air Act regulation. In 1977 the precautionary "endanger" standard was placed in all of the major standard-setting provisions to govern the threshold determination about whether to regulate. The House did reiterate, however, that the purpose of all the major sections of the Act was to encourage the development of new technology. H.R. Rep. No. 294, 95th Cong., 1st Sess. 50-51 (1977). Congress's concern in 1977 with the health risks posed by a variety of hazardous air pollutants raises the question of whether EPA was somehow supposed to be especially solicitous of health, even in exercising the wide latitude in "policy judgment" Judge Leventhal said that the agency possessed in setting technology-based standards. The House report appears to suggest that it should. For another view, see Davis, Kurtock, Leape & Magill, The Clean Air Act Amendments of 1977: Away from Technology-Forcing? 2 Harv. Envtl. L. Rev. 1 (1978).

3. *Technology-forcing and the diesel case.* The court's views on technology-forcing in *Thomas* should be compared with its views on the availability of the trap oxidizer for light-duty vehicles in NRDC v. EPA (*Diesel I*), which is discussed in the *Thomas* case. In *Diesel I*, NRDC argued that EPA should set a graduated standard for particulates by imposing stricter and more costly requirements on low-polluting vehicles. The court rejected this claim by noting that a graduated standard would give the more loosely regulated, highly polluting models a regulatory advantage. The court also noted that Congress had imposed a unitary standard when it adopted emission limitations for gasoline-powered motor vehicles. Is the industry leader argument advanced in *Thomas* a replay of NRDC's argument in *Diesel I*? *Thomas* allowed EPA to base its standards on an industry-wide average that took "balancing" into account. Is this consistent with *Diesel I*?

Diesel I also upheld EPA standards requiring the use of a trap oxidizer, again on scanty evidence that they could be produced in time. The standard was delayed in 1984 because of continuing problems with this technology. 49 Fed. Reg. 3,010 (1984). Manufacturers then stopped making diesel passenger automobiles and blamed their decision on EPA's standards. See 14 Envt. Rep. (BNA): Current Developments 2186 (1984). The trap oxidizer saga is not yet over. Manufacturers presently claim they can meet EPA's 1991 standards for trucks without using a trap oxidizer. 19 Envt. Rep. (BNA): Current Developments 395 (1988). Whether the technology can be developed is still in doubt. Operators of public transit buses have petitioned EPA to roll back the 1991 standards because of trap oxidizer problems. See also 52 Fed. Reg. 21,075 (1987) (EPA proposes delay in particulate standards for light-duty diesel trucks).

What does all this say about technology-forcing? Proposals are presently before EPA to allow manufacturers of heavy-duty vehicles to meet the diesel standards through banking and trading emission reductions. Is this a reasonable way to implement technology-forcing? Refiners may also be required to lower the sulfur content of diesel fuel, which will make the diesel standard easier to meet. 18 Envt. Rep. (BNA): Current Developments 2287 (1988).

4. *Technology-based standards and ambient conditions.* What is the connection between the severity of the injury that particulates may cause and the stringency of technology-based standards? Congress did not distinguish between taking health risks into account in determining whether to regulate at all and taking health risks into account in determining how strict to make the standard. Health thus becomes another factor to consider, along with technological exigencies, costs, and (if §202(a)(3)(A)(iii) applies) safety, energy consumption, and noise.

Another line of reasoning supports taking impacts on health into account in setting technology-based standards by addressing the concept of technology-

forcing itself. Setting a technology-forcing standard necessarily involves judgments about how hard and how rapidly to press for improved emission controls.
Assessing the importance of rapid developments requires considering the health
risks technology is being "forced" to reduce. A precise formulation of this point
appeared in Sierra Club v. Costle, 657 F.2d 298 (D.C. Cir. 1981), in which
Judge Wald speculated that the Administrator cannot decide meaningfully how
much marginal pollution reduction to require at very high levels of control —
at which each new increment of pollution control secures much less pollution
reduction than the preceding one — without examining whether the small pollution control gain is worth its high cost in terms of health protection "purchased." Thus marginal investment in pollution control becomes a surrogate
dollar measure of the marginal health gains that progressively stricter regulation
might "buy." Judge Wald was addressing the problem of how strict EPA could
make NSPS for coal-fired electrical generating plants under §111, but her point
applies here. Even if the statute does not explicitly require that health be considered in setting technology-based standards, it may be impossible for the Administrator to exclude it entirely from his judgment.

5. *Judicial review of technology-forcing.* In *Thomas,* the court applied the
traditional arbitrary and capricious standard of judicial review and did not vary
it because of the technology-forcing issues presented by the diesel standards. The
court took a different approach in *Diesel I.* It held that reviewing courts should
demand a more thorough and persuasive agency justification for its technology-
forcing regulations if the lead time is short, if all of the technology is not available, and if compliance with the agency's decision depends upon advances at the
frontier of scientific knowledge.

Diesel I approved a more indulgent judicial review standard when EPA
regulated potentially harmful pollutants because this decision required a large
element of policy choice that could not be "demonstrably" correct. Does it make
sense for a court to be more indulgent when fewer facts are available, as in cases
when EPA decisions on the NAAQS are reviewed, and less indulgent when
factually rich engineering feasibility determinations are made?

The *Diesel I* approach may be foreclosed by *Chevron,* on which *Thomas*
relied. If this approach is not foreclosed, does the history of the Clean Air Act
suggest a different standard of judicial review for technology-forcing?

c.   Federal Quality Control and Enforcement of Vehicle Standards

Motor vehicle emissions standards must be enforced to be effective, and
here EPA's record is mixed. Although catalytic converters are required to last for
50,000 miles or five years, §202(d)(1), data show that properly maintained cars
exceed federal standards by 30,000 miles and are well over the federal standards
during their expected lifetimes. Part of the problem is with federal enforcement,
which has been severely cut back in recent years. Since 1980, for example, EPA's

recall investigations of light duty vehicles have been reduced by 67 percent. Walsh, *supra*, at 57.

Certification of prototype vehicles. The Clean Air Act requires each new vehicle sold to be certified that it meets emissions standards. To obtain federal certification, a manufacturer must submit a prototype of its new model vehicles to EPA for testing. See §206(a). If the prototype meets the emissions standards, EPA provides a certificate of conformity approving the prototype for mass production. The actual testing is ordinarily performed by the manufacturer itself, in accordance with detailed test procedures, although EPA may conduct confirmatory tests itself. The difficulty with the certification program is that it must deal with prototype cars, which may even be hand-made, in an artificial environment that assumes very careful maintenance, perfect driving conditions, and the like. As a result, cars that pass the prototype test may not perform well in use, and modifications in the test procedure are required. For criticism of the certification program see Regulating the Automobile, *supra*, at 90 (manufacturers can obtain waivers, postponements or changes to avoid plant closings that would follow a sales ban on production).

Assembly line testing. If a sample of vehicles taken off the assembly line should fail an emissions test, EPA may revoke the certificate of conformity. The Act makes plain the manufacturers' right to obtain judicial review of an EPA decision to revoke a certificate of conformity. §206(b)(2)(B)(i)-(iv).

In United States v. Chrysler Corp., 591 F.2d 958 (D.C. Cir. 1979) the court held that although the Plymouth Valiants and Dodge Darts involved plainly met emissions standards, the parts installed in these autos were not precisely the same as those named in the certificates of conformity and therefore the government was entitled to the civil penalties it had assessed earlier against Chrysler (591 F.2d at 960).

Recalls. The Clean Air Act authorizes EPA to recall entire classes of vehicles when "a substantial number of any class or category of vehicles or engines, although properly maintained, do not conform to" applicable standards. §207(c). General Motors Corp. v. Ruckelshaus, 742 F.2d 1561 (D.C. Cir. 1984) (en banc), *cert. denied*, 471 U.S. 1074 (1985), held that EPA could interpret this language to provide for "classwide remedies of classwide defects." EPA could thus require manufacturers to recall and repair all members of a recall class even though some vehicles would have exceeded their natural lives. The court disapproved an EPA plan that allowed a manufacturer to offset pollution from a nonconforming class by attaining more-than-required emissions from future model years. The court held that offsets would not remedy the nonconformity of the recall vehicles. It concluded that Center for Auto Safety v. Ruckelshaus, 7457 F.2d 1 (D.C. Cir. 1984), requires recall and repair as the only statutory remedy for nonconformity.

To be eligible for recall, vehicles must be properly maintained and used. When can a manufacturer argue that the automobile owner is responsible for excessive emissions? See Chrysler Corp. v. EPA, 631 F.2d 865 (D.C. Cir.) *cert. denied*, 449 U.S. 1021 (1980): "If design defects make 'proper maintenance' so

difficult that even Chrysler dealers do not perform it, then such 'proper maintenance' is beyond the reach of the average car owner. Use of a laboratory-pure
standard of 'proper maintenance' is contrary to the 'actual use' standard of the
Act." 631 F.2d at 889.

Tampering and fuel-switching. Under §203 of the Act, EPA may also prosecute manufacturers, dealers, service facilities, and fleet owners (e.g., car rental
companies, large corporations, and city governments) that disconnect or tamper
with pollution control devices or use leaded fuel in catalyst-equipped vehicles.
Tampering is extensive. An EPA survey found 22 percent of vehicles tampered
and 29 percent arguably tampered. R. Greco, Motor Vehicle Tampering Survey
1984 (EPA, 1984). Tampering is inevitable with a bolt-on technology like the
catalytic converter. Is there any way to prevent it in a do-it-yourself society?

Defect warranty. Section 207(a) requires manufacturers to provide purchasers with defect warranties that cover the design and workmanship of emissions control components. The warranty remains in effect for the statutory useful
life of the vehicle. If a covered defect causes the vehicle to exceed the emissions
standards during that period, the manufacturer must make the necessary repairs
at no cost to the owner. Manufacturers also must warrant (for two years or 24,000
miles) that if a vehicle that has been maintained and used in accordance with
the manufacturer's instructions fails an emissions test in a properly enforced state
inspection and maintenance program, the manufacturer will repair the vehicle
at no cost to the owner. §207(b). These provisions create a warranty relationship
between the manufacturer and the vehicle owner, but importantly, EPA has the
power to enforce the warranty provision and to prosecute manufacturers who fail
to honor valid claims (40 C.F.R. §85). See Motor Vehicle Manufacturers Association v. Costle, 647 F.2d 675 (6th Cir. 1981).

Automotive Parts Rebuilders Assn. v. EPA, 720 F.2d 142 (D.C. Cir.
1983), upheld EPA's requirement that manufacturers warrant all components
affecting emissions rather than the narrower category of all parts integral to emissions for the first 24-month or 24,000-mile warranty period. EPA could also
require manufacturers liable for the failure of dealers to honor or redress warranty
claims because Congress intended manufacturers to be liable for a broad performance warranty. Specialty Equipment Market Assn. v. Ruckelshaus, 720 F.2d
124 (D.C. Cir. 1983), upheld EPA regulations governing the certification of
after-market parts under §207(a)(2). The court held in part that the scope of the
certification program could extend to parts affecting emissions as well as primary
parts. See Ostrov, Controlling Automobile Pollution Through Manufacturers'
Performance Warranties, 61 U. Det. J. Urb. L. 65 (1983).

d.   Alternatives to the Internal Combustion Engine and Technology-Forcing

Recall that some critics argued that the manufacturers' choice of the catalytic converter was a problem-plagued, exceedingly timid response to the mandate of technology-forcing and that it delayed for many years the development

of more imaginative solutions to the vehicle emissions problem. The converter increased engine output of NO_x and in its early years appeared to increase sulfates, enmeshing EPA in doubt and delay for many months. See L. Lynn, Designing Public Policy 326-365 (1982).

Alternative engines and technologies. Attention focused for some time on the development of alternative engines. Stratified charge, fuel-injected, electric, gas turbine-powered, and rotary engines can meet statutory emissions standards without the use of catalytic converters. Stratified charge, fuel-injected, and rotary internal combustion engines have considerably better emissions performance, in some cases without necessitating add-on pollution controls.

Electric cars emit no pollutants, are quieter, and conserve petroleum-based fuels. However, the lead batteries used in most prototypes are heavy, low in power output, and have a range of 50 miles or less between charges. Although they could be recharged during times of day when power plant demand is low, electric vehicles nevertheless would increase power plant total loadings and electric power utilization inefficiencies.

The development of alternative engines has waned as attention has been directed toward improvements in the internal combustion engine noted earlier. Some claim that the automobile has been reinvented in the last 15 years. The following excerpt describes an important new lean-combustion system that is under development:

> An important engine emission control system under development is the lean combustion system. This system uses a closed-loop microprocessor in conjunction with lean mixture sensor and an oxidation catalyst. This alternate emission control approach achieves good fuel economy (potential 10-15 percent improvement) and also meets the emission standards. . . . In this lean operating region, the engine needs a different sensor design to provide feedback, and also a highly turbulent fast-burn combustion system so that slow flame speed and misfires do not cause emissions and driveability problems. Toyota has developed and marketed such a system but not yet in the United States. [Air Pollution, The Automobile, and Public Health, *supra*, at 48.]

In 1969 the Justice Department brought suit against the Big Four (GM, Ford, Chrysler, and American Motors), charging them with conspiring to eliminate competition in the development of vehicle emissions control devices. The result of this unsavory episode was a consent decree that, until 1981, restrained the Big Four from entering into joint ventures to develop emissions control technologies. Under a relaxation of the consent decree obtained by the Reagan Administration (the Carter Administration favored the same relaxation), the companies may now cross-license, pool patents, publicize research efforts, and otherwise coordinate their emissions control research. 12 Envt. Rep. (BNA): Current Developments 856 (1981); 12 Envt. Rep. (BNA): Current Developments 963 (1981). Do you think this relaxation of anti-trust policy will improve the manufacturers' performance in emissions control? John Kenneth Galbraith has argued, in The New Industrial State (1967), that the complex technologies that underpin the auto industry (and, indeed, all of modern industrial society) need long lead times for product development and a guaranteed consumer response once marketing begins. Does Galbraith's theory explain Detroit's behavior? Does it suggest a better emissions control policy?

Fuel economy standards. Congress has chosen the path of strict, detailed regulation to achieve its mobile source emissions reductions goals. Minimum miles per gallon (mpg) rules are part of this strategy, and Congress legislated a corporate average fuel economy (CAFE) in the Automobile Fuel Efficiency Act of 1980, 15 U.S.C. §§2001-2112. The law provides civil penalties for violations. §2008. Substantial progress was made under the law until the Reagan Administration, which slowed fuel economy improvement. The Bush Administration reversed a Reagan decision for more slowdown soon after taking office. For discussion of the program see Regulating the Automobile, *supra*, ch. 6. Gas guzzler taxes are also added to each car that fails to achieve a given fuel economy. Internal Revenue Code, §1016(d).

Alternative fuels. The use of alternative fuels as a means of reducing motor vehicle emissions has received considerable attention in recent years. Methanol and natural gas are receiving the most attention. Interest in these fuels has increased because of their potential for reducing emissions, especially ozone emissions, and because their manufacture would use surplus agricultural crops. Studies so far indicate that the impact of the use of these fuels on emissions is uncertain. Ozone formation may be depressed, but the extent to which this occurs may vary by metropolitan area. These fuels also create new hazards. Methanol is both toxic and flammable and natural gas also has flammability problems. See Congressional Research Service, Alternative Fuel for Motor Vehicles: Some Environmental Issues (1988). EPA has established emission standards for methanol-powered vehicles. 19 Envt. Rep. (BNA): Current Developments 2339 (1989). Ethanol, another alternative fuel, may produce less emissions of carbon monoxide. Congressional Research Service, Ethanol Fuel and Global Warming (1989).

Emission fees. Section 205 authorizes EPA to impose a penalty of "not more than" $10,000 on each new motor vehicle that does not meet federal emissions standards. In 1975, a law student proposed using §205 to impose a penalty that would reflect the social costs imposed by each noncomplying vehicle. The penalty, as best it could be calculated, would include the health, property, and other environmental injuries that excess emissions would cause (or the amount the manufacturer should have spent on the vehicle to attain the standard). The vehicles could continue to be sold as long as the incentive penalty was paid for each vehicle marketed. Book Review, 5 Ecology L.Q. 212, 219 (1975). Roger Strelow, then EPA Assistant Administrator for Air Programs, picked up on the student's idea but was unsuccessful in getting the agency to adopt the proposal. Strelow estimated that the "emissions fees" would range from a few dollars to over $300 per vehicle (Strelow, A Solution for Auto Pollution, Washington Post, Jan. 2, 1977, at C-8, col. 3).

Similar but more elaborate vehicular emissions fee proposals have also been suggested. See F. Anderson, A. Kneese, P. Reed, R. Stevenson & S. Taylor, Environmental Improvement through Economic Incentives 56 (1977); Willis & White, Government Policies toward Automotive Emissions Control, in Approaches to Controlling Air Pollution 348 (A. Friedlaender ed. 1978); J. Krier & E. Ursin, Pollution and Policy 96, 193-195, 284-287 (1977) (Los Angeles smog tax). The argument for such proposals focuses on their flexibility, economic efficiency, and superiority in inducing desired behavioral changes without detailed regulation.

Costs and benefits. Substantial uncertainty still exists about both the extent of harm caused by mobile source air pollution and the extent of public support for a radical improvement in air quality if pollution control means high-priced autos or severe additional economic impacts on a vital industry that has been ailing for several years. For an argument that the costs of control exceed the benefits see Regulating the Automobile, *supra,* at 109-115. Would a "two-car strategy" by which low-emissions vehicles would be required to be sold in heavily polluted areas, be more cost-effective? See L. Lave & G. Omenn, Clearing the Air 33 (1981).

2.   Performance Standards for New Stationary Sources

The Clean Air Act also provides for the setting of technology-limited standards applicable to new and modified stationary sources that increase air pollution or emit a new air pollutant. See the definition of a new source in §111(a)(2). Is there a threshold? The extension of "new source" review to modified sources is critical because it sweeps changes in operation in existing sources into new source review programs. EPA has defined modification as "any physical or operational change to an existing facility." 40 C.F.R. §60.14(a). How far does this stretch? See National-Southwire Aluminum Co. v. EPA, 838 F.2d 935 (6th Cir. 1988) (turning off pollution control equipment is modification); Hawaiian Electric Co. v. EPA, 723 F.2d 1440 (9th Cir. 1984) (change to fuel containing more sulfur than allowed by existing permit is modification).

The idea of using uniform national emissions standards dates back to the hearings on the 1967 amendments. The Senate bill did not distinguish between new and existing sources. The reasons offered in support of emissions standards included (1) the unreliability of ambient standards (enforcement, inability of regional monitors to pick up local "hot spots"), (2) elimination of regional pollution havens, (3) the inability of states to take necessary action, (4) the rapidity with which emissions standards could be adopted, (5) simplicity of enforcement, (6) due consideration of economic and technical factors, (7) the mobile source standards provided useful experience on which to pattern stationary source standards, and (8) atmospheric transport of pollutants to distant polluted areas would be reduced. Air Pollution: Hearings on S1821-0-A before Subcomm. on Air and Water Pollution of the Senate Comm. on Public Works, 90th Cong., 1st Sess. (pt. III), 762, 766-767, 791-793, 1153-1156 (1967). What counterarguments do you imagine were offered?

Read §111. What steps does this section require in setting new source performance standards? For an authoritative analysis of §111, see D. Currie, Air Pollution, ch. 3 (1981), and Currie, Direct Federal Regulation of Stationary Sources under the Clean Air Act, 128 U. Pa. L. Rev. 1389 (1980).

Technology-forcing and NSPS. Are §111 NSPS technology-forcing? The §111 requirement that technology be "adequately demonstrated," taking various costs into account, seems on its face to preclude technology-forcing that would require a higher level of performance than current technology is capable of producing. Is technology-forcing relegated to the §111(j) seven-year waiver for use of innovative emission control technology?

Earlier cases do not shed much light on technology-forcing under §111. Portland Cement Association v. Ruckelshaus, 486 F.2d 375 (D.C. Cir. 1973), indicated that Congress did not require a technology to be in routine use before it could be adopted. To be "adequately demonstrated" meant to be "available" at a future date when the technology may reasonably be expected to be installed and to work: "Section 111 looks toward what may fairly be projected for the regulated future, rather than the state of the art at present" (486 F.2d at 391-392). This is hardly an explicit mandate for technology-forcing since there is no hint that EPA could add a "margin for striving" on top of its forecast of routine technological development. See also National Lime Association v. EPA, 627 F.2d 416 (D.C. Cir. 1980)(remand of lime and lime hydrate industry NSPS because EPA failed to show that the standard was "achievable" for the industry as a whole). This decision, reminiscent of the court's acceptance of the worst-car approach in the diesel emissions case, again narrows the concept of technology-forcing in setting NSPS. See generally D. Currie, Air Pollution §3.10 (1981); Currie, Direct Federal Regulation of Stationary Sources under the Clean Air Act, 128 U. Pa. L. Rev. 1389, 1412-1417 (1980); Davis, Kurtock, Leape & Magill, The Clean Air Act Amendments of 1977: Away from Technology-Forcing? 2 Harv. Envtl. L. Rev. 1, 16 (1978). As a matter of law, which do you think permits EPA to "force" technological development more vigorously — §202(a), at issue in the diesel emissions case, or §111?

NSPS and existing sources. Read §111(d) carefully. What gap in the Clean Air Act scheme is the subsection designed to plug? Does §111(d) give EPA added flexibility to choose among the ambient, hazardous (§112), nondeterioration, and new source standards? EPA has dragged its feet in implementing this provision, and has approved plans for existing sources in only a few states. See D. Currie, *supra*, §§3.19-32.25.

NSPS for coal-fired electrical generating facilities. Sierra Club v. Costle, 657 F.2d 298 (D.C. Cir. 1981), sustained the most complex and controversial NSPS EPA has ever set. The old standard allowed emissions of 1.2 lbs. of SO_2 for every million (M) British Thermal Units (Btu) of heat the coal could produce when burned (1.2 lbs/MBtu). This standard could be met simply by burning coal that was naturally low in sulfur content. Under the new standard, SO_2 emissions were limited to a maximum of 1.2 lbs/MBtu, and a 90 percent reduction of potential uncontrolled SO_2 emissions is required except when emissions to the atmosphere are less than 0.60 lbs/MBtu. When SO_2 emissions are less than 0.60 lbs/MBtu, potential emissions must be reduced by no less than 70 percent. As a result, the NSPS requirements for percentage reduction of SO_2 removal vary on a sliding scale ranging from a minimum of 70 percent to a maximum of 90 percent. The 70 percent floor necessarily means that utilities will have to employ some form of flue gas desulfurization (or "scrubbing") technology. In wet scrubbing, exhaust gases in the stack are sprayed with absorbent chemicals, which react with the SO_2 in the stack to form a solid sludge that can then be removed and disposed of on land. To justify the sliding scale standard, however, EPA had to justify use of a type of SO_2 removal performed with little or no wet chemical in-stack sprays. Called "dry scrubbing," this technology was potentially cheaper but had never been regularly used in any plant anywhere in the country.

The standard is aimed at coal-fired power plants, which then produced half the electricity, two-thirds of the SO_2, and one-fourth of the particulate matter emitted in the United States — some 360,000 tons of particulates per day. Yet by 1982 this figure would have been 58 percent higher in the absence of environmental controls. Instead, by 1982, 88 scrubbers had already been installed, at a cost of over $4 billion. The scrubber requirement sustained in the decision will drive costs still higher by the 1990s. Bennett, Comments, 9 Envtl. Poly. & L. 85 (1982). Do the health and environmental injuries caused by SO_2 justify this investment? The standard also pits West against East because it requires that the emissions from low sulfur western coal be scrubbed despite the very low SO_2 levels the burning of western coal produces.

Amendment in 1977 of the language of §111(a)(1) precipitated the new standards sustained in Sierra Club v. Costle. Does §111(a)(1) mandate scrubbing? May the standard be met by limiting the hours or levels of plant operation? Burning untreated low sulfur coal? The spare language of the statute does not provide an answer to these and similar questions, which were answered in the carefully-constructed legislative history.

Some critics believe that the scrubber-based NSPS for coal-fired power plants will cost billions more than standards that can be achieved primarily by coal washing and by burning low sulfur coal. See, e.g., B. Ackerman & W. Hassler, Clean Coal/Dirty Air or How The Clean Air Act Became a Multibillion-Dollar Bailout for High-Sulfur Coal Producers and What Should Be Done about It (1982), and their article Beyond the New Deal: Coal and the Clean Air Act, 89 Yale L.J. 1466 (1980). Ackerman and Hassler think that the statute and its legislative history allow EPA to adopt a standard that can be met solely by burning low sulfur coal. They argue that while Congress sometimes inadvisedly may mandate that an agency adopt an explicit solution to a problem (e.g., removing a certain percentage of SO_2 via scrubbers), EPA was not explicitly bound to adopt such a solution here because the legislative history is ambiguous. The price of EPA's decision is dirtier air, billions of dollars for scrubbers, and an effective subsidy to eastern high sulfur coal interests. Such a decision, they maintain, should be imposed only when a statute is crystal clear and its legislative history unambiguous. Only §125, the authors contend, clearly authorizes regional favoritism, and that section mandates a very different approach than that which EPA adopted under §111 (Clean Coal/Dirty Air, at 42-58, 104-109).

Ackerman and Hassler are probably wrong that an "unholy alliance" of eastern coal producers and environmentalists failed to obtain a statute and legislative history that enacted their preferences into law. The alliance succeeded, but it did not succeed by much. The texts of the crucial House-Senate conference committee report, completed at 2:20 A.M. on the day both houses adopted the 1977 amendents, and the clarifying statement the same drowsy staff members prepared later that day while the Congress was voting, certainly reflect the issues and the tug of war that occurred, but as Ackerman and Hassler argue, the texts produced do not clearly reveal who won. A participant in this hectic process told one of the editors of this casebook that none of the legislators, even the conference participants, saw their explanation for the new §111 until after they made it law. Perhaps it is enough to quote Chancellor Bismark, who reportedly said, "one should not inquire closely how legislation and sausages are made."

To avoid wasteful decisions, Ackerman and Hassler urge a return to New Deal-type administration in which an agency like EPA would have broad leeway to fashion a least-cost standard in the public interest after interagency consultation and presumably with White House leadership. Recall the need for interagency coordination of authority to control human exposure to lead. Is the need as great here? Or is the problem the opposite — that Congress should have set the standard itself? For such an argument, see Schoenbrod, Goals Statutes or Rules Statutes: The Case of the Clean Air Act, 30 U.C.L.A.L. Rev. 740 (1983). For EPA's criticism of Ackerman and Hassler, see Smith & Randle, Comment on Beyond the New Deal, 90 Yale L.J. 1381 (1981), and the authors' reaction to this comment, Beyond the New Deal: Reply, 90 Yale L.J. 1412 (1981). For another attack on the standard, see also Navarro, The 1977 Clean Air Act Amendments: Energy, Environmental, Economic, and Distributional Impacts, 29 Pub. Poly. 121 (1981); for a defense of the standard, see Trisko, Universal Scrubbing: Cleaning the Air, 84 W. Va. L. Rev. 983 (1982).

East vs. West. Some believe that the structure of the Clean Air Act betrays how the populous East, the cities, and the large corporations were able to impose heavy environmental control costs on the West, rural areas, and small businesses. See B. Pashigian, The Political Economy of the Clean Air Act: Regional Self-Interest in Environmental Legislation 3 (Center for the Study of American Business, 1982). Pashigian examined regional gross annual air pollution abatement costs between 1973 and 1977 and found that the Pacific, mountain, and south central states paid considerably more per dollar's worth of goods produced for emissions control than did New England and the middle Atlantic and north central states (The Political Economy of the Clean Air Act, at 13). See also W. Tucker, Progress and Privilege: America in the Age of Environmentalism (1982) (environmentalism favors the rich, the aristocratic, and the large corporations). For a contrary view that the East has always sought to develop the West economically as a colonial "sacrifice area" to serve eastern markets, with consequent destruction of western environmental amenities, see R. Lamm & M. McCarthy, The Angry West (1982). See also Regional Conflict and National Policy (K. Price ed. 1982).

Judging by the brouhaha over the NSPS for coal-burning power plants, one would think that virtually all new plants would be governed by the standards. But the NSPS set only a minimum to which additional SO_2 reduction may be added in order to meet the further requirements of the non-attainment and PSD programs. Their controls for new sources supersede NSPS (see sections G and H *infra*). NSPS apply to units of 250 MBtu per hour and up. Controlled at 1.2 lbs/MBtu SO_2, such a unit would still emit 300 lbs/hr. of SO_2, easily meeting the requirement for 1,000 lbs. a day of controlled emissions so that the PSD or non-attainment programs would apply.

Cost-effective control at old rather than new sources. New coal-burning power plants meeting NSPS will not outnumber their far dirtier predecessors for three or more decades. The marginal costs of high levels of SO_2 removal at new plants far exceed the marginal costs of high levels of SO_2 emissions controls at existing plants. Since under the current standard some 10 percent of total capital investment by electrical utilities will be spent on SO_2 control (about $33.4 billion), would it make better sense to spend some of that money on SO_2 control at existing plants? The Congressional Budget Office estimated that if total national SO_2 emissions were fixed at the amount projected to be emitted under the NSPS standard (21 million tons a year) and if the utilities themselves were allowed to decide which new or old sources to control to meet this quota, control costs might be 75 percent less per ton of SO_2 removed, even though old sources would be removing additional SO_2 emissions on top of existing SIP obligations. Undoubtedly they would do this primarily by burning low sulfur coal, which they are permitted to do. Congressional Budget Office, The Clean Air Act, the Electric Utilities, and the Coal Market xviii, xxi (1982).

The wisdom of the Clean Air Act's excessive reliance on new source emissions controls once again is called into question. The Act creates an enormous incentive to keep the older, dirtier plants in operation as long as possible. Further, state public utility commissions do not allow electrical utilities to put the capital costs of new plant construction into their rate bases until the facility becomes operational, a period of 8 to 12 years. But utilities *are* permitted to pass on rising fuel costs almost immediately to their consumers, thus creating a bias toward keeping old oil- and gas-burning plants in operation rather than constructing NSPS-burdened plants. Should Congress preempt state utility commission rate-making to take care of this problem? Is there precedent for this kind of congressional action?

Multiple emissions points, bubbles, and efficiency. A power *plant* may consist of several boiler *units*, each of which emits pollutants and is presently subject to NSPS. Other industrial subcategories subject to NSPS may also emit pollutants from several locations within a plant. For NSPS purposes, should the entire plant be considered the source, or should each piece of emissions-generating equipment within the plant be considered a source? See §111(a)(3).

The appropriate units on which to impose the regulatory standard is an issue that will appear again in other Clean Air Act provisions. The issue is crucial because under the wider definition of "source," EPA could allow plant operators more leeway to decide the level of control at individual units, thereby promoting economic efficiency. Such leeway could reduce a plant operator's costs significantly because marginal emissions control costs vary widely among pieces of plant equipment that emit the same pollutants.

EPA attempted to adopt a wider, "dual" definition under which both particular pieces of equipment *and* a combination of such pieces of equipment, i.e., an entire plant, would be considered sources (40 Fed. Reg. 58,416). To determine the emissions allowable at a particular plant, EPA imagined it to be covered by a high "bubble," with only one emissions point at the top. That one source, but not the individual contributing units beneath the bubble, would be subject to the NSPS. Studies of internal bubbles have found that substantial cost savings are possible. Hahn & Hester, Where Did All the Markets Go? An Analysis of EPA's Emissions Trading Program, 6 Yale J. Reg. 109 (1989). Plant operators would presumably strive to reduce emissions the most in the units for which control was the cheapest, until the marginal investment for every pound of emissions controlled at all units would be equal. The NSPS bubble policy was invalidated in ASARCO v. EPA, 578 F.2d 319 (D.C. Cir. 1978). The court was troubled that the broader definition of "source" would have permitted any in-plant rebuilding or modifications that did not increase overall plantwide increase in emissions to elude or "net out" of the NSPS requirements, retarding the application of new technology that met the strict NSPS standards and therefore delaying the improvement in air quality, which the court said was the purpose of §111.

The same court accepted the plantwide definition for purposes of the PSD program in Alabama Power Co. v. Costle, 636 F.2d 323 (D.C. Cir. 1980). The court held that EPA may define the term "source" so as best to serve a particular program's purposes. Later, in the *Chevron* case, reproduced *supra* at Chapter 2, the Supreme Court upheld the use of the bubble for modified sources in non-attainment areas and indicated its disapproval of the ASARCO case.

EPA has now reinstated the bubble under certain circumstances for the NSPS program. See 17 Envt. Rep. (BNA): Current Developments 2151 (1987). EPA has also authorized compliance bubbles for new source standards. This bubble does not allow the source to escape NSPS review, but does allow the source under designated safeguards to average emissions from emissions sources within the plant for purposes of determining compliance with the NSPS. See 50 Fed. Reg. 3,688 (1985) (proposed for Illinois powerplant); 52 Fed. Reg. 28,946 (1987) (bubble adopted). For discussion of compliance bubbles see R. Liroff, Reforming Air Pollution Regulation: The Toil and Trouble of EPA's Bubble 110-117 (1986). We will give close attention to EPA's attempts to interpret the Clean Air Act in such a way that emitters could reduce costs while maintaining the same overall total level of emissions.

F. STATE IMPLEMENTATION PLANS

The Clean Air Act requires each state to prepare, and EPA to approve, a state implementation plan (SIP). As noted in the overview of the Clean Air Act in section C, the SIP is not a true plan as that term is commonly understood. Because the SIP contains the state's strategy for meeting and maintaining ambient standards, it is the heart of the state Clean Air Act program. Its most important components are existing stationary source emissions limitations and the transportation control plans discussed in section G. The SIP does not actually include the national uniform emission standards established by EPA for new stationary sources or motor vehicles; however, a state may assume implementation and enforcement of the standards if EPA approves. A SIP must provide for preconstruction review of a new stationary source to ensure that it will not interfere with attaining or maintaining the ambient standards. See §§111(c), 110(a)(4).

Compliance with the ambient standards is determined geographically within the air quality control regions (AQCRs). See §107. Metropolitan areas are usually designated as air quality control regions, and some urban AQCRs are interstate. Does the statute expressly provide authority to create interstate AQCRs? Although different problems face "clean air" and "dirty air" areas, the 1970 Act made no distinction among types of AQCRs based on the severity of air pollution within them. The 1977 amendments corrected this flaw by dividing the country into non-attainment areas, where air quality standards have not been met, and "nondegradation" areas, where the quality of the air is better than the ambient standards require. The different control strategies for these two types of regions are elaborated on in sections G and H. For now, the essential point to understand is that each state is responsible for meeting the ambient standards within its air quality control regions and that the SIP details the means the state will use to attain compliance.

The statutory requirements for SIPs are found in §110 of the Clean Air Act. Section 110(a)(2)(B) applies to existing sources, requiring SIPs to contain "emission limitations . . . and such other measures as may be necessary" to meet and maintain the national air quality standards. Although SIPs must be approved by EPA, the Supreme Court has made it clear that the Clean Air Act leaves the choice of emissions limitations for existing sources to the states as long as the combination of measures selected will achieve compliance with the NAAQS:

> The Act gives . . . [EPA] no authority to question the wisdom of a State's choices of emissions limitations if they are part of a plan which satisfies the standards of §110(a)(2). . . . Thus, so long as the ultimate effect of a State's choice of emission limitations is compliance with the national standards for ambient air, the state is at liberty to adopt whatever mix of emission limitations it deems best suited to its particular situation. [Train v. Natural Resources Defense Council, Inc., 421 U.S. 60, 79 (1975).]

Train v. Natural Resources Defense Council, Inc. created problems for the administration of the 1970 Act. Many states simply provided for compliance with the ambient standards by the statutory deadline and did not attempt to ensure interim improvement in air quality prior to the compliance date. The 1977 amendments addressed this problem by requiring "reasonable" annual progress prior to the compliance date.

Although the Clean Air Act requires SIPs to contain emission limitations, it also authorizes such other measures "as may be necessary." Some of the other "necessary" measures are specified, such as transportation control plans. Some are not. Must a state rely primarily on emissions limitations on existing sources, or may it rely on other techniques to meet the ambient standards? Are any other techniques forbidden under the Clean Air Act scheme? The issue of other measures was considered in several lower federal court cases, and the majority holding is illustrated by Natural Resources Defense Council, Inc. v. EPA, 489 F.2d 390 (5th Cir. 1974), rev'd on other grounds, Train v. Natural Resources Defense Council, Inc., 421 U.S. 60 (1975), quoted above. Georgia had submitted a SIP under which allowable emissions varied with the height of the plant smokestack. More emissions were allowed for plants with higher stacks, a technique for compliance by dispersion; tall stacks help meet the ambient standards in an air quality region by dispersing pollutants elsewhere.

The court, with some exceptions, rejected the use of dispersion techniques to meet air quality standards, adopting what it called the "broad" approach to the Act. This approach viewed the Act in its entirety and held that "emission reduction is clearly the preferred control method." The court rejected a "narrow" approach, which would have focused on the objectives of the Act and would have allowed any control strategy to be used provided the ambient standards were met. Two other circuit courts extended the Fifth Circuit rationale to "intermittent" controls, disapproving the strategies of reducing operations at the source or switching to less-polluting fuel when atmospheric conditions cause high pollution levels. Big River Electric Corp. v. EPA, 523 F.2d 16 (6th Cir. 1975); Kennecott Copper Corp. v. Train, 526 F.2d 1149 (9th Cir. 1975).

For several years a lively debate went on over the "tall stacks" strategy and other dispersion techniques, in which environmentalists, led by the Natural Resources Defense Council, were pitted against EPA, industry, and other federal agencies such as the Department of Energy and the Tennessee Valley Authority. See, e.g., Ayres, Enforcement of Air Pollution Controls on Stationary Sources under the Clean Air Amendments of 1970, 4 Ecology L.Q. 441 (1975). The 1977 amendments resolved the dispersion techniques controversy in favor of the environmentalists' position. Section 123 provides that the "degree of emission limitation" is not to be affected by stack height in excess of "good engineering practice" or by any dispersion technique. "Dispersion technique" is defined to mean "any intermittent or supplemental control of air pollutants varying with atmospheric conditions." In addition, §302(K) defines an emission limitation as a requirement that "limits the quantity, rate, or concentration of emission of air pollutants on a continuous basis." See generally R. Melnick, Regulation and the Courts, ch. 5 (1983).

Some plant operators have argued that they can be allowed to avoid air quality violations during episodes of high pollution by closing the plant or by switching to less-polluting fuels strategies rejected by the courts in the mid-1970s. Should the 1977 amendments be interpreted to prohibit these strategies? Are there circumstances when the "dilution is not the solution to pollution" maxim is wrong? Note carefully how the 1977 amendments and the reliance on emissions limitations affect a state's SIP strategy, as defined by the *Train* case. The degree of emission limitation chosen for existing sources will determine the flexibility a state has in allowing new sources to locate in its area. New sources can only be allowed if they "trade" emissions with existing sources. For discussion of this problem, see section G *infra*.

A NOTE ON TALL STACKS

The tall stack issue is important to implementation of SIPs because it determines the extent to which polluters can comply with emission limitations through dispersion rather than by installing pollution controls. Tall stacks are also an issue in the acid rain debate. A small group of Ohio power plants with tall stacks, for example, are claimed to produce much of the acid rain that falls in the northeast. Note that §123 does not prohibit the building of tall stacks. It merely limits the extent to which a polluter can take credit for tall stacks in meeting its emission limitations.

Implementing the tall stack limitations imposed by §123 was long delayed, and EPA's tall stack rule was subject to two judicial appeals. A major issue in the tall stack rule is the "control first" issue. The issue is complex and arises because §123 defines "good engineering practice" as that height "necessary" to ensure that emissions will not cause local "excessive concentration" due to atmospheric downwash from "nearby" structures or terrain. This is an attempt to resolve the tension between prohibiting dispersion that causes pollution outside the local region and at the same time prohibiting "downwash" locally from terrain and structures that can create unhealthy local "hot spots."

Sierra Club v. EPA, 719 F.2d 436 (D.C. Cir. 1983), *cert. denied*, 468 U.S. 1204 (1984), affirmed most of EPA's tall stack regulations but held that EPA must adopt an absolute, health-based standard in defining excessive concentrations. This ruling created a new problem, as the court pointed out in its next opinion on the tall stack regulations:

> The mandate to develop an absolute test revealed an issue that did not exist [before]. . . . Ground-level concentrations are obviously a function not only of stack height and other elements mentioned in [the statute's definition of good engineering practice] . . . , but also of the emissions emerging at the top of the stack.

Once "excessive" emissions are defined in absolute terms, the stack height "*necessary*" to avoid those concentrations on the ground will obviously vary with a source's actual emissions. . . .

Although the parties disagree as to how much the assumed emissions rate affects any computation of credit-worthy stack height, they agree on the direction of the impact: high assumed emissions rates entail relatively generous stack credits (and thus relatively high emissions rates), low assumptions the opposite. [NRDC v. Thomas, 838 F.2d 1224, 1234 (D.C. Cir.), *cert. denied*, 109 S. Ct. 219, 250 (1988).]

In its amended regulation, which was challenged in *Thomas*, EPA defined the assumed emissions rate for purposes of emissions credit within its formula as the emissions rate specified by a SIP or the actual emissions rate. NRDC argued that the emissions rate should be that which would result from a source's using all "available methods," which was dubbed the "control-first" approach. The NRDC approach would clearly mean that emissions rates for purposes of calculating emissions credit would be lower than they would be under the EPA standard, with the result (as noted above) that the determination of "necessary" height to avoid excessive concentrations would also be lower.

The court in *Thomas* rejected NRDC's argument, noting it would have a substantial impact on the emissions rate that would emerge after the stack height credit was calculated. The court examined the statutory language and legislative history and held that Congress did not intend so drastic a reduction in emissions rates when it adopted §123. NRDC argued that the word "necessary" in the statute supported its approach but the court disagreed, noting that the word necessary is "not always used in its most rigid sense."

Like other important control issues in the Clean Air Act, the stack height issue was decided through statutory interpretation. Do you agree with the court's holding? What might or should Congress do to further address the "control-first" problem? Is this another technology-forcing issue? See Note, Good Engineering Practice and the Tall Stack Rules: Judicial Disregard of the EPA's Delegated Duties, 36 J. Urb. & Contemp. L. 213 (1989).

1.   *Approving State Implementation Plans*

The Clean Air Act requires EPA approval of SIPs, and approval is based on a list of requirements contained in §110. The 1970 Act centralized review of the state plans in the federal courts of appeal. All questions concerning SIPs are to be reviewed when the plan is first promulgated. See §307(b)(1). This centralized and "up-front" review process was intended to prevent polluters from challenging SIPs later in the day, when enforcement proceedings were brought for violations of the Act.

The discretion conferred on EPA in the review of state plans as they affect existing sources raised a critical problem under the Act. Polluters argued, successfully in some lower federal courts, that emissions limitations could be set aside or modified if they were not economically or technologically feasible. This problem arises at several points in the administration of the Clean Air Act. How it was resolved in the context of state implementation plans is indicated by the following Supreme Court case.

UNION ELECTRIC CO. v. EPA
427 U.S. 246 (1976)

Mr. Justice MARSHALL delivered the opinion of the Court.

After the Administrator of the Environmental Protection Agency (EPA) approves a state implementation plan under the Clean Air Act, the plan may be challenged in a court of appeals within 30 days, or after 30 days have run if newly discovered or available information justifies subsequent review. We must decide whether the operator of a regulated emission source, in a petition for review of an EPA-approved state plan filed after the original 30-day appeal period, can raise the claim that it is economically or technologically infeasible to comply with the plan.

I

We have addressed the history and provisions of the Clean Air Amendments of 1970 in detail in Train v. Natural Resources Defense Council (NRDC), 421 U.S. 60 (1975), and will not repeat that discussion here. Suffice it to say that the Amendments reflect congressional dissatisfaction with the progress of existing air pollution programs and a determination to "tak[e] a stick to the States," id., at 64, in order to guarantee the prompt attainment and maintenance of specified air quality standards. The heart of the Amendments is the requirement that each State formulate, subject to EPA approval, an implementation plan designed to achieve national primary ambient air quality standards — those necessary to protect the public health — "as expeditiously as practicable but . . . in no case later than three years from the date of approval of such plan." §110(a)(2)(A). The plan must also provide for the attainment of national secondary ambient air quality standards — those necessary to protect the public welfare — within a "reasonable time." Each State is given wide discretion in formulating its plan, and the Act provides that the Administrator "shall approve" the proposed plan if it has been adopted after public notice and hearing and if it meets eight specified criteria. §110(a)(2).

On April 30, 1971, the Administrator promulgated national primary and secondary standards for six air pollutants he found to have an adverse effect on the public health and welfare. Included among them was sulfur dioxide, at issue here. After the promulgation of the national standards, the State of Missouri formulated its implementation plan and submitted it for approval. Since sulfur dioxide levels exceeded national primary standards in only one of the State's five air quality regions — the Metropolitan St. Louis Interstate region — the Missouri plan concentrated on a control strategy and regulations to lower emissions in that area. The plan's emission limitations were effective at once, but the State retained authority to grant variances to particular sources that could not immediately comply. The Administrator approved the plan on May 31, 1972.

Petitioner is an electric utility company servicing the St. Louis metropolitan area, large portions of Missouri, and parts of Illinois and Iowa. Its three coal-fired generating plants in the metropolitan St. Louis area are subject to the sulfur dioxide restrictions in the Missouri implementation plan. Petitioner did not seek review of the Administrator's approval of the plan within 30 days, as it was entitled to do under §307(b)(1) of the Act, but rather applied to the appropriate state and county agencies for variances from the emission limitations affecting its three plants. Petitioner received one-year variances, which could be extended upon reapplication. The variances on two of petitioner's three plants had expired and petitioner was applying for extensions when, on May 31, 1974, the Administrator notified petitioner that sulfur dioxide emissions from its plants violated the emission limitations contained in the Missouri plan. Shortly thereafter petitioner filed a petition in the Court of Appeals for the Eighth Circuit for review of the Administrator's 1972 approval of the Missouri implementation plan.

Section 307(b)(1) allows petitions for review to be filed in an appropriate court of appeals more than 30 days after the Administrator's approval of an implementation plan only if the petition is "based solely on grounds arising after such 30th day." Petitioner claimed to meet this requirement by asserting, inter alia, that various economic and technological difficulties had arisen more than 30 days after the Administrator's approval and that these difficulties made compliance with the emission limitations impossible.[4]

The court held that "only matters which, if known to the Administrator at the time of his action [in approving a state implementation plan], would justify setting aside that action are properly reviewable after the initial 30 day review period." 515 F.2d 206, 216 (1975). Since, in the court's view, claims of economic and technological infeasibility could not properly provide a basis for the Administrator's rejecting a plan, such claims could not serve at any time as the basis for a court's overturning an approval plan. Accordingly, insofar as petitioner's claim of newly discovered or available information was grounded on an assertion of economic and technological infeasibility, the court held itself to be without jurisdiction to consider the petition for review, and so dismissed the petition. In so holding the Court of Appeals considered and rejected the contrary or partially contrary holdings of three other Circuits. On the other hand, the Eighth Circuit

---

4. The Court of Appeals also found that no claim was stated by petitioner's assertion that the Missouri standards exceeded those necessary for compliance with the national standards because, the court held, the States are free to adopt stricter standards than the national standards under §116 of the Clean Air Act, 515 F.2d, at 220. While certiorari was not sought on this question, it has been briefed for us and we find it necessary to resolve it in deciding this case.

found support for its position in the decisions of several other Circuits. We granted certiorari to resolve the conflict among the Circuits, 423 U.S. 821 (1975), and we now affirm.

II

A . . .

[The Court held that if "new grounds" are alleged for an appeal more than 30 days after the approval or promulgation of a SIP, "they must be such that, had they been known at the time the plan was presented to the Administrator for approval, it would have been an abuse of discretion for the Administrator to approve the plan."]

B

Since a reviewing court — regardless of when the petition for review is filed — may consider claims of economic and technological infeasibility only if the Administrator may consider such claims in approving or rejecting a state implementation plan, we must address ourselves to the scope of the Administrator's responsibility. The Administrator's position is that he has no power whatsoever to reject a state implementation plan on the ground that it is economically or technologically infeasible, and we have previously accorded great deference to the Administrator's construction of the Clean Air Act. After surveying the relevant provisions of the Clean Air Amendments of 1970 and their legislative history, we agree that Congress intended claims of economic and technological infeasibility to be wholly foreign to the Administrator's consideration of a state implementation plan.

As we have previously recognized, the 1970 Amendments to the Clean Air Act were a drastic remedy to what was perceived as a serious and otherwise uncheckable problem of air pollution. The Amendments place the primary responsibility for formulating pollution control strategies on the States, but nonetheless subject the States to strict minimum compliance requirements. These requirements are of a "technology-forcing character" and are expressly designed to force regulated sources to develop pollution control devices that might at the time appear to be economically or technologically infeasible.

This approach is apparent on the face of §110(a)(2). The provision sets out eight criteria that an implementation plan must satisfy, and provides that if these criteria are met and if the plan was adopted after reasonable notice and hearing, the Administrator "shall approve" the proposed state plan. The mandatory "shall" makes it quite clear that the Administrator is not to be concerned with factors other than those specified, and none of the eight factors appears to permit consideration of technological or economic infeasibility. Nonetheless, if a basis is to be found for allowing the Administrator to consider such claims, it must be among the eight criteria, and so it is here that the argument is focused.

It is suggested that consideration of claims of technological and economic infeasibility is required by the first criterion that the primary air quality standards be met "as expeditiously as practicable but . . . in no case later than three years . . ." and that the secondary air quality standards be met within a "reasonable time." §110(a)(2)(A). The argument is that what is "practicable" or "reasonable" cannot be determined without assessing whether what is proposed is possible. This argument does not survive analysis.

Section 110(a)(2)(A)'s three-year deadline for achieving primary air quality standards is central to the Amendments' regulatory scheme and, as both the language and the legislative history of the requirement make clear, it leaves no room for claims of technological or economic infeasibility. The 1970 congressional debate on the Amendments centered on whether technology forcing was necessary and desirable in framing and attaining air quality standards sufficient to protect the public health, standards later termed primary standards. The House version of the Amendments was quite moderate in approach, requiring only that health-related standards be met "within a reasonable time." H.R. 17255, 91st Cong., 2d Sess., §108(c)(1)(C)(i) (1970). The Senate bill, on the other hand, flatly required that, possible or not, health-related standards be met "within three years." S. 4358, 91st Cong., 2d Sess., §111(a)(2)(A) (1970).

The Senate's stiff requirement was intended to foreclose the claims of emission sources that it would be economically or technologically infeasible for them to achieve emission limitations sufficient to protect the public health within the specified time. As Senator Muskie, manager of the Senate bill, explained to his chamber:

> "The first responsibility of Congress is not the making of technological or economic judgments or even to be limited by what is or appears to be technologically or economically feasible. Our responsibility is to establish what the public interest requires to protect the health of persons. This may mean that people and industries will be asked to do what seems to be impossible at the present time." [116 Cong. Rec. 32901-32902 (1970).]

This position reflected that of the Senate committee:

> In the Committee discussions, considerable concern was expressed regarding the use of the concept of technical feasibility as the basis of ambient air standards. The Committee determined that 1) the health of people is more important than the question of whether the early achievement of ambient air quality standards protective of health is technically feasible; and 2) the growth of pollution load in many areas, even with application of available technology, would still be deleterious to public health.
>
> Therefore, the Committee determined that existing sources of pollutants either should meet the standard of the law or be closed down. . . . [S. Rep. No. 91-1196, pp. 2-3 (1970).]

The Conference Committee and, ultimately, the entire Congress accepted the Senate's three-year mandate for the achievement of primary air quality standards, and the clear import of that decision is that the Administrator must approve a plan that provides for attainment of the primary standards in three years even if attainment does not appear feasible. In rejecting the House's version of reasonableness, however, the conferees strengthened the Senate version. The Conference Committee made clear that the States could not procrastinate until the deadline approached. Rather, the primary standards had to be met in less than three years if possible; they had to be met "as expeditiously as practicable." §110(a)(2)(A). Whatever room there is for considering claims of infeasibility in the attainment of primary standards must lie in this phrase, which is, of course, relevant only in evaluating those implementation plans that attempt to achieve the primary standard in less than three years.

It is argued that when such a state plan calls for proceeding more rapidly than economics and the available technology appear to allow, the plan must be rejected as not "practicable." Whether this is a correct reading of §110(a)(2)(A) depends on how that section's "as expeditiously as practicable" phrase is characterized. The Administrator's position is that §110(a)(2)(A) sets only a minimum standard that the States may exceed in their discretion, so that he has no power to reject an infeasible state plan that surpasses the minimum federal requirements — a plan that reflects a state decision to engage in technology forcing on its own and to proceed more expeditiously than is practicable. On the other hand, petitioner and amici supporting its position argue that §110(a)(2)(A) sets a mandatory standard that the States must meet precisely, and conclude that the Administrator may reject a plan for being too strict as well as for being too lax. Since the arguments supporting this theory are also made to show that the Administrator must reject a state plan that provides for achieving more than the secondary air quality standards require, we defer consideration of this question in order to outline the development and content of the secondary standards provision of §110(a)(2)(A).

Secondary air quality standards, those necessary to protect the public welfare, were subject to far less legislative debate than the primary standards. The House version of the Amendments treated welfare-related standards together with health-related standards, and required both to be met "within a reasonable time." The Senate bill, on the other hand, treated health- and welfare-related standards separately and did not require that welfare-related standards be met in any particular time at all, although the Committee Report expressed the desire that they be met "as rapidly as possible." S. Rep. No. 91-1196, p. 11 (1970). The final Amendments also separated welfare-related standards from health-related standards, labeled them secondary air quality standards, and adopted the House's requirement that they be met within a "reasonable time." §§109(b), 110(a)(2)(A). Thus, technology forcing is not expressly required in achieving standards to protect the public welfare.

It does not necessarily follow, however, that the Administrator may consider claims of impossibility in assessing a state plan for achieving secondary standards. As with plans designed to achieve primary standards in less than three years, the scope of the Administrator's power to reject a plan depends on whether the State itself may decide to engage in technology forcing and adopt a plan more stringent than federal law demands.[7]

Amici Appalachian Power Co. et al. argue that the Amendments do not give such broad power to the States. They claim that the States are precluded from submitting implementation plans more stringent than federal law demands by §110(a)(2)'s second criterion that the plan contain such control devices "as may be necessary" to achieve the primary and secondary air quality standards. §110(a)(2)(B). The contention is that an overly restrictive plan is not "necessary" for attainment of the national standards and so must be rejected by the Administrator.[9]

The principal support for this theory of amici lies in the fact that while the House and Senate versions of §110(a)(2) both expressly provided that the States could submit for the Administrator's approval plans that were stricter than the national standards required, see H.R. 17255, 91st Cong., 2d Sess., §108(c) (1970); S. 4358, 91st Cong., 2d Sess., §111(a)(1) (1970), the section as enacted contains no such express language. Amici argue that the Conference Committee must have decided to require state implementation plans simply — and precisely — to meet the national standards. The argument of amici proves too much. A Conference Committee lacks power to make substantive changes on matters about which both Houses agree. Here the Conference Report expressly notes that both the Senate and House bills would allow States to submit plans more stringent than the national standards demand, and offers no suggestion that the Conference bill intended to change that result, even if it could. H.R. Conf. Rep. No. 91-1783, p. 45 (1970). And while the final language of §110(a)(2)(B) may be less explicit than the versions originally approved by the House and the Senate, the most natural reading of the "as may be necessary" phrase in context is simply that the Administrator must assure that the minimal, or "necessary," requirements are met, not that he detect and reject any state plan more demanding than federal law requires.

We read the "as may be necessary" requirement of §110(a)(2)(B) to demand only that the implementation plan submitted by the State meet the "minimum

---

7.   A different question would be presented if the Administrator drafted the plan himself pursuant to §110(c). Cf. District of Columbia v. Train, 521 F.2d 971 (D.C. 1975); South Terminal Corp. v. EPA, 504 F.2d 646 (1st Cir. 1974). Whether claims of economic or technical infeasibility must be considered by the Administrator in drafting an implementation plan is a question we do not reach.

9.   Amici not only argue that the Administrator must reject state plans that attempt to attain the primary standards more rapidly than "practicable" or the secondary standards in less than a "reasonable time," but also that he must reject state implementation plans that call for more quantitative emission controls than those necessary to meet the national primary and secondary standards. This argument adds nothing to deciding whether claims of economic or technological infeasibility can be raised. If quantitatively stiffer standards are barred, all plans containing them must be rejected, whether infeasible or not. In any case, as we make clear below, the States may adopt such more rigorous emission standards, and the Administrator must approve plans containing them if the minimum federal requirements are satisfied.

conditions" of the Amendments.[13] Train v. NRDC, 421 U.S., at 71 n.11. Beyond that, if a State makes the legislative determination that it desires a particular air quality by a certain date and that it is willing to force technology to attain it — or lose a certain industry if attainment is not possible — such a determination is fully consistent with the structure and purpose of the Amendments, and §110(a)(2)(B) provides no basis for the EPA Administrator to object to the determination on the ground of infeasibility.[14] See Train v. NRDC, *supra,* at 79.

In sum, we have concluded that claims of economic or technological infeasibility may not be considered by the Administrator in evaluating a state requirement that primary ambient air quality standards be met in the mandatory three years. And, since we further conclude that the States may submit implementation plans more stringent than federal law requires and that the Administrator must approve such plans if they meet the minimum requirements of §110(a)(2), it follows that the language of §110(a)(2)(B) provides no basis for the Administrator ever to reject a state implementation plan on the ground that it is economically or technologically infeasible. Accordingly, a court of appeals reviewing an approved plan under §307(b)(1) cannot set it aside on those grounds, no matter when they are raised.

III

Our conclusion is bolstered by recognition that the Amendments do allow claims of technological and economic infeasibility to be raised in situations where consideration of such claims will not substantially interfere with the primary congressional purpose of prompt attainment of the national air quality standards. Thus, we do not hold that claims of infeasibility are never of relevance in the formulation of an implementation plan or that sources unable to comply with emission limitations must inevitably be shut down.

Perhaps the most important forum for consideration of claims of economic and technological infeasibility is before the state agency formulating the implementation plan. So long as the national standards are met, the State may select whatever mix of control devices it desires, and industries with particular economic or technological problems may seek special treatment in the plan itself. More-

13. Economic and technological factors may be relevant in determining whether the minimum conditions are met. Thus, the Administrator may consider whether it is economically or technologically possible for the state plan to require more rapid progress than it does. If he determines that it is, he may reject the plan as not meeting the requirement that primary standards be achieved "as expeditiously as practicable" or as failing to provide for attaining secondary standards within "a reasonable time."

14. In a literal sense, of course, no plan is infeasible since offending sources always have the option of shutting down if they cannot otherwise comply with the standard of the law. Thus, there is no need for the Administrator to reject an economically or technologically "infeasible" state plan on the ground that anticipated noncompliance will cause the State to fall short of the national standards. Sources objecting to such a state scheme must seek their relief from the State.

over, if the industry is not exempted from, or accommodated by, the original plan, it may obtain a variance, as petitioner did in this case; and the variance, if granted after notice and a hearing, may be submitted to the EPA as a revision of the plan. Lastly, an industry denied an exemption from the implementation plan, or denied a subsequent variance, may be able to take its claims of economic or technological infeasibility to the state courts.[16] . . .

[The court then discusses several alternatives available under the 1970 Act for delaying achievement of the ambient standards or for allowing EPA or the federal courts to grant compliance extensions for individual sources. These *federal* "escape hatches," although modified, were retained in the 1977 amendments; they are discussed in the Notes and in section I, *infra* (federal enforcement).]

In short, the Amendments offer ample [state and federal] opportunity for consideration of claims of technological and economic infeasibility. Always, however, care is taken that consideration of such claims will not interfere substantially with the primary goal of prompt attainment of the national standards. Allowing such claims to be raised by appealing the Administrator's approval of an implementation plan, as petitioner suggests, would frustrate congressional intent. It would permit a proposed plan to be struck down as infeasible before it is given a chance to work, even though Congress clearly contemplated that some plans would be infeasible when proposed. And it would permit the Administrator or a federal court to reject a State's legislative choices in regulating air pollution, even though Congress plainly left with the States, so long as the national standards were met, the power to determine which sources would be burdened by regulation and to what extent. Technology forcing is a concept somewhat new to our national experience and it necessarily entails certain risks. But Congress considered those risks in passing the 1970 Amendments and decided that the dangers posed by uncontrolled air pollution made them worth taking. Petitioner's theory would render that considered legislative judgment a nullity, and that is a result we refuse to reach.

Affirmed.

[Justice POWELL and the Chief Justice, concurring, agreed with the majority's interpretation of the Act but believed that it might lead to economically disastrous consequences.]

16. Of course, the Amendments do not *require* the States to formulate their implementation plans with deference to claims of technological or economic infeasibility, to grant variances on those or any other grounds, or to provide judicial review of such actions. Consistent with Congress' recognition of the primary role of the States in controlling air pollution, the Amendments leave all such decisions to the States, which have typically responded in the manner described in the text.

NOTES AND QUESTIONS

1. *Cost blindness in* Union Electric. Are you convinced by the Court's statutory analysis in *Union Electric?* Would the Court reach a different result today, now that the compliance dates for meeting the ambient standards have been extended by the 1977 amendments? Does it make a difference that EPA has dropped secondary standards for some pollutants and that the secondary standards for other pollutants are the same as the primary standards? The Court found several points in the SIP decisionmaking process at which economic and technological considerations could be taken into account. What are they? See also the general SIP deadline delay provision, §110(e).

Bleicher, Economic and Technological Feasibility in Clean Air Act Enforcement against Stationary Sources, 89 Harv. L. Rev. 316 (1975), suggests that the claims made by the company in *Union Electric* raise "reasonableness" problems in two ways. An emission limitation may be unreasonably high as applied to an individual polluter, and it may also unfairly distribute the compliance burden among existing pollution sources. Which claim did the company make in *Union Electric?* Is either a valid defense? See generally Huber, Electricity and the Environment: In Search of Regulatory Authority, 100 Harv. L. Rev. 1002 (1987).

2. *Emitter options for obtaining acceptable emissions limitations.* As the Court indicates, a number of options exist for individual polluters to elude or delay compliance with emissions limitations contained in state plans. First, several means exist for an individual source to obtain a more relaxed emissions limitation without delaying overall SIP compliance. The earliest and strategically most effective opportunity, of course, is when the state selects the region-wide combination of emissions limitations for all sources that will achieve the SIP goals within the statutory deadlines. If a source fails to obtain an emissions limitation acceptable to it when the SIP is first prepared, it may seek a variance from the state pollution control agency under state legislation authorizing variances. A state variance usually operates as an amendment of the SIP. The SIPs as published in the Federal Register contain emissions limitations and compliance schedules for major existing sources of pollution. A variance is a revision of the compliance schedule for an existing source and so is a revision of the SIP. The Court also says a party may take its claim of infeasibility to a state court. An Illinois court invalidated portions of the state SIP because technological and economic feasibility had not been considered as required by state law. In Illinois v. Celotex Corp., 516 F. Supp. 716 (C.D. Ill. 1981), the federal district court held that it would not enforce the invalidated SIP provisions. Is the policy of *Union Electric* subverted by this decision?

The Supreme Court held in Natural Resources Defense Council v. Train, 421 U.S. 60 (1975), that EPA could also approve a state variance as an amendment of the SIP under §110(a)(3). A variance could be approved only if it did not cause a violation of an ambient standard or prevent a state from meeting the

SIP compliance deadline. Congress adopted provisions in 1977 authorizing delayed compliance by existing sources, see §113(d), but the plan revision alternative may have survived. See United States Steel Corp. v. EPA, 612 F.2d 56 (2d Cir. 1980).

The Supreme Court left this issue open, but it is now clear that a nonconforming source may not raise a defense of economic and technological infeasibility late in the SIP implementation process, when an enforcement action is brought. Navistar Internatl. Transp. Corp. v. EPA, 858 F.2d 282 (6th Cir. 1988); Natural Resources Defense Council, Inc. v. Thomas, 705 F. Supp. 1 (D.D.C. 1988).

A question remains whether the Administrator or the federal courts can take economic and technical infeasibility into account in fashioning administrative and judicial enforcement orders under §§113(a), 113(b), and 113(d). This and other questions regarding federal Clean Air Act enforcement authority are taken up below in section I.

3. *The "bubble" policy for existing sources.* EPA has encouraged states to take compliance costs into account when an existing source can identify less costly means of achieving its SIP emissions limitations. Under EPA's "bubble" policy, a source with multiple emission points (e.g., stacks, vents, tubes, and ports), each of which is already subject to specific emissions limitations requirements in an EPA-approved SIP, may propose to meet its total SIP emissions control requirements for a given pollutant that is subject to ambient standards with a mix of controls that is different from the combination mandated by its existing SIP obligations.

To decide whether to take advantage of the policy, a source would imagine all of its emission points to be beneath an enormous bubble, as plants are placed under the NSPS bubble (see p. 231 *supra*). If the total emissions allowed to escape through one imaginary vent at the top of the bubble were projected to be equal to or less than the total of approved emissions from all emissions points, the source might be able to obtain state and EPA approval of a SIP amendment, allowing a cost-saving adjustment in its mix of total emissions controls. The same air quality impact would be achieved, but at less expense, by placing relatively more control on emissions points with low marginal costs of control and less on emissions points with high costs. Futhermore, under appropriate conditions, a company could bubble several plants, rather than just emissions points within a single plant. Can you imagine what these conditions might be?

EPA's bubble policy for existing sources was first published in 1979 and revised in a new policy guide late in 1986 that also applies to other similar programs, such as the emissions trading policy that applies to new sources in non-attainment areas. 51 Fed. Reg. 43,814 (1986).

Recall that the definition of a "source" in the §111 NSPS provision led to the invalidation of the bubble policy for new sources. Does a similar definition inhibit implementation of a bubble policy for existing sources? Reread §110, which applies to state implementation plans, carefully, and recall that case-by-case bubbles are implemented as amendments to the SIP.

A review of existing source bubbles indicates they are not used frequently. Hahn & Hester, Where Did All the Markets Go? An Analysis of EPA's Emissions Trading Program, 6 Yale J. Reg. 109 (1989) (200 bubbles through 1985). The evidence on their impact on air quality is mixed, with some reports indicating they do not decrease emissions. Id. at 129. For a review of a number of actual bubbles which concludes that "paper trades" in some cases may actually have increased rather than decreased emissions see Liroff, Reforming Air Pollution Regulation: The Toil and Trouble of EPA's Bubble, ch. 4 (1986). For more discussion of "paper trades" and other problems in the emissions trading policy see p. 261 *infra*.

4. *Red tape, ambient versus technology-based standards, permits, and certainty.* Generic approval of state bubbles is one of a number of reforms that might remedy a serious deficiency in the Clean Air Act: Each SIP change must go through lengthy reviews on both state and federal levels. Pedersen, Why the Clean Air Act Works Badly, 129 U. Pa. L. Rev. 1059, 1093 (1981), notes that minor requests pile up at EPA regional offices, whereas permits for important new construction projects may be processed rapidly by the state agencies. Pedersen, at the time Deputy General Counsel of the EPA, recommends consolidation of all ambient-based SIP approvals with all technology-based new source standard approvals into a single fixed-term permit for each regulated source. If the permit is issued by the state, EPA would have a short time to veto it; otherwise, it would go into effect automatically. States would also be able to update SIPs without additional delays at EPA. In addition to breaking the SIP approval logjam so that the Act can take more rapid account of expanding knowledge of emissions impacts, the Pedersen proposal would help mesh fundamentally inconsistent Clean Air Act policies and procedures for ambient standards enforced in the SIP process and technology-based standards like NSPS and NESHAP enforced via permits. Currently a source that obtains a permit, including a permit for a major new source in a PSD or non-attainment area (see sections G and H *infra*), is still vulnerable to additional SIP requirements that the permit does not reflect. Pedersen's fixed-term, combined permit provides certainty, even if scientific understanding of pollution changes rapidly and is rapidly reflected in the SIP. Certainty for dischargers, in fact, is one of the dominant objectives of his proposal. It also provides a settled pool of pollution rights that can be bought and sold between sources under the emissions trading program of which bubbles are a part.

Is fixed-term certainty for emitters consistent with rapidly changing scientific understanding of pollution effects? Consider the following:

> [W]e must put aside the dominating idea that the legal system is to be designed essentially to institutionalize stability and security. Probably nothing is more urgently required in environmental management than institutions for controlled instability. Environmental law is principally needed to deal with a rapidly changing world: one of rising public standards; of newly discovered evidence of hazard; of rapid proliferation of novel and dangerous substances; and of a fast changing technology for environmental amelioration. In such a world, the old idea of a stable

and predictable regulatory agency, patiently negotiating solutions that will then be fixed and unquestionable for years, or even decades, is hopelessly outdated. A mixture of legal techniques designed to destabilize arrangements that have become too secure — precisely what is needed for a milieu in which rapid change is the central feature. [Sax, A General Survey of the Problem, in Science for Better Environment 753, 755-756 (Science Council of Japan ed. 1976).]

Who is right, Pedersen or Sax? Does Sax conclude with a perfect description of the contemporary Clean Air Act?

2.   Monitoring and Modeling

The AQCRs may contain hundreds of existing sources of stationary pollution. The contribution of each existing source to air quality must be determined, so that emission controls can be adopted for the source. Regions must be classified as "non-attainment" or "attainment" to determine which set of Clean Air Act controls applies. EPA must determine how much of a reduction in pollution from each criteria pollutant is necessary to achieve the ambient standards. EPA has developed air quality monitoring and modeling techniques to make these determinations. See pp. 154-156 *infra*. The Act expressly authorizes the use of monitoring and modeling in the designation of non-attainment areas (§171(2)). The accuracy and reliability of the models used by EPA in the SIP process has been challenged in several cases. Although the courts have generally deferred to EPA's selection of modeling techniques, in a few cases EPA's application of these models to air quality problems has been set aside.

What modeling strategy should be used? The selection of a modeling strategy in the SIP process raises critical problems. EPA at first used the simple "rollback" model; this practice was approved in Texas v. EPA, 499 F.2d 289 (5th Cir. 1974). The court held that the rollback model was "neutral" because "it establishes as a starting point the commonsensical proposition that pollutants will be reduced proportionately to reductions in their chemical precursors." Id. at 301. This was a heroic assumption, as the contribution of different sources to pollution varies and a simplistic uniform proportionate rollback is hardly "neutral."

EPA has now adopted more sophisticated diffusion models, one of which was closely examined in Cleveland Electric Illuminating Co. v. EPA, 572 F.2d 1150 (6th Cir.), *cert. denied*, 435 U.S. 996 (1978). The model was used by EPA in developing a SIP for Ohio. Ohio had refused to prepare its own SIP, so EPA prepared one for it under §110(c)(1). Neither the availability of more advanced models, nor the existence of monitoring data inconsistent with the model's predictions, nor evidence that the model systematically overpredicted emissions was sufficient to enable the court to find that use of the model was arbitrary or capricious. Compare Northern Great Plains Resource Council v. EPA, 645 F.2d 1349 (9th Cir. 1981).

An attack was made on the MAXT-24 (Second Maximum 24-Hour Dispersion Model with Terrain Adjustments), which EPA had developed for rural areas, in Cincinnati Gas & Electric Co. v. EPA, 578 F.2d 660 (6th Cir. 1978), *cert. denied*, 439 U.S. 1114 (1979). The court upheld the use made of the model despite an objection that the model did not take sufficient account of the effect of hilly terrain on pollution dispersion. Although not satisfied that EPA had fully considered this problem, the court held that the terrain adjustment in the model was not arbitrary or capricious. See also New York v. EPA, 710 F.2d 1200 (6th Cir. 1983) (upholding model used as basis for relaxing sulfur dioxide emission limitations).

Other Sixth Circuit cases have rejected EPA models. Columbus & Southern Ohio Electric Co. v. Costle, 638 F.2d 910 (6th Cir. 1980) rejected modeling assumptions EPA made concerning weather stability conditions. The court noted that an EPA conference and expert studies had suggested alternative modeling methods and remanded to EPA to develop a better methodology; the court later held that EPA had not subsequently undertaken a reconsideration of this defect in the model. See also Alabama Power v. Costle, 636 F.2d 323, 381-388 (D.C. Cir. 1979), and Citizens against the Refinery's Effects v. EPA, 643 F.2d 178 (4th Cir. 1981).

Ohio v. EPA, 784 F.2d 224 (6th Cir. 1986), rejected EPA's use of its CRSTER model to determine emission limitations for two power plants. The CRSTER model is a single source model for hot buoyant stack emissions, especially from power plants and furnaces. A number of northeastern states brought suit claiming EPA violated the Act by revising emission limitations based on the CRSTER model without showing that these limitations would ensure attainment of the sulfur dioxide NAAQS.

The court held it was arbitrary for EPA to rely on the model without testing the model against actual monitoring data from the two plants. The court held that the model's unimpressive validation studies made it suspect, and that site-specific factors that EPA had not taken into account were critical to its validity. Note the tension in this situation between the use of models as compared with the use of data secured through monitoring. EPA obviously preferred the use of the model because it was less expensive than monitoring. Should the court defer to EPA in this situation? See Connecticut v. EPA, 696 F.2d 147 (2d Cir. 1982) (deferring to EPA's use of CRSTER model). See also California ex rel. California Air Resources Board v. EPA, 774 P.2d 1437 (9th Cir. 1985) (upholding modeling assumptions in state SIPs). For discussion see McMahon & Hinkle, State of Ohio v. EPA: Does the Sixth Circuit Have a New Standard for Its Review of the EPA's Use of Air Quality Monitoring?, 18 U. Toledo L. Rev. 569 (1987).

The statute authorizes EPA to use monitoring or modeling in the designation of AQCRs as PSD or non-attainment areas. The agency need not base its designation on actual rather than model-predicted air quality. PPG Industries, Inc. v. Costle, 630 F.2d 462 (6th Cir. 1980) (but holding that modeling based on erroneous data.) Compare South Terminal Corp. v. EPA, 504 F.2d 646 (1st Cir. 1974) (monitoring inaccurate), with Mission Industrial v. EPA, 547 F.2d 123 (1st Cir. 1976) (model upheld despite high margin of random error).

Air quality modeling also determines the size of an AQCR. Assume that EPA has decided to designate an entire county as a non-attainment area for air quality control purposes. An objection is made that existing sources that create air pollution are located in the northwestern part of the county and that only this part of the county should be designated as a non-attainment area. This argument was made but rejected in United States Steel Corp. v. EPA, 605 F.2d 283 (7th Cir. 1979):

> This argument assumes that the designation process is designed to define those areas in which the principal offending sources are contained. The statute does not expressly state the standards or methods by which areas are to be designated. Although one method would be to designate the areas containing the principal offenders as non-attainment, another approach would be to look simply at the expected air quality throughout a region and designate noncomplying areas, regardless of the origin of the noncompliance, as "non-attainment." The EPA has clearly adopted the latter approach. [605 F.2d at 292.]

EPA has advanced several reasons for taking this approach. What do you suppose they are? How is EPA to decide how much of an area surrounding the polluting sources should be included? Does modeling help with this problem?

May EPA base an AQCR designation on predicted growth in pollution as well as on present air quality? The statute bases designation on "maintenance" as well as achievement of the ambient standards (§197(d)(1)(B)). Is this requirement relevant to your answer? See PPG Industries, Inc. v. Costle, 630 F.2d 462 (6th Cir. 1980), upholding EPA's interpretation of this section to mean that it allows consideration "projected future violations" as the basis for a non-attainment area designation. How would EPA use modeling to predict the impact on air pollution from future growth? And why do you suppose that utility companies brought most of the litigation challenging EPA modeling procedures? For discussion, see Kramer, Air Quality Modeling: Judicial, Legislative and Administrative Reactions, 5 Colum. J. Envtl. L. 236 (1979); 84 A.L.R. Fed 710 (1987).

G.   NON-ATTAINMENT: THE SPECIAL PROBLEMS OF DIRTY AIR AREAS

Congress primarily had the air quality problems of industrialized urban areas in mind when it enacted the 1970 Clean Air Act Amendments. Unfortunately, the statutory deadlines for cleaning up these areas were unrealistic. Congress extended compliance deadlines in 1977, but the extensions did not help and a large number of urban areas were still non-attainment as the 1980s ended. The problem was aggravated by congressional failure during this period to reauthorize the Act and address the serious compliance problems that the non-attainment areas present.

EPA's compliance efforts. As the original 1975-1977 deadlines for compliance under the 1970 Act approached, it was clear that many areas would not be able to meet their SIP objectives for one or even several pollutants. The failure was caused in part by the inadequacy of some SIPs, the intransigence of some sources, inadequate federal and state enforcement, litigation that delayed the implementation of some state regulations, and what a congressional report called "the overall complexities of air pollution control." National Commission on Air Quality, To Breathe Clean Air 112 (1981).

But the real problems lay in the technical and economic challenge of effective pollution control in badly polluted areas. For SO_x or TSP, the primary causes of missed deadlines were high concentrations of sources in industrialized eastern and midwestern areas (thus requiring a larger percentage reduction by each source), and the difficulties of adequately controlling emissions at large smelters and electrical generating facilities located primarily in the West.

The main reasons the deadlines for mobile source pollutant ambient standards were missed are more complex. First, the SIP deadlines were hopelessly optimistic in view of the magnitude of the ozone (photochemical oxidant) and CO problem in some urban areas. Second, Congress extended the deadlines for achieving the 1975 and 1976 emissions standards for new vehicles into the late 1970s. Even if the states had the will, the Act only allowed California to set its own emissions standards for new vehicles. Instead, to control mobile source emissions the statute thrust the states back on secondary strategies such as dispersing traffic, providing incentives not to drive or to take mass transit, policing the performance of new car emissions control systems through inspection and maintenance programs, and (in theory more than in practice) setting retrofit standards for older vehicles. Third, the secondary techniques directly affected the driving public, sometimes in ways that drivers viewed as exceedingly restrictive. As a result, these nontechnological control alternatives crumbled one by one under the political reality of the average American's daily dependence on the automobile.

Against this backdrop, EPA attempted to provide for new industrial growth with its 1975 "offset" program. This program allowed new sources to build in non-attainment areas if they could offset their new emissions by cutting back emissions at other existing facilities or by paying other existing sources to reduce emissions. EPA also confronted the automobile head-on. For example, EPA promulgated and the Ninth Circuit approved draconian gas rationing regulations for Los Angeles, explaining that attaining the ambient standards for some mobile source pollutants would require an 82 percent reduction in summer automobile traffic in the city. City of Santa Rosa v. EPA, 534 F.2d 150 (9th Cir. 1976). The rules were subsequently withdrawn.

The 1977 amendments. To avoid such steps in other cases, EPA sought direct legislative relief from the mid-1970s SIP deadlines, and its offset policy provided Congress with a focus for its 1977 non-attainment amendments to the Clean Air Act. See Currie, Relaxation of Implementation Plans under the 1977 Clean Air Act Amendments, 78 Mich. L. Rev. 155, 185-186 (1979). In the 1977 amendments Congress gave EPA and regulated sources the delays they sought but in return tightened up SIP implementation and enforcement in non-attainment areas and codified the offset policy. Before continuing, you should review the brief summary of the 1977 non-attainment provisions provided in section C *supra*.

1.   The Non-Attainment Problem: Ozone and Carbon Monoxide

Excessive concentrations of ozone (smog) and carbon monoxide are the major non-attainment problems in urban areas today:

> Ozone formation in the atmosphere is a complex process involving a number of different pollutants and conditions. It is generally agreed that volatile organic compounds (VOCs) and nitrogen oxides are the major precursors to ozone. The major sources of VOCs are industrial processes (40%), transportation (40%), and nonindustrial uses of solvents (15%). Major sources of nitrogen oxides are electricity and industrial boilers (47%), industrial process heaters (3%), and transportation (48%). [Congressional Research Serv. (Envt. & Natural Resources Policy Div.), Clean Air Act: Ozone Nonattainment 3 (1988).]

Hydrocarbons (HC) are an important VOC. EPA at one time had a NAAQS for HC but withdrew it because it could not be implemented in practice.

The multiple sources of ozone precursors make control difficult:

> The relationship between ozone and its precursors is complex. Reducing emission of VOCs or NO_x may or may not produce a decrease in ozone concentrations, depending on the mix of pollutants that is present. Reducing NO_x can even increase ozone concentrations, in some instances. The effect of emission control on ozone concentrations depends on meteorological conditions, the absolute and relative amounts of VOCs and NO_x emitted in a particular area, and the background concentrations of ozone and its precursors that are present. Every urban area has a different balance between VOCs and NO_x. Furthermore, day-to-day variability in emissions levels, background VOC and NO_x concentrations and wind patterns leads to day-to-day variations in the balance between VOCs and NO_x in each area. [U.S. Office of Technology Assessment, Urban Ozone and the Clean Air Act 58 (1988).]

The ozone non-attainment problem varies tremendously around the country. Three groupings are possible:

> Central and Southern California, where the air quality standard is exceeded over entire metropolitan areas for days, and sometimes weeks at a time.
> Houston and the New York area, where exceedances occur over most of the metropolitan areas on up to a dozen or so occasions per year for one or a few days each.
> The rest of the country, where exceedances occur in parts of metropolitan areas on a handful of occasions per year, seldom, if ever, lasting more than a day or two each. [Congressional Research Serv. (Envt. & Natural Resources Policy Div.), Ozone/Carbon Monoxide Nonattainment: Is It What It Seems to Be? 13, 14 (1988).]

In addition, exposure to ozone varies significantly during different times of the day and health effects are minimized because much of the population is indoor most of the time, where ozone does not penetrate. Id. at 9-13. The conclusion is that exceedances in metropolitan areas may overstate the ozone health problem. What does this say about the cost of ozone controls, which are estimated at between $5.8 and $6.8 billion per year by 1993? See Urban Ozone and the Clean Air Act, *supra*, at 106.

Carbon monoxide is different:

> Carbon monoxide, unlike ozone, is an emitted pollutant. It is a product of combustion of all materials containing carbon and is thus emitted by power plants, furnaces, fires of all sorts, and engines. In urban areas, engines in motor vehicles are the largest single source category. . . .
>
> For the most part, CO exceedances occur in "hot spots" of high concentration near major traffic arteries and intersections. . . .
>
> [Warm weather increases ozone emissions, but cold weather increases CO emissions, CO migrates indoors while ozone does not, and the health effects of CO differ.] The basic effect is a reduction in the oxygen carrying capacity of the blood, leading to heart problems and depression of the central nervous system. The extent of effect is a function of the concentration of CO and the length of time exposed. CO is a cumulative poison. . . .
>
> [O]utdoor levels of CO are of relatively greater health concern to a fairly well-defined group of people — those whose jobs require them to work in the areas of high concentration. . . .
>
> [T]his view would lend greater significance to the issue of cost effectiveness of strategies and somewhat less to the issue of overall attainment as soon as possible. For example, attention to the occupational exposure of workers would address acute health needs, while cost effectiveness considerations would imply a long term approach to both indoor and outdoor emission sources. There would be less relative need for fast, area-wide response measures with high social and economic costs such as some transportation controls and technology-forcing emission standards. [Ozone/Carbon Monoxide Non-attainment, *supra*, at 17, 18).]

2.   Non-Attainment Area Plans and Sanctions

The 1977 amendments introduced a complicated Part D of the Act that provides specific requirements for non-attainment plans. The most important new provisions for stationary sources were the emissions offset program and the requirement for more stringent emission controls. These are discussed later in this section. Other important provisions governed controls over motor vehicles, termed mobile sources. Ozone standard compliance deadlines were extended to the end of 1987, and Congress extended them once more by resolution until the end of 1988. To enforce the non-attainment plan provisions, Congress authorized EPA to withhold federal funds for highways and to impose a ban on the construction of new stationary sources of pollution.

How the non-attainment plan process works can be illustrated by reviewing the process of developing and implementing a non-attainment plan for ozone:

1) First, the extent and severity of the local air quality problem is determined by monitoring ambient ozone concentrations. . . .

2) [The next step] is an inventory of VOC and NO$_x$ emissions that covers both stationary and mobile sources. . . . [This requires an] estimate of current emissions of both precursors . . . [and] changes that are anticipated to occur in the future without additional local control efforts. . . .

3) The next step is to use a mathematical model to predict how much emissions will have to be reduced (in addition to reductions that will be achieved through federally-implemented control programs) to meet the ozone standard. . . .

4) Each nonattainment area must develop a control strategy that allocates the required emissions reductions among sources in the area, and then design programs to carry out the strategy. . . . [The regulations required for the SIP are then approved through the state regulatory process and sent to EPA for approval. The plan is then implemented and revised as necessary.] [Urban Ozone and the Clean Air Act, *supra*, at 120-121.]

This report analyzed the following source-specific control strategies:

Reasonably Available Control Technology, which the Act requires as the basis for emissions limitations for stationary sources in non-attainment areas;

Adoption by EPA of new Control Technique Guidelines (CTGs) for several existing stationary sources of VOC;

Establishment of new federally regulated controls on selected stationary VOC sources;

Onboard technology on motor vehicles to capture gasoline vapor during refueling;

Advanced "Stage II" control devices on gas pumps to capture gasoline vapor during motor vehicle refueling;

Inspection and maintenance (I & M) programs for motor vehicles to test the performance of catalytic converters;

More stringent exhaust emissions standards for gasoline highway vehicles;

New federal restrictions on fuel volatility; and

The use of methanol instead of gasoline as a fuel for vehicles in centrally owned fleets. Id. at 79.

The report found that RACT and fuel volatility control would produce over half the expected reduction in emissions from these measures by 1993 as compared with 1985 levels. Id. at 81. Cost per ton of VOC removed was between $2,900 and $7,200 for RACT but only between $320 and $700 for limits on fuel volatility.

NOTES AND QUESTIONS

1. *The implementation problem.* Differences in the cost-effectiveness of different control strategies and the complexity of controlling ozone formation complicate the development of a successful implementation plan. Should Congress deal with this problem by making control priorities and selection depend on the severity of the ozone problem? On cost-effectiveness? Does this mean we

need separate and carefully tailored programs for places like Los Angeles and New York, where the ozone problem is most serious?

Reviews of non-attainment plan implementation efforts have revealed serious drawbacks. These include incomplete and inadequate emissions inventories, underestimating the extent of required controls, difficulties at the state level in issuing stationary source regulations, poor control over emissions growth, and a lack of leadership and political will to solve the problem. See GAO, Air Pollution: Ozone Attainment Requires Long-Term Solutions to Solve Complex Problems (1988), and Urban Ozone and the Clean Air Act, *supra*, at 122-128. Are these defects in implementation readily cured? What pressures do they place on EPA and the states? On citizen groups seeking to enforce the requirements of the Act?

2. *Federal options when SIPs are inadequately implemented.* EPA can assume direct responsibility for promulgating a SIP, for enforcing an already approved SIP, or for both when a SIP is inadequate or is inadequately implemented. See §§110(c)(1) and 113(a)(2). But EPA would quickly overtax its resources if it took complete charge of administering and enforcing major SIP requirements on the local level, even for a short time. Thus the urge to find some way *both* to select the precise means by which the states were to meet the Clean Air Act deadlines *and* to require state and local governmental personnel to carry them out. See McCarthy v. Thomas, 18 Envt. L. Rep. 21025 (D. Ariz. 1988), where the court held that EPA had not demonstrated it was impossible for it to meet a court-imposed deadline for a federal implementation plan for Maricopa County, which includes Phoenix.

A guiding premise of the Clean Air Act has been that the federal government will not interfere with the state's choice of SIP components, so long as the components chosen enable the state to achieve the ambient standards in time to meet the statutory deadlines. The least intrusive federal option is to refuse to approve a proposed SIP, or to withdraw prior approval because the SIP no longer meets one or more §110(a)(2) requirements; then the state must propose alternative, stricter measures to avoid further EPA disapproval and possible sanctions. See Arizona v. Thomas, 829 F.2d 834 (9th Cir. 1987) (upholding EPA's disapproval of Arizona SIP for failure to meet CO standard); Michigan v. Thomas, 805 F.2d 176 (6th Cir. 1986) (EPA has broad discretion in defining RACT).

When the 1982 deadlines were not met, and when they were not met again in 1987, EPA granted and some courts sustained generous conditional approvals to large portions of noncomplying SIPs, although the Act did not authorize conditional approvals. See Reed, Circuit Courts Endorse Conditional SIP Approval, Connecticut's Construction Ban Restored, 12 Envtl. L. Rep. (Envtl. L. Inst.) 10,055 (1982).

Abramovitz v. EPA, 832 F.2d 1071 (9th Cir. 1987), undercut the validity of conditional approvals. The court ordered EPA to disapprove a SIP for the Los Angeles area and impose new source construction bans. It also held that EPA must disapprove a SIP that does not show attainment of the ozone standard by the compliance date and "face up to implementing the measures which are to be triggered by failure to meet attainment requirements." EPA had earlier pro-posed a new round of planning for areas that did not meet attainment in the near term and to reserve sanctions, as it had done previously, for states that failed to submit adequate plans. Abramovitz casts doubt on this proposal. See GAO, EPA's Ozone Policy Is a Positive Step but Needs More Legal Authority (1988).

3. *Federal sanctions.* Repeated state refusals to prepare an adequate SIP may force EPA to invoke stiffer sanctions. The 1977 amendments imposed a ban on new construction of major stationary sources in non-attainment areas if the state did not have an EPA-approved SIP in place after mid-1979 and if the SIP did not attain the ambient standards by 1983. See §§110(a)(2)(I) and 172(a)(1). Other measures empowered EPA to withhold the states' sewage treatment (§316) and transportation funding (§176(a)) if the submission and compliance deadlines were not met.

EPA interpreted its obligation to impose sanctions narrowly. It ruled it would not impose construction bans on new sources solely for a failure to achieve standards by the statutory attainment dates. Areas that had received final approval of a 1979 SIP would be given an additional year following a notice of deficiency to attain the standards. 48 Fed. Reg. 98,606 (1983). Dressman v. Costle, 759 F.2d 548 (6th Cir. 1985) ruled that EPA had authority to bar the construction of new stationary sources of ozone pollution in counties that did not have an approved SIP or I & M programs.

EPA was equally unenthusiastic about the funding cutoff provisions, but applied them to states that had not enacted legislation to implement I & M programs. See Mountain States Legal Foundation v. Costle, 630 F.2d 754 (10th Cir. 1980), *cert. denied,* 450 U.S. 1050 (1981); Pacific Legal Foundation v. Costle, 627 F.2d 917 (9th Cir. 1980), *cert. denied,* 450 U.S. 914 (1981). See also Delaware Valley Citizens' Council for Clean Air v. Pennsylvania, 553 F. Supp. 869 (E.D. Pa.) (state held in contempt when legislature refused to appro-priate funds for I & M program), *denial of motions to modify and stay aff'd,* 674 F.2d 976 (3d Cir.), *civil contempt order and injunction aff'd,* 678 F.2d 470 (3d Cir. 1982). Delaware Valley Citizens Council for Clean Air v. Pennsylvania, 762 F.2d 272 (3d Cir. 1985), held that a state court may not invalidate a federally mandated I & M program.

Sanctions have also been imposed in a number of recent cases through citizens suits that have sought to force compliance with the non-attainment plan provisions. See p. 178 *supra.* In some of these cases the courts imposed deadlines on states that had not adopted required control strategies. See American Lung Assn. v. Kean, 871 F.2d 219 (3d Cir. 1989).

Federalism-based Tenth Amendment challenges to sanctions arose when National League of Cities v. Usery, 426 U.S. 833 (1976) was law. But see United States v. Ohio Department of Safety, 635 F.2d 1195 (6th Cir. 1980), *cert. denied,* 451 U.S. 949 (1981) (upholding EPA enforcement action against state refusing to deny registration to vehicles not passing I & M inspection). Garcia v. Metro-politan Transit Authority, 469 U.S. 528 (1985) overruled *National League* and held that the only recourse of the states against federal legislation based on the commerce power, like the Clean Air Act, is through their political representation in Congress.

4. *Redesignating non-attainment areas.* Some states have attempted to escape non-attainment area requirements by redesignating these areas to attainment status. Ohio v. Ruckelshaus, 776 F.2d 1333(6th Cir. 1985), *cert. denied,* 106 S. Ct. 2889 (1986), upheld EPA's refusal to allow redesignation of an upwind county that is de jure a part of the Cleveland non-attainment area. Compare Illinois State Chamber of Commerce v. EPA, 775 F.2d 1141 (7th Cir. 1985) (reversing as inconsistent with prior implementation policy EPA's refusal to allow redesignation of two ozone non-attainment areas because they contributed to non-attainment in nearby Chicago.) See Reed, When Is an Area That Is Attainment Not an Attainment Area, 16 Envtl. L. Rep. (Envtl. L. Inst.) 10041 (1986).

3.   Controlling Emissions from Vehicles in Non-Attainment Areas

A critical element in EPA's pre-1977 mobile source strategy was the Transportation Control Plan (TCP), through which it sought in some areas to impose dramatic and even draconian controls on automobile usage. The key to the TCP is reducing the use of the automobile through a variety of controls ranging from encouraging carpooling to improvements in public mass transit. These measures are known as Transportation Control Measures (TCMs).

The 1977 amendments curtailed federal authority to control mobile source pollution through transportation control plans (TCPs). In addition to earlier legislation that prohibited EPA from promulgating parking surcharges and from spending federal funds to regulate or tax parking facilities, Congress gave the states until 1987 to achieve the ambient air quality standards for ozone and CO and suspended existing TCP provisions for private vehicle retrofit, gas rationing, parking supply reduction, and bridge tolls. The 1977 Act did not say that these or similar TCP measures could be required again when EPA reviewed the second generation of SIPs due in 1979. Moreover, the 1977 legislation prohibited the imposition of federal controls on indirect sources that attract large numbers of vehicles. The statute did provide for fund cutoffs and project disapprovals by federal agencies if the SIP was not approved, or thereafter if a project did not conform to the relevant SIP.

The SIPs of states that were granted until 1987 to achieve the ozone or CO ambient standards had to include a "specific schedule" for imposition of an auto emissions control inspection and maintenance program. After the 1977 amendments, I & M programs became the principal TCP strategy. The states persuaded EPA that they should be allowed to rely heavily on the emissions reductions the federal vehicle emissions standards were supposed to achieve in order to meet the 1983 and 1987 compliance deadlines. But we have already seen that despite federal authority to certify, test, and recall vehicles, enforce warranty provisions, and prosecute persons who tamper with pollution control devices or use unleaded fuels, the performance of emissions controls falls off rapidly soon after vehicles are put into service.

Review again the measures for achieving ozone standards attainment, p. 254 *supra*. Which of these are mobile-related, and which seem most likely to succeed?

NOTES AND QUESTIONS

1. *The efficiency of I & M.* I & M programs have been very much at the center of political and legal controversy over the implementation of non-attainment plans. Yet a recent report indicates that in the group of accepted control strategies listed earlier, enhanced I & M programs will account for only 10 percent of VOC reductions by 1993 at a cost of between $2500 and $5100 per ton of VOC removed. Urban Ozone and the Clean Air Act, *supra* at 81, 112. These findings support an earlier cautious evaluation of these programs:

> Mandatory inspection and repair strategies designed to reduce emissions from vehicles in actual use . . . are only marginally effective, are costly, and require substantial administrative effort. They should be used only in those few highly polluted metropolitan areas where even slight reductions in emissions must be taken advantage of to avoid serious health hazards. [F. Grad, A. Rosenthal, L. Rockett, J. Fay, J. Heywood, J. Kain, G. Ingram, D. Harrison & T. Teitenberg, The Automobile and the Regulation of Its Impact on the Environment 431 (1975).]

Many cities and states vigorously oppose I & M. Some of their objections challenge the data regarding the potential overall reductions I & M can achieve, its cost-effectiveness, and the accuracy with which it can identify offending vehicles. Other objections are harder to meet. One of these questions the need for I & M as stricter federal emissions standards and fuel efficiency requirements come into effect. Further, new vehicles are equipped with more advanced emissions control technology that is more reliable, less vulnerable to tampering or disconnection, and more expensive and difficult to inspect. In response to EPA regulations, manufacturers have made idle mixture and choke adjustments impossible to carry out without removing the carburetor and using special tools. Yet even these advanced systems can fail.

Evaluations continue to be critical of I & M programs. M. Walsh, Critical Analysis of the Federal Motor Vehicle Control Program 73-81 (1988) notes that effective I & M programs can reduce HC and CO emissions by 25 percent but reports a number of implementation problems. These include decentralized implementation to private garages using manual analyzers and the abuse of waivers that excuse motorists from repairs when costs are too high. Walsh also recommends the extension of I & M programs to nitrogen oxides and particulates. See also GAO, Vehicle Emissions Inspection and Maintenance Program Is behind Schedule (1985); Ostrov, Inspection and Maintenance of Automotive Pollution Controls: A Decade-Long Struggle among Congress, EPA and the States, 9 Harv. Envtl. L. Rev. 139 (1984).

2. *Gasoline vapor recovery.* Another control strategy that has attracted attention because of its impact on motoring costs is the recovery of gasoline vapor hydrocarbon VOCs that escape during refueling. Vapor escape from uncontrolled refueling contributes close to a billion pounds of VOCs per year, but this is only 2 percent of total VOC emissions. One report notes:

> There are three basic ways to reduce the amount of gasoline vapor which enters the atmosphere through refueling:
>
> — reduce the gasoline's volatility;
> — capture the gasoline vapors in a container "on board" the vehicle; and
> — capture the gasoline vapors by routing them back to the station's main tank (called Stage II controls, where Stage I recovers vapors when the station's main storage tanks are filled).
>
> Each of these options has advantages and disadvantages. The costs are high and flow to consumers through different industries. Response times differ, as do relative efficiencies and ease of administration. As a result, political pressures have been high, and EPA and the [Reagan] Administration have been reluctant to make the ultimate commitment by promulgating regulation. [Congressional Research Serv. (Envt. & Natural Resources Policy Div.), Clean Air Act: Gasoline Vapor Recovery 4 (1988).]

EPA has proposed regulations for gasoline volatility and onboard controls, and some states have adopted Stage II controls for gasoline stations, but the control option issue is not yet resolved. See American Lung Assn. v. Kean, 871 F.2d 319 (3d Cir. 1989) (upholding court-imposed schedule requiring New Jersey to adopt Stage II controls).

3. *Land use and transportation control measures.* If I & M and other emissions reduction measures do not succeed in attaining air quality standards in the urban areas that do not meet the ozone standard, the states will have to adopt additional land use and transportation control measures. Each of these may become the focus of struggle over the need for the measure, its stringency, and the speed with which it must be implemented, reminiscent of the controversial experiment with federal land use controls that the 1970 Act appeared to authorize. See Mandelker & Rothschild, The Role of Land-Use Controls in Combating Air Pollution under the Clean Air Act of 1970, 3 Ecology L.Q. 235 (1973).

The adoption and implementation of plans with transportation control measures (TCMs) have continued since the 1977 amendments, but have lost momentum because of fuel price decreases, reductions in federal grants for mass transit and the reluctance of local governments to fund transit operating costs. Congressional Research Serv., The Role of Transportation Controls in Urban Air Quality 21 (1988). This report estimates reductions in precursor ozone emissions from TCMs at only from one to three percent and notes the problems they present:

> TCMs require major investments of institutional time, talent, and management. They are immensely detailed. They deal with each major employer in the planning

260 Chapter III. Protecting the Air Resource

area for work schedules, carpooling programs, and incentive programs for employee use of public transit. They deal with red light synchronization on dozens of main arteries, and congestion at hundreds of intersections. They address bus routes and schedules, bicycle lanes, shopping center layouts, transportation networks, sites and institutional arrangements for fringe parking, and various ways to entice people out of their cars. [Id. at 20.]

A number of recent cases brought to compel compliance with the Act's non-attainment provisions have attempted to compel the adoption of TCMs. See Note 3, *supra*. But see Council of Commuter Organizations v. Thomas (II), 799 F.2d 879 (2d Cir. 1986) (New York City can maintain rather than improve public transit as measure to meet "basic transportation needs" as required by Act).

4. *A federal plan for Los Angeles?* The *Abramovitz* decision, *supra*, led EPA late in 1988 to publish a notice of rulemaking in which it candidly discussed the hard choices required in adopting a federal implementation plan for the Los Angeles area that would bring it into attainment. 53 Fed. Reg. 49,494 (1988). The notice discusses a variety of controls on stationary sources such as those described earlier, as well as land use and transportation controls. EPA had earlier imposed a construction ban on the area. 19 Envt. Rep. (BNA): Current Developments 755 (1988).

As the Notice points out, a plan that would achieve attainment in five years would have to ban all except electrified vehicles and "would deny access to employment to all but those capable of working at home or commuting to work by mass transit, vanpool, electric vehicle, bicycle, or foot." Id. at 49,513. The Notice points out that the average commuting trip in the area is 20 miles. In addition, a five-year plan would have to secure an 80 to 90 percent reduction in VOCs from existing sources and "prohibit economic growth of any kind." Id. at 49,514.

The regional planning agency for the area later adopted a regional Air Quality Management Plan that proposes land use measures, such as requirements for a jobs-housing balance in new development that would reduce commuting. 19 Envt. Rep. (BNA): Current Developments 2523 (1989). Implementation of the plan is far from assured, and the EPA Notice discusses ways in which a federal plan can supplement local efforts. Id. at 49,515-49,518. Yet, as EPA ultimately notes, it cannot implement many of the measures in the regional plan because many of them, such as "land use measures, incentive based transportation control measures (TCMs), and long-range transit planning," require local commitment and initiative. Id. at 49,518. For discussion of the plan see Salvesen, Seeing Through the Smog in LA, Urban Land, Vol. 48, No. 6, at 36 (1989).

5. *Indirect source review.* The 1977 amendments expressly eliminated federal measures that attempt to improve air quality through land use controls on the spacing and location of facilities that attract large numbers of vehicles. These "indirect sources" include highways, airports, parking garages and lots, shopping centers, and large office and apartment buildings. EPA may not promulgate and enforce its own indirect source review (ISR) as part of a SIP, except for federally

assisted projects such as highways, airports, and office buildings; nor may EPA disapprove a SIP because it does not include an ISR program. States are free to adopt ISRs if they wish. To stress the point, the phrase "land use and transportation controls," formerly used in §110(a)(2)(B) to describe a category of SIP components, was reduced to "transportation controls."

In proscribing ISR, Congress's rationale was plain: severely polluted cities might find that the Clean Air Act had effectively transferred land use siting decisions away from local government, which had traditionally exercised them, and to the federal EPA. EPA could then enforce single-purpose air-quality-based planning and zoning, potentially with locally disruptive social and economic impacts. H.R. Rep. No. 294, 95th Cong., 1st Sess. 1301 (1977).

Some states had already placed ISRs in their SIPs prior to 1977. To get them out, did a state have to demonstrate that without the ISR it could still attain the ambient standards by the 1983 or 1987 deadlines? The EPA thought not, but the Second Circuit disagreed. Further, the court said that if a state balked after EPA refused to let it drop the ISR, "the Administrator's remedy would be to enforce the state ISR." Manchester Environmental Coalition v. EPA, 612 F.2d 56, 59 (2d Cir. 1979). But Connecticut ultimately did succeed in getting EPA to approve its revocation of ISR. Connecticut Fund for the Environment v. EPA, 672 F.2d 998, 1012 (2d Cir. 1982).

All facilities that could be subjected to parking supply reductions — parking lots, garages, and other existing off-street facilities — are clearly excluded from EPA-imposed control. But the Act makes it equally clear that EPA could impose controls on new or existing on-street parking and other "transportation control measures" (§110(a)(5)(C), (E); §110(a)(2)(B)). Do exclusive bus and car pool lanes and other traffic flow improvement strategies that involve modifying highways or highway use (e.g., bike lanes) fit the definition for indirect sources?

4. Controlling Emissions from Stationary Sources in Non-Attainment Areas

a. Emissions Trading and Offsets

Since 1977, new sources have continued to bear the heaviest cleanup burden under the Act. Major new or modified stationary sources must obtain a permit and meet a new technology-based emissions standard defined by the "lowest achievable emissions rate" (LAER) for the applying facility. LAER was intended to be the strictest of the Clean Air Act's technology-based standards, stricter than the "best available control technology" (BACT) applicable in clean air areas, which in turn is stricter than the NSPS.

To relieve some of the pressure on new sources seeking to locate in non-attainment areas, EPA's offsets policy was incorporated in the 1977 amendments. If a second generation SIP does not require existing sources to reduce emissions enough to accommodate new construction without causing the ambient standards to be exceeded, the new source must secure, from whatever currently emitting sources it can, a reduction in emissions more than sufficient to offset the new emissions from the proposed facility. This type of emissions trading is called an extra-source offset to distinguish it from "bubbles" for existing sources, which are called intra-source offsets. See p. 246 *supra*. Note that a "new" source is defined to include a "modified" source.

EPA's Emissions Trading Policy Statement defines an extra-source offset:

> In *nonattainment* areas, major new stationary sources and major modifications are subject to a preconstruction permit requirement that they secure sufficient surplus emission reductions to more than "offset" their emissions. This requirement is designed to allow industrial growth in nonattainment areas without interfering with attainment and maintenance of ambient air quality standards. [51 Fed. Reg. 43,814, 43,839 (1986).]

One of the problems with extra-source offsets is whether they represent real reductions in emissions or whether they are spurious. The next case considers this issue. In this case, a citizens' group opposed plans to locate the second largest oil refinery ever built on the east coast at Portsmouth, Virginia. This lawsuit focused on the anticipated increase in HC emissions, which were already excessive in the area, and which were then governed by a now-repealed NAAQS. The case arose under an earlier Interpretive Ruling that preceded the Emissions Trading Policy, but the issues also arise under the new Policy even though hydrocarbons are no longer governed by a NAAQS.

Other potential environmental problems also made the Portsmouth refinery controversial from the beginning. The nearby Elizabeth River was already heavily polluted and water supplies strained; fuel facilities caused some 800 spills a year. The Interior Department called the refinery site one of the most undesirable on the east coast. Local officials welcomed the prospect of several hundred new jobs and a $5 million annual increase in income from property taxes. See Sulzberger, Refinery Prompts Classic Battle of Energy v. Ecology, N.Y. Times, Aug. 7, 1979, at 1, col. 4.

CITIZENS AGAINST THE REFINERY'S EFFECTS v. EPA
643 F.2d 183 (4th Cir. 1981)

K. K. HALL, Circuit Judge.

Citizens Against the Refinery's Effects (CARE) appeals from a final ruling by the Administrator of the Environmental Protection Agency (EPA) approving the Virginia State Implementation Plan (SIP) for reducing hydrocarbon pollutants. The plan requires the Virginia Highway Department to decrease usage of a certain type of asphalt, thereby reducing hydrocarbon pollution by more than enough to offset expected pollution from the Hampton Roads Energy Company's (HREC) proposed refinery. We affirm the action of the administrator in approving the state plan. . . .

[Before the 1977 amendments] [t]he Clean Air Act created a no-growth environment in areas where the clean air requirements had not been attained. EPA recognized the need to develop a program that encouraged attainment of clean air standards without discouraging economic growth. Thus the agency proposed an Interpretive Ruling in 1976 which allowed the states to develop an "offset program" within the State Implementation Plans. 41 Fed. Reg. 55,524 (1976). The offset program, later codified by Congress in the 1977 Amendments to the Clean Air Act, permits the states to develop plans which allow construction of new pollution sources where accompanied by a corresponding reduction in an existing pollution source. In effect, a new emitting facility can be built if an existing pollution source decreases its emissions or ceases operations as long as a positive net air quality benefit occurs.

If the proposed factory will emit carbon monoxide, sulfur dioxide, or particulates, the EPA requires that the offsetting pollution source be within the immediate vicinity of the new plant. The other two pollutants, hydrocarbons and nitrogen oxide, are less "site-specific," and thus the ruling permits the offsetting source to locate anywhere within a broad vicinity of the new source.

The offset program has two other important requirements. First, a base time period must be determined in which to calculate how much reduction is needed in existing pollutants to offset the new source. This base period is defined as the first year of the SIP or, where the state has not yet developed a SIP, as the year in which a construction permit application is filed. Second, the offset program requires that the new source adopt the Lowest Achievable Emissions Rate (LAER) using the most modern technology available in the industry.

The Refinery

HREC proposes to build a petroleum refinery and offloading facility in Portsmouth, Virginia. Portsmouth has been unable to reduce air pollution enough to attain the national standard for one pollutant, photochemical oxidants, which is created when hydrocarbons are released into the atmosphere and react with other substances. Since a refinery is a major source of hydrocarbons, the Clean Air Act prevents construction of the HREC plant until the area attains the national standard.

In 1975, HREC applied to the Virginia State Air Pollution Control Board (VSAPCB) for a refinery construction permit. The permit was issued by the VSAPCB on October 8, 1975, extended and reissued on October 5, 1977 after a full public hearing, modified on August 8, 1978, and extended again on September 27, 1979. The VSAPCB, in an effort to help HREC meet the clean air requirements, proposed to use the offset ruling to comply with the Clean Air Act.

On November 28, 1977, the VSAPCB submitted a State Implementation Plan to EPA which included the HREC permit. The Virginia Board proposed to offset the new HREC hydrocarbon pollution by reducing the amount of cutback asphalt[5] used for road paving operations in three highway districts by the Virginia Department of Highways.[6] By switching from "cutback" to "emulsified" asphalt, the state can reduce hydrocarbon pollutants by the amount necessary to offset the pollutants from the proposed refinery.

EPA requested some changes in the state plan, including certain monitoring changes and verification from the Virginia Attorney General that the offset program was legally enforceable. The plan was transmitted by the EPA Region III director to EPA headquarters on September 9, 1978. Notices of the proposed plan were published . . . [and] [n]umerous comments were received, including several from CARE. The EPA administrator carefully considered the comments and approved the Virginia offset plan on January 31, 1980. . . .

We reject the CARE challenges to the state plan. . . .

The Geographic Area

CARE contends that the state plan should not have been approved by EPA since the three highway-district area where cutback usage will be reduced to offset refinery emissions was artificially developed by the state. The ruling permits a broad area (usually within one AQCR) to be used as the offset basis.

The ruling does not specify how to determine the area, nor provide a standard procedure for defining the geographic area. Here the Virginia Board originally proposed to use four highway districts comprising one-half the state as the offset area. When this was found to be much more than necessary to offset pollution expected from the refinery, the state changed it to one highway district plus nine additional counties. Later the proposed plan was again revised to include a geographic area of three highway districts.

The agency action in approving the use of three highway districts was neither arbitrary, capricious, nor outside the statute. First, Congress intended that the states and the EPA be given flexibility in designing and implementing SIPs. Such flexibility allows the states to make reasoned choices as to which areas may be used to offset new pollution and how the plan is to be implemented. Second, the offset program was initiated to encourage economic growth in the state. Thus a state plan designed to reduce highway department pollution in order to attract another industry is a reasonable contribution to economic growth without a corresponding increase in pollution. Third, to be sensibly administered the offset plan had to be divided into districts which could be monitored by the highway department. Use of any areas other than highway districts would be unwieldy and difficult to administer. Fourth, the scientific understanding of ozone pollution is not advanced to the point where exact air transport may be predicted.

5. "Cutback" asphalt has a petroleum base which gives off great amounts of hydrocarbons. "Emulsified" asphalt uses a water base which evaporates, giving off no hydrocarbons.
6. The three highway districts so designated comprise almost the entire eastern one-third of the state. This area cuts across four of the seven Virginia Air Quality Control Regions (AQCR).

Designation of the broad area in which hydrocarbons may be transported is well within the discretion and expertise of the agency. . . .

The Legally Binding Plan

For several years, Virginia has pursued a policy of shifting from cutback asphalt to the less expensive emulsified asphalt in road-paving operations. The policy was initiated in an effort to save money, and was totally unrelated to a State Implementation Plan. Because of this policy, CARE argues that hydrocarbon emissions were decreasing independent of this SIP and therefore are not a proper offset against the refinery. They argue that there is not, in effect, an actual reduction in pollution.

The Virginia voluntary plan is not enforceable and therefore is not in compliance with the 1976 Interpretive Ruling which requires that the offset program be enforceable. 41 Fed. Reg. 55,526 (1976). The EPA, in approving the state plan, obtained a letter from the Deputy Attorney General of Virginia in which he stated that the requisites had been satisfied for establishing and enforcing the plan with the Department of Highways. Without such authority, no decrease in asphalt-produced pollution is guaranteed.[8] In contrast to the voluntary plan, the offset plan guarantees a reduction in pollution resulting from road paving operations. . . . [The court also held that EPA had selected an appropriate base year and had adopted a satisfactory LAER.]

NOTES AND QUESTIONS

1. *Creating emission reduction credits.* EPA's revised Emission Trading Policy Statement applies to offsets. 51 Fed. Reg. 43,814 (1986). The revised Statement tightens emissions trading in non-attainment areas that lack a demonstrated plan to achieve attainment. Emissions trading is allowed in these areas only if it produces a net air quality benefit that will produce additional interim progress toward attaining the national standards. The key issue in trading is the creation of emission reduction credits:

> Emission reduction credits (ERCs) are the common currency of all trading activity. ERCs may be created by reductions from either stationary, area, or mobile sources. To assure that emissions trades do not contravene relevant requirements of the Clean Air Act, only reductions which are *surplus*, *enforceable*, *permanent*, and *quantifiable* can qualify as ERCs and be banked or used in an emissions trade. [51 Fed. Reg. 43,814, 43,831 (1986).]

---

8. Despite the fact that the voluntary plan has been in force for several years, 1977 was the year of the highest consumption of cutback asphalt.

Does the emissions trade in CARE meet these requirements?

What about the CARE decision? EPA studies in the early 1970s revealed that water-based paving asphalt was rapidly replacing petroleum-based asphalt for energy conservation and cost reasons. By 1977 EPA had recognized water-based asphalt paving as a minimum "reasonably available control technology" (RACT) that existing sources of air pollution might adopt (see Control of Volatile Organic Compounds from Use of Cutback Asphalt (1977) (EPA Pub. No. 450/2-77-037)), yet EPA did not require states to impose RACT in non-attainment areas until 1979. See §172(b)(3). Under the CARE decision, Virginia and other resourceful states could generously offer as "legally binding" offsets reduced petroleum-based asphalt use between 1976 and 1979 even though water-based asphalt was cheaper, offered a better energy conservation strategy, was a readily available, soon-to-be-required emission control technology, and was destined for highway use whether or not Clean Air Act offsets were created.

Can a source use emission reduction credits created by the shutdown of another plant? The policy statement allows this if their use is subject to "stringent qualitative review" to ensure consistency with SIP planning goals, such as avoidance of double-counting and shifting demand. 51 Fed. Reg. 43,814, 43,841 (1986). Motivation is not a factor, but there must be a showing that there was an application to make the shutdown state-enforceable through a banking mechanism prior to the time the shutdown occurred. Why? The same rules apply to curtailments.

2. *The offset area.* The three highway districts involved in the offset spanned most of the eastern, mainly rural, third of the state and cut across four Air Quality Control Regions (AQCRs). Unperturbed by Virginia's far-flung search for offsets, the court allowed it to include highways selected from any area into which HC might in time be transported, rather than confining the offsets to the urban area around the new source. Yet the Interpretive Ruling favored keeping offsets at least within the same AQCR as the proposed source and HC offsets in particular within 85 miles of urban areas (because photochemical oxidants form where both HC and NO_x are abundant, i.e., urban concentrations) (41 Fed. Reg. 55,524, 55,527, 55,558-55,559).

The current policy provides:

> Since the ambient impact of . . . [VOCs such as hydrocarbons or NO_x] is areawide rather than localized, one pound of increased emissions will be balanced in ambient effect by one pound of decreased emissions within the same broad area, and the precise location . . . ordinarily does not matter. . . . [T]rades may therefore be treated as equal in ambient effect where all sources involved in the trade are located in the same control strategy demonstration area or the state otherwise shows such source to be sufficiently close that a "pound-for-pound" trade can be justified. [51 Fed. Reg. 43,814, 43,843, 43,844 (1986).]

Does this regulation support the holding in the CARE case? Is it more or less lenient than the similar requirement in the ruling in effect at the time of that case? Note that for other pollutants policy requires a demonstration through designated approved methods that there is "ambient equivalence" in pound-for-pound trades. Id. at 43,844, 43,845. Why are these other pollutants, which include particulate matter, SO_2, CO, and lead treated differently?

3. *Offsets and economic efficiency.* Assuming that the ambient standards have already determined optimal emissions levels overall, do you agree that in theory offsets will eventually produce an economically efficient allocation of emissions reductions among emitting sources in an area? Consider the following:

> The offset price is set by the parties. In theory, the price range would be between the cost of the reducer's (seller's) abatement and the purchaser's potential cost of abatement equipment to prevent its emissions. It is assumed each polluter will hold his rights until the offset price is greater than his costs of emission abatement. If the price of an offset is more than the cost of abatement, the rational profit-motivated decision would be to abate emissions and sell an offset. Theoretically, trading would continue until each polluter's cost of an additional reduction would equal the cost of an additional offset right. Prices would reach this equilibrium because each polluter would reduce pollution by purchasing abatement equipment until the next (marginal) reduction would be equally as costly as purchasing the right to emit pollutants. Limiting the amount of offsets through control of the supply of pollution rights would ensure that the equilibrium price would be relatively high, stimulating voluntary reductions. The allocation of rights would be economically efficient when no source could benefit from a trade without greater cost to another source. [Note, Regulating with a Carrot: Experimenting with Incentives for Clean Air, 31 Buffalo L. Rev. 193, 204-205 (1982).]

See also T. Tietenberg, Emissions Trading 16-30 (1985).

4. *Establishing a dependable and fair supply of marketable offsets.* Note the serious problems associated with establishing the total of allowable emissions for an area (the "pool" of emissions, or the "market"), so that offsets trading can begin. Yet without a fixed, dependable base of allowable emissions, emitters understandably will be reluctant to purchase offsets at high prices, only to find offsets plentiful and cheap the next day. Sources that can provide relatively cheap offsets (i.e., sources with inherently low emissions reductions costs) do not want to part with their emissions rights because they fear that tomorrow they will need them themselves or because offsets may increase greatly in value. An EPA-approved SIP relaxation would automatically create new offset possibilities, and a SIP constriction would potentially extinguish them. In markets in which the government prints new money or restricts money supply, prices fluctuate and the outcomes of economic transactions become less predictable. Offset transactions are sensitive to the same risks. For discussion of abuse of power by sellers of ERCs see Tietenberg, *supra*, ch. 6.

Offset constriction may occur through RACT. In non-attainment areas, emission reductions must reduce baseline emissions, defined as the lower of either SIP-approved emissions or RACT, the emissions control required in these areas by §172(b)(3). If the state had earlier allowed sources to emit a greater quantity of emissions than RACT allows, such existing sources may suddenly find that the cheap emissions reduction potential they had "banked" has been wiped out by operation of the minimum RACT requirements. Difficulties in negotiating the applicable RACT have also impeded emission trading. See *United States v. National Steel Co.*, 767 F.2d 176 (6th Cir. 1985); *National Steel Corp., Great Lakes Steel Division v. Gorsuch*, 700 F.2d 314 (6th Cir. 1983).

5. *The "lowest achievable emissions rate" requirement.* The non-attainment provisions require major new sources to install equipment achieving the lowest emissions rate possible. This technology-limited requirement, defined as the "lowest achievable emissions rate" (LAER), is to be determined exclusively by the states, case by case, for each permit. Read the definition of LAER in §171(3).

Theoretically, LAER sets the strictest level of control technology required by the Clean Air Act. But the National Commission on Air Quality found that the states generally have set LAER at or near NSPS, despite EPA efforts to influence the process through control techniques guidance documents and informal jawboning. To Breathe Clean Air, at 138-139 (1981). The Commission consequently recommended that LAER be abolished and replaced with BACT (see pp. 276-280 *infra*), with minor exceptions.

If the offsets policy is in effect, why should LAER be required? Recall that NSPS would also apply. With the offsets policy in effect, are even NSPS necessary? In fact, if total areawide annual emissions quotas are set at levels adequate to ensure "reasonable further progress" and eventual attainment of the ambient standards and if offsets within the quota can be freely bought and sold is there need for any additional regulatory controls at all?

A NOTE ON OFFSET THEORY VERSUS OFFSET PRACTICE

The basic theory of offsets is appealing. An emitting source that wishes to locate or expand in an area finds other existing sources willing to reduce emissions for a price. Because of the ambient standards and the greater than one-for-one offset reductions, a slowly dwindling total pool of emissions rights is established in the region. Emitters buy and sell these rights depending on how costly it is for them to control pollution. EPA is content because it has not retarded industrial growth and is making progress toward the SIP deadlines. Business and economists are reasonably happy because although the total amount of pollution rights has been arbitrarily fixed without regard to economic efficiency, the marginal costs of controlling emissions will become approximately equal across all sources emitting the offset pollution. The sources that can control emissions most cheaply are making the greatest emissions reductions.

The experience with emissions trading has not entirely lived up to these expectations. One estimate is that approximately 2,000 sources used emissions trading through 1986. Hahn & Hester, Where Did All the Markets Go? An Analysis of EPA's Emissions Trading Program, 6 Yale J. Reg. 109, 119 (1989). Although this is below expectations, cost savings appear to be substantial. See Tietenberg, *supra*, ch. 2.

Uncertainties in the process may have inhibited emissions trading. These include uncertainties about baselines, about a firm's current emission levels, and about future control requirements that may wipe out what once was an emission surplus. Many state emission inventories are also unrealistically high, so that allowable emission rates for individual sources may exceed actual rates. This leads to "paper trades." Paper trades occur when emission credits are traded that never really existed or that would have happened anyway. An emission credit resulting from a shutdown is an example. So is an emission credit that results when plant-controlled emissions are lower than RACT. For discussion of these problems see R. Liroff, Reforming Air Pollution Regulation: The Toil and Trouble of EPA's Bubble (1986); Dudek & Palmisano, Emissions Trading: Why Is This Thoroughbred Hobbled?, 13 Colum. J. Envtl. L. 217 (1988).

Problems in emissions trading can be remedied to some extent through creation of a state or local offsets "bank." The bank purchases offsets and holds them until an applicant needs them. Even banks cannot be helpful when markets are especially slow to develop because of low demand, as in the industrially declining Northeast. Note, Regulating with a Carrot: Experimenting with Incentives for Clean Air, 31 Buffalo L. Rev. 193, 207 (1982). EPA's policy statement provides detailed regulations for emissions banks, but few have developed so far although "informal" banks are operating in some areas. See Hahn & Hester, *supra*, at 129-132. If trades work best when there is some leniency in criteria that govern them, but if leniency interferes with improving air quality, how should EPA deal with this problem? Is this an issue for Congress?

b.   "Netting Out" in Dirty Air Areas

To understand how another form of emissions trading occurs, recall that a "modification" of an existing source that increases its emissions is subject to the emission limitations applicable to new sources in non-attainment areas, such as LAER. In a form of emissions trading known as "netting," a modified existing source can avoid having to comply with these requirements:

> [A] company can avoid or reduce these requirements when it compensates for those [emissions] increases by reducing emissions from other points within that source and thereby earning ERCs. Because this trading approach causes the net emissions from the entire source to stay at the same level as they were before the modifications, it is commonly known as *netting*. [R. Liroff, Reforming Air Pollution Regulation: The Toil and Trouble of EPA's Bubble 6 (1986).]

A source that nets does not escape the Act entirely. It must still comply with NSPS requirements, with emissions standards for hazardous pollutants and with preconstruction review requirements. 51 Fed. Reg. 43,814, 43,830 (1986).

The Supreme Court eventually upheld a netting out regulation that was adopted early in the Reagan Administration:

CHEVRON, U.S.A., INC. v. NATURAL RESOURCES
DEFENSE COUNCIL, INC.
457 U.S. 837 (1984)

[Page 128 *supra*]

NOTES AND QUESTIONS

1. A *new view on judicial review*. *Chevron* stands primarily as a strong
judicial statement by the Supreme Court on the need for deference to agency
interpretation of statutes rather than as a critical reading of the Clean Air Act. Is
it also one more rebuke to the judicial activism of the District of Columbia Court
of Appeals in environmental litigation? See also Belsky, Environmental Policy
Law in the 1980's: Shifting Back the Burden of Proof, 12 Ecology L.Q. 1 (1984),
which is a useful foil to probe the "Zeitgeist" of the District of Columbia Court
of Appeals's attitude toward judicial review. For additional discussion of *Chevron*, see Stukane, EPA's Bubble Concept after Chevron v. NRDC: Who Is to
Guard the Guards Themselves?, 17 Nat. Resources L. 647 (1985) and Chapter
2 of this book.

2. *Was the Court right?* Do you agree with the Court's handling of the text
of the statute and the legislative history? Would Congress have enacted a stringent new source review program if it was aware that the cleanup required by the
program could be dodged with ease through the bubble?

What do you think of the Court's holding that economic development is
the principal statutory purpose of the non-attainment program? This interpretation has little support in the legislative history. It was advanced by industry in
the *Chevron* case and then picked up in the brief of the United States Solicitor
General. Could this have influenced the Court?

3. *Netting out in practice*. Netting out has easily been the most popular
form of emissions trading. An estimated 900 sources used netting in 1984, the
only year for which data are available, and cost savings are substantial. Hahn &
Hester, *supra*, at 132-136. Neither does netting appear to have much effect on
environmental quality, primarily because the non-attainment problem in those
areas is due principally to mobile sources. R. Liroff, *supra*, at 132. But note that
netting is an internal trade by the same source. It does not affect markets for
external trades and may actually dampen the market for these trades if a source
can accomplish the same objective internally.

A NOTE ON EMISSIONS TRADING AND THE REFORM OF
THE CLEAN AIR ACT THROUGH THE USE OF
MARKET INCENTIVES

The primary motivation behind the various forms of emissions trading is
to permit plant managers greater choice in deciding how to reduce emissions, so

that they can take advantage of the fact, well understood by environmental economists, that the marginal costs of reducing emissions vary considerably among different types of installations in the same plant, among the same types of installations in different plants, and even among the same types of installations in the same plants. The economists argue that if left alone plant managers would choose to reduce emissions the most in plant components for which marginal emissions control costs are the lowest. If called upon later to make still more reductions, managers would reexamine the marginal emissions control costs for the various pieces of equipment and again make the cheapest reduction. Ultimately, cost-sensitive managers would act so as to equate all marginal emissions control costs throughout entire plants (and, if allowed, over several plants, a region, or the nation). This, the economist concludes, is a better management strategy because the required emissions reductions will have been purchased at the lowest possible cost, freeing the money saved from less efficient approaches for income-producing investment elsewhere.

If different legal requirements apply to the different units in a plant, the manager is deprived of the opportunity to make these cost-minimizing choices. Depending on the legal standard applied, required emissions control investments may vary enormously from one piece of equipment to the next, raising the total investment required to achieve the same amount of emissions reductions.

The policy argument against bubbling has salience as well. Since avoiding NSPS or non-attainment review would allow an existing plant to continue to pollute at the same level while expanding or rebuilding, the bubble and kindred schemes create an incentive to keep an old plant in operation long past its optimal lifetime and discourage opening plants in new areas. Thus two very important national goals — one environmental and one economic — are frustrated: (1) as a general rule, new plants emit less pollution than existing ones, by substantial margins; (2) new plants are more productive because they are built to reflect changing markets, population shifts, resource and labor supplies, and competitive opportunity.

"Controlled trading" to "emissions trading." Together, the various forms of emissions trading would bring about a fundamental reform of the Clean Air Act scheme. Their ultimate goal is to freeze the total emissions quota legally permitted under the Clean Air Act and then to allow emitters maximum leeway to select the combination of emissions reductions or bargains for reductions that minimizes costs nationwide. The idea of developing an overall policy to link the common conceptual underpinnings of bubbles, offsets, netting out, and banking originated in the Carter Administration (in which it was called "controlled trading") was the brainchild of William Drayton, who served as Assistant EPA Administrator for Planning and Management.

When the Reagan Administration took office in 1981, one of the very few Carter Administration initiatives to be retained and expanded at EPA was controlled trading. The emissions trading policy of course cannot modify directly the command-and-control regulatory style of the Clean Air Act. Is it time to amend the Act explicitly to authorize full bubbling? If you were a member of a congressional subcommittee charged with developing the amendments, how far would you be willing to go?

Replacing command-and-control regulation with an incentive-based economic approach. Would you be willing to abandon current Clean Air Act strategies and substitute a new strategy that relies primarily on the economics-based approach? The theoretical advantages to economics-based approaches are considerable. Review the arguments discussed in Chapter 1, at pp. 28-43. Economists have long argued that the Clean Air Act pursues costly, misbegotten ends through even more inept means. See, e.g., R. Crandall, Controlling Industrial Pollution (1983). Practical proposals for management of environmental resources through pricing schemes now have a respectable history. See the proposals discussed in F. Anderson, A. Kneese, P. Reed, R. Stevenson & S. Taylor, Environmental Improvement through Economic Incentives (1977). See also Controlling Industrial Pollution, *supra*, at 156-170, and Noll, The Feasibility of Marketable Emissions Permits in the United States, in Public Sector Economics (J. Finsinger ed. 1983); W. Baumol & W. Oates, The Theory of Environmental Policy 135 (1975); J. Dales, Pollution, Property, and Prices (1968); Economics of the Environment (1972) (R. Dorfman & N. Dorfman eds.); A. Kneese & C. Schultze, Pollution, Prices, and Public Policy (1975); C. Schultze, The Public Use of Private Interest (1977); Ruff, The Economic Common Sense of Pollution, Pub. Interest, Spring 1970, at 69. But see Rose-Ackerman, Effluent Charges: A Critique, 6 Canadian J. Econ. 512 (1973).

Proposals that carry applied microeconomic theory to its logical conclusion go even further. A pure emissions fee would not be based on achieving predetermined levels of ambient air quality; rather, it would be set by comparing the dollar value of the *marginal* (additional, or incremental) damage to health and welfare caused by the last unit of pollutant emitted with the emitter's *marginal* investment in emissions control equipment that will abate that additional unit of pollution. (*Total* damage and *total* costs are different; they are the *sum* of the damage and costs associated with each separate ton of pollutant emitted. Note also that marginal damage equals marginal benefits measured as reduced pollution damage.) The fee for each unit of pollutant emitted should be set equal to the dollar amount at which the marginal damage and marginal abatement costs are equal. In Figure 3-5, for example, as Plant 1's SO_x emissions go up (right to left) to hypothetical maximum uncontrolled emissions of 100 tons, the marginal health and other environmental injury expressed in dollars increases with each marginal ton of emissions (MD). Why may the marginal injury be greater, rather than the same, for the last tons emitted? But as Plant 1 installs more emissions control equipment or otherwise reduces sulfur emissions, its marginal costs of controlling each additional ton rise (MC, left to right). The MC curve becomes especially steep as it approaches very low emissions levels. Do you see why? Note carefully that the MD curve also plots the marginal benefits (MB) of increased abatement when read as reduced damages from left to right. Economists traditionally label this curve for the benefits it plots. At X, marginal damage equals marginal abatement cost. The emissions fee should be set equal to $1,000 per

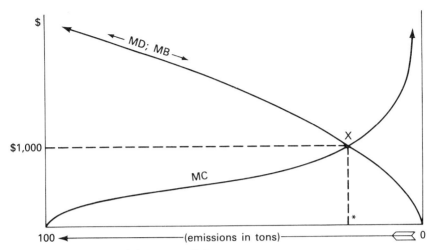

*Tenth ton emitted; ninetieth ton controlled.

FIGURE 3-5
Plant 1: SO$_x$ Emissions

ton — no more, no less. A higher fee would reduce emissions and cause more
to be spent on pollution control, but the additional pollution control costs would
exceed the additional benefits (in terms of reduced damage) from the increased
abatement. A lower fee would not stimulate Plant 1 to control all possible tons
of pollutant for which abatement is cheaper than the injury the emissions inflict.

What other information does the MD or MB curve provide? Does it represent the willingness of receptors to "bribe" Plant 1 to reduce emissions? Does
it also represent the investment receptors should be willing to make to avoid
injury themselves? Sometimes it will be cheaper for the receptors to take measures to reduce pollution injury (e.g., relocate out of the area or stay indoors)
than it is for the emitter to install expensive pollution control equipment. How
should the costs to receptors of avoiding health damage be taken into account in
the pure approach? Note how steep the MD curve is when pollution levels are
very low. Why might the first ton hurt so much? The last so little? Abatement
may proceed in phases, as large units of pollution control equipment are added,
one after the other, so that the MC curve becomes a staircase. What difference
might this make to how the pure emissions fee is set?

Of course, the practical problems of calculating the dollar value of marginal damage and marginal abatement costs for individual sources in thousands
of specific settings around the country are overwhelming. The pure emissions
fee, therefore, remains more of an ideal — a teacher's device — than a concrete
proposal for legislative action. A more practical variant, *averaging* marginal
abatement cost across entire categories of emitters, has attracted numerous proponents. They maintain that the average marginal control costs for key emitting
industries can be determined with reasonable accuracy, so that a charge can be

estimated that, if imposed, will cause abatement expenditures to rise to the necessary level while minimizing the cost or achieving predetermined ambient air quality standards; then an emissions fee can be uniformly applied by category. Further, on the injury side, even the most serious fee system advocates concede the difficulty of computing regional or national environmental injury associated with varying pollution levels and accept a legislative determination of the level of air quality to be sought.

Notwithstanding the theoretical appeal of the emissions fee approach and the luster of its list of impressive advocates, Congress has shown almost no interest in it. See S. Kelman, What Price Incentives? Economists and the Environment (1981), and Kelman, Economics and the Environmental Muddle, Pub. Interest, Summer 1981, at 106. Compare the approach of emissions quota strategies based on land use controls. Mandelker & Sherry, Emissions Quota Strategies as an Air Pollution Control Technique, 5 Ecology L.Q. 401 (1976). Do the land use control and economics-based strategies have anything to offer each other? See D. Mandelker, Environment and Equity (1981).

H.   PREVENTION OF SIGNIFICANT DETERIORATION

1.   Origins and Purposes

Lurking in the background in the late 1960s and early 1970s, while Congress developed the principal elements of contemporary air pollution control policy, was the troublesome issue of what to do about the large areas of the nation that already enjoyed air cleaner than that required by the ambient standards — some 80 percent of the nation's land area. Was the air over these areas to be allowed to deteriorate to the ambient standards?

Congress did not address the nondegradation issue forthrightly until 1977. In the meantime, the initiative passed to the courts and EPA. Motivated primarily to protect the unique vistas in the western national parks, the Sierra Club brought suit in 1972. The Club adopted a simple legal argument: Congress plainly stated in §101 that a purpose of the Clean Air Act was to "protect and enhance" air resources. The Sierra Club thought that EPA had to take Congress at its cryptic word.

Relying on §101, legislative history from the 1960s, and prior federal commitments to maintain existing air quality, the federal district court in Washington, D.C., held that EPA had a nondiscretionary duty to adopt measures that would improve air quality and prevent all but nonsignificant deterioration of existing high air quality levels. The circuit court affirmed without issuing an opinion, and the Supreme Court also affirmed, without opinion, dividing 4 to 4 on the issue. Sierra Club v. Ruckelshaus, 344 F. Supp. 253 (D.D.C. 1972), *aff'd per curiam without opinion* (D.C. Cir. 1972), *aff'd by an equally divided Court*, 412 U.S. 541 (1973). The nondegradation policy undercuts *uniform* ambient air quality standards by creating literally hundreds of air quality zones in which existing air quality must be maintained. This has been called a tertiary air quality standard. Do you see why?

The purpose of PSD. As the search for an acceptable PSD program expanded in the middle and late 1970s, the conceptual bases for PSD underwent steady improvement:

> The PSD program that emerged from Congress in the 1977 Amendments was intended to address a number of concerns. These included the following:
>
> — While the primary ambient air quality standards were intended to protect against adverse health effects with an adequate margin of safety, Congress felt there was some justification to maintain the quality of air that was already cleaner than required by the standards in order to protect against effects on public health. Debate in Congress on the health-based rationale for the PSD program centered on whether the primary ambient standards would be sufficiently stringent to protect against all known or suspected health effects associated with ambient concentrations of pollutants.
>
> — It was believed by Congress that limiting pollution in certain areas to levels below the air quality standards and applying best available control technology to sources also would limit the total amount of pollutants entering the atmosphere. This in turn would reduce adverse effects such as acid rain and impaired visibility resulting from the long-range transport and transformation of pollutants. Limiting the amounts of pollutants transported to areas not attaining the standards would assist those areas in meeting the standards.
>
> — Congress believed that visibility and other air-quality-related values should receive special protection. Visibility, particularly in pristine areas of the West, was perceived as a national resource that should be preserved.
>
> — Congress believed that a national program applied uniformly to maintain clean air in specified areas would enable states wishing to maintain good air to compete for industrial expansion with other states without needing to trade off air quality. There was strong support among some states for a program that would prevent air quality from becoming a bargaining chip in this process.
>
> — Congress also intended that the burden of controlling pollution should be equalized among less industrialized and more industrialized areas. It was argued that some prohibition on emissions growth in clean air areas was needed to prevent industry from moving out of industrialized areas into clean air areas where fewer pollution controls would be needed. A constraint on emissions growth in clean air areas was perceived as necessary if the industrialized states were to maintain their economic base when competing against states with cleaner air for new growth.
>
> — Congress also intended that the program be administered by the states with minimum federal involvement. [National Commission on Air Quality, To Breathe Clean Air 148 (1981). This summary is based on a remarkable "brief" written by the House subcommittee staff in support of the PSD program. See H.R. Rep. No. 294, 95th Cong., 1st Sess. 103-141 (1977).]

While traditionally, preservation efforts have centered on the protection of environmentally sensitive land areas, by the middle of the twentieth century the accelerated pace of urbanization and industrialization had created such widespread despoliation of shared air and water resources that major efforts were mounted to control environmental pollution. As these programs matured, not only were efforts increasingly bent toward abating existing pollution, but a new opportunity was created for extension of the conservation ethic to unpolluted air and water resources. If it is appropriate to preserve wilderness and other geomorphically unique land areas, is it not equally desirable to prevent the deterioration of airsheds and waterways that now enjoy pure air and clean water? The nondegradation policy, which provides a clear affirmative answer to the question, thus represents a new embodiment of the same conservation ethic that underlies most of the recent generation of environmental legislation. It is no coincidence that such a policy was adopted administratively by EPA in the mid-1960s almost simultaneously with a renewed congressional commitment to preservation of wild and scenic areas.

The nondegradation policy is necessitated by the historical evidence that, unless restrained by some external force or internal command, mankind incessantly exploits and ultimately despoils or destroys natural environments. The simple idea on which the policy is based is the recognition that somewhere in the frenzied pursuit of more material possessions and a higher living standard it is morally necessary to think about what kind of world will be passed along to future generations. It is a sobering thought to reflect on the possibility that nature may not continue to exist as we know it. While the nondegradation principle does not rely solely on philosophical grounds for its justification, it will be apparent in examining the process by which the policy has been adopted and refined that at several key decision points the ethical force of the idea best explains the actions taken. [Hines, A Decade of Nondegradation Policy in Congress and the Courts: The Erratic Pursuit of Clean Air and Clean Water, 62 Iowa L. Rev. 643, 645, 649 (1977).]

The regulatory program for PSD. Neither the Clean Air Act, the legislative history, nor Sierra Club v. Ruckelshaus gave EPA the slightest hint about how to design a practical regulatory program for prevention of significant deterioration. Menaced by claims that full implementation of the court's decision would halt industrial growth, particularly in the Southwest, and afraid to act decisively because of what it felt were shallow legal precedents favoring nondegradation, EPA equivocated. It proposed four very different schemes for public comment (38 Fed. Reg. 18,986). In late 1974, the EPA adopted final regulations, based on its fourth option (39 Fed. Reg. 42,510). After the regulations had successfully survived attack from environmental and industrial groups and several states (Sierra Club v. EPA, 540 F. 2d 1114 (D.C. Cir. 1976)), Congress finally acted. See §§160-169A (part C of Title I). The new PSD program was based on the final EPA rules, but it went much further in mandating stringent protection for the Golden Circle of national parks, wilderness areas, and other specially protected natural and recreational areas in the Southwest.

In the summer of 1978 a second set of PSD guidelines appeared (43 Fed. Reg. 26,380), which was immediately subjected to another lawsuit challenging dozens of the specific interpretations of part C EPA had made. The reviewing court took the unusual step of writing a lengthy preliminary opinion (Alabama Power v. Costle, 606 F. 2d 1068 (D.C. Cir. 1979)), followed a few months later by a still lengthier final opinion, a kind of environmental lawyer's PSD hornbook (636 F. 2d 323 (D.C. Cir. 1979)). Alabama Power v. Costle reshaped the PSD program to an appreciable extent. Do you see advantages in having courts issue preliminary opinions when detailed statutes that raise complex scientific and technical issues are being reviewed? See Leventhal, Environmental Decision Making and the Role of the Courts, 122 U. Pa. L. Rev. 509, 546 (1974). To implement *Alabama Power*, EPA revised its regulations a third time (45 Fed. Reg. 52,676), but the Alabama Power litigation is not fully resolved as EPA has not revised its regulations as provided in a settlement agreement.

2.   The Current PSD Program: An Overview

The following excerpt describes the highlights of the current PSD program. When reading this excerpt keep in mind that the PSD program is nationwide. An Air Quality Control Region can be a PSD area for one or more pollutants even though it is a non-attainment area for other pollutants, and no part of the country is non-attainment for all pollutants. No significant reclassifications have been made to Class III, so that an area is either Class I or Class II. The TSP standard has been replaced by a PM-10 standard for small particulates. Thirty states had assumed delegated authority to administer the program as of July 1, 1988.

For the PSD regulations see 40 C.F.R. §52.21. For a thorough review of the program see Oren, Prevention of Significant Deterioration: Control-Compelling v. Site-Shifting, 74 Iowa L. Rev. 1 (1988).

NATIONAL RESEARCH COUNCIL OF THE NATIONAL ACADEMY OF SCIENCES, ON PREVENTION OF SIGNIFICANT DETERIORATION OF AIR QUALITY
5-18 (1981)

In the Clean Air Act Amendments of 1977, Congress specified the initial classification of lands for PSD purposes. Certain lands, where existing good air quality is deemed to be of national importance, were designated Class I and may not be reclassified. These mandatory Class I areas include all international parks, national wilderness areas larger than 5,000 acres, national memorial parks larger than 5,000 acres, and national parks larger than 6,000 acres that were in existence when the amendments were passed. . . . In addition, Congress provided that any other areas that had been redesignated Class I under EPA's previous PSD regulations would remain Class I; these areas, however, are subject to reclassification. All other areas to which the PSD provisions apply were initially designated Class II. . . . [The Act provides procedures for reclassification to Class III.]

Defining Significant Deterioration

The Act defines significant deterioration due to the presence of sulfur dioxide (SO_2) and total suspended particulate matter (TSP) by setting maximum allowable increases over baseline concentrations (increments) for these pollutants for

each of the three classes of land, subject to the restriction that the allowed increases may not result in concentrations that exceed either the primary or the
secondary NAAQS. Increments for SO$_2$ and TSP called the Set I pollutants are
defined for both a long-term (annual) average concentration and maximum concentrations over short periods of time (Table 3-2). The 24-hour and 3-hour maxima and standards may be exceeded once per year.

As a result of the decision in Alabama Power v. Costle, the baseline concentration includes (a) the ambient concentration resulting from actual emissions from existing sources at the time of the first application for a permit to
construct a major emitting facility in a PSD area, and (b) the projected emissions
from major stationary sources that began construction before January 6, 1975,
but had not begun operation by the time of the first permit application. Baseline
conditions also account for natural phenomena that affect air quality.

Contributions to ambient concentrations of SO$_2$ and TSP from certain
sources are not to be taken into account in determining the extent to which the
increments have been consumed. Exemptions are provided for emissions from
plants that are required by law to convert from oil or natural gas to coal and from
new sources located outside the United States. In addition, concentrations of
TSP resulting from temporary construction activities are not counted against the
increments. The exemption of these sources is one reason why simply measuring
changes in ambient concentrations over a period of time cannot be the basis of
a procedure to determine compliance.

The 1977 amendments also require EPA to devise means for preventing
significant deterioration of air quality from other pollutants regulated under the
Act. [These are called the Set II pollutants and EPA has proposed increments
for nitrogen oxides.]

PRECONSTRUCTION REVIEW

To assess the potential consequences of emissions from new sources for
ambient air quality and the consumption of increments, proposed sources of
pollution must be reviewed before construction. However, not all sources are
subject to preconstruction review for PSD purposes. Only major stationary
sources or major modifications to existing stationary sources in areas in which
the PSD provisions apply are subject to review. As a result of the decision in
Alabama Power v. Costle, a major source located in a nonattainment area is not
subject to PSD review even if emissions from the source adversely affect air
quality in a PSD area, unless the affected PSD area and the source are in different
states.

There are two classes of major stationary sources. In one class are all stationary sources that emit or have the potential to emit 250 or more tons per year
of any pollutant regulated under the Act. In the other class are any stationary
sources from a list of 28 types of industrial facilities that emit or have the potential to emit 100 tons or more per year of any regulated pollutant. . . . [Section
169(1) contains the list, which includes, e.g., large fossil fuel-fired steam electric

TABLE 3-2

NAAQS for SO$_2$ and TSP and Maximum Allowable Increases in Concentrations over the Baseline in PSD Areas (μg/m^3)

Pollutant	Maximum Allowable Increases			NAAQS	
	Class I	Class II	Class III	Primary	Secondary
Particulate Matter					
Annual geometric mean	5	19	37	75	60
24-hour maximum*	10	37	75	260	150
Sulfur Dioxide					
Annual arithmetic mean	2	20	40	80	—
24-hour maximum*	5	91	182	365	—
3-hour maximum*	25	512	700	—	1,300

*Short-term maxima may be exceeded no more than once per year.

plants, Kraft pulp mills, Portland cement plants, iron and steel plants, lime plants, smelters, etc.]

In EPA's earlier regulations, the potential for a source to emit pollutants was to be judged without taking into account any air pollution control equipment. The decision in *Alabama Power* overturned this interpretation, and thus potential to emit now means the maximum capacity of a source to emit pollutants under its actual physical and operational design, which includes any air pollution control equipment. The decision means that some new sources that otherwise would have been subject to preconstruction review will now be treated as nonmajor sources, not subject to preconstruction review but included in the inventory of sources whose emissions contribute to the consumption of increments.

Major modifications of existing sources are defined as physical or operational changes that result in a significant net increase in emissions of any pollutant regulated under the Act. Regulations specify what a significant increase is for each pollutant. For example, a significant increase in the emission rate of SO$_2$ is 40 tons per year; of asbestos, 0.007 tons per year (45 Fed. Reg. 52,732, August 7, 1980).

Stationary point sources that are not large enough to be classified as major sources and distributed sources such as urban growth associated with major sources, including emissions from mobile sources that accompany this growth, are not subject to preconstruction review; however, changes in air quality due to emissions from such sources are to be counted against the increments. It is up to the permitting authorities to maintain inventories of the nonmajor sources as well as the major sources and to assess the effects of emissions from both major and nonmajor sources.

MODELING THE CONSEQUENCES OF EMISSIONS

The consequences of emissions on ambient concentrations of pollutants and on air quality related values must be predicted before facilities are built if deterioration of air quality is to be avoided. Air quality models . . . are the only tools available for this purpose. Implementing the PSD provisions therefore depends strongly on modeling capabilities. . . .

EMISSION LIMITATIONS FOR MAJOR PSD SOURCES

Major stationary sources in PSD areas are required to limit emissions of each pollutant subject to regulation under the Act by using the best available control technology (BACT). The permitting authority is to determine what control technology is best and available for each specific case, taking into account energy, environmental, and economic impacts and other costs. If a source qualifies as a major one for any regulated pollutant, BACT must be applied for all regulated pollutants. The results of modeling are often important determinants in the determination of emission limitations. . . . [T]he BACT requirement is at least as stringent as an applicable NSPS, but in general is not as stringent as the LAER requirement to which the new source would be subject in a nonattainment area. In some circumstances, of course, BACT could be as stringent as LAER. Vermont, for example, has adopted a PSD SIP that requires the same emission limitation in both nonattainment and PSD areas.

Nonmajor stationary sources are exempted from preconstruction review and are not required to use BACT. These sources are, however, subject to applicable NSPS.

THE AQRV [AIR QUALITY-RELATED VALUES] TEST FOR CLASS I AREAS

To represent the national interest in Class I areas that encompass federal lands, federal officials have been given special roles in the preconstruction review of proposed facilities that may affect those lands. Under the Act, the federal land manager and the federal official who is directly responsible for managing federal land in a Class I area have an affirmative responsibility to protect AQRVs in that land. One way of discharging that responsibility is to determine whether a proposed major source will adversely affect those values. The federal land manager is the secretary of the department with authority over the federal land in question. Other than visibility, the Act does not specify what AQRVs are.

Even if Class I increments have not been consumed and a proposed new source would not cause or contribute to concentrations of pollutants that exceed the increments, a construction permit cannot be issued if the federal land manager demonstrates to the satisfaction of the state that the proposed facility would nonetheless have adverse consequences for AQRV on the federal lands in question.

Conversely, when Class I increments have been consumed or when a proposed source would cause or contribute to concentrations of pollutants that do exceed the increments, a permit may still be issued if the applicant can demonstrate to the satisfaction of the federal land manager that the emissions from the facility will not have adverse consequences for AQRVs on federal lands in the Class I area. The burden of proof in these circumstances is on the applicant. When such waivers of the Class I increments are granted, the Act specifies new maximum allowable increases over ambient concentrations, which are the same as the increments for Class II areas except for the 3-hour maximum for SO_2 [which is 325 µg/m^3]. . . .

The Act provides another procedure for obtaining relief from the increments. The applicant must demonstrate to the satisfaction of the governor that the facility cannot be built because of the 24-hour and 3-hour SO_2 increments and, in the case of a federal mandatory Class I area, that a variance will not adversely affect AQRVs. If the governor is convinced and if the federal land manager concurs, the state may grant a variance of the SO_2 increment and issue a permit subject to the maximum allowable increases listed in . . . [§165(d)(2)(D)(iii)]. If the federal land manager does not concur with the findings of the governor, the recommendations of the governor and the federal land manager are to be submitted to the President, who may approve the governor's recommendation for an SO_2 variance if the President finds it to be in the national interest.

Neither the AQRV test nor waivers and variances are applicable to Class II and III areas.

Visibility Protection in Mandatory Class I Areas

Section 169A of the Act establishes as part of the PSD provisions a national goal of both preventing future impairment of visibility in mandatory Class I areas and remedying existing impairment due to man-made pollution. Visibility protection against degradation in the future is to be accomplished through the PSD provisions for review of new sources. Remedying existing impairment requires retrofitting emission control equipment to existing sources that adversely affect visibility.

Regulations to implement Section 169A (45 Fed. Reg. 80,084, December 2, 1980) require the 36 states containing mandatory Class I areas where visibility has been identified as an important value to revise their SIPs in three ways: they must add provisions for using the best available retrofit technology (BART) on certain installations of existing major sources; they must adopt certain measures to supplement new source review programs regarding visibility; and they must identify and evaluate long-term strategies for achieving the national goal.

Under the visibility regulations, the state authority is required to make a determination of BART for each existing major stationary source that may reasonably be suspected of causing or contributing to visibility impairment in a mandatory Class I area. The state is required to consult with the appropriate federal land manager in identifying sources and determining BART. The determination of BART is to take into account the costs of compliance, the energy and (nonatmospheric) environmental impacts of retrofitting, existing control equipment, the remaining useful life of the facility, and the degree of improvement in visibility that may be expected to result from the application of the technology. Sources 15 years old or older at the time of passage of the 1977 amendments are exempted from the retrofit program. . . .

Determining Compliance

Compliance with the PSD program is enforced through emission limitations specified in permits to construct facilities rather than through monitoring changes in ambient air quality. There are several reasons for this emphasis. First, the emission limitations are binding on the individual operators. A facility that exceeds its emission limitation is readily identified by stack gas monitoring, for example, whereas it may be difficult if not impossible to determine the extent to which a specific source may be responsible when an increment is exceeded. Second, changes in ambient concentrations represented by the short-term increments not only challenge the state of the art of measurement but also may be masked by temporal variations in concentrations arising from natural sources or from sources in the baseline.

Moreover, actual changes in ambient air quality may not be directly related to consumption of increments. A number of restrictions in the PSD program can cause differences between the calculated status of increments and actual changes in ambient concentrations of pollutants. Certain sources — both major and nonmajor — are exempted from the PSD program. Furthermore, current regulations require that modeling computations use stack heights for facilities according to the rule of good engineering practice [40 C.F.R. §52.21(h)]. In many circumstances, the actual heights of stacks at which pollutants are emitted to the air are greater than the GEP height, which is a function of the linear dimensions of the plant. Tall stacks help prevent ambient concentrations that would cause Class II or Class III increments to be exceeded or that would violate the NAAQS in the vicinity of large facilities by enhancing dispersion of the emitted pollutants. Dispersal, however, may exacerbate PSD problems in distant Class I areas, since the higher the point of emission, the greater the distance from the stack that pollutants are transported through the air and the greater the time for gaseous emissions to undergo physical and chemical transformations in the atmosphere.

A NOTE ON APPLYING PSD IN URBAN AREAS: THE PROBLEM OF PSD-NON-ATTAINMENT OVERLAP

It should be clear by now that both PSD and non-attainment requirements are applied on the basis of individual pollutants. Even a highly developed urban area can be a Class II PSD area, despite serious non-attainment problems, if ambient levels of a single criteria pollutant fall under the national standards.

There will be many cases in which a major new plant wants to locate in an area that is non-attainment for one pollutant but is PSD for others. The photochemical oxidant (ozone) standard is violated over large regions, especially in the Northeast. Violations of the TSP standard are more limited but still are common in industrialized areas. By contrast, CO and NO_x violations are rare. Thus a plant seeking to locate in an industrialized zone quite commonly will have to undergo non-attainment review for ozone and HC and PSD review for CO, NO_x and, possibly SO_2. Many times, this will mean obtaining a state permit for non-attainment but a federal one for PSD.

In urban "clean air" areas, a new source like an oil refinery is likely to affect a nearby "dirty air" area. It could conceivably cause the SO_2 non-attainment status of a nearby area to worsen, even if the area is a PSD area for SO_2. If this were the case, would the refinery have to obtain offsets?

A source comes under non-attainment review only for the particular pollutants for which non-attainment violations exist and only if the proposed plant exceeds the size cutoff for each of those pollutants. But PSD review occurs for all pollutants subject to regulation under the Clean Air Act that will be emitted by a major facility in any amount, so long as one pollutant exceeds the 100/250-ton PSD trigger emissions levels. See §§165(a)(4) and 169(1). EPA originally tried to limit PSD review to those pollutants emitted by the facility that met the statutory threshold requirement, but this approach was voided by *Alabama Power*. EPA must apply PSD review and BACT to each pollutant regulated for any purpose under any provision of the Clean Air Act, not just SO_2 and TSP (636 F.2d at 403).

3.   The Intermountain Power Project Proposal: Applying PSD in the Southwest

The problem that follows is intended to raise the major issues that arise in the application of the PSD program to an actual proposal for a large power plant to be sited in the Southwest. Assume that the facts stated still apply. A Postscript at the end of the next section explains what actually happened to the proposal. The following is the situation as it was at the time of the application.

In the mid-1970s a group of publicly owned electric utilities in Utah and in six California cities, including Los Angeles, began to think of constructing an enormous coal-fired electrical generating plant at a remote site in southern Utah. Called the Intermountain Power Project (IPP), the 3,000 megawatt (MW) plant would have been the largest ever constructed in the Western hemisphere. The IPP was to consist of four identical 750 MW units. Construction on the first unit would begin as soon as approvals could be obtained and would be completed in the middle to late 1980s. The remaining three units would begin operation at successive one-year intervals.

The IPP was not the only major power plant planned for construction in the region. Large population centers throughout the West were hoping to obtain much of their future power from a series of remote "mine mouth" facilities like

IPP, to be constructed in the coal-rich Southwest. The cost of transporting the coal to the urban centers was far greater than the cost of transmitting electricity by high tension lines, and the lines brought no air pollution with them to the already polluted coastal urban areas. The IPP's daily requirement of 22,000 tons of coal would be supplied from nearby underground mines via a new 64-mile-long railroad. Two 84-car unit trains would shuttle ceaselessly transporting the coal.

The IPP would provide 75 percent of the electrical needs of the participating Utah utilities and one third of the requirements of the California cities. It would enable its sponsors to retire older, less efficient gas and oil-fired generating facilities. It would provide jobs for 2,000 coal miners and 550 plant employees. Annual state and local tax revenues would probably reach $30 to $40 million.

The site selected was in the Salt Wash — an arid, undeveloped region 16 miles northwest of the small town of Hanksville, Utah. While remote and in many ways unappealing, Salt Wash is approximately 10 miles northeast of the 222,000-acre Capitol Reef National Park, 40 miles west of the larger Canyonlands National Park, and 70 miles west of the 65,000-acre Arches National Park. It is also near several other scenic areas under state or federal consideration for greater protection, e.g., Glen Canyon National Recreation Area, 45 miles to the southeast. Portions of a national forest and a proposed wilderness area also lie within sight of Salt Wash.

Although the coal that the IPP would burn was low in sulfur, its heat content was low and its fly ash content high. Formidable amounts of SO_2, TSP, and NO_x would be discharged each day. With the technology proposed by its managers, the completed four-unit plant, after removing 99.75 percent of the fly ash, would still discharge just under 5 tons per day of particulates and, after 90 percent of the SO_2 was removed with flue gas desulfurization scrubbers, would still discharge daily more than 44 tons of SO_2 and 137 tons of nitrogen oxides.

Year-long monitoring data compiled by the IPP indicated that for the entire region, including Salt Wash and the surrounding national parks and other federal lands, the background levels of SO_2 concentrations were very low — well under 13 $\mu g/m^3$, whether averaged over a year, a day, or even over periods as short as 3 hours. Monitors showed the annual average of background concentrations of particulate matter to be 19 $\mu g/m^3$, with 24-hour averages reaching 90 $\mu g/m^3$ on as many as 73 days a year around the Salt Wash site and in national parks like Capitol Reef. The increased 24-hour natural concentrations were due to windblown dust.

Two 430 MW units of the Utah Power and Light Hunter Plant began operation in 1978 and 1980. The plant is located approximately 50 miles north of Salt Wash. Construction began on Unit 1 in March 1975 and on Unit 2 in March 1977. A third 430 MW unit is scheduled to begin operation in 1983; its construction began in 1980. Because prevailing winds blow southwest to northeast, the plant contributes minimally to background levels of SO_2 or TSP and only occasionally to short-term concentrations in the parks to the south or east of Salt Wash. The IPP emissions would be well dispersed before they combined with Hunter's emissions to the northeast. No other major existing or proposed SO_2 or TSP sources lie within 70 miles of Salt Wash, although the huge Four Corners power plant complex is located almost 200 miles to the southeast in the extreme northeast corner of New Mexico.

Models predicted the increased ambient pollutant levels that would probably be caused by the construction of the IPP. For SO_2, initial estimates indicated that IPP would increase concentrations near the Salt Wash site by 7 $\mu g/m^3$ annual arithmetic mean. The highest 24-hour SO_2 estimated concentration was 76 $\mu g/m^3$. The 3-hour maximum at the site, it was initially believed, would never exceed 512 $\mu g/m^3$. For particulates, modeling showed that the IPP would increase emissions near Salt Wash by no more than 19 $\mu g/m^3$ annual geometric mean and that no 24-hour maximum would exceed 37 $\mu g/m^3$. No 3-hour particulate concentration predictions were made.

Further, it appeared that Capitol Reef National Park would experience an SO_2 increase of 0.4 $\mu g/m^3$ annual arithmetic mean, a maximum annual 3-hour SO_2 concentration of 69 $\mu g/m^3$, and a 3-hour SO_2 concentration over 25 $\mu g/m^3$ on 12 days of the year. The 24-hour SO_2 maximum was estimated to reach 8.7 $\mu g/m^3$ and to be over 5 $\mu g/m^3$ on 7 days of the year. The maximum 24-hour particulate concentration would be 1.7 $\mu g/m^3$ and the annual arithmetic mean less than 0.1 $\mu g/m^3$. No other national park or federal special use area would be measurably affected by the projected emissions.

A full analysis of climate, terrain, soils, vegetation, visibility, and other air quality-related values was undertaken. The plant, its stacks, or its smoke plumes would be visible within Capitol Reef, Fishlake National Forest, and the Hondu Primitive Area. The primitive area had been proposed for federal wilderness protection. The plant itself could not be seen from within Capitol Reef, although its two tall stacks would be visible along foot trails to high peaks within the park. Ordinarily, visibility at Capitol Reef is 87 miles; the distance across the park itself is 66 miles. Naturally occurring haze and windblown dust reduce visibility in the area to less than 40 miles approximately 70 days a year and to less than 20 miles approximately 45 days a year. Studies estimate the IPP would reduce visibility on clear air days from 87 to 82 miles 2 to 3 percent of the time. These decreases ordinarily would occur in the early morning or late evening, when higher moisture levels are present. Visibility reduction would also occur on the other federal lands from which the plant would be visible.

Basing your analysis on the NAS excerpt and the PSD provisions of the Clean Air Act, address the PSD issues that arise in connection with the IPP's PSD permit application *before* reading the following notes and questions.

NOTES AND QUESTIONS

1. *"Major" facilities and "potential to emit."* Is the IPP a "major" facility? Is PSD review triggered by uncontrolled or controlled emission levels? For the IPP, does it matter? As the NAS excerpt indicates, *Alabama Power* disposed of

this issue (636 F.2d at 352-355). Some 4,000 facilities a year would have been reviewed under the EPA "uncontrolled" emissions definition invalidated in *Alabama Power*, but under the court ruling only about 165 would be subject to PSD review. J. Quarles, Federal Regulation of New Industrial Plants, Envt. Rep. (BNA) Monograph No. 28 at 10 (1979). See United States v. Louisiana-Pacific Corp., 682 F. Supp. 1122, 1141 (D. Colo. 1987) (EPA may not base "potential to emit" on operation not contemplated by design of plant).

Does the PSD program also apply to pollutants like heavy metals and minerals that the IPP will emit in small quantities? Consult the NAS excerpt and *Alabama Power*, 636 F.2d at 403-406 (de minimis quantities of such pollutants are exempted by regulation). Contrast the non-attainment program, which applies only to whichever of five named pollutants exceed the 100/250 ton cutoff levels. Can you fathom the air quality protection logic, if any, that moved Congress to adopt these divergent approaches? For other issues raised by the PSD definition of "source," see *Alabama Power*, 636 F.2d at 394-399.

2. *Plant location*. Will the IPP plant be located in an area to which the PSD program applies? See §§165(a). As a result of *Alabama Power*, a facility must be located in a PSD or unclassifiable area in the same state as the area in which it will degrade air quality. In reality, this is almost no limitation at all — virtually every area in the nation is classified PSD for one or more criteria pollutants, and this is all it takes to trigger PSD review. But the problem of out-of-state facilities is quite serious, and *Alabama Power* blocks reaching over a state boundary to apply the PSD requirements, no matter how severely the proposed facility impairs air quality in a neighboring state. Are interstate impacts likely in areas downwind of the IPP?

For some proposed plants, even quite local impacts such as increment consumption, plume blight, or odor may occasionally be separated from their cause by a state boundary. Sources like the IPP, which are in the intermediate range — 60 to 120 miles — are more likely to be out of state because of the greater distances involved, yet state-of-the-art air quality modeling and monitoring is already adequate to trace sulfate haze to them (D. A. Latimer, Power Plant Impacts on Air Quality and Visibility: Siting and Emissions Control Implications (Systems Applications, Inc., for EPA, 1979) (EF 79-101)). Even distant new sources 200 to 300 miles away could possibly be linked to local loss of air quality sufficient to trigger PSD. The impact of a handful of copper smelters in southern Arizona and New Mexico on air quality in the Utah and Colorado national parks appears to be fairly well established. Distant sources will continue to pose the largest threat to the PSD program in the Four Corners region (where New Mexico, Arizona, Utah, and Colorado meet) through the end of the century — not new local sources planned for construction in the region.

The *Alabama Power* court tried to give solace by pointing out the many other Clean Air Act provisions that could be invoked to combat interstate pollution (636 F.2d at 366). After studying these provisions (at pp. 303-312 *infra*) you may want to consider whether the interstate pollution provisions are an adequate surrogate for full PSD review. See Oren, *supra*, at 88. Does visibility protection (§169A) afford a way around the narrow *Alabama Power* interpretation?

3. *The baselines and increment consumption.* Do the SO_2 and TSP levels monitored by the IPP constitute the baselines for the project area? Or were the baselines already established? What sources of pollution must be counted in the IPP baselines? What sources instead count toward increment consumption? Review the dates on which construction commenced for the units of the Hunter Plant. See §169(4). The Hunter Plant may be close enough to IPP for its baselines to apply at Salt Wash and in the parks. A lot is at stake: if one of the Hunter units had triggered the baseline determinations in areas of joint impact years before the IPP application was filed, increment consumption could have begun already.

What purpose, if any, would be served by allowing baseline determinations to be postponed until the time of the first PSD permit application? The EPA could see none and tried to fix the baseline determination date at August 7, 1977, the date of enactment of the 1977 amendments. The *Alabama Power* court disagreed with EPA's reading of the statute and mandated the "first-applicant" policy (636 F.2d at 374-376). Baseline is triggered by an application only in the state in which the plant is located. How does this affect the IPP problem? See 40 C.F.R. 52.21(b)(15)(i). Note that baseline variability determines how much additional air pollution is available. Does this have the perverse effect of shifting growth to the cleanest areas?

Several idiosyncrasies of PSD increment protection conceivably help the IPP. Review the NAS excerpt on the exclusion from increment consumption of foreign sources, for example, lead smelters in Mexico (§163(c)(1)(D)), major sources required to convert from oil or gas to coal under 1974 federal legislation (§163(c)(1)(A)), temporary emissions increases caused by construction projects (§163(c)(1)(C)), and emissions caused by smokestack heights in excess of good engineering practice. See also *Alabama Power*, 636 F.2d at 361-370, 376-381, 409. More generally, in view of the numerous exclusions from and inclusions in increment consumption, of what practical use are monitoring data in determining increment consumption? See 636 F.2d at 371-373.

Assuming that the IPP air quality impact areas do not overlap with the Hunter Plant areas, the IPP as the first applicant for a permit will determine the baselines and the project may consume all the increments, subject only to a decision by Utah to save some portion of the increments for use by new emitters. If another applicant expects to file for a PSD permit soon after the IPP, is it entitled to a comparative hearing on its entitlement to some of the remaining increment? See Ashbacker Radio Corp. v. FCC, 326 U.S. 327 (1946). EPA and most states currently allocate the available remaining increments on a first-come, first-served basis. Should marketable emissions permits be used instead?

4. *IPP's exceedance of the SO_2 increments.* Will the IPP violate the Class I 24-hour and 3-hour maximum increments for SO_2 in Capitol Reef National Park? If so, may the IPP still be issued its permit? Read §165(d)(2)(C) and (D). The variance provision of §165(d)(2)(D) was included in the 1977 amendments

specifically for the purpose of allowing the Utah governor or the president to approve the IPP. Utah's two senators had filibustered against the Clean Air Act Amendments in 1976 and had blocked their passage. The waiver and variance provisions were enacted to avoid similar problems in 1977. See Note, Prevention of Significant Deterioration of Air Quality: The Clean Air Amendments of 1977 and Utah's Power Generating Industry, 1977 Utah L. Rev. 775, 778-779, 787.

Note §165(d)(2)(C)(ii), which empowers the Federal Land Manager (see §302(i)) to block issuance of a PSD permit when AQRVs are impaired in a Class I area, *even if the Class I increments are not exceeded*. Visibility protection is addressed by this provision, as well as the certification procedure, the variance provision, and a separate visibility program. See §169A. The issue of visibility impairment was critical to the fate of the original IPP proposal and will receive careful attention below.

Modeling done after the passage of the 1977 amendments indicated that IPP could not meet the Class II increments applicable in the region around Salt Wash. Can the IPP obtain a "variance" for its Class II increment exceedances? Could IPP obtain the necessary gubernatorial and legislative approvals from the state of Utah for redesignation of Salt Wash as a Class III area? Could it obtain the approvals from the Secretary of the Interior? See §164(a).

5. *Monitoring, modeling, and the rationality of the PSD baseline increment analysis.* Do you think that the indeterminacy of the baseline increment requirements makes a charade of PSD analysis? Since the goal of PSD is limiting actual increases in pollution to "insignificant" amounts, one would expect that the administration of the PSD increment system would be relatively straightforward. Regulators would monitor existing pollution levels, first to establish baselines and then to keep tabs on deteriorating conditions as time passes. Using air quality models, they would predict any increases in ambient pollution expected to result from a major new facility, to make sure that if built it would not exceed the increments. This in fact was EPA's approach under the 1973 PSD program it adopted in response to Sierra Club v. Ruckelshaus.

But as the NAS excerpt explains, under the 1977 amendments the baseline and the increments are computed from a mishmash of monitoring data and regulatory fiats about hypothetical and actual emissions that must be (or cannot be) counted, depending on the statute and the regulations. The result is that actual air quality in PSD areas bears little resemblance to what the regulatory accounting system says it is. The baseline is as much a creature of law as of science. The unavailability of data with which to establish the baselines from the start and the inability of monitoring technology to keep track of actual increment consumption persuaded Congress to place less reliance on monitoring actual air quality and more on inventing administratively reliable techniques for selecting baselines and allocating increments to applicants. Any monitoring data that do exist could prove to be an embarrassment. Note, however, that actual impairment of AQCRs such as visibility in Class I areas must be prevented without exception.

EPA has attempted to overcome these problems through modeling, and the PSD regulations incorporate its guidelines on air quality models. The difficulty is that modeling capability is far from perfect, see pp. 154-156 *supra*. Oren, *supra*, at 40-43 points out that modeling is least successful in situations where increment exceedance is likely. Modeling for small increases, such as those for Class I areas, is difficult, models for complex terrain are primitive, and modeling can be deficient when multiple sources threaten an exceedance. Assume two sources are proposed for locations close together, and that an exceedance will occur only if the emissions of these two plans coincide in time and place. "Deciding when this will occur, though, strains the capabilities of modeling." Id. at 41.

Despite these problems, the courts have been deferential to the efforts of EPA and the states to overcome the shortcomings of models. See *Alabama Power*, 636 F.2d at 381-388, and Citizens against the Refinery's Effects v. EPA, 643 F.2d 178 (4th Cir. 1981). Forced to wrestle with the problem of monitoring data that directly contradicted the results produced by two EPA models, one circuit court sustained EPA's reliance on the uncorrected models in issuing a PSD permit. Northern Great Plains Resource Council v. EPA, 645 F.2d 1349 (9th Cir. 1981). PSD permit holders must also conduct post-construction monitoring, presumably to correct errors in the predicted level of increment consumption and to help EPA refine its models.

6. *The definition of "source" and "modification" in the PSD program.* Although the issue has no bearing on the IPP's initial PSD clearance, the court in *Alabama Power* construed "source" and "modification" in such a way as to include some new construction and exempt other construction from the reach of the PSD program. Consider an existing plant to which a new unit will be added. What level of emissions will subject the additional facility to PSD? What if an old unit (e.g., a boiler) is retired at the same time the new unit is put into operation? In such a case, can the overall plant "net out" of PSD review if total plant emissions then are equal to or less than what they were before?

The court in *Alabama Power* held that any modification that increased emissions to *any* extent (except for de minimis increases) required PSD review, invalidating an EPA regulation that limited PSD review to the same 100- or 250-ton-per-year threshold Congress established for facilities falling under the rubric "major emitting facility" (636 F.2d at 400). The ruling is important because most cases in which permits are required are modifications. See United States v. Chevron, U.S.A., Inc., 639 F. Supp. 770 (W.D. Tex. 1985) (shutting off pollution control system is modification covered by PSD).

But *Alabama Power* also determined that PSD review does not apply to any modification — usually a plant expansion — that does *not* increase net plant emissions. In other words, *Alabama Power* held that major plants in PSD areas were "sources" that could bubble their emissions from all equipment, plantwide (636 F.2d at 399-402). Of what consequence to PSD review is the fact the IPP will consist of four separate units?

7. *The BACT determination.* Read §169(3). Do the SO$_2$ and TSP emissions controls that the IPP proposes to install meet the "best available control

technology" standard required of all major new facilities sited in PSD areas? See §165(a)(4) and §169(3). Must a high percentage of NO$_x$ control be achieved as well, although no NO$_x$ increments have as yet been determined? Recall that the TSP standard has been replaced with a standard for fine particulates.

The administration of the BACT requirement has been lenient, and most BACT determinations were no stricter than NSPS, which set a floor for the BACT determination. In a number of instances, state and regional EPA offices established BACT for categories of sources, rather than for individual sources. Many BACT determinations did not assess alternative technologies or take into account the environmental, energy, and economic consequences (other than direct operating costs) of proposed controls.

EPA has now tightened BACT control determinations by requiring that BACT must be set at the most stringent level achieved by a similar source unless the applicant can show that this level is unachievable. See 18 Envt. Rep. (BNA): Current Developments 2427 (1988) (industry criticism). EPA studies of BACT determinations also show that "[a]pproximately half the BACT determinations for sulfur dioxide and two-fifths of the BACT decisions for particulate matter between 1981 and 1984 were tighter than the applicable NSPS." Oren, *supra*, at 33. The result was a 24 percent reduction in particulate emissions and a 19 percent reduction in sulfur dioxide emissions beyond what the NSPS would have required.

Some critics still claim that BACT determinations make inefficient use of the reserve of "pollution rights" represented by the increments. Do you see how? They exacerbate a basic flaw of the Clean Air Act by putting the heaviest cleanup burden on the newest sources. Further, like other technology-limited emissions standards, BACT already has built-in tendencies to be economically inefficient; it restricts emissions control options and thus causes wide discrepancies between the marginal costs of control among sources. Atkinson & Lewis, Determination and Implementation of Optimal Air Quality Standards, 3 J. Envtl. Econ. Mgmt. 363 (1976). The more major PSD sources vary with respect to size, type, and operation, the less efficient BACT is likely to be. To take efficiency into account, could the legal standard of availability (B "Available" CT) be defined to subject candidates for BACT to the same marginal control costs?

Does the statute rule out switching fuel or reducing or interrupting operations to meet BACT? Compare NSPS. Could visibility protection requirements, for example, intermittent meteorologically determined emissions and plume controls, be imposed as part of BACT?

During the perennial debates over Clean Air Act reform, critics of multiple technology-based standards propose BACT as a replacement for the existing Clean Air Act emissions standards. Thus, NSPS, LAER, and BART would disappear; a uniform BACT requirement would be inserted in their place. See, e.g., National Environmental Development Association, Clean Air Project, The Clean Air Act and Industrial Growth 28-29 (1981). Do you think BACT is well enough defined at present to play the broader role? What changes would you suggest?

Before addressing the visibility problems the IPP may cause, consider the statutory program for the regulation of visibility, which is discussed in section 4 below.

A Postscript: What Actually Happened to the IPP Salt Wash Proposal

During the summer of 1977, the IPP's sponsors realized that the Salt Wash site might not comply with the proposed PSD amendments to the Clean Air Act. They took their case to Congress and obtained a variance provision tailor-made for the IPP. See §165(d)(2)(D); Protection of Parklands, *supra*, at 378-379. Their effort, however, was misplaced because further modeling indicated that the plant could not comply with the Act at Capitol Reef, Canyonlands National Park, or Glen Canyon Recreation Area, even with the variance.

With trouble brewing for Salt Wash, a task force created by the governor of Utah and the Secretary of the Interior was instructed to review the available alternative sites for the facility. In December 1977, the Secretary of the Interior, Cecil Andrus, wrote the IPP that "[t]he Department will not approve a power-plant site for the proposed IPP project which would require a variance to the requirements of the Clean Air Act when a comparable alternative site is available that does not require a variance." The more generous Class II increments could have applied if Andrus had been willing to determine that visibility or other AQRVs would not be impaired in Capitol Reef or other Class I areas if the plant were built. See §165(d)(2)(D). Hence Andrus used the variance denial as leverage to force a relocation of the plant; such a denial would have had to have been based on visibility impairment alone.

In April 1978, the IPP co-sponsors indicated that they would be willing to study a site at Lynndyl, Utah, 100 miles northwest of the original site, although Salt Wash remained their first choice. Almost two years later, the Department of the Interior, EPA, and the IPP agreed on the Lynndyl site, and a PSD permit was issued in June 1980. Despite some local opposition, construction began on the $5.8 billion project in early 1981 and a 1500 megawatt plant is now in operation.

Groundbreaking did not signal the end of problems for the IPP. Utah Power & Light (UP & L), a private utility, originally had obtained a 25 percent interest in the project. In 1982, as energy demand fell in Utah (as did demand in virtually all other areas of the nation), UP & L recognized that its projected energy needs far outpaced actual demand. To protect the company's bond rating, UP & L attempted to reduce its commitment drastically, to 4 percent. After a heated debate in which smaller participating public utilities in Utah received various concessions from UP & L, the sponsors agreed in 1983 to a 50 percent reduction in plant size. Under the present scheme, more than 80 percent of the power produced will belong to California, thus highlighting the coastal cities' "mine mouth" southwestern electrical power strategy.

The IPP project also had a substantial impact on the sparsely populated area in which it was located. For discussion of the program under which the project entered into contracts with local governments to alleviate its impact on the area see Zillman, Controlling Boomtown Development: Lessons From the Intermountain Power Project, 21 Land & Water L. Rev. 1, 325 (1986).

4. The Visibility Program

1. *The values at stake.* The spacious western sky is a striking natural and cultural asset of the United States. As captured by early landscape artists, it played an important role in mobilizing public support for the national park system. For example, the artist Thomas Moran was a member of the 1871 survey party of Yellowstone and was later commissioned by the Santa Fe Railroad to paint a series of now-classic paintings of the Grand Canyon, which Steven Mather used to popularize the national park system. Read this description of Moran's landscapes: "The sun is never passive but kindles brilliant fires in the clouds or on the walls of strange eroded canyons." Taylor, A Land for Landscapes, in The American Land 39-40 (1979). However, it must be noted that William Ashley, the first documented explorer to navigate a substantial part of the Colorado River, found Flaming Gorge "gloomy." D. Lavender, Colorado River Country 35 (1982).

The annual median visual range in the Rocky Mountain states still exceeds 100 miles in most areas, as opposed to 9 to 25 miles in regions east of the Mississippi River and south of the Great Lakes. National Park Service, Air Quality in the National Parks 2-10, 2-12 (1988). The mean annual visual range in some areas approaches 125 miles. Although good visibility primarily means good visual range, as an integrated aesthetic experience it also involves contrast (the relative brightness of features in view) and discoloration (pollution-induced shifts in the wavelengths of atmospheric light). Loss of contrast and discoloration are important in the East, even if distant horizons are not perceptible. See Kahaner, Something in the Air, Wilderness, Winter, 1988, at 19.

2. *Explaining and measuring visibility impairment.* Particles and gases impair visibility by scattering or absorbing light. The largest contribution to reduced visibility occurs from the breaking up and scattering of light by airborne particles. The chief light-absorbing aerosol is soot, which often is the cause of plume blight or general visibility reduction in urban areas. Light scattering depends on particle size; the best scatterers are the smaller particles, which present more surface area per unit of weight. For example, allowing 10 $\mu g/m^3$ of relatively coarse particles with diameters greater than 2.5 microns to be emitted where the visual range is 80 miles would reduce visibility to 67 miles, a 16 percent reduction. But the same amount by weight of secondary sulfate aerosols, especially efficient light scatterers, would reduce visual range to 27 miles, a 66 percent reduction. (National Research Council of the National Academy of Sciences, On Prevention of Significant Deterioration of Air Quality, *supra*, at 47). The only gaseous pollutant that is a significant absorber of light is NO_2, which by absorbing blue light produces a brownish discoloration in smokestack plumes.

Research on visibility has established fairly exact quantitative relationships between range, contrast, and discoloration and ambient pollutant concentrations. Monitoring and measuring visibility precisely, however, is not the same as valuing it for safety, aesthetic, and regulatory purposes. What is it worth to an observer to be able to see towering red rock formations a hundred miles distant? To someone who will never see the view but who still values its existence? To the nation who values the view for its symbolic value? Researchers' efforts to answer these questions in an objective fashion suggest how difficult, if not impossible, the task is.

Social scientists have attempted to establish the public's willingness to pay for preserving or restoring good visibility by showing interviewees photographs of polluted western vistas and eliciting money bids. See Brookshire, Ives & Schulze, The Valuation of Aesthetic Preferences, 3 J. Envtl. Econ. & Mgmt. 325 (1976), and Schulze, d'Arge & Brookshire, Valuing Environmental Commodities: Some Recent Experiments, 57 Land Econ. 151 (1981). See also Sloane & White, Visibility: An Evolving Issue, 20 Envtl. Sci. & Technology 760 (1986) (discussing recent improvements in measuring and modeling visibility). Is it important in placing a value on visibility that "the visual experience is instantaneous . . . [and] [u]nlike health effects . . . neither cumulative nor averaged over time"? Id. at 765.

3. *Types of visibility impairment.* Pollution impairs visibility in three ways, each of which presents a different regulatory challenge. Plume blight from a single source such as a coal-fired power plant is the most obvious. For the first twenty or so miles downwind (assuming a steady 6 mph wind), light scattering by fly ash and discoloration by NO_2 dominate. Thereafter, the transformation of colorless SO_2 to sulfate particles occurs, so that sulfates and NO_2 determine the visible character of the plume. Beyond 90 miles sulfates usually dominate, and the plume becomes steadily less distinguishable to observers. Yet the first astronauts reported that the plume from the Four Corners Power Plant in northeastern New Mexico was the most strikingly visible human artifact they saw from their space capsule; the plume stretched northeast for over a thousand miles.

At the opposite extreme, thoroughly diffused "older" pollutants may cause a second form of visibility-impairing pollution: large-scale regional haze. Sulfates are the chief culprit, although a myriad of other pollutants also contribute to haze. Diffused haze attributable to distant sources may be the eventual undoing of the visibility program in the Southwest, not local sources like the IPP. In the southwestern national parks, 90 percent of regional sulfate haze originates hundreds of miles outside the region, chiefly at copper smelters in southern Arizona, southern New Mexico, western Texas, and possibly in the Los Angeles area. Southwestern haze has intensified over time as the West has developed.

A third visibility-impairing phenomenon, intermediate between plumes and regional hazes, are small pockets of haze that form in valleys or around other land forms, usually in layer-cake bands of discoloration. Secondary aerosols dominate, although NO_2 probably adds to the layered effect. Urban smog, eastern high humidity hazes, and pollution pockets brought about by unique western geological features (especially high terrain) belong to this category.

4. *Visibility and other air quality-related values.* The Clean Air Act protects visibility through a two-tier scheme. A state must deny a permit to a new source even though Class I increments are not violated if the source will have an "adverse impact" on "air quality-related values" (AQRV). Neither term is defined in the Act. See §165(d). Conversely, a source that would violate the increments may obtain a permit if it can show that AQVR are not violated. Visibility is the principal air quality-related value that must be reviewed under §165 before a major new source can be sited near a Class I area. For the definition of "adverse impact" see 40 C.F.R. §51.301(a).

The AQRV provision has had little effect. No source has been denied a permit under this section, and only seven sources have been given permits despite increment violations. One commentator claims the reason is that the Class I increments are a poor indicator of park damage because they assume that all damage comes from new sources of pollution rather than from a cumulative impact of new and existing sources. Oren, The Protection of Parklands from Air Pollution: A Look at Current Policy, 13 Harv. Envtl. L. Rev. 313, 366 (1989). Oren also argues that the statutory failure to define "adverse impact" causes state and federal governments to avoid the "political land mines" involved in using this test." Id. at 373. Does IPP have an adverse impact on AQRV?

5. *Reasonable progress, BART, and integral vistas.* A separate visibility protection program not technically part of PSD is provided by §169A for mandatory Class I areas in which EPA lists areas where visibility is an important value. All but two of the mandatory Class I areas are on the EPA list. States must identify existing "major stationary sources" that affect visibility in the listed areas and these sources must install "best available retrofit technology" (BART) if built after 1962. No source has yet been affected by this requirement because no source has been linked with visibility impairment.

The second part of §169A requires states to adopt long-term strategies for making "reasonable progress" toward a national goal of remedying and preventing impairment of visibility from air pollution in mandatory Class I areas. EPA rules to implement this program require consideration of the effects on visibility of pollutants that cause violations in non-attainment areas. 40 C.F.R. §307. They also require states to consider the impact of proposed major stationary sources on "integral vistas." These are views looking out from a Class I area declared by the Federal Land Manager to be an important part of visitor experience. Finally, a permit that might affect visibility in a federally owned Class I area may only be issued after consideration of comments by the Federal Land Manager and explanation of why the project will not have an adverse impact on visibility. See 52 Fed. Reg. 28,547 (1985) (explaining program).

This program has also been hobbled. EPA rules permit states to allow new sources that affect visibility if they decide their economic development is more important. Monitoring and modeling difficulties led EPA to limit its efforts to plume blight rather than regional haze, and it has not extended §169A to states without Class I areas but with sources that might affect visibility in these areas. Finally, no integral vistas were designated.

Dissatisfaction with the EPA program led to litigation which was settled in 1982 when EPA agreed to prepare plans for states whose visibility programs were found inadequate. Most of the states where the §169A "reasonable progress" requirements apply did not adopt satisfactory plans. EPA has now adopted a rule for these states specifying a number of actions for inclusion in their SIPs that are necessary to satisfy the "reasonable progress" requirement. 52 Fed. Reg. 45,132 (1987). One integral vista was designated in Maine, and states have designated two others. But EPA decided again that it found no instance in which application of BART was necessary.

6. *The IPP and integral vistas.* Does it matter that the IPP plant, its stacks, or its smoke plumes can be seen from within Capitol Reef and other areas? The boundaries of some Class I areas were drawn to include a relatively small "sample" of a vastly larger, visible area that was intended to be part of the experience for which the area was established. For example, the view from Yovimpa Point in Bryce Canyon National Park sweeps across over 70,000 square miles of land outside the park. Should an integral vista be established for Capitol Reef? What is the statutory basis for the integral vista regulations? Before you answer, consider §169A(e).

Is the integral vista protection process the only way EPA can protect visibility impaired by what one sees outside a mandatory Class I area? Protecting a few scenic panoramas that encompass breathtaking distances raises a different issue from the constantly visible plant-cum-plume of the IPP, located only a few miles from Capitol Reef. Prevailing winds would probably blow the plume into the area often enough that such a site would have an "adverse effect" on visibility entirely within the area. But even if the plume did not affect visibility *in* the area often enough or severely enough to "impair" it, is the nearby eyesore prohibited nevertheless? What does §165(d)(2)(B) mean by charging the responsible official to protect the visibility "of" Class I lands? Would it make more sense to abandon the Class I increment system and rely exclusively on the §165 AQRV review and §169A?

Like other Clean Air Act problems, visibility requires more than a local solution. The following case indicates what happened when plaintiffs brought suit to compel EPA to adopt a regional haze strategy:

STATE OF VERMONT v. THOMAS
850 F. 2d 99 (2d Cir. 1988)

ALTIMARI, Circuit Judge:
Petitioners, the State of Vermont, Conservation Law Foundation of New England, Inc., and Vermont Natural Resources Council, seek review, pursuant to §307(b)(1), of a final ruling of respondent, the Environmental Protection Agency ("EPA"), taking "no action" on those portions of Vermont's state imple-

mentation plan ("state implementation plan" or "SIP") addressing "regional haze" submitted under section 169A of the Clean Air Act of 1970. Because we agree with respondent Lee Thomas, Administrator of the EPA (the "Administrator"), that current regulations do not encompass federally enforceable measures to alleviate "regional haze," we deny the petition for review.

Background . . .

At issue in this case are the 1977 amendments to the Act which directed EPA, in pertinent part, to adopt regulations protecting visibility in certain national parklands and wilderness areas, designated as "class I Federal areas." Clean Air Act §169A; see id. §162(a) (defining class I areas to include international parks, national wilderness areas exceeding 5,000 acres, national memorial parks exceeding 5,000 acres, and national parks exceeding 6,000 acres). Class I areas were singled out by Congress as requiring special protection in view of the aesthetic importance of visibility to the continued enjoyment and preservation of the country's scenic vistas. Accordingly, Congress set as a "national goal the prevention of any future, and the remedying of any existing impairment of visibility . . . resulting from man-made air pollution" in class I areas, §169A(a)(1), and directed EPA to provide guidelines for the states in order "to assure . . . reasonable progress toward meeting the national goal" of visibility enhancement in those areas. Id. §169A(a)(4),(b).

Pursuant to its authority under section 169A of the Act, EPA promulgated regulations in 1980 designed to "establish long-range goals, a planning process, and implementation procedures" toward achieving the national visibility goal. 45 Fed. Reg. 80,084 (codified at 40 C.F.R. §51.300 et seq.). Specifically, EPA determined that visibility impairment is of two types: 1) "plume blight," i.e., traceable streams of smoke, dust or colored gas emanating from single sources or small groups of sources; and 2) "regional haze," i.e., widespread, homogeneous haze from a multitude of sources which impairs visibility in large areas, often for hundreds of miles from the sources of the pollution. Of the two types of air pollution, EPA recognized that plume blight obviously was more susceptible to identification, measurement and thus control. The more vexing problem of how to alleviate regional haze was, in EPA's view, subject to certain scientific and technical limitations. Consequently, the 1980 regulations adopted a "phased approach to visibility protection." Id. at 80,085. Under "Phase I" of the program, EPA regulations targeted plume blight while deferring for "future phases" the complexities of regional haze and urban plumes. Id. at 80,085-86. "Phase II" would address regional haze once monitoring and other scientific techniques progressed to a point that EPA could develop a regulatory program for that type of impairment. Id. at 80,087.

The effect of the 1980 regulations was to require the 36 states containing class I areas to revise their SIPs to implement a visibility protection program, consistent with the new regulations, to assure reasonable progress toward section

169A's national visibility goal. The regulations mandated that each of the affected states' SIPs contain, inter alia, a "long-term (10-15 years) strategy" to combat
visibility impairment in each class I area. 40 C.F.R. §51.306(a) (1987).

In April 1986, Vermont submitted to EPA its proposed plan addressing
visibility impairment at the Lye Brook National Wilderness Area, a 12,000 acre
mountain plateau in the southern portion of the Green Mountain National Forest and the state's only class I area. As indicated in Vermont's 300-page SIP, the
Lye Brook area is afflicted with summertime haze that has drastically reduced
visibility by as much as 40 percent since the mid 1950s. The Vermont plan
contained extensive technical analysis demonstrating that Lye Brook's visibility
impairment is due primarily to sulfur dioxide pollution originating from out-of-
state sources, e.g., power plants and coal and oil company factories. Vermont
found that sulfate particle emissions from a multitude of sources located in 8
upwind states — Ohio, Pennsylvania, West Virginia, Kentucky, Tennessee, Illinois, Indiana, and Michigan — were principally responsible for the haze blan-
keting Lye Brook during the summer months.

Vermont's SIP concluded that while adequate in-state measures to prevent
plume blight were already in place, a reduction program aimed at out-of-state
sulfate emissions would be necessary to assure reasonable progress toward the
national visibility goal. Consequently, Vermont proposed a federally enforceable
"long-term strategy" to combat the effects of regional haze at Lye Brook. The
long-term strategy included a summertime ambient sulfate standard and a 48-
state emissions reduction plan in order to meet the air quality standard by 1995.
In addition, Vermont asked EPA to disapprove and revise the SIPs of the eight
upwind states which were the major contributors to visibility impairment at Lye
Brook, see Clean Air Act §110(c)(1)(B) ("[t]he Administrator shall . . . set[ ] forth
an implementation plan . . . for a State if . . . the plan . . . submitted for such
State is determined by the Administrator not to be in accordance with the requirements of this section"), and also asked that four of these states not containing class I areas (Ohio, Illinois, Indiana, and Pennsylvania) be added to the list
of 36 states required to submit visibility plans.

In December 1986, EPA issued a proposed ruling on Vermont's SIP. 51
Fed. Reg. 43,389. EPA agreed with Vermont's assessment that visibility impairment at Lye Brook is due predominantly to regional haze caused by out-of-state
sulfur dioxide emissions. Id. at 43,391. Nevertheless, EPA proposed taking "no
action" on those portions of Vermont's SIP addressing regional haze "because
EPA has yet to establish requirements for strategies relating to regional haze." Id.
at 43,392. EPA objected to Vermont's program as dictating a single solution to
a national problem without the benefit of EPA regulations implementing a Phase
II regional haze program.

In July 1987, EPA issued its final ruling on Vermont's proposal. 52 Fed.
Reg. 26,973. While EPA approved limited portions of Vermont's SIP complying
with existing plume blight regulations under section 169A of the Act, EPA decided to take "no action" on those parts of the SIP aimed at controlling regional
haze. EPA also denied Vermont's request to disapprove the SIPs of the eight

upwind states as well as its request to add four states to the list of states required to submit visibility protection plans for class I areas. In explaining its "no action" ruling, EPA concluded that Vermont's proposal establishing an ambient sulfate standard and its long-term strategy for emissions reduction throughout the continental United States were outside the scope of EPA's existing regulations. EPA viewed as federally enforceable only those portions of a state implementation plan submitted in response to regulations promulgated by the agency. According to EPA, Vermont's regional haze measures could not become federal rules "until such time as EPA decides to promulgate a national regional haze program." Id. at 26,974. . . .

Discussion

Petitioners argue that EPA's refusal to approve Vermont's SIP in its entirety violates both EPA's own regulations and the Clean Air Act, and accordingly seek reversal of EPA's ruling as an administrative action "not in accordance with law." §307(d)(9)(A); 5 U.S.C. §706(2)(A). Specifically, petitioners contend that the 1980 regulations encompass measures to alleviate regional haze and that EPA's contrary interpretation of its regulations is inconsistent with the terms and the underlying purposes of the Clean Air Act. For the reasons that follow, we disagree. . . .

[The court held that its scope of review was limited, that it must "give great deference" to EPA's interpretation of the statute, and that it would reverse EPA's ruling only if it was "plainly unreasonable."]

We begin with the statute itself. Section 169A of the Clean Air Act directs EPA to promulgate regulations requiring states containing class I areas to adopt through their SIPs long-term strategies assuring reasonable progress toward meeting the national visibility goal. §169A(b). Pursuant to this legislative mandate, in 1980 EPA issued regulations providing that each SIP include a long-term strategy designed to remedy any existing, and prevent any future, impairment of visibility in class I areas. 40 C.F.R. §51.306(a) (1987).

Vermont claims that its long-term strategy addressing regional haze fits within the purview of the 1980 regulations and must be approved by EPA. See Clean Air Act §110(a)(2)(J) ("Administrator shall approve [the SIP] . . . if he determines that . . . it meets the requirements" of, inter alia, section 169A). The Administrator responds by arguing that the 1980 regulations do not cover regional haze impairment and that measures addressing that type of impairment are not required by section 169A and therefore cannot be part of a federally enforceable SIP. See id. §110(d)) (federally enforceable SIP is one which "implements the *requirements*" of the statute) (emphasis added).

In support of its interpretation of the 1980 regulations, EPA cites the preamble to the final regulations in which EPA explained its adoption of a "phased approach" to visibility protection in class I areas. The preamble indicates that "Phase I" of the program "[r]equire[s] control of impairment that can be traced to a single existing stationary facility or small group of . . . facilities" while "[f]uture phases will . . . address[ ] more complex problems such as regional haze and urban plumes." 45 Fed. Reg. 80,085-86. Although petitioners concede that action on regional haze was deferred for future phases of the visibility program, they nonetheless argue that the 1980 regulations were intended to allow, as technologies improved, for the evolution of long-term strategies combating regional haze. We disagree.

It is one thing to recognize that the regulatory mechanism put into place by the 1980 regulations anticipated long-term strategies designed to alleviate regional haze, see 45 Fed. Reg. 34,764 ("[e]ven though we are calling these . . . regulations 'Phase I of the visibility protection program,' the basic structure . . . will remain constant for all phases"); it is quite another to suggest that the 1980 regulations actually authorized states containing class I areas to implement regional haze measures through federally enforceable SIPs. Petitioners would have us ignore the preamble language in favor of the "plain meaning" of the regulations. But see New York State Commission on Cable Television v. FCC, 571 F.2d 95, 98 (2d Cir.), cert. denied, 439 U.S. 820 (1978) ("[m]ere incantation of the plain meaning rule, without placing the language to be construed in its proper framework, cannot substitute for a meaningful analysis"). Respondents correctly note, however, that no "plain meaning" to regulate regional haze can be discerned from the face of the regulations. Consequently, having looked to the preamble to determine the scope of the 1980 regulations, we find that EPA intended to limit the regulations to plume blight.

Petitioners also contend that even in the absence of EPA regulatory "guidelines" addressing regional haze, Clean Air Act §169A(b)(1), the Act imposes upon states an independent duty to develop visibility protection standards to assure "reasonable progress" toward achieving the national visibility goal. While it is certainly true that the actual implementation of visibility protection measures is the responsibility of the states, the statute and its legislative history make clear that Congress charged EPA with the responsibility through its rulemaking power to ensure attainment of the national goal. Id. §169A(a)(4); H.R. Rep. No. 294, 95th Cong., 1st Sess. 206, reprinted in 1977 U.S. Code Cong. & Admin. News 1077, 1285. Without EPA rulemaking on regional haze, therefore, Vermont's proposed interstate measures are outside the scope of the regulations and thus are not subject to federal enforcement under the Act.

Since Vermont's regional haze measures were not required to be included in its SIP, we believe that EPA's "no action" response was appropriate. Petitioners maintain, however, that EPA's "no action" ruling deprives Vermont of a definitive decision on the merits of its proposal and violates section 110 of the Act. See §110(a)(2) (Administrator "shall . . . approve or disapprove" proposed SIP). We have held previously that the Clean Air Act should not be read to permit only outright approval or disapproval of state plans so long as EPA's action was reasonable. In this case, the effect of EPA's ruling was to "keep [Vermont's] measures out of the Federally enforceable SIP." 52 Fed. Reg. 26,976 (1987). EPA explained its action in this regard as an attempt to "avoid the appearance of a premature judgment as to [the measures'] ultimate approvability, and [to] prevent confusion regarding their present enforceability as a matter of state law." Id. Given that Vermont was free to adopt within its borders air quality standards more stringent than federal law requires, 42 U.S.C. §7416, it is evident that EPA's "no action" ruling — as opposed to outright rejection of Vermont's regional haze measures — was more than reasonable.

We recognize, of course, that without federal enforcement of Vermont's plan, little, if any, progress will be made on regional haze at Lye Brook. While this is indeed lamentable, until such time as a federal regional haze program is in place, Vermont may not impose its standards on upwind states. See Air Pollution Control District v. EPA, 739 F.2d 1071, 1087-88 (6th Cir. 1984) (downwind state's air quality standards that are more stringent than national standards do not require upwind state to alter its otherwise valid SIP); Connecticut v. EPA, 656 F.2d 902, 909 (2d Cir. 1981) (same); see also Clean Air Act §110(a)(2)(E)(i). Consequently, we find that EPA's denial of Vermont's request to disapprove the SIPs of the eight upwind states contributing to visibility impairment at Lye Brook was in accordance with federal law, see Clean Air Act §110(c)(1)(B) (providing that EPA may revise SIP if it is not in compliance with requirements of the Act), and likewise that EPA's refusal to add four regional haze producing states to those now required to develop class I visibility protection programs was reasonable in view of the limited scope of the 1980 regulations.

Finally, we note that, more than ten years after the enactment of section 169A, there still is no national program addressing regional haze. We are sympathetic to petitioners' argument that something must be done soon. EPA's assurances of future action on regional haze are little comfort to Vermont and visitors to Lye Brook. We can only hope that EPA will act quickly in furtherance of the national visibility goal. In the meantime, Vermont can pursue an alternative remedy, namely, the filing with EPA of a petition for rulemaking under the Administrative Procedure Act, 5 U.S.C §553(e), with eventual judicial review in the D.C. Circuit. Section 307(b)(1). In any event, we are convinced that the issues raised by the petition in the instant case are best left to the national rulemaking process rather than to an SIP approval proceeding.

Conclusion

For all of the foregoing reasons, the petition for review is denied.

NOTES AND QUESTIONS

1. *Compelling EPA to act.* Reread the Train case, p. 174 *supra*, in which the court held that EPA was required to adopt a NAAQS for lead. Then review

the material earlier in this section on the history of the PSD program. On what basis did the court mandate EPA to adopt a lead NAAQS? A PSD program? Was the statutory basis for this result any stronger than it was in the Vermont case? If so, why do you suppose the court refused to mandate EPA to adopt a regional haze program? See also Maine v. Thomas, 874 F.2d 883 (1st Cir. 1989). The court dismissed a suit brought to compel EPA to adopt regulations for regional haze as unripe and held that plaintiffs should have challenged the original 1980 regulation in which EPA adopted a visibility program.

The Vermont case is the converse of the usual federalism problem that arises under the Clean Air Act, which is created when EPA tries to make the states adopt more stringent requirements. What explains Vermont's decision to force EPA to act on the visibility problem? Would Vermont sources pay the cost of a regional haze strategy? Is the decision consistent with the federalism concepts embedded in the Act? To what extent are these concepts implicit in the Vermont case, and what are they? See generally Fayad, The Clean Air Act: New Horizons for National Parks in Our Common Lands 293 (D. Simon ed. 1988).

2. *Regulating regional haze.* How difficult would it be to regulate regional haze? Sloane & White, *supra*, point out:

> Regional haze . . . is easier to model [than plume blight. . . . [But] regional haze is much more difficult to trace to specific emission sources because of the chemical diversity of these sources and because of mixing and reaction of emissions. [Id at 764.]

The authors also note that "the mathematical models designed to simulate visibility effects are built from air pollution models that describe the evolution of aerosol and NO_2 concentrations" and suffer from the same obstacles and uncertainties. Id. at 765. Is modeling the Achilles' heel of the Clean Air Act program? Modeling problems are also an obstacle in the design of programs to control acid rain, which are discussed in the next section.

A NOTE ON A FINAL EVALUATION OF THE PSD PROGRAM

Professor Oren, in Prevention of Significant Deterioration, *supra*, provides a thorough criticism of the PSD program as now implemented.

> [An] appropriate way to analyze the program is to see it as functioning in two different ways. First, the program aims at "control compelling": that is, it is intended to force pollution sources to improve their pollution controls or change their production processes to cut emissions. . . .
> A control-compelling program may to some extent influence where sources decide to locate. . . . The PSD program, though, influences siting . . . [through] site-shifting. The increments are the primary tools of site-shifting. . . .

There has been substantial question about whether the PSD program ac-
complishes either control-compelling or site-shifting. Some empirical evidence on
the question is now available thanks to a series of studies directed by Leigh Hayes
of the Radian Corporation . . . between 1982 and the present. These show that
considerable control-compelling, but relatively minor site-shifting, has occurred
within the first decade of the program. . . .

The case-by-case BACT review appears clearly to be control-compelling by
cutting emissions from new sources below what might otherwise be the case. . . .
The Hayes studies also indicate that the increments play at least some role in
control-compelling. In some instances, the permitting agency has obliged an applicant to reduce proposed emissions because modeling reveals that the source
would consume all or most of an increment. . . . [But] the site-shifting that has
occurred has been relatively minor. [Id. at 29-31, 34, 36.]

Professor Oren reviews and rejects a number of reasons that might support
a site-shifting strategy, such as the preservation of economic growth opportunities, and concludes that the control-compelling features of PSD are justified but
the site-shifting features are not. He claims, for example, that site-shifting "will
increasingly distort source location and control technology determinations." Id.
at 112. How could this happen? Is it enough of an answer that the PSD program
implements an "ethical imperative" to preserve clean air areas from further degradation? See also Tobi, Balancing Economic Growth and Air Quality: Prevention of Significant Deterioration and the Protection of Florida's Future, 1 J. Land
Use & Envtl. L. 25 (1985).

Do the PSD and visibility programs for parklands have a different justification? Professor Oren, in Protection of Parklands, *supra* at 344-354, argues that
the PSD program is justified for parks as a measure of ecosystem protection. He
differentiates the program as used for this purpose from the program as used
elsewhere, where its objective is to prevent negative health and welfare effects.
Is this distinction supportable?

But Professor Oren concludes that the PSD program as applied to parks
has had limited success:

No systematic attempt seems to have been made yet to determine the impact
of PSD near the parks. The limited evidence available presents what is at best a
mixed picture. There is some anecdotal evidence that the National Park Service,
by commenting on prospective sources near the parks, has at times prompted per-
mit-granting agencies to be stricter than would otherwise be the case. The Class I
increments seem to be playing little role, however. There are almost no recorded
instances in which modeling has shown that a prospective source would exceed an
allowable Class I increment. [Id. at 355.]

What should the response be to this criticism? Would it be better simply
to tighten the NAAQS generally and then abandon the PSD and visibility programs as unnecessary? What effect would this have on source location and economic opportunities nationally? Assume you decide to keep the PSD and
visibility programs for the national parks? How would you change them?

I. SPECIAL ISSUES IN THE CLEAN AIR ACT

1. Interstate Pollution

The Clean Air Act assumes that local, easily identifiable sources cause most air pollution problems and that an adequate SIP will enable a state to achieve the ambient standards. This section discusses problems of nondegradation (PSD), interstate transport, and acid rain that cast doubt on these congressional assumptions. Air pollution does not respect political boundaries. A downwind state may suffer injury from air pollution originating in a nearby or even a distant state, yet it may be unable to design a SIP that at a reasonable cost can achieve the federal ambient standards through controls on its own sources alone.

Only two sections of the Clean Air Act directly address interstate air pollution. In brief, §110(a)(2)(E) requires that a SIP prohibit emissions from stationary (but not mobile) sources that prevent attainment of the ambient standards or "interfere with" PSD or visibility protection measures in other states. Section 126 requires a state to notify other states of existing or proposed major sources that may contribute significantly to the downwind state's air pollution problems. It authorizes receptor states to petition EPA to take steps to abate existing emissions and to prevent the construction of new sources that would violate §110(a)(2)(E). Section 126 confers authority on EPA to take the necessary enforcement actions.

NEW YORK v. EPA
852 F.2d 574 (D.C. Cir. 1988)

SENTELLE, Circuit Judge:

Petitioners challenge the Environmental Protection Agency's (EPA) denial of petitions filed by three eastern states under section 126(b) of the Clean Air Act ("the Act"). We find that the EPA denial of these petitions is based on a reasonable interpretation of the relevant statutes and is not arbitrary or capricious. We therefore deny the petitions, with the exception of the petition of the state of New York which we remand to the Agency for the submission of new data.

I. Background . . .

The requirements of §110 include provisions dealing with certain types of interstate air pollution. Obviously, air movement across state borders is inevitable and the Act does not purport to bar interstate pollution but rather requires each SIP

to contain measures [for interstate pollution]. [Here the court quoted the requirements of §110(a)(2)(E), and then discussed the petition process contained in
§126.] . . .

The administrative decision challenged herein involved EPA's disposition
of petitions under section 126(b) filed by Pennsylvania, New York and Maine.
Separate section 126 petitions filed by the three states in 1980 and 1981 alleged
violations of NAAQS and impaired visibility within the borders of each state,
substantially attributable to the cumulative impact of SO_2 emissions in seven
mid-western states. In the atmosphere, SO_2 gas is transformed into tiny particles known as sulfate. Thus the above-referenced EPA NAAQS for SO_2 and
particulate matter are both implicated in this instance by the same pollution
sources.

The initial petition, filed by Pennsylvania on December 19, 1980, sought
a determination that 38 specific sources in Ohio and West Virginia prevented
attainment and maintenance of the SO_2 ambient standards in four Pennsylvania
counties and its southwestern air quality region. On December 22, 1980 and
January 16, 1981, New York filed nine petitions alleging that 19 specific sources
in the states of Illinois, Indiana, Michigan, Ohio, Tennessee and West Virginia
were preventing attainment and maintenance of the TSP standard in New York.
EPA consolidated the petitions and scheduled a hearing for June 18 and 19,
1981. Two weeks before the hearing, Pennsylvania supplemented its petition
and expanded its allegations to include all major emitters of SO_2 in Ohio,
West Virginia, Illinois, Indiana and Kentucky. At the hearing, New York submitted a list of 59 sources and later amended its petition to include all sources
of SO_2 and particulates under SIPs in the six states it originally named and
Kentucky.

After the hearing, Maine filed its petition on October 7, 1981, alleging
that SO_2 derived sulfate particulates were interfering with its ability to prevent
significant deterioration (PSD) and protect visibility as required by §§160-169A
(Part C requirements incorporated by reference in §110(a)(2)(E)(i)(II). Maine
alleged that a "regional haze" at Acadia National Park was the responsibility
of all "SO_2 sources in the seven mid-western states cited by New York and
Pennsylvania" and confessed an inability to trace the effects to any specific
source or list of sources. The further proceedings on the three petitions were
consolidated.

After extensive proceedings on the three petitions, including an eleven
month comment period which closed in May of 1982, the three petitioning
states sued in United States District Court seeking an order requiring EPA to
decide the petitions. That court ordered EPA to render a decision on the petitions
within 60 days. State of New York v. Ruckelshaus, 21 Envt. Rep. Cas. (BNA)
1721 (D.D.C. October 5, 1984). On December 10, 1984, EPA published a
denial of each state's petition. 49 Fed. Reg. 48,152, 48,157. The states then
filed these petitions for review pursuant to the judicial review section of the
Clean Air Act. 42 U.S.C. §7607.

II. *Analysis*

A. EPA's Duty Under Section 126(b)

EPA has interpreted §126(b) as requiring that four elements be met before relief will be provided. Those elements are: (1) Section 126(b) provides relief with respect to only those pollutants for which National Ambient Air Quality Standards have been set or PSD or visibility measures required; (2) Section 126(b) provides redress for violations alleged to have occurred in specified geographic areas; (3) Section 126(b) provides relief with respect to interstate pollution that results in the violation of an NAAQS or PSD increment, or interferes with required SIP measures to protect visibility; and (4) Where an NAAQS or PSD increment or proscribed visibility impairment occurs, the out-of-state source or sources must make a significant contribution to the levels of pollution causing that violation or impairment. 49 Fed. Reg. 34,856-58.

Petitioners argue that §126(b) provides a statutory mechanism to implement an affirmative duty, created by §110(a)(2), to review existing SIPs to determine whether the SIPs are adequate to prevent impermissible interstate impacts. Specifically, Petitioners contend that the filing of their section 126(b) petitions immediately obliged EPA to take the investigatory steps necessary to determine whether the SIPs in all named upwind states were in compliance with §110(a)(2)(E).

Section 110(a)(2)(E) prescribes substantive standards against which the interstate impacts of SIPs must be judged. The Administrator contends that his responsibility to evaluate SIPs for compliance with §110(a)(2)(E) is linked to his review of an otherwise required submission by a state. In other words, the Administrator contends that §110(a)(2)(E) does not require reevaluation and revision of existing SIPs, and that a section 126(b) petition does not trigger such review. We agree.

Petitioners' argument centers on the contention that the substantive inquiry under §126(b) is the same as that under §110(a)(2). If indeed it is the same substantive inquiry, and we will assume for these purposes it is, then the language of §126(b) supports the Administrator's interpretation of §110(a)(2)(E).

The language of §126(b) is quite specific and focuses on "major sources," not the validity of a state's SIP: "Any State or political subdivision may petition the Administrator for a finding that any major source emits or would emit any air pollution in violation of the prohibition of section 110(a)(2)(E)(i) of this title." §126(b) (emphasis added). The elements EPA has derived from §126(b) are reasonable and therefore, this Court will not disturb EPA's interpretation. [Citing *Chevron.*]

Congress specified that the Administrator take final action on a section 126(b) petition very quickly: "Within 60 days after receipt of any petition under this subsection and after public hearing, the Administrator shall make such a finding or deny the petition." §126(b) (emphasis added). Under Petitioners' theory, once a section 126(b) petition has been filed, the Administrator would be required to engage in an entire array of investigative duties. In particular, the Administrator would be required to undertake a full-scale investigation of the adequacy of the SIPs of all states named in the petition for all pollutants involved, to conduct whatever data-gathering and research is necessary to either prove Petitioners' claims or affirmatively disprove their allegations, and to develop whatever new air pollution models are necessary to confirm or affirmatively disprove Petitioners' modeling theories, as well as conducting a public hearing, analyzing the evidence presented by all interested parties, proposing a determination, considering all comments submitted and promulgating a final rule — all within 60 days of receipt of the petition.[1] It is reasonable to conclude that Congress did not intend that the Administrator be required to perform all these duties in such a short period of time in the absence of the clearest expression. See *Chevron*.

In addition, the language of §110(a)(2) resists Petitioners' interpretation and conversely, lends support to the Administrator's. Section 110(a)(2) contains no language expressly directing the Administrator to reevaluate existing SIPs. When Congress has intended to establish a requirement for direct EPA action it has said so. In 1977, Congress explicitly ordered the promulgation of EPA regulations addressing a variety of matters, including new source performance standards, noncompliance penalties, stack height credit, and visibility protection requirements. The statute also directs EPA to undertake other actions, including periodic reassessments of existing ambient standards and new source performance standards.

In one instance Congress specifically directed EPA to investigate the adequacy of existing SIPs. Section 124 of the Act, which is entitled "Assurance of adequacy of State plans," expressly requires EPA to review the adequacy of existing plans with regard to dependence by major fuel burning sources on petroleum products and natural gas. That section, unlike §110(a)(2)(E), sets up a procedure for accomplishing the task. Again, where Congress wanted EPA to review the adequacy of existing SIPs, it said so. Against that backdrop, Congress' silence in §110(a)(2)(E) is significant.

Not only is §110(a)(2)(E) itself devoid of any requirement for direct action by the EPA, but the legislative history is similarly barren. *If* any Congressional intent can be divined from this silence, it must be an intent *not* to require affirmative action. If Congressional intent cannot be determined then we must defer to EPA's construction of the statute so long as it is a permissible one. *Chevron*. . . .

The Administrator's review of various SIP revisions submitted by states is an ongoing process, and under the Administrator's interpretation the prohibition of §110(a)(2)(E) is one of the requirements that must be met before he can approve any initial SIP or revision. Because the Administrator's construction of

---

1. With the possibility of extension pursuant to section 307(d)(10), 42 U.S.C. §7607 (d)(10).

§110(a)(2) is consistent with the plain language of that provision and is a reasonable one, this Court must accept it.

B.   THE PETITIONS

Petitioners' position before this Court so thoroughly relied on their misconception that §§110 and 126 of the Act imposed a duty on the EPA to review SIPs that the affirmance of the Administrator's interpretation of those statutes is largely dispositive of the issues argued before us; nonetheless, we will address the Agency's treatment of each state's petition. In none of the three instances was the denial arbitrary or capricious.

MAINE

Maine presented evidence that, under certain weather conditions, sulfate particles transported from seven mid-western states caused the formation of "regional haze" that impairs visibility at Acadia National Park, an area where visibility is specially protected under §169A of the Act. EPA denied the petition because "Maine had not adopted the required visibility measures contained in the Federal regulations; moreover, such visibility measures at this time do not address regional haze." 49 Fed. Reg. 48,153; see State of Vermont v. Thomas, 850 F.2d 99 (2d Cir. June 23, 1988) (current regulations do not encompass federally enforceable measures to alleviate "regional haze").

Because Maine's claims in this proceeding concern only the problem of regional haze, Maine has not presented any claim which falls within the ambit of §126(b), which incorporates the substantive standard of §110(a)(2)(E). In other words, Maine does not allege that major sources in any other states are interfering with visibility measures contained in its SIP — its SIP does not contain regional haze visibility measures. Maine has failed to make even a threshold showing of entitlement under §126(b). Therefore, EPA properly denied Maine's petition.

PENNSYLVANIA

Pennsylvania's challenge to EPA's action on its petition is now directed to three particular areas in south-western Pennsylvania. The sole question is whether EPA was justified in not concluding that SO_2 emissions from major sources in Ohio and West Virginia prevented attainment or maintenance by Pennsylvania of the NAAQS for SO_2 in the subject areas.

The three areas are located in the West Virginia-Ohio border area (Border area), the Beaver Valley Air Basin (Beaver Valley area) and the Monongahela Valley Air Basin (Monongahela Valley area). Pennsylvania submitted no actual monitoring data showing violations of the SO_2 standards in the Border area. It relied on a modeling study (Cramer Study), commissioned by the EPA, which purported to predict violations in that area. The state argues that the Cramer Study represents the best modeling techniques available.

Because the Border area was not included in the original area of the Cramer Study, EPA contends that the results for that area are subject to several problems. Although violations of the SO_2 standard were predicted, the results were only "preliminary" due to questionable meteorological assumptions and questions regarding the accuracy of the emissions inventories for the out-of-state sources used in the model. In fact, the author of the Cramer Study conceded that additional work would be needed before firm results could be obtained. EPA thoroughly analyzed the Cramer Study and its applicability to the Border area and concluded that it did not provide a reasonable basis for determining that SO_2 violations were occurring in that area.

It is well established that when a court is reviewing predictions within an agency's area of special expertise, at the frontiers of science, the "court must generally be at its most deferential." Baltimore Gas & Electric Co. v. NRDC, 462 U.S. 87, 103 (1983). . . . Acceptance or rejection of a particular air pollution model and the results obtained from it are interpretations of scientific evidence. This Court cannot say that the Administrator's rejection of the Cramer Study was in any way unreasonable.

The Cramer Study did not predict a violation in the Beaver Valley area and Pennsylvania submitted no monitoring data showing an actual violation. It was therefore reasonable for the EPA to deny the section 126(b) petition with regard to the Beaver Valley Area.

Pennsylvania failed to submit any monitoring data showing an actual violation in the Monongahela Valley area. The Cramer Study predicted a violation at one site in that area, which was one of the areas covered by the original study. However, EPA estimated that more than 80% of the SO_2 contributing to the predicted violation would come from Pennsylvania sources, and that therefore the out-of-state sources did not "significantly contribute" to the violation. Once again this Court is being asked to second-guess the scientific judgments of the EPA. Once again, we are at our "most deferential." Baltimore Gas, 462 U.S. at 103. And, once again, we cannot say that the EPA's assessment of the scientific evidence was unreasonable. Therefore, Pennsylvania's petition will be denied.

NEW YORK

On July 1, 1987, EPA promulgated a new national ambient air quality standard for particulate matter which replaces the previous TSP standards. EPA contended in its brief that New York's claim had been mooted by this change and that, therefore, New York's petition should be dismissed.

However, at oral argument, EPA raised no objection to a remand for submission of new data rather than dismissal with leave to re-petition. Therefore, we remand New York's petition (and New York's petition only) for submission of new data relevant to the new NAAQS.

III. Conclusion

The Administrator's interpretation of §110(a)(2)(E) and §126(b) is consistent with the statutory language and is reasonable. The section 126(b) petitions of Maine and Pennsylvania were properly rejected by the EPA; accordingly, we deny Maine's and Pennsylvania's petitions for review. New York's petition is remanded for reconsideration in light of the revised TSP NAAQS.

It is so ordered.

GINSBURG, Ruth B., Circuit Judge, concurring: [Judge Ginsburg briefly concurred with the majority opinion and concluded that "[t]he judiciary, therefore, is not the proper place in which to urge alteration of the Agency's course.]

NOTES AND QUESTIONS

1. *Interstate pollution.* The Clean Air Act was premised on the attainment of national air quality standards in local areas and did not address interstate pollution, which has become a serious problem. Acid rain, an issue discussed later in this section, is one interstate pollution problem. Regional haze, the issue raised in the *Vermont* case, p. 295 *supra*, is another.

Interstate air pollution problems also occur where state boundaries pass through or near urban areas. Practically all of the major air pollutants may travel the short distances involved. Urban intergovernmental conflict over the responsibility for pollution abatement has gone on for decades in most major interstate urban areas, usually without successful resolution. Congress added §§110(a)(2)(E) and 126 to deal with interstate pollution problems, but EPA and the courts have substantially limited their effectiveness.

2. *Issues in New York v. Thomas.* What is the relationship between §§110(a)(2)(E) and 126? If EPA need not examine existing SIPs to determine compliance with §110(a)(2)(E) but need only proceed in §126 proceedings, are complaining downwind states left with access only to cumbersome case-by-case proceedings? Earlier cases took the same position on this issue. See Connecticut v. EPA, 656 F.2d 902 (2d Cir. 1981) (§126 primarily intended as means for resolving interstate disputes when SIP under revision); Connecticut v. EPA (*Connecticut Fund I*), 696 F.2d 147 (2d Cir. 1982) (upholding EPA's approval of New York SIP without responding to Connecticut's §126 petition alleging violation of interstate provisions).

What contribution must an upwind state make to downwind state pollution to violate §§110(a)(2)(E) and 126? The New York case adopted the "significant contribution" rule and held that a 20 percent contribution from outside sources to Pennsylvania pollution was not enough. Is this a proper reading of the statute?

The issue received more attention in Air Pollution Control District of Jefferson County v. EPA, 739 F.2d 1071 (6th Cir. 1984). The court noted the difficulties in determining interstate equities in air pollution. It observed that the broad reading of the interstate pollution provisions adopted by Jefferson County would prohibit nearly all interstate pollution. A narrow reading would "allow only the most extreme instances of air pollution to come under scrutiny." Id. at 1090. The court adopted the "significant contribution" test, although it was not specifically incorporated in §110(a)(2)(E). It relied on the inclusion of this phrase in §126(a). But see *Connecticut Fund I, supra,* (no violation of interstate pollution section when impact on nearby state of another state's revision of its SIP is minimal); New York v. EPA, 710 F.2d 1200 (6th Cir. 1983) (accord).

Assume Downwind State A believes that SO_2 emissions from an aggregate of several sources in Upwind State B are preventing it from attaining the SO_2 NAAQS. Can State A successfully bring a §126 petition against State B? If not, what must it show?

3. NAAQS *violations and growth issues.* Note that the interstate pollution sections apply only to NAAQS attainment and maintenance. What does this do to local "margins of growth"?

The leading case is the *Jefferson County* case, *supra.* The Jefferson County District, which includes Louisville, Kentucky, petitioned EPA under §126. It argued that SO_2 emission limits approved by EPA for a power plant across the Ohio River in Indiana prevented the attainment and maintenance of the SO_2 NAAQS in Jefferson County. The County had not attained the SO_2 NAAQS. The District also claimed the Indiana power plant emission limits would interfere with the County's efforts to prevent significant deterioration of air quality once the SO_2 NAAQS were attained. The emission limits approved for the Indiana power plant were several times higher than the emission limits approved for a power plant that was the major producer of SO_2 in Jefferson County. EPA rejected the §126 petition and the Jefferson County District appealed.

The Jefferson County District noted the Kentucky SIP included a margin of growth for the county by adopting emission limits for SO_2 more stringent than the NAAQS required. This margin of growth would allow additional industrial development in Jefferson County without violating the NAAQS. Because the Indiana power plant contributed 47 percent of the secondary SO_2 NAAQS in some parts of Jefferson County, the District claimed the County's margin of growth had been "stolen" by the power plant to the County's economic disadvantage.

The court rejected this argument. It accepted EPA's argument that the Jefferson County margin of growth established a local air quality standard more stringent than the national standard. EPA argued that the interstate pollution provisions only prohibited attainment or maintenance of the national air quality standards. The court noted that because Jefferson County had not yet attained the SO_2 NAAQS "the asserted margin of growth is necessarily conjectural." Id. at 1088. It held that national uniformity in the interpretation of the Act was especially important in applying the interstate pollution provisions.

Do you agree with the court's interpretation? What other interpretation would you adopt? What interstate equities do you see? Consider the following:

> Interstate equity requires that the burden of reducing interstate pollution be allocated fairly among the states involved. Some of the factors that must be considered in defining interstate equity are whether existing or new sources are involved, whether the source state's SIP contains stringent or lax emission standards, whether emission standards are being violated in the source state, the extent to which sources in the receiving state contribute to NAAQS non-attainment there, and whether the contributions by sources in the receiving states are due to violations of emissions standards or to lax standards. [Silverstein, Interstate Air Pollution: Unresolved Issues, 3 Harv. Envtl. L. Rev. 291 (1979).]

The court in *Connecticut Fund (I)*, *supra*, considered but did not fully decide these issues.

4. *PSD and baselines*. Assume downwind State A has attained the NAAQS for SO_2 and so is subject to the PSD program for that pollutant. Now assume that no applications for new or modified sources that emit SO_2 have been filed in State A. May upwind State B approve a SIP that will cause increased emissions of SO_2 that destroy its PSD status? In answering this question, recall that a duty to conduct a PSD analysis is not triggered until an application is filed.

Connecticut Fund (I) recognized but did not decide this issue, though it noted that a downwind PSD state could protect its PSD status through the interstate pollution sections if it adopted voluntary measures to reinforce its PSD designation. But see New York v. EPA, 716 F.2d 440 (7th Cir. 1983) (no duty to conduct PSD analysis until application filed). What is the effect of the *Jefferson County* case, *supra*, on this problem?

5. *Once again, modeling*. Long-range transport is the cause of interstate pollution, but the Reagan Administration undercut implementation of the interstate pollution provisions by recognizing modeling results only for a range of fifty kilometers. 49 Fed. Reg. 34,863 (1984). The courts upheld EPA's use of short-range models in the interstate pollution cases, see *Connecticut Fund (I)* and *Jefferson County*, *supra*. Note the holding on the modeling problem in New York v. Thomas. Does it reinforce EPA's position on models?

Despite EPA's intransigence on long-range modeling, many claim that reliable long-range models have been available for some time. But see Schwartz, Acid Deposition: Unraveling a Regional Phenomenon, 243 Science 753 (1989) (criticizing long-range models for acid deposition). New York had argued as early as 1981 in a §126 petition that reliable long-range models were available:

> [T]here are numerous long-range air pollution transport models which could have been used by EPA to predict the impact of such sources on both sulfur dioxide and particulate levels in the downwind states. EPA itself has stated that models capable of estimating the impact of SO_2 emissions on ground level particulate matter concentrations have been developed and are now being evaluated by EPA as part of an overall revision to the modeling guidelines. 46 Fed. Reg. 37,645 (1981). [Memorandum of Law in Support of Petition for Interstate Pollution Abatement 41 (December 31, 1981).]

New York added that "the long-range impacts complained of here may also be traced by air parcel trajectory analysis, analysis of monitoring data, analysis of meteorology data, satellite tracking of air masses, and by procedures which combine such methods" (Memorandum, at 43). See also Bass, Modeling Long Range Transport and Diffusion, in Research Guidelines for Regional Modeling of Fine Particulates, Acid Deposition and Visibility (EPA Pub. No. II-D-50(F) No. 16) (report of a workshop held at Port Deposit, Maryland, Oct. 29-Nov. 1, 1979). Reread the section on models, p. 154 *supra*. Should EPA be more or less cautious when it uses models to resolve interstate pollution disputes? See Note, Interstate Air Pollution: Over a Decade of Ineffective Regulation, 64 Chi.-Kent L. Rev. 619 (1988).

2.   The Acid Rain Controversy

The problem of controlling acid precipitation and deposition has come front and center as one of the most important issues facing Congress under the Clean Air Act. The problem surfaced in the United States in the 1970s as the second most severe environmental threat posed by fossil fuel-fired power plants. (Worldwide carbon dioxide buildup is potentially worse.) The outcry in the media hides serious uncertainties about the acid rain phenomenon, its effects, and its cure. This section reviews the acid rain problem and proposed remedies that require revisions in the Clean Air Act.

1. *What acid rain is.* Emissions of SO_2 and NO_x gases are eventually transformed by chemical reactions to fine sulfate and nitrate particles. Although the transformation process begins soon after emission, it may last several days. Sulfates and nitrates may be transported hundreds or even thousands of miles upon prevailing winds. Sulfuric and nitric acid forms when rain, snow, fog, and dew combine with the sulfate and nitrate aerosols, or when precipitation or surface waters combine with particles deposited dry upon the ground. The long-range transport and deposition (wet or dry) of sulfates and nitrates have come to be called, a little imprecisely, "acid rain."

Acid rain usually results from well-mixed emissions from numerous sources located hundreds of miles upwind. Over two-thirds of the acid produced is the product of coal combustion in power plants and smelter operations. Vehicular pollution also contributes to the problem.

> While the overall chemistry leading to the formation of acid rain is reasonably well defined, important questions remain regarding the underlying dynamics of that process. For example, defining the reaction pathways — sometimes termed transformation processes — for SO_2 and NO_x and establishing the conditions under which specific pathways produce acidic compounds is important in evaluating the efficacy of various emissions reduction scenarios. If the amount of sulfate produced by a pathway is proportional to the amount of sulfur dioxide in the atmosphere, then reducing the level of sulfur dioxide emissions will reduce proportionately the amount of sulfate formed. But, if the reaction process is oxidant-limited, then the availability of ozone may become the dominant pathway for acid formation. [J. Reegens & R. Rycroft, The Acid Rain Controversy 43 (1988).]

In addition to debate over the linearity or non-linearity of the relationship between precursor gases and sulfate formation, there is also considerable uncertainty over source-receptor relationships. The northeastern states, where the acid rain problem is particularly severe, believe that the predominant cause of the problem is the concentration of old electric power plants in the Ohio River Valley and its environs. Existing plants that have never been subjected to NSPS emit five to seven times the amount of SO_2 allowed from comparable new sources (National Commission on Air Quality, To Breathe Clean Air 242 (1981)). Twenty-one of the oldest of these are located in Ohio alone.

But the models available to help determine this relationship are imperfect. See, e.g., Venkatram & Karamchandani, Source-Receptor Relationships: A Look at Acid Deposition Modeling, 20 Envtl. Sci. & Technology 1084 (1986), and the discussion of modeling in the section on interstate transport, *supra*.

The federal government has been conducting an extensive research program on acid rain, but reports issued during the Reagan Administration downplayed the issue and came under heavy criticism. See National Acid Precipitation Assessment Program, Interim Assessment: The Causes and Effects of Acidic Precipitation (1988); Acid Rain Controversy, *supra*, at 53-58 (reporting criticisms).

2. *The effects of acid rain.* The harmful effects of acid rain were first noticed in Scandinavia in the 1960s, then later in Canada and the Adirondack Mountains of upstate New York. Studies are beginning to implicate other regions of this country and Canada as both recipients and sources. The cumulative effects of acid rain may kill fish and other aquatic life in lakes and streams, decrease forest and crop productivity (by both direct leaf blight and leaching of soil nutrients), and damage buildings and metals. Acidified runoff apparently also leaches toxic elements and compounds from rocks, soils, and even pipes into drinking water supplies. Sulfate and nitrate particulate mists can severely impair visibility in the Northeast and the Southwest.

Uncertainties also surround the question of the damage caused by acid rain:

> Scientists are certain that transported air pollutants have caused *some* damage. At issue is the severity of the damage, whether it is fairly localized or widespread, and which resources are affected. For example, there is little question that acid deposition damages lakes, and ozone harms crops. The uncertainties revolve around *how many* lakes and streams and *what quantity* of crops. For these and other resources, the *risks* of extensive damage over large parts of the United States are substantial. . . .
>
> For certain concerns, such as the extent of damage to forests from acid deposition, the uncertainties are so large that it is difficult to describe the patterns or magnitude of risk. [Office of Technology Assessment, Acid Rain and Transported Air Pollutants 32 (1984).]

See also Woodman & Cowling, Airborne Chemicals and Forest Health, 21 Envtl. Sci. & Technology 120 (1987); Stumm, Sigg & Schnoor, Aquatic Chemistry of Acid Deposition, 21 Envtl. Sci. & Technology 8 (1987).

Cost-benefit analysis. Like every other program aimed at reducing air pollution, programs for acid rain have been subject to economic cost-benefit analysis. Here is one cost estimate from an impartial source:

> Proposals in Congress have targeted utility emissions. Although estimates vary, a typical proposal would target reductions in utility SO₂ of 10 million tons at an estimated cost of $30-$60 billion. . . .
>
> [T]he cost could result in "rate shock" for some Midwest utilities, depending on how they or the State governments choose to implement the reductions. If utilities choose a capital-intensive means of meeting reduction requirements, such as . . . scrubbers, rate shock in the first year of the program could reach 15% in extreme cases (then declining). If switching facilities to lower-sulfur coal was chosen, the rate impact could be much less, at least in the short term. . . .
>
> [W]ithout a cost-sharing mechanism, ten States would bear 80-90% of the cost of a 10-million ton SO₂ reduction. . . . [These are midwestern states but Pennsylvania, West Virginia and Tennessee are also included.] The uneven effect on rates, along with the substantial cost of the program, has resulted in various cost-sharing proposals being suggested. [Congressional Research Service (Envtl. & Natural Resources Policy Div.) Acid Rain: Issues in the 101st Congress 4-5 (1989).]

There is general agreement that the annual costs of a politically and economically achievable 10 million-ton reduction in sulfur dioxide emissions, which is 40 percent, would cost from three to six billion dollars annually in the foreseeable future. Cost-benefit analysis based on these costs is difficult primarily because of uncertainties on the benefits side. See Crocker & Regens, Acid Deposition Control — A Benefit-Cost Analysis: Its Prospects and Limits, 19 Envtl. Sci. & Technology 112 (1985) ("major errors of omission and commission" possible). See also Congressional Budget Office, Curbing Acid Rain: Cost, Budget, and Coal-Market Effects (1986).

Program strategies. Most legislative proposals have focused on reducing acid rain through a rollback of precursor emissions. These proposals raise the following issues:

> *Issue 1: Which pollutants should be regulated?* [B]oth SO₂ and NOₓ emissions are acid rain precursors. . . . Approximately two-thirds of the total acidity found in precipitation in the Adirondacks and New England is believed to be from SO₂, and one-third is from NOₓ. For this reason most proposals focus on SO₂, at least initially. But the NOₓ contribution is growing steadily, and perhaps at some point NOₓ controls will be required as well. . . .
>
> *Issue 2: How large will emission reductions have to be?* . . . It is estimated that reduction to 10 to 30 [kilograms per hectacre per year] will protect sensitive ecosystems. . . . Achieving a reduction to 20 kg/h/yr requires a 50 percent reduction in SO₂ emissions, assuming a linear rollback. Applying this percentage to projected emissions in the United States in the year 2000 gives a required reduction of 13.4 million tons per year. . . .
>
> *Issue 3: What technological approach for reducing emissions will be required?* [T]o what extent should emission sources be required to employ particular abatement technologies — chiefly . . ."scrubbing"? Or should sources be allowed to reduce emissions by any method they desire?

The great attraction of allowing sources to choose the method of emission reduction is that it reduces cost, for an alternative to scrubbing would be selected only if it was less expensive. At present the most likely substitute is switching from a high- to a low-sulfur coal. [Harrington, Breaking the Deadlock on Acid Rain Control, Resources, Fall 1988, at 1, 2.]

A related issue is whether specific emission reduction strategies should be proposed for states, or whether they should be given emission quotas with the option to choose any reduction strategy that meets the quota. What are the advantages and disadvantages of each approach? The Department of Energy sponsors a clean-coal technology program that subsidizes 50 percent of the cost of technology development. DOE made $1.3 billion in technology grants in 1988, 19 Envt. Rep. (BNA): Current Developments 1125 (1988), and President Bush has recommended additional funding. Id. at 2252 (1989). Is this a sufficient alternative to an acid rain strategy?

Naturally, the distributive impacts of an acid rain emissions reduction program have stirred up a political hornet's nest:

> The politics of acid rain pits nation against nation, the Midwest against East and West, and state against state. It storms within states. It sets industry against industry and erodes trust among the party regulars. Such discord . . . blows unequally across the states, because federal proposals to reduce emissions have an uneven economic impact. . . . [Davis, Acid Rain: No Truce Is in Sight in the Eight-Year War between the States, Governing, Dec. 1988, at 50.]

What is it in the proposals for emission reductions that creates the war between the states? Can anything be done about it? What variables in the analysis of the acid rain problem affect the distributive impact of an emission reduction program? For example, do assumptions about linearity affect distributive impact? See also Blackwood, A Conceptual Framework for an Acid Rain Control Program, 19 Envtl. L. Rep. (Envtl. L. Inst.) 10166 (1989); Stanfield, The Acid Rainmakers, 18 Natl. J. 1500 (1986).

International solutions. Canada is seriously concerned about the impact of acid rain on its lakes and forests. One estimate is that one out of ten Canadian jobs depends on the forests. Canadian officials estimate that about 60 percent of the acid rain that falls on Canada comes from the United States and that it contributes 4 times as much SO_2 and 11 times as much NO_x to Canada's eastern provinces as the United States receives from Canada. 12 Envt. Rep. (BNA): Current Developments 648 (1981). See House of Commons Subcommittee on Acid Rain of the Standing Committee on Fisheries and Forestry, Still Waters: The Chilling Reality of Acid Rain 92 (1981) (urging American action).

Section 115 of the Clean Air Act addresses international air pollution. Paradoxically, it affords Canada a somewhat stronger ground to attack Ohio River Valley sulfate pollution than it affords New York. Do you see why? The section's requirement that the foreign country give the United States equal treatment is met by Can. Rev. Stat., ch. 47, 21.2

Administrator Costle attempted to invoke §115 in 1980, during the Carter Administration, but when the Reagan Administration took office EPA Administrator Gorsuch rejected Costle's findings. New York v. Thomas, 802 F.2d 443 (D.C. Cir. 1986), *cert. denied*, 107 S. Ct. 3196 (1987), held that letters from Costle to the Secretary of State and a United States Senator stating that the United States is partially responsible for acid rain damage in Canada did not trigger §115 duties, which require the EPA to identify responsible states and issue appropriate SIP revisions. Costle wrote the letters instead of identifying the states that caused the pollution and proposing SIP revisions. Judge (now Justice) Scalia concluded that his successor was not bound because the action was a rule that could be promulgated only through APA notice and comment procedures.

The Reagan Administration also frustrated diplomatic efforts with Canada to resolve the acid rain controversy. In 1982 the Administration stopped work on transboundary solutions to the acid rain problem, claiming that more research was necessary. The United States did not attend a 1984 conference called by Canada that produced a Declaration on Acid Rain. Canada decided to mandate substantial sulfur dioxide reductions on its own.

President Reagan, under intense pressure during a summit conference with the Canadian Prime Minister, finally appointed a Special Envoy on Acid Rain who, with his Canadian counterpart, produced a joint report. D. Lewis & W. Davis, United States & Canadian Joint Report of the Special Envoys on Acid Rain (1986). The report committed the United States to acceptance of the transboundary pollution problem, but diluted this commitment by stating that current emission control technology was too costly and provided only a limited number of options. To resolve this problem the Administration committed itself to a $5 billion research partnership in clean coal technology that would reduce emissions from high sulfur coal, which America has in abundance.

For additional discussion of transboundary pollution problems see Steiner, The North American Acid Rain Problem: Applying International Legal Principles Economically Without Burdening Bilateral Relations, 12 Suffolk Transnatl. L.J. 1 (1988); Note, Our Neighbor's Keeper? The U.S. and Canada: Coping with Transboundary Air Pollution, 9 Fordham Internatl. L.J. 159 (1985).

NOTES AND QUESTIONS

1. *Policy choices*. More than any other issue, the acid rain issue highlights the difficulties of making the Clean Air Act work because of the important distributive judgments that must be made in the design of an acid rain program. In addition to the inter-regional issues, serious distributive problems are raised by the impact on utility rates and thus on state and regional economies. These impacts raise serious questions about the distribution of costs and benefits in the clean air program. Solutions are made more difficult by uncertainties over such issues as the variables that affect interstate transport and the extent and nature of the benefits to be gained from an emissions reduction program.

With all this in mind, how would you design an acid rain control program? Congress may well adopt an emissions reduction program as an overlay on existing programs under the Clean Air Act. Is this the best solution? Note also that nitrogen oxides may play an increasingly important role in acid rain formation. Should this be another reason for tightening controls on motor vehicle emissions? Does the acid rain controversy suggest that the time has come for a comprehensive look at air quality programs rather than piecemeal patching?

2. *State programs.* In the absence of definitive action from Congress, several states have adopted acid rain control programs:

> Wisconsin's is among the most successful. The first bill, passed in 1983, merely capped emissions from five utilities. Subsequent reduction, to comply with the Clean Air Act, was largely achieved by switching fuels, explains Richard H. Osa of the Milwaukee-based Wisconsin Electric Power Co. Burning lower-sulfur coal required several million dollars worth of changes in the company's pollution control devices.
>
> In 1985, state legislators approved a tougher law calling for 50 percent reduction of sulfur dioxide emissions from utilities by 1993. The law also set a voluntary emission reduction standard for other industries, including the state's many paper mills, heavy emitters of sulfur dioxide. Osa says the law, based on recommendations from a committee of business people, consumers and environmentalists, "sought a level of control that could be reached without resorting to retrofitting old plants with scrubbers." [War between the States, *supra*, at 52.]

The state acid rain laws are the first example, apart from California's exemption for motor vehicle emission controls, of states taking a tougher stance on clean air than Congress. What does this say about the "national uniformity" assumptions behind the Clean Air Act? Should Congress simply leave the acid rain control issue to the states? For discussion of Minnesota's acid rain control program see Roberts, Acid Rain Regulation: Federal Failure and State Success, 8 Va. J. Nat. Resources L. 1, 35-60 (1988).

3. The literature on acid rain is substantial and growing. For readings in addition to those cited earlier see C. Park, Acid Rain: Rhetoric and Reality (1987); The Acid Rain Debate (E. Yanarella & R. Ihara eds. 1985); G. Wetstone & A. Rosencranz, Acid Rain in Europe and North America (1983); Comment, Front Doors, Back Doors and Trapdoors to Acid Rain Control, 7 U.C.L.A.J. Envtl. L. & Poly. 97 (1987). For a summary of the issue as of that time and a good collection of readings see House Comm. on Energy & Commerce, Acid Rain: A Survey of Data and Current Analyses (1984).

3.   *Enforcement*

This chapter has emphasized the substantive requirements of the Clean Air Act. Enforcement is the last step in the Act's complex federal-state implementation scheme. Although environmental attorneys spend a good deal of their time on enforcement actions involving individual sources, enforcement is treated briefly in this chapter because cases and statutes are less important to enforcement than the unwritten rules of prosecutorial discretion: "Enforcement is always a dark figure of administrative law, and informed judgments about it require a closer look at the files than is afforded by conventional legal research." W. Rodgers, Environmental Law 351 (1977).

Enforcement of all pollution laws, including the Clean Air Act, has increased substantially since the early years of the Reagan Administration following management improvements adopted by EPA in 1984. EPA, FY 1988 Enforcement Accomplishments Report (1988). President Bush's EPA Administrator, William Reilly, has also made enforcement a top priority. Ask as you proceed to what extent the legal process can "rewrite" the Clean Air Act through enforcement discretion, case settlement, and judges' power to fashion compliance decrees. For a discussion of enforcement of the Clean Water Act, see Chapter 4.

The framework for coordinated federal and state enforcement. The enforcement of pollution legislation creates complicated administrative problems. The states have the first opportunity and the primary responsibility to enforce the statute. They are continuously involved in scores of enforcement actions, creating an important subfield of environmental law. See, e.g., Conoco, Inc. v. Department of Health, 651 P.2d 125 (Okla. 1982). See Currie, Illinois Pollution Law Enforcement, 70 NW. U.L. Rev. 389 (1975); Note, The Role of the Michigan Attorney General in Consumer and Environmental Protection, 72 Mich. L. Rev. 1030 (1974); National Association of Attorneys-General, Power, Duties and Operations of State Attorneys-General 341-348 (1977).

Yet Congress also expected that vigorous federal enforcement would occur under §113, to correct what it perceived as state unwillingness to get tough with its industrial sources. State officials often refer to federal enforcement as their "gorilla in the closet." EPA's enforcement relationship with the states is governed by a Policy Framework for State/EPA Enforcement Agreements (Rev. 1986). EPA regional offices and the states negotiate enforcement agreements each year that provide criteria for enforcement and compliance programs. See also Comment, State/Federal Enforcement of the Clean Air Act and other Federal Pollution Laws: Federal Overfiling on State Enforcement Proceedings, 1987 B.Y.U.L. Rev. 1085. The agency completed development of an Inspector Training and Development Program in 1988. An earlier report had criticized state and federal inspections. GAO, Air Pollution: Environmental Protection Agency's Inspections of Stationary Sources (1985). EPA has also issued a number of other guidance documents and strategies for state and federal compliance efforts. See also C. Russell, W. Harrington & W. Vaughan, Enforcing Pollution Control Laws (1986).

In theory, EPA refers all enforcement cases to the Lands and Natural Resources Division of the Department of Justice, following the practice of virtually all federal agencies for which the Department provides representation. In practice, the EPA Office of Enforcement conducts some enforcement actions itself and participates heavily in most of the actions brought by Justice Department lawyers. The U.S. Attorneys in the field, EPA regional offices, and state and local counsel and program staff are also involved or consulted.

Relations between EPA and the Justice Department have never been smooth and occasionally are stormy. The EPA argues that its own attorneys should decide which cases merit vigorous prosecution and that its specialized lawyers are better prepared to handle scientifically and technically complex cases than the Department's lawyers. Further, it argues that integrated EPA enforcement would promote consistency of result between administrative and judicial enforcement. The Department counters that as a "client" agency EPA should focus on preparing enforcement cases, especially on hiring and training specialists in detection and surveillance ("gumshoes"), modeled on the Treasury Department agents who go into the field to detect lawbreakers. The tension between the Department and EPA resulted in a joint Memorandum of Understanding, codified in part by §305 of the 1977 amendments, which guarantees that if prompt departmental representation in an enforcement action is not provided, EPA may bring the action itself and that EPA lawyers will be allowed to participate in actions prosecuted by the Department.

Delayed compliance orders. The Supreme Court in its earlier decision in *Union Electric* said that technological or economic infeasibility could be taken into account by EPA in fashioning a federal administrative compliance order (427 U.S. at 267-268). Responding to this dictum, EPA initially exercised its discretion under the statutory enforcement provision, §113, to authorize delayed compliance by existing sources subject to enforcement orders.

Congress reacted in the 1977 amendments by restricting EPA's discretion and creating the delayed compliance order (DCO) (§113(d)). Section 113(d) authorizes a DCO for any source "unable to comply" with a SIP but limits the extension to a maximum of three years after the date for final compliance with the ambient standards. The DCO provision has not yet received extensive judicial consideration. But see Bethlehem Steel Corp. v. EPA, 638 F.2d 994 (7th Cir. 1980) ("arbitrary and capricious" standard applied to EPA disapproval of DCO). Administrative orders, authorized by §113(a), are not used extensively in Clean Air Act enforcement.

The controversial steel amendment, developed by the government-industry-citizen Tripartite Steel Commission, allows the steel companies to delay compliance until 1985. Steel Compliance Extension Act of 1981, Pub. L. No. 97-23, 95 Stat. 139, *amending* §172(b)(2). Money saved is to be applied to plant modernization. Compliance consent decrees must be negotiated with each steelmaker. Further, §119 provides for extended compliance orders for primary non-ferrous smelters. The EPA regulations governing the award of NSO were invalidated in part in Kennecott Corp. v. EPA, 684 F.2d 1007 (D.C. Cir. 1982). Section 113 also contains several other special authorizations for delayed compliance, including DCOs for sources using innovative pollution control technology and for energy sources converting to coal.

Civil money penalties. The problem of widespread noncompliance was high on the agenda when Congress enacted the 1977 Clean Air Act Amendments. Thousands of sources had not yet managed to comply, and hundreds of others had not even begun to try. In response, Congress first gave EPA authority to seek civil money penalties in court, as a more expeditious alternative to existing enforcement provisions. See generally Olds, Unkovic & Lewin, Thoughts on the Role of Penalties in the Enforcement of the Clean Air and Clean Water Acts, 17 Duq. L. Rev. 1 (1978-1979). Civil penalties have turned out to be important enforcement tools.

The courts continue to impose substantial civil penalties. See, e.g., United States v. SCM Corp, 667 F. Supp. 1110 (D.C. Md. 1987) (stressing size of business, apparent footdragging and seriousness of violation in assessing $350,000 penalty for 30 days violation); United States v. Chevron, U.S.A, Inc., 639 F. Supp. 770 (W.D. Tex. 1985) (imposing $4.5 million penalty against major corporation for long-continued and egregious violations). EPA also continues to negotiate consent decrees that contain substantial penalties. See, e.g., 18 Envt. Rep. (BNA): Current Developments 2266 (1988) ($1.5 million).

Are there punitive aspects to these penalties that raise due process problems? Criminal due process may be necessary if the penalty is at base a criminal sanction. Despite this problem, civil money penalties usually survive constitutional attack. See F. Anderson, A. Kneese, P. Reed, R. Stevenson & S. Taylor, Environmental Improvement through Economic Incentives 123-128 (1977), and Note, Deterring Air Polluters through Economically Efficient Sanctions: A Proposal for Amending the Clean Air Act, 32 Stan. L. Rev. 807, 820 (1980) (concluding that civil penalties do not deter noncompliance).

The §120 economic non-compliance penalties. In a unique federal experiment with economic penalties, Congress enacted §120 to authorize penalties computed to be equal to the violator's economic benefit from non-compliance, on the theory that if sources insisted on delay they would do so "on their own time." Congress hoped to place polluters on the same economic footing as those who had limited their emissions through increased anti-pollution expenditures. It also hoped that the penalties would increase administrative flexibility in enforcing the Act, by serving as a middle ground between stiff criminal sanctions or shutdown of noncomplying facilities. The penalty must include at least the quarterly equivalents of capital costs, operating costs, and maintenance expenses avoided as a result of noncompliance (§120(d)(2)).

Delay in complying with standards has always been the Achilles' heel of pollution control schemes that are prospective in effect and do not penalize past pollution. See, e.g., United States v. West Penn Power Co., 460 F. Supp. 1305 (W.D. Penn. 1978) (further delay in installing SO_2 scrubber merited injunctive relief; civil penalties denied). Delay almost always was richly rewarded. As long as it could resist enforcement, a source could invest the money it would have spent on non-productive pollution control equipment to produce more income. Delays sometimes required outlays for attorneys' fees, but these were only a fraction of the cost of compliance or of the income that could be earned.

The idea for §120 was taken from a similar approach that was funded by EPA but was conceived and refined by the state of Connecticut during the mid-1970s. Douglas Costle, soon to become EPA Administrator in the Carter Administration, headed the state's environmental protection agency. His assistant, William Drayton, a future Assistant EPA Administrator, developed the noncompliance penalty concept. Mindful of precedent, they carefully prepared a six-volume "how-to-do-it" manual and brought it to Washington with them. EPA, Economic Law Enforcement, Strengthening Environmental Law Enforcement: Air Pollution (Connecticut Enforcement Project, 1975).

EPA took three years to promulgate the lengthy §120 regulations. Duquesne Light Co. v. EPA (I), 698 F.2d 456 (D.C. Cir. 1983) upheld the regulations in almost all respects. A sequel to that case considered the application of the regulations in a compliance situation that presented important policy problems and raised questions concerning the role of the penalty as an economic deterrent:

DUQUESNE LIGHT CO. v. EPA (II)
791 F.2d 959 (D.C. Cir. 1986)

MIKVA, Circuit Judge:

I

In Duquesne Light Co. v. Environmental Protection Agency, 698 F.2d 456 (D.C. Cir. 1983) (*Duquesne I*), this court considered twenty consolidated petitions for review of regulations promulgated by the Environmental Protection Agency (EPA) pursuant to the Clean Air Act Amendments of 1977. Those regulations provide a model for the assessment of penalties against entities that fail to comply with the Clear Air Act's pollution limitations. The penalties that the model calls for are designed to recoup the economic benefits those entities derive by failing to comply with the Clean Air Act's requirements. In *Duquesne I* we upheld the penalty assessment model's propriety in most respects. However, briefing was deferred on those issues that we hoped the parties would settle through negotiations. See *Duquesne I* at 461 n.1. Two of those deferred issues were settled. Today we decide the remaining issue: the legality of the model used for calculating noncompliance penalties assessed against regulated utilities. Although the question is not entirely free from doubt, we are satisfied that the EPA's regulations comply with the statutory mandate under which they were adopted.

II

The Clean Air Act ("Act"), provides for national standards on the level of air pollutants. Act §109. These standards are implemented through a procedure that limits permissible emissions from stationary sources, including power plants operated by public utilities. Act §110. The Act also provides for penalties for noncompliance. Section 120(d)(2) of the Act, added by the 1977 Amendments, authorizes the EPA to sanction polluters by assessing penalties designed to alter their economic behavior by changing the costs of emitting pollutants in violation of the applicable air quality standards. . . . [B]y removing the economic benefits of noncompliance with the Act, Congress hoped to place polluters on the same economic footing as those who had limited their emissions through increased anti-pollution expenditures. [Duquesne I at 461; see generally id. at 461-465.]

Section 120 of the Act specifically provides that

The amount of the penalty which shall be assessed and collected with respect to any source under this section shall be equal to — (A) the amount determined by the Administrator . . . which is no less than the economic value which a delay in compliance beyond July 1, 1979, may have for the owner of such source, including the quarterly equivalent of the capital costs of compliance and debt service over a normal amortization period, . . . operation and maintenance costs forgone as a result of noncompliance, and any additional economic value which such a delay may have for the owner or operator of such source. . . .

§120(d)(2).

In 1980 the EPA adopted regulations implementing §120. 45 Fed. Reg. 50,086 (1980) (codified at 40 C.F.R. §§66.1 to 67.43 and appendices). The regulations provide that "[a]ll noncompliance penalties shall be calculated in accordance with the Technical Support Document and the Manual." 40 C.F.R. §66.21(a). That document in turn provides that "[f]or the purposes of noncompliance penalties, the economic value, or savings, from noncompliance is defined to have two components: (1) the return which can be earned on the capital costs of pollution control equipment whose purchase has been delayed, and (2) the operating and maintenance costs avoided as a result of not having installed the equipment and the return on these savings." Noncompliance Penalties, Technical Support Document, 45 Fed. Reg. at 50,123. It is readily apparent that the penalty assessment model set forth in the EPA's regulations is primarily based on the factors mentioned in the authorizing statute.

III

A

Our standard of review is provided by section 307(d)(9) of the Act. . . . With that standard in mind, we now evaluate the petitioners' challenge to the EPA regulations.

The dispute in this case concerns the propriety of applying the EPA's §120 penalty assessment model, upheld by this court in its general application, see Duquesne I, to regulated utilities. Petitioners here, regulated public utilities, urge this court to set aside the EPA regulations governing penalty assessment insofar as they apply to them. They claim that the EPA, to comply with §120's mandate, must devise a special penalty calculation model for public utilities.

Petitioners argue that Congress' overarching desire in enacting §120 was to ensure that polluters would be economically "indifferent" between polluting and paying the statutory penalty, on the one hand, and installing pollution control equipment, on the other. According to petitioners, penalties under §120 should equal an amount that will have the same negative economic effect on the polluters as would complying with the Act's requirements. That is, penalties should be equal to the benefit or "economic value" of noncompliance. Petitioners assert that they suffer much more from a penalty than they would from incurring the same amount of pollution-control costs. Thus, they claim that applying a penalty-assessment model that equates economic value with savings frustrates Congress' plan that firms should be indifferent between penalties and compliance, at least with respect to public utilities. Such a penalty-assessment model allegedly misapplies §120's requirement that penalties be set equal to economic value.

The petitioners' argument turns on the peculiar way in which costs are borne by regulated utilities. Public utility regulators govern the extent and manner in which public utilities are allowed to recover costs from their ratepayers. Petitioners assert that public utility regulatory bodies allow expenditures on pollution control equipment to be included in a utility's rate base and periodic costs to be passed through as expenses. Thus, the financial impact of complying with the Act's emission standards is assertedly very small for public utilities that are permitted to recover their expenditures on pollution control equipment.

The regulatory treatment of fines imposed pursuant to §120 will, according to petitioners, be very different. Although no such fines have in fact been incurred, petitioners believe that utility regulators will not allow §120 penalties to be included in the rate base or passed through to the ratepayers as expenses. (The National Association of Regulatory Utility Commissioners, *amicus curiae* here, endorses this prediction.) Based on the disparate regulatory treatment of actual expenditures on pollution-control equipment and fines for noncompliance, petitioners argue that, for public utilities, the economic value of noncompliance is less than the direct cost avoided by noncompliance. Therefore, petitioners assert, a penalty commensurably lower will engender the desired indifference. Petitioners conclude that the differential impact on their finances of fines and costs requires the EPA to develop a special penalty-assessment model for public utilities. Only by using a special model, argue the petitioners, will Congress's goal of "economic indifference" be achieved.

Petitioners' challenge to the §120 regulations is misconceived. Petitioners go on at great length about Congress' desire to assure, via the §120 penalties, that firms would be economically indifferent between polluting and complying with the Act. Although petitioners' conclusions about §120 are incorrect, they are essentially correct in describing its thrust. As we said in *Duquesne I*, "Congress hoped to place polluters on the same economic footing as those who had limited their emissions through increased anti-pollution expenditures." Id. at 463. Section 120 itself speaks of the "economic value" of noncompliance. It is not much of a leap to conclude that if the economic value of noncompliance is to be used in setting the noncompliance penalty, Congress desired to render polluters indifferent to obeying or disobeying the Act. If §120 merely authorized the EPA to come up with penalties that would remove the economic incentive to continue polluting, the utilities might successfully argue that a penalty equal to the full cost avoided by failing to comply exceeds the statutory authorization.

What the petitioners fail to come to terms with, however, is the specific statutory mandate to include certain elements in the calculation of economic value. The statute specifies that "the capital costs of compliance" and "operation and maintenance costs foregone" are to be included in the §120 penalty. The penalty-assessment model adopted by the EPA specifically includes these costs. We decline to hold that EPA regulations that follow the clear terms of the stature are arbitrary and capricious or contrary to law, even if the results may be more onerous for some polluters than for others.

Even if section 120 were not so clear as to the elements that are properly included in calculating noncompliance penalties, we think the petitioners would have an uphill battle. The legislative history of §120 makes clear that Congress believed that §120 penalties would have the sure and certain effect of eliminating any incentive to avoid compliance.

Representative Henry Waxman, a member of the conference committee that produced the Amendments, explained §120 as follows:

> In order to speed compliance by industry, we are enacting a penalty applicable to each major source which will be equal to the economic value of noncompliance with emission limitations. No longer will . . . our major utilities . . . be able to reap an economic windfall from polluting the air. No longer will they find it cheaper to send their lawyers into court instead of purchasing and installing the necessary pollution control equipment.

3 A Legislative History of the Clean Air Act Amendments of 1977 335-36 (House Consideration of the Conference Committee Report, Aug. 4, 1977). Assessing a penalty equal to costs foregone will assure that no incentive remains to delay compliance. That a lesser penalty might have done the job is irrelevant; a penalty equal to the cost avoided will always produce at least indifference.

Moreover, section 120 does not say, as the petitioners sometimes seem to argue, that noncompliance penalties should produce economic indifference. Rather, the section states as its general principle the idea that penalties should be "no less" than the "economic value" of noncompliance. It is not at all clear that economic value can be equated with the amount by which profits are reduced by incurring compliance expenditures. (Even petitioners do not suggest that this measure of economic value would be appropriate for firms selling in a competitive market. See *infra* part III B.) The calculation of profits is complicated, and the legislative history strongly suggests that economic value was understood as being a measure of costs foregone rather than net loss. That the Congress' use of "economic value" clashes somewhat with its allegedly primary goal of ensuring economic indifference is not a fatal flaw in the legislative scheme.

Thus, we think the penalty-assessment model adopted by the EPA accurately reflects the mandate of the Amendments' legislative history. Bearing in mind that agency interpretations of ambiguous statutes are to be upheld if they are permissible, we do not think the EPA's regulations would be impermissible even if section 120 were less specific. See *Chevron*. It strains credulity to believe that in adopting regulations that not only track the statute's terms so closely but also clearly achieve Congress' desire to assure compliance with the Act the EPA may have acted in an arbitrary or capricious manner or exceeded its statutory authority.

B

We pause to make clear that petitioners' argument about the unique economic circumstances of regulated public utilities has not been lost on us. The court understands clearly that it is the *differential* impact of fines and costs on public utilities that is at the heart of petitioners' complaint. According to the petitioners, economic indifference is achieved for an unregulated firm when fine and cost are equal. Because the unregulated firm can pass through to its customers an *equal proportion* of its various sorts of expenses (i.e., the demand schedule faced by the firm is independent of its costs), it does not matter what that proportion in fact is or how it compares with the proportion of expenses that another firm, perhaps facing a different competitive environment, may be able to pass through.

Put another way, an unregulated monopolistic firm will be able to pass on to its customers a large fraction of any added expenses it is forced to bear. Conversely, a firm selling into a competitive market (a price-taker) will be forced to absorb expenses. Thus, for unregulated firms across the competitive spectrum, the effect of pollution control expenses and §120 penalties of equivalent amount will be the same. Although the net benefit of noncompliance for a monopolist is not as great as the costs foregone, neither is the net cost of paying a penalty as great as the penalty.

This is not the case with public utilities. If Congress had mandated economic indifference in the sense that petitioners suggest, petitioners would be right that the unique circumstance of public utilities would merit unique treatment. Where petitioners' analysis fails, however, is in premising their argument on an incorrect notion of economic indifference. Congress understood the economic value of noncompliance to be roughly equivalent to the direct costs avoided by failing to comply. It is not for us to rewrite the statute and its legislative history to conform to petitioners' understanding of economics. If public utilities really benefit so little by failing to comply and suffer so much by bearing §120 fines, it is open to them to comply with the Act and avoid the problem alto-

gether. Alternatively, petitioners are of course free to seek to have the Act amended to take explicit account of their unique circumstances.

IV

The Amendments and their legislative history make it clear that Congress was
not constructing an econometric model when it fashioned section 120. Rather,
Congress fashioned a new sanctioning mechanism to push polluters into compliance with the substantive provisions of the Act. That the sanction chosen may
have an asymmetric effect on public utilities does not make it less applicable or
less suited to furthering Congress' will. Applying the EPA's section 120 noncompliance penalties to public utilities is proper. It is well past time to put into effect
the penalty assessment mechanism ordered by Congress. Accordingly, the petitioners' challenge is dismissed and the regulations at issue are affirmed.

It is so ordered.

NOTES AND QUESTIONS

1. *Economic noncompliance penalties.* Reread the discussion of emissions
fees, p. 272 *supra.* To what extent does the economic noncompliance penalty,
as interpreted in *Duquesne II*, implement this proposal for enforcing air quality
standards? Is it perhaps better, as a matter of policy, that polluters not be entirely
"indifferent" to the choice between pollution and compliance through payment
of a civil money penalty?

Other decisions made by EPA in its regulations also affect the extent to
which the penalty is based on the economic impact on the noncomplying polluter. In order to assess a penalty, as required by §120(d), based on the "economic
value" of delay, EPA constructed a mathematical penalty calculation model. In
Duquesne I industry petitioners challenged a number of assumptions made in
the model, including EPA's decision to base rate of return on equity on industry
averages rather than the recent investment history of the polluting firm. The
court upheld EPA, noting its argument that "the past performance of an
individual firm may have been influenced by non-recurring factors and that the
industry-wide averages can be verified far more easily." Id. at 483. Is this holding
consistent with the theory of *Duquesne II*?

Discretion in assessing the penalty is provided in other provisions of the
regulations. For example, sources unable to comply with emission limitations
for reasons beyond their control are exempted from the penalty. §120(a)(2)(B)(iv).
EPA initially implemented this exemption by listing seven factors it would consider beyond the control of a source. In *Duquesne I* the court struck down this
regulation as contrary to the legislative history. Id. at 476-477. It held that EPA
must include in its factors a provision that allows it "in its discretion" to exempt
sources to "prevent inequity."

EPA responded to this holding by authorizing a source to claim the inability to comply exemption without regard to whether the cause fit any preconceived category. 50 Fed. Reg. 36,732 (1985). Is this response sufficient? The court rejected an industry argument in *Duquesne I* that §120 mandated including a "safety valve" that would allow sources to show that the individual facts of a case warrant individualized treatment. The court held that §120 "does not suggest a general exemption." Id. at 485. How much agency discretion remains in the administration of §120? See Perellis, Noncompliance Penalties under Section 120 of the Clean Air Act, 16 Nat. Resources Law. 499 (1983).

2. *Technological infeasibility.* Recall that technological infeasibility is not a defense to the enforcement of state implementation plans. See p. 237 *supra.* In its regulations EPA denied a §120 exemption for technological infeasibility because of the technology-forcing character of the Act but recognized it was difficult to assess a penalty when the technology necessary to bring a source into compliance was not available. EPA's compromise was "to deny an exemption for technological infeasibility but to calculate the penalties to ensure that sources doing their best to surmount existing technology will not be assessed any penalties." Id. at 476. The court upheld this rule as "a reasonable balance of statutory goals." Do you agree? Does it provide an incentive to polluters to avoid SIP compliance and fight out a technology-effort defense in court?

See also United States v. Ford Motor Co., 814 F.2d 1099 (6th Cir. 1987), *cert. denied*, 108 S. Ct. 83 (1988), holding that a properly adopted emission limitation is enforceable even though a state changes its views on its technological or economic feasibility. Is this correct?

3. *Citizen enforcement against individual sources.* The Clean Air Act citizens' suit provision states that any person may bring a civil action to enforce an emissions standard or a limitation or order issued by the EPA Administrator or a state. Section 304(a)(1). Concurrent government enforcement generally has not preempted citizens' suit enforcement. See Baughman v. Bradford Coal Co., 592 F.2d 215 (3d Cir.), *cert. denied*, 441 U.S. 961 (1979) (state and federal relief did not substantially overlap; citizens could not intervene as a matter of right in the state proceedings); and Gardeski v. Colonial Sand & Stone Co., 501 F. Supp. 1159 (S.D.N.Y. 1980) (state failure to prosecute diligently).

If EPA brings an action to enforce a single standard against a stationary source, does this bar a private suit to enforce another standard against the same source? See §120(b)(4)(B) and Maryland Waste Coalition v. SCM Corp., 616 F. Supp. 1474 (D. Md. 1985), holding that a holding to this effect would be contrary to the purpose of the citizen suit provision. Do you see any problems with this kind of dual enforcement? See Polebaum & Slater, Preclusion of Citizen Environmental Enforcement Litigation by Agency Action, 16 Envtl. L. Rep. (Envtl. L. Inst.) 10013 (1986).

Citizens' suits cannot be used to compel government agencies to enforce the Act. In a §304 suit to compel EPA to investigate alleged SIP violations, the Fifth Circuit said that the "principle of almost absolute discretion in initiating enforcement action should apply with equal force to the decision to take the preliminary investigatory steps that would provide the basis for enforcement action." City of Seabrook v. Costle, 659 F.2d 1371, 1374 (5th Cir. 1981). But see Save the Valley, Inc. v. Ruckelshaus, 565 F. Supp. 709 (D.D.C. 1983) (finding mandatory duty to deny construction permit to source that does not have required PSD permit).

4. *The criminal enforcement provisions: prosecution of "white collar crime"?* Criminal fines and imprisonment are prescribed for "knowingly" violating the Clean Air Act's basic regulatory sections or making false statements under its reporting requirements (§113(c)). The EPA has emphasized false reporting of emissions data. See, e.g., United States v. Felsen, 648 F.2d 681 (10th Cir. 1981) (affirming conviction of auto dealer who falsely stated that autos he imported met U.S. emissions and safety requirements).

Should knowing violation of Clean Air Act emissions limitations be prosecuted as well? Or do such violations fall into the area of "white collar crime" for which injunctions and civil penalties are more appropriate remedies? For a thorough discussion of corporate crime see K. Brickey, Corporate Criminal Liability (1984).

5. *Contractor listing.* The federal government purchases an enormous amount of goods from private industry. If a source is convicted for a pollution violation under §113(c)(1), federal agencies must observe a mandatory ban on all federal contracting with that source. See §306(a). Further, under §306(b) violators who have not been criminally convicted may be "blacklisted" under appropriate presidential guidelines. See Exec. Order No. 11,738, 44 Fed. Reg. 6,910. Courts have upheld the authority to list noncriminal violators. See, e.g., United States v. Interlake, 432 F. Supp. 987 (N.D. Ill. 1977).

Since 1986 EPA has significantly increased its use of contractor listing to bar the federal government from awarding contracts, grants or loans to contractors that have demonstrated a pattern of noncompliance with the Clean Air and Water Acts. See Lee & Slaughter, Government Contractors and Environmental Litigation, 19 Envt. Rep. (BNA): Current Developments 2138 (1989).

6. *Is the Act what its enforcers say it is?* In theory, prompt achievement of each and every emissions limitation is vital to the Clean Air Act scheme. Any adjustment of a source's responsibilities has to be made with an eye to the impact of the change on other sources and on overall Clean Air Act objectives. A relaxation here must be counterbalanced by a tightening there, if SIP deadlines are to be met.

This rigidity creates a dilemma. On the one hand, broad enforcement discretion could be used as a safety valve to relieve the inequities created by the strict statutory scheme. See Leventhal, Environmental Decision Making and the Role of the Courts, 122 U. Pa. L. Rev. 509 (1974). On the other, the exercise of enforcement discretion is dominated by lawyers, who are not as sensitive to programmatic objectives as they are to the triability of the case, their overall caseloads, the peculiarities of the local forum, and politics. A U.S. Attorney may convince the Department of Justice that a complex air enforcement case will sap resources or will be treated unsympathetically by the judge if the source is a major local business. He may even harbor ambitions of running for office and may not want to be involved with an unpopular case. Should the exercise of discretion to enforce be restricted by EPA rule? See K. Davis, Discretionary Justice (1970). Two excellent student notes also touch upon this issue. Note, Implementation Problems in Institutional Reform Litigation, 91 Harv. L. Rev. 428 (1977); Note, Judicial Control of Systemic Inadequacies in Federal Administrative Enforcement, 88 Yale L.J. 407 (1978).

Is it possible that two Clean Air Acts exist, one produced by officials and experts based on the permits and standards required under the Act as written, and another created by lawyers that is the result of the actual emissions levels permitted by enforcement policy? Suppose you were unaware of the provisions of the Clean Air Act and were given only the numerical emissions levels that regulation actually compels sources to achieve today. Do you think that you could even come close to inferring the contents of the statute that regulates those emissions levels?

IV

PROTECTING THE WATER RESOURCE

The river must have been wonderful when he was young. The shad would run up it in the spring and there was a run of salmon also. Now it had an oily odor from the cotton mills upstream.

J. P. Marquand, Wickford Point 92-93 (1939)

A. INTRODUCTION: WHAT IS WATER POLLUTION?

COUNCIL ON ENVIRONMENTAL QUALITY, NINTH ANNUAL REPORT
91-92, 96, 98-99, 108 (1978)

National Patterns of Water Quality

CONDITIONS

In a recent summary of state reports to the Congress prepared according to requirements of Section 305(b) of the Clean Water Act, the Environmental Protection Agency indicated that 95 percent of the 246 hydrological drainage basins in the United States were affected by water pollution in 1977. This summary figure oversimplifies the situation, however. A basin identified as "affected" may not be affected in its entirety; pollution may be limited to one or two short segments. On the other hand, the failure to report a problem does not necessarily mean that the basin is free of pollution; it may simply mean that monitoring data are lacking. This lack of data is particularly true of potential carcinogens or other toxic pollutants.

The nation's most widespread water quality problems, as perceived by state officials, are high levels of nutrients, bacterial pollution, high concentrations of suspended sediment, and heavy loading of oxygen-demanding material and consequent oxygen depletion in streams.

Another nationwide system for reporting water quality is the National Stream Quality Accounting Network of the U.S. Geological Survey. In operation since 1974, NASQAN collects uniform data at the downstream ends of 349 hydrologic accounting units. Data are taken at or near the mouths of all major U.S. rivers and their principal tributaries.

There are important differences between NASQAN and the state reports on water quality patterns. First, reporting is based on different hydrologic subdivisions of the United States. Second, states report problems anywhere in a basin, whereas NASQAN reports on the downstream ends of the accounting units (basins). The result is that state summaries tend to represent the worst condition in each basin, and NASQAN data generally represent downstream conditions, masking out the best and the worst streams in most areas. Further, problems identified by the states are not clearly and uniformly defined, whereas NASQAN reports pollutant concentrations uniformly.

Despite the differences, the two systems generally agree on nationwide patterns of water quality as represented by nitrogen and phosphorus and by bacterial pollution. . . . Unfortunately, NASQAN data on sediment and oxygen are too few to provide a comparison with the state data.

Excessive levels of nitrogen and phosphorus cause serious problems because these nutrients accelerate algal growth, which is part of eutrophication.

The patterns of high nutrient concentrations reflect the influence of the farm belt; fertilizer and livestock wastes are principal sources of nitrogen and phosphorus. Nutrient levels are also high in urban industrialized regions, such as the Northeast and the Great Lakes, where the common sources are municipal sewage, urban runoff, and industrial wastes.

Major sources of bacterial pollution are improperly treated sewage, sewer overflows, poorly operated septic systems, ships and boats, and livestock. Water bodies with excessive fecal bacterial levels cannot be used for swimming, boating, and fishing because of threat of waterborne disease. Coliform, fecal coliform, and fecal streptococcal bacterial counts are commonly used as the principal indicators of bacterial pollution. Coliform bacteria, though not harmful in themselves, indicate the possible presence of pathogens that are a hazard to health.

There are differences in results from the two reporting systems (the states and NASQAN), but again the overall national patterns are similar. . . . [T]he worst bacterial pollution problems are in areas of high human or livestock population, such as the Northeast and the Ohio, lower Missouri, and Mississippi River basins. Problems are least in the Great Plains, the High Plains, the Northwest, and the Atlantic Coastal Plains, where population densities are generally low.

CHANGES

Many of the pollution facilities built during the past decade are just beginning to operate. Evaluation of their effectiveness requires good uniform data on plant performance and water quality. Fortunately, improved data networks are now providing the means for judging water quality changes, and they will continue to improve in the future.

So far, uniform water quality data exist for only 3 years, so it is premature to characterize trends definitively. But it is encouraging that bacteria levels improved through the third year.

Figure 2-5 [not reproduced here] shows fecal coliform levels from measurements at NASQAN stations during the 1975-77 water years. "Violation rates" are the percentage of measurements in which concentrations of fecal coliform bacteria exceeded the recommended maximum for safe swimming, which many states and CEQ define as greater than 200 cells per 100 milliliters of water. (There is no legal uniform national standard; standards vary with water use and local laws and standards sometimes differ from nationally recommended criteria.) Patterns of improvement are apparent in several populous regions, particularly in the industrial urban belt south of the Great Lakes.

For other pollutants, no similar patterns of improvement are yet apparent. Levels of suspended material, nutrients, oil and grease, oxygen-demanding substances, and other materials should decline as pollution control becomes more effective. Nonpoint sources are largely responsible for some of these substances.

Specific Problems and Solutions

INDUSTRIAL POINT SOURCES

IMPACTS

According to state reports industrial discharges affect 72 percent of the basins in the country. A regional breakdown is shown in Table 4-1 and the basins in Figure 4-1. The Northeast and Great Lakes regions are most affected by industrial discharges, with impacts on 88 percent of the basins compared to 65 percent for the rest of the nation. In the Southwest only 23 percent of the basins were affected by industrial discharges.

Oxygen depletion, excessive suspended material, oil and grease, heavy metals, and toxic chemicals are common industrial pollution problems. Particular industries generate thermal pollution and pH problems: for example, discharges of cooling water from electric powerplants can warm receiving waters enough to affect aquatic life significantly.

Specific pollutants from industrial discharges vary with location. In the Northeast, Great Lakes, and North Central regions where heavy industries are centered, effluents containing high concentrations of toxic metals and other industrial chemicals are common. In these regions states reported heavy metals present in 55 percent of the basins and other toxic pollutants in 40 percent of the basins, compared to only 23 percent and 15 percent, respectively, for the rest of the country.

A classic illustration of the effects of heavy industry on water quality is the

TABLE 4-1
Point Source Pollution by Region 1977

Region	Number of Basins	Percentage Affected[1] by Type of Source		
		Industrial	Municipal	Combined Sewer Overflow
Northeast	40	95	95	60
Southeast	47	74	91	17
Great Lakes	41	80	95	37
North Central	35	74	86	6
South Central	30	70	100	0
Southwest	22	23	64	0
Northwest	22	55	73	14
Islands	9	89	100	0
Total	246	72	89	20

[1]In whole or in part.

Source: U.S. Environmental Protection Agency, *National Water Quality Inventory: 1977 Report to Congress* (Washington, D.C.: U.S. Government Printing Office, 1978).

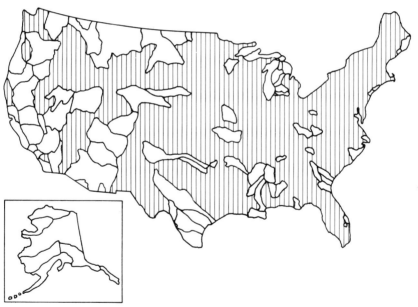

[1]In whole or in part.

FIGURE 4-1
Basins Affected by Industrial Discharges 1977

Source: U.S. Environmental Protection Agency, National Water Quality Inventory: 1977 Report to Congress (Washington, D.C.: U.S. Government Printing Office, 1978).

severe degradation of the Mahoning River as it passes through Warren and Youngstown, Ohio, both major steel centers. In this stretch of river there are large increases in lead, zinc, and phenols, all toxic pollutants at levels that can severely affect aquatic life. . . . As plants along the river begin treating waste water, improvement is expected. . . .

July 1, 1977, was the statutory deadline for industrial dischargers to meet effluent limitations based on "best practicable control technology" unless other federal or state regulations require stricter controls. Approximately 81 percent of the 3,798 major industrial dischargers complied on time; 724 did not. By February 1978, the number of noncompliers was 627. EPA targeted the worst 300 offenders for civil or criminal enforcement actions. . . .

In fiscal year 1977, EPA and the states conducted 6,880 sampling inspections and 15,639 nonsampling inspections. EPA issued 1,128 administrative enforcement orders, referred 115 cases to the Department of Justice, and collected $15.6 million in penalties and fines for noncompliance.

MUNICIPAL POINT SOURCES

IMPACTS

State reports noted adverse effects on water quality from municipal discharges in 89 percent of the basins in the country. . . . As expected, the more populous regions generally have more basins that are affected. Yet even in the sparsely populated Southwest, 64 percent reported pollution from municipal discharges. Most of the pollution was caused by inadequate treatment or overloaded treatment plants. The states expect that much of the problem will be resolved as federally funded treatment facilities are constructed. As discussed below, however, operation of these plants could be a significant problem.

The pollutants most often observed at unacceptable levels in municipal discharges are fecal coliform bacteria, oxygen-demanding materials, and phosphorus and nitrogen. Municipal discharges can also contain an excess of suspended sediments or dissolved solids as well as heavy metals and toxic organic compounds.

Combined sewer overflows can severely degrade water quality. When rainfall runoff is added to normal sewage flows in systems with combined storm and sanitary sewers, sewage treatment plants generally cannot handle the flow, and much of it bypasses treatment. Combined overflow discharges contain bacteria, nutrients, oxygen-demanding loads, suspended sediment, heavy metals, and oil and grease.

JOHNSON, WATER-QUALITY ISSUES: FACTORS AFFECTING GROUND-WATER QUALITY

United States Geological Survey, Water Supply Paper 2325, National Water Summary 1986, 76-81

Effects of Human Activities on Ground-Water Systems

GROUND-WATER PUMPAGE

Large withdrawals of ground water have profoundly altered the flow systems and geochemical conditions of some of the major aquifers in the United States. The decline of ground-water levels due to pumping from wells has caused changes in the location and size of some recharge areas, large reductions in natural discharge, and in some parts of the arid West, major losses in aquifer storage. The hydrologic response of aquifers to pumping from wells was explained concisely for the first time by Theis (1940) and is summarized briefly here. Theis noted that aquifer response is determined by the distance from the pumped wells to the localities of recharge and natural discharge and by the character of the cone of depression in the aquifer (an area of reduced hydraulic head surrounding a pumped well), which depends upon the values of transmissivity and storage coefficient. He further noted that "all water discharged by wells is balanced by a loss of water somewhere." Initially, some water always is withdrawn from storage in the aquifer. As pumping rates and the number of wells increase, cones of depression tend to coalesce and form broad areas of lowered water levels. If there are nearby recharge or discharge areas, water will be diverted from these areas instead of withdrawing additional water from storage. The lowered water levels create hydraulic gradients that tend to induce more recharge into the aquifer, often by expansion in the size of the recharge area, and to decrease the rate of aquifer discharge. Reduced streamflow or lowered lake levels may be the result. Thus, for an extensively developed aquifer, the location of the recharge and discharge areas may be different from those that existed before development.

The location of recharge areas can be very important in the protection of aquifers from water-quality degradation. Consequently, it should never be assumed that recharge and discharge areas are the same under all hydrologic conditions because those areas move dynamically in response to pumping and other hydrological changes in the aquifer system. The ground-water divides that separate ground-water basins also move in response to recharge or pumping patterns. The natural ground-water divides may correspond to a topographic or river-basin divide, but after the aquifer is developed the new divides may not.

To illustrate these changes, the following discussion examines two of the most extensively developed ground-water systems in the United States — the Central Valley aquifer system in California and the Floridan aquifer system. . . .

CENTRAL VALLEY AQUIFER SYSTEM

The most intensive and longest term development of ground water in the United States has occurred in the Central Valley of California, primarily in the San Joaquin Valley. Pumpage from wells, mostly for irrigation, averaged about 10 bgd (billion gallons per day) between 1961 and 1977. This amount is more than five times the estimated predevelopment recharge rate of 1.8 bgd (Williamson and others, 1987).

The Central Valley's aquifer system is composed of alluvial deposits of sand, gravel, silt, and clay with minor amounts of volcanic deposits. Before development began, most recharge was supplied by infiltration of streamflow at the heads of alluvial fans at the edges of the foothills that surround the Valley. Then ground water moved towards the center of the valley and discharged as evapotranspiration and seepage to streams (Fig. 4-2). Pumpage increased steadily throughout the 1940s, 1950s, and 1960s, primarily in the San Joaquin Valley. This caused ground-water levels to decline hundreds of feet and changed the pattern of ground-water circulation over a large area. An example of the changes in ground-water flow after development in the western part of the San Joaquin Valley is shown in Figure 4-2B.

The estimated present-day recharge is more than five times the predevelopment recharge, and it is provided mainly by infiltration from irrigated lands that are largely supplied by imported surface waters and pumpage (Williamson and others, 1987). However, the amount of present-day recharge is less than the amount of water discharged from the aquifer system, which is primarily by pumpage. Thus, valley-wide some water continues to be removed from storage resulting in continued lowering of water levels even though some parts of the aquifer system are experiencing water-level rises owing to localized decreases in pumpage and to increased application of imported surface water for irrigation.

The large decline in water levels in the Central Valley, particularly in the San Joaquin Valley, has caused permanent compaction of subsurface clays, which has resulted in a loss of ground-water storage and a lowering of the land surface (Ireland and others, 1984). Although the vertical permeability of the clays has probably been decreased by compaction, the vertical hydraulic connection across the aquifer system has actually increased owing to the construction of about 100,000 wells with long sections of screen or perforated casing (Williamson and others, 1987). These multiscreen wells also provide the potential for mixing of waters from different sand and gravel layers because the wells enable ground water to flow between the sand and gravel layers that are separated by layers of less permeable silt and clay.

This example illustrates several ways in which human activities can affect the ground water of a region. Recharge and discharge areas can be changed by ground-water development. As a result of extensive ground-water development, the former discharge area of the shallow aquifer in the San Joaquin Valley now is largely a recharge area. Most post-development recharge is supplied by irriga-

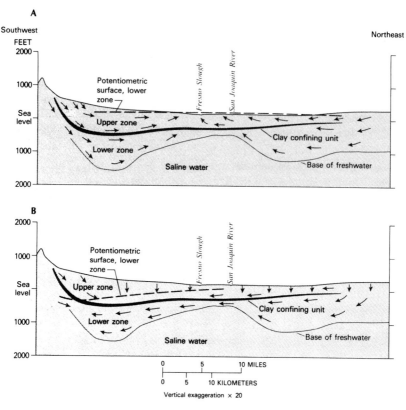

FIGURE 4-2

Comparison of Ground-Water-Flow Conditions before and after Development in the San Joaquin Valley, California.

A, Before development, about 1900; B, after development, 1966. Note change in potentiometric surface of lower zone. Arrows show general direction of ground-water flow.

(*Source:* Modified from Bull and Miller, 1975, fig. 20.)

tion return flow rather than infiltration of stream-flow in upland areas; most ground-water discharge is pumpage (Williamson and others, 1987). These changes in the ground-water-flow system may redirect poor-quality water in some areas towards pumping centers. This includes the movement of saline water found beneath the freshwater in the Central Valley (Fig. 4-2) and poor-quality water found above, or within, the fresh ground water. For example, shallow water along the west side of the San Joaquin Valley, which has dissolved solids ranging from 1,000 to 5,000 mg/L, has a potential to move towards pumping centers because of changes in the ground-water flow system. In addition, water quality in the shallow aquifer is being changed by irrigation return flow. Fertilizers and pesticides have been leached by irrigation water and are present in small amounts in the shallow aquifer in the Central Valley. A widely used nematodicide has been found in ground water in every county in the San Joaquin Valley (Bertoldi and Sun, 1986, p. 11). In parts of the San Joaquin Valley, selenium, which is believed to be essential to human and animal nutrition in minute amounts but which can be toxic at relatively low concentrations, is being leached from seleniferous soil by applied irrigation waters, and eventually this might cause an increase in selenium concentration in the shallow ground water in the western side of the San Joaquin Valley. The downward hydraulic gradient due to pumping and the increased hydraulic connection among individual aquifer layers (provided by multilayer-screened wells) creates an opportunity for poor-quality water to move from shallow aquifers into deep aquifers. Because of the increase in the recharge area in the Central Valley, accidental spills of toxic chemicals or applied fertilizers and pesticides have a greater potential to contaminate ground water.

FLORIDAN AQUIFER SYSTEM

The Floridan aquifer system, which underlies all of Florida, the southern part of Georgia, and small parts of adjoining Alabama and South Carolina, is the most extensively pumped ground-water system east of the Mississippi River. About 3 bgd is withdrawn from the Floridan. It is the principal source of public, industrial, and agricultural water supply in the southeastern United States, except in south Florida where it contains saline water (Bush and Johnston, 1987). High average rainfall (about 53 inches per year), with little surface runoff, provides abundant recharge to the Floridan. The Floridan contains thick beds of highly permeable limestone, and transmissivity generally is very high. Individual wells yielding several thousand gallons per minute are common.

Development has not greatly altered the flow system of the Floridan. Overall, pumpage from wells is balanced by increased recharge and decreased discharge from the aquifer system and the change in storage has been negligible. The dominant feature of the Floridan's flow system, both before and after development, is discharge from springs. Currently, pumpage is less than 20 percent of the recharge rate; however, the pumpage is distributed unevenly throughout the Floridan aquifer system (Bush and Johnston, 1987). Large withdrawals have caused long-term water-level declines in three broad areas: the western panhandle of Florida; west-central Florida, southeast of Tampa; and a coastal strip extending from Hilton Head, S.C., to Jacksonville, Fla., and 50 to 80 miles inland. All three areas are located where the Floridan is confined by thick clay beds and are distant from the outcrop (recharge) areas. About 500 Mgal/d is pumped from the Floridan in the Hilton Head-Jacksonville coastal area (Krause and Randolph, 1987). . . .

CONTAMINANTS IN GROUND WATER

Ground-water contamination refers to any degradation of ground-water quality resulting from human activities. To provide guidance for water use, the U.S. Environmental Protection Agency (1986a,b) established water-quality criteria (see National Drinking-Water Regulations, in Supplementary Information section of this volume) that include —

> *Recommended concentration limits* for certain, not particularly harmful constituents, such as chloride, iron, and dissolved solids.
> *Maximum permissible concentrations* for highly toxic substances, such as some pesticides, certain metals, and radionuclides.

The most serious problems of ground-water contamination generally have resulted from the introduction into the ground water of organic chemicals (especially pesticide residues or byproducts, oils, phenols, and solvents) and metals (especially chromium, lead, and mercury) from a variety of human activities. Fortunately, serious ground-water contamination has occurred in only a small part of the Nation's ground-water supply. However, such contamination often is in areas of heaviest ground-water use. Cleaning up an extensively contaminated aquifer is expensive and time consuming; the best cleanup strategy may be difficult to determine because of the complexities of the hydrogeologic framework and ground-water flow system. Clearly, the high costs and uncertain results of aquifer cleanup make the prevention of ground-water contamination whenever possible a very desirable national goal (Conservation Foundation, 1987, p. 13).

SOURCES OF CONTAMINANTS

Contaminants may enter freshwater aquifers from at least 33 generic sources (Office of Technology Assessment, 1984, p. 43). These sources may be classified broadly as either point or nonpoint sources. Point sources are derived from localized areas (a few acres or less in size) and include

Landfills (industrial and municipal)
Surface impoundments (lagoons, pits, and ponds)
Underground storage tanks (petroleum, toxic chemicals, and wastes)
Spills of chemicals, oil, or brine during transport or transfer operations
Injection wells (hazardous waste and brine disposal) or abandoned oil wells

The first four point sources are considered to be major contamination problems by the EPA (U.S. Environmental Protection Agency, 1984, p. 13) on the basis of information supplied by State agencies. However, EPA stated (p. 16) that "information on the current extent of contamination is far from adequate to quantify the severity of the problem."

Nonpoint sources actually consist of activities or processes that introduce contaminants over a broad area, rather than in a specific area. Nonpoint sources can range in size from several acres to hundreds of square miles and can consist of multiple point sources, such as septic tank drainfields. Significant nonpoint sources include

Agricultural pesticides and fertilizers
Septic tank drainfields and cesspools
Encroachment of saline water
Road salt applications
Animal feed lots
Mining operations

The above nonpoint sources also were indicated as being intermediate significant contamination problems (U.S. Environmental Protection Agency, 1984, p. 13).

Contaminants can enter aquifers by five basic mechanisms as illustrated in Figure 4-3 below.

Downward percolation to the water table from a surface source. Liquids from surface impoundments or spills infiltrate the ground and percolate downward to the water table. Infiltration of precipitation or runoff into landfills dissolves chemicals and metals and collects bacteria that results in a liquid called "leachate," which percolates downward to the water table. In a similar manner, precipitation dissolves pesticides and de-icing road salts from agricultural lands and highway rights-of-way and transports these nonpoint-source contaminants downward to the water table.

Downward percolation to the water table from sources in the shallow subsurface. This mechanism operates in a manner similar to the one described above except that the source is located below the land surface. Sources include leaking petroleum and chemical storage tanks and buried wastes.

Leakage from a source below the water table. The most common examples of this mechanism are brine leakage from abandoned oil wells and poorly constructed injection wells. In the latter situation, fluid wastes that are intended to be emplaced in a deep saline aquifer leak into a shallow freshwater aquifer due to defects, such as casing breaks or poor grouting, in an injection well.

Intrusion of naturally occurring saline water into freshwater aquifers as a result of pumping from wells. Intrusion may occur by lateral movement of salty water towards wells or by "upconing" of saline water located beneath pumping wells. In either situation, the cause is a reduction of hydraulic heads due to withdrawals and creation of a hydraulic gradient from the saline-water source towards wells tapping a freshwater aquifer.

Movement of contaminants between aquifers by short-circuiting natural flow paths. . . . [A] short-circuiting mechanism might occur in a well or along a natural geologic feature such as a fault. In either situation, the well or fault zone acts as a conduit for transmitting poor-quality water from one aquifer to another. Movement via wells might occur either outside the well casing in an unsealed annulus or inside the casing of a well open to more than one aquifer through screens or perforations. Examples of this type of contamination are given

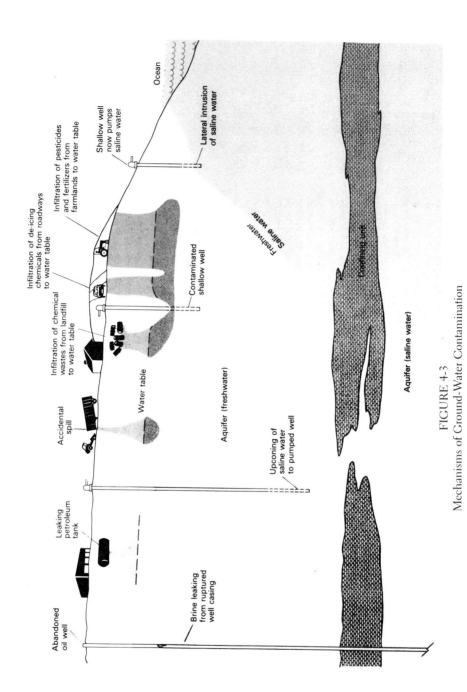

FIGURE 4-3
Mechanisms of Ground-Water Contamination

in the previous discussion of the Central Valley in California and in the article "Coal-Tar Derivatives in the Prairie du Chien-Jordan Aquifer, St. Louis Park, Minnesota." Short-circuiting along faults occurs because the fault zone is more permeable than the confining unit separating two aquifers. Pumping from a fresh-water aquifer might induce poor-quality water to move from a contaminated or saline aquifer into the freshwater aquifer. An example of contamination by this mechanism is given in the previous discussion of the Floridan aquifer system.

MOVEMENT OF CONTAMINANTS THROUGH AQUIFERS

After entering the aquifer, contaminants dissolved in ground water (solutes) will move in the direction of the prevailing hydraulic gradient. This process of contaminant transport by flowing ground water is termed "advection." Variations in permeability, as in a sequence of sand and silt layers, will cause the moving front of contaminants to be irregular — the higher permeability sands generally will contain contaminants farthest from the source because water containing the solutes moves faster in the sands than in the less permeable silts. Local variations in flow velocity on the scale of individual sand grains or rock particles cause dispersion of the solutes. The dispersion process causes dilution of solute concentrations in the direction of ground-water flow and, to a lesser extent, perpendicular to the flow direction. Dilution of solutes due to dispersion is controlled by the flow velocity, which, in turn, is a function of local variations in aquifer characteristics. Solutes also can be diluted by molecular diffusion and by some of the chemical processes previously discussed. Solutes in ground water that move slowly along deep flow paths have greater opportunity for diffusion and attachment to earth materials (sorption) than the solutes in shallow ground water that moves faster along short flow paths. On the other hand, contaminated water following deep flow paths has the potential to invade a much greater volume of aquifer.

Liquids that do not mix with water are termed "immiscible." Contaminants that are immiscible in water, such as petroleum, will be separated from the flowing ground water by a distinct boundary (or interface), and their movement is governed by pressures along the interface. Frequently, immiscible contaminants occur in discrete pockets within ground water. These pockets move in response to gravity and in response to pressures exerted on them through the surrounding water. Liquids that are less dense than water, such as gasoline, will tend to accumulate as a layer just above the water table. More dense liquids, including many organic liquids such as chloroform and bromoform, will tend to move downward through the ground water and accumulate as a layer just above a confining bed.

NOTES AND QUESTIONS

1. How is water quality measured? As the two previous readings suggest, pollution is measured by selecting certain parameters to characterize water qual-

ity. The first step in any measurement is monitoring, the collection of scientifically credible water samples. The data is then assessed to compare the present
state of the stream with its condition in the past. The usual measure is background. Background is either the complete absence of a pollutant or "[i]n the
case of naturally occurring substances like dissolved oxygen, background may be
that which can be expected in the complete absence of a causative effect being
monitored, e.g., a wastewater discharge." Orlob, Technical Considerations in
Data Collection and Interpretation — Surface Water Quality, in National Academy of Sciences, National Water Quality Monitoring and Assessment: Report of
Colloquium Sponsored by the Water Science and Technology Board, May 21-
22, 1986 18, 20 (1987).

2. How well are we doing in reducing water pollution? In part, the answer
depends on whether the question refers to specific lakes and streams or aggregate
data. We have a great deal of data, but scientists still find it difficult to answer
basic questions such as, have DO levels improved for a given stream reach? Since
the passage of the Clean Water Act, there have been dramatic improvements in
specific streams, although the introduction of new substances can cancel the
effect of removing old substances. For example, salmon returned to the Hudson
River after sewage discharges were curtailed, but they cannot be eaten because
of high PCB levels. In 1979, the Council on Environmental Quality concluded
that the data suggest that "water quality in the United States, while not showing
vast improvement since the early 1970s, is at least not getting worse." Council
on Environmental Quality, Tenth Annual Report 75 (1979). A 1982 counter-
Council on Environmental Quality report, State of the Environment 1982: A
Report from the Conservation Foundation (1982), reached a similar conclusion.
Nationwide, it found "little change in water quality for the past seven years" with
regard to the five conventional pollutants: dissolved oxygen, bacteria, suspended
solids, total dissolved solids, and nutrients (State of the Environment 1982, at
97). One reason that water quality levels have remained relatively constant over
the years is that reductions in point source discharges have not been matched by
non-point source reductions. Environmental Protection Agency, National Water
Quality Inventory — 1986 Report to Congress reported that 76 percent of impaired lake acres, 65 percent of impaired stream miles and 45 percent of impaired
estuary square miles came from non-point sources. Data on toxic pollutants are
harder to come by because they are not in the National Stream Quality Accounting Network (NASQAN) so we may not always be measuring the right indicators.
In 1986 Congress appropriated money to the United States Geological Survey to
test and refine the NAWQA program. One of the reasons was the complexity of
choosing the target pollutants to measure. There are over 60,000 synthetic organic compounds but only a few can be systematically measured, so serious
pollution may remain undetected. "As an example, industrial wastewaters have
been under continuous scrutiny for a set of specific priority pollutants since
1977. Yet, examination of some broad spectrum results . . . shows that many
other potentially toxic organic compounds may be occurring more frequently
than the organic priority pollutants." R. Hirsh, W. Alley & W. Wilber, Concepts

For a National Water-Quality Assessment Program, 17 (U.S. Geological Survey Circular 1021, 1988).

3. When is a stream polluted? "Just as there is no single measure of human health, there is no single measure of water quality. Rather, there are dozens of specific physical, chemical, and biological characteristics of the nation's waters." Council on Environmental Quality, Sixth Annual Report 348 (1975). Thus a definition of pollution must be relative. But relative to what? To natural background conditions in a body of water? To the survivability of species that are proxies for some notion of ecosystem stability? To human uses of the water? Which definition of pollution does the Clean Water Act adopt? Does it in fact adopt a single definition? The Act's definition of pollution has been praised by environmentalists because it includes nonquantifiable costs and risks. Nonetheless, this definition was strongly criticized by the National Water Commission in 1973:

When Is Water Polluted?

Pollution can be defined in alternative ways which have markedly different implications for the Nation's effort to improve water quality. One view of pollution is expressed in the Federal Water Pollution Control Act Amendments of 1972, which defines "pollution" as "man-made or man-induced alteration of the chemical, physical, biological, and radiological integrity of water." Thus, natural water quality appears to be regarded as a norm from which any deviation constitutes pollution. This is not a good standard on which to base the definition of pollution. In some places water is naturally toxic, naturally hot, naturally turbid, naturally radioactive, or naturally acid or alkaline. Some lakes are naturally choked with algae, and the eutrophication of lakes is a natural process in their aging. Oil seeps in large quantity occur in nature. Heavy sediment loads occur naturally in many flowing streams. Man-induced changes due to discharges of specific chemicals can actually improve the usefulness of water, for example, where wastes which contain lime neutralize the excess natural acidity of streams, or where nutrients are needed to support aquatic life. Conservation of marine species that are heavily used as a source of food for many may require replacement of nutrients in the marine environment to maintain the food chain.

If the purpose of the 1972 Act's definition of pollution were just to bring within the ambit of the control program all discharges of substances potentially harmful to water quality, its breadth of scope would be commendable. However, this all-encompassing definition does not merely expand the jurisdiction of the control program: it is an integral component of a water quality policy which is designed ultimately to prevent all use of water bodies for waste disposal. The 1972 Act establishes 1985 as a tentative target date for achievement of this "no discharge" goal.

Such a goal is unrealistic. Tolerance of foreign materials in water varies greatly among different water uses. The ranking of purposes for which water is used in terms of the quality levels required in natural watercourses might be represented as follows: (1) preservation of the natural environment, as in the "wild river" program; (2) water contact sports, such as swimming and water-skiing; (3) use as a source of a potable domestic water supply; (4) preservation of aquatic life; (5) noncontact recreational uses, such as boating; (6) agricultural use, such as irrigation and livestock watering; (7) industrial use; (8) navigation; (9) disposal and transport of wastes. Only use (1) requires natural water quality. In all other cases water quality different from that which would exist in nature will adequately support the desired uses. In fact, natural water itself often is unfit to satisfy important uses, and a requirement that all water discharged after use be distilled would not assure water of useful quality.

The Commission believes adoption of "no discharge" as a national goal for water quality management is no more sound than would be the establishment of a "no development" goal for controlling land use. First, the "no discharge" policy ignores the functional interrelationships among environmental resources and places man in absolute opposition to natural processes of runoff and drainage. Second, the maximum degree of industrial or sewage treatment process changes cannot eliminate all wastes which are now discharged to water. Forbidding the disposal of these wastes in water inevitably will result in their disposal in the air or on land, but with no assurance that such disposal alternatives are either environmentally or economically preferable to disposal in water. Third, the no discharge policy assumes that restoration and preservation of natural water quality is of higher value than any other use of the resource. This assumption will not pass the tests commonly applied to determine how or whether resources should be used. The costs of achieving the social objective of pure water are so great that they surely will necessitate a cutback or postponement of other worthy domestic programs. An examination of relative priorities among social goals is in order. In the Commission's view, a reduction in waste disposal beyond that necessary to protect existing or anticipated future uses of receiving water would create costs unrelated to any social benefit and would result in needless expenditures and a waste of other resources such as air, land, minerals, and energy. Absolutely pure water simply is not necessary for many uses, and these include uses such as recreation and fish propagation. Adoption of a no discharge policy thus amounts to the imputation of an extravagant social value to an abstract concept of water purity; a value the Commission is convinced the American people would not endorse if the associated costs and effect on other resources were fully appreciated and the policy alternatives clearly understood.

The danger of setting the restoration of natural water quality as a national goal lies not merely in its conceptual unsoundness, but in its potential for doing long-term harm to the pollution control effort. Like other oversimplified solutions to complex social problems, this policy holds out a promise of "natural" water it cannot redeem. Water quality regulation which loses touch with the reasons people value water is hopelessly adrift and eventually will founder. When it does, the attendant loss of public confidence will make it more difficult to marshall public support to reestablish a program with rational objectives.

In the Commission's view, pollution should be defined in a functional and dynamic manner by saying that *water is polluted if it is not of sufficiently high quality to be suitable for the highest uses people wish to make of it at present or in the future.* Such uses should be determined by responsible public authorities. Under this approach, maintenance of natural water quality is necessary only where some use of the resource requires it. This is not to say that the pollution control program ought to ignore any man-induced alteration of water quality. Rather, the goal of the control program should be to regulate those changes to achieve and maintain a quality sufficient to sustain the uses people wish to make of the water now or in the future.

It is this relative theory of pollution upon which was based the national water quality standards program introduced by the Water Quality Act of 1965. This legislation fostered the establishment of receiving water standards for nearly all of the Nation's surface waters. [Final Report of the National Water Commission, Water Policies for the Future 69-70 (1973).]

See also Giannes & Peskin, The Distribution of the Costs of Federal Water Pollution Control Policy, 56 Land Econ. 85 (1980), and W. Baumol & W. Oates, Economics, Environmental Policy, and the Quality of Life 211-212 (1979).

4. What should be the objective of water pollution control policy? Our current objective is the virtual elimination of pollution. This is a defensible goal for the discharge of toxic substances that present short- and long-run threats to human health. But is this a defensible goal for the discharge of non-toxic pollutants? Human health problems may be caused by many discharges, but are these problems different from the ones caused from air pollution, since exposure is almost always involuntary with respect to air pollution but is often voluntary with respect to water pollution? Water pollution generally is a problem of having voluntary uses of a stream foreclosed by what is in the stream. See Cost-Benefit Analysis & Water Pollution Policy (H. Peskin & E. Seskin eds. 1975). This generally holds true even for many discharges of toxic pollutants because humans are exposed to the pollutant by eating fish or shellfish that have ingested the pollutant. What consequences follow from defining water pollution primarily as a water use problem? Should we follow a rational strategy that first eliminates the sources of pollution that can be cheaply and easily removed and second subjects further removal increments to a cost-benefit analysis or a conservative strategy that seeks to eliminate all discharges, to avoid any risks? B. Ackerman, S. Ackerman, J. Sawyer & D. Henderson, The Uncertain Search for Environmental Quality (1974), is an excellent study of pollution control strategies on the Delaware River. It concludes that the costs of reducing conventional pollutants were excessive compared with the benefits and that the strategies failed to reduce discharges of the toxic pollutants. See also Milliman, Can Water Pollution Policy Be Efficient?, 2 Cato J. 165 (1982). A study of the benefits of improving surface water quality attempted to calculate the value of increasing the amount of fishable waters by the application of Best Practicable Technology (BPT). Prior to 1972, there were about 30.6 million acres of fishable fresh waters in the United States. A. Kneese, Measuring the Benefits of Clean Air and Clean Water (1984) found that the application of BPT would add an additional 100,000 acres of fishable water. The study next estimated the increase in fishing that this improvement would produce; the number was put at between 307 and 683 million dollars. Finally, contingent valuation studies were run to estimate the benefits of increased boatable and swimmable as well as fishable water. The result yields large numbers:

> There are about 80 million households in the United States. Assume that the sample results imply that to have high-quality recreational waters throughout the country there is an annual willingness to pay of $200 per household. This would imply a total willingness to pay of $16 billion. . . . This would divide about equally between user and nonuser values. At first this might seem out of line with the value of well under the billion dollars that was calculated for recreational fishing. But this is not necessarily the case. . . . [T]hat estimate is for a relatively small

increase in the nation's fishable waters over the actual conditions in the early 1970s, and the estimate from the national survey is the value people attach to making and *maintaining* the whole of the nation's fresh waters of high recreational quality where the alternative is almost total degradation of most of the nation's watercourses. In other words, both the baselines and routes of benefit accrual considered are different in the two studies. A somewhat closer comparison, though still not a perfect one, is between the survey's reported willingness to pay for an improvement from boatable to fishable water ($42 per household, or 3.4 billion) and the largest value found in the fishing study for essentially complete cleanup (in fishing terms) of the nation's *fresh* water — roughly $1 billion. [Id. at 103.]

Do studies such as these justify the estimated $200 billion that have been spent on water pollution control? United States Environmental Protection Agency, The Cost of Clean Air and Clean Water: Report to Congress (1984).

B.   BACKGROUND OF WATER POLLUTION REGULATION

In 1607, the first English colonists in the Chesapeake Bay region drew their drinking water from the often-brackish James River estuary, which ebbed and flowed past the shores of the swampy island that was to be called Jamestown. In doing so, they exposed themselves to disease-carrying bacteria from their own wastes (according to a theory of a twentieth century historian) and subjected themselves to gradual salt poisoning from the brackish water. Those who sickened and died may have been the first recorded victims of water pollution in the Bay. [F. Capper, G. Power & F. Shivers, Jr., Governing Chesapeake Waters: A History of Water Quality Controls on Chesapeake Bay, 1607-1972 (1983), citing C. Earle, Environment, Disease and Mortality in Early Virginia, in The Chesapeake in the Seventeenth Century 96 (T. Tate & D. Ammorman eds. 1979).]

1.   Nineteenth Century Water Pollution Problems and Legal Responses

Water pollution is largely a function of available waste disposal technology. In the nineteenth century, industries disposed untreated wastes directly in water bodies, subject only to minimal restrictions, and the technology for disposing of human wastes was even more primitive. In his classic study of the development of water pollution control institutions in Wisconsin, Water Purity: A Study in Legal Control of Natural Resources 49 (1961), Professor Earl Finbar Murphy notes that the first early prohibitions against practices such as throwing animal carcasses into a stream "were to defend industries from self-destruction." Industrial waste disposal practices continued virtually unrestrained until after World War II because industrial pollution was not seen as a major threat. Initial efforts were concentrated on human wastes. Tarr, McCurley & Yosie, The Development and Impact of Urban Wastewater Technology: Changing Concepts of Water Quality Control, 1850-1930, in Pollution and Reform in American Cities, 1870-1930, at 63 (M. Melosi ed. 1980), trace the decline in the use of cesspool, privy vault, and scavenger systems, their replacement by sanitary sewers, and the emergence of a water pollution problem with which our country is still struggling:

> The spread of water polluted with fecal matter created serious health hazards and grave concern. Putrefying fecal matter was believed to be especially objectionable and productive of "dangerous gases" and "unwholesome vapors." Public health officials viewed overflowing cesspools with water closet connections as a dangerous threat to a healthful environment. . . .
>
> The health and nuisance problems caused by running water and the consequent adoption of water closets and other water-using fixtures led to a search for devices to make the wastewater disposal system more efficient. These innovations were intended to modify the existing system rather than replace it entirely. Three methods were widely adopted: the pail system, the earth closet, and the odorless pit — all of which had distinct limitations. . . .
>
> As use of water closets increased and cesspool and privy nuisance grew, citizens demanded that they be permitted to connect their water closets to existing stormwater sewers. . . . The modern concept of a water-carriage system designed for the removal of human excreta originated in England in the 1840s, although versions of this technology had existed for centuries. In the 1850s, English authorities decided to construct a system of brick sewers, called the combined system, that would carry both household wastes and stormwater. The water-carriage system of waste removal had a number of characteristics that sharply differentiated it from the cesspool-privy vault-scavenger system. First of all, it was capital-intensive rather than labor-intensive and required the construction of large public works. Second, the new system employed batch, rather than individual, collection. It also removed waste automatically through the plumbing, which eliminated the need for humans to remove the wastes from the immediate premises. The third critical characteristic was that the system depended on municipal maintenance and responsibility, not upon individual action.
>
> Arguments over adoption of the water-carriage system focused on economic considerations, health factors, and questions of comparative urban advantage. Water-carriage systems — along with water supply systems — represented the most expensive capital projects undertaken by nineteenth-century municipalities. However, the advocates of the water-carriage system argued that costs were less and benefits greater compared to annual charges for collection under the cesspool-privy vault-scavenger system. . . .
>
> The perceived benefits of sewerage in fact so clearly outweighed the costs that the nation's cities undertook a great wave of sewer-building activity in the late nineteenth and early twentieth centuries, beginning in the 1870s. The first year for which aggregate figures are available is 1890, when the U.S. Census recorded 8,199 miles of all types of sewers (data for cities with more than 10,000 population); by 1909, the mileage had increased to 24,972 (data for cities with more than 30,000 population), a near threefold increase in mileage or from 1,795 persons per mile of sewer to 825 persons per mile. . . .
>
> Health benefits, however, were often less impressive than anticipated. In Baltimore, where it had been predicted that a "good sewerage system" would reduce

typhoid death rates from 40 to between 4 and 8 per 100,000 population, the decline was actually only from 24.9 to 20.7. What had not been predicted, except by a few solitary voices, was the rise in typhoid death rates for cities that drew their water supplies from streams or lakes into which other cities discharged their raw sewage. Of course, this effect applied whether or not a city had a sewerage system.

Water-carriage technology had been implemented because of expectations of health benefits, but it was now found to produce serious repercussions for downstream or neighboring cities. Typhoid death rates in these cities soared, as upstream or lake cities constructed sewerage systems and discharged their raw sewage into the streams or lakes from which downstream cities drew their water supplies. Some of the more striking examples were Atlanta, Pittsburgh, Trenton, and Toledo, all of whom had constructed sewerage systems in the last twenty years of the nineteenth century but also had experienced rises in typhoid death rates during the same years. Mortality rates in these cities reached levels as high as 100 to 144 per 100,000. Engineers and city officials traditionally viewed waterways as the natural vehicles for wastes under the old assumption that running water purified itself and that the dilution would eliminate hazard. The adverse health effects in downstream cities clearly exposed the limitations of this theory. In addition to the negative health effects, the use of waterways for disposal of raw sewage created nuisances, restricted water use for manufacturing purposes, and reduced recreational possibilities.

One logical source of relief for municipalities and individuals suffering from the health and nuisance effects of sewage-polluted waterways was the courts. In the absence of any specific legislative statutes governing water pollution, the common-law doctrine of nuisance prevailed, used by the courts to restrain any "unreasonable" use of property that damaged others. In regard to water quality, nuisance law emphasized the rights of lower riparian owners to water "with quality unimpaired and quantity undiminished." In actual practice, however, courts usually maintained that lower riparian owners could not expect water of absolute purity since such a doctrine would prohibit all upstream use. While the law theoretically had potential for reducing water pollution, it was most slow and cumbersome, hedged around with difficulties in the judicial process and vagaries in interpretation. [Pollution and Reform in American Cities, 1870-1930, at 64, 68, 70.]

F. Capper, G. Power & F. Shivers, Jr., report that Baltimore, Maryland, was the first city to treat its wastes for purposes other than protecting its own water supply, as Chicago was forced to do, or protecting downstream riparians:

> It was to protect the oyster industry from perceived public health threats. The ultimate concern of the oyster interests was not that oysters would be killed or that people would get sick from eating contaminated oysters. It was that people would associate oysters from the Bay with sewage from Baltimore, make the connection to the recently established and highly publicized link between oysters and sewage-borne disease, and then stop buying Maryland oysters. What was controlling was whether *people would think* that oysters from the Bay were tainted. [Governing Chesapeake Waters: A History of Water Quality Controls on Chesapeake Bay, 1607-1972, at 62.]

Private and public suits seeking relief from allegedly harmful discharges could be based on the interference with riparian rights, if a water use was impaired, or the common law of nuisance, if the use of land was impaired, e.g., Bowman v. Humphrey, 124 Iowa 744, 100 N.W. 854 (1904). Originally, some states adopted the "natural flow" rule of riparian rights, which gave downstream riparians (those who own land adjacent to a stream) the right to the flow of the stream, undiminished in quantity and quality. There are cases affording riparians relief under this theory (e.g. City of Richmond v. Test, 18 Ind. App. 482, 48 N.E. 610 (1897)), but most states adopted the "reasonable use" rule of riparian rights, which allows a greater range of uses and diversions compared with the natural flow theory and was thought to be more in harmony with the national policy of promoting industrial growth. The reasonable use rule allowed courts to incorporate the nuisance concept that a discharge was unreasonable only if it exceeded background conditions in the area. Davis, Theories of Water Pollution Litigation, 1971 Wis. L. Rev. 738, is a comprehensive analysis of nuisance and riparian rights cases. The reasonable use rule was especially favorable to cities because the courts in some states recognized that cities had a right to use waters for the discharge of wastes so long as the discharge did not constitute a public nuisance. See, e.g., City of Hampton v. Watson, 119 Va. 95, 89 S.E. 81 (1916).

2.   The Twentieth Century Evolution of Federal Water Pollution Control Policy

Until after World War II, pollution control was assumed to be a local and state responsibility. In Chapter 3 we traced the evolution of the shift from local and state to federal responsibility in air pollution regulation. The shift is similar in water pollution, although the federal interest in the quality of navigable waters antedates its interest in air pollution. Federal water pollution control policy has moved through three stages: (1) post hoc federal actions against those who have discharged substances into navigable waters; (2) a federal-state effort to dedicate different waters to varying levels of waste assimilation, with federal enforcement as a last resort; and (3) a federal effort to eliminate all pollution by imposing technology-forcing standards on effluents discharged, as opposed to setting standards for the quality of receiving waters, with state enforcement of federal policy. The technology-forcing, effluent limitations policy to eliminate pollution was put in place in 1972 and remains the basis of the program. Suitability for a given use, however, remains the measure of the extent of pollution and the technology-based regulation remains controversial. The lack of attention to water quality standards has been criticized because technology-based standards are inefficient and provide insufficient incentives for officials to be concerned with real improvements in water quality. Pedersen, Turning the Tide on Water Quality, 15 Ecology L.Q. 69 (1988) advocates a "bubble approach" to water quality: states would be required to prepare water quality standard attainment plans for EPA approval, but would be allowed to allocate the control burdens as they chose.

a.   Post Hoc Actions against Discharges

Because of the federal government's traditional interest in the protection of navigation, federal water pollution control legislation existed long before air pollution legislation. The oldest surviving statute of current interest is §13 of the Rivers and Harbors Act of 1899. This simple statute, which grew out of efforts to regulate potential obstructions to navigation, prohibits the discharge of "any refuse matter of any kind or description whatever other than that flowing from streets and sewers and passing therefrom in a liquid state," without a permit from the Secretary of the Army (33 U.S.C. §407). This statute, which was virtually unenforced for discharges that did not actually threaten to decrease the navigable capacity of rivers and harbors, was dramatically revived between 1966 and 1970 as a potential cornerstone of a federal water pollution control program. First, the Supreme Court held that refuse included valuable as well as valueless substances discharged into navigable waters when navigable capacity was not even threatened. United States v. Standard Oil Co., 384 U.S. 224 (1966) (commercial aviation fuel). Second, in 1970 a House subcommittee issued a report pointing out that the Rivers and Harbors Action provided for citizen enforcement by allowing qui tam actions. A qui tam action is a common law action that antedates the development of professional police forces, allowing individuals to prosecute crimes and to keep one half of any fines recovered. Staff of Subcomm. on Conservation and Natural Resources, House Comm. on Government Operations, 91st Cong., 2d Sess., Qui Tam Actions and the 1899 Refuse Act: Citizen Lawsuits against Polluters of the Nation's Waterways (1970).

For a brief period in 1971, the Nixon Administration intended to make the Act the basis for a comprehensive discharge permit program, a feature lacking in then-existing federal laws (described below), but the passage of the Federal Water Pollution Control Act Amendments of 1972 aborted this stopgap program. See Rodgers, Industrial Water Pollution and the Refuse Act: A Second Chance for Water Quality, 119 U. Pa. L. Rev. 761 (1971). Druley, The Refuse Act of 1899, 2 Envt. Rep. (BNA), Monograph No. 11 (1972), is a complete discussion of the proposed program. The theory that the Act allowed qui tam actions was rejected in Connecticut Action Now, Inc. v. Roberts Plating Co., 457 F.2d 81 (2d Cir. 1972).

b.   Water Use Zoning

After the states solved some of their more immediate public health problems, they began to take a more comprehensive approach to water pollution control and started to develop water quality standards. These standards, which were the centerpiece of the state abatement programs, focused on the quality of the receiving medium, not the effluent discharged into the medium. Standards defined the parameters of certain qualities — pH, heat, suspended solids and dissolved oxygen — for given uses of water. Until 1948, as we outlined above, the federal government's role in pollution control was limited to special problems, such as refuse discharged into navigable waters and oil spills. The Federal Water Pollution Control Act of 1948 modestly expanded the federal government's role. The Surgeon General was authorized to conduct investigations, to make grants to state and local agencies for research, and to make loans for the construction of treatment works. He could declare interstate pollution a public nuisance, but the necessary investigation to determine if a nuisance in fact existed could not begin unless the local agency authorized it. The federal government's promulgation of a model state pollution control law in 1950 did stimulate state efforts to adopt water quality standards, and in 1956 federal efforts were strengthened when Congress began to subsidize the construction of sewage treatment works. See Wilson, Legal Aspects of Water Pollution Control, in U.S. Department of Health, Education and Welfare, Proceedings: The National Conference on Water Pollution 354, 364-369 (1961). State pollution control statutes are described in Currie, State Pollution Statutes, 48 U. Chi. L. Rev. 27 (1981), and R. Beck and P. Goplerud, Water Pollution and Water Quality Legal Resources, 3 Water and Water Rights, Appendix I (R. Clark 3d ed. 1988).

By the end of the 1950s, the official analysis of the pollution problem voiced by legislators and technical organizations was still that water pollution was primarily a local problem (see, e.g., Advisory Commission on Intergovernmental Relations, Metropolitan America: Challenge to Federalism 47 (1966)), but the reality was that a consensus was emerging among key legislators that would expand the federal role from abatement to prevention. See Federal-State Relations in Transition: Implications for Environmental Policy, A Report Prepared by the Congressional Research Service of the Library of Congress for the Comm. on Environment and Public Works, S. Rep. No. 52, 87th Cong., 2d Sess. 3-32 (1962). Planners long had urged that the river basin was the appropriate control unit. Between 1935 and 1948 the Ohio River Valley states negotiated a compact to create the Ohio River Valley Sanitation Commission, which required primary treatment from all municipal sewage systems along the river. See E. Cleary, The ORSANCO Story: Water Quality Management in the Ohio Valley under an Interstate Compact (1967). Northern states, which had so-so track records for cleaning up their waters, became increasingly concerned that southern and western states were trying to lure industry with low water quality standards, and thus the industrialized states began to support the idea of minimum standards for federal water quality. See D. Carr, Death of Sweet Waters: The Politics of Pollution (1967). A similar tolerance — or even preference — among the large firms in an industry for federal regulation as a means of eliminating competition from smaller firms was first noted in G. Kolko, The Triumph of Conservatism (1960), and this observation was applied to the pollution field in W. Tucker, Progress and Privilege: America in the Age of Environmentalism (1982). In recent years, critics of environmental controls have expanded on the inter-regional impacts of pollution controls and argued that domestic environmental regulations put United States firms at a competitive disadvantage in the global market, but there is little evidence to support this hypothesis. See H. J.

Leonard, Are Environmental Regulations Driving U.S. Industry Overseas? (1984) and Pollution and the Struggle for the World Product: Multinational Corporations, Environment, and International Comparative Advantage (1988).

At the important National Conference on Water Pollution in 1959, the Assistant Surgeon General offered the following reason for the emergence of water pollution as a national problem:

> Prior to 1940, there was a somewhat orderly transition from a rural to an industrial economy. Cities were still separate entities, generally with appreciable distances between shocks of pollution. Industries were in or near cities. Pollution, for the most part, was natural organic materials with concentrations of biological contaminants. Improvements in water treatment and extension of waste treatment kept the scales reasonably in balance. Excessive pollution, where it occurred, was still largely localized and over short stretches of streams.
>
> Since 1940, three major influences aggravate the pollution situation. All three are World War II related:
>
> 1. There was a fantastically increased tempo in the transition to metropolitan and industrial development — the formation of gigantic metropolitan complexes extending hundreds of miles generally following major watercourses. Industries go where there is water and populations build up where there is industry.
>
> 2. There was practically no construction of municipal or industrial waste treatment works over the period 1940 to 1947. Men and materials were needed for the war effort.
>
> 3. The avalanche of technological progress brought with it a whole array of new-type contaminants, such as synthetic chemicals and radioactive wastes. Production and use of such materials continue upward at substantial rates. [Hollis, The Water Pollution Image, in Proceedings of the National Conference on Water Pollution 30, 32 (1961).]

The necessity of a strong federal role in water pollution control was confirmed in 1965 and 1966. The Water Quality Act of 1965, 79 Stat. 903, required all states to enact water quality standards for interstate navigable waters and provided for a cumbersome "talk show" enforcement process. Judicial action was a last resort, and the federal government could only convene a conference, a long investigation of pollution problems and remedies, if the pollution substantially endangered the health of citizens in another state or if substantial injury would result to those attempting to market shellfish in interstate commerce. If the governor of an injured state so requested, the federal government had to call a conference; if the pollution was wholly intrastate, the governor had the sole right to determine if a federal conference would be convened. The 1966 amendments increased the federal contribution to sewage treatment plants and began to fund water quality planning programs (80 Stat. 1246).

The heart of the 1965 Act's regulatory program was water quality standards. States were required to enact standards for all interstate navigable waters, although many states already had such standards in place. As described by Professor N. William Hines, water quality standards zone a stream so that, when appropriate, its assimilative uses are allocated for different reaches of the stream:

> The water quality standards . . . involve three essential components: First, a determination is made concerning the present and future uses to be made of each body or stretch of interstate water. Public hearings are required as a part of the decision-making process regarding use designations. Second, the specific water quality characteristics allowed or required for such uses must be identified and descriptive or numerical values established for each of them. These so-called water quality criteria include such matters as dissolved oxygen, temperature, chlorides, phenols, alkalinity, salinity, alkalinity-acidity balance, hardness, number of coliforms, sedimentation, and suspended solids or turbidity. The establishment of such criteria in relation to every reach of interstate waters provides a ready measure for evaluating the quality of these waters. The third component of the standards is a precise, detailed plan for achieving and preserving the criteria established, including such ingredients as preventive steps, construction schedules, enforcement actions, surveillance and monitoring. [Hines, Controlling Industrial Water Pollution: Color the Problem Green, 9 B.C. Indus. & Com. L. Rev. 553, 585-586 (1968).]

Professor Hines has written the standard analysis of the evolution of federal water pollution control policy, Nor Any Drop to Drink: Public Regulation of Water Quality; Part I: State Pollution Control Programs, 52 Iowa L. Rev. 186 (1966); Part II: Interstate Arrangements for Pollution Control, 52 Iowa L. Rev. 432 (1966); and Part III: The Federal Effort, 52 Iowa L. Rev. 799 (1967).

c.   The Clean Water Act: An Overview

(1)   Goals

In 1972 Congress concluded that the water quality approach was not working. The amendments departed from the 1965-1966 legislation in three major aspects. First, the goal of no pollution discharges was substituted for the goal of calibrating discharges to water use. Second, a two-tiered system of technology-based effluent limitations supplemented existing water quality standards. Third, the federal role in setting water pollution policy was made primary, and the states were reduced to the role of agents implementing federal policy, if they passed a qualifying state program. J. Quarles, Cleaning Up America: An Insider's View of the Environmental Protection Agency 151-161 (1976), contains an account of the efforts of the Nixon White House to force Congress to reconsider the legislation because of the cost to the federal government and to private industry. President Nixon initially vetoed the legislation because, after Congress refused to give him what he considered adequate authority to control federal spending, he felt the legislation would cost the federal government too much. But the Senate overrode the veto 52 to 12. In the Senate debate over the conference bill, which ultimately was enacted, Senator Muskie likened water pollution to cancer and offered the following explanation for a control-at-any-cost strategy:

> Can we afford clean water? Can we afford rivers and lakes and streams and oceans which continue to make possible life on this planet? Can we afford life

itself? Those questions were never asked as we destroyed the waters of our Nation, and they deserve no answers as we finally move to restore and renew them. These questions answer themselves. [Senate Consideration of the Report of the Conference Comm., Oct. 4, 1972, reprinted in Senate Comm. on Public Works, 1 Legislative History of the Water Pollution Control Act Amendments of 1972, S. Rep. No. 1, 93d Cong., 1st Sess. 164 (1973) (hereinafter cited as 1972 Legislative History).]

The structure of the Clean Water Act can be analyzed in terms of multiple levels of commands. First, the lofty objective of §101, 33 U.S.C. §1251, is "to restore and maintain the chemical, physical and biological integrity of the Nation's waters." Only slightly less lofty is the national goal "that the discharge of pollutants into navigable waters be eliminated by 1985" and the 1983 interim goal "that wherever attainable" waters be made fishable and swimmable. These goals were to be achieved by means of a number of more specific policies, such as the reduction of toxic pollutants and the encouragement of areawide waste treatment facilities. The national objective and the interim goal are not directly enforceable; rather, Congress chose to achieve these goals indirectly, through the effluent limitation standards.

But the standards may be objectives in and of themselves:

> The Congressional debate makes it clear that supporters of the 1972 amendments saw them as an explicit rejection of ambient water quality standards, either as a feasible basis for determining effluent reduction or as a basis for enforcement. Rather, if technology allows an effluent limitation to be achieved, it should be done. [Freeman, Air and Water Pollution Policy, in Current Issues in U.S. Environmental Policy 12, 48 (1978).]

It is easy to understand the theory of enforceable commands. What is the theory of non-enforceable objectives, goals, and policies? Initially, the use of goals helped commit Congress to the effluent limitation policy because the goals were seen as modifiable. The Clean Water Act provided for the creation of a National Commission on Water Quality to assess the impact of the Act and to recommend midcourse corrections. The Commission's reports recommended the somewhat inconsistent approaches of keeping the 1983 interim goal but redefining the 1985 no-discharge goal to stress conservation and reuse and extending deadlines and incorporating other flexibility devices into the law. Report to the Congress by the National Commission on Water Quality (1976).

The major environmentalist argument for non-enforceable goals has been that they help hold Congress's and regulators' feet to the fire.

(2)   Structure

The Clean Water Act divides pollution into two fundamental categories: pollution emanating from point and non-point sources. The legal definition of a point source is complicated, but initially it can be defined as a confined discharge. Point sources are subjected to a two-level reduction standard that seeks to force the adoption of effluent reduction technology and squeeze out consideration of the costs versus the benefits of effluent reduction. Non-point sources are less amenable to add-on technologies because they require behavior adjustments in land use activities — such as agriculture, mining, forestry, and construction — that cause run-off into streams. Point sources were initially broken down into municipal sewage treatment plants and industrial discharges. Both types of point sources had to apply for a permit issued either by the federal government or a qualified state program. Publicly owned sewage treatments got the benefit of grants, whereas private facilities got only indirect subsidies such as tax abatements. Initially, all non-toxic industrial sources of pollution except heat were to be treated equally. The standards for toxic pollutants were to be based on health effects rather than on possible levels of effluent reduction.

Point sources may be subject to five different effluent limitations, administered through the National Pollutant Discharge Elimination System (NPDES). The NPDES system makes the Clean Water Act much simpler to administer than the Clean Air Act because everything that comes out of a pipe, and more, is subject to a permit system. Under the "new federalism" in vogue in the early 1970s, states were permitted to administer their own programs if they met federal standards. NPDES permits establish the effluent limitations a discharger must meet and the deadline for meeting them. Section 402(b)(1)(B), 33 U.S.C. §1342(b)(1)(B), authorizes permits for up to five years, and the EPA generally issues full five-year permits subject to modification or revocation for cause. Permit procedures are described in R. Zener, Guide to Federal Environmental Law 76-85 (1981). Section 511(c)(1), 33 U.S.C. §1371(c)(1), exempts all NPDES permits from NEPA except for sewage treatment plant grants and new source discharge permits (see Guide to Federal Environmental Law, at 86-89). Although §402 does not contain the phrase "on the record," which the Supreme Court has suggested is the best evidence of congressional intent to require an adjudicatory hearing, it has been held that the issuance of an NPDES permit by the EPA is a quasi-judicial proceeding and that an on-the-record hearing is required. Marathon Oil Co. v. EPA, 564 F.2d 1253 (9th Cir. 1977). Zemansky & Zerbe, Adjudicatory Hearings as Part of the NPDES Hearing Process, 9 Ecology L.Q. 1 (1980), is an empirical study of the federal hearing process. Federal regulations for federally issued NPDES permits can be found at 40 C.F.R. §124.71.

The most important effluent limitations are the two-step technology-forcing standards imposed on sewage treatment plants and industrial sources. Originally, sewage treatment plants had to provide secondary treatment by 1977 and had to use the best practicable level of technology over the life of the works by July 1, 1983 (§301(b)(1)(B), 33 U.S.C. §1311(b)(1)(B)), but this deadline was repealed in 1981. Likewise, all existing industrial dischargers had to use the best practicable control technology currently available (BPT) by 1977 and the higher best available technology economically achievable (BAT) by 1983 (§301(b)(1)(A)). The 1977 amendments extended the deadline for BAT to July 1, 1984, and, more importantly, divided pollutants into three classes: conventional, nonconventional, and toxic. BAT is still required for nonconventional and toxic pollutants, but conventional pollutants are subject to a less rigorous standard. As of 1983, the BAT program was focused entirely on toxic pollutants. In 1987, Congress extended the deadline for compliance to March 31, 1989. Section 301(b)(2)(D). EPA defines "conventional" pollutants as: biochemical oxygen-demanding substances (BOD), total suspended solids, fecal coliform bacteria, pH, and oil and grease. These characteristics are typically influenced by wastes discharged from municipal sewage plants, food processing plants, and pulp and paper mills. The Clean Water Act of 1977 requires that EPA review existing BAT limits for conventional pollutants and incorporate any revisions into new BCT (best conventional technology) standards. The new BCT limitations for pollutants must be at least as stringent as the BPT limits required for the 1977 deadline. However, any additional removal must be subject to a cost-effectiveness test. EPA will compare the cost of BAT levels of pollutant reduction in an industry with costs for removing the same pollutants at a publicly owned treatment works. EPA will compare the cost for an industrial source to remove an additional pound of pollutant above the BPT level with the cost for a POTW (publicly owned treatment works) to remove an additional pound of pollutant above the same level. If the cost to the industry is less than the cost to the POTW, the additional level of control for the industrial source will be considered reasonable and will be incorporated into the BCT standards.

In addition to BPT and BAT, there are new source performance standards similar to those in the Clean Air Act (described in Chapter 3); water quality-related standards when technology forcing is not enough to meet applicable water quality standards (§303(d), 33 U.S.C. §1313(d)); standards for toxic pollutants, and pretreatment standards for industries that discharge pollutants into publicly owned sewage treatment works (§307(b)(1), 33 U.S.C. §1317(b)(1)).

The Water Quality Act of 1987, Pub. L. No. 100-4 (Feb. 4, 1987) (codified in scattered sections of 33 U.S.C. §§1251 et seq.), made a number of changes in the Clean Water Act, but left the basic structure of the Act untouched. The Water Quality Act of 1987 extends the deadlines for compliance with a variety of effluent limitations and allows modifications, subject to relatively strict standards, of some best available technology (BAT) requirements. The Act also permits a limited modification of water quality limitations. Congress addressed the subject of ocean dumping, which has been a continuing source of controversy; imposed increased treatment requirements; and attempted to reduce the amount of toxic pollutants dumped into municipal sewage systems. Title II construction grants were continued through fiscal 1990, but the program is being phased out. The 1987 Amendments substituted a revolving loan program initially funded by federal grants and loans. All federal funding for sewage plants is to end in 1994.

End-of-the-pipe controls are the primary but not the exclusive thrust of the Clean Water Act. In addition to the NPDES program, the Act mandates three different land use planning processes. Section 303(e) requires a continuous state basin planning process for all navigable waters in the state to support the NPDES program:

Under the regulations and guidelines for section 303(e) planning, all river basins within a state are classified as either water quality or effluent limitation segments. EPA's 1974 Water Strategy Paper described the significance of this classification for basin planning. If 1977 water quality standards can be met by application of the "best practicable" technology for industries and secondary treatment for municipal plants, then the segment will be classified as an effluent limitation segment. When this technological base is insufficient for attaining the 1977 water quality standard, the segment will be categorized as a water quality limited segment. If any doubt arises as to the category in which a segment belongs, the question will be resolved in favor of the water quality limited segment classification, subject to change. The basic planning elements of the section 303(e) process will vary depending upon the classification of the respective basin segments under either the "water quality" or "effluent limitation" categories.

Under the regulatory scheme for the effluent limitation segments consideration must be given to the inventory and ranking of significant dischargers, the schedule of compliance for significant dischargers, the assessment of municipal needs for waste treatment controls, residual waste controls, recommendations for water quality standards revisions, relationships with other planning processes including section 201, section 208, and other federal environmental management planning programs, appropriate monitoring and surveillance programs, and intergovernmental cooperation for water quality management. [Phillips, Developments in Water Quality and Land Use Planning: Problems in the Application of the Federal Water Pollution Control Act Amendments of 1972, 10 Urb. L. Ann. 43, 78-79 (1975).]

In theory, §303 basin plans control the other two processes. Section 208, 33 U.S.C. §1288, requires areawide plans primarily for non-point sources, and §201, 33 U.S.C. §1281, requires a planning process for waste treatment facilities and alternative waste management techniques to ensure that the proposed management strategy is cost-effective.

The control of non-point sources of pollution was left primarily to the state through the §208 planning process. Basically, non-point sources of pollution are land uses that cause pollution. The Act divided states into planning areas. The governor of each state had to designate areas having substantial water quality control problems and select a regional planning agency, controlled by local governments, to formulate §208 plans. The plans had to contain land use regulations to control non-point sources, an identification of all waste treatment works necessary to meet municipal and industrial needs for a 20-year period and a planning program for the location of point sources of pollution. The relationship between §208 and the NPDES program was never clearly defined. Jungman, Areawide Planning under the Federal Water Pollution Control Act Amendments of 1972: Intergovernmental and Land Use Implications, 54 Tex. L. Rev. 1047, 1057-1058 (1976). In 1987 Congress added Section 319 to the Act which requires that states identify waters threatened by non-point sources of pollution and prepare four-year watershed-based management programs to control non-point source pollution.

Hazardous waste and oil spills are treated in a separate section of the Act, §311, 33 U.S.C. §1321. Both on- and off-shore facility operators and vessel

owners are liable without fault for the costs of cleaning up spills and for civil
and criminal penalties. The standard has been described as "strict liability with
limitations." United States v. West of England Ship Owners Mutual Protection
& Indemnification Association (Luxembourg), 872 F.2d 1192, 1197 (5th Cir.
1989). The Limitation of Liability Act, 46 U.S.C. §§181-189, limits a vessel's
liability to its post-spill value. Section 311 retains the concept of limited liability
but ups the amount of potential liability unless the government proves that the
vessel operator or owner or those in privity with him were willfully negligent or
engaged in willful misconduct. The government can recover up to $50,000,000
from an on- or off-shore facility operator; the greater of $125 per gross ton or
$125,000 against an inland oil barge; and the greater of $150 per gross ton or
$250,000 against a vessel carrying oil as a cargo. There are four narrow defenses:
act of God; act of war; negligence by the United States; and an act or omission
by a third party, e.g., Hollywood Marine, Inc. v. United States, 625 F.2d 524,
cert. denied, 451 U.S. 994 (1981) and United States v. M/V Sam, 681 F.2d 432
(5th Cir. 1982), *cert. denied,* 462 U.S. 1132 (1983). A vessel is liable if its action
was a contributing or proximate cause of a spill. See *West of England Ship
Owners Mutual Protection & Indemnification Association, supra.* (vessel which
navigated outside channel and struck a wreck liable because spill was foreseeable). See generally Note, Oil Spills and Cleanup Bills: Federal Recovery of Oil
Spill Cleanup Costs, 93 Harv. L. Rev. 1761, 1766-1767 (1980). A series of spills
in 1989 has revived interest in this section and in the natural resources damages
assessment standards developed under Superfund. See pages 665 to 681 *infra.*

C.   FEDERAL JURISDICTION

1.   *Constitutional Power to Regulate Water Pollution*

All federal environmental regulation must be grounded in an enumerated
power of the Constitution, but water pollution presents a constitutional issue
different from those raised by all other pollution control programs. The most
obvious source of federal power to regulate water pollution is the commerce
clause, article 1, §8. Since the Supreme Court's decision in Wickard v. Filburn,
317 U.S. 111 (1942), Congress's power to regulate commerce extends both to
interstate and intrastate activities that in the aggregate might have a substantial
effect on interstate commerce. Any form of water pollution would seem to meet
this liberal, perhaps limitless, test for the requisite constitutional nexus between
an activity and the commerce clause power. See Soper, The Constitutional
Framework of Environmental Law, in Federal Environmental Law 20 (E. Dolgin & T. Guilbert eds. 1974).

However, because of the peculiar and complex history of federal regulation
of water resources use, the issue of federal regulation of water pollution is not

solely one of constitutional power. Historically, Congress has refrained from exercising the full extent of its regulatory power under the commerce clause. Throughout most of this country's history, Congress has contained federal power over water resources to "navigable waters." Navigability defines (1) admiralty jurisdiction, (2) federal regulation of private use of water resources, (3) the allocation of the titles to submerged lands between the states and the federal government and their respective patentees, and (4) the determination of the waters to which public use rights attach under state law. The standard of navigability varies depending on the purpose for which it is defined. Originally, navigable waters were uniformly defined as those affected by the ebb and flow of the tide. Public rights, such as commercial navigation, regardless of who claimed the bed and banks, and admiralty jurisdiction attached. This limited definition served English interests in navigation perfectly well, and it was not until this country began the great migration west that the definition became disfunctional. After a long political and scholarly debate, the Supreme Court extended admiralty jurisdiction to fresh as well as to tidal navigable waters. The Propeller Genesee Chief v. Fitzhugh, 53 U.S. (12 How.) 443 (1851). See Conover, The Abandonment of the "Tidewater" Concept of Admiralty Jurisdiction in the United States, 38 Or. L. Rev. 34 (1958). The leading definition of navigability for an expanding nation was given in The Daniel Ball, 77 U.S. (10 Wall.) 557 (1870). Waters are "navigable in fact . . . when they form in their ordinary condition by themselves, or by uniting with other waters, a continued highway" in the chain of interstate and foreign commerce.

Space does not permit us to trace the course by which the concept of navigability was stretched from the 1930s to the 1950s to accommodate claims for increased federal regulatory power and the flood control program of the New Deal. Suffice it to say that by the time of the enactment of the Clean Water Act the pertinent issue was the narrower one of whether Congress intended to limit federal jurisdiction to navigable waters by adopting the historic, limited definition, as interpreted by the courts, or if it intended to assert the full reach of commerce clause jurisdiction permitted by Wickard v. Filburn, 317 U.S. 111 (1942), and Heart of Atlanta Motel, Inc. v. United States, 379 U.S. 241 (1964). The Clean Water Act speaks of preventing the discharge of pollutants into "navigable waters," and §402 speaks of permits for the discharge of pollutants into navigable waters. Navigable waters are defined in §502, 33 U.S.C. §1362(7), as "the waters of the United States, including the territorial seas." Does this definition expand the historic definition of navigability, and does Congress have the constitutional power to do so? United States v. Ashland Oil & Transportation Co., 504 F.2d 1317 (6th Cir. 1974), answered both of these questions yes. Ashland Oil was indicted for failing to report an oil spill under §311, 33 U.S.C. §1321(b)(5), into navigable waters. The oil was spilled into a non-navigable tributary (twice removed) of a river, the Green River in Kentucky, which was navigable in fact. The court held that Congress did intend to exercise the full extent of its power under the commerce clause and that Congress had ample authority to control water pollution:

The government in this case, however, pins its argument primarily upon the wider concept that water pollution is subject to Congressional restraint because it affects commerce in innumerable ways and because it affects the health and welfare of the nation, Wickard v. Filburn, 317 U.S. 111, 63 S. Ct. 82, 87 L. Ed. 122 (1942). The statute lends some weight to the government's argument by its many references (some of which we have quoted above) to aspects of pollution control which have no possible direct bearing on navigability. Congressional concern in the 1972 Act with the impact of pollution upon fishing for commercial purposes or upon bathing and fishing and boating for recreational purposes of interstate travelers, and for the needs of towns, cities, industries and farms for unpolluted water for both health and commerce supports this broader concept. Congress, as indicated above, intended to exercise its full constitutional powers, and we are required to give effect to that intention. McCulloch v. Maryland, 17 U.S. (4 Wheat.) 316, 423, 4 L. Ed. 579 (1819); United States v. Appalachian Power Co., 311 U.S. 377, 423-429, 61 S. Ct. 291, 85 L. Ed. 243 (1940); United States v. Darby, 312 U.S. 100, 115, 61 S. Ct. 451, 85 L. Ed. 609 (1941). [504 F.2d at 1328.]

For its answer to the first question, the court relied heavily on a statement Congressman Dingell introduced into the record (118 Cong. Rec. 33,756-33,757 (1972)). This statement of congressional intent has been accepted as decisive:

Third, the conference bill defines the term "navigable waters" broadly for water quality purposes (502(7)). It means all "the waters of the United States" in a geographical sense. It does not mean "navigable waters of the United States" in the technical sense as we sometimes see in some laws.

The new and broader definition is in line with more recent judicial opinions which have substantially expanded that limited view of navigability — derived from the *Daniel Ball* case (77 U.S. 557, 563) — to include waterways which would be "susceptible of being used . . . with reasonable improvement," as well as those waterways which include sections presently obstructed by falls, rapids, sand bars, currents, floating debris, et cetera. United States v. Utah, 283 U.S. 64 (1931); United States v. Appalachian Electric Power Co., 331 U.S. 377, 407-410, 416 (1940); Wisconsin Public Service Corp. v. Federal Power Commission, 147 F.2d 743 (C.A. 7, 1945); *cert. denied*, 325 U.S. 880; Wisconsin v. Federal Power Commission, 214 F.2d 334 (C.A. 7, 1954) *cert. denied*, 348 U.S. 883 (1954); Namekagon Hydro Co. v. Federal Power Commission, 216 F.2d 509 (C.A. 7, 1954); Puente de Reynosa, S.A. v. City of McAllen, 357 F.2d 43, 50-51 (C.A. 5, 1966); Rochester Gas and Electric Corp. v. Federal Power Commission, 344 F.2d 594 (C.A. 2, 1965); The Montello, 37 U.S. (20 Wall.) 430, 441-42 (1874); Economy Light & Power Co. v. United States, 256 U.S. 113 (1921).

The U.S. Constitution contains no mention of navigable waters. The authority of Congress over navigable waters is based on the Constitution's grant to Congress of "Power . . . To regulate commerce with Foreign Nations and among the several States. . . . (art. I, sec. 8, clause 3). Gibbons v. Ogden, 22 U.S. (9 Wheat.) 1 (1824). Although most interstate commerce 150 years ago was accomplished on waterways, there is no requirement in the Constitution that the waterway must cross a State boundary in order to be within the interstate commerce power of the Federal Government. Rather, it is enough that the waterway serves as a link in the chain of commerce among the States as it flows in the various channels of transportation — highways, railroads, air traffic, radio and postal communication, waterways, et cetera. The "gist of the Federal test" is the waterway's use "as a highway," not whether it is "part of a navigable interstate or international commercial highway." Utah v. United States, 403 U.S. 9, 11 (1971); U.S. v. Underwood, 4 ERC 1305, 1309 (D.C., Md., Fla., Tampa Div., June 8, 1972).

Thus, this new definition clearly encompasses all water bodies including main streams and their tributaries, for water quality purposes. No longer are the old, narrow definitions of navigability, as determined by the Corps of Engineers, going to govern matters covered by this bill. Indeed, the conference report states on page 144: "The conferees fully intend that the term navigable waters be given the broadest possible constitutional interpretation unencumbered by agency determinations which have been made or may be made for administrative purposes." [House Consideration of the Report of the Conference Comm., Oct. 4, 1972, reprinted in 1972 Legislative History, at 250-251 (1973) (statement of Rep. Dingell).]

NOTES AND QUESTIONS ON THE JURISDICTION OF THE CLEAN WATER ACT

1. *Tributaries.* United States v. Phelps Dodge Corp., 391 F. Supp. 1181 (D. Ariz. 1975), rejected the argument that 33 U.S.C. §1362(7)'s definition of "navigable waters" was void for vagueness. After *Ashland Oil* and *Phelps Dodge*, must limitations on the Act's coverage be based on lack of congressional intent, not on a lack of constitutional power to regulate? Although the answer seems to be yes, defendants continue to challenge EPA's jurisdiction in two fact situations, discharges into remote tributaries of historically navigable waters and into wetlands. A direct discharge into a tributary of a river that is navigable in fact is a violation of the Act, regardless of the tributary's remoteness, whether it is named or not and whether the flow is constant or intermittent. See United States v. Texas Pipeline Co., 611 F.2d 345 (10th Cir. 1979); Ward v. Coleman, 598 F.2d 1187 (10th Cir. 1979), *rev'd on other grounds sub nom.* United States v. Ward, 448 U.S. 242, *reh'g denied*, 448 U.S. 916 (1980); and *Phelps Dodge, supra.* See also Harleysville Mutual Insurance Co. v. United States, 16 Envt. Rep. Cas. (BNA) 1103 (Ct. Cl. 1981) (refusal to dismiss third-party defendant who spilled heating oil that EPA alleged would have reached a remote tributary of Delaware River had agency not cleaned up the spill). But cf. Buttrey v. United States, 19 Envt. Rep. Cas. (BNA) 2074 (E.D. La. 1983).

Quivira Mining Co. v. United States, 765 F.2d 126 (10th Cir. 1985), upheld the EPA's power to require NPDES permits for a New Mexico uranium mining facility that discharged into an arroyo and creek in part because pollutants could reach a navigable-in-fact stream through underground aquifers fed by the two non-navigable-in-fact watercourses. Pursuant to its internal waste stream rule, 40 C.F.R. §122.45(h) (1986), EPA regulates the discharges from a utility's internal treatment facility into settling ponds. The ponds allow suspended solids to settle out before the wastes are discharged into a reservoir. The utility argues that EPA lacks the authority to adopt the rule because internal waste streams are not "waters of the United States." What result? See Texas Municipal

Power Agency v. Administrator of the United States Environmental Protection Agency, 836 F.2d 1482 (5th Cir. 1988).

2. *Groundwater.* Although the Act's coverage of surface waters seems unlimited, the same cannot be said about groundwater. In the late 1960s and early 1970s, most public, legislative, and regulatory efforts were focused on surface water pollution. Congress basically left whatever state regulatory programs existed in place as it began to deal with groundwater pollution. Five separate statutes, The Clean Water Act, the Safe Drinking Water Act, the Resource and Recovery Conservation Act, the Comprehensive Environmental Response, Compensation and Liability Act, and the Toxic Substances Control Act, deal with groundwater, but regulation is piecemeal. See Chapter 5. This is important because one effect of the Clean Air and Water Acts is to create pressures for land and subsurface disposal of wastes that were formerly spewed into the air or water media. As this fact began to be appreciated, and as there was more and more evidence of groundwater pollution, protection of groundwater emerged in 1979-1980 as a major environmental problem. Interim Report on Groundwater Contamination: Environmental Protection Agency Oversight, Twenty-Fifth Report by the House Comm. on Government Operations, 96th Cong., 2d Sess. 3-4 (1980), summarizes the consensus about the nature of the problem and federal regulatory efforts prior to 1980:

> Scientists have recently learned that many manmade and naturally occurring toxic materials which are dumped into the ground do not break down but are stored and eventually transported under the subsurface to areas where they may poison drinking water wells, and eventually, lakes and streams. Because of the slow movement of ground water, this pollution can remain undetected for decades. That has led to the erroneous and shortsighted belief that the ground is a bottomless sponge, which could soak up any material poured into it, clean it, and store it for future use. That costly misperception has now been proven wrong.
>
> The Federal effort to control ground water pollution will be more carefully reviewed in future Committee reports. To date the Federal effort has been haphazard and ineffective, despite numerous Federal statutes already on the books allowing EPA to take additional action to protect this vital resource. As Representative Peter H. Kostmayer (D-Pa.) pointed out at the subcommittee's hearings, EPA has not fully tested those powers.

EPA's powers, at least as interpreted by the courts, are perhaps not as broad as Congressman Kostmayer thought. Groundwater is not explicitly dealt with in the Clean Water Act. EPA's authority rests on two sections and an expansive reading of the definition of navigable waters. Section 402(b)(1)(D), 33 U.S.C. §1342(b)(1)(D), prohibits the EPA Administrator from approving a state NPDES permit program unless the state has adequate authority to control the disposal of pollutants into wells, and §402(a)(3), 33 U.S.C. §1342(a)(3), provides that EPA programs for non-approved states shall be subject to the same terms, conditions, and requirements as state permit programs. Nonetheless, the leading case of Exxon Corp. v. Train, 554 F.2d 1310 (5th Cir. 1977), holds that EPA lacks the authority to control the disposal of wastes into deep wells that are unconnected to surface waters. Congress, the court concluded, did not know enough about groundwater pollution to attempt comprehensive federal regulation and therefore decided to leave regulation up to the states. There is contrary authority in the Seventh Circuit, U.S. Steel Corp. v. Train, 556 F.2d 822 (7th Cir. 1977), but EPA chose not to continue to press its authority under the Clean Water Act and shifted its attention to two acts passed in 1974 and 1976. The Safe Drinking Water Act of 1974 and the Resource Conservation and Recovery Act of 1976 are currently the primary federal regulatory authority for the control of groundwater pollution. There is some authority for the proposition, however, that EPA has jurisdiction over deep well disposal schemes that would "flow into or otherwise affect surface waters." United States v. GAF Corp., 389 F. Supp. 1379, 1383 (S.D. Tex. 1975). The relationship among the federal acts is discussed in Tripp & Jaffe, Preventing Groundwater Pollution: Toward a Coordinated Strategy to Protect Critical Recharge Zones, 3 Harv. Envtl. L. Rev. 1 (1979) and Wood, Regulating Discharges into Groundwater: The Crucial Link in Pollution Control under the Clean Water Act, 12 Harv. Envtl. L. Rev. 569 (1988). McClellan Ecological Seepage Situation v. Weinberger, 707 F. Supp. 1182 (E.D. Cal. 1988), allowed the plaintiff to engage in additional discovery to "establish that the groundwater is naturally connected to surface waters that constitute 'navigable waters' under the Clean Water Act" as opposed to isolated groundwater. Consider United States v. Riverside Bayview Homes, p. 370 *infra*. Is the court's distinction between connected and isolated groundwater tenable in light of the Court's holding?

EPA Administrator William Ruckelshaus made groundwater quality protection a high agency priority in 1983 and 1984. The agency's Ground-Water Protection Strategy (August, 1984) concluded that states and local governments have the principal role in groundwater protection with the federal government playing secondary roles such as program coordination and financial support. The strategy recommended a differential protection approach to the coordination of federal groundwater protection programs. Aquifers are divided into three classes. Class I groundwaters are those which are highly vulnerable to contamination and are irreplaceable or ecologically vital; Class II groundwaters are those that are either dedicated to drinking water supply or suitable for that purpose and do not fall within classes I or III; and Class III groundwaters are those with a TDS level over 10,000 mg/l or are so contaminated that they cannot be purified by methods reasonably employed in public water systems. See also United States Environmental Protection Agency, Guidelines for Ground-Water Classification under the EPA Ground-Water Protection Strategy (November 1986). A national policy forum endorsed the EPA's conclusion that groundwater protection was primarily a state responsibility, in part because of the need to control consumptive withdrawals and to coordinate ground and surface water management. It also endorsed the general concept of aquifer classification, but cautioned that such a system should not "allow large areas to be expendable as dumps for civilization's wastes." The forum went beyond EPA's strategy and called for a more aggressive national groundwater protection policy. Groundwater Protection

(Conservation Foundation 1987) urged the adoption of legislation that establishes strong non-degradation national goals and requires each state to adopt a comprehensive groundwater management program. Various bills have been introduced, but to date Congress has supported only increased funding for federal and state groundwater research. Existing state programs are surveyed in T. Henderson, J. Trauberman & T. Gallagher, Groundwater Strategies for State Action (Envtl. Law Inst. 1984). See also Symposium, Groundwater Protection in the Great Lakes Region — Chi.-Kent L. Rev. — (1990).

For an ambitious attempt to exercise state power over an entire groundwater ecosystem, the New Jersey Pine Barrens, see New Jersey Builders Association v. Department of Environmental Protection, 169 N.J. Super. 76, 404 A.2d 320 (App. Div.), *petition for cert. denied*, 81 N.J. 402, 408 A.2d 796 (1979).

3. *Interagency comity.* Interagency comity also may be a basis for a statutory exclusion. In Train v. Colorado Public Interest Research Group, 426 U.S. 1, (1976), the Supreme Court held that radioactive materials were not a "pollutant" within the meaning of the Act. Although the term "pollutant" as defined in the Act includes "radioactive materials," the Administrator of the EPA specifically excluded radioactive materials from EPA's regulatory program to avoid duplicating the Atomic Energy Commission's functions. The Court upheld the Administrator's decision because nuclear waste material was subject to regulation by the AEC and by its successor, the Nuclear Regulatory Commission. The NRC regulates the production, possession, and use of three types of radioactive materials — source material, special nuclear material, and byproduct material — and establishes the maximum permissible releases of such materials into the environment. Therefore, the court concluded, the Administrator could exclude such materials from the jurisdiction of the FWPCA.

4. *Federalism and the Clean Water Act.* Does the Clean Water Act apply to the federal government? The Federal Water Pollution Control Act Amendments of 1972 were silent on the question of whether to apply the Act to federal facilities, and in 1976 the Supreme Court held that states could apply their substantive standards but not their procedures to federal facilities. EPA v. California ex rel. State Water Resources Control Board, 426 U.S. 200 (1976). Congress was not happy with the Court's resolution of the federalism issue, and a new section was added to the Clean Water Act in 1977 subjecting federal facilities to all federal, state, or local procedural and substantive requirements. The only defense to federal facility compliance is congressional failure to approve a presidential budget request for the necessary funds (§313(a), 33 U.S.C. §1323(a)). A creative use of §313 was rebuffed in United States ex rel. Tennessee Valley Authority v. Tennessee Water Quality Control Board, 12 Envtl. L. Rep. (Envtl. L. Inst.) 20,740 (M.D. Tenn. 1982). Opponents of a Tennessee Valley Authority diversion argued that the diversion of waters through a flume would cause the degradation of high quality recreation waters, but the court held that §313 was not applicable because there was no discharge or runoff of pollutants. The decision was affirmed on appeal. The court held that "[s]ince EPA does not require discharge permits from dam operators under section 402(a), the states

may not do so under section 402(b)." 717 F.2d 922, 999 (6th Cir. 1983), *cert. denied*, 466 U.S. 937 (1984). The term "requirements" has been narrowly construed to mean "an objective administratively predetermined effluent standard or limitation or administrative order upon which to measure prohibitive levels of water pollution." State of New York v. United States, 620 F. Supp. 374, 384 (E.D. N.Y. 1985), as opposed to general nuisance-like prohibitions in state statutes, McClellan Ecological Seepage Situation v. Weinberger, 707 F. Supp. 1182, (E.D. Cal. 1988). A recent GAO study found that "[f]ederal facilities' rate of noncompliance during fiscal years 1986 and 1987 was twice the rate of that of private industrial facilities nationwide. On average 20 percent . . . of the 150 major federal facilities were in noncompliance with priority NPDES requirements during any given quarter of the 2-year period." United States General Accounting Office, Water Pollution: Stronger Enforcement Needed to Improve Compliance at Federal Facilities 23 (1988). See also Lotz, Federal Facility Provisions for Federal Environmental Statutes: Waiver of Sovereign Immunity for "Requirements" and Fines and Penalties, 31 Air Force L. Rev. 31 (1989).

In the 1987 Clean Water Act Amendments, Congress exercised its plenary power over Indians and classified Indian tribes as states for the purpose of the Act, removing any remaining ambiguity about the duty of tribes to comply with the Act and to enforce it. 33 U.S.C. §1377. To qualify to administer the NPDES permit program, the tribes must have a "governing body carrying out substantial governmental duties and powers." Rivers are usually not confined to reservation boundaries, and tribal jurisdiction is limited to waters subject to tribal rights, water rights held in trust for the tribe by the United States, held by an individual Indian, or otherwise within the boundary of the reservation. This prohibits the states from applying their water quality requirements to waters subject to tribal jurisdiction. State of Washington, Department of Ecology v. United States Environmental Protection Agency, 752 F.2d 1465 (9th Cir. 1985) (state may not impose RCRA regulations on tribe). The ramifications of *Department of Ecology* are discussed in Royster and SnowArrow Fausett, Control of the Reservation Environment: Tribal Primacy, Federal Delegation and the Limits of State Intervention, 64 Wash. L. Rev. 581 (1989).

Wetlands Jurisdiction

Federal jurisdiction over wetlands is sufficiently complex to merit extended treatment. Until 1968, the federal government did not regulate dredging and filling in navigable waters landward of harbor lines fixed by the U.S. Army Corps of Engineers. Because dredge and fill activities can in fact cause pollution and other environmental damage, after considerable controversy the Corps of Engineers began to expand its jurisdiction. The relationship between EPA and the Corps of Engineers, which retains dredge and fill jurisdiction under the Clean Water Act, is considered in more detail at pp. 445 to 456 *infra*. Corps regulations define navigable waters as those waters "conventionally of the United States that are subject to the ebb and flow of the tide shoreward to the mean high water mark," but waters of the United States were expanded to include submerged lands (wetlands) landward of the mean high tide line. 33 C.F.R. §323.2(c)-(e) defines adjacent wetlands as follows:

> (c) The term "wetlands" means those areas that are inundated or saturated by surface or ground water at a frequency and duration sufficient to support, and that under normal circumstances do support, a prevalence of vegetation typically adapted for life in saturated soil conditions. Wetlands generally include swamps, marshes, bogs and similar areas.
>
> (d) The term "adjacent" means bordering, contiguous, or neighboring. Wetlands separated from other waters of the United States by man-made dikes or barriers, natural river berms, beach dunes and the like are "adjacent wetlands."
>
> (e) The term "natural lake" means a standing body of open water that occurs in a natural depression fed by one or more streams and from which a stream may flow, that occurs due to the widening or natural blockage of a river or stream, or that occurs in an isolated natural depression that is not a part of a surface river or stream.

This definition potentially encompasses many real estate developments and mining activities, and litigation over the Corps' jurisdiction has been intense. Many developers and others have found to their great surprise that a proposed or completed development that filled wetlands with demolition debris and sand was illegal because it lacked the necessary Corps of Engineers permit. See Conservation Council v. Costanzo, 398 F. Supp. 653 (E.D.N.C.), aff'd, 528 F.2d 250 (4th Cir. 1975), which holds that wetlands subject to periodic tidal inundation are subject to the Act, even though the flooding is so infrequent that biological communities in surrounding waters are not dependent on the wetland's contribution. See also United States v. Holland, 373 F. Supp. 665 (M.D. Fla. 1974) (mangrove swamp); United States v. Bradshaw, 541 F. Supp. 880 (D. Md. 1981); and United States v. Weisman, 489 F. Supp. 1331 (M.D. Fla. 1980) (road on flat-top floodplain in wetland forest). Fresh water wetlands contiguous to navigable waters are also within the definition. American Dredging Co. v. Dutchyshyn, 480 F. Supp. 957 (E.D. Pa.), aff'd without opinion, 614 F.2d 769 (3d Cir. 1979).

Those who conduct land development activities adjacent to coastal waters or inland waters that are clearly navigable arguably have some notice that the activity is subject to federal regulation, but the Act reaches more isolated inland wetlands. United States v. Byrd, 609 F.2d 1204 (7th Cir. 1979), enjoined a fill in a 3,000 acre freshwater lake wholly within Indiana because interstate travelers visited the lake, fish removed from the lake were sold in interstate commerce, and water was withdrawn to produce crops and products sold in interstate commerce. The defendant introduced evidence at trial to prove that the wetlands were not inundated by the lake because of a natural barrier situation between the lake and wetlands. The district court held that the evidence failed to show a natural barrier, but the Seventh Circuit went further and suggested that the wetlands would be covered by the Act so long as they were contiguous, regardless of whether they were inundated; destruction of the wetlands could impair the lake's attraction to travelers, thereby indirectly affecting the flow of interstate commerce. As the definition of "wetlands" has expanded, developers have used more ingenious arguments to escape the §404 process. In 1977, the Corps changed the definition of "wetlands vegetation" from that which "requires saturated soil conditions" to that which is "typically adapted for life in saturated soil conditions." Avoyelles Sportsmen's League, Inc. v. Alexander, 511 F. Supp. 278 (W.D. La. 1981), rejected an argument that §404 wetlands should be confined to an area containing trees that can survive in inundated or saturated soils almost 100 percent of the time:

> We find absolutely no basis for the contention that the words "for life" mean that "wetlands" vegetation must spend all of its life in inundated or saturated soils. We hold that the word means simply the ability to live, to exist, to tolerate. Only the latter interpretation is consistent with the balance of the clause in which "for life" appears; with the rest of the definition and with the purpose of the 1977 revision. If the meaning of "wetlands" is to be restricted in this manner, there was no need to revise in 1977. We agree with plaintiffs that the words "vegetation typically adapted for life in saturated soil conditions" includes all vegetation which is capable of and does adapt regardless of a mechanism it might employ to do so. The scientific evidence establishes that there is little or no dispute regarding which vegetable species are intolerant. The only discernable disputes occurred in the degree of tolerance assigned to each tolerant species by different scientific experts. These disputes are more a matter of semantics than actual differences of opinion because the definitional standards for the classifications VT [very tolerant], T [tolerant], and ST [somewhat tolerant] differed. However they all had a common characteristic — they were all tolerant to a greater or lesser degree. None were intolerant. We hold that all species except the intolerant species are wetland species. We hold in fact that the very purpose of the revision was to close a technical loophole which might include many species which are truly aquatic by adaption but do not require saturated soil from a biological standpoint for their growth and reproduction. Certainly this broader interpretation was the intent of the drafters of the 1977 revision.

>> At the same time, we have changed our description of the vegetation involved by focusing on vegetation "typically adapted for life in saturated soil conditions." The old definition of "freshwater wetlands" provided a technical "loophole" by describing the vegetation as that which requires saturated soil conditions for growth and reproduction, *thereby excluding many forms of truly aquatic vegetation that are prevalent in an inundated or saturated area, but that do not require saturated soil from a biological standpoint for their growth and reproduction.*

> Fed. Reg., Vol. 42, No. 138, at p. 37128 (1977) (emphasis ours). [511 F.2d at 289-290.]

The decision was reversed on appeal because EPA's final wetlands determination that limited wetlands to areas of vegetation that required rather than simply tolerated saturated soil conditions was not arbitrary and capricious. Avoyelles Sportsmen's League, Inc. v. Marsh, 715 F.2d 897 (5th Cir. 1983). The landowners challenged the agency's wetlands determination methodology as procedurally defective and substantively wrong. The methodology was classified as an "interpretive" fleshing out of the Corps's 1977 modification of the definition of wetlands and thus was upheld against arguments that the agency had failed to follow the Administrative Procedure Act's notice-and-comment procedures, that the methodology was unreasonable and unfair, and that the final determination was an unlawful delegation of congressional power. On the merits, the court concluded:

> The essence of the landowners' challenge to the EPA's final wetlands determination concerned the legal issues described above, in particular the use of the new methodology. To a limited extent, the landowners have also disputed some of the agency's factual findings. Our review of the administrative record in this case does not indicate that the EPA's findings were arbitrary or capricious.
>
> While the EPA found that approximately eighty percent of the Lake Long Tract was a wetland, the district court found that over ninety percent of the tract was a wetland. The court and the agency reach different conclusions because they held differing beliefs about whether Tensas and Dundee soils were wetlands soils. The EPA's conclusion that areas made up of these two soils should be excluded from the wetlands area was based on the report of the agency's soil expert. [715 F.2d at 917.]

Was the appeal a victory for the would-be soybean farmer? The court held that clearing the wetland areas with bulldozer and backhoe and redepositing the materials in sloughs during the leveling constituted a point source of pollution because the defendants "collected into windrows and piles material that may ultimately have found its way back into the waters" (715 F.2d at 922). Thus a §404 permit was required. Does *Avoyelles* foreclose subsequent plaintiffs from arguing that areas containing vegetation that merely tolerates saturated soils should be classified as wetlands? The Act exempts normal farming operations but not activities that put the altered area to a new use and impair the flow of navigable waters. 33 U.S.C. §1344(f). This so-called recapture provision effectively prevents farmers from bringing large tracts of newly drained land into production. *Avoyelles, supra*; United States v. Huebner, 752 F.2d 1325 (7th Cir. 1985); and United States v. Akers, 785 F.2d 814 (9th Cir. 1986).

UNITED STATES v. RIVERSIDE BAYVIEW HOMES, INC.
474 U.S. 121 (1985)

Justice WHITE delivered the opinion of the Court.

This case presents the question whether the Clean Water Act, 33 U.S.C. §1251 et seq., together with certain regulations promulgated under its authority by the Army Corps of Engineers, authorizes the Corps to require landowners to obtain permits from the Corps before discharging fill material into wetlands adjacent to navigable bodies of water and their tributaries.

I

The relevant provisions of the Clean Water Act originated in the Federal Water Pollution Control Act Amendments of 1972, 86 Stat. 816, and have remained essentially unchanged since that time. Under §§301 and 502 of the Act, 33 U.S.C. §§1311 and 1362, any discharge of dredged or fill materials into "navigable waters" — defined as the "waters of the United States" — is forbidden unless authorized by a permit issued by the Corps of Engineers pursuant to §404, 33 U.S.C. §1344. After initially construing the Act to cover only waters navigable in fact, in 1975 the Corps issued interim final regulations redefining "the waters of the United States" to include not only actually navigable waters but also tributaries of such waters, interstate waters and their tributaries, and nonnavigable intrastate waters whose use or misuse could affect interstate commerce. 40 Fed. Reg. 31,320 (1975). More importantly for present purposes, the Corps construed the Act to cover all "freshwater wetlands" that were adjacent to other covered waters. A "freshwater wetland" was defined as an area that is "periodically inundated" and is "normally characterized by the prevalence of vegetation that requires saturated soil conditions for growth and reproduction." 33 C.F.R. §209.120(d)(2)(h) (1976). In 1977, the Corps refined its definition of wetlands by eliminating the reference to periodic inundation and making other minor changes. The 1977 definition read as follows:

> The term "wetlands" means those areas that are inundated or saturated by surface or ground water at a frequency and duration sufficient to support, and that under normal circumstances do support, a prevalence of vegetation typically adapted for life in saturated soil conditions. Wetlands generally include swamps, marshes, bogs and similar areas.

33 C.F.R. §323.2(c) (1978). In 1982, the 1977 regulations were replaced by substantively identical regulations that remain in force today. See 33 C.F.R. §323.2 (1985).

Respondent Riverside Bayview Homes, Inc. (hereafter respondent), owns 80 acres of low-lying, marshy land near the shores of Lake St. Clair in Macomb County, Michigan. In 1976, respondent began to place fill materials on its property as part of its preparations for construction of a housing development. The Corps of Engineers, believing that the property was an "adjacent wetland" under the 1975 regulation defining "waters of the United States," filed suit in the United States District Court for the Eastern District of Michigan, seeking to enjoin respondent from filling the property without the permission of the Corps.

[The District Court initially held that some of Riverside's property below 575.5 feet above sea level was a wetland, and the Court of Appeals remanded for consideration of the effect of the intervening 1977 amendments to the regulation. On remand, the District Court again held the property to be a wetland subject to the Corps' permit authority, but the Sixth Circuit construed the Corps' regulations to exclude from the category of adjacent wetlands — and hence from that of "waters of the United States" — wetlands that were not subject to flooding by adjacent navigable waters at a frequency sufficient to support the growth of aquatic vegetation because this interpretation was consistent with Congressional intent and to avoid finding that a taking of private property without just compensation had occurred.] We now reverse.

II

The question whether the Corps of Engineers may demand that respondent obtain a permit before placing fill material on its property is primarily one of regulatory and statutory interpretation: we must determine whether respondent's property is an "adjacent wetland" within the meaning of the applicable regulation, and, if so, whether the Corps' jurisdiction over "navigable waters" gives it statutory authority to regulate discharges of fill material into such a wetland. In this connection, we first consider the Court of Appeals' position that the Corps' regulatory authority under the statute and its implementing regulations must be narrowly construed to avoid a taking without just compensation in violation of the Fifth Amendment.

We have frequently suggested that governmental land-use regulation may under extreme circumstances amount to a "taking" of the affected property. . . . We have made it quite clear that the mere assertion of regulatory jurisdiction by a governmental body does not constitute a regulatory taking. See Hodel v. Virginia Surface Mining & Reclamation Assn., 452 U.S. 264, 293-297, 101 S. Ct. 2352, 2369-71, 69 L. Ed. 2d 1 (1981). The reasons are obvious. A requirement that a person obtain a permit before engaging in a certain use of his or her property does not itself "take" the property in any sense: after all, the very existence of a permit system implies that permission may be granted, leaving the landowner free to use the property as desired. Moreover, even if the permit is denied, there may be other viable uses available to the owner. Only when a permit is denied and the effect of the denial is to prevent "economically viable" use of the land in question can it be said that a taking has occurred.

If neither the imposition of the permit requirement itself nor the denial of a permit necessarily constitutes a taking, it follows that the Court of Appeals erred in concluding that a narrow reading of the Corps' regulatory jurisdiction over wetlands was "necessary" to avoid "a serious taking problem." 729 F.2d, at 398. . . .

III

Purged of its spurious constitutional overtones, the question whether the regulation at issue requires respondent to obtain a permit before filing its property is an easy one. The regulation extends the Corps' authority under §404 to all wetlands adjacent to navigable or interstate waters and their tributaries. Wetlands, in turn, are defined as lands that are "inundated *or saturated* by surface *or ground water* at a frequency and duration sufficient to support, and that under normal circumstances do support, a prevalence of vegetation typically adapted for life in saturated soil conditions." 33 CFR §323.2(c) (1985) (emphasis added). The plain language of the regulation refutes the Court of Appeals' conclusion that inundation or "frequent flooding" by the adjacent body of water is a *sine qua non* of a wetland under the regulation. Indeed, the regulation could hardly state more clearly that saturation by either surface or ground water is sufficient to bring an area within the category of wetlands, provided that the saturation is sufficient to and does support wetland vegetation.

The history of the regulation underscores the absence of any requirement of inundation. The interim final regulation that the current regulation replaced explicitly included a requirement of "periodi[c] inundation." 33 C.F.R. §209.120(d)(2)(h) (1976). In deleting the reference to "periodic inundation" from the regulation as finally promulgated, the Corps explained that it was repudiating the interpretation of that language "as requiring inundation over a record period of years." 42 Fed. Reg. 37,128. In fashioning its own requirement of "frequent flooding" the Court of Appeals improperly reintroduced into the regulation precisely what the Corps had excised.

Without the nonexistent requirement of frequent flooding, the regulatory definition of adjacent wetlands covers the property here. The District Court found that respondent's property was "characterized by the presence of vegetation that requires saturated soil conditions for growth and reproduction," App. to Pet. for Cert. 24a, and that the source of the saturated soil conditions on the property was ground water. There is no plausible suggestion that these findings are clearly erroneous, and they plainly bring the property within the category of wetlands as defined by the current regulations. In addition, the court found that the wetland located on respondent's property was adjacent to a body of navigable water, since the area characterized by saturated soil conditions and wetland vegetation extended beyond the boundary of respondent's property to Black Creek, a navigable waterway. Again, the court's finding is not clearly erroneous. Together, these findings establish that respondent's property is a wetland adjacent to a navigable waterway. Hence, it is part of the "waters of the United States" as defined by 33 CFR §323.2 (1985), and if the regulation itself is valid as a construction of the term "waters of the United States" as used in the Clean Water Act, a question which we now address, the property falls within the scope of the Corps' jurisdiction over "navigable waters" under §404 of the Act.

IV

A

An agency's construction of a statute it is charged with enforcing is entitled to deference if it is reasonable and not in conflict with the expressed intent of Congress. Chemical Manufacturers Assn. v. Natural Resources Defense Council, Inc., 470 U.S. —, —, 105 S. Ct. 1102, —, 84 L. Ed. 2d 90 (1985); Chevron, U.S.A., Inc. v. Natural Resources Defense Council, Inc., 467 U.S. —, —, 104 S. Ct. 2778, —, 81 L. Ed. 2d 694 (1984). Accordingly, our review is limited to the question whether it is reasonable, in light of the language, policies, and legislative history of the Act for the Corps to exercise jurisdiction over wetlands adjacent to but not regularly flooded by rivers, streams, and other hydrographic features more conventionally identifiable as "waters."

On a purely linguistic level, it may appear unreasonable to classify "lands," wet or otherwise, as "waters." Such a simplistic response, however, does justice neither to the problem faced by the Corps in defining the scope of its authority under §404(a) nor to the realities of the problem of water pollution that the Clean Water Act was intended to combat. In determining the limits of its power to regulate discharges under the Act, the Corps must necessarily choose some point at which water ends and land begins. Our common experience tells us that this is often no easy task: the transition from water to solid ground is not necessarily or even typically an abrupt one. Rather, between open waters and dry land may lie shallows, marshes, mudflats, swamps, bogs — in short, a huge array of areas that are not wholly aquatic but nevertheless fall far short of being dry land. Where on this continuum to find the limit of "waters" is far from obvious.

Faced with such a problem of defining the bounds of its regulatory authority, an agency may appropriately look to the legislative history and underlying policies of its statutory grants of authority. Neither of these sources provides unambiguous guidance for the Corps in this case, but together they do support the reasonableness of the Corps' approach of defining adjacent wetlands as "waters" within the meaning of §404(a). Section 404 originated as part of the Federal Water Pollution Control Act Amendments of 1972, which constituted a comprehensive legislative attempt "to restore and maintain the chemical, physical, and biological integrity of the Nation's waters." CWA §101, 33 U.S.C. §1251. This objective incorporated a broad, systemic view of the goal of maintaining and improving water quality: as the House Report on the legislation put it, "the word 'integrity' . . . refers to a condition in which the natural structure and function of ecosystems is maintained." H.R. Rep. No. 92-911, p. 76 (1972). Protection of aquatic ecosystems, Congress recognized, demanded broad federal authority to control pollution, for "[w]ater moves in hydrologic cycles and it is essential that discharge of pollutants be controlled at the source." S. Rep. No. 92-414, p. 77 (1972), U.S. Code Cong. & Admin. News 1972, pp. 3668, 3742.

In keeping with these views, Congress chose to define the waters covered by the Act broadly. Although the Act prohibits discharges into "navigable waters," see CWA §§301(a), 404(a), 502(12), 33 U.S.C. §§1311(a), 1344(a), 1362(12), the Act's definition of "navigable waters" as "the waters of the United States" makes it clear that the term "navigable" as used in the Act is of limited import. In adopting this definition of "navigable waters," Congress evidently intended to repudiate limits that had been placed on federal regulation by earlier water pollution control statutes and to exercise its powers under the Commerce Clause to regulate at least some waters that would not be deemed "navigable" under the classical understanding of that term. See S. Conf. Rep. No. 92-1236, p. 144 (1972); 118 Cong. Rec. 33,756-33,757 (1972) (statement of Rep. Dingell).

Of course, it is one thing to recognize that Congress intended to allow regulation of waters that might not satisfy traditional tests of navigability; it is another to assert that Congress intended to abandon traditional notions of "waters" and include in that term "wetlands" as well. Nonetheless, the evident breadth of congressional concern for protection of water quality and aquatic ecosystems suggests that it is reasonable for the Corps to interpret the term "waters" to encompass wetlands adjacent to waters as more conventionally defined. Following the lead of the Environmental Protection Agency, see 38 Fed. Reg. 10,834 (1973), the Corps has determined that wetlands adjacent to navigable waters do as a general matter play a key role in protecting and enhancing water quality:

> The regulation of activities that cause water pollution cannot rely on . . . artificial lines . . . but must focus on all waters that together form the entire aquatic system. Water moves in hydrologic cycles, and the pollution of this part of the aquatic system, regardless of whether it is above or below an ordinary high water mark, or mean high tide line, will affect the water quality of the other waters within that aquatic system. For this reason, the landward limit of Federal jurisdiction under Section 404 must include any adjacent wetlands that form the border of or are in reasonable proximity to other waters of the United States, as these wetlands are part of this aquatic system.

42 Fed. Reg. 37,128 (1977).

We cannot say that the Corps' conclusion that adjacent wetlands are inseparably bound up with the "waters" of the United States — based as it is on the Corps' and EPA's technical expertise — is unreasonable. In view of the breadth of federal regulatory authority contemplated by the Act itself and the inherent difficulties of defining precise bounds to regulable waters, the Corps' ecological judgment about the relationship between waters and their adjacent wetlands provides an adequate basis for a legal judgment that adjacent wetlands may be defined as waters under the Act.

This holds true even for wetlands that are not the result of flooding or permeation by water having its source in adjacent bodies of open water. The Corps has concluded that wetlands may affect the water quality of adjacent lakes, rivers, and streams even when the waters of those bodies do not actually inundate the wetlands. For example, wetlands that are not flooded by adjacent waters may still tend to drain into those waters. In such circumstances, the Corps has concluded that wetlands may serve to filter and purify water draining into adjacent bodies of water, see 33 C.F.R. §320.4(b)(2)(vii) (1985), and to slow the flow of surface runoff into lakes, rivers, and streams and thus prevent flooding and erosion, see §§320.4(b)(2)(iv) and (v). In addition, adjacent wetlands may "serve significant natural biological functions, including food chain production, general habitat, and nesting, spawning, rearing and resting sites for aquatic . . . species." 33 C.F.R. §320.4(b)(2)(i) (1985). In short, the Corps has concluded that wetlands adjacent to lakes, rivers, streams and other bodies of water may function as integral parts of the aquatic environment even when the moisture creating the wetlands does not find its source in the adjacent bodies of water. Again, we cannot say that the Corps' judgment on these matters is unreasonable, and we therefore conclude that a definition of "waters of the United States" encompassing all wetlands adjacent to other bodies of water over which the Corps has jurisdiction is a permissible interpretation of the Act. Because respondent's property is part of a wetland that actually abuts on a navigable water-way, respondent was required to have a permit in this case.

B

Following promulgation of the Corps' interim final regulations in 1975, the Corps' assertion of authority under §404 over waters not actually navigable engendered some congressional opposition. The controversy came to a head during Congress' consideration of the Clean Water Act of 1977, a major piece of legislation aimed at achieving "interim improvements within the existing framework" of the Clean Water Act. H.R. Rep. No. 95-139, pp. 1-2 (1977). In the end, however, as we shall explain, Congress acquiesced in the administrative construction.

Critics of the Corps' permit program attempted to insert limitations on the Corps' §404 jurisdiction into the 1977 legislation: the House bill as reported out of committee proposed a redefinition of "navigable waters" that would have limited the Corps' authority under §404 to waters navigable in fact and their adjacent wetlands (defined as wetlands periodically inundated by contiguous navigable waters). H.R. 3199, 95th Cong., 1st Sess., §16 (1977). The bill reported by the Senate Committee on Environment and Public Works, by contrast, contained no redefinition of the scope of the "navigable waters" covered by §404, and dealt with the perceived problem of overregulation by the Corps by exempting certain activities (primarily agricultural) from the permit requirement and by providing for assumption of some of the Corps' regulatory duties by federally approved state programs. S. 1952, 95th Cong., 1st Sess., §49(b) (1977). On the floor of the Senate, however, an amendment was proposed limiting the scope of "navigable waters" along the lines set forth in the House bill. 123 Cong. Rec. 26,710-26,711 (1977).

In both chambers, debate on the proposals to narrow the definition of navigable waters centered largely on the issue of wetlands preservation. See id., at 10,426-10,432 (House debate); id., at 26,710-26,729 (Senate debate). Proponents of a more limited §404 jurisdiction contended that the Corps' assertion of jurisdiction over wetlands and other nonnavigable "waters" had far exceeded what Congress had intended in enacting §404. Opponents of the proposed changes argued that a narrower definition of "navigable waters" for purposes of §404 would exclude vast stretches of crucial wetlands from the Corps' jurisdiction, with detrimental effects on wetlands ecosystems, water quality, and the aquatic environment generally. The debate, particularly in the Senate, was lengthy. In the House, the debate ended with the adoption of a narrowed definition of "waters"; but in the Senate the limiting amendment was defeated and the old definition retained. The Conference Committee adopted the Senate's approach: efforts to narrow the definition of "waters" were abandoned; the legislation as ultimately passed, in the words of Senator Baker "retain[ed] the comprehensive jurisdiction over the Nation's waters exercised in the 1972 Federal Water Pollution Control Act.". . .

We are thus persuaded that the language, policies, and history of the Clean Water Act compel a finding that the Corps has acted reasonably in interpreting the Act to require permits for the discharge of fill material into wetlands adjacent to the "waters of the United States.". . .

2.   Point and Non-Point Sources

The Clean Water Act divides pollution sources into two categories: point and non-point. There is, of course, no biological rationale for this division. For example, pesticide residues are just as harmful if they are discharged into a river from a chemical company's outfall as they are when they enter drinking water supplies as the result of agricultural runoff. The reason for the distinction is technological and political, and the legal consequences are great. If a source is a point source, an NPDES permit must be obtained and the discharger is subject to the applicable technology-forcing effluent limitations. Congress expressed great faith in the ability of engineers to limit what came out of pipes but less faith in the ability of engineers to fix non-point source pollution:

> There is no effective way as yet, other than land use control, by which you can intercept that runoff and control it in the way that you do a point source. We have not yet developed technology to deal with that kind of a problem. We need to find ways to deal with it, because a great quantity of pollutants is discharged by runoff, not only from agriculture but from construction sites, from streets, from parking lots, and so on, and we have to be concerned with developing controls for them. [Senate Debate on S. 2770, Nov. 2, 1971, reported in 1972 Legislative History, at 1315.]

As the above statement indicates, the solution to non-point pollution involves a complicated mix of institutional and technical factors. To move aggressively against non-point sources of pollution, the federal government would have had to have mandated new local land use control and agricultural practices standards. In 1972 Congress was unwilling to do this directly, so it attempted to address local land use and agricultural management indirectly by shifting the responsibility for non-point pollution control to the states, subject to federal planning in standards. The mandated planning process established §208, 33 U.S.C. §1288, and related sections have been a continuing source of controversy; they are discussed in detail at pp. 384-386 *infra*.

EPA perceived from the beginning that what came out of a pipe did not exhaust the definition of point source, as the next case shows, but it chose not to specify the extent of "non-outfall" point sources. There are relatively few statutory exemptions for point source dischargers. The original major one is for secondary oil and gas recovery operations, 33 U.S.C. §1362(6)(B). As a result of Congress's failure to delineate more clearly the reach of the concept of point source, EPA sought to exempt the most controversial potential non-pipe point sources from the NPDES permit program. These sources included all silvicultural point sources, all confined animal feedlots, and all irrigation return flows from less than 3,000 acres. Natural Resources Defense Council, Inc. v. Costle, 568 F.2d 1369 (D.C. Cir. 1977), rejected EPA's argument that regulation of these sources was administratively unfeasible and invalidated the regulations. The court did hold, however, that EPA could introduce flexibility into its program by issuing general areawide permits for classes of point source dischargers. In 1977 Congress eased EPA's regulatory burden by categorically exempting "return flows from irrigated agriculture" (33 U.S.C. §1362(14)). See United States v. Frezzo Brothers, 642 F.2d 59 (3d Cir. 1981). States remain free to deal with agricultural return flows through the §208 process or their own NPDES permit programs except that the Administrator is prohibited from directly or indirectly requiring any state to subject return flows to a permit program. 33 U.S.C. §1342(l)(1). This is a serious omission and is subject to mounting criticism as the side effects of irrigated agriculture become clearer. In 1982 scientists discovered toxic levels of selenium, a naturally occurring trace element, in the Kesterson National Wildlife Refuge in the Central Valley of California. See page 337 *supra*. Since that time the Department of Interior has identified other areas in the West where trace elements have accumulated in irrigation drainage sinks and in wild life refuges. A National Academy of Sciences Committee — formed to advise the Bureau of Reclamation in its cleanup program — has recommended that the return flow exemption be repealed as part of a broader effort to integrate water quantity and quality law. Committee on Irrigation-Induced Water Quality Problems, Water Science and Technology Board, Commission of Physical Sciences, Mathematics and Resources, National Research Council, Irrigation-Induced Water Quality Problems: What Can Be Learned from the San Joaquin Valley Experience? (National Academy Press, 1989).

UNITED STATES v. EARTH SCIENCES, INC.
599 F.2d 368 (10th Cir. 1979)

The government appeals the district court's conclusion that the FWPCA exempts all mining activities from point sources regulation. Earth Sciences cross-appeals, and defends the trial court's decision on the alternative grounds that Earth Sciences' overflows were not from a "point source," the stream involved in this case was not a "navigable water" under the Act, no person made a "discharge" of the pollutant at issue here, and the government suit was precluded by a prior choice to pursue administrative remedies.

The events which gave rise to this action occurred at Earth Sciences' gold leaching operation on the Rito Seco Creek in Costilla County, Colorado, and were stipulated by the parties. Gold leaching is a process whereby a toxic substance, here a sodium cyanide-sodium hydroxide water solution, is sprayed over a "heap" of gold ore, separating the gold from the ore. The leachate solution is then collected and the gold extracted for commercial sale. The center of Earth Sciences' operation is a 3½- to 4-acre pile of gold ore on top of an impermeable

plastic membrane and 12 inches of sand constructed with a gradual slope, causing the leachate solution to funnel to one end into a small fiberglass-lined pool,
called the primary sump. The solution is pumped from the primary sump into
a processing trailer where the gold is removed, and then back onto the heap or
into the primary sump. A 168,000-gallon reserve sump is available to catch
excess leachate or runoff in emergency situations. The entire operation consists
of several open excavations lined with plastic membrane, the processing trailer
and pumps, all designed to be a closed system without any pollutant discharge.

Warm April temperatures caused faster melting than expected of a blanket
of snow covering the heap, filling the primary and reserve sumps to capacity.
This caused a one- to five-gallon-per-minute discharge of the sodium cyanide-
sodium hydroxide leachate solution in the Rito Seco Creek for about a six-hour
period. The solution is stipulated to be a pollutant under the FWPCA. Earth
Sciences did not report the discharge to either state or federal environmental
authorities.

A few days later the Colorado Division of Wildlife received a report of dead
fish on the Rito Seco, causing a state inspector and two other wildlife employees
to visit the Earth Sciences site. The inspector interviewed Earth Sciences employees and verified that a discharge had occurred. . . .

Because the FWPCA encourages use of approved state enforcement procedures, 33 U.S.C. §§1316(c) and 1319(a)(1), the Environmental Protection
Agency (EPA) requested the Colorado Department of Health to act to prevent
further discharges. The state notified Earth Sciences it had violated Colo. Rev.
Stat. §25-8-501 (1973), which requires a permit to discharge pollutants, and
Colo. Rev. Stat. §25-8-601(2) (1973), allowing for criminal penalties if a discharge is not reported. Colorado ordered Earth Sciences to cease and desist from
further illegal discharges and to "perform any work necessary to prevent future
unauthorized discharges" or stop its operation. . . .

Apparently the EPA decided the Colorado enforcement was insufficient
and issued its own notice of violation and cease and desist order under 33 U.S.C.
§1319(a)(3). . . .

The EPA notice informed Earth Sciences the cyanide solution discharges
violated 33 U.S.C. §1311(a), because Earth Sciences had not applied for and
been granted a permit to discharge pollutants under 33 U.S.C. §1342. The
notice identified an open ditch between the reserve sump and the Rito Seco
Creek as a point source, defined in 33 U.S.C. §1362(14) as

> any discernible, confined and discrete conveyance, including but not limited to
> any pipe, ditch, channel, tunnel, conduit, well, discrete fissure, container, rolling
> stock, concentrated animal feeding operation, or vessel or other floating craft, from
> which pollutants are or may be discharged. This term does not include return flows
> from irrigated agriculture.

Contrasted with the state order, the EPA order was substantially more detailed
and required Earth Sciences submit a plan to assure future discharges would not
occur.

Five days after the EPA order was issued, a sampling team of two EPA employees visited the Earth Sciences site. Groundwater seeps of approximately one gallon per minute were observed below the sumps running toward the Rito Seco and partially gathering into pools near the creek. Samples taken from two of these pools were found to contain cyanide.

Earth Sciences' compliance with the EPA order reaffirmed the capacity of the reserve sump system against maximum recorded precipitation, and identified several steps Earth Sciences would take to divert the natural runoff away from the leaching facilities. Earth Sciences also assured the EPA it would monitor groundwater seeps around the sumps and the quality and quantity of the runoff.

Soon thereafter the United States filed suit, alleging Earth Sciences committed three separate violations of FWPCA, one each time the reserve sump overflowed and one as a result of the tests on the water collected from the groundwater seeps. All three violations were asserted under 33 U.S.C. §1311(a). . . .

Because nonpoint sources of pollution, such as oil and gas runoffs caused by rainfall on the highways, are virtually impossible to isolate to one polluter, no permit or regulatory system was established as to them. Rather, the EPA is instructed under 33 U.S.C. §1314(f) to develop

> (1) guidelines for identifying and evaluating the nature and extent of nonpoint sources of pollutants, and (2) processes, procedures, and methods to control pollution resulting from —
> (A) agricultural and silvicultural activities, including runoff from fields and crops and forest lands;
> (B) mining activities, including runoff and siltation from new, currently operating, and abandoned surface and underground mines;
> (C) all construction activity, including runoff from the facilities resulting from such construction; . . .

Based on its reading of the legislative history, the district court interpreted §1314(f) as exempting those activities listed in (2) from the FWPCA enforcement provisions, due to their character as nonpoint source polluters. After the court decided Earth Sciences' gold leaching facility was a mining activity, dismissal of the government's suit followed because the government no longer had any enforcement power under §1311(a) to bring a civil action. Appellant United States contends the district court's conclusion is an incorrect interpretation of the law.

I

The United States argues discharges from mining activities often may be from nonpoint sources, but it is possible pollutants will be conveyed through a point source and be subject to regulation under the Act. Initially, the government argues, the definition of a point source does not exclude mining activity; the district court interpolated an exemption from the structure of §1314(f). The United States contends that if Congress wanted to exempt all activities in

§1314(f)(2) because they are listed after subpart (1), it would not have done so ambiguously by placing the exemption in a general instruction section of the statute. It further points out that Congress rejected an amendment that would have explicitly regulated mining discharges from point sources, because it was duplicative of the Act's general regulatory provisions. Congress also debated and eventually adopted an amendment exempting irrigation discharges because those would have been included under general point source regulations. Congressional intent behind FWPCA was to eliminate "discharge of pollutants into the navigable waters" of the United States by 1985. 33 U.S.C. §1251. The EPA was instructed to promulgate regulations within a year governing effluent limitations for point source regulation. 33 U.S.C. §1314(b). Because the agency had not issued those regulations within a year, a suit was brought forcing them to do so, the result being that a federal district court established a timetable for EPA compliance. Natural Resources Defense Council, Inc. v. Train, 6 E.R.C. 1033 (D.D.C. 1973), aff'd in part, rev'd in part on other grounds, 510 F.2d 692 (1975). That court order included mining activities as a category for EPA regulations.

In fact the EPA has promulgated extensive regulations covering mining, 40 C.F.R. pt. 434, 436 and 440 (1977), and more than 6,000 discharge permits have been applied for or received by mining operations. . . .

In a suit challenging the EPA's authority to exclude all silvicultural and certain agricultural discharges from point source regulation, two of the categories listed in §1314(f), the United States Court of Appeals for the District of Columbia held, "The wording of the statute, legislative history, and precedents are clear: the EPA Administrator does not have authority to exempt categories of point sources from the permit requirements of §402." Natural Resources Defense Council, Inc. v. Costle, 568 F.2d 1369, 1377 (1977). The D.C. Circuit agreed with the district court in that case "that the power to define point and nonpoint sources is vested in EPA and should be reviewed by the court only after opportunity for full agency review and examination." . . .

Any time a comprehensive Congressional regulatory program is enacted the legislative history is relevant for determining Congressional intent. In another context we have noted the legislative history behind the FWPCA "does not help us much." American Petroleum Inst. v. EPA, 540 F.2d 1023, 1027 (10th Cir. 1976), cert. denied, 430 U.S. 922 (1977). But in our view the government has the better of the arguments on legislative history.

We are impressed by the rejection of the proposed Hechler amendment on mine water wastes, as being based upon the view mining was already covered by the proposed Act (See Staff of Senate Comm. on Public Works, 93d Cong., 1st Sess., A Legislative History of the Water Pollution Control Act Amendments of 1972, 530-535 (Comm. Print 1973)); the debate and later adoption of the irrigation water exception from the definition of point sources in 33 U.S.C. §1362(14) as being necessary to prevent it from being covered by the permit requirements (Id. 651-653); and the fact the FWPCA's permit program superceded the Refuse Act's permit program while preserving its general prohibition against unpermitted discharges (33 U.S.C. §§1342(a)(5), 1371(a)). The Refuse Act has been held to prevent unpermitted discharges of mining wastes. See Reserve Mining Co. v. EPA, 514 F.2d 492, 529-532 (8th Cir. 1975), *modified*, 529 F.2d 181 (1976); United States v. Valley Camp Coal Co., 480 F.2d 616 (4th Cir. 1973).

The legislative history indicates to us Congress was classifying nonpoint source pollution as disparate runoff caused primarily by rainfall around activities that employ or cause pollutants. . . .

Beginning with the Congressional intent to eliminate pollution from the nation's waters by 1985, the FWPCA was designed to regulate to the fullest extent possible those sources emitting pollution into rivers, streams and lakes. The touch-stone of the regulatory scheme is that those needing to use the waters for waste distribution must seek and obtain a permit to discharge that waste, with the quantity and quality of the discharge regulated. The concept of a point source was designed to further this scheme by embracing the broadest possible definition of any identifiable conveyance from which pollutants might enter the waters of the United States. It is clear from the legislative history Congress would have regulated so-called nonpoint sources if a workable method could have been derived; it instructed the EPA to study the problem and come up with a solution.

We believe it contravenes the intent of FWPCA and the structure of the statute to exempt from regulation any activity that emits pollution from an identifiable point. Therefore, we hold the district court erred interpreting 33 U.S.C. §1314(f) as enumerating nonpoint source exemptions from FWPCA enforcement regulations. Mining and the other categories listed in §1314(f)(2) may involve discharges from both point and nonpoint sources, and those from point sources are subject to regulation.

NOTES AND QUESTIONS

1. *Earth Sciences* was followed in Sierra Club v. Abston Construction Co., 620 F.2d 41 (5th Cir. 1980), which held that a mine operator was liable for spoil piles that caused pollution after rainfall ultimately carried pollutants into navigable waters through erosion-created ditches and gullies. See also United States v. Oxford Royal Mushroom Products, Inc. 487 F. Supp. 852 (E.D. Pa. 1980) (self-contained spray irrigation waste treatment system that leaked because too much waste water was sprayed on absorbing field). In 1987 Congress added the following amendment to Section 402. 33 U.S.C. §1342 (1)(2):

> The Administrator shall not require a permit under this section, nor shall the Administrator directly or indirectly require any State to require a permit, for discharges of stormwater runoff from mining operations or oil and gas exploration . . . , composed entirely of flows which are from conveyances or systems of conveyances (including but not limited to pipes, conduits, ditches, and channels) used for collecting and conveying precipitation runoff and which are not contaminated

by contact with, any overburden, raw material, intermediate products, finished product, byproducts, or waste products located on the site of such operations

Does it reverse *Earth Sciences*?

2. Which of the following might be a point source? A dredge and fill operation conducted by heavy equipment? See Avoyelles Sportsmen's League v. Alexander, 473 F. Supp. 525 (W.D. La. 1979), and United States v. Weisman, 489 F. Supp. 1331 (M.D. Fla. 1980). A deep waste injection well? See Exxon v. Train, 554 F.2d 1310 (5th Cir. 1977). A hydroelectric dam that threatens to lower oxygen levels downstream? This issue was first raised in South Carolina Wildlife Federation v. Alexander, 457 F. Supp. 118 (D.S.C. 1978). The issue was first resolved in National Wildlife Federation v. Gorsuch, 530 F. Supp. 1291, (D.D.C. 1982), which held that the Administrator of the federal EPA had violated a nondiscretionary duty to designate dams as point sources of pollution under §402 of the Clean Water Act, but the decision was reversed on appeal. 693 F.2d 156 (D.C. Cir. 1982). Judge Wald, writing for a unanimous panel, held that EPA reasonably refused to classify dams as point sources of pollution. Neither the statutory nor the legislative definitions of "pollutant" or "pollution" were found inconsistent with EPA's decision. The district court had relied heavily on the zero discharge goal of the Act to support its construction of the Act, but the District of Columbia Circuit Court of Appeals found that the goal was not a legal command because "Congress recognized that the substantive provisions of the Act fall short of completely achieving the announced goals of the Act." The Court also concluded that "Congress did not want to interfere any more than necessary with state water management of which dams are an important component." Section 101(g), 33 U.S.C. §1251, added in 1977 — the Wallop Amendment, proposed by Senator Wallop of Wyoming — was cited in support of this conclusion. Section 101(g) provides: "[I]t is the policy of Congress that the authority of each state to allocate quantities of water within its jurisdiction shall not be superceded, abrogated, or otherwise impaired. . . ." Effective regulation of dam-caused pollution was found to be too tied up with non-point sources and water management programs not concerned with water quality to augur well for effective control through NPDES permits. See also Missouri ex rel. Ashcroft v. Department of the Army, 672 F.2d 1297 (8th Cir. 1982), which summarily affirmed a district court finding, 526 F. Supp. 660 (W.D. Mo. 1980), that a Corps of Engineers dam that discharged oxygen depleted water did not cause pollution.

A district court refused to apply *Gorsuch* to the discharge of dead fish killed by the turbines of a pumped storage plant, National Wildlife Federation v. Consumers Power Co., 657 F. Supp. 989 (W.D. Mich. 1987). but the court of appeals found that the two cases were the same because neither involved the "addition of any pollutant to navigable waters within the meaning of Section 502(12), 33 U.S.C. §1362(12)(A). 862 F.2d 580 (6th Cir. 1988). The court suggested that the issue would be best addressed by the Federal Energy Regulatory commission, which licenses the plant.

A NOTE ON THE §208 PROGRAM

Section 208 areawide plans are, on paper, the core of the water pollution abatement program, but the program has not fulfilled its promise. Section 208 allocates planning authority among federal, state, and local officials in a multi-step process. First, subject to EPA approval and after consultation with local officials, the governor must specially designate areas with "substantial water quality control problems" and must select an areawide planning agency for each designated area (e.g., the Councils of Governments). The state serves as the planning agency for nondesignated areas. See Natural Resources Defense Council, Inc. v. Costle, 568 F.2d 1369 (D.C. Cir. 1977). Second, each agency must develop a plan ("management strategy") that identifies pollution control techniques and the institutions through which the comprehensive management scheme will be carried out, such as zoning, PUDs (planned unit developments), easements, economic incentives, subsidies and intergovernmental agreements. See generally R. Ellickson & A. Tarlock, Land Use Controls (1981). Third, EPA must approve the plan and the local management agency selected to implement the plan. However, unlike the SIPs studied in Chapter 3, EPA cannot write its own §208 plan if the state's plan is inadequate.

Subject to a rigorous timetable, the plan includes controls of both point and non-point source discharges. It covers the location and construction of facilities under §201 (construction grant program), area NPDES permits, groundwater protection, and financial and managerial measures necessary to execute the plan. The completed §208 areawide plan is then incorporated in the §303(e) state plan.

The §208 mandate is a monument to systematic, rational processes. Based on a correct assessment of water quality problems, §208 proceeds relentlessly to specify logical solutions: build treatment capacity only where needed; issue NPDES permits only where water quality will be protected; use appropriate non-technology-based land use controls to curtail non-point urban, agricultural, construction, and silvicultural runoff; attack needs on a "problem-shed" basis. But the §208 program is at odds with two major premises that underlie the federal water pollution control program. First, §208 planning was delegated to regional agencies rather than to the state agencies responsible for administering the NPDES program. Second, §208 introduced a planning process at odds with the technological pollution control requirements Congress mandated to clean up the nation's waters. Hostility to the program inside EPA and a number of implementation problems weakened the §208 planning effort. These problems included the short time frame allowed for the planning process, erratic federal funding, lack of adequate data, and intergovernmental conflicts at the regional level. State water pollution control agencies objected to the delegation of authority at the regional level and ultimately convinced EPA to allow the state agencies to exert substantial control over the regional water quality planning process.

The regulatory program proved most controversial. The Act can be interpreted to require a §208 land use control program regulating any "facility" affecting the discharge of water pollution. Since the regulatory program was to be administered by a regional agency, local governments resisted this displacement of their regulatory authority over land use. EPA responded to local government resistance by authorizing the delegation of regulatory authority to local governments and by downplaying the land use control component.

The other elements of the §208 plan proved equally difficult to implement. Planning for treatment plants often came only after major funding and site location decisions had been made. Sewage grant funding is discussed at pp. 457-461 *infra*. Thus, local and regional efforts to manage growth were undercut by the Clean Water Act, which creates a developmental bias by limiting the issue in waste treatment facility approval to where the plants and pipes should go — never touching the issue of whether plants and pipes were to be constructed at all. In addition to the sources cited in the introduction to this chapter, see Environmental Law Institute, Legal and Institutional Approaches to Water Quality Management Planning and Implementation (EPA, 1977); Note, Sewers, Clean Water, and Planned Growth: Restructuring the Federal Pollution Abatement Effort, 86 Yale L.J. 733 (1977); Quarles, Federal Regulation of New Industrial Plants, 10 Envt. Rep. (BNA) Monograph No. 28 (1979); Tripp, Tensions and Conflicts in Federal Pollution Control and Water Resource Policy, 14 Harv. J. on Legis. 225 (1977); Wilkins, The Implementation of Water Pollution Control Measures — Section 208 of the Water Pollution Control Act Amendments, 15 Land & Water L. Rev. 479 (1980).

Regional §208 agencies did address non-point water pollution problems, but non-point source pollution is politically difficult to remedy. Legislative authority for non-point pollution control often is either nonexistent or inadequate. See generally Uchtmann & Seitz, Options for Controlling Nonpoint Source Water Pollutants, A Legal Perspective, 19 Nat. Resources J. 587 (1979). Agricultural interests resisted the application of non-point controls to farming even though water runoff from agricultural pursuits is a major water pollution source in many areas. See Note, Agricultural Nonpoint Source Water Pollution Control under Sections 208 and 303 of the Clean Water Act: Has Forty Years of Experience Taught Us Anything? 54 N.D.L. Rev. 589 (1978). Section 208 requires EPA to adopt the best management practice guidelines, and §208(j) establishes a cooperative program between EPA and the Department of Agriculture to fund non-point management practices through the Soil Conservation Service. A BPM is a control measure for slowing, retaining, or absorbing pollutants produced by non-point surface run-off. See generally Farming & Groundwater: An Introduction (Agricultural Law & Policy Institute Issues Booklet No. 1 (1988)) and Sivas, Groundwater Protection From Agricultural Activities: Policies For Protection, 7 Stan. Envtl. L.J. 117 (1987-1988). What little legal precedent exists supports the use of agricultural land use controls. See Woodbury County Soil Conservation District v. Ortner, 279 N.W.2d 276 (Iowa 1979), noted in 65 Iowa L. Rev. 1035 (1980), which holds that a soil conservation district order requiring farmer to adopt erosion control practices is not a taking. The liability of an occupier of land for soil erosion is discussed in Note, Moser v. Thorpe

Sales Corporation, 312 N.W.2d 881 (Iowa 1981): The Protection of Farmland from Poor Farming Practices, 27 S.D.L. Rev. 513 (1982). See generally 1 J. Juergensmeyer & J. Wadley, Agricultural Law §7.10.3 (1982), for a discussion of the operations of the Soil Conservation Service.

Despite these difficulties, EPA responded to congressional criticism late in the Carter Administration by redirecting the program to non-point pollution problems. All of the §208 plans have now been approved, but the program seemed finished as both the Carter and Reagan Administrations recommended termination. Congress rescued it in 1981 with continued funding, but the program is currently moribund.

The Water Quality Act of 1987 mounts a new non-point source initiative. The Act establishes a national policy to control non-point sources of pollution "in an expeditious manner so as to enable the goals of this Act to be met through the control of both point and non-point sources of pollution." H.R. Conference Report No. 1004, 99th Cong., 2d Sess. 143 (1986). Section 319 requires that states identify waters threatened by non-point sources of pollution and prepare four-year watershed-based management programs to control non-point source pollution. The 319 program is linked to neither the water quality planning programs nor the water quality standards maintenance program. Four hundred million dollars is authorized over four years for state grants to implement agricultural and urban non-point source management programs. EPA approval is subject to vigorous deadlines. The program must identify the BAT management practices that the state will adopt, including the regulatory and non-regulatory programs, and establish a schedule containing annual milestones. The Act returns to the 1960s concept of the management conference to deal with interstate non-point source pollution. The same technique is used for estuarine pollution. Section 320. See generally Davidson, Little Waters: The Relationship between Water Pollution and Agricultural Drainage, 17 Envtl. L. Rep. (News and Analysis) 10, 074 (1987) and Thinking about Nonpoint Sources of Water Pollution and South Dakota Agriculture, 34 S.D.L. Rev. 20 (1989).

The critical implementation question is whether §319 requires states to adopt a regulatory program for controlling nonpoint pollution or whether it requires only a process for the consideration of nonpoint pollution problems at the state level. Congressional debate on §319 indicates that Congress did not intend a federal program that would require states to adopt regulatory controls. The division of the nonpoint source program into separate assessment report and management report stages, and the delegation of authority to EPA to revise only the assessment report, confirms this interpretation. Senator Mitchell emphasized the different role of EPA at each stage when he explained that §319 "does not provide for Federal intervention in State and local planning decisions." He added that the legislation does not "direct" states to adopt regulatory programs for the control of nonpoint pollution. "If a State decides that it does not want a program to control nonpoint pollution, that is it." [133 Cong. Rec. S 1698 (daily ed. 1987).]

Congress did include a federal consistency provision in §319 that may provide an important incentive to state participation in the non-point source program. The federal consistency provision in §319 is a form of "reverse federal preemption" similar to the federal consistency provision contained in the National Coastal Zone Management Act. The federal consistency provision in §319 requires states to identify federal financial assistance programs and development projects to determine whether they are consistent with their non-point source programs.

D.   WATER QUALITY STANDARDS: THEORY AND CURRENT FUNCTION

As discussed in the introduction to this chapter, water quality standards were the heart of the pre-1972 federal regulatory program. A Senate report on the predecessor of the 1972 Federal Water Pollution Control Act Amendments, the proposed Federal Water Pollution Control Act Amendments of 1971, explained the theory of the 1965 Act:

> The standards are intended to function in two ways:
> 1. As a measure of performance, the standards are expected to establish the maximum level of pollution allowable in interstate waters.
> 2. The standards also are intended to provide an avenue of legal action against polluters. If the wastes discharged by polluters reduce water quality below the standards, actions may be begun against the polluters. [S. Rep. No. 414, 92d Cong., 1st Sess. 4 (1971).]

The theory did not work out. States dragged their feet in submitting standards, and enforcement was nil. By 1971, despite considerable efforts by the states to control pollution through water quality standards, Congress concluded that this approach was hopelessly flawed and that a switch to effluent limitations was necessary. Senate Report 411 went on to pinpoint the major flaw in a receiving water quality approach: "Water quality standards, in addition to their deficiencies in relying on the assimilative capacity of receiving waters, often cannot be translated into effluent limitations — defendable by court tests because of the imprecision of models for water quality and the effects of effluents in most waters" (Senate Report 414, at 18).

Many members of the Senate wanted to drop the water quality standards approach entirely, but in the end the Senate accepted a House amendment to continue and expand the program. Thus, the BPT and BAT effluent limitations were superimposed on the existing interstate standards and additional standards were required for interstate waters. The House defended the superimposition on

the ground that enforcement of effluent limitations would be strengthened, not
weakened:

> Section 301(b)(1)(C) requires that water quality standards shall be achieved
> not later than July 1, 1977. The water quality standard requirements are not in-
> tended to be in lieu of the technological requirements for 1977 but are required to
> be the basis for water quality control if they are more stringent than the effluent
> limitations determined by "best practicable control technology currently available."
> For example, if there are a multitude of point sources on a given stretch of water,
> the potential of exceeding the water quality standards exists even though each point
> source is meeting best practicable control technology. If "best practicable control
> technology" in this or in any other situation is inadequate to meet the water quality
> standards, the managers clearly intend that each point source shall be required to
> meet effluent limitations which would be consistent with the applicable water qual-
> ity standard. [1972 Legislative History, at 246 (remarks of Mr. Harsha).]

The best that the Senate could do was to direct the EPA in the Senate Conference Report to give priority to implementing the effluent limitations and
NPDES programs at the expense of the standards process (1972 Legislative History, at 171).

EPA was faithful to the Senate's directive, but the standard-setting process
has gone forward. Standards are based on water quality criteria promulgated by
the EPA. The basic document is the 1976 "Red Book," EPA, Quality Criteria
for Water (Office of Water and Hazardous Materials, 1976). As the result of
litigation between EPA and the Natural Resources Defense Council, EPA agreed
to publish criteria documents for 64 of the 65 toxic pollutants listed under
§307(a)(1), 33 U.S.C. §1317(a)(1) (45 Fed. Reg. 79,318). Under the 1987
Amendments, when a state revises its water quality standards, it must adopt specific numerical criteria for priority toxic pollutants; the states are required to
adopt water quality criteria published under §304(a) for these pollutants if the
discharge or presence of such pollutants could reasonably be expected to interfere
with the state's designated water uses. If water quality criteria have not been
published for the pollutants in question, the state must adopt criteria based on
biological monitoring or assessment methods. Section 308(d). States must list
those streams where applicable water quality standards cannot be expected to be
met because of the presence of toxic pollutants, and thus there will be insufficient water quality to ensure protection of health, public water supplies, agricultural and industrial uses, marine recreational uses, and the protection and
propagation of marine life. If the state fails to act, the Administrator may implement the necessary requirements and control strategies.

Red Book criteria are used for all other pollutants. Because water quality
standards constitute an additional level of effluent reduction to which a
discharger may be subject, the question of what standards apply on a given
reach of stream is very important, as the next case and the Notes following it
illustrate.

MISSISSIPPI COMMISSION ON NATURAL RESOURCES v. COSTLE
625 F.2d 1269 (5th Cir. 1980)

FAY, Circuit Judge:

The Mississippi Commission on Natural Resources (Commission) challenges the authority of the United States Environmental Protection Agency (EPA) to promulgate a water quality standard on dissolved oxygen for Mississippi. The Commission filed a complaint seeking a declaratory judgment that EPA's rejection of the state standard and promulgation of a federal standard were arbitrary, capricious, and beyond EPA's authority. The Commission sought a preliminary and permanent injunction against enforcement of EPA's standard. The district court granted the preliminary injunction. After cross-motions for summary judgment, the court granted judgment to EPA and dissolved the preliminary injunction. The Commission appeals pursuant to 28 U.S.C. §1291 (1976). We affirm the district court. . . .

. . . EPA can promulgate standards if the state does not set standards consistent with the Act or whenever EPA determines that another "standard is necessary to meet the requirements of [the Act]." State standards are reviewed every three years. 33 U.S.C. §1313 (1976). NPDES permits must contain not only any effluent limitations set by EPA and the states, but also any more stringent limits necessary to reach the water quality standards. Id. §1311(b). If EPA determines that limits on discharges from a source or group of sources are insufficient for the water quality set for that area, it can, after hearing, set effluent limitations designed to reach that standard. Id. §1312. In addition, EPA must develop and publish "criteria for water quality accurately reflecting the latest scientific knowledge." Id. §1314.

II.   Facts

The dispute in this case arises from EPA's refusal to approve the Mississippi water quality standard for dissolved oxygen (DO) and EPA's subsequent promulgation of a DO standard. Dissolved oxygen is necessary for the protection and propagation of fish and aquatic life, and is generally measured in milligrams per liter (mg/l).

In 1946, the Mississippi Game and Fish Commission adopted a regulation requiring a minimum average DO concentration of 3.0 mg/l and an instantaneous minimum of 2.5 mg/l. Under this standard, the DO concentration could drop as low as 2.5 so long as compensating periods at higher concentrations raised the daily average to 3.0 mg/l.

In response to state and federal legislation, the Commission adopted standards on January 17, 1967 requiring a minimum daily average DO of 4.0 mg/

l. The 1972 amendments to the Act allowed preexisting water quality standards to remain in effect upon approval by EPA. 33 U.S.C. §1313(a)(1)-(2) (1976). These standards were approved in October, 1972.

On January 18, 1973, EPA advised the Commission that it was time for the triennial review of its standards. After public hearings, the Commission submitted to EPA a DO standard of not less than an average of 5.0 mg/l, but allowing a level of 4.0 mg/l during periods with extremely low water levels.[2] The low flow standard applies to days with the lowest water level that occurs for seven consecutive days in ten years (7 days Q 10). On May 15, 1973, EPA approved the Commission's water quality standards, stating they were in "full compliance with the 1972 Amendments to the Federal Water Pollution Control Act."

As noted above, one of EPA's duties under the amendments is to develop and publish "criteria for water quality accurately reflecting the latest scientific knowledge." 33 U.S.C. §1314(a)(1) (1976). These criteria were to be published one year after October 18, 1972 and from time to time thereafter. Id. EPA gave notice of the availability of Quality Criteria for Water, also called the Red Book, on October 26, 1973. It thereafter became EPA's policy to request a state to justify its standards whenever the state submitted for approval water quality criteria less stringent than those in the Red Book.

In 1976, at the time for Mississippi's triennial review, EPA conferred with the Commission about upgrading its DO standard. Although the likelihood of the 7 day Q 10 rate's occurring for seven straight days is only once in ten years, that particular low flow rate actually occurs for significant periods virtually every year. In addition, the 4.0 mg/l 7 day Q 10 standard is an average, which therefore allows the DO level to fall below 4.0 on numerous occasions each year. Higher DO concentrations reduce crowding of fish and the resulting susceptibility to disease and toxicants. Adult fish generally are more tolerant of lower DO levels than juvenile forms. Lower levels also interfere with fish spawning.

The Commission forwarded to EPA for comment a proposed standard which required 5.0 mg/l with an instantaneous minimum of 4.0 mg/l, but allowed the DO to range between 5.0 and 4.0 for short periods. The Commission also proposed a higher standard of 5.0 mg/l for shellfish harvesting areas. In March, 1977, the Commission held hearings on the proposal. EPA advised that the proposal appeared to meet the Act's requirements. The Commission, how-

---

2.   The Mississippi standard reads as follows:

Dissolved Oxygen: For diversified warm-water biota, including game fish, daily dissolved oxygen concentration shall be maintained at a minimum of not less than 4.0 mg/l during the low 7-day, one-in-ten years flow. However, at all greater flows dissolved oxygen shall be maintained at not less than 5.0 mg/l, assuming there are normal seasonal and daily variations above this level; except that under extreme conditions, with the same stipulations as to seasonal and daily variations, the dissolved oxygen level may range between 5.0 mg/l and 4.0 mg/l for short periods of time, provided that the water quality is maintained in favorable conditions in all other respects.

That the 4.0 concentration is an average is clear from documents supplied to EPA by the Commission. Record, Appendix C, at 208.

ever, abandoned the proposal and on April 22, 1977, submitted to EPA its existing 5.0 mg/l − 4.0 mg/l 7 days Q 10 standard.

On June 9, 1977, EPA notified the Commission that it questioned the adequacy of the DO criteria. Specifically, Mississippi's DO standard was the only one in its region below 5.0 for 7 day Q 10 conditions, and it was below the 5.0 mg/l criteria established in the Red Book. In accordance with its policy, EPA requested justification for the lower standard. The Commission sent its report on July 21. Pending review of the report, EPA disapproved the DO criteria. On August 24, 1977, EPA notified the Commission that it found Mississippi's justification unpersuasive. EPA gave the Commission until October 24, 1977 to promulgate an appropriate standard. EPA recommended a daily average of 5.0 mg/l and a minimum of 4.0 mg/l.

The Commission reconsidered its standard in September, 1977, and decided the state's standard was in the public interest.

EPA found this action insufficient and on July 13, 1978, proposed a DO standard of 5.0 mg/l at all times. In September, 1978, two public hearings were held in Mississippi as part of the rulemaking process. In response to public comment, EPA revised its proposed rule and adopted the less stringent standard of 5.0 mg/l daily average with an instantaneous minimum of not less than 4.0 mg/l. This standard, which was promulgated April 24, 1979, was very similar to the one initially proposed and then abandoned by the Commission when the 1976 triennial review began.

The Commission then filed this action for an injunction and declaratory judgment.

III.   The Commission's Position

The Commission argues that EPA exceeded its powers both in its disapproval of the state DO criteria and in its promulgation of a federal standard. As to the disapproval, the Commission emphasizes that Congress intended for the states to have primary responsibility in setting water quality standards. The Commission reasons that EPA therefore cannot substitute its judgment for the state's unless the state standard is arbitrary, capricious, or totally unreasonable. According to the Commission, since the same standard was approved in 1973, it cannot be disapproved now. Furthermore, EPA can only disapprove standards that fail to meet the requirements of the Act. The Commission argues that EPA is enforcing its policies as though they were the Act's requirements. In addition, the Commission claims that EPA improperly failed to consider economic factors in evaluating the DO criteria and that EPA ignored and misinterpreted evidence presented at hearings.

The Commission also attacks EPA's promulgation of its own standard. Because EPA did not promulgate the standard within ninety days, it therefore, according to the Commission, lost the power to act. The Commission also claims that nothing in the record supports a 4.0 mg/l instantaneous minimum. The standards in nearby states are irrelevant. The Commission asserts that Mississippi's flat topography and subtropical summer climate result in naturally low DO concentrations. According to the Commission, Congress intended for the individual states to account for these regional variations in setting criteria and did not intend for these differences to be ignored for the sake of bureaucratic uniformity.

IV.   The District Court's Order

The district court acknowledged that states are given the first opportunity to establish water quality standards, but held that states were not given unfettered discretion. Although the court agreed that EPA had missed its deadline for promulgating the standard, it disagreed on the result that produced. The court held that section 706 of the Administrative Procedures Act (APA) required consideration of whether the state had been prejudiced by delay, and held that no prejudice had been shown. The court addressed the state's substantive challenges to EPA's decisions and held that the agency's actions were justifiable and reasonable, not arbitrary or capricious. . . .

For EPA to promulgate a water quality standard, it must determine that the state's standard "is not consistent with the applicable requirements of [the Act]" or that "a revised or new standard is necessary to meet the requirements of [the Act]" 33 U.S.C. §1313(c)(3), (c)(4)(B) (1976). Review is therefore centered around two issues: first, whether EPA's disapproval of Mississippi's DO standard was proper; and second, whether EPA properly promulgated the substitute standard. The relevant statutory, substantive, and procedural aspects of each issue will be considered.

VI.   Disapproval of Mississippi's Standard

A.   SCOPE OF AUTHORITY

The Commission contends that EPA exceeded its statutory authority by tipping the balance of federal and state power created by Congress in the FWPCA. The Commission argues that EPA may substitute its judgment only if a state fails to act or acts irresponsibly. Furthermore, the Commission asserts that EPA misconstrues its authority as allowing disapprovals of standards that do not meet the requirements of EPA policy instead of those not meeting the requirements of the Act.

Congress did place primary authority for establishing water quality standards with the states. . . . [T]he legislative history reflects congressional concern that the Act not place in the hands of a federal administrator absolute power over zoning watershed areas. The varied topographies and climates in the country call for varied water quality solutions.

Despite this primary allocation of power, the states are not given unreviewable discretion to set water quality standards. All water quality standards must be submitted to the federal Administrator. 33 U.S.C. §1313(c)(2) (1976). The state must review its standards at least once every three years and make the results of the review available to the Administrator. Id. §1313(c)(1). EPA is given the final voice on the standard's adequacy:

> If the Administrator determines that any such revised or new standard is not consistent with the applicable requirements of this chapter, he shall not later than the ninetieth day after the date of submission of such standard notify the State and specify the changes to meet such requirements. If such changes are not adopted by the State within ninety days after the date of notification, the Administrator shall promulgate such standard pursuant to paragraph (4) of this subsection.

Id. §1313(c)(3). In addition, EPA can override state water quality standards by changing the effluent limits in NPDES permits whenever a source interferes with water quality. Id. §1312.

EPA's role also is more dominant when water quality criteria are in question. Although the designation of uses and the setting of criteria are interrelating chores, the specification of a waterway as one for fishing, swimming, or public water supply is closely tied to the zoning power Congress wanted left with the states. The criteria set for a specific use are more amenable to uniformity. Congress recognized this distinction by placing with EPA the duty to develop and publish water quality criteria reflecting the latest scientific knowledge shortly after the amendment's passage and periodically thereafter. Id. §1314(a)(1). EPA correctly points out that by leaving intact the Mississippi use designations it has acted in the manner least intrusive of state prerogatives. Nothing indicates a congressional intent to restrict EPA's review of state standards to the issue of whether the state acted arbitrarily or capriciously. The FWPCA requires EPA to determine whether the standard is "consistent with" the Act's requirements. The Commission argues that the Administrator has improperly construed his power as authorizing disapproval of state standards that do not meet EPA policy as embodied in the Red Book.

The statute enumerates the following requirements for water quality standards:

> Such standards shall be such as to protect the public health or welfare, enhance the quality of water and serve the purposes of this chapter. Such standards shall be established taking into consideration their use and value for public water supplies, propagation of fish and wildlife, recreational purposes, and agricultural, industrial, and other purposes, and also taking into consideration their use and value for navigation.

33 U.S.C. §1313(c)(2) (1976). One purpose of the Act is "the national goal that wherever attainable, an interim goal of water quality which provides for the protection and propagation of fish, shellfish, and wildlife and provides for recreation in and on the water be achieved by July 1, 1983." Id. §1251(a)(2). The EPA Administrator did not improperly construe his authority by interpreting the FWPCA as allowing him to translate these broad statutory guidelines and goals into specifics that could be used to evaluate a state's standard. One "requirement of the Act" is that EPA formulate these policies for water quality criteria. Id. §1314(a)(1). It was not unreasonable for the EPA Administrator to interpret the Act as allowing him to require states to justify standards not in conformance with the criteria policy. . . .

We conclude that EPA did not exceed its statutory authority in disapproving the state water quality standard. . . .

With a position that contains both procedural and substantive elements, the Commission argues that EPA's approval of the 5.0 − 4.0 7 day Q 10 standard in 1973 estops EPA's disapproval of it now and renders EPA's action unreasonable. This position overlooks the congressional goal of attaining fishable and swimmable waters by 1983. Triennial review of state standards is a means of evolving and upgrading water quality standards. In addition, the Act authorizes EPA to set standards whenever the Administrator determines that a revised standard is necessary to meet the FWPCA's requirements. 33 U.S.C. §1313(c)(4)(B) (1976). If EPA were bound by its prior approvals, this power would be meaningless. We also note that the prior approval in this case was before the statutory deadline for developing criteria under §1314 and before the Red Book was published.

The Commission asserts that EPA failed to consider all relevant factors by excluding economic considerations in setting the DO criteria. EPA determined that while economic factors are to be considered in designating uses, those factors are irrelevant to the scientific and technical factors to be considered in setting criteria to meet those uses. 44 Fed. Reg. 25,223, -24, -26 (April 30, 1979). When criteria cannot be attained because of economic factors, EPA states that the particular water can be designated for a less restrictive use, a process called "downgrading." Id. at 25,224. The Commission argues that the statute's requirement that "use and value" be considered in setting standards makes economic factors relevant to both the designation of uses and the setting of criteria. 33 U.S.C. §1313(c)(2) (1976). Furthermore, it claims that EPA's policies against downgrading make its suggested solution illusory.

We note at the outset that EPA states it did examine the economic impact of its criteria and "concluded that a significant impact [was] not likely to occur." 44 Fed. Reg. at 25,225-26. Nevertheless, we are convinced that EPA's construction is correct. See E. I. du Pont de Nemours & Co. v. Train, 430 U.S. 112, at 134-35. Congress itself separated use and criteria and stated that "the water quality criteria for such waters [shall be] based on such uses." 33 U.S.C. §1313(c)(2) (1976). The statute requires EPA to develop criteria "reflecting the latest *scientific* knowledge." Id. §1314(a)(1) (emphasis added). The interpretation that criteria were based exclusively on scientific data predates the 1972 amendments. Water Quality Criteria vii (1968). Furthermore, when Congress wanted economics and cost to be considered, it explicitly required it. See 33 U.S.C. §§1311(b)(2)(A), 1312(b), 1314(b) (1976).

EPA policy does permit downgrading when "substantial and widespread adverse economic and social impact" would otherwise result. 40 C.F.R. §130.17(c)(3) (1978) (now codified at id. §35.1550(c)(3) (1979)). General downgrading is not possible in this case, however, because Mississippi has the same standard for all uses. Furthermore, the statute requires that waters be at least fishable and swimmable "wherever attainable." 33 U.S.C. §1251(1)(2). Mississippi's lowest use is fishable water. EPA does all downgrading for particular stream segments, see 43 Fed. Reg. 43,741 (Sept. 27, 1978), and suggested this course to the Commission in its disapproval letter. Record, Appendix C, at 222.

The Commission also argues that EPA's disapproval was a clear error of judgment. EPA has determined that most fishable waters require a DO concentration of 5.0 mg/l. Quality Criteria for Water 224 (1976). It determined that the fish species in Mississippi, as throughout the South, would be adversely affected by a 4.0 mg/l average during the stressful low flow periods. Record, Appendix C, at 221-23. EPA cited laboratory and field studies supporting its position. Its disapproval of the state standard was not arbitrary or capricious.

VII.   *Promulgation of the Substitute Standard*

A.   The New DO Criteria

Because EPA's disapproval of the DO standard was proper, it was within the scope of the Administrator's authority to promulgate a substitute standard. The question is whether the EPA was arbitrary or capricious in promulgating the DO criteria.

Mississippi wants its waters to support a diversified fish population. See note 2 *supra*. By weight, about 85% of the Mississippi fish can be classified as course or rough fish, such as catfish, carp, drum, buffalo, and shad. Nevertheless, the waters also include higher oxygen demanding gamefish, such as bass, (large mouth, spotted, white, and striped), white perch, bream, crappie, flounder, redfish, speckled trout, white trout, sheephead, croaker, blue gills, and red ear sunfish. Data cited by EPA in both its disapproval and as support for its standard "point very strongly to 5 [mg/l] as the lower limit of dissolved oxygen, if the complex is to maintain a desirable fish faunae under natural river conditions." Record, vol. V, at Exh. 73. Testimony and data of experts based on laboratory and field studies support EPA's position that a 5.0 mg/l concentration is needed to support a balanced and diverse fish population and that 4.0 mg/l is the lowest safe level. In addition, fish are subject to more stress as water temperatures rise, a condition usually occuring during low flow periods. Record, Appendix A, at 18-19.

The EPA's DO criteria was not a clear error in judgment. Furthermore, EPA did not arbitrarily promulgate its 5.0 mg/l criteria without considering the Mississippi situation. After reviewing the statements from the public hearings, EPA promulgated a lower standard that allows an instantaneous minimum of 4.0 mg/l. EPA did not act in an arbitrary or capricious manner.

Water quality standards. Whenever the state revises or adopts new water quality standards, a new section, §303(c)(2)(B), requires that states adopt specific numerical criteria for Table 1 toxic pollutants.

NOTES AND QUESTIONS

1. See also Kentucky v. Train, 9 Envt. Rep. Cas. (BNA) 1280 (E.D. Ky 1976), which holds that the state cannot limit the waters for which interstate standards will be set to a map ("Streams of Kentucky") because standards must be set for all waters of the United States. See generally Gaba, Federal Supervision of State Water Quality Standards under the Clean Water Act, 36 Vand. L. Rev. 1167 (1983).

2. In *Mississippi Commission on Natural Resources*, the state acted to protect the interests of its dischargers in lower water quality standards. A discharger may also be directly affected by water quality standards that are imposed in an NPDES permit. The permit must include conditions that require that both the technological and receiving water quality standards be met. Thus, the discharger must meet the stricter of the two. Homestake Mining Co. v. EPA, 477 F. Supp. 1279 (D.S.D. 1979), involved a challenge by a mining company to high water quality standards set by the state to protect as a permanent cold water trout fishery a reach of the stream into which the company discharged. Homestake's principal argument was that South Dakota law could not give the state the discretion to ignore social and economic factors in setting water quality standards. Relying in part on *Union Electric*, p. 237 *supra*, the court held that the state could condition the NPDES permit on compliance with higher state standards:

> South Dakota's water quality standards simply establish more stringent standards than those required by the Act. The statute itself and the case law make it clear that the states can adopt more stringent standards and can force technology. Under §§301 and 510 of the FWPCA, EPA had no power to disapprove these standards and was required to include them in the NPDES permit. South Dakota was not required to consider economic and social factors and thus its failure to do so does not invalidate its water quality standards. Even though it may be much more difficult for plaintiff to comply with South Dakota's standards than it would be to comply with the Act's standards, South Dakota had the power to adopt the stricter standards and EPA's approval of those standards was not arbitrary and capricious or violative of the Act. [477 F. Supp. at 1284.]

Homestake also relied on §302, 33 U.S.C. §1312, which allows the EPA Administrator to set water quality-related effluent limitations when technology-based effluent limitations do not provide sufficient protection for "public water supplies, agricultural and industrial uses, and the protection and propagation of a balanced population of shellfish, fish and wildlife, and allow recreational opportunities." Before a water quality effluent limitation can be established, §302 requires that the Administrator hold a public hearing to consider the costs and benefits of the proposed limitation. EPA held no such hearing before approving South Dakota's standards. Was the district court correct in holding that §302 did not bar South Dakota from setting its receiving water standards without any consideration of the relationship between the costs and the benefits of trout preservation? The court relied in part on the EPA General Counsel's opinion:

> A decision by EPA's General Counsel, Robert Zener, dealt with the question regarding the applicability of §302. The question presented in that decision was whether state-established effluent limitations, which are more stringent than BAT, are subject to the hearing requirement of §302. In that instance the permit holder argued that §302 amends §301(b)(1)(C) by requiring EPA to follow the provisions of §302 before imposing effluent limitations based on water quality standards which are more stringent than BAT. In rejecting this argument EPA's General Counsel held that there was no interconnection between §301(b)(1)(C) and §302. The opinion goes on to point out that under §301(b)(1)(C) the effluent limitations are established by individual examination of the waterway and that the hearing under §302 to consider costs and benefits is not necessary. Based upon this and other factors, EPA's General Counsel determined that EPA must apply the water quality standards without resort to a §302 cost-benefit analysis. [Homestake Mining Co. v. EPA, 477 F. Supp. at 1285-1286.]

3. Section 401, 33 U.S.C. §1341, provides another avenue for a state to incorporate its water quality standards into an NPDES or other permit. Any applicant for a federal license or permit must obtain state certification that any discharge into navigable waters will comply with the effluent and water quality sstandards of the Act. See pages 786 to 788 *infra* for a brief discussion of the history of Section 401. Section 401 certification is in addition to any other necessary federal permits such as a §404 permit from the Corps of Engineers. Monongahela Power Co. v. Marsh, 809 F.2d 41 (D.C. Cir. 1987), *cert. denied*, 484 U.S. 816 (1987). The Federal Energy Regulatory Commission has been one of the most recalitrant federal agencies with respect to 401 certification, but City of Fredericksburg v. FERC, 856 F.2d 1109 (4th Cir. 1989), disciplines the commission. A federal power licensee refused to file a 401 application with the state, and FERC exempted the applicant because the state jefused to issue its certification within the statutory period. The Fourth Circuit remanded the license because the statute gives states the discretion to prescribe certification procedures and thus Virginia correctly refused to respond to FERC. Discharge has been broadly interpreted. Power Authority of New York v. Williams, 101 App. Div. 2d 259, 475 N.Y.S.2d 901 (1984), holds that Section 401 certification is required to transfer water from an upper to lower reservoir when water temperature would be changed. The major question surrounding Section 401 is the extent to which a state may include water quality related conditions not directly found in effluent limitations and water quality standards. Arnold Irrigation Co. v. Department of

Environmental Quality, 79 Or. App. 136, 717 P.2d 377, *reh'g denied*, 301 Or. 765, 726 P.2d 377 (1986), holds that the state could not require a Federal Energy Regulatory Commission licensee to comply with a county land use plan without a greater showing of water quality effects:

> That EQC erred in affirming the denial of the certificate does not resolve this case. Although the state could not deny the certificate on the grounds stated, 33 USC §1341(d) does allow it to place limitations on the certificate if the limitations are
>
>> necessary to assure that any applicant for a Federal license or permit will comply with any applicable effluent limitations and other limitations, under section 1311 or 1312 of this title, standard of performance under section 1316 of this title, or prohibition, effluent standard, or pretreatment standard under section 1317 of this title, and with *any other appropriate requirement of State law* set forth in such certification. . . . (Emphasis supplied.)
>
> Any limitation that the state imposes becomes a condition on any federal license or permit issued pursuant to the certification.
>
> Although the emphasized language does not allow DEQ to consider land use and other issues outside the CWA in deciding whether to approve certification applications, it may be able to consider those factors in deciding what limitations to place on the certificate. Because the question of the relevance of land use regulations to limitations on a certificate is certain to arise on remand, we discuss it here.
>
> The legislative history of the phrase in question is minimal. The conference committee which developed the final version of the bill added it; there was nothing precisely comparable previously. The committee's report says only that under this provision "a State may attach to any Federally issued license or permit such conditions as may be necessary to assure compliance with water quality standards in that State." That statement gives little additional hint of Congress' intent. We believe, however, that there are sufficient indications of what kinds of other state requirements Congress considered "appropriate" for DEQ and EQC to use.
>
> We look first at the purpose of the act and at what Congress could have said but did not. The purpose of CWA is "to restore and maintain the . . . integrity of the Nation's waters." 33 U.S.C. §1251(a). Under the act, primary responsibility for determining what constitutes the integrity of the nation's waters and what is necessary to restore and maintain that integrity is with the states. The act requires the states to exercise their responsibility by adopting water quality standards under 33 USC §1313 and to base those standards on the uses which the states wish to encourage. The specific effluent limitations and performance standards provided in other sections of the act are designed to achieve the quality standards of section 1313. Certainly, section 1313 water quality standards are appropriate limitations in determining what limits to place on a certificate.
>
> The section 1313 standards are not, however, the only water quality standards which states may enforce; the states have inherent authority, independently of the CWA, to protect and plan the use of their waters. Congress did not make the section 1313 standards the exclusive water quality criteria which the states may use in placing limitations on section 1341 certificates. If Congress had intended to do so, it could have specifically mentioned those standards in section 1341(d), but it did not. Rather, it allowed the states to enforce *all* water quality-related statutes and rules through the states' authority to place limitations on section 1341 certificates. Congress thereby required federal licensing authorities to respect all state

water quality laws in licensing projects involving discharges to navigable streams. "[A]ny other appropriate requirement of State law" is thus a Congressional recognition of all state action related to water quality and Congressional authorization to the states to consider those actions in imposing limitations on CWA certificates. It does not, however, allow limitations which are not related to water quality.

Although it functions as a federal agent in issuing certificates of compliance, DEQ is a state agency and must comply with state law to the extent that federal law does not supersede it. That law requires DEQ to act, with respect to programs affecting land use, in compliance with the statewide land use goals and in a manner compatible with acknowledged comprehensive plans. ORS 197.180(1). DEQ therefore must include limitations reflecting the goals and plans in section 1341 certificates to the maximum extent that the CWA allows — that is, to the extent that they have any relationship to water quality. Only if a goal or plan provision has absolutely no relationship to water quality would it not be an "other appropriate requirement of State law." In that case, and only in that case, would the CWA override DEQ's obligations under ORS 197.180(1).

We cannot say at this point what land use provisions would relate to water quality. Many uses of land may affect water quality, even if they do not immediately result in direct discharges to the state's waters. Part of the goals and plans clearly relate to water quality — Goal 6 most obviously — but others may also have a significant, if indirect, impact. Limitations on development or on other uses of land near waters may fit into the category. The precise determination is for DEQ in the first instance. [717 P.2d at 1278-1279]

See also Flax v. Ash, 142 Misc. 2d 828, 538 N.Y.S.2d 891 (S. Ct. 1988). Would a diversion licensed under state law require §401 certification if it would reduce the assmilative capacity of a stream? See generally Davis, Protecting Waste Assimilation Stream Flows by the Law of Water Allocation, Nuisance and Public Trust, and by Environmental Statute, 28 Nat. Resources J. 357 (1988).

4. If the state does not challenge EPA guidelines and the state has not yet applied the standard in an NPDES permit, can a discharger who is concerned about the potential impact of a standard challenge the standard? The answer to this question is quite complicated and potentially frustrating for all interested parties. First, §303, which continues the pre-1972 water quality standards plans, contemplates a closed bargaining process between the state and the EPA over the adequacy of state standards. The Clean Water Act contains no express statutory procedure that allows an interested party to challenge directly a federally approved or disapproved standard. Because §§402(a)(1) and 510 require EPA, where it has NPDES authority, to incorporate compliance with state standards into any permits issued, one might suppose that a challenge to a federal NPDES permit would be the proper place to challenge a state standard. Not so, holds U.S. Steel v. Train, 556 F.2d 822 (7th Cir. 1977). Because the standards are state standards, the court is without jurisdiction to hear the challenge. To U.S. Steel's argument that Indiana law did not provide for judicial review of its standards, the court suggested that the plaintiff raise its due process objections in a direct federal action against the responsible state official. U.S. Steel would not, of course, preclude a water quality standard challenge in an NPDES permit proceeding in a state that has NPDES authority.

U.S. Steel suggests that an interested party may obtain pre-enforcement review of a water quality standard by a direct action against the federal or state official at any time after federal approval or disapproval of the standard. In recent years, federal courts have sanctioned pre-enforcement review of crystallized federal rules on the theory that the regulated party's interest in planning its affairs with certainty outweighs the agency's interest in being able to control the timing of enforcement of a regulation. But a final order or agency action is still required before a court will review an agency decision. Recall that in Abbott Laboratories v. Gardner, 387 U.S. 136 (1967), p. 109 *supra*, the court substituted a functional, flexible balancing test to determine if a matter was "ripe" for judicial review for the old "final order" rule. Ripeness problems exist for regulations such as water quality standards, as opposed to effluent limitations, which have an uncertain impact on individual dischargers. In Commonwealth Edison Co. v. Train, 649 F.2d 481 (7th Cir. 1980), the utility wanted to challenge EPA's anti-degradation guideline (discussed in Note 5, below) because it thought that the guideline jeopardized its ability to secure NPDES permits for existing facilities and to site new ones. The guideline was found not to be ripe for review because it was only the first step in an ongoing process:

> None of these minimum criteria preclude degradation. It may be, for example, that a state may determine that a new plant in a given area may discharge without affecting existing uses. Similarly, a state may conclude that economic and social development necessitates limited degradation of high quality waters. Even in situations involving national resource waters where no degradation can be allowed, the anti-degradation policy will not necessarily injure utilities. First, each state must determine which waters are to be classified as national resource waters. If a plant does not discharge into a national resource water, it obviously will not be affected. More fundamentally, it cannot be said with any certainty that the prohibition of any degradation of national resource waters will necessarily prohibit new dischargers. A state would have the option of applying more stringent controls to existing dischargers or otherwise limit pollution so that a new plant would be able to discharge without lowering water quality. It is quite possible, therefore, that the anti-degradation policy, when implemented into a water quality plan by the states, will inflict no injury on utilities.
>
> The anti-degradation regulation is merely the first step in an ongoing administrative process which has not yet resulted in an order requiring compliance by utilities. Thus, even if the issue of the validity of the regulations is a purely legal one which will not be aided by development of a factual record, the absence of a coercive order directed at utilities makes the issues in this case unfit for judicial determination. Bethlehem Steel Corp. v. U.S. Environmental Protection Agency, 536 F.2d 156, 161 (7th Cir. 1976). [649 F.2d at 485.]

The Seventh Circuit was concerned with the hardship to Commonwealth Edison and identified two certain review points: federal approval of state standards or federal approval of a state §208 plan. Suppose Illinois set higher water quality standards than those required by federal law. What federal action is there for a federal court to review?

5. Section 303(d) of the Clean Water Act requires that states identify waters where effluent limitations standards are not stringent enough to achieve an applicable water quality standard. The EPA must then set total maximum daily loads for specified pollutants for these waters. The theory behind §303(d) was explained in House debates, where the theory originated and was incorporated into the final bill in conference:

> Section 303 contains provisions for the identification of waters where the technological standards are not stringent enough to implement applicable water quality standards. For these waterways, the States are required to establish load limits which are to be approved by the Administrator. These load limits would indicate, for those pollutants which are suitable for such calculations, the maximum quantity which can be discharged into the water and still not result in a violation of the water quality standards. It is believed that this information is needed for planning and enforcement and the managers expect that the States and the Administrator will be diligent and will make these studies in a timely fashion. [1972 Legislative History, at 246.]

States have been slow to set total maximum daily loads (TMDLs), due to lack of funds and the problems of multiple source allocations, and the EPA did not push the states during the 1980s. General Accounting Office, Water Pollution: More EPA Action Needed to Improve the Quality of Heavily Polluted Waters (January, 1989). Scott v. City of Hammond, 741 F.2d 992 (7th Cir. 1984) holds that if a state fails to set TMDLs after a prolonged period of time, this is, in effect, a determination that no TMDLs are necessary. EPA must then approve or disapprove the submission and set its own, if the agency disapproves the state's determination.

The TMDLs are to be allocated — by criteria that have never been specified — through the NPDES process. The leading TMDL case is Environmental Defense Fund, Inc. v. Costle, 657 F.2d 275 (D.C. Cir. 1981), which arose from a challenge to a twenty-plus-year effort to control the salinity of the Colorado River. Salinity is caused by salt loading as the river passes over soils or rocks containing soluble salts and from the concentration of these salts as the flow is reduced by diversions. To complicate matters, about half of the salt load is produced by natural causes and half from human activities, mainly irrigation return flows which leach soils. In November 1976 EPA approved standards set by the seven upper and lower Colorado River Basin states, which included: (1) the goal of maintaining salinity concentrations below 1972 levels, (2) specific numerical criteria for three monitoring stations on the Colorado, and (3) written provisions telling how the states *as a whole* would meet the goal. The Environmental Defense Fund (EDF) challenged the standards on a number of grounds, all of which were rejected. Applying the "arbitrary and capricious" standard, the court held that numerical criteria did not have to be set for each state; that the implementation plan proposed by EPA was adequate; that EPA did not have to revise the standards in light of new information; that the continuous planning process required under §303 was adequate and that the agency did not violate §102(2)(E) of NEPA by refusing to study on-farm management changes as an alternative to the program proposed by EPA and the Bureau of Reclamation; and that the agency failed to set total maximum daily loads. On the first and last arguments, the court concluded:

IV.   Claim One

In Claim One, EDF alleged that the approved water quality standards for salinity, including the implementation plans, failed to comply with the requirements of the Clean Water Act and the Water Quality Act of 1965. EDF also claimed that EPA's approval of the standards in November 1976 was arbitrary and capricious, as well as an abuse of discretion under Sections 303(a) and 303(b) of the Clean Water Act. 33 U.S.C. §§1313(a) and (b). EDF also challenged EPA's action on two related grounds. First, EDF asserted that establishment of specific numeric criteria was required for each basin state (including the four basin states within the upper basin). Second, EDF contended that the plan for the implementation of the standards, as adopted by each basin state, was based upon unrealistic assumptions, relied upon insufficient control methods, and contained "patently" ineffective provisions.

In its approval of the water quality standards, EPA was found by the district court to have acted in complete compliance with the Clean Water Act. The court correctly found EPA's actions to be sufficiently explained in the record, and determined that EPA had acted reasonably, and neither arbitrarily nor capriciously in approving the standards. EPA's actions, in approving the standards, had a rational basis in the administrative record and were not contrary to the provisions of the Clean Water Act.

A.   Sufficiency of the Numeric Criteria

Pursuant to EPA regulation, each basin state adopted salinity standards which included: specific numeric criteria for three stations in the River's lower main stem, narrative provisions, and other factual information, with the goal of maintaining salinity concentrations below 1972 levels. Included also was a water quality monitoring and analysis program which was consistent with EPA's basin-wide approach to the salinity problem. EPA, after a public comment period, approved the standards in 1976.

EPA's review of the standards must ensure that they were consistent with the applicable requirements of the FWPCA, as in effect immediately prior to the date of the enactment of the FWPCA Amendments of 1972. Clean Water Act §§303(a)(1), 303(a)(2), and 303(a)(3)(B). See Montgomery Environmental Coalition v. Costle, 646 F.2d 568, at 592, 593 (D.C. Cir. 1980). This reference back mandated that the state standards were to be evaluated, by EPA, under the provisions of the Water Quality Act of 1965. The test for the adequacy of the standards under the 1965 Act directed that the standards were "to protect the public health or welfare, enhance the quality of water, and serve the purposes of [the] Act." §10(c)(3).

EDF asserted below that separate numeric criteria were to be established in each basin state and that a failure to do so created a set of salinity standards with no accountability. The district court found that "EDF has not pointed the court to any section of the Clean Water Act that would require the establishment of separate numerical criteria in any basin state." Environmental Defense Fund, Inc. v. Costle, 13 Envir. Rep. (BNA) 1867, 1871 (D.D.C. Oct. 3, 1979). EDF also fails to cite any persuasive authority to this court.

Here, EDF details several reasons which it argues necessitates judicial disapproval and corrective remand of the salinity standards. EDF first contends that the Clean Water Act and corresponding EPA regulations provide that numeric criteria are needed in each of the seven states. To the contrary, neither the Act itself nor the regulations require that any numeric criteria be established. Water quality criteria may be, and often are, totally narrative. EPA's 1974 salinity regulation directed that salinity should be viewed by the states as a basinwide problem, and that numeric criteria be adopted for "appropriate points" on the River, to aid in the maintenance of lower main stem salinity at pre-1972 levels. 40 C.F.R. §§120.5(b), 120.5(c)(1), and 120.5(c)(2) (1974). The regulation, with its requirement of numeric levels at "appropriate points," was promulgated after careful agency study and with complete cognizance of EPA's obligation to protect the public health or welfare, enhance the water quality, and serve the 1965 Act's relevant purposes. If the establishment of numeric criteria in each state became legally mandated after thorough EPA study and review of its statutory obligations, EPA would have been duty bound to promulgate appropriate regulations.

The district court found the narrative and three numeric criteria to be sufficient to meet the 1965 Act's test of adequacy. We agree. The selection of the three points for numeric standards to supplement the narrative provisions is consistent with the basinwide approach and is fully explained in the record. . . .

VI.   Claim Three

EDF asserted in Claim Three that EPA failed to promulgate total maximum daily loads ("TMDL's") for salinity, in violation of Section 303(d) of the Clean Water Act. The district court correctly found the Claim to be without merit.

Section 303(d) involves a complex statutory scheme which requires the states to identify waters where point source controls alone will be insufficient to implement the water quality standards applicable to such waters. The Section obligates the states to establish the TMDL's in accordance with a priority ranking based upon both the severity of the pollution and the water's designated uses. The TMDL's set the maximum amount of a pollutant which can be contributed into a stream segment without causing a violation of the water quality standards. The TMDL's can then be allocated by insertion in NPDES permits, among the various point source dischargers upon the stream segment, taking into account nonpoint source impacts as well.

The states are to submit the respective TMDL calculations for EPA approval, Section 303(d)(2), within one hundred and eighty days of the date of the Administrator's publication of the initial Section 304 identification of the respective pollutants. EPA is to review the TMDL identification and levels, and either approve or disapprove them as appropriate. Id. EPA approval will then result in the incorporation of the TMDL's into the state water quality management plans under Section 303(e). Disapproval, on the other hand, mandates the identification and establishment of TMDL's, by EPA, which are determined to be necessary to implement the applicable water quality standards.

EDF avers that the waters were not properly identified and the proper TMDL's were not correctly established. Thus EPA must be ordered to exercise its mandatory duties of identification of insufficient waters and TMDL establishment. The district court based its finding that this contention is without merit upon two reasons. First, the court ruled that the request for such an order was premature because EPA did not identify such pollutants until December 28, 1978, 43 Fed. Reg. 60,662. Therefore, the states' duty to submit TMDL calculations, as the court noted, did not arise until June 28, 1979. Section 303(d)(2). See Homestake Mining Co. v. U.S.E.P.A., 477 F. Supp. 1279 (D.S.D. 1979). Since EPA did not have the occasion to approve or disapprove the state TMDL submissions prior to the time of EDF's filing of its motion for summary judgment, we agree that this claim is premature. Thus, it would be improper for us to review EPA's action or alleged inaction at this time. In addition, as the state defendants note, the court would be required to review the states' priority rankings before it could properly review EPA's decision not to establish TMDL's for a specific pollutant such as salinity.

The district court also relied upon the fact that the salinity standards are currently being met. EDF correctly argued below that TMDL's are occasionally employed to prevent *anticipated* violations of the water quality criteria. The court countered this observation, however, by finding that average salinity levels had been decreasing since 1972, and there was no likelihood of any anticipated violations in the immediate future. Hence, the court ruled that an order directing EPA to establish salinity TMDL's in the basin states would not be warranted. We agree. If salinity concentrations were to rise and future violations were anticipated, the states or EPA, in their respective review processes, could establish TMDL's as necessary to comply with Section 303(d).

Our affirmance of this Claim is further strengthened by the record evidence which indicates that under two percent of the salinity concentration is currently subject to the Section 402 NPDES permit program. Thus, the effect of placing TMDL's for salinity upon the specific numeric criteria is minimal at best. EPA and the states have acted reasonably and in compliance given our limited standard of review under Section 706(1) of the APA. However, we admonish EPA to approve or disapprove such identification, prioritization, and load limits within the requisite statutory framework and time limits. While review of EPA's action is now premature, we urge EPA to carefully heed the statutory deadlines in the future. [657 F.2d at 287-288, 294-295.]

The Colorado River is a major source of water supply for agricultural uses within the seven basin states and for growing urban centers such as Denver and Los Angeles just outside the basin. The river's supply is fully allocated under the "law of the river," which includes interstate compacts, Supreme Court decisions, and acts of Congress. See Meyers, The Colorado River, 19 Stan. L. Rev. 1 (1966). Salinity issues are intertwined with the broader problems of the allocation of the River since a strict, non-technology based salinity control program could limit future diversions in Colorado, New Mexico, Utah and Wyoming. T. Miller, G. Weatherford & J. Thorson, The Salty Colorado (The Conservation Foundation, 1986) explores these issues and contains a useful discussion of the different estimates of the seriousness or relative lack thereof of the problem. Do you understand EDF's strategy for reducing salinity? Do you understand why the basin states oppose it? How would EDF's strategy have been implemented? How will EPA's approved strategy be implemented? Can it be? See generally P. Fradkin, A River No More: The Colorado River and the West (1981), and N. Hundley, Water and the West: The Colorado River Compact and the Politics of Water in the American West (1975).

Section 302(b)(2) allows a discharger to obtain a variance if he can demonstrate that although the technology or other control strategy is available to meet the water quality related effluent limitation, "there is no reasonable relationship between the economic and social costs and the benefits to be obtained (including attainment of the objective of this chapter)."

6. The Clean Air Act's application to a given pollution source generally turns on whether the source is located in a clean or a dirty area. The water quality standards program adopted pursuant to the Clean Water Act makes a similar division between clean and dirty water, but less turns on the distinction because in implementing the Act the consistent emphasis has been on the promulgation of uniform effluent limitations. The development of the anti-degradation policy has largely been a matter of agency discretion, see Hobbs and Raley, Water Quality versus Water Quantity: A Delicate Balance, 34 Rocky Mt. M. L. Inst. 24-1, 24-20–24-24 (1988), but Congress seems to have ratified the policy in the 1987 Amendments to the Clean Water Act. 33 U.S.C. §1313(d)(4)(B). 40 C.F.R. §35.131.12 sets forth EPA's non-degradation policy with respect to clean streams:

> (e) The State shall develop and adopt a statewide antidegradation policy and identify the methods for implementing such policy pursuant to this subpart. The antidegradation policy and implementation methods shall, at a minimum, be consistent with the following:
> (1) Existing instream water uses shall be maintained and protected. No further water quality degradation which would interfere with or become injurious to existing instream water uses is allowable.
> (2) Where the quality of the waters exceed levels necessary to support propagation of fish, shellfish, and wildlife and recreation in and on the water, that quality shall be maintained and protected unless the State finds, after full satisfaction of the intergovernmental coordination and public participation provisions of the State's continuing planning process, that allowing lower water quality is necessary to accommodate important economic or social development in the area in which the waters are located. In allowing such degradation or lower water quality, the State shall assure water quality adequate to protect existing uses fully. Further, the State shall assure that there shall be achieved the highest statutory and regulatory requirements for all new and existing point sources and all cost-effective and reasonable best management practices for nonpoint source control.
> (3) Where high quality waters constitute an outstanding National resource, such as waters of National and State parks and wildlife refuges and waters of exceptional recreational or ecological significance, that water quality shall be maintained and protected.

33 U.S.C. §1313(d)(4)(B), added in 1987, prohibits a state from lowering the TMDL loads for a stream where the quality equals or exceeds the level necessary to attain applicable water quality standards unless the revision "is subject to and consistent with the antidegradation policy established under this section." The section appears to adopt EPA's antidegradation policy. S. Rep. No. 50, 99th Conf., 1st. Sess. 4-7 (1985). See generally Hines, A Decade of Non-Degradation Policy in Congress and the Courts: The Erratic Pursuit of Clean Air and Clean Water, 62 Iowa L. Rev. 643 (1977), for a valuable history of the evolution of EPA's nondegradation policy for water. See also Comment, The Federal Water Pollution Control Act's Antidegradation Policy and Its Application to Groundwater, 20 U.S.F.L. Rev. 633 (1986).

7. There are no national groundwater aquifer standards. The federal En-

vironmental Protection Agency sets only end of the tap drinking water standards. The agency has set maximum contaminant levels (MCLs) and maximum contaminant level goals (MCLGs). The former take into account both health and technical feasibility; the latter are set at a level, often zero, at which there will be no harmful health effects. States have relied upon these standards to establish groundwater standards. This has major implications for RCRA and for Superfund clean up standards. See Chapter 5, pp. 662 to 663. Strict as MCLs and MCLGs are, these standards do not adequately protect all groundwater uses. GAO, Groundwater Protection: The Use of Drinking Water Standards by the States 9 (1988) cautions:

> Groundwater has several uses besides drinking. It is used to irrigate crops and water livestock. It affects the habitat of aquatic life because it flows into bodies of surface water. Applying drinking water standards to groundwater could jeopardize other uses that require standards higher than those for drinking. We compared EPA maximum contaminant levels with guidelines for other uses published separately by EPA and the National Academy of Sciences. We found that EPA maximum contaminant levels are at least as stringent as all published guidelines for livestock watering and irrigation and therefore would protect these uses. However, we found that the MCLs for 17 substances are less stringent than EPA and NAS aquatic life guidelines and therefore would not always protect aquatic life. Using the same techniques outlined in the previous section, we examined how often the cells exceeded the more stringent of the MCLs and aquatic life guidelines. Whereas we had found earlier that 91.8 percent of the cells met the MCLs, we next found that when the aquatic life guidelines are substituted for the MCLs (for those substances that have an aquatic life guideline that is more stringent than its MCL), 66.9 percent of the cells met the recommended levels. A decision to apply EPA maximum contaminant levels as groundwater standards, without allowing for greater stringency when local conditions warrant it (such as in ecosystems that are sensitive to these particular substances or that are in areas of high groundwater recharge with low surface water dilution) could jeopardize sensitive species of aquatic life.

8. Can a downstream state impose its own higher water quality standard against an upstream state? A dispute between North Carolina and Tennessee provides some answers to this question and raises more questions. An old paper mill on the Pigeon River, 26 miles upstream from the state border, withdraws the average flow and returns it to the stream with dissolved solids that turn it a murky brown. Tennessee, which had narrative color standards, objected because of aesthetic and fish and wildlife considerations. Since a state cannot directly impose its standards on another, see International Paper Co. v. Ouelette, 479 U.S. 481 (1987) page 760 *infra*, Tennessee asked North Carolina to revise its standards to conform to its vision of the river. Each state and the EPA constructed color removal models to determine the percentages of removal necessary to meet Tennessee's standards. Tennessee and the EPA put the percentage at 80 and 89, but North Carolina put the figure at 55. In 1981, the plant's NPDES permit expired and North Carolina started to issue a new one which included aesthetic-based water quality standards, but at a North Carolina hearing Tennessee ob-

jected that the permit still required less than 75 removal because it was based largely on economic considerations. Tennessee had better luck with the EPA, which ultimately objected to the permit:

> On July 18, 1985, EPA notified North Carolina that the May 14th permit would be considered to be a proposed permit as defined in the regulations. This was done because North Carolina had not complied with either the Memorandum of Agreement (MOA) or the EPA regulations in that it had not provided EPA with a proposed final permit prior to issuance. On August 6, 1985, the EPA formally objected to the May 14th permit on the grounds that it:
> 1) Did not assure compliance with water quality color standards under 33 U.S.C. §1311(b)(1)(C), and did not, with certain qualifications, insure a 50 color count standard 26 miles downstream;
> 2) Did not unequivocally require Champion to comply with color standards; and
> 3) Was not an adequate response to Tennessee's objections to the permit for the reasons stated just above.

Interestingly, neither North Carolina nor the mill requested a public hearing on the objections. Because of this, EPA simply informed the parties that it had assumed permitting authority. The mill immediately challenged the action as ultra vires. Champion International Paper Co. v. EPA, 850 F.2d 182 (4th Cir. 1988) holds that "§1342(d) now allows the EPA to take jurisdiction and issue a permit in the event of an impasse between a state and the EPA administrator." See Note, The Dilemma of the Downstream Plaintiff in an Interstate Water Pollution Case, 37 Buffalo L. Rev. 257 (1988-89). The reviewability of the EPA action is further discussed on page 471 *infra*.

E.   ESTABLISHMENT OF EFFLUENT LIMITATIONS AND DEFENSES TO COMPLIANCE: INTRODUCTION

The heart of the Clean Water Act is subchapter III, which allows the federal government to impose effluent limitatons on point source discharges. Effluent limitations specify (1) the numerical limits on the discharge from individual units of production, (2) maximum daily and 30-day average permissible concentrations in unit waste streams of listed pollutants, and (3) specific treatment and process modification designs that must be employed. The limitations are especially important for new plants. R. Zener, Guide to Federal Environmental Law 96 (1981). The Act makes two crucial distinctions. First, sources are divided, as they are in the Clean Air Act, between existing and new. Second, pollutants are divided into five categories for purposes of standard-setting and compliance dead-lines: (1) conventional pollutants, generally those that are biodegradable; (2) toxic pollutants, those that are not biodegradable and create a risk of substantial hu-man health impairment; (3) nonconventional, non-toxic pollutants; (4) heat, which is treated as a separate category because its adverse impacts are more site-specific than those of the first three categories; and (5) the disposal of dredge and fill spoil. The importance of effluent limitations was strengthened by the "anti-backsliding" policy incorporated into the 1987 Amendments to the Clean Water Act. Subject to exceptions, "a permit may not be renewed, reissued, or modified on the basis of effluent guidelines promulgated . . . subsequent to the original issuance of the permit, to contain effluent limitations which are less stringent than the comparable effluent limitations in the previous permit." 33 U.S.C. §1342(o). A permit may be modified if the plant has been modified to justify less stringent limitations, the original permit was based on technical or legal mistakes, or new information justifies less stringent limitations. The permittee may also show that less stringent limitations are justified by "events over which the permittee has no control and for which there is no reasonably available rem-edy" or "the permittee has installed the processes necessary to meet the original limitations but has been unable to achieve them." The exceptions do not apply to revised waste load allocations or to alternative grounds for translating water quality standards into effluent limitations unless the revised allocations result in a decrease in the amount of pollutant discharge.

Effluent limitatons are set by EPA for subclasses of an industry. EPA's stan-dards are developed by looking at the existing state of the art in an industry and potential advances in waste treatment technology. This approach leads the agen-cy to set performance standards that are often in fact design standards, which has led to charges within and without industry that the standards impede economic efficiency because they discourage or prohibit the adoption of the least costly treatment alternative. See Note, Technology-Based Emission and Effluent Standards and the Achievement of Ambient Environmental Standards, 91 Yale L.J. 792 (1982). Once the regulations for a subclass become final, the regula-tions are floors — not ceilings — that must be incorporated into all NPDES permits.

Effluent limitations have been challenged at two stages: Industry trade as-sociations have challenged industry or subclass regulations, and individual dis-chargers have challenged the application of the regulations to them in their NPDES permits. A discharge in excess of the amount specified in an NPDES permit is a violation of the Act and subjects the discharger to the enforcement actions discussed in section I.

The Act speaks both to EPA, telling it what it must consider in setting standards, and to dischargers and other interested parties, specifying the proce-dures for judicial review of various EPA actions. The Act does not specifically list the defenses a discharger or other interested party may raise to regulations and permits. Defenses must be inferred from the Act. Dischargers have usually asserted one of the following four defenses: (1) lack of scientific justification, a defense that allows the adequacy of EPA models, agency knowledge of the relevant technical literature, and the agency's inferences and conclusions to be questioned; (2) economic impossibility, a defense that argues that the industry or particular facility cannot comply with a standard and make a decent profit; (3) technical impossibility, a defense that argues that there is no proven technology to meet the mandated effluent reductions or that EPA's specified technology will not work; and (4) unfavorable cost-benefit ratio, a defense that argues that the costs of compliance exceed the benefits — the discharger concedes that it can afford to comply with the limitations and the technology to do so exists but argues that it is economically inefficient to insist on full compliance.

Before the Act could be implemented, it was necessary to decide whether EPA could set uniform effluent guidelines that bound all permittees or whether any EPA guidelines could be varied on a case-by-case basis in an individual NPDES permit. See Note, The EPA's Power to Establish National Effluent Limitations for Existing Water Pollution Sources, 125 U. Pa. L. Rev. 120 (1976), and Parenteau & Tauman, The Effluent Limitations Controversy, 6 Ecology L.Q. 1 (1976). The next case sets forth the Supreme Court's resolution of this issue.

E. I. DU PONT DE NEMOURS & CO. v. TRAIN
430 U.S. 112 (1977)

Mr. Justice STEVENS delivered the opinion of the Court.

Inorganic chemical manufacturing plants operated by the eight petitioners in Nos. 75-978 and 75-1473 discharge various pollutants into the Nation's waters and therefore are "point sources" within the meaning of the Federal Water Pollution Control Act (Act), as added and amended by §2 of the Federal Water Pollution Control Act Amendments of 1972, 33 U.S.C. §1251 et seq. The Environmental Protection Agency has promulgated industrywide regulations imposing three sets of precise limitations on petitioners' discharges. The first two impose progressively higher levels of pollution control on existing point sources after July 1, 1977, and after July 1, 1983, respectively. The third set imposes limits on "new sources" that may be constructed in the future.

These cases present three important questions of statutory construction: (1) whether EPA has the authority under §301 of the Act to issue industrywide regulations limiting discharges by existing plants; (2) whether the Court of Appeals, which admittedly is authorized to review the standards for new sources, also has jurisdiction under §509 to review the regulations concerning existing plants; and (3) whether the new-source standards issued under §306 must allow variances for individual plants. . . .

THE STATUTE

The statute, enacted on October 18, 1972, authorized a series of steps to be taken to achieve the goal of eliminating all discharges of pollutants into the Nation's waters by 1985, §101(a)(1).

The first steps required by the Act are described in §304, which directs the Administrator to develop and publish various kinds of technical data to provide guidance in carrying out responsibilities imposed by other sections of the Act. . . . Section 304(b) goes into great detail concerning the contents of these regulations. They must identify the degree of effluent reduction attainable through use of the best practicable or best available technology for a class of plants. The guidelines must also "specify factors to be taken into account" in determining the control measures applicable to point sources within these classes. A list of factors to be considered then follows. The Administrator was also directed to develop and publish, within one year, elaborate criteria for water quality accurately reflecting the most current scientific knowledge and also technical information on factors necessary to restore and maintain water quality. §304(a). . . .

Section 306 directs the Administrator to publish within 90 days a list of categories of sources discharging pollutants and, within one year thereafter, to publish regulations establishing national standards of performance for new sources within each category. Section 306 contains no provision for exceptions from the standards for individual plants; on the contrary, subsection (e) expressly makes it unlawful to operate a new source in violation of the applicable standard of performance after its effective date. The statute provides that the new-source standards shall reflect the greatest degree of effluent reduction achievable through application of the best available demonstrated control technology.

Section 301(b) defines the effluent limitations that shall be achieved by existing point sources in two states. . . .

Section 301(c) authorizes the Administrator to grant variances from the 1983 limitations. Section 301(e) states that effluent limitations established pursuant to §301 shall be applied to all point sources. . . .

THE REGULATIONS

The various deadlines imposed on the Administrator were too ambitious for him to meet. For that reason, the procedure which he followed in adopting the regulations applicable to the inorganic chemical industry and to other classes of point sources is somewhat different from that apparently contemplated by the statute. Specifically, as will appear, he did not adopt guidelines pursuant to §304 before defining the effluent limitations for existing sources described in §301(b) or the national standards for new sources described in §306. This case illustrates the approach the Administrator followed in implementing the Act. EPA began by engaging a private contractor to prepare a Development Document. This document provided a detailed technical study of pollution control in the industry. The study first divided the industry into categories. For each category, present levels of pollution were measured and plants with exemplary pollution control were investigated. Based on this information, other technical data, and economic studies, a determination was made of the degree of pollution control which could be achieved by the various levels of technology mandated by the statute. The study was made available to the public and circulated to interested persons. It formed the basis of "effluent limitation guideline" regulations issued by EPA after receiving public comment on proposed regulations. These regulations divide the industry into 22 subcategories. Within each subcategory, precise numerical limits are set for various pollutants. The regulations for each subcategory contain a variance clause, applicable only to the 1977 limitations.

THE ISSUES

The broad outlines of the parties' respective theories may be stated briefly. EPA contends that §301(b) authorizes it to issue regulations establishing effluent limitations for classes of plants. The permits granted under §402, in EPA's view, simply incorporate these across-the-board limitations, except for the limited variances allowed by the regulations themselves and by §301(c). The §304(b) guidelines, according to EPA, were intended to guide it in later establishing §301 effluent-limitation regulations. Because the process proved more time consuming than Congress assumed when it established this new two-stage process, EPA condensed the two stages into a single regulation.

In contrast, petitioners contend that §301 is not an independent source of authority for setting effluent limitations by regulation. Instead, §301 is seen as merely a description of the effluent limitations which are set for each plant on an individual basis during the permit-issuance process. Under the industry view, the §304 guidelines serve the function of guiding the permit issuer in setting the effluent limitations. . . .

I

We think §301 itself is the key to the problem. The statutory language concerning the 1983 limitations, in particular, leaves no doubt that these limitations are to be set by regulation. Subsection (b)(2)(A) of §301 states that by 1983 "effluent limitations *for categories and classes* of point sources" are to be achieved which will require "application of the best available technology economically achievable *for such category or class.*" (Emphasis added.) These effluent limitations are to require elimination of all discharges if "such elimination is technologically and economically achievable for a *category or class* of point sources." (Emphasis added.) This is "language difficult to reconcile with the view that individual effluent limitations are to be set when each permit is issued." American Meat Institute v. EPA, 526 F.2d 442, 450 (C.A. 7 1975). The statute thus focuses expressly on the characteristics of the "category or class" rather than the characteristics of individual point sources. Normally, such classwide determinations would be made by regulation, not in the course of issuing a permit to one member of the class.[17]

Thus, we find that §301 unambiguously provides for the use of regulations to establish the 1983 effluent limitations. Different language is used in §301 with respect to the 1977 limitations. Here, the statute speaks of "effluent limitations for point sources," rather than "effluent limitations for categories and classes of point sources." Nothing elsewhere in the Act, however, suggests any radical difference in the mechanism used to impose limitations for the 1977 and 1983 deadlines. See American Iron & Steel Institute v. EPA, 526 F.2d 1027, 1042 n.32 (C.A. 3 1975). For instance, there is no indication in either §301 or §304 that the §304 guidelines play a different role in setting 1977 limitations. Moreover, it would be highly anomalous if the 1983 regulations and the new-source standards were directly reviewable in the Court of Appeals, while the 1977 regulations based on the same administrative record were reviewable only in the District Court. The magnitude and highly technical character of the administrative record involved with these regulations makes it almost inconceivable that Congress would have required duplicate review in the first instance by different courts. We conclude that the statute authorizes the 1977 limitations as well as the 1983 limitations to be set by regulation, so long as some allowance is made for variations in individual plants, as EPA has done by including a variance clause in its 1977 limitations.

The question of the form of §301 limitations is tied to the question whether the Act requires the Administrator or the permit issuer to establish the limitations. Section 301 does not itself answer this question, for it speaks only in the passive voice of the achievement and establishment of the limitations. But other parts of the statute leave little doubt on this score. Section 304(b) states that "[f]or the purpose of adopting or revising effluent limitations . . . the Administrator shall" issue guideline regulations; while the judicial-review section. . . .

This legislative history supports our reading of §301 and makes it clear that the §304 guidelines are not merely aimed at guiding the discretion of permit issuers in setting limitations for individual plants.

What, then, is the function of the §304(b) guidelines? As we noted earlier, §304(b) requires EPA to identify the amount of effluent reduction attainable through use of the best practicable or available technology and to "specify factors

17.   Furthermore, §301(c) provides that the 1983 limitations may be modified if the owner of a plant shows that "such modified requirements (1) will represent the maximum use of technology within the economic capability of the owner or operator; and (2) will result in reasonable further progress toward the elimination of the discharge of pollutants." This provision shows that the §301(b) limitations for 1983 are to be established prior to consideration of the characteristics of the individual plant. American Iron & Steel Institute v. EPA, *supra*, at 1037 n.15. Moreover, it shows that the term "best technology economically achievable" does not refer to any individual plant. Otherwise, it would be impossible for this "economically achievable" technology to be beyond the individual owner's "economic capability."

to be taken into account" in determining the pollution control methods "to be applicable to point sources . . . within such categories or classes." These guidelines are to be issued "[f]or the purpose of adopting or revising effluent limitations under this Act." As we read it, §304 requires that the guidelines survey the practicable or available pollution-control technology for an industry and assess its effectiveness. The guidelines are then to describe the methodology EPA intends to use in the §301 regulations to determine the effluent limitations for particular plants.

Consequently, we hold that EPA has the authority to issue regulations setting forth uniform effluent limitations for categories of plants.

II

Our holding that §301 does authorize the Administrator to promulgate effluent limitations for classes and categories of existing point sources necessarily resolves the jurisdictional issue as well. For, as we have already pointed out, §509(b)(1) provides that "[r]eview of the Administrator's action . . . in approving or promulgating any effluent limitation or other limitation under section 301, 302, or 306, . . . may be had by any interested person in the Circuit Court of Appeals of the United States for the Federal judicial district in which such person resides or transacts such business. . . ."

III

The remaining issue in this case concerns new plants. Under §306, EPA is to promulgate "regulations establishing Federal standards of performance for new sources. . . ." §306(b)(1)(B). A "standard of performance" is a "standard for the control of the discharge of pollutants which reflects the greatest degree of effluent reduction which the Administrator determines to be achievable through application of the best available demonstrated control technology, . . . including, where practicable, a standard permitting no discharge of pollutants." §306(a)(1). In setting the standard, "[t]he Administrator may distinguish among classes, types, and sizes within categories of new sources . . . and shall consider the type of process employed (including whether batch or continuous)." §306(b)(2). As the House Report states, the standard must reflect the best technology for "that category of sources, and for class, types, and sizes within categories." H.R. Rep. No. 92-911, p. 111 (1972). Leg. Hist. 798.

The Court of Appeals held: "Neither the Act nor the regulations contain any variance provision for new sources. The rule of presumptive applicability applies to new sources as well as existing sources. On remand EPA should come forward with some limited escape mechanism for new sources." *Du Pont II*, 541 F.2d, at 1028. The court's rationale was that "[p]rovisions for variances, modifications, and exceptions are appropriate to the regulatory process." Ibid.

The question, however, is not what a court thinks is generally appropriate to the regulatory process; it is what Congress intended for *these* regulations. It is clear that Congress intended these regulations to be absolute prohibitions. The use of the word "standards" implies as much. So does the description of the preferred standard as one "permitting *no* discharge of pollutants." (Emphasis added.) It is "unlawful for *any* owner or operator of *any* new source to operate such source in violation of any standard of performance applicable to such source." §306(e) (emphasis added). In striking contrast to §301(c), there is no statutory provision for variances, and a variance provision would be inappropriate in a standard that was intended to insure national uniformity and "maximum feasible control of new sources." S. Rep. No. 92-414, p. 58 (1971), Leg. Hist. 1476.

EPA v. NATIONAL CRUSHED STONE ASSOCIATION
449 U.S. 64 (1980)

Justice WHITE delivered the opinion of the Court.

In April and July 1977, the Environmental Protection Agency (EPA), acting under the Federal Water Pollution Control Act Amendments of 1972 (Act), 33 U.S.C. §1251 et seq., promulgated pollution discharge limitations for the coal mining industry and for that portion of the mineral mining and processing industry comprising the crushed stone, construction sand, and gravel categories. Although the Act does not expressly authorize or require variances from the 1977 limitation, each set of regulations contained a variance provision. . . .

To obtain a variance from the 1977 uniform discharge limitations a discharger must demonstrate that the "factors relating to the equipment or facilities involved, the process applied, or other such factors relating to such discharger are fundamentally different from the factors considered in the establishment of the guidelines." Although a greater than normal cost of implementation will be considered in acting on a request for a variance, economic ability to meet the costs will not be considered. A variance, therefore, will not be granted on the basis of the applicant's economic inability to meet the costs of implementing the uniform standard.

The Court of Appeals for the Fourth Circuit rejected this position [601 F.2d 111 (4th Cir. 1979)]. . . .

We granted certiorari to resolve the conflict between the decision below and Weyerhaeuser Co. v. Costle, 191 U. S. App. D.C. 309, 590 F.2d 1011 (1978), in which the variance provision was upheld. . . .

Section 301(c) of the Act explicitly provides for modifying the 1987 (BAT) effluent limitations with respect to individual point sources. A variance under §301(c) may be obtained upon a showing "that such modified requirements (1) will represent the maximum use of technology within the economic capability of the owner or operator; and (2) will result in reasonable further progress toward elimination of the discharge of pollutants." Thus, the economic ability of the individual operator to meet the costs of effluent reductions may in some circumstances justify granting a variance from the 1987 limitations.

No such explicit variance provision exists with respect to BPT standards, but in E. I. du Pont de Nemours v. Train, 430 U.S. 112 (1977), we indicated that a variance provision was a necessary aspect of BPT limitations applicable by regulations to classes and categories of point sources. 430 U.S., at 128. The issue in this case is whether the BPT variance provision must allow consideration of the economic capability of an individual discharger to afford the costs of the BPT limitation. For the reasons that follow, our answer is in the negative.

II

The plain language of the statute does not support the position taken by the Court of Appeals. Section 301(c) is limited on its face to modifications of the 1987 BAT limitations. It says nothing about relief from the 1977 BPT requirements. Nor does the language of the Act support the position that although §301(c) is not itself applicable to BPT standards, it requires that the affordability of the prescribed 1977 technology be considered in BPT variance decisions. This would be a logical reading of the statute only if the factors listed in §301(c) bore a substantial relationship to the considerations underlying the 1977 limitations as they do to those controlling the 1987 regulations. This is not the case.

The two factors listed in §301(c) — "maximum use of technology within the economic capability of the owner or operator" and "reasonable further progress toward the elimination of the discharge of pollutants" — parallel the general definition of BAT standards as limitations that "require application of the best available technology economically achievable for such category or class, which will result in reasonable further progress toward . . . eliminating the discharge of all pollutants. . . ." §301(b)(2). A §301(c) variance, thus, creates for a particular point source a BAT standard that represents for it the same sort of economic and technological commitment as the general BAT standard creates for the class. As with the general BAT standard, the variance assumes that the 1977 BPT has been met by the point source and that the modification represents a commitment of the maximum resources economically possible to the ultimate goal of eliminating all polluting discharges. No one who can afford the best available technology can secure a variance.

There is no similar connection between §301(c) and the considerations underlying the establishment of the 1977 BPT limitations. First, §301(c)'s requirement of "reasonable further progress" must have reference to some prior standard. BPT serves as the prior standard with respect to BAT. There is, however, no comparable, prior standard with respect to BPT limitations. Second, BPT limitations do not require an industrial category to commit the maximum economic resources possible to pollution control, even if affordable. Those point sources already using a satisfactory pollution control technology need take no additional steps at all. The §301(c) variance factor, the "maximum use of technology within the economic capability of the owner or operator," would therefore be inapposite in the BPT context. It would not have the same effect there that it has with the respect to BAT's, i.e., it would not apply the general requirements to an individual point source.

More importantly, to allow a variance based on the maximum technology affordable by the point source, even if that technology fails to meet BPT effluent limitations, would undercut the purpose and function of BPT limitations. Rather than the 1987 requirement of the best measures economically and technologically feasible, the statutory provisions for 1977 contemplate regulations prohibiting discharges from any point source in excess of the effluent produced by the best practicable technology currently available in the industry. . . .

. . . To allow a variance based on the economic capability and not to require adherence to the prescribed minimum technology would permit the employment of the very practices that the Administrator had rejected in establishing the best practicable technology currently in use in the industry. . . .

The Administrator's present interpretation of the language of the statute is amply supported by the legislative history, which persuades us that Congress understood that the economic capability provision of §301(c) was limited to BAT variances; that Congress foresaw and accepted the economic hardship, including the closing of some plants, that effluent limitations would cause; and that Congress took certain steps to alleviate this hardship, steps which did not include allowing a BPT variance based on economic capability.[18] . . . Instead of economic variances, Congress specifically added two other provisions to address the problem of economic hardship.

First, provision was made for low-cost loans to small businesses to help them meet the cost of technological improvements. §8, amending 15 U.S.C. §636. The Conference Report described the provision as authorizing the Small Business Administration "to make loans to assist small business concerns . . . if the Administrator determines that the concern is likely to suffer substantial economic injury without such assistance." 1 Leg. Hist. 153. . . .

Second, an employee protection provision was added, giving EPA authority to investigate any plant's claim that it must cut back production or close down

---

18. Since any variance provision will permit nonuniformity with the general BPT standard for a given category, we cannot attribute much weight to those passages in the legislative history, to which the Government points, that express a desire and expectation that "each polluter within a category or class of industrial sources . . . achieve nationally uniform effluent limitations based on 'best practicable technology no later than July 1, 1977.'" See 1 Leg. Hist. 162 (statement of Sen. Muskie). See also, e.g., 1 Leg. Hist. 170, 1 Leg. Hist. 302, 309 (Conference Report); 1 Leg. Hist. 787 (Report of House Committee on Public Works). Moreover, EPA has itself stated that a variance does not represent an exception to BPT or BAT limitations, but rather sets an individualized BPT or BAT limitation for that point source: "No discharge . . . may be excused from the Act's requirement to meet BPT [and] BAT . . . through this variance clause. A discharger may instead receive an individualized definition of such a limitation or standard where the nationally prescribed limit is shown to be more or less stringent than appropriate for the discharger under the Act." 44 Fed. Reg. 32893. Therefore, expressions of an intent that "all" point sources meet BPT standards by 1977 do not necessarily support the Government's argument.

because of pollution control regulations. §507(e), 33 U.S.C. §1367(e). This provision had two purposes: to allow EPA constantly to monitor the economic effect on industry of pollution control rules and to undercut economic threats by industry that would create pressure to relax effluent limitation rules.

Congress addressed the variance issue in 1987. See pages 442 to 443 *infra*.

WEYERHAEUSER CO. v. COSTLE
590 F. 2d 1011 (D.C. Cir. 1978)

[The pulp paper mill industry challenged EPA's BPT standards. After describing the rule-making process and extensively discussing the scope of review, the court concluded that it should examine the fairness of the agency's procedures and determine, with due respect to the problems of scientific uncertainty, whether the agency's judgment was reasonable in the light of its explanations and factual record. One final explanation for one standard for one subpart of the industry was found to be inadequate judged by this standard. The court next addressed the variance issue and reached the conclusion affirmed by the Supreme Court in *National Crushed Stone*, p. 386 *supra*. The court's description of the pulp and paper waste disposal process and its disposition of the industry's two major challenges to the regulations follow.]

B

To make paper from trees is an old art; to do it without water pollution is a new science. In papermaking, logs or wooden chips must be ground up or "cooked" in one of several processes until only cellulose pulp is left. The pulp is bleached and made into various types and grades of paper. The cooking solutions and wash water that are left contain a variety of chemicals produced during "cooking" and other processes, including acids and large quantities of dissolved cellulose-breakdown products. Indeed, in some pulping processes, more of the wood is discarded in the waste water than is used to make paper. Appendix (App.) 2116. EPA has selected three parameters for measuring the pollutant content of the industry's effluent, all of which have been used extensively in this and other industries' measurements: total suspended solids (TSS), biochemical oxygen demand (BOD), and pH.[5] TSS reflects the total amount of solids in solution, while

---

5.   Zinc is also a pollution parameter measure for industry subcategories that use it in their processes. Zinc effluent limitations have not been challenged.

The term "parameter" has been used to describe BOD, TSS, pH, and similar measures because of their function. In mathematics, a parameter is defined as an "arbitrary constant" —

BOD reflects the amount of biodegradable material in solution, and pH measures the acidity of the solution.[6]

EPA has divided this segment of the industry into 16 subcategories, and further subdivided it into 66 subdivisions, for the purposes of its rulemaking effort. As noted, some of petitioners' challenges concern all of the regulations for the whole industry, while other challenges are directed to regulations for particular industry subcategories. Actually, of the 16 subcategories in the whole industry, only three — the three that use some form of the "sulfite process" — have evoked particularized challenges. The reaction of sulfite mill operators stems from the limitations' greater economic impact on them. That impact in turn results from the fact that the sulfite process creates one of the highest pollution loads of any industrial process, and certainly the highest within the pulping industry. In fact, the Act's legislative history focused in particular on injury to shellfish in rivers and bays caused by sulfite wastes. A Legislative History of the Water Pollution Control Act Amendments of 1972 718-21 (1973) [hereinafter referred to as *Legislative History*]. Because the sulfite process is central in this case, we describe it in greater detail.

In the sulfite process, wooden chips are "cooked" in hot solutions of sulphurous acid and other chemicals. The cooking dissolves the binding agent in the wood (lignin) and also a good deal of the cellulose. The end product is cellulose pulp and an acid solution called spent sulfite liquor (SSL). There are two types of sulfite processes. In the papergrade sulfite process, which produces cellulose pulp for paper, the cellulose does not need to be very pure, and moderate steps suffice for cooking and separating pulp from SSL. In the dissolving sulfite process, aimed at making the raw cellulose base for materials such as cellophane and rayon, the cellulose must be pure, so the cooking and separation of the SSL are more complete and extra bleaching of the pulp is performed.

The sulfite process results in SSL and other potential pollution solutions

---

a variable that keeps a constant role in a formula as it takes on different (arbitrary) numerical values. For example, in the formula for a parabola ($y = ax^2 + b$), the horizontal or "x" variable is a parameter because it keeps a constant role in the formula while different numerical values are plugged in to calculate different vertical or "y" levels. For all EPA regulations, BOD and the like keep a constant role — what they are, and how they are measured, stay the same — even as they take on different numerical values for the acceptable level in each industrial category depending on the available technology for that category.

6.   As the Second Circuit recently noted, "Biochemical Oxygen Demand is not strictly speaking a pollutant at all." C & H Sugar Co. v. EPA, 553 F.2d 280, 282 n.7 (2d Cir. 1977). BOD is a measure of how much oxygen is used by organisms in water that break down biodegradable pollutants. As such, it indicates how much dissolved oxygen in the water will be used in fermenting the wastes. It is important because that fermentation process is capable of depleting so much of the water's oxygen supply that fish and other life in the water asphyxiate. The BOD level is also important because it correlates with the level of harmful organic chemicals. Accordingly, effluent with high BOD can cause damage even when dumped into waters that have more than ample amounts of dissolved oxygen. The same is true of pH: effluent high in toxic acids may cause damage even when dumped into sea water, whose salts buffer its pH level. It is well recognized that EPA can use pollution parameters that are not harmful in themselves, but act as indicators of harm. See American Paper Inst. v. Train, 177 U.S. App. D.C. 181, 202, 543 F.2d 328, 349, *cert. dismissed*, 429 U.S. 967 (1976) (color can be used as a pollution parameter).

containing acids, dissolved cellulose break-down products, and many types of organic compounds. These solutions receive various kinds of waste treatment. SSL is evaporated and burned in "SSL recovery," eliminating the water pollution potential and producing usable heat and sometimes reusable chemicals. The non-SSL waste solutions are pumped into sedimentation tanks where some of the suspended solids settle out of solution. The solutions are then pumped into other tanks and lagoons for secondary or "biological" treatment, in which bacteria are grown in the solutions to feed on and break down the waste. Eventually, the water is drained from the bacteria-laden solutions by a variety of methods. After draining, the caked solid or "sludge" that is left is incinerated or used for landfill. . . .

1

Some of the paper mills that must meet the effluent limitations under review discharge their effluents into the Pacific Ocean. Petitioners contend that the ocean can dilute or naturally treat effluent, and that EPA must take this capacity of the ocean ("receiving water capacity") into account in a variety of ways. They urge what they term "common sense," i.e., that because the amounts of pollutant involved are small in comparison to bodies of water as vast as Puget Sound or the Pacific Ocean, they should not have to spend heavily on treatment equipment, or to increase their energy requirements and sludge levels, in order to treat wastes that the ocean could dilute or absorb.[41]

EPA's secondary response to this claim was that pollution is far from harmless, even when disposed of in the largest bodies of water. As congressional testimony indicated, the Great Lakes, Puget Sound, and even areas of the Atlantic Ocean have been seriously injured by water pollution. Even if the ocean can handle ordinary wastes, ocean life may be vulnerable to toxic compounds that typically accompany those wastes. In the main, however, EPA simply asserted that the issue of receiving water capacity could not be raised in setting effluent limitations because Congress had ruled it out. We have examined the previous legislation in this area, and the 1972 Act's wording, legislative history, and policies, as underscored by its 1977 amendments. These sources, which were thoroughly analyzed in a recent opinion of the administrator of the Agency, fully support EPA's construction of the Act. They make clear that based on long experience, and aware of the limits of technological knowledge and administrative

41.   Apart from this simple "common sense" version of the argument, there is a more sophisticated economic version called the "optimal pollution" theory. This economic theory contends that there is a level or type of pollution that, while technologically capable of being controlled, is uneconomic to treat because the benefit from treatment is small and the cost of treatment is large. See generally W. Baxter, People or Penguins: The Case for Optimal Pollution (1974); B. Ackerman, S. Rose-Ackerman, J. Sawyer & D. Henderson, The Uncertain Search for Environmental Quality (1974). These economic theories are premised on a view that we have both adequate information about the effects of pollution to set an optimal test, and adequate political and administrative flexibility to keep polluters at that level once we allow any pollution to go untreated. As discussed in this section, it appears that Congress doubted these premises.

flexibility, Congress made the deliberate decision to rule out arguments based on receiving water capacity. . . .

Moreover, by eliminating the issue of the capacity of particular bodies of receiving water, Congress made nationwide uniformity in effluent regulation possible. Congress considered uniformity vital to free the states from the temptation of relaxing local limitations in order to woo or keep industrial facilities. In addition, national uniformity made pollution clean-up possible without engaging in the divisive task of favoring some regions of the country over others.

More fundamentally, the new approach implemented changing views as to the relative rights of the public and of industrial polluters. Hitherto, the right of the polluter was pre-eminent, unless the damage caused by pollution could be proved. Henceforth, the right of the public to a clean environment would be pre-eminent, unless pollution treatment was impractical or unachievable. The Senate Committee declared that "[t]he use of any river, lake, stream or ocean as a waste treatment system is unacceptable" — regardless of the measurable impact of the waste on the body of water in question. Legislative History at 1425 (Senate Report). The Conference Report stated that the Act "specifically bans pollution dilution as an alternative to waste treatment." Id. at 284. This new view of relative rights was based in part on the hard-nosed assessment of our scientific ignorance: "we know so little about the ultimate consequences of injection of new matter into water that [the Act requires] a presumption of pollution. . . ." Id. at 1332 (remarks of Sen. Buckley). It also was based on the widely shared conviction that the nation's quality of life depended on its natural bounty, and that it was worth incurring heavy cost to preserve that bounty for future generations. . . .

The Act was passed with an expectation of "mid-course corrections," Legislative History, at 175 (statement of Sen. Muskie), and in 1977 Congress amended the Act, although generally holding to the same tack set five years earlier. Pub. L. No. 95-217, 91 Stat. 1584. Notably, during those five years, representatives of the paper industry had appeared before Congress and urged it to *change* the Act and to incorporate receiving water capacity as a consideration. See, e.g., Hearings before the Subcomm. on Environmental Pollution of the Senate Comm. on Environment and Public Works, 95th Cong., 1st Sess., pt. 3, at 193, 195, 540. Nonetheless, Congress was satisfied with this element of the statutory scheme. . . .

2

Petitioners also challenge EPA's manner of assessing two factors that all parties agree must be considered: cost and non-water quality environmental impacts. They contend that the Agency should have more carefully balanced costs versus the effluent reduction benefits of the regulations, and that it should have also balanced those benefits against the non-water quality environmental impacts to arrive at a "net" environmental benefit conclusion. Petitioners base their arguments on certain comments made by the Conferees for the Act, see note 52 *infra*, and on the fact that the Act lists non-water quality environmental impacts as a factor the Agency must "take into account."

In order to discuss petitioners' challenges, we must first identify the relevant statutory standard. Section 304(b)(1)(B) of the Act, 33 U.S.C. §1314(b)(1)(B), identifies the factors bearing on BPCTCA in two groups. First, the factors shall "include consideration of the total cost of application of technology in relation to the effluent reduction benefits to be achieved from such application," and second, they "shall also take into account the age of equipment and facilities involved, the process employed, the engineering aspects of the application of various types of control techniques, process changes, non-water quality environmental impact (including energy requirements), and such other factors as the Administrator deems appropriate[.]"

The first group consists of two factors that EPA must compare: total cost versus effluent reduction benefits. We shall call these the "comparison factors." The other group is a list of many factors that EPA must "take into account:" age, process, engineering aspects, process changes, environmental impacts (including energy), and any others EPA deems appropriate. We shall call these the "consideration factors." Notably, section 304(b)(2)(B) of the Act, 33 U.S.C. §1314(b)(2)(B), which delineates the factors relevant to setting 1983 BATEA limitations, tracks the 1977 BPCTCA provision before us except in one regard: in the 1983 section, *all* factors, including costs and benefits, are consideration factors, and no factors are separated out for comparison.

Based on our examination of the statutory language and the legislative history, we conclude that Congress mandated a particular structure and weight for the 1977 comparison factors, that is to say, a "limited" balancing test.[52] In contrast, Congress did not mandate any particular structure or weight for the many consideration factors. Rather, it left EPA with discretion to decide how to account for the consideration factors, and how much weight to give each factor. In response to these divergent congressional approaches, we conclude that, on the one hand, we should examine EPA's treatment of cost and benefit under the 1977 standard to assure that the Agency complied with Congress' "limited" balancing directive. See note 52 *supra*. On the other hand, our scrutiny of the Agency's treatment of the several consideration factors seeks to assure that the

---

52.   Senator Muskie described the "limited" balancing test:

The modification of subsection 304(b)(1) is intended to clarify what is meant by the term "practicable." The balancing test between total cost and effluent reduction benefits is intended to limit the application of technology only where the additional degree of effluent reduction is wholly out of proportion to the costs of achieving such marginal level of reduction for any class or category of sources.

The Conferees agreed upon this limited cost-benefit analysis in order to maintain uniformity within a class and category of point sources subject to effluent limitations, and to avoid imposing on the Administrator any requirement to consider the location of sources within a category or to ascertain water quality impact of effluent controls, or to determine the economic impact of controls on any individual plant in a single community.

Legislative History, at 170 (emphasis added).

Agency informed itself as to their magnitude, and reached its own express and considered conclusion about their bearing. More particularly, we do not believe that EPA is required to use any specific structure such as a balancing test in assessing the consideration factors, nor do we believe that EPA is required to give each consideration factor any specific weight.

Our conclusions are based initially on the section's wording and apparent logic. By singling out two factors (the comparison factors) for separate treatment, and by requiring that they be considered "in relation to" each other, Congress elevated them to a level of greater attention and rigor. Moreover, the comparison factors are a closed set of two, making it possible to have a definite structure and weight in considering them and preventing extraneous factors from intruding on the balance.

By contrast, the statute directs the Agency only to "take into account" the consideration factors, without prescribing any structure for EPA's deliberations. As to this latter group of factors, the section cannot logically be interpreted to impose on EPA a specific structure of consideration or set of weights because it gave EPA authority to "upset" any such structure by exercising its discretion to add new factors to the mix. Instead, the listing of factors seems aimed at noting all of the matters that Congress considered worthy of study before making limitation decisions, without preventing EPA from identifying other factors that it considers worthy of study. So long as EPA pays some attention to the congressionally specified factors, the section on its face lets EPA relate the various factors as it deems necessary. . . .

Judicial decisions have carefully observed that the cost and benefit factors require more rigorous EPA consideration of cost versus benefit in the 1977 standards than in the 1983 standards. *American Paper Inst., supra,* 177 U.S. App. D.C. at 191, 543 F.2d at 338 (cost-benefit balancing in 1977, not in 1983); accord *American Frozen Food Inst., supra,* 176 U.S. App. D.C. at 117, 539 F.2d at 119; *American Meat Inst., supra,* 526 F.2d at 462-63. . . .

A

Petitioners do not challenge the cost-benefit analysis for the whole industry. They do, however, challenge the analysis for the sulfite sector, contending that EPA used an "overall" instead of an "incremental" method of balancing, and that its figures on the cost of BPCTCA for the dissolving sulfite subcategory were underestimates. We uphold EPA's determination against both contentions.

EPA's approach was similar to the one we upheld in *American Paper Inst., supra,* 177 U.S. App. D.C. at 191-92, 543 F.2d at 338-39. The Agency assessed the costs of internal and external effluent treatment measures, not only for the industry, but also for each subcategory. This included a separate cost assessment for the sulfite subcategories. App. 2380-83. An economic analysis was prepared to determine the impact of the costs on the industry. App. 1211-448. It found that the industry as a whole would readily absorb the cost of compliance with the 1977 standards, estimated at $1.6 billion. Out of 270 mills employing

120,000 people, eight mills would likely be closed and 1800 people laid off. The Agency noted that the impact on the three heavily polluting sulfite subcategories would be the greatest. Of less than 30 sulfite mills, three would probably close, resulting in 550 people being laid off.

Against these costs, EPA balanced the main effluent reduction benefit: overall 5,000 fewer tons per day of BOD discharged into the nation's waters. EPA refined this balance by calculating the cost per pound of BOD removed for each subcategory. App. 2478-79. Although sulfite mills must make large investments in waste treatment facilities, the cost-benefit balance is favorable for the limitations on these mills, because of the large volume of waste they produce and thus the greater treatment efficiency.

Petitioners' first contention is that EPA not only should have calculated the overall cost-benefit balance, but also should have made an "incremental" calculation of that balance. More precisely, they contend that EPA must undertake to measure the costs and benefits of each additional increment of waste treatment control, from bare minimum up to complete pollution removal. In support of this contention, they point to Senator Muskie's description of cost-benefit balancing, which suggests a focus on the "additional degree" or "marginal" amount of effluent reduction. See note 52 *supra*. Petitioners concede that we accepted EPA's calculation of the overall cost-benefit balance, without any further marginal or incremental analysis, in *American Paper Inst.*, *supra*, 543 F.2d at 338. Nonetheless, they suggest that the present case can be distinguished, because in these proceedings, unlike in *American Paper Inst.*, industry representatives submitted an incremental breakdown of costs and benefits to the Agency.

The failure of *American Paper Inst.* to require EPA to perform its own incremental analysis is justified for a number of reasons beyond some oversight on the part of paper industry petitioners in that case. While EPA has no discretion to avoid cost-benefit balancing for its 1977 standards, it does have some discretion to decide how it will perform the cost-benefit balancing task. "[E]ven with th[e] 1977 standard, the cost of compliance was not a factor to be given primary importance," *American Iron & Steel Inst.*, *supra*, 526 F.2d at 1051, and, as such, cost need not be balanced against benefits with pinpoint precision. A requirement that EPA perform the elaborate task of calculating incremental balances would bog the Agency down in burdensome proceedings on a relatively subsidiary task. Hence, the Agency need not on its own undertake more than a net cost-benefit balancing to fulfill its obligation under section 304.

However, when an incremental analysis has been performed by industry and submitted to EPA, it is worthy of scrutiny by the Agency, for it may "avoid the risk of hidden imbalances between cost and benefit." Id. at 1076 n.19 (Adams, J., concurring). If such a "hidden imbalance" were revealed here, and if the Agency had ignored it, we might remand for further consideration. But in this case the incremental analysis proffered by industry showed that the last and most expensive increment of BOD treated in sulfite mills cost less than $.15 per pound of BOD removed, which is below the average cost of treatment in most of the industry's subcategories. App. 3545-51B. We would be reluctant to find that EPA had ignored a "hidden imbalance" when the most unfavorable incremental cost-benefit balance that is challenged falls well within the range of averages for the industry as a whole.

NOTES AND QUESTIONS

Is the following language from BASF Wyandotte Corp. v. Costle, 598 F. 2d 637 (1st Cir. 1979), inconsistent with *Weyerhaeuser?*

> Congress "self-consciously made the legislative determination that the health and safety gains that achievement of the Act's aspirations would bring to future generations will in some cases outweigh the economic dislocation it causes to the present generation." *Weyerhaeuser*, at 1037. The obligation the Act imposes on EPA is only to perform a limited cost-benefit balancing to make sure that costs are not "wholly out of proportion" to the benefits achieved. A Legislative History of the Water Pollution Control Act Amendments of 1972 170 (1973) (statement of Senator Muskie); *Weyerhaeuser*, at 1045 n.52. Thus, the balancing is a relatively subsidiary task and need not be precise. *Weyerhaeuser* at 1049. The Agency has considerable discretion to decide how to go about considering costs and benefits and need not "perform the elaborate task of calculating incremental balances" of marginal costs and benefits. Id. . . . We agree with the *Weyerhaeuser* court that "when an incremental analysis has been performed by industry and submitted to EPA, it is worthy of scrutiny by the Agency." [Id. at] 1048. Du Pont's study, indicating rapidly increasing costs for removal of incremental amounts of pollutants, certainly was "worthy of scrutiny," and we assume that EPA did not ignore it. Largely through no fault of du Pont's, however, the study tested a carbon absorption model very different from the one that formed the basis for EPA's costs estimates. Most notably, du Pont studied contact times of 22, 44 and 66 minutes whereas EPA prepared costs estimates for systems with contact times of 60, 300, 600, and 750 minutes. Generally the longer the effluent remains in contact with the carbon, the more efficient the treatment will be. We are not prepared to say that the du Pont study demonstrates that incremental costs of EPA's model system were wholly out of proportion to incremental benefits, nor will we require EPA explicitly to respond to every study submitted by commenters. [598 F. 2d at 656-657.]

Within the framework of welfare economics, can a case be made against incremental cost-benefit analyses? If one factor is the costs of administering economic rationality, is the case still as strong? See Note, Cost-Benefit Analysis and the Federal Water Pollution Control Act Amendments of 1972: A Proposal for Congressional Action, 67 Iowa L. Rev. 1057 (1982). Consider the comments of Christopher DeMuth, the Office of Management and Budget's point man on the Clean Water Act under Executive Order 12,291, reported in 13 Envt. Rep. (BNA): Current Developments, 1575 (1983).

> EPA's test of economic achievability for effluent guidelines under the Clean Water Act has been a thorn in DeMuth's side, according to EPA officials, who said in some cases the statute forces regulations that are not cost-effective. They said that, if a rule does not make a company go out of business, it basically is considered achievable.

"The important thing is to keep a degree of cost-effectiveness across industries," he said, explaining that, if a rule costs one industry $1,000 to remove a pound of pollution and costs another $100 for an equivalent pound, "we must be doing something wrong."

Further, he said, it is especially difficult to assess benefits of pollution removal when most of the pollution already has been removed.

"It doesn't make any sense on one waterway to be spending $100 a pound [to remove pollution] at one point and to be spending $1,000 at another." The Water Act was not written with Executive Order 12291 in mind, DeMuth commented. [13 Envt. Rep. (BNA): Current Developments, at 1575.]

A NOTE ON BPT AND BAT DEFENSES

1. *Du Pont* upholds EPA's discretion to promulgate uniform, national effluent standards, and *National Crushed Stone* sets the ground rules for BPT variances. However, national EPA regulations remain open to the challenge that they are unauthorized or arbitrary. In a series of suits brought by trade associations, effluent limitations were attacked as ultra vires or as scientifically unjustified. Among the more important issues related to compliance defenses that have been litigated are:

a. Can EPA adopt BPT standards that can be met only by in-plant modifications? American Petroleum Institute v. EPA, 540 F. 2d 1023 (10th Cir. 1976), *cert denied sub. nom.* Exxon Corp. v. EPA, 430 U.S. 922 (1977), rejected the argument that BPT technologies were restricted to end-of-the-pipe treatment systems, in part because the standard was based on pollution control practices that were widespread within the industry.

b. *American Petroleum Institute* also settled an argument between industries and EPA about whether the regulations must establish effluent limitations over a range of numbers or whether the agency could use only single numbers. The court upheld the agency's discretion to use single numbers, and that construction of the Act was affirmed in *Du Pont*.

Trustees for Alaska v. EPA, 749 F. 2d 549 (9th Cir. 1984), holds that the EPA must include turbidity effluent limitations in placer mining permits. EPA sets mass effluent limitations by multiplying the maximum concentration level of the pollutant times water flow to prevent dischargers from avoiding compliance by dilution. A zero discharge BAT standard was upheld in Kennecott v. EPA, 780 F. 2d 445 (4th Cir. 1985), *cert denied*, 479 U.S. 814 (1986). An NPDES permit holder cannot raise an upset defense in a citizen enforcement action. *Marathon Oil*, p. 357 *supra*, requires that the permit holder seek an administrative modification of the permit. Sierra Club v. Union Oil Co., 813 F. 2d 1480 (9th Cir. 1987), *vacated*, 108 S. Ct. 1102 (1988), *opinion on remand*, 716 F. Supp. 429 (N.D. Cal. 1989).

c. *Weyerhaeuser* holds that the 1972 amendments foreclose a permit applicant from arguing that he should receive credit in his NPDES permit if he discharges into clean or relatively clean water. Accord American Petroleum Institute v. EPA, 858 F. 2d 261 (5th Cir. 1988) (product substitution appropriate

BAT even though the existing technology, "toxic-carrying" diesel drilling mud, carries no environmental threat when discharged in small quantities because impact on receiving water is not relevant). See also Natural Resources Defense Council, Inc. v. EPA, 863 F.2d 1420 (9th Cir. 1988). Crown Simpson Pulp Co. v. Costle, 642 F.2d 323 (9th Cir. 1981), *opinion on remand from* 445 U.S. 193 (1980), *cert. denied*, 454 U.S. 1053 (1982) (p. 357 *infra*), holds that receiving water quality is not a fundamentally "different" factor to be considered by EPA in granting a BPT variance. But cf. Association of Pacific Fisheries v. EPA, 615 F.2d 794 (9th Cir. 1980). The BPT regulations for the Preserved Seafood Point Source Category require that all wastes be screened, collected, and either deposited in landfills or barged out to sea at ocean sites from one half to two and one half miles from the plant. The general practice of the industry is to grind the wastes and discharge them at the shore. EPA's regulations are based on studies that show inadequate tidal dispersion near major processing centers in Alaska. Is this regulation technology-based rather than water quality-based? Is the agency's cost-benefit analysis deficient because it fails to consider grinding, which the industry maintains either eliminates the same environmental harms sought to be minimized by screening and poses the same environmental risks as screening? But does the issue end there? Any effluent limitations must be based on assumptions about water quality. For example, must the agency make express provisions for excursions (situations in which effluent limitations are intentionally exceeded for reasons beyond the control of the permittee)? Corn Refiners Association v. Costle, 594 F.2d 1223 (8th Cir. 1979), holds that EPA does not have to do so when it includes such a possibility in the database on which the regulations rest:

> The parties' arguments can be briefly stated. Petitioners note that the Federal Water Pollution Control Act Amendments of 1972 (the Act), 33 U.S.C. §1251 et seq., requires point sources of pollution to utilize the "best practicable control technology currently available" (BPCTCA) prior to 1984. 33 U.S.C. §1311(b)(1)(A); see note 3, *supra*. Even in a mill employing properly operating BPCTCA technology, however, excursions may occur from time to time. Therefore, by failing to provide that excursions do not constitute violations of the effluent limitation regulations, EPA may be actually imposing on petitioners a standard which is greater than that imposed by the Act.
>
> EPA counters with a number of arguments why including an express provision excusing excursions would frustrate, or at least not further, the policies underlying the Act.
>
> The parties' arguments largely track the rationales of two recent, and conflicting, decisions. In Marathon Oil Co. v. Environmental Protection Agency, 564 F.2d 1253 (9th Cir. 1977), the court overturned EPA's refusal to include excursion provisions in individual effluent limitation permits issued to several oil companies with respect to both offshore oil platforms and onshore facilities. However, in Weyerhaeuser Co. v. Costle, 590 F.2d 1011 (1978), the court upheld EPA's industry-wide effluent limitation regulations for the bleached paper industry against a challenge that they were deficient because they did not include express provisions regarding excursions. . . .
>
> We are thus faced with a rather clear conflict in the circuits on this matter. After weighing the arguments on both sides, we agree with EPA and the District of Columbia Circuit's decision in *Weyerhaeuser* that no express provision regarding excursions is required.

We begin by noting that there is substantial force to petitioner's argument that EPA's regulations seemingly require petitioners to do the impossible — i.e., to prevent excursions which, by their very nature, can occur even in a properly operated facility meeting BPCTCA standards. Against this hardship, however, we must weigh the effect which a decision requiring excursion provisions in the regulations or individual permits would have on the important policies underlying the Act.

First, we note that a decision requiring EPA to make provisions for excursions might hamper EPA's ability to "force technology." Weyerhaeuser Co. v. Costle, *supra*, 590 F.2d at 1057. That is, Congress intended effluent limitations to compel plants to improve their antipollution performance, even when technological innovation is required, id. 191 U.S. App. D.C. at 359, 590 F.2d at 1061, thus furthering Congress' ultimate goal of entirely eliminating the discharge of pollutants into the nation's waters. 33 U.S.C. §1251. Denying excursion provisions justifiably compels the industry to develop the technological capability necessary to avoid excessive discharges.

Second, the compulsory inclusion of excursion provisions can lead to serious problems of enforcement. It is axiomatic that Congress intended enforcement of the Act to be "swift and direct." A Legislative History of the Water Pollution Control Act Amendments of 1972, Senate Committee on Public Works, 93d Cong., 1st Sess. at 1483 (1973). Enforcement is "swift and direct" when the case turns on the sharply defined question whether the plant discharged more pollutant than allowed under the simple numerical standards contained in the effluent discharge regulations. Excursion provisions cannot, however, be properly framed in simple numerical terms and must therefore be stated in more complex terms relating to questions of fault and justification. As the *Weyerhaeuser* court noted, once such an excursion provision is promulgated, the outcome of an enforcement proceeding "depends on murky determinations concerning the sequence of events in the plant, whether those events would have been avoidable if other equipment had been installed, and whether the discharge was within the intent of the excursion provision. Consequently, what Congress planned as a simple proceeding suitable for summary judgments would become a form of inquest into the nature of system malfunction." 191 U.S. App. D.C. at 356, 590 F.2d at 1058.

Third, petitioners' argument that excursions must be dealt with by regulations rather than left to administrative discretion overlooks the fact that some degree of administrative discretion is inevitable in these situations. The very nature of excursions and the virtually infinite number of causes of excursions make it impossible to foresee all problems which may arise and deal with them in particularized regulations. In short, at some point, violations of regulatory limits due to wholly unforeseen and uncontrollable occurrences must be a matter for administrative discretion rather than advance administrative regulation. Id. . . . Where the line is to be drawn between situations governed by a general rule and situations to be handled on a case-by-case basis is largely a matter for EPA to decide and we are persuaded that here it has drawn the line at a permissible place. [594 F.2d at 1225-1226.]

d. In setting BPT and BAT regulations, can EPA base the regulations solely on the performance of the best plants, or must all plants be considered in setting an effluent limitation? Hooker Chemicals & Plastics Corp. v. Train, 537 F.2d 620 (2d Cir. 1976), holds that the agency correctly limited the range of plants because the legislative history supported the use of "the average of the best existing performance." *National Crushed Stone* affirms this holding. Chemical Manufacturers Association v. EPA, 870 F.2d 177, 207-211 (5th Cir. 1989) followed these cases to hold that EPA could base BPT for the organic chemical, plastics and synthetic fiber industry on its use by 99 out of 304 plants and further could use the practice of 71 plants as the "average of the best" and need not distinguish between cold and warm weather plants. Cold weather area plants could apply biological treatment as well as warm weather ones by design and operations changes.

Kennecott v. EPA, 780 F.2d 445 4th Cir. (1985) *cert. denied*, 479 U.S. 814 (1986), summarized and applied the law of interindustry technology transfer:

> The model technology may exist at a plant not within the primary base metals industry. Congress contemplated that EPA might use technology from other industries to establish the Best Available Technology. *Reynolds Metals*, 760 F.2d at 562. Progress would be slowed if EPA were invariably limited to treatment schemes already in force at the plants which are the subject of the rulemaking. Congress envisioned the scanning of broader horizons and asked EPA to survey related industries and current research to find technologies which might be used to decrease the discharge of pollutants. Leg. Hist. at 170.
>
> To determine that technology from one industry can be applied to another, the agency must:
>   (1) show that the transfer technology is available outside the industry;
>   (2) determine that the technology is transferable to the industry;
>   (3) make a reasonable prediction that the technology if used in the industry will be capable of removing the increment required by the effluent standards.
> Tanners' Council of America, Inc. v. Train, 540 F.2d 1188, 1192 (4th Cir. 1976) (using the standard set out by the Eighth Circuit in CPC International Inc. v. Train, 515 F.2d 1032, 1048 (8th Cir. 1975).
>
> EPA has demonstrated that sulfide precipitation — a process it terms "familiar" and "well established" — is available outside the primary base metals industry and that the technology is transferable to that industry. The agency notes that "the low solubility of metal sulfides" has made sulfide precipitation a more effective treatment than the conventional lime and settle process. We do not think it disqualifying that the Ashio plant, for example, uses sulfide precipitation to produce an end product rather than to clean its wastewater, so long as the process adequately reduces pollutant concentrations in wastewater. Again, granting the agency a proper measure of deference in technical judgments, it was not arbitrary for EPA to decide that sulfide precipitation would remove pollutants to the degree required by the effluent limitations.
>
> Kennecott discusses two other differences between the sulfide precipitation process at the model plants and the process at the primary base metals plants. Kennecott points out that the Ashio plant treats wastewater in batches, while the primary base metals plants treat wastewater continuously. EPA answers that the choice of the batch or continuous processes affects only cost, not effectiveness, and that study demonstrates the installation and operation of sulfide precipitation is economically achievable.
>
> Kennecott also notes that all three model plants use sulfide pretreatment, rather than sulfide polishing. Again, EPA believes that the difference is irrelevant; whether sulfide precipitation is the step before or after L, S & F will not affect the achievability of the desired effluent limitations. The critical matter, in the agency's judgment, is the application of the proper amount of precipitant and the maintenance of proper levels of pH, factors entirely independent of the timing of wastewater treatment.
>
> We hold that EPA had a reasonable basis for deciding that the sulfide pre-

cipitation technology is transferable. We are unable to conclude the agency acted arbitrarily or capriciously in selecting sulfide precipitation as part of the Best Available Technology for the primary base metals industry. [Id. at 453-454.]

See also Chemical Manufacturers Association, *supra*, at 208-210 and 239-240 for a discussion of the agency's discretion to reject technologies as unachieveable and to exclude a single exceedance of daily limitations in deciding that a plant can meet a BAT technology.

2. In setting BAT effluent limitations, EPA has often prescribed technologies that were not in fact in use in any plant within the United States. Is such a technology nonetheless still available? See American Frozen Food Institute v. Train, 539 F.2d 107 (D.C. Cir. 1976). A technology is not per se unavailable just because it is not in use in any plant, but agency's burden of justification increases. In Hooker Chemicals & Plastics Corp. v. Train, 537 F.2d 620 (2d Cir. 1976), the court found that the agency's record was inadequate on the issue of feasibility because EPA had failed to specify adequately the facts underlying its conclusion that technologies would become commercially feasible and thus available. In American Petroleum Institute v. EPA, 540 F.2d 1023 (10th Cir. 1976), cert. denied sub nom. Exxon Corp. v. EPA, 430 U.S. 922 (1977), the plaintiffs secured a remand on the issue of whether a particular BAT technology, carbon absorption, was in fact available. The case was easy because EPA conceded that further development of the technology was necessary before a high degree of effectiveness in large scale operations could be shown. In addition, the record offered by the agency in support of its decision contained shifting and conflicting rationales for the decision.

The strongest case for EPA would be to devise a mathematical model of a hypothetical waste treatment plant built based on the best technology in use at that time and then convince a company to build a model plant. If the model plant met the EPA standard, it would be difficult for industry to show that the technology was not technically available. See CPC International, Inc. v. Train, 540 F.2d 1329 (8th Cir. 1976), in which the wet corn milling industry was faced with a plant that met BOD_5 standards and was thus reduced to the unsuccessful argument that the capital and operating costs were excessive. American Iron & Steel Institute v. EPA, 526 F.2d 1027 (3d Cir. 1975), *motions granted*, 560 F.2d 589, 568 F.2d 284, *cert. denied*, 435 U.S. 914 (1978), allows EPA to assume that technology can be transferred in setting standards. Obviously, the weaker industry's scientific case, the slimmer the chances of a reversal. See, e.g., American Meat Institute v. EPA, 526 F.2d 442 (7th Cir. 1975), in which the plaintiff argued that EPA's BPT standards that required waste water lagoons could not be achieved on a year-round basis. Basically, the argument was that seasonal changes would impair the efficiency of the required lagoons to break down wastes both in winter and in summer, but the court found that for the anaerobic lagoons (where organic matter is consumed by bacteria that do not require free oxygen) the industry's objections were not supported by sufficient data because the drop in efficiency caused by cold temperatures would be counteracted by the heat of incoming waste water. A similar conclusion was reached with respect to EPA's conclusion that ice would not impair the functioning of aerobic lagoons (where organic matter is mostly consumed by bacteria that do need oxygen) in cold weather, but only on the ground that EPA's record was insufficient under the "substantial evidence on the record as a whole" test but adequate under the "arbitrary and capricious" standard.

3. The function of cost in effluent limitations is not specified in the legislative history, other than some general evidence that Congress contemplated a greater use of cost-benefit calculations in BPT rather than BAT regulations. American Petroleum Institute v. EPA, 661 F.2d 340 (5th Cir. 1981), remanded an EPA BPT standard that required that all water produced from on-shore oil wells that discharged into coastal waters be reinjected because there was too great a difference between EPA and industry cost studies. On remand the agency stuck to reinjection as the BAT standard for new wells but delayed requiring existing wells to be retrofitted because it needed to study the technological feasibility and costs of the technology. Natural Resources Defense Council, Inc. v. EPA, 863 F.2d 1420 (9th Cir. 1988) partially disagreed with EPA:

> Technology-based limitations under BAT must be both technologically available and economically achievable. See 33 U.S.C. §1314(b)(2)(B). To be technologically available, it is sufficient that the best operating facilities can achieve the limitation. See Association of Pac. Fisheries v. EPA, 615 F.2d 794, 816-17 (9th Cir. 1980). To demonstrate economic achievability, no formal balancing of costs and benefits is required, see id. at 817-18; Reynolds Metals Co. v. EPA, 760 F.2d 549, 565 (4th Cir. 1985); BAT should represent "a commitment of the maximum resources economically possible to the ultimate goal of eliminating all polluting discharges." See EPA v. National Crushed Stone Assn., 449 U.S. 64, 74, 101 S. Ct. 295, 302, 66 L. Ed.2d 268 (1980). EPA has considerable discretion in weighing the costs of BAT. American Iron and Steel Inst. v. EPA, 526 F.2d 1027, 1052 (3d Cir. 1975), *amended in part on other grounds,* 560 F.2d 589 (3d Cir. 1977).
>
> There is no serious question that reinjection is technologically feasible at the present time. The record indicates that existing offshore operations in California and Alaska use reinjection technology. As we have seen, the proposed national guidelines would require it for new sources. The ostensible bar to reinjection becoming BAT for all existing sources is economic. The EPA maintains that it has insufficient information on the cost of retrofitting existing platforms in the Gulf with reinjection technology.
>
> EPA's contention that it lacks substantial information on the economic feasibility of retrofitting existing sources with reinjection technology is not supported by the record. The record contains several studies detailing the technology required for retrofitting existing offshore facilities with reinjection capability. See J.A. 254-62 (study prepared by Offshore Operators Committee); J.A. 335-52 ("Development Document for Effluent Limitations Guidelines and Standards for the Offshore Segment of the Oil and Gas Point Source Category," prepared by EPA); Supp. J.A. 1-27; 28-85 (studies prepared for the EPA). The focus of these studies is on the cost of retrofitting existing platforms.
>
> These studies do not agree about the precise costs of retrofitting. Their estimates vary. However, the Act does not require a precise calculation of BAT costs.

It requires that, in addition to other factors, the EPA "take into account" the cost of BAT. 33 U.S.C. §1314(b)(2)(B). In BASF Wyandotte Corp. v. Costle, 598 F.2d 637, 656-57 (1st Cir. 1979), the court stated that, in determining "best practicable control technology" (BPT), a level of control in which cost is a more significant factor than in BAT, EPA is not required to perform a precise measurement of cost; instead, "EPA needed to develop no more than a rough idea of the costs the industry would incur." Id. at 657. Congress made cost a more significant factor in establishing BPT than in establishing BAT, since in defining BPT it required a balancing of costs and benefits. It follows that EPA need make only a reasonable cost estimate in setting BAT. Compare 33 U.S.C. §1314(b)(2)(B) (in establishing BAT, EPA should "take into account" the cost) with §1314(b)(1)(B) (in establishing BPT, EPA must consider "the total cost of application of technology in relation to the effluent reduction benefits to be achieved").

The legislative history of the Act supports our conclusion that EPA should not delay requiring technologically feasible limitations as BAT in order to wait for precise cost figures. Senator Muskie, during Senate consideration of the conference report, stated that although cost should be a factor in determining BAT, "no balancing test will be required," and that the Administrator should be bound by a test of "reasonableness." Committee on Public Works, 92nd Cong., 1st Sess., Report on S. 2770, reprinted in A Legislative History of the Water Pollution Control Act Amendments of 1972, 161, 170 (hereinafter "Leg. Hist."). Senator Muskie continued that the reasonableness of what is economically achievable "should reflect an evaluation of what needs to be done to move toward the elimination of the discharge of pollutants and what is achievable through the application of available technology — without regard for cost." Id. The House Public Works Committee stated that the consideration of cost in determining BAT requires only "economic viability at the level sufficient to reasonably justify the making of investments in such new facilities." H.R. Rep. No. 911, 92nd Cong., 2d Sess., 103 (1972), reprinted in Leg. Hist. 753, 789.

On the basis of this record, we are thus unable to agree with the EPA that it could not have made a reasonable estimate of the economic effect of requiring that reinjection is BAT. The studies contained in the record, which include both agency and industry studies, analyze in considerable detail the cost of retrofitting existing platforms with reinjection technology. These studies evaluate the costs of retrofitting model platforms of different sizes, in different water depths and geographic locations; the studies consider the capital and maintenance costs of this technology. Given this detailed and developed record, we find that EPA had sufficient information to make a reasonable estimate of the costs of retrofitting existing platforms with reinjection technology.

The issue, however, is whether the agency was required to make such an estimate from the record before it and conclude that reinjection is BAT for existing sources. Because of circumstances peculiar to this case, we do not hold that the agency acted arbitrarily or capriciously in waiting for further information. This is because the question of whether EPA should make reinjection of produced water BAT for the sources covered by this permit is intertwined with the development of national effluent discharge limitations.

The recent "anti-backsliding" amendment to the Act is designed to prevent "backsliding" from limitations in BPJ permits to less stringent limitations which may be established under the forthcoming national effluent limitation guidelines. It prohibits a permit containing effluent limitations issued under a BPJ determination from being "renewed, reissued, or modified on the basis of effluent guidelines promulgated under [the national rulemaking] . . . subsequent to the original issuance of such permit," if the permit would contain effluent limitations which are "less stringent than the comparable limitations in the previous permit." 33 U.S.C.A. §1342(o)(1) (West Supp.1988). See id. at section 1342(o)(2) (exceptions to the general "anti-backsliding" prohibition). If the EPA were to require as BAT the retrofitting of all drilling sources for reinjection of produced water in the Gulf of Mexico, and, the eventual national standards were less stringent in any respect, there would be an inconsistency between BAT for Gulf drilling and BAT for the rest of the nation's off-shore drilling. This inconsistency would lack any apparent scientific or equitable basis. If, on the other hand, the eventual national standards embody more stringent standards than this permit requires, this permit can be reopened and its standards made more stringent. See 51 Fed. Reg. at 24,922, II(A)(3)(d). Given the large commitment of resources that would be necessary to begin retrofitting, the values of certainty and uniformity inherent in the congressional scheme take on added significance. There is a justification for some delay in this situation in order to ensure that the produced water limitation in the Gulf conforms with the national standard. [Id. at 1427.]

However, the court concluded that the agency did not act arbitrarily because it was in the process of adopting national effluent limitations and under the 1987 anti-back sliding amendments, see p. 408 *supra*, there was a possibility that the national standards might be less stringent than those adopted for the Gulf of Mexico, so the delay was justified.

4. In many cases, compliance with the best available technology is very costly, perhaps prohibitively so, leaving the industry with the choice of closing down or seeking administrative relief. Hobson's choices such as this put severe pressures on pollution control agencies to grant such relief, but the agency runs the risk of citizens' suits charging abuse of discretion. Ideally, BAT standards should provide incentives for industry to find cheaper methods of effluent reduction. La Pierre, Technology-Forcing and Federal Environmental Protection Statutes, 62 Iowa L. Rev. 771 (1977), is an enlightening introduction to the possible effects of BAT standards on waste reduction strategy decisions. Is the following solution consistent with the Act?

5. Recall the discussion of EPA's bubble policy for air, pp. 269-270 *supra*. The first water bubble was applied in February 1983 when U.S. Steel and the Natural Resources Defense Council, Inc., reached agreement in a suit over the interim effluent limitations for iron and steel. NRDC's lawyer, Alan S. Miller, said that NRDC still considered the bubble illegal but approved its use because the "overall settlement will result in substantial effluent reductions." EPA's bubble policy in effect at the time of the suit allowed a plant with multiple outfalls to discharge pollutants that exceeded the applicable effluent limitations at one outlet in exchange for an equivalent reduction at another point, but the settlement allowed the bubble only if certain water quality standards were met and the effluent exchange resulted in a net reduction in the total mass of pollution traded. See 13 Envt. Rep. (BNA) Current Developments 2005, 2005-2006 (1983). Krueger, The Iron and Steel Industry Consent Decree: Implementing the Bubble Policy under the Clean Water Act, 4 Va. J. Nat. Resources L. 155 (1984), analyzes the "bubble" consent decree and resulting EPA regulations.

AMERICAN PAPER INSTITUTE v. EPA
660 F.2d 954 (4th Cir. 1981)

ERVIN, Circuit Judge.

The petitioners in these consolidated cases seek judicial review of the actions of the Administrator of the Environmental Protection Agency (EPA) in issuing regulations pursuant to section 304(b)(4)(B) of the Clean Water Act ("the Act") promulgating effluent water limitations controlling conventional pollutants from private industrial sources in accordance with section 301(b)(2)(E) of the Act. This court is vested with the responsibility and authority for making a pre-enforcement examination of the EPA guidelines by section 509(b)(1)(E) of the Act.

Although the petitioners challenge the best conventional technology (BCT) regulations issued pursuant to section 304(b)(4)(B), their primary objection is to the methodology used by the Administrator in promulgating the regulations. In particular, the petitioners contend that Congress in section 304(b)(4)(B) mandated that EPA incorporate two main factors in its methodology for determining BCT: an industry cost-effectiveness test and a test that compares the cost for private industry to reduce its effluent levels with that incurred by publicly owned treatment works (POTWs) for a similar purpose. The petitioners assert that EPA considered only the latter factor and that EPA's benchmark for this latter factor was arbitrary and capricious. . . .

While the parties disagree over precisely what Congress intended to do when it enacted the 1977 amendments to the Act and draw markedly different conclusions from the language of the amendments and the legislative history, it is clear that Congress felt that the results produced by the BPT had provided a high degree of water quality improvement, and that in some instances, BAT for conventional pollutants about which much was known might require treatment not deemed necessary to meet the 1983 water quality goals of the Act. Concern was expressed about requiring "treatment for treatment's sake," and there was much discussion about comparing the cost of treatment with the benefits obtained from the reductions achieved.

Out of this came the development of a new standard, best conventional pollutant control technology (BCT). The new requirement was described by one Senate-House conferee as "the equivalent of best practical technology or something a little bit better, even as far as best available technology in some circumstances."

In directing EPA to promulgate regulations concerning BCT standards, Congress passed section 304(b)(4)(B) of the Act, which provides in part:

> Factors relating to the assessment of best conventional pollutant control technology (including measures and practices) shall include consideration of the reasonableness of the relationship between the costs of attaining a reduction in effluents and the effluent reduction benefits derived, and the comparison of the cost and level

of reduction of such pollutants from the discharge from publicly owned treatment works to the cost and level of reduction of such pollutants from a class or category of industrial sources, and shall take into account the age of equipment and facilities involved, the process employed, the engineering aspects of the application of various types of control techniques, process changes, non-water quality environment impact (including energy requirements), and such other factors as the Administrator deems appropriate. 33 U.S.C. §1314(b)(4)(B).

In addition, in section 73 of the 1977 amendments, Congress directed EPA to "review every effluent guideline promulgated prior to the enactment of this Act which is final or interim final." This required review of all outstanding BAT limitations for conventional pollutants for all secondary industrial sources within 90 days after the effective date of the amendments.

Pursuant to this Congressional directive, EPA proceeded to carry out its duties. On August 23, 1978, proposed rules were published relating to 13 secondary industry categories. These rules also contained a methodology for determining the reasonableness of any proposed effluent limitation under the BCT criteria. Critical comments were received, and on April 2, 1979, a notice was published indicating that the use of two additional documents was being considered for the data contained therein and that such data might be used in the future for computing the costs and levels of pollutants from POTWs. EPA published its final BCT determinations on August 29, 1979, and the petitioners filed these petitions on May 9, 1980, thus presenting these final regulations for our review.

II. Analysis

A. Cost Effectiveness Test

EPA's position is that Congress did not require it to utilize an industry cost-effectiveness test, but instead only mandated a POTW cost comparison standard in arriving at BCT regulations for industry. In interpreting section 304(b)(4)(B), EPA concludes that the proposed effluent guidelines are not required to pass two reasonableness tests. In support of its position, EPA reads the seemingly dual requirements of section 304(b)(4)(B) as one, commanding only a consideration of reasonableness. It contends that the second clause in the relevant portion of section 304(b)(4)(B) sets forth the benchmark of reasonableness — a comparison of the proposed BCT cost and level of effluent reduction for industry to the cost and level of reduction from the discharge of POTWs.

We are unable to accept this suggested statutory interpretation. When faced with such a question, our starting point for discerning congressional intent is the words of the statute itself. . . . The law which empowers EPA to act directs that EPA's effluent regulations "shall . . . specify factors to be taken into account in determining the best conventional pollutant control technology measures and practices to comply with section 1311(b)(2)(E) of this title to be applicable to any point source (other than publicly owned treatment works) within such categories or classes." 33 U.S.C. §1314(b)(4)(B). Congress did not leave EPA free to select these factors. The statute continues:

> Factors relating to the assessment of best conventional pollutant control technology . . . *shall* include consideration of the reasonableness of the relationship between the costs of attaining a reduction in effluents and the effluent reduction benefits derived, *and* the comparison of the cost and level of reduction of such pollutants from the discharge from publicly owned treatment works to the cost and level of reduction of such pollutants from a class or category of industrial sources. Id. (emphasis added).

We find the language of this statute to be clear and straightforward. We thus find no reason to resort to additional rules of statutory construction or to rely on the legislative history, which has minimum probative value because of the numerous conflicts contained therein.

EPA's construction of section 304(b)(4)(B) is contrary to the plain meaning of the words contained therein. EPA ignores the mandatory language of the law ("shall"), disregards the conjunctive ("and"), and completely eliminates the first factor. By its own admission, the agency made no effort to determine what it would cost an affected industry to remove a pound of pollutant past the BPT level nor did it compare the cost of such removal with the benefits derived from the removal, as specifically required by statute. . . .

This court has made it clear that EPA must be held to a standard of at least literal compliance with the language of a statute which it is authorized to implement. . . . Where, as here, the language of the Act is unambiguous and EPA has failed to comply with its directives, we must grant the petitions to set aside the regulations involved and remand the regulations to EPA for reconsideration. On remand EPA is to develop an industry cost-effectiveness test in accordance with the provisions of section 304(b)(4)(B), employ that test in a manner consistent with the statute, and re-examine all existing BCT regulations to ensure that they are not inconsistent with the proper employment of this industry cost-effectiveness test.

B.   POTW Comparison Test

The petitioners also challenge the action of EPA in the formation and application of the POTW comparison test. They argue that EPA erred in using an incremental approach, i.e., one going beyond the cost of normal secondary treatment for POTWs, in arriving at a POTW benchmark. They also contend that even if EPA were permitted to use an incremental POTW comparison, it acted arbitrarily and capriciously because the increment was too large to comply with congressional intent. The petitioners also object to the POTW cost data as being inadequate and statistically unreliable. We reject each of these challenges, except the one directed to the errors in the cost data. . . .

The petitioners specifically argue that EPA erred in concluding that it was appropriate to consider the cost of upgrading POTWs beyond secondary treatment. The petitioners object to the POTW benchmark for several reasons because: (1) secondary treatment is the only specifically defined treatment level that POTWs are required by law to meet; (2) advanced secondary treatment (AST), the increment which EPA chose, was not in existence when Congress enacted section 304 of the Act; and (3) the legislative history indicates that the POTW benchmark should be based on the average cost of normal secondary treatment.

We reject the petitioners' contentions. Section 304(b)(4)(B) explicitly authorizes EPA in establishing BCT limitations to compare "the cost and level of reduction of such pollutants from the discharge from publicly owned treatment works to the cost and level of reduction of such pollutants from a class or category of industrial sources." This controlling statute unequivocally directs EPA to employ a POTW comparison test. Contrary to the suggestions, we find nothing on the face of the statute or in the legislative history to suggest that Congress intended for EPA to use a specific POTW benchmark. Although Congress specifically directed the use of this comparison test, it did not issue any instructions as to how EPA was to structure or administer the test.

EPA considered a number of ways in which a POTW test could be formulated. 43 Fed. Reg. 37,572 (1978). One of the suggestions was that the POTW benchmark be based on the average pollutant removal costs for secondary treatment at POTWs, i.e., the increment from no treatment to secondary treatment. 43 Fed. Reg. 37,572 (1978). In addition to looking at average POTW costs for secondary treatment, EPA considered various incremental approaches below secondary treatment. EPA rejected these proposals primarily because it felt that a proper POTW benchmark should be one roughly paralleling that with which it is to be compared — the industrial increment from BPT to BAT. Whereas industry was required to be at a BPT level in 1977, POTWs were required to have met effluent limitations based upon secondary treatment by 1977. EPA believed that a relevant basis of comparison for POTWs would be at an incremental level beyond secondary treatment since BCT would be at a level at least equal to BPT and in many cases beyond BPT. EPA considered several such increments. After a careful consideration of various alternatives, EPA adopted a test employing a comparison of the cost of upgrading POTWs from secondary treatment levels. The selection of this upgrade comparison does not do violence to the language of the statute, and we do not find it to be arbitrary or capricious.

2

Not only do the petitioners object to an incremental POTW benchmark, but they also object specifically to the use of the increment from secondary to AST as being too costly. In essence, the petitioners contend that even if EPA were permitted to use an incremental POTW benchmark, it should have used a narrower increment, one that more closely straddles the marginal cost of secondary treatment. . . .

EPA initially proposed comparing the incremental costs of removal from industrial plants with the incremental costs of removal from POTWs of a similar flow. EPA based its proposal on separate and distinct technologies for small and large POTWs and arrived at POTW cost-effectiveness ratios at an increment progressing from normal secondary treatment at 30 mg/l each of BOD and TSS to better secondary treatment defined as 12 mg/l each of BOD and TSS. 43 Fed. Reg. 37,571-72 (1978).

Both the Corn Refiners Association, Inc. (hereinafter the Corn Refiners) and the Council on Wage & Price Stability (CWPS) made suggestions on the calculation of an incremental POTW cost standard. The Corn Refiners condemned the proposed incremental flow reduction from 30 mg/l to 12 mg/l as too unrealistic and objected that such a reduction was based on chemical addition technology which encompasses higher costs than some other methods because of its higher purchase, storage, and disposal costs. The Corn Refiners recommended using a POTW increment based on an improved sedimentation technology. Memorandum: "Comments on the Agency's Proposed 'BCT' Limitations," from Corn Refiners Association, Inc. to EPA (Dec. 7, 1978) at 33-40, App. at 498-505. The Corn Refiners also recommended using POTW incremental costs based on a microscreen filtration technology. Id. at 50-55, App. at 515-20.

Unlike the Corn Refiners, the CWPS did not object to the proposed increments as being too large or too unrealistic. The CWPS' recommendations were aimed at achieving the same level of cleanup that EPA had proposed at a lower overall cost. Instead of EPA using a flow basis of comparison, the CWPS recommended that EPA utilize a flow weighted average of marginal costs for POTWs "computed as the weighted average of the incremental cost per pound removed by POTWs of different size, where the weighing factor is the number of plants operating at a particular flow rate multiplied by that flow rate." Comments of the Council on Wage & Price Stability to EPA (Dec. 7, 1978) at 8, 21, App. at 447, 459. The CWPS also recommended that EPA use as its basis a different technology from that proposed. The CWPS suggested a technology based on increases in sedimentation area; yet, it is not clear as to the sources on which CWPS relies.

As indicated by the above comments of the Corn Refiners and the CWPS, there may be any number of increments based on slightly different technology or slightly different sizes of a given technology that EPA could have used. It is clear from the record that EPA was not oblivious to these comments. Instead of using POTW cost reasonableness figures based on specific separate and distinct technologies employed by small and large POTWs, as it had proposed initially, in its final rules, EPA used a single POTW cost reasonableness figure based on the average of all cost-effective technologies used by POTWs operating beyond secondary treatment, but employing basic secondary treatment technology.

We cannot conclude that EPA acted arbitrarily and capriciously in choosing AST as the increment beyond secondary treatment for the POTW benchmark. While EPA sought to use an increment that narrowly straddled secondary treatment, i.e., one that closely approximated marginal cost, and although it admitted its failure to find the narrowest increment that would have more closely approximated marginal cost, there is no statutory mandate requiring EPA to use an increment that equals marginal cost.

EPA has rationally justified its use of the AST increment. AST is the "knee-of-the-curve" point, the maximum cost-effective level of control for POTWs. The increment from secondary treatment to AST for POTWs was also determined by EPA to be roughly analogous to the industrial increment from BPT to BAT. While comments received by EPA have suggested that there may have been a narrower increment that EPA could have used, the suggestions by the commentators imply that EPA would have had to limit itself to a specific POTW technology to arrive at a smaller increment.

We are unwilling to place a straitjacket on EPA to so limit its decision making process. We find that EPA made its decision on its POTW comparison after it fully considered various alternatives, and that its decision is rationally based. We thus conclude that EPA's choice of an increment for POTWs from secondary treatment to AST was neither arbitrary nor capricious.

NOTES AND QUESTIONS

1. The final regulations for the organic chemicals, plastics, and synthetic fiber industry, the main source of conventional discharges, define BPT as process controls, in-plant treatment, and secondary clarification followed by biological treatment. Compliance will require a 10 percent increase above current industry costs to remove an addition 108 million pounds. Compliance costs would be $76.6 million per year after an initial capital investment of $215.8 million. Industry removal costs will rise from 38 to 71 cents per pound. Industry argues that "whether EPA labels its regulations BPT or BCT" the Act requires a "knee of the curve" test and that the BPT/BCT rules are not cost-effective under this test. How would you frame EPA's response? What is the difference between BPT and BCT? Is it determinative in this case? See Chemical Manufacturers Association v. EPA, 870 F.2d 177, 203- 207 (5th Cir. 1989).

2. The issues in *Weyerhaeuser* and *American Paper Institute* revolve on the question of which, if any, cost increments should be used in analyzing the cost-effectiveness of different pollution control technologies. Consider the following example:

Technology	Total Cost	Total Pollution Control	Incremental Cost	Average Cost
A	$ 2	10	.20	.20
B	4	16	.33	.25
C	8	19	1.33	.42
D	11	20	3.00	.55

In this example, incremental cost is the cost of going from the previous to the next most stringent technology, e.g., from A to B. Notice that total pollution control benefits do not increase proportionately with cost. They are nonlinear because they usually are in the real world. The marginal cost of additional technology is not shown on the chart but it is higher than incremental cost. For example, the marginal cost of technology D is $4.00. Why is the marginal cost always higher than the incremental cost?

3. EPA took considerable time to adopt a final rule for determining BCT that would comply with the *American Paper* decision. A final rule was adopted in July 1986. 41 Fed. Reg. 24,974 (1986). Here is its explanation of the POTW test and industry cost-effectiveness test it finally adopted:

> 2. *POTW Test*
>
> To "pass" the POTW test, the cost per pound of conventional pollutant removed by industrial dischargers in upgrading from BPT to the candidate BCT must be less than the cost per pound of conventional pollutant removed in upgrading POTWs from secondary treatment to advanced secondary treatment. . . . [The POTW benchmark is $0.25 per pound for industries whose cost is based on long-term performance data and $.014 for industries whose performance is not based on long-term performance data.]
>
> 3. *Industry Cost-Effectiveness Test*
>
> Candidate technologies must also "pass" the industry cost-effectiveness test. For each industry subcategory, EPA computes a ration of two incremental costs. The first is the cost per pound removed by the BCT candidate technology relative to BPT; the second is the cost per pound removed by BPT relative to no treatment (i.e., the second cost compares raw wasteload to pollutant load after application of BPT).
>
> The ratio of the first cost divided by the second cost is a measure of the candidate technology's cost-effectiveness. . . . [The benchmark for industries whose ratio is based on long-performance data is 1.29. For industries whose ratio is not based on long-performance data the ratio is .68.]
>
> 4. *BCT Determination*
>
> EPA will evaluate both the POTW test and the industry cost-effectiveness test as measures of reasonableness. The most stringent technology option that "passes" these tests provides the basis for setting BCT. [Id. at 24,976.]

Review the chart in Note 2. Did EPA adopt average cost or incremental cost as the basis for determining the cost-effectiveness of a BCT technology? Is the cost-effectiveness test for BCT determination consistent with *American Paper*?

F. TOXIC POLLUTANTS

In the mid-1970s, the regulation of toxic chemicals emerged as a major environmental priority. The discharge of toxic pollutants was recognized as a special problem in the Federal Water Pollution Control Amendments of 1972. What is the basis for classifying a pollutant as toxic versus conventional? EPA's authority to make the decision based on the presence of "indicators," carriers of toxic pollutants, regardless of whether pollutants had previously been classified as conventional or nonconventional was upheld in American Petroleum Institute v. EPA, 858 F.2d 261, 261-263, n.2 (5th Cir. 1988) (diesel oil could be classified as toxic although grease and oil classified as conventional). Section 307, 33 U.S.C. §1317, adopted a health-based approach to toxic pollutants. A list of toxic pollutants was to be published by EPA, and effluent standards were to be set on the basis of toxicity, persistence, degradability, the importance of affected organisms, and the nature and extent of the effect on such organisms. This approach failed. A statement of the House conferees, based on a more detailed staff memorandum of the Subcommittee on Investigations and Review of the Committee on Public Works and Transportation issued during the consideration of the Clean Water Act of 1977 explained:

> The principal regulatory mechanism for the control of toxics in Public Law 92-500 as originally enacted was contained in section 307(a), which set forth the requirement for toxic effluent standards to be issued for toxic pollutants identified by the Administrator. Frankly, it has failed.
>
> Procedural requirements have proven insurmountable for the Agency, to the point where only six toxic chemicals — aldrin/dieldrin, endrin, DDT, toxaphene, benzidine and PCB's — have been regulated. Six chemicals in 5 years.
>
> The Agency's problems have included uncertainty with respect to the intended breadth of the regulatory effort, lack of toxicological and biological data for many chemicals, and scientific disputes over what amount of a "toxic" pollutant . . . can be considered as "safe." But far and away the most severe single problem has been the formal, cumbersome rulemaking process.
>
> The result of the failure to regulate toxics has been litigation leading to the consent decree ratified by the court in NRDC against Train, which in effect has placed the toxics control program under the administration of the court. The court mandated that effluent guidelines based on Best Available Technology (BAT) be developed for 65 pollutants by December 31, 1979. [Report on Resolution Providing for Consideration of Conference Report on H.R. 3199, Clean Water Act of 1977, reported in A Legislative History of the Clean Water Act of 1977: A Continuation of the Legislative History of the Federal Water Pollution Control Act, 95th Cong., 2d Sess. 327 (1978) (hereinafter cited as 1977 Legislative History).]

The "Flannery decree," Natural Resources Defense Council v. Train, 8 Envt. Rep. Case (BNA) 2120 (D.D.C. 1976), rev'd in part on other grounds sub nom. Natural Resources Defense Council, Inc. v. Costle, 561 F.2d 904 (D.C. Cir. 1977), which Congress adopted as the model for a new toxic pollutant regulatory strategy, substituted technology-based effluent standards for health-based ones. The decree required EPA to develop technology-based BAT standards for 21 industry categories covering 65 toxic or potentially toxic pollutants in order to establish water quality criteria indicating safe levels of the pollutants. It also required the agency to identify segments of rivers and lakes where the water quality criteria would not be achieved after industry dischargers attained BAT and then to develop even tighter effluent limitations for discharges to those bodies of water.

> The conferees intend the Administrator to have the widest latitude in adding pollutants to the list of toxic pollutants under section 307. He will not be required to justify the relative advantages of listing one pollutant or group of pollutants over another. In determining the toxicity of pollutants, the Administrator must consider the definition of toxic pollutants contained in section 502(13). While he would similarly have latitude in deleting pollutants, no pollutant listed in House Report 95-30 should be deleted without a clear finding that delisting will not compromise adequate control over the discharge of toxic pollutants. Review of the Administrator's action will be in the courts of appeals pursuant to section 509.
>
> Moreover, it should be obvious that the fact that a pollutant listed under section 307(a) has oxygen demanding or other characteristics similar to those of conventional pollutants shall not affect the status of such pollutant as a toxic pollutant.
>
> This provision is not intended to require extensive documentation of toxicity as is the case of toxic effluent standards. It is intended to be more closely akin to the general concept of the 1971 act — that is, that ecological protection will more likely be achieved through the elimination of discharge of all pollutants rather than requiring that the Government bear the burden of establishing a precise relationship between each pollutant in each effluent stream to a particular receiving water quality impact.
>
> The control requirement for any pollutant placed on the toxic list is still best available technology unless the Administrator determines that there is sufficient information on toxicity to establish a separate nationwide effluent standard for that pollutant.
>
> That is an important distinction. The toxic effluent limitation is a best available technology-based control requirement. A toxic effluent standard is a control requirement based on an established relationship between a toxic pollutant and a receiving water/ecosystem impact. A best available technology effluent limitation applies to industrial classes and categories. A toxic effluent standard applies to the pollutant per se, and cannot be exceeded by any source of that pollutant unless the Administrator makes a separate categorical determination. Thus, for example, toxic effluent standards must be achieved by all municipal treatment plants, whereas best available technology limits apply to industrial point source categories. [1977 Legislative History, at 459-460.]

See generally Hall, The Control of Toxic Pollutants under the Federal Water Pollution Control Act Amendments of 1972, 63 Iowa L. Rev. 609 (1978). The implementation of §307 is examined in Chapter 5, pp. 567-568 *infra*. See generally Gaba, Informal Rulemaking by Settlement Agreement, 73 Geo. L.J. 1241 (1985).

After the 1977 amendments, the EPA allowed variances for indirect toxic dischargers, those subject to pre-treatment standards, if the discharger's situation was fundamentally different from its industrial class. Section 301(l), added in 1977, provided: "The Administrator may not modify any requirement of this section as it applies to any specific pollutant which is on the toxic pollutant list under section 1317(a)(1) of this title." Chemical Manufacturers Association v.

Natural Resources Defense Council, Inc., 470 U.S. 116 (1985) held EPA's decision to grant variances was within its discretion:

> Section 301(l) states that EPA may not "modify" any requirement of §301 insofar as toxic materials are concerned. EPA insists that §301(l) prohibits only those modifications expressly permitted by other provisions of §301, namely, those that §301(c) and §301(g) would allow on economic or water-quality grounds. Section 301(l), it is urged, does not address the very different issue of FDF variances. This view of the agency charged with administering the statute is entitled to considerable deference; and to sustain it, we need not find that it is the only permissible construction that EPA might have adopted but only that EPA's understanding of this very "complex statute" is a sufficiently rational one to preclude a court from substituting its judgment for that of EPA. Train v. NRDC, 421 U.S. 60, 75, 87, 95 S. Ct. 1470, 1480, 1485, 43 L. Ed. 2d 731 (1975); see also Chevron, U.S.A., Inc. v. NRDC, 467 U.S. 837 (1984). Of course, if Congress has clearly expressed an intent contrary to that of the Agency, our duty is to enforce the will of Congress. . . .

In 1987 Congress ratified *Chemical Manufacturers Association*. 33 U.S.C. §1311(n) now provides in part:

Fundamentally different factors

(1)   GENERAL RULE

The Administrator, with the concurrence of the State, may establish an alternative requirement under subsection (b)(2) of this section or section 1317(b) of this title for a facility that modifies the requirements of national effluent limitation guidelines or categorical pretreatment standards that would otherwise be applicable to such facility, if the owner or operator of such facility demonstrates to the satisfaction of the Administrator that—

(A)   the facility is fundamentally different with respect to the factors (other than cost) specified in section 1314(b) or 1314(g) of this title and considered by the Administrator in establishing such national effluent limitation guidelines or categorical pretreatment standards;

(B)   the application —

(i)   is based solely on information and supporting data submitted to the Administrator during the rule-making for establishment of the applicable national effluent limitation guidelines or categorical pretreatment standard specifically raising the factors that are fundamentally different for such facility; or

(ii)   is based on information and supporting data referred to in clause (i) and information and supporting data the applicant did not have a reasonable opportunity to submit during such rulemaking;

(C)   the alternative requirement is no less stringent than justified by the fundamental difference; and

(D)   the alternative requirement will not result in a nonwater quality environmental impact which is markedly more adverse than the impact considered by the Administrator in establishing such national effluent limitation guideline or categorical pretreatment standard.

Otherwise, all dischargers of toxic pollutants for which effluent limitations have been established should have been in compliance by March 31, 1989. 33

U.S.C. §1311(b). EPA established its BAT regulations by taking the long-term average of toxics discharged by the best plants and multiplying it by a variability factor to account for variation among plants. Because some discharges cannot be measured by existing procedures, EPA set an analytical minimum of 10 parts per million and assumed that toxics were always present at this level. The net effect was to raise the long-term average discharge figure and thus to raise the effluent limitations. EPA's methodology was upheld in Chemical Manufacturers Association v. EPA, 870 F.2d 177, 226-233 (5th Cir. 1989). The methodology presents a nice enforcement problem which the court ducked by invoking the ripeness doctrine:

> DuPont and Hardwicke assert that the BAT limitations for some toxics are very close to their minimum analytical values. The petitioners argue that a non-detect reading should be considered zero for enforcement purposes.
>
> Although the EPA states in its brief that, to be consistent with its approach in calculating the BAT limitations, "it would be reasonable" to treat non-detect values as the analytical minimum, it is not clear that the Agency has adopted this position as its policy, for neither the regulations nor the development documents address it.
>
> The issue presented is therefore not ripe for review. In Abbott Laboratories v. Gardner, the Supreme Court stated that the doctrine of ripeness is intended to prevent the courts from entangling themselves in premature abstract discussions of administrative policies, and "to protect agencies from judicial interference until an administrative decision has been formalized and its effects felt in a concrete way by the challenging parties." To further these purposes, the Supreme Court held that whether a controversy is "ripe" requires a court "to evaluate both the fitness of the issues for judicial decision and the hardship to the parties of withholding court consideration."
>
> Because the EPA has not formally adopted a position our discussion of the validity of what it might do would be merely advisory. Withholding court consideration will not result in substantial hardship to the petitioners because enforcement proceedings have not taken place. If there is any merit to their argument, the issue can be addressed in enforcement proceedings. Finally, "the possibility that the petitioner may have to make capital budgeting decisions under a cloud of uncertainty" does not amount to the requisite hardship when the petitioners do not face sanctions for non-compliance.[229] [870 F.2d at 233.]

G.   SPECIAL POLLUTANTS

1.   Thermal Pollution

In the mid-1960s, many large scale nuclear and fossil fuel electric generating plants were constructed or proposed by utilities. In the pre-1973 OPEC oil embargo days, exponential projections in the growth of electricity demand were common. One of the early major environmental issues in the 1960s was the effect of discharge of large amounts of heat into aquatic environments. Some

---

229.   NRDC v. EPA, 859 F.2d 156, 166 (D.C. Cir. 1988).

studies estimated that by 1979 one-sixth of the nation's fresh water runoff would be required for cooling and condensing uses and that 100 percent of some eastern streams would pass through various power plants during periods of low flow. A case holding that the Atomic Energy Commission (subsequently the Nuclear Regulatory Commission) lacked jurisdiction over thermal pollution, New Hampshire v. AEC, 406 F.2d 170 (1st Cir. 1969), prompted Congress to amend the Federal Water Pollution Control Act in 1970 to require that an applicant for a federal permit prove that there was reasonable assurance that the activity would not violate applicable state water quality standards. The current version of the 1970 amendment is §401 of the Clean Water Act, 33 U.S.C. §1341. C. Meyers & A. Tarlock, Selected Legal and Economic Aspects of Environmental Protection 365-381 (1971), reviews early federal and state responses to the thermal pollution problem. The technology exists to prevent once-through cooling; the most widely employed method is the cooling tower. But heat is different from other pollutants because its adverse impact on water quality is site-specific. For this reason, heat is treated differently from all other pollutants in the Clean Water Act.

Section 316, 33 U.S.C. §1326(b), assumes that closed-cycle cooling will be the best practicable and best available technology for both old and new facilities. EPA's ultimate reliance on closed-cycle cooling was forged out of an intense dispute among the TVA, the states of Alabama and Tennessee, and the EPA, which ended when the authority agreed to install cooling towers on all its proposed nuclear plants. See R. Durant, When Government Regulates Itself: EPA, TVA, and Pollution Control in the 1970s (1985). However, §316(a) allows once-through cooling if the discharger demonstrates that "such discharge (taking into account the interaction of such thermal component with other pollutants), . . . will assure the protection and propagation of a balanced, indigenous population of shellfish, fish and wildlife." EPA regulations initially required existing plants to retrofit with cooling towers, ponds, or lakes but limited new plants to either cooling towers or ponds. The electric power industry challenged the regulations arguing that the cost of compliance was excessive compared with the benefits. See Appalachian Power Co. v. Train, 545 F.2d 1351 (4th Cir. 1976), and Appalachian Power Co. v. EPA, 671 F.2d 801 (4th Cir. 1982). The present law of §316(a) variances comes from the epic battle to prevent the construction of the Seabrook, New Hampshire, nuclear plant. After the EPA Administrator granted a variance, overruling the regional administrator, without an adjudicatory hearing, the First Circuit held that §316(a) requires an adjudicatory hearing because of the nature of the variance proceeding and that the Administrator's use of a technical staff panel to resolve the question of species tolerance to heat violated §556(e) of the Administrative Procedure Act's prohibition against the use of extra-record evidence. Seacoast Anti-Pollution League v. Costle, 572 F.2d 872 (1st Cir.), cert. denied sub nom. Public Service Co. v. Seacoast Anti-Pollution League, 439 U.S. 824 (1978). On remand, the First Circuit held that the Administrator's revised decision procedure was valid and found that the decision to grant the variance was supported by substantial evidence. Seacoast Anti-Pollution League v. Costle, 597 F. 2d 306 (1st Cir. 1979).

2.   *Dredge and Fill*

a.   The Problem

The environmental movement has focused a great deal of attention on the value, aesthetic and otherwise, of wetlands. Throughout most of our history, marshes and swamps have been considered health menaces, and much effort, supported by national and state land grant laws, was devoted to draining and filling these lands. One half of the 215 million areas that existed at the time of European settlement were drained and filled, and 400,000 acres of wetlands are destroyed each year. At the national level, the nation's chief construction agency, the U.S. Corps of Engineers, acquired jurisdiction over many wetlands in the late nineteenth century for the purpose of navigation protection. The Corps historically exercised this jurisdiction by allowing all dredging and filling that did not impair the navigable capacity of rivers and harbors. Starting in 1970, the Corps was given expanded jurisdiction to consider environmental values in its permit decisions and expanded jurisdiction over wetlands adjacent to water bodies. Thus, the Corps, one of the nation's creatures of pork barrel politics — and therefore a popular environmental villain — found itself with the additional mission of assessing the environmental impact of much important land development activity. In 1972, §404 of the Clean Water Act, 33 U.S.C. §1344, expanded EPA's role in regulating dredge and fill activities, but the Corps retained primary jurisdiction over the permit approval process.

The ability of the Corps to include environmental protection within its developmental mission has been questioned, but there is no doubt that the Corps has made major adjustments in its procedures to accommodate environmental values. See Power, The Fox in the Chicken Coop: The Regulatory Program of the U.S. Army Corps of Engineers, 63 Va. L. Rev. 503 (1977). Still, Corps regulation of dredge and fill permits has been a major source of controversy. At the center is the question of the Corps' jurisdiction. The expansion of commerce clause jurisdiction to almost all surface waters (see pp. 360 to 364 *supra*) swept in associated wetlands as well. Environmentalists initially argued that the Corps was too lax. Land developers, farmers, and water users saw the issue differently and attempted to persuade the Reagan Administration to limit Corps jurisdiction. The stakes were high. A proposed definition of navigability limited to waters used for interstate commerce in their natural conditions would remove about 85 percent of the nation's wetlands, about 126 million acres, from federal jurisdiction. Statement of Jay D. Hair, National Wildlife Federation, before the Senate Comm. on Environment and Public Works, Subcomm. on Environmental Pollution, 97th Cong. 2d Sess. 1045 (1982). Opponents of wetlands regulation lost the battle to return the Corps to its pre-Clean Water Act jurisdiction. Today, we are moving to a "no net loss" standard for wetlands maintenance. The Conservation Foundation, Protecting America's Wetlands: An Action Agenda (1989). This standard will not prohibit all conversion but would emphasize mitigation by restoration and the creation of new wetlands. Federal agencies are concentrating on the creation of new wetlands, and restoration experiments are underway. See D. Salversen, Wetland Mitigation (1989).

b.   The Evolution of EPA/U.S. Army Corps Regulation

In the late 1960s the Corps itself began to change its mission in response to increasing congressional pressure. The agency's power to do so was confirmed in Zabel v. Tabb, 430 F.2d 199 (5th Cir. 1970), cert. denied, 401 U.S. 910 (1971). Section 10 of the Rivers and Harbors Act, 33 U.S.C. §403, requires a permit for fills and other activities in navigable waters. The Fifth Circuit held that any doubts about the Corps's ability to deny a §10 permit for environmental reasons had been resolved by the passage of the Fish and Wildlife Coordination Act and NEPA. Zabel took on even greater legal significance as the definition of navigable waters moved landward after a district court held that the definition of navigable waters in §404 of the Clean Water Act had the same meaning as the definition in the Clean Water Act generally. Natural Resources Defense Council, Inc. v. Callaway, 392 F. Supp. 685 (D.D.C. 1975). The Corps soon found itself with even more power over both coastal and inland agricultural, land development, and mining activities. An interjurisdictional dispute between EPA and the Corps was resolved by Congress in 1972 with the enactment of §404 of the Clean Water Act, and the 1977 amendments expanded EPA's powers. The Corps may issue either site-specific permits or nationwide permits for classes of activities, such as pipeline crossings, that have minimal separate or cumulative impacts.

The Corps continues to issue dredge and fill permits, but EPA can set disposal site criteria under §404(b) and veto any permit that will have an unreasonable adverse effect upon water supplies, fish, wildlife, or recreation areas. §404(c). Creppel v. United States Army Corps of Engineers, 19 ELR 20134 (E.D. La. 1988) holds that the plain language and legislative history make it clear that "no economic arguments require consideration." William Reilly, President George Bush's EPA Administrator, caused a great stir in the West when he reversed his regional administrator and allowed Region 10 to begin proceedings to veto a 404 permit for the Two Forks Dam. The dam is the source of bitter controversy between environmentalists and the Denver Water Board, which sees the dam as necessary to give the city adequate water reserves. Western States Water No. 778, April 14, 1989. See generally Blumm, The Clean Water Act's Section 404 Permit Program Enters Its Adolescence: An Institutional and Programmatic Perspective, 8 Ecology L.Q. 409, 437-442 (1980) and Focus: Clean

Water Act Section 404, 60 U. Colo. L. Rev. 685 (1989); and W. Want, Law of Federal Wetlands Regulation (1989).

Section 402 of the Clean Water Act, 33 U.S.C. §1342, has been interpreted to require trial-type hearings for NPDES permits. Buttrey v. United States, 690 F.2d 1170 (5th Cir. 1982), *cert. denied*, 461 S. Ct. 927 (1983) holds that §404 does not require a trial-type hearing because Congress "consciously chose to use the simplified permit procedures that the Corps had developed in administering the existing dredge and fill permit program." Does a developer denied a permit have a due process right to a trial-type hearing? The distinction between formal and informal proceedings may not always matter. The District of Columbia Circuit Court of Appeals has rendered many decisions that partially collapse the formal-informal hearing or proceeding distinction in order to expand citizens' rights of participation. National Wildlife Federation v. Marsh, 568 F. Supp. 985 (D.D.C. 1983), applies these decisions to §404 proceedings. The court set aside a §404 permit issued for a refinery in Hampton Roads, Virginia (see p. 262 *supra*) because "the informal adjudicatory process under section 404 of the CWA, the opportunity to comment and the right to a hearing both necessarily require that the Army present for public scrutiny the rationale and pivotal data underlying its proposed action *before* the close of the comment and hearing period. Unfortunately, that requirement was not satisfied in the administrative proceeding here" (568 F. Supp. at 994). Initially, the refinery was justified because it would fulfill the nation's energy needs, but after the stabilization of world oil prices in response to reduced demand, savings in transportation costs became the rationale. This shift was contained in a "Staff Evaluation" that was prepared *after* the close of the administrative record. A §404 permit applicant does not, however, have a right to an informal hearing unless it requests one during the comment period. AJA Associates v. Corps of Engineers, 817 F.2d 1070 (3d Cir. 1987).

Because of the scope of the delegated authority and the geographical reach of the program, it is difficult to determine whether a given activity requires a §404 permit, and the standards for the issuance of §404 permits are open-ended. And the §404 process may trigger NEPA. California ex rel. Van de Kamp v. Marsh, 687 F. Supp. 495 (N.D. Cal. 1988).

There are no minimum standards that entitle an applicant to a permit as a matter of right. A disappointed applicant must contest the jurisdiction of the Corps (see pp. 367 to 377 *supra*), argue that denial of the permit is a taking of property without due process of law, argue that the denial was arbitrary (e.g., Smithwick v. Alexander, 17 Envt. Rep. Cas. (BNA) 2126 (E.D.N.C. 1981), *aff'd*, 673 F.2d 1317 (4th Cir. 1981)), or argue that the Corps is estopped to deny the permit. As a general matter, the federal government may not be estopped when acting in a sovereign capacity, Federal Crop Insurance Corp. v. Merrill, 332 U.S. 380 (1947), although the Supreme Court has left open the question of whether estoppel applies to federal proprietary actions or to the affirmative misconduct of federal agents. Schwieker v. Hansen, 450 U.S. 785 (1981) and Heckler v. Community Health Services, 467 U.S. 51 (1984). Several cases have raised the defense when the Corps issued a permit and later revoked it when it was initially unsure of its jurisdiction, Buccaneer Point Estates, 17 Envt. Rep. Cas. (BNA) 1973 (S.D. Fla. 1982), or its authority, but the courts have refused to apply the doctrine. "The act of granting a §404 permit is unquestionably an exercise of the government's sovereign power to protect the public interest." Deltona Corp. v. Alexander, 682 F.2d 888 (11th cir. 1982). See also United States v. Schoenborn, 860 F.2d 1448 (8th Cir. 1988).

c.   Substantive Criteria

The scope of the Corps' discretion to determine whether a permit is in the public interest is considerable. 33 C.F.R. §320.4 allows the Corps to consider 12 general policies:

> All factors which may be relevant to the proposal must be considered including the cumulative effects thereof: among those are conservation, economics, aesthetics, general environmental concerns, wetlands, historic properties, fish and wildlife values, flood hazards, floodplain values, land use, navigation, shore erosion and accretion, recreation, water supply and conservation, water quality, energy needs, safety, food and fiber production, mineral needs, considerations of property ownership and, in general, the needs and welfare of the people.

See Parish and Morgan, History, Practice and Emerging Problems of Wetlands Regulation: Reconsidering Section 404 of the Clean Water Act, 17 Land & Water L. Rev. 43, 62 (1982). What is the difference between §404 and NEPA balancing?

The most litigated substantive criteria is the Corps' water-dependency standard. Before a non-water-dependent activity can be approved, the Corps must determine whether an alternative site is available that would cause less damage to wetlands. 40 C.F.R. §230.10(a). Initially, the courts held that the water-dependency criterion could not be given priority over other factors, Atlantic LTD v. Hudson, 574 F. Supp. 1381, 19 Envt. Rep. Cas. (BNA) (E.D. Va. 1983). Bersani v. Robichard, 850 F.2d 36 (2d Cir. 1988), cert. denied, 109 S. Ct. 1556 (1989) suggests that the factor may be determinative in a large number of cases. Edward DeBartolo Corporation purchased an 80-acre site with about 50 acres of wetland sometime before 1982 to construct a regional shopping center. DeBartolo sold the site to Pyramid in 1983. Until July of that year, an alternative upland site was available, but then a competitor purchased it. Location theory requires a minimum population within an exclusive radius to support these centers. After lengthy proceedings, the Director of Civil Works in Washington reversed the district engineer and granted the permit because the competitor removed the alternative site from the market. In contrast, EPA vetoed the permit concluding that Pyramid had not overcome the presumption that an alternative existed. The district court rejected Pyramid's argument that EPA could not consider alternative sites in assessing the environmental impact of the project because the policy was consistent with the purpose of the Act. Bersani v. United States, 674 F.Supp. 405 (S.D.N.Y. 1987):

> Under Pyramid's analysis, however, the only relevant portions of the 404(b)(1) guidelines are those which directly pertain to the five resources listed in Section 404(c). The court rejects Pyramid's contention that the fact that Section 403(c) and Section 404(b) are concerned with a greater number of environmental factors than is Section 404(c) limits the manner in which the EPA may determine the effect on the 404(c) resources, including the use of the practicable alternatives test. Both the 404(b)(1) guidelines and the Section 403 criteria, upon which they are patterned, provide a means to evaluate the desirability of discharges into the aquatic environment. Applying these standards to a proposed discharge in a particular context does no violence to the policy underlying the Act. These guidelines provide a useful tool for evaluating discharges into the aquatic environment. Furthermore, the fact that Section 403(c) explicitly allows an agency to consider a certain factor does not necessarily mean that the absence of such a provision in Section 404(c) precludes consideration of that factor. Instead, use of these criteria makes the general standard workable. Moreover, the EPA did not use the Section 404(b)(1) guidelines to find an unacceptable adverse impact on any resource not specified in Section 404(c). The unacceptability of the site was determined with respect to wildlife, a category explicitly enumerated thereunder.

On appeal Pyramid tried a more technical attack on the decision:

> We turn next to the issue of whether EPA's interpretation of the 404(b)(1) guidelines is entitled to the deference usually accorded an agency with regard to its interpretation of regulations it is charged with administering, see EPA v. National Crushed Stone Assn., 449 U.S. 64, 83 (1980), and participated in formulating. See also United States v. Hescorp, Heavy Equip. Sales Corp., 801 F.2d 70, 76 (2d Cir.), cert. denied, 107 S. Ct. 672 (1986). The district court implied in its decision that.it was according EPA such deference in examining its market entry approach.
>   Pyramid contends that such deference was unwarranted because two agencies — EPA and the Corps — developed and administered the regulations, and the Corps reached a different conclusion from that of EPA on the market entry issue. It asserts that, contrary to EPA's market entry approach, the "Corps' position is that the availability should be determined as of the time an application is under review." Pyramid points out that under §404(b) the regulations are to be developed by EPA "in conjunction with" the Secretary of the Army (who acts through the Corps). It cites General Elec. Co. v. Gilbert, 429 U.S. 125, 144-45 (1976), for the proposition that a court must use its own judgment in construing a regulation when two agencies with responsibility for administering it reach divergent conclusions. It also contends that the Corps has greater experience with and expertise in assessing the "availability" of alternatives than EPA, because it is the Corps that makes the initial decision on thousands of applications while EPA reviews under §404(c) only rarely. Furthermore, Pyramid claims that the availability analysis implicates zoning, economic and financial issues, not environmental ones.
>   In response, EPA asserts that the Corps did not take a developed opposing policy position on the issue of what time is relevant in the "practicable alternatives" analysis. The reason for this is that the Corps, acting through General Wall, based

its decision primarily on its finding that Pyramid's mitigation proposal was workable. EPA also asserts, on the issue of its expertise, that its "selective and most infrequent invocation" of its veto power underscores EPA's "seriousness" about using the veto. Finally, EPA asserts that the Act's legislative history indicates that Congress intended EPA to have the "final word" on any disputes with the Corps.

While none of EPA's assertions is entirely persuasive, there also are difficulties with Pyramid's position. It is undeniable, for example, that Wall in fact did find that the North Attleboro site was "unavailable" and thus it appears that the Corps tacitly was applying a time-of-application test. On the other hand, it is possible that Wall believed that Pyramid did not enter the market until after NED had purchased the North Attleboro site. Accordingly, Wall may have found the alternative site "unavailable" under the market entry approach. Pyramid's and EPA's other arguments similarly cut both ways or are inconclusive.

Even if we are not thoroughly persuaded that EPA's interpretation was entitled to deference, however, we nevertheless conclude that the district court's decision in its favor must be upheld. As Pyramid itself points out (to the detriment of its argument), the issue of the standards of review of the district court and of our Court.

The standard of review for the district court in this case is that the court shall set aside EPA's findings, conclusions or actions only if they are "arbitrary, capricious, an abuse of discretion, or otherwise not in accordance with law." Administrative Procedure Act §10(e), 5 U.S.C. §706(2)(A) (1982). As stated by the Supreme Court in Motor Vehicle Mfrs. Assn. v. State Farm Mut. Auto. Ins. Co., 463 U.S. 29 (1983),

> [A] reviewing court may not set aside an agency rule that is rational, based on consideration of the relevant factors, and within the scope of the authority delegated to the agency by the statute. . . . The scope of review under the 'arbitrary and capricious' standard is narrow and a court is not to substitute its judgment for that of the agency. Nevertheless, the agency must examine the relevant data and articulate a satisfactory explanation for its action including a 'rational connection between the facts found and the choice made.'

Id. at 42-43 (quoting Burlington Truck Lines, Inc. v. United States, 371 U.S. 156, 168 (1962)).

Applying these standards, we are convinced that EPA's market entry interpretation was reasonable, and therefore was neither "arbitrary and capricious" nor "not in accordance with law." We therefore hold that the district court correctly found that EPA's interpretation of the regulations was reasonable. [850 F.2d at 45-46]

Van Abbema v. Fornell, 807 F.2d 633 (7th Cir. 1986), reviewed the issuance of a permit for a coal-loading facility in a historic district. The court agreed with the Corps that an environmental impact statement was not necessary but vacated the permit and remanded it for further consideration because the public interest review was inadequate. The Corps had not adequately justified the economic benefits of the facility in light of the environmental costs and had not adequately explored the economic feasibility of alternative loading sites. The limits of §404 review are illustrated by Mall Properties, Inc. v. Marsh, 672 F. Supp. 561 (D. Mass. 1987), aff'd, 841 F.2d 440 (1st Cir. 1988), cert. denied,

109 U.S. 128 (1988), which held that a permit for a shopping center may not be denied to protect the economic position of existing businesses:

> The present case is analogous to *Metropolitan Edison* [p. 826 *infra*]. As discussed earlier, Section 404 and Section 10 are, like NEPA, concerned with the physical environment. When there is a reasonably close causal relationship between a change in the physical environment and economic factors, the Corps may consider those factors in its public interest review. *Metropolitan Edison*, however, indicated that the Corps may not properly consider and give significant weight to other economic factors in deciding whether to issue a permit pursuant to Section 404 or Section 10.
>
> Similarly, once again contrary to defendants' contentions, the Court of Appeals for the First Circuit decision in Sierra Club v. Marsh, 769 F.2d 868 (1st Cir. 1985), is also compatible with the conclusion that economic factors are cognizable by the Corps only if they are adequately related to impacts on the physical environment.
>
> *Sierra Club* involved the question whether a cargo port and a causeway that Maine planned to build at Sears Island would "significantly affect the environment" and, therefore, under NEPA, require an EIS. [Environmental Impact Statement] Id. at 870. The First Circuit found "serious omission" in the Corps' decision not to require an EIS, namely, the "failure to consider adequately the fact that building a port and causeway may lead to the further industrial development of Sears Island, *and* that further development will significantly affect the environment." Id. at 877 (emphasis added). As the Court of Appeals later elaborated, the Corps had before it evidence that industrial development of the island would lead to "2,750 new jobs in a town with a population of under 2,500 . . . , increased traffic . . . , additional lost scallop beds and clam flats, more soil erosion and aesthetic harm, a need for additional waste disposal and water supply, [and] an added threat to water quality. . . ." Id. at 880. Thus, in *Sierra Club* the evidence indicated that construction causing a change in the environment would cause industrial development which would further impact the environment in significant respects. It was not an economic impact alone — but rather its relationship to the environment — which the Corps was directed to consider.
>
> Thus *Sierra Club*, like *Metropolitan Edison*, suggests that there must be a reasonably close link between economic factors and the physical environment for the Corps to be legitimately concerned about those economic factors in performing its function under NEPA. Once again, a comparable conclusion is required when the Corps is operating under Section 404 or Section 10.
>
> As described previously, the purposes and policies of Section 404 and Section 10, the relevant provisions of the statutes and regulations, and the case law all indicate that the Corps may not rely upon economic factors which are not proximately related to changes in the physical environment in denying a dredge or fill permit. Therefore, because the Corps gave significant weight to economic factors not related to changes in physical environment in this case, its decision was not in accordance with Section 404 or Section 10.

If the Corps classifies an activity as water-dependent, the court will defer to the agency as long as the record adequately explains the Corps' reasons. For example, Friends of the Earth v. Hintz, 800 F.2d 822 (9th Cir. 1986), held that a log export storage yard on 17 acres of mudflats met the agency's water dependency criteria, although log storage is ordinarily not water-dependent, because the yard was an integral part of an export facility. Houck, Hard Choices: The Analysis of Alternatives under Section 404 of the Clean Water Act and Similar Environmental Laws, 60 U. Colo. L. Rev. 773 (1989) critically examines the consideration of alternatives and recommends that the water-dependency test be "dispositive." See generally Seltzer & Steinberg, Wetlands and Private Development, 12 Colum. J. Envtl. L. 159 (1987), for further discussion of the issues raised in the preceding cases.

The denial of a permit to drain and fill wetlands inevitably raises a taking question because all productive uses of land may be foreclosed. The Supreme Court's taking law took an important new turn in 1987 when the Court decided three land use taking cases. First English Evangelical Lutheran Church of Glendale v. County of Los Angeles, 107 S. Ct. 2378 (1987) and Nollan v. California Coastal Commission, 107 S. Ct. 3141 (1987). Although these cases primarily restated prior law, they will definitely affect and may even modify existing taking doctrines as they relate to environmental land use regulations. The other of the 1987 cases, Keystone Bituminous Coal Association v. DeBenedictus, 480 U.S. 470 (1987), adopted a two-part taking test. Land use regulations must (1) advance a legitimate governmental interest and (2) leave the landowner with an economically viable use of his land. This test cuts both ways as it applies to wetlands regulation. The environmental purpose of wetlands regulations should convince courts that they advance governmental interests, but the almost total restriction on land use that is imposed may lead a court to find a taking. See Florida Rock Indus. v. United States, 791 F.2d 893 (1986), cert. denied, 479 U.S. 1053 (1987). The taking issue is further complicated when the landowner asserts the right to fill navigable waters subject to the public trust or the federal or state navigation servitude. Compare Kaiser Aetna v. United States, 444 U.S. 164 (1979) with Orion Corp. v. State, 109 Wash. 2d 621, 747 P.2d 1062 (1987), cert. denied, 108 S. Ct. 1996 (1988). In Orion, the state classified 5,600 acres of tidelands as an estuarine sanctuary after a long struggle to develop a large tract of tidal lands, and the developer challenged the regulation as a taking. The Washington State supreme court applied both the 1987 takings trilogy and the public trust doctrine to deny the claim. "Orion had no right to make any use of this property that would substantially impair the public rights of navigation and fishing. . . . Orion never had the right to dredge and fill its tidelands. . . ." The court, however, remanded the issue to determine if the creation of the sanctuary precluded reasonable uses consistent with the public trust. State power is bolstered by the U.S. Supreme Court's decision in Phillips Petroleum Co. v. Mississippi, 108 S. Ct. 791 (1988), which holds that the public trust extends to tidal but non-navigable waters because the states have historically been granted title to submerged tidal lands. Justice White noted that these lands "share those 'geological, chemical and environmental' qualities that make lands beneath tidal waters unique."

The remedy in a §404 violation can be restoration, e.g., United States v. Bradshaw, 541 F. Supp. 884 (D. Md. 1982). Tull v. U.S., 481 U.S. 412 (1987), held that a §404 enforcement action for substantial civil penalties and injunctive relief triggers a Seventh Amendment right to a jury trial because "[t]he legislative history of the Act reveals that Congress wanted the district court to consider the need for retribution and deterrence, in addition to restitution, when it imposed civil penalties." A defendant does not, however, have a right to jury assessment of the amount of the penalty.

A NOTE ON OTHER STATUTORY CONSTRAINTS ON DREDGING AND FILLING

1. A few cases have tried to use §10* to block the construction of public works projects. Section 10 was originally enacted in 1889 in response to a Supreme Court decision holding that there was no federal common law prohibition against the obstruction of navigable waters by private parties. Willamette Iron Bridge Co. v. Hatch, 125 U.S. 1 (1888). The 1899 version requires the consent of Congress for the construction of "any bridge, dam, dike, or causeway" on navigable waters. Section 10 was invoked to block an expressway along the east bank of the Hudson River in one of the early "remand theory" cases, Citizens Committee for the Hudson Valley v. Volpe, 302 F. Supp. 1083 (S.D.N.Y.), aff'd, 425 F.2d 97 (2d Cir.), cert. denied sub nom. Parker v. Citizens Committee for the Hudson Valley, 400 U.S. 949 (1970), but subsequent cases refused to follow Hudson Valley and held that intrusions into navigable waters required only a §404 permit. In Hart & Miller Islands Area Environmental Group v. Corps of Engineers, 621 F.2d 1281 (4th Cir. 1980), the plaintiffs challenged the construction of a diked disposal area in Chesapeake Bay to contain dredge spoil that would have otherwise been dumped in the open waters of the bay. After a full review of the legislative history and precedents, the court held that the Corps had correctly limited §10 to structures that completely span a waterway since only those pose a risk of completely blocking a navigable waterway. The court found that the legislative history of the 1972 amendments showed a congressional intent to treat diked disposal areas through the §404 process. Cf. Sierra Club v. Morton, 400 F. Supp. 610 (N.D. Cal. 1975), aff'd in part, rev'd in part sub nom. Sierra Club v. Andrus, 610 F.2d 581 (9th Cir. 1979), which applied §10 to block an intensely controversial water diversion project that would have routed northern California water around the Sacramento-San Joaquin Delta in a peripheral canal. Section 10 was held applicable because a navigable capacity of a river would be impaired. The Supreme Court did not reach the merits, but it reversed on the ground that §10 created no implied right of action. California v. Sierra Club, 451 U.S. 287 (1981). The district court required a finding that the

*Navigability under §10 is defined by the more restrictive The Daniel Ball test, 77 U.S. (10 Wall.) 557 (1871), discussed at p. 361 supra, not the broader "navigable waters of the United States" test used for §404. See Minnehaha Creek Watershed District v. Hoffman, 597 F.2d 617 (8th Cir. 1979) (Lake Minnetonka, in the middle of Minneapolis, navigable under §404 but not §10).

navigable capacity of the river would be impaired, but the Ninth Circuit required no finding of impaired navigability. The impact of applying the Rivers and Harbors Act to water diversions is explored in Proctor, Section 10 of the Rivers and Harbors Act and Western Water Allocations — Are All Western Waters up a Creek without a Permit? 10 B.C. Envtl. Aff. L. Rev. 111 (1982). The canal was ultimately blocked by a referendum in June 1982.

Harmon Cove Condominium Association, Inc. v. Marsh, 815 F. 2d 949 (3d Cir. 1987), held that neither §10 of the Rivers and Harbors Act nor §404 of the Clean Water Act imposes a duty on the Secretary, enforceable by mandamus, to enforce compliance with the conditions of a dredge and fill permit. The court also refused to find an implied private right of action for permit violations.

2. Another statute that must be considered by the Corps of Engineers is the Fish and Wildlife Coordination Act (FWCA). Lake Erie Alliance v. Corps of Engineers, 526 F. Supp. 1063 (W.D. Pa. 1981), describes the statute and the duties it imposes on the Corps in issuing §404 permits:

> Count Five of the complaint alleges that the defendants drew up the draft and final impact statements and issued the permit to U.S. Steel in violation of the Fish and Wildlife Coordination Act of 1934, 15 U.S.C. §661, et seq., the Migratory Bird Act, 16 U.S.C. §701, et seq. and the Corps' regulations. The Fish and Wildlife Coordination Act is intended to encourage cooperation between the Secretary of the Interior and other federal, state and public or private agencies in conserving wild life resources while expanding the national economy. 16 U.S.C. §661. The Act requires that:
>
> > (a) . . . [w]henever the waters of any stream or other body of water are proposed or authorized to be impounded, diverted, the channel deepened, or the stream or other body of water otherwise controlled or modified for any purpose whatever, . . . by any department or agency of the United States, or by any public or private agency under Federal permit or license, such department or agency first shall consult with the United States Fish and Wildlife Service, Department of the Interior, and with the head of the agency exercising administration over the wildlife resources of the particular State wherein the impoundment, diversion, or other control facility is to be constructed with a view to the conservation of wildlife resources and preventing loss of and damage to such resources as well as providing for the development and improvement thereof in connection with such water-resource development.
> >
> > (b) . . . In furtherance of such purposes, the reports and recommendations of the Secretary of the Interior on the wildlife aspects of such projects . . . shall be made an integral part of any report prepared or submitted by any agency of the Federal Government responsible for engineering surveys and construction of such projects when such reports are presented to the Congress or to any agency or person having the authority . . . to authorize the construction of water-resource, development projects. . . . The reporting officers in project reports of the Federal agencies shall give full consideration to the report and recommendations of the Secretary of the Interior and to any report of the State agency on the wildlife aspects of such projects, and the project plan shall include such justifiable means and measures for wildlife purposes as the reporting agency finds should be adopted to obtain maximum overall project benefits. 16 U.S.C. §662.

The Corps' regulations reiterate the requirement that they consult with the Regional Director, U.S. Fish and Wildlife Service, and the head of the state agency responsible for fish and wildlife and give great weight to their views in evaluating the application. The regulations provide that the applicant will be urged to modify his proposal to eliminate or mitigate any damage to such resources, and in appropriate cases a permit may be conditioned to accomplish this purpose. 33 C.F.R. §320.4(c)

Plaintiffs argue that this Act was violated because defendants ignored State and Federal agency requests that the final EIS definitively display in maps the areas of the plant site which will remain completely undeveloped. The fact that the defendants issued the permit and refused to withdraw it despite the recommendations of the U.S. Fish and Wildlife Service and the Pennsylvania Agencies is a violation of the Fish and Wildlife Coordination Act according to the plaintiffs. Plaintiffs do not consider this issue proper for summary judgment since there is a dispute as to whether the U.S. Fish and Wildlife Service supported the wildlife management plan developed by a private consulting firm. This dispute is not critical to the question of whether the defendants consulted with the Secretary of the U.S. Fish and Wildlife Service, with the head of the appropriate state agencies, made their reports an integral part of the Corps report, and gave their reports and recommendations full consideration as required by the Act.

The EIS indicates that the statutory and regulatory procedures were followed. There is no requirement that the Corps follow the advice of the State or Federal agencies or adopt their positions. Plaintiffs are arguing that the final decision was wrong because a Pennsylvania agency recommended against it. Review of the merits of the agency's proposed action is not required by NEPA. One circuit court has stated that "[t]he project, when finished, may be a complete blunder — NEPA insists that it be a knowledgeable blunder." Matsumato v. Brinegar [568 F.2d 289 (9th Cir. 1978)].

The administrative record and the final EIS support defendants' positions that they did not violate either the Fish and Wildlife Coordination Act or the Migratory Bird Act. See, Administrative Record, Vols. 1, 2 and 3; EIS, Vol. II, pp. 2-991 through 2-1071; EIS, Vol. III, pp. 4-838, 5-61, and 6-120 through 6-129. Representatives of federal and state fish and wildlife organizations were consulted early in the review process and contacts were maintained throughout the permitting process. The end result of all these consultations was the development of the fish and wildlife management plan for the lakefront site by the consulting firm of Fahringer, McCarty, Grey, Inc. Administrative Record. Vol. 113. The U.S. Fish and Wildlife Service and the Ohio Department of Natural Resources wholly supported the Wildlife Management Plan developed by Fahringer, McCarty & Grey, Inc. All fish and wildlife resource agencies except the Pennsylvania Fish and Game Commissions agreed that the effect of culverting Turkey Creek culvert upon fish and wildlife would be minimal.

The fact that the Pennsylvania Game and Fish Commission opposed issuance of the permit does not mean that the Corps did not give "full consideration" of "great weight" to the views of that agency. It only shows that they gave greater weight to the views of the majority of the agencies and experts which studied the effects the plant would have on wildlife. [526 F. Supp. at 1080-1081.]

The failure to listen can sometimes be fatal. Sierra Club v. Corps of Engineers, 697 F.2d 297 (2d Cir. 1982), *affirming* 541 F. Supp. 1367 (S.D.N.Y. 1982), held that the Corps issuance of a §404 permit for a Hudson River landfill for the intensely controversial Westway highway in New York City was arbitrary

because the record "discloses that at every level of review the Corps simply ignored the views of sister agencies that were, by law, to be accorded 'great weight.'
The evidence amply warranted the district court's finding that the Corps never
made a serious attempt to discover, or to make a decision based on, reliable
fisheries information." NEPA and FWCA issues are often interrelated. However,
NEPA statements must only be filed for major federal actions, but FWCA consultation is triggered by actions that do not meet the threshold for an environmental impact statement. In addition, the mitigation duties imposed by the
FWCA may be greater than those imposed by NEPA. Compare Veiluva, The
Fish and Wildlife Coordination Act in Environmental Litigation, 9 Ecology
L.Q. 489 (1980), with Note, Environmental Protection under the Fish and
Wildlife Coordination Act: The Road Not Taken, 2 Va. J. Nat. Resources L. 53
(1982).

3. Another limitation on the Corps' §404 authority is the Endangered Species Act, 16 U.S.C. §1536(a)(2), which requires that all federal agencies insure
that their actions will not jeopardize the continued existence of a species listed
as threatened or endangered. Once a federal action is found to jeopardize a listed
species, the agency has an absolute mandate to prevent the destruction of the
species, TVA v. Hill, 437 U.S. 153 (1978), unless a cabinet level committee
exempts the species from the Act. 16 U.S.C. §1536(e)-(h). See Riverside Irrigation District v. Andrews, 568 F. Supp. 583 (D. Colo. 1983), aff'd, 758 F.2d
508 (10th Cir. 1985) (dam developer may not discharge sand and gravel pursuant
to a national permit during the construction of a dam because the operation of
the dam and the altered water flow might have an adverse impact on whooping
crane habitat 250 to 300 miles downstream). The agencies' duties to protect
species are well outlined in Roosevelt Campobello International Park Commission v. EPA, 684 F.2d 1041 (1st Cir. 1982). See generally Tarlock, The Endangered Species Act and Western Water Rights, 20 Land & Water L. Rev. 1 (1985).

4. Many §404 permits for large projects will trigger NEPA. Suppose that
the impact statement is found inadequate. Does it follow that the §404 permit
decision is invalid? Is the standard of review the same for the permit and the
impact statement? Consider the following quotation from Sierra Club v. Sigler,
695 F.2d 957 (5th Cir. 1983). The court found that the impact statement for a
deep water port, which required a §404 permit, was inadequate because it failed
to include a worst-case analysis of a supertanker spill, so relevant costs were
slighted:

> It is apparent to us that the skewed FEIS [Federal Environmental Impact
> Statement] tainted the Colonel's permit decisionmaking process preventing the
> "careful weighing of all [relevant] factors" necessary in the "general balancing pro-
> cess" required by Corps regulations. Important and significant environmental costs
> were omitted from the FEIS and therefore were not considered by the Colonel in
> his permit decision. Since the Corps' decision was not made "according to law," it
> must be reversed. The FEIS must be redone to consider the costs of bulk com-
> modities activities it extols, and the permit decision by the Corps is reversed and
> remanded to the Corps for reconsideration in light of the corrected FEIS. We, of

course, may not and do not express an opinion on the merits of the permits. The Corps may reach the same decision, but only after considering an adequate FEIS. If that decision is procedurally adequate under NEPA and Corps regulations, it will pass judicial muster. [695 F.2d at 983.]

H.   MUNICIPAL SEWAGE AND OCEAN DUMPING

1.   *The Construction Grant Program*

Title II of the Clean Water Act, 33 U.S.C. §§2181-2197, has attempted to reduce municipal discharges of pollution through a subsidy program that finances the construction of POTWs (publicly owned treatment plants) that meet a national state-of-the-art standard (secondary treatment) and are cost-effective. Initially, the federal government paid up to 75 percent of the cost of a conventional plant and up to 85 percent of the cost of an innovative or alternative facility, but in 1984 Congress decreased the federal share to 55 percent for conventional plants and 75 percent for innovative and alternative ones. Industrial wastes discharged into POTWs were originally subject to both pre-treatment standards and special user fees called industrial cost recovery. In 1980 industrial cost recovery was ended because the program did not work, having generated only about 2 percent of average waste water treatment revenue. See Donahue, What's Right and Wrong with Industrial Cost Recovery, 47 Am. Pub. Works Assn. Rptr. 15 (1980).

Section 307, 33 U.S.C. §1317, authorizes the promulgation of pre-treatment standards. The standards were reviewed in National Association of Metal Finishers v. EPA, 719 F.2d 624 (3d Cir. 1983), and Ford Motor Co. v. EPA, 718 F.2d 55 (3d Cir. 1983). *National Metal Finishers* approved of many EPA regulations and remanded others. The statutory rationale for pre-treatment standards is to prevent industrial discharges that interfere with plant operation or are incompatible with a plant. EPA regulations were found inconsistent with this purpose because they did not require proof of cause in fact. One of the most controversial aspects of indirect discharge regulation is the agency's removal credits policy. EPA allows POTWs removal credits for wastes adequately treated by a manufacturer that has an approved pretreatment plan before they are discharged into the system, and *National Metal Finishers* held that such credits were consistent with the Act. EPA then relaxed the pre-treatment rules, but these were overturned because the agency had not issued sludge regulations which were required by "the statute's command for a comprehensive framework to regulate the disposal and utilization of sludge. . . ." Natural Resources Defense Council v. EPA, 790 F.2d 289 (3d Cir.), *cert. denied*, 479 U.S. 1084 (1987). Congress ratified the decision in the Water Quality Act of 1987. 33 U.S.C. §1345. See generally, Gold, EPA's Pretreatment Program, 16 B.C. Envtl. Aff. L. Rev. 459

(1989). EPA and state agencies are prohibited from issuing removal credits after August 31, 1987 until EPA issues the sludge regulations. Armco Inc. v. EPA, 869 F.2d 975 (6th Cir. 1989).

Chemical Manufacturers Association v. EPA, 870 F.2d 177, 245-247 (5th Cir. 1989) reviewed the agency's calculation of the BAT pretreatment standards:

> In adopting the "BAT comparison" approach to defining "pass through," the EPA explained that it sought to satisfy two competing congressional objectives:
>
>> That standards for indirect dischargers be equivalent to standards for direct dischargers, and that the treatment capability and performance of the POTW be recognized and taken into account in regulating the discharge of pollutants from indirect dischargers.[292]
>
> The EPA explained that it had determined, after considering alternative methods, that its approach of comparing average percent removal rates to determine pass through was the best solution to the inherent difficulty of measuring the effectiveness of POTW's treatment of toxic pollutants. The difficulty stems from the fact that the concentration of toxic pollutants in POTWs' influent is much lower than that in industry treatment systems because the industrial dischargers' wastewater mixes in the POTW system with wastewater from other sources that does not contain toxic pollutants. As a result of this dilution, the POTWs' influent concentrations of toxics may already be nearly undetectable by present methods — even though the mass of toxic pollutants has not been reduced. The concentration of toxic pollutants in effluent may therefore be undetected, even if the POTWs' treatment is not, in actuality, very effective in reducing the mass of toxic pollutants.
>
> The EPA explained that it had rejected the alternatives of direct comparison of effluent concentrations[293] and a percent differential approach[294] to measuring pass through because both approaches tended to overestimate the effectiveness of POTW treatment and therefore created an unacceptable risk that toxic pollutants were in fact passing through POTWs.[295]
>
> The EPA concluded that the approach of comparing average percent re-

---

292.   48 Fed. Reg. 11,841.

293.   The EPA determined that a comparison between the effluent concentrations of POTWs and industrial facilities was inappropriate due to two major factors: (1) the unique problems posed by the dilution that results from commingling industrial with non-industrial wastewater within POTWs; and (2) the more complicated nature of the POTWs' effluent, resulting from contributions from various industries. These factors were found likely to render the POTW effluent-pollutant concentration lower than that for direct dischargers — even if the pollutant's mass exceeded the amount allowed for any single direct discharger. 46 Fed. Reg. at 9415-16.

294.   The EPA considered, but ultimately rejected, the "percent differential approach" to calculating "pass through." The percent differential approach would have found "pass through" only when the average percent removed by a direct discharger using BAT exceeded POTW removals by a specified percent. This approach is based on the assumption that a removal difference of less than a certain percent may not reflect differences in treatment efficiency, but may reflect only analytical variability of low concentrations typically found in end-of-pipe biological systems. See 48 Fed. Reg. 11,841-42 (EPA proposed five percent differential in 1983); 51 Fed. Reg. 44,090 (EPA proposed in 1985 to increase five percent differential to ten percent, but ultimately decided to adhere to present approach of comparing average percent removal rates). The Agency explained that the percent differential approach was unsatisfactory because it was difficult, using that method, to determine whether levels substantially below the analytical detection limit result from POTW treatment or from mere dilution, since the data were derived from samples demonstrating pollutants at or below the detection limits. 52 Fed. Reg. 42,545.

moval rates "is unbiased in that it does not favor either overregulation or underregulation in determining which pollutants are regulated at PSES."[296] CMA objects that if the EPA applied this direct comparison, it would find pass through, and therefore impose pretreatment standards, even if POTWs achieved a 96.2% removal rate for a particular toxic pollutant, so long as the EPA predicts that plants complying with BAT can achieve slightly greater removal — even 96.3%.

Given the EPA's well-founded concern that the effects of dilution may cause the effectiveness of POTW treatment to be overstated, we cannot conclude that the EPA's method of determining pass through is arbitrary. As we have stated, "At first blush, it may be unclear why dilution can be a problem. One might believe that the proper goal of a treatment system is to produce water 'so clean' that pollutants are present in only immeasurably small amounts. This is usually, but not always the case. Certain pollutants are dangerous even in immeasurably small concentrations."[297]

CMA also maintains that the EPA arbitrarily assumed that certain pollutants that were not detected in POTW effluent were present at the minimum analytical level. Because the minimum analytical level is then used to calculate removal, CMA asserts that some pollutants may be subject to PSES even if POTWs' actual percent removal is higher than the BAT percent removal of the same pollutant.

The EPA has explained, however, that its practice of assigning the minimum analytic value to certain pollutants that did not appear at detectable levels in POTW effluent is also designed to compensate for the effects of dilution. The Agency explained:

> The conservative approach of adopting the 'detection' limit or the analytical threshold as the effluent value for such measurements has the effect of underestimating the POTW's percent removal. . . . In many cases, in fact, both POTW and BAT treatment systems with relatively [low] influent concentrations yielded effluent measurements below detection, and the resulting percent removals were not true measures of treatment effectiveness, but rather were functions of influent concentrations. . . . The POTW might be achieving as high a percent removal as the BAT level technology, but there was no basis for determining whether this was so or not.[298]

The EPA reasonably concluded that due to the effects of dilution on influent concentrations, the "non-detects" or "ND" values (indicating effluent concentrations too low to measure) derived from POTWs with low influent concentrations of priority toxic pollutants did not necessarily demonstrate that the pollutants had been effectively treated and removed from the effluent.[299]

We hold that the EPA reasonably adopted the conservative methodology of assigning the minimum analytical value to certain pollutants that yielded "ND" values in effluent concentrations in order to account for the possibility that, because of the effects of dilution on influent concentrations, priority toxics are present in POTW effluent at levels far greater than can presently be measured. We further

---

295. EPA concluded that to allow even a few pollutants to go unregulated based on a percent differential could have significant consequences in terms of the number of pounds of unregulated toxic pollutants discharged. Dev. Doc. VI-32, reprinted in Joint App. at 3688.

296. 52 Fed. Reg. 42,545.

297. Texas Municipal Power Agency v. EPA, 836 F.2d at 1489 n.38; see also Weyerhaeuser Co. v. Costle, 590 F.2d at 1041; National Assn. of Metal Finishers v. EPA, 719 F.2d at 651 n.38; Cerro Copper Products Co. v. Ruckelshaus, 766 F.2d at 1069.

298. 52 Fed. Reg. 42,546.

299. 52 Fed. Reg. 42,545-46.

note that the EPA has taken reasonable steps to reduce the likelihood of underestimating the effectiveness of POTW removals.[300]

2.   The EPA's Methodology in Assuming an Absence of "Pass Through" Based on POTW Averages

NRDC argues that the EPA's pass-through methodology in practice tends to overestimate the amount of toxic pollutants removed by POTWs. Originally, the EPA had proposed to find pass through whenever it had insufficient POTW data to make a comparison with BAT removal; this position was supported by NRDC. The EPA then revised its position and decided to assume an absence of pass through for three toxic pollutants — bis(2 chloroisopropyl)ether, acrylonitrile, and 3, 4 benzofluoroanthene — on the basis of POTW removal averages. NRDC argues that the EPA's new position is inconsistent with §307(b)(1) of the Clean Water Act, which reads: "Pretreatment standards . . . shall be established to prevent the discharge of any pollutant through treatment works . . . which are publicly owned, which pollutant interferes with, passes through, or otherwise is incompatible with such works."[301] NRDC further alleges that the EPA committed analytical errors in its calculation of average POTW removal. The EPA decided to calculate the overall average of BAT and POTW removal rates rather than average daily rates. This, NRDC alleges, tends to merge spike concentrations of individual pollutants into the base flow and thus determines a plant's average removal, rather than a plant's consistent, daily removal capability.

The EPA responds to NRDC's argument that determining the average POTW removal rate for purposes of determining pass through is inconsistent with the Clean Water Act by correctly noting that its regulations meet Congress' mandate that the EPA establish pretreatment standards for pollutants which pass through. Since Congress provided no criteria by which the EPA is to determine when a pollutant "passes through" a POTW untreated, the establishment of pass-through criteria is left to the Administrator's discretion. In reviewing the Administrator's interpretation of the phrase "pass through," we must accord the Administrator a presumption of regularity.[302] While we must "reject administrative constructions that are contrary to clear congressional intent,"[303] we must nonetheless accord the EPA deference if it is within the limits of its authority to interpret that statute.

The EPA has chosen to define pass through by reference to the average

---

300.   The EPA explained that in selecting appropriate data for the "pass through" comparison, it deleted very low influent data from its analysis and used data from POTWs only if their influent level was at least ten times the analytical minimum level or at least 100 µg/1. This editing criterion, which was also used to select data for establishing BAT limitations, assesses more accurately the POTWs' removal rate. The EPA explained that when influent concentration is below this level, effluent concentrations below the pollutants' analytical threshold often may be achieved using less than BAT level treatment. This "editing criterion helps to insure that BAT effluent limitations generally reflect the technical capability of BAT level treatment rather than low influent concentrations." 52 Fed. Reg. 42,546.

More than half (24) of the pollutants subject to PSES were identified based on this editing criterion. For the remainder (16), influent data above the "ten times the detection limit" are unavailable due to POTW dilution. For these pollutants, EPA relied instead on data procured after using a 20 µg/l cutoff for POTW influent concentrations — the standard originally used to calculate pass through in the Agency's 1983 proposal. Id.

301.   33 U.S.C. §1317(b)(1).

302.   Citizens to Preserve Overton Park, 401 U.S. at 405, 91 S. Ct. at 818; NRDC v. EPA, 790 F.2d 289, 297 (3d Cir. 1986).

303.   Chevron, U.S.A., Inc. v. NRDC, 467 U.S. at 843 n.9, 104 S. Ct. at 2781 n.9.

amount of toxic pollutants removed by the POTW. NRDC would rather have the EPA determine pass through on a daily consistent basis. We hold that the EPA's decision to define pass through based on POTW average removal does not violate the CWA. Due to the fact that industrial waste entering a POTW is mixed with other municipal wastes, such as sewage, it is impossible to trace a given influent stream through the POTW. It would therefore be impossible for the EPA to accurately determine what percentage of waste a POTW was removing on a daily basis, since this requires a direct comparison of influent concentration to effluent concentration. As a result of this analytical difficulty, the EPA has chosen the reasonable and available step of evaluating POTW performance on an average basis. Given the factual situation and analytical uncertainty in this area, we find this to be an acceptable interpretation of §307(b)(1) of the CWA.

Title II has generally been an endless source of controversy. The main problems are cost, lack of cost-effectiveness, and lack of coordination between Title II and other land use and environmental objectives. It is estimated that $120 billion will be required to meet Clean Water Act goals by the year 2000, but demand has always exceeded appropriated funds. Title II survived an attempt by President Nixon to impound congressionally allotted funds. Train v. City of New York, 420 U.S. 35 (1975). Congress subsequently enacted the Congressional Budget Impoundment and Control Act of 1974, 33 U.S.C. §§1282(a)(1)-(2). See Fisher, The Authorization-Appropriation Process in Congress: Formal Rules and Informal Practices, 29 Cath. U.L. Rev. 51 (1979). The constitutionality of this act has been called in question by the Supreme Court's invalidation of one-house legislative vetoes. INS v. Chadha, 462 U.S. 919 (1983).

In 1987 Congress responded to the mounting budget deficit and continuing criticisims that Title II was not cost effective by ending construction grants after 1994. Instead of relying on federal grants, states are encouraged to set up revolving loan funds. These loan funds will initially be supported by federal grants, 33 U.S.C. §§1381-1384, but they are expected to become self-supporting permanent funds. States have expressed some initial concern that the funds will not pay their administrative costs and that EPA's use of letters of credit rather than lump sum payments will not generate sufficient funds.

EPA retains considerable discretion to ensure that Title II grants meet federal goals, but there has been litigation over the agency's exercise of this discretion. See, e.g., California v. EPA, 689 F.2d 217 (D.C. Cir. 1982) (proposed plant not cost-effective). A major source of conflict between local units of government and the EPA is §204(b)(1)(A), 33 U.S.C. §1284(b)(1)(A), which requires that each POTW operator have an adequate system of user charges. This section has been sustained against a tenth amendment challenge (Middlesex County Utility Authority v. Borough of Sayreville, 690 F.2d 358 (3d Cir. 1982)), but other arguments remain open. See City of New Brunswick v. Borough of Miltown, 686 F.2d 120 (3d Cir. 1982), and Hotel Employers Association v. Gorsuch, 669 F.2d 1305 (9th Cir. 1982). See also Pacific Legal Foundation v. Quarles, 440 F. Supp. 316 (C.D. Cal. 1977), aff'd sub nom. Kilroy v. Quarles, 614 F.2d 255 (9th Cir. 1980) (NEPA does not apply to treatment charges).

The environmental impacts of the sewer grant program have been a source of continuing controversy. An early charge against the program was that funds were disbursed in such a way that only part of a watercourse's sewage was treated, so that often there was no net improvement in water quality. Title II and other sections of the Clean Water Act try to make the grants more cost-effective by requiring that states have a priority schedule for POTWs based on the relative severity of a pollution problem; that a planned facility be in conformity with the regional §208 plan (§204(a)(1), 33 U.S.C. §1284(a)(1)); and that Title II grants are subject to NEPA. See Bosco v. Beck, 475 F. Supp. 1029 (D.N.J. 1979), aff'd, 614 F.2d 769 (3d Cir. 1980). However, problems remain in coordinating Title II grants with local land use planning and control programs. In many areas, EPA requirements that a POTW have sufficient reserve capacity to accommodate future growth led to facility overbuilding. Courts have upheld EPA's discretion to refuse to fund a facility with too much reserve capacity (State of Maryland ex rel. Burch v. Costle, 452 F. Supp. 1154 (D.D.C. 1978)), and after October 1, 1984, subject to certain exceptions, EPA can only fund plants with a capacity adequate to serve the residential, commercial, and industrial needs of the area in question as of the date of the grant. For earlier litigation involving suits by developers against EPA for failure to fund facilities with adequate reserve capacity, see Chesapeake Bay Village, Inc. v. Costle, 502 F. Supp. 213 (D. Md. 1980), and Smoke Rise Inc. v. Washington Suburban Sanitary Commission, 400 F. Supp. 1369 (D. Md. 1975), aff'd sub nom. Donhoe Construction Co. v. Montgomery County, 567 F.2d 603 (4th Cir. 1977). Although EPA has become more sensitive to the relationship between Title II and growth management, courts have not always agreed that the agency has the power to use Title II to decide where growth should or should not occur. See Cape May Greene, Inc. v. Warren, 698 F.2d 179 (3d Cir. 1983) and Shanty Town Associates v. EPA, 843 F.2d 787 (4th Cir. 1988) (sewer service may be restricted to floodplain).

Other problems with Title II include the §211, 33 U.S.C. §1291, prohibition against the use of Title II funds for collection systems unless the system is part of the placement or major rehabilitation of an existing system or the system is a new one in an existing community. Further, Title II funds may not be used to treat discharges from combined sanitary and storm runoff sewers or to construct new combined systems. There have also been federalism conflicts about who is responsible for administering the grants. See Sylves, Congress, EPA, the States and the Fight to Decentralize Water-Pollution-Grant Policy, in Environmental Policy Implementation: Planning and Management Options and Their Consequences 109 (D. Mann ed. 1982).

2.   Ocean Discharge of Effluents:
A Continuing Controversy

The direct discharge of partially treated effluents into the oceans is a continuing source of controversy under the Clean Water Act. Many experts estimate that secondary treatment is unnecessary and that billions of dollars can be saved in POTW construction costs with little or no compromise of water quality by allowing coastal municipalities to discharge partially treated effluents into the ocean. But others disagree, arguing that ocean discharges are in direct conflict with §101(a)(1)'s objective that "the discharge of pollutants into the navigable waters be eliminated by 1985." Initially, EPA treated ocean and other discharges equally and categorized municipal dischargers with all other dischargers, prohibiting the discharge of untreated wastewater. This policy was challenged in *Pacific Legal Foundation v. Quarles*, 440 F. Supp. 316 (C.D. Calif. 1977). EPA had ordered Los Angeles to apply secondary treatment to all effluent and to cease dumping sludge into the ocean under §301(b)(1)(B). The plaintiffs argued that §403 and the Marine Protection, Research, and Sanctuaries Act, 42 U.S.C. §§1431-1434, authorized EPA to grant permits for the discharge of untreated effluent, but the court disagreed:

> Surely, when Congress adopted a regulatory philosophy of strict end-of-pipe regulation, if an exception was intended for ocean polluters or deep ocean outfalls such an exception would have been specifically referred to in either the statutory language or the legislative history. The court is satisfied that a reasonable interpretation of the Water Act requires that Section 301 and Section 403 apply *concurrently* to all ocean pollution within the jurisdictions of the Act, i.e., to obtain an NPDES permit an ocean polluter must meet both the technological control requirements of Section 301 and the ocean degradation criteria of Section 403. [440 F. Supp. at 326 (emphasis in original).]

In 1977 Congress amended §301(h), 33 U.S.C. §1311(h), to allow municipalities a variance from the secondary treatment standard if they could demonstrate that "the modification will not interfere with protection of public water supplies and the attainment or maintenance of that water which assures the protection of public water supplies and the protection and propagation of a balanced, indigenous population of fish, shellfish, and wildlife, and allows recreational activities, in and on the water, will not require additional controls on any other source, assures enforcement of all applicable pretreatment requirements, and assures that there will be no substantial increase in the volume of the discharge." S. Rep. No. 95-370, reprinted in U.S. Code Cong. & Admin. News 4326, 4369 (1977). The 1987 amendments require the Administrator to consider the effects of combinations of different pollutants on water quality before granting any modification, 33 U.S.C. §1311(h)(2), and the discharge must have received at least primary treatment, defined as the removal of 30 percent of BOD and suspended solids, and must meet applicable water quality standards beyond a mixing zone. §1311(h)(9). The section makes it very difficult to obtain a modification in saline estuarine waters. All outfalls that require an NPDES permit must renew their permits every five years (§301(h), §402(a), (b)(1)(B)). In 1981 the application period under §301(j)(1)(A) (nine months) was reopened for one year, starting December 30, 1981. Congress's primary motive was construction costs savings. Eight hundred communities were eligible for the variance; if all were granted — an unlikely event — $12 billion in construction funds could be saved. See H.R. No. 97-270, reprinted in U.S. Code Cong. & Admin. News 2629, 2645 (1981).

Rite-Research Improves the Environment v. Costle, 650 F.2d 1312 (5th Cir. 1981), holds that a citizens' group has standing to challenge EPA's refusal to approve a city's (Miami in this instance) application for planning funds for a deep ocean outfall. In Natural Resources Defense Council, Inc. v. EPA, 656 F.2d 768 (D.C. Cir. 1981), the court held that §301(h) does allow unrestricted discharge of effluents into the ocean because the regulations "restrict the discharge of sewage by limiting the availability of a variance to a class of applicants which does not include all coastal municipalities." The court also rejected the argument that EPA must set a minimum depth standard for the location of outfalls:

> Depth was a subject of concern to Congress in its consideration of section 1311(h). The statute itself uses the word "deep." The Conference Committee Report states that "[d]epth is a key factor in determining the amount of circulation in waters of the territorial sea or contiguous zone." 3 Leg. Hist. at 259. NRDC cites several appearances of the expression "deep marine discharge," e.g., 3 Leg. Hist. 257, or "deep marine outfalls," e.g., 3 Leg. Hist. 320. NRDC also cites a letter from the Assistant Administrator for Water and Hazardous Materials stating that the Agency interprets section 1311(h) to apply to " . . . outfalls into very deep waters . . . ," 3 Leg. Hist. 449.
>
> A citation to legislative history which mentions the word "deep" is not helpful in defining the content of the statutory term. It amounts to mere repetition. "Very deep" is no more helpful. The question remains, what is "deep"? . . .
>
> We are convinced that the word "deep" in section 1311(h) does not refer to any uniform minimum depth in feet. Depth is not an independent controlling factor because it is but one factor which must be taken into account. The Agency must consider depth, but it must also consider offshore distance, geological characteristics, and tidal movements. 3 Leg. Hist. 259. The interpretation urged on the court by NRDC elevates depth to the status of a controlling factor. The Administrator's interpretation treats depth as one factor in the environmental calculus set up in section 1311(h). We hold that this is a reasonable and proper interpretation. [656 F.2d at 778.]

Finally, the court held that a literal interpretation of the regulations allowed primary treatment plants to be eligible for the waiver. The 1981 amendments reverse this and only allow plants that have achieved secondary treatment to apply for a waiver. EPA is currently processing requests for waivers at a cautious pace. The first waivers the agency granted were for cities on the west coast. See Dalpra, Secondary Treatment Waivers Issued, Controversy Continues, 53 Water Pollution Control 1554 (1981), but relatively few variances have been granted.

Ocean dumping of sewage sludge has also generated controversy. By 1982, only New York City continued to dump sludge into the ocean, but the practice is being phased out there. Title II requires more treatment and thus more sludge is generated; as a result, east coast communities are being forced to find alternative disposal methods for dewatered sludge because EPA has consistently viewed the Marine Protection Research and Sanctuaries Act (MPRSA) as banning all ocean dumping of sludge. In City of New York v. EPA, 17 Envt. Rep. Cas. (BNA) 1181 (S.D.N.Y. 1981), the court agreed with New York City's view that the Act only bars dumping that unreasonably degrades the environment. New York dumps 260 tons of dry sewage a day into an area known as the New York Bight, located approximately 12 miles east of Sandy Hook, New Jersey. New York originally had planned to start land application of dried sludge as an interim alternate disposal method. As planning for this project proceeded, it was estimated over $200 million would be needed to take care of disposal costs for eight years, and the environmental effects of a project of this magnitude were unknown. Still, EPA threatened to revoke New York City's ocean dumping permit. The court held that §1412(a) of the Act prohibits "only such dumping as unreasonably endangers the environment. The term reasonable inherently connotes a weighing of all the relevant circumstances. By enumerating several factors that inevitably conflict, such as the need for dumping and its effect upon the environment, and requiring the Administration to consider them, the Act forces EPA to balance the statutory factors" (17 Envt. Rep. Cas. (BNA) at 1186). The court concluded that New York's continued dumping would not significantly degrade the environment and that a cessation of dumping would not improve it. The court ordered EPA to give New York City a chance to prove its claims that under the current statute it should be allowed to continue ocean dumping.

Further litigation on ocean dumping in the New York Bight includes National Wildlife Federation v. Gorsuch, 744 F.2d 963 (3d Cir. 1984), and National Wildlife Federation v. Ruckelshaus, 21 Envt. Rep. Cas. (BNA) 1776 (D.N.J. 1983). See also Zeppetello, National and International Regulation of Ocean Dumping: The Mandate to Terminate Marine Disposal of Contaminated Sewage Sludge, 12 Ecology L.Q. 619 (1985) and Bakalian, Regulation and Control of United States Ocean Dumping: A Decade of Progress, an Appraisal for the Future, 8 Harv. Envtl. L. Rev. 193 (1984). New York continued to dump sludge under the 1981 order, but in 1988, in response to a summer of concern over ocean debris, Congress enacted a ban on ocean dumping, which prohibited sludge dumping after 1989 unless a municipality entered into an agreement with EPA to end the practice. 33 U.S.C. §1345. On June 23, 1989 New York City along with Westchester County reached a tentative agreement with the EPA to end ocean dumping by 1992. The New York Times, Saturday, June 24, 1989, p. 9, col. 4. The non-ocean options are landfilling, land spreading, drying, composting, and incineration. Naturally, ocean dumping is the least costly solution; incineration and composting are the costliest. For an early effort to compare the benefits and costs of the different options see C. Menzie, F. Babin, J. Cura & G. Mariami, Assessment for Future Environmental Problems — Ocean Dumping (EPA Contract 68-02-3724, 1983).

A NOTE ON CHOOSING THE RIGHT FORUM FOR
JUDICIAL REVIEW OF FEDERAL AND STATE
IMPLEMENTATION DECISIONS

Choosing the right court to review an implementation decision is not always easy. Section 509, 33 U.S.C. §1369, reprinted below, lists actions that will be reviewed in an appropriate court of appeals and provides that other actions will be reviewed, when jurisdiction exists, in a federal district court. Ideally, court of appeals review would seem appropriate when there is a full and exclusive administrative record (Currie & Goodman, Judicial Review of Federal Administrative Action: The Quest for the Optimum Forum, 75 Colum. L. Rev. 1 (1975)), but environmental issues are not always presented in a procedurally optimal manner. See Currie, Judicial Review under Federal Pollution Laws, 62 Iowa L. Rev. 1221 (1977).

In part, §509 provides:

> (b)(1) Review of the Administrator's action (A) in promulgating any standard of performance under section 306, (B) in making any determination pursuant to section 306(b)(1)(C), (C) in promulgating any effluent standard, prohibition, or pretreatment standard under section 307, (D) in making any determination as to a State permit program submitted under section 402(b), (E) in approving or promulgating any effluent limitation or other limitation under sections 301, 302, or 306, and (F) in issuing or denying any permit under section 402, may be had by any interested person in the Circuit Court of Appeals of the United States for the Federal judicial district in which such person resides or transacts such business upon application by such person. Any such application shall be made within ninety days from the date of such determination, approval, promulgation, issuance or denial, or after such date only if such application is based solely on grounds which arose after such ninetieth day.
>
> (2) Action of the Administrator with respect to which review could have been obtained under paragraph (1) of this subsection shall not be subject to judicial review in any civil or criminal proceeding for enforcement.
>
> (c) In any judicial proceeding brought under subsection (b) of this section in which review is sought of a determination under this Act required to be made on the record after notice and opportunity for hearing, if any party applies to the court for leave to adduce additional evidence, and shows to the satisfaction of the court that such additional evidence is material and that there were reasonable grounds for the failure to adduce such evidence in the proceeding before the Administrator, the court may order such additional evidence (and evidence in rebuttal thereof) to be taken before the Administrator, in such manner and upon such terms and conditions as the court may deem proper. The Administrator may modify his findings as to the facts, or make new findings, by reason of the additional evidence so taken and he shall file such modified or new findings, and his recommendation, if any, for the modification or setting aside of his original determination, with the return of such additional evidence.

CROWN SIMPSON PULP CO. v. COSTLE
445 U.S. 193 (1980)

Per Curiam.

Pursuant to §301 of the Federal Water Pollution Control Act (Act), as added by the Federal Water Pollution Control Act Amendments of 1972, and amended by the Clean Water Act of 1977, the Environmental Protection Agency (EPA) promulgates regulations limiting the amount of effluent that can be discharged into navigable waters from a category or class of point sources of pollution. Requirements for particular plants or mills are implemented through National Pollutant Discharge Elimination System (NPDES) permits. EPA issues NPDES permits directly except in those States authorized by EPA to issue permits through their own programs. §§402(b), 402(c) of the Act. EPA is notified of the actions taken by state permit-issuing authorities and may veto the issuance of any permit by state authorities by objecting in writing within 90 days. §402(d)(2). This case presents the question of whether the EPA's action denying a variance and disapproving effluent restrictions contained in a permit issued by an authorized state agency is directly reviewable in the United States Court of Appeals under §509(b) of the Act.[2]

Petitioners operate bleached kraft pulpmills which discharge pollutants into the Pacific Ocean near Eureka, Cal. In 1976, they sought NPDES permits from the California Regional Water Resources Board, North Coast Region (Regional Board). The Director of EPA's Region IX Enforcement Division objected to the permits proposed by the Regional Board. Petitioners sought direct review of the EPA's action in the Court of Appeals for the Ninth Circuit. Those direct review proceedings were stayed pending action by the California State Water Resources Control Board (State Board). The State Board set aside the orders of the Regional Board and proposed to issue new permits in their stead. App. to Pet. for Cert. 54. It granted petitioners' requests for variances from EPA's effluent limitations for Biochemical Oxygen Demand (BOD) and pH, but established alternative effluent limitations for BOD and pH to apply in case EPA disapproved the variances in the proposed permits. EPA denied the requested variances and vetoed the permits to the extent that they exempted petitioners from full compliance with the BOD and pH effluent limitations. Petitioners brought a direct review action in the Ninth Circuit, which was consolidated with the actions which they had individually filed earlier. The Court of Appeals dismissed the petitions for lack of jurisdiction. 599 F.2d 897 (1979). It concluded that it had no jurisdiction under §509(b)(1)(E) of the Act, which provides for review in the courts of appeals of actions "approving or promulgating any effluent limitation

---

2. Section 402 was amended in 1977, after the permits in the present case were vetoed, to give EPA the power, which it did not then have, to issue its own permit if the State fails to meet EPA's objection within a specified time. §402(d)(4) of the Act, as added. We do not consider the impact, if any, of this amendment on the jurisdictional issue presented herein.

or other limitation. . . ." The Court of Appeals found this subsection inapplicable since EPA did not approve or promulgate anything when it rejected a proposed permit. 599 F. 2d, at 902. Further, the court found that the subsection applied to effluent limitations affecting categories of point sources rather than to decisions affecting particular plants only. Ibid.

The court also found jurisdiction lacking under §509(b)(1)(F) of the Act, which provides for review in the courts of appeals of EPA actions "in issuing or denying any permit under [§402 of the Act]. . . ." The court recognized that in States where EPA itself administers the permit program, this subsection unquestionably provides for direct review in the courts of appeals. 599 F. 2d, at 903. However, because California administers its own permit-issuing program, EPA in the present case did no more than veto an NPDES permit proposed by the state authority. The Court of Appeals found that under its decision in Washington v. EPA, 573 F. 2d 583 (1978) (*Scott Paper*), EPA's veto of a state-issued permit did not constitute "issuing or denying" a permit and therefore did not clothe the court with jurisdiction.

District Judge Renfrew, sitting by designation, concurred in the majority's analysis of §509(b)(1)(E), and also agreed that the §509(b)(1)(F) question was foreclosed by *Scott Paper*. 599 F. 2d, at 905. However, Judge Renfrew, believing that *Scott Paper* was wrongly decided, urged the Court of Appeals to take the present case en banc in order to consider overruling that decision. He argued that vesting jurisdiction in the courts of appeals under §509(b)(1)(F) would best comport with the congressional goal of ensuring prompt resolution of challenges to EPA's actions and would recognize that EPA's veto of a state-issued permit is functionally similar to its denial of a permit in States which do not administer an approved permit-issuing program.

We agree with the concurring opinion and hold that the Court of Appeals had jurisdiction over this action under §509(b)(1)(F). When EPA, as here, objects to effluent limitations contained in a state-issued permit, the precise effect of its action is to "den[y]" a permit within the meaning of §509(b)(1)(F). Under the contrary construction of the Court of Appeals, denials of NPDES permits would be reviewable at different levels of the federal-court system depending on the fortuitous circumstance of whether the State in which the case arose was or was not authorized to issue permits. Moreover, the additional level of judicial review in those States with permit-issuing authority would likely cause delays in resolving disputes under the Act. Absent a far clearer expression of congressional intent, we are unwilling to read the Act as creating such a seemingly irrational bifurcated system.[9] We therefore grant the petition for certiorari, reverse the

---

9. Our holding is consistent with the approach taken by the Court of Appeals for the Sixth Circuit, Republic Steel Corp. v. Costle, 581 F. 2d 1228, 1230, n. 1 (1978), *cert. denied*, 440 U.S. 909 (1979); Ford Motor Co. v. EPA, 567 F. 2d 661, 668 (1977), and with dicta in the Second and Ninth Circuits, Mianus River Preservation Comm. v. Administrator, EPA, 541 F. 2d 899, 909 (C.A. 2 1976); Shell Oil Co. v. Train, 585 F. 2d 408, 412 (C.A. 9 1978). The Court of Appeals in the present case relied on decisions holding that the EPA's failure to object to a state-

judgement of the Court of Appeals, and remand the case for further proceedings consistent with this opinion.

NOTES AND QUESTIONS

1. District of Columbia v. Schramm, 631 F.2d 854 (D.C. Cir. 1980), holds that the court is without jurisdiction to hear a challenge to EPA's decision not to veto a permit for a sewage treatment plant that discharged into a creek that runs through the District of Columbia:

> The bill that emerged from the conference committee and became the Clean Water Act featured provisions of H.R. 11896 that gave the states the primary responsibility for issuing NPDES permits. The bill also made the EPA approval of state programs meeting the statutory requirements mandatory rather than discretionary, as in S. 2770. In addition, the final version incorporated the waiver provisions of the House and Senate bills, thereby permitting the EPA to waive the notification requirement under section 1342(e) and to waive its right to veto an application for failure to follow the guidelines under section 1342(d)(3).
>
> These provisions reflect the desire of Congress to put the regulatory burden on the states and to give the Agency broad discretion in administering the program. As Representative James Wright stated in describing the NPDES permit process,
>
>> If the Administrator determines that a State has the authority to issue permits consistent with the act, he shall approve the submitted program. In that event, the States, under State law, could issue State discharge permits. These would be State, not Federal actions. . . .
>>   . . . The managers expect the Administrator to use this authority [over state programs] judiciously; it is their intent that the act be administered in such a manner that the abilities of the States to control their own permit programs will be developed and strengthened. They look for and expect State and local interest, initiative, and personnel to provide a much more effective program than that which would result from control in the regional offices of the Environmental Protecton Agency.
>
> 118 Cong. Rec. 33761 (1972), reprinted in 1 Legislative History 262 (remarks of Rep. Wright).
>
> This legislative history compels the conclusion that the Agency's decision not to review or to veto a state's action on an NPDES permit application is "committed to agency discretion by law." 5 U.S.C. §701(a)(2) (1976). Although section 701(a)(2) has a narrow scope, see Citizens to Preserve Overton Park, Inc. v. Volpe, 401 U.S. 402 (1971), it applies here, where "'the statutes are drawn in such broad terms that . . . there is no law to apply.'" Id. at 410, 91 S. Ct. at 821 (quoting S. Rep. No. 752, 79th Cong., 1st Sess. 26 (1945)). The Clean Water Act allows the

---

issued permit is not reviewable in the courts of appeals under §509. Save the Bay, Inc. v. Administrator, EPA, 556 F.2d 1282 (C.A. 5 1977); Mianus River Preservation Comm., *supra.* However, those cases may be distinguishable because EPA's failure to object, as opposed to its affirmative veto of a state-issued permit, would not necessarily amount to "Administrator's action" within the meaning of §509(b)(1).

EPA to choose whether to participate in the application for a state NPDES permit. The Act also gives the EPA freedom to waive notice of the application and to waive any violations in the permit. Certain guidelines apply to the application process, but these guidelines do not bind the Agency in its supervisory role of monitoring state permits. In reaching substantially the same conclusion, the Court of Appeals for the Fifth Circuit noted that

> the legislative history makes very clear that Congress intended EPA to retain discretion to decline to veto a permit even after the agency found some violation of applicable guidelines. That legislative history, more explicit and unequivocal than generally found, leans in almost every expression toward minimal federal intervention when a state plan has been approved.
>   . . . In light of the pervasiveness of this theme, . . . and the conferral of broad discretion to waive review of individual permits, we conclude that Congress intended to allow the Administrator to consider the significance of any guideline violations in terms of the overall goal of the [Act]. . . .

Save the Bay, Inc. v. EPA, 556 F.2d 1282, 1294 (5th Cir. 1977).[12] . . .
    Granting federal court review of the Agency's actions in cases such as this one would upset the federal-state balance struck by Congress: it would allow parties to create a basis for federal jurisdiction when federal involvement is merely secondary. As the Ninth Circuit stated in Shell Oil Co. v. Train, 585 F.2d 408 (9th Cir. 1978),

> a holding that statutorily sanctioned advice by the EPA to a state constitutes final federal agency action reviewable in the federal courts would permit an applicant, dissatisfied with a decision of a state board, to circumvent the appellate process envisioned by the statute and bestow jurisdiction upon a federal court simply by alleging coercion or undue influence.

Id. at 414. See generally Note, Jurisdiction to Review Informal EPA Influence upon State Decisionmaking under the Federal Water Pollution Control Act, 92 Harv. L. Rev. 1814 (1979). Such a result would be unacceptable. Therefore, we hold that the Agency's actions regarding Maryland's approval of the NPDES permit for the plant are not reviewable in federal court. [631 F.2d at 860-861.]

    2. Are any of the following actions reviewable under §509? The EPA Administrator's approval of water quality standards? See Bethlehem Steel Co. v.

---

    12.   The Court of Appeals for the Second Circuit has agreed with this view of the Administrator's discretion under the Clean Water Act:

> Neither the [Clean Water Act] nor its legislative history provide any clear direction to the Administrator as to when he should or should not reject any particular State permit that he finds does not conform with the guidelines and regulations under the Act. It would appear that the option to take no action, even when a permit does not conform, is committed to the Administrator's almost unfettered discretion. See Greater New York Hospital Assoc. v. Matthews, 536 F.2d 494 (2d Cir. 1976).

Mianus River Presevation Comm. v. Administrator, EPA, 541 F.2d 899, 909 n.24 (2d Cir. 1976).
    The court in Save the Bay recognized two possible grounds for limited judicial review of the EPA's decision not to veto a state permit: failure by the Agency even to consider violations of guidelines in deciding not to veto a permit and consideration of impermissible factors in reaching its decision, 556 F.2d at 1295-96. We doubt that Congress intended federal court review in these situations. Nonetheless, since neither of these situations has been shown to be present here, we do not reach issue.

EPA, 538 F.2d 513 (2d Cir. 1976). An EPA compliance order requiring a city to stop discharging wastes into navigable waters in violation of its NPDES permit? See City of Baton Rouge v. EPA, 620 F.2d 478 (5th Cir. 1980). A failure to obtain state certification under §401 (pp. 397-399 *supra*)? Mobil Oil v. Kelly, 426 F. Supp 230 (S.D. Ala. 1976). A utility applies to the federal EPA for an NPDES permit; EPA issues a notice of final determination that will become the final permit unless an adjudicatory hearing is granted within 30 days. Because the permit requires a 90 percent reduction in thermal discharges, the utility files for an adjudicatory hearing, which is granted; by this time EPA has approved the state NPDES program, with the agreement that all adjudicatory hearings for permits issued before the approval date will be defended by the federal EPA. Does the federal EPA still have jurisdiction, and in which federal court is review of this issue proper? See Central Hudson Gas & Electric Corp. v. EPA, 587 F.2d 549 (2d Cir. 1978). EPA objects to a series of state NPDES permits because some of them violate federal and state antidegradation policies. The state modifies the permits to meet EPA's objections, but an industry group seeks federal circuit court of appeals review to challenge EPA's authority both to object and to promulgate an antidegradation policy for the states. Does a circuit court have subject matter jurisdiction under 33 U.S.C. §1369(b)(1)(F) to review either of these challenges? If it does, is either one of these challenges ripe for review? American Paper Institute v. EPA, — F.2d — (7th Cir. 1989). After 1977, EPA has the authority to issue its own permit when it assumes jurisdiction. 33 U.S.C. §1342(d)(2)(A). Review the Pigeon River dispute between Tennessee and North Carolina, p. 407 *supra*. After EPA notifies a state that it is assuming permitting authority, can an industry in that state object to the administrator's action before EPA issues a permit, in a district court, in a circuit court of appeals? Champion International Corp. v. EPA, 850 F.2d 182 (4th Cir. 1988).

3. In theory, an administrative agency's decision *not* to act is as much a decision as a decision that has reached the "final action" stage. However, the distinction between review of a failure to act and final agency action is important because the citizens' suit provision of the Clean Air and Clean Water Acts confers jurisdiction over the former to district courts, whereas circuit courts of appeals have jurisdiction over the latter. Sometimes it may be difficult to determine the nature of a suit. See Pacific Legal Foundation v. Costle, 18 Envt. Rep. Cas. (BNA) 1133 (E.D. Cal. 1981). In California, EPA imposed a construction ban on federal highway and sewer projects after the state failed to adopt a revised SIP with vehicle inspection and maintenance. Previous litigation can be found in 14 Envt. Rep. Cas. (BNA) 2121 (E.D. Cal.), *aff'd*, 627 F.2d 917 (9th Cir. 1980), *cert. denied*, 450 U.S. 914 (1981). The court held that the legality of the construction ban was reviewable in the circuit court because it was a final agency action and that the failure of EPA to promulgate a revised SIP was reviewable in the district court because it was an allegation of a failure to perform a nondiscretionary duty. But, the court held, the Administrator had discharged that duty by imposing a construction ban and thus the legality of the ban under the Administrative Procedure Act was not reviewable because that was a final agency

action, reviewable in the court of appeals! Thus EPA was entitled to summary judgment. 18 Envt. Rep. Cas. (BNA) 1146 (E.D. Cal. 1981).

I.   ENFORCEMENT

Implementation of a statute as comprehensive as the Clean Water Act ultimately depends on voluntary compliance with its commands. DiMento, Can Social Science Explain Organizational Noncompliance with Environmental Law?, 45 J. Social Issues 109 (1989), reviews the literature on the relationship between enforcement and corporate compliance. Compliance is often aided by the knowledge that permit or standard violations will be subject to enforcement actions. Section 309, 33 U.S.C. §1319, contemplates, consistent with the "creative federalism" approach of the statute, that the primary enforcement responsibility for the NPDES permit program will rest with the states, with the federal EPA serving as a backstop. After a state has a qualified program, the federal Administrator "shall," based "on any information available to him," notify the affected state of an NPDES permit or effluent limitation violation. If the state fails to institute an enforcement action within 30 days after notice, the Administrator shall either issue a compliance order or begin a civil action. However, United States v. Cargill, Inc., 508 F. Supp. 734 (D. Del. 1981), holds that the federal EPA may bring a concurrent enforcement action, at least when the federal government is not a party to the state proceeding and is seeking a remedy different from that sought by the state. Accord United States v. Town of Lowell, Ind., 637 F. Supp. 254 (N.D. Ind. 1985). See also State Water Control Board v. Washington Suburban Sanitary Commission, 654 F.2d 802 (D.C. Cir. 1981), cert. denied sub nom. Prince George's County v. United States, 454 U.S. 1082 (1981). Compare United States v. ITT Rayonier, Inc., 627 F.2d 996 (9th Cir. 1980) (collateral estoppel bars EPA from litigating issue resolved in state court proceeding).

Section 309, 33 U.S.C. §1319 contemplates four possible sanctions against a violator of NPDES permit conditions or effluent limitations: (1) compliance orders, which set a timetable for correcting the violation; (2) civil actions for equitable relief or money damages; (3) civil penalties of up to $25,000 per day per violator; (4) criminal penalties imposed against any person who willfully or negligently violates permit conditions or effluent limitations. A "person" is defined in §309(c) to include "any responsible corporate officer." A first offender may be subject to a fine of from $2,500 to $25,000 for each day of the violation, or imprisonment. For second offenders, the maximum fine jumps to $50,000 and the maximum prison term is two years. See Schneider, Criminal Enforcement of Federal Water Pollution Laws in an Era of Deregulation, 73 J. Crim. L. & Criminology 642 (1982). The agency has the traditional prosecutorial discretion to choose between criminal and civil enforcement. K.W. Thompson

Tool Co., Inc. v. United States, 836 F. 2d 721 (1st Cir. 1988)(decision to institute criminal proceedings within discretionary exemption to federal Tort Claims Act). As environmental programs have matured, the case for criminal enforcement becomes stronger because violations are more reprehensible. Convictions and prison sentences are becoming common. See McMurry & Ramsey, Environmental Crime: The Use of Criminal Sanctions in Enforcing Environmental Laws, 19 Loyola of Los Angeles L. Rev. 1133 (1986). The sentencing guidelines established by the United States Sentencing Commission[1] apply to environmental crimes. For example, a violation of the Clean Water Act is a Basic Level Offense 24 which carries a mandatory prison sentence for first offenders where a knowing violation places another in imminent danger regardless of any resulting death or serious bodily injury. See United States v. Protex, — F. 2d — (10th Cir. 1989). Colt Industries, Inc. v. United States, 11 Cl. Ct. 140 (1986), held that §309 civil penalties constitute non-tax deductible fines.

Agencies generally view judicial or formal administrative enforcement proceedings as a last resort. A typical statement of the "last resort" policy can be found in draft memoranda from EPA Administrator Anne M. Burford, General Operating Procedures for Civil Enforcement Program, 13 Envt. Rep. (BNA): Current Developments 78 (1982). Not surprisingly, a massive early empirical study of water pollution enforcement prepared for the National Commission on Water Quality, W. Irwin et al., The Water Pollution Control Act of 1972, Institutional Assessment, Enforcement (1975) (2 vols.), found that states prefer graduated enforcement processes that stress cooperation with dischargers, generous compliance opportunities, and negotiation over technical and economic feasibility issues but that the federal EPA took a somewhat harder enforcement line.

Congressional surveillance of EPA is a major source of enforcement monitoring. See Hearings on S. 777, S. 2652, and S. 97-H.R. 582 before the Subcomm. on Pollution of the Comm. on Environment and Public Works, 97th Cong., 2d Sess. (1982), and House Comm. on Public Works and Transportation, Implementation of the Federal Water Pollution Control Act, Report by the Subcomm. on Oversight and Review, House Comm. on Public Works and Transpiration, H.R. Rep. No. 71, 96th Cong., 2d Sess. (1981). A particularly noteworthy example of congressional surveillance occurred in December 1982 when two congressional committees cited the EPA Administrator for contempt for her failure to respond to subpoenas in connection with "Superfund" enforcement.

1. Access to Information

In some cases, evidence of a violation is fairly straightforward — a harmful discharge occurs without an NPDES permit. See United States v. Earth Sci-

---

1. Mistretta v. United States, 488 U.S. — (1989) (holding that the Sentencing Reform Act of 1984 is not an invalid delegation of judicial power to the Sentencing Commission).

ences, p. 378 *supra*. However, in other cases sophisticated information about the discharge and the quality of the receiving waters in question has to be collected. By and large, the Clean Water Act seeks to shift the costs of monitoring compliance to the discharger. A particularly dramatic example of this is §311(b)(5), 33 U.S.C. §1321(b)(5), which requires that any person in charge of a vessel or offshore facility that discharges oil or a hazardous substance in harmful quantities "shall, as soon as he has knowledge of any discharge . . . immediately notify the appropriate agency of the United States government." Section 309, 33 U.S.C. §1319, imposes substantial monitoring and reporting requirements on all NPDES discharges:

(A) the Administrator shall require the owner or operator of any point source to (i) establish and maintain such records, (ii) make such reports, (iii) install, use, and maintain such monitoring equipment or methods (including where appropriate, biological monitoring methods), (iv) sample such effluents (in accordance with such methods, at such locations, at such intervals, and in such manner as the Administrator shall prescribe), and (v) provide such other information as he may reasonably require; and

(B) the Administrator or his authorized representative, upon presentation of his credentials —

(i)   shall have the right of entry to, upon, or through any premises in which an effluent source is located or in which any records required to be maintained under clause (A) of this subsection are located, and

(ii)   may at reasonable times have access to and copy any records, inspect any monitoring equipment or method required under clause (A), and sample any effluents which the owner or operator of such source is required to sample under such clause.

(b)   Any records, reports or information obtained under this section (1) shall, in the case of effluent data, be related to any applicable effluent limitations, toxic, pretreatment, or new source performance standards, and (2) shall be available to the public, except that upon a showing satisfactory to the Administrator by any person that records, reports, or information, or particular part thereof (other than effluent data), to which the Administrator has access under this section, if made public would divulge methods or processes entitled to protection as trade secrets of such person, the Administrator shall consider such record, report, or information, or particular portion thereof confidential in accordance with the purposes of section 1905 of Title 18, except that such record, report, or information may be disclosed to other officers, employees, or authorized representatives of the United States concerned with carrying out this chapter or when relevant in any proceeding under this chapter.

(c)   Each State may develop and submit to the Administrator procedures under State law for inspection, monitoring, and entry with respect to point sources located in such State. If the Administrator finds that the procedures and the law of any State relating to inspection, monitoring, and entry are applicable to at least the same extent as those required by this section, such State is authorized to apply and enforce its procedures for inspection, monitoring, and entry with respect to point sources located in such State (except with respect to point sources owned or operated by the United States).

See Mobil Oil Co. v. EPA, 18 Envt. Rep. Cas. (BNA) 2031 (N.D. Ill. 1982).

Facility inspection is often necessary to determine if a violation is occurring. Both as a matter of statute and constitutional law, EPA has greater discretion to conduct warrantless searches of industrial plants because a plant owner has a lower expectation of privacy than a private home dweller. Donovan v. Dewey, 452 U.S. 594 (1981). Dow Chemical Co. v. United States, 476 U.S. 227 (1986), illustrates the search and seizure problems that an agency may face if it fails to obtain a search warrant. In 1977 EPA made an in-plant inspection of Dow Chemical Company's 2,080-acre Midland, Michigan, plant to check the powerhouses for possible air quality violations. The agency decided that a second inspection was necessary and informed Dow that it intended to take aerial photographs of the facility; Dow objected. Rather than obtain a civil search warrant, EPA contracted with a private concern to take sophisticated photographs of the facility. Dow sued, claiming that the flight and the photographs constituted *both* an unreasonable search and an unconstitutional taking of trade secrets. Writing for a five justice majority, Chief Justice Burger held that the plant did not fall within the curtilage doctrine and thus Dow had no reasonable expectation of privacy. "[O]pen areas of an industrial plant complex with numerous plant structures spread over an area of 2,000 acres are not analogous to the 'curtilage' of a dwelling for the purposes of aerial surveillance."

Other constitutional guarantees may apply to enforcement actions. Prior to 1978, §311(b)(4), 33 U.S.C. §1321(b)(4), prohibited the discharge of oil in "quantities . . . that will be harmful to the public health and welfare of the United States." In 1978 this language was changed to "such quantities as *may* be harmful." Harmful discharges are defined as any discharges that cause "a film or sheen upon or discoloration of the surface of the water." 40 C.F.R. §110.3. Is the "visible sheen" test authorized by the pre-1978 §311(b)(4)? If the test is authorized, is it void for vagueness? The statutory authority for the constitutionality of the test was upheld in United States v. Boyd, 491 F.2d 1163 (9th Cir. 1973), but cf. United States v. Chevron Oil Co., 583 F.2d 1357 (5th Cir. 1978). An oil well in a Louisiana lake discharged from 21 to 42 gallons of oil because of a vent malfunction. About one half of the oil was recovered, but because there was a sheen Chevron notified the Coast Guard of the spill. Chevron's marine biologist testified that the spill had no harmful effect on the lake environment, and this evidence was accepted and not contradicted by the United States. The court held that the defendant must be allowed to prove that the spill is not harmful because otherwise the standard would exceed the scope of congressionally delegated authority: "By 'not harmful' we mean only that the quantity of oil spilled was de minimis, not that a harmful quantity was spilled but fortunately did not *actually* cause any harm." 583 F.2d at 1363 (original emphasis). Accord United States v. Chotin Transportation Co., 649 F. Supp. 356 (S.D. Ohio 1986). See also United States v. Healy Tibbitts Construction Co., 713 F.2d 1469 (9th Cir. 1983) (due process does not require a hearing with respect to district commander's initial determination of a prima facie violation of sheen test, although district commander is superior to the hearing officer because the subsequent hearing was not tainted by command influence).

Is *Chevron* still good law? A person who causes a harmful spill is liable, subject to limitations, for cleanup costs and for civil penalties of not more than $5,000 per violation. In addition, failure to notify is a crime punishable by a maximum fine of $10,000 or one year in prison. Section 311(b)(5) provides that the information "shall not be used against any such person in a criminal case, except for prosecution for perjury or giving a false statement." Of course, the information may be the basis of a civil penalty. In United States v. Ward, 448 U.S. 242 (1980), the defendant argued that these penalties were in fact criminal and thus the privilege against self-incrimination applied to individuals, as opposed to situations involving corporate discharges. The court accepted the principle that congressional classification of a penalty is not conclusive but found that these penalties were civil because Congress intended to remedy past wrongs rather than to punish wrongdoers.

2. *Judicial Discretion to Fashion Remedies For Statutory Violations*

WEINBERGER v. ROMERO-BARCELO
456 U.S. 306 (1982)

[The plaintiffs, including the governor of Puerto Rico, sued to enjoin the United States Navy from conducting bombing operations because pilots sometimes missed land-based targets and dropped bombs, a defined pollutant under 33 U.S.C. §1362(6) (regarding munitions), into navigable waters around the island of Puerto Rico. The Navy refused to obtain an NPDES permit. No federal or state effluent limitations for bombs existed. The district court found that the bombs caused no damage to the quality of the water and refused to enjoin the operation. 478 F. Supp. 646 (D.P.R. 1979). The court of appeals reversed on the ground that the district court had no discretion to balance the equities when the statute was violated. 643 F.2d 835 (1st Cir. 1981).]

II

It goes without saying that an injunction is an equitable remedy. It "is not a remedy which issues as of course," Harrisonville v. U.S. Dickey Clay Mfg. Co., 289 U.S. 334, 338 (1933), or "to restrain an act the injurious consequences of which are merely trifling." Consolidated Canal Co. v. Mesa Canal Co., 177 U.S. 296, 302 (1900). An injunction should issue only where the intervention of a court of equity "is essential in order effectually to protect property rights against injuries otherwise irremediable." Cavanaugh v. Looney, 248 U.S. 453, 456 (1919). The Court has repeatedly held that the basis for injunctive relief in the federal courts has always been irreparable injury and the inadequacy of legal remedies. . . .

Where plaintiff and defendant present competing claims of injury, the traditional function of equity has been to arrive at a "nice adjustment and reconciliation" between the competing claims. In such cases, the court "balances the conveniences of the parties and possible injuries to them according as they may be affected by the granting or withholding of the injunction." Yakus v. United States, 321 U.S. 414, 440 (1944). "The essence of equity has been the power of the chancellor to do equity and to mold each decree to the necessities of the particular case. Flexibility rather than rigidity has distinguished it." Hecht Co. v. Bowles, *supra*, 321 U.S. [321], at 329 [1944].

In exercising their sound discretion, courts of equity should pay particular regard for the public consequences in employing the extraordinary remedy of injunction. . . .

The grant of jurisdiction to insure compliance with a statute hardly suggests an absolute duty to do so under any and all circumstances, and a federal judge sitting as chancellor is not mechanically obligated to grant an injunction for every violation of law. TVA v. Hill, 437 U.S. 153, 193 (1978).

These commonplace considerations applicable to cases in which injunctions are sought in the federal courts reflect a "practice with a background of several hundred years of history," a practice of which Congress is assuredly well aware. Of course, Congress may intervene and guide or control the exercise of the courts' discretion, but we do not lightly assume that Congress has intended to depart from established principles. . . .

In TVA v. Hill, we held that Congress had foreclosed the exercise of the usual discretion possessed by a court of equity. There, we thought that "one would be hard pressed to find a statutory provision whose terms were any plainer" than that before us. 437 U.S., at 173. The statute involved, the Endangered Species Act, 87 Stat. 884, 16 U.S.C. §1531 et seq., required the district court to enjoin completion of the Tellico Dam in order to preserve the snail darter, a species of perch. The purpose and language of the statute under consideration in *Hill*, not the bare fact of a statutory violation, compelled that conclusion. Section 1536 of the Act requires federal agencies to "insure that actions authorized, funded, or carried out by them do not jeopardize the continued existence of [any] endangered species . . . or result in the destruction or modification of habitat of such species which is determined . . . to be critical." The statute thus contains a flat ban on the destruction of critical habitats.

It was conceded in *Hill* that completion of the dam would eliminate an endangered species by destroying its critical habitat. Refusal to enjoin the action would have ignored the "explicit provisions of the Endangered Species Act." 437 U.S., at 173. Congress, it appeared to us, had chosen the snail darter over the dam. The purpose and language of the statute limited the remedies available to the district court; only an injunction could vindicate the objectives of the Act.

That is not the case here. An injunction is not the only means of ensuring compliance. The FWPCA itself, for example, provides for fines and criminal penalties. 33 U.S.C. §1319(c) and (d). Respondents suggest that failure to enjoin the Navy will undermine the integrity of the permit process by allowing the statutory violation to continue. The integrity of the nation's waters, however, not the permit process, is the purpose of the FWPCA.[7] As Congress explained, the objective of the FWPCA is to "restore and maintain the chemical, physical and biological integrity of the Nation's waters." 33 U.S.C. §1251(a).

This purpose is to be achieved by compliance with the Act, including compliance with the permit requirements. Here, however, the discharge of ordnance had not polluted the waters, and, although the District Court declined to enjoin the discharges, it neither ignored the statutory violation nor undercut the purpose and function of the permit system. The court ordered the Navy to apply for a permit.[9] It temporarily, not permanently, allowed the Navy to continue its activities without a permit.

In *Hill*, we also noted that none of the limited "hardship exemptions" of the Endangered Species Act would "even remotely apply to the Tellico Project." 437 U.S., at 188. The prohibition of the FWPCA against discharge of pollutants, in contrast, can be overcome by the very permit the Navy was ordered to seek. The Senate Report to the 1972 Amendments explains that it was enacting the permit program because "the Committee recognizes the impracticality of any effort to halt all pollution immediately." S. Rep. 92-414, 92d Cong., 1st Sess. 43 (1971), U.S. Code Cong. & Admin. News 1972, p. 3709. That the scheme as a whole contemplates the exercise of discretion and balancing of equities militates against the conclusion that Congress intended to deny courts their traditional equitable discretion in enforcing the statute.

Other aspects of the statutory scheme also suggest that Congress did not intend to deny courts the discretion to rely on remedies other than an immediate prohibitory injunction. Although the ultimate objective of the FWPCA is to eliminate all discharges of pollutants into the navigable waters by 1985, the statute sets forth a scheme of phased compliance. As enacted, it called for the achievement of the "best practicable control technology currently available" by July 1, 1977 and the "best available technology economically achievable" by July

---

7.   The objective of this statute is in some respects similar to that sought in nuisance suits, where courts have fully exercised their equitable discretion and ingenuity in ordering remedies. E.g., Spur Ind. Inc. v. Del E. Webb Development Co., 108 Ariz. 178, 494 P.2d 700 (1972); Boomer v. Atlantic Cement Co., 26 N.Y.2d 219, 309 N.Y.S.2d 312, 257 N.E.2d 870 (1970).

9.   The Navy applied for an NPDES permit in December, 1979. In May, 1981, the EPA issued a draft NPDES permit and a notice of intent to issue that permit. The FWPCA requires a certification of compliance with state water quality standards before the EPA may issue an NPDES permit. 33 U.S.C. §1341(a). The Environmental Quality Board of the Commonwealth of Puerto Rico denied the Navy a water quality certificate in connection with this application for an NPDES in June, 1981. In February, 1982, the Environmental Quality Board denied the Navy's reconsideration request and announced it was adhering to its original ruling. In a letter dated April 9, 1982, the Solicitor General informed the Clerk of the Court that the Navy has filed an action challenging the denial of the water quality certificate. United States of America v. Commonwealth of Puerto Rico, No. 82-0726 (D.P.R.).

1, 1983. 33 U.S.C. §1311(b) (Supp. IV 1970). This scheme of phased compliance further suggests that this is a statute in which Congress envisioned, rather than curtailed, the exercise of discretion.[11]

The FWPCA directs the Administrator of the EPA to seek an injunction to restrain immediately discharges of pollutants he finds to be presenting "an imminent and substantial endangerment of the health of persons or to the welfare of persons." 33 U.S.C. §1364(a). This rule of immediate cessation, however, is limited to the indicated class of violations. For other kinds of violations, the FWPCA authorizes the Administrator of the EPA "to commence a civil action for appropriate relief, including a permanent or temporary injunction, for any violation for which he is authorized to issue a compliance order. . . ." 33 U.S.C. §1319(b). The provision makes clear that Congress did not anticipate that all discharges would be immediately enjoined. Consistent with this view, the administrative practice has not been to request immediate cessation orders. "Rather, enforcement actions typically result, by consent or otherwise, in a remedial order setting out a detailed schedule of compliance designed to cure the identified violation of the Act." Brief for United States 17. . . . Here, again, the statutory scheme contemplates equitable consideration.

Both the Court of Appeals and respondents attach particular weight to the provision of the FWPCA permitting the President to exempt Federal facilities from compliance with the permit requirements. 33 U.S.C. §1323. They suggest that this provision indicates Congressional intent to limit the court's discretion. According to respondents, the exemption provision evidences Congress' determination that only paramount national interests justify failure to comply and that only the President should make this judgment.

We do not construe the provision so broadly. We read the FWPCA as permitting the exercise of a court's equitable discretion, whether the source of pollution is a private party or a federal agency, to order relief that will achieve *compliance* with the Act. The exemption serves a different and complementary purpose, that of permitting *noncompliance* by federal agencies in extraordinary circumstances. Exec. Order No. 12088, 43 Fed. Reg. 47,707, 47,709 (1978), which implements the exemption authority, requires the federal agency requesting such an exemption to certify that it cannot meet the applicable pollution standards. "Exemptions are granted by the President only if the conflict between pollution control standards and crucial federal activities cannot be resolved

---

11. We have, however, held some standards related to phased compliance to be absolute. See EPA v. National Crushed Stone Association, 449 U.S. 64 (1980). In Middlesex County Sewerage Authority v. National Sea Clammers Assn., 453 U.S. 1 (1981), we concluded that the federal common law of nuisance was preempted by the FWPCA and other similar acts: "In the absence of strong indicia of a contrary congressional intent, we are compelled to conclude that Congress provided precisely the remedies it considered appropriate." 453 U.S., at 15. . . . But, as we have also observed in construing this Act, "The question . . . is not what a court thinks is generally appropriate to the regulatory processes, it is what Congress intended. . . ." E. I. Du Pont de Nemours & Co. v. Train, 430 U.S. 112, 138 (1977). Here we do not read the FWPCA as intending to abolish the courts' equitable discretion in ordering remedies.

through the development of a practicable remedial program." Brief for United States 25, n.30.

Should the Navy receive a permit here, there would be no need to invoke the machinery of the Presidential exemption. If not, this course remains open. The exemption provision would enable the President, believing paramount national interests so require, to authorize discharges which the district court has enjoined. Reading the statute to permit the exercise of a court's equitable discretion in no way eliminates the role of the exemption provision in the statutory scheme.

Like the language and structure of the Act, the legislative history does not suggest that Congress intended to deny courts their traditional equitable discretion. Congress passed the 1972 Amendments because it recognized that "the national effort to abate and control water pollution has been inadequate in every vital aspect." S. Rep. No. 92-414, 92d Cong., 1st Sess. 7, U.S. Code Cong. & Admin. News, p. 3674. . . .

The exercise of equitable discretion, which must include the ability to deny as well as grant injunctive relief, can fully protect the range of public interests at issue at this stage in the proceedings. The District Court did not face a situation in which a permit would very likely not issue and the requirements and objective of the statute could therefore not be vindicated if discharges were permitted to continue. Should it become clear that no permit will be issued and that compliance with the FWPCA will not be forthcoming, the statutory scheme and purpose would require the court to reconsider the balance it has struck.

Because Congress, in enacting FWPCA, has not foreclosed the exercise of equitable discretion, the proper standard for appellate review is whether the district court abused its discretion in denying an immediate cessation order while the Navy applied for a permit. We reverse and remand to Court of Appeals for proceedings consistent with this opinion.

NOTES AND QUESTIONS

The attorney who won the "snail darter" case, TVA v. Hill, 437 U.S. 153 (1978), argues: "When a court in equity is confronted on the merits with a continuing violation of statutory law, it has no discretion or authority to balance the equities so as to permit that violation to continue." Plater, Statutory Violations and Equitable Discretion, 70 Calif. L. Rev. 524, 527 (1982). See also Farber, Equitable Discretion, Legal Duties and Environmental Injunctions, 45 U. Pitt. L. Rev. 513 (1984). Judged by this standard, is Romero-Barcelo incorrectly decided? Is Professor Plater's rule constitutionally required? If a discharger applies for a BPT variance, is denied, and is subsequently subject to an enforcement action for violating the applicable effluent limitations, can the discharger use Romero-Barcelo as a defense in the enforcement action? See United States v. Louisiana-Pacific Corp., 18 Envt. Rep. Cas. (BNA) 2020 (N.D. Cal. 1982).

Romero-Barcelo was applied and qualified in Amoco Production Co. v. Village of Gambell, 107 S. Ct. 1396 (1987). The Court refused to enjoin an offshore oil and gas lease as a violation of the Alaska National Interest Lands Conservation Act, 16 U.S.C. §3120(a)(3)(C). An injunction was not warranted because the Act did not prohibit all federal resource development, and a presumption that a violation of the Act caused irreparable damage was contrary to traditional equitable principles. However, the Court noted that "the balance of harms will usually favor the issuance of an injunction to protect the environment."

A NOTE ON NONCOMPLIANCE WITH TREATMENT REQUIREMENTS

In an era of shrinking municipal revenues, the problem of complying with treatment standards for POTW discharges soon may become a major concern. Initially §301(b)(1)(B), 33 U.S.C. §1311(b)(1)(B), and §304(d)(1), 33 U.S.C. §1314(d)(1), required all POTWs to meet secondary treatment requirements by July 1, 1977. It soon became clear that only a few communities would be able to meet this goal. In the 1977 amendments Congress added §301(i), which allows communities that were constructing or planning to build new treatment works to seek a time extension. The EPA was authorized to grant variances to July 1, 1983. The 1981 amendments move this deadline back to July 1, 1988. Not surprisingly, Montgomery Environmental Coalition, Inc. v. EPA, 711 F.2d 420, 19 ERC 1169 (D.C. Cir. 1983), holds that the agency may issue a permit to a sewage treatment facility that is in violation of the Act:

> The logical implication of petitioners' view of the Act — that violators cannot *obtain* NPDES permits — is that violators likewise cannot *retain* their permits. Yet this interpretation, which would require EPA to revoke the permit of a violator, would render the compliance order provisions of section 309 meaningless. Furthermore, petitioners' interpretation of the Act ignores the fact that municipal sewage treatment plants simply cannot be shut down for violations of the Act; countervailing considerations of public health require that treatment facilities continue to operate. [19 ERC at 1171]

See also Natural Resources Defense Council, Inc. v. EPA, 656 F.2d 768 (D.C. Cir. 1981) (regulations for municipal variances were "effluent limitations" and thus were reviewable in the court of appeals).

Absent the granting of a variance, the EPA has started enforcement action against some communities that are not in compliance with treatment standards. If a municipality is not in compliance with applicable standards, what decree can a court enter? Require a bond election to be held? Prohibit all new hookups? Shut down the POTW? Put the city in receivership?

State Water Control Board v. Train, 559 F.2d 921 (4th Cir. 1977), holds that EPA can enforce secondary treatment standards regardless of the availability of Title II funds. The state of Virginia brought an action seeking a declaratory judgment that §301(b)(1)(B) standards did not apply to communities that had not received Title II funding. Looking to the statute and its legislative history, the court found the requirements imposed by the Clean Water Act were clear: EPA can enforce the standards regardless of the availability of federal funding. The court continued:

> More importantly, Congress actually declined to write the statute as appellant would now have us construe it. During hearings on the House bill, William Ruckelshaus, then head of EPA, and appellee Train, then Chairman of the Council on Environmental Quality, urged that the Act permit extension of the 1977 deadline in cases where, despite good faith efforts, compliance is impossible. Significantly, Mr. Ruckelshaus also recommended that "the secondary treatment requirement [of §301(b)(1)(B)] should only apply to projects for which new Federal grants are provided." The bill which the House subsequently passed empowered EPA to extend the 1977 deadline for up to two years in cases where compliance is physically or legally impossible; but, despite the recommendation of Mr. Ruckelshaus, it did not limit the applicability of Section 301(b)(1)(B) to those facilities receiving federal assistance. Moreover, even the provision authorizing case-by-case extension of the deadline was later deleted without comment by the Conference Committee. This clearly provides strong support for the conclusion that Congress meant for the July 1, 1977 deadline to be rigid and that it did not intend that sewage treatment plants not receiving timely federal grants should be exempt from that deadline. [9 F.2d at 925.]

Often, the remedy will be a compliance schedule. What is the next step? See United States v. City of Detroit, 476 F. Supp. 512 (E.D. Mich. 1979). In early 1977, EPA filed suit over Detroit's failure to maintain effluent quality standards, and Detroit agreed to make significant improvements in its treatment works. The city found compliance with the agreed improvement schedule difficult, and EPA reinstated its action. The court appointed Detroit's mayor as a Special Administrator of the city's treatment system and ordered him to supervise its rehabilitation. The court acknowledged that under Michigan law the mayor was elected in part to supervise the city's treatment facilities. The court stated that by appointing the mayor to the position of Special Administrator he would be receiving special powers:

> The present situation does require that to the powers that the Mayor presently possesses as Detroit's chief executive there be added such powers as may be entrusted to him by this court. There is thus conjoined in one person, Mayor Coleman A. Young, both the traditional powers of his office and the extraordinary powers inherent in this appointment to bring about compliance. These powers will enable him to act decisively and swiftly to bring about needed results; in their exercise, where needed, he is not responsible to the Water Board, the Civil Service Commission, the Common Council, suburban governments, or the State of Michigan, but only to this court. [476 F. Supp. at 521.]

Subsequent litigation illustrates the difficulty with judicially funded decrees. Title II moneys allotted to a state must be used within one year, or the Administrator must allocate these unobligated funds to other states. 33 U.S.C. §1285(b)(1). Regarding the possible loss of allocated funds, Michigan law provides that if it is likely that a fundable priority project will not obtain an obligation of allotted funds, the state will "bypass" the project in favor of the next priority project that can be timely funded. After it appeared that Detroit's proposed sewage projects were priority projects but were unlikely to satisfy the criteria for obtaining an EPA commitment for fiscal year 1981, the district court entered an order reserving the state's allotted but unobligated funds for Detroit. The order was challenged by a county that would have obtained funds but for the court's order. The Sixth Circuit held that the order violated "the constitutional separation of powers between the three branches of our government" and that "the EPA was effectively foreclosed from fulfilling its obligation . . . to immediately reallocate the unobligated funds to the other states"; therefore "Michigan was effectively precluded from certifying by-pass projects to the EPA to achieve timely obligation of allotted funds." United States v. Wayne County Department of Health, 19 Envt. Rep. Cas. (BNA) 2090, 2096 (6th Cir. 1983). For further litigation on Detroit's efforts to clean up its act, see City of Detroit v. Michigan, 803 F.2d 1411 (6th Cir. 1986).

The court chose an alternate enforcement remedy in United States v. City of Providence, 492 F. Supp. 602 (D.R.I. 1980). Providence was in the same situation as Detroit; it was unable to meet the effluent standards that had been agreed to in an earlier consent decree. Initially the court refused to modify the agreement, leaving the city open to a previously stipulated $2,500-per-day non-compliance penalty. The court then ruled that the city was in civil contempt. However, the court declined to assess any penalties against Providence, ruling that such action would not serve any useful purpose. The court gave the city another chance to bring its treatment works up to agreed-upon standards, but the court also issued a warning to city officials that they could be required specifically to comply with provisions of the consent decree if the city did not. Is a court-ordered receivership the final step? See generally Comment, Court-Created Receivership Emerging as Remedy for Persistent Non-Compliance with Environmental Laws, 10 Envtl. L. Rep. (Envtl. L. Inst. 10,059 (1980)).

State courts have also started to enforce effluent standards. In Sewerage Commission v. State Department of Natural Resources, 98 Wis. 2d 464, 297 N.W.2d 40 (Ct. App. 1980), vacated, 102 Wis. 2d 613, 307 N.W.2d 189 (Wis. 1981), the court ordered state effluent standards enforced against several municipal sewerage districts.* The sewerage districts argued that the state standards

---

*The Wisconsin Supreme Court did not decide this case on its merits. It ruled that according to Wisconsin administrative law the sewerage commissions had waived their right to a judicial review of Department of Natural Resources' action. The court ordered the trial court to reconsider the Department of Natural Resources' counterclaim for forfeitures.

were stricter than what federal law required and therefore were unenforceable. The court ruled that the Clean Water Act required that state standards be consistent with federal law; regardless of federal deadlines, the court concluded, the state could order compliance at an earlier date.

See generally Note, Municipal Compliance With the Clean Water Act, 90 W. Va. L. Rev. 595 (1987-1988); Feliciano, National Municipal Policy and Strategy: Tightening the Screws, 52 J. Water Pollution Control 3 (1980), and Guthrie, Polvi & Lyons, Implementation of EPA's Municipal Compliance Program, 52 J. Water Pollution Control 2090 (1980).

QUESTION: A city builds a new treatment system in the 1970s to replace an old one, but the new one fails. EPA then sues the city to enforce the NPDES permit and all parties agree that a new facility will be built. To reduce flows into the plan while reconstruction is underway, EPA allows the city to disconnect a tunnel, which discharges directly into a river, from the system and use it for storm water overflows on the condition that these flows could be rediverted back into the system at some future date to prevent pollution. The plan allows the direct discharges of untreated dry weather groundwater flows based on the assumption that this will produce about 17 pounds per day of toxic priority pollutants. By 1987, the numbers are 30-78 pounds per day and EPA orders the city to remedy the situation by rediverting these flows into the new system which has excess treatment capacity or show that a rediversion is impractical. Should a court grant a permanent injunction? See United States v. City of Niagara Falls, 706 F. Supp. 1053 (W.D.N.Y. 1989). Review *Romero-Barcelo*, p. 476 *supra*.

3.   Private Enforcement of Statutory Violations

MIDDLESEX COUNTY SEWERAGE AUTHORITY v. NATIONAL SEA CLAMMERS ASSOCIATION
453 U.S. 1 (1981)

[This case can be found at p. 740 *infra*.]

NOTES ON CITIZEN INITIATION OF ENFORCEMENT ACTION

1. The Court's inability to articulate a clear theory of the role of implied rights of action in statutory schemes has been much noted, e.g., Manning, Middlesex County Sewerage Authority v. National Sea Clammers Association: Implied Private Rights of Action for Damages under the Federal Water Pollution Control Act Amendments of 1972, 12 Envtl. L. 197 (1981). The Court's current position is that courts lack the power to fashion common law remedies for specific statutory violations unless Congress specifically grants that power. Is this

position mandated by the Constitution? Most commentators agree that the answer is no because federal courts have long asserted the power to create substantive federal common law rights to protect federal interests protected by Congress. See Haried, Implied Causes of Action: A Product of Statutory Construction or the Federal Common Law Power? 51 U. Colo. L. Rev. 355 (1980), and Frankel, Implied Rights of Action, 67 Va. L. Rev. 553, 565-570 (1981). If the issue is not lack of constitutional power but rather judicial discretion, the case for the Court's current restrictive standard for implied rights of action must rest on the unstated premise that a liberal standard will result in excessive or inefficient enforcement of federal regulatory schemes. Assuming that pollution compliance resources are scarce, how would one measure whether allowing a private right of action for standard violations is efficient or inefficient?

2. Section 505, 33 U.S.C. §1365, allows citizens' suits against both polluters and the Administrator to compel performance of "any act or duty under this Act which is not discretionary." Most suits to force the Administrator to perform a nondiscretionary duty have failed because of the plaintiff's failure to give the required 60 days' notice. The main use of the provision has been to force the Administrator to comply with statutorily mandated deadlines, e.g., Commonwealth of Pennsylvania, Department of Environmental Resources v. EPA, 618 F.2d 991 (3d Cir. 1980), and Natural Resources Defense Council, Inc. v. Train, 510 F.2d 692 (D.C. Cir. 1974).

There is legislative history to support the proposition that "enforcement duties" are included within the term "nondiscretionary duties" (1972 Legislative History, at 1499), but the law on this subject is not clear. Section 1319(a)(3) requires that the Administrator shall issue a compliance once he finds a violation of the Act. In South Carolina Wildlife Federation v. Alexander, 457 F. Supp 118 (D.S.C. 1978), the court held that this duty is nondiscretionary. Compare Sierra Club v. Train, 557 F.2d 485 (5th Cir. 1977) and Susquehanna Valley Alliance v. Three Mile Island Nuclear Reactor, 619 F.2d 231 (3d Cir.), cert. denied, 449 U.S. 1096 (1980). The most recent case to consider the issue, Dubois v. Thomas, 820 F.2d 943 (8th Cir. 1987), concluded that the structure of the Act and the legislative history supported EPA's position that its duties were discretionary. The court focused on the phrase "is authorized to commence a civil action" in Section 309(b) and Section 505(a)(1) because the creation of a private right of action "was not intended to enable citizens to commandeer the federal enforcement machinery." The Committee report was found capable of two reasonable interpretations, despite the Muskie statement that the duty was mandatory, because it could be read to mean either that the duty to act was mandatory but that the administrator had discretion how to act or that the agency had the discretion to decide whether to act at all. Thus, under Chevron, U.S.A. v. Natural Resources Defense Council, p. 128 supra, the agency's position was entitled to deference. Is Heckler v. Chaney, 470 U.S. 821 (1985), which holds that agency decisions not to take enforcement action are presumptively immune from judicial review, relevant? Andreen, Beyond Words of Exhortation: The Congressional Prescription for Vigorous Federal Enforcement of the Clean

Water Act, 55 Geo. Wash. L. Rev. 202, 250 (1987) argues that "[t]he legislative history of the Clean Water Act clearly demonstrates that Congress never meant to create a loophole through which the EPA could defeat a citizen suit seeking compulsory administrative enforcement simply by refusing to issue a finding of a violation." Compare Bloomquist, Rethinking the Citizen as Prosecutor Model of Environmental Enforcement under the Clean Water Act: Some Overlooked Problems of Outcome Independent Values, 22 Ga. L. Rev. 337 (1988). Professor Bloomquist, a former attorney for a citizen suit defendant, constructs a process model to criticize the prosecutorial discretion delegated to private citizens by the Clean Water Act.

Section 505 adopts the test of standing announced in Sierra Club v. Morton, 405 U.S. 727 (1972). Traditional citizens' associations have usually been given standing (Loveladies Property Owners Association v. Raab, 430 F. Supp. 276, (D.N.J. 1975), aff'd without op., 547 F.2d 1162 (3d Cir. 1976), cert. denied, 432 U.S. 906 (1977); Rite-Research Improves the Environment, Inc. v. Costle, 650 F.2d 1312 (5th Cir. 1981)), but a contractor with a municipal authority has been held not to have standing to compel the Administrator to require the authority to submit an industrial cost recovery system as required by EPA regulations. J. E. Brenneman Co. v. Schramm, 473 F. Supp. 1316 (E.D. Pa. 1979).

At the time §505 was passed, Sierra Club v. Morton represented the constitutional law of standing. Since Sierra Club the Supreme Court apparently has expanded the list of constitutional elements of standing, as well as having rearticulated traditional nonconstitutional prudential concerns about the exercise of federal jurisdiction. See Chapter 2, at pp. 88-107 supra. Gonzales v. Gorsuch, 688 F.2d 1263 (9th Cir. 1982), illustrates the problems that the developing law may pose for plaintiffs. In Gonzales, the plaintiff sued the Administrator on the theory that the expenditure of §208 funds by the designated local planning agency in the San Francisco Bay area was illegal because the funds were not earmarked for water pollution-related purposes. The district court held that the plaintiff had standing but denied the requested relief on the merits (Gonzales v. Costle, 463 F. Supp. 335 (N.D. Cal. 1978)), but the Ninth Circuit affirmed on the ground that the plaintiff lacked standing. Judge Kennedy conceded that as a user of San Francisco Bay the plaintiff had the requisite personal stake in the outcome of the controversy but held that he failed to meet the redressability requirement. The concurring opinion of Judge Wallace is an especially enlightening discussion of the power of Congress to confer standing on public interest plaintiffs.

A coordinated effort by public interest organizations is underway to bring §505 citizen actions against companies alleged to be in violation of the Clean Water Act. These cases have raised (or re-raised) the issue of standing for organizations that fail to allege the requisite injury in fact. Courts have followed a Second Circuit case that requires that plaintiffs allege that the use of the affected waters by plaintiffs would be impaired. Sierra Club v. SMC Corp., 747 F.2d 99 (2d Cir. 1984)(complaint dismissed for lack of standing because Sierra Club refused to identify specific members that used affected waters). Accord Sierra Club v. Kerr-McGee Corp., 23 ERC 1685 (N.D. La. 1985). Plaintiffs have thus thrown in affidavits of actual injury for good measure. Friends of the Earth v. Consolidated Rail Corp., 768 F.2d 57 (2d Cir. 1985); SPIRG v. Georgia-Pacific Corp., 615 F. Supp. 1419 (D.N.J. 1985). Defendants have unsuccessfully raised other objections to standing. Defendants have argued that Article III requires plaintiffs to allege an injury "fairly traceable" to the violations in question, see Allen v. Wright, 104 S. Ct. 3315 (1984), but courts have concluded that this would be contrary to the intent of §505 because it would preclude most citizen suits unless the direct impact of the discharge was great or the waterway very small. SPIRG of New Jersey v. Tenneco Polymers, Inc., 602 F. Supp. 1394 (D.N.J. 1985). Defendants have also urged that the redressability requirement of Simon v. Eastern Kentucky Welfare Rights Organization, p. 97 *supra* precludes standing when the impact of the pollution on a watercourse is so small that remedying the discharge will not change the nature of water uses in the area; courts, however, have reasoned that the Clean Water Act presumes that unlawful discharges reduce water quality, and thus the argument is without merit. But cf. City of Las Vegas v. Clark County, 755 F.2d 697 (9th Cir. 1985).

Often a federal or state enforcement proceeding is pending when a §505 suit is brought, and the courts have begun to work out the relationship between §505 suits and other proceedings. SPIRG of New Jersey v. Tenneco Polymers, Inc., *supra*, holds that a citizens' group may challenge an NPDES violation even though the company had "actively cooperated" with EPA enforcement. Section 505(b)(1)(B) was not a bar because the EPA proceedings were not the substantial equivalent of a federal court proceeding and the citizens had no opportunity to participate in the proceedings. Accord SPIRG v. Fritzsch Dodge & Olcott, Inc., 759 F.2d 1131 (3d Cir. 1985). Cf. United States v. Hooker Chemicals & Plastics Corp., 749 F.2d 968 (2d Cir. 1984), which denied intervention in a settlement between EPA and the company because the intervenors failed to show inadequate representation. Sierra Club v. Chevron, U.S.A., Inc., 834 F.2d 1517 (9th Cir. 1987), declined to follow the Third Circuit's approach, which would allow some administrative actions to bar citizen suits, and instead adopted the Second Circuit's position in Friends of the Earth v. Consolidated Rail Corp., *supra*, in which the court held that the statute plainly bars citizen suits only when there is a pending judicial enforcement action.

Section 505 does not authorize citizen suits for wholly past violations. Circuit courts of appeal had split on the issue, but the Supreme Court held that the language of §505, which permits suits against NPDES permit-holders "alleged to be in violation" of the permit, limits suits to continuous or intermittent violations. Plaintiff must either allege that there is an ongoing violation or that there is a reasonable likelihood that past violations will continue. The Court adopted the First Circuit's construction of §505, Pawtuxet Cove Marina, Inc. v. Ciba-Geigy Corp., 807 F.2d 1089 (1st Cir. 1986), *cert. denied*, 108 S. Ct. 484 (1987), and rejected the Fourth Circuit's reading of the section, Chesapeake Bay Foundation, Inc. v. Gwaltney of Smithfield, 791 F.2d 304 (4th Cir. 1986).

Gwaltney of Smithfield v. Chesapeake Bay Foundation, Inc., 108 S. Ct. 376 (1987). See Note, Citizen Suits and Civil Penalties under the Clean Water Act, 85 Mich. L. Rev. 1656 (1987), for a discussion of the different approaches among the circuits. On remand, the court of appeals held that the plaintiff may prevail "either (1) by proving violations that continue on or after the date the complaint is filed, or (2) by adducing evidence from which a reasonable trier of fact could find a likelihood or recurrence in intermittent or sporadic violations." Chesapeake Bay Foundation v. Gwaltney, 844 F.2d 170 (4th. Cir. 1988). Accord Sierra Club v. Union Oil Co., 853 F.2d 667 (9th Cir. 1988). Is the installation of pollution control equipment or the adoption of other remedial strategies a sufficient defense to a §505 suit?

Justice Scalia suggested that the adoption of remedial measures "that clearly eliminate the cause of the violation" prevents a court from concluding that there is a continuous violation. Is a sporadic violation a sufficient basis for a suit? EPA effluent levels are set on the assumption that they will be met 95 to 99 percent of the time. Sierra Club v. Shell Oil Co., 817 F.2d 1169 (5th Cir.), *cert. denied*, 108 S. Ct. 501 (1987), *reh'g denied*, 108 S. Ct. 1065 (1988), held that permit compliance rates above 95 percent do not put a company in violation of an NPDES permit. See generally J. Miller, Citizen Suits: Private Enforcement of Federal Pollution Control Laws (1987); and Note, The Rise of Citizen-Suit Enforcement in Environmental Law: Reconciling Private and Public Attorney General, 81 NW. U.L. Rev. 220 (1987). Note, Statute of Limitation for Citizen Suits under the Clean Water Act, 72 Cornell L. Rev. 195 (1986), argues that courts should apply the generic five-year federal statute of limitations for the recovery of penalties, 42 U.S.C. §2462, to citizen suits. Sierra Club v. Chevron, U.S.A., Inc., *supra*, adopts this analysis.

3. If a specific statute does not give an individual the right to compel an official to initiate action, the law provides little relief for individuals dissatisfied with an exercise of prosecutorial discretion, e.g., Bass Anglers Sportsman Society v. U.S. Steel Corp., 324 F. Supp. 412 (S.D. Ala.), *aff'd*, 447 F.2d 1304 (5th Cir. 1971). Occasionally the courts have held that a decision not to proceed with a permissible enforcement action is subject to judicial review. However, the scope of review is narrow, and the courts have not gone beyond requiring a statement of reasons justifying the decision not to proceed further. In holding that the Secretary of Labor had to submit a statement justifying his decision not to bring a civil action to set aside an election under the Labor-Management Reporting and Disclosure Act of 1959, the Supreme Court wrote:

> Except in what must be a rare case, the court's review should be confined to examination of the "reasons" statement, and the determination whether the statement without more evinces that the Secretary's decision is so irrational as to constitute the decision arbitrary and capricious. Thus, review may not extend to cognizance or trial of a complaining member's challenges to the factual basis for the Secretary's conclusion. [Dunlop v. Bachowski, 421 U.S. 560, 572-573 (1975).]

Dunlop seems to have been undercut by Heckler v. Chaney, 470 U.S. 821 (1985), discussed in Note 2 *supra*.

Of course, the agency's discretion to impose a substantial penalty also would seem protected from judicial review except in exceptional cases. For an analogous decision under the Clean Water Act, see Rite-Research Improves the Environment, Inc. v. Costle, 650 F.2d 1312 (5th Cir. 1981).

4. If the requisite notice is not given, *National Sea Clammers* would seem to make it clear that a plaintiff could not proceed under the federal mandamus statute, 28 U.S.C. §1361. See also City of Highland Park v. Train, 519 F.2d 681 (7th Cir. 1975), which reached the same conclusion on the ground that mandamus is not available if an adequate legal remedy exists, one such remedy being the mother of §505, §304 of the Clean Air Act, 33 U.S.C. §1314.

5. Public participation in NPDES permit hearings may aid enforcement by allowing interested parties to urge compliance deadlines and permit conditions that can be monitored. EPA does, however, have considerable discretion to structure hearings. Costle v. Pacific Legal Foundation, 445 U.S. 198 (1980), upheld regulations that conditioned the availability of public hearings on the filing of a proper request and limited adjudicatory hearings to disputed issues of material facts identified by interested parties.

V

CONTROLLING TOXIC AND
HAZARDOUS SUBSTANCES

Chapters 3 and 4 examined the Clean Air Act and Clean Water Act, two comprehensive regulatory statutes that emphasize pollution of two specific environmental media. Yet environmental law also attacks pollution by focusing on the dangers presented by specific pollutants. Some 20 federal statutes and 6 agencies are involved in attempting to regulate the release of hazardous substances into all the environmental media: air, water, lifeforms, landforms, and foodstuffs. Federal environmental statutes might be easier to understand if they were limited either to the receiving media or to the pollutants themselves, but for a number of scientific, practical, and administrative reasons, an overlapping approach has prevailed under federal law.

By the mid-1970s, the problem of hazardous substances had caused a fundamental change in the way policymakers thought about environmental legislation. In broad terms, Congress enacted the Clean Air and Clean Water Acts in 1970 and 1972 believing that the core of the pollution problem was that a fairly small number of environmental pollutants that were present in large quantities caused limited harm to large numbers of people (e.g., SO_2 was a respiratory irritant; waterborne bacteria caused infectious diseases). Only a few situations seemed to exist in which a few persons were threatened with severe harm because they were being exposed to small quantities of a few pollutants (e.g., a heavy metal in the air or water might cause cancer; SO_2 could cause emphysema in sensitive population groups). Brief statutory provisions were added, almost as an afterthought, to handle pollutants that could not be adequately regulated under the principal ambient and technology-limited water and air act provisions. Shortly thereafter, however, policymakers began to realize that their perspective on the pollution problem might be wrong — that hundreds or thousands of environmental contaminants could exist that might cause severe harm to large numbers of persons if exposure even to trace quantities occurred over long enough periods of time, no matter what the pathway of exposure.

These observations raise the problem, which will be with us throughout this chapter, of how a "hazardous" or "toxic" pollutant is any different from the pollutants encountered in Chapters 3 and 4. No easy solution exists because conventional pollutants may be hazardous under some circumstances. In general, a pollutant may irritate the skin or mucous membranes, may depress the functions of the nervous system, may damage blood, liver, kidney, or brain cells, may interfere with important enzyme systems, or may cause damage to the reproductive system. Most effects of this type are reversible, and generally when the exposure stops the individual gradually returns to normal. To take a simple example, alcohol-induced central nervous system depression disappears a few hours after a person stops drinking. The effects of many conventional pollutants are reversible under most conditions of exposure. But essentially nonreversible effects may also occur, sometimes after prolonged exposure at low levels. Examples include severe tissue damage or scars from acid or alkali burns, mutations that are passed on to succeeding generations, teratogens that deform the developing fetus — and cancer. Because of the great public concern about cancer and the substantial amount of information about it, cancer risk is a recurrent theme throughout this chapter.

The hazardous substances problem seemed to rise suddenly on Congress's legislative agenda in the mid-1970s, much like the wider environmental crisis burst into prominence in 1970. But hazardous substances have always been a serious concern. Primitive societies had to learn which foods were safe to eat and which would cause illness or death. The early physicians Galen and Hippocrates devoted attention to the treatment of accidental and deliberate poisonings. It is suspected that in ancient Rome the use of lead plumbing, leaded pottery glazes, and the addition of a lead-containing substance to wine contributed to Rome's fall. Recent concern is based more on degree than on kind. The expansion of the chemical industry after World War II produced thousands of new chemicals, most of which are organic (carbon-containing) compounds. Because life itself is based in part on carbon compounds, interference by newly invented carbon compounds with evolutionary ones may play havoc with human life processes if exposure occurs.

Over nine million chemicals appear in the registry of the American Chemical Society. The registry expands at a rate of around 10,000 new entries per week. Over 100,000 chemicals are in commercial use, but only 3,000 are commonly used. Yet attention has focused on the comparatively few pesticides, heavy metals, packaging materials, and industrial substances that have been regulated after intense scientific scrutiny and proceedings lasting as long as seven years. The precise number of chemicals that are dangerous is not yet known.

The key questions then are: What compounds are dangerous to humans in the quantities in which they are likely to be encountered? What regulatory responses are appropriate? In particular, how are prolonged low-level, low-risk exposures to chemicals to be addressed? Many hazardous compounds are capable of inducing disease or causing death, but the effects of everyday low level exposures on human health are extremely difficult to determine. The Surgeon General has stated: "We believe that toxic chemicals are adding to the disease burden of the United States in a significant, although as yet not precisely defined, way.

In addition we believe that this problem will become more important in the years ahead." Senate Comm. on Environment and Public Works, 96th Cong., 2d Sess., Health Effects of Toxic Pollution: A Report from the Surgeon General iii (Comm. Print 1980). The uncertainty that caused the Surgeon General to state that the problem is not "precisely defined" presents the major issue awaiting you in this chapter.

A.   DEFINING THE PROBLEM: RISK AND UNCERTAINTY

1.   *The Nature of Environmental Risk*

PAGE, A GENERIC VIEW OF TOXIC CHEMICALS AND SIMILAR RISKS
7 Ecology L.Q. 207, 207-223 (1978)

A new type of environmental problem is emerging which differs in nature from the more familiar pollution and resource depletion problems. This type of problem, which may be called *environmental risk*,[1] has rapidly increased in importance over the last few decades and may indeed become the dominant type of environmental problem. Environmental risk problems are exemplified by: the risk of leakage and contamination in the disposal of nuclear wastes; the production of synthetic chemicals which may be toxic, carcinogenic, mutagenic, or teratogenic; the risk of ozone depletion due to fluorocarbon emissions by supersonic transports; and the danger presented by recombinant DNA of the creation and escape of a new disease against which mankind has no natural defense. [Environmental risk possesses nine characteristics, all discussed below. The first four emphasize scientific uncertainty and often are the focus of cost-benefit analysis. The remaining five concern regulatory management of risk.] . . .

Ignorance of mechanism is the first characteristic of environmental risk problems. The present state of knowledge of the mechanisms by which a risk is effected is both limited and limiting. Ignorance of mechanism may be present at any number of levels of risk creation, from the generation of the hazard (e.g., the release of radiation from the nuclear fuel cycle) or transmission of the hazard's effect (e.g., dispersion of radiation in the ambient environment or food chain) to an organism's response to exposure, particularly health-related re-

---

1.   "Environmental risk" will be defined specifically in terms of nine characteristics discussed *infra*. "Risk" has several distinct meanings depending on its usage. In "environmental risk," the term draws attention to the potential adverse consequences, for which the underlying probability may be highly uncertain. In this usage one speaks of the risk of cigarette smoking, the risk of war, benefit-risk analysis, but the chance, not risk, of winning the Irish Sweepstakes.

sponses (e.g., sensitivity to "hot particles" and other forms of radiation). The mechanisms of generation, transmission, and response are understood so poorly that any management of these problems is truly decision making under pervasive uncertainty. . . .

The *potential for catastrophic costs* is the second common characteristic of environmental risk. What little is known about mechanism in each case establishes that each is a gamble with high stakes. But what is not known about mechanism precludes specification of just how catastrophic and likely the costs might be. Ignorance of mechanism colors the next two characteristics as well.

The third characteristic is a *relatively modest benefit* associated with the environmental risk gamble. Although some may feel that the benefits of nuclear power and recombinant DNA are not small compared with the potential cost, there appears to be at some level a strong asymmetry between potential costs and benefits, for all four examples, and for most other environmental risks. For nuclear power there is the asymmetrical gamble of a little more shielding and a little more care in waste disposal for a little lower probability of radiation release. Similarly, for recombinant DNA there is the gamble of a little more care in experimental procedures for a little lower chance that a newly created disease will escape. The situation with spray cans and ozone depletion is more clear cut. The benefits of fluorocarbons can be directly measured in markets in terms of a cheaper and finer spray compared with the alternatives, which include pump spray. These benefits accrue regardless of the potential effects of the fluorocarbons on the ozone layer. They appear modest indeed compared with the potentially catastrophic costs which might result from ozone depletion. Corrrespondingly, for the potentially toxic chemical Red Dye No. 40, the benefit is the cosmetic effect the color provides in foods. Again this benefit is modest compared with the potential of the chemical as a carcinogen. This asymmetry in the orders of magnitude of potential costs and benefits has important implications for environmental decision making in terms of the degree of proof necessary to warrant precautionary action.

An environmental risk gamble may be thought of as a seesaw with the potential costs on one side of the pivot and the potential benefits on the other. The distances from the pivot represent the relative magnitudes of benefits and costs. Figure 5-1 illustrates the freon propellant example. The distance from zero to B represents the benefit of the convenience of using propellants. Foregoing this convenience is the cost of opting out of the gamble. The distance from zero to C-B represents the net cost of taking the gamble and losing. The net cost is the potential, relatively large "catastrophic" cost reduced by the comparatively small benefit of using propellants that will accrue even if propellants do deplete the ozone.

In Figure 5-1 the potential costs, due to their greater magnitude, are considerably farther from the pivot than the modest benefits. If both hypotheses were of equal weight the seesaw would tip toward the potentially great loss. Common sense then suggests that the gamble is too risky to undertake.

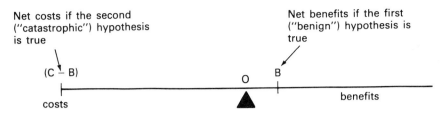

Net costs if the second   Net benefits if the first
("catastrophic") hypothesis   ("benign") hypothesis is
is true   true

$(C - B)$ O   B

costs   benefits

FIGURE 5-1
Net Costs and Benefits Associated with Two Hypotheses

However, there is a dilemma. There often are reasons to believe that the probabilities of the safe and catastrophic hypotheses are not equal and that the catastrophic outcome is considerably less likely than the favorable outcome. For many potentially toxic chemicals, and for nuclear power, ozone depletion, and recombinant DNA, what little is known about mechanism suggests that the probability of the catastrophic outcome is low, much lower than the probability of the favorable outcome. Just how low is impossible to say with confidence, because of the incomplete knowledge of mechanism. Due to the fragmentary knowledge of mechanism, the likelihood of the catastrophic hypothesis cannot be determined objectively, but must be assessed subjectively, based upon whatever knowledge is available.

Low subjective probability of the catastrophic outcome is the fourth characteristic of environmental risk. Common sense suggests that the low subjective probability of the catastrophic costs should be taken into account in balancing costs and benefits. In terms of the seesaw illustration, the probabilities of the benign and catastrophic hypotheses can be thought of as weights placed upon the seesaw at distances from the pivot equal to the magnitude of the respective potential costs and benefits. A heavy weight close to the pivot can more than balance a light weight farther from the pivot. With a low subjective probability of the catastrophic outcome and a high subjective probability of the favorable outcome, it is no longer clear which way the seesaw will tip. The fourth characteristic, low subjective probability of the potential catastrophe, introduces a second asymmetry which tends to counterbalance the asymmetry of potential high costs and modest benefits.

Whether the greater likelihood of the favorable outcome compensates for its smaller relative size is a fundamental question of environmental risk management. In the extreme case, the problem is called a "zero-infinity dilemma": a virtually zero probability of a virtually infinite catastrophe.

In the seesaw illustration, common sense may suggest that an environmental risk is worth taking as long as the seesaw, with the probability weights added, tips in the direction of the benign hypothesis. This interpretation is formally equivalent to the expected value criterion, which says that a gamble is worth taking only if the product of the benefits and their likelihood is greater than the product of the adverse outcome and its likelihood. The analogy to the seesaw is used to suggest that the expected value criterion has some natural appeal as a way of balancing potential costs and benefits and their probabilities.

There are obvious limitations to the expected value criterion. It focuses on outcomes rather than processes; because of the uncertainties involved it may be difficult or even impossible to estimate the magnitudes of the outcomes or their probabilities. The various uncertainties surrounding the quantification of costs, benefits, and probabilities are illustrated in Figure 5-2. The range of uncertainty associated with benefits, represented by a, is the uncertainty of *efficacy*. In the freon propellant example, it is not clear how well freon works as a propellant. The corresponding range of uncertainty associated with *costs*, represented by b, is typically much larger than the uncertainty of efficacy. In addition, there is uncertainty as to the *likelihood* of each hypothesis (c and d).

The uncertainties surrounding the potential costs, benefits, and probabilities often are so strong that the decision maker avoids numerical quantification altogether. Even so, the magnitudes of the costs, benefits, and probabilities are essential considerations in environmental risk decision making, and informal estimations of costs, benefits, and probabilities cannot be avoided. Moreover, a decision to forego a final verdict on a chemical's use and to allow, or prevent, its use pending the collection of more information, is still a decision made under uncertainty. . . .

The five remaining characteristics common to environmental risk problems bear more directly on the institutional problems encountered in their management. The first of these is the *internal transfer of benefits* associated with these risks. In the case of freon propellants, the benefits — added convenience and possibly lower manufacturing costs — are transferred through markets and reflected in product prices. The economic term for costs and benefits thus transferred is "internal."

In contrast to an internal transfer, the adverse effects of environmental risk gambles usually are transferred directly through the environment rather than through the market. A direct, non-market transfer of an effect is called an economic externality. The *external transfer of costs* is the sixth characteristic of en-

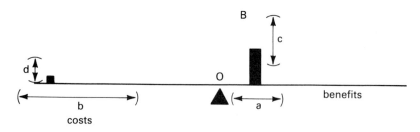

FIGURE 5-2
Costs and Benefits Weighted by Probability

vironmental risk. The failure of markets to internalize these potentially catastrophic costs is the primary reason for regulation of environmental risk problems.

The asymmetry between internal benefits and external costs, added to the asymmetry of the potential magnitudes of costs and benefits ("zero-infinity dilemma"), increases the strain on institutional management of environmental risk. The market failure associated with environmental risk is likely to be more severe than if both benefits and potential costs were external and offsetting, with the same group receiving the benefits also bearing risks.

The seventh characteristic of environmental risk, *collective risk*, is also related to the environmental transfer of effect. A risk is collective when it is borne by many people simultaneously. Since environmental transfer often means a diffusion of effect, major environmental risk problems have the potential to affect millions of people at the same time. The effectiveness of insurance, liability law, and other traditional compensatory mechanisms in protecting against loss resulting from risk is limited in the case of collective risk. The larger the potential loss and the more widespread its effects, the more difficult it is to insure. Society is more averse to collectcive risks than to individual risks, which often are managed through insurance markets.

The eighth characteristic of environmental risk is *latency*, the extended delay between the initiation of a hazard, or exposure to it, and the manifestation of its effect. For many carcinogens, the latency is from 20 to 30 years. Indeed, the mutagenic effect of a chemical may not show up for several generations. As a result of latency, those bearing environmental risks may not be the ones enjoying the benefits of the decision. Moreover, in most cases, latency is sufficiently long and the risk sufficiently diffuse so that the risk is borne involuntarily, if not unknowingly. Since an acute, or short-term, effect usually is much easier to discover and trace than a chronic, or long-term effect, long latencies increase the likelihood that the potential effects of environmental risks will be masked by other factors.

The ninth characteristic of environmental risk is *irreversibility*. Even when an effect is theoretically reversible, as a practical matter there are important elements of irreversibility when reversal of the effect inescapably requires a long time, especially when reversal entails a high cost in addition to a long time. Irreversibility can be essentially absolute, as is the case with plutonium's half-life of 24,000 years. It can also be measured on a scale of tens of generations, as is the case with mutagens. In the freon propellant example, the stratospheric effects of ozone depletion might last a hundred years after fluorocarbon emissions are stopped. Within this essentially irreversible period of stratospheric change, however, the resulting climate modification could produce further irreversible effects, such as species extinction.

The last two characteristics, latency and irreversibility of effect, have profound ethical and institutional implications. They raise questions concerning fair distributions of risk over time and how institutions can be designed to anticipate adverse effects, rather than merely to react to existing, known effects. . . .

2.   Cancer, the Environment, and Lifestyle

Some scientists now believe that 90 percent of human cancer may have "environmental" origins, i.e., nonhereditary origins such as diet, lifestyle, and type of work. Other scientists strongly disagree with this conclusion because demonstrating the precise connection between various cancers and their nonhereditary causes is fraught with enormous difficulty. Trying to link cancer to a cause illustrates Talbot Page's conclusion that uncertainty makes environmental risk decisions a high-stakes gamble with the health of thousands or even millions of individuals. The "zero-infinity dilemma" has perplexed many a regulator who fears that failure to act may permit a cancer epidemic to occur.

L. ROBERTS, CANCER TODAY: ORIGINS, PREVENTION, AND TREATMENT
1-11 (1984)

Although the incidence and mortality rates for lung cancer have soared during the last 50 years, the age-adjusted rates for cancers at most other sites have remained steady or declined.[1] For some cancers, this reflects a drop in the incidence, or the number of new cancer cases; for others, the striking improvements in the cure rate for certain cancers.

Cancer takes many forms, striking different types of cells in diverse parts of the body. Each cancer runs its own distinctive course. For instance, although cancer usually appears as a tumor — a visible mass of cancer cells — in leukemia the malignant cells largely remain dispersed throughout the body in the blood and bone marrow.

All of these cancers, however, share the same fundamental properties. Cancer is a breakdown of the orderly process of cell growth and differentiation. It seems to begin with a change in a single cell, presumably a mutation in that cell's genetic apparatus. This change transforms the cell profoundly; it begins to divide without restraint, failing to differentiate into its mature form. Eventually, this altered cell will give rise to billions of other aberrant cells, cancer cells, that invade and destroy nearby tissues. As the colony grows, some of these cells will break off, or metastasize, and be carried by the blood or lymph stream to remote parts of the body where they will invade other tissues as well. . . .

The Biology of Cancer

In the early 1970s, cancer research was galvanized by the discovery of oncogenes, specific genes that can trigger a cell's unbridled growth. Since that time,

---

1.   The actual number of people who develop and die of cancer has increased throughout this period, largely because a major segment of the population is reaching the age when cancers usually develop.

close to 30 of these cancer genes have been isolated from both human and ani-mal cells. In laboratory experiments, the activity of a single one of them is often sufficient to transform normal cells to cancer cells.

In the past few years, molecular biologists have been able to decipher the genetic code of these cancer genes. To their surprise, they found that the onco-genes are remarkably similar, if not identical, to benign genes that are normally present within the cell. It now appears that each cell contains certain normal genes that when activated or altered in some way can start the cell on the path to cancer. Many cancer researchers suspect that all agents of cancer — radiation, chemicals, and viruses — act upon these genes, somehow releasing their malig-nant potential. . . .

There is a new sense of optimism pervading cancer hospitals and research laboratories. Scientific advances of the past few decades have brought steady increases in the cancer survival rate. It is estimated that nearly 50 percent of all patients diagnosed with cancer in 1984 will be cured. A decade ago, the figure was 40 percent. . . .

Yet [c]ancer is still a disease of tragic dimensions. One of every four Amer-icans will develop cancer and one in five will die of it, if current incidence and mortality rates remain the same. It is the second largest cause of death in this country, exceeded only by heart disease. In 1984, there will be 870,000 new cases of cancer and 450,000 cancer deaths, approximately 20 percent of all deaths this year.

Half of all cancer deaths will result from malignancies of the lung, colon and rectum, breast, and pancreas. Lung cancer, which is closely tied to tobacco consumption, alone accounts for over 20 percent of all cancer deaths. Among men, it is the largest cause of cancer death; among women, the second largest (see Figure 5-3).

This work is just beginning; many questions remain. It is still not clear whether oncogenes are involved in all or just some cancers. Nor is it known how they fit into the overall scheme of carcinogenesis, which in humans is a complex process involving many discrete steps and often taking 20 years. While the acti-vation of an oncogene may be a necessary part of this process, it is not sufficient to induce human cancer. . . .

Although McClintock and others were doing work relevant to understand-ing cancer decades ago, the technology needed to confirm their ideas and tie them to the disease process has been available only for the past 10 years or so. Without recombinant DNA and other genetic technologies, most recent research in molecular biology could not have proceeded. It is these technologies that have enabled researchers for the first time to isolate and study a single gene from among the tens of thousands contained in a human cell. . . .

Diet and Cancer

Even before the discovery of oncogenes, it was thought that cancer, at least in some of its manifestations, was the product of the interaction of genes and the

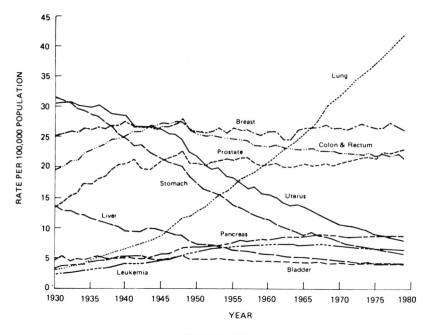

FIGURE 5-3

Age-adjusted Cancer Death Rates by Site, United States, 1930–1979

(*Source:* American Cancer Society, Cancer Facts and Figures 1984.)

environment. Certain agents, such as ultraviolet and ionizing radiation, some chemicals, and some viruses, can initiate cancer, presumably by causing a genetic mutation. From recent work, it is tempting to think that the mutation occurs on an oncogene. Still other external or environmental agents can promote or facilitate the process of carcinogenesis without actually inducing it.

There is now widespread agreement that roughly 85 percent of all cancers are caused by broad environmental factors, including lifestyle patterns. The rest, presumably, have a hereditary basis, or else arise from spontaneous metabolic events. Identifying the environmental factors in cancer, however, has not been easy. At this stage, viruses appear to play only a minor role in human cancers. Occupational chemicals are thought to be responsible for 4 percent of all cancers; environmental chemicals for an estimated 2 percent. Tobacco is by far the largest documented cause of cancer, accounting for roughly 30 percent of all cancers in lungs and some other sites.

Recently, epidemiological studies similar to those that uncovered an association between smoking and cancer have detected a link between the foods that people eat and the cancers that afflict them. Overall, dietary factors are thought to be responsible for another 30 percent of the cancer incidence in the United States, which could mean that a substantial portion of those cancers may be preventable.

With a few exceptions, the studies have not turned up specific culprits — certain foods or constituents of foods that cause cancer. Nor does the major problem appear to be food additives or contaminants. Rather, . . . cancer risk is associated with certain broad dietary patterns and the consumption of major nutrients. Specifically, a diet high in fats and fatty meats seems to carry a risk of cancer. Salt-cured, salt-pickled, and highly spiced foods are also suspect. On the other hand, the consumption of high-fiber grains, vegetables, and fruits seems to protect against cancer. In short, cancer risk appears to be a matter of dietary choice, of the balance and proportion of nutrients in the diet, as well as of methods of food preparation.

The case against diet is still circumstantial. These epidemiological studies have revealed broad associations, not causality. Further laboratory and clinical studies are necessary to determine exactly how diet contributes to cancer. For instance, the specific dietary constituents that may be responsible for observed carcinogenic or protective effects are not known, nor are their mechanisms of action. Nonetheless, several federal agencies have decided that the weight of evidence is strong enough to suggest that the public modify its eating habits in accordance with the findings of these studies.

This is not to imply that a modification in diet would elicit a reduction in cancer incidence similar to the one that would result if smoking were eliminated. Studies to date have made it abundantly clear that the relationship of diet to cancer is exceedingly complex. The risk factors in diet cannot simply be eliminated; some of the dietary constituents that seem to pose greatest cancer risk are essential human nutrients.

In addition, . . . it has become increasingly clear from another line of inquiry that natural mutagens and carcinogens are ubiquitous throughout the human diet, occurring in common vegetables, fruits, meats, nuts, and beverages. Conversely, some natural substances, such as the precursor of vitamin A and the mineral selenium, appear to be anticarcinogens, capable of preventing the process of malignant transformation in laboratory studies.

At this stage, the potency of most of the natural carcinogens and the magnitude of risk they pose to human health have not been determined, nor is it known if and how they might interact with anticarcinogens in the diet. What does seem clear, however, is that it will not be possible to specify a risk-free diet.

Cancer researchers generally agree that adoption of a low-risk diet should help to prevent some cancers. The exact benefit to be gained, however, cannot be predicted until the biological mechanisms underlying the association between diet and cancer are better understood. . . .

. . . Traditionally, the government has acted through its regulatory policies to minimize human exposure to harmful substances in foods. It has set standards for food additives and natural contaminants, as well as for pesticide residues and other industrial chemicals that might enter the food supply. Now that foods themselves, not the substances added to them, appear to pose the greatest cancer risk, this regulatory approach no longer appears sufficient, although it is certainly a vital element of any food safety policy. Indeed, the most effective strategy for

preventing cancer may simply be to provide information that will help consumers make intelligent dietary decisions, giving them an increasing share of the
responsibility for their own protection. . . .

3.   *Pinning Down Risk: Separating Risk Assessment from Risk Management*

COMMITTEE ON INSTITUTIONAL MEANS FOR
ASSESSMENT OF RISKS TO PUBLIC HEALTH,
COMMISSION ON LIFE SCIENCES, NATIONAL
RESEARCH COUNCIL, RISK ASSESSMENT IN THE
FEDERAL GOVERNMENT: MANAGING THE PROCESS
18-347 (1983)

Risk Assessment and Risk Management

We use *risk assessment* to mean the characterization of the potential adverse
health effects of human exposures to environmental hazards. Risk assessments
include several elements: description of the potential adverse health effects based
on an evaluation of results of epidemiologic, clinical, toxicologic, and environmental research; extrapolation from those results to predict the type and estimate
the extent of health effects in humans under given conditions of exposure; judgments as to the number and characteristics of persons exposed at various inten-
sities and durations; and summary judgments on the existence and overall
magnitude of the public-health problem. Risk assessment also includes characterization of the uncertainties inherent in the process of inferring risk. . . .

The Committee uses the term *risk management* to describe the process of
evaluating alternative regulatory actions and selecting among them. Risk management, which is carried out by regulatory agencies under various legislative
mandates, is an agency decision-making process that entails consideration of
political, social, economic, and engineering information with risk-related information to develop, analyze, and compare regulatory options and to select the
appropriate regulatory response to a potential chronic health hazard. The selection process necessarily requires the use of value judgments on such issues as the
acceptability of risk and the reasonableness of the costs of control. . . .

Scientific Basis for Risk Assessment

STEP 1. HAZARD IDENTIFICATION . . .

EPIDEMIOLOGIC DATA

Well-conducted epidemiologic studies that show a positive association between an agent and a disease are accepted as the most convincing evidence about

human risk. This evidence is, however, difficult to accumulate; often the risk is low, the number of persons exposed is small, the latent period between exposure and disease is long, and exposures are mixed and multiple. Thus, epidemiologic data require careful interpretation. Even if these problems are solved satisfactorily, the preponderance of chemicals in the environment has not been studied with epidemiologic methods, and we would not wish to release newly produced substances only to discover years later that they were powerful carcinogenic agents. These limitations require reliance on less direct evidence that a health hazard exists.

ANIMAL-BIOASSAY DATA

The most commonly available data in hazard identification are those obtained from animal bioassays. The inference that results from animal experiments are applicable to humans is fundamental to toxicologic research; this premise underlies much of experimental biology and medicine and is logically extended to the experimental observation of carcinogenic effects. Despite the apparent validity of such inferences and their acceptability by most cancer researchers, there are no doubt occasions in which observations in animals may be of highly uncertain relevance to humans.

Consistently positive results in the two sexes and in several strains and species and higher incidences at higher doses constitute the best evidence of carcinogenicity. More often than not, however, such data are not available. Instead, because of the nature of the effect and the limits of detection of animal tests as they are usually conducted, experimental data leading to a positive finding sometimes barely exceed a statistical threshold and may involve tumor types of uncertain relation to human carcinogenesis. Interpretation of some animal data may therefore be difficult. Notwithstanding uncertainties associated with interpretation of some animal tests, they have, in general, proved to be reliable indicators of carcinogenic properties and will continue to play a pivotal role in efforts to identify carcinogens.

SHORT-TERM STUDIES

Considerable experimental evidence supports the proposition that most chemical carcinogens are mutagens and that many mutagens are carcinogens. As a result, a positive response in a mutagenicity assay is supportive evidence that the agent tested is likely to be carcinogenic. Such data, in the absence of a positive animal bioassay, are rarely, if ever, sufficient to support a conclusion that an agent is carcinogenic. Because short-term tests are rapid and inexpensive, they are valuable for screening chemicals for potential carcinogenicity and lending additional support to observations from animal and epidemiologic investigations.

COMPARISONS OF MOLECULAR STRUCTURE

Comparison of an agent's chemical or physical properties with those of known carcinogens provides some evidence of potential carcinogenicity. Experimental data support such associations for a few structural classes; however, such studies are best used to identify potential carcinogens for further investigation and may be useful in priority-setting for carcinogenicity testing.

STEP 2. DOSE-RESPONSE ASSESSMENT

In a small number of instances, epidemiologic data permit a dose-response relation to be developed directly from observations of exposure and health effects in humans. If epidemiologic data are available, extrapolations from the exposures observed in the study to lower exposures experienced by the general population are often necessary. Such extrapolations introduce uncertainty into the estimates of risk for the general population. Uncertainties also arise because the general population includes some people, such as children, who may be more susceptible than people in the sample from which the epidemiologic data were developed.

The absence of useful human data is common for most chemicals being assessed for carcinogenic effect, and dose-response assessment usually entails evaluating tests that were performed on rats or mice. The tests, however, typically have been designed for hazard identification, rather than for determining dose-response relations. Under current testing practice, one group of animals is given the highest dose that can be tolerated, a second group is exposed at half that dose, and a control group is not exposed. (The use of high doses is necessary to maximize the sensitivity of the study for determining whether the agent being tested has carcinogenic potential.) . . .

The testing of chemicals at high doses has been challenged by some scientists who argue that metabolism of chemicals differs at high and low doses; i.e., high doses may overwhelm normal detoxification mechanisms and provide results that would not occur at the lower doses to which humans are exposed. An additional factor that is often raised to challenge the validity of animal data to indicate effects in man is that metabolic differences among animal species should be considered when animal test results are analyzed. Metabolic differences can have important effects on the validity of extrapolating from animals to man if, for example, the actual carcinogen is a metabolite of the administered chemical and the animals tested differ markedly from humans in their production of that metabolite. A related point is that the actual dose of carcinogen reaching the affected tissue or organ is usually not known; thus, dose-response information, of necessity, is based on administered dose and not tissue dose. Although data of these types would certainly improve the basis for extrapolating from high to low doses and from one species to another, they are difficult to acquire and often unavailable.

Regulators are interested in doses to which humans might be exposed, and such doses usually are much lower than those administered in animal studies.

Therefore, dose-response assessment often requires extrapolating an expected response curve over a wide range of doses from one or two actual data points. In addition, differences in size and metabolic rates between man and laboratory animals require that doses used experimentally be converted to reflect these differences.

LOW-DOSE EXTRAPOLATION

One may extrapolate to low doses by fitting a mathematical model to animal dose-response data and using the model to predict risks at lower doses corresponding to those experienced by humans. At present, the true shape of the dose-response curve at doses several orders of magnitude below the observation range cannot be determined experimentally. Even the largest study on record — the ED_{01} study involving 24,000 animals — was designed only to measure the dose corresponding to a 1% increase in tumor incidence. However, regulatory agencies are often concerned about much lower risks (1 in 100,000 to 1 in 1,000). Several methods have been developed to extrapolate from high doses to low doses that would correspond to risk of such magnitudes. A difficulty with low-dose extrapolation is that a number of the extrapolation methods fit the data from animal experiments reasonably well, and it is impossible to distinguish their validity on the basis of goodness of fit. (From a mathematical point of view, distinguishing among these models on the basis of their fit with experimental data would require an extremely large experiment; from a practical point of view, it is probably impossible.) As Figure 5-4 shows, the dose-response curves derived with different models diverge substantially in the dose range of interest to regulators. Thus, low-dose extrapolation must be more than a curve-fitting exercise, and considerations of biological plausibility must be taken into account.

Although the five models shown in Figure 5-4 may fit experimental data equally well, they are not equally plausible biologically. Most persons in the field would agree that the supralinear model can be disregarded, because it is very difficult to conceive of a biologic mechanism that would give rise to this type of low-dose response. The threshold model is based on the assumption that below a particular dose (the "threshold" dose of a given carcinogen) there is no adverse effect. This concept is plausible but not now confirmable. The ED_{01} study showed an apparent threshold for bladder cancers caused by 2-acetylaminofluorene; when the data were replotted on a scale giving greater resolution, the number of bladder tumors consistently increased with dose, even at the lowest doses, and no threshold was detected. Another aspect of the debate over thresholds for inducing carcinogenic effects is the argument that agents that act through genotoxic mechanisms are not likely to have a threshold, whereas agents whose effects are mediated by epigenetic mechanisms are possibly more likely to have a threshold. The latter argument is also currently open to scientific challenge. Finally, apparent thresholds observable in animal bioassays cannot be equated with thresholds for entire populations. Even if a threshold exists for individuals, a single threshold would probably not be applicable to the whole population. . . .

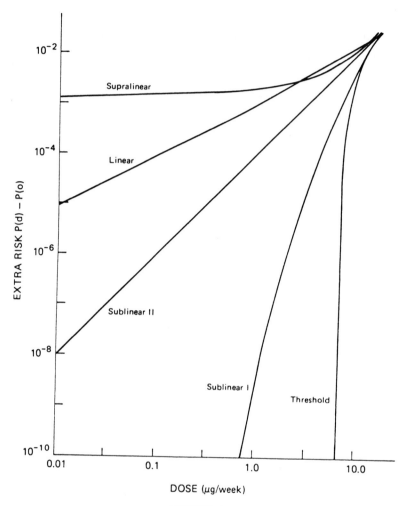

FIGURE 5-4

Results of Alternative Extrapolation Models for the Same
Experimental Data

Note: Dose-response functions were developed (Crump, forthcoming) for data
from a benzopyrene carcinogenesis experiment with mice conducted by Lee
and O'Neill (1971).

Step 3. Exposure Assessment

The first task of an exposure assessment is the determination of he concentration of the chemical to which humans are exposed. This may be known
from direct measurement, but more typically exposure data are incomplete and
must be estimated. . . .

. . . In the community environment, the ambient concentrations of chemicals to which people may be exposed can be estimated from emission rates only if the transport and conversion processes are known. Alternative engineering control options require different estimates of the reduction in exposure that may be achieved. For new chemicals with no measurement data at all, rough estimates of exposure are necessary. Some chemical agents are of concern because they are present in foods or may be absorbed when a consumer product is used. Assessments of exposure to such agents are complicated by variations in diet and personal habits among different groups in the population. . . .

Another important aspect of exposure assessment is the determination of which groups in the population may be exposed to a chemical agent; some groups may be especially susceptible to adverse health effects. Pregnant women, very young and very old people, and persons with impaired health may be particularly important in exposure assessment. The importance of exposures to a mixture of carcinogens is another factor that needs to be considered in assessing human exposures. For example, exposure to cigarette smoke and asbestos gives an incidence of cancer that is much greater than anticipated from carcinogenicity data on each substance individually. Because data detecting such synergistic effects are often unavailable, they are often ignored or accounted for by the use of various safety factors.

STEP 4. RISK CHARACTERIZATION

Risk characterization, the estimate of the magnitude of the public-health problem, involves no additional scientific knowledge or concepts. However, the exercise of judgment in the aggregation of population groups with varied sensitivity and different exposure may affect the estimate.

Scientific and Policy Judgments in Risk Assessment

The uncertainties inherent in risk assessment can be grouped in two general categories: missing or ambiguous information on a particular substance and gaps in current scientific theory. When scientific uncertainty is encountered in the risk assessment process, inferential bridges are needed to allow the process to continue. The Committee has defined the points in the risk assessment process where such inferences must be made as *components*. The judgments made by the scientist/risk assessor for each component of risk assessment often entail a choice among several scientifically plausible options; the Committee has designated these *inference options*. . . .

A key premise of the proponents of institutional separation of risk assessment is that removal of risk assessment from the regulatory agencies will result in a clear demarcation of the science and policy aspects of regulatory decision-making. However, policy considerations inevitably affect, and perhaps determine, some of the choices among the inference options. . . . [The Committee then addressed these critical inference options, stating that there were twenty-five components for choice (especially whether to rely on positive or negative animal data, and whether to count all types of benign tumors as evidence of carcinogenicity). The Committee identified 13 components for dose-response assessment (especially high to low dose extrapolation, interspecies dose conversion, and choice of sensitive or less sensitive experimental animal species). It addressed numerous components for exposure assessment (e.g., media propagation models, frequency, duration, and rates of intake, contact, and absorption) and for risk characterization. It concluded:]

BASIS FOR SELECTING INFERENCE OPTIONS

The Committee has presented some of the more familiar, and possibly more controversial, components of risk assessment. A review of the list of components reveals that many components lack definitive scientific answers, that the degree of scientific consensus concerning the best answer varies (some are more controversial among scientists than others), and that the inference options available for each component differ in their degree of conservatism. . . .

That a scientist makes the choices does not render the judgments devoid of policy implications. Scientists differ in their opinions of the validity of various options, even if they are not consciously choosing to be more or less conservative. In considering whether to use data from the most sensitive experimental animals for risk assessment, a scientist may be influenced by the species, strains, and gender of the animals tested, the characteristics of the tumor, and the conditions of the experiment. A scientist's weighting of these variables may not easily be expressed explicitly, and the result is a mixture of fact, experience (often called intuition), and personal values that cannot be disentangled easily. As a result, the choice made may be perceived by the scientist as based primarily on informed scientific judgment. From a regulatory official's point of view, the same choice may appear to be a value decision as to how conservative regulatory policy should be, given the lack of a decisive empirical basis for choice.

A risk assessor, in the absence of a clear indication based on science, could choose a particular approach (e.g., the use of an extrapolation model) solely on the basis of the degree to which it is conservative, i.e., on the basis of its policy implications. Furthermore, a desire to err on the side of overprotection of public health by increasing the estimate of risk could lead an assessor to choose the most conservative assumptions throughout the process for components on which science does not indicate a preferred choice. Such judgments made in risk assessment are designated *risk assessment policy*, that is, policy related to and subservient to the scientific content of the process, in contrast with policy invoked to guide risk management decisions, which has political, social, and economic determinants.

When inference options are chosen primarily on the basis of policy, risk management considerations (the desire to regulate or not to regulate) may influence the choices made by the assessors. The influence can be generic or ad hoc;

i.e., assessments for *all* chemicals would consistently use the more or less conservative inference options, depending on the *overall* policy orientation of the
agency ("generic"), or assessments would vary from chemical to chemical, with
more conservative options being chosen for substances that the agency wishes to
regulate and less conservative options being chosen for substances that the agency does not wish to regulate. (The desire to regulate or not would presumably
stem from substance-specific economic and social considerations.) The possible
influence of risk management considerations, whether real or perceived, on the
policy choices made in risk assessment has led to reform proposals (reviewed later
in this report) that would separate risk assessment activities from the regulatory
agencies. . . .

Risk Assessment and Regulatory Decision-Making

The regulatory process can be initiated in many ways. Each regulatory agency
typically has jurisdiction over a large number of substances, but circumstances
force an allocation of resources to a few at a time. The decision as to which
substances to regulate is based, at least in part, on the degree of hazard. Thus,
some notion of relative hazard (implicit or explicit, internally generated or imposed by outside groups) is necessary. Critics of federal regulation have contended that the agencies have not set their priorities sensibly. In general, agency risk
assessments for priority-setting have been more informal, less systematic, and
less visible than those for establishing regulatory controls.

Agenda-setting involves decisions about which substances should be selected (and often in what order) for more intense formal regulatory review. All
programs face this problem, but it assumes different configurations: some programs cover a finite and known set of chemicals that must be reviewed, so the
order of the regulatory reviews is the key question, and the primary job of the
risk assessor is to help the agency implement a worst-first approach. For example,
EPA's pesticides program has long had lists of suspect pesticide ingredients, and
agency officials have had to decide which ones warrant formal consideration of
cancellation or of new controls. An agency's agenda may also respond to private-
sector initiatives (in the case of approval of new drugs or pesticides), conform to
statutory directives, or react to new evidence of hazards previously unrecognized
or thought to be less serious. This agenda formation phase, too, involves elements of risk assessment by the agency, the Congress, or private-sector entities;
that is, there must be some assessment, however informal, that indicates reason
for concern.

For many items on an agency's regulatory agenda, hazard identification
alone will support a conclusion that a chemical presents little or no risk to human health and should be removed from regulatory consideration, at least until
new data warrant renewed concern. If a chemical is found to be potentially
dangerous in the hazard-identification step, it could then be taken through the
steps of dose-response assessment, exposure assessment, and risk characteriza-

tion. At any of these steps, the evaluation might indicate that a substance poses little or no risk and therefore can be removed from regulatory consideration until new data indicate a need for reevaluation.

Chemicals that are judged to present appreciable risks to health are candidates for regulatory action, and an agency will begin to develop options for regulating exposures. Regulatory options usually involve specific product or process changes and typically need to be based on extensive engineering and technical knowledge of the affected industry. Evaluation of the regulatory options includes recomputation of the predicted risk, in accord with altered expectations of exposure intensity or numbers of persons exposed.

Many of the activities of regulatory agencies do not conform to this sequential approach. However, regardless of the sequence of steps and the number of steps used to determine whether regulatory action is warranted, risk assessment serves at least two major functions in regulatory decisions: first, it provides an initial assessment of risks, and, if the risk is judged to be important enough to warrant regulatory action, it is used to evaluate the effects of different regulatory options on exposure. In addition, it may be used to set priorities for regulatory consideration and for further toxicity testing.

These varied functions place different requirements on risk assessors, and a single risk assessment method may not be sufficient. A risk assessment to establish testing priorities may appropriately incorporate many worst-case assumptions if there are data gaps, because research should be directed at substances with the most crucial gaps; but such assumptions may be inappropriate for analyzing regulatory controls, particularly if the regulator must ensure that controls do not place undue strains on the economy. In establishing regulatory priorities, the same inference options should be chosen for all chemicals, because the main point of the analysis is to make useful risk comparisons so that agency resources will be used rationally. However, this approach, which may be reasonable for priority-setting, may have to yield to more sophisticated and detailed scientific arguments when a substance's commercial life is at stake and the agency's decision may be challenged in court. Furthermore, the available resources and the resulting analytic care devoted to a risk assessment for deciding regulatory policy are likely to be much greater for analyzing control actions for a single substance than for setting priorities.

NOTES AND QUESTIONS

Competing theories of cancer causation. Beginning in the 1950s, the United States began an all-out effort to find *the* cause of cancer and *a* cure. Reports soon appeared that researchers were closing in on the cause of cancer, suspected to be viruses. With the end in sight, Congress and the American Cancer Society provided millions of dollars for research. The cause and cure did not materialize, but by the 1970s some were blaming environmental exposure to industrial chemicals for causing cancer, although the cellular mechanism remained a mystery. All along evidence was accumulating that implicated smoking as a cause of lung cancer and other health problems such as heart disease. Then in the early 1980s scientists concluded that lifestyle and diet were the major determinants of cancer incidence.

Throughout this progression through the pathogenic, environmental, and behavioral hypotheses of cancer causation, researchers maintained that reducing or eliminating cancer would require understanding its cause on the molecular level. Optimistic reports of an imminent cure for cancer have become a staple of American journalism. A 1983 New York Times report, excerpted at length in the first edition of this casebook, reported that scientists would understand how cancer is caused "by the end of the year or shortly thereafter," and a cure would soon follow. Boffey, New Findings About Cancer Raising Hope, N.Y. Times, Feb. 20, 1983, at 1, col. 6. Today, the optimistic reports focus on genetically engineered oncotoxin molecules that will kill cancer cells and "perhaps" the AIDS virus. Rovner, "Magic" Molecules to Kill Cancer, Washington Post, Mar. 22, 1988, Health, p. 7, col. 1. Does the excerpt by Roberts, *supra*, reflect this optimism? Is optimism warranted?

Smoking. Smoking is by far the single most important preventable cause of death in the United States. Tobacco smoke contains 43 chemical carcinogens. In 1985 smoking accounted for 87 percent of lung cancer deaths, 82 percent of chronic obstructive pulmonary disease, 21 percent of coronary heart disease, and 18 percent of strokes. In 1985, 390,000 deaths (one in six) were attributable to smoking — 18 percent more than predicted, although from 1965 to 1987 smokers declined from 40 to 29 percent of the adult population. Lung cancer rates increased two- to fourfold among men in the period 1965-1986, but the rate for women 45 or older rose four to sevenfold. By 1986 lung cancer had overtaken breast cancer as the leading cause of cancer among women. Women's risk of lung cancer has also caught up with the risk to men. Yet while men are giving up smoking in substantial numbers, smoking among women has declined only slightly. Report of the Surgeon General, Reducing the Health Consequences of Smoking (1989). The risk to exposed non-smokers is also significant. See National Research Council, Environmental Tobacco Smoke (1986).

Federal law requires package labeling to warn smokers of health risks. As of mid-1988 more than 320 local governments had regulated smoking in public places — a threefold increase in three years. Report of the Surgeon General, *supra*. Something of a victory in a suit for damages against a cigarette manufacturer was obtained in Cipollone v. Liggett Group, Inc., 683 F. Supp. 1487 (D.N.J. 1988), although the circuit court partially reversed. The district court held that the issues of whether a duty existed to warn smokers prior to the 1966 federal labeling law, whether the manufacturer gave express safety warranties prior to 1966, and whether the manufacturer made false representations or intentionally concealed facts about smoking risks, could go to a jury. Smokers, however, have lost the vast majority of damage actions. Thus, considering the enormous risk, smoking remains one of the least effectively controlled environmental and lifestyle problems.

A cancer "epidemic"? The stringency of hazardous substances regulation is often justified as an attempt to prevent a cancer epidemic. If the cancer risk has been unduly exaggerated, support for the costly regulatory programs that are the focus of this chapter will be significantly undercut. The issue hinges upon whether an unexplained increase in the incidence of cancer (the number of new cases) is in fact occurring, and on this issue experts are divided.

No one questions that cancer now accounts for a greater percentage of deaths than it once did. The accepted explanation for the increase is that because fewer persons died young of infectious diseases after "miracle" drugs were discovered, they lived long enough to die of cancer or heart disease. A relatively stable cancer rate for the past 25 years seemed to confirm this hypothesis.

In 1980 researchers at the National Cancer Institute (NCI) detected what they believed to be a 9 percent increase in cancer in white males and a 14 percent increase in white females over the period 1969 to 1976 — a possible 10,000 new cancer cases a year. They had adjusted their data to correct for the increasing longevity of the United States population. Pollack & Horm, Trends in Cancer Incidence and Mortality in the United States: 1969-76, 64 J. Natl. Cancer Inst. 1091 (1980). Yet other NCI epidemiologists concluded that but for smoking, cancer incidence would actually be decreasing (Devesa & Silverman, Cancer Incidence and Mortality Trends in the United States: 1934-74, 60 J. Natl. Cancer Inst. 545 (1978)). The Director of Science Policy at NCI concluded that less than half of the increased incidence of cancer could be explained by smoking. He found that between 1969 and 1976, occupationally related cancers had increased by 25 percent in white workers. Culliton, Government Says Cancer Rate Is Increasing, 209 Science 998 (1980). A federal interagency committee endorsed the basic conclusions of Pollack, Horm & Schneiderman, Toxic Substances Strategy Committee, Toxic Chemicals and Public Protection: A Report to the President (1980). Later, two prominent British epidemiologists concluded that the data "do not . . . suggest that the United States is beginning to experience an epidemic of cancer due to new factors." Doll & Peto, The Causes of Cancer: Quantitative Estimates of Avoidable Risks of Cancer in the United States Today, 66 J. Natl. Cancer Inst. 1191 (1981). Others expect a cancer epidemic in the 1990s when high-risk chemicals will have had ample time to reach humans through the environment and ample time for their long latency periods to lapse. Large quantities of high-risk chemicals were not manufactured until the 1960s. Davis & Magee, Cancer and Industrial Chemical Production, 206 Science 1356 (1980); Davis, Bridbord & Schneiderman, Cancer Prevention: Assessing Causes, Exposures, and Recent Trends in Mortality for U.S. Males 1968-1978, 2 Teratogenesis, Carcinogenesis & Mutagenesis 105 (1982).

Too great a focus on the national cancer rate may mask increases in the cancer rate in small groups of persons exposed to carcinogens. The evidence correlating occupational and environmental exposures to particular chemicals with site-specific cancers improves steadily and does reveal, if not epidemics, outbreaks of cancer. Many occupational correlations exist: mesothelioma (cancer of the lung lining) with asbestos; angiosarcoma (liver cancer) with polyvinylchloride; leukemia with benzene; lung and thyroid cancer with low-level radiation;

TABLE 5-1
Cancer Deaths in the United States

Attribution	Percent
Diet	35
Tobacco	30
Infection (speculative)	10
Sexual/reproductive behavior	7
Occupational	4
Alcohol	3
Geophysical (sunlight, radiation)	3
Pollution	2
Other and unknown	6

Source: Based on Doll & Peto, The Causes of Cancer: Quantitative Estimates of Avoidable Risks of Cancer in the United States Today, 66 J. of the Natl. Cancer Inst. (1981) (Table 20).

stomach cancer with ethylene oxide and dichloride (hospitals and laboratories); and bowel and rectal cancer with paint and coating manufacture.

Dietary factors. What does Table 5-1 suggest should be the prevailing strategy for reducing cancer mortality in the United States? The current federal strategy relies on bans and controls under the regulatory statutes administered by the Food and Drug Administration, the Environmental Protection Agency, the Occupational Safety and Health Administration, the Consumer Product Safety Commission, the Department of Agriculture, and a few others. This approach might work to control cancer from smoking. What problems do you anticipate? How feasible is direct regulation of other lifestyle and dietary factors?

The Roberts excerpt suggests that the human body is awash in naturally occurring carcinogens and mutagens. Human sources add only the tiniest increments. Dietary intake of natural toxicants is likely to be seven grams a day (not milligrams or micrograms), 10,000 times more than intake of manufactured pesticides. Ames, Dietary Carcinogens and Anticarcinogens, 221 Science 1256, 1258 (1983). What foods contain natural carcinogens? In addition to animal fat, coffee, pepper, potatoes, and browned foods, consider also mushrooms, celery, spinach, herbal teas, and alfalfa sprouts. Health food devotees, take note. Further, cancer is thwarted by vigorous natural cell repair mechanisms and cancer-inhibiting chemicals in common foods which contain vitamin E, carotene, Selenium, and ascorbic and uric acid. Id. at 1259.

Is the point then to select foods carefully, do not smoke or drink, stay well, be celibate, and largely forget environmental and occupational regulation? Perhaps the industrial contribution to the problem of cancer is too tiny, nature's role too large, and personal choice too determinative to justify much regulatory activity at all. Does this also invalidate the one-hit theory of cancer (one molecule of carcinogen can initiate cancer by striking a single body cell)? Does it suggest that regulators re-examine their assumption that no threshold dose exists for regulated carcinogens? Is it possible to conduct meaningful cancer risk assessments in light of these data?

In the 1940s and 1950s, the FDA regulated the composition of processed foods, such as cheeses, jams, and mayonnaise. Should such regulation be reinstituted today? Professor Richard Merrill, former General Counsel of the FDA, has suggested shifting the emphasis away from the regulation of dietary carcinogens (the "pollution control approach") to requiring labels on foods which cannot practically be eliminated from the diet, as Congress did for saccharin. Merrill, Reducing Diet-Induced Cancer through Federal Regulation: Opportunities and Obstacles, 38 Vand. L. Rev. 513 (1985). Yet fruits and vegetables are difficult to label. Their naturally occurring carcinogen content may vary seasonally and regionally. Further, many persons have a strong attachment to certain foods. They might not respect or heed the advice, possibly because of confusing labels and "information overload." Because of the variety of foods containing natural carcinogens, the FDA concluded that many, perhaps most, supermarket foods would require lengthy labels. 44 Fed. Reg. 59,513 (1979).

Chemicals, carcinogens, and regulatory action. Of the roughly 9 million known chemicals, over 70,000 are in commercial use. The EPA lists about 3,500 chemicals as under active consideration in the agency's regulatory programs. For comparison, the Food and Drug Administration's food program covers 2,000 chemicals. While fewer than 30 agents are definitely linked with cancer in humans, some 1,500 substances are carcinogenic according to animal tests. Only about 7,000 of the 9 million known substances have been tested for carcinogenicity. Risk Assessment in the Federal Government, *supra* at 11-12.

The EPA has regulated six hazardous air pollutants (including one noncarcinogen) but lists ten as needing regulation. The agency's regulation of waterborne toxicants is complicated but likewise remains incomplete; it covers 126 chemicals in 65 industrial categories, of which 29 involve carcinogens. Eighty-three drinking water toxicants are intended for regulation, but only 51 are in the process of being regulated. Final regulations exist for only nine chemicals, six of which are likely carcinogens. Of 81 carcinogenic active pesticide ingredients, EPA has not acted on 47. Twenty-eight inert ingredients may be carcinogenic but remain unregulated. Of other new or existing chemicals, 38 chemicals or chemical classes are suspect carcinogens, but the agency prepared risk assessments on only 21; four have been identified for "accelerated review"; and actual regulatory action remains "limited." Under the federal hazardous waste site and spill cleanup program, 717 hazardous substances have been listed, of which EPA has identified 191 as potential carcinogens. Agencywide, 57 full carcinogenic risk assessments have been prepared. Office of Technology Assessment, Identifying and Regulating Carcinogens 12-15 (1987).

"Mega-mouse" experiments. Federal regulation relies overwhelmingly on rodent bioassay data. For example, of 57 chemicals that have been fully evaluated by the EPA Carcinogen Assessment Group, 40 had sufficient animal data; nine, sufficient human and animal data; and eight, other types of data. As of 1987 the 191 potential carcinogens covered by the federal "Superfund" hazard-

ous waste site cleanup law (see p. 613 *infra*) represents something of an exception, in that while animal and human data implicate 130 and 14 substances,
respectively, 40 of these chemicals were deemed suspect because of their molecular similarity to known carcinogens. Office of Technology Assessment, Identifying and Regulating Carcinogens 15-16 (1987).

The low risks associated with most regulated carcinogens creates the need
for the controversial leaps of faith involved in risk assessment inference options.
To demonstrate low-level cancer risk, regulators have somehow to extrapolate
from the high-dose region of the dose-response curve of an actual animal experiment where tumor rates run 5 to 50 percent to the low-dose region of a hypothetical human dose-response curve where there is a projected incidence of one
cancer per 100 thousand to 100 million people. Id. at 55. To show incontrovert-
ibly (95 percent confidence) that a low dose of one substance causes fewer than
one cancer in a million subjects would require 6 million test animals. Because
of the assumptions which must be made in order to rely on smaller experiments (still involving hundreds or thousands of test animals), the major models
differ by a factor of 100,000 on the dose size which creates a risk of one cancer per million subjects. The impact of conservative assumptions may therefore
be quite large. Doniger, Federal Regulaton of Vinyl Chloride: A Short Course
in the Law and Policy of Toxic Substances Control, 7 Ecology L.Q. 497, 512
(1978).

Some scientists are not willing to accept the chain of inferences upon
which a conclusion that a substance is carcinogenic depends — animal evidence, large-dose experiments, the one-hit no-threshold theory, and the like.
They think better evidence should support such an inference, somewhat like the
law imposes the "best evidence" rule. For example, some scientists view the
"rebutttable presumption against registration" (RPAR), now called Special Review (see p. 576 *infra*), which empowers EPA under the Federal Insecticide,
Fungicide, and Rodenticide Act to cast the burden of proof of a pesticide's safety
on its manufacturer, as being based upon "bad science" because under EPA rules
the appearance of non-malignant tumors in laboratory animals exposed to the
pesticide will be taken as evidence of potential human carcinogenicity. Cancers
are malignant tumors, yet the biological mechanisms producing malignant and
non-malignant tumors are very similar. "Good science" would only accept malignant tumors as a valid basis for inferring the pesticide's cancer-causing properties. The choices to be made in establishing risk assessment guidelines have
led Professor Latin to conclude that risk assessment necessarily contains as much
policy making as science and thus should not be left entirely to scientists. Latin,
Good Science, Bad Regulations, and Toxic Risk Assessment, 5 Yale J. on Reg.
89 (1988).

Categorizing cancer controls. Cancers may be viewed as falling in three
categories:

a. Self-induced cancer: the most victims, strong data on causation (e.g.,
smoking, diet).

b. Workplace cancer: many victims, adequate data (e.g., asbestos, benzene, PVC).

c. General environmental cancer: as yet few victims, weakest data (e.g., pesticides, air pollution, nuclear power).

Paradoxically, category c has received the most regulatory attention and category a the least, with category b somewhere in between. Why? Do the chemical companies and utilities lack the political clout of tobacco companies? Is it harder for a chemical company to ascertain its self-interest? Did the chemical manufacturers make a basic tactical mistake by calling for affirmative governmental proof that chemicals cause cancer before regulating them, rather than arguing that whatever the risks, workers have consented to them in return for higher wages? Does the minimum legislation in category a show that Congress is not as paternalistic as some may think? The public may be willing to accept voluntary over involuntary risks by a factor of 1,000 (three orders of magnitude): "We are loath to let others do unto us what we happily do to ourselves." Starr, Social Benefit versus Technological Risk, 165 Science 1232, 1235 (1969). See also Tversky & Kahneman, The Framing of Decisions and the Psychology of Choice, 211 Science 453 (1981), and Schelling, The Life You Save May Be Your Own, in Problems in Public Expenditure Analysis 127 (S. Chase ed. 1967).

Framing the issues. We are about to enter the thicket of hazardous substances law. Keep in mind the questions asked above, and the following: To what extent will economic markets and common law liability provide sufficient incentives to keep hazardous substances in check? Would shifting the burden of proof from an injured plaintiff to the generator of a hazardous substance correct other shortcomings you may perceive? Would other changes in the common law have to be made (e.g., in statutes of limitations, strict liability, joint and several liability, and measures of damages)? Or is a strict zero-risk regulatory requirement necessary to prevent harm from known human carcinogens? Animal carcinogens? Other hazardous substances? Should the regulatory decision depend, based on the best quantified estimate possible, on whether risks, injuries, and other costs exceed the benefits of further use of the substance in question? Should new and existing substances be handled differently? Should the burden rest on the agency to prove risk, or should an agency be able to require that a suspect substance be strictly contained or removed from commerce pending a demonstration that satisfies the agency that the substance is safe? Should compounds be examined generically by chemical family, hundreds at a time, or does prudence dictate a substance-by-substance approach? How might insurance and social welfare programs be used to combat the problem?

Simplistic solutions (e.g., "to ban risks") would impose an enormous economic burden, even if only a small percentage of the chemicals in production posed health risks. Chemicals provide massive benefits and play a huge role in the economies of the United States, other industrialized countries, and increasingly, the developing world. Chemical sales gross over $120 billion a year. The pharmaceutical, plastics, and organic and inorganic chemical manufacturing industries are based directly on the invention and use of chemicals. Other industries, such as agriculture and electronics, are highly dependent on the availability of modern chemicals. The petroleum refining, metals, and paper industries are major sources of exposure to chemical byproducts — exposures that are costly to control. Such hazardous chemicals as asbestos, vinyl chloride, and benzene have extremely diverse, high-volume, high-profit uses. Many chemicals confer health benefits as well, in the form of drugs, disinfectants, and medical products.

What use would you make of risk assessment in risk management? Does the distinction between risk assessment and risk management make sense in light of the numerous value and policy choices ("inference options") an assessor faces?

"Rational" quantitative risk management approaches would enable policymakers to permit all exposure levels for which the benefits exceed the costs. But plotting the dose-response curve on which such approaches depend is confounded by uncertainty in the data. See Dore, A Commentary on the Use of Epidemiological Evidence in Demonstrating Cause-in-Fact, 7 Harv. Envtl. L. Rev. 429 (1983), and Hall & Silbergeld, Reappraising Epidemiology: A Response to Mr. Dore, id. at 444. Consider the government's best effort to establish the dose-response relationship for the risk of saccharin-induced bladder cancer, as a result of a controversy in the late 1970s over the Food and Drug Administration's proposed ban on saccharin soft drink additives. Between 600 and 700 cancers a year were predicted, a useful number in itself for policy-making purposes, except that this figure was derived from studies that gave cancer incidence estimates ranging from 0.0007 to 3,640 cases a year — a difference of a factor of 5 million. National Academy of Sciences, Saccharin: Technical Assessment of Risks and Benefits 3-72, Table 3-8 (1978). But see Latin, The "Significance" of Toxic Health Risks: An Essay on Legal Decisionmaking under Uncertainty, 10 Ecology L.Q. 339, 371 (1982).

A NOTE ON MEASUREMENT AND DETECTION

Rapid improvement in chemical analyses for measuring and detecting substances in extremely low concentrations has revolutionized the field of risk management, much like Leeuwenhoek's powerful lenses and Galileo's telescope revolutionized the fields of microscopy and astronomy in the seventeenth century. Sensitive equipment and chemical procedures now enable researchers to detect toxicants whose presence might not even have been suspected in past years. The most frequently used methods are mass spectrometry and gas and liquid chromatography; a fully equipped test laboratory may cost $2 million and separate tests from $10,000 to $100,000. See U.S. Office of Technology Assessment, Environmental Contaminants in Food ch. 8 (1979), and Council on Environmental Quality, Tenth Annual Report 238 (1979). The new technology thus may force regulators to act, and it may soon enable them to set enforceable standards in the part-per-billion (ppb) and even the part-per-trillion (ppt) range.

The measurement of dioxins illustrates the point. For many years, one dioxin (2,3,7,8-tetrachlorodibenzo-p) has been known to be present in small quantities in Agent Orange, a herbicide used by the U.S. Army to clear jungle undergrowth during the Vietnam War. As one court put it, "it is undisputed that dioxin is the most acutely toxic substance yet synthesized by man." United States

v. Vertac, 489 F. Supp. 870, 876 (E.D. Ark. 1980). Even extremely low concentrations of dioxin caused concern, so that measurements that revealed that dioxin was present at the ppb and ppt levels in the soil around a plant where Agent Orange was manufactured led to a judicial order mandating cleanup of the site (489 F. Supp. at 876). In 1983, the discovery of dioxin residues in soils and oiled roadbeds in Missouri resulted in the complete abandonment of the small town of Times Beach and of several other areas.

Sensitive measurements enabled EPA to set the dioxin residue content standard at 1 ppb for the herbicide 2,4,5-T. An EPA scientific panel stated that the level at which dioxin had no observable effects was 1 ppt. None of this would be possible without measurement devices so sensitive as to tax one's credulity: "One expert said that the existence of one part per trillion was analogous to comparing the width of a hair to the distance between the earth and the moon" (489 F. Supp. at 881). Nevertheless, the accuracy of dioxin measurements, like that for many trace contaminants, continues to be uncertain: "The search for . . . [dioxin] in the environmental samples is probably the most difficult and thorough one ever taken" (Crummett, Measurement Near the Limit of Detection, 1979 Annals N.Y. Acad. Sci. 43, 45).

Dioxin residues might be expected to turn up at very low concentrations in the immediate vicinity of their manufacture or application. But improved measurement technology has vastly expanded the zones of risk. The evidence now suggests that small quantities of dioxins in fact are formed in many ordinary types of combustion. Scientists have detected dioxins in the ppb to the ppt range in power plant emissions, vehicle mufflers, and fireplaces — and in cigarette smoke and charcoal-broiled steaks. Bumb et al., Trace Chemistries of Fire: A Source of Chlorinated Dioxins, 210 Science 385 (1980).

Doubt that safe thresholds exist for dioxins and other trace toxicants thrusts sensitive detection methods into a controversial role in the administration of statutes that require zero-risk or low-risk regulation. Does the presence of potent substances at extremely low levels in the general environment without apparent ill effects suggest the need for a reexamination of the threshold theory? For example, dioxins appear in very small quantities in human adipose tissue, fish, and milk. Kimbrough & Houk, Effects of Chlorinated Dibenzodioxins, in Solving Hazardous Waste Problems: Learning from Dioxins (J.H. Exner, ed. 1987). While documented effects on humans include skin disease (chloracne), immune dysfunction, and neural and kidney toxicity, dioxins have been shown to cause cancer, malformation, and reproductive disorders only in laboratory animals. Environmental Protection Agency, A Cancer Risk-specific Dose Estimate for 2,3,7,8-TCDD (1988); Suskind & Hertzberg, Human Health Effects of 2,4,5-T and its Toxic Contaminants, 251 J. Am. Med. Assoc. 2372 (1984).

On occasion, regulation has worked to improve the sensitivity of measurement techniques, not vice versa, creating a new type of environmental technology-forcing. The Food, Drug, and Cosmetic Act, 21 U.S.C. §301, provides that a carcinogenic new animal drug may be approved for use in animals raised for human consumption if "no residue" of the drug can be "found" in meat products. To implement this requirement, the federal Food and Drug Administration must prescribe how sensitive the measurement method has to be to "find" residues. §512(d)(1)(H). As increasingly powerful analytic methods appeared, the FDA was pushed into a quandary: must it always prescribe the most sensitive methods? If so virtually all the drugs in question would have to be banned because the foods would contain minute drug residues that could be detected by the new analytic techniques. Or could the agency discharge its statutory obligation to specify measurement techniques by requiring that before marketing their products meat suppliers must supply measurements showing that residue levels in fact are so low that the human risk of cancer is negligible, i.e., a lifetime risk of cancer of from zero to one in a million?

First, the agency would specify a sensitivity-of-measurement approach that would allow a carcinogenic ingredient to be added to animal feed if no residues of that ingredient would be detectable by an FDA-approved analytical method that is sensitive enough to detect any level of residue representing a lifetime excess human cancer risk of more than one in a million. Then it would be up to the food producers to supply the measurements that showed that product residues did not exceed the "safe" levels. For potent carcinogens, the suppliers would obviously have to develop or locate very sensitive measurement equipment. See R. Merrill & P. Hutt, Food and Drug Law 496-506 (1980).

The FDA's use of this approach with food dyes was struck down in Public Citizen v. Young, 831 F.2d 1108 (D.C. Cir. 1987). The court relied on an "extraordinarily rigid" legislative history. The EPA nevertheless has proposed using the same de minimis approach in regulating certain pesticides used in food production. 53 Fed. Reg. 41,104 (Oct. 19, 1988).

Do you agree with the FDA and EPA sensitivity of measurement approach, which ensures that the technology of measurement is good enough for safety's sake, but not so good that it requires virtually all new carcinogenic animal drugs to be kept off the market? In view of substantial measurement error ranges (plus or minus a factor of 10, 100, or more), can a quantitative risk assessment be accurately performed for carcinogens at such low exposures and for such extreme odds (1 in 1 million)?

B.   RISK AND THE COMMON LAW

The common law offers many forms of relief to a plaintiff who can prove that the defendant has caused or is causing actual harm: damages, injunctions, and other equitable relief. But what about the plaintiff who is merely endangered and cannot yet show any actual harm? This section addresses the relief the common law offers to persons who are threatened but not yet injured by the low-probability, delayed, but potentially serious harms that hazardous substances may cause. This issue is part of the large problem of common law relief from environmental disruption in general, a subject Chapter 6 treats in detail.

VILLAGE OF WILSONVILLE v. SCA SERVICES, INC.
86 Ill. 2d 1, 426 N.E.2d 824 (1981)

[The plaintiffs sued to enjoin the operation of the defendant's chemical waste disposal site on the grounds that it presented a public nuisance and hazard. The trial court agreed, ordering the defendant to close the site, remove the wastes and the contaminated soil, and restore the site to its former condition. The appeals court affirmed (77 Ill. App. 3rd 618, 396 N.E.2d 552), as did the Illinois Supreme Court, in this opinion.]

CLARK, Justice. . . .

The defendant has operated a chemical-waste landfill since 1977. The site comprises approximately 130 acres, 90 of which are within the village limits of the plaintiff village. The remaining 40 acres are adjacent to the village. The defendant enters into agreements with generators of toxic chemical waste to haul the waste away from the generators' locations. The defendant then delivers it to the Wilsonville site, tests random samples of chemical waste, and then deposits the waste in trenches. There are seven trenches at the site. Each one is approximately 15 feet deep, 50 feet wide, and 250 to 350 feet long. Approximately 95% of the waste materials were buried in 55-gallon steel drums, and the remainder is contained in double-wall paper bags. After the materials are deposited in the trenches, uncompacted clay is placed between groups of containers and a minimum of one foot of clay is placed between the top drum and the top clay level of the trench.

The site is bordered on the east, west, and south by farmland and on the north by the village. The entire site, the village, and much of the surrounding area is located above the abandoned Superior Coal Mine No. 4, which operated from 1917 to 1954. The No. 6 seam of the mine was exploited in this area at a depth of 312 feet. The mining method used to extract coal was the room-and-panel method, whereby about 50% of the coal is left in pillars which provide some support for the earth above the mine. There was testimony at trial by Dr. Nolan Augenbaugh, chairman of the Department of Mining, Petroleum and Geological Engineering at the University of Missouri at Rolla, that pillar failure can occur in any mine where there is a readjustment of stress. . . .

. . . There are still 73 water wells in the village, some of which are used to water gardens or wash cars. At least one well is used to water pets, and another is used for drinking water. . . .

The materials deposited at the site include polychlorinated biphenyls (PCBs), a neurotoxic, possibly carcinogenic chemical which it has been illegal to produce in this country since 1979. Due to the extensive use of PCBs in electrical equipment such as transformers, capacitors, and heat-transfer systems, and in hydraulic systems, any PCBs that were produced legally now have to be disposed of when they are no longer in use. PCBs have been stored at the site in liquid, solid and semi-solid form. Additionally, there are a number of now-empty drums which had once contained PCBs, which are also buried at the site. Other materials buried at the site in large quantities are solid cyanide, a substance known as $C_{5, 6}$, paint sludge, asbestos, pesticides, mercury, and arsenic. Considerable evidence was adduced to show that these and other substances deposited at the site are extremely toxic to human beings. Some of the adverse reactions which could result from exposure to these materials are pulmonary diseases, cancer, brain damage, and birth defects.

The general geologic profile of the site shows a surface layer of about 10 feet of loess (wind-blown silt and clay material), under which lies 40 to 65 feet of glacial till. In the till material there is a thin sand layer of a few inches to approximately two feet. Some ground water has been found in the sand layer. All trenches dug at the site have between 10 to 15 feet of glacial till below them. The glacial till is reported to be very dense and is not very permeable. Thus liquids do not travel through it quickly. . . .

[The court then examined at length the testimony presented by a parade of expert witnesses for both sides in the 104-day trial. It found no reason to disturb the findings of the trial court that some chemical wastes at the site had spilled from the metal drums and paper bags in which they were transported to the site, that explosions and fires might result from the interaction of chemicals there, that the chemicals might overflow the trenches at the site or migrate down to groundwater becuase of the permeable nature of the soil, and that infiltration into groundwater and migration of wastes could be hastened by subsidence in the abandoned mine beneath the site. The defendant relied particularly on the testimony of Raymond Harbison, a pharmacology professor at Vanderbilt University and consultant to the federal EPA, who offered the opinion that the site was the most advanced scientific landfill in the country and that the "absolute confinement" of the materials to the site rendered the interaction of the chemicals an impossibility, but the Illinois Supreme Court would not fault the trial court for discounting Harbison's testimony in the light of the other evidence presented.]

The trial court herein concluded that defendant's chemical-waste-disposal site constitutes both a private and a public nuisance. Professor Prosser has defined a private nuisance as "a civil wrong, based on a disturbance of rights in land" (Prosser, Torts sec. 86, at 572 (4th ed. 1971)), and a public nuisance as "an act or omission 'which obstructs or causes inconvenience or damage to the public in the exercise of rights common to all Her Majesty's subjects.'" (Prosser, Torts sec. 88, at 583 (4th ed. 1971) quoting, Stephen, General View of the Criminal Law of England 105 (1890)). . . . Prosser has also quoted the following, more precise definition of a public nuisance: "'A common or public nuisance is the doing of or the failure to do something that injuriously affects the safety, health or morals of the public, or works some substantial annoyance, inconvenience or injury to the public.'" (Prosser, Torts sec. 88, at 583 n.29 (4th ed. 1971), quoting Commonwealth v. South Covington & Cincinnati Street Ry. Co. (1918), 181 Ky. 459, 463, 205 S.W. 581, 583.) It is generally conceded that a nuisance is remediable by injunction or a suit for damages. . . .

[The court then found that Illinois nuisance law requires that before the trial court can find that a prospective nuisance exists, it must balance the social utility of the defendant's activity against the plaintiffs' right to use their property without suffering deleterious effects. The trial court did in fact conduct such a balancing process here, contrary to the defendant's assertions.] The defendant's next contention is that the courts below were in error when they failed to require a showing of a substantial risk of certain and extreme future harm before enjoining operation of the defendant's site. We deem it necessary to explain that a *prospective* nuisance is a fit candidate for injunctive relief. Prosser states:

> Both public and private nuisances require some substantial interference with the interest involved. Since nuisance is a common subject of equity jurisdiction, the damage against which an injunction is asked is often merely threatened or potential; but even in such cases, there must be at least a threat of a substantial invasion of the plaintiff's interests.

(Prosser, Torts sec. 87, at 577 (4th ed. 1971).) The defendant does not dispute this proposition; it does, however, argue that the trial court did not follow the proper standard for determining when a prospective nuisance may be enjoined. The defendant argues that the proper standard to be used is that an injunction is proper only if there is a "dangerous probability" that the threatened or potential injury will occur. (See Restatement (Second) of Torts sec. 933(1), at 561, comment b (1979).) The defendant further argues that the appellate court looked only at the potential consequences of not enjoining the operation of the site as a nuisance and not at the likelihood of whether harm would occur. The defendant assigns error on this basis.

We agree with the defendant's statement of the law, but not with its urged application to the facts of this case. Again, Professor Prosser has offered a concise commentary. He has stated that

> One distinguishing feature of equitable relief is that it may be granted upon the threat of harm which has not yet occurred. The defendant may be restrained from entering upon an activity where it is highly probable that it will lead to a nuisance, although if the possibility is merely uncertain or contingent he may be left to his remedy after the nuisance has occurred.

(Prosser, Torts sec. 90, at 603 (4th ed. 1971).) This view is in accord with Illinois law. (. . . Fink v. Board of Trustees (1966), 71 Ill. App. 2d 276, 281-82, 218 N.E.2d 240). In *Fink* the plaintiff sought to enjoin construction of a dam and also the discharge of sewage effluent in a watercourse which flowed past plaintiffs' property. Construction of the dam was not enjoined, but the discharge of effluent was prospectively enjoined. The court stated:

> While, as a general proposition, an injunction will be granted only to restrain an actual, existing nuisance, a court of equity may enjoin a threatened or anticipated nuisance, where it clearly appears that a nuisance will necessarily result from the contemplated act or thing which it is sought to enjoin. This is particularly true where the proof shows that the apprehension of material injury is well grounded upon a state of facts from which it appears that the danger is real and immediate. While care should be used in granting injunctions to avoid prospective injuries, there is no requirement that the court must wait until the injury occurs before granting relief.

(71 Ill. App. 2d 226, 281-82, 218 N.E.2d 240.) We agree.

In this case there can be no doubt but that it is highly probable that the chemical-waste-disposal site will bring about a substantial injury. Without again reviewing the extensive evidence adduced at trial, we think it is sufficiently clear that it is highly probable that the instant site will constitute a public nuisance if, through either an explosive interaction, migration, subsidence, or the "bathtub effect," the highly toxic chemical wastes deposited at the site escape and contaminate the air, water, or ground around the site. That such an event will occur was positively attested to by several expert witnesses. A court does not have to wait for it to happen before it can enjoin such a result. Additionally, the fact is that the condition of a nuisance is already present at the site due to the location of the site and the manner in which it has been operated. Thus, it is only the damage which is prospective. Under these circumstances, if a court can prevent any damage from occurring, it should do so.

The defendant next asserts that error occurred in the courts below when they failed to defer to the IEPA and the USEPA, as well as when they failed to give weight to the permits issued by the IEPA. This assertion has no merit, however, because the data relied upon by the IEPA in deciding to issue a permit to the defendant were data collected by the defendant, data which have been proved at trial to be inaccurate. In particular, defendant's experts concluded that any subsidence at the site would be negligible. The IEPA (as well as the USEPA) adopted this inaccurate conclusion in deciding to issue a permit to the defendant. . . .

The next issue we consider is whether the trial court erroneously granted a permanent injunction. The defendant argues first that the courts below granted injunctive relief without proof that the alleged injury is both substantial and certain to occur. We have already addressed this question in discussing whether relief may be granted for a prospective nuisance. We will not unduly prolong this already lengthy opinion with duplicate discussion. The second argument raised is that the courts below did not balance the equities in deciding to enjoin the defendant from continuing to operate the waste-disposal site. Defendant cites Harrison v. Indiana Auto Shredders Co. (7th Cir. 1975), 528 F.2d 1107, for the proposition that the court must balance the relative harm and benefit to the plaintiff and defendant before a court may enjoin a nuisance. (528 F.2d 1107, 1109.) . . .

In *Harrison*, an auto shredder operated its business in a residential neighborhood in Indianapolis. There was considerable testimony from nonexperts that the shredder created too much noise, vibration, and air pollution in the forms of dust and debris. The defendant shredder company defended on the ground that while difficulties in starting up the operation had occurred, it had taken steps, and would do whatever further was necessary, to abate the nuisance. Several experts testified that the noise, vibration, and pollution were well within permissible State and local standards. After a 30-day trial, the court issued a permanent injunction ordering the shredder to cease operations and awarded permanent and punitive damages to the plaintiffs for the diminution in value of their property. The trial court conceded that the shredder performed a "very real social function" in disposing of and recycling old automobiles, but concluded that the machine ought to be somewhere else. (528 F.2d 1107, 1119.) The court of appeals agreed that the shredder's effect upon the quality of life in the neighborhood entitled the plaintiffs to some form of equitable relief and damages. The court did not, however, view the complete cessation of operations as appropriate to the facts presented. The court stated:

> Reasonableness is the standard by which the court should fashion its relief in ordinary nuisance cases, . . . and reasonableness is also the appropriate standard for relief from environmental nuisance. Ordinarily a permanent injunction will not lie unless (1) either the polluter seriously and imminently threatens the public health or (2) he causes non-health injuries that are substantial and the business cannot be operated to avoid the injuries apprehended. Thus the particular situation facts of each pollution nuisance case will determine whether a permanent injunction should be issued.

(528 F.2d 1107, 1123.) The court concluded in *Harrison* that since the defendant was not in violation of any relevant zoning standards, and since the shredder did not pose an imminent hazard to the public health, the defendant should not be prevented from continuing to operate. The court then ordered that the defendant be permitted a reasonable time to "launder its objectionable features." 528 F.2d 1107, 1125.

This case is readily distinguishable for the reason that the gist of this case is that the defendant is engaged in an extremely hazardous undertaking at an unsuitable location, which seriously and imminently poses a threat to the public health. We are acutely aware that the service provided by the defendant is a valuable and necessary one. We also know that it is preferable to have chemical-waste-disposal sites than to have illegal dumping in rivers, streams, and deserted areas. But a site such as defendant's, if it is to do the job it is intended to do, must be located in a secure place, where it will pose no threat to health or life, now, or in the future. This site was intended to be a *permanent* disposal site for the deposit of extremely hazardous chemical-waste materials. Yet this site is located above an abandoned tunneled mine where subsidence is occurring several years ahead of when it was anticipated. Also, the permeability-coefficient samples taken by defendant's experts, though not conclusive alone, indicate that the soil is more permeable at the site than expected. Moreover, the spillage, odors, and dust caused by the presence of the disposal site indicate why it was inadvisable to locate the site so near the plaintiff village.

Therefore, we conclude that in fashioning relief in this case the trial court did balance relative hardship to be caused to the plaintiffs and defendant, and did fashion reasonable relief when it ordered the exhumation of all material from the site and the reclamation of the surrounding area. The instant site is akin to Mr. Justice Sutherland's observation that "Nuisance may be merely a right thing in a wrong place — like a pig in the parlor instead of the barnyard." Village of Euclid v. Ambler Realty Co. (1926), 272 U.S. 365, 388.

We are also cognizant of amicus USEPA's suggestion in its brief and affidavits filed with the appellate court which urge that we remand to the circuit court so that alternatives to closure of the site and exhumation of the waste materials may be considered. The USEPA states:

> Heavy equipment may damage drums, releasing wastes and possibly causing gaseous emissions, fires, and explosions. Repackaging and transporting damaged drums also risks releasing wastes. Workers performing the exhumation face dangers from contact with or inhalation of wastes; these risks cannot be completely eliminated with protective clothing and breathing apparatus. Nearby residents may also be endangered.

It is ironic that the host of horribles mentioned by the USEPA in support of keeping the site open includes some of the same hazards which the plaintiffs have raised as reasons in favor of closing the site.

The USEPA continues that while it is not suggesting a specific alternative remedy to closure, possible alternative remedies exist:

> A proper cap of low permeability can ensure that little or no rain water can infiltrate the site, and thus that little leachate will be formed. Leachate-collection sumps can also be installed to remove whatever leachate is formed. Ground water monitoring can generally detect any migration of waste constituents, and counterpumping of contaminated ground water (or other measures) can protect against further migration.

We note, however, that the USEPA does not suggest how the location of the disposal site above an abandoned tunneled mine and the effects of subsidence can be overcome. . . .

Affirmed and remanded.

RYAN, Justice, concurring. . . .

. . . I am concerned that the holding of *Fink* quoted by the majority, (86 Ill.2d at 26, 426 N.E.2d at 836), may be an unnecessarily narrow view of the test for enjoining prospective tortious conduct in general. . . . I believe that there are situations where the harm that is potential is so devastating that equity should afford relief even though the possibility of the harmful result occurring is uncertain or contingent. The Restatement's position applicable to preventative injunctive relief in general is that "[t]he more serious the impending harm, the less justification there is for taking the chances that are involved in pronouncing the harm too remote." (Restatement (Second) of Torts sec. 933, at 561, comment b (1979).) If the harm that may result is severe, a lesser possibility of it occurring should be required to support injunctive relief. Conversely, if the potential harm is less severe, a greater possibility that it will happen should be required. Also, in the balancing of competing interests, a court may find a situation where the potential harm is such that a plaintiff will be left to his remedy at law if the possibility of it occurring is slight. This balancing test allows the court to consider a wider range of factors and avoids the anomalous result possible under a more restrictive alternative where a person engaged in an ultrahazardous activity with potentially catastrophic results would be allowed to continue until he has driven an entire community to the brink of certain disaster. A court of equity need not wait so long to provide relief.

Although the "dangerous probability" test has certainly been met in this case, I would be willing to enjoin the activity on a showing of probability of occurrence substantially less than that which the facts presented to this court reveal, due to the extremely hazardous nature of the chemicals being dumped and the potentially catastrophic results.

NOTES AND QUESTIONS

1. To obtain injunctive relief in a nuisance action, the plaintiff typically must make at least these three showings: (1) that a tort has been committed or one is threatened, (2) that an adequate remedy is not otherwise available (e.g., damages), and (3) that the balance of convenience or social utility, assessed in the light of the overall public interest, favors the injunction. *Wilsonville* addressed all three, but the second deserves closer attention. An oft-cited student note states:

> [To obtain an injunction] . . . the plaintiff must show that there is not an adequate remedy at law. It is generally accepted that the legal remedy is not adequate if the plaintiff will suffer imminent irreparable injury of a substantial nature unless he is protected by the injunction's restraining effect. Irreparable harm is, inter alia, damage which, from the nature of the act or from the circumstances of the parties, cannot be adequately compensated for or for which there exists no certain pecuniary standard for measurement. . . .
>
> The imminence doctrine consists of two requirements, both of which act to limit the granting of an injunction to abate an anticipated nuisance. First, there must be a threat that harm will occur in the immediate future. Second, it is generally stated that equity will not interfere if the thing that is sought to be restrained is not a nuisance per se and will not necessarily become a nuisance, depending on the use, manner of operation or other circumstances. Unfortunately, there is considerable disagreement among the courts as to the required degree of certainty that the anticipated harm will result. Although this makes generalization difficult, it would appear that as a majority rule the substance of this second requirement is that in order for the threatened harm, and hence the nuisance, to be imminent, one must establish that the anticipated harm is "practically certain" to result from the act which he seeks to enjoin. [Note, Imminent Irreparable Injury: A Need for Reform, 45 S. Cal. L. Rev. 1025, 1030-1032 (1972).]

Does the *Wilsonville* court aply this version of the black-letter law? Which is the sounder test of the power to issue injunctions to enjoin risky hazardous waste disposal practices — the traditional rule that the court applies and the Restatement (Second) of Torts apparently endorses (§933), or the approach of Judge Ryan's concurring opinion? Why should courts stop short of enjoining low-probability, delayed harm? Does economist Talbot Page's risk "seesaw" (see p. 495 *supra*) state a better standard for injunctions than the *Wilsonville* majority? The dissent? Apply the majority's traditional approach and the appellate court approach to the following: (1) an ax poised to fall on your wrist, (2) exposure to smallpox, and (3) exposure to asbestos dust.

The traditional view was restated in *Wilsonville*, but nevertheless one of the editors of this casebook believes that the *Wilsonville* court's "summary of the evidence and the law leaves little doubt that courts now have more discretion to resolve the uncertainty issue in the public's favor when hazardous wastes are involved" (Tarlock, Anywhere but Here: An Introduction to State Control of Hazardous Waste Facility Location, 2 U.C.L.A.J. Envtl. L. & Poly. 1, 21 (1982)). Do you agree? Compare Green v. Castle Concrete Co., 181 Colo. 309, 509 P.2d 588 (Colo. 1973) (new limestone quarry held not to be a nuisance because actual substantial harm was still uncertain).

2. Is it significant that the site in *Wilsonville* was fully authorized under state and federal law? In Green v. Castle Concrete Co., *supra*, the quarry could not be held to be a public nuisance, in the court's opinion, because the site was zoned for quarrying and the facility was in compliance with other state regulations. Whether or not federal and Illinois agencies were factually correct about the Wilsonville site, it could be argued that state and federal statutes had already preempted the issue of whether the site could continue to operate and had committed it to technical agency expertise. But the court never mentions preemption. Why? For a discussion of whether federal pollution statutes preempt common law remedies, see p. 752 *infra*. If common law recovery is not preempted, should not the court at least defer to the state agency under the doctrine of primary jurisdiction?

3. Historically, abatement of a public nuisance was an action at law. Only under unusual circumstances — for example, when the remedy of abatement at law by indictment was too slow to prevent an imminent hazard — would courts of equity, sitting without a jury, give relief for a public nuisance. Relief was to be given in cases in which "there was imminent danger of irreparable mischief before the tardiness of the law could reach it" (City of Georgetown v. Alexandria Canal Co., 37 U.S. 91, 98 (1838)). The basic rule was that a court of equity had no jurisdiction over crimes, and public nuisances were normally prosecuted as crimes. The reluctance of the Chancellor to intervene was predicated on the absence of a jury (2 Story's Equity Jurisprudence §§1251, 1252 (14th ed., 1918)). When evidence of injury to the public was conflicting or doubtful, equity would not intervene but would leave the issue of fact to trial by jury. Should courts show a similar reluctance today? See Mugler v. Kansas, 123 U.S. 623, 673 (1887), and Chapter 6, at p. 745.

4. Why did the plaintiffs win the battle of the experts? The witnesses for federal and state governments were as well or better qualified than the plaintiffs' witnesses. Moreover, the Wilsonville site had been heralded as one of the most modern, safest chemical waste disposal facilities in the country, a site to which unsafely disposed-of wastes that had been exhumed elsewhere should be sent. The fully permitted site had been under constant federal and state surveillance since its inception. The Illinois Attorney General intervened on the plaintiffs' side (to the embarrassment of the Illinois EPA) only after local groups made angry entreaties — and stoned trucks delivering PCB wastes to Wilsonville from

a waste site cleanup operation conducted by the U.S. Coast Guard in nearby Missouri.

Do you think the *Wilsonville* case presented any particularly difficult problems of proof? What problems of proof might have arisen if the plaintiffs had sought damages for injuries already caused? We will address the problem of proof in common law actions to prevent environmental disruption in Chapter 6. Regulation of hazardous waste disposal facilities is addressed in this chapter.

5. In Sterling v. Velsicol Corp., 855 F.2d 1188 (6th Cir. 1988), plaintiffs established defendant's liability for a wide variety of nervous, respiratory, digestive, dermal, liver, and optic injuries sustained as a result of drinking and using wellwater contaminated by eleven organic chemical toxicants, including benzene and carbon tetrachloride. The chemicals had contaminated the groundwater because of defendant's negligent operation of a nearby hazardous waste disposal site. Unlike the plaintiff in *Wilsonville*, the plaintiffs in *Sterling* had already sustained a variety of personal injuries. Thus the issue was measure of damages, and as to both type and extent of injury, the plaintiffs found rough going in the appeals court. The court stated that to recover money damages plaintiffs must show to "a reasonable medical certainty" that the contaminated water caused bodily harm. Damages may not be "speculative or conjectural" and may not be based on a mere "probability" or "likelihood," especially for diseases which may be "the product of a variety of causes and inflict society at random, often with no known specific origin." Id. at 1200. How does this test compare to the test in *Wilsonville?*

While finding proximate causation, the court applied the reasonable medical certainty test to reduce or deny a wide variety of money damages allowed by the district court. Awards for injuries already incurred, including kidney cancer, liver damage, nervous system impairment, and optic atrophy, were remanded for reduction. The mere risk of cancer and kidney and liver diseases was held noncompensable. The risk here was 25-30 percent, not the required 50-plus percent (i.e., "more probable than not"). Fear of increased risk of cancer was "clearly" a present injury and compensable, but only for "reasonable" fear. The district court awards were drastically reduced (e.g., from $250,000 to $18,000 for plaintiff Johnson). Damages for immune system impairment and learning disorders were denied entirely, because no generally accepted scientific theory of causation exists for these injuries. The court denied damage awards for post-traumatic stress disorder, holding that drinking the contaminated water was not sufficiently stressful and that no recurring fear existed. The awards for reduced property values did survive, however. Why was the injunction in *Wilsonville* relatively easy to obtain, in comparison to the difficulties the plaintiffs in *Sterling* encountered with the measure of damages for actual and future injury to human health? Does threat to property values seem more important than that to human health?

6. *Wilsonville* could not have been decided in Utah. Adopting a model state statute drafted for the Chemical Manufacturers Association by one of the editors of this casebook, Utah alone has expressly foreclosed its courts from enjoining the construction or operation of a hazardous waste disposal facility that conforms to the state's hazardous waste facility siting statute. Under the Utah

statute, landowners or users are limited to seeking two types of relief: (1) compensation in an inverse condemnation action for loss of property value or use at the time a facility is constructed and (2) the incremental damages caused by a subsequent "modification" in the approved design or operation of the facility (Utah Code Ann. §26-14a-7). The Utah statute is unclear about whether damages for personal injury may be recovered in the latter type of action. Does this statute unconstitutionally foreclose potential plaintiffs' right to bring an action at common law? See Duke Power Co. v. Carolina Environmental Study Group, 438 U.S. 59 (1978); San Diego Gas & Electric Co. v. City of San Diego, 450 U.S. 621 (1981); and First English Evangelical Lutheran Church of Glendale v. County of Los Angeles, 107 S. Ct. 2378 (1987), which holds that the Constitution allows the recovery of damages for temporary takings.

C.   LEGISLATIVE AND ADMINISTRATIVE DETERMINATIONS OF RISK

Legislation may go far beyond the common law in authorizing the abatement of dangers posed by hazardous substances. A state or federal enactment must be able to survive constitutional scrutiny — occasionally environmental statutes encounter constitutional objections — but the courts generally have affirmed that state and federal legislatures have vast leeway to pursue environmental objectives. Of course, Congress must act under an enumerated power (for environmental legislation, almost invariably the commerce clause) and a state legislature under its police powers. Regulatory statutes may have to undergo judicial scrutiny to assure the courts that a minimum rational nexus exists between the perceived harm and its statutory cure. Nor may such measures work a confiscatory taking without due process compensation, and strict environmental statutes occasionally succumb to this attack. See Soper, The Constitutional Framework of Enviromental Law, in Federal Environmental Law 20 (E. Dolgin & T. Guilbert eds. 1974).

A more challenging issue concerns just how far Congress intended to leave common law standards behind when it forged ahead with legislation designed to control speculative risks to health and the environment. The issue was raised in two landmark cases decided one year apart by two federal circuit courts of appeals. In each case, brief federal statutes authorized the abatement of conditions that "endangered" the public health. In each, the strict common law approach denying abatement of risks was first embraced by the majority of a three-judge panel and then rejected on fuller consideration en banc. The opinion of the Eighth Circuit in United States v. Reserve Mining Co. is excerpted here. The District of Columbia Circuit decision in Ethyl Corp. v. EPA, 541 F.2d 1 (D.C. Cir. 1976), no less a landmark, is discussed in the notes that follow the Reserve Mining excerpt.

Reserve Mining is one of the key court decisions that shaped the development of environmental law. It contains all of the elements of high drama — allegations of suppressed government research reports, the sudden appearance of startling new evidence, intergovernmental and intercourt rivalries, bureaucratic ineptitude, a classic confrontation between "good" and "bad" science, pressure from dedicated citizen activists, and the usual sharply focused issues pitting economic development against environmental quality. See R. Bartlett, The Reserve Mining Controversy: Science, Technology, and Environmental Quality (1980).

The Reserve Mining dispute began far afield from health risk regulation. Prior to the allegation that the mine tailings (the crushed rock residue discarded in the mining process) that Reserve discharged into Lake Superior contained cancer-causing fibers, administrative and judicial proceedings focused on the "green water" phenomenon, which the tailings discharge caused. Turbid water, the lake's protectors argued, impaired the aesthetic quality of a priceless natural resource, and the resultant algal growth threatened to destroy the fragile lake ecosystem, which was dependent to a critical extent on the extreme clarity and cold temperature of its waters. In the first proceeding, a federally initiated interstate conference, the evidence against Reserve seemed weak because aesthetic impairment was not generally perceived as a basis for shutting down a vital industry, and the ecological evidence on issues such as impairment of fish species was largely inferential and circumstantial. Some experts seemed to suggest that the lake's problems were attributable to a natural process of aging (The Reserve Mining Controversy: Science, Technology, and Environmental Quality, *supra*, at 77).

Between 1968 and 1972, pressure for state or federal action increased, but the scientific evidence remained inadequate to sustain a legal remedy. The first judicial proceeding, Reserve Mining Co. v. Minnesota Pollution Control Agency, 2 Envt. Rep. Cas. (BNA) 1135 (Lake Cty., Minn., Dist. Ct. 1970), *aff'd in part, rev'd in part*, 294 Minn. 300, 200 N.W.2d 142 (1972), grew out of Reserve's challenge to the state of Minnesota's compliance with a requirement of the Department of Interior that state water quality standards for interstate waters contain an anti-degradation clause. Minnesota raised as an affirmative defense the allegation that Reserve was causing a public nuisance and asked for a reasonable abatement schedule. The trial judge held (and Minnesota conceded) that the anti-degradation clause applied only to *new* discharges. The court also said that "with respect to possible future 'potential contamination' the evidence is in such conflict that the court would have to indulge in speculation in order to make a finding as to such future possibility. The court is precluded under law from indulging in such speculation" (2 Envt. Rep. Cas. (BNA) at 1141). The court refused to order an immediate cessation of Reserve's operations, but it did accept scientific testimony that the continuation of the discharge, "if continued over a long period of time, might result in the material deterioration of the water quality of Lake Superior" (id.).

This litigation threw the matter back to negotiations between Reserve and the state of Minnesota. The remedial issue initially centered on an offer by Reserve to inject the tailings by pipe deep into the lake, creating a reef 150 feet below its surface. Environmentalists, the Minnesota Pollution Control Agency, and the state of Wisconsin objected to the deep pipe plan and proposed the remedy that ultimately was adopted — disposal on land. As the federal and state governments hardened their opposition to any use of the lake as a waste sink, Reserve hardened its objections to the on-land proposals on cost grounds. Compromise and negotiation became impossible, and the issue moved to the federal courts.

At this point, the case for ending the discharges seemed destined to fail. Only the nondegradation policy, uncertain ecological impairment, and aesthetic blight favored the plaintiffs. In late 1972, however, a remarkable thing happened to change the course of the plaintiffs' case — and the course of environmental law. By chance, a professor of geology from the University of Wisconsin at Superior remarked to the president of the Save Lake Superior Association that magnified photographs of the chemical structure of minerals contained in Reserve's ore showed that they bore a resemblance to asbestos fibers. This remark changed the nature of the case overnight. Concern over the subtle, long-term changes in the lake's ecosystem was replaced by a single and powerful public health concern: the risk that discharges of asbestiform taconite fibers might cause cancer. Thus cancer became a proxy for the other environmental insults Lake Superior had received, and the nature of the proof offered changed dramatically. Like an environmental Jarndyce v. Jarndyce (the endless probate case in Dickens's novel, Bleak House), controversies continue today over Reserve's water and air discharges.

RESERVE MINING CO. v. EPA
514 F.2d 492 (8th Cir. 1975) (en banc)

BRIGHT, Circuit Judge. . . .

I.   Introduction

A.   SUMMARY OF CONTROVERSY

In 1947, Reserve Mining Company (Reserve), then contemplating a venture in which it would mine low-grade iron ore ("taconite") present in Minnesota's Mesabi Iron Range and process the ore into iron-rich pellets at facilities bordering on Lake Superior, received a permit from the State of Minnesota to discharge the wastes (called "tailings") from its processing operations into the lake.

Reserve commenced the processing of taconite ore in Silver Bay, Minnesota, in 1955, and that operation continues today. Taconite mined near Babbitt, Minnesota, is shipped by rail some 47 miles to the Silver Bay "beneficiating" plant where it is concentrated into pellets containing some 65 percent iron ore. The process involves crushing the taconite into fine granules, separating out the metallic iron with huge magnets, and flushing the residual tailings into Lake Superior. The tailings enter the lake as a slurry of approximately 1.5 percent solids. The slurry acts as a heavy density current bearing the bulk of the suspended particles to the lake bottom. In this manner, approximately 67,000 tons of tailings are discharged daily.

The states and the United States commenced efforts to procure abatement of these discharges as early as mid-1969. These efforts, however, produced only an unsuccessful series of administrative conferences and unsuccessful state court proceedings. The instant litigation commenced on February 2, 1972, when the United States — joined eventually by the States of Minnesota, Wisconsin, and Michigan and by various environmental groups — filed a complaint alleging that Reserve's discharge of tailings into Lake Superior violated §407 of the Rivers and Harbors Act of 1889 (33 U.S.C. §401 et seq. (1970)), §1160 of the pre-1972 Federal Water Pollution Control Act (FWPCA) (33 U.S.C. §1151 et seq. (1970)), and the federal common law of public nuisance.

Until June 8, 1973, the case was essentially a water pollution abatement case, but on that date the focus of the controversy shifted to the public health impact of the tailings discharge and Reserve's emissions into the ambient air. Arguing the health issue in the district court, plaintiffs maintained that the taconite ore mined by Reserve contained an asbestiform variety of the amphibole mineral cummingtonite-grunerite, and that the processing of the ore resulted in the discharge into the air and water of mineral fibers substantially identical and in some instances identical to amosite asbestos. This contention raised an immediate health issue, since inhalation of asbestos at occupational levels of exposure is associated with an increased incidence of various forms of cancer.

Although it is undisputed that Reserve discharges significant amounts of waste tailings into Lake Superior and dust into the Silver Bay air, the parties vigorously contest the precise physical properties of the discharge, their biological effects, and, with respect to the water discharge, the issue of whether a significant proportion of the discharge, instead of flowing to the lake bottom with the density current, disperses throughout the lake. Plaintiffs attempted to show that a substantial amount of the fibers discharged by Reserve could be classified as amosite asbestos, and that these fibers could be traced in the ambient air of Silver Bay and surrounding communities and in the drinking water of Duluth and other communities drawing water from the lake. Reserve countered that its cummingtonite-grunerite does not have a fibrous form and is otherwise distinguishable from amosite asbestos. It further maintained that the discharges do not pose any cognizable hazard to health and that, in any event, with respect to the discharge into water, the tailings largely settle to the bottom of the lake in the "great trough" area as initially planned.

The evidence presented on these points was extensive and complex. Hearings on a motion for a preliminary injunction were consolidated with the trial on the merits and during the nine-month period of 139 days of trial, the trial court heard more than 100 witnesses and received over 1,600 exhibits. . . .

On April 20, 1974, the district court entered an order closing Reserve's Silver Bay facility. In an abbreviated memorandum opinion, the court held that Reserve's water discharge violated federal water pollution laws and that its air emissions violated state air pollution regulations, and that both the air and water discharges constituted common law nuisances. The court's decision, in part, rested on these core findings:

> The discharge into the air substantially endangers the health of the people of Silver Bay and surrounding communities as far away as the eastern shore in Wisconsin.
>
> The discharge into the water substantially endangers the health of people who procure their drinking water from the western arm of Lake Superior including the communities of Beaver Bay, Two Harbors, Cloquet, Duluth [Minnesota], and Superior, Wisconsin. [380 F. Supp. at 16.]

The district court issued an extensive supplemental memorandum on May 11, 1974,[12] expanding on its earlier findings of fact and conclusions of law. . . . [A] panel of this court stayed the injunction[13] and subsequently requested the district court to fully dispose of the litigation and enter final judgment. This court, sitting en banc, heard the merits of several consolidated appeals at the December 1974 session. . . .

The initial, crucial question for our evaluation and resolution focuses upon the alleged hazard to public health attributable to Reserve's discharges into the air and water. . . .

[In deciding to stay the district court's injunction, we] thought one proposition evident: "[A]lthough Reserve's discharges represent a possible medical danger, they have not in this case proven to amount to a health hazard. The discharges may or may not result in detrimental health effects, but, for the present, that is simply unknown." [498 F. 2d. at 1082.]

On the basis of the foregoing we forecast that Reserve would likely prevail on the merits of the health issue. We limited this forecast to the single issue before us whether Reserve's plant should be closed immediately because of a "substantial danger" to health. . . .

As will be evident from the discussion that follows, we adhere to our preliminary assessment that the evidence is insufficient to support the kind of demonstrable danger to the public health that would justify the immediate closing of Reserve's operations. We now address the basic question of whether the discharges pose any risk to public health and, if so, whether the risk is one which is legally cognizable. This inquiry demands separate attention to the discharge into the air of Silver Bay and the discharge into Lake Superior.

12.   United States v. Reserve Mining Co., 380 F. Supp. 11, 21 (D. Minn. 1974).
13.   Reserve Mining Co. v. United States, 498 F.2d 1073 (8th Cir. 1974).

II.   Health Issue

A.   The Discharge into Air

As we noted in our stay opinion, much of the scientific knowledge regarding asbestos disease pathology derives from epidemiological studies of asbestos workers occupationally exposed to and inhaling high levels of asbestos dust. Studies of workers naturally exposed to asbestos dust have shown "excess" cancer deaths[21] and a significant incidence of asbestosis.[22] The principal excess cancers are cancer of the lung, the pleura (mesothelioma) and gastrointestinal tract ("gi" cancer). . . .

Several principles of asbestos-related disease pathology emerge from these occupational studies. One principle relates to the so-called 20-year rule, meaning that there is a latent period of cancer development of at least 20 years. Another basic principle is the importance of initial exposure, demonstrated by significant increases in the incidence of cancer even among asbestos manufacturing workers employed for less than three months (although the incidence of disease does increase upon longer exposure). Finally, these studies indicate that threshold values and dose response relationships, although probably operative with respect to asbestos-induced cancer, are not quantifiable on the basis of existing data.

Additionally, some studies implicate asbestos as a possible pathogenic agent in circumstances of exposure less severe than occupational levels. For example, several studies indicate that mesothelioma, a rare but particularly lethal cancer frequently associated with asbestos exposure, has been found in persons experiencing a low level of asbestos exposure.[26] Although Dr. Selikoff acknowledged that these studies of lower-level exposure involve certain methodological difficulties and rest "on much less firm ground" than the occupational studies, he expressed the opinion that they should be considered in the assessment of risks posed by an asbestos discharge.

---

21.   "Excess" cancer deaths refers to an incidence of *observed* cancer deaths among a segment of the population exposed to a certain agent greater than that *expected* from a general population not similarly exposed. The expected incidence of cancer is usually determined by reference to national cancer statistics.

22.   Asbestosis, a respiratory disease, is a diffuse scarring of the lung resulting from the inhalation of asbestos dust.

26.   Dr. Selikoff described some of this research. A study of mesothelioma victims in the northwestern portion of Cape Province, South Africa, in an area where there are many crocidolite asbestos mines and mills, found that in approximately one-half the deaths the only asbestos exposure was that resulting from residence in an area where there was a mine or mill. A study of mesothelioma victims in Hamburg, Germany, showed rates of mesothelioma of nine per ten thousand and one per ten thousand in two districts which had an asbestos factory, and no occurrence of the disease in the one district without such a factory. A study of 76 cases of mesothelioma drawn from the files of a London hospital showed that, of 45 victims who had not worked with asbestos, nine had simply lived in the household of an asbestos worker, 11 had lived within one-half mile of an asbestos plant. Finally, a study of 42 mesothelioma victims drawn from the files of the Pennsylvania Department of Health revealed that, of 22 victims who had not been occupationally exposed, three had lived in the household of an asbestos worker and eight had lived within one-half mile of an asbestos plant. . . .

At issue in the present case is the similarity of the circumstances of Rserve's discharge into the air to those cirumstances known to result in asbestos-related disease. This inquiry may be divided into two stages: first, circumstances relating to the nature of the discharge and, second, circumstances relating to the level of the discharge (and resulting level of exposure).

1.   THE NATURE OF THE DISCHARGE

The comparability of the nature of Reserve's discharge to the nature of the discharge in known disease situations raises two principal questions. The first is whether the discharged fibers are identical or substantially identical to fibers known to cause disease; the second is whether the length of the fibers discharged is a relevant factor in assessing pathogenic effect. The district court found that Reserve's discharge includes known pathogenic fibers and that a lower risk to health could not be assigned to this discharge for reasons of fiber length.

On the first question — the issue of the identity of the fibers — the argument focuses on whether the ore mined by Reserve contains (and yields wastes during processing consistent with) amosite asbestos. The inquiry is critical because studies demonstrate that amosite, at least in occupational settings, may serve as a carcinogenic (cancer-producing) agent. . . .

The trial court heard extensive evidence as to the chemistry, crystallography and morphology of the cummingtonite-grunerite present in the mined ore. This evidence demonstrated that, at the level of the individual fiber, a portion of Reserve's cummingtonite-grunerite cannot be meaningfully distinguished from amosite asbestos. . . .

The second question, that of fiber length, reflects a current dispute among scientists as to whether "short" fibers (i.e., fibers less than five microns in length) have any pathogenic effect. Most of the fibers detected in Reserve's discharges may be termed "short." . . .

Presented with this conflicting and uncertain evidence from animal experimentation, and the fact that there are no human epidemiological studies bearing on the issue, the district court concluded that short fibers could not be assigned a lower relative risk than long fibers. This conclusion comports with the uncertain state of scientific knowledge. . . .

2.   THE LEVEL OF EXPOSURE

The second major step in the inquiry of the health aspects of Reserve's air emissions is an assessment of the amount of the discharge and the resulting level of exposure. Two principal issues are raised: first, what in fact is the level of exposure; second, does that level present a cognizable risk to health? The district court found the level "significant" and comparable to the levels associated with disease in nonoccupational contexts.

The first issue was addressed at length in our stay opinion. We noted there the great difficulties in attempted fiber counts and the uncertainties in measurement which necessarily resulted. Commenting on these difficulties, Dr. Brown stated that the fiber counts of the air and water samples could establish only the presence of fibers and not any particular amount, i.e., such a count establishes only a qualitative, and not a quantitative, proposition. The district court recognized these difficulties in counting fibers and observed that "[t]he most that can be gained from the Court [ordered] air study is the very roughest approximation of fiber levels." 380 F. Supp. at 49. . . .

Given the presence of excess fibers, we must now assess the effects of this exposure on the public. We note first, as we did in the stay opinion, that the exposure here cannot be equated with the factory exposures which have been clearly linked to excess cancers and asbestosis. Our inquiry, however, does not end there. Asbestos-related disease, as noted earlier, has been associated with exposure levels considerably less than normal occupational exposure. The studies indicating that mesothelioma is associated with the lower levels of exposure typical of residence near an asbestos mine or mill or in the household of an asbestos worker are of significance. Although these studies do not possess the methodological strengths of the occupational studies, they must be considered in the medical evaluation of Reserve's discharge into the air.

Of course, it is still not possible to directly equate the exposure in Silver Bay with the exposure patterns in these nonoccupational studies. The studies typically do not attempt to quantify the level of exposure and, as noted above, it is not possible to assess with any precision the exposure level in Silver Bay; thus, exposure levels may be compared only on the most general basis. Furthermore, it is questionable whether Reserve's operations may be equated with those of an asbestos mine or mill; for, while we concur in the trial court's finding that Reserve discharges fibers similar, and in some cases, identical to amosite asbestos, it is also true, as testified by plaintiffs' own witnesses, that only a portion of Reserve's discharge may be so characterized. . . .

3.   CONCLUSION

Plaintiffs' hypothesis that Reserve's air emissions represent a significant threat to the public health touches numerous scientific disciplines, and an overall evaluation demands broad scientific understanding. We think it significant that Dr. Brown, an impartial witness whose court-appointed task was to address the health issue in its entirety, joined with plaintiffs' witnesses in viewing as reasonable the hypothesis that Reserve's discharges present a threat to public health. Although, as we noted in our stay opinion, Dr. Brown found the evidence insufficient to make a scientific probability statement as to whether adverse health consequences would in fact ensue, he expressed a public health concern over the continued long-term emission of fibers into the air. . . .

B.   THE DISCHARGE INTO WATER

The claim that Reserve's discharge of tailings into Lake Superior causes a hazard to public health raises many of the same uncertainties present with respect to the discharge into air. Thus, the previous discussion of fiber identity and fiber size is also applicable to the water discharge. In two respects, however, the discharge into water raises added uncertainties: first, whether the ingestion of fibers, as compared with their inhalation, poses any danger whatsoever; and second, should ingestion pose a danger, whether the exposure resulting from Reserve's discharge may be said to present a legally cognizable risk to health.

1. INGESTION OF FIBERS AS A DANGER TO HEALTH

All epidemiological studies which associate asbestos fibers with harm to health are based upon inhalation of these fibers by humans. Thus, although medical opinion agrees that fibers entering the respiratory tract can interact with body tissues and produce disease, it is unknown whether the same can be said of fibers entering the digestive tract. If asbestos fibers do not interact with digestive tissue, they are presumably eliminated as waste without harmful effect upon the body.

The evidence bearing upon possible harm from ingestion of fibers falls into three areas: first, the court-sponsored tissue study, designed to measure whether asbestos fibers are present in the tissues of long-time Duluth residents; second, animal experiments designed to measure whether, as a biological phenomenon, fibers can penetrate the gastrointestinal mucosa and thus interact with body tissues; third, the increased incidence of gastrointestinal cancer among workers occupationally exposed to asbestos, and the hypothesis that this increase may be due to the ingestion of fibers initially inhaled.

a. The Tissue Study

Recognizing the complete lack of any direct evidence (epidemiological or otherwise) on the issue of whether the ingestion of fibers poses a risk, the trial court directed that a tissue study be conducted to determine whether the tissues of long-time Duluth residents contain any residue of asbestoslike fibers.

The study sought to analyze by electron microscope the tissues of recently deceased Duluth residents who had ingested Duluth water for at least 15 years; that is, approximately since the beginning of Reserve's operations. As a "control" check on results, tissue samples were obtained from the deceased residents of Houston, Texas, where the water is free of asbestos fibers. Although this study was necessarily expedited, plaintiffs' principal medical witness, Dr. Selikoff, testified to the sound design of the study and expressed his belief that it would yield significant information.

One of the court-appointed experts, Dr. Frederick Pooley, in explaining the results of the study, stated that he found that the tissues of the Duluth residents were virtually free of any fibers which could be attributed to the Reserve discharge. . . . After negative results had been actually obtained, however, plaintiffs argued, and the district court agreed, that because the specimens of tissue represented only a microscopically minute body area, the actual presence of fibers may have been overlooked.

We note that this limitation had not seemed dispositive prior to the study when Dr. Selikoff commented:

> I would think we should find some fibers there. We're looking for needles in a haystack, but that's all right, we should find needles in the haystack with all the difficulties of the study, the technical difficulties, if we examine sufficiently large numbers of samples in some instances we should find some fibers there.

The district court decided, and we agree, that the study cannot be deemed conclusive in exonerating the ingestion of fibers in Lake Superior water as a hazard. The negative results must, however, be given some weight in assessing the probabilities of harm from Reserve's discharge into water. The results also weigh heavily in indicating that no emergency or imminent hazard to health exists. Thus, while this study crucially bears on the determination of whether it is necessary to close Reserve down immediately, the negative results do not dispose of the broader issue of whether the ingestion of fibers poses some danger to public health justifying abatement on less immediate terms.

b.   Animal Studies and Penetration of the Gastrointestinal Mucosa

At a somewhat more theoretical level, the determination of whether ingested fibers can penetrate the gastrointestinal mucosa bears on the issue of harm through ingestion. If penetration is biologically impossible, then presumably the interaction of the fibers with body tissues will not occur.

This medical issue has been investigated through experiments with animals which, unfortunately, have produced conflicting results. . . . On this conflicting scientific evidence, Dr. Brown testified that the Westlake and Pontrefact studies provide some support for the hypothesis that asbestos fibers can penetrate the gastrointestinal mucosa.[46] . . .

c.   Excess Gastrointestinal Cancer among the Occupationally Exposed

The affirmative evidence supporting the proposition that the ingestion of fibers poses a danger to health focuses on the increased rate of gastrointestinal cancer among workers occupationally exposed to asbestos dust. Plaintiffs'

---

46.   We note from the record that while attempts to induce tumors in experimental animals through the inhalation of fibers have succeeded, attempts to induce tumors by ingestion have generally failed. Reserve witness Dr. Smith ventured the opinion, based on such studies, that there is no *proof* that the ingestion of fibers causes cancer in man. The failure to induce animal tumors by ingestion cannot be dispositive on the issue of whether the ingestion of fibers poses a risk to humans. This is because, as a general matter, animal cancer susceptibility is not directly equivalent to human experience, and, more particularly, because the studies so far undertaken may be criticized for various shortcomings in experimental design. Thus, one of Reserve's own witnesses, Dr. Wright, testified that at least one of the studies may be criticized for using too few animals over too brief an experimental time.

experts attribute this excess incidence of gastrointestinal cancer to a theory that the asbestos workers first inhaled the asbestos dust and thereafter coughed up and swallowed the asbestos particles.

The attribution of health harm from ingestion rests upon a theoretical basis. As Dr. Selikoff explained, there are several possible explanations for the increased evidence of gastrointestinal cancer, some of which do not involve ingestion. Moreover, as noted previously, the excess rates of gastrointestinal cancer are generally "modest," and substantially lower than the excess rates of mesothelioma and lung cancer associated with inhalation of asbestos dust. Also, the experts advised that an analysis of a small exposed population may produce statistically "unstable" results.

The existence of an excess rate of gastrointestinal cancer among asbestos workers is a matter of concern. The theory that excess cancers may be attributed to the ingestion of asbestos fibers rests on a tenable medical hypothesis. Indeed, Dr. Selikoff testified that ingestion is the "probable" route accounting for the excess in gastrointestinal cancer. The occupational studies support the proposition that the ingestion of asbestos fibers can result in harm to health.

2.   LEVEL OF EXPOSURE VIA INGESTION

The second primary uncertainty with respect to ingestion involves the attempt to assess whether the level of exposure from drinking water is hazardous. Of course, this inquiry is handicapped by the great variation in fiber counts, and Dr. Brown's admonition that only a qualitative, and not a quantitative, statement can be made about the presence of fibers.

In spite of these difficulties, the district court found that the level of exposure resulting from the drinking of Duluth water was "comparable" to that found to cause gastrointestinal cancer in asbestos workers. 380 F. Supp. at 48. The court drew this finding from an elaborate calculation by Dr. Nicholson in which he attempted to make a statistical comparison between the fibers probably ingested by an asbestos worker subject to an excess risk of gastrointestinal cancer with the probable number of amphibole fibers ingested by a Duluth resident over a period of 18 years. . . .

The Nicholson comparison, although evidentially weak, must be considered with other evidence. The record does show that the ingestion of asbestos fibers poses some risk to health, but to an undetermined degree. Given these circumstances, Dr. Brown testified that the possibility of a future excess incidence of cancer attributable to the discharge cannot be ignored:[50]

---

50.   Since Lake Superior affords water supplies to an estimated 200,000 people of Duluth and other North Shore Minnesota municipalities, as well as Superior, Wisconsin, we think it is essential that the facts regarding the present disease effects of the discharge be accurately stated.

As our review below demonstrates, we conclude that there is no evidence on a scientific or medical basis showing that Duluth residents experience an excess rate of cancer attributable to Reserve's discharge. . . .

> . . . I would say that it is conceivable that gastrointestinal cancers can develop from the ingestion of asbestos, and what I don't know, Your Honor, is just how low that level of ingestion must be before the likelihood of GI cancer becomes so remote as to be, for all intents and purposes, ignored as a real live possibility.

We quote at length Dr. Brown's testimony expressing the medical concern appropriate to the continued discharge of asbestos fibers into Lake Superior:

> [*Dr. Brown*]   After some degree of exposure to the literature and to the testimony given in this trial I would say that the scientific evidence that I have seen is not complete in terms of allowing me to draw a conclusion one way or another concerning the problem of a public health hazard in the water in Lake Superior.
>
> Q.   [The court].   Would you define the difference between what you say is scientific proof and medical proof, and then maybe I will give you another kind of proof that I have to live with here and we will see where we are going?
>
> A.   Well, science requires a level of proof which is pretty high. That is, we do not accept as truth things that seem to be casually associated, a cause casually associated with an effect. We have erected certain statistical barriers which force us to come to conclusions based on probability, and Dr. Taylor used those terms. He used .05 per cent, he used things like .01 per cent, criteria which generally are accepted in the scientific community as levels which are consistent with or from which you can conclude that there is some cause and effect relationship.
>
> Q.   All right. Now, scientific proof for what purpose? Doesn't the quantum of proof vary with the purpose? Now, I haven't really asked you this before, but wouldn't scientists be satisfied for one purpose and not another, or is that when you stop and put on your medical hat then, after you get a certain quantum of proof?
>
> A.   Well, as a scientist, sir, I would say that there are many questions which have been raised in this trial which would provide me with a hypothesis which I would like to see pursued. This is in the abstract scientific sense of an interesting intellectual question for which there is suggestive evidence.
>
> Now, when I turn, however, to the medical side of things, Your Honor, I am faced with the fact that I am convinced that asbestos fibers can cause cancer, I am faced with the fact that I have concluded that the size of the fibers is not particularly helpful in allowing me to decide whether a given fiber is or is not carcinogenic.
>
> As a medical person, sir, I think that I have to err, if err I do, on the side of what is best for the greatest number. And having concluded or having come to the conclusions that I have given you, the carcinogenicity of asbestos, I can come to no conclusion, sir, other than that the fibers should not be present in the drinking water of the people of the North Shore.

C.   Conclusion

The preceding extensive discussiosn of the evidence demonstrates that the medical and scientific conclusions here in dispute clearly lie "on the frontiers of scientific knowledge." Industrial Union Department, AFL-CIO v. Hodgson, 499 F.2d 467, 474 (1974). The trial court, not having any proof of actual harm, was faced with a consideration of 1) the probabilities of any health harm and 2) the consequences, if any, should the harm actually occur. See Carolina Environmental Study Group v. United States, 510 F.2d 796 at 799 (D.C. Cir., Jan. 21, 1975). [The court briefly referred with approval to the risk analysis developed by Judge Skelly Wright in dissent in the three-judge decision in Ethyl Corporation v. Environmental Protection Agency (D.C. Cir. 1975), rev'd, 541 F.2d 1 (D.C. Cir. 1976) (en banc), *cert. denied*, 426 U.S. 941 (1977).] . . .

These concepts of potential harm, whether they be assessed as "probabilities and consequences" or "risk and harm," necessarily must apply in a determination of whether any relief should be given in cases of this kind in which proof with certainty is impossible. The district court, although not following a precise probabilities-consequences analysis, did consider the medical and scientific evidence bearing on both the probability of harm and the consequences should the hypothesis advanced by the plaintiffs prove to be valid.

In assessing probabilities in this case, it cannot be said that the probability of harm is more likely than not. Moreover, the level of probability does not readily convert into a prediction of consequences. On this record it cannot be forecast that the rates of cancer will increase from drinking Lake Superior water or breathing Silver Bay air. The best that can be said is that the existence of this asbestos contaminant in air and water gives rise to a reasonable medical concern for the public health. The public's exposure to asbestos fibers in air and water creates some health risk. Such a contaminant should be removed.

As we demonstrate in the following sections of the opinion, the existence of this risk to the public justifies an injunction decree requiring abatement of the health hazard on reasonable terms as a precautionary and preventive measure to protect the public health.

III.   Discharge into the Air

[The court then held that the district court properly found that Reserve had violated one state statute and three separate air pollution regulations, including a requirement for 99 percent particulate removal. The court also affirmed the district court's finding that Reserve's emissions could be enjoined as a public nuisance, but it rejected the district court's view that the federal common law of nuisance was a basis for relief.]

IV.   Federal Water Pollution Control Act

The district court found that Reserve's discharge into Lake Superior violated §§1160(c)(5) and (g)(1) of the Federal Water Pollution Control Act. (FWPCA).[65] 380 F. Supp. at 16. These two provisions authorize an action by the United

---

65.   33 U.S.C. §1151 et seq. (1970), as amended, 33 U.S.C. §1251 et seq. (Supp. 1974). The amendments, passed in 1972, are not applicable to this litigation. . . .

States to secure abatement of water discharges in interstate waters where the discharges violate state water quality standards and "endanger . . . the health or welfare of persons." §1160(g)(1).

Minnesota has adopted water quality standards — Minnesota Water Pollution Control Regulation 15 (WPC 15) — in conformity with the FWPCA. . . . WPC 15 incorporates selected Minnesota statutory provisions into the water quality standards, including the policy of "protection of the public health" contained in Minn. Stat. Ann. §155.42 and a definition of "pollution" contained in Minn. Stat. Ann. §115.01(5) as contamination which renders waters "impure so as to be actually or *potentially harmful or detrimental or injurious to public health,* safety or welfare. . . ." (Emphasis added.)

The evidence shows Reserve's water discharge to be "potentially harmful" to the public health. As such, these discharges pollute the waters of Lake Superior in violation of the Minnesota water quality standards.

An action under the FWPCA requires proof of an additional element. The United States must establish that the water pollution which is violative of state water quality standards is also "endangering the health or welfare of persons."

In this review, we must determine whether "endangering" within the meaning of the FWPCA encompasses the potential harm to public health in the degree shown here.

Provisions of the FWPCA are aimed at the prevention as well as the cure of water pollution. The initial sentence of the FWPCA reads: "The purpose of this chapter is to enhance the quality and value of our water resources and to establish a national policy for the prevention, control, and abatement of water pollution." (33 U.S.C. §1151(a).) The term "endangering," as used by Congress in §1160(g)(1), connotes a lesser risk of harm than the phrase "imminent and substantial endangerment to the health of persons" as used by Congress in the 1972 amendments to the FWPCA. 33 U.S.C. §1364 (Supp. 1974).[70]

In the context of this environmental legislation, we believe that Congress used the term "endangering" in a precautionary or preventive sense, and, therefore, evidence of potential harm as well as actual harm comes within the purview of that term. We are fortified in this view by the flexible provisions for injunctive relief which permit a court "to enter such judgment and orders enforcing such judgment as the public interest and the equities of the case may require." 33 U.S.C. §1160(c)(5). . . .

Although the Supreme Court has not interpreted the concept of "endangering" in the context of an environmental lawsuit, it has emphasized the importance of giving environmental legislation a "common-sense" interpretation. Mr. Justice Douglas, writing for the Court, said:

---

70. The 1972 amendments to the FWPCA grant the Administrator of the Environmental Protection Agency emergency powers to file suit for an immediate injunction where pollution is "presenting an imminent and substantial endangerment to the health of persons." 33 U.S.C. §1364 (Supp. 1974). Compare 33 U.S.C. §1161(d) (1970).

> This case comes to us at a time in the Nation's history when there is greater concern than ever over pollution — one of the main threats to our free-flowing rivers and to our lakes as well. . . . [W]hatever may be said of the rule of strict construction, it cannot provide a substitute for common sense, precedent, and legislative history. [United States v. Standard Oil Co., 384 U.S. 224, 225 (1966).]

See United States v. Republic Steel Corp., 362 U.S. 482, 491 (1960).

The record shows that Reserve is discharging a substance into Lake Superior waters which under an acceptable but unproved medical theory may be considered as carcinogenic. As previously discussed, this discharge gives rise to a reasonable medical concern over the public health. We sustain the district court's determination that Reserve's discharge into Lake Superior constitutes pollution of waters "endangering the health or welfare of persons" within the terms of §§1160(c)(5) and (g)(1) of the Federal Water Pollution Control Act and is subject to abatement.[71] . . .

VII. Remedy

As we have demonstrated, Reserve's air and water discharges pose a danger to the public health and justify judicial action of a preventive nature.

In fashioning relief in a case such as this involving a possibility of future harm, a court should strike a proper balance between the benefits conferred and the hazards created by Reserve's facility. In its pleadings Reserve directs our attention to the benefits arising from its operations [which included a $350 million capital investment, construction of two company towns, support of 3,367 employees on an annual payroll of almost $32 million, and payment of substantial state and local taxes. Reserve's mine alone was producing 10 million tons of taconite a year, 12 percent of total U.S. production]. . . .

The district court justified its immediate closure of Reserve's facility by characterizing Reserve's discharges as "substantially" endangering the health of persons breathing air and drinking water containing the asbestos-like fibers contained in Reserve's discharges. 380 F. Supp. at 16. The term "substantially" in no way measures the danger in terms of either probabilities or consequences. Yet such an assessment seems essential in fashioning a judicial remedy.

Concededly, the trial court considered many appropriate factors in arriving at a remedy, such as a) the nature of the anticipated harm, b) the burden on Reserve and its employees from the issuance of the injunction, c) the financial

---

71. We are not here concerned with standards applied to abatement of a nuisance under non-statutory common law doctrines. In most common law nuisance cases involving alleged harmful health effects some present harm or at least an immediate threat of harm must be established. See New Jersey v. New York City, 283 U.S. 473 (1931); Arizona Copper Co. v. Gillespie, 230 U.S. 46 (1913); Georgia v. Tennessee Copper Co., 206 U.S. 230 (1907); Missouri v. Illinois, 200 U.S. 496 (1906). But see Harris Stanley Coal & Land Co. v. Chesapeake & O. Ry. Co., 154 F.2d 450 (6th Cir.), cert. denied, 329 U.S. 761 (1946). . . .

ability of Reserve to convert to other methods of waste disposal, and d) a margin of safety for the public.

An additional crucial element necessary for a proper assessment of the health hazard rests upon a proper analysis of the probabilities of harm. . . .

With respect to the water, these probabilities must be deemed low for they do not rest on a history of past health harm attributable to ingestion but on a medical theory implicating the ingestion of asbestos fibers as a causative factor in increasing the rates of gastrointestinal cancer among asbestos workers. With respect to air, the assessment of the risk of harm rests on a higher degree of proof, a correlation between inhalation of asbestos dust and subsequent illness. But here, too, the hazard cannot be measured in terms of predictability, but the assessment must be made without direct proof. But, the hazard in both the air and water can be measured in only the most general terms as a concern for the public health resting upon a reasonable medical theory. Serious consequences could result if the hypothesis on which it is based should ultimately prove true. . . .

In addition to the health risk posed by Reserve's discharges, the district court premised its immediate termination of the discharges upon Reserve's persistent refusal to implement a reasonable alternative plan for on-land disposal of tailings.

During these appeal proceedings, Reserve has indicated its willingness to deposit its tailings on land and to properly filter its air emissions. At oral argument, Reserve advised us of a willingness to spend 243 million dollars in plant alterations and construction to halt its pollution of air and water. Reserve's offer to continue operations and proceed to construction of land disposal facilities for its tailings, if permitted to do so by the State of Minnesota, when viewed in conjunction with the uncertain quality of the health risk created by Reserve's discharges, weighs heavily against a ruling which closes Reserve's plant immediately.

Indeed, the intervening union argues, with some persuasiveness, that ill health effects resulting from the prolonged unemployment of the head of the family on a closing of the Reserve facility may be more certain than the harm from drinking Lake Superior water or breathing Silver Bay air.

Furthermore, Congress has generally geared its national environmental policy to allowing polluting industries a reasonable period of time to make adjustments in their efforts to conform to federal standards. In the absence of proof of a reasonable risk of imminent or actual harm, a legal standard requiring immediate cessation of industrial operations will cause unnecessary economic loss, including unemployment, and, in a case such as this, jeopardize a continuing domestic source of critical metals without conferring adequate countervailing benefits.

We believe that on this record the district court abused its discretion by immediately closing this major industrial plant. In this case, the risk of harm to the public is potential, not imminent or certain, and Reserve says it earnestly seeks a practical way to abate the pollution. A remedy should be fashioned which will serve the ultimate public weal by insuring clean air, clean water, and continued jobs in an industry vital to the nation's welfare. . . .

A. The Discharge into Water

Reserve shall be given a reasonable time to stop discharging its wastes into Lake Superior. A reasonable time includes the time necessary for Minnesota to act on Reserve's present application to dispose of its tailings at Milepost 7 (Lax Lake site) or to come to agreement on some other site acceptable to both Reserve and the state. Assuming agreement and designation of an appropriate land disposal site, Reserve is entitled to a reasonable turn-around time to construct the necessary facilities and accomplish a changeover in the means of disposing of its taconite wastes.

We cannot now precisely measure this time. Minnesota must assume the obligation of acting with great expedition in ruling on Reserve's pending application or otherwise determining that it shall, or that it shall not, afford a site acceptable to Reserve. We suggest, but do not determine, that with expedited procedures a final administrative decision should be reached within one year after a final appellate decision in this case.

Upon receiving a permit from the State of Minnesota, Reserve must utilize every reasonable effort to expedite the construction of new facilities. If the parties cannot agree on the duration of a reasonable turn-around time, either party may apply to the district court for a time-table which can be incorporated in the injunction decree, subject to our review.

Should Minnesota and Reserve be unable to agree on an on-land disposal site within this reasonable time period, Reserve, Armco and Republic Steel must be given a reasonable period of time thereafter to phase out the Silver Bay facility. In the interests of delineating the rights of the parties to the fullest extent possible, this additional period of time is set at one year after Minnesota's final administrative determination that it will offer Reserve no site acceptable to Reserve for on-land disposal of tailings. . . .

B. Air Emissions

Pending final action by Minnesota on the present permit application, Reserve must promptly take all steps necessary to comply with Minnesota law applicable to its air emissions, as outlined in this opinion. . . .

. . . Reserve must use such available technology as will reduce the asbestos fiber count in the ambient air at Silver Bay below a medically significant level. According to the record in this case, controls may be deemed adequate which will reduce the fiber count to the level ordinarily found in the ambient air of a control city such as St. Paul.

We wish to make it clear that we view the air emission as presenting a hazard of greater significance than the water discharge. Accordingly, pending a determination of whether Reserve will be allowed to construct an on-land disposal site or will close its operations, Reserve must immediately proceed with the planning and implementation of such emission controls as may be reasonably and practically effectuated under the circumstances. . . .

Additionally, the district court should take proper steps to ensure that filtered water remains available in affected communities to the same extent as is now provided by the Corps of Engineers, although not necessarily at the expense of the Corps.

Finally, this court deems it appropriate to suggest that the national interest now calls upon Minnesota and Reserve to exercise a zeal equivalent to that displayed in this litigation to arrive at an appropriate location for an on-land disposal site for Reserve's tailings and thus permit an important segment of the national steel industry, employing several thousand people, to continue in production. As we have already noted, we believe this controversy can be resolved in a manner that will purify the air and water without destroying jobs. . . .

[Twenty-five days after issuing the above decision, the court issued the following:]

Order on Remand

For reasons stated below, we find it necessary to issue this special order on remand to protect the integrity of the processes of this court.

We filed our detailed and carefully drawn, unanimous en banc opinion [above] in these cases on March 14, 1975. Although these cases remained exclusively in our jurisdiction subject to any request for consideration by any of the parties and before issuance of any mandate, the district court called the parties and other persons together for a hearing the very next day, March 15, 1975. After learning of this hearing through news dispatches published in the daily press, we requested that the clerk of the district court furnish each member of the en banc court with a transcript of the hearing.

We have reviewed this transcript. We can only characterize the district court proceedings of March 15 as irregular. Indeed, since no mandate had yet been issued from this court to the district court, the various orders, directions to parties, suggestions to the Governor of Minnesota, members of Congress, and the Minnesota State Legislature, and all other actions taken by the trial judge at these proceedings are a complete nullity. . . .

We have an additional concern over the actions of the district court judge at that hearing. The judge initiated steps which appear to be in conflict with the express language of this court's opinion of March 14, 1975. Moreover, the district court judge and counsel for certain of the plaintiffs suggested in that hearing that Reserve Mining Company will be able to continue its present discharges for seven to ten years as a consequence of our modification of the district court's injunction. We made no such prediction nor authorized any unnecessary delay in abatement of air and water discharges. . . .

NOTES AND QUESTIONS

1. Although the outcomes are similar, the legal standards adopted in *Wilsonville* and *Reserve Mining* are quite different. Could the danger factually documented in *Reserve Mining* have justified injunctive relief under the *Wilsonville* standard? The dissent in *Wilsonville*? Why are the courts more reluctant to enjoin health risks as common law nuisances than they are to enjoin them under an "endangerment" statute? Why is direct legislative approval important?

Do you agree that "it is more important in a democracy that the public have the decision it wants, rationally or irrationally, right or wrong, than that the 'correct' decision be made" (Green, Limitations on the Implementation of Technology Assessment, 14 Atomic Energy L.J. 59, 82 (1972))? Many judges feel that the courts are constrained by a more objective standard and may not "legislate" their notions of the general will. This is particularly true of the causal nexus and the proof of damage or substantial threat the common law historically has required. Is there a way to base judicial intervention on something more than a judicial "policy decision" to enjoin health risks? See Gelpe & Tarlock, The Uses of Scientific Information in Environmental Decision Making, 48 S. Cal. L. Rev. 371, 381 n.21c, 412-427 (1974).

What of the legislature that in its pursuit of greater safety appears to take leave of direct causation entirely? Does the public policy justification suffice, even if the causal nexus between risk and harm or between risk creation and the regulatee's activities is virtually non-existent? Justice Powell thought that the retroactive effect of the Black Lung Benefits Act of 1972, which required coal mine operators to pay into a fund to compensate miners afflicted with chronic black lung disease that they might have contracted years earlier working in another operator's mine, was "highly questionable" in the light of "the Fifth Amendment guarantee against arbitrary, irrational, or discriminatory legislation" (Usery v. Turner Elkhorn Mining Co., 428 U.S. 1, 40 (1975)). But neither he nor the majority, which also discussed the issue (428 U.S. at 24), was willing to hold the legislative scheme excessive or irrational. In Industrial union Department, AFL-CIO v. American Petroleum Institute, 448 U.S. 607 (1980), Justice Rehnquist used the delegation doctrine to argue that a statute empowering the Occupational Health and Safety Administration (OSHA) to tighten the workplace exposure standard for benzene (a human carcinogen) if "reasonably necessary or appropriate" to assure that "to the extent feasible" no worker would suffer material health impairment was unconstitutionally vague on the crucial issue of whether the agency had to weigh the costs against the benefits before tightening the standard. He pressed his attack against the same statute shortly thereafter in American Textile Manufacturers Institute v. Donovan, 452 U.S. 490 (1981):

> The words "to the extent feasible" . . . mask a fundamental policy disagreement in Congress. I have no doubt that if Congress had been required to choose whether

> to mandate, permit, or prohibit [OSHA] from engaging in a cost-benefit analysis, there would have been no bill for the President to sign. [452 U.S. at 546 (Chief Justice Burger concurring).]

If Congress enacts a broad precautionary statute that leaves the hard decisions to the administrative agencies, the most significant ideological, scientific, and economic issues still remain to be thrashed out before the responsible agency. The traditional wisdom of the separation of powers doctrine holds that an administrative agency should be as apolitical as possible, a repository of expertise and specialization for the efficient execution of policies set by the legislature. This formal model came under stress as regulation became one of the central realms of political choice in post-World War II American society. The adjustment has been a shaky success, although most writing on the missions of agencies tends to submerge the political dimension. See Anderson, Human Welfare and the Administered Society: Federal Regulation in the 1970s to Protect Health, Safety, and the Environment, in Environmental and Occupational Medicine 835, 848-851, 854-860 (W. Rom ed. 1983). Has overdelegation in the precautionary statutes created a political crisis? Yes, says Schoenbrod, Goals Statutes or Rules Statutes: The Case of the Clean Air Act, 30 U.C.L.A.L. Rev. 201 (1983).

2. The decision in Ethyl Corp. v. EPA, 541 F.2d 1 (D.C. Cir. 1976), sheds additional light on the meaning of statutory "endangerment." At issue in *Ethyl* was a provision of the Clean Air Act that authorized the Administrator of EPA to regulate gasoline additives if their emissions products "will endanger the public health or welfare" ($211(c)(1)(A)). After rule-making proceedings in which EPA reviewed a number of inconclusive scientific studies that indicated that lead emissions harmed the health of urban populations, particularly children, the Administrator determined that leaded gasoline emissions presented "a significant risk of harm," thereby endangering the public health within the meaning of the statute. The Administrator set standards requiring an annual reduction in the lead content of gasoline.

You are already aware of the scientific uncertainty surrounding the potential impact of lead emissions on human health from your consideration of the 1978 rule-making proceeding in which EPA set a uniform ambient air quality standard for lead. See Chapter 3 at pp. 172-200. As in *Reserve Mining* and *Lead Industries*, the court in *Ethyl* had to wrestle with the significance of different pathways of exposure (lead inhalation vs. ingestion), of applying results obtained from occupational studies at high levels of exposure to the general population, which experiences lower exposure levels, of important methodological shortcomings in all of the studies, of focusing on the most vulnerable population group (children) instead of the general population, and of the relative contribution that other possible sources of lead may add to the total danger experienced.

Thus in *Ethyl* and *Reserve Mining*, applying the "endanger" standards of the relevant statutes to the available data presented very much the same problem. Regarding the meaning of the critical statutory language, Judge Wright wrote:

Case law and dictionary definition agree that endanger means something less than actual harm. When one is endangered, harm is *threatened*; no actual injury need ever occur. Thus, for example, a town may be "endangered" by a threatening plague or hurricane and yet emerge from the danger completely unscathed. A statute allowing for regulation in the face of danger is, necessarily, a precautionary statute. Regulatory action may be taken before the threatened harm occurs; indeed, the very existence of such precautionary legislation would seem to *demand* that regulatory action precede, and, optimally, prevent, the perceived threat. As should be apparent, the "will endanger" language of Section 211(c)(1)(A) makes it such a precautionary statute.

    The Administrator read it as such, interpreting "will endanger" to mean "presents a significant risk of harm." We agree with the Administrator's interpretation. . . .

    . . . While the dictionary admittedly settles on "probable" as its measure of danger, we believe a more sophisticated case-by-case analysis is appropriate. Danger, the Administrator recognized, is not set by a fixed probability of harm, but rather is composed of reciprocal elements of risk and harm, or probability and severity. Cf. Carolina Environmental Study Group v. United States, 510 F.2d 796, 799 (1975); Reserve Mining Co. v. EPA, *supra*, 514 F.2d at 519-520. That is to say, the public health may properly be found endangered both by a lesser risk of a greater harm and by a greater risk of a lesser harm.[32] Danger depends upon the relation between the risk and harm presented by each case, and cannot legitimately be pegged to "probable" harm, regardless of whether that harm be great or small. [541 F.2d at 13-18.]

Which formulation of the standard common to the statutes do you find clearer — the one offered by Judge Bright (p. 540 *supra*), by Judge Wright, or by Talbot Page (p. 494 *supra*)? Notice that the key words — harm, danger, risk, probability, severity, magnitude — are not always used in the same way; a few are even used interchangeably. The result of considering both the *probability* that actual harm will eventually occur and the *magnitude* or severity of that harm if it does occur sometimes is called "risk," but sometimes it is also called "danger." This alone would not be unduly confusing were it not that "risk" is sometimes used, e.g., by Judge Wright, to mean only "probability." The important thing to keep clear, as Judge Wright indicates, is that "danger . . . is not set by a fixed probability of harm, but rather is composed of reciprocal elements of . . . probability and severity" (*Ethyl*, 541 F.2d at 18). See also Natural Resources Defense Council, Inc. v. NRC, 685 F.2d 459, 478 n.100 (D.C. Cir.) (*Vermont Yankee II*), rev'd sub nom. Baltimore Gas & Electric Co. v. Natural Resources Defense Council, Inc., 462 U.S. 87 (1983).

---

    32.   This proposition must be confined to reasonable limits, however. In Carolina Enviromental Study Group. v. United States, 510 F.2d 796 (1975), a division of this court found the possibility of a Class 9 nuclear reactor disaster, a disaster of ultimate severity and horrible consequences, to be so low that the Atomic Energy Commission's minimal consideration of the effects of such a disaster in an environmental impact statement prepared for a new reactor was sufficient. Likewise, even the absolute certainty of de minimis harm might not justify government action. Under §211 the threatened harm must be sufficiently significant to justify health-based regulation of national impact. Ultimately, of course, whether a particular combination of slight risk and great harm, or great risk and slight harm, constitutes a danger must depend on the facts of each case.

3. If danger or risk depends on two interdependent factors, probability and magnitude of harm, and neither factor can be considered in isolation, then what is the court in *Reserve Mining* doing when, in addressing the remedies to be applied, it reassesses the "probabilities of harm" and then refuses to sustain the trial court's injunction? Is it incorrectly applying its own analytic framework by permitting the timing of relief to hinge on probability alone? If so, should Reserve Mining have been immediately enjoined from all activities that endangered public health? If not, what better reasoning would support the relief the court in fact did order? Compare Henderson & Pearson, Implementing Federal Environmental Policies: The Limits of Aspirational Commands, 78 Colum. L. Rev. 1429, 1543-1456 (1978).

A second problem exists with the *Reserve Mining* court's approach to the relief granted. To justify delaying relief rather than granting an immediate injunction, the court repeatedly contrasted the "potential" threat to the public health it found to exist with an "imminent" danger to public health. The implication is that only an "imminent" hazard merits immediate relief, and Reserve's discharges did not present one. Yet is it correct to say that the danger in *Reserve* was not imminent? Strictly speaking, the danger already existed, did it not? Had it been many years earlier and Reserve Mining had been almost ready to open the mine and dump the first load of tailings into the lake, the danger could have been imminent. But at the time of the decision the danger existed, and the statute said nothing about showing imminent *harm* before relief could be granted. See Note, *Reserve Mining* — The Standard of Proof Required to Enjoin an Environmental Hazard to the Public Health, 59 Minn. L. Rev. 893 (1975).

The statute in *Reserve Mining* authorizes such relief "as the public interest and the equities of the case require" (33 U.S.C. §1160(c)(5)). Does this mean that the court is free to trade off the factors ("equities") traditionally balanced against each other in deciding whether to grant an equitable injunction at common law (e.g., in a nuisance suit), or must the court apply a formula more favorable to the plaintiff because *statutory* equitable relief has been authorized? Holding for the traditional view, see Weinberger v. Romero-Barcelo, 454 U.S. 813 (1982), excerpted at p. 476 *supra*. For criticism of *Romero-Barcelo* (the Clean Water Act mandates the award of an injunction when necessary permits have not been obtained; the Act is not simply "nuisance writ large"), see Petruzzi & Thomas, Equitable Discretion under the Federal Water Pollution Control Act: Weinberger v. Romero-Barcelo, 11 Ecology L.Q. 73 (1983).

Assume that a group of plaintiffs come forward who live near the mine and drink Lake Superior water and they have the types of cancers that Reserve's asbestiform emissions and effluents conceivably could cause. Should they be able to recover damages at common law relying on a *Reserve*-type risk analysis? Compare the *Sterling* case, *supra* at 528. Can a right to recover damages be implied from Reserve's violation of statutes? See Chapter 6, at p. 476, and Note, Toxic Substance Contamination: The Risk-Benefit Approach to Causation Analysis, 14 U. Mich. J.L. Reform 53 (1980).

4. Despite numerous similarities, a very important difference exists between *Reserve Mining* and *Ethyl*. In *Reserve Mining* the courts directly interpreted and applied the "endanger" standard. In *Ethyl* the EPA Administrator interpreted and applied the statute. The court of appeals in *Ethyl* merely reviewed the Administrator's decision to make sure that it was not arbitrary and capricious and that it had a rational basis in the evidence.

Regarding agency decisionmaking under a precautionary statute, the *Ethyl* court said:

> Where a statute is precautionary in nature, the evidence difficult to come by, uncertain, or conflicting because it is on the frontiers of scientific knowledge, the regulations designed to protect the public health, and the decision that of an expert administrator, we will not demand rigorous step-by-step proof of cause and effect. Such proof may be impossible to obtain if the precautionary purpose of the statute is to be served. Of course, we are not suggesting that the Administrator has the power to act on hunches or wild guesses. . . . The Administrator may apply his expertise to draw conclusions from suspected, but not completely substantiated, relationships between facts, from trends among facts, from theoretical projections from imperfect data, from probative preliminary data not yet certifiable as "fact," and the like. We believe that a conclusion so drawn — a risk assessment — may, if rational, form the basis for health-related regulations under the "will endanger" language of Section 211.[58] [541 F.2d at 28.]

58. It bears emphasis that what is herein described as "assessment of risk" is neither unprecedented nor unique to this area of law. To the contrary, assessment of risk is a normal part of judicial and administrative fact-finding. Thus EPA is not attempting to expand its powers; rather, petitioners seek to constrict the usual flexibility of the fact-finding process. Petitioners argue that the Administrator must decide that lead emissions "will endanger" the public health solely on "facts," or, in the words of the division majority, by a "chain of scientific facts or reasoning leading [the Administrator] ineluctably to this conclusion. . . ." Petitioners demand sole reliance on *scientific* facts, on evidence that reputable scientific techniques certify as certain. Typically, a scientist will not so certify evidence unless the probability of error, by standard statistical measurement, is less than 5%. That is, scientific fact is at least 95% certain.

Such certainty has never characterized the judicial or the administrative process. It may be that the "beyond a reasonable doubt" standard of criminal law demands 95% certainty. But the standard of ordinary civil litigation, a preponderance of the evidence, demands only 51% certainty. A jury may weigh conflicting evidence and certify as adjudicative (although not scientific) fact that which it believes is more likely than not. Since *Reserve Mining* was adjudicated in court, this standard applied to the court's fact-finding. Inherently, such a standard is flexible; inherently, it allows the fact-finder to assess risks, to measure probabilities, to make subjective judgments. Nonetheless, the ultimate finding will be treated, at law, as fact and will be affirmed if based on substantial evidence, or, if made by a judge, not clearly erroneous.

The standard before administrative agencies is no less flexible. Agencies are not limited to scientific fact, to 95% certainties. Rather, they have at least the same fact-finding powers as a jury, particularly when, as here, they are engaged in rule-making. "Looking to the future, and commanded by Congress to make policy, a rule-making agency necessarily deals less with "evidentiary" disputes than with normative conflicts, projections from imperfect data, experiments and simulations, educated predictions, differing assessments of possible risks, and the like." Amoco Oil Co. v. EPA, 501 F.2d at 735. An agency's finding of fact differs from that of a jury or trial judge primarily in that it is accorded more deference by a reviewing court. Thus, as a matter of administrative law, the Administrator found *as fact* that lead emissions "will endanger" the public health. That in so doing he did not have to rely solely on proved scientific fact is inherent in

Footnote 58 to *Ethyl* is an excellent statement of the jurisprudence of risk assessment. You may want to review the materials on risk assessment, *supra* at 502-509, at this time. The footnote also raises again the issue of good versus bad science. To a "good" scientist, a judicial or administrative conclusion that a fact exists would be a bad scientific conclusion that the same fact exists if, to use the *Ethyl*'s terminology, only a 51 to 94 percent certainty accompanied the administrative or judicial determination. Is it meaningful to speculate whether an adjudicative fact is "good" or "bad" science? Is it science at all? If not, what difference does it make? The court's explanation of the standard of judicial review applicable in *Ethyl* has already been set out in Chapter 2 at p. 124.

5. *Reserve Mining* and *Ethyl* have decisively influenced judicial interpretation of practically all the regulatory statutes that attempt to protect health and the environment before actual harm occurs. Indeed, the rationale that they provide stretches across the breadth of pollution control legislation, from the provisions contained in all the major pollution control statutes for direct abatement by court action when the federal government can show that "imminent and substantial endangerment" to health and the environment exists, to the threshold showing of danger necessary to trigger regulation under conventional ambient and emissions standards provisions. In 1977 Congress incorporated the *Reserve Mining-Ethyl* approach to risk management into the major regulatory provisions of the Clean Air Act: ambient air quality standards (§108), new source performance standards (§111), new vehicle emissions standards (§202), regulation of fuels and fuel additives (§211), and aircraft emissions standards (§231). These sections now authorize regulation of pollutants that "endanger" the public. Explicitly endorsing the decision, the House report made plain that the *Ethyl* approach should now guide the Administrator in selecting pollutants for regulation (H.R. Rep. No. 294, 95th Cong., 1st Sess. 43-51 (1977)). Do you think risk analysis could serve to unify the widely disparate principles and standards of modern environmental law?

6. In 1970, before a decade of precautionary environmental legislation, Professor James Krier wrote that "burden of proof rules at present have an inevitable bias against protection of the environment. . . ." Environmental Litigation and the Burden of Proof, in Law and the Environment 105, 107 (M. Baldwin & J. Page eds. 1970). Why was this? Is the effect of the precautionary approach of *Reserve Mining*, *Ethyl*, and the many precautionary statutes enacted in the 1970s to put the burden of proving safety on risk-creating enterprises? If so, has the precautionary approach fundamentally changed the economic and social relationship between risk-creating enterprises and those who bear the risks? Can

---

the requirements of legal fact-finding. Petitioners' assertions of the need to rely on "fact" confuse the two terminologies. We must deal with the terminology of law, not science. At law, unless the administrative or judicial task is peculiarly factual in nature, or Congress expressly commands a more rigorous finding, assessment of risks as herein described typifies both the administrative and the judicial fact-finding function, and is not the novel or unprecedented theory that petitioners contend.

you predict confidently what defendants would have to show in *Reserve Mining* in order to continue to discharge or emit asbestiform fibers indefinitely?

Much of the rest of this chapter concerns federal regulatory statutes that go quite far in shifting the burden of proving safety to risk-generating enterprises. For each statute, Congress had to answer two basic questions: (1) What showing of risk by the agency will suffice to place the burden of avoiding regulation on risk-creating enterprises? (2) What showing will enable such enterprises to escape regulation? You may recognize that these questions are very similar to those the courts must answer in trials at law: (1) What proof must the plaintiff offer before the burden of going forward with contrary evidence shifts to the defendant? Is a mere prima facie showing of injury appropriate to shift the burden of producing contradictory evidence to the risk-generating enterprise? (2) What must the defendant show or do to escape liability?

In a sense, the only major task still awaiting your attention in this chapter is that of grasping the specific techniques by which Congress and EPA place various suspect compounds, processes, wastes, and the like within the prohibitions of the statutes with a minimum of fuss and bother and then make them stick.

Shakespeare had Iago speak these words to explain his scheme to get even with Othello:

> I know not if't be true;
> But I, for mere suspicion in that kind,
> Will do as if for surety.
>
> Othello, act 1. sc. iii, lines 493-498

Has society now adopted Iago's philosophy?

A POSTSCRIPT ON SUBSEQUENT EVENTS IN THE RESERVE MINING AND ETHYL CONTROVERSIES

Reserve Mining. In the opinion excerpted above, the circuit court did not set a firm deadline for ending the discharges into Lake Superior; rather, it ordered the state and Reserve to resolve their differences and come up with an acceptable land disposal plan within "a reasonable time." The state authorities refused to give Reserve a permit for the site at Mile Post 7; they favored an alternate site farther inland at Mile Post 20. In the summer of 1976, the federal district court gave the parties one year to reach agreement on a site or it would shut down the mine. United States v. Reserve Mining Co., 417 F. Supp. 789 (D. Minn.), *aff'd*, 543 F.2d 1210 (8th Cir. 1976). Prodded by state court opinions directing the state to grant permits for the Mile Post 7 site, the parties agreed that Reserve would construct the facility at Mile Post 7 and end all discharges to the lake by the spring of 1980. Reserve met its deadline. However, in 1983 production needs forced Reserve to overflow the Mile Post 7 pond. The state pollution control agency set a discharge limitation of 1 million fibers per liter of water, over Reserve's request for a 15 million fiber per liter standard. Reserve challenged the one million fibers per liter limit and prevailed. Reserve Mining Co. v. Minnesota Pollution Control Agency, 364 N.W. 2d 411, 415 (Minn. 1985). Still, as a result of further proceedings Reserve entered into an agreement in 1985 to accept the one million fiber limit and to construct a $1.5 million filtration plant, utilizing the best available technology for control of filtered discharges. 16 Envt. Rep. (BNA): Current Developments 132 (1985).

The problem of providing safe drinking water has also been addressed in subsequent litigation. In 1976, the federal district court ordered Reserve to pay for an Army Corps of Engineers program to filter drinking water for use in the North Shore cities that took their water from Lake Superior. United States v. Reserve Mining Co., 408 F. Supp. 1212 (D. Minn.), 423 F. Supp. 759 (D. Minn. 1976). Four communities built water filtration systems, for which the state paid (except for Duluth's). Reserve reimbursed the state for $1.1 million of construction expenses incurred and paid another $740,000 directly to Duluth for building its own system. In order to reduce the emission of asbestiform fibers into the air, Reserve spent approximately $370 million on the installation of electrostatic precipitators and bag-house filters.

District Court Judge Miles Lord, whose distaste for the circuit court's handling of the case was obvious, was forced to relinquish jurisdiction of the controversy. In 1976 the circuit court found that Judge Lord had disregarded its earlier decision and had shown "gross bias" against Reserve. Judge Lord at one point assessed a $100,000 fine against Reserve without notice or hearing, stating that Reserve's repeated misrepresentations made a hearing a waste of time. Reserve Mining Co. v. Lord, 529 F. 2d 181 (8th Cir. 1976) (en banc). Does this fifteen-year sequence of events argue for or against judicial resolution of pollution problems and judicial supervision of solutions?

Controversy has continued over the release of asbestiform fibers into the air. In 1985 the Minnesota Health Department released a preliminary study suggesting a potentially dangerous link between asbestos fibers from taconite mining and thickening of the pleural lining of the lung. Duluth News Tribune & Herald, March 3, 1985, at 1A, col. 2. The study of chest x-rays from four cities in the Mesobi Iron Range, the area involved in Reserve, found the incidence of pleural thickening was from 13 to 36 percent, as compared to 1 to 10 percent normally found in areas of the country with no major source of asbestos. Id. The state health department arranged for a panel of national experts to examine the x-rays and determine whether the abnormal pleural thickening was attributable to asbestos fibers in the ambient air. Duluth News Tribune & Herald, Mar. 9, 1985 at 1A, col. 1. In April 1985, the panel concluded that neither the region's air pollution monoitoring data nor the chest x-rays supported the contention that a public health problem existed with regional air quality. Duluth News Tribune & Herald, Apr. 13, 1985 at 1A, col. 5.

Ethyl. Despite the en banc court decision upholding EPA regulations, by September 1976 the leaded gasoline regulations were still not being enforced because of EPA concern that they might contribute to a fuel shortage and because of lingering uncertainty about the economic feasibility of the regulations. The EPA eliminated all interim phasedown levels except the 0.8 gram per gallon (gpg) standard that was due to take effect January 1, 1978, and put off the date on which the final 0.5 gpg standard was to take effect until October 1, 1979 (41 Fed. Reg. 42,675). Small refineries obtained less stringent standards because they faced relatively higher capital costs. See 44 Fed. Reg. 63,103. The standards were further delayed for various reasons. 10 Envt. Rep. (BNA): Current Developments 232 (1979). The EPA resumed enforcement of the 0.8 gpg standard in October 1979 and of the 0.5 gpg standard a year later (except, of course, for small refineries) (44 Fed. Reg. 53,144).

Meanwhile, various studies appeared that showed that combustion of lead-containing fuels was the principal source of lead in the environment, that the blood lead level of urban children directly correlated with the lead content of gasoline, and that high blood lead levels caused psychological and behavioral problems in urban children. See Billick, Relation of Pediatric Blood Levels to Lead in Gasoline, 34 Envtl. Health Perspectives 213 (1980); Needleman, Deficits in Psychological and Classroom Performance of Children with Elevated Dentine Lead Levels, 300 New Eng. J. Med. 689 (1979). Science and economics, when mixed, proved politically potent. Billick, a researcher at the Department of Housing and Urban Development, appears to have lost his job because of findings that embarrassed the Reagan Administration at a time when EPA was considering a relaxation in the standards (Washington Post, July 29, 1982, §A, at 21, col. 6).

In February 1982, in response to the political climate favoring less regulation and to evidence that the increased use of unleaded gasoline in automobiles equipped with catalytic converters had substantially lessened overall lead emissions, EPA announced that it was considering either relaxing or eliminating the lead standards (47 Fed. Reg. 7,812). In July 1982, EPA announced that the accumulated data on injury from inhaled lead showed that relaxation of the regulations was not warranted and withdrew its proposal. 13 Envt. Rep. (BNA): Current Developments 541 (1982). Reliable Washington sources reported that President Reagan personally urged Administrator Anne M. Burford to retain the strict standards after he had received a telephone call from newspaper columnist George Will, who argued strenuously that lead emissions were harming young children. In October 1982, new regulations set a 1.1 gpg standard for all leaded gasoline, abandoning the approach of the earlier standards, which pooled (i.e., averaged) the lead content of the combined production of leaded and unleaded gasoline. The pooled standards had given the refiners an incentive to increase production of unleaded gasoline; by 1982 this incentive was unnecessary because the market for unleaded gasoline was secure.

In March 1985, the EPA again approved stricter phase-down regulations. The regulations set a 0.50 gpg standard for all leaded gasoline after mid-1985 and a 0.10 gpg after January 1, 1986. See 50 Fed. Reg. 9,397. To facilitate industry transition to the stricter standards, the EPA established a temporary "banking" system (50 Fed. Reg. 1,328). Refiners could bank lead use rights equal to the amount their gasoline's actual lead content fell below the standard. These rights could be withdrawn later, e.g., to bring a refiner into compliance with the stricter standards, or the banking refiner could sell rights to another refiner. The EPA has proposed a total ban on leaded gasoline; however, action on a final regulation has been delayed because of a requirement in the 1985 farm bill that EPA test agricultural equipment. 17 Envt. Rep. (BNA): Current Developments 432 (1986).

With stricter standards in place, debate focused on enforcement. The General Accounting Office reported that the EPA had failed to investigate numerous violations of lead content standards and the banking system. 17 Envt. Rep. (BNA): Current Developments 819 (1986). That same year EPA obtained $40 million in penalties from four companies for violations of both lead content standards and the banking system. 17 Envt. Rep. (BNA): Current Developments 1296 (1986). See also 18 Envt. Rep. (BNA): Current Developments 465 (1987).

In 1987 EPA concluded that a sharp reduction in ambient lead levels since 1976 was the direct result of the increased use of unleaded gasoline and the phasedown of lead in gasoline. 17 Envt. Rep. (BNA): Current Developments 2117 (1987). In 1988 the United States Geological Survey concluded that the dramatic decline in lead pollution of major rivers resulted from the lead-in-gasoline phaseout. 19 Envt. Rep. (BNA): Current Developments 1090 (1988).

D. HAZARDOUS SUBSTANCES IN THE AIR AND WATER

The federal Clean Air Act and Clean Water Act are discussed in Chapters 3 and 4, but their special provisions for hazardous emissions and effluents belong conceptually among the special legislative measures that Congress has adopted for regulating hazardous substances. In this section, keep these questions in mind: How do the special hazard prevention provisions differ from the rest of the air and water pollution control provisions? How do they interact with those provisions?

1. Emissions Standards for Hazardous Air Pollutants

When Congress enacted the 1970 Clean Air Act, it viewed the regulation of hazardous emissions as a unique problem meriting a limited statutory solution. Eschewing traditional ambient air quality and emissions standards approaches, Congress required stringent national emissions standards for each substance that exposed an individual to a risk of death or serious bodily harm, and refused to give the states flexibility in implementing them. This stringent approach put high compliance costs and health protection on a collision course, as the following case shows.

NATURAL RESOURCES DEFENSE COUNCIL v. U.S.E.P.A.
824 F. 2d 1146 (D.C. Cir. 1987)

BORK, Circuit Judge:

Current scientific knowledge does not permit a finding that there is a completely safe level of human exposure to carcinogenic agents. The Administrator of the Environmental Protection Agency, however, is charged with regulating hazardous pollutants, including carcinogens, under section 112 of the Clean Air Act by setting emission standards "at the level which in his judgment provides an ample margin of safety to protect the public health." 42 U.S.C. §7412(b)(1)(B) (1982). We address here the question of the extent of the Administrator's authority under this delegation in setting emission standards for carcinogenic pollutants.

Petitioner Natural Resources Defense Council ("NRDC") contends that the Administrator must base a decision under section 112 exclusively on health-related factors and, therefore, that the uncertainty about the effects of carcinogenic agents requires the Administrator to prohibit all emissions. The Administrator argues that in the face of this uncertainty he is authorized to set standards that require emission reduction to the lowest level attainable by best available control technology whenever that level is below that at which harm to humans has been demonstrated. We find no support for either position in the language or legislative history of the Clean Air Act. We therefore grant the petition for review and remand to the Administrator for reconsideration in light of this opinion.

I

Section 112 of the Clean Air Act provides for regulation of hazardous air pollutants, which the statute defines as "air pollutant[s] to which no ambient air quality standard is applicable and which in the judgment of the Administrator cause[ ], or contribute[ ] to, air pollution which may reasonably be anticipated to result in an increase in mortality or an increase in serious irreversible, or incapacitating reversible, illness." 42 U.S.C. §7412(a)(1) (1982). The statute requires the Administrator to publish a list containing each hazardous pollutant for which he intends to adopt an emission standard, to publish proposed regulations and a notice of public hearing for each such pollutant, and then, within a specified period, either to promulgate an emission standard or to make a finding that the particular agent is not a hazardous air pollutant. See id. §7412(b)(1)(B). The statute directs the Administrator to set an emission standard promulgated under section 112 "at the level which in his judgment provides an ample margin of safety to protect the public health." Id.

This case concerns vinyl chloride regulations. Vinyl chloride is a gaseous synthetic chemical used in the manufacture of plastics and is a strong carcinogen. In late 1975, the Administrator issued a notice of proposed rulemaking to establish an emission standard for vinyl chloride. 40 Fed. Reg. 59,532 (1975). In the notice, the EPA asserted that available data linked vinyl chloride to carcinogenic, as well as some noncarcinogenic, disorders and that "[r]easonable extrapolations" from this data suggested "that present ambient levels of vinyl chloride may cause or contribute to . . . [such] disorders." Id. at 59,533. The EPA also noted that vinyl chloride is "an apparent non-threshold pollutant," which means that it appears to create a risk to health at all non-zero levels of emission. Scientific uncertainty, due to the unavailability of dose-response data and the twenty-year latency period between initial exposure to vinyl chloride and the occurrence of disease, makes it impossible to establish any definite threshold level below which there are no adverse effects to human health. Id. at 59,533-34. The notice also stated the "EPA's position that for a carcinogen it should be assumed, in the absence of strong evidence to the contrary, that there is no atmospheric concentration that poses absolutely no public health risk." Id. at 59,534.

Because of this assumption, the EPA concluded that it was faced with two alternative interpretations of its duty under section 112. First, the EPA determined that section 112 might require a complete prohibition of emissions of non-threshold pollutants because a "zero emission limitation would be the only emission standard which would offer absolute safety from ambient exposure." 40 Fed. Reg. at 59,534. The EPA found this alternative "neither desirable nor necessary" because "[c]omplete prohibition of all emissions could require closure of an entire industry," a cost the EPA found "extremely high for elimination of a risk to health that is of unknown dimensions." Id.

The EPA stated the second alternative as follows:

> An alternative interpretation of section 112 is that it authorizes setting emission standards that require emission reduction to the lowest level achievable by use of the best available control technology in cases involving apparent non-threshold pollutants, where complete emission prohibition would result in widespread industry closure and EPA has determined that the cost of such closure would be grossly disproportionate to the benefits of removing the risk that would remain after imposition of the best available control technology.

Id. The EPA adopted this alternative on the belief that it would "produce the most stringent regulation of hazardous air pollutants short of requiring a complete prohibition in all cases." Id.

On October 21, 1976, the EPA promulgated final emission standards for vinyl chloride which were based solely on the level attainable by the best available control technology. 41 Fed. Reg. 46,560 (1976). The EPA determined that this standard would reduce unregulated emissions by 95 percent. Id. With respect to the effect of the standard on health, the EPA stated that it had assessed the risk to health at ambient levels of exposure by extrapolating from dose-response data at higher levels of exposure and then made the following findings:

> EPA found that the rate of initiation of liver angiosarcoma among [the 4.6 million] people living around uncontrolled plants is expected to range from less than one to ten cases of liver angiosarcoma per year of exposure to vinyl chloride. . . . Vinyl chloride is also estimated to produce an equal number of primary cancers at other sites, for a total of somewhere between less than one and twenty cases of cancer per year of exposure among residents around plants. The number of thse effects is expected to be reduced at least in proportion to the reduction in the ambient annual average vinyl chloride concentration, which is expected to be 5 percent of the uncontrolled levels after the standard is implemented.

Id. The EPA did not state whether this risk to health is significant or not. Nor did the EPA explain the relationship between this risk to health and its duty to set an emission standard which will provide an "ample margin of safety."

The Environmental Defense Fund ("EDF") filed suit challenging the standard on the ground that section 112 requires the Administrator to rely exclusively on health and prohibits consideration of cost and technology. The EDF and the EPA settled the suit, however, upon the EPA's agreement to propose new and more stringent standards for vinyl chloride and to establish an ultimate goal of zero emissions.

The EPA satisfied its obligations under the settlement agreement by proposing new regulations on June 2, 1977. While the proposal sought to impose more strict regulation by requiring sources subject to a 10 parts per million ("ppm") limit to reduce emissions to 5 ppm, and by establishing an aspirational goal of zero emissions, the EPA made it clear that it considered its previous regulations valid and reemphasized its view that the inability scientifically to identify a threshold of adverse effects did not require prohibition of all emissions, but rather permitted regulation at the level of best available technology. 42 Fed. Reg. 28,154 (1977). The EPA received comments on the proposal, but took no final action for more than seven years. On January 9, 1985, the EPA withdrew the proposal. Noting that certain aspects of the proposed regulations imposed "unreasonable" costs and that no control technology "has been demonstrated to significantly and consistently reduce emissions to a level below that required by the current standard," 50 Fed. Reg. 1182, 1184 (1985), the EPA concluded that it should abandon the 1977 proposal and propose in its place only minor revisions to the 1976 regulations.

This petition for review followed. . . .

III

The NRDC's challenge to the EPA's withdrawal of the 1977 amendments is simple: because the statute adopts an exclusive focus on considerations of health, the Administrator must set a zero level of emissions when he cannot determine that there is a level below which no harm will occur. . . .

. . . We find no support in the text or legislative history for the proposition that Congress intended to require a complete prohibition of emissions whenever the EPA cannot determine a threshold level for a hazardous pollutant. Instead, there is strong evidence that Congress considered such a requirement and rejected it.

Section 112 commands the Administrator to set an "emission standard" for a particular "hazardous air pollutant" which in his "judgement" will provide an "ample margin of safety." Congress' use of the term "ample margin of safety" is inconsistent with the NRDC's position that the Administrator has no discretion in the face of uncertainty. The statute nowhere defines "ample margin of safety." The Senate Report, however, in discussing a similar requirement in the context of setting ambient air standards under section 109 of the Act, explained the purpose of the "margin of safety" standard as one of affording "a *reasonable* degree of protection . . . against hazards which research has not yet identified." S. Rep. No. 1196, 91st Cong., 2d Sess. 10 (1970) (emphasis added). This view comports with the historical use of the term in engineering as "a safety factor : . . . meant to compensate for uncertainties and variabilities." See Hall, The Control of Toxic Pollutants under the Federal Water Pollution Control Act Amendments of 1972, 63 Iowa L. Rev. 609, 629 (1978). Furthermore, in a discussion of the use of identical language in the Federal Water Pollution Control Act, this court has recognized that, in discharging the responsibility to assure "an ample margin of safety," the Administrator faces "a difficult task, indeed, a veritable paradox — calling as it does for knowledge of that which is unknown — [but] . . . the term 'margin of safety' is Congress's directive that means be found to carry out the task and to reconcile the paradox." Environmental Defense Fund v. EPA, 598 F.2d 62, 81 (D.C. Cir. 1978). . . .

The only arguable support for the NRDC's position is a passage in the summary of the provisions of the conference agreement attached to Senator Muskie's statement during the post-conference debate on the Clean Air Act:

> The standards must be set to provide an ample margin of safety to protect the public health. This could mean, effectively, that a plant could be required to close because of the absence of control techniques. It could include emission standards which allow for no measurable emissions.

Senate Consideration of the Report of the Conference Committee, Exhibit 1 to Statement of Sen. Muskie, Congressional Research Service of the Library of Congress, 93d Cong., 2d Sess., 1 A Legislative History of the Clean Air Amendments of 1970 at 133 (Comm. Print 1974). This statement does not, as the NRDC supposes, mean that the Administrator must set a zero-emission level for all non-threshold pollutants. On its face, the statement means only that, in certain conditions, there may be plant closings and sometimes zero emissions may be required. Senator Muskie did not say this would invariably be so when scientific uncertainty existed. His statement confirms that the Administrator is *permitted* to set a zero-emission level for some pollutants; it does not hold that the Administrator is invariably *required* to do so whenever there is some scientific uncertainty. . . .

IV

We turn now to the question whether the Administrator's chosen method for setting emission levels above zero is consistent with congressional intent. The Administrator's position is that he may set an emission level for non-threshold pollutants at the lowest level achievable by best available control technology when that level is anywhere below the level of demonstrated harm and the cost of setting a lower level is grossly disproportionate to the benefits of removing the remaining risk. The NRDC argues that this standard is arbitrary and capricious because the EPA is never permitted to consider cost and technological feasibility under section 112 but instead is limited to consideration of health-based factors. Thus, before addressing the Administrator's method of using cost and technological feasibility in this case, we must determine whether he may consider cost and technological feasibility at all. . . .

A

On its face, section 112 does not indicate that Congress intended to preclude consideration of any factor. Though the phrase "to protect the public health" evinces an intent to make health the primary consideration, there is no indication of the factors the Administrator may or may not consider in determining, in his "judgment," what level of emissions will provide "an ample margin of safety." Instead, the language used, and the absence of any specific limitation, gives the clear impression that the Administrator has some discretion in determining what, if any, additional factors he will consider in setting an emission standard.

B

The petitioner argues that the legislative history makes clear Congress' intent to foreclose reliance on non-health-based considerations in setting standards under section 112. We find, however, that the legislative history can be characterized only as ambiguous. . . .

C

The petitioner argues next that a finding that section 112 does not preclude consideration of cost and technological feasibility would render the Clean Air

Act structurally incoherent and would be inconsistent with the Supreme Court's interpretation of section 110 of the Act, see Union Electric Co. v. EPA, 427 U.S. 246 (1976), and this court's interpretation of section 109 of the Act, see Lead Indus. Assn. v. EPA, 647 F.2d 1130 (D.C. Cir.), cert. denied, 449 U.S. 1042 (1980), as precluding consideration of these factors. We do not believe that our decision here is inconsistent with either the holding or the statutory interpretation in either case. . . .

In *Union Electric*, the Court addressed the issue of whether the Administrator could reject a state implementation plan submitted for approval under section 110 of the Clean Air Act on the ground that the plan was not economically or technologically feasible. The Court noted that section 110 sets out eight criteria that a state plan must meet and further provides that if these criteria are met, and if the state adopted the plan after notice and a hearing, the Administrator "shall" approve the plan. 427 U.S. at 257. The Court then held that "[t]he mandatory 'shall' makes it quite clear that the Administrator is not to be concerned with factors other than those specified, . . . and none of the eight factors appears to permit consideration of technological or economic infeasibility." Id. (citation omitted). In a footnote to this statement, the Court found its position bolstered by a "[c]omparison of the eight criteria of §110(a)(2)" with other provisions of the Act which expressly permit consideration of cost and technological feasibility. Id. at 257 n.5. The Court concluded that "[w]here Congress intended the Administrator to be concerned about economic and technological infeasibility, it expressly so provided." Id. We simply do not, as the NRDC does, read these statements as announcing the broad rule that an agency may never consider cost and technological feasibility, under any delegation of authority, and for any purpose, unless Congress specifically provides that the agency is authorized to consider these factors. At most, we believe that these statements stand for the proposition that when Congress has specifically directed an agency to consider certain factors, the agency may not consider unspecified factors. Because Congress chose not to limit specifically the factors the Administrator may consider in section 112, this discussion in *Union Electric* is not on point here. The factors that the Administrator may consider under section 112 could conceivably include all of the specific factors listed in other parts of the Act if necessary "to protect the public health."

A similar analysis distinguishes this court's reasoning in *Lead Industries*. In *Lead Industries*, we held that the Administrator is not required to consider cost and technology under the mandate in section 109 of the Clean Air Act to promulgate primary air quality standards which "allow[ ] an adequate margin of safety . . . to protect the public health." 42 U.S.C. §7409(b)(1) (1982). The NRDC argues that the decision in *Lead Industries*, which involved the more permissive language "adequate," rather than "ample," "margin of safety," compels the conclusion that section 112 precludes consideration of economic and technological feasibility. We think not.

The *Lead Industries* court did note that the statute on its face does not allow consideration of technological or economic feasibility, but the court based its decision that section 109 does not allow consideration of these factors in part on structural aspects of the ambient air pollution provisions that are not present here. First, besides "allowing an adequate margin of safety," ambient air standards set under section 109(b) must be based on "air quality criteria," which section 108 defines as comprising several elements, all related to health. See 42 U.S.C. §7408(a)(2)(A), (B), & (C) (1982). The court reasoned that the exclusion of economic and technological feasibility considerations from air quality criteria also foreclosed reliance on such factors in setting the ambient air quality standards based on those criteria. 647 F.2d at 1149 n.37. The court also relied on the fact that state implementation plans, the means of enforcement of ambient air standards, could not take into account economic and technological feasibility if such consideration interfered with the timely attainment of ambient air standards, and that the Administrator could not consider such feasibility factors in deciding whether to approve the state plans. Id.; see 42 U.S.C. §7410 (1982). This provided further grounds for the court to believe that Congress simply did not intend the economics of pollution control to be considered in the scheme of ambient air regulations. See 647 F.2d at 1149 n.37. . . .

The substantive standard imposed under the hazardous air pollutants provisions of section 112, by contrast with sections 109 and 110, is not based on criteria that enumerate specific factors to consider and pointedly exclude feasibility. Section 112(b)(1)'s command "to provide an ample margin of safety to protect the public health" is self-contained, and the absence of enumerated criteria may well evince a congressional intent for the Administrator to supply reasonable ones. Further, section 112, in marked contrast to the regime of ambient air standards, operates through nationally enforced standards; the state plans are permissive and may not interfere with national enforcement of any hazardous pollutant standard. 42 U.S.C. §7412(d) (1982). No detailed provisions preclusive of technological and economic considerations govern the state plans allowed under section 112; indeed, the Administrator must delegate enforcement and implementation authority to the state (subject to his continuing ability to enforce national standards) if he finds the state plan "adequate." Id. Thus, nothing in the scheme of state implementation plans under section 112 demonstrates disfavor for feasibility considerations, and this further distinguishes section 112 from the *Lead Industries* court's interpretation of section 109. . . .

V

Since we cannot discern clear congressional intent to preclude consideration of cost and technological feasibility in setting emission standards under section 112, we necessarily find that the Administrator may consider these factors. We must next determine whether the Administrator's use of these factors in this case is "based on a permissible construction of the statute." Chevron v. Natural Resources Defense Council, Inc., 467 U.S. 837, 843 (1984). We must uphold the Administrator's construction if it represents "a reasonable policy choice for the agency to make." Id. We cannot, however, affirm an agency interpretation found to be "arbitrary, capricious, or manifestly contrary to the statute." Id. at 844. Nor can we affirm if "it appears from the statute or its legislative history that the accommodation [chosen] is not one that Congress would have sanctioned." United States v. Shimer, 367 U.S. 374, 383 (1961).

Our role on review of an action taken pursuant to section 112 is generally a limited one. Because the regulation of carcinogenic agents raises questions "on the frontiers of scientific knowledge," Industrial Union Dept., AFL-CIO v. Hodgson, 499 F.2d 467, 474 (D.C. Cir. 1974), we have recognized that the Administrator's decision in this area "will depend to a greater extent upon policy judgments" to which we must accord considerable deference. Id. . . . Despite this deferential standard, we find that the Administrator has ventured into a zone of impermissible action. The Administrator has not exercised his expertise to determine an acceptable risk to health. To the contrary, in the face of uncertainty about risks to health, he has simply substituted technological feasibility for health as the primary consideration under Section 112. Because this action is contrary to clearly discernible congressional intent, we grant the petition for review.

. . . [T]he Administrator has determined that . . . [the "ample margin of safety"] standard is met whenever he sets "emission standards that require emission reduction to the lowest level achievable by use of the best available control technology in cases involving apparent nonthreshold pollutants where complete emission prohibition would result in widespread industry closure and EPA has determined that the cost of such closure would be grossly disproportionate to the benefits of removing the risk that would remain after imposition of the best available control technology." 40 Fed. Reg. 59,532, 59,534 (1975).

Thus, in setting emission standards for carcinogenic pollutants, the Administrator has decided to determine first the level of emissions attainable by best available control technology. He will then determine the costs of setting the standard below that level and balance those costs against the risk to health below the level of feasibility. If the costs are greater than the reduction in risk, then he will set the standard at the level of feasibility. This exercise, in the Administrator's view, will always produce an "ample margin of safety."

If there was any doubt that the Administrator had substituted technological feasibility for health as the primary consideration in setting emission standards under section 112, that doubt was dispelled by counsel for the EPA at oral argument. In response to a question from the court regarding a carcinogenic pollutant known to cause certain harm at 100 ppm, counsel stated that the Administrator could set an emission level at 99 ppm if that was the lowest feasible level and the costs of reducing the level below 99 ppm would be grossly disproportionate to the reduction in risk to health. Given the strong inference that harm would also certainly result at 99 ppm, the Administrator appears to have concluded that the "ample margin of safety" standard does not require any finding that a level of emissions is "safe." Instead, the Administrator need only find that the costs of control are greater than the reduction in risk to health. We disagree.

We find that the congressional mandate to provide "an ample margin of safety" "to protect the public health" requires the Administrator to make an initial determination of what is "safe." This determination must be based exclusively upon the Administrator's determination of the risk to health at a particular emission level. Because the Administrator in this case did not make any finding of the risk to health, the question of how that determination is to be made is not before us. We do wish to note, however, that the Administrator's decision does not require a finding that "safe" means "risk-free," see Industrial Union Dept. v. American Petroleum Inst., 448 U.S. 607, 642 (1980), or a finding that the determination is free from uncertainty. Instead, we find only that the Administrator's decision must be based upon an expert judgment with regard to the level of emission that will result in an "acceptable" risk to health. In this regard, the Administrator must determine what inferences should be drawn from available scientific data and decide what risks are acceptable in the world in which we live. This determination must be based solely upon the risk to health. The Administrator cannot under any circumstances consider cost and technological feasibility at this stage of the analysis. The latter factors have no relevance to the preliminary determination of what is safe. Of course, if the Administrator cannot find that there is an acceptable risk at any level, then the Administrator must set the level at zero. . . .

. . . In determining what is an "ample margin" the Administrator may, and perhaps must, take into account the inherent limitations of risk assessment and the limited scientific knowledge of the effects of exposure to carcinogens at various levels, and may therefore decide to set the level below that previously determined to be "safe." This is especially true when a straight line extrapolation from known risks is used to estimate risks to health at levels of exposure for which no data is available. This method, which is based upon the results of exposure at fairly high levels of the hazardous pollutants, will show some risk at every level because of the rules of arithmetic rather than because of any knowledge. In fact the risk at a certain point on the extrapolated line may have no relationship to reality; there is no particular reason to think that the actual line of the incidence of harm is represented by a straight line. Thus, by its nature the finding of risk is uncertain and the Administrator must use his discretion to meet the statutory mandate. It is only at this point of the regulatory process that the Administrator may set the emission standard at the lowest level that is technologically feasible. In fact, this is, we believe, precisely the type of policy choice that Congress envisioned when it directed the Administrator to provide an "ample margin of safety." Once "safety" is assured, the Administrator should be free to diminish as much of the statistically determined risk as possible by setting the standard at the lowest feasible level. Because consideration of these factors at this stage is clearly intended "to protect the public health," it is fully consistent with the Administrator's mandate under section 112.

We wish to reiterate the limited nature of our holding in this case because it is not the court's intention to bind the Administrator to any specific method of determining what is "safe" or what constitutes an "ample margin." We hold only that the Administrator cannot consider cost and technological feasibility in determining what is "safe." This determination must be based solely upon the risk to health. The issues of whether the Administrator can proceed on a case-by-case basis, what support the Administrator must provide for the determination of what is "safe," or what other factors may be considered, are issues that must be resolved after the Administrator has reached a decision upon reconsideration of the decision withdrawing the proposed 1977 amendments. . . .

NOTES AND QUESTIONS

1. The remand to EPA for "timely reconsideration" of the vinyl chloride rule had produced no EPA response two years after the court decision and is not likely to for some time. However, the agency is developing a revised §112 public health protection standard with an ample safety margin for benzene and radionuclides. The plaintiff NRDC has concluded for the time being that benzene and radionuclides pose greater health risks and therefore deserve priority at the EPA. Natural Resources Defense Council, Inc. v. United States Environmental Protection Agency, 695 F. Supp. 48 (D.D.C. 1988). For proposed rule making see 53 Fed. Reg. 28,496 (July 28, 1988) (benzene) and 54 Fed. Reg. 9612 (March 7, 1989) (radionuclides). The deadline for both final rules is August 31, 1989. Each proposal asks for comments on approaches that range from a lifetime risk of cancer (for benzene) of one in 170 to one in a million.

2. The EPA has listed seven carcinogens as hazardous air pollutants and issued emission standards for six carcinogens: asbestos, vinyl chloride, benzene, radionuclides, and arsenic. Beryllium has also been listed and regulated, although not for carcinogenic effects. EPA listed coke oven emissions and proposed emissions standards in March 1987 but has not issued them in final form.

EPA has indicated an intent to list another 10 substances, including chromium, carbon tetrachloride, chloroform, and ethylene oxide. According to EPA, an intent to list a substance as a hazardous pollutant does not legally bind the agency as does a listing decision. In a pending suit NRDC contends that EPA is required to list a substance immediately if it has been determined to cause serious irreversible illness and if EPA has determined that it is a hazardous air pollutant. NRDC v. Thomas, No. 86 CIV0603 (CSH) (S.D.N.Y.).

The Clean Air Act provides EPA one year in which to issue regulations after a substance is listed. The EPA met this deadline only in the case of vinyl chloride. From the date of listing to final action, EPA has taken an average of four years for the six carcinogens for which there are final rules. Four of these carcinogens were regulated or listed under legal pressure: asbestos, vinyl chloride, radionuclides, and arsenic.

For the five substances regulated primarily for carcinogenic effects, EPA has relied on human evidence of carcinogenicity (asbestos, vinyl chloride, benzene, radionuclides, and arsenic). For eight of the ten substances EPA intends to regulate, it has relied on animal bioassays for evidence of carcinogenicity. For chromium and cadmium, it has both animal and human evidence of carcino-genicity.

3. Do you see why EPA has dragged its feet in developing NESHAP? In addition to the "ample margin of safety" problem, EPA also thought that the requirement for evidence that the pollutant may "reasonably be anticipated to result" in an increase in death or serious illness imposed a burden heavier than that imposed by the endangerment standards sprinkled throughout the rest of the Clean Air Act. Setting a §112 standard would involve the agency in the protract-ed problems of proof of risk from low-level, chronic exposures. The EPA was reluctant to tie up time and effort in implementing a provision that imposes a heavy procedural burden on the agency, deflects it from more cost-effective reg-ulation under the ambient and emissions standard provisions (especially NSPS), and requires single substances (rather than groups of substances or industries) to be regulated.

4. In 1977 Congress added §112(e), which, like a parallel provision for NSPS, allows EPA to set a "design, equipment, work practice, or operational standard" when it is not feasible to set a conventional numerical emissions stan-dard. Congress enacted this amendment to anticipate the problem addressed in Adamo Wrecking Co. v. United States, 434 U.S. 275 (1978), in which the Su-preme Court held that the authority to set "emissions standards" under §112 did not include authority to set a design or operational standard. At issue in the case was EPA's 1973 work practice standard requiring the wetdown of asbestos insu-lation in old buildings before demolition.

The Court's stingy interpretation of "emissions standards" did little harm because of Congress's prompt action in reversing *Adamo*. Some felt, however, that the Court was led to construe the statute as it did to avoid a serious consti-tutional issue that still overshadows the Clean Air Act. Section 307(b)(1) now requires that judicial review of most Clean Air Act standards (including §112 standards) be sought within only 60 days of promulgation. Section 307(b)(2) then forecloses substantive judicial review of the standard in any subsequent enforce-ment proceeding. Restricting judicial review has been upheld in certain con-texts, such as wartime emergency price controls. Yakus v. United States, 321 U.S. 414 (1944). How do you think the issue of sixty-day Clean Air Act judicial review should be decided if it subsequently cannot be avoided by the Court?

2.   Toxic Effluent Control under the Clean Water Act: Of Balancing and Margins of Safety

Toxic effluent standards are set either according to the procedures con-tained in Clean Water Act §307(a)(2) with a NESHAP-like strictness and "an ample margin of safety," or they may be set as industry-wide technology-based effluent limitations under §§301 and 304. The latter allow the agency to use informal rule-making and the somewhat relaxed formal rule-making procedures of §307(a)(2). Review pp. 407-443 in Chapter 4. Section 307 codifies a 1976 settlement that put EPA on a strict schedule to develop toxic effluent standards. Natural Resources Defense Council, Inc. v. Gorsuch, 12 Envtl. L. Rep. (Envtl. L. Inst.) 20,570 (D.D.C. 1982), holds that EPA must adhere to the 1976 "Flannery decree" schedule despite the 1977 amendments.

The adoption of the "Flannery decree" was challenged by various companies and trade associations as being outside the court's power, but the District of Columbia Circuit Court of Appeals upheld the decree. Citizens for a Better Environment v. Gorsuch, — F.2d —, 19 Envt. Rep. Cas. (BNA) 2057 (D.C. Cir. 1983). The challengers argued that each provision of a consent decree must necessarily remedy a specific statutory violation for the decree to be valid and that, consequently, the "Flannery decree" impermissibly infringed on EPA's discretion to implement §307. The court first held that a district court has the power to enter a consent decree without first determining that a statutory violation has occurred, so long as the decree is fair and consistent with the purpose of the relevant statute. The second challenge was based on Vermont Yankee Nuclear Power Corp. v. Natural Resources Defense Council, Inc., 435 U.S. 519 (1978), p. 141 *supra*, which curtailed judicial imposition of extra procedures on agencies. *Vermont Yankee* did not, in the Court's opinion, either prescribe the content of EPA's regulations or direct EPA to enforce the regulations in any particular way. Finally, the court found that during the debates on the 1977 amendments to the Clean Water Act, Congress sanctioned the limited infringement on the agency's discretion the decree imposes (123 Cong. Rec. 39,181 (1977)).

What defenses are open to a discharger challenging a regulation based on a risk assessment? Two companion cases decided under the pre-1977 §307 answer this question, "Very few, if any." Environmental Defense Fund, Inc. v. EPA, 598 F.2d 62 (D.C. Cir. 1978), upheld the agency's power virtually to prohibit the discharge of PCBs. Hercules, Inc. v. EPA, 598 F.2d 91 (D.C. Cir. 1978), upheld health-based standards for chlorinated hydrocarbon pesticides, toxaphene and endrin, which were alleged to be carcinogenic.

The manufacture of PCBs — some 209 flame-resistant compounds used in electrical equipment and as plasticizers, adhesives, and textile coatings — has been prohibited since 1978, but some 150 million pounds of PCBs are now dispersed in the air and water; twice that amount is located in landfills; and five times that amount is still in use in industrial equipment. In Environmental Defense Fund, Inc. v. EPA, industry argued that the regulations lacked an adequate scientific basis because the record consisted in large part of studies involving related substances with more chlorinated PCBs than those discharged by the industry objectors. They argued that EPA had to demonstrate the toxicity of each regulated chemical "through studies demonstrating a clear line of causation between a particular chemical and harm to the public health or the environment." The court interpreted "ample margin of safety" to mean that EPA had a mandate "'to take into account and compensate for uncertainties and lack of precise predictions in the area of forecasting the effects of toxic pollutants'" (598 F.2d at 81). Applying the substantial evidence standard, the court said that industry's arguments were foreclosed by the "ample margin of safety" standard and the need to defer to the scientific expertise of the agency, quoting and discussing *Ethyl, Reserve Mining,* and the pesticide cases (pp. 571-577 *infra*). For a sketch of concepts very similar to the "ample margin of safety," see *Lead Industries* (ambient air quality standard for lead), at p. 190 *supra,* Natural Resources Defense Council, Inc. v. EPA, 655 F.2d 318 (D.C. Cir. 1981) (diesel car emissions standards), and NESHAP.

Hercules, Inc. v. EPA rejected manufacturers' arguments that EPA could not set standards for pesticides discharged into only two water bodies by relying on laboratory tests on aquatic organisms not found in those waters. EPA set the standards for two site-specific discharges through rule-making. The court also rejected the argument that §307 required EPA to consider economic and technological factors in setting the standards. Was the court correct? Recall EPA's handling of the same issue under the NESHAP provision of the Clean Air Act. What are the comparative advantages of the alternative pollutant-by-pollutant technology-based approaches of §307? See BASF Wyandotte Corp. v. Costle, 598 F.2d 637 (1st Cir. 1979). See also Weyerhaeuser v. Costle, 590 F.2d 1011, 1042 (D.C. Cir. 1978).

Discharges of radionuclides cannot be regulated under §307 as they are under NESHAP in the Clean Air Act. See §301(f). See Train v. Colorado Public Interest Research Group, 426 U.S. 1 (1976), which holds that despite §301(f) the Nuclear Regulatory Commission, not EPA, regulates any discharges involving special nuclear, source, and byproduct material under the Atomic Energy Act. Compare Clean Air Act §122.

Section 301(*l*) of the Clean Water Act provides that "[t]he Administrator may not modify" any statutory requirement under §301 that applies to a toxic pollutant listed under §307. Should a "fundamentally-different-factor" variance for municipal POTW pre-treatment standards that would permit the discharge of toxic pollutants be considered a modification of a pre-treatment standard to which §301 applies? Or is it simply the creation of a more appropriate standard based on factors previously overlooked by the Administrator? See National Association of Metal Finishers v. EPA, 719 F.2d 624, 645-646 (3d Cir. 1983).

E.   PREVENTING THE ENTRY OF TOXIC SUBSTANCES INTO THE STREAM OF COMMERCE

More can be done to control hazardous substances than merely bringing common law actions to enjoin a nuisance or setting emissions and effluent standards, using the classic approach of the Clean Air and Clean Water Acts. Commerce in substances that are hazardous or that pollute may be restricted or banned entirely. A less disruptive strategy embodying this policy allows a product to be marketed until its hazards become known and then restricts its marketing or use only so far as necessary to protect the public. A more aggressive strategy restricts or forbids commerce in all substances that are shown by pre-market screening to be likely to subject the public to unacceptable hazards. Federal regulation of pesticides exemplifies the former approach, whereas the latter approach was adopted in the Toxic Substances Control Act of 1976, which purports to screen all existing and new toxic substances of every kind. Each approach will now be examined in turn.

1. Pesticide Regulation: Federal Bellwether for Controlling Pollution at Its Source

Modern agriculture is heavily dependent on two chemical technologies: fertilizers and pesticides. Some 40,000 registered pesticides contain 600 active ingredients. Of the 1 billion pounds of pesticides sold annually in the United States, 80 percent are used in agriculture, 15 percent in industry and government, and 5 percent in homes. General Accounting Office, Carcinogens: EPA's Formidable Task to Assess and Regulate Their Risk 10 (1986).

The application of large amounts of chemical pesticides (a generic name for three different classes of chemicals and compounds: fungicides, insecticides, and rodenticides) became controversial after the publication of Rachel Carson's book Silent Spring (1962). Her book touched off a reevaluation of one of the most widely hailed benefits of World War II technology, synthetic organic pesticides. Initially, environmentalists focused their attention on eliminating the use of DDT. Out of the DDT cancellation proceeding emerged many of the core concepts that continue to control the assessment of toxic chemicals because that proceeding first illustrated the use of cancer risk as a proxy for other environmental injuries.

The rich statutory, regulatory, and judicial law of pesticides control could justify chapter-length (or indeed book-length) treatment. Earlier casebooks did treat pesticide control in great detail. The interconnections between food and drug law and pesticide control law offer interesting possibilities for study. Pesticide regulation remains controversial today. Every few months, the continued registration of what was previously believed to be a safe pesticide is challenged. Nevertheless, other areas of environmental law are now the battleground for resolving contemporary risk assessment and management issues, many of which first appeared in the field of pesticides control. Treatment here will be largely historical.

The pesticide regulatory experience is a classic example of the box into which risk assessment placed regulators. As screening procedures increased in sophistication and sensitivity, so did indicators that risks were present. See the Note on measurement and detection at p. 517 *supra*. Does this mean that every pesticide that triggers a determination that some risk is present should be taken off the market? What conceivable defenses are there to such a risk trigger approach? EPA has chosen, for a variety of reasons, to concentrate on minimizing the use of cancer-causing pesticides, but one can ask if this is in fact the right focus. Congress has mandated that EPA screen pesticides for public health risks. But once a pesticide has been screened, it can be marketed, and the decision about how much can be used is up to the applicator. This philosophy is consistent with a theory of regulation limited to the correction of market failures, but a substantial question exists about whether health screening is the right strategy to minimize crop and other pest damage.

In addition to laying the foundation for risk assessment, the regulatory experience with pesticides has important lessons for environmental law. Pesticide use is supported by a powerful constituency of industry, agricultural associations, and much (but not all) of the agricultural research establishment. Not surprisingly, Congress has tried to balance EPA's power to protect public health against extensive duties to consider the economic benefits of pesticide use. EPA has broad authority to take both risks and economic impacts into account, with the result that its political legitimacy remains fragile in this area.

The constituency has produced a compromise regulatory strategy that, in the opinion of some, makes it difficult for EPA to deal with the real issue. Insects and other pesticide targets develop immunities, so that applicators constantly must use more chemicals. To break this environmentally destructive cycle, it has been argued that Integrated Pest Management (IPM) be used. IPM is a set of strategies that mix chemical and nonchemical alternatives to minimize pest damage. IPM requires forced participation of holdouts in an area, much like compulsory unitization allows a majority of oil and gas interest holders to bind the minority, ensuring that an oil pool will not be exploited too rapidly. Those wishing to pursue IPM and the mixed regulatory strategies it entails might start with National Academy of Sciences, Pest Control: An Assessment of Present and Alternative Technologies (1975) (5 vols.), and D. Pimentel & J. Perkins, Pest Control: Cultural and Environmental Aspects (1980). Dunning, Pests, Poisons, and the Living Law: The Control of Pesticides in California's Imperial Valley, 2 Ecology L.Q. 633 (1972), contains a useful discussion of the legal ramifications of IPM. IPM may be an idea whose time has come. The movement for less chemically-dependent crop raising techniques is gaining momentum, see National Research Council (Board on Agriculture), Alternative Agriculture (1989). See also United States Environmental Protection Agency Science Advisory Board, Future Risk: Research Strategies For the 1990s (1988) which recommends that EPA shift its strategies from end of the pipe controls to the reduction of all sources of pollution.

a. The Evolution of Pesticide Regulations: From Classic Consumer Protection to DDT

Pesticides were first regulated in 1910 to prevent consumer fraud after users complained of adulterated goods (Insecticide Act of 1910, Pub. L. No. 61-152,

36 Stat. 331). In 1947 Congress responded to the increasing use of more sophisticated, synthetic compounds by passing the Federal Insecticide, Fungicide and
Rodenticide Act (FIFRA) 7 U.S.C. §§136-136y (1988). The Food, Drug, and
Cosmetic Act (FD & CA) and FIFRA relied largely on the same model: Drugs
and pesticides should be efficacious; any public health or "environmental" problems are caused by misuse, which labeling will prevent. Under FIFRA, the
Department of Agriculture was required to register all pesticides; the chief restriction on entry to the market was labeling requirements explaining how to use the
compound effectively and safely. Until 1964, a pesticide to which the Department of Agriculture objected could be registered under protest. Once a pesticide
was registered, it could be marketed unless the registration was suspended under
an interim administrative procedure, pending the initiation of lengthy proceedings to cancel the registration.

The Department's administration of FIFRA was examined and found
wanting when public attention focused on DDT. See Rodgers, The Persistent
Problem of the Persistent Pesticides: A Lesson in Environmental Law, 70 Colum. L. Rev. 567 (1970). In 1969 the Environmental Defense Fund asked the
Department to suspend the registration of DDT. A 1964 amendment to FIFRA
required the agency to suspend a registration if necessary to prevent an "imminent hazard." The Secretary responded by refusing to suspend the registration of
the major use of DDT, the suppression of cotton pests. (A pesticide is registered,
not by chemical compound, but by use.) The Department issued notices to
cancel four minor uses and promised additional notices after further study. In
the interim, two significant events occurred. The administration of FIFRA was
given to the newly created EPA, and the District of Columbia Circuit Court of
Appeals held that the Administrator had a duty to suspend a registration when a
substantial question of an "imminent hazard" existed. Environmental Defense
Fund, Inc. v. Ruckelshaus, 439 F.2d 584 (D.C. Cir. 1971). The litigation growing out of the DDT controversy provides a case study in the power and limits of
appellate courts to control an agency agenda and to structure the agency's discretion within the constraints of separation of powers principles. The crucial
opinions in addition to Environmental Defense Fund, Inc. v. Ruckelshaus are
Environmental Defense Fund, Inc. v. Hardin, 428 F.2d 1093 (D.C. Cir. 1970);
Wellford v. Ruckelshaus, 439 F.2d 598 (D.C. Cir. 1971); and Environmental
Defense Fund, Inc. v. EPA 465 F.2d 528 (D.C. Cir. 1972).

The DDT cancellation hearing began on August 17, 1971, before a hearing examiner on loan from the Department of the Interior. His primary experience had been in mine accident inquiries. By this time, the focus of public
concern and of the administrative proceeding against DDT had shifted from
general environmental damage to carcinogenicity, although Carson's Silent
Spring had focused entirely on ecosystem effects. The hearing examiner found
that DDT was neither carcinogenic nor mutagenic and that it did not have a
deleterious effect on freshwater fish, estuarine organisms, wild birds, or other
wildlife. He refused to recommend cancellation. After finding that DDT did
present significant risks and balancing all of the risks and benefits of DDT use,

EPA Administrator William Ruckelshaus issued an opinion canceling almost all of the registrations of the pesticide. His decision was sustained on appeal, in part because the head of the agency can ignore the decision of the hearing examiner when the issue involves a policy judgment. Environmental Defense Fund, Inc. v. EPA, 489 F.2d 1247 (D.C. Cir. 1973). See generally McGarity, Substantive and Procedural Discretion in Administrative Resolution of Science Policy Questions: Regulating Carcinogens in EPA and OSHA, 67 Geo. L.J. 729 (1979).

The DDT opinion paved the way for the agency to use evidence of tumors in laboratory animals as the basis for risk assessment. Industry chose to try to rebut the laboratory evidence primarily with the argument that a human health hazard could be found only on the basis of epidemiological evidence. In short, as soon as people contract cancer, the pesticide registration can be canceled. The Administrator rejected this argument because the persistence and biomagnification of pesticides in the food chain were a cause for concern. The long-term effects of DDT were unknown; evidence that high levels of DDT caused tumors in laboratory mice was sufficient to warrant the conclusion that the pesticide was a potential carcinogen (37 Fed. Reg. 13,369, 13,371).

b.   The Current Law

In 1972 Congress amended FIFRA with the Federal Environmental Pesticide Control Act (FEPCA). FEPCA carries forward the consumer protection philosophy of FIFRA but supplements it with public health regulation for more subtle risks. FEPCA requires that the risks and benefits of pesticide use be considered at four stages of decisionmaking (registration, restricted registration, cancellation, and suspension), but the definition of risk and benefit is not the same at each stage. See generally Spector, Regulation of Pesticides by the Environmental Protection Agency, 5 Ecology L.Q. 223 (1976).

Registration. EPA must register a pesticide if the Administrator determines that its chemical composition seems to justify the efficacy claims made for it, that the manufacturer has complied with FEPCA labeling and data submission requirements, and that the pesticide will not cause "unreasonable adverse effects on the environment" when used as intended and "in accordance with widespread and commonly recognized practice" (§136a(c)(5)). The term "unreasonable adverse effects on the environment" is defined by the statute to mean "any unreasonable risk to man or the environment, taking into account the economic, social, and environmental costs and benefits of the use of any pesticide" (7 U.S.C. §136(bb)). A pesticide may either be registered for general or restricted use. A pesticide may be registered for restricted use if the Administrator determines that acute dermal or inhalation toxicity may result from misuse or that without additional restrictions use may cause unreasonable adverse effects on the environment (§136a(d)). In 1978 Congress allowed EPA to grant conditional registrations for pesticides that are "identical or substantially similar" to registered pesticides and that do not significantly increase the risk of any unreasonable adverse effects in the environment (§136a(c)(7)).

How is "unreasonableness" to be determined? FEPCA requires a fuller balancing of costs and benefits than do other environmental statutes. The balancing stops just short of a formal cost-benefit analysis. See Rodgers, Benefits, Costs, and Risks: Oversight of Health and Environmental Decisionmaking, 4 Harv. Envtl. L. Rev. 191, 207 (1980). There is a tension between a full balancing and the EPA policy of using sensitive cancer triggers to determine risk. Earlier drafts of the legislation required a showing of substantial adverse effects before registration could be denied, but the more environmentally oriented Senate Commerce Committee changed the language to the present formula to ensure that a court would not hold "that a 'substantial' level of adversity must be reached before the Environmental protection Agency invokes the necessary balancing of risk versus benefit in determining whether a pesticide ought to be registered" (Senate Comm. on Commerce, Federal Environmental Pesticide Control Act of 1972, S. Rep. No. 970, 92d Cong., 2d Sess. 10 (1972)).

FEPCA clearly requires EPA to consider the benefits of pesticide use, and the statute has been amended several times to enlarge the role of the Department of Agriculture in the decisionmaking process. Although EPA is not required to do so, it has tried to adapt formal cost-benefit analysis for application in pesticide decisions. See Office of Pesticide Programs, Office of Water and Hazardous Materials, A Benefit-Cost System for Chemical Pesticides (1975). Judicial consideration of EPA benefit decisions is unenlightening (e.g., Environmental Defense Fund, Inc. v. EPA, 510 F.2d 1292, 1302-1303 (D.C. Cir. 1975)), and nagging unresolved issues remain regarding whether the agency knows how to develop and apply benefit data. For example, the first pesticide to complete the RPAR process (see p. 576 *infra*) was chlorobenzilate, primarily used to control citrus rust mites. EPA refused to cancel most uses because the failure to control the mite in Florida, Texas, and California would have significant adverse effects on fruit size, appearance, crop yield, and treestock stamina. A National Academy of Sciences (NAS) study found in a subsequent independent literature search that the Department of Agriculture, which has a formal role in supplying benefit data, had failed to bring to EPA's attention "eight additional studies of the effect of chemical miticides on citrus yields. None of these additional studies . . . found a statistically significant difference in yields between sprayed and unsprayed plots that could be attributed to rust mites" (National Academy of Sciences, Regulating Pesticides 192 (1980)). More startling, the NAS committee concluded that estimated increased pest control costs from canceling the uses of chlorobenzilate would range between $2.4 and 9.2 million per year rather than $57 million a year, as EPA had projected (Regulating Pesticides, at 209-210).

Cancellation and suspension. FIFRA guarantees the registrant of a pesticide a fullblown adjudicatory hearing before cancellation, which may take place whenever it appears that "a pesticide or its labeling or other material required to be submitted does not comply with . . . [this Act] or when used in accordance with widespread and commonly recognized practice, [the pesticide] . . . generally causes unreasonable adverse effects on the environment" (§136d(b)). If the Administrator determines that an "imminent hazard" is posed by continued use during the time required for cancellation, the agency may immediately suspend the pesticide's registration (§136(d)(c)(1)). The test for imminent hazard is whether "unreasonable adverse effects on the environment," the familiar criterion for initial registration and for cancellation, are likely to result during the interim period unless suspension occurs. (§136(l),(bb)).

The burden of proof in suspension proceedings. The first judicial interpretations of FIFRA focused on its suspension provisions. These cases set the tone for the courts' interpretation of other provisions of FIFRA as well. Although the courts initially intimated that suspension should be reserved for substantial irreparable harm to the public, after 1970 they came to the position that for a suspension only a preliminary assessment indicating possible public harm was required. The decision to suspend would be upheld if it was supported by respectable scientific authority. Environmental Defense Fund, Inc. v. EPA, 465 F.2d 528 (D.C. Cir. 1972). This interpretation effectively placed the burden of proving the safety of a pesticide on the registrant. This was made explicit in suspension proceedings for the pesticides heptachlor and chlorodane. EPA regulations placed the burden of going forward on the agency and the burden of persuasion on the registrant:

> In urging that the ultimate burden of proof in a suspension proceeding rests on the Administrator, Velsicol and USDA assert that the suspension decision is a drastic step differing fundamentally from both the registration and cancellation decisions made under FIFRA. But we have already cautioned that the "imminent hazard" requisite for suspension is not limited to a concept of crisis: "It is enough if there is *substantial likelihood* that serious harm will be experienced during the year or two required in any realistic projection of the administrative process."[15] "FIFRA confers broad discretion" on the Administrator to find facts and "to set policy in the public interest." Wellford v. Ruckelshaus, 439 F.2d 598, 601 1971). This broad discretion was conferred on the implicit assumption that interim action may be necessary to protect against the risk of harm to the environment and public health while a fuller factual record is developed in the cancellation proceeding. This avenue of protective relief would be effectively foreclosed if we accepted Velsicol's argument that the Administrator must *prove* imminent hazard — apparently in some sense of weight of the evidence going beyond substantial likelihood. But as we have already pointed out, the basic statutory directive requires affirmance of the Administrator's decision if supported by substantial evidence, and this requires "something less than the weight of the evidence." We reject that renewed invitation to exercise increased substantive control over the agency decision process. [Environmental Defense Fund, Inc. v. EPA, 548 F.2d 998, 1004-1005 (D.C. Cir. 1976), *cert. denied*, 431 U.S. 925 (1977).]

15. EDF v. EPA, 510 F.2d at 1297, quoting EDF v. EPA, 465 F.2d at 540.
Our en banc decision in Ethyl Corp. v. EPA, 541 F.2d 1 at 16, n.28 (1976), *cert. denied*, 426 U.S. 941 (1976), considered this standard as more rigorous than the standard involved in *Ethyl*; we have not sought to engage in a comparative analysis of the differences that may be discernible in these two statutory standards, but have rested with applying the "substantial likelihood" standard to the facts of this case.

See generally Note, Pesticide Regulation: Risk Assessment and Burden of Proof, 45 Geo. Wash. L. Rev. 1066 (1977). Agency-manufacturer settlements of cancellation proceedings are subject to a reasonableness standard. National Coalition Against the Misuse of Pesticides v. EPA, 867 F.2d 636 (D.C. Cir. 1989).

Cancellation and the "rebuttable presumption against registration" (RPAR). The leading DDT case that first established the liberal burden rule in suspension proceedings, Environmental Defenses Fund, Inc. v. Ruckelshaus, also set the tone for cancellation proceedings as well. The court interpreted FIFRA to require the Administrator to commence a cancellation proceeding whenever there exists a "substantial question" about the hazards to health caused by a registered pesticide. Under the court's new, liberal definition of "health hazard," the agency would have no great difficulty launching cancellation proceedings. The difficulty came in establishing workable guidelines for the health hazards that would "trigger" cancellation and in bringing the long adjudicatory proceedings to a successful conclusion. To aid it in achieving both these objectives, in 1975 EPA issued a policy statement that declared that a rebuttable presumption against registration (RPAR) would arise if certain types of data suggested that the pesticide was acutely or chronically toxic or no effective emergency treatment was available in case of human exposure. Evidence of chronic toxicity that would trigger the RPAR included, in addition to epidemiological data, acceptance of mutagenic or benign tumorigenic effects discovered through animal experiments. This policy not only formalized the acceptance of animal experiment data on carcinogenicity but ignored for precautionary purposes the distinction between benign and malignant tumors. Any tumors in laboratory animals potentially would trigger an RPAR (40 Fed. Reg. 28,242). In 1985, EPA renamed the RPAR "Special Review." 40 C.F.R. §154.7. The concept remains the same, but third parties may now initiate a second look at a compound. See D. Stever, Law of Chemical Regulation and Hazardous Waste §303(2)(a)(ii) (1986).

In 1976, EPA published a broader and more polished statement of its RPAR "cancer principles," indicating that it intended to apply them not only in pesticide regulation but in its remaining regulatory programs as well (41 Fed. Reg. 21,402). Note that EPA was careful not to propose that its principles be adopted as binding rules. The 1976 "interim" guidelines recognize four types of evidence of carcinogenicity: (1) epidemiological studies in humans confirmed with animal tests (the "best evidence"), (2) animal tests in which malignant tumors appear, including benign tumors recognized as early stages of malignancy ("substantial evidence"), (3) indirect tests of tumorigenic activity and animal tests revealing only non-life-shortening benign tumors ("suggestive evidence"), and (4) studies relating chemical structure to carcinogenicity ("ancillary evidence"). The significance that these types of evidence may carry in a decision to register or cancel a pesticide is more likely to turn on EPA's assessment of overall risks and benefits than merely on the evidence of carcinogenicity. Recall that EPA could still permit even a known human carcinogen to be registered if it determined that the benefits of its use outweighed its health risks. The courts have responded sympathetically to EPA's attempt to "prejudge" the acceptability of various categories of evidence before a particular pesticide has even been singled out for cancellation proceedings. See Environmental Defense Fund, Inc. v. EPA, 548 F.2d 9989, 1006-1007 (D.C. Cir. 1976).

"Old" pesticides, indemnification, and disposal. The FIFRA has been amended four times since 1972, but its basic statutory structure was established in 1947 and 1972 (FEPCA). The 1988 amendments, however, did address three significant problems in FIFRA implementation. Pub. L. No. 100-532, 102 Stat. 2654 (1988). Approximately 50,000 "old" pesticides had been registered under the permissive pre-1972 requirements. Examination of all these pesticides proved impossible by the 1976 deadline imposed by FEPCA. The EPA believed it would take a decade or more to re-register them. In fact, EPA has been able to identify data needs on only 25 pesticides a year; thus a mere handful of re-registered "final standards" has been issued. The 1988 FIFRA amendments set a nine-year re-registration schedule, provided funding through $150 million in fees to be collected from registrants, shifted numerous tasks to registrants, and streamlined the process. Approximately one-third of old registrations probably will not be renewed.

The 1972 law, FEPCA, required EPA to indemnify producers, distributors, and others for economic loss when EPA cancelled or suspended a registration. Claims for two suspended and cancelled pesticides, 2,4,5-T/silvex and ethylene dibromide (EDB), totalled $30 millon. The third and last suspended and cancelled pesticide, dinoseb, may involve another $40 million in claims. Senate Comm. on Agriculture, Nutrition, and Forestry, Report on the FIFRA Reform Act of 1988, S. Rep. No. 346, 100th Cong., 2d Sess. 7 (1988). To eliminate the chilling effect on regulation caused by assessing these sums against the EPA operating budget, the 1988 amendments transferred liability to the Federal Judgment Fund, an existing fund that relies on general appropriations to pay claims against the federal government. §15(b)(1). Other minor changes made indemnification harder to obtain. Also, prior to the 1988 amendments FIFRA required the EPA to bear the costs of disposing of cancelled pesticides. Disposal cost some $195 million for the three products mentioned above. The amendments shifted responsibility for disposal to the pesticide industry. See generally Ferguson and Gray, 1988 FIFRA Amendments: A Major Step in Pesticide Regulation, 19 Envtl. L. Rep. (Envtl. L. Inst.) — News and Analysis 10070 (1989).

Many local communities are enacting stricter pesticide controls, reflecting dissatisfaction with federal and state regulation. These ordinances face a high risk of state and federal preemption. See Pesticide Public Policy Committee v. Village of Wauconda, 117 Ill.2d 107, 510 N.E.2d 858 (1987).

A NOTE ON FEDERAL GENERIC CANCER POLICIES FOR REGULATING CARCINOGENS

The primary motivation behind "generic" agency cancer policies is to create a uniform systematic agency approach to cancer risk assessment. These policies were also necessitated by the tortuous proceedings that exposed the agencies to claims that lawyers, not scientists, are the real authors of agency cancer policies and "cancer principles." Before the generic approaches were adopted, federal regulatory resources were stretched thin trying to reestablish in separate administrative proceedings that a scientific basis existed for the various methodological short cuts for inferring a human cancer risk (e.g., use of animal data, not human data). Months or years could pass while an agency laboriously went through the same defense of its methodology for the hearing officer (often the same one), who was obligated to allow manufacturers to make the same attacks on agency methodology that they had made in prior proceedings on other substances. The generic approach would enable an agency to provide its answers to disputed fundamental questions in advance of particular proceedings as guidance to its own decisionmakers, regulatees, and public participants.

The generic policies have roughly the same content and codify the approach to risk assessment set out *supra* at pp. 502-510. The nine "cancer principles" listed by EPA in the proceedings to cancel registration for the pesticides aldrin and dieldrin are illustrative:

1. A carcinogen is any agent which increases tumor induction in man or animals.
2. Well-established criteria exist for distinguishing between benign and malignant tumors; however, even the induction of benign tumors is sufficient to characterize a chemical as a carcinogen.
3. The majority of human cancers are caused by avoidable exposure to carcinogens.
4. While chemicals can be carcinogenic agents, only a small percentage actually are.
5. Carcinogenesis is characterized by its irreversibility and long latency period following the initial exposure to the carcinogenic agent.
6. There is great variation in individual susceptibility to carcinogens.
7. The concept of a "threshold" exposure level for a carcinogenic agent has no practical significance because there is no valid method for establishing such a level.
8. A carciniogenic agent may be identified through analysis of tumor induction results with laboratory animals exposed to the agent, or on a post hoc basis by properly conducted epidemiological studies.
9. Any substance which produces tumors in animals must be considered a carcinogenic hazard to man if the results were achieved according to the established parameters of a valid carcinogenesis test. [Office of Technology Assessment, Identifying and Regulating Carcinogens 33 (1987).]

Uniform principles for agency cancer risk assessment have a long history. As early as the 1950s the Food and Drug Administration set guidelines for toxicity assessment, although the FDA has never explicitly specified uniform guidelines for interpreting carcinogenicity data. For the FDA's current guidelines on conducting animal toxicity tests, see the FDA's "Red Book," Principles for the Safety Assessment of Direct Food Additives and Color Additives Used in Food (1982).

With its 1976 interim guidelines EPA became the first federal agency to set out systematic criteria for evaluating potential human carcinogens in subsequent regulatory proceedings. The EPA's revised Guidelines for Cancer Risk Assessment appear at 51 Fed. Reg. 33,992 (1986). The EPA simultaneously published uniform guidelines for exposure assessment (51 Fed. Reg. 34,042), health risk assessment of suspect developmental toxicants (51 Fed. Reg. 34,028), and mutagenicity risk assessment (51 Fed. Reg. 34,006).

The Occupational Safety and Health Administration (OSHA) and the Consumer Product Safety Commission (CPSC) developed their own cancer policies. As with the 1976 EPA "interim" guidelines, the CPSC elected not to try to adopt its cancer policy through notice-and-comment rule-making, a procedural mistake invalidated in Dow Chemical Co. v. Blum, 467 F. Supp. 892 (D.D.C. 1979). The CPSC withdrew these guidelines and now applies the generic government-wide policy adopted by the Office of Science and Technology Policy in 1985, *infra*. OSHA did take the more arduous route of rule-making. The informal public hearing on its proposed rules lasted six weeks. The rule-making record eventually grew to 250,000 pages. To state and explain the final policy required almost 300 pages in the Federal Register. 45 Fed. Reg. 5,001 (1980). The result remains an extremely useful statement of the methodology of cancer regulation, but litigation and the Reagan Administration's lack of enthusiasm for the approach caused OSHA to vacillate over the regulations. Although the regulations have never actually been withdrawn permanently, they have been amended several times.

The Carter Administration began an effort to develop guidelines that would be applied throughout all the federal agencies with authority to regulate carcinogens. Council on Environmental Quality, Ninth Annual Report 209-210 (1978). In 1981 the Reagan Administration attacked the generic approach through a task force on regulatory relief chaired by then-Vice President George Bush. This assault coincided with a dismal episode in the history of EPA. Under Administrator Anne Gorsuch Burford, application of a cancer policy did not fare well. John Todhunter, Assistant EPA Administrator for Pesticides and Toxic Substances, attempted to scuttle regulation of formaldehyde. Assistant Administrator Rita Lavelle attacked regulation of trichloroethylene. Nevertheless, in the Executive Office of the President an effort continued to carry forward the formulation of a government-wide generic carcinogen policy which was begun in the Carter Administration. By 1985 the effort produced an extensive summary of the state of various scientific fields involving carcinogen risk assessment, including discussion of the assumptions used in risk assessment and a statement of rudimentary principles. U.S. Office of Science and Technology Policy, Chemical Carcinogens: A Review of the Science and Its Associated Principles, 50 Fed. Reg. 10,372 (March 14, 1985).

A student of the agencies' carcinogen policies discerns three types: presumption-rebuttal, weight-of-the-evidence, and leave-it-to-the-scientists. M.E. Rushefsky, Making Cancer Policy (1986). The OSHA policy represents the presumption-rebuttal approach. This policy approach uses the regulatory process to establish presumptions and sets stringent conditions on when and how these presumptions may be rebutted. The OSTP policy and the carcinogen risk assessment guidelines of EPA take a weight-of-the-evidence approach, in which all relevant data are used. A weight-of-the-evidence approach is more flexible, and, when implemented by the agencies, is more open to considering negative data on carcinogenicity. The OSHA policy restricted the circumstances in which negative data could be considered. In the third approach, leave-it-to-the-scientists, a separate body conducts risk assessments — the clearest separation of risk assessment from risk management. According to Rushefsky, only proposals exist for creating centralized science panels for developing or reviewing risk assessments of this type. Industry groups support proposals to centralize risk assessments, while labor, public interest, and environmental organizations oppose them. Industry groups also endorse the weight-of-the-evidence approach. Labor, public interest, and environmental organizations want regulatory agencies to act on limited positive evidence.

Should the generic cancer policy approach be expanded? Some administrative law specialists maintain that this type of rule-making increases agency consistency, public understanding, and efficiency in resolving individual cases, saves money, avoids relitigation of issues, provides an accessible procedure for diverse interests to make their views known, clarifies agency policy, and enhances the predictability of agency decisions (McGarity, Substantive and Procedural Discretion in Administrative Resolution of Science Policy Questions: Regulating Carcinogens in EPA and OSHA, 67 Geo. L.J. 729 (1979); R. Merrill, Federal Regulation of Cancer-Causing Chemicals (pt. 1) 100-101 in Report to the Administrative Conference of the United States, 1982. Potential disadvantages include oversimplification, inappropriate mixing of scientific knowledge with risk assessment policy, overallocation of agency resources to guideline development, and the freezing of science. A serious question also exists whether an agency may limit an evidentiary hearing (or avoid it entirely) by promulgating general decisional criteria, the applicability of which in individual cases cannot be disputed on the facts. Such "administrative summary judgment" may prejudge issues that can only be addressed meaningfully in proceedings to regulate individual chemicals.

2.   Toxic Chemicals and Other Substances

a.   Trade Secrets and Information Property

Both TSCA and FIFRA require the submission of enormous quantities of technical data. Under the Trade Secrets Act, the Freedom of Information Act, the common law, and various other statutory provisions, proprietary information — trade secrets, confidential business information, or privileged information — in general receives rather complete protection. TSCA and FIFRA remove this protection from data bearing upon health and safety that has been submitted for regulatory purposes. See TSCA §14(a) and FIFRA §136h(d). Brief mention of these explicit directives is warranted because they have caused great concern in the chemical industry and have stimulated the expansion of a complex subfield of environmental law. See McGarity & Shapiro, The Trade Secret Status of Health and Safety Testing Information: Reforming Agency Disclosure Policies, 93 Harv. L. Rev. 837 (1980).

Under FIFRA a pesticide registrant must mark and separately submit required trade secrets and commercial or financial information (§136h(a)). The Administrator has discretion in applying the statutory protections and exclusions to the data submitted, subject to judicial review of a decision to disclose after notice to the registrant (§136h(b), (d)(1)). See Mobay Chemical Corp. v. Costle, 447 F. Supp. 811 (W.D. Mo.), *appeal dismissed*, 439 U.S. 320, *reh'g denied*, 440 U.S. 940 (1978) (protected status depends on a case-by-case analysis), and Chevron Chemical Co. v. Costle, 443 F. Supp. 1024 (N.D. Cal. 1978) (trade secret status confirmed, balancing the factors of the cost of developing the data, its value to the owner and to competitors, the extent to which the data was not independently available, and the extent to which the owner itself had maintained confidentiality). Both statutes provide stiff penalties for willful disclosure by agency personnel. TSCA permits disclosure of health and safety studies of a chemical which has already been marketed or which poses an unreasonable risk of injury to health or the environment. Like FIFRA, TSCA does not permit release of data about manufacturing or processing or the proportions of chemical mixtures. Manifold problems attend the designation and segregation of protected information and the management of these requirements. See McGarity & Shapiro, *supra*, at 879, and S. Rep. No. 551, 97th Cong., 2d Sess. 8-11, 50-52 (1982).

Both statutes permit subsequent reliance on data submitted in connection with earlier health and safety studies, but with protections accorded the company that first generated the information. Under TSCA, for a five-year period a manufacturer may obtain EPA-adjudicated "fair and equitable" reimbursement from companies that rely upon its test results in their own submission to EPA (§4(c)(3)). Under FIFRA, a more complex exclusive use and compensation scheme depends on how long the information has existed — for 10 years post-1978, no use; for the next 15 years, compensated use.

The Supreme Court has twice had to address the FIFRA provisions. In Ruckelshaus v. Monsanto, 467 U.S. 986 (1984), Monsanto's $23.6 million worth of health and environmental data regarding potential commercial pesticides were held to be property susceptible to taking under the Fifth Amendment, although they were intangible trade secrets. EPA's use of the data to evaluate the registrations of other applicants, and the agency's disclosure of the data to qualified members of the public, could not be a taking under the pre-1972 law, but could be a taking from 1972 until the 1978 Federal Pesticide Act amended FIFRA. However, under those amendments once again use and disclosure are not now takings. The test is whether under the three statutory schemes Monsanto could have had a reasonable, investment-backed expectation that EPA would keep the data confidential beyond the limits prescribed in the statutes themselves. Held, pre-1972, no; 1972-78, yes; post-1978, no. A company that submits data does so willingly to obtain permission to market its products under a valid regulatory scheme. The Court precluded injunctive relief to protect the 1972-1978 data by holding that the data were taken for public use. An adequate remedy, compensation, was available under the Tucker Act. Monsanto also attacked on constitutional grounds the FIFRA requirement that if a competitor relies on one's data in the 15-year period following its submission, compensation must be paid. FIFRA requires that if the parties cannot agree on the compensation amount, either may initiate an unreviewable binding arbitration. The Court held that the issue was not ripe because no arbitration proceeding had yet been conducted. A year later, however, in Thomas v. Union Carbide Agricultural Products Co., 473 U.S. 568 (1985), the Court held that FIFRA's arbitration requirement is not an unconstitutional delegation of judicial power to the executive branch.

b.   Federal Toxic Substances Control Act

Introduction. Although thousands of pesticides are regulated under FIFRA, they constitute but a small fraction of the millions of chemical compounds in existence. In 1976 Congress enacted generic legislation empowering EPA to regulate the manufacture of most of the remaining unregulated chemical substances, based on the risks they pose to health or the environment. Toxic Substances Control Act, Pub. L. No. 94-469, 90 Stat. 2003 (codified at 15 U.S.C. §§2601-2629) (TSCA). Under TSCA, EPA is supposed to review each new chemical marketed annually, as well as the approximately 55,000 chemicals in commerce shortly after TSCA was enacted, to determine if they "may present an unreasonable risk of injury to health or the environment" (§4(a)(1)(A)(i)). Exempted from TSCA are pesticides, drugs, food products, cosmetics, and most nuclear materials; these are otherwise regulated. Also exempt are tobacco products, firearms, and ammunition because political lobbies were powerful enough to obtain their exclusion (§3(2)(A)). TSCA therefore represents the closest thing to a comprehensive chemical substance control statute that Congress has ever enacted.

TSCA is unusual in a number of respects. First, no federal statute since the 1930s has visited the possibility of sudden, complete regulation upon a major industry. Approximately 11,500 establishments employing 1.1 million persons produced or distributed chemicals worth more than 5 percent of the nation's gross national product. Council on Environmental Quality, Thirteenth Annual Report 115 (1982). Second, TSCA is unusual as an environmental statute because rather than controlling the use of products or the disposal of wastes, its emphasis falls high in the stream of commerce, at the pre-manufacture phase. As a product safety law, TSCA more closely resembles FIFRA and the Federal Food, Drug, and Cosmetic Act (FD & CA) than, for example, the Clean Air and the Clean Water Acts or the Consumer Product Safety Act, although TSCA requires neither affirmative agency approval before marketing (as does FD & CA) nor a licensing-type process (as does FIFRA).

Third, TSCA's "action-forcing" provisions setting deadlines and authorizing citizens' suits have not been as effective as similar provisions were in promoting the vigorous implementation of the major pollution control statutes. TSCA has been disappointing to its proponents, who do not believe that its testing and pre-manufacture review provisions have improved chemical product safety. Indeed, the three most important issues that these materials address are whether TSCA succeeds as a legal device for shifting the burden of proof of safety to chemical manufacturers, whether Congress really did intend EPA to screen thousands of chemicals rather than control just the handful that present the greatest risks, and whether the test of "unreasonable risk," which appears 38 times in TSCA, can be applied with a balanced emphasis on health protection and economic productivity.

As with FIFRA, much TSCA law lies in the particulars of its administrative application. Thus space limitations prevent us from examining TSCA in detail; however, do not be misled by this summary treatment into concluding that TSCA does not belong in the first rank of the environmental regulatory statutes.

The statutory framework and implementation of the Act. The TSCA scheme, though itself lengthy, is not difficult to summarize: For new chemical substances, subject to some important exemptions, TSCA requires that manufacturers or others engaging in commerce in a new chemical, or making a significant new use of an existing chemical, give EPA pre-manufacturing notice (PMN) of data and test results regarding the chemical. EPA then determines if the new chemical presents an unreasonable risk or if testing must be done (§5). EPA must compile an inventory of chemicals already in commerce, and EPA has undertaken to see if the chemicals on the inventory meet the standard of no unreasonable risk. Manufacturers or others who put chemicals in commerce must perform tests on both new or existing chemical substances and mixtures if EPA determines that they present unreasonable risks or that existing information is insufficient to allow an informed preliminary assessment to be made (§4). Ample enforcement authority empowers the Administrator to limit or forbid the manufacture of both new and existing chemicals that studies have shown present an unreasonable risk to health or the environment (§6). These provisions were intended to put the burden of proof on the manufacturer whenever EPA raises the issue of a chemical's safety. In theory, this burden may be very difficult to discharge. In practice, the picture is still more complex. Critics feel that EPA still assumes most of the burden of showing that a chemical presents an unreasonable risk, rather than using TSCA's numerous techniques for requiring the manufacturer to demonstrate safety.

Pre-manufacturing notice for new chemicals. The Administrator must be notified at least 90 days before a new chemical, i.e., one not on the inventory of existing chemicals, is manufactured or processed and before an existing chemical is applied to a "significant new use" (§4(a)(1)(A), (B)). The notice of intent to manufacture or make a significant new use may have to be accompanied by existing data and, in theory at least, new information. For the specific requirements, see §§8(a)(2); 5(b)(1), (2); 5(d)(1)(B), (C). For notice and trade secrets protection requirements, see §§5(d)(2), (14). If the data submitted to EPA are insufficient to permit a reasoned conclusion about health and environmental risks or if allowing commerce in the chemical may present an unreasonable risk, the Administrator may issue an administrative order or seek a court injunction to limit or prohibit use (§5(e)).

Because of their low production volume and low exposure potential, EPA exempts manufacturers of new chemicals in quantities of 1,000 kg or less from full pre-manufacture notification review. Qualified manufacturers are subject to a simplified 21-day review with reduced information requirements. The rule affects approximately 20 percent of new chemicals. Exemption from Notification Allowed for New Chemicals Made in Small Amounts, 16 Envt. Rep. (BNA): Current Developments 56 (1985). See also EPA, 6 TSCA Chemicals-in-Progress Bulletin, No. 2 at 2 (1985).

The EPA's performance in implementing the PMN requirements has not been impressive. EPA issued final PMN regulations years behind schedule (48 Fed. Reg. 21,722). For several years most PMNs contained no toxicity data at all. Only a handful of chemicals has been subjected to §5(e) orders requiring the production of additional data, although a few companies have withdrawn PMNs in anticipation of such orders. The Reagan Administration adopted a "voluntary" approach to TSCA compliance; EPA reported that 28 companies voluntarily took control actions. EPA, 3 TSCA Chemicals-in-Progress Bulletin, No. 2, at 11 (1982). Nevertheless, in 1988, in the largest non-PCB penalty ever assessed under TSCA §5, EPA and the BASF Corp. entered into a settlement agreement in which BASF agreed to pay $1.28 million for allegedly importing chemicals without PMN. BASF to Pay Record $1.28 Million Fine to Settle TSCA Complaint on New Chemicals, 19 Envt. Rep. (BNA): Current Developments 2531 (1988). In addition, EPA and AT&T entered into a 1987 consent agreement in which AT&T agreed to pay a $1 million fine for violating the PMN provisions. EPA, 8 TSCA Chemicals-in-Progress Bulletin, No. 3, at 2 (1987). EPA has filed four TSCA §5 complaints, but says that it plans to file 24 more PMN cases. 19 Envt. Rep. at 971.

Screening and regulating existing chemicals. Some 55,000 chemicals and chemical groups were listed before the inventory of existing chemicals was formally closed in 1980. The original inventory appears at 45 Fed. Reg. 49,974. The inventory must be supplemented to include all new chemicals for which PMN notices are filed. Although the Act does not specifically state that EPA must systematically study this backlog to determine which chemicals may pose an unreasonable risk, the inventory requirement would be pointless without such a review.

In the four years after TSCA was enacted, EPA placed less emphasis on assessing the potential risks of existing chemicals and on controlling those that might present an unreasonable risk than on other TSCA mandates. More recently, EPA has listed 102 chemicals as required by the §8(d) health and safety reporting rule. 52 Fed. Reg. 16,022 (1987). EPA also proposed to require manufacturers and processors of 73 chemicals to test them for health effects and chemical fate, 52 Fed. Reg. 20,333 (1987), but such testing would primarily benefit the agency's RCRA program. EPA, 8 TSCA Chemicals-in-Progress Bulletin, No. 3, at 5 (1987).

Over 1,000 inventoried chemicals have been screened, but only a handful have received more than cursory attention. The EPA reviews tend to be very thorough, and very protracted — it may take two years or more to assess a chemical. The agency undertakes an exhaustive search of the published literature on a chemical, going back thirty to fifty years in some cases. EPA has indicated that it will undertake at most two or three regulatory actions a year that are intended to ban or limit the manufacture of a substance. See, e.g., 43 Fed. Reg. 11,318 (chlorofluorocarbon propellants in aerosol containers). Since 1978 EPA has taken steps to implement TSCA's ban on the manufacture and use of polychlorinated biphenyls.

The issuance of test rules. The most intensive testing requirements for potentially injurious chemicals — new and old — are provided in §4 of TSCA. EPA may mandate a series of particular tests if it believes that they are necessary to determine the safety of a chemical substance. Once a test is completed, EPA may carry out its PMN duties under §5 or make a determination of unreasonable risk under §6 and promulgate rules limiting or banning the chemical's use. The tests required under §4 are referred to collectively as the chemical's test "rule" because TSCA specifies notice-and-comment rule-making procedures.

Behind each test rule are "standards for the development of test data for such substance or mixture" (§4(b)(1)(B)). The standards must be reviewed and amended if necessary every 12 months, which implies that EPA must first promulgate generic standards governing test rules. Such standards may then be required as needed in each of the chemical-by-chemical test rules.* Section 4 specifies a not-surprising list of effects (e.g., carcinogenesis, mutagenesis), characteristics (e.g., acute and chronic toxicity), and methodologies that may be used in formulating standards (§4(b)(2)(A), (b)(1)).

To help EPA set priorities, §4(e) created an Interagency Testing Committee (ITC), which lists chemicals for priority testing after informal rule-making. After listing, the Administrator has one year either to propose a test rule or to publish reasons for not doing so. The Administrator may also list a chemical after hybrid rule-making (§5(b)(4)). What is the connection between the Administrator's list and the ITC list? For six years EPA did not finally promulgate a single generic test standard or a single test rule, although the first ITC list appeared in 1977. Standards were proposed in 1979 (44 Fed. Reg. 27,334, 27,347, 44,054), but EPA decided not to finalize them because of the controversy they engendered and because the agency was not challenged when it proposed test rules without

---

*Note the possible confusion between the test "rule" and generic standards potentially applicable to scores of separate test rules for individual chemicals. These broad standards would also be produced in notice-and-comment rule-making and therefore would also be "rules." Indeed, generic test standards are far more like most "rules" (guidelines, regulations, standards, procedures) than are EPA's case-by-case chemical test protocols, but Congress did not see fit to give the individualized test requirements some other name and neither has EPA. So "rules" they are.

first promulgating generic standards. EPA has made standards available in un-published guidelines to industry (47 Fed. Reg. 33,001).

In the early 1980s, the EPA entered into voluntary testing agreements negotiated with industry instead of promulgating final test rules (48 Fed. Reg. 54,836). NRDC v. EPA, 595 F. Supp. 1255, 1270 (S.D.N.Y. 1984), held that these negotiated agreements did not satisfy §4 testing requirements and ordered the EPA to issue final test rules for chlorinated benzenes by mid-1986, which EPA did. 51 Fed. Reg. 11,728. By 1988 EPA promulgated final test rules for eight other chemicals: anthroquinone (52 Fed. Reg. 21,028), biphenyls (52 Fed. Reg. 19,087), diethylenetrianmine (52 Fed. Reg. 3,238), fluoroalkenes (52 Fed. Reg. 21,530), a fractional chemical (52 Fed. Reg. 2,527), hydroquinone (52 Fed. Reg. 19,870), and mesityle oxide (52 Fed. Reg. 19,093).

Regulation. If the results of testing, PMN review, or screening of the inventory of existing chemicals indicates that there is a "reasonable basis to conclude" that the commerce in a chemical "presents or will present" an unreasonable risk to health or the environment, the Administrator may impose a variety of restraints on the marketing of a chemical: absolute bans, production quotas, bans or limitations on particular uses or at certain concentrations, labeling requirements, and the like (§6(a)). See also §6(b). The restraint is subject to hybrid rule-making. See §§6(c) and 19(c).

In addition to applying the substantial evidence test here, TSCA also applies it to §4 test rules, to the listing of hazardous substances by the Administrator under §5(b)(4), and to the rules for PCBs under §6(e). But the Act applies the more relaxed "arbitrary and capricious" standard to all other reviewable actions under TSCA, including priority listing of a hazardous substance, PMN new uses, and information gathering under §8. Can you fathom the rationale for adoption of different rule-making procedures and standards of judicial review for similar TSCA determinations?

If time is of the essence, a §6 rule may be made effective almost immediately (§§5(f)(2), 6(d)(2)(B)). An absolute ban may be obtained only through an administrative order or federal district court process for an injunction (§5(f)(3)). If even faster action seems necessary, the Administrator may file a civil action for immediate seizure or other relief if a chemical will present "an imminent and unreasonable risk of serious or widespread injury to health or the environment" before a rule under §6 can protect against such a risk (§7). Such imminent hazard provisions appear in all major federal environmental pollution statutes.

The meaning of "unreasonable risk" in TSCA. TSCA specifically regulates the production, use, and disposal of polychlorinated biphenyls (PCBs), the only chemicals singled out by name for special attention in the Act. PCBs have long been used for their chemical stability, fire resistance, and electrical resistance properties. They are frequently used in electrical transformers and capacitors. The EPA estimates that up to 400 million pounds of PCBs have entered the environment. Approximately twenty-five to thirty percent of this amount is a direct source of contamination for wildlife and humans, and PCBs are extremely toxic to humans and wildlife. Experimental animals developed tumors after eating diets that included concentrations of PCBs as low as 100 parts per million. PCBs may adversely affect enzyme production, thereby interfering with the treatment of diseases in humans. Concentrations below one part per billion are believed to impair reproduction of aquatic invertebrates and fish. Because PCBs bioaccumulate in fish, fish-eating mammals run a special risk of adverse effects.

Aside from certain specific, carefully regulated exceptions for PCB use in transformer service, mining equipment, heat transfer and hydraulic systems, copy paper, pigments, electromagnet service, natural gas pipeline compressors, microscope mounts, and research and development — all of which illustrate the wide commercial value of PCBs — TSCA §6(e) permits PCBs to be used only in a totally enclosed manner. The statute completely prohibits the manufacture, processing, and sale of PCBs. All manufacture was to have ended in January 1, 1979. Processing and distribution ended six months later, subject to one-year exemptions when unreasonable risk would not result and when good faith efforts to find PCB substitutes were going forward.

Regarding unenclosed PCB uses, the Administrator may define "enclosed" and "unenclosed" and may authorize unenclosed PCB uses that "present no unreasonable risk of injury to health or the environment," the familiar standard for virtually all regulatory actions under TSCA. EPA regulations approved many unenclosed but "reasonable-risk" uses until mid-1984 and extended PCB use for carbonless copy paper indefinitely. These regulations were reviewed in Environmental Defense Fund v. EPA, 636 F.2d 1267 (D.C. Cir. 1980), the principal TSCA case to reach the federal appellate courts. The court upheld EPA's use of §6(c)(1) criteria, including adverse economic impacts, in determining unreasonable risk of injury under §6(e)(2)(B). The most important non-totally-enclosed use regulations at issue in the challenge covered electrical transformer maintenance and conversion to PCB-free dielectric fluids. For example, the court found the Administrator's refusal to force more rapid conversion of some 1,000 railway transformers, as a result of his trading-off of the hazards of fire, explosion, and environmental contamination against rail service curtailment and the $90 million cost of immediate conversion, satisfied the TSCA "no unreasonable risk" standard. Citing the EPA's inadequate rationale, the court did, however, remand both the EPA's rules permitting continued use of fluids containing only 50 parts per million of PCBs and certain permissive EPA definitions for "totally enclosed" uses in non-railroad transformers, capacitors, and electromagnets. The 1984 uncontrolled PCB rule may be amended. See 52 Fed. Reg. 25,838 (1987) (excluding decontaminated equipment, redefining recycled PCBs); 49 Fed. Reg. 29,625 (1984) (redefining "totally enclosed" and clarifying "significant exposure").

Despite the express PCB phase-out, TSCA's treatment of PCBs under §6(e) does not differ very much from its treatment of any other chemical that presents an "unreasonable risk" under the flexible provisions of §6(a). Compare FIFRA's standard of "unreasonable adverse effects" to TSCA's "unreasonable risk" standard. Are benefits and costs weighed in different ways under the two statutes?

Time after time TSCA instructs the Administrator and judges to apply the standard of "unreasonable risk of injury to health or the environment" in making decisions. The phrase appears in the Act no less than 38 times. If "unreasonable risk" is suspected or determined to be present, the Administrator may:

— require testing and studies (§4(a), (b));
— place a chemical on a list for priority attention (§4(e));
— require pre-manufacture testing of new chemicals (§5(b)(2)(B)) and prepare a list of them (§5(b)(4));
— prevent manufacture of new chemicals pending completion of studies (§5(e)(1)(A)(ii)(I));
— regulate chemicals through bans, use limitations, production quotas, etc. (§6);
— regulate imminent hazards (§7);
— request regulation by other agencies (§9);
— make rules governing disclosure of confidential data (§14);
— act on citizens' petitions (§21).

The Environmental Defense Fund strongly objected to allowing EPA to determine how stringent to make its PCB ban exemptions by applying the same §6(c)(1) criteria it uses to determine "unreasonable risk" in promulgating rules for any other chemical under TSCA — but to no avail. Should the "unreasonable risk" test be uniform, or should it vary with the circumstances of its application? For example, should "unreasonable risk" be strictly construed in considering whether to ban a chemical from commerce but relaxed when the only issue is whether more studies should be performed?

"Significant" and "serious" risk. Other sections apply slightly different standards to agency determinations under TSCA. Section 4(f) is one of the most important. Under it, the Administrator has a nondiscretionary duty to take action within six months under other TSCA provisions if available data indicate that "there may be a reasonable basis to conclude that a chemical substance or mixture presents or will present a significant risk of serious or widespread harm to human beings from cancer, gene mutations, or birth defects." With the important exception of purely environmental effects, EPA apparently once thought the "significant risk" standard much stricter than the "unreasonable risk" standard just discussed, attempting to insulate itself from the "action-forcing" deadline by interpreting §4(f) to apply to situations that require a crash effort to remedy a very serious hazard to public health. See Ashford, Ryan & Caldart, A Hard Look at Federal Regulation of Formaldehyde: A Departure from Reasoned Decision-making, 7 Harv. Envtl. L. Rev. 297 (1983). Do you think EPA correctly interpreted the §4(f) action-forcing mandate? If so, when should §7(f) be invoked to control an imminently hazardous chemical, i.e., one that "presents an imminent and unreasonable risk of serious or widespread injury to health or the environment?

Coordinating TSCA's provisions. There may be redundancies in TSCA's testing, listing, and regulatory provisions.

Testing: EPA may use §§4(a), 5(e), and 6(a)(4) to require testing.

Listing: Sections 4(e) (the Interagency Testing Committee's list), 5(b)(4) (the Administrator's list), and §8(b) (inventory) all authorize listing.

Regulation: Sections 6(a) and (b), 7 (imminent hazard), and 5(e) (regulation pending development of information) provide for the direct regulation of chemicals. Section 4(f) sets a 180-day deadline for beginning regulation under §§5, 6, and 7.

TSCA *and the burden of proof.* Before TSCA, the production of a new but potentially dangerous chemical not otherwise regulated could only be enjoined if the government or some other plaintiff could prove that a legal wrong — e.g., a tort such as negligence or a tort or crime such as public nuisance — had occurred and that the manufacturer's action threatened to cause imminent irreparable harm of a substantial nature. In civil trials the "burden of proof," that is, persuading the trier of fact that the plaintiff's interpretation of the facts was more probably true than not true, always rested on the plaintiff. TSCA is considered to have permanently placed the burden of persuasion on the manufacturer. Under TSCA, the manufacturer will have to prove to the satisfaction of EPA that it was more probably true than not that its chemical does not present an unreasonable risk of injury to health and the environment.

The standard of proof — more probable than not, or, to borrow Judge Wright's phrasing, at least 51 percent — applicable in trials at law is rather like the standard that the Administrator applies to factual determinations under TSCA, although it would probably be inaccurate to equate them narrowly. Furthermore, the standards of judicial review applicable to the Administrator's decision — "substantial evidence" support in the record of absence of "arbitrary or capricious" reasoning — are consistent with the more-probable-than-not standard. They also are more deferential than the standard an appellate court would apply in reviewing a lower court's decision, as Judge Wright lucidly explained in footnote 58 of the *Ethyl* opinion, the text of which appears at p. 551 *supra*.

Thus it is not precisely correct to say that TSCA assumes that a chemical is "guilty" until proven "innocent." See Hearings on S. 776 before the Subcomm. on Commerce, 94th Cong., 1st Sess. 193 (1975) (testimony of CEQ Chairman Russell Peterson). The criminal standard of proof "beyond a reasonable doubt" has never had to be met by plaintiffs in civil chemical injury trials — nor any other civil trials, for that matter. Neither must manufacturers now prove "beyond a reasonable doubt" under TSCA that their chemicals do not present unreasonable risks. Conversely, EPA does not now have to determine that a scientifically acceptable, proven chain of causation links the chemical with its effects. Such a determination would require proof capable of meeting the "beyond a reasonable doubt" standard before EPA could act. Yet the logic of federal risk regulation, established in *Reserve Mining, Ethyl,* and their judicial and legislative progeny, pointedly rejects this view. EPA need *not* meet the scientific standards of 95 percent or better probability before regulating — a standard tantamount to the criminal law standard.

Can you construct a similar analysis of the hazardous pollutant provisions of the Clean Air and the Clean Water Acts and FIFRA? The great majority of environmental statutes do not explicitly address the burden of proof issue. Yet examining a statute like TSCA in terms of evidentiary burdens and trial procedures may be useful in understanding what Congress intended in the statute and also in analyzing the roles to be played by the agency and by affected parties in the regulatory process. The analogy should not be forced beyond its useful limits, however, nor should it be used to shoehorn congressional policy into the constraining mold of judicial proof. With this caveat, such a comparative analysis may be used, for example, to establish a framework for critiquing judicial interpretation of a precautionary statute's purposes and procedures. See Latin, The "Significance" of Toxic Risks: An Essay on Legal Decisionmaking under Uncertainty, 10 Ecology L.Q. 339 (1982). Latin argues that the Supreme Court's "reductionist" approach to the burden of proof under scientific uncertainty in the Occupational Safety and Health Act in its decision invalidating a stricter workplace benzene exposure standard, Industrial Union Department, AFL-CIO v. American Petroleum Institute, 448 U.S. 607 (1980), seriously misinterpreted the Act. Latin argues for an approach to proof under precautionary health statutes that fulfills Congress's underlying burden-shifting approach to legal resolution of scientific uncertainty, using *Reserve Mining* as a model.

NOTE ON OZONE DEPLETION

The depletion of the stratospheric ozone layer, which blocks the entry of harmful ultraviolet rays, is perhaps the most serious immediate global pollution problem. See generally J. Brunnee, Acid and Ozone Layer Depletion (1988); Ogden, The Montreal Protocol: Confronting the Threat to Earth's Ozone Layer, 63 Wash. L. Rev. 997 (1988) and Lobos, Thinning Air, Better Beware, 6 Dick. L. Rev. 89 (1987). Chlorofluorocarbons (CFCs) and halon releases have been identified as the agents that break down the ozone layer by releasing chlorine, bromine, and nitrogen molecules that strip away the third oxygen atom in ozone, which is extremely unstable, converting it from O_3 to O_2, oxygen. As one would expect, experts differ over the magnitude of the problem, but unlike kthe global climate debate, the ozone depletion debate seems to be only about the rate of harmful depletion. Evidence is rapidly accumulating that the problem has been underestimated. The harmful effects are the risk of increased skin cancer and crop destruction or damage. Ozone depletion has also been linked to global climate change because ozone and the gases that deplete the layer are greenhouse gases.

Regulatory solutions are complex because the destructive releases come from a variety of highly valuable consumer and industrial products used throughout the world. As with all trade-related environmental problems, there are strong incentives for countries to resist total CFC and halogen bans to promote economic development. For example, France, Japan and the USSR are concerned that the United States has too great a competitive advantage in benign product substitutes. However, the problem is not hopeless because effective unilateral or multilateral action has the potential to respond with considerable effectiveness to the problem. The European Economic Community, Japan, and the United States control 95 percent of the world's CFC production and 85 percent of its consumption. At the national level, most aerosol products used in food, drugs, or cosmetics have been banned under the Federal Food, Drug and Cosmetic Act. 21 C.F.R. §2.125. Other aerosols have been banned under the Toxic Substances Control Act, 15 U.S.C. §§2601 et seq., and the Clean Air Act, 42 U.S.C. §§7450-7459, but the chemicals are still produced and used in a wide variety of products such as solvents, refrigeration, air conditioning, and foams for domestic and foreign consumption and remain subject to regulation under these acts. Section 157 of the Clean Air Act, 42 U.S.C. §7457(b) authorizes EPA to regulate the production of CFC and halons that "may reasonably be anticipated to affect the stratosphere," but the agency initially resisted the use of this authority because it determined that substitutes were too expensive and difficult to produce.

In recent years, there is a growing consensus among international lawyers that the historic concept of absolute territorial sovereignty must be modified by the nuisance-based principle that no state should permit its territory to be used to injure another state, see Williams, Public International Law Governing International Pollution, 13 Queensland L. Rev. 112 (1984), and that states should cooperate to protect the environment. See generally L. Caldwell, Concepts in the Development of International Environmental Policies, International Environmental Law (1974) and L. Caldwell, International Environmental Policy: Emergence and Dimensions (1984). Whether or not this has become a norm of international law is still the subject of some speculation, but this principle was recognized at the 1972 Stockholm Conference, which produced the United Nations Environmental Programme. In March 1985, the Vienna Convention for the Protection of the Ozone Layer was adopted as a result of the program and opened for signature. U.N. Document UNEP/1G.53/Rev. 1. This has been hailed as the first international anticipatory approach to a problem. The issue is how the CFC and halon production and consumption reduction burden will be allocated among nations. The issue involves conflicts between both the most technologically advanced nations and those close behind as well as the usual developed versus developing world tensions.

The September 16, 1987, Montreal Protocol on Substances that Deplete the Ozone Layer, opened for signature Sept. 16, 1987, reprinted in 26 I.L.M. 1550 and 52 Fed. Reg. 239, 46,515 (1987), begins to address the allocation issue. The Protocol covers CFC and halons either alone or in a mixture but excludes products that incorporate the defined controlled substancs. The basic objective of the Protocol for CFCs is to freeze consumption at 1986 levels and to reduce consumption and production by 1999 to 50 percent of the 1986 base. In contrast, halon consumption is frozen starting in 1992 because there are no known substitutes. Groups of "controlled substances" are identified and within each group any mix may be used if the total ozone depletion potential does not exceed specified limits. There are, however, no effective enforcement provisions, a problem common to international environmental efforts. See Levy, International Law and the Chernobyl Accident: Reflections on an Important but Imperfect System, 36 Kan. L. Rev. 81 (1987). However, many experts think existing trade controls and the market will provide a sufficient incentive to enforce the Protocol as substitutes make banned products less and less attractive. J. Brunee, *supra*, at 251-252.

Nations that consume less than 0.3 kilograms per capita may delay compliance with this standard for ten years. It has been estimated that this base period calculation variance will allow some developing countries to increase their consumption by 50 percent and may undermine the 50 percent reduction goal. See Note, The Montreal Protocol on Substances that Deplete the Ozone Layer: Can It Keep Us All from Needing Hats, Sunglasses, and Suntan Lotion, 11 Hastings Int. and Comparative L. Rev. 509, 523-528 (1988). To create incentives for developing country participation, it may require subsidies to ensure that substitute technologies are transferred at the same cost as existing ones. Further, the Protocol bans trade between participating and non-participating parties except for those in compliance with the Protocol. This could have a substantial effect on the economies of the People's Republic of China and India, which are not parties, and are developing stronger consumer economies. There is a reservation clause, however, that allows a country to object to a listed chemical that may not be imported from a nonparty. Article 5 urges the developed nations to provide developing nations with subsidies, credits, and other incentives to use substitute products and technologies, but the article is not binding on the parties.

To implement the Montreal Protocol, the EPA has allocated production and consumption rights among producers by a 1986 baseline. Consumption is defined in the Protocol production as imports minus exports. Exports are not directly banned; article 4 only urges the parties to "discourage" exports. However, their inclusion in the consumption calculation will create discentives to export, because exports will be counted against the amount a party may allocate to domestic consumption. Production rights are apportioned among producers based on 1986 production, and consumption rights are based on the 1986 production allocation minus a proportionate share of the 1986 exports. A system of transferable production and consumption rights among the 15 to 20 producers has been created. For example, a producer who wants to convert his potential production rights into actual ones must obtain consumption rights in the same amount. This can be done by exporting the controlled substance. Doniger, Global Emergency (Does the Montreal Protocol Go Far Enough?), Envtl. Forum, 24 July-August (1988) is a critical analysis of the limits of EPA's implementation of the Protocol.

Events are moving quite rapidly and may overtake the approaches outlined above. The Protocol contains provisions to allow new chemicals to be added and for the depletion potential of the chemicals to be revised upwards. In March of 1989 the EEC announced its intention to eliminate the production and use of the most harmful CFCs by the end of the century. Legislation has been introduced to cap domestic production and phase out 95 percent of CFCs within a few years or even phase out the production and use of ozone-depleting chemicals entirely. Led by E. I. du Pont de Nemours & Company, industry is investing substantial sums in replacement substances, but issues such as the potential windfall profits that will be created among the five major domestic producers by the regulatory scarcity in CFC production must be resolved. Former President Reagan's proposed 1990 budget proposed to tax windfall profits by allowing the EPA to impose permit fees and auction production rights at fair market value instead of the present regulations, which allocate rights based on past production and consumption. Would such a charge be an unconstitutional delegation of the power to tax? See Skinner v. Mid-America Pipeline Co., 109 S. Ct. 1726 (1989).

3.   Comparing the Benefits and the Costs of Hazardous Substances Control

After assessing health risks, an agency must go on to make its risk management decisions (see the excerpt at pp. 502-510 *supra*). Risk management necessarily raises the issue of how (or whether) the agency will trade off health benefits against the added economic costs of hazardous substances control. We have now examined a number of attempts by courts, legislatures, and regulatory agencies to adjust to the fact that reducing risks ordinarily increases economic costs, sometimes quite steeply. In *Wilsonville*, the court took the costs and benefits of closing the hazardous waste disposal site into account in enjoining the further operation of the facility (p. 519 *supra*). In *Reserve Mining* and *Ethyl*, the statutes applied in those cases merely required abatement if public health was "endangered," without explicitly requiring the high costs involved to be taken into account in any particular manner, if at all. But in *Reserve Mining* the court explicitly took the economic costs of enjoining Reserve's taconite discharges into Lake Superior into account in fashioning delayed injunctive relief (p. 543 *supra*), and in *Ethyl* EPA took costs into account in scheduling the phase-in of its gasoline lead content standards (p. 554 *supra*). In setting national emissions standards for hazardous air pollutants under §112 of the Clean Air Act, EPA appears constrained to exclude costs from consideration, but the court in NRDC v. EPA gave the agency some leeway to consider costs (p. 557 *supra*). The Clean Water Act explicitly contemplates that costs be considered in setting hazardous effluent discharge limits under the best available technology (BAT) standard, but not for hazardous discharge standards set under the more exacting provisions of §307(a)(2) (p. 567 *supra*). Under FIFRA, the EPA Administrator must explicitly compare the benefits and the costs of canceling the registration of an economic poison and give substantial weight to economic impacts (p. 573 *supra*). The criterion of "unreasonable risk" under the Toxic Substance Control Act also requires that costs be taken into account in promulgating test rules, in restricting or forbidding the marketing of a chemical, or in implementing many other TSCA provisions (p. 582 *supra*). As the following excerpt explains, agencies other than EPA face equally difficult cost-benefit problems under their risk management statutes.

Do these cases and statutory provisions and other provisions in federal statutes reveal a consistent pattern in the treatment of the costs and benefits of risk reduction? Professor Richard Merrill, former general counsel of the Food and Drug Administration (FDA), has written in his study of federal regulation of carcinogens:

> The criteria for regulatory decision making embodied in current legislation fall into three broad categories. A very few statutes mandate a "no risk" policy, which means that the administering agency must attempt to prevent human exposure to any carcinogen. Other laws, either expressly or through administrative construction, focus exclusively on the issue of risk but essentially direct the agency to regulate only significant risks. A third, much broader class of laws directs the administering agency to allow other criteria to moderate its efforts to protect human health. These criteria may be limited to the technological capability of an industry to reduce exposure, or they may include a wider range of consequences of regulation. While the laws within this last category vary widely, they all in some fashion permit regulators to determine how much safety should be required. . . .
>
> To be sure, the nearly thirty statutes under which Federal agencies regulate carcinogens seem to express different degrees of concern about risks to human health and about the weight to be given economic costs in determining control levels for toxic agents. This diversity has several explanations. The laws were enacted at different times. More recent statutes reflect increased Congressional sensitivity to economic costs and describe in more detail the factors an agency shall consider in setting control levels. The laws originated with, and remain under the influence of, different political constituencies. One would expect that legislation drafted by the House Agriculture Committee would reflect greater concern about economic costs of restrictions on pesticide use than laws designed to protect worker health sponsored by the Senate Committee on Labor and Public Welfare. Perhaps most important, none of the laws was enacted for the sole purpose of controlling cancer risks; rather, each is addressed to a particular medium or commercial activity that may present several kinds of health hazards. [R. Merrill, Federal Regulation of Cancer-Causing Chemicals, Report to the Administrative Conference of the United States 22-32 (1982).]

To Professor Merrill's final category belongs standard setting for carcinogens and other hazardous substances under the Clean Water Act, the Safe Drinking Water Act, the Toxic Substances Control Act, and the Federal Hazardous Substances Act. Where in Professor Merrill's taxonomy do the statutory provisions discussed in *Reserve Mining* and *Ethyl* belong?

Professor Rodgers categorizes agency approaches somewhat differently: the cost-oblivious model ("heretic"), the cost-effective model ("nominal convert"), the cost-sensitive model ("practicing parishioner"), and the strict cost-benefit model ("high priest"). What do you suppose the "practicing parishioner" agency does? Rodgers, Benefits, Costs, and Risks: Oversight of Health and Environmental Decision Making, 4 Harv. Envtl. L. Rev. 191 (1980).

Assuming the statutes permitted it, would cost-benefit analysis, uniformly applied by the half dozen or so federal agencies administering the hazardous substances control statutes, improve federal regulation by bringing rigor and consistency to the decision of how much to make the trade-off between risk reduction and economic cost?

> Two premises underlie the demand for systematic analysis of the effects of regulatory action as an integral part of decision making. The first is the prosaic belief that rational choicemaking ought to be based on full awareness of the consequences. The second is the now vivid awareness, long ago illuminated by the discipline of economics, that society's resources are limited, and that the allocation of a portion of those resources to one objective necessarily displaces others. This perception is implicit in statutory directives to control risks that are unreasonable or to take into account specified collateral effects of regulation. [Federal Regulation of Cancer-Causing Chemicals, at 102.]

Former EPA Administrator William Ruckelshaus holds the "strong belief" that all social regulatory agencies should be given a "common statutory formula" under which risks and benefits of toxic substances and their substitutes would be traded off, based on the same criteria. He acknowledged that legislative change "in the current climate" would be "difficult" to obtain. Science, Risk, and Public Policy, address to the National Academy of Sciences, June 22, 1983, Vital Speeches of the Day 612, 613 (1983).

This casebook discusses formal cost-benefit analysis in Chapter 1, at p. 43, and in Chapter 7, at p. 869. Briefly, formal cost-benefit analysis assumes that one can (1) identify correctly and put accurate money prices on the social benefits of an activity (e.g., producing a product, building a public works project, regulating a dangerous substance), and (2) identify and price the things ("costs") whose value or alternative uses must be reduced to produce the benefits (e.g., raw materials, the natural environment, capital, and labor), so that one can (3) predict quantitatively the net posture of the activity, which may be expressed either as a ratio of benefits to costs or as the net increase in social utility one hopes to maximize. In the context of hazardous substances regulation, this means that the agency must compute costs, including compliance costs (capital equipment, maintenance, monitoring, etc.), the social benefits lost when products are removed from the market, and arguably the transactions costs incurred by the agency in promulgating the regulation. Then the agency must undertake the harder task of placing a money value on benefits, e.g., the health injuries averted (cancer, mutations, diseases, other systemic disorders) and environmental degradation avoided.* Because these harms obviously have no established market prices that can be inserted into the agency's computations, studies must be performed to develop surrogate prices by imputing to affected individuals their

---

*Note that the words "benefit" and "cost" require that the context of their usage be clearly stated. Otherwise, the "benefits" of reduced health risks may be confused with the economic "costs" of abatement or the "benefits" of not regulating an activity may be entered on the "benefits" side of the analysis rather than on the "costs" side, where they belong.

willingness to pay to avoid these costs (e.g., from the payments they make for medical treatment or to move away from a hazardous neighborhood) or their willingness to be paid to risk harm (e.g., hazardous duty pay, reduced rent). The "willingness-to-pay" criterion is the device by which economists try to ensure that "priceless" items are valued by the same method as is used for articles in everyday commerce.

Although not essential to the method, cost-benefit analysis implies that regulatory tasks should be ranked and that those regulations that show the highest cost-benefit ratios should be undertaken first, on the theory that limited government resources should be applied first to tasks yielding the highest marginal return in public health and environmental protection. See Grabowski & Vernon, Estimating the Effects of Regulation on Innovation: An International Comparative Analysis of the Pharmaceutical Industry, 1 J.L. & Econ. 133 (1978). Further, cost-benefit analysis is not the same as cost-effectiveness analysis, which serves the allied but more limited purpose of ensuring that the agency selects the least costly method for attaining a predetermined goal. More cost-effective solutions produce better cost-benefit ratios. Do you see why? Finally, the term "cost-benefit analysis" is frequently replaced by the term "risk-benefit analysis" when hazardous substances regulation is involved, reflecting the fact that risks are the "costs" normally regulated, rather than well-established harms. For a definition stressing that risk-benefit analysis stops short of fully aggregating costs and benefits into dollars, see Zeckhauser, Measuring Risks and Benefits of Food Safety Decisions, 38 Vanderbilt L. Rev. 539, 545 (1985). See generally E. Crouch & R. Wilson, Risk-Benefit Analysis (1982); Cost-Benefit Analysis and Environmental Regulations: Politics, Ethics, and Methods (D. Schwartzmen, R. Liroff & K. Croke eds. 1982); M. Douglas & A. Wildavsky, Risk and Culture 164 (1982).

The proponents of formal cost-benefit analysis have become increasingly persuasive in the face of costly and sometimes wasteful regulatory strategies. Academic commentators have long urged the federal government to make fuller use of cost-benefit or risk-benefit analysis in enacting new statutes, taking regulatory actions, and conducting program evaluations. Federal agencies have usually contained an office of economic analysis, in which practitioners plied their trade, but with minimal impact on agency regulations. During the Ford and Carter Administrations, however, the White House required executive branch agencies to begin making cost-benefit comparisons when promulgating major new regulations (Exec. Order No. 12,291, 46 Fed. Reg. 13,193, reprinted in 5 U.S.C. §601). This order was vigorously pursued by the Reagan Administration, through a government-wide regulatory oversight group led by Vice President George Bush. The Reagan approach, which endorsed cost-benefit analysis, was amplified in Regulatory Program of the United States Government, April 1, 1987-March 31, 1988. See DeMuth & Ginsberg, White House Review of Agency Rulemaking, 99 Harv. L. Rev. 1075 (1986); Note, Regulatory Analyses and Judicial Review of Informal Rulemaking, 91 Yale L.J. 739 (1982).

Keep in mind that despite the White House initiatives, no federal agency regulating hazardous substances currently employs classical cost-benefit analysis to decide whether or how strictly to regulate, although several statutes arguably would permit agencies to adopt this practice. The EPA approach to regulating cancer-causing pesticides under FIFRA comes close, but it still falls far short of the economists' theoretical ideal. To maintain its still-growing support for adoption as the decisionmaking tool sine qua non in federal regulatory programs, cost-benefit analysis must overcome several severe limitations. These limitations apply even to the less formal versions of cost-benefit analysis that several agencies employ to adjust to the unique challenges presented by hazardous substances. The limitations also highlight the basic policy conflicts that occur, whatever the decisional tools it may want to use, when a highly industrialized society that is permeated with risk-laden substances, activities, and forms of energy attempts to understand them systematically and to bring them under strict control.

Most of the issues raised with respect to cost-benefit analysis concern its treatment of the costs of exposure to hazardous substances, although even deciding whether a "benefit" (e.g., an artificial sweetener or cheap energy) is universally viewed as a "benefit" rather than a "cost" does arise. As Amory Lovins asked, "is an artful new kind of synthetic dessert a benefit or a disgrace?" (Cost-Risk-Benefit Assessments in Energy Policy, 45 Geo. Wash. L. Rev. 911, 912 n.5 (1977).) Consider the problem of inventorying all relevant costs and benefits correctly. The benefit of workdays saved by disease prevention should be counted. Likewise, the lives of children and other nonwage-earners are indisputably valuable, although the traditional cost-benefit analysis focused only on wage losses averted. But should the benefits also include a dollar estimate of the reduced need for special diets for patients? Special or extra household help? Transportation costs to obtain medical treatment? Should victims' anxieties, nervous system disorders, genetic injury, and reduced sexual functions be "priced"? At what price? The cost of treatment and counseling alone? Important effects may be neglected or deliberately ignored, especially when the full range of health and environmental impacts are difficult to predict in relation to type, quantity, and time of injury. The temptation to exclude "remote" effects is abetted by the high administrative costs incurred in identifying and computing them, the possibility that quantifying a speculative but potentially disastrous factor might tip the scales against an activity with definite immediate economic benefits, and the reluctance to include factors for which a firm causal nexus with the harm regulated has not yet been established.

Even if the costs and benefits have been identified adequately, they may be extremely difficult to quantify as you have already seen. Recall the lack of dose-response relationships for many carcinogens. Often the best one can say about the benefits of carcinogen control at a given exposure level is that the number of cancers varies with a range of several orders of magnitude (factors of ten). If a quantitative risk assessment of numbers of deaths, diseases, injuries, and other impacts cannot be made, they cannot be assigned more than a range of dollar values (e.g., "the health injury averted by this regulation may be between $1 million and $10 billion"). See A. Ferguson & E. LeVeen, The Benefits of Health and Safety Regulation (1981), and Quantitative Risk Assessment in Regulation (L. Lave ed. 1982).

A particularly sensitive area of risk quantification concerns the dollar value of losing (or saving) a human life as a consequence of regulation. Note that the valuation problem is similar for loss of an endangered species or a symbolic or unique aesthetic resource. What is a human life worth? Must it be valued in dollars for regulatory cost-benefit comparisons to proceed? Agencies are understandably uneasy about overtly assigning a dollar value to human life in their cost-benefit analyses, but those that do not do so overtly do so impliedly because there is no other way to reduce the costs and benefits of life-saving regulation to a common money measure. One survey of agency cost-benefit assessments shows a low boundary of $70,000 and a high boundary of $132 million for the value of a human life, apparently with the most widely accepted single value hovering around $1-2 million. C. Gilette & T. Hopkins, Federal Agency Valuations of Human Life, Report to the Administrative Conference of the U.S. 1, 3 (July 7, 1988). See M. Bailey, Reducing Risks to Life: Measurement of the Benefits 52 (1980); Sagoff, On Markets for Risk, 41 Md. L. Rev. 755, 767 (1982).

Professor Dorfman has suggested a refinement: Express all non-health-related costs and benefits in dollars, but reduce all health-related costs (e.g., cases of disease and injury, days of restricted activity, unpleasant odors, etc.) to the common unit of lives saved (or lost) by regulating (or refusing to regulate), without ever assigning a dollar value to health-related factors. This approach would create two bases for cost-benefit comparisons: dollars and lives. Decisionmakers would then decide whether or how strictly to regulate by comparing both dollar costs averted and lives saved (Methods of Policy Analysis, in 2 National Research Council, Decision Making in the Environmental Protection Agency, part B, at 82, 89 (1977)). Would adopting this suggestion improve cost-benefit analysis?

An implication of Professor Dorfman's "compromise" is that cost-benefit analysis makes good sense when guns and butter, books and televisions, food and clothes, and other conventional goods present us with ordinary choices about which we are willing to give up in order to have the other, but this is much less true when health, safety, and life itself are involved. Yet consistent application of the economic view, critics feel, has caused policy analysts progressively to view arms, legs, and life, air, water, and silence, and physical integrity, survival, and the stock of "life-givens" (e.g., genes) as part of a smoothly interchangeable mix, in which dollar evaluations allow regulators to trade off hats, cars, and desserts against items that are entirely different in nature. By virtue of the increasing power to create new ways to exchange health and safety for economic gain and through growing knowledge of the nature and magnitudes of impacts, we can apply the economic view more expansively than ever before. But can we add some of these "goods" to the mix without rethinking social decisionmaking theory?

Professor Tribe thinks not. He carries the implications of this reasoning forward, while preserving a quantitative approach, by asserting that it might be possible eventually to develop a complex set of mathematical relationships between or among health, aesthetics, the environment, productivity, and other values that more adequately reflect the discontinuities and relationships actually experienced as part of human preferences, mathematical relationships that intuitively resist reduction to a few simple, commensurable terms. This approach would avoid the tendency of economics "to reduce complex structures to an unstructured set of components rendered comparable by simple exchange rates or indifference functions." Tribe, Policy Science: Analysis or Ideology? 2 Phil. & Pub. Affairs 66, 87 (1972). Would Tribe's approach still be cost-benefit analysis?

The selection of an appropriate discount rate raises additional issues. In formal cost-benefit analysis, whenever a benefit of regulation is to be enjoyed sometime in the future, its future value is deflated or "discounted" to its present value. The benefits of regulation may be worth a great deal at some future time to us or to persons yet unborn, but since our present enjoyment of a future benefit exists only as an expectation, and since for a host of reasons we may never actually enjoy the benefit, the theory is that we will want to value it less now. The long-standing controversy over the low discount rates applied to the benefits of public works projects has been overshadowed by the more recent controversy over the high discount rates (around 10 percent) applied to the potential costs of leaving hazardous chemicals unregulated. The issue is important to cost-benefit analysis of health and safety regulation because the injuries caused by some chemicals may not be realized for generations, or even centuries. As a National Academy of Sciences report points out, if the discount rate were 5 percent, one toxic poisoning case in 1975 would be valued the same as 1,733 cases in 200 years, or the same as the world population in 450 years. Decision Making for Regulating Chemicals in the Environment 43 (1975). For an argument for abandoning the strict discount rate approach, see T. Page, Conservation and Economic Efficiency (1978). Yet would not complete abandonment of discounting require that persons living forego enormous benefits to protect unborn generations from uncertain risks? How can the living strike an appropriate bargain with the unborn? See J. Rawls, A Theory of Justice 284 (1970).

The recipients of a regulatory benefit may not be the same persons who pay the costs. Cost-benefit mismatch takes on poignancy in the context of hazardous substances, when refusing regulation may mean that workers and others must bear the risk of serious disease or injury in order to continue to produce luxury items, attractive packaging, and products with long shelf lives.

Under traditional cost-benefit analysis, a redistribution of costs and benefits is appropriate if it yields a net positive benefit or if the redistributional effects of the change can be regarded as "beneficial." Are there constitutional constraints on the use of cost-benefit analysis? Is the problem beyond constitutional solution? See M. Baram, Regulation of Health, Safety and Environmental Quality and the Use of Cost-Benefit Analysis 34, Report to the Administrative Conference of the United States (1979). See also Cost-Benefit Analysis of Social Regulation, in Reforming Regulation pt. 6 (T. Clark, M. Kosters & J. Miller eds. 1980).

Are values served by current laws that transcend the primary goals of cost-benefit analysis? Consider the following:

The principal value informing public law for the workplace and the environment — as well as private behavior — may be *autonomy*, not *efficiency*. Public policy, then, may not represent an attempt to increase welfare, utility, or "satisfaction." It may represent our attempt, rather, to control the conditions under which we pursue happiness — the conditions under which we lead out lives. . . .

An efficient society promotes the ability of the individuals in it to satisfy their wants and desires; it promotes freedom in the sense that refers to an individual's welfare. This sense of freedom — "negative" freedom or freedom from interference in one's pursuit of happiness — has no necessary connection with autonomy. Freedom, in this sense, has to do with getting what you want or doing as you like; autonomy, on the other hand, consists in your ability to get or to do these things on your own, without being beholden to any other person, without accepting favors, and without having the important background decisions made by somebody else. . . .

E. F. Schumacher, in his book Small Is Beautiful, hit upon a formula which appeals to a vast constituency. We need not argue whether small is efficient, whether, for example, solar and wind power may generate more electricity more safely and cheaply than nuclear reactors. That question, I believe, is somewhat beside the point. Small is not beautiful because it is efficient; it is beautiful because it encourages autonomy. . . .

Economists who believe that much of our behavior under risk is irrational might take another view of it were they to consider that it may be motivated, not by fear, but by resentment. The problem, then, would be to explain, not why we fear some dangers more than others but why we resent some dangers more than others. One answer is plain. We resent risks imposed upon us, as members of the public, by those who seek, in doing so, to achieve economic ends. We resent these risks because those who subject us to them treat us not as ends in ourselves but as means to the production of some economic goal such as efficiency or wealth. This is not a value system to which many of us would subscribe, for society or for ourselves; yet it seems to be imposed upon us by those who take an economic view of regulatory policy. Accordingly, people who resent being subjected to technological risks, e.g., dangers associated with nuclear technology, become even more angry when they are told that the risks to the public are small in relation to the benefits. They resent these risks even though they acknowledge that they face greater dangers quite casually, for example, when they drive their cars. . . .

Cost-benefit analysis, then, cannot be justified as a means of achieving the public's primary goal, for that goal may not be efficiency; it may be autonomy. People want to determine the background level of risk; they do not want the working conditions of their lives to be determined by others. It does not matter how cost-beneficial risks are; it is a question, rather, of who controls them. [Sagoff, On Markets for Risk, 41 Md. L. Rev. 755, 761-764 (1982).]

Compare the view that any tradeoff approach that weighs toxicant reduction against economic and technological considerations is "fundamentally flawed," because when applied to "matters of intense personal interest" such as risk to life and highly-valued environmental amenities, such tradeoffs ignore the "almost universal recognition that citizens of this country have a 'right' to a healthy environment and workplace, at least insofar as the societal pursuit of that right is not technologically impossible or prohibitively expensive." McGarity, Media-Quality, Technology, and Cost-Benefit Balancing Strategies for Health and Environmental Regulation, 46 L. & Contemp. Prob. 159, 161 (1983).

In light of the foregoing observations, which of the following comments do you agree with the most?

I

We should not underestimate either the complexity of importance of estimating intangible costs and benefits. . . . In some cases, it may be best to avoid quantifying some intangibles as long as possible, carrying them along instead in the form of a written paragraph of description. Maybe we will find that the intangible considerations point toward the same decision as the more easily quantified attributes. Maybe one or a few of them can be adequately handled by a decision maker without resort to quantification. . . . [But] [w]e will find no escape from the numbers. . . . Ultimately the final decision will implicitly quantify a host of intangibles; there are no incommensurables when decisions are made in the real world. [E. Stokey & R. Zeckhauser, A Primer for Policy Analysis 5 (1978).]

II

Highly formalized methods of benefit-cost analysis can seldom be used for making decisions about regulating chemicals in the environment. Thus the development of such methods should not have high priority. . . . Value judgments about noncommensurate factors in a decision such as life, health, aesthetics, and equity should be explicitly dealt with by the politically responsible decision makers and not hidden in purportedly objective data and analysis. [Committee on Principles of Decision-Making for Regulating Chemicals in the Environment, Decision-Making for Regulating Chemicals in the Environment 7 (National Academy of Sciences, 1975).]

III

The limitations on the usefulness of benefit/cost analysis in the context of health, safety, and environmental regulatory decision making are so severe that they militate against its use altogether. [2 Regulatory Reform: Hearings before the Subcomm. on Oversight and Investigations of the Comm. on Interstate and Foreign Commerce, 94th Cong., 2d Sess. 515 (1976).]

F.   PREVENTING HARM FROM HAZARDOUS WASTES

Chemical waste dumps have long been known to be dangerous. Just how dangerous and numerous they are was fully appreciated only in the mid-1970s. For decades, large quantities of dangerous residues, largely from industrial processes, have been accumulating on generators' premises or at dump sites to which the wastes have been transported. The wastes include acids and bases, synthetic organic compounds such as pesticides and phenols, fuel byproducts, toxic metals, flammable compounds and explosives, radioactive materials, and infectious organic materials from hospitals and scientific laboratories. As time has passed, storage containers, ponds, and burial grounds have been adversely affected by corrosion, breakage, natural processes, and acts of vandalism, so that the waste material has begun to disperse in ground and surface waters, in the soil, and in the air. The original generator or disposal site operator in the meantime may have died, gone out of business, or conveyed the site to another person. Records revealing the composition of the wastes may have been lost or destroyed, if they ever existed.

Loosed in the environment, waste chemicals often display a deathly versatility. They may explode, ignite, or bring instant death from inhalation of their fumes. But more often they work indirectly and incrementally, just as other toxic substances do, insinuating themselves slowly, revealing themselves through mild symptoms, which are usually attributable to another, far less offensive, source. Human exposure occurs via direct contact with the skin, inhalation, or ingestion of drinking water and food in which toxicants may be reconcentrated. The numbers of persons and environmental systems threatened are high, although incidents of actual harm are not yet numerous. Potential impacts on human health range from acute and chronic impacts on the respiratory, nervous, alimentary, and urological systems to cancer, infant deformity, and permanent genetic impairment, as in the case of other toxic substances.

The problem at the Love Canal near Niagara Falls, New York, illustrates the issue. Until the early 1940s the Hooker Chemical Company used a mile-long abandoned hydroelectric canal about 40 feet deep and 20 yards wide as a dump for some 20,000 tons of wastes from its operations in Niagara Falls. Initially, over 80 compounds were thought to have been disposed of in Love Canal, including several potential carcinogens. Present were benzene, PCBs, and several pesticides. One of these pesticides, TCP, produces trace quantities of dioxin. Other disposal sites were also identified nearby. In all, perhaps 300 chemicals were disposed of in the vicinity of Niagara Falls — a total of 352 million tons of industrial wastes.

The Love Canal site eventually was abandoned and bulldozed over. In 1953 Hooker sold it to the Niagara Falls Board of Education for one dollar. The Board promptly built a school and playground in the middle of the site, and over a hundred residences were built near the school. Health problems had plagued residents of the Love Canal area for years, although dumping had ceased forty years earlier. Some of the afflictions that occurred in persons living near Love Canal included cancer, spontaneous abortion, malformed fetal organ systems, skin disorders, neurological, kidney, and liver disorders, hyperactivity, and suicide. These reached a high in 1977, coinciding with the appearance in surface depressions and basements of chemicals that had "floated up" on several years' accumulation of heavy rains and snows that had gathered in the clay-lined canal beneath. See M. Brown, Laying Waste (1980). . . .

Annually the U.S. produces in excess of 264 million metric tons of hazardous waste, enough to fill the New Orleans Superdome 1,500 times over. Some six billion tons have accumulated since 1950. National Geographic, Mar., 1984, at 325. The annual cost by 1990 of complying with federal requirements for safe disposal of new hazardous wastes will probably fall in between $4.2 and

$9.4 billion. Christopher Harris, William L. Want, and Morris A. Ward, Hazardous Waste 93 (1987).

The following excerpt makes clear why the hazardous waste disposal problem is largely a groundwater protection problem. Groundwater trapped in underground aquifers supplies one quarter of all fresh water used in the United States. The "most pernicious" consequence of land disposal is that improperly maintained waste sites have caused hundreds of drinking water wells to be closed. H.R. Rep. No. 1491, 94th Cong., 2d Sess. 89 (1976). Of the federal government's first list of 418 waste sites meriting priority attention, 347 were listed for their groundwater impacts. Even if human exposure can be anticipated and prevented by restricting use, the loss of usable groundwater is the highest price that must be paid for careless waste disposal. Millions of dollars' worth of this natural resource have been lost.

JOHNSON, WATER-QUALITY ISSUES: FACTORS AFFECTING GROUND-WATER QUALITY CONTAMINATION OF GROUND WATER BY TOXIC CHEMICALS
United States Geological Survey, Water Supply Paper, National Water Summary 1976-81

[See chapter 4, p. 336 *supra*.]

1.   The Federal Framework for Hazardous Waste Control

Hazardous wastes have been controlled piecemeal by local, state, and federal law for many decades. In particular, public nuisance laws and emergency health protection measures were used. A few states adopted more comprehensive legislation, as discussed later. Tort suits also acted as a deterrent to negligent hazardous waste disposal. In the 1970s, however, the inadequacy of the predominantly local or stopgap strategies caused Congress to act.

There are three basic strategies for the minimization of the risks created by hazardous wastes; (1) treatment, storage, or disposal; (2) process changes, to reduce the volume of the waste stream; and (3) resource recovery, e.g., recycling. Congress has thus far adopted only the first strategy. It assumed that little could be done to reduce the volume of waste generated if we want to preserve the benefits of the chemical era. Further, Congress did not want to mandate the adoption of the specific technologies used in resource recovery. However, there is a broad consensus emerging that the second and third strategies represent the best long-term options. States such as California and Illinois have enacted statutes that sharply constrain the use of land disposal (e.g., Ill. Rev. Stat. ch. 111-1/2, §§1022(h), 1039(f) and are even considering the preclusion of land disposal entirely. See also Yanggen & Amrheim, Groundwater Quality Regulation: Existing Governmental Authority and Recommended Roles, 14 Colum. J. Envtl. L. 1 (1989).

a.   The Resource Conservation and Recovery Act

In responding to the hazardous waste problem, Congress relied on the same strategy it had used many times in attacking other pollution problems: enactment of a comprehensive, complex scheme of direct regulation. Subpart C of the Resource Conservation and Recovery Act (RCRA), 42 U.S.C. §§6901-6991i, is in many ways the most evolved application of the regulatory paradigm for pollution control ever enacted by Congress. It is also the last to date. Since RCRA became law in October 1976 (following TSCA by only ten days), Congress has refrained from enacting additional comprehensive regulatory schemes for environmental protection, although RCRA was significantly amended in 1984. See generally C. Harris, W. Want, and M. Ward, *supra*. Several thousand pages of regulations have been proposed or promulgated under RCRA. Environmental practitioners in this field are treated to an unrelenting diet of regulatory negotiation and textual exegesis. Frankly, RCRA is not for everyone.

Touted as a comprehensive, closed "cradle to grave" system, RCRA provides for the formal identification of wastes as hazardous, written manifests tracking all waste shipments, and certification, through a permit system, that performance standards for safe treatment, storage, and disposal are being met. As in other environmental statutes, states may run their own hazardous waste programs so long as they satisfy or exceed minimum EPA requirements. Otherwise, EPA will administer them, although EPA has no discretion to choose to run a state program that meets federal requirements. §3006(b).

Identifying and listing hazardous wastes. The trigger for regulatory action under RCRA is formal designation of a solid waste as hazardous. Thus a "hazardous" waste must first be a "solid" waste. See §1004(27). Two procedures are available for designating a waste as hazardous. §3001(b)(1). The first, followed by some states and by some countries in Europe in their own statutes, is the least complex because it simply requires a generator to consult a list to see if a substance is regulated. A waste is hazardous when EPA determines after informal rulemaking that the waste meets one or more of three criteria (it contains already-listed constituents; it is acutely toxic; or it possesses one or more of four characteristics: ignitability, corrosivity, reactivity, or toxicity) (40 C.F.R. §261.11). The second requires the generator to test unlisted wastes to determine if they possess dangerous characteristics. If the tests confirm the hazard, the wastes must be accounted for through the RCRA system.

The EPA first proposed to put most of the burden of identifying wastes on the generators but soon switched to listing as the predominant strategy for bringing wastes into the RCRA scheme. See 45 Fed. Reg. 33,105, 33,108-33,110 (generator-identified wastes). Testing by generators for toxicity, carcinogenicity, mutagenicity, teratogenicity, and phytotoxicity was in general impractical. Instead EPA listed the constituents of hazardous waste streams that have been shown in reputable scientific studies to have toxic, carcinogenic, mutagenic, or teratogenic effects on human or other forms of life and generally required that these waste streams be managed under RCRA. Because industrial wastes tend to be generated in complex mixtures of many separate substances, the agency has listed scores of hazardous waste streams, typical waste sources, and hazardous waste generating processes, as well as about 455 specific hazardous substances. The composition of the lists changes as new data prompts the listing or delisting of particular wastes. Hazardous Waste Treatment Council v. EPA, 19 Envtl. L. Rep. (Envtl. L. Inst.) 20059 (D.C. Cir. 1988), held that EPA improperly decided not to list waste oil under RCRA.

RCRA appears to authorize informal rule making, initiated by the generator, as the exclusive means of delisting a waste process or an individual substance (§7006). The guidelines allow a generator to show that a specific waste generated by an individual facility is not hazardous because of plant-specific variations in raw materials, processes, or other factors (e.g., our pickle liquor waste does not contain cyanide as pickle liquors usually do from plants like ours, so please delist our plant only). See 40 C.F.R. §260.20-22.

Transportation of wastes. EPA estimates that generators dispose of 75 percent of wastes on-site. Other estimates run higher, but if a generator contracts for waste services, for each waste shipment it must originate a detailed paper manifest, select responsible transporters, specify a fully permitted facility to which delivery is to be made, and report irregularities if receipt is not confirmed (§3003). Transporters must meet rigorous requirements to ensure that wastes remain within the regulated waste handling system. "Midnight dumping" by "gypsy haulers" was the target of §3003. Owners — not merely operators — of any link in the chain of handlers are directly bound by RCRA. §3005.

The implementation of §3003 must be consistent with the requirements of the Hazardous Materials Transportation Act of 1975, which attempts to unify federal oversight of the transport by all modes of all types of hazardous materials. §3003(b). The 1984 amendments to RCRA added a provision regulating the export of hazardous wastes. §6938. It provides that no person may export hazardous wastes to another country unless the government of that country has agreed to accept them or the shipment complies with the terms of an agreement between the United States and that country regarding the export of hazardous waste. §6938(a). See 51 Fed. Reg. 28,664 (final rule).

Standards for treatment, storage, and disposal facilities. In the long run the statute's most important provisions will almost certainly be those that establish the permit system for on- or off-site treatment, storage, and disposal (TSD) (§3005). To obtain a permit, a facility operator must comply with detailed regulations for incineration, landfills, chemical treatment, liquids restrictions, site location (away from wetlands and other critical areas), groundwater and leachate monitoring, fencing and warning signs, special employee training and emergency procedures, and final site closure. The regulations adopt a two-pronged approach. They prescribe design and operation standards aimed at preventing waste releases during the life of the facility and (generally) for 30 years thereafter. In addition, they establish performance standards for groundwater protection implemented through monitoring and, if necessary, corrective action.

In 1984, Congress amended RCRA. Pub. L. 98-616, title I, §101(a), Nov. 8, 1984, 98 Stat. 3224. Congress was dissatisfied with the progress of the EPA in promulgating regulations to implement the Act, and the 1984 amendments make detailed decisions about the design and operation of hazardous waste treatment, storage, and disposal facilities. In brief, the Hazardous and Solid Waste Amendments of 1984 apply the same technology-forcing approach of the Clean Air and Clean Water Acts to RCRA. The primary features of the new legislation are as follows. (1) The lowering of the threshold for small quantity generators subject to regulation (§6921(d)). The EPA has issued regulations for generators producing more than one hundred but less than one thousand kilograms per month. 51 Fed. Reg. 10,146. (2) The generator must certify on the manifest that it has a program to reduce the volume, quantity, or toxicity of wastes "to the degree determined by the generator to be economically practicable . . ." (§6922(b)). (3) The placement of bulk or noncontainerized liquid hazardous waste in landfills is prohibited (§6924(c)). (4) The land disposal of all hazardous wastes is prohibited 32 months after November 8, 1984, subject to exceptions. Land disposal may be permitted if the Administrator determines that "the prohibition on one or more methods of land disposal . . . is not required to protect human health and the environment for so long as the waste remains hazardous" (§6924(d)). See 51 Fed. Reg. 40,572 (final rules). Deep well injections may continue, but the Administrator must review deep well disposal and promulgate regulations prohibiting the use of deep well disposal by 1989 if he determines that disposal may not protect human health and the environment so long as the waste remains hazardous (§6924(f)(12)). (5) All new landfills or surface impoundments (and lateral expansions) are required to have double liners. Variances however, are possible (§6924(o)(2)). (6) Existing surface impoundments must comply with the double liner and other minimum technological requirements (§6925(j)(1)). See 53 Fed. Reg. 24,717. (7) Underground storage tanks are regulated (§6991). Leaking underground storage tanks (LUSTs) have been identified as a major problem, and the amendments regulate both waste and product storage tanks, subject to exemptions. The regulations implementing many of these sections can be found in 40 C.F.R. Part 264.

United Technologies Corp. v. EPA, 821 F.2d 714 (D.C. Cir. 1987), upheld a variety of EPA regulations implementing the 1984 amendments to RCRA, including a broad definition of hazardous waste facility. The functional equivalency doctrine was applied to hold that EPA is not required to prepare an environmental impact statement (under the National Environmental Policy Act, see Chapter 7) for a RCRA permit. Alabamians for a Clean Environment v. EPA, 26 Envt. Rep. Cas. (BNA) 2116 (N.D. Ala. 1987). A suit to enjoin EPA from forcing a hazardous waste facility to comply with RCRA standards because the states, not the federal government, have jurisdiction over their territories was dismissed as "totally devoid of merit." "The RCRA easily passes constitutional muster as an exercise of congressional power under the commerce clause." United States v. Rogers, 26 Envt. Rep. Cas. (BNA) 2046 (D. Minn. 1987).

RCRA repeatedly requires standards "necessary to protect human health and the environment." See RCRA §§3002, 3003, and 3004. The House's version of the bill required standards that would "reasonably" protect health and the environment. (H.R. No. 14,496, 94th Cong., 2d Sess. (1976)). In the House-Senate compromise, this word was dropped. Does the statutory standard require zero discharge?

Landfill leachate is at the heart of public fears about hazardous waste disposal. A major purpose of EPA's regulations is to prevent another incident like Love Canal. Liner systems must be designed to prevent migration of wastes into adjacent soils or groundwater or surface water during facility life and during a post-closure period, generally 30 years. Surface impoundments, landfills, and land treatment facilities are required to have a monitoring program that can determine the facility's impact on groundwater, although the Administrator may exempt facilities from these requirements case-by-case if it can be shown that there is a reasonable certainty that there will be no migration of hazardous constituents. §6924(p). The groundwater protection requirements crucially depend on the assumption that leachate reaching groundwater can and will be detected and removed through corrective action, e.g., pumping. In brief, response may escalate through three tiers. First, simple detection monitoring must take place in the uppermost groundwater for the life of the facility plus (normally) 30 years. Second, if leachate does reach groundwater, more extensive compliance monitoring must begin, and EPA will specify ambient tolerances for the contaminated groundwater. Finally, if ambient tolerances are exceeded, corrective action must be begun, e.g., construction of slurry wells and counter pumping. Under the 1984 amendments, corrective action must be taken for all releases of hazardous waste or constituents from any facility, regardless of when the waste was placed there. §6924(u). Corrective action may be required beyond the facility's boundary. §6924(v).

Note that sites existing at the time RCRA was passed were not expected to shut down immediately until they could meet RCRA standards. EPA reasoned that wastes that would accumulate or be disposed of illegally would pose a greater danger than they would if they were placed even in substandard existing disposal facilities. Under interim disposal guidelines authorized by RCRA, the facilities could continue to operate so long as they notified EPA of their existence and complied with minimum interim requirements. A facility could operate at the level and in the fashion that existed when interim status was granted. Yet interim status is not like a preexisting use that has been "grandfathered," as when rezoning raises land use standards. The interim permit does not create a vested right to permanent operation at the interim status level.

The 1984 amendments require EPA or a state administering an authorized hazardous waste program to determine whether to issue a final (or "Part B") permit to incinerator facilities by November 8, 1989 and to non-incinerator facilities by November 8, 1992 for permit applications submitted before late 1984. §6925(c)(2). A facility may lose interim status if not granted a final permit within this time period. A land disposal facility that had not submitted an application for a final permit by late 1984 will lose its interim status unless it does so within a year of the date on which the facility first becomes subject to a final permit requirement. §6925(e)(3). See 51 Fed. Reg. 4,128. Interim status facilities are subject to the same groundwater protection requirements as new facilities. §6925(i). EPA has to decide whether to grant final permits on 16 of 264 operating land disposal facilities by March 31, 1989. 19 Envt. Rep. (BNA): Current Developments 1461 (1988). Georgia is the only state authorized to issue a final permit, because it is the only state approved by EPA to oversee corrective action plans.

Under RCRA a facility is more like a nuclear generating plant than a conventional landfill. Unless the operator demonstrates that unauthorized entry cannot cause damage, a facility must either have a permanent barrier or a 24-hour surveillance system. Facilities must be inspected under an EPA facility inspection plan. Facility personnel are required to have sufficient expertise to carry out their assigned tasks safely. Facility operators must have a contingency plan to be followed whenever there is a release that would threaten human health or the environment.

Both closure and post-closure plans must be integrated with the administration of Superfund (see p. 614 *infra*). To close a facility, landfills must be covered, storage and treatment facilities must be decontaminated, and the hazardous wastes must be removed from the facility. The post-closure plan must include an extended period of groundwater monitoring activities, maintenance activities to ensure the integrity of the final groundcover or containment structures, and the name and address of the person who should be contacted during the post-closure period. The most important post-closure notice requirement concerns deed restriction. Although the EPA regulations do not put it quite this way, post-closure status in effect creates an easement or restrictive covenant that runs with land that contains a closed hazardous waste facility. The restriction placed in the deed to the property pursuant to the applicable state recording act must inform subsequent purchasers that the facility is under post-closure RCRA status. The post-closure restriction may be released only if all wastes, waste residues, and contaminated soils are removed from the facility.

Building on the general tort law principle that a landowner who maintains a dangerous condition may be liable after the land has been transferred, regulations require the operator of an interim status facility to maintain a trust fund, surety bond, or bank letters of credit to cover the costs of post-closure activities. See, e.g., Department of Environmental Protection v. Ventron Corp., 94 N.J. 254, 463 A.2d 893 (1983), and Philadelphia Chewing Gum Corp. v. Commonwealth, 35 Pa. Commw. Ct. 443, 387 A.2d 142 (1978), *aff'd sub nom.* National Wood Preservers, Inc. v. Commonwealth, 489 Pa. 221 414 A.2d 37 (1980). Corrective action funds are not required. In brief, proposed regulations would allow a trust fund to be built up over the life of the facility or 20 years, whichever is shorter. The other two alternatives must be payable directly to the EPA regional administrator, and unlike the trust fund, these cannot be built up over a period of years. In addition to financial guarantees, operators are required to obtain liability insurance.

Enforcement. Just as RCRA gives the states the opportunity to run their own hazardous waste control programs, it gives an approved state the first opportunity to enforce the Act against its violators. The state has 30 days to take action; after 30 days, EPA may enforce state requirements as if EPA never had relinquished the program to the state. §3008(a)(2). Informal warnings aside, EPA may choose to enforce via an administrative compliance order or a civil suit. §3008(a)(1). EPA may seek temporary or permanent injunctions, criminal penalties, civil penalties up to $25,000 per day of violation of an administrative order, and other appropriate relief. See §3008(a)(3). Under criminal penalties added by the 1984 amendments, a person who knowingly violates the statute may be subject to a fine of not more than $50,000 per day of violation and from two to five years in prison. These penalties are doubled in the case of a second conviction. §6928(d). A person who knowingly violates the statute and knows that by doing so he or she places another person in imminent danger of death or serious bodily harm can be fined up to $250,000 and imprisoned for up to 15 years. §6928(e). A corporation that violates this subsection can be fined up to $1 million. The longest jail sentence ever imposed for an environmental crime was three years for disposing of hazardous wastes without a RCRA permit and making false statements. United States v. Harwell, No. 85-28R (N.D. Ga. 1987). RCRA includes a conventional citizens' suit provision under which, after appropriate notice, "any person" may sue violators and government agencies and officials for failure to perform nondiscretionary duties. See §7002(a). In addition, EPA may bring suit to enjoin an action presenting an "imminent and substantial endangerment to health or the environment." §6973(a).

b.   The Insurance Provisions of RCRA

The strict regulatory scheme of RCRA is supposed to prevent the release of wastes from licensed disposal facilities. But if the regulatory program fails despite all precautions, Congress has attempted to ensure that owners and operators will be able to pay for cleanup and to compensate for injuries by empowering EPA to impose "necessary or desirable" financial responsibility requirements. §3004(a)(6). Out of the 1,451 active land disposal facilities nationwide, 956 were to close as of early 1988 because they were unable to certify compliance with RCRA's financial responsibility and groundwater monitoring requirements. U.S. General Accounting Office, New Approach Needed to Manage the Resource Conservation and Recovery Act 39 (1988). The mandatory insurance requirements EPA has imposed are comprehensive; all RCRA regulatory safeguards are backed up by parallel insurance requirements. Regulations require evidence of financial responsibility for third party liability resulting from operations during facility life (including reimbursing the federal government or other party undertaking cleanup) and for the estimated costs of closing the facility and monitoring and maintaining it for 30 years after closure. Under a proposed rule, owners and operators of municipal landfills would also be required to demonstrate financial responsibility for corrective action for known releases. 53 Fed. Reg. 33,314 (1988). In addition to insurance, to demonstrate financial responsibility, letters of credit, surety bonds, trust funds and corporate guarantees may also be used. 53 Fed. Reg. 33,938 (1988). The insurance must cover all property damage and personal injury claims that could normally be brought under state law, subject to exclusions for damage caused by acts of war, injuries covered by workers' compensation or disability benefits, or intentional injuries (40 C.F.R. §264.147(a) (1988)) (owners or operators must demonstrate liability coverage for bodily injury and property damage to third parties resulting from facility operation); Id., §264.146(a) (closure and post-closure financial assurance requirements). Regulations also require insuring for the costs of corrective action if groundwater beyond a facility shows more than background levels of specified contaminants (47 Fed. Reg. 32,274, 32,279).

The regulations distinguish between sudden, one-time releases resulting from spills, explosions, or breaches in containment material and non-sudden releases, such as gradual seepage into groundwater. The owner or operator must maintain liability insurance for sudden releases in the amount of $1 million per occurrence, with an annual aggregate of at least $2 million (Id., §264.147(a)). Non-sudden releases are more prevalent and may be continuous or continual. For reasons that will emerge below, insurers, have been reluctant to cover non-sudden occurrences; hence EPA has moved slowly in requiring insurance for non-sudden releases. An owner or operator must insure for $3 million per non-sudden "occurrence" (i.e., discovery of leakage), with an annual aggregate of at least $6 million. Id., §264.147(b). This requirement was applied to facilities with annual sales of $10 million or more beginning in 1980, to facilities in the $5 to $10 million range in late 1983, and to smaller facilities in 1984. One policy may be written to cover both sudden and non-sudden releases for at least $4 million per occurrence, with an annual aggregate of at least $8 million. If lower than average risk levels exist, the Administrator may lower the coverage requirements in particular cases. Id., §264.147(c). The maximum annual insurance coverage currently available is $12.5 million. U.S. General Accounting Office, Hazardous Waste: Issues Surrounding Insurance Availability 3 (1988).

The distinction between sudden and non-sudden occurrences developed from the insurance industry's response to polluters' needs for wider coverage as their liability expanded in the 1960s and 1970s. Prior to the late 1960s, comprehensive general liability (CGL) policies were written to cover both sudden and gradual environmental impairment. In the late 1960s and early 1970s, however, the increased number of pollution problems led insurance companies to adopt the "pollution exclusion," which dropped CGL coverage for "bodily injury or property damage arising out of the discharge, dispersal, release, or escape of smoke, vapors, soot fumes, acids, alkalines, toxic chemicals, liquids, gases, waste materials, irritants, contaminants, or pollutants onto or upon the land, atmosphere, or watercourse, unless the discharge, dispersal, release or escape is sudden or accidental" (Meyer, Compensating Hazardous Waste Victims: RCRA Insurance Regulations and a Not So "Super" Fund, 11 Envtl. L. 689, 710 (1981).

The CGL sudden occurrence contract covers claims arising out of an incident taking place during the policy year, regardless of when those claims are presented. But the strict "occurrence" basis of the CGL policy renders it inappropriate for full pollution protection because typically it is written for one year only. Pollution incidents of long duration make it impossible to say when the "occurrence" took place. Some other solution seems necessary. Or do you think a satisfactory solution is to require all of the insurance policies that applied sometime during the period of seepage or escape to pay a share, viewing the entire period as one "occurrence"? This approach was adopted in Keene Corp. v. Insurance Co. of North America, 667 F.2d 1034 (D.C. Cir. 1981), cert. denied, 455 U.S. 1007 (1982), in which the court held that the development of asbestos-related disease, from first inhalation of asbestos fibers to the manifestation of the disease, as much as thirty to forty years later, constituted an "occurrence" under each of the insurance policies in effect during the thirty-to-forty year period.

Another approach became available in the mid-1970s, when about a dozen domestic and foreign brokers and companies began offering high-limit insurance for non-sudden pollution occurrences under the "claims made" environmental impairment liability (EIL) policy developed by the London insurance market. EIL covers "claims made" during the policy year, no matter when the incident giving rise to the claims occurred (with certain limits). If a slow leak or accumulated asbestos exposure leads to a claim in 1995, for example, it does not matter that the problem may already be decades old. An EIL policy valid for 1995 will cover the claim. Deductibles and premiums may be as high as $5 million each. The demand for EIL coverage increased steadily in the early 1980s, but recent figures indicate that EIL coverage may be declining. Insurance Availability, supra, at 19. The present availability of insurance is quite limited. See Abraham, Environmental Liability and the Limits of Insurance, 88 Colum. L. Rev. 942 (1988). Most insurers have stopped issuing new policies covering pollution-related damages since the mid-1980s, citing their increased potential liability under federal environmental statutes. Id. at 2. Presently there is only one insurance organization that actively markets pollution insurance. Id. at 3.

The gap in insurance coverage is being filled by risk-retention groups formed by financial brokers and trade associations. (This type of insurance is authorized by Section 210 of SARA). Two groups, Hypercept and Environmental Protection Insurance Company (EPIC), began operating in late 1987 and offer insurance to small to mid-sized companies. A third group that planned to insure 30 to 100 Fortune 500 companies was unable to gather the initial capital required to start operations. The effectiveness of risk-retention groups in meeting industry's pollution insurance needs remains to be seen. Id. at 25-26.

Which type of insurance would best serve the RCRA scheme? The insurance companies have much to gain from the "claims made" approach. They find it difficult, particularly in times of inflation or rapid change in statutory cleanup or compensation law, to set premiums adequate to cover pollution incidents of long duration. How should the insurer compute the current premium for unspecified liabilities that may not materialize for 30 years? Further, state insurance regulation requires insurers to base future rates on past experience, eliminating "speculation" in premiums. This may tempt insurers to continue using the CGL approach.

The claims made approach enables insurers to accumulate reserves gradually to cover claims for the long-latency diseases that slow discharges might cause. Rates can be adjusted up or down rather quickly as experience with the policies develops because claims are covered by the policy currently in force rather than one for which the premiums were set years or decades earlier. What disadvantages do you see flowing from the adoption of a claims made approach?

The author of the following excerpt stated that the points he makes raise "a number of interesting questions" about the "proliferation of financial responsibility requirements" in environmental laws. How would you rebut his four criticisms? Or do you agree with them?

> First, the extent of the current and proposed requirements and their correlation with the key stages of EPA facility regulation — operating life, closure, and post-closure — suggests the possibility that EPA and others may view insurers providing evidence of financial responsibility as de facto regulators of insured facilities, as substitutes or surrogates for active EPA or state regulation.
>
> From a public policy standpoint, such a perception would be disaster: It would invite further cutbacks in EPA funding, and impose upon insurers a role they neither desire nor are equipped to fulfill. Moreover, experience with financial responsibility requirements in other contexts has shown that they cannnot operate as substitutes for public regulation of inherently hazardous industries.
>
> For example, even though airline operators are subject to financial responsibility regulations, we would not consider abandoning FAA airworthiness certification of aircraft. Similarly, despite compulsory compensation protection for workers, we would not relieve employers of their statutory obligations to provide a safe workplace.
>
> In addition, the profit-maximizing instincts of the 900 or so casualty insurers competing in interstate commerce would subvert any effort to convert them into a regulatory monolith. For insurers, loss prevention is an incident of profitable underwriting, subject to cost restraints imposed by competition, rather than an end in itself. And even if insurers were compelled by law to enforce government-decreed safety standards against their insureds, how would these standards be enforced against the large and growing number of self-insured operators?
>
> Second, EPA's financial responsibility requirements are a formidable regulatory weapon, enforced not through administrative or judicial process, from whose judgments an appeal may be taken, but by the marketplace, whose judgments, from which there is no appeal, can mean economic ruin. The requirements place in the hand of insurers the power to foreclose or void, on *economic* grounds that may bear little relationship to statutory criteria for or the social utility of a given facility, what should be a *regulatory* judgment as to the fitness of a given operator to receive a permit. . . .

Third, from the perspective of those subject to them, EPA's financial responsibility requirements are an imposing entry barrier to competition in the waste management business. They automatically convert what should be a competitively neutral element — insurance — into a potent weapon for large self-insured firms to wield against smaller current or would-be competitors who must purchase commercial coverage, and they will do more to encourage oligopoly in the waste management industry than would an exemption from the antitrust laws. It was not coincidence that the strongest advocates of EPA's initial financial responsibility rules were the self-insured giants of the petroleum, chemical and waste management industries. . . .

Fourth, as financial responsibility requirements proliferate, the implicit delegation of quasi-regulatory authority to surrogates creates pressures to impose — by regulation — the same duties upon the surrogates as were assumed by government. Thus we had early forms of the EPA's "facility liability endorsement" which sought to rewrite the terms and conditions of underlying insurance policies; we now have members of the [insurance] industry proposing amendments to RCRA to permit financial responsibility insurers to perform government safety inspections; and we have yet to deal with Superfund's financial responsibility provisions, which would make insurers' legal responsibilities coextensive with those of facility owners by overriding insurers' contractual defenses to liability. [Cheek, Financial Responsibility Requirements under RCRA: Insurance Coverage for and beyond the Grave, Hazardous Wastes, Superfund, and Toxic Substances 132-134 (ALI-ABA Committee on Continuing Professional Education ed. 1982).]

See also Cheek, Risk-Spreaders or Risk Eliminators? An Insurer's Perspective on the Liability and Financial Responsibility Provisions of RCRA and CERCLA, 2 Va. J. Nat. Resources L. 131, 149 (1982); Pfennigstorf, Insurance of Environmental Risks: Recent Developments in Environmental Law Symposium 57 (P. Schroth ed. 1982). For another view, see Ferreira, Promoting Safety through Insurance, in Social Regulation: Strategies for Reform 267, 276-277 (E. Bardach & R. Kagan eds. 1982); Comment, Liability Insurance Coverage for Superfund claims: A Modest Proposal, 53 Mo. L. Rev. 289, 304-06 (1988).

2.   Dangerous Existing Sites: Of Deep Pockets, Orphans, and Superfunds

RCRA's regulatory scheme is prospective only. While RCRA may be successful at preventing harm from active and new disposal facilities, many inactive or abandoned dump sites still threaten health and natural systems. The larger chemical companies have cooperated with the cleanup effort, but sites no longer receiving wastes often are still difficult to get cleaned up. Some key generators, transporters, or owners have gone out of business; others quickly enter bankruptcy petitions upon being confronted with the problems they have caused. The nature or quantity of wastes may be impossible to establish because records may have been lost or destroyed, if any existed at all. Judges are reluctant to assign responsibility to solvent "good actors" who have a prior connection with the site when site mismanagement seems to be the fault of a subsequent bad actor, even if the malefactor is penniless or has vanished entirely.

Some sites are true "orphan" sites: no one knows who operated or used them. A few sites clearly are the work of "midnight dumpers" or "gypsy haulers," who significantly lowered their overhead costs by treating unoccupied land as a waste commons. As a result, estimates of the extent of the problem vary so widely that they cannot be trusted. Conservation Foundation, The State of the Environment 145-146 (1982). The EPA's estimate that there are about 27,000 sites contaminated with hazardous wastes has been challenged by a congressional report that puts the figure at 130,340. General Accounting Office, Superfund, Extent of Nation's Problem Still Unknown (1988). A 1985 Office of Technology Assessment report, Superfund Strategy, estimated that at least 10,000 sites — in contrast to EPA's estimate of 2,000 — were serious enough to require cleanup. The OTA estimated the cleanup cost at $100 billion and the time to do it 50 years. Id. at 3. A report by Standard and Poor for the insurance industry puts the total eventual cost at $700 billion. Dimond, the $700 Billion Cleaning Bill, Insurance Review, January, 1989, p. 30.

a.   The Superfund: History, Purpose, and Structure

The Comprehensive Environmental Response, Compensation, and Liability Act (CERCLA)* represents Congress's effort to rectify decades of careless waste disposal practices. The basic idea of CERCLA is simple: it places responsibility for cleaning up sites on the responsible parties but provides seed money for federal cleanups and site study. The implementation of these concepts, however, has proved anything but simple. Part of the problem stems from the genesis of the Act. CERCLA was patched together during the last days of the Carter administration, although Congress had been considering far-reaching legislation for three years. The draft legislation included liability rules drawn from the Clean Water Act's oil spill provisions and other federal remedial and corrective legislation. It also included an ambitious compensation scheme for property, victims, and natural resources. Except for natural resources damage compensation, this approach was abandoned after the 1980 election because of concern over the inflationary impact of the proposal. At the last minute, the Senate bypassed the conference procedures and presented the House with a quickly worked out compromise. As a result, there is little conventional legislative history. A court commented acerbically on this "virtually incomprehensible" legislation

---

*The Comprehensive Environmental Response, Compensation, and Liability Act was originally passed in 1980. The Act was subsequently amended by the Superfund Amendments and Reauthorization Act in 1986 (SARA). The current citation for the two Acts, which are collectively referred to as CERCLA, is 31 U.S.C. §§9601-9675. "CERCLA as amended by SARA (please forgive our heavy use of acronyms, but it is unavoidable because the full names of the statutes are both cumbersome and uninformative." United States v. Fisher, 864 F.2d 434, — (7th Cir. 1988) (Posner, J.).

that has achieved a "quirky notoriety" and stated that CERCLA resembled King Minos' labyrinth in ancient Crete. See In re Acushnet River & New Bedford Harbor Proceedings Re Alleged PCB Pollution, 675 F. Supp. 22, 25-26, n.2 (D. Mass. 1987). See also Dedham Water Co. v. Cumberland Farms Dairy, Inc., 805 F.2d 1074 (1st Cir. 1986) (legislative history shrouded with mystery); United States v. Mottolo, 605 F. Supp. 898, 902 (D.N.H. 1985) (well-deserved notoriety).

CERCLA contemplates both short- and long-term responses at the worst sites to eliminate immediate threats to human health and to minimize future risks. The statute creates a federal trust fund (Superfund) to pay for government responses and provides a mechanism for the government to sue potentially responsible parties (PRPs) for these costs in order to replenish the fund. Ultimate responsibility is placed on the entities that used the sites. CERCLA §104, 42 U.S.C. §9604, authorizes EPA to recover both "removal" and "remedial" costs. Removal costs are short-term responses to an emergency, usually a spill or a leaking site. Remedial costs are long-term cleanup costs. There is a history of successful emergency responses to accidents such as spills, but the implementation of long-term risk minimization at Superfund sites has proved particularly difficult. Only a few sites have been cleaned up, and estimates about what the existing fund can accomplish are pessimistic. No remedial action may be undertaken unless the state in which the release occurs has entered into a contract or cooperative agreement with EPA that provides assurance that the state will maintain all future removal and remedial actions. The state must also agree to pay a minimum of 10 percent of the cost of a cleanup. 42 U.S.C. §9604(c)(3). In addition to these expenditures, §106 authorizes the Department of Justice to bring actions where an "imminent and substantial endangerment to the public health or welfare or the environment" exists. 42 U.S.C. §9606.

The statute requires the preparation of a National Contingency Plan (NCP), which must include "criteria for determining priorities among releases or threatened releases . . . for the purpose of taking remedial action." 42 U.S.C. §9605. The EPA met this mandate by establishing a list of hazardous sites, the National Priority List (NPL). In 1989 the NPL included 1,175 sites ranked by hazard.

Once the EPA expends fund monies for a removal or remedial action, it may recover these costs from four classes of "potentially responsible parties" (PRPs): (1) owners or operators of vessels or facilities that contain hazardous substances, (2) owners or operators of a facility at the time of disposal, (3) persons who arranged for disposal, and (4) any person who accepted hazardous substances for transport or disposal. 42 U.S.C. §9607. The Superfund Amendments and Reauthorization Act of 1986 (SARA) creates a lien against PRPs in favor of the federal government for any response costs it incurs, but the lien is subject to liens perfected under state law before notice of the federal lien is filed. 42 U.S.C. §9607(1).

CERCLA may have been poorly drafted, but this poor draftsmanship has not kept the courts from imposing sweeping liability on the PRPs. Liability is strict and joint and several; a PRP's nexus with the site may be very slight, and liability will still attach. Hence the government need make only a rudimentary prima facie case: it must prove only that the site is a "facility," that there is a "release" from the facility, that the government has incurred response costs, and that the defendant is one of the persons on whom liability is imposed. Recent cases have added a fifth possible element: consistency with the NCP. The CER-CLA liability net is wide and tight. As a result, the Act raises a number of basic fairness questions that must be balanced against the congressional desire for fast cleanups by those responsible for the hazards.

Any thoughts that CERCLA would become a fast-moving juggernaut with which the federal government would terrorize the PRPs were dispelled by EPA's administration of the statute. EPA initially dragged its feet and subordinated congressional directives to political influence.

Between mid-1981 and mid-1983, internal dissension, reduced staffing and funding, and several reorganizations impaired operations throughout the EPA. The inability of the CERCLA program to establish a record of accomplishment is due in large part to this unfortunate period. Moreover, the current approach to CER-CLA implementation has been forged as a reaction to the politically discredited managerial strategy which then prevailed.

The strategy that contributed to the resignation or firing of more than fifteen EPA officials attempted to use program delays and private cleanup agreements to keep Fund expenditures low so that Congress would not need to reauthorize the Fund in 1985. This approach was supposed to curb inflationary spending and obviate the need for another federal public works program.

The National Contingency Plan was to have been revised within six months of CERCLA's enactment. Many months passed before a court order forced EPA to promulgate the plan. The Fund, meanwhile, accumulated unspent revenues. The EPA defended its actions as necessary to ensure that limited funds would be spent at deserving sites and to allow its staff time to negotiate for cleanup by responsible parties.

Critics charged that the EPA had relaxed cleanup requirements as an inducement to private parties to clean up sites themselves, had agreed to cost-reimbursement settlements short of what the Fund should recover under the statute, had allowed politics to interfere with the proper administration of the Fund, and, in general, had failed to follow acceptable management practices. On instructions from the White House, EPA Administrator Anne Gorsuch claimed executive privilege and refused to share enforcement documents with House subcommittees. In response, the House of Representatives voted for the first time in history to hold an agency head in contempt of Congress. The head of the CERCLA program was later convicted of perjury in connection with her testimony before a congressional committee and of obstructing congressional investigations.

Under Administrator Gorsuch, the agency experienced unprecedented managerial dissension. In fairness, a chronic tension between "program" and "enforcement" functions, never satisfactorily resolved in the Agency's fifteen years of existence, caused some of the difficulty. Yet this longstanding tension alone was inadequate to explain three chaotic reorganizations within one year.

CERCLA program officials are now keenly aware that Congress is vigilant concerning Superfund abuse. This political backdrop helps explain EPA's current wariness toward negotiation. But negotiation done improperly need not rule out negotiation done properly. In retrospect, the discarded negotiation strategy seems

almost quixotic; however much the Agency was committed to holding down inflationary spending and promoting cooperative problem-solving with the private sector, the site problem was enormous and private willingness to solve it was limited.
Failure of an all-carrot-and-no-stick approach was certain. [Anderson, Negotiation
and Informal Agency Action: The Case of Superfund, 1985 Duke L. J. 261, 279-
282.]

In the post-Gorsuch era the CERCLA program was administered ultra-
cautiously because of the harsh criticism even non-culpable officials had received in the press and in Congress. As EPA began to grapple with the problem
of remedy selection and the issue of how clean a cleaned-up site would have to
be, it transformed CERCLA, perhaps inadvertently, into a quasi-regulatory statute. Cleanup decisionmaking became more cumbersome and protracted as the
EPA deliberately limited the wide discretion Congress originally gave.

EPA created a lengthy site and remedy evaluation process. The Remedial
Investigation/Feasibility Study (RI/FS) determines the extent of the threat posed
by the release and sets out a proposed remedy. Congress confirmed and extended
the RI/FS in the 1986 amendments (SARA). SARA also codified many other
EPA policies established in guidance documents, e.g., cleanup standards imported from regulatory pollution control statutes (see A Note on How Clean is
Clean *infra*, at p. 662) and agency negotiation policy. See A Note on Negotiation *infra*, at p. 642.

SARA also authorized more revenues. The Hazardous Substance Response Trust Fund, 42 U.S.C. §9611, was renamed the Hazardous Substance
Superfund and authorized at $8.5 billion for five years. The fund is replenished
by taxes on chemical feedstocks, on certain imported substances from chemical
feedstocks, and on domestic and imported petroleum; by a new corporate environmental tax equal to .12 percent of an alternative minimum taxable income
in excess of $2 million annually; and by other sources, such as Superfund inter-
est and cleanup reimbursement. See generally Carlson and Bausell, Financing
Superfund: An Evaluation of Alternative Tax Mechanisms, 27 Nat. Resources
J. 103 (1987). With individual surface and groundwater cleanups costing $21-
30 million, continuing to spend the $8.5 billion fund at the current rate could
leave half of the NPL sites without remediation.

The evolution of Superfund into a regulatory program is also illustrated by
SARA's increased public participation opportunities. EPA must establish procedures for the participation of interested persons in the development of the administrative record on which EPA will base the selection of removal and
remedial options. 42 U.S.C. §9613(k). The agency must provide public notice,
accompanied by a brief analysis of the cleanup plan for proposed remedial actions and any alternative plans considered, a reasonable opportunity to comment, an opportunity for a public meeting in the affected area, a response to
significant written public comments, and a statement of the basis and purpose
of the selected action. Public participation rights for short-term removal actions
are less extensive. If EPA brings a §106 abatement action or a §107 cost recovery
suit against PRPs or sues under the Resource Conservation and Recovery Act

(RCRA), any person claiming an interest in the subject matter of the suit who is not being adequately represented by existing parties may intervene as a matter of right. 42 U.S.C. §9613(i). See Stringfellow v. Concerned Neighbors in Action, 480 U.S. 370 (1987), which holds that a district court order denying intervention as a matter of right in a CERCLA action brought by the United States but allowing permissive intervention subject to conditions is not immediately appealable. See generally Friedman, Judicial Review under the Superfund Amendments: Will Parties Have Meaningful Input to the Remedy Selection Process?, 14 Colum. J. Envtl. L. 187 (1989).

Within SARA is a significant, freestanding act titled the Emergency Planning and Community Right-to-Know Act, SARA Title III, 42 U.S.C. §§11001-11050. In response to the Bhopal disaster at Union Carbide's plant in India, Congress required local and federal governments and industry to prepare emergency response plans and to disclose the manufacture or use of hazardous chemicals. Some 30,000 companies must report annually the number of pounds of some 329 chemicals released to the environment, subject to threshold quantities. The first report, for 1987, indicated that 10.4 billion pounds of toxic substances were released into water, 2.7 billion pounds to the air, 3.9 billion pounds to landfills and pits, and 3.3 billion pounds to treatment and disposal facilities. Weiskopf, EPA Finds Pollution Unacceptably High, Washington Post, April 13, 1989, p. A33, col. 4. The information is available publicly, and environmental groups have seen that the press is fully informed. Companies must send the information to local fire departments, local emergency planning committees, and state emergency resource commissions so that they can plan and take appropriate action in the event of an emergency. Citizens may sue for failure to implement these provisions. The EPA has fined 25 companies from $5,000 to $721,000 for failure to comply. 10 TSCA Chemicals-in-Progress Bulletin 9 (February, 1989). Public interest in this new "right-to-know law" runs high. See, e.g., Shabecoff, Industry to Give Vast New Data on Toxic Perils, New York Times, Sunday, February 14, 1988, p. 1, col. 1. Industry has responded slowly, in part by petitioning to delist select chemicals. See A.L. Laboratories v. EPA, 674 F. Supp. 894 (D.D.C. 1987).

SARA also extends the applications of CERCLA to ongoing treatment, storage, and disposal facilities as well as to abandoned or orphaned sites. Ongoing facilities are primarily regulated by RCRA and state siting acts, but CERCLA contains a modest federal siting policy, creating a complicated RCRA-CERCLA interface, as they say in Washington. For example, the EPA may not take any remedial action in a state that has failed to enter into a federal-state cooperative agreement that ensures that there will be adequate capacity for the treatment or secure disposal of all hazardous wastes reasonably expected to be generated within a twenty-year period. 42 U.S.C. §9604(c)(9). A facility may not receive wastes from a Superfund site unless the facility is in full compliance with RCRA. 42 U.S.C. §9621(d)(3). The relationship between this off-site policy and the prior EPA off-site policy is discussed in Chemical Waste Management, Inc. v. Environmental Protection Agency, 673 F. Supp. 1043 (D. Kan. 1987). SARA removes doubts about EPA authority to enter property, doubts created by Outboard Marine Corp. v. Thomas, 773 F.2d 883 (7th Cir. 1985), *vacated and remanded sub nom.* Thomas v. Outboard Marine Corp., 107 S. Ct. 638 (1986), by expressly authorizing the EPA to enter and inspect property to decide what action, if any, to take at a site. 42 U.S.C. §9604(e).

Two useful sources of background information on CERCLA are Developments in the Law — Toxic Waste Litigation, 99 Harv. L. Rev. 1458 (1986), which is a comprehensive survey of the subject; and Alexander, CERCLA 1980-1985: A Research Guide, 13 Ecology L.Q. 311 (1986), which is an annotated bibliography of the Superfund literature.

b.   Potentially Responsible Parties: Liability, Site Nexus, and Cost Recovery

UNITED STATES v. MONSANTO CO.
858 F.2d 160 (4th Cir. 1988)

Before WIDENER, SPROUSE and ERVIN, Circuit Judges.

SPROUSE, Circuit Judge:

Oscar Seidenberg and Harvey Hutchinson (the site-owners) and Allied Corporation, Monsanto Company, and EM Industries, Inc. (the generator defendants),[1] appeal from the district court's entry of summary judgment holding them liable to the United States and the State of South Carolina (the governments) under section 107(a) of the Comprehensive Environmental Response, Compensation, and Liability Act of 1980 (CERCLA). 42 U.S.C.A. §9607(a) (West Supp. 1987). The court determined that the defendants were liable jointly and severally for $1,813,624 in response costs accrued from the partial removal of hazardous waste from a disposal facility located near Columbia, South Carolina. The court declined, however, to assess prejudgment interest against the defendants. We affirm the district court's liability holdings, but we vacate and remand for reconsideration its denial of prejudgment interest.

I

In 1972, Seidenberg and Hutchinson leased a four-acre tract of land they owned to the Columbia Organic Chemical Company (COCC), a South Carolina chemical manufacturing corporation. The property, located along Bluff Road near Columbia, South Carolina, consisted of a small warehouse and surrounding areas. The lease was verbal, on a month-to-month basis, and according to the site-owners' deposition testimony, was executed for the sole purpose of allow-

---

1.   Originally a named generator defendant in this case, Aquair Corporation has entered into a settlement agreement with the plaintiffs.

ing COCC to store raw materials and finished products in the warehouse. Seidenberg and Hutchinson received monthly lease payments of $200, which increased to $350 by 1980.

In the mid-1970s, COCC expanded its business to include the brokering and recycling of chemical waste generated by third parties. It used the Bluff Road site as a waste storage and disposal facility for its new operations. In 1976, COCC's principals incorporated South Carolina Recycling and Disposal Inc. (SCRDI), for the purpose of assuming COCC's waste-handling business, and the site-owners began accepting lease payments from SCRDI.

SCRDI contracted with numerous off-site waste producers for the transport, recycling, and disposal of chemical and other waste. Among these producers were agencies of the federal government and South Carolina,[2] and various private entities including the three generator defendants in this litigation. Although SCRDI operated other disposal sites, it deposited much of the waste it received at the Bluff Road facility. The waste stored at Bluff Road contained many chemical substances that federal law defines as "hazardous."

Between 1976 and 1980, SCRDI haphazardly deposited more than 7,000 fifty-five gallon drums of chemical waste on the four-acre Bluff Road site. It placed waste laden drums and containers wherever there was space, often without pallets to protect them from the damp ground. It stacked drums on top of one another without regard to the chemical compatibility of their contents. It maintained no documented safety procedures and kept no inventory of the stored chemicals. Over time many of the drums rusted, rotted, and otherwise deteriorated. Hazardous substances leaked from the decaying drums and oozed into the ground. The substances commingled with incompatible chemicals that had escaped from other containers, generating noxious fumes, fires, and explosions.

On October 26, 1977, a toxic cloud formed when chemicals leaking from rusted drums reacted with rainwater. Twelve responding firemen were hospitalized.[3] Again, on July 24, 1979, an explosion and fire resulted when chemicals stored in glass jars leaked onto drums containing incompatible substances. SCRDI's site manager could not identify the substances that caused the explosion, making the fire difficult to extinguish.

In 1980, the Environmental Protection Agency (EPA) inspected the Bluff Road site. Its investigation revealed that the facility was filled well beyond its capacity with chemical waste. The number of drums and the reckless manner in which they were stacked precluded access to various areas in the site. Many of the drums observed were unlabeled, or their labels had become unreadable

---

2.   The federal instrumentalities that contracted with SCRDI included the Environmental Protection Agency, the Army, the Air Force, and the Center for Disease Control. The South Carolina Department of Health and Environmental Control also contracted with SCRDI for waste disposal.

3.   This incident sparked substantial publicity, and the site-owners concede that as of June 1977 they were aware of hazardous waste disposal activities taking place on their Bluff Road property.

from exposure, rendering it impossible to identify their contents. The EPA concluded that the site posed "a major fire hazard."

Later that year, the United States filed suit under section 7003 of the Resource Conservation and Recovery Act, 42 U.S.C. §6973, against SCRDI, COCC, and Oscar Seidenberg. The complaint was filed before the December 11, 1980, effective date of CERCLA, and it sought only injunctive relief. Thereafter, the State of South Carolina intervened as a plaintiff in the pending action.

In the course of discovery, the governments identified a number of waste generators, including the generator defendants in this appeal, that had contracted with SCRDI for waste disposal. The governments notified the generators that they were potentially responsible for the costs of cleanup at Bluff Road under section 107(a) of the newly-enacted CERCLA. As a result of these contacts, the governments executed individual settlement agreements with twelve of the identified off-site producers. The generator defendants, however, declined to settle.

Using funds received from the settlements, the governments contracted with Triangle Resource Industries (TRI) to conduct a partial surface cleanup at the site. The contract required RAD Services, Inc., a subsidiary of TRI, to remove 75% of the drums found there and to keep a log of the removed drums. RAD completed its partial cleanup operation in October 1982. The log it prepared documented that it had removed containers and drums bearing the labels or markings of each of the three generator defendants.

The EPA reinspected the site after the first phase of the cleanup had been completed. The inspection revealed that closed drums and containers labeled with the insignia of each of the three generator defendants remained at the site. The EPA also collected samples of surface water, soil, and sediment from the site. Laboratory tests of the samples disclosed that several hazardous substances contained in the waste the generator defendants had shipped to the site remained present at the site.

Thereafter, South Carolina completed the remaining 25% of the surface cleanup. It used federal funds from the Hazardous Substances Response Trust Fund (Superfund), 42 U.S.C. §9631, as well as state money from the South Carolina Hazardous Waste Contingency Fund, S.C. Code Ann. §44-56-160, and in-kind contribution of other state funds to match the federal contribution.

In 1982, the governments filed an amended complaint, adding the three generator defendants and site-owner Harvey Hutchinson, and including claims under section 107(a) of CERCLA against all of the non-settling defendants. The governments alleged that the generator defendants and site-owners were jointly and severally liable under section 107(a) for the costs expended completing the surface cleanup at Bluff Road.

In response, the site-owners contended that they were innocent absentee landlords unaware of and unconnected to the waste disposal activities that took place on their land. They maintained that their lease with COCC did not allow COCC (or SCRDI) to store chemical waste on the premises, but they admitted that they became aware of waste storage in 1977 and accepted lease payments until 1980.

The generator defendants likewise denied liability for the governments' response costs. Among other defenses, they claimed that none of their specific waste materials contributed to the hazardous conditions at Bluff Road, and that retroactive imposition of CERCLA liability on them was unconstitutional. They also asserted that they could establish an affirmative defense to CERCLA liability under section 107(b)(3), 42. U.S.C. §9607(b)(3), by showing that the harm at the site was caused solely through the conduct of unrelated third parties. All parties thereafter moved for summary judgment.

After an evidentiary hearing, the district court granted the governments' summary judgment motion on CERCLA liability. The court found that all of the defendants were responsible parties under section 107(a), and that none of them had presented sufficient evidence to support an affirmative defense under section 107(b). The court further concluded that the environmental harm at Bluff Road was "indivisible," and it held all of the defendants jointly and severally liable for the governments' response costs. United States v. South Carolina Recycling & Disposal, Inc., 653 F. Supp. 984 (D.S.C. 1984) (*SCRDI*).

As to the site-owners' liability, the court found it sufficient that they owned the Bluff Road site at the time hazardous substances were deposited there. Id. at 993 (interpreting 42 U.S.C.A. §9607(a)(2) (West Supp. 1987)). It rejected their contentions that Congress did not intend to subject "innocent" landowners to CERCLA liability. The court similarly found summary judgment appropriate against the generator defendants because it was undisputed that (1) they shipped hazardous substances to the Bluff Road facility; (2) hazardous substances "like" those present in the generator defendants' waste were found at the facility; and (3) there had been a release of hazardous substances at the site. *SCRDI*, 653 F. Supp. at 991-93 (interpreting 42 U.S.C.A. §9607(a)(3) (West Supp. 1987)). In this context, the court rejected the generator defendants' arguments that the governments had to prove that their specific waste contributed to the harm at the site, and it found their constitutional contentions to be "without force." *SCRDI*, 653 F. Supp. at 992-93, 995-98. Finally, since none of the defendants challenged the governments' itemized accounting of response costs, the court ordered them to pay the full $1,813,624 that had been requested. Id. at 1009, 1014. It refused, however, to add prejudgment interest to the amount owed. Id. at 1009. This appeal followed.

II

The site-owners and the generator defendants first contest the imposition of CERCLA liability vel non, and they challenge the propriety of summary judgment in light of the evidence presented to the trial court. The site-owners also reassert the "innocent landowner" defense that the district court rejected, and claim that the court erroneously precluded them from presenting evidence of a valid affirmative defense under section 107(b)(3), 42 U.S.C. §9607(b)(3). The generator defendants likewise repeat their arguments based on the governments' failure to establish a nexus between their specific waste and the harm at the site. They also claim that the trial court ignored material factual issues relevant to affirmative defenses to liability. We address these contentions sequentially, but pause briefly to review the structure of CERCLA's liability scheme.

In CERCLA, Congress established "an array of mechanisms to combat the increasingly serious problem of hazardous substance releases." Dedham Water Co. v. Cumberland Farms Dairy, Inc., 805 F.2d 1074, 1078 (1st Cir. 1986). Section 107(a) of the statute sets forth the principal mechanism for recovery of costs expended in the cleanup of waste disposal facilities. At the time the district court entered judgment,[9] section 107(a) provided in pertinent part:

(a) Covered persons; scope

Notwithstanding any other provision or rule of law, and subject only to the defenses set forth in subsection (b) of this section . . .

> (2)   any person who at the time of disposal of any hazardous substance owned or operated any facility at which such hazardous substances were disposed of, [and]
>
> (3)   any person who by contract, agreement, or otherwise arranged for disposal or treatment, or arranged with a transporter for transport for disposal or treatment, of hazardous substances owned or possessed by such person, by any other party or entity, at any facility owned or operated by another party or entity and containing such hazardous substances, and
>
> (4)   . . . from which there is a release, or a threatened release which causes the incurrence of response costs, of a hazardous substance, shall be liable for —
>
> > (A)   all costs of removal or remedial action incurred by the United States Government or a State not inconsistent with the national contingency plan.

42 U.S.C.A. §9607(a) (West Supp. 1987).

In our view, the plain language of section 107(a) clearly defines the scope of intended liability under the statute and the elements of proof necessary to establish it. We agree with the overwhelming body of precedent that has interpreted section 107(a) as establishing a strict liability scheme.[11] Further, in light of the evidence presented here, we are persuaded that the district court correctly held that the governments satisfied all the elements of section 107(a) liability as to both the site-owners and the generator defendants.

---

9.   Congress amended section 107(a) in 1986, Pub. L. No. 99-499, 100 Stat. 1628-30, 1692, 1693, 1705-06 (1986), but the changes are not material to the issues presented in this part of the appeal.

11.   See, e.g., Levin Metals Corp. v. Parr-Richmond Terminal Co., 799 F.2d 1312, 1316 (9th Cir. 1986); New York v. Shore Realty Corp., 759 F.2d 1032, 1042 (2d Cir. 1985); Violet v. Picillo, 648 F. Supp. 1283, 1290 (D.R.I. 1986) (and cases cited therein); see also United States v. Northeastern Pharmaceutical & Chemical Co., 810 F.2d 726, 732 n.3 (8th Cir. 1986), cert. denied, — U.S. —, 108 S. Ct. 146, 98 L. Ed. 2d 102 (1987) (dictum).

In addition to the unanimous judicial viewpoint that Congress intended CERCLA liability to be strict, we observe that CERCLA section 101(32), 42 U.S.C.A. §9601(32) (West Supp.

A.   SITE-OWNERS' LIABILITY

In light of the strict liability imposed by section 107(a), we cannot agree with the site-owners' contention that they are not within the class of owners Congress intended to hold liable. The traditional elements of tort culpability on which the site-owners rely simply are absent from the statute. The plain language of section 107(a)(2) extends liability to owners of waste facilities regardless of their degree of participation in the subsequent disposal of hazardous waste.

Under section 107(a)(2), *any* person who owned a facility at a time when hazardous substances were deposited there may be held liable for all costs of removal or remedial action if a release or threatened release[12] of a hazardous substance occurs. The site-owners do not dispute their ownership of the Bluff Road facility, or the fact that releases occurred there during their period of ownership. Under these circumstances, all the prerequisites to section 107(a) liability have been satisfied.[13] See *Shore Realty*, 759 F.2d at 1043-44 (site-owner held liable under CERCLA section 107(a)(1) even though he did not contribute to the presence or cause the release of hazardous substances at the facility).[14]

1987), provides that the standard of liability applicable to CERCLA actions shall be that which governs actions under section 311 of the Clean Water Act, 33 U.S.C. §1321. In Steuart Transportation Co. v. Allied Towing Corp., 596 F.2d 609, 613 (4th Cir. 1979), we held that the standard of liability under section 311 is strict liability.

12.   The statute defines "release" to include "any spilling, leaking, pumping, pouring, emitting, emptying, discharging, injecting, escaping, leaching, dumping, or disposing into the environment (including the abandonment or discarding of barrels, containers, and other closed receptacles containing any hazardous substance or pollutant or contaminant)." 42 U.S.C.A. §9601(22) (West Supp. 1987).

13.   The site-owners' relative degree of fault would, of course, be relevant in any subsequent action for contribution brought pursuant to 42 U.S.C.A. §9613(f) (West Supp. 1987). Congress, in the Superfund Amendments and Reauthorization Act of 1986, Pub. L. 99-499, §113, 100 Stat. 1613, 1647 (1986) [hereafter SARA], established a right of contribution in favor of defendants sued under CERCLA section 107(a). Section 113(f)(1) provides:

> Any person may seek contribution from any other person who is liable or potentially liable under section 9607(a) of this title, during or following any civil action under section 9606 of this title or under section 9607(a) of this title. Such claims shall be brought in accordance with this section and the Federal Rules of Civil Procedure, and shall be governed by Federal law. In resolving contribution claims, the court may allocate response costs among liable parties using such equitable factors as the court determines are appropriate. Nothing in this subsection shall diminish the right of any person to bring an action for contribution in the absence of a civil action under section 9606 or section 9607 of this title.

42 U.S.C.A. §9613(f) (West Supp. 1987). The legislative history of this amendment suggests that in arriving at an equitable allocation of costs, a court may consider, among other things, the degree of involvement by parties in the generation, transportation, treatment, storage, or disposal of hazardous substances. H.R. Rep. No. 253(III), 99th Cong., 1st Sess. 19 (1985), reprinted in 1986 U.S. Code Cong. & Admin. News 2835, 3038, 3042.

14.   Congress, in section 101(35) of SARA, acknowledged that landowners may affirmatively avoid liability if they can prove they did not know and had no reason to know that hazardous substances were disposed of on their land *at the time they acquired title or possession.* 42 U.S.C.A. §9601(35) (West Supp. 1987). This explicitly drafted exception further signals Congress' intent to impose liability on landowners who cannot satisfy its express requirements.

The site-owners nonetheless contend that the district court's grant of summary judgment improperly denied them the opportunity to present an affirmative defense under section 107(b)(3). Section 107(b)(3) sets forth a limited affirmative defense based on the complete absence of causation. See *Shore Realty*, 759 F.2d at 1044. It requires proof that the release or threatened release of hazardous substances and resulting damages were caused solely by "a third party other than . . . one whose act or omission occurs in connection with a contractual relationship, existing directly or indirectly, with the defendant. . . ." 42 U.S.C. §9607(b)(3). A second element of the defense requires proof that the defendant "took precautions against foreseeable acts or omissions of any such third party and the consequences that could foreseeably result from such acts or omissions." Id. We agree with the district court that under no view of the evidence could the site-owners satisfy either of these proof requirements.

First, the site-owners could not establish the absence of a direct or indirect contractual relationship necessary to maintain the affirmative defense. They concede they entered into a lease agreement with COCC. They accepted rent from COCC, and after SCRDI was incorporated, they accepted rent from SCRDI. See United States v. Northernaire Plating Co., 670 F. Supp. 742, 747-48 (W.D. Mich. 1987) (owner who leased facility to disposing party could not assert affirmative defense). Second, the site-owners presented no evidence that they took precautionary action against the foreseeable conduct of COCC or SCRDI. They argued to the trial court that, although they were aware COCC was a chemical manufacturing company, they were completely ignorant of all waste disposal activities at Bluff Road before 1977. They maintained that they never inspected the site prior to that time. In our view, the statute does not sanction such willful or negligent blindness on the part of absentee owners. The district court committed no error in entering summary judgment against the site-owners.

B.   GENERATOR DEFENDANTS' LIABILITY

The generator defendants first contend that the district court misinterpreted section 107(a)(3) because it failed to read into the statute a requirement that the governments prove a nexus between the waste they sent to the site and the resulting environmental harm. They maintain that the statutory phrase "containing such hazardous substances" requires proof that the specific substances they generated and sent to the site were present at the facility at the time of release. The district court held, however, that the statute was satisfied by proof that hazardous substances "like" those contained in the generator defendants' waste were found at the site. *SCRDI*, 653 F. Supp. at 991-92. We agree with the district court's interpretation.

Reduced of surplus language, sections 107(a)(3) and (4) impose liability on off-site waste generators who:

> arranged for disposal . . . of hazardous substances . . . at any facility . . . *containing such hazardous substances* . . . from which there is a release . . . of a hazardous substance.

42 U.S.C.A. §§9607(a)(3), (4) (West Supp. 1987) (emphasis supplied). In our view, the plain meaning of the adjective "such" in the phrase "containing such hazardous substances" is "[a]like, similar, of the like kind." *Black's Law Dictionary* 1284 (5th ed. 1979). As used in the statute, the phrase "such hazardous substances" denotes hazardous substances alike, similar, or of a like kind to those that were present in a generator defendant's waste or that could have been produced by the mixture of the defendant's waste with other waste present at the site. It does not mean that the plaintiff must trace the ownership of each generic chemical compound found at a site. Absent proof that a generator defendant's specific waste remained at a facility at the time of release, a showing of chemical similarity between hazardous substances is sufficient.[15]

The overall structure of CERCLA's liability provisions also militates against the generator defendants' "proof of ownership" argument. In *Shore Realty*, the Second Circuit held with respect to site-owners that requiring proof of ownership at any time later than the time of disposal would go far toward rendering the section 107(b) defenses superfluous. *Shore Realty*, 759 F.2d at 1044. We agree with the court's reading of the statute and conclude that its reasoning applies equally to the generator defendants' contentions. As the statute provides — "[n]otwithstanding any other provision or rule of law" — liability under section 107(a) is "subject *only* to the defenses set forth" in section 107(b). 42 U.S.C.A. §9607(a) (West Supp. 1987) (emphasis added). Each of the three defenses[16] established in section 107(b) "carves out from liability an exception based on causation." *Shore Realty*, 759 F.2d at 1044. Congress has, therefore, allocated the burden of disproving causation to the defendant who profited from the generation and inexpensive disposal of hazardous waste. We decline to interpret the statute in a way that would neutralize the force of Congress' intent.[17]

Finally, the purpose underlying CERCLA's liability provisions counsels

---

15. CERCLA plaintiffs need not perform exhaustive chemical analyses of hazardous substances found at a disposal site. See *SCRDI*, 653 F. Supp. at 993 n.6. They must, however, present evidence that a generator defendant's waste was shipped to a site and that hazardous substances similar to those contained in the defendant's waste remained present at the time of release. The defendant, of course, may in turn present evidence of an affirmative defense to liability.

16. In addition to the limited third-party defense discussed above, sections 107(b)(1) and (2) respectively allow defendants to avoid liability by proving that the release and resulting damages were "caused solely" by an act of God or an act of war. 42 U.S.C. §9607(b)(1), (2).

17. In fact, Congress specifically declined to include a similar nexus requirement in CERCLA. As the Second Circuit in *Shore Realty* observed, an early House version of what ultimately became section 107(a) limited liability to "any person who caused or contributed to the release or threatened release." 759 F.2d at 1044 (quoting H.R. Rep. 7020, 96th Cong., 2d Sess. §3071(a) (1980), reprinted in 2 A Legislative History of the Comprehensive Environmental Response, Compensation and Liability Act of 1980 at 438. As ultimately enacted after House and Senate compromise, however, CERCLA "imposed liability on classes of persons without reference to whether they caused or contributed to the release or threat of release." *Shore Realty*, 759 F.2d at 1044. The legislature thus eliminated the element of causation from the plaintiff's liability case. Id.; see also United States v. Bliss, 667 F. Supp. 1298, 1309 (E.D. Mo. 1987) ("traditional tort notions, such as proximate cause, do not apply"); Violet v. Picillo, 648 F. Supp. 1283, 1290-93 (D.R.I. 1986) (minimal causal nexus); United States v. Conservation Chemical Co., 619 F. Supp. 162, 190 (W.D. Mo. 1985); United States v. Wade, 577 F. Supp. 1326, 1331-34 (E.D. Pa. 1983).

against the generator defendants' argument. Throughout the statute's legislative history, there appears the recurring theme of facilitating prompt action to remedy the environmental blight of unscrupulous waste disposal.[18] In deleting causation language from section 107(a), we assume, as have many other courts, that Congress knew of the synergistic and migratory capacities of leaking chemical waste, and the technological infeasibility of tracing improperly disposed waste to its source.[19] In view of this, we will not frustrate the statute's salutary goals by engrafting a "proof of ownership" requirement, which in practice, would be as onerous as the language Congress saw fit to delete. See United States v. Wade, 577 F. Supp. 1326, 1332 (E.D. Pa. 1983) ("To require a plaintiff under CERCLA to 'fingerprint' wastes is to eviscerate the statute.").

The generator defendants next argue that the trial court ignored evidence that established genuine factual issues as to the existence of an affirmative defense to liability. They maintain that summary judgment was inappropriate because they presented some evidence that all of their waste had been removed from Bluff Road prior to cleanup. We agree with the trial court, however, that the materials on which the generator defendants rely were insufficient to create a genuine issue of material fact.

The generator defendants offered only conclusory allegations, principally based "on information and belief," that their waste, originally deposited at Bluff Road, was at some time prior to 1979 transported from that facility to other sites operated by SCRDI.[20] To withstand summary judgment under section 107(b)(3), however, the generator defendants had to produce specific evidence creating a genuine issue that all of their waste was removed from the site prior to the release of hazardous substances there. See 42 U.S.C. §9607(b)(3).[21] In light of the un-

18.   The legislative history underlying the Superfund Amendments and Reauthorization Act of 1986 echoed this theme with even greater force than that underlying CERCLA's original enactment in 1980.

19.   In advancing their arduous proof requirements, the generator defendants make little mention of the fact that leaking chemicals may combine to form new compounds or escape into the atmosphere before proper response action can be taken. See cases cited *supra* note 17.

20.   The generator defendants offered the following materials:

1.   An officer of the company that oversaw the final cleanup at Bluff Road testified that he did not know whether drums bearing Allied's label actually contained Allied's waste when they were removed from the site.

2.   An officer of EM Industries averred that SCRDI assured him prior to 1980 that none of EM Industries' waste had been deposited at Bluff Road.

3.   An officer of Monsanto averred that two of his employees inspected the site in 1979, and while they "did not explore all areas of the site, upon information and belief they did not observe any drums of material taken from [Monsanto's plant]."

4.   An officer of Allied averred that SCRDI's site manager at Bluff Road told him in 1979 that all of Allied's waste was removed from the site before 1977.

None of these largely second-hand allegations were supported by evidence tending to show that any of the generators' waste materials were actually taken away from the site. "The mere existence of a scintilla of evidence in support of the [nonmoving party's] position will be insufficient [to avoid summary judgment]; there must be evidence on which the [finder of fact] could reasonably find for the [nonmoving party]." Anderson v. Liberty Lobby, Inc., 477 U.S. 242, 106 S. Ct. 2505, 2512, 91 L. Ed. 2d 202 (1986).

21.   Had they produced such evidence, it would have created an issue as to whether the "release or threat of release of a hazardous substance and the damages resulting therefrom were caused solely by . . . an act or omission of a third party." 42 U.S.C. §9607(b)(3).

controverted proof that containers bearing each of the defendants' markings remained present at the site at the time of cleanup and the fact that hazardous substances chemically similar to those contained in the generators' waste were found, the generator defendants' affidavits and deposition testimony simply failed to establish complete removal as a genuine issue. See Celotex v. Catrett, 477 U.S. 317, 106 S. Ct. 2548, 91 L. Ed. 2d 265 (1986) (summary judgment appropriately granted against nonmoving party who failed to produce evidence supporting an element essential to its case on which it bore burden of proof at trial).

III

The appellants next challenge the district court's imposition of joint and several liability for the governments' response costs.[22] The court concluded that joint and several liability was appropriate because the environmental harm at Bluff Road was "indivisible" and the appellants had "failed to meet their burden of proving otherwise." SCRDI, 653 F. Supp. at 994. We agree with its conclusion.

While CERCLA does not mandate the imposition of joint and several liability, it permits it in cases of indivisible harm. See Shore Realty, 759 F.2d at 1042 n.13; United States v. ChemDyne, 572 F. Supp. 802, 810-11 (S.D. Ohio 1983). In each case, the court must consider traditional and evolving principles of federal common law,[23] which Congress has left to the courts to supply interstitially.

Under common law rules, when two or more persons act independently to cause a single harm for which there is a reasonable basis of apportionment according to the contribution of each, each is held liable only for the portion of harm that he causes. When such persons cause a single and indivisible harm, however, they are held liable jointly and severally for the entire harm. Id. (citing Restatement (Second) of Torts §433A (1965)). We think these principles, as reflected in the Restatement (Second) of Torts, represent the correct and uniform federal rules applicable to CERCLA cases.

---

22. The site-owners limit their joint and several liability argument to the contention that it is inequitable under the circumstances of this case, i.e., their limited degree of participation in waste disposal activities at Bluff Road. As we havae stated, however, such equitable factors are relevant in subsequent actions for contribution. They are not pertinent to the question of joint and several liability, which focuses principally on the divisibility among responsible parties of the harm to the environment.

23. As many courts have noted, a proposed requirement that joint and several liability be imposed in all CERCLA cases was deleted from the final version of the bill. See, e.g., Chem-Dyne 572 F. Supp. at 806. "The deletion," however, "was not intended as a rejection of joint and several liability," but rather "to have the scope of liability determined under common law principles." Id. at 808. We adopt the Chem-Dyne court's thorough discussion of CERCLA's legislative history with respect to joint and several liability. We note that the approach taken in Chem-Dyne was subsequently confirmed as correct by Congress in its consideration of SARA's contribution provisions. See H.R. Rep. No. 253(I), 99th Cong. 2d Sess., 79-80 (1985), reprinted in 1986 U.S. Code Cong. & Admin. News at 2835, 2861-62.

Section 433A of the Restatement provides:

(1) Damages for harm are to be apportioned among two or more causes where
        (a)   there are distinct harms, or
        (b)   there is a reasonable basis for determining the contribution of each
    cause to a single harm.
(2) Damages for any other harm cannot be apportioned among two or more causes.

Restatement (Second) of Torts §433A (1965).

Placing their argument into the Restatement framework, the generator defendants concede that the environmental damage at Bluff Road constituted a
"single harm," but contend that there was a reasonable basis for apportioning the
harm. They observe that each of the off-site generators with whom SCRDI contracted sent a potentially identifiable volume of waste to the Bluff Road site, and
they maintain that liability should have been apportioned according to the volume they deposited as compared to the total volume disposed of there by all
parties. In light of the conditions at Bluff Road, we cannot accept this method
as a basis for apportionment.

The generator defendants bore the burden of establishing a reasonable basis
for apportioning liability among responsible parties. *Chem-Dyne*, 572 F. Supp.
at 810; Restatement (Second) of Torts §433B (1965).[24] To meet this burden, the
generator defendants had to establish that the environmental harm at Bluff Road
was divisible among responsible parties. They presented no evidence, however,
showing a relationship between waste volume, the release of hazardous substances, and the harm at the site.[25] Further, in light of the commingling of
hazardous substances, the district court could not have reasonably apportioned
liability without some evidence disclosing the individual and interactive qualities
of the substances deposited there. Common sense counsels that a million gallons
of certain substances could be mixed together without significant consequences,
whereas a few pints of others improperly mixed could result in disastrous con-

---

24. Section 433(B)(2) of the Restatement provides:

    Where the tortious conduct of two or more actors has combined to bring about
harm to the plaintiff, and one or more of the actors seeks to limit his liability on the
ground that the harm is capable of apportionment among them, the burden of proof as to
the apportionment is upon each such actor.

Restatement (Second) of Torts §433(B)(2) (1965).
25. At minimum, such evidence was crucial to demonstrate that a volumetric apportionment scheme was reasonable. The governments presented considerable evidence identifying
numerous hazardous substances found at Bluff Road. An EPA investigator reported, for example,
that in the first cleanup phase RAD Services encountered substances "in every hazard class,
including explosives such as crystallized dynamite and nitroglycerine. Numerous examples were
found of oxidizers, flammable, and nonflammable liquids, poisons, corrosives, containerized
gases, and even a small amount of radioactive material." Under these circumstances, volumetric
apportionment based on the overall quantity of waste, as opposed to the quantity and quality of
hazardous substances contained in the waste would have made little sense.

sequences.[26] Under other circumstances proportionate volumes of hazardous substances may well be probative of contributory harm.[27] In this case, however, volume could not establish the effective contribution of each waste generator to the harm at the Bluff Road site.

Although we find no error in the trial court's imposition of joint and several liability, we share the appellants' concern that they not be ultimately responsible for reimbursing more than their just portion of the governments' response costs.[28] In its refusal to apportion liability, the district court likewise recognized the validity of their demand that they not be required to shoulder a disproportionate amount of the costs. It ruled, however, that making the governments whole for response costs was the primary consideration and that cost allocation was a matter "more appropriately considered in an action for contribution between responsible parties after plaintiff has been made whole." SCRDI, 653 F. Supp. at 996 & n.8. Had we sat in place of the district court, we would have ruled as it did on the apportionment issue, but may well have retained the action to dispose of the contribution questions. See 42 U.S.C.A. §9613(f) (West Supp. 1987). That procedural course, however, was committed to the trial court's discretion and we find no abuse of it. As we have stated, the defendants still have the right to sue responsible parties for contribution, and in that action they may assert both legal and equitable theories of cost allocation.[29]

IV

The generator defendants raise numerous constitutional challenges to the district court's interpretation and application of CERCLA. They contend that the im-

---

26.   We agree with the district court that evidence disclosing the relative toxicity, migratory potential, and synergistic capacity of the hazardous substances at the site would be relevant to establishing divisibility of harm.

27.   Volumetric contributions provide a reasonable basis for apportioning liability only if it can be reasonably assumed, or it has been demonstrated, that independent factors had no substantial effect on the harm to the environment. Cf. Restatement (Second) of Torts §433A comment d, illustrations 4, 5 (1965).

28.   The final judgment holds the defendants liable for slightly less than half of the total costs incurred in the cleanup, while it appears that the generator defendants collectively produced approximately 22% of the waste that SCRDI handled. Other evidence indicates that agencies of the federal government produced more waste than did generator defendant Monsanto, and suggests that the amounts contributed by the settling parties do not bear a strictly proportionate relationship to the total costs of cleaning the facility. We note, however, that a substantial portion of the final judgment is aattributable to litigation costs. We also observe that the EPA has contributed upwards of $50,000 to the Bluff Road cleanup, and that any further claims against the EPA and other responsible government instrumentalities may be resolved in a contribution action pursuant to CERCLA secton 113(f).

29.   Contrary to the generator defendants' request, it would be premature for us to interpret the effect of settlement on the rights of nonsettling parties in contribution actions under CERCLA section 113(f)(2), 42 U.S.C.A. §9613(f)(2) (West Supp. 1987). We observe, however, that the possibility this subsection precludes contribution actions against settling parties signals legislative policy to encourage settlement in CERCLA cleanup actions. At the same time, we

position of "disproportionate" liability without proof of causation violated constitutional limitations on retroactive statutory application and that it converted CERCLA into a bill of attainder and an *ex post facto* law. They further assert, along with the site-owners, that the trial court's construction of CERCLA infringed their substantive due process rights. . . .

Many courts have concluded that Congress intended CERCLA's liability provisions to apply retroactively to pre-enactment disposal activities of off-site waste generators. They have held uniformly that retroactive operation survives the Supreme Court's tests for due process validity.[31] We agree with their analyses.

In Usery v. Turner Elkhorn Mining Co., 428 U.S. 1 (1976), the Supreme Court, in a different context, rejected a due process challenge to the retroactive operation of the liability provisions in the Black Lung Benefits Act of 1972. The Court stated that "a presumption of constitutionality" attaches to "legislative Acts adjusting the burdens and benefits of economic life," and that "the burden is on one complaining of a due process violation to establish that the legislature has acted in an arbitrary and irrational way." Id. at 15. It reasoned that although the Act imposed new liability for disabilities developed prior to its enactment, its operation was "justified as a rational measure to spread the costs of the employees' disabilities to those who have profited from the fruits of their labor." Id. at 18.

The reasoning of *Turner Elkhorn* applies with great force to the retroactivity contentions advanced here. While the generator defendants profited from inexpensive waste disposal methods that may have been technically "legal" prior to CERCLA's enactment, it was certainly foreseeable at the time that improper disposal could cause enormous damage to the environment. CERCLA operates remedially to spread the costs of responding to improper waste disposal among all parties that played a role in creating the hazardous conditions. Where those conditions are indivisible, joint and several liability is logical, and it works to ensure complete cost recovery. We do not think these consequences are "particularly harsh and oppressive," United States Trust Co. v. New Jersey, 431 U.S. 1, 17 n.13 (1977) (retrospective civil liability not unconstitutional unless it is particularly harsh and oppressive), and we agree with the Eighth Circuit that retroactive application of CERCLA does not violate due process. United States v. Northeastern Pharmaceutical & Chemical Co., Inc., 810 F.2d 726, 734 (8th Cir. 1986), *cert. denied*, 108 S. Ct. 146 (1987).

Nor does the imposition of strict, joint and several liability convert CER-

---

recognize that the language of CERCLA's new contribution provisions reveals Congress' concern that the relative culpability of each responsible party may be considered in determining the proportionate share of costs each must bear.

31. See, e.g., United States v. Northeastern Pharmaceutical & Chemical Co., Inc., 810 F.2d 726, 732-34 (8th Cir. 1986), *cert. denied*, — U.S. —, 108 S. Ct. 146, 98 L. Ed. 2d 102 (1987) (NEPACCO); United States v. Hooker Chemicals & Plastics Corp., 680 F. Supp. 546 (W.D.N.Y. 1988); United States v. Shell Oil Co., 605 F. Supp. 1064, 1069-73 (D. Colo. 1985). These decisions hold that CERCLA's legislative history and the past-tense language of section 107(a) evince congressional intent to apply CERCLA retroactively.

CLA into a bill of attainder or an *ex post facto* law. United States v. Conservation Chemical Co., 619 F. Supp. 162, 214 (W.D. Mo. 1985); United States v. Tyson, 25 Envt. Rep. Cas. (BNA) 1897 (E.D. Pa. 1986). The infliction of punishment, either legislatively or retrospectively, is a sine qua non of legislation that runs afoul of these constitutional prohibitions. See Nixon v. Administrator of General Services, 433 U.S. 425, 473-84 (1977) (bill of attainder analysis); Weaver v. Graham, 450 U.S. 24, 28-30 (1981) (ex post facto law analysis). CERCLA does not exact punishment. Rather it creates a reimbursement obligation on any person judicially determined responsible for the costs of remedying hazardous conditions at a waste disposal facility. The restitution of cleanup costs was not intended to operate, nor does it operate in fact, as a criminal penalty or a punitive deterrent. Cf. Tull v. United States, 481 U.S. 412 (1987) (distinguishing civil penalties under Clean Water Act from equitable remedy of restitution). Moreover, as this case amply demonstrates, Congress did not impose that obligation automatically on a legislatively defined class of persons.[33]

V

The United States contends on cross-appeal that the district court erred in denying its request for prejudgment interest on its response costs. At the time the court issued its decision, CERCLA contained no explicit provision for the award of prejudgment interest. Since then, however, Congress has added the following language to section 107(a):

> The amounts recoverable in an action under this section shall include interest on the amounts recoverable under subparagraphs (A) through (D). Such interest shall accrue from the later of (i) the date payment of a specified amount is demanded in writing, or (ii) the date of the expenditure concerned. The rate of interest on the outstanding unpaid balance of the amounts recoverable under this section shall be the same rate as is specified for interest on investments of the Hazardous Substance Superfund established under subchapter A of chapter 98 of Title 26. For purposes of applying such amendments to interest under this subsection, the term "comparable maturity" shall be determined with reference to the date on which interest accruing under this subsection commences.

42 U.S.C.A. 9607(a) (West Supp. 1987). Because of this addition to the law, we look to the Supreme Court's decision in Bradley v. Richmond School Board, 416 U.S. 696 (1974), for the principles controlling application of later-enacted amendments to previously accrued statutory liability. We conclude under *Brad-*

---

33. The existence of joint and several liability in cases of indivisible harm does not transform an otherwise constitutional obligation into one that exacts punishment. "Where there are opportunities for contribution . . . as well as for joinder or impleader of responsible parties (Fed. R. Civ. P. Rules 14, 20 and 21), it can hardly be said that imposition of joint and several liability would be unconstitutional." *Conservation Chemical*, 619 F. Supp. at 214-15.

ley that the case must be remanded for reconsideration of the interest question pursuant to the terms of amended statute. . . .

VI

In view of the above, the judgment of the district court as to the CERCLA liability of the site-owners and generator defendants is affirmed. The case is remanded, however, for reconsideration of the question of prejudgment interest.

Affirmed in part, vacated in part, and remanded.

WIDENER, Circuit Judge, concurring and dissenting:

I concur in the majority opinion in all respects save its decision not to require the district court to treat the issue of allocation of costs of cleanup among the various defendants and, as to that, I respectfully dissent. While it may be true that a subsequent suit for contribution may adequately apportion the damages among the defendants, I am of opinion that the district court, as a court of equity, is required to retain jurisdiction and answer that question now.

So far as I know, it is now and has been the general law without any variance that when a court of equity has jurisdiction it "will decide all matters in dispute and decree complete relief," e.g., Alexander v. Hillman, 296 U.S. 222, 242 (1935), see Pomeroy's Equity Jurisprudence, 3d Ed (1905) §181, 231, and that a court of equity should dispose of a case "so as to end litigation, not to foster it; to diminish suits, not to multiply them." Payne v. Hook, 74 U.S. (7 Wall) 425, 432 (1869). . . .

I see great danger in postponing the ultimate apportioning of the damages to a later day. As an example, a small generator which deposited a few gallons of relatively innocuous waste liquid at a site is jointly and severally liable for the entire cost of cleanup under this decision. And with that I agree. If that generator were readily available and solvent, however, the government might well, and probably would, proceed against him first in collecting its judgment. The vagaries of and delays in his subsequent suit for contribution might result in needless financial disaster. I do not see this as a desired or even permissible result.

The statute involved, 42 U.S.C. 9613(f)(1), provides that "[a]*ny person* may seek contribution from any other person who is liable or potentially liable under section 9607(a) of this title during or following any civil action under section 9606 of this title or under section 9607(a) of this title." (Italics added.) Thus, the statute plainly provides that discretion with respect to contribution is not in the district court to consider relief or not as the majority opinion holds; rather, it is in the generator to seek relief, for "any person" certainly includes the generators of the waste. So, since the matter was brought before the district court, that court had no discretion but to decide the question.[1] To repeat, the

---

1. In the unlikely event that there was not sufficient evidence before the district court, it should simply have required more evidence to be taken, or should [have] on remand should my view have prevailed.

discretion is in the party to make the claim, not in the district court to defer decision. While I agree that the claims may be asserted in a separate action, if they are asserted in the main case they must be decided. . . .

Not only do the statute and federal procedural law require the course I have suggested, I think that the interests of justice as well as judicial economy are best served by proceeding in that manner.

NOTES AND QUESTIONS

Joint and several liability. Since United States v. Chem-Dyne, 572 F. Supp. 802 (S.D. Ohio 1983), joint and several liability has been universally accepted by the courts and has formed the cornerstone of EPA's implementation of CERCLA. *Monsanto* follows this trend, but note that the Supreme Court has yet to confirm joint and several CERCLA liability. How does CERCLA joint and several liability differ from the common law doctrine? Is the imposition of joint and several liability on PRPs fair and efficient?

Contribution. When CERCLA was first enacted, the statute was silent on joint and several liability and on how contribution was to be handled. Apparently the sponsors wanted both of these issues to be handled under traditional and evolving principles of common law. But the state common law of joint and several liability was contradictory. No right of contribution existed at common law; states conferred it by statute. Anderson, Natural Resources Damages, Superfund, and the Courts, 16 B.C. Envtl. Aff. L. Rev. 405, 432-434 (1989). Early federal district court cases called for a federal common law of joint and several liability and contribution under CERCLA, see, e.g., Colorado v. ASARCO, 616 F. Supp. 822 (D. Colo. 1985), but prior to SARA, CERCLA §107(a)(4)(B) began to emerge as a possible statutory basis for contribution. This section makes all PRPs liable to any person who has incurred response costs consistent with the NCP. §9607(a)(4)(B). See Walls v. Waste Resource Corp., 761 F.2d 311 (6th Cir. 1985). In 1986 SARA explicitly created a right of contribution, but Congress did not set out criteria for apportionment. The court is to apply "Federal law" and "such equitable factors as the court deems appropriate." §9613(f). Three sources of law thus remain somewhat in tension: (1) federal common law, (2) §107(a)(4)(B), 42 U.S.C. §9607(a)(4)(B), and (3) 42 U.S.C. §9613(f). See generally, Comment, Contribution under CERCLA: Judicial Treatment after SARA, 14 Colum. J. Envtl. L. 267 (1989); Comment, Federal Common Law of Contribution under the 1986 CERCLA Amendments, 14 Ecology L.Q. 365 (1987).

The source of the right of contribution may be important. For example, §107(a)(4)(B) makes a PRP liable for response costs, incurred by any person, that are consistent with the NCP. This creates an implied private right of action by third party PRP plaintiffs against third party defendants. A third party claim can be dismissed under this section if the third party plaintiff has not incurred the necessary response costs, Levin Metals Corp. v. Parr-Richmond Terminal Co., 608 F. Supp. 1272 (N.D. Cal. 1985), but incurring response costs is not a pre-requisite for impleading a third party for federal common law contribution. United States v. New Castle County, 642 F. Supp. 1270 (D. Del. 1986).

As *Monsanto* indicates, the trial court has to make a decision whether to go ahead and hear the PRPs' contribution claims even if liability for the entire cleanup can be imposed on one or a few PRPs. See also United States v. String-fellow, 661 F. Supp. 1053, 1060 (C.D. Cal. 1987). In general the federal gov-ernment favors a two-action approach, that is, it wants to exit CERCLA cases once it has recovered its full response costs from a single (or a few) jointly and severally liable deep-pocket PRPs. The full array of PRPs is then left to fight over respective shares in a subsequent contribution action brought by the unlucky deep-pocket PRPs. In his *Monsanto* dissent, Judge Widener maintained that CERCLA and equity required a one-action approach, in which shares are allo-cated among the full array of PRPs at the same time the government's cost re-covery is determined, as was done in Allied Corp. v. Acme Solvents Reclaiming, Inc., 691 F. Supp. 1100 (N.D. Ill. 1988). Which approach do you favor? Does the presence in *Monsanto* of federal and state PRPs affect your answer? Does the EPA possess special expertise valuable to the court in allocating shares? Are con-tribution defendants jointly and severally liable to contribution plaintiffs? If not, in suing recalcitrant PRPs, the cooperative settling PRPs would be deprived of the principal tool EPA has in forcing PRPs to bargain. See U.S. v. Conservation Chemical Co., 619 F. Supp. 162, 176 (W.D. Mo. 1985), depriving contribution plaintiffs of this benefit.

Assume that a court has already held that a single indivisible injury exists and thus joint and several liability is warranted. What basis for assigning shares then exists when a contribution action is filed? *Monsanto* suggests that assigning shares based on the fraction of the total volume of wastes deposited at the site is too simplistic. Yet the majority of settlements among PRPs are based on volume. For the volumetric approach, see U.S. v. South Carolina Recycling and Dis-posal, Inc., 653 F. Supp. 984 (D.S.C. 1984); U.S. v. Ottati & Goss, Inc., 630 F. Supp. 1361 (D.N.H. 1986). Rejecting the volumetric approach, see O'Neil v. Picillo, 682 F. Supp. 706, 725 (D.R.I. 1988). Courts might consider total amount, toxicity, involvement, degree of care exercised, and cooperativeness in equitably assigning shares. What other factors are relevant? A defendant con-victed of roadside dumping could not seek contribution from others also indict-ed. U.S. v. Ward, 618 F. Supp. 884 (E.D.N.C. 1985).

Note that in *Monsanto*, only surface cleanup was at issue and still over $3.5 million had been spent. The subsurface (i.e., groundwater) cleanup at Bluff Road is still in the RI/FS preparation stage, but estimates are that it will cost an additional $7-17 million. Groundwater cleanups will intensify the debate over contribution, because they will be much more expensive.

Causation. Under *Monsanto* what causal nexus must exist between the health risk the site presents and a PRP's involvement at the site? Traditional cause-in-fact? Any causal nexus at all? The court says that the mere presence at the site of chemicals of the same type that defendant deposited is enough. Can such a test survive constitutional challenge? The court thought so. Could the owner of a jar of copper pennies found at the site be held liable as a PRP if free copper, a CERCLA hazardous waste, is found in the site? What if Monsanto and Allied had been able to show that their wastes had been removed from the site prior to 1979? The court implied that they might not be held to be PRPs. See Dedham Water Co. v. Cumberland Farms, Inc., 689 F. Supp. 1223 (D. Mass. 1988) (no causal connection between release and incurrence of response costs). The decision was reversed on appeal, 889 F.2d 1148 (1st Cir. 1989), *reh'g denied*, because the district court failed to consider "whether defendant's releases (or threatened releases) might nonetheless have caused plaintiff to incur 'response costs' even though those releases did not in fact contaminate the wells." Should all generators whose wastes are removed from sites escape CERCLA liability? In Artisan Water Co. v. Government of New Castle County, 659 F. Supp. 1269 (D. Del. 1987), the court declined to apply the strict traditional "but for" rule of causation ("but for" the presence of defendant's waste, the release would not have occurred) and imposed a federal common law requirement that the defendant's conduct, along with other contributing causes, still be "a material element and substantial factor" in causing the release. Id. at 1282-1283. Is this test consistent with *Monsanto*? Should the courts include in the emerging federal common law of causation a breach-of-containment rule? Intact drums contribute little if any overall risk; effectively, there is no "release." Percolation of escaped liquid wastes into the soil and synergistic interactions of leaked chemicals cause the majority of problems. Compare Ohio v. Interior Dept., excerpted *infra* at 665 (D.C. Cir. 1989) which appears to endorse the Department's adoption of common law causation standards for natural resource damage assessments because CERCLA was ambiguous.

Potentially Responsible Parties (PRPs). The courts have given §107(a), 42 U.S.C. §9607, a broad reading in order to reach the widest possible array of parties responsible for creating dangerous conditions at hazardous waste disposal sites.

Piercing the corporate veil. Suppose a company forms a subsidiary to purchase the assets of a corporation with potential CERCLA liability for the purpose of avoiding CERCLA liability. The formation of a wholly-owned undercapitalized subsidiary whose day-to-day operations are controlled by the parent is an easy case for imposing liability on the parent. For example, in State v. Bunker Hill Co., 635 F. Supp. 665 (D. Idaho 1986), a parent who capitalized a subsidiary at $1,110 and received $27,000,000 in dividends was deemed an owner or operator. The cases hold that CERCLA requires a uniform rule to determine when the corporate veil may be pierced, but the standard for doing so remains unclear. In re Alleged PCB Pollution, 675 F. Supp. 22 (D. Mass. 1987), rejected the argument of the federal government and the state of Massachusetts that the veil should be pierced as soon as the parent's involvement transcends a pure investment relationship. Instead, the district court held that the federal common law is based on the factors traditionally considered by state courts. These factors include: (1) inadequate capitalization in light of the purposes for which the corporation organized, (2) extensive control by the parent shareholders, (3) intermingling of subsidiary and parent accounts and property, (4) failure to observe the formalities of separateness, such as separate records, (5) diversion of funds from the subsidiary to the parent, and (6) existence of nonfunctioning officers or directors. The formation of a subsidiary to avoid "liability through the corporate form, without more, is not a wrong that equity's hand must right." For a dissenting view that the above analysis ignores "the corporate form without an express congressional directive" see Joslyn Manufacturing Corp. v. T.L. James & Co., 696 F. Supp. 222 (W.D. La. 1988), aff'd, — F.2d — (5th Cir. 1990). See generally Note, Piercing the Corporate Law Veil: The Alter Ego Doctrine under Federal Common Law, 95 Harv. L. Rev. 853 (1982).

"Arranging for disposal." To further the goal of shifting cleanup costs to responsible parties, courts have defined "arranging for disposal" liberally. Owning shareholders who manage a company or corporate officers who arrange for the disposal of hazardous waste are liable as "owners and operators." United States v. Conservation Chemical Co., 610 F. Supp. 152 (W.D. Mo. 1985). A corporate employee or officer may also be liable under §107(a)(3) as a person who arranges for the transportation or disposal of hazardous wastes. United States v. Northeastern Pharmaceutical & Chemical Co., 810 F.2d at 743-744, held that a plant supervisor who was also a corporate officer and shareholder was liable because he personally participated in conduct that violated CERCLA. The sale of waste products that contain hazardous substances also falls within the section. See, e.g., United States v. Ward, 618 F. Supp. 884 (E.D.N.C. 1985) (PCB-laden waste oil), and United States v. Conservation Chemical Co., 619 F. Supp. at 237-240 (fly ash used to neutralize wastes from other generators); and United States v. Aceto Agricultural Chemicals Corp., 872 F.2d 1373 (8th Cir. 1989) (pesticide manufacturer who supplied active ingredients to formulator and supervised production of commercial grade product). Courts have recognized limited exceptions for the sale of useful products that are sold to a party who incorporates it into the product which is released into the environment, e.g., Florida Power & Light Co. v. Allis Chalmers Corp., 27 Envt. Rep. Cas. (BNA) 1558 (S.D. Fla. 1988).

Financial institutions as PRPs. Does a bank's interest in property on which it has loaned money ever make the bank a PRP? Section 101(20)(A) exempts "a person, who, without participating in the management of a vessel or facility, holds indicia of ownership to protect his security interest in the vessel or facility." 42 U.S.C. §9601(20)(A). This section would seem to protect mortgagees from liability, regardless of whether a state has adopted the lien, title, or intermediate theory of a mortgage, at least until the mortgagor defaults and the mortgagee forecloses or otherwise acquires possession and control over the property. The liability of a lender after default has been litigated in two cases. The first, United States v. Mirabile, 15 Envtl. L. Rep. (Envtl. L. Inst.) 20,992, 20,996 (E.D. Pa. 1985), held that a lender who foreclosed and purchased at the sale but refused to accept a sheriff's deed until it was able to sell the property four months later was not an owner: "Regardless of the nature of the title received by ABT, its actions with respect to the foreclosure were plainly undertaken in an effort to protect its security interest in the property." Maryland Bank & Trust Co., 632 F. Supp. 573 (D. Md. 1986), held that a lender who foreclosed and purchased was liable when hazardous wastes were discovered and EPA cleaned up the property. "MB & T purchased the property at the foreclosure sale not to protect its security interest, but to protect its investment," and held title for four years. 632 F. Supp. at 579. The legislative history indicates that Congress intended to protect banks that hold mortgages in the 13 states governed by the common law of mortgages, under which the financial institution actually holds title to the property while the mortgage is in force.

> The interpretation of section 101(20)(A) urged upon the Court by MB & T runs counter to the policies underlying CERCLA. Under the scenario put forward by the bank, the federal government alone would shoulder the cost of cleaning up the site, while the former mortgagee-turned-owner would benefit from the clean-up by the increased value of the now-unpolluted land. At the foreclosure sale, the mortgagee could acquire the property cheaply. All other prospective purchasers would be faced with potential CERCLA liability, and would shy away from the sale. Yet once the property has been cleared at the taxpayers' expense and becomes marketable, the mortgagee-turned-owner would be in a position to sell the site at a profit.
>
> In essence, the defendant's position would convert CERCLA into an insurance scheme for financial institutions, protecting them against possible losses due to the security of loans with polluted properties. Mortgagees, however, already have the means to protect themselves, by making prudent loans. Financial institutions are in a position to investigate and discover potential problems in their secured properties. For many lending institutions, such research is routine. CERCLA will not absolve them from responsibility for their mistakes of judgment. [632 F. Supp. at 580.]

Are *MB & T* and *Mirabile* consistent? Should post-foreclosure liability depend on the amount of time that the lender holds the property? See generally Comment, The Impact of the 1986 Superfund Amendments and Reauthorization Act on the Commercial Lending Industry: A Critical Assessment, 41 U. Miami L. Rev. 879 (1987). Should the threshold of lender liability be high or low? Compare Note, Interpreting the Meaning of Lender Management under Section 101(20)(a) of CERCLA, 98 Yale L.J. 925 (1989) with Burkhart, Lender/Owners and CERCLA: Title and Liability, 25 Harv. J. on Legis. 317 (1988). In a rather cryptic opinion, the Fifth Circuit included a lender in a group of defendants who had participated in the development of a subdivision over contaminated property. Tanglewood East Homeowners v. Charles-Thomas, Inc., 849 F.2d 1568 (5th Cir. 1988).

Governments as PRPs. In *Monsanto*, the EPA, the Army and Air Force, the Federal Center for Disease Control, and the state health and environment agency all contributed wastes to the site. Are units of federal, state, and local governments liable under CERCLA just like private PRPs? See 42 U.S.C.

§9601(21) (defining "person"); §9607(a); §9620. If a unit of federal government is liable, then should its share be taken from the federal Superfund? Could, say, the Air Force be held jointly and severally liable for the entire cleanup cost and be forced to seek contribution from other private and governmental PRPs?

Note that as a result of *Monsanto* the federal PRPs' shares are first financed by the federal Superfund, then shifted to the private PRPs, until the private PRPs sue the federal PRPs in a contribution action to recover their shares. All this may take years and creates an incentive for the plaintiff U.S. to argue for a much-delayed contribution action, because though it is plaintiff today, it could be defendant tomorrow. To short-circuit this problem, and remove the conflict of interest, should not the courts treat the federal shares as partial defenses to the government's attempt to recover all costs from private PRPs, rather than as counterclaims for contribution or recompense? The federal plaintiff's liability may well be an equitable reason why the government should not recover fully in its initial cost recovery action. See Light, United States v. Monsanto: Inconsistency in the Government's Position on the Trimming of CERCLA Contribution Claims, 19 Envtl. L. Rep. (Envtl. L. Inst.) — News and Analysis 10163, 10165 (1989).

SARA expressly includes states and units of local government in the definition of facility owners. Artisan Water Co. v. Government of New Castle County, 659 F. Supp. 1269, 1280-1281 (D. Del. 1987), held that a county that purchased a site, title to which was held by the state, and used third party contractors to operate it, was liable as an owner. A pre-SARA case that found that Congress did not intend to abrogate the state's Eleventh Amendment immunity was vacated and remanded after SARA. United States v. Union Gas Co., 792 F.2d 372 (3d Cir. 1986), *vacated and remanded sub nom.* Union Gas Co. v. Pennsylvania, — U.S. — (1987). The circuit court of appeals held that SARA did abrogate the state's immunity, 832 F.2d 1343 (3d Cir. 1987), and the Supreme Court affirmed. Pennsylvania v. Union Gas Co., — U.S. — (1989). Justice Brennan reasoned that Section 101(20)(D), discussed below, was a clear expression of congressional intent to treat states as owners or operators except in very narrow circumstances and that the Commerce Clause empowered Congress to abrogate a state's Eleventh Amendment sovereign immunity. Definitional sections 101(20)(A) and (D), 42 U.S.C. §§9601(20)(A), (D), provide a limited shelter for states and units of local government that have involuntarily acquired property as a result of foreclosure of a tax lien, bankruptcy, or other escheat mechanism. These entities are only liable if they contribute to the release of hazardous substances.

What is a facility? As is apparent from the following excerpt from United States v. Northeastern Pharmaceutical Co., 810 F.2d 727, 743 (8th Cir. 1986), "facility" includes more than the usual image of a leaking dump site:

> CERCLA defines the term "facility" in part as "any site or area where a hazardous substance has been deposited, stored, disposed of, or placed, or otherwise come to be located." CERCLA §101(9)(B), 42 U.S.C. §9601(9)(B); see New York v. Shore Realty Corp., 759 F.2d 1032, 1043 n.15 (2d Cir. 1985). The term "facility" should

be construed very broadly to include "virtually any place at which hazardous wastes have been dumped, or otherwise disposed of." United States v. Ward, 618 F. Supp. at 895 (definition of "facility" includes roadsides where hazardous waste was dumped); see also United States v. Conservation Chemical Co., 619 F. Supp. at 185 (stereotypical waste disposal facility); New York v. General Electric Co., 592 F. Supp. 291, 296 (N.D.N.Y. 1984) (dragstrip); United States v. Metate Asbestos Corp., 584 F. Supp. 1143, 1148 (D. Ariz. 1984) (real estate subdivision). In the present case, however, the place where the hazardous substances were disposed of and where the government has concentrated its cleanup efforts is in the Denney farm site, not the NEPACCO plant. The Denney farm site is the "facility." Because NEPACCO, Lee and Michaels did not own or operate the Denney farm site, they cannot be held liable as the "owners or operators" of a "facility" where hazardous substsances are located under CERCLA §107(a)(1), 42 U.S.C. §9607(a)(1). [Id. at 743.]

Superfund includes a federal discovery rule; see p. 727, Chapter 6, *infra*. Can a worker who alleges injury from exposure to asbestos in the workplace invoke the statute that requires a release "into the environment from a facility?" Covalt v. Carey Canada, Inc., 860 F.2d 1434 (7th Cir. 1988).

CERCLA and common law inter-landowner liability. CERCLA, SARA, and the expansion of the common law duty to disclose material facts in connection with the sale of property move the seller of property in the direction of full disclosure of the existence of hazardous wastes on the property. See Johnson v. Davis, 480 So. 2d 624 (Fla. 1985); and Note, Hazardous Waste and the Innocent Purchaser, 38 Fla. L. Rev. 253 (1986). In addition, brokers who misrepresent the condition of the property may be liable to buyers. Sheehy v. Lipton Industries, Inc., 24 Mass. App. 188, 507 N.E.2d 781 (Mass. App. Ct. 1987), *reh'g denied*, 400 Mass. 1103, 509 N.E.2d 1201 (1987). CERCLA recognizes the possibility of an innocent landowner defense, but most Superfund lawyers doubt that such a person exists. Section 107(b)(3) exempts acts or omissions of third parties other than those that occur in the context of a contractual relationship. SARA added §101(35)(A), which defines a contractual relationship as a land contract, deed, or any other instrument transferring title or possession of real property unless "[a]t the time the defendant acquired the facility the defendant did not know and had no reason to know that any hazardous substance . . . was disposed of on, in, or at the facility." Does CERCLA demand a uniform rule of indemnity among PRPs? Mardan v. C.G.C. Music, Ltd., 804 F.2d 1454 (9th Cir. 1986), found no need for a uniform federal rule.

States are beginning to intervene in transactions involving potentially contaminated land. Many states now require some form of disclosure by the seller. New Jersey, in a much noted statute, goes further and requires that sellers of certain classes of industrial property clean up the property prior to transfer. N.J. Stat. Ann. 13:1K-6 to -13.

Defenses. With PRP, ownership, waste, facility, release, and cause defined so broadly, and under strict, joint, and several liability, are there any effective defenses left at all for the hapless PRP? Very, very few. See generally Glass, Superfund and SARA: Are There Any Defenses Left?, 12 Harv. Envtl. L. Rev.

385 (1988). Section 107(b), 42 U.S.C. §9607(b), provides three narrow affirmative defenses to liability, and the courts also have recognized equitable defenses. Mardan Corp. v. C.G.C. Music, Ltd., 804 F.2d 1454 (9th Cir. 1986). These affirmative defenses "essentially serve to shift the burden of proof of causation to the defendants. This causation scheme encourages defendants to mark and dispose of their hazardous waste with the greatest care; the defenses discourage defendants from carelessly allowing their wastes to run into one large, unidentifiable morass at the waste site, confident in the knowledge that the government must identify the wastes and prove causation." Violet v. Picillo, 648 F. Supp. 1283, 1293 (D.R.I. 1986).

United States v. Stringfellow, 661 F. Supp. 1053, 1061 (C.D. Cal. 1987), illustrates the limited availability of §107 defenses:

> . . . [W]hen claiming a defense under section 107(b), the defendants must show that the act or omission was caused *solely* by an act of God, an act of War, or a third party. The defendants raised the act of God defense under section 107(b)(1) and the third party defense under section 107(b)(3).
>
> The defendants contend that the heavy rainfall in 1969 and 1979 was a natural disaster which constituted an act of God. However, the Court finds that the rains were not the kind of "exceptional" natural phenomena to which the narrow act of God defense of section 107(b)(1) applies. The rains were foreseeable based on normal climatic conditions and any harm caused by the rain could have been prevented through design of proper drainage channels. Furthermore, the rains were not the *sole* cause of the release. Therefore, the Court concludes that the rains were not sufficient to establish an act of God defense pursuant to CERCLA section 107(b)(1).
>
> In addition, the defendants allege that the third party defense under section 107(b)(3) applies because the cause of the release was the negligent and reckless conduct of the State of California. However, section 107(b)(3) provides a defense to liability only where a totally unrelated third party is the *sole* cause of the release or threatened release of a hazardous substance. The Court concludes that there were multiple causes of the release and threats of release at the Stringfellow site. Therefore, the third party defense of section 107(b) does not apply in the instant action.

In Wagner Seed Co. v. Daggett, 800 F.2d 310 (2d Cir. 1986), EPA brought a §106 imminent and substantial endangerment order in connection with a spill caused by a bolt of lightning that struck a chemical warehouse. The warehouse owner argued that compliance with the order would be a violation of due process because it was not a responsible party. The court held that the party could raise a good faith defense prior to the imposition of fines and in dictum noted: "In an ordinary situation a third party would exist who would be a 'responsible party.' . . . But where an act of God defense is successful there is no third party — there is only EPA and Wagner — and reimbursement from EPA is doubtful." 800 F.2d at 316-317.

Courts have held that an owner that knows about the harmful consequences of disposal practices undertaken by third parties in a contractual relationship with it must take precautions to prevent a release and thus cannot invoke the third party defense. United States v. Tyson, 17 Envtl. L. Rep. (Envtl. L. Inst.) 20527 (E.D. Pa. 1986). The exclusion for persons in a contractual relationship precludes employees and independent contractors such as transporters from invoking the third party defense, United States v. Ward, 618 F. Supp. 884 (E.D.N.C. 1985), even in the case of a transporter who takes the waste to a different site without the generator's knowledge, United States v. Conservation Chemical Co., 619 F. Supp. 162 (W.D. Mo. 1985). Lessors, United States v. Northernaire Plating Co., 670 F. Supp. 742 (W.D. Mich. 1987), and subsequent purchasers, see State of New York v. Shore Realty Corp., are similarly precluded from invoking the defense. The third party defense has also been rejected when a facility operator sells recycled hazardous wastes, but one court has said that "mere sales of chemicals to an entity other than a hazardous dump site simply are not within the statute's contemplation." State of New York v. General Electric, 592 F. Supp. 291 (N.D.N.Y. 1984).

Question: X Corp. owns a wood processing facility that ends up on the National Priorities List (NPL). Y Corp., a supplier of a wood treatment chemical, builds an additional plant to X Corp's specifications and supplies it with its requirements of that chemical. If both are joined in an action brought by the government, can X Corp. obtain contribution against Y Corp? See Edward Hines Lumber Co. v. Vulcan Materials Co., 861 F.2d 155 (7th Cir. 1988).

A NOTE ON NEGOTIATION

In *Monsanto* a dozen generators settled with the government and avoided litigation. Defendants Aquair and Eaton, both corporations, settled before the litigation was completed. Settlement agreements with these 14 PRPs totalled about $1,990,000. Negotiation is expected to produce a second agreement for the $7-17 million groundwater cleanup. Other settlements are more ambitious. In early 1989, 34 PRPs agreed to spend $24 million cleaning up the fifth-ranked NPL site at Woburn, Massachusetts. The largest settlement, *Petro Processors*, obligates ten PRPs to clean up two sites in Louisiana over a fifteen-year period at a cost of $60 million. Some 550 Superfund settlements have been reached since 1980; however, the pace has picked up since SARA. Since 1986, EPA has obtained settlements for 128 removals, 51 longer-term remedies, and 139 RI/FS preparations, for a total of $600 million committed by PRPs for site work. Clean Sites, Making Superfund Work 14 (1989). The solid successes of the Superfund program to date are codified in these agreements.

The pace of CERCLA cleanups has been slow. Only 43 NPL sites have been cleaned up, although EPA has already committed $4 billion to scores of site cleanups. Id. at 2. EPA projects an annual cleanup rate of 25-30 sites per year, but its ability to meet this target is doubtful. In order to accelerate cleanup, the choice seems to be between giving the agency even more money or increasing the number of negotiated private cleanups.

SARA authorized the EPA to enter into settlement agreements. 42 U.S.C. §9622. EPA has responded to SARA by issuing a number of formal and informal guidance documents to its personnel to encourage more receptivity to negotiated settlements and to reduce the incentives for parties to refuse to settle. See the EPA's Settlement Policy, 50 Fed. Reg. 5,034; Streamlining the CERCLA Process, Envtl. L. Rep.: Regulations 35014 (6-87) (internal Guidance Memorandum).

The essence of Superfund practice today is meetings and negotiation toward agreement on the terms of a consent decree, which is the legally required vehicle for a negotiated cleanup or cost-sharing agreement. §9622(d). Litigation and legal analysis occupy only a small fraction of Superfund lawyers' time.

Existing negotiation processes follow two basic models, with frequent overlap and variation. Most negotiated cleanups involve a committee of a few PRPs, corporate technical staff, and, of course, all manner of lawyers. The participants exchange information and negotiate a draft settlement. See Anderson, Negotiation and Informal Agency Action: The Case of Superfund, 1985 Duke L.J. 261, 285-286. Some negotiated settlements are the product of a unique institution, Clean Sites, Inc., a non-profit corporation that seeks to take responsibility for a limited number of sites, to "coalesce" potentially responsible parties around a cost-sharing agreement (Clean Sites even has a Vice-President for Coalescing), and to carry out cleanups. One of the casebook authors has prepared a more sweeping negotiation alternative that relies on third party conveners. The theory is that a neutral third party would be better able to inspire PRP confidence than EPA and therefore would expedite the process. EPA would be a full party to the negotiation along with PRPs and citizen groups. See Anderson, ibid, and Anderson, Superfund and Negotiation, 5 Envtl. Impact Assessment Rev. 295 (1985). See also Grad, Alternative Dispute Resolution in Environmental Law, 14 Colum. J. Envtl. L. 157 (1989).

Consent decrees for remedial actions may include covenants not to sue should future problems develop at the site, provided that such covenants are "in the public interest" and "would expedite the response." 42 U.S.C. §9622(f)(1)(A) and (B). Section 9622(f)(6) of 42 U.S.C. requires that covenants not to sue have a reopener clause for releases or threats of releases that arise "out of conditions which were unknown at the time" that EPA certified the remedial action was complete. As a matter of policy, EPA also includes reopeners for conditions based on new information received by the agency after the remedial action has been completed. The EPA may also enter into covenants not to sue with no reopener clauses for off-site treatment in a RCRA-approved facility for the destruction or permanent immobilization of the waste (42 U.S.C. §§9622(f)(2)(A)-(B)). No covenant can take effect until the agency certifies that a remedial action has been completed in accordance with the state law. 42 U.S.C. §9622(b)(3). In a codification of existing Department of Justice regulations, SARA requires the Attorney General to provide opportunities for public comment on proposed settlements or consent decrees in §106 abatement actions or §107 cost recovery actions. 42 U.S.C. §9622(a). EPA also has the discretion to issue a Non-Binding Preliminary Allocation of Responsibility (NBAR), which cannot be introduced as evidence in any judicial proceeding. 42 U.S.C. §9622(e)(3)(c). PRP liability releases have proved to be one of the most difficult problems in settlement negotiations. EPA policy on issues such as reopener clauses and the acceptance of mixed PRP and trust fund settlements is evolving rapidly.

Despite SARA, industry lawyers argue that there are still insufficient incentives for settlement. The problems lie both in the structure of CERCLA and SARA and in EPA's implementation of its settlement policy. Agency policy makes it more attractive for industry to enter into reimbursement rather than cleanup settlements. EPA may enter into consent decrees with PRPs, but it takes a long time to secure the internal consensus necessary for agency approval. A difficult sticking-point has been the large number of de minimis PRPs who individually generate a small percentage of the overall waste volume at a site. To reduce site negotiations to manageable proportions, SARA authorized early de minimis settlements ("buyouts") in which the de minimis parties pay a premium and obtain an EPA covenant not to sue in return. §9622(g). The EPA's detailed guidance on this provision causes regional personnel to proceed slowly with de minimis settlements. See 52 Fed. Reg. 24,333 (June 30, 1987). As of late 1988, EPA had recovered only 10 percent of its outlays. J. Acton, Understanding Superfund: A Progress Report (Rand Corp., 1989).

c.   The Role of the EPA: Is CERCLA "Regulatory"?

The preceding section focused on the liability of parties potentially responsible for the costs of cleanup. The circuit courts have confirmed that Superfund made the broadest possible array of the parties who are even minimally involved with a site strictly and jointly and severally liable for the complete cost of cleanup. SARA's legislative history re-enforces this trend. See generally, Environmental Law Reporter, Superfund Deskbook (1986). Ordinarily, the EPA brings the recovery action. But can others recover who have spent money cleaning up sites? Can anyone other than EPA pick a site to be cleaned up? What physical remedial measures must be taken, and how clean must a cleaned-up site be? Must parties always wait out the slow EPA approval process before getting down to work? Or, since liability is so sweeping, can EPA summarily order private parties to carry out or pay for EPA's preferred cleanup? Many important questions remain about the orchestration of the Superfund program. The EPA is supposed to conduct, but with so many players, a slow tempo, expensive tickets, and a critical audience, the Superfund remains Congress's unfinished symphony.

CADILLAC FAIRVIEW/CALIFORNIA v.
DOW CHEMICAL CO.
840 F.2d 691 (9th Cir. 1988)

Before CHAMBER, WALLACE and POOLE, Circuit Judges.
WALLACE, Circuit Judge:
. . . Cadillac Fairview's complaint alleges that it is the owner of certain real property (the Site) located in Torrance, California. Cadillac Fairview pur-

chased the Site from CC & F Western Development Co., Inc. (Western) in 1976. It later learned that hazardous substances had been deposited at the Site, and that these substances had migrated into the underlying soil. Cadillac Fairview conducted chemical tests and analyses at the Site, which indicated that the presence of various hazardous substances in the soil threatened to cause substantial environmental and health problems. State officials requested Cadillac Fairview to undertake certain steps to protect neighborhood residents from illnesses that might result from contact with the hazardous substances. Pursuant to the state's request, Cadillac Fairview hired engineers to conduct chemical testing at the Site to evaluate the hazards posed by the substances, erected a fence around the Site, employed a guard service to secure the Site from trespassers, and posted bilingual "no trespassing" signs at the Site. These measures allegedly cost Cadillac Fairview in excess of $70,000.

According to the complaint, the federal government acquired the Site in 1942 and constructed a rubber-producing plant on it. The government contracted with Dow to operate the facility and authorized Dow to dump hazardous by-products from the facility at the Site. In 1955, Shell acquired the Site from the government. During the period of its ownership, Shell allegedly deposited hazardous substances at the Site and took no measures to prevent the release of those substances into the environment.

Shell owned the Site until 1972. It was then owned successively by defendants International Property Development Co. (International) and by Western. Defendant Cabot, Cabot & Forbes (CCF) is the successor in interest to International and Western. None of the latter defendants are parties to this appeal.

Cadillac Fairview sued the federal defendants, Dow, and Shell in district court under CERCLA §107(a), 42 U.S.C. §9607(a), to recover its costs of responding to the hazardous substances. Cadillac Fairview also requested a declaration that any cleanup costs or other damages resulting from the presence of the hazardous substances should be borne only by Dow, Shell, the federal defendants, or others who owned the property at the time of the dumping or who were responsible for such dumping. Finally, it requested an injunction requiring Dow, Shell, CC & F, and the GSA to remove hazardous wastes from the Site. Cadillac Fairview also brought state law claims against various defendants.

On the motions of Dow and Shell, the district court dismissed Cadillac Fairview's CERCLA claims for failure to state a claim upon which relief could be granted, and dismissed the pendent state law claims for lack of jurisdiction. The district court certified its order for immediate appeal under section 1292(b). The federal defendants' motion for summary judgment was granted, and the judgment certified for appeal under Fed. R. Civ. P. 54(b). We consolidated the appeals. . . .

Section 107(a)(2)(B) expressly creates a private claim against any person who owned or operated a facility at the time hazardous substances were disposed of at the facility for recovery of necessary costs of responding to the hazardous substances incurred consistent with the national recovery plan. NL Industries, Inc. v. Kaplan, 792 F.2d 896, 898 (9th Cir. 1986) (*NL Industries*). Cadillac Fairview alleged that it incurred "necessary costs" of response within the meaning of section 107(a), and that Dow, Shell, and the federal defendants owned or operated the Site at the time that hazardous substances were deposited there. Despite these allegations, the district court dismissed Cadillac Fairview's suit against the private defendants for failure to state a claim under section 107(a).

The district judge based his decision to dismiss Cadillac Fairview's damages claims on its failure to await governmental action with respect to the Site before bringing suit. The court held that in order for a private response action to be "consistent with the national contingency plan," it must be "initiated and coordinated by a governmental entity, and not by a private individual acting alone." The court also stated that the costs incurred by Cadillac Fairview were not compensable response costs under section 107 because they did not constitute "cleanup costs" within the meaning of the national contingency plan.

In defense of the district court's ruling, Dow argues that a private action under section 107(a) must be preceded by federal governmental action with respect to the property in question. This argument ignores our holdings in [Wickland Oil Terminals v. ASARCO, 792 F.2d 887 (9th Cir. 1986)] and NL Industries. In Wickland, we rejected the defendant's argument that in order to incur costs "consistent with the national contingency plan," a private party must act pursuant to federal governmental authorization. 792 F.2d at 891-92. Though the national contingency plan describes the role of lead agencies in examining information and determining appropriate responses to environmental hazards, id. at 891, we held that such provisions do not constrain private parties seeking to recover response costs under section 107(a). Id. at 892. We concluded that this reading of section 107(a) was supported both by "the lack of any procedure whereby a private party could seek to obtain prior governmental approval of a cleanup program" and by CERCLA's broad remedial purpose to promote private enforcement actions "independent of governmental actions financed by Superfund." Id. at 892. In NL Industries, we reaffirmed our holding in Wickland, and rejected the argument that response costs cannot be deemed "necessary" in the absence of lead agency approval of the cleanup. 792 F.2d at 898. Because Dow's contention that action by the federal government or by a lead agency is a necessary prerequisite to a private response action under section 107(a) is indistinguishable from the arguments rejected in Wickland and NL Industries, we need not consider it further.

Shell makes a different argument in support of the district court's ruling. Shell argues that although no *federal* involvement is necessary, some significant *state* or *local* governmental action must precede a response action for which recovery is possible under section 107(a). It then argues that the state's action in requesting Cadillac Fairview to undertake certain measures with regard to the Site in the present case is too insubstantial to constitute "significant" governmental involvement.

Shell, however, cites no authority for the proposition that significant state or local governmental action is a necessary prerequisite to a private action under section 107(a). Nor is there any mention of such a requirement in either section 107 or in the national contingency plan. We are thus reluctant to read a state or local governmental action requirement into the statute absent some strong indication that Congress intended that private parties await action by a state or local government before commencing a response action. Our examination of CERCLA's provisions leads us to conclude that significant state or local governmental action need not precede a response action for that action to be either "necessary" or "consistent with the national contingency plan."

First, there is nothing in the plain language of section 107(a) that indicates that a party seeking to recover its costs of response must await approval of or action by a state or local governmental entity. In contrast, CERCLA §111(a)(2), 42 U.S.C. §9611(a)(2), specifically provides that necessary costs may be recovered from the Superfund only if such costs are approved under the national contingency plan and certified by the responsible federal official. The absence of an approval or certification requirement in section 107(a) justifies the inference that parties not seeking reimbursement from the Superfund need not obtain prior governmental approval for their response action to be "necessary" or "consistent with the national contingency plan" under section 107(a).

Second, the statute fails to provide any mechanism through which a party could seek approval from state or local entities or prompt such entities to undertake significant action with respect to a contaminated facility. In *Wickland*, we observed that the lack of any procedure in CERCLA by which a private party could seek prior governmental approval of a cleanup program indicated that such approval was not a prerequisite to an action under section 107(a). See 792 F.2d at 892. We find that reasoning persuasive here. Neither CERCLA nor the national contingency plan describes a procedure whereby a private party could coordinate its response efforts with those of a local or state government or seek the approval of state or local governmental entities before commencing a response action. Indeed, there is no indication in the statute that prior approval or action by a state or local government is either necessary or desirable.

Finally, we observe that requiring significant state or local governmental action with regard to facilities described in section 107 would result in requiring these governmental entities to devote their limited resources to this procedure. There is no indication in the statute that Congress contemplated placing this burden on state and local governments.

Dow argues that without preliminary governmental action, a defendant can be forced to pay for cleanup actions that are inadequate or ill-conceived. This argument ignores the plain language of the statute. Section 107(a) does not allow recovery of any and all costs of response that a private party incurs. To recover costs under section 107(a), the party undertaking the response action must prove that the costs it incurred were "necessary" and that it incurred those costs in a manner "consistent with the national contingency plan." A response action is consistent with the plan for purposes of section 107 only if it satisfies criteria set forth in pertinent regulations. See, e.g., 40 C.F.R. §300.71(a)(2) (1986). Under this statutory and regulatory scheme, the question whether a response action is necessary and consistent with the criteria set forth in the contingency plan is a factual one to be determined at the damages stage of a section 107(a) action, rather than by the mechanism of prior governmental approval. Dow and Shell will have ample opportunity at trial to express their concern that the costs incurred by Cadillac Fairview in this case were unnecessary or inconsistent with the national contingency plan.

Dow's doubts regarding the wisdom of allowing section 107(a) response actions to proceed without governmental authorization should be addressed to Congress rather than to the courts. The plain language of section 107(a) compels us to reject an interpretation of CERCLA that would create a significant obstacle to private response actions not contemplated by Congress. We conclude, therefore, that the district court erred in ruling that some governmental entity must authorize and initiate a response action for that action to be necessary and consistent with the national contingency plan. . . .

Cadillac Fairview also pleaded a section 107(a) claim for damages against the federal defendants on the basis of their prior ownership of the Site. The federal defendants asserted various defenses to Cadillac Fairview's claim, including a defense of sovereign immunity. Because the district court held that Cadillac Fairview's failure to allege prior governmental action with regard to the Site entitled the federal defendants to judgment as a matter of law, it did not address the federal defendants' other defenses in its ruling. Because we hold that prior governmental action is not a prerequisite to a 107(a) suit, we reverse the summary judgment and remand the damages claim against the federal defendants for further consideration. . . .

Cadillac Fairview also pleaded a claim for injunctive relief ordering Dow, Shell, CC & F, and the federal defendants to undertake appropriate response actions with respect to the Site in a manner consistent with the national contingency plan. Cadillac Fairview predicated this claim on its request for declaratory relief. The district court dismissed the claims for injunctive relief, holding that no private cause of action for injunctive relief exists under CERCLA. Cadillac Fairview argues that our holding in *Wickland* establishes a right to injunctive relief under CERCLA.

In *Wickland*, the district court predicated its dismissal of Wickland's suit for injunctive relief on its ruling that Wickland was not entitled to declaratory relief. 792 F.2d at 893. Because we held that the dismissal of Wickland's claims for declaratory relief was improper, we reversed the dismissal of Wickland's claims for injunctive relief to allow the court to give further consideration to this claim. Id. We did not hold thereby that a private action for injunctive relief exists under CERCLA; we merely remanded the claim to the district court to allow the court to examine the question in the first instance.

In the present case, the district court fully considered the question whether CERCLA establishes a private right of action for injunctive relief. The district court examined CERCLA's provisions and found that the only private remedy provided in CERCLA is the private cause of action for response costs described in section 107(a). Under section 107(a), the United States, a State, an Indian Tribe, or any other person may recover necessary costs of response incurred consistent with the national contingency plan. There is no mention of a right to injunctive relief in section 107(a). In contrast, under section 106(a), the President may require the Attorney General to seek injunctive relief "when the President determines that there may be an imminent and substantial endangerment to the public health or welfare or the environment." 42 U.S.C. §9606(a). The district court concluded that the failure to provide for injunctive relief in section 107(a), coupled with the absence of any provision for a private right of action under section 106(a), mandated the conclusion that Congress did not intend to create a private cause of action for injunctive relief under CERCLA.

We find convincing the inference that the district court drew from construing sections 106 and 107 together. Section 107(a) allows the United States, States, Indian tribes, and other persons to recover their necessary costs of response from owners and operators as defined by section 107(a)(2), but makes no mention of injunctive relief. Section 106(a), by contrast, expressly grants the President authority to seek injunctive relief under limited circumstances. We agree with the Second Circuit that to imply a private right of action for injunctive relief into section 107(a) would render the express grant of injunctive authority in section 106(a) redundant. State of New York v. Shore Realty Corp., 759 F.2d 1032, 1049 (2d Cir. 1985). Moreover, to allow parties entitled to damages under section 107(a) to seek injunctive relief under that section would enable such parties to bypass the specific limitations on the President's authority to seek injunctive relief described in section 106(a). We find this result inconsistent with the plain language of the statute.

We conclude, therefore, that CERCLA §107(a) does not provide for a private right to injunctive relief against owners and operators as defined by section 107(a)(2). Sections 106(a) and 107(a) indicate that when Congress wished to provide for injunctive relief under CERCLA, it knew how to do so and did so expressly. The district court's dismissal of Cadillac Fairview's claims for injunctive relief against Dow, Shell, CC & F, and the federal defendants is affirmed. . . .

SOLID STATE CIRCUITS, INC. v. U.S.E.P.A.
812 F.2d 383 (8th Cir. 1987)

HEANEY, Circuit Judge.

In this appeal, appellants challenge the district court's finding that the punitive damages provision of the Comprehensive Environmental Response, Compensation, and Liability Act (CERCLA), 42 U.S.C. §9607(c)(3), does not violate their due process rights. We affirm.

I. Factual Background

On March 6, 1985, after two months of negotiations, the United States Environmental Protection Agency (EPA) issued a clean-up order to Solid State Circuits, Inc. (Solid State) and Paradyne Corporation (Paradyne) pursuant to section 106(a) of CERCLA, 42 U.S.C. §9606(a). The order contained factual findings including: (1) from April, 1968, to October, 1973, Solid State conducted manufacturing operations in a leased building in Republic, Missouri; (2) Solid State used trichloroethylene (TCE) and a copper based plating solution in its operation, and stored the used chemicals in an unlined pit in the basement of a building at the site; (3) TCE and copper are harmful to humans; (4) in 1982, corporate ownership of Solid State was transferred to Paradyne; (5) recent soil and groundwater samples from the vicinity of the site show TCE and copper contamination; (6) the contamination poses a threat to the drinking water of Republic, Missouri, the aquifers underlying the site, and the health of humans and animals in the vicinity. The order concluded that Solid State's handling of the TCE and copper was the cause of the contamination and the chemicals posed an "imminent and substantial endangerment to the public health, welfare, or the environment." [§106(a)] The order directed Solid State and Paradyne, as responsible parties, to obtain access to contaminated areas, to provide security at the facility, to submit a detailed clean-up plan to the EPA, and to notify the EPA within two days of their intent to comply with the order. No party contends that either applicable EPA regulations or CERCLA provided for an administrative hearing at which the findings of fact or conclusions of law in the order could have been challenged.

On March 14, 1985, Solid State and Paradyne filed suit in federal district court to enjoin the EPA from enforcing the order, from assessing daily penalties for failure to comply with the order, and from assessing treble damages for failing to comply with the order. . . .

On April 18, 1985, the EPA, pursuant to section 104 of CERCLA, 42 U.S.C. §9604, began the clean-up it had ordered Paradyne and Solid State to perform. The clean-up was completed by November of 1985.

On May 20, 1985, the EPA moved to dismiss the suit by Paradyne and Solid State. The EPA argued that the court had no jurisdiction to review the merits of an order issued pursuant to section 106 of CERCLA because the statute does not provide for pre-enforcement review of such orders. In addition, the EPA argued that since it had begun its own clean-up of the site, it would not seek to enforce its order or to collect daily penalties for noncompliance. . . .

The district court agreed it lacked subject matter jurisdiction to engage in pre-enforcement review of the merits of an order issued by the EPA pursuant to section 106 of CERCLA. Thus, the court refused to address the merits of Paradyne's and Solid State's defenses to the order. The court also agreed that the EPA's commencement of the clean-up rendered Paradyne's and Solid State's request for an injunction prohibiting the EPA from seeking to enforce its order or to collect penalties for non-compliance moot.[1] The court, however, found it had

---

1. We agree with the district court's decision that it lacked jurisdiction to review the merits of an EPA clean-up order prior to an attempt by the EPA to enforce it. See, e.g., Wagner Seed Co. v. Daggett, 800 F.2d 310, 314-15 (2d Cir. 1986) (finding no pre-enforcement review); Wheaton Industries v. United States, 781 F.2d 354, 356-57 (3d Cir. 1986) (same). The October, 1986, amendments to CERCLA confirm Congress' intent to preclude pre-enforcement review. See Superfund Amendments and Reauthorization Act of 1986, Pub. L. No. 99-499, 1986 U.S. Code Cong. & Admin. News (100 Stat.) 1649-50 (to be codified at 42 U.S.C. §9613(h)).

jurisdiction to consider the claim by Paradyne and Solid Staste relating to the constitutionality of that portion of CERCLA's statutory scheme subjecting them to treble damages for failing to comply with the EPA's order. . . .

Proceeding to the merits of the constitutional claim [after finding that claim ripe for review[2]], the court held that there is no violation of due process in the application of the CERCLA statutory scheme, adopting the conclusions of recent opinions in Wagner Electric Corp. v. Thomas, 612 F. Supp. 736 (D. Kan. 1985), and United States v. Reilly Tar & Chemical Corp., 606 F. Supp. 412 (D. Minn. 1985). Thus, the court refused to enjoin the EPA from seeking to assess treble damages against Paradyne and Solid State pursuant to section 107(c)(3) of CERCLA. Paradyne and Solid State appeal the district court's ruling only with respect to the due process issue.

II.   The Statutory Scheme of CERCLA

Recognizing the grave consequences arising from delays in cleaning up hazardous waste sites, Congress gave the EPA authority to direct clean-up operations prior to a final judicial determination of the rights and liabilities of the parties affected. Thus, if the EPA has determined that a hazardous substance has been or is likely to be released at a facililty, and has issued an order to the responsible party directing clean-up operations, it has several enforcement options available.

First, the EPA may bring an action in federal district court seeking an order directing compliance with its order using the contempt powers of the court as a sanction for non-compliance. See CERCLA §106(a), 42 U.S.C. §9606(a). Second, it may bring an action in federal district court seeking to impose fines of up to $5,000 a day for non-compliance. See CERCLA §106(b), 42 U.S.C. §9606(b). Finally, if the EPA determines that a release of a hazardous substance may pose an imminent and substantial danger to the public health or welfare and that the responsible parties will not properly respond, it may arrange for the required clean-up itself and pay for it using funds from the Hazardous Substance Response Trust Fund (Superfund) created as part of CERCLA. See CERCLA §104(a), 42 U.S.C. §9604(a) (authorizing the EPA to conduct clean-up); CERCLA §221, 42 U.S.C. §9631 (creating Superfund); CERCLA §111(a), 42 U.S.C. §9611(a) (authorizing the EPA to pay clean-up costs from the Superfund). ∘

Since Superfund money is limited, Congress clearly intended private parties to assume clean-up responsibility. In addition, it sought to ensure that responsible parties would not delay clean-up activities until the EPA felt it necessary to perform the required work itself. Thus, in addition to allowing the EPA to bring an action for actual costs incurred by the Superfund in conducting the clean-up, see CERCLA §107(a), 42 U.S.C. §9607(a), Congress established

---

2.   We agree with the district court's holding on the ripeness issue. See Wagner Electric Corp. v. Thomas, 612 F. Supp. 736, 741 (D. Kan. 1985) (finding issue ripe for review); Aminoil, Inc. v. United States, 599 F. Supp. 69, 72 (C.D. Cal. 1984) (*Aminoil I*) (same).

a cause of action allowing the EPA, in its discretion, to bring a claim in federal district court to recover up to three times the amount of any costs incurred by the Superfund from any person who is liable for a release or threatened release of a hazardous substance and who fails without sufficient cause to properly comply with the EPA's order. See CERCLA §107(c)(3), 42 U.S.C. §9607(c)(3).

III.   Analysis

Because neither CERCLA nor applicable EPA regulations or practice provides for a pre-enforcement hearing at which the merits of the EPA's order could be tested, Paradyne and Solid State argue that the statutory scheme of CERCLA violates their right to due process by depriving them of any meaningful opportunity to test the validity of the EPA's order "without incurring the prospect of debilitating or confiscatory penalties." Brown & Williamson Tobacco Corp. v. Engman, 527 F.2d 1115, 1119 (2d Cir. 1975), *cert. denied*, 426 U.S. 911 (1976).

In essence, Paradyne and Solid State argue that upon receiving the EPA order they found themselves stuck between a rock and a hard place. They assert that, under the statutory scheme, if they had chosen to comply with the EPA's order and were later found to have a valid defense to liability, they would have been forced to bring an action against the responsible party in order to obtain reimbursement for the clean-up. If the responsible party could not have been located or determined or had turned out to be judgment proof, they would have been forced to bear the cost of a clean-up for which they were not liable. On the other hand, if Paradyne and Solid State had refused to comply, they would have been exposed to the possibility of treble liability under CERCLA §107(c)(3).[9] In addition, Paradyne and Solid State contend that even if the EPA did not bring an action for treble damages, they would still have had to carry the potential treble liability on all public financing disclosures for an indefinite period because, at the time the EPA issued its order, there was no statute of limitations on EPA cost recovery actions. Paradyne and Solid State contend this "Hobson's choice" between compliance and potential treble liability effectively prevents a challenge to an EPA order.

The due process argument has its origins in Ex Parte Young, 209 U.S. 123, 28 S. Ct. (1908). That case establishes that a statutory scheme violates due process if "the penalties for disobedience are by fines so enormous and impris-

---

9.   Although coming too late to do them any good, the hardship posed by the dilemma Paradyne and Solid State supposedly faced upon being served with the clean-up order has been ameliorated significantly by the recent amendments to CERCLA. Section 106(b) of CERCLA has been amended to allow a person who receives and complies with a clean-up order a right of action against the Superfund for costs incurred in performing the required clean-up provided certain conditions are met. [citing 42 USC §9606 (a)(2)] . . .

Thus, we note that, in the future, parties wishing to avoid treble liability may apparently perform any required clean-up, with the assurances that if recovery is unavailable from a third party and they are not a responsible party, recovery may be had from the Superfund.

onment so severe as to intimidate [an affected party] from resorting to the courts to test the validity of the legislation." Id. at 209 U.S. 147. It concludes that in such a situation "the result is the same as if the law in terms prohibited the [affected party] from seeking judicial construction of laws which deeply affect its rights." Id.

Paradyne and Solid State, however, acknowledge that the constitutional requirements of Ex Parte Young are met if the challenged statutory scheme may be interpreted so that no penalty is imposed if the challenging party has reasonable grounds to contest the validity or applicability of an administrative order.

Expansion of the Ex Parte Young doctrine to preclude imposition of statutory penalties if the plaintiff has reasonable grounds to contest the validity or applicability of an administrative order is important in this case because the challenged treble damage provision of CERCLA provides:

> If any person who is liable for a release or threat of release of a hazardous substance fails *without sufficient cause* to properly provide removal or remedial action upon order of the President pursuant to section 9604 or 9606 of this title, such person may be liable to the United States for punitive damages in an amount at least equal to, and not more than three times, the amount of any costs incurred by the Fund as a result of such failure to take proper action.

CERCLA §107(c)(3), 42 U.S.C. §9607(c)(3) (emphasis added).

Thus, this case presents the question whether the sufficient cause defense provided in CERCLA §107(c)(3) affords adequate protection against imposition of the treble damage penalty to allow a challenge to an EPA clean-up order as required by Ex Parte Young and its progeny.

Paradyne and Solid State argue that the sufficient cause defense provides adequate protection only if it is interpreted to encompass a subjective good faith belief in the invalidity or inapplicability of an EPA clean-up order. In support of their position, they point to Aminoil, Inc. v. United States, 646 F. Supp. 294 (C.D. Cal. 1986) (*Aminoil II*). In that case, the court stated:

> [T]he phrase "sufficient cause" should be interpreted to mean a "good faith" defense. Under such an interpretation, plaintiffs are sufficiently protected against the threat of punitive damages under §9607(c)(3). Punitive damages may only be assessed where the Government proves that plaintiffs have refused to comply with the order in bad faith. For example, if the Government can prove that plaintiffs have challenged the merits of the order simply for the purpose of delay, punitive damages should be assessed. Consequently, the risk that plaintiffs would forego a valid challenge to the order would not offend Due Process principles.

Id. at 299.

Thus, Paradyne and Solid State contend that only by adopting an interpretation similar to that enunciated in *Aminoil II* can this Court find the treble damage provision constitutional.

The EPA, on the other hand, urges us to interpret sufficient cause as encompassing an objective standard arguing that:

> As a federal agency, EPA must be presumed to act correctly, and ultimately review of the administrative order must be on an arbitrary and capricious standard. Thus, only a reasonable belief that the agency acted arbitrarily and capriciously in issuing the order would be sufficient cause for non-compliance.

Brief of Appellee at 31 n.15.

The EPA cites *Wagner Electric Corp. v. Thomas*, 612 F. Supp. 736 (D. Kan. 1985), as supporting an objective good faith standard. *Wagner Electric* construes the "reasonable grounds" language of Oklahoma Operating Co. v. Love, 252 U.S. at 338, 40 S. Ct. at 340, as requiring that "one must assert an objectively good faith challenge to [an] administrative action before one may invoke the protections of Ex Parte Young." *Wagner Electric*, 612 F. Supp. at 745.

As a matter of constitutional law, we believe that the label "objective" or "subjective" is not as important as the functional significance of the standard. To put it another way, to pass constitutional requirements, the standard must provide parties served with EPA clean-up orders a real and meaningful opportunity to test the validity of the order. At the same time, the standard must protect the government's interest in encouraging parties to conduct clean-ups promptly and in promoting settlements once the EPA has performed clean-ups itself so as to avoid using resources necessary to respond to threats posed by hazardous waste on litigation to replenish the Superfund. We are, therefore, convinced that "sufficient cause" as used in CERCLA §107(c)(3) may be constitutionally interpreted to mean that treble damages may not be assessed if the party opposing such damages had an objectively reasonable basis for believing that the EPA's order was either invalid or inapplicable to it.[11]

---

11.   We note . . . that the legislative history of the recent CERCLA Amendments states:

The phrase "without sufficient cause" is currently set forth as a defense to liability for treble damages in section 107(c)(3) of CERCLA. The government has argued and the courts have interpreted this phrase to mean that a party will not be liable for treble damages for failing to comply with an EPA order when the party has a reasonable good faith belief that it has a valid defense to that order. See Wagner Electric Corp. v. Thomas, [612 F. Supp. 736] No. 85-2212-0 (D. Kan. June 20, 1985); United States v. Reilly Tar & Chemical Corp., 606 F. Supp. 412, 421 (D. Minn. 1985).

   To avoid potential unfairness that might arise from the limitation on the timing of review of section 106 orders, this amendment expressly extends the "sufficient cause" defense to the penalty provision in section 106. The amendment contemplates that the phrase "sufficient cause" will continue to be interpreted to preclude the assessment of penalties or treble damages when a party can establish that it has a reasonable belief that it was not liable under CERCLA or that the required response action was inconsistent with the national contingency plan. The court must base its evaluation of the defendant's belief on the objective evidence of the reasonableness and good faith of that belief. Given the importance of EPA orders to the success of the CERCLA program, courts should carefully scrutinize assertions of "sufficient cause" and accept such a defense only where a party can demonstrate by objective evidence the reasonableness and good faith of a challenge to an EPA order.

   The amendment also contemplates that courts will continue to interpret "sufficient cause" to encompass other situations where the equities require that no penalties or treble damages be assessed.

H.R. Rep. No. 253(I) 99th Cong., 2d Sess. 82, *reprinted in* 1986 U.S. Code Cong. & Admin. News 2835, 2864.

Under this standard, a court assessing the objective reasonableness of a party's challenge to a clean-up order must keep in mind that the EPA is presumed to have acted correctly, and its decision to issue such an order may be found erroneous only if it acted arbitrarily or capriciously. Thus, in order to establish the objective reasonableness of a challenge to an EPA clean-up order, a party must show that the applicable provisions of CERCLA, EPA regulations and policy statements, and any formal or informal hearings or guidance the EPA may provide, give rise to an objectively reasonable belief in the invalidity or inapplicability of the clean-up order. We note, however, that in some instances, CERCLA itself is silent or ambiguous, and the EPA has failed to promulgate regulations or to issue position statements that could allow a party to weigh in advance the probability that the clean-up order is valid or applicable. Absent such guidance, it will also be difficult for a court to determine the reasonableness of a challenge to the order notwithstanding the presumption of validity an agency order enjoys.

In such instances, therefore, it would be patently unreasonable and inequitable for a court to require a challenging party to prove the reasonableness of its challenge to avoid imposition of treble damages. Thus, we hold that if neither CERCLA nor applicable EPA regulations or policy statements provides the challenging party with meaningful guidance as to the validity or applicability of the EPA order, Ex Parte Young and its progeny require that the burden rest with the EPA to show that the challenging party lacked an objectionably reasonble belief in the validity or applicability of a clean-up order.

Although shifting the burden may seem onerous, we agree with the *Wagner Electric* court that the EPA could greatly limit sufficient cause defenses by issuing regulations and policy statements and by providing for informal hearings that would enable a party to better determine the validity and applicability of an EPA order prior to the time it must decide whether to comply with a clean-up order or risk treble damages. By providing such guidance at an early stage, the EPA will best protect the interests of all concerned and promote faster, more efficient clean-ups while making certain liability for clean-ups remains with those responsible. Accordingly, we affirm.

NOTES AND QUESTIONS

The EPA approach to site cleanup. The EPA has elaborately detailed plans for cleaning up sites. Some of its requirements appear in the NCP and other rules and notices in the Federal Register, but the bulk of the EPA plan for CERCLA must be pieced together from hundreds of pages of informal Guidance Memoranda and handbooks. It taxes the ability of Superfund lawyers to keep

---

Thus, it appears from the last sentence of the quoted passage that Congress intended courts to remain flexible and to refuse to award the EPA punitive damages if to do so would be patently unjust in light of the public and governmental interests at stake. We fully expect that as the EPA and the courts face concrete cost recovery and treble damage cases, section 107(c)(3) of CERCLA will develop accordingly.

track of what guidance EPA has proposed, finalized, withdrawn, and amended in this gray world of policy making. Anderson, Negotiation and Informal Agency Action: The Case of Superfund, 1985 Duke L.J. 261, 287-297.

Site rank on the NPL is determined by EPA's Hazard Ranking System (HRS). Rank is non-reviewable because it is merely one means by which EPA sets priorities. Eagle-Picher Industries v. EPA 759 F.2d 905 (D.C. Cir. 1985). No constitutional right to a hearing exists before a PRP's site is placed on the NPL. SCA Services of Indiana v. Thomas, 634 F. Supp. 355 (N.D. Ind. 1986).

The EPA prepares for every NPL site an elaborate study of site conditions and cleanup options, which is called the Remedial Investigation and Feasibility Study (RI/FS). The process usually takes two or more years and is expensive ($1 million for a study is not uncommon). SARA set an action-forcing target of only 92 RI/FSs a year, 42 U.S.C. §9616(d), but the agency cannot meet this goal. Because the RI/FS is an EPA condition for any site remediation, the RI/FS process is a major CERCLA bottleneck. A few private PRPs have been permitted to prepare RI/FS to agency specifications under strict controls. The RI/FS applies "Applicable and Relevant and Appropriate Regulatory Standards" (ARARS) from other environmental programs. 42 U.S.C. §9621(d)(2). Effluent and ambient standards borrowed from a dozen or more federal and state regulatory programs apply. See Note on How Clean is Clean, p. 662 *infra*.

Once the RI/FS is prepared, EPA's preferred remedy is documented in a record of decision (ROD). The PRPs are given an opportunity to negotiate a consent decree under which they can carry out the cleanups. 42 U.S.C. §§9622(a)-(d), (g). See A Note on Negotiation, *supra*.

If negotiations fail, the EPA can issue an administrative order mandating cleanup (§§104, 106), carry out the cleanup, sue to compel cleanup (§106(a)), and negotiate or sue under §107 for the remedial costs (§§107, 122).

"*Any person*" can recover response costs "*not inconsistent with*" the NCP. The federal government is not entirely in charge, however, as *Cadillac-Fairview* indicates. Other units of government and the PRPs may try to move at a different pace or may prefer a different cleanup strategy than EPA. States, municipalities, interstate bodies, and individuals are among the "persons" who can recover under §107(a)(4)(B), 42 U.S.C. §9607(a)(4)(B). CERCLA defines person very broadly. §101(2), 42 U.S.C. §9601(21).

Consistency with the NCP was addressed in State of New York v. Shore Realty Corp., 759 F.2d 1032, 1045-1047 (2d Cir. 1985), which affirmed the state's right to recover and largely agrees with the *Cadillac Fairview* approach to the role of the EPA:

> Shore also argues that, because the Shore Road site is not on the NPL, the State's action is inconsistent with the NCP and thus Shore cannot be found liable under section 9607(a). This argument is not frivolous. Nevertheless, we hold that inclusion on the NPL is not a requirement for the State to recover its response costs.
>
> The State claims that, while NPL listing may be a requirement for the use of Superfund money, it is not a requisite to liability under section 9607. See New

York v. General Electric Co., 592 F. Supp. 291, 303-04 (N.D.N.Y. 1984). The State relies on the reasoning of several district courts that have held that liability under section 9607 is independent of the scope of section 9611, which governs the expenditure of Superfund monies, and by extension, section 9604, which governs federal cleanup efforts. See, e.g., id.; United States v. Northeastern Pharmaceutical & Chemical Co., 579 F. Supp. 823, 850-51 (W.D. Mo. 1984); United States v. Wade, 577 F. Supp. 1326, 1334-36 (E.D. Pa. 1983). These courts have reasoned that CERCLA authorizes a bifurcated approach to the problem of hazardous waste cleanup, by distinguishing between the scope of direct federal action with Superfund resources and the liability of polluters under section 9607. While implicitly accepting that Superfund monies can be spent only on sites included on the NPL, they conclude that this limitation does not apply to section 9607. And it is true that the relevant limitation on Superfund spending is that it be "consistent with" the NCP, 42 U.S.C. §9604(a), while under section 9607(a)(4)(A), liability is limited to response costs "not inconsistent with" the NCP. This analysis, however, is not so compelling as might be; the distinction between section 9604 and section 9607 blurs for two reasons. First, as we noted above, Congress envisioned section 9607 as a means of reimbursement of monies spent by government on cleanup pursuant to section 9604. The money that the federal government presumably would be spending is Superfund money. That is to say, Congress may have seen section 9607 as equal in scope to sections 9604 and 9611. Second, it is difficult to accept the State's argument that section 9607's statement "[n]otwithstanding any other provision or rule of law" supports the distinction. Shore's argument is not based on implying limitations on the scope of section 9604 into section 9607 but on an interpretation of "not inconsistent with" the NCP under section 9607 itself.

Still, we reject Shore's argument. Instead of distinguishing between the scope of section 9607 and the scope of section 9604, we hold that NPL listing is not a general requirement under the NCP. We see the NPL as a limitation on remedial, or long-term, actions — as opposed to removal, or short-term, actions — particularly federally funded remedial actions. The provisions requiring the establishment of NPL criteria and listing appear to limit their own application to remedial actions. Section 9605(8)(A) requires EPA to include in the NCP "criteria for determining priorities among releases or threatened releases . . . for the purpose of taking remedial action and, to the extent practicable taking into account the potential urgency of such action, for the purpose of taking removal action." And section 9605(8)(B), which requires EPA to draw up the NPL, refers to "priorities for remedial action." Accord 126 Cong. Rec. 30,933 (statement of Sen. Randolph) 40 C.F.R. §300.68(a) (1984). . . .

Moreover, limiting the scope of NPL listing as a requirement for response action is consistent with the purpose of CERCLA. The NPL is a relatively short list when compared with the huge number of hazardous waste facilities Congress sought to clean up. And it makes sense for the federal government to limit only those long-term — remedial — efforts that are federally funded. We hold that Congress intended that, while federally funded remedial efforts be focused solely on those sites on the NPL, states have more flexibility when acting on their own. See Pinole Point Properties, Inc. v. Bethlehem Steel Corp., 596 F. Supp. 283, 290 (N.D. Cal. 1984).

Finally, we reject Shore's argument that the State's response costs are not recoverable because the State has failed to comply with the NCP by not obtaining EPA authorization, nor making a firm commitment to provide further funding for remedial implementation nor submitting an estimate of costs. See 40 C.F.R. §300.62(1984) (describing the states' role in joint federal-state response actions). EPA designed the regulatory scheme — the NCP — focusing on federal and joint federal-state efforts. See, e.g., id. §300.6 (defining "lead agency"). Shore apparently is arguing that EPA has ruled that the State cannot act on its own and seek liability under CERCLA. We disagree. Congress envisioned states' using their own resources for cleanup and recovering those costs from polluters under section 9607(a)(4)(A). . . . [Id. at 1047.]

The early district court decisions split over whether there must be a governmentally authorized cleanup before a PRP can bring a §107(a)(4)(B) action. The cases that required government approval concluded that such approval was a fair accommodation of the public interest in a prompt cleanup and the interests of the PRPs. Those that did not require approval read CERCLA to impose cleanup responsibility on the PRPs without placing a financial burden on the government. These early cases are collected and discussed in Fischel v. Westinghouse Electric Corp., 23 Envt. Rep. Cas. (BNA) 1239 (M.D. Pa. 1985). See generally Gaba, Recovering Hazardous Waste Cleanup Costs: The Private Cause of Action under CERCLA, 13 Ecology L.Q. 181 (1986). Artisan Water Co. v. Government of New Castle County, 659 F. Supp. 1269, 1291-1298 (D. Del. 1987), held that the provision of alternative water supplies was not consistent with the NCP because the response did not bring the site into compliance with applicable environmental and public health requirements.

Citizen enforcement. Theoretically, a well-funded environmental group, as a "person" under §107(a)(4)(B), could clean up a site consistent with the NCP and recover its costs; however, such groups are not nearly well enough funded to make this a general practice. Environmentalists would prefer to act as "private attorneys-general" and bring citizen suits for mandatory injunctive orders compelling PRPs to clean up sites themselves. Yet *Cadillac-Fairview* holds that the statute confers no private right of action against PRPs for injunctive relief. Is this holding correct? If it is, should §106(a), 42 U.S.C. §9606(a), be amended to confer on private citizens Superfund cleanup enforcement authority? See MacMillan and Miller, Flaws of RCRA Amendments Can Be Minimized, Legal Times, Jan. 30, 1984, at 12, col. 3 (such citizen suits would complicate waste cleanups). Congress refused to add this power to SARA on the theory that the very broad citizens' suit provision added to RCRA in 1984, 42 U.S.C. §6972, permits citizen suits against PRPs who have contributed to a site that may present an "imminent and substantial endangerment to health or the environment." See also discussion *infra* at pp. 660. The legislative history of SARA indicates that this RCRA provision may be applicable to many Superfund sites. Still, SARA §310, 42 U.S.C. §9659, did authorize citizen suits against EPA and other federal and local agencies that will enable citizens to play a watchdog role in enforcing statutory deadlines and challenging cleanup risk assessments, standards, and remedial decisions. The details of the provision are virtually identical to the provisions of citizens' suits in other environmental regulatory statutes. Attorneys' fees are recoverable. Environmental Law Reporter, Superfund Handbook 13, 46-47 (1986).

In light of the 1984 changes to RCRA, the 1986 changes in CERCLA, and the interpretations of CERCLA in *Cadillac Fairview* and *Shore Realty*, is EPA in charge or not? Should not sites at least be on the NPL for anyone to recover response costs? The EPA thinks it very important that it have the final say as to the adequacy of the cleanup. Do these cases condone "runaway" state, municipal, and individual cleanup efforts? Is the distinction that *Shore Realty* makes between short-term and long-term remedies valid?

Unilateral administrative orders: the key to future enforcement? The increased use of unilateral administrative orders is expected to play the key role in the EPA strategy for enforcing Superfund. While more site cleanups have been scheduled, less fund revenues are available to perform them than were available before 1989. Unilateral orders remove the need for fund revenues. Congress and the public are increasingly critical of the pace of Superfund cleanups. More cleanups can be scheduled if the PRPs are made responsible for them. Finally, the President has emphasized stepped-up Superfund enforcement by specifically requiring PRPs to pay for cleanups. See generally, Mays, Who's Afraid of CER-CLA §106 Administrative Orders? Envt. Rep. (BNA) — Analysis and Perspective 1926 (Jan. 27, 1989).

Through an administrative order EPA can require the PRPs to carry out the federal remedy of choice, based on the EPA RI/FS and record of decision. The agency can specify the precise behavior it expects, as if the PRPs were subject to a regulatory regime. As *Solid State Circuits* indicates, EPA provides an opportunity only for an informal conference with regional personnel to discuss the PRPs' objections to the order, which may require the expenditure of millions. SARA provided that a PRP who complies with a unilateral administrative order may sue for reimbursement from the federal fund if it can show that it is not liable for response costs or that EPA abused its discretion in selecting its preferred remedy. 42 U.S.C. §9606(b)(2). But if a PRP refuses to carry out a unilateral administrative order, EPA may sue and possibly obtain fines of not more than $25,000 per day of violation and punitive damages of three times the costs incurred by the federal fund as a result of PRP refusal to carry out the order. 42 U.S.C. §§9606(b)(1) and 9607(c)(3).

Is *Solid State Circuits* correct to require district courts to apply an objective "reasonable cause" standard in deciding whether PRPs can escape these onerous penalties when they refuse to comply immediately with an EPA administrative order? The PRPs would prefer the more subjective *Aminoil II* standard. Which standard is correct as a matter of law? *Aminoil II* would require the government to prove bad faith in order to justify imposition of the full penalties. But is the *Solid State Circuits* approach unfair? Do not the omissions, ambiguities, and contradictions in CERCLA and SARA, the NCP, and the plethora of Guidance Memoranda virtually guarantee that PRPs can prove an objectively reasonable belief that the EPA order is flawed? If so, will the penalty provisions retain any teeth at all if other courts apply *Solid State Circuits*? Yet even after *Solid State Circuits*, would you as prudent counsel ever advise your client to refuse to comply with an order? Would your advice change if you knew that EPA could not afford to clean up the site if you refuse? Re-read §107(c)(3), 42 U.S.C. §9607(a)(3). If you resist the order what steps would you take to improve your chances when you are sued later?

EPA could greatly improve its position if it created some kind of pre-enforcement administrative hearing procedure for PRPs who want to dispute the terms of an order. Why has EPA steadfastly refused? SARA limits judicial review of response actions, presumably including §106 administrative orders, to the administrative record. SARA requires rule making to specify exactly what the record must contain. These rules must provide notice, an opportunity to comment, and public meeting procedures for interested persons, so that they can participate from the beginning in the EPA's selection of response measures. 42 U.S.C. §§9613(a-k). If properly implemented, are these requirements not enough to satisfy constitutional requirements for due process toward PRPs? See United States v. Hardage, 663 F. Supp. 1280 (W.D. Okla. 1987), which holds that when EPA seeks a court-ordered cleanup under §106(a) judicial review is de novo and is not limited to the administrative record.

"Imminent and substantial endangerment": trigger for lawsuits and administrative orders? Recent cases like *Solid State Circuits* address objections to the harshness of the penalty provisions of unilateral administrative orders. Yet extensive reliance on §106, 42 U.S.C. §9606(a), raises additional questions that first arose during the Carter and Reagan administrations. You may be surprised to learn that the first major federal strategy for cleanup of waste sites was based on §7003 of RCRA and §106 of CERCLA. The language of the two provisions is virtually identical. Arguing that §7003 codified and expanded the common law and empowered the United States to sue in federal district courts for mandatory relief, in 1979 the Justice Department brought over 50 suits, identified over 100 additional sites for possible action, and placed some 1,850 more sites under investigation. See Note, Using RCRA's Imminent Hazard Provision in Hazardous Waste Emergencies, 9 Ecology L.Q. 599 (1981). In 1980 the emphasis shifted to §106 of Superfund. It seems inconceivable that the Justice Department could bring up to two thousand sites into litigation under §106, but this was the plan: sue them all, and try to negotiate private cleanup consent decrees. The enactment of Superfund, and the Reagan Administration's preference for negotiated solutions, caused this lawsuit-dominated approach to fade into the background.

The authority both to bring lawsuits and to issue unilateral administrative orders depends upon whether a site presents an "imminent and substantial endangerment to the public health or welfare or the environment" because of an actual or threatened release of hazardous substances. §106(a), 42 U.S.C. §9606(a). What does this phrase mean? Is it broad enough to authorize a lawsuit or an administrative order at every site on the NPL? See U.S. v. Reilly Tar & Chemical Corp., 546 F. Supp. 1100 (D. Minn. 1982).

The first provision using the language of "imminent and substantial endangerment" appeared in the Air Quality Act of 1967, §108(k), 42 U.S.C. §1857(k). Congress explained that this provision was intended to cover widespread mortal danger to persons (S. Rep. No. 403, 90th Cong., 1st Sess. 31 (1967); H.R. Rep. No. 728, 90th Cong., 1st Sess. 19 (1967). Section 108(k) was never invoked in an air pollution emergency. The "imminent hazard" provisions of current air and water pollution control legislation, i.e., §303 of the 1970

Clean Air Act and §504 of the Federal Water Pollution Control Act Amendments of 1972, took their language directly from §108(k) of the 1967 Air Quality Act, although their legislative histories add nothing to Congress's earlier gloss on §108(k).

In late 1971, EPA moved swiftly under the imminent hazard provision of the Clean Air Act to shut down the major sources of air pollution in highly industrialized Birmingham, Alabama. At 1:45 A.M. of the fourth day of extraordinarily severe air pollution, a federal district judge granted EPA an ex parte temporary restraining order ordering curtailment of operations by Birmingham's major industrial air polluters. United States v. U.S. Steel Corp., No. 71-1041 (S.D. Ala., filed November 18, 1971). Contemporaneous explanations of the purposes of §303 confirmed the then-prevailing interpretation of §303 as applicable only to sudden, acute pollution emergencies. See A Review of the Implementation of Various Provisions of the Clean Air Act of 1970: Hearing before the Subcomm. on Public Health and the Environment of the House Comm. on Interstate and Foreign Commerce, 92d Cong., 1st Sess. (1971).

Until the Justice Department unveiled its §7003 program, EPA interpreted all imminent hazard provisions as being applicable to infrequent, exceptional, Birmingham-type emergencies. See generally Note, The Emergency Powers in the Environmental Protection Statutes: A Suggestion for a Unified Emergency Provision, 3 Harv. Envtl. L. Rev. 298 (1979). This was true despite indications in the legislative history of the Safe Drinking Water Act (SDWA) emergency provision that it, at least, was intended to cover more than just Birmingham-type emergencies. See 42 U.S.C. §300i and H.R. Rep. No. 1185, 93rd Cong., 2d Sess. 35-36 (1974). In the late 1970s, EPA began to soften its view, and in 1979 the Justice Department began to interpret §7003 broadly, despite the lack of direct legislative history supporting its interpretation.

Is the EPA correct to give "imminent and substantial endangerment" the broadest possible reading? We have encountered the endangerment standard before in the discussion of *Reserve Mining* and *Ethyl*. Actual harm need not be shown; rather, the plaintiff must show only a significant "risk" or "danger," determined by discounting the magnitude of harm threatened by the probability that it will occur. Yet in the statutory standards applied in *Reserve Mining* and *Ethyl* Congress did not require that the danger be "imminent" or "substantial," words that another court said are "concepts with rich statutory and judicial histories." United States v. Diamond Shamrock, 12 Envtl. L. Rep. (Envtl. L. Inst.) 20,819 (N.D. Ohio 1981). A Senate committee report indicated that §7003 "incorporates the legal theories used for centuries to assess liability for creating a public nuisance . . . and to determine appropriate remedies . . . attached to terms such as 'imminent' and 'substantial,'" although the report went on to indicate that the legislative history of modern statutes should also be used in interpreting §7003. S. Rep. No. 172, 96th Cong., 1st Sess. 15 (1979).

Which way do these "rich histories" cut? Does the "imminent and substantial endangerment" standard merely adopt unchanged the old common law standard for injunctive relief from a prospective nuisance? There is some suggestion of this in *Reserve Mining,* in which the court noted that "the term 'en-dangering' connotes a lessser risk of harm than the 'imminent and substantial endangerment'" phrase as used in the "emergency powers" section of the 1972 Federal Water Pollution Control Act Amendments and that the common law required "an immediate threat of harm" before a nuisance could be abated (514 F.2d at 529 n.71). The *Ethyl* court agreed (541 F.2d at 20 n.36). This of course does not necessarily mean that the *Reserve Mining* and *Ethyl* courts concluded that the "imminent and substantial endangerment" standard adopts the common law test of "imminent irreparable injury of a substantial nature," discussed at p. 526 *supra.* Yet if "imminent and substantial endangerment" is an easier standard for the government to meet than the common law standard, how much easier is it? How much harder than the straight "endangerment" standard?

The condition that an endangerment be "substantial," according to the legislative history of the SDWA, merely means that it must be more than de minimis in degree. Do you agree? The condition that an endangerment be "imminent" presents a harder problem: An "imminent" endangerment can readily be understood to be one that threatens harm within a few hours or days, a meaning that would square well with the scope of the "emergency" provisions, as *Reserve Mining* and *Ethyl* seem to suggest. Do you agree that "logically, it is senseless to tie the immediacy of relief to the imminence of harm, because in many cases harm occurring far in the future will be attributable to present events"? Note, *Reserve Mining* — The Standard of Proof Required to Enjoin an Environmental Hazard to Public Health, 59 Minn. L. Rev. 893, 919 (1975). Support for this analysis can be found in Environmental Defense Fund, Inc. v. Ruckelshaus, 439 F.2d 584 (D.C. Cir. 1971). See generally Mintz, Abandoned Hazardous Waste Sites and the RCRA Imminent Hazard Provision: Some Suggestions for a Sound Judicial Construction, 11 Harv. Envtl. L. Rev. 247 (1987).

Additional issues confront the EPA before it can rely upon unilateral administrative orders as freely as it can §104 and §107 orders. Does §106 incorporate the same concepts of strict, joint, and several liability and causation as do §§104 and 107? Liability under §106 may not be joint and several, if United States v. Stringfellow, 20 Envt. Rep. Cas. (BNA) 1905, 1910 (C.D. Cal. 1984) is followed.

A NOTE ON HOW CLEAN IS CLEAN

Evolution of SARA Standards. CERCLA did not originally contain clean-up standards. See Comment, Superfund and the National Contingency Plan: How Dirty Is "Dirty"? How Clean Is "Clean"?, 12 Ecology L.Q. 89 (1984). In 1985, EPA issued a regulation that addressed the issue of "how clean is clean." The agency obligated itself to meet certain environmental standards in a variety of situations. 50 Fed. Reg. 47912 (1985). Section 121 of SARA, 42 U.S.C. §9621, curtails the discretion of EPA to set cleanup standards on a site-by-site basis and adopts stringent risk-protection and technology-forcing standards that apply to all Fund-financed and private cleanups. SARA relies on the incorporation of other "applicable or relevant and appropriate requirements" (ARARs), but the rigidity of its approach creates a number of uncertainties and may mandate inefficient cleanup strategies. Congress did not address the fundamental questions about the long-term cleanup goals and processes of Superfund. Instead, Section 121 responded to intense lobbying by environmental and industry groups and attempted to strike a balance among (1) technology-forcing, (2) the implementation of health-based standards and (3) cost effectiveness considerations. The balance was clearly struck in favor of the environmental community.

Section 121 requires EPA to select cost-effective cleanup responses, but it subordinates cost-benefit analyses to public health and environmental protection goals. This subordination of cost considerations to health and environmental goals is reflected in two major constraints imposed on EPA's selection of remedial actions: (1) "actions in which treatment . . . permanently and significantly reduces the volume, toxicity or mobility of the hazardous substances, pollutants, and contaminants . . . are to be preferred over remedial actions not involving such treatment," and (2) off-site transport and disposal "without such treatment should be the least favored alternative remedial action where practicable treatment technologies are available." 42 U.S.C. §9621(b). Moreover, actions may be chosen regardless of whether they have been successful in practice at another site. 42 U.S.C. §9621(b)(2). The Act does not adopt the technology-forcing approaches of the Clean Air and Water acts in large part because Congress and the environmental community did not want to lock the agency into low levels of treatment technology.

Role of State Standards. SARA's general cleanup standard for remedial actions is tied to standards adopted under other federal and state environmental laws. At a minimum, all remedial actions must obtain a degree of cleanup that assures protection of human health and the environment, is cost-effective, and utilizes permanent solutions. 42 U.S.C. §9621(b)(1)(G). If another federal standard or a more stringent standard under a state environmental or facility siting law is "legally applicable," the level of control attained by the remedial action must "at least" attain the standard. 42 U.S.C. §9621(d)(2)(a)(ii). The statute, however, does not define which standards or other federal and state laws are "legally applicable." The legislative history indicates that a statutory standard is legally applicable if the statute "subjects to regulation" a hazardous substance, even though the statute does not "apply directly to the situation involved at the hazardous waste site." H.R. Rep. No. 253, 99th Cong., 1st Sess. pt. 5, at 53 (1985). In addition, the cleanup must attain other standards that are "relevant and appropriate" under the circumstances of the release or threatened release. This language gives the EPA the discretion to choose among potentially applicable standards. ARARs are not themselves standards but a source of standards. EPA is currently attempting to flesh out the meaning of this term. The agency is debating, for example, whether the Safe Drinking Water Act's maximum contaminant level goals (MCLGs) or more lenient MCLs are "relevant and appropriate" to releases that threaten to pollute public drinking water supplies.

EPA's present practice is to adopt the three-part agency classification of groundwater, Environmental Protection Agency, Ground-Water Protection Strategy (Aug. 1984) and Final Draft Guidelines for Ground-water Classification under the EPA Ground-Water Protection Strategy (Dec. 1986), and to rely in part on the Safe Drinking Water Act MCLs and state standards. The result is that the standards are applied to the groundwater under the CERCLA site but not at the facility boundary or the tap. Thus, contaminated groundwater that is potentially usable for public drinking water supplies must be restored or protected so that it can be used for this purpose. See Weisshaar and Gray, Groundwater Cleanup under Superfund: A New Ballgame, 2 Toxics L. Rep. (BNA) No. 4, at p. 105 (June 24, 1987).

Integration of RCRA and CERCLA. RCRA's groundwater protection standards will be the most likely "legally applicable" standards. RCRA permits a site owner to avoid the standards normally applicable to disposal facilities by demonstrating, on a case-by-case basis, that some alternative level of control at a particular point in the groundwater will fully protect public health and the environment. If the owner can carry this burden, he must then meet an "alternative concentration limit" (ACL) that will be sufficiently stringent to protect health and the environment at that site. 40 C.F.R. §264.94(b). RCRA ACLs may not be used to establish alternative concentration limits in Superfund cleanups if, subject to limited exceptions, the remedial process assumes human exposure beyond the boundaries of a site. 42 U.S.C. §9621(d)(2)(B). EPA may select a remedial action, however, that does not attain a level or standard of control at least equivalent to legally applicable or relevant criteria if it finds that (1) the remedial action is part of a larger remedial plan that will attain the required standard, (2) compliance will result in increased health and environmental risks compared with alternative options, (3) compliance is technically impracticable, (4) through the use of another method or approach the action will attain an equivalent standard of performance, (5) the state has not consistently applied the standard it seeks to require, or (6) section 104 Fund balancing suggests that the monies necessary to meet the standard would be more effectively spent to protect public health and the environment at other sites. 42 U.S.C. §9621(d)(4)(A-F). State and local governments may enforce legally applicable or relevant and appropriate standards in federal court, though they may not require a permit for removal or remedial actions conducted entirely on site.

One of the major goals of Section 121 is to force the adoption of nationally consistent rational cleanup standards, but EPA's selection of cleanup remedies has been criticized by a staff member of the Office of Technology Assessment in testimony before the Subcommittee on Investigations and Oversight of the House Committee on Public Works and Transportation. The testimony may be found in Hirschhorn, Superfund: Congress Asks, Is It Working?, 2 Toxics L. Rep. (BNA) 1281 (April 20, 1988). A study of all 1987 RODs concluded "EPA's selection of remedies and cleanup levels are virtually indistinguishable from the flawed decisions that plagued the early years of the program." Environmental Defense Fund, Hazardous Waste Treatment Council, National Audubon Society, National Wildlife Federation, Natural Resources Defense Council, Sierra Club, U.S. PIRG, Right Train, Wrong Track: Failed Leadership in the Super- fund Cleanup Program 1 (1988). For a discussion of the processes and technical problems of setting cleanup standards, see Hazardous Waste Site Management: Water Quality Issues, Report on a Colloquium Sponsored by the Water, Sci- ence, and Technology Board of the National Academy of Sciences (Feb. 19-20, 1987) (National Academy Press, 1988).

d. Natural Resources Damages

OHIO v. INTERIOR DEPARTMENT
800 F.2d 432 (D.C. Cir. 1989)

WALD, Chief Judge, and ROBINSON and MIKVA, Circuit Judges.

Petitioners are 10 states, three environmental organizations ("State and En- vironmental Petitioners"), a chemical industry trade association, a manufactur- ing company and a utility company ("Industry Petitioners"), who seek review of regulations promulgated by the Department of the Interior ("DOI" or "Interior") pursuant to §301(c)(1)-(3) of the Comprehensive Environmental Response, Compensation and Liability Act of 1980 ("CERCLA" or the "Act"), as amended, 42 U.S.C. §9651(c). The regulations govern the recovery of money damages from persons responsible for spills and leaks of oil and hazardous substances, to compensate for injuries such releases inflict on natural resources.[2] Damages may be recovered by state and in some cases the federal governments, as trustees for those natural resources.

Petitioners challenge many aspects of those regulations. State and Envi- ronmental Petitioners raise ten issues, all of which essentially focus on the reg- ulations' alleged undervaluation of the damages recoverable from parties responsible for hazardous materials spills that despoil natural resources. Industry Petitioners attack the regulations from a different vantage point, claiming they will permit or encourage overstated damages. In addition, three public interest organizations ("Environmental Intervenors") defend the regulations from the at- tacks of Industry Petitioners, and a collection of corporations and industry groups ("Industry Intervenors") defend the regulations from the attacks of State and En- vironmental Petitioners.

We hold that the regulation limiting damages recoverable by government trustees for harmed natural resources to "the lesser of" (a) the cost of restoring or replacing the equivalent of an injured resource, or (b) the lost use value of the resource is directly contrary to the clearly expressed intent of Congress and is therefore invalid. We also hold that the regulation prescribing a hierarchy of methodologies by which the lost-use value of natural resources may be mea-

---

2. The natural resource damage regulations are codified at 43 C.F.R. §§11.10-11.93 (1987).

sured, which focuses exclusively on the market values for such resources when market values are available, is not a reasonable interpretation of the statute. We remand the record to DOI for a clarification of its interpretation of its own regulations concerning the applicability of the CERCLA natural resource damage provisions to privately owned land that is managed or controlled by a federal, state or local government. We reject all other challenges to Interior's regulations.

I.   Background

A.   STATUTORY BACKGROUND

CERCLA, popularly known as Superfund, was enacted in 1980. Pub. L. No. 96-510, 94 Stat. 2767 (1980). Congress amended it in 1986, in the Superfund Amendments and Reauthorization Act ("SARA"), Pub. L. No. 99-499, 100 Stat. 1613 (1986). Unless otherwise specified, references to CERCLA in this opinion refer to the statute as amended. . . .

The relevant provisions of CERCLA in this case, however, go beyond the mere removal or remedying of spills. CERCLA provides that responsible parties may be held liable for "damages for injury to, destruction of, or loss of natural resources, including the reasonable costs of assessing such injury, destruction, or loss resulting from such a release." §107(a)(c), 42 U.S.C. §9607(a)(C). Liability is to "the United States Government and to any State for natural resources within the State or belonging to, managed by, controlled by, or appertaining to such State." §107(f)(1), 42 U.S.C. §9607(f)(1).[3] The Act provides for the designation of federal and state "trustees" who are authorized to assess natural resource damages and press claims for the recovery of such damages, both under CERCLA and under §311 of the Federal Water Pollution Control Act (commonly referred to as the "Clean Water Act"), 33 U.S.C. §1321. CERCLA §107(f)(2), 42 U.S.C. §9607(f)(2).

Congress conferred on the President (who in turn delegated to Interior) the responsibility for promulgating regulations governing the assessment of damages for natural resource injuries resulting from releases of hazardous substances or oil, for the purposes of CERCLA and the Clean Water Act's §311(f)(4)-(5) oil and hazardous substance natural resource damages provisions, 33 U.S.C. §1321(f)(4)-(5). These regulations originally were required to be in place by December 1982. §301(c), 42 U.S.C. §9651(c). CERCLA prescribed the creation of two types of procedures for conducting natural resources damages assessments. The regulations were to specify (a) "standard procedures for simplified assessments requiring minimal field observation" (the "Type A" rules), and (b) "alternative protocols for conducting assessments in individual cases" (the "Type B" rules). §301(c)(2), 42 U.S.C. §9651(c)(2). Both the Type A and the Type B rules

---

3.   Liability may also be to an Indian tribe for certain resources. §107(f)(1), 42 U.S.C. §9607(f)(1).

were to "identify the best available procedures to determine such damages." Id. The regulations must be reviewed and revised as appropriate every two years. §301(c)(3), 42 U.S.C. §9651(c)(3). Under the Act, a trustee seeking damages is not required to resort to the Type A or Type B procedures, but CERCLA as amended provides that any assessment performed in accordance with the prescribed procedure is entitled to a rebuttable presumption of accuracy in a proceeding to recover damages from a responsible party. §107(f)(2)(C), 42 U.S.C. §9607(f)(2)(C).

In August 1986, Interior published a final rule containing the Type B regulations for natural resource damage assessments, the subject of this lawsuit. Shortly thereafter, in October 1986, Congress adopted SARA, amending the natural resources damages provisions of CERCLA in several respects. For example, SARA provided that assessments performed by state as well as federal trustees were entitled to a rebuttable presumption, it provided for the recovery of prejudgment interest on damage awards, and it proscribed "double recovery" for natural resources damages. §§107(f)(2)(C), 107(a), 107(f)(1), 42 U.S.C. §§9607(f)(2)(C), 9607(a), 9607(f)(1). SARA also amended §301(c) to require Interior to adopt any necessary conforming amendments to its natural resource damage assessment regulations within six months of the effective date of the amendments, "[n]otwithstanding the failure of the President to promulgate the regulations required under this subsection on the required [December 1982] date." §301(c)(1), 42 U.S.C. §9651(c)(1).

B.   The Natural Resource Damage Assessment Regulations

. . . Ultimately, on August 1, 1986, Interior published a final rule containing general natural resource damage assessment regulations as well as the Type B rules challenged in the present case. 51 Fed. Reg. 27,674 (1986) (codified at 43 C.F.R. §§11.10-11.93 (1987)).

The assessment process established by the Type B regulations has four phases. In the "preassessment phase," a trustee that has become aware of a release of hazardous substances or oil makers an initial determination whether natural resources may have been affected. If further action is deemed warranted, the trustee enters the "assessment plan phase," in which an assessment strategy is mapped out. Next comes the "assessment phase," in which the trustee establishes whether there was in fact an injury to natural resources, quantifies the extent of the injury, and ascertains the appropriate dollar-amount of damages caused by the release. Finally, in the "post-assessment phase," the trustee assembles a report documenting the assessment process and presents the responsible party with a demand for payment of damages. See 51 Fed. Reg. at 27,726-27.

The August 1986 regulations were promptly challenged by state governments, environmental groups, industrial corporations, and an industry group.

Shortly after the issuance of the August 1986 regulations, Congress amended CERCLA by enacting SARA. As noted above, SARA gave Interior six months in which to conform its natural resource damage assessment rules to the amended statute. In response to SARA, Interior issued revised rules (following notice and comment) in February 1988. 53 Fed. Reg. 5,166 (1988). A state government and an environmental group filed additional challenges to these revised rules, which this court consolidated with the original case.

Interior's formulation of Type A rules (governing simplified damage assessments) was handled in a separate rule-making proceeding. Following notice and comment, a set of Type A rules was issued as a final rule in March 1987, 52 Fed. Reg. 9,042 (1987). The Type A rules are the subject of a separate petition for review, which was briefed and argued simultaneously with the present case and is decided today in State of Colorado v. Department of the Interior, No. 87-1265 [30 ERC 1044] (D.C. Cir. July 14, 1989).

II. Standard of Review

In reviewing an agency's interpretation of a statute, we first determine "whether Congress has directly spoken to the precise question at issue." Chevron U.S.A., Inc. v. Natural Resources Defense Council, Inc., 467 U.S. 837, 842 (1984). If so, then both Interior and this court "must give effect to the unambiguously expressed intent of Congress." Chevron, 467 U.S. at 842-43; accord NLRB v. United Food & Com. Workers Union Local 23, 108 S. Ct. 413, 421 (1987). This is "Step One" of Chevron analysis.

Whether Congress has made its intent clear and unambiguous does not depend on whether a particular phrase of the statutory text standing all alone resolves the matter. Rather, the court must look beyond "the particular statutory language at issue" and examine "the language and design of the statute as a whole." K Mart Corp. v. Cartier, Inc., 108 S. Ct. 1811, 1817 (1988). "It is a fundamental canon of statutory construction that the words of a statute must be read in their context and with a view to their place in the overall statutory scheme." Davis v. Michigan Dept. of Treasury, 109 S. Ct. 1500, 1504 (1989). Moreover, as the Supreme Court indicated in Chevron and has reiterated since then, the reviewing court must "employ[ ] traditional tools of statutory construction" — including, when appropriate, legislative history — to determine whether Congress "had an intention on the precise question at issue." Chevron, 467 U.S. at 843 n.9; accord United Food & Com. Workers Union, 108 S. Ct. at 421; INS v. Cardoza-Fonseca, 480 U.S. 421, 446-48 (1987). If the court, having studied the statutory text, structure and history, is left with the unmistakable conclusion that Congress had an intention on the precise question at issue, "that intention is the law and must be given effect." Chevron, 467 U.S. at 843 n.9.

If, on the other hand, the statute is ambiguous or is silent on a particular issue, this court must assume that Congress implicitly delegated to the agency the power to make policy choices that " 'represent[ ] a reasonable accommodation of conflicting policies that were committed to the agency's care by the statute.' " Chevron, 467 U.S. at 844-45, quoting United States v. Shimer, 367 U.S. 374, 383 (1961). In that event, the court must defer to the agency's interpretation of the statute so long as it is reasonable and consistent with the statutory purpose. Id. This is "Step Two" of *Chevron* analysis.

We first take up the ten issues raised by State and Environmental Petitioners, followed by the one issue raised by Industry Petitioners.

III.   The "Lesser-of" Rule

The most significant issue in this case concerns the validity of the regulation providing that damages for despoilment of natural resources shall be "the *lesser of*: restoration or replacement costs; or diminution of use values." 43 C.F.R. §11.35(b)(2) (1987) (emphasis added).

State and Environmental Petitioners challenge Interior's "lesser of" rule, insisting that CERCLA requires damages to be at least sufficient to pay the cost in every case of restoring, replacing or acquiring the equivalent of the damaged resource (hereinafter referred to short-handedly as "restoration"). Because in some — probably a majority of — cases lost use-value will be lower than the cost of restoration, Interior's rule will result in damages awards too small to pay for the costs or restoration. Petitioners point to a section of CERCLA providing that recovered damages must be spent only on restoration as evidence that Congress intended restoration cost-based damages to be the norm. As further proof of such a norm, the same section goes on to state that the measure of damages "shall not be limited by" the sums which can be used for restoration. Petitioners maintain that the "shall not be limited by" language clearly establishes restoration costs as a "floor" measure of damages. Petitioners also rely on the legislative history of CERCLA and of SARA, claiming that it reinforces the sense of the text and documents Congress' primary emphasis on restoration of natural resources. In particular, they point to a House report on SARA, insisting that it, together with the other statutory indicators, proves conclusively that Congress intended restoration costs to be a minimum measure of damages in natural resource cases.

Interior defends its rule by arguing that CERCLA does not prescribe any floor for damages but instead leaves to Interior the decision of what the measure of damages will be. DOI acknowledges that all recovered damages must be spent on restoration but argues that the amount recovered from the responsible parties need not be sufficient to complete the job. DOI suggests two alternative meanings of the "shall not be limited by" phrase that do not construe it as a damages floor. Finally, DOI arguees that the legislative history, like the statutory text, is ambiguous and that Interior's rule for measuring damages is a reasonable one.

Although our resolution of the dispute submerges us in the minutiae of CERCLA text and legislative materials, we initially stress the enormous practical significance of the "lesser of" rule. A hypothetical example will illustrate the point: imagine a hazardous substance spill that kills a rookery of fur seals and destroys a habitat for seabirds at a sealife reserve. The lost use value of the seals and seabird habitat would be measured by the market value of the fur seals' pelts (which would be approximately $15 each)[4] plus the selling price per acre of land comparable in value to that on which the spoiled bird habitat was located.[5] Even if, as likely, that use value turns out to be far less than the cost of restoring the rookery and seabird habitat, it would nonetheless be the only measure of damages eligible for the presumption of recoverability under the Interior rule.

After examining the language and purpose of CERCLA, as well as its legislative history, we conclude that Interior's "lesser of" rule is directly contrary to the expressed intent of Congress.

A. The Contours of "the Precise Question at Issue"

Commencing our *Chevron* analysis, we must first decide exactly what "the precise question at issue" is in the present case. *Chevron*, 467 U.S. at 842. Much depends on accurately identifying that issue so as to decide whether Congress has "directly spoken" on it; if so, under *Chevron's* "Step One" we must give effect to that unambiguously expressed intent. If not, we proceed instead to "Step Two" and determine whether Interior's construction of CERCLA is reasonable and consistent with the statutory purpose.

State and Environmental Petitioners posit that the precise question at issue in this case is what measure of damages must be applied in natural resource damage actions. They argue that Congress *did* address the precise question at issue by deciding that damages must at a minimum encompass the full cost of restoration in every case. See Pet. Br. 18-22. Therefore, petitioners say, this court must strike down the "lesser of" rule on *Chevron* Step One grounds.

Interior also assumes that the precise question at issue here is what measure of damages must be applied in natural resource damage actions. Interior's position, however, is that Congress did *not* definitively address that question. See Resp. Br. 25-27; 51 Fed. Reg. 27,705. To support this view, Interior points out that Congress did not choose a particular measure of damages, opting instead to authorize the President to draft regulations governing the assessment of damages. §301(c)(2), 42 U.S.C. §9651(c)(2) (regulations shall "identify the best available procedures to determine . . . damages" and shall "take into consideration" certain listed factors, among others). Since Congress delegated the matter to the President (who turned it over to DOI), DOI argues that this case is governed by *Chevron* Step Two and that its "lesser of" rule must be upheld if not unreasonable or inconsistent with the statutory purpose.

We find both parties' arguments flawed in one important respect. Both fail to properly describe the "precise question at issue" in the "lesser-of" rule. That

---

4. See U.S. Dept. of the Interior, "Measuring Damages to Coastal and Marine Natural Resources," vol. 1 at p. V-37 (mandating $15 figure for valuation under Type A rules); see also 52 Fed. Reg. 9,092 (1987) (stating that $15 value is consistent with valuation principles of Type B rules).

5. See Interagency Land Acquisition Conference, "Uniform Appraisal Standards for Federal Land Acquisitions" 9 (1973), Joint Appendix ("J.A.") 273; see also 43 C.F.R. §11.83(c)(2).

question is not what measure of damages should apply in any or all cases which are brought under the Act. As to that larger question, Interior is obviously correct in asserting that Congress delegated to it a considerable measure of discretion in formulating a standard. See §301(c)(2), 42 U.S.C. §9651(c)(2). The precise question here is a far more discrete one: whether DOI is entitled to treat use value and restoration cost as having equal presumptive legitimacy as a measure of damages.[6]

Interior's "lesser of" rule operates on the premise that, as the cost of a restoration project goes up relative to the value of the injured resource, at some point it becomes wasteful to require responsible parties to pay the full cost of restoration. See 51 Fed. Reg. at 27,704-05; 50 Fed. Reg. at 52,141. The logic behind the rule is the same logic that prevents an individual from paying $8,000 to repair a collision-damaged car that was worth only $5,000 before the collision. Just as a prudent individual would sell the damaged car for scrap and then spend $5,000 on a used car in similar condition, DOI's rule requires a polluter to pay a sum equal to the diminution in the use value of a resource whenever that sum is less than restoration cost. What is significant about Interior's rule is the point at which it deems restoration "inefficient." Interior chose to draw the line not at the point where restoration becomes practically impossible, nor at the point where the cost of restoration becomes grossly disproportionate to the use value of the resource, but rather at the point where restoration cost exceeds — by any amount, however small — the use value of the resource. Thus, while we agree with DOI that CERCLA permits it to establish a rule exempting responsible parties *in some cases* from having to pay the full cost of restoration of natural resources,[7] we also agree with Petitioners that it does not permit Interior to draw the line on an automatic "which costs less" basis.

---

6. Although this formulation of the precise question at issue might be viewed as a narrow one, we remind that the *Chevron* Court itself cast the precise question at issue in that case in narrow terms as well. *Chevron* concerned the validity of an EPA regulation that treated all pollution-emitting devices within a given industrial grouping as though they were encased in a single "bubble," for purposes of deciding whether the installation or modification of one such device triggered a statutory requirement that a permit be obtained "for the construction and operation of new or modified stationary sources." 467 U.S. at 839-40. The *Chevron* Court did not ask whether Congress addressed the question of what is a "stationary source [ ]" within the meaning of the amended Clean Air Act, 42 U.S.C. §7502(b)(6). Rather, it asked whether "Congress . . . actually ha[d] an intent regarding *the applicability of the bubble concept to the permit program.*" 467 U.S. at 845 (emphasis added).

7. This can be inferred from §301(c)(2) of CERCLA. First, that provision delegates to the President the duty to formulate a measure of damages, which suggests some degree of latitude in deciding what measure shall apply. Second, it states that the regulations "shall take into consideration factors including, but not limited to, replacement value, use value, and ability of the ecosystem or resource to recover." §301(c)(2), 42 U.S.C. §9651(c)(2). That suggests that DOI is permitted to apply use value in some cases and restoration cost in others (and both in yet others). See also 132 Cong. Rec. H9613 (daily ed. Oct. 8, 1986) (statement of Rep. Jones) ("Where, of course, restoration is technically impossible or the costs thereof are grossly disproportionate to the value of the resources to society as a whole, then other valuation measures, both market and nonmarket, must be used." (Scholars agree that recovery of full restoration cost in every case, no matter how large the sum is, is not required by CERCLA. See Anderson, Natural Resource Damages, Superfund, and the Courts, 16 B.C. Envtl. Aff. L. Rev. 405, 446 (1989); Cross,

Interior's "lesser of" rule squarely rejects the concept of any clearly expressed congressional preference for recovering the full cost of restoration from responsible parties. The challenged regulation treats the two alternative measures of damages, restoration cost and use value, as though the choice between them were a matter of complete indifference from the statutory point of view; thus, in any given case, the rule makes damages turn solely on whichever standard is less expensive. (An analogy would be a government procurement rule that dictated the purchase of the lowest-priced goods, regardless of whether they were domestically made or imported.) If Congress, however, in enacting CERCLA, clearly expressed an intention that DOI's damage measurement rules incorporate a distinct preference for restoration cost over use value, then the "lesser of" rule is inconsistent with that intent. Congress' expressed preference would mean that restoration cost must normally be preferred over use value despite use value being the "lesser" figure, except in unusual situations where the disadvantages or expenses were extreme. (Returning to our analogy, the lowest-price procurement rule would be invalid under *Chevron* Step One if it were promulgated under a statute clearly mandating a preference for domestic goods.) Based on the discussion that follows, we conclude that CERCLA unambiguously mandates a distinct preference for using restoration cost as the measure of damages, and so precludes a "lesser of" rule which totally ignores that preference.

B.   TEST AND STRUCTURE OF CERCLA

CERCLA provides that parties responsible for hazardous substance releases "shall be liable for . . . damages for injury to, destruction of, or loss of natural resources, including the reasonable costs of assessing such injury, destruction, or loss resulting from such a release." §107(a)(C), 42 U.S.C. §9607(a)(C). The Regulations promulgated pursuant to §107(a)(C) are to identify procedures for measuring damages that "shall take into consideration factors including, but not limited to, replacement value, use value, and ability of the ecosystem or resource to recover." §301(c)(2), 42 U.S.C. §9651(c)(2). While CERCLA thus empowers DOI to formulate a measure of damages, several other provisions of the Act make it clear that replacement costs and use value are not to be accorded equal presumptive legitimacy in the process.

1.   SECTION 107(f)(1) AND THE MEASURE OF DAMAGES

The strongest linguistic evidence of Congress' intent to establish a distinct preference for restoration cost as the measure of damages is contained in

---

Natural Resource Damage Valuation, 42 Vand. L. Rev. 269, 301, 329 (1989); Breen, CERCLA's Natural Resource Damage Provisions: What Do We Know So Far?, 14 Envtl. L. Rep. 10,304, 10,309-10 (1984). DOI obviously has some latitude in deciding which measure applies in a given case: the rule might for instance hinge on the relationship between restoration cost and use value (e.g., damages are limited to three-times the amount of use value), or it might hinge on the ability of the resource to recover (e.g., use value is the measure whenever restoration is infeasible). DOI has not, however, fashioned its rules along these lines.

§107(f)(1) of CERCLA. That section states that natural resource damages recovered by a government trustee are "for use only to restore, replace, or acquire the equivalent of such natural resources." 42 U.S.C. §9607(f)(1). It goes on to state: "The measure of damages in any action under [§107(a)(C)] shall not be limited by the sums which can be used to restore or replace such resources." Id.[8]

a. Limitation on Uses of Recovered Damages

By mandating the use of all damages to restore the injured resources, Congress underscored in §107(f)(1) its paramount restorative purpose for imposing damages at all. It would be odd indeed for a Congress so insistent that all damages be spent on restoration to allow a "lesser" measure of damages than the cost restoration in the majority of cases. Only two possible inferences about congressional intent could explain the anomaly: Either Congress intended trustees to commence restoration projects only to abandon them for lack of funds, or Congress expected taxpayers to pick up the rest of the tab. The first theory is contrary to Congress' intent to effect a "make-whole" remedy of complete restoration,[9] and the second is contrary to a basic purpose of the CERCLA natural resource damage provisions — that polluters bear the costs of their polluting activities.[10] It is far more logical to presume that Congress intended responsible parties to be liable for damages in an amount sufficient to accomplish its restorative aims. Interior's rule, on the other hand, assumes that Congress purposely

---

8. Although at first glance these two sentences might seem inconsistent, a closer look reveals that the missing link is the absence of the phrase "or acquire the equivalent" in the latter sentence. This suggests (and the legislative history confirms) that damages recovered in excess of restoration or replacement costs must be spent on acquiring the equivalent of lost resources. See H.R. Rep. No. 253(IV), 99th Cong., 1st Sess. 50 (1985). . . .

9. See, e.g., 132 Cong. Rec. at H9613 (daily ed. Oct. 8, 1986) ("[The] purpose of the regime, rather, is to make whole the natural resources that suffer injury from releases of hazardous substances." (remarks of Rep. Jones); 126 Cong. Rec. 30942 (1980) ("[W]e do not want damage to natural resources to await the workings of that [common-law tort litigation] process; we want prompt, full compensation in such cases so we can replant trees in the park. . . .") (remarks of Sen. Mitchell). Underscoring its intent to accomplish full restoration, Congress in 1980 provided that government trustees could recover restoration costs from Superfund whenever efforts to reecover from responsible parties failed (for example, in a secret "midnight dumping" case where the responsible party cannot be determined, or where the responsible party is insolvent). See §111(c)(2), (b)(2)(A), 42 U.S.C. §9611(c)(2), (b)(2)(A); see *infra* note 11.

10. See, e.g., S. .Rep. No. 848, 96th Cong., 2d Sess. 13 (1980):

> The goal of assuring that those who caused chemical harm bear the costs of that harm is addressed in the reported legislation by the imposition of liability. Strict liability, the foundation of S. 1480, assures that those who benefit financially from a commercial activity internalize the health and environmental costs of that activity into the costs of doing business.

See also id. at 31 ("Since C. 1480 is designed to assure that products reflect their true costs, the bill is at its most efficient when such actual costs [imposed by hazardous substance releases] are calculated to the penny."); 126 Cong. Rec. 30941 (1980) ("The guiding principle of those who wrote S. 1480 was that those found responsible for harm caused by chemical contamination should pay the costs of that harm.") (remarks of Sen. Mitchell).

formulated a statutory scheme that would doom to failure its goals of restoration in a majority of cases.[11]

In this connection, it should be noted that Interior makes no claim that a "use value" measure will provide enough money to pay for *any* of the three uses to which all damages must be assigned: restoration, replacement *or acquisition of an equivalent resource.* Nor could Interior make such a claim, because its "lesser of" rule not only calculates use value quite differently from restoration or replacement cost but it also fails to link measurement of use value in any way to the cost of acquiring an equivalent resource. For example, Interior could not possibly maintain that reovering $15 per pelt for the fur seals killed by a hazardous substance release would enable the purchase of an "equivalent" number of fur seals.

b. The "Shall Not Be Limited By" Language

The same section of CERCLA that mandates the expenditures of all damages on restoration (again a short-hand reference to all three listed uses of damages) provides that the measure of damages "shall not be limited by" restoration costs. §107(f)(1), 42 U.S.C. §9607(f)(1). This provision obviously reflects Congress' apparent concern that its restorative purpose for imposing damages not be construed as making restoration cost a damages ceiling.[12] But the explicit command that damages "shall not be limited by" restoration costs also carries in it an implicit assumption that restoration cost will serve as the basic measure of damages in many if not most CERCLA cases. It would be markedly inconsistent with the restorative thrust of the whole section to limit restoration-based damages, as Interior's rule does, to a minuscule number of cases where restoration is cheaper than paying for lost use.[13]

---

11. DOI states that federal or state agencies "are not precluded from supplementing damage funds with other monies to restore, replace, or enhance the injured natural resource." 51 Fed. Reg. 27,705. Those "other monies," however, cannot come from Superfund, as the enactment of SARA in 1986 cut off the availability of Superfund money for restoration of injured natural resources. See SARA §517(a), Pub. L. No. 99-499, 100 Stat. 1772 (1986), codified at 26 U.S.C. §9507(c)(1)(A)(ii) (Superfund money to be available "only" to carry out the purposes of, inter alia, "section 111(c) of CERCLA . . . *other than paragraphs (1) and (2) thereof*") (emphasis added); cf. CERCLA §111(c)(2), 42 U.S.C. 9611(c)(2) (providing for Superfund expenditures on restoration of injured resources).

12. Interior's regulations provide that, when restoration costs are the "lesser" of the two possible measures, the trustee may recover not only restoration costs but also damages for "the diminution of use values during the period of time required to obtain restoration or replacement." 43 C.F.R. §11.84(g)(1).

13. Commentators are unanimous in predicting that applying the "lesser of" rule will invariably favor the use value standard. See, e.g., Cross, *supra* note 7, at 307 ("Only about five percent of some resources, such as plants and animals, possess an established economic value."); Anderson, *supra* note 7, at 442; Kenison, Buchholz & Mulligan, State Actions for Natural Resource Damages: Enforcement of the Public Trust, 17 Envtl. L. Rep. 10,437-39 (1987). The Anderson article points out that Interior's own strict definition of what "uses" will be recognized for damage purposes guarantees that "lost use" will almost always be the chosen measure. Anderson, *supra*, at 442.

2.   INTERIOR'S READING OF CERCLA §§301 AND 107

In the face of §107's clear preference for restoration as the basic measure of natural resource damages, DOI and Industry Intervenors advance "ambiguities" in the language of §§301 and 107, asserting that those ambiguities are sufficient to permit Interior to promulgate the "lesser of" rule under *Chevron* Step Two.

a.   The "Take Into Consideration" Language

First, Interior argues that the "take into consideration" language of §301(c)(2) delegates to Interior the decision of whether and how restoration cost should be taken into consideration. Resp. Br. 25-27; 51 Fed. Reg. 27,705. We have acknowledged that CERCLA does confer on DOI discretion in fashioning the measure of damages; indeed, if §301(c)(2) were the only instruction Congress had given, DOI's argument would be a strong one. But the reality is that Interior's discretion is cabined by Congress' determination, as evidenced by the statutory text discussed above, that the measure of damages reflect a preference for restoration cost, at least where restoration is feasible and can be performed at a cost not grossly disproportionate to the use value of the resource. Thus, while DOI is correct in pointing to the "take into consideration" language as hinting at a measure of latitutde on the part of DOI, the degree of latitude conferred by Congress is not infinite.

b.   The Assessment Costs Language

Industry Intervenors argue that the reference in §107(a)(C) to including assessment costs in damages awards indicates, by the principle of *expressio unius est exclusio alterius*, that Congress intended only the one narrow daparture from common-law damage measurement standards.[14] But this crabbed reading ignores the existence of §301(c)(2), which states that the factors to be taken into account by the regulations "includ[e] but [are] not limited to" replacement cost and use value. Under the common law, the Industry Intervenors would have us believe, there are no other factors to consider. In light of §301(c)(2), the *expressio unius* argument, at best a canon for constructing statutes in the absence of more definite guidance within the four corners of the act itself, loses force. We do not think Congress' mere mention of assessment costs in §107(a)(C) implicitly excludes all other non-common-law components of damages.

---

14.   Industry Intervenors advance a related argument, to the effect that Congress' choice of the word "damages" in §107(a)(C) should be read to incorporate the common-law meaning of the term. In the first place, this argument loads a great deal of baggage onto an everyday word which has long since transcended its origins and is now defined in Webster's Dictionary as "compensation in money imposed by law for loss or injury." Webster's New Collegiate Dictionary 286 (1977). Moreover, as our examination of CERCLA's legislative history indicates, Congress' dissatisfaction with the common law provided a central motivation for enacting CERCLA.

c.   The "Shall Not Be Limited By" Language

Interior and Industry Intervenors propose several alternative readings of the "shall not be limited by" language of §107(f)(1) in an effort to show that Congress did not unambiguously express a preference for restoration cost as the basic measure of CERCLA natural resource damages. None of their various constructions is plausible, however.

They first contend that the phrase "shall not be limited by" dictates not the measure of damages but the uses to which damages must be put. Industry Intervenors argue that Congress' "primary purpose" in this portion of §107(f) was "to describe the appropriate uses of the natural resource damages *once they are recovered*, while making sure that section 107(f) did not contradict the scope of recovery set forth in section 107(a)(C)." Ind. Int. Br. 16 (emphasis in original). This is a difficult argument to understand, let alone accept. First, the notion that a sentence beginning with the words, "The measure of damages . . . shall . . ." refers only to the *uses* of damages rather than the proper *measure* of damages is counterintuitive, especially when the sentence immediately preceding it expressly refers to the *uses* of damages. Second, we fail to see why Congress need be concerned that §107(f)(1) would "contradict the scope of recovery set forth in" §107(a)(C). The latter section simply imposes liability for "damages" for injury or loss to natural resources (including asessment costs). Any conflict with subsection (f)(1) is of Industry's own making; it arises only if, as Industry does, one reads a common-law limitation into the word "damages." See *supra* note 14. The whole argument strikes us as circular. Indeed, the fact that subsection (f)(1) itself explicitly cross-references subsection (a)(C) as the source of liability indicates Congress' conscious design to read the two subsections as compatible and complementary: liability for "damages" is established in subsection (a)(C), while subsection (f)(1) orders DOI not to place a restoration-cost ceiling on the "measure of damages." Industry Intervenors' caution that subsection (f)(1) should not be read "to supplant the measure of damages established in" subsection (a)(C), Ind. Int. Br. 17, is superfluous: subsection (a)(C) does not purport to set a measure of damages, while subsection (f)(1) contains an explicit command regarding "[t]he measure of damages in any action under" subsection (a)(C).[15] . . .

3.   SUPERFUND PROVISIONS

CERCLA's Superfund provisions lend additional weight to our conclusion that Interior's "lesser of" rule is not true to the statute. In CERCLA as originally

---

15.   Industry Intervenors tried rephrasing the point at oral argument, but without success. Counsel argued that the "measure of damages" provision of §107(f)(1) does not expand on the "categories of recoverable cost" set forth in §107(a)(C). This of course harks back to the expressio unius treatment accorded §107(a)(C)'s mention of assessment costs, which we find unconvincing for reasons already stated. At any rate, §107(a)(C) makes no mention of "categories of recoverable cost" or anything of the sort. Industry Intervenors' attempt to identify an ambiguity in this aspect of the statute fails.

enacted, public trustees could rely on Superfund money to pay for restoration in cases where they could not recover money from the polluters themselves (for example, where the responsible party had become insolvent, or where the responsible party had engaged in secret dumping and thus could not be identified).[17] SARA cut off the availability of Superfund money for natural resource restoration in 1986,[18] but the statutory provisions governing Superfund remain on the books and provide evidence of Congress' intent to require responsible parties to pay restoration costs. Under CERCLA, Superfund monies can be spent to redress harm to natural resources only to (1) assess the extent of the damages, and to (2) finance government trustees' "efforts in the restoration, rehabilitation, or replacement or acquiring the equivalent of any natural resources injured, destroyed, or lost as a result of a release of a hazardous substance." §111(c)(1)-(2), 42 U.S.C. §9611(c)(1)-(2). The statute, though, bars a trustee from obtaining Superfund money until it has first "exhausted all administrative and judicial remedies to *recover the amount of such claim* from persons who may be liable" under §107 as responsible parties. §111(b)(2)(A), 42 U.S.C. §9611(b)(2)(A) (emphasis added). Interior's "lesser of" rule, however, means that in the majority of cases, the trustee *cannot* "recover the amount of such claim" from the responsible parties since use-based damages will be less.[19] So once again, Interior's rule appears to be out of sync with the statutory scheme and with CERCLA's decided emphasis on making polluters pay for restoration of spoiled resources. . . .

---

17.   See S. Rep. No. 848, *supra* note 10, at 13 (purpose of fund is to finance response actions "where a liable party does not clean up, cannot be found, or cannot pay the costs of cleanup and compensation"); id. at 16 (existing statutes are inadequate "to deal with abandoned and inactive sites or with new cases of 'midnight dumping' onto the ground"); id. at 80 (purpose of fund is "to assure prompt payment of valid claims where the claimant has ben unable to obtain satisfaction from a liable party"); 126 Cong. Rec. 30932 (1980) (fund to pay cleanup costs and mitigate damages "where a liable party does not clean up or cannot be found") (remarks of Sen. Randolph).

18.   See *supra* note 11.

19.   CERCLA's legislative history supports this interpretation. The Senate CERCLA report states:

> Monies from the Fund should be available to a State or the appropriate Federal agencies for use to restore, rehabilitate, or acquire the equivalent of such resources which have been injured, lost or destroyed. It should be noted, however, that in a case where the election to pursue an action in court is chosen, the measure of such resource damages shall not be limited to the sums which can be used to restore or replace such resources.

S. Rep. No. 848, *supra* note 10, at 84-85.

Industry Intervenors dismiss this passage in the Senate report as "address[ing] a component of the bill that was never passed." Ind. Int. Br. 16. This is untrue. Although subsections (a)(2)(D) and (a)(2)(E) of §4 of S. 1480 were never passed, the right of state and federal government trustees to recover was expressly authorized "under subsection (a)(2)(C) of this section" — the one subsection of the three that was eventually enacted in CERCLA. S. 1480, §4(b), reprinted in 1 Senate Comm. on Environment and Public Works, 97th Cong., 2d Sess., A Legislative History of the Comprehensive Environmental Response, Compensation and Liability Act of 1980 488 (Comm. Print 1983) [hereinafter "Legislative History"]. The passage in the Senate report addresses subsection (C), not subsections (D) and (E).

6. CERCLA and the clean water act

The "lesser of" rule is also inconsistent with §311(f)(4) and (5) of the Clean Water Act, to which Interior's natural resource damage regulations are applicable in accordance with §301(c)(1) of CERCLA. Section 311 of the Clean Water Act provides that damages recoverable for releases of hazardous substances or oil covered by the CWA "shall include any costs or expenses incurred by the Federal Government or any State government in the restoration or replacement of natural resources damaged or destroyed." 33 U.S.C. §1321(f)(5).[22] Thus, the CWA expressly establishes restoration cost as the standard measure of damages.[23] . . .

C. Legislative History of CERCLA

The text and structure of CERCLA indicate clearly to us that Congress intended restoration costs to be the basic measure of recovery for harm to natural resources. We next examine the legislative history of CERCLA to ascertain if there are any countervailing indications to our conclusion and also to check on Interior's assertions that certain parts of the history are inconsistent with our conclusion and so render the statute ambiguous within the meaning of *Chevron*. Far from finding these arguments persuasive, we conclude that the legislative history of CERCLA — both in its original enactment in 1980 and in its amendment and reenactment in 1986 — reinforces our interpretations of the text. . . .

XIII.   *Contingent Valuation*

A. The Regulatory Background

When a natural resource is injured by a discharge of oil or release of a hazardous substance, an authorized official[60] assesses the damages resulting.[61] DOI has prescribed methodologies for estimating in any such instance the amount of money to be sought as recompense. Either DOI's restoration methodology[62] or one of its use methodologies[63] must be employed in calculations of damages.[64] The issue we now address concerns one of the latter.

---

22.   Subsections 311(f)(4) and (f)(5) were added to the Federal Water Pollution Control Act in 1977. Pub. L. No. 95-217, §58(g), 91 Stat. 1566 (1977).

23.   See Commonwealth of Puerto Rico v. S.S. Zoe Colocotroni, 628 F.2d 652, 673 [15 ERC 1675] (1st Cir. 1980), *cert. denied*, 450 U.S. 912 (1981).

60.   "'Authorized official' means the Federal or State official to whom is delegated the authority to act on behalf of the Federal or State agency designated as trustee, or an official designated by an Indian tribe, pursuant to section 126(d) of CERCLA, to perform a natural resource damage assessment." 43 C.F.R. §11.14(d) (1988). See also CERCLA §107(f)(2), 42 U.S.C. §9607(f)(2) (Supp. IV 1986).

61.   43 C.F.R. §11.80(a)(1) (1988).

62.   Id. §11.81.

63.   Id. §11.83.

64.   Id. §11.80(c).

DOI's natural resource damage assessment regulations define "use value" as

> the value to the public of recreational or other public uses of the resource, as measured by changes in consumer surplus, any fees or other payments collectable by the government or Indian tribe for a private party's use of the natural resource, and any economic rent accruing to a private party because the government or Indian tribe does not charge a fee or price for the use of the resource.[65]

The regulations provide several approaches to use valuation. When the injured resource is traded in a market, the lost use value is the diminution in market price.[66] When that is not precisely the case, but similar resources are traded in a market, an appraisal technique may be utilized to determine damages.[67] When, however, neither of these two situations obtains, nonmarketed resource methodologies are available.[68] One of these is "contingent valuation" (CV), the subject of controversy here.

The CV process "includes all techniques that set up hypothetical markets to elicit an individual's economic valuation of a natural resource."[69] CV involves a series of interviews with individuals for the purpose of ascertaining the values they respectively attach to particular changes in particular resources. Among the several formats available to an interviewer in developing the hypothetical scenario embodied in a CV survey are direct questioning, by which the interviewer learns how much the interviewee is willing to pay for the resource; bidding formats, for example, the interviewee is asked whether he or she would pay a given amount for a resource and, depending upon the response, the bid is set higher or lower until a final price is derived; and a "take or leave it" format, in which the interviewee decides whether or not he or she is willing to pay a designated amount of money for the resource.[70] CV methodology thus enables ascertainment of individually-expressed values for different levels of quality of resources, and dollar values of individuals' changes in well-being.[71] The regulations also

---

65.   Id. §11.83(b)(1).
66.   Id. §11.83(c)(1).
67.   Id. §11.83(c)(2).
68.   Id. §11.83(d).
69.   Id. §11.83(d)(5)(i).
70.   Type B Technical Information Document; "Techniques to Measure Damages to Natural Resources," DOI CERCLA 301 Project (1987) at 2-35-2-36, J.A. 850-851 [hereinafter Type B Technical Information Document]. This document was prepared by DOI to accompany the Type B rules. See Natural Resource Damage Assessments, Final Rule, 51 Fed. Reg. 27,720 (1986).

See also R. Bishop & T. Heberlein, The Contingent Valuation Method (paper presented at National Workshop on Non-Market Valuations Methods and Their Use in Environmental Planning, University of Canterbury, New Zealand (December 2-5, 1985)) (discussing bidding game, open-ended question, payment-card, dichotomous-choice and contingent ranking formats) at 7-11, J.A. 3017-302?.

71.   Type B Technical Information Document, *supra* note 70, at 2-31, 2-32, J.A. 846, 847.

sanction resort to CV methodology in determining "option"[72] and "existence"[73] values.[74]

Industry petitioners'[75] complaint is limited to DOI's inclusion of CV in its assessment methodology.[76] They claim fatal departures from CERCLA on grounds that CV methodology is inharmonious with common law damage assessment principles, and is considerably less than a "best available procedure."[77] These petitioners further charge that DOI's extension of CERCLA's rebuttable presumption to CV assessments is arbitrary and capricious, and violative of the due process rights of a potentially responsible party. We find none of these challenges persuasive.

B.   CONSISTENCY WITH CERCLA

Industry petitioners point out that at common law there can be no recovery for speculative injuries, and they contend that CV methodology is at odds with that principle. CV methodology, they say, is rife with speculation, amounting to no more than ordinary public opinion polling.

We have already noted our disagreement with the proposition that the strictures of the common law apply to CERCLA.[78] That much of industry petitioners' argument to the contrary thus fades away. CERCLA does, however, require utilization of the "best available procedure" for determinations of damages flowing from destruction of or injury to natural resources,[79] and industry petitioners

---

72.   Option value is the dollar amount an individual is willing to pay although he or she is not currently using a resource but wishes to reserve the option to use that resource in a certain state of being in the future. Final Rule, *supra* note 70, 51 Fed. Reg. at 27,692, 27,721. For example, an individual who does not plan to use a beach or visit the Grand Canyon may nevertheless place some value on preservation of the resource in its natural state for personal enjoyment in the event of a later change of mind.

73.   Existence value is the dollar amount an individual is willing to pay although he or she does not plan to use the resource, either at present or in the future. The payment is for the knowledge that the resource will continue to exist in a given state of being. Final Rule, *supra* note 70, 51 Fed. Reg. at 27,692, 27,721. Though lacking any interest in personally enjoying the resource, an individual may attach some value to it because he or she may wish to have the resource available for others to enjoy.

74.   43 C.F.R. §11.84(d)(5)(i) (1988).

75.   Industry petitioners are the Chemical Manufacturers Association, the Dana Corporation, and the Public Service Electric and Gas Company. The Chemical Manufacturers Association consists of 75 national and multinational corporations producing chemicals. The Dana Corporation, a manufacturer, has 44 American subsidiaries and affiliates, and 116 foreign subsidiaries and affiliates. Public Service Electric and Gas Company is a utility licensed to supply electricity and gas in New Jersey, and has two subsidiaries.

76.   We have found DOI's current hierarchy of use values inconsistent with CERCLA. See Part VI *supra*. This does not affect the manner in which the CV methodology operates, or whether it produces sufficiently accurate results to be included in the regulations.

77.   Industry petitioners also contend that DOI's natural resource damage assessment regulations are invalid to the extent that they authorize resort to CV methodology for purposes of calculating option and existence values. These they assert, are nonuse values, and as such are not allowable under CERCLA. It suffices to point out that we have already rejected this conclusion. Option and existence values are non-consumptive values compensable under the terms of CERCLA.

78.   See Part III(c)(3)(a) *supra*.

79.   CERCLA §301(c)(2), 42 U.S.C. §9651(c)(2) (1982).

insist that CV methodology is too flawed to qualify as such. In their eyes, the CV process is imprecise, is untested, and has a built-in-bias and a propensity to produce overestimation.

It cannot be gainsaid that DOI's decision to adopt CV was made intelligently and cautiously. DOI scrutinized a vast array of position papers and discussions addressing the use of CV. It recognized and acknowledged that CV needs to be "properly structured and professionally applied." It eliminated a feature of CV, as originally proposed, that might have resulted in overly high assessments. We find DOI's promulgation of CV methodology reasonable and consistent with congressional intent, and therefore worthy of deference.

NOTES AND QUESTIONS

1. The Department's "type A" rules, which apply to short term releases in marine and coastal environments, were challenged in a companion case, Colorado v. Interior Dept., 800 F.2d 881 (D.C. Cir. 1989). The court upheld the limited scope of the rules because Interior had sufficient information to devise a computer model for damage assessment. The selection of lost use as the measure of damages was remanded for the reasons set out in the principal case.

2. Interior defended its lost rule as the correct application of the principles of efficiency. Do you see why? Do you agree with the court's reason for the rejection of this defense? "The fatal flaw of Interior's approach . . . is that it assumes that natural resources are fungible goods, just like any other, and that the value to society can be accurately measured in every case. . . ." — F.2d at —. Environmental intervenors challenged Interior's use of a 10 percent discount rate to calculate the present value of expected future injury because discounting undervalues the potential long-term resource damages. Specifically, they argued that because the value of scarce resources will rise in the future, there is too much uncertainty to permit the establishment of an accurate discount rate. The court rejected this challenge because the regulations provide that the trustee performing the assessment must take into account the possibility that restoration costs will rise faster than the general price level. Is this analysis consistent with the court's rejection of Interior's efficiency defense for lost value?

3. After the D.C. Circuit opinion in *Ohio*, economists have informally proposed the following new rule for DOI adoption: if restoration cost is less than the diminution in use value narrowly defined, then the value of the natural resource damage is equal to restoration cost. If restoration cost exceeds lost use value alone, but is less than the "total loss in value" as now construed by the court, then the damage is equal to restoration cost. Otherwise, the damage is equal to the sum of lost use and nonuse value. This rule, it is suggested, would give operational meaning to the court's view that DOI might ". . . establish some class of cases where other considerations — i.e., infeasibility of restoration or grossly disproportionate cost to use value — warrant a different standard." Do you agree that this is the best approach for DOI to take?

A NOTE ON STRATEGIC BANKRUPTCY

Bankruptcy provides some relief from CERCLA liability. The principal goal of bankruptcy law is to provide an orderly distribution of the debtor's asssets to creditors. Basically, secured creditors are paid first and then classes of unsecured creditors share what assets, if any, are left. An individual or a corporate PRP may file for bankruptcy. An individual debtor has a choice of liquidating his assets and seeking a discharge from unsatisfied pre-bankruptcy debts or reorganizing. Discharge gives the debtor a fresh start. See Jackson, The Fresh Start Policy in Bankruptcy Law, 98 Harv. L. Rev. 1393 (1985). Corporations that liquidate cannot obtain a discharge, although their limited liability achieves the same purpose. After a petition for bankruptcy is filed, all creditor collections are automatically stayed. "Burdensome" property may be abandoned by the trustee. Under the Bankruptcy Code, the "commencement or continuation of an action or proceeding by a government unit to enforce such government unit's police or regulatory power" and the "enforcement of a judgment, other than a money judgment, obtained in an action or proceeding by a governmental unit to enforce such governmental unit's police or regulatory power" are exempt from the automatic stay provision. 11 U.S.C. §362(b)(4).

State and federal cleanup orders threaten to disrupt the scheme of bankruptcy priorities. If the trustee must comply with an order, the cleanup burden is shifted to the unsecured creditors. If the trustee need not comply with the order, the costs of cleanup are shifted back to the state. In neither case does the polluter pay. As you review the developing law, discussed below, ask yourself what incentives or disincentives for compliance and enforcement are created by the decisions.

Ohio v. Kovacs, 469 U.S. 274 (1985), stayed state enforcement of a cleanup order for a site at which a state receiver had been appointed. Ohio had obtained an injunction requiring cleanup and $75,000 in wildlife damages against the chief executive officer and stockholder of Chem-Dyne Corp. A receiver was appointed when Kovacs failed to comply with the injunction; after part of the cleanup had been completed, Kovacs filed for bankruptcy. The Court held that the injunction was not within the automatic stay exemption because it was a nonexempt claim for money damages. Justice White indicated that a pre-bankruptcy fine would not be discharged because such fines are preserved in the statute and that an injunction to prevent the further treatment of disposal of toxic wastes also would not be discharged.

Kovacs distinguished an earlier circuit court of appeals decision, Penn Terra v. Department of Environmental Resources, 733 F.2d 267 (3d Cir. 1984), which enforced an injunction against a facility that required it to clean up pre-filing violations of the applicable law. The court reasoned that the injunction was not a money judgment, although most commentators argue that Congress intended to treat corrective injunctions as money judgments. Accord In re Commonwealth Oil Refining Co., 805 F.2d 1175 (5th Cir. 1986), *cert. denied*, 107 S. Ct. 3228 (1987) (RCRA enforcement action). See Baird and Jackson, *Kovacs* and Toxic Wastes in Bankruptcy, 36 Stan. L. Rev. 1199 (1984). As one writer has remarked, "The goal of orderly distribution of estate assets is disrupted by permitting the state to enforce an injunction requiring expenditure of estate assets not in the ordinary course of business and outside the system of priorities set up by Congress. Assets expended in compliance with the injunction would be removed from the estate and would be unavailable to other creditors; indeed, compliance could deplete the estate entirely." Sward, Resolving Conflicts between Bankruptcy Law and the State Police Power, 1987 Wis. L. Rev. 403, 428. Nonetheless, a district court has applied this distinction to hold that CERCLA response and remedial actions are immune from the automatic stay provision because they are police power actions. United States v. Nicolet, Inc., 27 Envt. Rep. Cas. (BNA) 1078 (E.D. Pa. 1988).

Strategic bankruptcy was also limited by a second Supreme Court case. The court of appeals had refused to allow a trustee to abandon a site because it was "burdensome" to the debtor under §535 of the 1978 Act. In re Quanta Resources, 739 F.2d 912 (3d Cir. 1984). The Supreme Court affirmed in Midlantic Natl. Bank v. New Jersey Dept. of Envtl. Protection, 106 S. Ct. 755 (1986):

> Before the 1978 revisions of the Bankruptcy Code, the trustee's abandonment power had been limited by a judicially developed doctrine intended to protect legitimate state or federal interests. This was made clear by the few relevant cases. In Ottenheimer v. Whitaker, 198 F.2d 289 (CA4 1952), the Court of Appeals concluded that a bankruptcy trustee, in liquidating the estate of a barge company, could not abandon several barges when the abandonment would have obstructed a navigable passage in violation of federal law. . . .
>
> Thus, when Congress enacted §554, there were well-recognized restrictions on a trustee's abandonment power. In codifying the judicially developed rule of abandonment, Congress also presumably included the established corollary that a trustee could not exercise his abandonment power in violation of certain state and federal laws. The normal rule of statutory construction is that if Congress intends for legislation to change the interpretation of a judicially created concept, it makes that intent specific. Edmonds v. Compagnie Generale Transatlantique, 443 U.S. 256, 266-267 (1979). The Court has followed this rule with particular care in construing the scope of bankruptcy codifications. If Congress wishes to grant the trustee an extraordinary exemption from non-bankruptcy law, "the intention would be clearly expressed, not left to be collected or inferred from disputable considerations of convenience in administering the estate of the bankrupt." Swarts v. Hammer, 194 U.S. 441, 444 (1904); see Palmer v. Massachusetts, 308 U.S. 79, 85 (1939) ("If this old and familiar power of the states [over local railroad service] was withdrawn when Congress gave district courts bankruptcy powers over railroads, we ought to find language fitting for so drastic a change"). Although these cases do not define for us the exact contours of the trustee's abandonment power, they do make clear that this power was subject to certain restrictions when Congress enacted §554(a).
>
> . . . Neither the Court nor Congress has granted a trustee in bankruptcy powers that would lend support to a right to abandon property in contravention of state or local laws designed to protect public health or safety. As we held last Term when the State of Ohio sought compensation for cleaning the toxic waste site of a bankrupt corporation:

> Finally, we do not question that anyone in possession of the site — whether it is [the debtor] or another in the event the receivership is liquidated and the trustee abandons the property, or a vendee from the receiver *or the bankruptcy trustee* — must comply with the environmental laws of the State of Ohio. Plainly, that person or firm may not maintain a nuisance, pollute the waters of the State, or refuse to remove the source of such conditions.

Ohio v. Kovacs, 469 U.S. 274, 285 (1985) (emphasis added).

Congress has repeatedly expressed its legislative determination that the trustee is not to have *carte blanche* to ignore non-bankruptcy law. . . .

In re Charles George and Reclamation Trust, 30 Bankr. 918 (Bankr. D. Mass. 1984), dismissed a bankruptcy action for cause under §107 because the site posed an immediate danger to public drinking water supplies. However, a bankruptcy court has allowed the abandonment of contaminated property when it did not pose an immediate threat to public health. In re Oklahoma Refining Co., 63 Bankr. 562 (Bankr. W.D. Okla. 1986).

Kovacs, Penn Terra, and *Midlantic* create a priority for the recovery of hazardous waste costs that have not yet been incurred. A balancing approach has been suggested to resolve this conflict between CERCLA and bankruptcy law. See, e.g., Hoffman, Environmental Protection and Bankruptcy Rehabilitation: Toward a Better Compromise, 11 Ecology L.Q. 671 (1984); and Note, Belly Up Down in the Dumps: Bankruptcy and Hazardous Waste Cleanup, 38 Vand. L. Rev. 1037 (1985). Other commentators, however, argue that the resolution will have to come from Congress. See, e.g., Klein, Hazardous Waste Liability and the Bankruptcy Code, 10 Harv. Envtl. L. Rev. 533 (1986); and Note, Cleaning Up Bankruptcy: Curbing Abuse of the Federal Bankruptcy Code by Industrial Polluters, 85 Colum. L. Rev. 870 (1985). Sward, Resolving Conflicts between Bankruptcy Law and the State Police Power, *supra*, discusses the factors to be considered in adding a new priority.

A NOTE ON FEDERAL PROTECTION OF DRINKING WATER

The Safe Drinking Water Act of 1974, 42 U.S.C. §300f-300j-q, established a federal regulatory system to ensure the safety of public drinking water systems. §300f(4). For a summary of the public health problems arising from the contamination of groundwater and drinking water see Okun, Philosophy of the Safe Drinking Water Act and Potable Reuse, 14 Envtl. Sci. & Technology 1293 (1980); General Accounting Office, Ground Water Overdrafting Must Be Controlled (1980); and Council on Environmental Quality, Contamination of Ground Water by Toxic Organic Chemicals (1981).

Drinking water standards. Under the Act, EPA must set maximum permissible levels for contaminants in drinking water (§300g-g-5). Not surprisingly, these provisions are accompanied by ample legislative history, detailed regulations, and the only significant litigation under the Act. The primary maximum contaminant levels (MCLs) for drinking water from public water systems include levels for microorganisms, turbidity, and organic and inorganic chemicals (including radionuclides), whereas the secondary standards are concerned with the color, odor, and appearance of the water. See 40 C.F.R. §141 (primary standards), and 40 C.F.R. §143 (secondary standards).

In 1986 Congress amended the Safe Drinking Water Act in an effort to force more aggressive EPA regulation of drinking water contaminants. See Gray, The Safe Drinking Water Act Amendments of 1986: Now a Tougher Act to Follow, 16 Envtl. L. Rep. (Envtl. L. Inst.) 10,338 (1986) and Note, The 1986 Amendments to the Safe Drinking Water Act and Their Effect on Groundwater, 40 Syracuse L. Rev. 893 (1989). The 1986 amendments require EPA to publish MCLs and promulgate National Primary Drinking Water Regulations (NPDWRs) for 83 listed contaminants by June 1989 (§300g-1(b)(1)). EPA must also publish a priority list every three years of contaminants "known or anticipated to occur in public water systems" which may require NPDWRs. §300g-1(b)(3)(A). NPDWRs establish monitoring and analytical requirements, recordkeeping, and notification, as well as filtration and disinfection standards. See 40 C.F.R. §141. Under the regulations an owner of a public water system that violates an NPDWR must notify the state authority and the persons served by the system of such violation. 40 C.F.R. §141.32. EPA delegates primary enforcement responsibility to the state, provided the state complies with EPA drinking water standards. 40 C.F.R. §142.10. Even in these primary enforcement states, however, the Act requires EPA to notify the responsible state if EPA finds a NPDWR violation and directs EPA to assume enforcement if the state fails to commence appropriate enforcement action. §300g-3(a)(1)(A).

A court has held that the Act does not regulate the discharge of pollutants into waterways and therefore does not provide a cause of action to a municipality whose drinking water supply was contaminated by a toxic chemicals discharge. City of Evansville v. Kentucky Liquid Recycling, 604 F.2d 1008 (7th Cir. 1979). See also United States v. Price, 523 F. Supp. 1055 (D.N.J. 1981), in which the court held that the imminent hazard provision of the Act authorizes broad relief, including the treatment of hazards and the provision of alternate water supplies. The court maintained that "the relief available under section 1431 [of SDWA] is broader than that available under section 7003 of RCRA." 523 F. Supp. at 1075.

Underground Injection Control (UIC). The Underground Injection Control (UIC) program is intended to prevent the endangerment of underground drinking water sources (42 U.S.C. §300h). Each state must establish an EPA-approved UIC control program; if state enforcement is law, EPA may assume enforcement, as it may enforce state implementation plans under the Clean Air Act. The UIC program regulations set injection well specifications and regulate radioactive and hazardous waste disposal wells, industrial and municipal wells within one quarter of a mile of an underground drinking water source, oil and natural gas recovery wells, and wells for the extraction of minerals and geothermal energy. 40 C.F.R. §122.32.

Under the UIC program, all injection wells require a permit. State plans must require that the applicant for the permit demonstrate that the injection will not endanger drinking water sources. §300h(b). Endangerment occurs "if such injection may result in the presence in underground water which supplies or can reasonably be expected to supply any public water system of any contaminant, and if the presence of such contaminant may result in such system's not complying with any national primary drinking regulations or may otherwise adversely affect the health of persons" (§300h). A state can exempt an aquifer or underground drinking water source if it is not a current source of drinking water, if it would be impractical to make it a source, or if it is unlikely that it will ever be used as a source because of the availability of other sources. 40 C.F.R. §146.

The UIC program, like the drinking water standards program, directs EPA, upon finding a violation of UIC regulations, to notify the state and issue an enforcement order if the state fails to take appropriate action. §300h-2(a)(1). Unlike the drinking water orders, EPA may assess penalties up to $125,000 directly. §300h-2(c)(2).

Sole source aquifer protection. The Act specially protects aquifers designated as the sole or principal source of drinking water for an area. After designation, federal financial assistance may not be committed to a project that may contaminate an aquifer through a recharge zone so as to create a significant public health hazard. §300(h)-3(e). Sole-source designation can be done on the Administrator's initiative or at the request of any other person. The Administrator's discretion to designate is very broad; see Montgomery County v. EPA, 662 F.2d 1040 (4th Cir. 1981) (seven drainage basins designated as a single aquifer).

As of January 1989, EPA has designated 41 sole source aquifers. A sole source aquifer is accorded increased protection if it is designated a Critical Aquifer Protection Area (CAPA). §300h-6. See also 40 C.F.R. §149 (listing criteria for CAPA designation. States with an approved comprehensive contamination management plan to protect a CAPA may receive up to 50 percent of their development and implementation costs from EPA. §300h-6(j). Plans approved under section 208 of the Clean Water Act qualify as comprehensive management plans. §300h-6(g).

The Safe Drinking Water Act also provides grants for state programs protecting wellhead areas from contaminants. §300h-7(a). EPA funds 50 to 90 percent of state development and implementation costs if a state wellhead protection program meets the requirements of §300h-7(a). §300h-7(k). In the spring of 1987, EPA announced it would fund 90 percent of state program costs for 1988 and at a rate decreasing 10 percent per year for each subsequent year the program continues. 52 Fed. Reg. 22,494 (June 22, 1987).

A *federal groundwater protection statute?* In recent years there has been much talk about the need for a federal groundwater strategy. Many laws regulate groundwater quality, but they do not add up to an adequate, comprehensive response to the long-standing use of aquifers as sinks. Water quality control is, in part, a function of water quantity, and the allocation of groundwater historically has been a state function. See generally Yanggen and Amrheim, Groundwater Quality Regulation: Existing Governmental Authority and Recommended Roles, 14 Colum. J. Envtl. L. 1 (1989). An ambitious state effort to limit groundwater pollution is described in Hopping & Preston, The Water Quality Assurance Act of 1983 — Florida's "Great Leap Forward" into Groundwater Protection and Hazardous Waste Management, 11 Fla. St. U.L. Rev. 599 (1983). Some states, e.g., the eastern states and Texas, allow virtually unlimited pumping under the common law "reasonable use" rule; other states, e.g., California, follow a theory of correlative rights that awards a proportionate share of the basin supply to overlying landowners; and still other western states allocate groundwater through the law of prior appropriation. This can produce stringent conservation regimes. Further complications abound, such as the application of the Restatement (Second) of Torts §858A and the law of negligence. See C. Meyers & A. D. Tarlock, Water Resource Management ch. 4 (1980). Some doubt about state primacy over water allocation has been cast by Sporhase v. Nebraska, 455 U.S. 975 (1983). *Sporhase* invalidated a portion of a Nebraska groundwater conservation statute that prohibited the export of water unless the host state granted reciprocal privileges. Western states had long argued, based on a 1908 Supreme Court opinion by Justice Holmes, that water was not subject to the commerce clause either because it was owned in trust for the public or because its uniqueness made the state's police power exclusive. *Sporhase* held that water is an article of interstate commerce, and it followed a long line of cases finding facially discriminatory state legislation unconstitutional. Even if an inter-agency and a federal-state program can be designed, the question of whether it is needed remains. Are public common law actions sufficient? To what extent do federal laws such as CERCLA supplant or supplement them? See City of Philadelphia v. Stepan Chemical Co., 544 F. Supp. 1135 (E.D. Pa. 1982). What relationship — ownership, use, or regulation — must the public plaintiff have to the groundwater to recover damages? See The S.S. Zoe Coloctroni, 628 F.2d 652 (1st Cir. 1980).

3. Transporting Hazardous Wastes and Siting Disposal Facilities: Federalism and the NIMBY Syndrome

The fear of more Love Canals and the reduction in approved hazardous waste disposal sites because of stringent RCRA permit requirements have led local governments to adopt measures restricting the transportation of hazardous wastes on their streets and forbidding the opening of new disposal facilities, a phenomenon called the NIMBY ("not in my back yard") syndrome. Recall the welcome local citizens gave the trucks hauling wastes to the new site in the *Wilsonville* case, p. 519 *supra*. In North Carolina, the malfeasors who at night dumped 35,000 gallons of PCBs along 200 miles of state highways were sent to prison. United States v. Ward, 676 F.2d 94 (4th Cir. 1982). But how to dispose of the many tons of contaminated soil they left became a much greater problem than finding and convicting the midnight dumpers. Protesters were unsuccessful in their suit to block the disposal. Residents of the small community near the proposed disposal site, unimpressed by the governor's assurances that this was the best of 99 sites examined statewide, staged massive demonstrations that attracted nationwide attention. Over 500 persons were arrested for obstructing disposal operations (Time, Nov. 1, 1982, at 29).

From a local perspective, hazardous waste disposal facilities provide all the disadvantages of airports, power plants, and highways and provide almost none of the advantages. The facilities are ugly, produce congestion, threaten public health and safety, and raise suspicions that local crops and products are tainted. But they provide few jobs, pay modest taxes, and do not produce obvious benefits such as energy or transportation.

Given the magnitude of the conflict the NIMBY problem engenders between lower and higher levels of government, one might have expected that Congress would preempt local control over waste transport and siting or at least provide an orderly procedure for resolving disputes. The Hazardous Materials Transportation Act, discussed in a Note at p. 692 *infra*, does provide for federal preemption unless the Department of Transportation determines that local regulations are adequate and do not burden commerce. For its part, RCRA does far less. There is no requirement that a state adopt procedures for site selection; states may administer the RCRA permit system after a site is selected. §3006. Other than prohibiting sites near seismic fault lines or within floodplains, RCRA merely requires each state to prepare an inventory of sites (40 C.F.R. §264.18). Thus the states are thrown back on their own devices to resolve one of the most challenging hazardous waste management problems.

What if a unit of local government absolutely bans any hazardous waste facilities within its borders?

> Absent an express legislative preemption, local units of government have great discretion to veto the entry of a hazardous-waste facility, because such a facility is just another land use to be regulated by applicable zoning ordinances. A persistent theme in local government and land-use law is that a community's first duty to its citizens is to protect their health and welfare. This theory of local self-interest has been sustained by the Supreme Court and state courts. As a result, it is difficult for courts to develop an effective law of local duties to consider extra-local interests. [Tarlock, Anywhere but Here: An Introduction to State Control of Hazardous-Waste Facility Location, 2 U.C.L.A.J. Envtl. L. & Poly. 1, 13 (1982).]

Sharon Steel Corp. v. City of Fairmont, 334 S.E.2d 616 (1985), held that a community may prohibit the permanent disposal of hazardous wastes as public nuisances — provided that the city can prove that permanent disposal is in fact a public nuisance — and that neither federal nor state law preempts the city's power.

Even absent preemption, some state courts have granted immunity from "host" state land use controls when the "intruder" is a unit of government or a licensed private entity, as a waste facility may well be. Based on a landmark New

Jersey case, Rutgers, The State University v. Piluso, 60 N.J. 142, 286 A.2d 697 (1972), some state courts apply a balancing analysis to determine if the intruder's interest in fact outweighs the host government's interest in protecting health and welfare. Other state courts start from the premise that host concerns are paramount but still balance interests. The many state court opinions that have invalidated exclusionary neighborhood zoning practices suggest additional approaches that would weigh heavily in favor of the "intruder": (1) a property owner denied the right to locate may have been denied substantive due process; (2) an exclusionary ordinance may be presumptively ultra vires (because zoning ordinances should mediate among uses, not exclude them); and (3) an exclusionary ordinance may be held to establish a prima facie case of unreasonable zoning and therefore shift the burden of showing reasonableness to the host. Which approach do you think should apply to hazardous waste sites: balancing, with a presumption favoring the local ban? Or should the presumption favor the facility? Is an analogy to exclusionary zoning apt? See Anywhere but Here: An Introduction to State Control of Hazardous-Waste Facility Location, *supra* at 13-20.

Almost thirty states have special siting legislation. Many of these new statutes preempt local land use controls, although many try to take the sting out of preemption by allowing local governments an extensive voice in state siting procedures. See Canter, Hazardous Waste Disposal and New State Siting Programs, 14 Nat. Res. Law. 421 (1982), and Tarlock, Land Use Issues in Hazardous Waste Facility Siting, 35 Land Use Law & Zoning Dig., No. 4, at 4 (April 1983). To date, arguments that preemption violates state home rule charters have been rejected by the courts, e.g., Clermont Environmental Reclamation Co. v. Wiederhold, 2 Ohio St. 3d 44, 442 N.E.2d 1278 (1982). For analysis of the 1981 New Jersey Major Hazardous Waste Facility Siting Act concluding that local communities have a de facto ability to obstruct unwanted facilities by making them too costly politically, see D. Morell & C. Magorian, Siting Hazardous Waste Facilities: Local Opposition and the Myth of Preemption (1982). A 1980 Massachusetts statute strictly limits the power of municipalities to regulate or zone out hazardous waste facilities in return for allowing local communities to negotiate cash and other "bribes" from the would-be TSD facility. Massachusetts's hazardous waste facility siting act was upheld against a challenge that it infringes on the home rule powers of cities. Town of Warren v. Hazardous Waste Site Safety Council, 392 Mass. 107, 466 N.E.2d 102 (1984). Local hazardous waste regulations were found preempted in Envirosafe Services of Idaho v. County of Owyhee, 112 Idaho 687, 735 P.2d 998 (Idaho 1987). See also Duffy, State Hazardous Waste Facility Siting: Easing the Process through Local Cooperation and Preemption, 11 Boston College Envtl. Aff. L. Rev. 755 (1985). The Thirteenth Annual Arlie House Conference on the Environment was devoted to Siting of Hazardous Waste Facilities and Transportation of Hazardous Substances: A Law and Policy Forum. The principal papers are printed in 17 Nat. Resources L. 428-532 (1984). Resolving Locational Conflict (R. Lake ed. 1987) is a collection of accounts of siting hazardous waste facilities and other similar locally undesirable land uses (LULUs).

A New Jersey law prohibited importation of wastes into that state. In Philadelphia v. New Jersey, 437 U.S. 617 (1978), the Supreme Court found wastes to be "articles of commerce" and castigated New Jersey for its "protectionist" attempt to erect a barrier against "interstate trade." Yet New Jersey was actually discriminating against in-state disposal businesses by barring them from accepting out-of-state customers, not discriminating in their favor, which is usually the case when the Supreme Court strikes down local ordinances. Are wastes "articles in commerce"? Should New Jersey be able to preserve its waste disposal capacity for its own future wastes, leaving other regions to work out their own waste disposal problems? If the state operates waste facilities itself, would the Court reach a different result? See Reeves v. Stake, 447 U.S. 429 (1980). But see also Washington State Building & Construction Trades Council v. Spellman, 684 F.2d 627 (9th Cir. 1982). In *Philadelphia*, the dissenters, Chief Justice Burger and Justice Rehnquist, thought New Jersey, already taxed in dealing with wastes generated in-state, had a paramount health interest. Why can't a state under its police power restrict the use of state resources as pollution sinks? Huron Portland Cement Co. v. City of Detroit, 362 U.S. 440 (1960). In Pacific Legal Foundation v. State Energy Resources Conservation & Development Commission, 103 S. Ct. 1713 (1983), the Supreme Court upheld against a federal preemption argument a state moratorium on nuclear power plant construction pending federal adoption of a high-level radioactive waste disposal plan found to be satisfactory by the California energy planning commission and the state legislature. The Court accepted the state's argument that the moratorium was based not on radiological health considerations, which were clearly preempted, but on the economic uncertainty that the failure of the federal government to resolve the waste disposal problem had created, making it impossible for California to engage in sound energy planning that would ensure a reliable energy supply in the future. Why could not New Jersey similarly bring order and certainty to its waste disposal planning efforts by excluding out-of-state wastes? Should not the dormant commerce clause claim invalidate the California statute as well?

The market participation doctrine exempts direct state participation in the market from dormant commerce clause scrutiny. White v. Massachusetts Council of Construction Employers, 460 U.S. 204 (1983). The state, however, cannot impose conditions on the sale of state-owned natural resources. South-Central Timber Development, Inc. v. Wunnicke, 467 U.S. 82 (1984), held that an Alaskan statute requiring that all timber purchased from the state be processed in-state violated the dormant commerce clause. Is a state law that bans out-of-state wastes from a state-owned landfill market participation or the imposition of unconstitutional conditions on a state-owned natural resource? County Commissioners of Charles County v. Stevens, 229 Md. 203, 473 A.2d 12 (1984); Evergreen Waste Systems, Inc. v. Metropolitan Service District, 643 F. Supp. 127 (D. Or. 1986); Lefrancois v. Rhode Island, 669 F. Supp. 1204 (D.R.I. 1987).

In a seminal article, Professor Herbert Wechsler suggested that the United States should not rely too heavily on judicial intervention to maintain the desired federal balance, indicating that political solutions enacted by Congress would be preferable. The Political Safeguards of Federalism: The Role of the State in the Composition and Selection of the National Government, 54 Colum. L. Rev. 543 (1954). Should the Court in *Philadelphia* have prudentially refrained from striking down the local ordinances, thereby leaving the legislatures free to preempt the local solutions if they liked? Should the Court's test under the dormant commerce clause be recast to allow state actions that are likely to secure a prominent place on the national political agenda and do not in fact deny out-of-state interests access to the political process? See Eule, Laying the Dormant Commerce Clause to Rest, 91 Yale L.J. 425 (1982); Tarlock, So It's not "Ours," Why Can't We Still Keep It?: A First Look at Sporhase v. Nebraska, 18 Land & Water L. Rev. 139 (1983). Compare J. Choper, Judicial Review and the National Political Process 208 (1980).

Philadelphia seems to turn its back on earlier Supreme Court cases affirming the power of a state to exclude or quarantine harmful items; it appears to endorse a per se rule of invalidity if a state statute facially denies out-of-state citizens access to use of in-state resources (in this case, land disposal space). But see American Can Co. v. Oregon Liquor Control Commission, 15 Or. App. 618, 517 P.2d 691 (1973) (requirement of returnable containers does not violate the dormant commerce clause), and Washington State Building & Construction Trades Council v. Spellman, 684 F.2d 627 (9th Cir. 1982) ("A challenge to bona fide safety regulations must overcome a strong presumption of validity"). Yet *American Can* has been criticized for its failure to apply the Supreme Court's balancing test (Note, State Environmental Protection Legislation and the Commerce Clause, 87 Harv. L. Rev. 1762 (1974)), and the Supreme Court has expressed its displeasure with reflexive state "incantations" of public health or safety. Kassel v. Consolidated Freightways, Inc., 450 U.S. 662, 670 (1981).

Addressing *Philadelphia*, Judge Richard A. Posner, a former University of Chicago law professor well versed in the principles of the Chicago school of economics, has written:

> [T]o pass laws that arbitrarily burden interstate commerce, by forbidding shipments merely because they originate out of state, violates the commerce clause . . . , and it is irrelevant that the traffic is in "bads" rather than goods. The efficient disposal of wastes is as much a part of economic activity as the production that yields the wastes as a byproduct, and to impede the interstate movement of those wastes is as inconsistent with the efficient allocation of resources as to impede the interstate movement of the product that yields them. [Illinois v. General Electric Co., 683 F.2d 206, 213 (7th Cir. 1982) (holding that an Illinois law barring the disposal of spent nuclear fuel used to generate power out of the state violates the commerce clause).]

Do you agree? See R. Posner, Economic Analysis of Law (1973). See also Stewart, Interstate Resource Conflicts: The Role of Federal Courts, 6 Harv. Envtl. L. Rev. 241, 248 (1982), arguing that the accommodation of state and federal interests in this context is an adjudicative function and thus the courts are well suited to this task, whereas Congress is not. The author further argues that the Supreme Court's per se rule is economically efficient because it strikes down interstate unilateral wealth transfers and that it would not be cost-effective to identify any exceptions. Compare J. Ely, Democracy and Distrust 83-84 (1980).

Note that both high-level and low-level nuclear waste disposal are subject to federal statutory regimes. [High Level] Nuclear Waste Policy Act of 1982 42 U.S.C. §§10,001-10,226 and Low Level Radioactive Waste Policy Act of 1980, 42 U.S.C. §§2001b-2021d. The latter approves interstate compacts that allow signing states to take collective action that would otherwise violate the dormant commerce clause (§2021).

A NOTE ON FEDERAL REGULATION OF THE TRANSPORTATION OF HAZARDOUS MATERIALS

Hazardous materials usually present the greatest risks while being handled, and increasing numbers of environmental lawyers are being called on to handle cases arising out of transportation accidents. Title I of the Transportation Safety Act of 1975, Pub. L. 93-633, 88 Stat. 2156, is the comprehensive Hazardous Materials Transportation ACT (HMTA), 49 U.S.C. §§1801-1812, a command-and-control statute authorizing strict performance, design, and information standards. Under HMTA, the Secretary of the Department of Transportation (DOT) may promulgate rules governing virtually all aspects of the transport of hazardous materials that meet the now-familiar standard of "unreasonable risk" to health, safety, or property when transported in commerce. §1802(2). In some 190 pages of the Code of Federal Regulations, the DOT more than fulfills HMTA's promise to regulate the "packing, repacking, handling, labeling, marking, placarding, routing (except with respect to pipelines) of hazardous materials" and the "manufacture, fabrication, marking, maintenance, reconditioning, repairing, or testing of a package or container" used in transport. §§1804(a), 1805; 49 C.F.R. §172. The Department has placed a great deal of emphasis on ensuring use of containers that will not leak or rupture in all the types or "modes" of transport through which they may pass (highway, rail, air, water, or pipeline). Vessels drilling for oil, firearms, and ammunition for personal use — you may have anticipated this — are exempted. For additional exemptions, see §1806.

DOT's hazardous materials regulations apply to the interstate transportation of all hazardous materials by rail, aircraft, and vessel, including "reportable quantities" under Superfund. 51 Fed. Reg. 42,174 (1986); 17 Envt. Rep. (BNA): Current Developments 1268-69 (1986). See also Keegan, Another Tangled Web: The New DOT "Reportable Quantity" Values, Hazardous Materials & Waste Mgmt. 32 (1987).

DOT requires carriers to give it written notice of route plans and other information relating to the transportation of radioactive materials. 53 Fed. Reg. 16,991 (1988). Subject to minor exceptions, the Act prohibits transport of radioactive materials on passenger airlines, a policy Congress adopted in reaction to a few well-publicized leakage accidents in the early 1970s. Several hundred un-suspecting passengers were exposed. See Kappelmann v. Delta Airlines, Inc., 539 F.2d 165 (D.C. Cir. 1976) (unsuccessful suit to force airlines to notify passengers if radioactive material is aboard), and Air Line Pilots Association v. Civil Aeronautics Board, 516 F.2d 1269 (2d Cir. 1975) (upholding CAB refusal to allow pilot and ground service union embargo of transport of hazardous materials by air).

The Secretary of DOT has broad quasi-judicial investigatory powers under HMTA, as well as administrative and judicial enforcement authority similar to that available to the Administrator of EPA under federal pollution statutes. It appears that no implied private right of action exists that would allow individuals or municipalities to sue under the HMTA to enforce its provisions. Borough of Ridgefield v. New York Susquehanna & Western RR, 17 Envt. Rep. (BNA): Current Developments 1845 (3d Cir. 1987). Civil penalties of up to $10,000 per violation, criminal panalties of up to $25,000 per violation and six years in jail, and punitive damages were authorized (§§1809(a), (b), 1810). The Act's unique preemption provision is discussed below.

The history of the evolution of HMTA and coordinated federal jurisdiction. HMTA was enacted to counteract the growing number of accidents involving hazardous substances, to coordinate DOT's rather independent modal subagencies, to lay the foundation for a container integrity-based regulatory scheme, and to strengthen enforcement authority. A huge amount of hazardous materials are transported each year — over 200 billion ton-miles of materials in over 600 thousand vehicles and vessels. A Review and Analysis of the Department of Transportation's Regulatory Program, Senate Comm. on Commerce, Science, and Transportation, Hazardous Materials Transportation, 96th Cong., 1st Sess. 10-11 (1979). In 1978 alone, 18,022 incidents were reported which accounted for 46 deaths and 1,130 injuries (Department of Transportation, Ninth Annual Report: Hazardous Materials Transportation 17, 20 (1978)). Typical are propane or chlorine tank car explosions or derailments.

Federal regulation of hazardous materials began in 1871 (explosions at sea), a responsibility the U.S. Coast Guard eventually acquired. Until the 1970s, regulation proceeded by accretion, with Congress slowly expanding the categories of substances to be regulated and specifying the modal transportation subunits of DOT that Congress wanted in charge. Eventually, a patchwork of inconsistent safety statutes emerged, which was administered by a powerful group of satrapes over whom DOT had little internal control: the Coast Guard, the Federal Highway Administration, the Federal Railway Administration, the Federal Avaiation Administration, and the Civil Aeronautics Board. The Department per se was left only the marine mode. The National Transportation Safety Board, a five-member investigatory body created in 1966 and strengthened in 1975 after a Nixon Administration-era scandal that almost undermined its apolitical independence, was empowered to act as something of an ombudsman with respect to the modal agencies, calling them to task if accidents that the Board investigated seemed to be due to some extent to lax federal regulation. But the

Board had no authority to provide the type of regulatory guidance HMTA authorized. For the history of federal hazardous materials transport, see S. Rep. No. 1192, 93d Cong., 2d Sess. 6, 7 (1974), and Note, Regulation of the Transportation of Hazardous Materials: A Critique and a Proposal, 5 Harv. Envtl. L. Rev. 345, 346-348 (1981). The DOT's Materials Transportation Board, created in 1975, was given overall authority to develop HMTA regulations and to police container integrity and intermodal transport, but the agencies still retain important consultative, inspection, and enforcement powers within their modes.

Although HMTA centralizes authority over hazardous materials transportation, the DOT's HMTA program overlaps with programs of four other agencies: EPA, the Nuclear Regulatory Commission (NRC), the Occupational Safety and Health Administration (OSHA), and the Interstate Commerce Commission (ICC). EPA's RCRA regulations must be consistent with HMTA regulations. See RCRA §3003(b). Both agencies have issued regulations (49 C.F.R. §§171-177, 40 C.F.R. §263) and have attempted to cooperate and define their respective responsibilities (45 Fed. Reg. 51,645). The Atomic Energy Act, 42 U.S.C. §2011, gives the NRC broad authority to control all aspects of the use of radioactive materials. As with EPA, DOT has worked to coordinate its authority with NRC's. See Note Regulation of the Transportation of Hazardous Materials: A Critique and a Proposal, 5 Harv. Envtl. L. Rev. 345, 352-353 (1981). Fulfilling its statutory mandate "to provide safe or healthful employment or places of employment" (29 U.S.C. §652(8)), OSHA has promulgated some transport workplace regulations that affect the transportation of hazardous materials. OSHA regulates the transportation of compressed gases, inflammable or combustible liquids, explosives and blasting agents, liquified petroleum gases, and anhydrous ammonia. See 29 C.F.R. §1990.101-1990.116. The Interstate Commerce Act, 49 U.S.C. §15,021, gives the ICC authority to regulate hazardous materials, but the Commission largely has deferred to DOT. See Note, Regulation of the Transportation of Hazardous Materials, *supra*, at 353, and Comment, Hazardous Wastes at the Crossroads: Federal and State Transit Rules Confront Legal Roadblocks, 12 Envtl. L. Rep. (Envtl. L. Inst.) 10,075 (1982). See also Bierlein, Increasing Complexity in the Regulation of Hazardous Materials Transportation, Transp. Prac. J. 68 (1986).

The special HMTA preemption provision. HMTA has a unique preemption provision that tests traditional preemption doctrines. Ordinarily, federal environmental statutes specify the extent to which state law is preempted. If there is uncertainty about whether a particular state law is preempted, the issue must be resolved in court. HMTA does specifically preempt any requirement of a state or its political subdivisions that is inconsistent with any provision of HMTA or any regulation issued under it (§112). But this section also goes on to state that the Secretary of Transportation may determine that a state or local requirement that is plainly inconsistent with HMTA or its regulations nevertheless is *not* preempted if the nonfederal requirement affords equal or greater protection to the public than HMTA and if it does not unreasonably burden commerce (§112(b)). Can Congress delegate the non-preemption decision to an administrative agency? A district court opinion by judge and former Columbia University law professor Abraham Sofaer indicates that it can, because the public safety and burden-on-commerce standards are sufficiently precise and involve DOT's special expertise (City of New York v. U.S. Department of Transportation, 539 F. Supp. 1237, 1252-1253 (S.D.N.Y. 1982), *rev'd on other grounds*, 715 F.2d 732 (2d Cir. 1983)).

The trend to a federally guided solution. After the passage of HMTA, states began to abandon their existing transport rules in favor of adopting the federal ones. Sensing that the problem is essentially national rather than local, a majority of the states have adopted part or all of the hazardous materials regulations promulgated by the MTB in 49 C.F.R. §§171-179. By 1981, 35 states had adopted the federal rules. Only five states — Florida, Indiana, Nevada, Oklahoma, and West Virgina — had not yet adopted any federal rules. If the trend continues, few areas of conflict between federal and state governments will exist at all.

In 1988, Ohio enacted what may be the toughest state law governing the transportation of hazardous materials. It requires rail and truck companies to provide emergency management officials with prior notice of shipments of any one of 180 designated chemicals. Transporters who fail to comply with these reporting requirements may be fined up to $10,000. Ohio ranks second in the United States in number of hazardous cargo accidents. 19 Envt. Rep. (BNA): Current Developments 306-07 (1988).

State and local government regulation of nuclear materials transport: a special case. In 1976 New York amended its health code to ban most shipments of radioactive materials through New York City. Brookhaven National Laboratories on Long Island was directly affected and asked the DOT to determine under §112 that HMTA preempted the New York ban. The Department refused to make this determination, explaining that no federal radioactive materials routing requirements had yet been promulgated that could preempt inconsistent state requirements. Immediately, state and local routing requirements proliferated across the nation.

In reaction, DOT promulgated HM-164, a detailed set of regulations specifying the interstate highway system as the approved route for radioactive materials transport. It also specified numerous safety measures for vehicles in transit. HM-164 then proceeded to deal with the New York problem by declaring that state time-of-transit restrictions, notification requirements, and urban bridge and tunnel bans were "inconsistent" with the HMTA regulations (46 Fed. Reg. 5298). In *City of New York supra*, Judge Sofaer held that DOT had failed to consider alternatives and risks, as required by the National Environmental Policy Act (see Chapter 7), but the Second Circuit disagreed, holding that it would be impractical for the Department to evaluate the alternatives and risks for each local transportation measure. Certiorari was denied.

The transportation of high-level radioactive wastes and spent fuel rods from civilian nuclear reactors presumably is governed by HM-164 and regulations of the NRC, but the full political and environmental dimensions of the problem are just emerging because high-level wastes from fuel recycling plants do not yet exist in large quantities (civilian spent fuel recycling has not yet begun in this country) and because spent fuel rods are retained in racks at nuclear plants as the United States tries to site a permanent underground disposal facility. U.S.C. §§10,101-10,226. The NRC has promulgated regulations purporting to ensure that the complex 15- to 100-ton shielded casks in which high-level wastes will be transported by truck or rail can survive any accidents to which they may be exposed along the way (10 C.F.R. §71). NRC has also published sabotage regulations for high-level waste transport (10 C.F.R. §73). See generally National Research Council, Social and Economic Aspects of Radioactive Waste Disposal (National Academy Press, 1984).

VI

THE ENVIRONMENT AND
THE COMMON LAW

This chapter explores the relationship between common law actions for damages to person and property and command and control environmental regulation. Historically, the function of the common law has been to redress civil wrongs between private parties. Corrective justice was done by holding a person liable who caused injury to another as the result of a breach of a legal duty. If actionable, environmental injuries to a person or to property were remedied by money damages or, less frequently, by injunctive relief. Statutory relief, when available, only filled the gaps left by the common law. By the twentieth century, as part of a wider movement promoting legislative solutions to social problems, Anglo-American legal systems had put in place some statutory regimes to prevent environmental harm. The common law had already proved to be too narrow, and judges were unwilling to fashion equitable remedies to deal comprehensively with the community-wide disruptions typical of environmental degradation. These simple early statutes had two characteristics that distinguished them from their common law origins. First, they were almost all prospective. Under them, courts denied damages but enjoined future harms if harm currently was being sustained. Second, the statutes redressed public rather than private wrongs. By the 1970s, Congress and state legislatures had enacted broader environmental protection measures, and the common law was reduced either to providing interim relief, pending likely regulation, or to filling the few remaining gaps in the statutes.

In the triumph of regulation, the statutory displacement of damages remedies occurred at a slower pace than the displacement of preventive injunctions. Legislatures were slow to provide compensation to wronged parties, whether from the public treasury or through a government-supervised transfer of funds from the persons responsible for harm. In the late 1970s, concern over toxic pollution revived interest in personal injury suits in conjunction with public actions to remedy pollution. However, suits to enforce environmental regulations are very much public actions and have not been interpreted to allow ancillary private damage actions. See, e.g., Lutz v. Chromateux, 725 F. Supp. 258 (M.D. Pa. 1989), which holds that citizen suit provisions of the Clean Water

Act, RCRA, and CERCLA do not allow any recovery for medical expenses of any kind.* For this reason, lawyers and politicians were often skeptical that the common law could provide adequate compensation for exposure to chemicals that did not result in immediate injuries, and there was great interest in administered compensation. See Trauberman, Compensating Victims of Toxic Substances Pollution: An Analysis of Existing Federal Statutes, 5 Harv. Envtl. L. Rev. 1 (1981). In the end, neither the plaintiff's bar nor the defense bar were interested in supplanting the common law and instead, "toxic torts" have become a major new branch of tort law. The relationship between the information generated by federal and state environmental regulatory law and common law duties is explored in Kanner, Future Trends in Toxic Tort Litigation, 20 Rutgers L.J. 667 (1989). This chapter begins with a brief survey of damage actions for injury to persons or property from environmental degradation and then considers the use of injunctions.

Environmental lawyers have taken two fundamentally conflicting positions on the role of the common law in promoting environmental quality. On the one hand, many commentators agree that the common law is a seriously flawed system for providing general environmental redress. On the other hand, many also think that there are distinct advantages in having common law judges decide environmental cases. For a recent articulation of the second point of view and a review of the literature, see Furrow, Governing Science: Private Risks and Private Remedies, 131 U. Pa. L. Rev. 1403 (1983). The second point of view is most persuasive when statutory schemes are judged to be inadequate, either because the statutes themselves do not reach a problem or because the statutes are not being vigorously implemented by regulatory agencies. The relationship among different methods of harm prevention and redress is addressed in Stewart, Crisis in Tort Law? The Institutional Perspective, 54 U. Chi. L. Rev. 184 (1987).

This chapter illustrates the difficulties created by the movement from common law to statute that has taken place over recent decades throughout the American legal system. As such, the materials that follow have applications far beyond the confines of environmental law. See G. Gilmore, The Ages of American Law 95 (1977). As one well-known judge noted, "The hydra-headed problem is how to synchronize the unguided missiles launched by the legislatures with an ongoing system of common law" (Traynor, Statutes Revolving in Common Law Orbits, 17 Cath. U.L. Rev. 401, 402 (1968)). Yet the possibilities for a fruitful, creative tension between common law and statute have been noted and encouraged by several outstanding scholars of our jurisprudence. See, e.g., Friendly, The Gap in Lawmaking — Judges Who Can't and Legislatures Who Won't, 63 Colum. L. Rev. 787 (1963); Landis, Statutes and the Sources of Law, in Harvard Legal Essays 213 (1934); Pound, Common Law and Legislation, 21 Harv. L. Rev. 383 (1908); Stone, The Common Law in the United States, 50

---

*State law may create a private right of action for those injured by the release of hazardous chemicals. Minn. Stat. Ann. §115B.05 (1). See Weber v. Gerads Development, No. C8-89-83 (Minn. Sup. Ct. accepted for review September 15, 1989).

Harv. L. Rev. 4 (1936). More recently, in searching for proper roles for courts in a statute-dominated era, Professor Calabresi has explored whether the common law courts should invalidate outmoded statutes that no longer fit within the wider fabric of American law. G. Calabresi, A Common Law for the Age of Statutes (1982).

A. COMMON LAW DAMAGES FOR ENVIRONMENTAL HARM

1. Liability at Common Law

FOLMAR v. ELLIOT COAL MINING CO.
441 Pa. 592, 272 A.2d 910 (1971)

POMEROY, Justice.

These are suits in trespass to recover damages for injury to plaintiffs' property allegedly caused by air pollution attributable to defendant's operation of its coal-cleaning plant. The trial court by its verdict found for the defendant in both cases and, as provided by Supreme Court Rule 1048, 12 P.S. Appendix, supported its verdict with findings of fact and conclusions of law. Plaintiffs' exceptions to the findings and conclusions were overruled, and these appeals followed.

The findings of fact, broadly stated, were as follows: The two appellants purchased their homes in 1931 and 1959, respectively. Both properties are located within 1500 feet of appellee's coal processing plant, which consists of crushers, conveyors, vibrating equipment, screens and picking tables. The plant has been operated by the appellee and its predecessor since 1948, and the appellants realized at the times of their respective purchases that the properties were located in an area generally used for industrial and coal mining purposes. As a result of complaints, appellee installed in 1962 an air cleaner, thermodryer and coal washing unit, and soon thereafter a dust collector and covered coal conveyor. Notwithstanding these measures, the appellee's coal cleaning operation has contributed to air pollution affecting the properties of appellants from 1962 to the time of trial. The appellee has employed specialists in the field of fuel and combustion air pollution who have conducted numerous tests. They have recommended the installation of a certain type of wet scrubber on the thermodryer as a means of reducing emission of dust from that source. This equipment will cost $20,000 to $30,000. The appellee has adopted the recommendation and "intends to either discontinue using the thermodryer or install the wet scrubber." "With the installation of the wet scrubber, defendant company will have done everything now known and economically feasible to eliminate any source of air pollution." The cleaning plant is an essential part of appellee's mining operations, and appellee is not in default in compliance with any requirements of the Air Pollution Control Commission.

The trial court concluded, as a matter of law, that the invasion of appellants' properties by coal dust from appellee's plant has not been substantial,[4] nor was it intentional or unreasonable; neither has the appellee been negligent in conducting its operations.[5]

Both the lower court and the parties have accepted §822 of the Restatement of Torts as the law governing this case. Our Court adopted that section in Waschak v. Moffat, 379 Pa. 441, 109 A.2d 310 (1954) and it is reproduced in full in the margin.[6] In essence, it provides that the owner of private property is entitled to damages due to injury occurring from a nontrespassory invasion of his premises if the defendant's conduct is the legal cause of the invasion and the invasion is (a) substantial, and (b) intentional and unreasonable, or unintentional negligent, reckless or ultrahazardous conduct. The appellants have not been able to satisfy the requirements of that section of the Restatement.

The primary question, as we view it, is whether the trial court was correct in concluding that the invasion of appellants' properties was not unreasonable when the condition could be cured by the installation of equipment which had not, at the time of trial, been installed. An actor's conduct is unreasonable under §822 of the Restatement, unless the utility of his conduct outweighs the gravity of the harm. Restatement of Torts, §826 (1939). Our Court has stated that the actor's conduct lacks utility if it is economically and technically possible to correct the harm and such steps are not taken. Burr v. Adam Eidemiller, 386 Pa. 416, 126 A.2d 403 (1956); see Herring v. H. W. Walker Co., 409 Pa. 126, 133, 185 A.2d 565 (1962). The limited record before us does not disclose when the

---

4. The finding as to substantiality, though below labeled a conclusion of law, is perhaps technically a finding of fact, since it is solely concerned with the quantity and quality of precipitation. The court did find as a fact that the invasion reduced the pleasant use and enjoyment of appellants' properties, and this is probably the "discomfort and annoyance" not amounting to substantial invasion which the court notes in its conclusions of law. Appellee deduces that these findings coalesce to produce a finding of fact that the invasion was not substantial. Based upon the abbreviated record presented and without opportunity to review the complete testimony, this seems to be a reasonable reading of the adjudication. In any event, the appellants are not bound by the lower court's finding of non-substantiality, since they have excepted to it as a conclusion of law.

5. The appellant did not except to the lower court's conclusion that the appellee had not been negligent in conducting its operations and does not contest that conclusion on this appeal.

6. Section 822 of the Restatement of Torts provides:

The actor is liable in an action for damages for a non-trespassory invasion of another's interest in the private use and enjoyment of land if

    (a)   the other has property rights and privileges in respect to the use or enjoyment interfered with; and

    (b)   the invasion is *substantial*; and

    (c)   the actor's conduct is a legal cause of the invasion; and

    (d)   the invasion is either

        (i)   *intentional* and *unreasonable*; or

        (ii)   unintentional and otherwise actionable under the rules governing liability for negligent, reckless or ultrahazardous conduct. [Emphasis ours.]

recommendations as to the wet scrubber were made or when this device became technically and economically feasible, or how long before trial the appellee had decided that it would either make the installation or discontinue its thermodryer. Since such facts are requisite to show an invasion was unreasonable and they have not been proven on the record, it can only be concluded that the appellants did not carry their burden of proof. It is clear, however, that the learned trial judge had before him sufficient facts to justify the legal conclusion that the invasion was not unreasonable: the major improvements in 1962, and the continuing attention to the problem thereafter, culminating in a decision to employ apparatus whereby the appellee "will have done everything now known and economically feasible to eliminate any source of air pollution."

Since, as indicated above, the posture of this case at the time of decision was an action at law for damages tried without a jury, the court was obligated to render a verdict for either the plaintiffs or defendant; the injunctive or conditional forms of equity decrees were not available. It is clear that the verdict for the appellee was based in part, at least, on its announced intention at trial to install a wet scrubber or abandon the thermodryer. Because the verdict was based in part on an expectation, however, the judgment thereon is not to be considered res judicata as to any damage subsequent to the date of the verdict in the event the appellee has not subsequently fulfilled that expectation or discontinued what otherwise might be considered an unreasonable invasion of the appellants' property.

Judgment affirmed.

CITIES SERVICE CO. v. STATE
312 So. 2d 799 (Fla. Dist. Ct. App. 1975)

GRIMES, Judge.

This is an interlocutory appeal from a partial summary judgment on liability entered against the appellant.

The appellant, Cities Service Company (Cities Service), operates a phosphate rock mine in Polk County. On December 3, 1971, a dam break occurred in one of Cities Service's settling ponds. As a result, approximately one billion gallons of phosphate slimes contained therein escaped into Whidden Creek and thence into the Peace River, thereby killing countless numbers of fish and inflicting other damage.

Appellee, The State of Florida (State), filed suit against Cities Service seeking injunctive relief as well as compensatory and punitive damages arising out of the dam break. The court granted an injunction for a limited period of time and struck the claim for punitive damages. Neither of these points are raised on this appeal. Later the court entered an order granting the State's motion for partial summary judgment on liability. The premise for this order was that Cities Service was liable without regard to negligence or fault for the damage occurring by reason of the escape of the phosphatic wastes into the public waters of the State of Florida.

The determination of this appeal necessarily requires the consideration of the doctrine of strict liability for the hazardous use of one's land which was first announced in Rylands v. Fletcher, 1868, L.R. 3 H.L. 330. In that case the defendants, who were millowners, had constructed a reservoir upon their land. The water broke through into the shaft of an abandoned coal mine and flooded along connecting passages into the adjoining mine of the plaintiff. When the case reached the Exchequer Chamber, Justice Blackburn said:

> We think that the true rule of law is that the person who for his own purposes brings on his land and collects and keeps there anything likely to do mischief if it escapes, must keep it at his peril, and if he does not do so he is prima facie answerable for all the damage which is the natural consequences of its escape.

This statement was limited in the House of Lords to the extent that Lord Cairns said that the principle applied only to a "non-natural" use of the defendant's land as distinguished from "any purpose for which it might in the ordinary course of the enjoyment of land be used."

Since that time there have been countless decisions both in England and America construing the application of this doctrine. Most of the early American decisions rejected the doctrine. However, the pendulum has now decidedly swung toward its acceptance. W. Prosser, The Law of Torts §78 (4th ed. 1971). According to Prosser, by 1971 the doctrine had been approved in principle by thirty jurisdictions with only seven states still rejecting the principle.

While the application of the doctrine has not been specifically passed upon by the appellate courts of Florida, an early Supreme Court case implies its acceptance. In Pensacola Gas Co. v. Pebbly (1889) 25 Fla. 381, 5 So. 593, the plaintiff claimed damages which resulted when a neighboring landowner constructed a gas works and allowed refuse to spill out onto the land and sink through the sand into the common water thereby polluting the plaintiff's well. The trial court apparently charged the members of the jury that the plaintiff would be entitled to a verdict if they determined that the plaintiff's wells were rendered unfit for use by the defendant without regard to the question of negligence. In affirming a judgment for the plaintiff, the Supreme Court said:

> The appellant gas company had the right to use the water in and about the gasworks as they pleased, but they had no right to allow the filthy water to escape from their premises, and to enter the land of their neighbors. It was the duty of the company to confine the refuse from their works so that it could not enter upon and injure their neighbors, and if they did so it was done at their peril; the escape of the refuse filthy water being in itself an evidence of negligence on the part of the gas company.

Among the cases cited for this proposition was Ball v. Nye, 99 Mass. 582, which was one of the early American decisions approving the strict liability doctrine of Rylands v. Fletcher. . . .

In early days it was important to encourage persons to use their land by whatever means were available for the purpose of commercial and industrial development. In a frontier society there was little likelihood that a dangerous use of land could cause damage to one's neighbor. Today our life has become more complex. Many areas are overcrowded, and even the non-negligent use of one's land can cause extensive damages to a neighbor's property. Though there are still many hazardous activities which are socially desirable, it now seems reasonable that they pay their own way. It is too much to ask an innocent neighbor to bear the burden thrust upon him as a consequence of an abnormal use of the land next door. The doctrine of Rylands v. Fletcher should be applied in Florida.

There remains, however, the serious question of whether the impounding of phosphate slime by Cities Service in connection with its mining operations is a non-natural use of the land. In opposition to the State's motion, Cities Service filed an affidavit of the manager of the plant where the dam break occurred. The affidavit points out that the property is peculiarly suitable for the mining of phosphate and that the central Florida area of which Polk County is the hub is the largest producer of phosphate rock in Florida. It further appears that Florida produced over 80% of the nation's marketable phosphate rock and one-third of the world production thereof in 1973. The affidavit goes on to explain that the storing of phosphate slimes in diked settling ponds is an essential part of the traditional method of mining phosphate rock. Hence, Cities Service argues that its mining operations were a natural and intended use of this particular land.

There have been many American cases which have passed upon the question of whether a particular use of the land was natural or non-natural for the purpose of applying the Rylands v. Fletcher doctrine. Thus, Prosser, *supra*, states at page 510:

> The conditions and activities to which the rule has been applied have followed the English pattern. They include water collected in quantity in a dangerous place, or allowed to percolate; explosives or inflammable liquids stored in quantity in the midst of a city; blasting; pile driving; crop dusting; the fumigation of part of a building with cyanide gas; drilling oil wells or operating refineries in thickly settled communities; an excavation letting in the sea; factories emitting smoke, dust or noxious gases in the midst of a town; roofs so constructed as to shed snow into a highway; and a dangerous party wall.
>
> On the other hand the conditions and activities to which the American courts have refused to apply Rylands v. Fletcher, whether they purport to accept or to reject the case in principle, have been with few exceptions what the English courts would regard as a "natural" use of land, and not within the rule at all. They include water in household pipes, the tank of a humidity system or authorized utility mains; gas in a meter, electric wiring in a machine shop, and gasoline in a filling station; a dam in the natural bed of a stream; ordinary steam boilers; an ordinary fire in a factory; an automobile; Bermuda grass on a railroad right of way; a small quantity of dynamite kept for sale in a Texas hardware store, barnyard spray in a farmhouse; a division fence; the wall of a house left standing after a fire; coal mining operations regarded as usual and normal; vibrations from ordinary building construction; earth moving operations in grading a hillside; the construction of a railroad tunnel; and even a runaway horse. There remain a few cases, including such things as water reservoirs or irrigation ditches in dry country, or properly conducted oil wells in Texas or Oklahoma, which are undoubtedly best explained upon the basis of a different community view which makes such things "natural"

to the particular locality. *The conclusion is, in short, that the American decisions, like the English ones, have applied the principle of Rylands v. Fletcher only to the thing out of place, the abnormally dangerous condition or activity which is not a "natural" one where it is.* [Emphasis supplied]

The American Law Institute has considered this question in §§519 and 520 of the Restatement of the Law of Torts (1938). These sections state:

§519.   Miscarriage of Ultrahazardous Activities Carefully Carried on

Except as stated in §§521-4, one who carries on an ultrahazardous activity is liable to another whose person, land or chattels the actor should recognize as likely to be harmed by the unpreventable miscarriage of the activity for harm resulting thereto from that which makes the activity ultrahazardous, although the utmost care is exercised to prevent the harm.

§520.   Definition of Ultrahazardous Activity

An activity is ultrahazardous if it
(a) necessarily involves a risk of serious harm to the person, land or chattels of others which cannot be eliminated by the exercise of the utmost care, and
(b) is not a matter of common usage.

Recognizing the evolving nature of the law in this area, the American Law Institute published Tentative Draft No. 10 in 1964 in which certain changes were recommended for §§519 and 520. Thus, in §519 and §520 the substitution of the words "abnormally dangerous" is suggested in place of the word "ultrahazardous." In §520, the following factors are said to be pertinent in determining whether an activity is abnormally dangerous:

(a) Whether the activity involves a high degree of risk of some harm to the person, land or chattels of others;
(b) Whether the harm which may result from it is likely to be great;
(c) Whether the risk cannot be eliminated by the exercise of reasonable care;
(d) Whether the activity is not a matter of common usage;
(e) Whether the activity is inappropriate to the place where it is carried on; and
(f) The value of the activity to the community.

Referring to these factors, F. James, The Law of Torts, Supp. to Vol. 2, §14.4 (1968), states:

The factors to be considered in marking off the area of strict liability are discussed in Comments g through k. One of them deserves special note, the value of the activity to the community. In a sense this factor has already been discounted in making the decision to impose strict liability on an activity. Thus in Comment b to Section 520 it is explained, in distinguishing strict liability from negligence:

The rule stated in §519 is applicable to an activity which is carried on with all reasonable care, and which is of such utility that the risk which is involved in it cannot be regarded as so great or so unreasonable as to make it negligence to carry on the activity at all. (See §282.) If the utility of the activity does not justify the risk which it creates, it may be negligence merely to carry it on, and the rule stated in this Section is not necessary to subject the defendant to liability for harm resulting from it.

The justification for strict liability, in other words, is that useful but dangerous activities must pay their own way (see text at 801; §16.9 at 933, *infra*). There is nothing in this reasoning which would exempt *very* useful activities from the rule, as is shown by the granting of compensation even where the activity is of such paramount importance to society that it justifies the exercise of eminent domain. And if the law were to embrace wholly the principle of strict liability and its underlying rationale, there would be no place for the consideration of this factor. But this is not the present case. Tort law today contains two opposing strains or principles, strict liability and liability based on fault. It is not surprising, therefore, that any attempt to draw a line between them (which is being done in Section 520) should contain factors which would be irrelevant if one principle or the other alone were being consistently pursued. At any rate this factor will probably continue to influence courts in fact for some time to come.

Some or all of the factors enumerated above recur in most of the cases involving the determination of whether a particular use is natural or non-natural. As applied to the instant case, the first four weigh in favor of the State while the last two favor Cities Service. As in many cases, there is much to be said for both sides.

In the final analysis, we are impressed by the magnitude of the activity and the attendant risk of enormous damage. The impounding of billions of gallons of phosphatic slimes behind earthen walls which are subject to breaking even with the exercise of the best of care strikes us as being both "ultrahazardous" and "abnormally dangerous," as the case may be. This is not clear water which is being impounded. Here, Cities Service introduced water into its mining operation which when combined with phosphatic wastes produced a phosphatic slime which had a high potential for damage to the environment. If a break occurred, it was to be expected that extensive damage would be visited upon property many miles away. In this case, the damage, in fact, extended almost to the mouth of the Peace River, which is far beyond the phosphate mining area described in the Cities Service affidavit. We conclude that the Cities Service slime reservoir constituted a non-natural use of the land such as to invoke the doctrine of strict liability.

Ordinarily, the determination of whether or not a particular structure or method of operation is natural or non-natural is one which would require the trial court's evaluation of all of the pertinent factors at a trial. However, we believe that in this case the liability may be properly determined by way of summary judgment. The occurrence of the calamity because of an act of God has always been recognized as an exception to the strict liability doctrine of Rylands v. Fletcher. But Cities Service has made no contention that the break in its dam was caused by an act of God. From the transcript of the testimony taken in connection with the injunction proceedings, it is evident that despite the best of care, earthen dams enclosing phosphate settling ponds do give way from time to time without explanation. All of the assertions of Cities Service relative to the need to maintain settling ponds in its mining operations, the suitability of the land for this purpose and the importance of phosphate to the community as well as to the world at large may be accepted at face value. Admitting the desirability of phosphate and the necessity of mining in this manner, the rights of adjoining landowners and the interests of the public in our environment require the imposition of a doctrine which places the burden upon the parties whose activity made it possible for the damages to occur.

Affirmed.

There seems to be little doubt that the land disposal of toxic chemicals without hydrologic studies are both ultrahazardous and abnormally dangerous activities. In imposing strict liability on the operator of landfill operated between 1964 and 1973 in rural Tennessee, a federal district court relied on the following factors:

> 1. There was a high decree of risk of some harm to the person, land or chattels of others, particularly after the 1967 USGS report;
> 2. There was a likelihood that the harm that results would be great, such as the increased risk of many diseases including cancer, and the destruction of plaintiffs' quality of life;
> 3. The inability to eliminate the risk by the exercise of reasonable care;
> 4. The extent to which the activity at the dump was not a matter of common usage and as a means of disposal violated the state of the art;
> 5. The inappropriateness of the location of the dump where it was carried out; and
> 6. The extent to which its value to the community (none) was outweighed by its dangerous attributes (great).
> [Sterling v. Velsicol Chemical Corp., 647 F. Supp. 303, 316 (W.D. Tenn. 1986), aff'd, 855 F.2d 1188, 192 (6th Cir. 1988).]

Accord Branch v. Western Petroleum, Inc., 657 P.2d 267 (Utah 1982) (driller strictly liable for seepage of toxic oil-drilling waste waters that contaminated domestic well).

FRADY v. PORTLAND GENERAL ELECTRIC CO.
55 Or. App. 344, 637 P.2d 1345 (1981)

WARREN, Judge.

This appeal involves seven consolidated actions for nuisance and trespass. Plaintiffs appeal the dismissal of their complaints.

Three of these actions were brought by plaintiffs who own real property located in the immediate vicinity of the Bethel Combustion Turbine Facility, which is owned and operated by defendant. The remaining four actions were brought by plaintiffs who reside on property near the facility. All the complaints allege that the facility began operating in 1973, and that when it is in operation it emits low frequency sound waves. The complaints of the plaintiffs who own property contain two counts, one in nuisance and one in trespass; both include allegations that the vibrations from the sound waves have damaged and continue to damage their homes, cause them to suffer from loss of sleep, emotional distress and mental strain, and interfere with their use and enjoyment of their property. One complaint contains a further allegation that those plaintiffs' dairy herd has been adversely affected. The complaints of the non-owner plaintiffs who reside on property near the facility contain only one count, alleging that the vibrations have caused and continue to cause them to suffer loss of sleep, emotional strain and mental distress. . . .

In order for the law to attach liability to the operation of a purported nuisance, the plaintiff must allege defendant's actions were intentional, negligent, reckless or an abnormally dangerous activity. Raymond v. Southern Pacific Co., 259 Or. 629, 634, 488 P. 2d 460 (1971). A trespass also requires that the intrusion be intentional, negligent or the result of ultrahazardous activity. Martin v. Union Pacific Railroad, 256 Or. 563, 565, 474 P. 2d 739 (1970).

Plaintiffs do not specifically allege that the damage of which they complain was caused by intentional, negligent or ultrahazardous activity. However, in Jacobson v. Crown Zellerbach, 273 Or. 15, 19, 539 P. 2d 641 (1975), the Supreme Court noted that "intentional" conduct is not limited to activity undertaken for the purpose of damaging another, but includes any act done with the knowledge that damage to another would result. In that case, the allegation that plaintiffs had notified defendant of the damage its trucks were causing was sufficient to allege knowledge on the part of defendant, which, if proved, would render its continued conduct intentional.

In this case, plaintiffs alleged that these same actions came to trial in April, 1978, a jury was empaneled and evidence was taken before plaintiffs' motion for nonsuit was granted. This could not have occurred unless the defendant appeared.

The significance of defendant's appearance is that it necessarily follows that it had notice of plaintiffs' damage claims as of the date of that appearance. Construing the complaints liberally, we conclude that, although the term "notice" does not appear, the plaintiffs have alleged facts from which notice as of April, 1978, must be inferred. Therefore, under the rule in Jacobson v. Crown Zellerbach, *supra*, the complaints contain a recitation of facts sufficient to state that defendant's conduct was intentional after that date.

We now address the arguments raised by defendant in the trial court in support of its motion to dismiss. Defendant argues that plaintiffs have alleged facts which would constitute a claim only for a public nuisance. This argument is based on the fact that to be free from excessive noise is a right common to the public, which is protected by law. An action against the perpetrator of a public nuisance can be brought only by the state, unless an individual can show special injury, different in kind from that suffered by the general public. Raymond v. Southern Pacific, *supra*, 259 Or. at 634, 488 P.2d 460; Prosser, Law of Torts §88 (4th ed. 1971). Defendant contends that plaintiffs have failed to plead special injury, because the damages they allege are the same as would be suffered by anyone in the area. Accordingly, they assert that plaintiffs have failed to state a private claim for public nuisance and the state, not these plaintiffs, is the real party in interest to bring this action.

Defendant is correct with regard to the complaints filed by the plaintiffs who reside on land near the facility but who are not landowners. Those plaintiffs only allege a public nuisance and plead injuries which are not different from those which would be suffered by anyone in the vicinity of the facility. Plaintiffs' proximity may make their inconvenience greater, but special injury must be different in kind, not merely degree. Smejkal v. Empire Lite-Rock, Inc., 274 Or. 571, 574, 547 P.2d 1363 (1976). The trial court's dismissal of these plaintiffs' complaints was proper.

The trial court erred, however, in dismissing the complaints of the plaintiffs who own land near the facility. These plaintiffs alleged physical damage to their property and interference with the use and enjoyment of it. When a public nuisance interferes with an individual's right to use and enjoy his real property, the individual suffers special injury and may bring an action against the perpetrator of the nuisance. Smejkal v. Empire Lite-Rock, Inc., *supra*, 274 Or. at 575, 547 P.2d 1363; Restatement (Second) of Torts §821C, comment e (1979). Furthermore, even when the nuisance would be classified as public, if it interferes with the use and enjoyment of land, the landowner may bring an action for either public or private nuisance. Restatement (Second) of Torts §821B, comment h (1979). We find the landowner plaintiffs have stated a claim and are real parties in interest.

These plaintiffs also argue that they have stated a claim in trespass. We do not construe their complaints as stating such a claim. In Martin et ux v. Reynolds Metals Co., 221 Or. 86, 342 P.2d 790 (1960), the Supreme Court wrote:

> Trespass and private nuisance are separate fields of tort liability relating to actionable interference with the possession of land. They may be distinguished by comparing the interest invaded; an actionable invasion of a possessor's interest in the exclusive possession of land is a trespass; an actionable invasion of a possessor's interest in the use and enjoyment of his land is a nuisance. . . . [221 Or. at 90, 342 P.2d 790.]

Plaintiffs' trespass counts are merely restatements of their nuisance counts. Plaintiffs have failed to allege any conduct on the part of defendant which would constitute a trespass as defined above. They allege no substantial interference with their possessory interest as distinct from their interest in the use and enjoyment of their property to warrant protection under the law of trespass. See Martin et ux v. Reynolds Metals Co., *supra*, 221 Or. at 96, 342 P.2d 790.

NOTES AND QUESTIONS

1. *Some questions.* Were the correct results reached in the three preceding cases? Why were so many different theories of liability involved? Do the courts' statements of the law square with their application of it?

What is the difference between trespass and nuisance? On certification from the federal district court, the Supreme Court of Washington held landowners could sue in trespass for microscopic airborne particles of heavy metals, undetectable by human senses, from a copper smelter. The smelter operator had the intent to commit a trespass because "intent to trespass may also include an act that the actor undertakes realizing that there is a high probability of injury to others and yet the actor behaves with disregard of those likely consequences." Prior law, including Martin v. Reynolds Metals Co., was interpreted to classify particles and substances that accumulate on land and do not pass away as trespasses. Transitory particles create nuisances only. However, the common law rule that the landowner need prove only nominal damages was found inappropriate, and the court required proof that the plaintiff suffered actual and substantial damage: "No useful purpose would be served by sanctioning actions for trespass by every landowner within a hundred miles of a manufacturing plant. Manufacturers would be harassed and the litigious few would cause the escalation of costs to the detriment of the many." A prescriptive easement defense was rejected because the trespass in the case was not open and notorious. Bradley v. American Smelting & Refining Co., 104 Wash. 2d 677, 709 P.2d 782 (1985). Would this analysis apply to a plume of polluted groundwater that migrates beneath plaintiff's land? See Sterling v. Velsicol Chemical Corp., 647 F. Supp. 303, 317-319 (W.D. Tenn. 1986), *aff'd*, 855 F.2d 1188, 1198 (6th Cir. 1988).

2. *Nuisance: What is it?* In *Folmar*, filing in trespass was correct pleading under Pennsylvania law, but isn't *Folmar* really a private nuisance action? Nuisance is a broad basis of liability for interferences with the enjoyment of land. The black-letter rules are easy to state (see p. 700 *supra*) but are hard to apply for two reasons. First, nuisance cases are very fact-sensitive, so that the precedent value of the cases is not high. Second, courts use two fundamentally different bases of liability in nuisance cases, with little appreciation of the tension between them. One, corrective justice, gives little weight to the utility of the defendant's conduct, but the other, a crude utilitarian cost-benefit analysis, compares the gravity of the plaintiff's harm with the utility of the defendant's conduct. See, e.g., Copart Industries, Inc. v. Consolidated Edison, 41 N.Y.2d 564, 362 N.E.2d 968, 394 N.Y.S.2d 169 (1977). The tension between these two theories of nuisance is explored in Epstein, Nuisance Law: Corrective Justice and Its Utilitarian Constraints, 8 J. Legal Stud. 49 (1979).

Is nuisance a tort? Courts and scholars assume so, although "nuisance" liability does not easily fit within one of the three heads of tort liability: negligence (lack of due care), intentional conduct (e.g., battery), or strict liability. Defendants often argue that an allegation of nuisance is an allegation of a lack of due care. However, most courts hold that a plaintiff need not prove that the defendant was negligent to recover in nuisance because in contrast with "negligence liability, liability in nuisance is predicated upon unreasonable injury rather than upon unreasonable conduct" (Wood v. Picillo, — R.I. — 443 A.2d 1244, 1247 (1982), *overruling* Rose v. Socony-Vacuum Corp., 54 R.I. 411, 173 A. 627 (1934)). Intentional conduct and strict liability seem to be better bases for liability because a defendant may still be liable even if he conducted his activity with due care. Is a finding that the defendant caused a nuisance always a finding that he acted intentionally?

Consider this problem: A breaks B's right arm; C breaks B's left arm. B sues C for battery. Can C defend on the ground that A had already degraded B, so that his (C's) conduct added only marginally to B's condition and thus was not so socially outrageous? Of course not; the usual defenses to intentional conduct are consent and privilege, never the character or physical condition of the plaintiff. But such a defense is in effect possible in a nuisance action because the character of the area is an important factor that courts consider in nuisance suits. See Restatement (Second) of Torts §828 (1979), *infra*. For example, if the defendant's type of use dominates in the neighborhood, it is much harder for a plaintiff to recover. In holding that a private windmill in a residential area of a seaside New Jersey community was a nuisance, the court wrote:

> [D]efendants' windmill constitutes an actionable nuisance. As indicated, the noise produced is offensive because of its character, volume and duration. It is a sound which is not only distinctive, but one which is louder than others and is more or less constant. Its intrusive quality is heightened because of the locality. The neighborhood is quiet and residential. It is well separated, not only from commercial sounds, but from the heavier residential traffic as well. Plaintiffs specifically chose the area because of these qualities and the proximity to the ocean. Sounds which are natural to this area — the sea, the shore birds, the ocean breeze — are soothing and welcome. The noise of the windmill, which would be unwelcome in most neighborhoods, is particularly alien here. [Rose v. Chaikin, 187 N.J. Super. 210, 453 A.2d 1378, 1382 (Ch. Div. 1982).]

Property scholars have characterized nuisance cases such as *Rose* as judicial zoning. See Beuscher & Morrison, Judicial Zoning through Recent Nuisance Cases, 1955 Wis. L. Rev. 440. Would it be useful to posit a fourth basis of the defendant's liability: a wrong guess about the suitability of a location for an activity? Or is this just another way of saying that nuisance is strict liability? Courts have considered this question but have not given a conclusive answer. Consider New Jersey v. Ventron, 94 N.J. 254, 463 A.2d 893 (1983).

3. *Nuisance: the requirement of a substantial physical invasion of plaintiff's interest*. Section 822 of the Restatement requires that a substantial invasion of a plaintiff's interest in land must be established in addition to unreasonable conduct. Was this also true in *Cities Service? Frady?* Will the plaintiffs in *Folmar* and *Frady* ultimately fail because they cannot meet the substantiality require-

ment? This threshold requirement has frustrated many environmental plaintiffs' claims because the injuries they allege are often minor but widely suffered or have to do with aesthetics or personal dignity rather than a tangible loss. What is the justification for the substantial injury requirement? See Ellickson, Alternatives to Zoning: Covenants, Nuisance Rules, and Fines as Land Use Controls, 40 U. Chi. L. Rev. 68, 757-758 (1973).

An allegation of a physical invasion is considered part of the prima facie nuisance case. This requirement generally precludes purely aesthetic injuries. The common law justified the rule that purely aesthetic injuries could not be a nuisance either because the law was too narrow — not subtle enough — to take these sensitivities into account or because any conclusion about what activity was an aesthetic nuisance would be arbitrary. The physical invasion requirement has been both affirmed and rejected by recent commentators. Compare Epstein, Nuisance Law: Corrective Justice and Its Utilitarian Constraints, 8 J. Legal Stud. 49, 60-63 (1979), with Ellickson, Alternatives to Zoning: Covenants, Nuisance Rules, and Fines as Land Use Controls, 40 U. Chi. L. Rev. at 731-732, *supra*. The argument that courts should change the common law in the light of more refined societal expectations voiced since the late 1960s has had very limited recognition by the courts. See Robie v. Lillis, 112 N.H. 492, 299 A.2d 155 (1972). However, courts do seem to be moving away from the physical invasion requirement when they apply a lowest common denominator test to an aesthetic nuisance. In holding that wrecked cars in a yard in a residential subdivision constituted a nuisance, the Virginia Supreme Court noted that "[f]reedom from discomfort and annoyance while using land, which inevitably involves an element of personal tastes and sensitivities, is often as important to a person as freedom from physical interruption with use of the land itself." Foley v. Harris, 286 S.E.2d 186, 190 (Va. 1982). See also Justice Abrahamson's pioneering opinion in Prah v. Maretti, 108 Wis. 2d 223, 321 N.W.2d 182 (1982), holding that an interference with solar access may be a nuisance.

4. *Intentional versus unintentional conduct and balancing the equities in nuisance.* The Restatement (Second) of Torts defines "intentional conduct" as either an activity undertaken for the express purpose of causing harm or conduct that the defendant knows is substantially certain to cause harm (§825). Were the defendant's emissions in *Folmar* an intentional tort? Should a person be under a duty to find out if his activity will cause environmental disruption? Does it make sense to apply the intentional-unintentional distinction in environmental pollution cases?

Why did the court in *Folmar* say that the "primary question" was the reasonableness of the defendants' conduct? Except for reckless and abnormally dangerous or ultrahazardous conduct, to which strict liability applies, the Restatement and the cases indicate that liability depends on essentially the same balancing analysis in all cases. A defendant may be liable for intentional unreasonable conduct or for unintentional negligent conduct. Negligence exists if the defendant has not behaved in a way that protects the plaintiff from unreasonable risks, and reasonableness is determined by balancing the risks created against the social utility of the defendant's conduct. Note that the concept of fault permeates this determination. See Restatement (Second) §§282-284.

Section 827 of the Restatement (Second) of Torts states the factors to be considered in deciding if the defendant's intentional conduct is reasonable because the utility of his conduct outweighs the gravity of the harm to the plaintiff (a test set out in §826(a)):

> (a) the extent of the harm involved,
> (b) the character of the harm involved,
> (c) the social value which the law attaches to the type of use or enjoyment invaded,
> (d) the suitability of the particular use or enjoyment invaded to the character of the locality,
> (e) the burden on the person harmed of avoiding the harm.

Section 828 of the Restatement sets forth the factors to be considered in assessing the utility of the defendant's conduct:

> (a) the social value that the law attaches to the primary purpose of the conduct;
> (b) the suitability of the conduct to the character of the locality; and
> (c) the impracticability of preventing or avoiding the invasion.

Was the defendant's conduct in *Folmar* unreasonable under §§827 and 828? Suppose a defendant's intentional behavior was reasonable under this balancing analysis. Should the plaintiff nevertheless be compensated for any harm he suffers as the result of the defendant's activities? Since 1979, the Restatement (Second) states that an intentional invasion is unreasonable not only if under §826(a) the utility of the defendant's conduct is outweighed by the gravity of the plaintiff's harm, but also if "the harm caused by the conduct is serious and the financial burden of compensating for this and similar harm to others would not make the continuation of the conduct not feasible" (§826(b)). What do you think of this policy? If the harm is serious, should a high-utility concern compensate for any harm, whatever the financial price? Compare the §826(b) approach with that of strict liability, under which intentionally conducting a dangerous activity of high social value that causes unavoidable harm results in liability, without regard to a defendant enterprise's continuing financial viability. But see Rabin, Nuisance Law: Rethinking Fundamental Assumptions, 63 Va. L. Rev. 1299, 1317-1318 (1977).

What is the relevance of the defendant's violation of a statutory pollution standard in determining the reasonableness of his conduct? For a suggestion that the plaintiff in such cases should be relieved of the burden of proving that the defendant's conduct constitutes nuisance or negligence, see Note, Water Quality Standards in Private Nuisance Actions, 79 Yale L.J. 102 (1969).

5. *Defenses: coming to the nuisance and hypersensitivity.* In *Folmar,* can a case be made for allowing one plaintiff to recover but not the other, based on their dates of arrival in the community? What is the significance of coming to the nuisance? Coming to the nuisance is sometimes recognized as a defense, at least to the scale of the activity as it existed when the plaintiff purchased nearby property. Its defenders argue that the defense promotes the mitigation of damages (Baxter & Altree, Legal Aspects of Airport Noise, 15 J. Law & Econ. 1 (1972), and Ellickson, Alternatives to Zoning: Covenants, Nuisance Rules, and Fines as Land Use Controls, 40 U. Chi. L. Rev. 68, 758-761 (1973)) or that it promotes economic efficiency by allowing the prior appropriation of a right to use an area. Note, An Economic Analysis of Land Use Conflicts, 21 Stan. L. Rev. 293 (1969), and Rothbard, Law, Property Rights, and Air Pollution, 2 Cato J. 55, 76-79 (1982). Critics of the defense argue that it is inconsistent with the plaintiff's legitimate right to be free from substantial interference with the enjoyment of his property. Consider the language of a federal district court judge in rejecting the defense in an air pollution nuisance suit against a steel mill:

Sharon argues that the doctrine of "coming to the nuisance" bars any recovery by Plaintiffs. This assertion is premised on the fact that the coke works was in operation when Plaintiffs moved into their residences near the coke works and, therefore, Plaintiffs assumed the risk of living near the nuisance.

This argument is untenable. Sharon relies upon an outdated doctrine that has never been recognized in West Virginia and which has been rejected by the majority of jurisdictions in which it had been previously adopted. The only West Virginia case to discuss this doctrine is Richards v. Ohio River Railroad Co., 56 W. Va. 592, 49 S.E. 385 (1904). Though the defense of coming to the nuisance was not raised in that case the court nevertheless discussed the issue and flatly rejected it saying "[i]f one comes to a nuisance, that does not debar him in legal proceedings for harm from it, or to restrain it." 56 W. Va. at 593, 49 S.E. 385. Though this statement is technically dictum, this Court believes West Virginia courts would follow it inasmuch as it represents the modern view. See Restatement 2d Torts §840(d); Prosser, Law of Torts, §91 (4th Ed. 1971). As the Supreme Court of Florida stated in Lawrence v. Eastern Airlines, Inc., 81 So. 2d 632, 634 (Fla. 1955):

The majority view rejects the doctrine of coming to the nuisance as an absolute defense to a nuisance action. Support for the majority view is found in the argument that the doctrine is out of place in modern society where people often have no real choices as to whether or not they will reside in an area adulterated by air pollution. In addition, the doctrine is contrary to public policy in the sense that it permits a defendant to condemn surrounding land to endure a perpetual nuisance simply because he was in the area first. Another reason given for rejecting the doctrine is that the owner of land subject to a nuisance will either have to bring suit before selling his land in order to attempt to receive the full value of the land or reconcile himself to accepting a depreciated price for the land since no purchaser would be willing to pay full value for land subject to a nuisance against which he is barred from bringing an action. [Patrick v. Sharon Steel Corp., 549 F. Supp. 1259, 1267 (N.D.W. Va. 1982).]

Hypersensitive plaintiffs, as opposed to those of ordinary tastes and suscep-
tibilities, are also denied protection by nuisance law. See DeBorde v. St. Michael
& All Angels Church, 272 S.C. 490, 252 S.E.2d 876 (1978); Lynn Open Air
Theater, Inc. v. Sea Crest Cadillac-Pontiac, Inc., 1 Mass. App. 186, 294
N.E.2d 473 (1973); and Amphitheaters, Inc. v. Portland Meadows, 184 Or. 336,
198 P.2d 847 (1948). What is the justification for hypersensitivity as a defense
to a nuisance action? Is it consistent with the general principle of torts that the
tort feasor takes his victim as he finds him? Should it be reevaluated in the light
of the fact that most environmental laws are designed to protect hypersensitive
persons from low-level exposures to various pollutants? In addition to these defenses, statutes of limitation may always be pleaded by a defendant. See Annot.,
19 A.L.R. 4th 456 (1983).

6. *An economic analysis of nuisances.* Nuisance liability can be analyzed
in economic terms. A polluter would be found to have acted unreasonably or
negligently if the marginal damage caused by his pollution exceeds his marginal
costs to control the pollution. If injuries and abatement costs are equal or abatement costs are greater than injury costs, the defendant would not be found liable.
Damages would be computed to encourage the defendant to equate marginal
damage and abatement costs. R. Stewart & J. Krier, Environmental Law and
Policy 225 (1978). Defining fault in this fashion would underline the "immo-
rality" of using limited resources in a less than optimal manner and would establish efficiency as an ethical as well as an economic norm, but no court has
yet explicitly endorsed this approach. What practical problems do you foresee in
applying it? Would cost comparisons at the margin provide a useful check on
the rationality of courts' nuisance and negligence liability determinations? On
the economic incentive provided by damage awards to control pollution in the
future?

7. *Negligence.* Straight negligence suits are not often used in environmental law, but negligence is often alleged as one of several bases of liability. Conduct
which gives rise to strict liability will generally be negligent as well, see Sterling
v. Velsicol Chemical Corp., 647 F. Supp. 303, 316-317 (W.D. Tenn. 1986),
aff'd, 855 F.2d 1188, 1198 (6th Cir. 1988), but negligence can play an important
role in cases seeking to hold persons other than the facility operator liable, e.g.,
Philip Morris, Inc. v. Emerson, 368 S.E.2d 268 (Va. 1988) (negligent retention
of independent contractor). Moreover, an understanding of the basis of liability
for negligent conduct is fundamental to understanding all modern theories of
liability. In a famous formulation, Judge Learned Hand wrote that the duty of
care one owes to others is a function of three variables: the probability of injury
occurring at all, the magnitude of injury if it does occur, and the burden of
preventing the injury. Judge Hand said: "Possibly it serves to bring this notion
into relief to state it in algebraic terms: if the probability be called P; the injury
L; and the burden B; liability depends upon whether . . . $B < PL$." United States
v. Carroll Towing, 159 F.2d 169, 173 (2d Cir. 1947). The burden of avoidance
(B) grows with the social utility of the defendant's conduct. How often will the
risks (PL) of an environmentally degrading activity unintentionally undertaken

outweigh its benefits? Compare Judge Hand's formulation to those appearing in the cases in Chapter 5 interpreting the precautionary regulation statutes. Might an expanded use of res ipsa loquitur help an environmental plaintiff surmount the limitations of negligence as a basis for relief? See Katz, The Function of Tort Liability in Technology Assessment, 38 U. Cin. L. Rev. 587 (1969).

8. *Beyond nuisance: strict liability for defective products and abnormally dangerous activities.* Cities Service notes the greater acceptance of strict liability for abnormally dangerous activities between the first and the second Restatements of Torts, reflecting the gradual acceptance and expansion of the doctrine in American tort law. Under both Restatements, the danger must be impossible to eliminate, even with the utmost care. The second Restatement does narrow the doctrine somewhat by requiring that the activity be inappropriate to its locale. Yet extensions of the doctrine in recent decades have caused a minor revolution in tort law. In his famous concurring opinion in Escola v. Coca Cola Bottling Co., 24 Cal. 2d 453, 195 P.2d 436, 440 (1944), Justice Traynor endorsed the following policy:

> Even if there is no negligence, public policy demands that responsibility be fixed wherever it will most effectively reduce the hazards to life and health inherent in defective products. . . . The cost of an injury and the loss of time or health may be an overwhelming misfortune to the person injured, and a needless one, for the risk of injury can be insured by the manufacturer and distributed among the public as a cost of doing business. [195 P.2d at 440.]

Subsequent decisions have extended strict liability to virtually all links in the chain of marketing, distribution, purchase, and use so long as the product in question is defective or unreasonably dangerous. Strict liability also has been applied to abnormally dangerous activities when the defective product and the chain-of-marketing restrictions do not apply, e.g., Langan v. Valicopters, 88 Wash. 2d 855, 567 P.2d 218 (1977) (crop dusting company liable for damages because activity not in common usage, although 287 aircraft were used locally for this purpose).

See generally M. Shapo, Public Regulation of Dangerous Products (1980); Levy & Ursin, Tort Law in California: At the Crossroads, 67 Calif. L. Rev. 497 (1979); Schwartz, Understanding Products Liability, 67 Calif. L. Rev. 435 (1979); Ursin, Judicial Creativity and Tort Law, 49 Geo. Wash. L. Rev. 229 (1981).

Should the "abnormally dangerous activity" doctrine of the Restatement (Second) be applied in environmental damage suits? What types of harms might be plausibly reached? Are toxic substances injuries particularly good candidates? Injury from the escape of hazardous wastes from dumps? Are hazardous wastes "products"? Are hazardous substances use and waste disposal "common usages"? What weight should be given to their value to the community? Of what relevance is the appropriateness of the activity to the place where handling or disposal occurs? See Gregory, Trespass to Nuisance to Absolute Liability, 37 Va. L.

Rev. 359 (1951), and Keeton, Trespass, Nuisance and Strict Liability, 59 Colum. L. Rev. 457 (1959).

9. *Strict liability in environmental cases?* Recall the discussion of economic efficiency in Chapter 1, at pp. 35-39. Welfare economics suggests a rationale for holding defendants strictly liable for broad categories of environmental harms without case-by-case balancing under the factors listed in Restatement (Second) §520. First, a cardinal premise of microeconomic theory is that markets will efficiently allocate resources only if prices reflect all the costs of doing business. Unregulated and uncontrolled environmental externalities may be internalized in a rough-and-ready way through court-awarded damages. Fault-based liability requires that non-negligent, reasonable injury be borne not by those whose personal satisfaction is enhanced by the products purchased but by injured plaintiffs and the environment itself, whereas rigorous strict liability would shift these liquidated environmental costs to the defendant.

Second, as a result of cost internalization, disrupters of environmental quality would have a stronger incentive than under fault liability rules to compare the costs of damage payments with the costs of abating the environmental pollution by switching product lines (e.g., redesigning a product to eliminate a hazardous chemical) or by reducing the level of use of damaging product inputs and production processes. See Calabresi & Hirschoff, Toward a Test for Strict Liability in Tort, 81 Yale L.J. 1055 (1972), arguing that strict liability should be imposed upon the party best able to make a cost-benefit analysis between accident costs and accident avoidance costs and then to act on that analysis. Third, corrective justice requires compensation, whether or not efficiency is served. The doctrine of strict liability at its core reflects the judgment that even if some harm is inevitable, the social value of some enterprises is greater than their costs, but if an enterprise's benefits exceed its costs, fundamental fairness requires at least that profits be net of any harms inflicted. Fourth, strict liability is simply easier to apply. Courts and parties can reduce transactions costs by focusing on causation and the measure of damages and eliminating the inquiry into fault, contributory negligence, and (in most cases) social utility. Finally, and most important, in the eyes of the California Supreme Court automatic no-fault liability would practically ensure that enterprises would obtain liability insurance to cover any environmental disruption they might cause. Premiums would cause prices to rise exactly as damage awards would, and the primary beneficiaries of "enterprise pools," the customers, would again bear the costs, as economic theory contemplates.

What arguments can be mounted against universal imposition of strict liability? First, the economic efficiency argument for strict liability ignores an important point: the defendant's environmental degradation is an externality only because the law has decreed that the plaintiff has the legal right to the resource the defendant needs. Take air, for example. The plaintiff needs it for breathing and the defendant needs it for emissions. Nature decrees that joint, non-exclusive use cannot occur for long without one or the other suffering harm. Why should the defendant be obligated to internalize the plaintiff's cost of breathing any more than plaintiff should be obligated to internalize the costs of the defendant's continuing to pollute? Economic efficiency might be just as well served by vesting the right to pollute in the defendant. Second, not all externalities are negative. Industrial facilities almost invariably generate positive externalities (benefits not captured through product prices) such as employment, family health care, and participation in community activities. Imposing strict liability on the defendant may cause it to shut down or reduce operations, resulting in the loss of these positive externalities. Damages awards traditionally are not reduced by the amount of the defendants' cost-free contributions to the plaintiffs' welfare. The concept of actions by enterprises against communities to recoup positive externalities is, at best, fanciful. Third, under existing doctrine, strict liability might require the defendant to pay damages greater than the cost to plaintiff of avoiding the injury in the first place. This result would be less cost-effective than fault-based liability, under which contributory negligence and post-harm loss minimization requirements may apply. Finally, fairness cuts two ways. The triumph of fault over more punitive bases of liability in the nineteenth century, was viewed as a moral victory, see Epstein, A Theory of Strict Liability, 2 J. Legal Stud. 151 (1973) and Causation and Corrective Justice, 8 J. Legal Stud. 391 (1979), at least until fault-based liability emerged as a device for shifting some of the costs of industrial entrepreneurship to the worker and the public. M. Horowitz, The Transformation of American Law: 1780-1860 ch. 3 (1977).

Strict liability seems fairest when — as between a faultless profit-making enterprise and a faultless but injured natural person — the only issue is which should bear a loss the former has caused. But what should be done for the second plaintiff in *Folmar*, who knowingly bought a house near the defendants' 11-year-old coal-processing plant? Is his economic status relevant? Can a parallel be made between this plaintiff and Jordan Baker, a character in Fitzgerald's The Great Gatsby, an ethically suspect young woman who has the following conversation with the novel's protagonist, Nick Carraway:

> "You're a rotten driver," I protested. "Either you ought to be more careful, or you oughtn't to drive at all."
> "I am careful."
> "No, you're not."
> "Well, other people are," she said lightly.
> "What's that got to do with it?"
> "They'll keep out of my way," she insisted. "It takes two to make an accident."
> [F. Scott Fitzgerald, The Great Gatsby 59 (1925).]

What about plaintiffs who know how to, but do not, minimize their environmental injuries? Is there any danger that strict liability damage suits might become so attractive that they would become the environmental equivalent of giving blood for money?

Clearly, strict liability does not provide an obvious common law panacea to all environmental problems. If strict liability is only appropriate sometimes, when is it appropriate? See J. Krier & R. Stewart, Environmental Law and Policy

225-233 (1977); Calabresi & Hirschoff, Toward a Test for Strict Liability in Torts, 81 Yale L.J. 1055 (1972); Posner, Strict Liability: A Comment, 2 J. Legal Stud. 205 (1973). Which of the various common law liability theories canvassed above is most likely to minimize the sum of abatement, damage, avoidance, and transactions costs?

Under the influence of CERCLA, courts are beginning to hold waste disposers strictly liable for injuries caused by disposal. For example, Sterling v. Velsicol Chemical Corp., 647 F. Supp. 303 (W.D. Tenn. 1986), held a chemical company liable for leakage from a hazardous waste site on theories of negligence, nuisance, trespass, and strict liability. Velsicol's liability was upheld on appeal. 855 F.2d 1188 (6th Cir. 1988). But cf. Anderson v. Cryovac, Inc., 862 F.2d 910, 921-922 (1st Cir. 1988).

10. *Private versus public nuisance. Frady* must go back to the trial court. At trial, what will the plaintiffs have to prove to succeed in their nuisance claim? Suppose the nuisance is only a public one. *Frady* correctly states the test for public nuisance. Historically, public nuisances were first infringements of the rights of the Crown and subsequently constituted "a large, miscellaneous and diversified group of minor criminal offenses, all of which involved some interference with the interests of the community at large — interests that were recognized as rights of the general public entitled to protection." 4 Restatement (Second) of Torts 88 (1979). By the sixteenth century, individual tort action for damages caused by a public nuisance was recognized, but plaintiffs still had to establish that the defendant committed a criminal offense. It was not clear if this meant conduct proscribed by the state as criminal or that any conduct found to be a public nuisance was a crime either at common law or by statute. Section 821B of the Restatement (Second) liberalized the law by making proof of criminal conduct only one of several relevant factors to consider:

> (2) Circumstances that may sustain a holding that an interference with a public right is unreasonable include the following:
> (a) Whether the conduct involves a significant interference with the public health, the public safety, the public peace, the public comfort or the public convenience, or
> (b) whether the conduct is proscribed by a statute, ordinance or administrative regulation, or
> (c) whether the conduct is of a continuing nature or has produced a permanent or long-lasting effect, and, as the actor knows or has reason to know, has a significant effect upon the public right.

Traditionally, public nuisance actions could be brought by public officials except when, as *Frady* indicates, individual injury different in kind (not merely in degree) from the rest of the community could be shown. Wayne County v. Tennessee Solid Waste Disposal Control Board, 756 S.W.2d 274 (Tenn. App. 1988). See Rothstein, Private Actions for Public Nuisance — The Standing Problem, 76 W. Va. L. Rev. 453 (1976). Restatement (Second) of Torts §821C(2)(c) (1979) extends standing to persons with "standing to sue as a representative of the general public, or as a citizen in a citizen's action or as a member of a class in a class action," but only for injunctions. What policies would this liberalization serve? Should standing be extended to damage actions? Under the Restatement, the requirement for an ownership interest in land is relaxed, so that general environmental harm may be enjoined. The remaining requirements for private nuisance, however, must still be met. See Bryson & Macbeth, Public Nuisance, The Restatement (Second) of Torts, and Environmental Law, 2 Ecology L.Q. 241, 255-264 (1972). Is a manufacturer liable for nuisances caused by the use of a product after it is sold? See Bloomington v. Westinghouse Electric Corp. — F.2d — , 30 ERC 1801 (7th Cir. 1989).

2.   Causation: Multiple Defendants and Alternative, Concert-of-Action, Enterprise, and Market Share Liability

Under conventional common law doctrines, the plaintiff must prove cause in fact, and this is next to impossible to do in toxic torts cases. Generally, the plaintiff carries the burden of persuading the trier of fact (ordinarily a jury) that but for a specific defendant's conduct he, the plaintiff, would not have been injured or threatened with imminent harm. The necessity to prove cause in fact

> reflects commonly held assumptions about causation as well as certain moral and political notions of responsibility, [and] tends to dominate the disposition of tort claims. Moreover, this rendition of but for causation coincides neatly with that of corpuscularian science [a Newtonian belief in universal mechanical laws]. Probabilistic linkage is distinguished from but for cause, but has a nebulous role in Anglo-American reasoning. Probabilistic notions correspond to the causal notions that modern science employs in that they are based on probabilistic evidence rather than simple deductively derived causal chains. Legal scholars have generally not assumed the existence of a singular causal power, nor have they used probabilistic notions in analyses of causation, but rather they have relied on the policy-laden concept of proximate cause to identify the bearer of liability. [Brennan, Causal Chains And Scientific Links: The Role of Scientific Uncertainty in Hazardous-Substance Litigation, 73 Cornell L. Rev. 469, 490 (1989).]

For a review of the full range of thinking about the relationship between rights, responsibility and causation see Symposium, Causation in the Law of Torts, 63 Chi.-Kent L. Rev. 397-680 (1987).

Courts have sometimes broadened the "but for" causation test to permit recovery when it is impossible to eliminate all causes except a single defendant's conduct. If a defendant's conduct was a substantial factor in bringing about injury or threat of injury, as, for example, when two fires set separately by A and B converge to destroy the plaintiff's house (and either fire alone would have been sufficient), both A and B may be liable, e.g., Anderson v. Minneapolis, St. P. & S.S.M. Ry., 146 Minn. 430, 179 N.W. 45 (Minn. 1920). Surrounding circumstances conducive to injury ordinarily will not defeat a cause of action unless they significantly erode the status of the defendant's conduct as a substantial causal factor, e.g., Stubbs v. City of Rochester, 226 N.E. 516, 124 N.E. 137 (1919). The effect of the substantial factor test may be to shift the burden of producing contrary evidence on causation to a group of defendants. Causation presents the same problem, whether the relief sought is damages or prospective relief, although the risk of various future harms may be difficult to show.

In many situations of environmental injury, it is impossible to satisfy either the "but for" or the "substantial factor" test for causation, although it seems clear that injury to many persons resulted one way or the other from the conduct of a group of defendants. Harder environmental causation problems await you because cause is central to the problem of redressing injuries alleged to result from exposure to toxic substances. These problems will be examined shortly. But first consider this question: Does the following case offer a viable solution to the multiple plaintiffs and defendants in environmental damage actions?

SINDELL v. ABBOTT LABORATORIES
26 Cal. 3d 588, 163 Cal. Rptr. 132, 607 P.2d 924 (1980), *cert. denied*, 449 U.S. 912 (1980).

[Before 1971, the defendants marketed a miscarriage preventive drug, diethylstilbesterol (DES), which may cause vaginal and cervical cancer. In 1971, the Food and Drug Administration ordered that the drug be removed from the market. The plaintiff's mother took the drug, and as a result of exposure to the drug before birth the plaintiff developed a malignant bladder tumor, which was removed by surgery. The plaintiff continued to suffer from precancerous vaginal and cervical growths that had to be monitored constantly by biopsy or coloscopy and promptly removed to prevent adenocarcinomas, i.e., cancerous growths. The plaintiff sought damages on the theory that the defendants were jointly and individually liable for marketing the drug without adequate labeling, testing, or monitoring of its effects. She alleged that the defendants were jointly liable regardless of the brand of DES used because all the defendants collaborated in testing, promoting, and marketing the drug.

To prove cause in fact, the plaintiff suggested three theories of liability: (1) the rule of Summers v. Tice, 33 Cal. 2d 80, 199 P.2d 1 (1948), (2) acts in concert, and (3) enterprise liability. *Summers* holds that if two defendants act negligently toward a plaintiff but only one act causes injury, the burden of proof shifts to the defendants to absolve themselves if they can. The court rejected the *Summers* approach because it requires at least a reasonable possibility that each defendant was responsible for the injury. The plaintiff's concert-of-action theory was based on industry-wide use of the same test data, promotional devices, and marketing techniques. In rejecting this theory, the court found no "tacit understanding or a common plan among defendants to fail to conduct adequate tests or give adequate warnings." Enterprise liability was based on the industry-wide adoption of an inadequate safety standard. Hall v. E. I. Du Pont de Nemours & Co., 345 F. Supp. 353 (E.D.N.Y. 1972), holds that individual manufacturers may be liable in this situation without proof of individual responsibility for an injury. After discussing a student note, Comment, DES and a Proposed Theory of Enterprise Liability, 46 Fordham L. Rev. 963 (1978), the court declined to apply *Hall* for two reasons: There was insufficient cooperation in the 200-member drug industry, as compared with the 6-member blasting cap industry involved in *Hall*, and the industry's safety standards were largely set by the federal Food and Drug Administration.

The court nonetheless held that the plaintiff had stated a cause of action and adopted a fourth theory of liability. Relying on Justice Traynor's celebrated concurring opinion in Escola v. Coca Cola Bottling Co., 24 Cal. 2d 453, 150 P.2d 436 (1944), Justice Mosk concluded that the defendants were better able to bear the costs of injuries resulting from the manufacture of a defective product and that thus a modified expansion of *Summers* was warranted:]

In our contemporary complex industrialized society, advances in science and technology create fungible goods which may harm consumers and which cannot be traced to any specific producer. The response of the courts can be either to adhere rigidly to prior doctrine, denying recovery to those injured by such products, or to fashion remedies to meet these changing needs. Just as Justice Traynor in his landmark concurring opinion in Escola v. Coca Cola Bottling Co. (1944) 24 Cal. 2d 453, 467-468 (150 P.2d 436), recognized that in an era of mass production and complex marketing methods the traditional standard of negligence was insufficient to govern the obligations of manufacturer to consumer, so should we acknowledge that some adaptation of the rules of causation and liability may be appropriate in these recurring circumstances. The Restatement comments that modification of the *Summers* rule may be necessary in a situation like that before us.

The most persuasive reason for finding plaintiff states a cause of action is that advanced in *Summers*: as between an innocent plaintiff and negligent defendants, the latter should bear the cost of the injury. Here, as in *Summers*, plaintiff is not at fault in failing to provide evidence of causation, and although the absence of such evidence is not attributable to the defendants either, their conduct in marketing a drug the effects of which are delayed for many years played a significant role in creating the unavailability of proof.

From a broader policy standpoint, defendants are better able to bear the cost of injury resulting from the manufacture of a defective product. As was said by Justice Traynor in *Escola*, "[t]he cost of an injury and the loss of time or health may be an overwhelming misfortune to the person injured, and a needless one, for the risk of injury can be insured by the manufacturer and distributed among the public as a cost of doing business." (24 Cal. 2d p. 462; see also Rest. 2d Torts, §402A, com. c, pp. 349-350.) The manufacturer is in the best position to discover and guard against defects in its products and to warn of harmful effects; thus, holding it liable for defects and failure to warn of harmful effects will provide an incentive to product safety. These considerations are particularly significant where medication is involved, for the consumer is virtually helpless to protect himself from serious, sometimes permanent, sometimes fatal, injuries caused by deleterious drugs.

Where, as here, all defendants produced a drug from an identical formula and the manufacturer of the DES which caused plaintiff's injuries cannot be identified through no fault of plaintiff, a modification of the rule of *Summers* is warranted. As we have seen, an undiluted *Summers* rationale is inappropriate to shift the burden of proof of causation to defendants because if we measure the chance that any particular manufacturer supplied the injury-causing product by the number of producers of DES, there is a possibility that none of the five defendants in this case produced the offending substance and that the responsible manufacturer, not named in the action, will escape liability.

But we approach the issue of causation from a different perspective: we hold it to be reasonable in the present context to measure the likelihood that any of the defendants supplied the product which allegedly injured plaintiff by the percentage which the DES sold by each of them for the purpose of preventing miscarriage bears to the entire production of the drug sold by all for that purpose. Plaintiff asserts in her briefs that Eli Lilly and Company and 5 or 6 other companies produced 90 percent of the DES marketed. If at trial this is established to be the fact, then there is a corresponding likelihood that this comparative handful of producers manufactured the DES which caused plaintiff's injuries, and only a 10 percent likelihood that the offending producer would escape liability.

If plaintiff joins in the action the manufacturers of a substantial share of the DES which her mother might have taken, the injustice of shifting the burden of proof to defendants to demonstrate that they could not have made the substance which injured plaintiff is significantly diminished. While 75 to 80 percent of the market is suggested as the requirement by the Fordham Comment we hold only that a substantial percentage is required.

The presence in the action of a substantial share of the appropriate market also provides a ready means to apportion damages among the defendants. Each defendant will be held liable for the proportion of the judgment represented by its share of that market unless it demonstrates that it could not have made the product which caused plaintiff's injuries. In the present case, as we have seen, one DES manufacturer was dismissed from the action upon filing a declaration that it had not manufactured DES until after plaintiff was born. Once plaintiff has met her burden of joining the required defendants, they in turn may cross-complaint against other DES manufacturers, not joined in the action, which they can allege might have supplied the injury-causing product.

Under this approach, each manufacturer's liability would approximate its responsibility for the injuries caused by its own products. Some minor discrepancy in the correlation between market share and liability is inevitable; therefore, a defendant may be held liable for a somewhat different percentage of the damage than its share of the appropriate market would justify. It is probably impossible, with the passage of time, to determine market share with mathematical exactitude. But just as a jury cannot be expected to determine the precise relationship between fault and liability in applying the doctrine of comparative fault or partial indemnity, the difficulty of apportioning damages among the defendant producers in exact relation to their market share does not seriously militate against the rule we adopt.

NOTES AND QUESTIONS

1. Sindell's *Influence.*. Compare Collins v. Eli Lilly & Co., 116 Wis. 2d 166, 342 N.W.2d 37 (1984), *cert. denied sub. nom.*, E. R. Squibb & Sons v. Collins, 469 U.S. 826 (1984), which allowed a plaintiff to sue any manufacturer of DES without proof of which of several manufacturers caused the harm because they all "contributed to the *risk* of injury to the public." Plaintiff need only allege that her mother took DES, the defendant marketed the type of DES taken by her mother or simply that the defendant produced DES as an anti-miscarriage drug to shift the burden to the defendant that plaintiff's mother could not have taken a pill manufactured by the defendant. Washington adopted an approach similar to *Sindell*, but allowed the defendant to reduce his liability if it could prove its exact market share. Martin v. Abbott Laboratories, 102 Wash. 2d 581, 689 P.2d 368 (1984). New York adopted market share liability in Hymowitz v. Eli Lilly & Co., 73 N.Y.2d 485, 541 N.Y.S.2d 941, 539 N.E.2d 1069 (1988) *sub nom.* Rexall Drug Co. v. Tigue, *cert. denied*, 110 S. Ct. 350 (1989). Liability was based on the "overall culpability" of DES manufacturers measured by the amount of risk to the public at large created by the manufacture of a dangerous product. The Supreme Court declined the manufacturers' invitation to consider whether the absence of a reasonable link between liability and injury violates due process of law. *Sindell* has not, however, swept the country. Courts have expressed concern over the probability of disproportionate liability, Payton v. Abbott Laboratories, 386 Mass. 540, 437 N.E. 2d 171 (1982), the difficulty of defining substantial market share, Zafft v. Eli Lilly & Co., 676 S.W.2d 241 (Mo. 1984). The argument that market share liability imposes disproportionate liability on defendants is developed in Wright, Causation in Tort Law, 73 Calif. L. Rev. 1735 (1985). The development of the doctrine is well summarized in In re Agent Orange Products Liability Litigation, 597 F. Supp. 740, 819-828 (E.D. N.Y. 1984).

The concept of proportional recovery based on the probability that defendant's conduct harmed the plaintiff has been widely but not uniformly endorsed, e.g., Delgado, Beyond *Sindell*: Relaxation of Cause-in-Fact Rules for Indeterminate Plaintiffs, 70 Calif. L. Rev. 881 (1982); Robinson, Multiple Causation in Tort Law: Reflections on the DES Cases, 68 Va. L. Rev. 713 (1982); Ursin, Judicial Creativity and Tort Law, 49 Geo. Wash. L. Rev. 229 (1981); Note, Market Share Liability: An Answer to the DES Causation Problem, 94 Harv. L. Rev. 668 (1981); Note, Refining Market Share Liability: Sindell v. Abbott Laboratories, 33 Stan. L. Rev. 937 (1981). For application of the theories advanced in *Sindell* to the hazardous waste dump problem, see Superfund §301(e) Study

Group report, at 46-71. However, market share liability has been criticized as unworkable, Epstein, Two Fallacies in the Law of Joint Torts, 73 Geo. L.J. 1377 (1985). Farber, Toxic Causation, 71 Minn. L. Rev. 1219 (1987) proposes a "most likely victim approach." As with proportional recovery, defendants who create a risk of injury would be liable, but victims with the highest probability of injury would receive full compensation and those with the lowest would receive nothing.

Further useful reading includes Barnett, Five Issues of Causation and Proof, 2 Cato J. 157 (1982); Best & Collins, Legal Issues in Pollution-Engendered Torts, 2 Cato J. 101 (1982); Green, The Causal Relation Issue in Negligence Law, 60 Mich. L. Rev. 543 (1962); Malone, Ruminations on Cause-in-Fact, 9 Stan. L. Rev. 60 (1956); Note, Judicial Attitudes towards Legal and Scientific Proof of Cancer Causation, 3 Colum. J. Envtl. L. 344 (1977); Note, Tort Actions for Cancer: Deterrence, Compensation, and Environmental Carcinogenesis, 90 Yale L.J. 840, 851-855 (1981); Note, Causation in Toxic Torts: Burdens of Proof, Standards of Persuasion, and Statistical Evidence, 96 Yale L.J. 376 (1986); Rabin, Environmental Liability and the Tort System, 24 Hous. L. Rev. 27 (1987)

2. *Joint and several liability.* When the activities of several actors combine to cause cumulative harm, is joint and several liability efficient and fair? Does it overdeter wealthy defendants and underdeter financially insolvent ones? Does it matter if the standard is negligence versus strict liability? See Rosenberg, Joint and Several Liability for Toxic Torts, 15 J. Hazardous Materials 219 (1987) and Wright, Allocating Liability Among Multiple Responsible Causes: A Principled Defense of Joint and Several Liability For Actual Harm and Risk Exposure, 21 U.C. Davis L. Rev. 1141 (1988). For an example of a water pollution case applying the rule that if the plaintiffs can prove injury and liability in relation to several tort feasors the burden shifts to the defendants to prove the degree of individual responsibility, see Michie v. National Steel Corp., Great Lakes Steel Division, 495 F.2d 213 (6th Cir. 1974). *Michie* and other cases allocating liability among multiple tort feasors are discussed in Kornhauser and Revesz, Sharing Damages among Multiple Tortfeasors, 98 Yale L.J. 831 (1989) and Note, Joint and Several Liability for Hazardous Waste Releases under Superfund, 68 Va. L. Rev. 1157, 1166-1170 (1982). As part of the recent tort reform movement, many states that have adopted comparative negligence have eliminated joint and several liability. See Note, 1986 Tort Reform Legislation: A Systematic Evaluation of Caps on Damages and Limitations on Joint and Several Liability, 73 Cornell L. Rev. 628 (1988). See further Twerski, The Joint Tort Feasor Legislative Revolt: A Rational Response to the Critics, 22 U.C. Davis L. Rev. 1125 (1989) and Wright, Throwing out the Baby with the Bathwater: A Reply to Professor Twerski, id. at 1147, and Professor Twerski's rejoinder, The Baby Swallowed the Bathwater: A Rejoinder to Professor Wright, id. at 1161.

3. Sindell *and environmental litigation.* What utility, if any, might the theories advanced in *Sindell* have for plaintiffs in environmental damage suits? Can any of the theories advanced in *Sindell* be used to shift the burden of proof

to the defendants? More broadly, should *Sindell* be expanded to accommodate plaintiffs in a wide variety of environmental damage suits? If so, the California Supreme Court's decision in *Sindell* may be for causation what its 1940 decision in *Escola* was for strict product liability. Recall the court's remarks regarding risk spreading. Which social policies are well served, and which disserved, by expanding the *Sindell* approach? See generally, Calabresi, Concerning Cause and the Law of Torts: An Essay for Harry Kalven, Jr., 73 U. Chi. L. Rev. 69 (1975).

Assume the following facts. In the state in which a toxic waste site is located the number of cases (the rate of incidence) of liver cancer per 100,000 persons has remained at 20 a year for the past two decades. In and near the town of Bristol, 100,000 persons have ingested or inhaled at least trace quantities of the substances released from the waste site, and the incidence of liver cancer among this population is 23 cases. No cases of the rare blood disorder have occurred statewide in the past ten years, and the national incidence is .1 per 100,000. Studies have shown that the substances to which the plaintiffs were exposed are weakly carcinogenic, mutagenic, and teratogenic. Liver cancer can be caused by at least one of the carcinogens escaping from the site, and another has been implicated in causing the blood disorder of the type plaintiff has contracted. In the light of these facts, what problems in proving causation will the plaintiffs face in their common law action? How is their problem different from that of the plaintiffs in *Sindell*? Would it be unfair to shift the burden to the defendants to show they did not cause the plaintiffs' injuries?

Suppose plaintiff wins $1 million in damages for his cancer, largely because the courts shifted the burden of proof to the defendants. Shortly thereafter, 20 other persons suffering from liver cancer file suit alleging exposure to the same hazardous releases. Should the burden again shift, so that the defendants have to prove which cancers were not caused by them, and if liability is found, should each class member's damages be comparable to plaintiff's? Is possible overinclusivity of remedy the price society must pay to make sure that the few whose cancers were caused by a dump are compensated for? Would such a result convert tort law from a mechanism for the adjudication of individual conduct into a mass social compensation system? Perhaps private or governmental general health insurance should continue to alleviate this problem. Yet, in the hazardous waste context, what disadvantages does general insurance create?

If all persons suffering from liver cancer recover damages, what will be the impact on the defendants' incentives to reduce the production of dangerous chemicals? Engage in loss prevention and safety research? Compete in world markets?

Consider the approach to this problem adopted in the following model statute drafted by the Environmental Law Institute:

§202(b) Where one or more among a group of persons or factors has caused or contributed to the exposure of an individual to a hazardous chemical substance or mixture, which exposure caused or contributed to a covered disease [one of the chronic hazardous waste-oriented diseases for which this statute authorizes compensation] in an individual, but the court determines that it is unreasonable and impractical for the individual to determine which persons or agents within the group have caused or have been a substantial factor in causing the covered disease, each joined person may be held liable for a share of the damages to the harmed individual which is proportionate to the risk, according to the best reasonably available estimates, that such person caused the covered disease, as compared with all persons or factors in the group, whether or not all such persons among the group are joined before the court. Provided that, in apportioning the damages among the various persons and factors, the trier of fact shall not consider the contributions to risk due to the conduct of . . . [the defendants' employees or agents or] the harmed individual, unless

   (i) the risk of such covered disease to the harmed individual resulted from the reckless, willful, or wanton misconduct of such individual; or

   (ii) the individual acted knowingly and voluntarily in encountering the risk of that particular form of covered disease from the hazardous chemical substance or mixture in question. In making this determination the trier of fact shall take the following factors into account:

    (aa) the amount and quality of information communicated to the individual concerning the specific risk involved, including such information that expressly or impliedly deemphasizes such risk;

    (bb) the ability of the individual to appreciate the risk involved from such information in light of the intelligence, understanding, comprehension, and judgment that the individual may be expected to possess under the circumstances; and

    (cc) whether it is fair under the particular circumstances to expect the individual to act upon that information to avoid or mitigate the risk of such covered disease.

[Trauberman, Statutory Reform of Toxic Torts: Relieving Legal, Scientific, and Economic Burdens on the Chemical Victim, 7 Harv. Envtl. L. Rev. 177, 260-261 (1983).]

Is this the correct way to resolve the overcompensation problem? The problems of the plaintiffs' assumption of risk or of contributory negligence? Under the model statute's approach, if the defendants in a toxic torts case were held liable, the amount of damages would be determined by dividing the total damage each plaintiff sustained by the number of persons who have been exposed and who have been determined from epidemiological data to be likely to contract liver cancer. For example, assume that about 100,000 local persons have been chronically exposed to the site's air and water pollution, that reliable epidemiological studies show that the nationwide "background" incidence of liver cancer cases is 20 per 100,000 persons and that chronic exposure to chemical compounds of the type escaping from the site is likely to increase the number of liver cancer cases by 3 per 100,000 persons exposed. (Thus, it is reasonable to conclude that there is a 13 percent probability that any particular individual's liver cancer was caused by the site. Do you see why?) Assume also that plaintiff's damages are determined to be $1 million. Under the model statute, plaintiff would actually recover just over $130,000. The rationale is that although three of the cancer cases that may occur would probably be caused by the defendant's releases, the court cannot identify which three with certainty. All victims who may come forward would have an equally plausible case. To allow all victims to recover their full damages would require the defendants to pay many times the damage they actually caused. Do you agree with this approach? See Posner, An Economic Approach to Legal Procedure and Judicial Administration, 2 J. Legal Stud. 399, 410 (1973). See also Rizzo & Arnold, Causal Apportionment in the Law of Torts: An Economic Theory, 80 Colum. L. Rev. 1399 (1980). Compare Note, Toxic Substance Contamination: The Risk-Benefit Approach to Causation Analysis, 14 J.L. Reform 53 (1980).

4. *The discovery rule.* A plaintiff who does prove a causal connection between exposure to a toxic substance and a resulting injury may still find that his action is barred by an applicable statute of limitations because cancer, neurological damage, and mutagenic and teratogenic injuries may have long latency periods. At common law, a cause of action accrues as of the date of the tort, but this rule is all but dead. States now follow a "discovery" rule. See Report on Statutes of Limitation Applicable to Actions Arising out of Hazardous Waste Disposal, in Superfund §301(e) Study Group, Injuries and Damages from Hazardous Wastes — Analysis and Improvement of Legal Remedies, 97th Cong., 2d Sess. (hereinafter cited as §301(e) Study Group report), Part 2 Appendices, at 13-77 (Comm. Print 1982), for a state-by-state survey of the statutes. New York was the last major state to adhere to the common law, but it adopted a discovery rule in 1986, CPLR §214-c. SARA, see p. 615, Chapter 5, *supra*, adopts a federal discovery rule for personal injury or property caused or contributed to by an exposure to a release from a facility covered by the Act. 42 U.S.C. §9658. The standard is whether the plaintiff knew or should have known that the injury or damage was caused in whole or in part by exposure to the release. Some discovery rules may still pose burdens for plaintiffs. For example, in some states the cause of action accrues when the plaintiff knows or should have known in the exercise of reasonable judgment that he has suffered a disease or injury, e.g., Conn. Gen. Stat. Ann. §§52-584. In other states, the plaintiff must not only discover the fact of an injury or disease but must discover or should discover its cause through the exercise of reasonable diligence. See, e.g., Warrington v. Charles Pfizer & Co., 274 Cal. App. 2d 564, 80 Cal. Rptr. 130 (1969); Witherell v. Weimer, 77 Ill. App. 3d 582, 396 N.E.2d 268 (1979); Dalton v. Dow Chemical Co., 280 Minn. 147, 158 N.W.2d 580 (1968). Suppose a California plaintiff discovers that she has a precancerous condition in 1972 caused by her mother's ingestion of DES. Between 1972 and 1978 plaintiff tries to discover the manufacturer, but the prescribing doctor has died. In 1978 plaintiff has a hysterectomy. Plaintiff does not file an action until after *Sindell*. California has a one-year statute of limitation plus the above described discovery rule. Is the suit barred? See Jolly v. Eli Lilly & Co., 44 Cal. 3d 1103, 245 Cal. Rptr. 658, 751 P.2d 923 (1988). Some 13 states, most notably Louisiana and New Jersey, toll the statute until the plaintiff realizes or should have realized both that he has been injured and that he has a cause of action against the entity that injured him, e.g., Graves

v. Church & Dwight Co., 115 N.J. 256, 558 A.2d 463 (1989); Anthony v. Abbott Laboratories, 490 A.2d 43 (R.I. 1985); Moran v. Napolitana, 71 N.J. 133, 363 A.2d 346 (1976).

AYERS v. JACKSON TOWNSHIP
106 N.J. 557, 525 A.2d 287 (1987)

[Three hundred and thirty-nine plaintiffs sued a township for injuries allegedly caused by contamination of an aquifer from a landfill. The jury returned a verdict for plaintiffs in the amount of $15,854,392.78 for impairment of the quality of life, emotional distress, and increased risk of cancer. The appellate division sustained the quality of life portion but set aside the damage award for emotional distress and the medical surveillance expenses for the increased cancer risk. The New Jersey Supreme Court sustained the quality of life award as pain and suffering but affirmed the reversal of the award for the other two categories. With respect to increased risk, the court wrote:]

I

Our evaluation of the enhanced risk and medical surveillance claims requires that we focus on a critical issue in the management of toxic tort litigation: at what stage in the evolution of a toxic injury should tort law intercede by requiring the responsible party to pay damages? . . . In the absence of statutory or administrative mechanisms for processing injury claims resulting from environmental contamination, courts have struggled to accommodate common-law tort doctrines to the peculiar characteristics of toxic-tort litigation. The overwhelming conclusion of the commentators who have evaluated the result is that the accommodation has failed, that common-law tort doctrines are ill-suited to the resolution of such injury claims, and that some form of statutorily-authorized compensation procedure is required if the injuries sustained by victims of chemical contamination are to be fairly redressed. See Ginsberg & Weiss, Common Law Liability for Toxic Torts: A Phantom Remedy, 9 Hofstra L. Rev. 859, 920-30 (1981) (hereinafter Ginsberg & Weiss); Rosenberg, "The Causal Connection in Mass Exposure Cases: A 'Public Law' Vision of the Tort System, 97 Harv. L. Rev. 851, 855-59 (1984) (hereinafter Rosenberg); Trauberman, Statutory Reform of 'Toxic Torts': Relieving Legal, Scientific, and Economic Burdens on the Chemical Victim, 7 Harv. Envtl. L. Rev. 177, 188-202 (1983) (hereinafter Trauberman); Developments in the Law — Toxic Waste Litigation, 99 Harv. L. Rev. 1458, 1602-31 (1986) (hereinafter "Developments — Toxic Waste); Note, The Inapplicability of Traditional Tort Analysis to Environmental Risks: The Example of Toxic Waste Pollution Victim Compensation, 35 Stan. L. Rev. 575, 581-88 (1983) (hereinafter Note, Traditional Tort Analysis). . . .

Although state statutes of limitations are invariably identified as procedural obstacles to mass exposure litigation, the extent of the problem posed by such statutes varies widely among jurisdictions. . . . CERCLA now pre-empts state statutes of limitation where they provide that the limitations period for personal-injury or property-damage suits prompted by exposure to hazardous substances starts on a date earlier than the "federally required commencement date." That term is defined as "the date plaintiff knew (or reasonably should have known) that the personal injury or property damages . . . were caused or contributed to by the hazardous substance . . . concerned." Superfund Amendments and Authorization Act of 1986, Pub. L. No. 99-499, 100 Stat. 1613, 1695-96, codified at 42 U.S.C.A. §9658 (West Supp. 1987).

The single controversy rule "requires that a party include in the action all related claims against an adversary and its failure to do so precludes the maintenance of a second action." Aetna Insurance Co. v. Gilchrist Brothers, Inc., 85 N.J. 550, 556-57, 428 A.2d 1254 (1981). The doctrine may bar recovery where, as here, suit is instituted to recover damages to compensate for the immediate consequences of toxic pollution, but the initiation of additional litigation depends upon when, if ever, physical injuries threatened by the pollution are manifested. . . .

. . . We concur with the principle advanced by the trial court, 189 N.J. Super. at 568, 461 A.2d 184, and endorsed by other federal and state courts, see Hagerty v. L & L Marine Servs., Inc., 788 F.2d 315, 320-21 (5th Cir.), *modified on other grounds*, 797 F.2d 256 (5th Cir. 1986); Eagle-Picher Indus. v. Cox, 481 So. 2d 517, 519-21 (Fla. Dist. Ct. App. 1985), that neither the statute of limitations nor the single controversy rule should bar timely causes of action in toxic-tort cases instituted after discovery of a disease or injury related to tortious conduct, although there has been prior litigation between the parties of different claims based on the same tortious conduct. . . .

By far the most difficult problem for plaintiffs to overcome in toxic tort litigation is the burden of proving causation. . . . Ordinarily, proof of causation requires the establishment of a sufficient nexus between the defendant's conduct and the plaintiff's injury. In toxic tort cases, the task of proving causation is invariably made more complex because of the long latency period of illnesses caused by carcinogens or other toxic chemicals. The fact that ten or twenty years or more may intervene between the exposure and the manifestation of disease highlights the practical difficulties encountered in the effort to prove causation. Moreover, the fact that segments of the entire population are afflicted by cancer and other toxically-induced diseases requires plaintiffs, years after their exposure, to counter the argument that other intervening exposures or forces were the "cause" of their injury. . . .

. . . The legal issue we must resolve, in the context of the jury's determination of defendant's liability under the Act, is whether the proof of an unquantified enhanced risk of illness or a need for medical surveillance is sufficient to justify compensation under the Tort Claims Act. In view of the acknowledged

difficulties of proving causation once evidence of disease is manifest, a determination of the compensability of post-exposure, pre-symptom injuries is particularly important in assessing the ability of tort law to redress the claims of
plaintiffs in toxic-tort litigation.

II

Much of the same evidence was material to both the enhanced risk and medical
surveillance claims. Dr. Dan Raviv, a geohydrologist, testified as to the movements and concentrations of the various chemical substances as they migrated
from the landfill toward plaintiffs' wells. Dr. Joseph Highland, a toxicologist,
applied Dr. Raviv's data and gave testimony concerning the level of exposure of
various plaintiffs. Dr. Highland also compiled toxicity profiles of the chemical
substances found in the wells, and testified concerning the health hazards posed
by the chemicals and the exposure levels at which adverse health effects had
been experimentally observed. According to Dr. Highland, four of the chemicals
were known to be carcinogenic, and at least four of the chemicals were capable
of adversely affecting the reproductive system or causing birth defects. Most of
the chemical substances could produce adverse effects on the liver and kidney,
as well as on the nervous system. For at least six of the chemicals, no data was
available regarding carcinogenic potential. He also testified that the exposure to
multiple chemical substances posed additional hazards to plaintiffs because of
the possibility of biological interaction among the chemicals that enhanced the
risk to plaintiffs.

   Dr. Highland testified that the Legler area residents, because of their exposure to toxic chemicals, had an increased risk of cancer; that unborn children
and infants were more susceptible to the disease because of their immature biological defense systems; and that the extent of the risk was variable with the
degree of exposure to the chemicals. Dr. Highland testified that *he could not
quantify the extent of the enhanced risk of cancer* because of the lack of scientific
information concerning the effect of the interaction of the various chemicals to
which plaintiffs were exposed. However, the jury could reasonably have inferred
from his testimony that the risk, although unquantified, was medically significant.

   Dr. Susan Daum, a physician affiliated with the Mount Sinai Hospital in
New York and specializing in the diagnosis and treatment of diseases induced by
toxic substances, testified that plaintiffs required a program of regular medical
surveillance. Acknowledging her reliance on the report of Dr. Highland, Dr.
Daum stated that plaintiffs' exposure to chemicals had produced "a reasonable
likelihood that they have now or will develop health consequences from this
exposure." . . .

   Although both the enhanced risk and medical surveillance claims are
based on Dr. Highland's testimony, supplemented by Dr. Daum's testimony in
the case of the surveillance claim, these claims seek redress for the invasion of

distinct and different interests. The enhanced risk claim seeks a damage award, not because of any expenditure of funds, but because plaintiffs contend that the unquantified injury to their health and life expectancy should be presently compensable, even though no evidence of disease is manifest. Defendant does not dispute the causal relationship between the plaintiffs' exposure to toxic chemicals and the plaintiffs' increased risk of diseases, but contends that the probability that plaintiffs will actually become ill from their exposure to chemicals is too remote to warrant compensation under principles of tort law.

By contrast, the claim for medical surveillance does not seek compensation for an unquantifiable injury, but rather seeks specific monetary damages measured by the cost of periodic medical examinations. The invasion for which redress is sought is the fact that plaintiffs have been advised to spend money for medical tests, a cost they would not have incurred absent their exposure to toxic chemicals. Defendant contends that the claim for medical surveillance damages cannot be sustained, as a matter of law, if the plaintiffs' enhanced risk of injury is not sufficiently probable to be compensable. In our view, however, recognition of the medical surveillance claim is not necessarily dependent on recognition of the enhanced risk claim.

III

The trial court declined to submit to the jury the issue of defendant's liability for the plaintiffs' increased risk of contracting cancer, kidney or liver damage, or other diseases associated with the chemicals that had migrated from the landfill to their wells. If the issue had not been withheld, the jury could have concluded from the evidence that most or all of the plaintiffs had a significantly but unquantifiably enhanced risk of the identified diseases, and that such enhanced risk was attributable to defendant's conduct.

A preliminary question is whether a significant exposure to toxic chemicals resulting in an enhanced risk of disease is an "injury" for the purposes of the Tort Claims Act. The Act defines injury to include "damage to or loss of property or any other injury that a person may suffer that would be actionable if inflicted by a private person." N.J.S.A. 59:1-3. We also note that the Restatement defines "injury" as "the invasion of any legally protected interest of another." Restatement (Second) of Torts §7(1) (1965):

> The word "injury" is used . . . to denote the fact that there has been an invasion of a legally protected interest which, if it were the legal consequence of a tortious act, would entitle the person suffering the invasion to maintain an action of tort. . . . The most usual form of injury is the infliction of some harm, but there may be an injury although no harm is done. [Id., Comment a.]

In our view, an enhanced risk of disease caused by significant exposure to toxic chemicals is clearly an "injury" under the Act. . . .

Except for a handful of cases involving traumatic torts causing presently discernible injuries in addition to an enhanced risk of future injuries, courts have generally been reluctant to recognize claims for potential but unrealized injury unless the proof that the injury will occur is substantial. . . .

Among the recent toxic tort cases rejecting liability for damages based on enhanced risk is Anderson v. W. R. Grace & Co., 628 F. Supp. 1219 (D. Mass. 1986). That case, recently settled for an undisclosed amount, see N.Y. Times, Sept. 23, 1986, at A16, col. 1, involved defendants' alleged chemical contamination of the groundwater in areas of Woburn, Massachusetts. See generally P. DiPerna, Cluster Mystery: Epidemic and the Children of Woburn, Mass. (1985) (containing background information on the Woburn case). Plaintiffs alleged that two wells supplying water to the City of Woburn drew upon the contaminated water, and that exposure to the contaminated water caused five deaths and severe personal injuries among plaintiffs. Among the claims for personal injuries dismissed before trial were plaintiff's claims for damages based on enhanced risk. Relying on the Massachusetts rule regarding prospective damages, the Anderson court reasoned that "recovery depends on establishing a 'reasonable probability' that the harm will occur." Id. at 1231 (citing Restatement (Second) of Torts §912 comment e). However, the Anderson court held that the plaintiffs failed to satisfy this threshold standard. They had not quantified their alleged enhanced risk: "Nothing in the present record indicates the magnitude of the increased risk or the diseases which plaintiffs may suffer." Id.

The court in Anderson explained that its reluctance to recognize the enhanced risk claims was based on two policy considerations. Its first concern was that recognition of the cause of action would create a flood of speculative lawsuits. Id. at 1232. In addition, the court stated:

> A further reason for denying plaintiffs' damages for the increased risk of future harm in this action is the inevitable inequity which would result if recovery were allowed. "To award damages based on a mere mathematical probability would significantly undercompensate those who actually do develop cancer and would be a windfall to those who do not." [Id., quoting Arnett v. Dow Chem. Corp., No. 729586, slip op. at 15 (Cal. Super. Ct. Mar. 21, 1983).]

The majority of courts that have considered the enhanced risk issue have agreed with the disposition of the District Court in Anderson. . . .

Other courts have acknowledged the propriety of the enhanced risk cause of action, but have emphasized the requirement that proof of future injury be reasonably certain. . . .

Additionally, several courts have permitted recovery for increased risk of disease, but only where the plaintiff exhibited some present manifestation of disease. See Jackson v. Johns-Manville Sales Corp., 781 F.2d 394, 412-13 (5th Cir.) (allowing recovery for increased risk of cancer where evidence indicated that due to asbestos exposure, plaintiff had greater than fifty percent chance of contracting cancer; "[o]nce the injury becomes actionable — once *some* effect appears — then the plaintiff is permitted to recover for all probable future manifestations as well"), *cert. denied,* — U.S. —, 106 S. Ct. 3339, 92 L. Ed. 2d 743 (1986). . . .

We observe that the overwhelming weight of the scholarship on this issue favors a right of recovery for tortious conduct that causes a significantly enhanced risk of injury. Gale & Goyer, "Recovery for Cancerphobia and Increased Risk of Cancer," 15 Cumb. L. Rev. 723 (1985); Ginsberg & Weiss, *supra,* 9 Hofstra L. Rev. 859; Rosenberg, *supra,* 97 Harv. L. Rev. 849; Trauberman, *supra,* 7 Harv. Envtl. L. Rev. 177; Note, Personal Injury Hazardous Waste Litigation: A Proposal for Tort Reform, 10 B.C. Envtl. Aff. L. Rev. 797 (1982-1983); Note, Increased Risk of Cancer as an Actionable Injury, 18 Ga. L. Rev. 563 (1984); Note, Traditional Tort Analysis, *supra,* 35 Stan L. Rev. 575; Note, Increased Risk of Disease From Hazardous Waste: A Proposal for Judicial Relief, 60 Wash. L. Rev. 635 (1985). For the most part, the commentators concede the inadequacy of common-law remedies for toxic-tort victims. Instead, they recommend statutory or administrative mechanisms that would permit compensation to be awarded on the basis of exposure and significant risk of disease, without the necessity of proving the existence of present injury.

Our disposition of this difficult and important issue requires that we choose between two alternatives, each having a potential for imposing unfair and undesirable consequences on the affected interests. A holding that recognizes a cause of action for unquantified enhanced risk claims exposes the tort system, and the public it serves, to the task of litigating vast numbers of claims for compensation based on threats of injuries that may never occur. It imposes on judges and juries the burden of assessing damages for the risk of potential disease, without clear guidelines to determine what level of compensation may be appropriate. It would undoubtedly increase already escalating insurance rates. It is clear that the recognition of an "enhanced risk" cause of action, particularly when the risk is unquantified, would generate substantial litigation that would be difficult to manage and resolve.

Our dissenting colleague, arguing in favor of recognizing a cause of action based on an unquantified claim of enhanced risk, points out that "courts have not allowed the difficulty of quantifying injury to prevent them from offering compensation for assault, trespass, emotional distress, invasion of privacy or damage to reputation." Although lawsuits grounded in one or more of these causes of action may involve claims for damages that are difficult to quantify, such damages are awarded on the basis of events that have occurred and can be proved at the time of trial. In contrast, the compensability of the enhanced risk claim depends upon the likelihood of an event that has not yet occurred and may never occur — the contracting of one or more diseases the risk of which has been enhanced by defendant's conduct. It is the highly contingent and speculative quality of an unquantified claim based on enhanced risk that renders it novel and difficult to manage and resolve. If such claims were to be litigated, juries would be asked to award damages for the enhanced risk of a disease that may never be contracted, without the benefit of expert testimony sufficient to establish the likelihood that the contingent event will ever occur.

On the other hand, denial of the enhanced-risk cause of action may mean that some of these plaintiffs will be unable to obtain compensation for their injury. Despite the collateral estoppel effect of the jury's finding that defendant's wrongful conduct caused the contamination of plaintiffs' wells, those who contract diseases in the future because of their exposure to chemicals in their well water may be unable to prove a causal relationship between such exposure and their disease. We have already adverted to the substantial difficulties encountered by plaintiffs in attempting to prove causation in toxic tort litigation. Dismissal of the enhanced risk claims may effectively preclude any recovery for injuries caused by exposure to chemicals in plaintiffs' wells because of the difficulty of proving that injuries manifested in the future were not the product of intervening events or causes. . . .

In deciding between recognition or non-recognition of plaintiffs' enhanced-risk claim, we feel constrained to choose the alternative that most closely reflects the legislative purpose in enacting the Tort Claims Act. We are conscious of the admonition that in construing the Act courts should "exercise restraint in the acceptance of novel causes of action against public entities." Comment, N.J.S.A. 59:2-1. In our view, the speculative nature of an unquantified enhanced risk claim, the difficulties inherent in adjudicating such claims, and the policies underlying the Tort Claims Act argue persuasively against the recognition of this cause of action. Accordingly, we decline to recognize plaintiffs' cause of action for the *unquantified* enhanced risk of disease, and affirm the judgment of the Appellate Division dismissing such claims. We need not and do not decide whether a claim based on enhanced risk of disease that is supported by testimony demonstrating that the onset of the disease is reasonably probable, see Coll v. Sherry, *supra*, 29 N.J. at 175, 148 A.2d 481, could be maintained under the Tort Claims Act.

IV

The claim for medical surveillance expenses stands on a different footing from the claim based on enhanced risk. It seeks to recover the cost of periodic medical examinations intended to monitor plaintiffs' health and facilitate early diagnosis and treatment of disease caused by plaintiffs' exposure to toxic chemicals. . . .

. . . It is inequitable for an individual, wrongfully exposed to dangerous toxic chemicals but unable to prove that disease is likely, to have to pay his own expenses when medical intervention is clearly reasonable and necessary. In other contexts, we have intervened to provide compensation for medical expenses even where the underlying disease was not compensable. In Procanik by Procanik v. Cillo, 97 N.J. 339, 478 A.2d 755 (1984), an action for "wrongful birth," we allowed compensation for medical expenses but disallowed the claims for pain and suffering and for a diminished childhood attributable to birth defects. In Schroeder v. Perkel, 87 N.J. 53, 432 A.2d 834 (1981), we upheld the claim of parents for incremental medical costs associated with raising a child who suffers from cystic fibrosis, without recognizing a "wrongful birth" cause of action based on that condition.

We find a helpful analogy in Reserve Mining Co. v. E.P.A., 514 F.2d 492 (8th Cir. 1975), where the issue was whether to grant injunctive relief compelling defendant to cease discharging wastes from its iron ore processing plant into the air of Silver Bay, Minnesota, and the waters of Lake Superior. . . .

Accordingly, we hold that the cost of medical surveillance is a compensable item of damages where the proofs demonstrate, through reliable expert testimony predicated upon the significance and extent of exposure to chemicals, the toxicity of the chemicals, the seriousness of the diseases for which individuals are at risk, the relative increase in the chance of onset of disease in those exposed, and the value of early diagnosis, that such surveillance to monitor the effect of exposure to toxic chemicals is reasonable and necessary. In our view, this holding is thoroughly consistent with our rejection of plaintiffs' claim for damages based on their enhanced risk of injury. That claim seeks damages for the impairment of plaintiffs' health, without proof of its likelihood, extent, or monetary value. In contrast, the medical surveillance claim seeks reimbursement for the specific dollar costs of periodic examinations that are medically necessary notwithstanding the fact that the extent of plaintiffs' impaired health is unquantified.

We find that the proofs in this case were sufficient to support the trial court's decision to submit the medical surveillance issue to the jury, and were sufficient to support the jury's verdict.

V

The medical surveillance issue was tried as if it were a conventional claim for compensatory damages susceptible to a jury verdict in a lump sum. The jury was so instructed by the trial court, and neither plaintiffs' nor defendant's request to charge on this issue sought a different instruction.

In the Appellate Division, defendant argued for the first time that a lump-sum damage award for medical surveillance was inappropriate. Defendant contended that if the court were to uphold all or any part of the medical surveillance award, it should "create an actuar[i]ally-sound fund, to which the plaintiffs may apply in the future for the cost of medical surveillance upon proof that those costs are not otherwise compensable . . . or after deduction of the amounts so reimbursed," and should leave to the trial court, on remand, the task of establishing "details of the creation and supervision of such a fund." Defendant contends that use of a fund to disburse medical surveillance benefits is particularly suitable for claims against public entities because of the requirements of the Tort Claims Act that judgments be reduced by the amount of payments from collateral sources. N.J.S.A. 59:9-2(e).

The indeterminate nature of damage claims in toxic-tort litigation suggests that the use of court-supervised funds to pay medical-surveillance claims as they accrue, rather than lump-sum verdicts, may provide a more efficient mechanism for compensating plaintiffs. A funded settlement was used in the Agent Orange litigation. In re "Agent Orange" Prod. Liab. Litig., 611 F. Supp. 1396, 1399 (E.D.N.Y. 1985), aff'd, 818 F.2d 194 (2d Cir. 1987). The use of insurance to fund future medical claims is frequently recommended by commentators. Ginsberg & Weiss, supra, 9 Hofstra L. Rev. at 928-40; Rosenberg, supra, 97 Harv. L. Rev. at 919-24; Trauberman, supra, 7 Harv. Envt'l L. Rev. at 237-46; Note, "Traditional Tort Analysis," supra, 35 Stan. L. Rev. at 614-16; Note, "Increased Risk of Disease from Hazardous Waste: A Proposal for Judicial Relief," supra, 60 Wash. L. Rev. at 648-52.

After oral argument we requested supplemental briefs from the parties on this issue. Plaintiffs contend that medical surveillance expenses are a customary item of compensatory damages; that a fund remedy would be unfair to plaintiffs and would impose severe administrative problems; and that the fund remedy might prove more expensive for defendants since improvements in medical technology could increase the long-term costs of medical surveillance. Defendant contends that a fund mechanism would insure that plaintiffs actually use the money for medical surveillance and would also provide a mechanism for crediting defendant with payments from collateral sources, as required by the Tort Claims Act.

In our view, the use of a court-supervised fund to administer medical-surveillance payments in mass exposure cases, particularly for claims under the Tort Claims Act, is a highly appropriate exercise of the Court's equitable powers. . . . Such a mechanism offers significant advantages over a lump-sum verdict. For Tort Claims Act cases, it provides a method for offsetting a defendant's liability by payments from collateral sources. Although the parties in this case sharply dispute the availability of insurance coverage for surveillance-type costs, a fund could provide a convenient method for establishing credits in the event insurance benefits were available for some, if not all, of the plaintiffs.

In addition, a fund would serve to limit the liability of defendants to the amount of expenses actually incurred. A lump-sum verdict attempts to estimate future expenses, but cannot predict the amounts that actually will be expended for medical purposes. Although conventional damage awards do not restrict plaintiffs in the use of money paid as compensatory damages, mass-exposure toxic-tort cases involve public interests not present in conventional tort litigation. The public health interest is served by a fund mechanism that encourages regular medical monitoring for victims of toxic exposure. Where public entities are defendants, a limitation of liability to amounts actually expended for medical surveillance tends to reduce insurance costs and taxes, objectives consistent with the legislature's admonition to avoid recognition of novel causes of action. Comment, N.J.S.A. 59:2-1. . . .

However, we decline to upset the jury verdict awarding medical-surveillance damages in this case. Such a result would be unfair to these plaintiffs, since the medical-surveillance issue was tried conventionally, and neither party requested the trial court to withhold from the jury the power to return a lump-sum verdict for each plaintiff in order that relief by way of a fund could be provided. Moreover, the jury verdict for medical-surveillance damages was based, as was the verdict for plaintiffs' other claims, on various factors distinguishing the individual plaintiffs, including age, and duration and extent of exposure to toxic chemicals. Accordingly, the verdict for medical-surveillance damages was in a specific amount for each of the plaintiffs, thereby limiting in this case the applicability of the fund concept, which contemplates an aggregate lump-sum award available to reimburse the medical-surveillance expenses of any plaintiff, without the constraint of individually-allocated limitations. We also recognize that the fund mechanism that we now endorse in toxic-tort cases is novel and represents a sharp break with our prevailing practice. In such circumstances, we have previously recognized the wisdom of limiting the application of a new rule of law or confining its application only to matters that arise after the rule has been announced. See Coons v. American Honda Motor Co., 96 N.J. 419, 476 A.2d 763 (1984), *cert. denied*, 469 U.S. 1123, 105 S. Ct. 808, 83 L. Ed. 2d 800 (1985). Under the circumstances, we think it would be inappropriate to impose this effective but novel procedure on these litigants at this late stage in litigation that has already been protracted and extensive. Accordingly, the judgment of the Appellate Division setting aside the jury verdict for medical surveillance damages is reversed and the jury verdict is reinstated. . . .

NOTES AND QUESTIONS

1. Was the court correct in declining to recognize the new tort of risk exposure? What would be the prima facie case for this new tort? See Wright, Causation, Responsibility, Risk, Probability, Naked Statistics, and Proof: Pruning the Bramble Bush by Clarifying the Concepts, 73 Iowa L. Rev. 1001, 1067-1071 (1988). How, if at all, would the new tort differ from a relaxed or probabalistic standard of cause in fact? Compare Sterling v. Velsicol Chemical Corp., 855 F.2d 1188, 1205-1206 (6th Cir. 1988). In a groundwater pollution case, the court characterized "cancerphobia" as "merely a specific type of mental anguish" compensable "where such distress is either foreseeable or is a natural consequence of, or reasonably expected to flow from, the present injury . . . the central focus of a court's inquiry in such a case is not on the underlying odds that future disease will in fact materialize." The court also upheld an award, based on nuisance, for impaired quality of life, but limited it to continuing residents of the affected area. Anderson v. W. R. Grace & Co., 628 F. Supp. 1219, 1226-1232 (D. Mass. 1986), on a motion for partial summary judgment, allowed plaintiffs to proceed with evidence that drinking contaminated groundwater in two municipal wells in Woburn, Massachusetts lowered their resistance to future diseases, caused cellular changes in their bodies which could manifest themselves in skin rashes, arthritis or cancer and caused them substantial emotional

distress. With respect to the increased risk of future injury, the court drew a distinction between future illnesses that stem from the same disease process as the illness plaintiffs presently allege and those that stem from different processes. The former may be recovered now, but no cause of action accrues for the latter until the injury manifests itself. Does it follow that plaintiff can invoke the discovery rule for the second category of future injury when and if it occurs? In the subsequent trial in the Woburn case, the jury found that no chemicals disposed of by the defendant prior to the time of the discovery that the two wells were contaminated contributed to the contamination. However, the case was remanded to allow plaintiffs to prove the defendants intentionally concealed a material report. Anderson v. Cryovac, Inc., 862 F. 2d 910 (1st Cir. 1988). Compare State, by Woyke v. Tonka Corp., 420 N.W. 2d 624 (Minn. App. 1984). A toy company allowed an employee, the plaintiff, to take home barrels of still bottom (oil) and obsolete paint which he used around his farm. Unknown to both the company and the employee, the barrels contained significant amounts of tricholorethelene, a listed hazardous substance, and plaintiff sued his employer for the improper disposal of hazardous wastes. He alleged property damage, personal injury, and the infliction of emotional distress under nuisance and negligence; Minnesota does not recognize a cause of action for increased risk of cancer. The intentional infliction of mental distress is an independent tort under Minnesota law, but the plaintiff must prove that the defendant's conduct was, inter alia, extreme and outrageous. In affirming a judgment not withstanding the verdict for emotional distress, the court reasoned that "[i]n the absence of a showing of knowledge by Tonka that the still-bottoms contained TCE, Tonka's behavior cannot be described as so atrocious that it offends notions of decency." Id. at 628.

2. The problems of toxic tort litigation are covered in M. Dore, Toxic Torts (1987). For a lucid inquiry into the jurisprudence of risk protection see Schroeder, Rights Against Risks, 86 Colum. L. Rev. 495 (1986).

B.   BEYOND EXISTING COMMON LAW: LEGISLATIVE INTERVENTION TO CHANGE OR SUPPLANT TORT COMPENSATION

1.   Statutory Cause of Action

Is the common law adequate to compensate the victims of toxic exposure? Many commentators and legislators answered this question no, see Ginsberg & Weiss, Common Law Liability for Toxic Torts: A Phantom Remedy, 9 Hofstra L. J. 859 (1981); Rosenberg, The Causal Connection in Mass Exposure Cases: A "Public Law" Vision of the Tort System, 97 Harv. L. Rev. 849 (1984) and

Symposium: Causation and Financial Compensation, 73 Geo. L.J. 1335 (1985), and urged that the common law be supplemented or supplanted by some form of administered compensation scheme with lowered causation requirements. Administered compensation was part of the original Superfund proposal, but Congress ducked the issue and passed it to a blue ribbon committee. The committee recommended a scheme modeled after workman's compensation, Superfund §301(e) Study Group, Injuries and Damages from Hazardous Wastes — Analysis and Improvement of Legal Remedies, 97th Cong., 2d Sess. (1982), and the issue remained on the political agenda until Congress rejected it in 1985. The schemes were based on Soble, A Proposal for the Administrative Compensation of Victims of Toxic Substance Pollution: A Model Act, 14 Harv. J. on Legis. 683 (1977), which in turn drew from an analysis of the Japanese experience with victim compensation by Professor Julian Gresser. See J. Gresser, K. Fujikura & A. Morishima, Environmental Law in Japan 55-132, 285-324 (1981). For other schemes see Trauberman, Compensating Victims of Toxic Substances Pollution: An Analysis of Existing Federal Statutes, 5 Harv. Envtl. L. Rev. 1 (1981) and Trauberman, Statutory Reform of Toxic Torts: Relieving Legal, Scientific, and Economic Burdens on the Chemical Victim, 7 Harv. Envtl. L. Rev. 177 (1983). For a recent version of a compensation scheme using a science panel see Brennan, Causal Chains and Statistical Links: The Role of Scientific Uncertainty in Hazardous Substance Litigation, 73 Cornell L. Rev. 469 (1989).

C.   PRIVATE ENFORCEMENT OF STATUTORY VIOLATIONS

Few problems have given the Supreme Court as much trouble as that of whether a federal statute creates implied private rights of action. Initially, the Court followed the common law rule that a statute creates private rights if the plaintiff is a member of the group protected by the statute. J. I. Case Co. v. Borak, 377 U.S. 426 (1964). As courts became more sensitive to the question of whether private rights were always consistent with centralized regulation, the common law presumption was modified by a four-factor test that considered whether the plaintiff was a special beneficiary of the statute, the legislative intent of the statute, the consistency of private remedies with the purpose of the statute, and the extent to which state law traditionally dealt with the remedy. Cort v. Ash, 422 U.S. 66 (1975). In recent years, the Court has erected a strong presumption against implied private rights unless there is clear legislative intent to create such rights. Sunstein, Section 1983 and the Private Enforcement of Federal Law, 49 U. Chi. L. Rev. 394, 411-415 (1982), explores the reasons for the Court's current doctrine. The next case applies the presumption against private implied rights of action to environmental law.

MIDDLESEX COUNTY SEWERAGE AUTHORITY v. NATIONAL SEA CLAMMERS ASSOCIATION
453 U.S. 1 (1981)

Justice POWELL delivered the opinion of the Court.

In this case, involving alleged damage to fishing grounds caused by discharges and ocean dumping of sewage and other waste, we are faced with questions concerning the availability of a damages remedy, based either on federal common law or on the provisions of two Acts — the Federal Water Pollution Control Act (FWPCA), as amended, 33 U.S.C. §1251 et seq., and the Marine Protection, Research, and Sanctuaries Act of 1972 (MPRSA), 33 U.S.C. §1401 et seq.

I

Respondents are an organization whose members harvest fish and shellfish off the coast of New York and New Jersey, and one individual member of that organization. In 1977, they brought suit in the United States District Court for the District of New Jersey against petitioners — various governmental entities and officials from New York, New Jersey and the Federal Government. Their complaint alleged that sewage, sewage "sludge," and other waste materials were being discharged into New York Harbor and the Hudson River by some of the respondents. In addition it complained of the dumping of such materials directly into the ocean from maritime vessels. The complaint alleged that, as a result of these activities, the Atlantic Ocean was becoming polluted, and it made special reference to a massive growth of algae said to have appeared offshore in 1976. It then stated that this pollution was causing the "collapse of the fishing, clamming and lobster industries which operate in the waters of the Atlantic Ocean."

Invoking a wide variety of legal theories, respondents sought injunctive and declaratory relief, $250 million in compensatory damages, and $250 million in punitive damages. The District Court granted summary judgment to petitioners on all counts of the complaint.

In holdings relevant here, the District Court rejected respondents' nuisance claim under federal common law, see Illinois v. Milwaukee, 406 U.S. 91 (1972), on the ground that such a cause of action is not available to private parties. With respect to the claims based on alleged violations of the FWPCA, the court noted that respondents had failed to comply with the 60-day notice requirement of the "citizen suit" provision in §505 of the Act, 33 U.S.C. §1365(b)(1)(A). This provision allows suits under the Act by private citizens, but authorizes only prospective relief, and the citizen plaintiffs first must give notice to the EPA, the State, and any alleged violator. Ibid. Because respondents did not give the requisite notice, the court refused to allow them to proceed with a claim under the Act independent of the citizen-suit provision and based on the general jurisdictional grant in 28 U.S.C. §1331. The court applied the same analysis to respondents' claims under the MPRSA, which contains similar citizen-suit and notice provisions. 33 U.S.C. §1415(g). Finally, the court rejected a possible claim of maritime tort, both because respondents had failed to plead such claim explicitly and because they had failed to comply with the procedural requirements of the federal and state tort claims acts.

The United States Court of Appeals for the Third Circuit reversed as to the claims based on the FWPCA, the MPRSA, the federal common law of nuisance, and maritime tort. With respect to the FWPCA, the court held that failure to comply with the 60-day notice provision in §505(b)(1)(A), 33 U.S.C. §1365(b)(1)(A), does not preclude suits under the Act in addition to the specific "citizen suits" authorized in §505. It based this conclusion on the savings clause in §505(e), 33 U.S.C. §1365(e), preserving "any right which any person (or class of persons) may have under any statute or common law to seek enforcement of any effluent standard or limitation or to seek any other relief." The Court of Appeals then went on to apply our precedents in the area of implied statutory rights of action, and concluded that "Congress intended to permit the federal courts to entertain a private cause of action implied from the terms of the [FWPCA]. . . ." . . .

II

It is unnecessary to discuss at length the principles set out in recent decisions concerning the recurring question whether Congress intended to create a private right of action under a federal statute without saying so explicitly. The key to the inquiry is the intent of the legislature. . . . We look first, of course, to the statutory language, particularly to the provisions made therein for enforcement and relief. Then we review the legislative history and other traditional aids of statutory interpretation to determine congressional intent.

These Acts contain unusually elaborate enforcement provisions, conferring authority to sue for this purpose both on government officials and private citizens. The FWPCA, for example, authorizes the EPA Administrator to respond to violations of the Act with compliance orders and civil suits. §309, 33 U.S.C. §1319. . . . In addition, under §509(b), 33 U.S.C. §1342(b)(7). In addition, under §509(b), 33 U.S.C. §1369(b) "any interested person" may seek judicial review in the United States Courts of Appeals of various particular actions by the Administrator, including establishment of effluent standards and issuance of permits for discharge of pollutants. . . .

In view of these elaborate enforcement provisions it cannot be assumed that Congress intended to authorize by implication additional judicial remedies for private citizens suing under MPRSA and FWPCA. As we stated in *Transamerica Mortgage Advisers*, "it is an elemental canon of statutory construction that where a statute expressly provides a particular remedy or remedies, a court must be chary of reading others into it." 444 U.S., at 19, 100 S. Ct., at 247. See also Touche Ross & Co. v. Redington, 442 U.S., at 571-574. In the absence of strong indicia of a contrary congressional intent, we are compelled to conclude that Congress provided precisely the remedies it considered appropriate.

[The Court then considered and foreclosed the possibility of 42 U.S.C. §1983 suits under Maine v. Thiboutot, 448 U.S. 1 (1980), to redress violations by state officials of rights created by federal statutes. The comprehensive enforcement scheme of the Clean Water Act demonstrated a congressional intent to preclude §1983 suits.]

Justice STEVENS, with whom Justice BLACKMUN joins, concurring in the judgment in part and dissenting in part.

I agree with the Court that the remedial provisions of the Clean Water Act and the MPRSA are "quite comprehensive." I cannot agree, however, with the Court's implicit conclusion that this determination ends the inquiry under Maine v. Thiboutot, *supra*. The question that must be answered in determining whether respondents may pursue their claims under §1983 is whether Congress intended that the remedies provided in the substantive statutes be exclusive. Because Congress did not expressly address this question in the statutes, the Court looks elsewhere for an answer and finds it in the comprehensive character of the express statutory remedies. I have no quarrel as a general matter with the proposition that a comprehensive remedial scheme can evidence a congressional decision to preclude other remedies. However, we must not lose sight of the fact that our evaluation of a statute's express remedies is merely a tool used to discern congressional intent; it is not an end in itself. No matter how comprehensive we may consider a statute's remedial scheme to be, Congress is at liberty to leave other remedial avenues open. Express statutory language or clear references in the legislative history will rebut whatever presumption of exclusivity arises from comprehensive remedial provisions. In my judgment, in these cases we are presented with both express statutory language and clear references in the legislative history indicating that Congress did not intend the express remedies in the Clean Water Act and the MPRSA to be exclusive.

Despite their comprehensive enforcement mechanisms, both statutes expressly preserve all legal remedies otherwise available. The statutes state in so many words that the authorization of an express remedy in the statute itself shall not give rise to an inference that Congress intended to foreclose other remedies. Thus, §505(e) of the Clean Water Act states: "Nothing in this section shall restrict any right which any person (or class of persons) may have under any statute or common law to seek enforcement of any effluent standard or limitation or to seek any other relief (including relief against the Administrator or a State agency)." 33 U.S.C. §1365(e). . . .

The legislative history of both statutes makes it clear that the savings clauses were intended to mean what they say. . . .

The Court, of course, discusses the savings clauses and this legislative history elsewhere in its opinion. In rejecting the Court of Appeals' conclusion, based in part on the savings clauses, that respondents may invoke implied rights of action under the Clean Water Act and the MPRSA, the Court finds it "doubtful" that the phrase "any statute" in the savings clauses refers to the very statutes in which the clauses appear. . . . Thus, the Court holds that the statutory phrase "any statute" does not refer to the Clean Water Act or the MPRSA; the Court apparently also holds that it does not refer to §1983, even though that statute clearly qualifies as "any *other* statute" or "any *other* law," within the meaning of the legislative history.

In my judgment, the Court has failed to uncover "a clear congressional mandate" to withdraw the §1983 remedy otherwise available to the respondents. . . .

Although I agree with the Court's holding that neither of these statutes implicitly authorizes a private damages remedy, I reach that conclusion by a different route. Under the traditional common-law analysis the primary question is whether the statute was enacted for the special benefit of a particular class of which the plaintiff is a member. As we have held in the past, "[t]hat question is answered by looking to the language of the statute itself." Cannon v. University of Chicago, 441 U.S. 677, 689.

The language of neither the Clean Water Act nor the MPRSA defines any such special class. Both the substantive provisions of these statutes and the breadth of their authorizations of citizen suits indicate that they were "enacted for the protection of the general public" *Cannon, supra*. Thus, even under the more liberal approach to implied rights of action represented by *Rigsby* and its antecedents, respondents cannot invoke implied private remedies under these statutes.

The conclusion required by the statutory language is fortified by the legislative history on which the Court relies. I agree that the legislative deliberations about civil remedies under the Clean Air Act illuminate the meaning of the Clean Water Act and the MPRSA — since these statutes were enacted only a short time later and had similar environmental objectives — and that those deliberations reveal a conscious congressional choice not to authorize a new statutory damages remedy. Accordingly, I agree with the conclusion reached by the Court in Part II-A of its opinion, but I respectfully dissent from the remainder of its judgment.

NOTES AND QUESTIONS

1. The Court's unsuccessful struggle to articulate a clear theory of the role of implied rights of action in statutory schemes has been much noted, e.g., Manning, Middlesex County Sewerage Authority v. National Sea Clammers Association: Implied Private Rights of Action for Damages under the Federal Water Pollution Control Act Amendments of 1972, 12 Envtl. L. 197 (1981). The Court's current position is that courts lack the power to fashion common law remedies for specific statutory violations unless Congress specifically grants that power. Is this position mandated by the Constitution? Most commentators think not because federal courts have long asserted the power to create substantive federal common law rights to protect federal interests recognized by Congress. See Harried, Implied Private Causes of Action: A Product of Statutory Construction or the Federal Common Law Power? 51 U. Colo. L. Rev. 355

(1980), and Frankel, Implied Rights of Action, 67 Va. L. Rev. 553, 565-570 (1981). If the issue is not lack of constitutional power but judicial discretion, the case for the Court's current restrictive standard for implied rights of action must rest on the unstated premise that the common law presumption of implied rights will result in excessive enforcement of federal regulatory schemes and thus promote the inefficient allocation of resources. How would one measure whether allowing a private right of action for pollution standard violations is efficient? See Landes & Posner, The Private Enforcement of Law, 4 J. Legal Stud. 1 (1975).

2. A similar problem has arisen under §311 of the Clean Water Act, the spill cleanup provision. The section contains liability limitations, and the government has tried to use maritime common law remedies to supplement the amounts recoverable under §311. Courts have held that §311 is the exclusive remedy, e.g., United States v. Dixie Carriers, 627 F.2d 736 (5th Cir. 1980), and In re Oswego Barge Corp., 664 F.2d 327 (2d Cir. 1981), reh'g denied, 673 F.2d 47 (2d Cir. 1982) (preemption of common law remedies for cleanup costs for domestic but not for foreign waters). Note, Oil Spills and Cleanup Bills: Federal Recovery of Oil Spill Cleanup Costs, 93 Harv. L. Rev. 1735 (1980), criticizes the cases and explores the options open to the states under the Act; the note also discusses a Supreme Court case, Askew v. American Waterways Operators, Inc., 411 U.S. 325 (1973), which holds that §311 does not preempt all state oil spill recovery statutes.

3. Today courts draw a distinction between the common law and legislation because each is thought to represent a distinct lawmaking process. Before the seventeenth century, less firm distinctions were drawn between judicial decisions and legislation; in this century, eminent legal scholars have rejected rigid, separation-of-powers-based distinctions between these two sources of law. The great Roscoe Pound argued for a return to the doctrine of the equity of statute, under which courts would receive a statute "fully into the body of law to be reasoned by analogy the same as any other rule of law . . . as of equal or coordinate authority . . . with judge made rules upon the same general subject" (Pound, Common Law Legislation, 21 Harv. L. Rev. 383, 385-386 (1908)). See the sources cited at p. 698 *supra* and Stewart & Sunstein, Public Programs and Private Rights, 95 Harv. L. Rev. 1193 (1982).

D.   CHOICE OF REMEDIES

If a continuing activity violates a plaintiff's common law rights, a court ordinarily may choose among four remedies: (1) abatement, (2) damages, (3) injunctive relief, and (4) declaratory relief. Abatement terminates the activity, whereas an injunction eliminates (at least in theory) only the offending aspect of the activity. See Comment, Nuisance as a Modern Mode of Land Use Control, 46 Wash.

L. Rev. 47, 75-92 (1970). Usually, a court frames the choice of remedies as one between damages and injunctive relief. The basic rationale for injunctive relief is that the remedy at law would be inadequate because the plaintiff's injury contains elements that cannot be expressed in monetary terms. The modern tort of nuisance grew out of an extension of the possessory assizes. These early writs protected a freeholder from loss of the freehold (disseisin), but not from interferences with the use of the freehold. The assize of nuisance filled this gap, and by the fifteenth century it was replaced with an action on the case for nuisance. The possessory origins of nuisance are important because until the nineteenth century land was presumed to be unique. Substantial invasions were therefore normally redressed by injunctions, not damages. In the late 1960s, the possibility of injunctive relief was attractive to environmental lawyers because common law nuisance actions remediable by injunction offered the possibility of a de facto common law class action, without the restrictions imposed by federal and state courts, on such actions. See Note, Class Actions and Mass Toxic Torts, 8 Colum. J. Envtl. L. 269 (1982). In addition, the problems of proving damage suffered by individual landowners and each defendant's contribution could be overcome by an injunction after proof was offered that the defendant had caused some harm and that the plaintiff had suffered some injury. Comment, Equity and the Eco-System: Can Injunctions Clear the Air? 68 Mich. L. Rev. 1254, 1263 (1970).

Injunction suits, however, foundered because courts of equity have the discretion to withhold injunctive relief and confine the plaintiff to the remedy at law through the use of the balance of the equities doctrine. Although an injunction was the presumed remedy for a nuisance, courts of equity have always had the power to withhold a remedy based on the facts of the case. This discretion became important in the nineteenth century. Negligence began to replace strict liability. The standard explanation for the rise of fault-based theories of liability is that courts adapted nuisance to the needs of an expanding industrial society for limitations on liability. As part of the move to trim landowner liability, courts began to find various procedural reasons for denying injunctive relief. Richard's Appeal, 57 Pa. 105 (1868), first announced the modern balancing test that compares the harm suffered by the plaintiff with the societal benefits that will be forgone if an injunction were issued. See Kurtz, Nineteenth Century Anti-Entrepreneurial Nuisance Injunctions — Avoiding the Chancellor, 17 Wm. & Mary L. Rev. 621 (1976). A 1928 article by a respected professor of equity summarized the results of a long and sometimes erratic doctrinal development and set forth the policy and the standards that have guided most courts since:

> The court should balance equities, including balancing hardships, in settling the terms of the injunction; the conduct of the respective parties with reference to the transaction is an important equity to be considered; the proportion of the use of plaintiff's property which will be lost if the injunction is denied may be compared with the proportion of use of defendant's property which the injunction

will destroy; the character of the uses may be considered, a use for residence pur-poses being accorded greater protection than a use for business; and, in cases where the result must be either the substantial loss of the entire use of either the plaintiff's or defendant's property, the mere pecuniary value of the respective properties is not decisive, but even in these cases the court cannot disregard the possible injury to the community. [McClintock, Discretion to Deny Injunction against Trespass and Nuisance, 12 Minn. L. Rev. 565, 583 (1928).]

The next two cases illustrate the two principal modern barriers to injunctive relief.

1.   *The Requirement of Imminent Irreparable Injury*

VILLAGE OF WILSONVILLE v. SCA SERVICES, INC.
86 Ill. 2d 1, 426 N.E.2d 824 (1981)

This case and accompanying notes can be found at p. 519 *supra*.

2.   *The Balancing of Equities*

BOOMER v. ATLANTIC CEMENT CO.
26 N.Y.2d 219, 257 N.E.2d 871, 309 N.Y.S.2d 312 (1970)

BERGAN, Judge.

Defendant operates a large cement plant near Albany. These are actions for injunction and damages by neighboring land owners alleging injury to prop-erty from dirt, smoke and vibration emanating from the plant. A nuisance has been found after trial, temporary damages have been allowed; but an injunction has been denied. . . .

. . . [T]here is now before the court private litigation in which individual property owners have sought specific relief from a single plant operation. The threshold question raised by the division of view on this appeal is whether the court should resolve the litigation between the parties now before it as equitably as seems possible; or whether, seeking promotion of the general public welfare, it should channel private litigation into broad public objectives.

A court performs its essential function when it decides the rights of parties before it. Its decision of private controversies may sometimes greatly affect public issues. Large questions of law are often resolved by the manner in which private litigation is decided. But this is normally an incident to the court's main function to settle controversy. It is a rare exercise of judicial power to use a decision in private litigation as a purposeful mechanism to achieve direct public objectives greatly beyond the rights and interests before the court. . . .

The ground for the denial of injunction, notwithstanding the finding both that there is a nuisance and that plaintiffs have been damaged substantially, is

the large disparity in economic consequences of the nuisance and of the injunction. This theory cannot, however, be sustained without overruling a doctrine
which has been consistently reaffirmed in several leading cases in this court and
which has never been disavowed here, namely that where a nuisance has been
found and where there has been any substantial damage shown by the party
complaining an injunction will be granted.

The rule in New York has been that such a nuisance will be enjoined
although marked disparity be shown in economic consequence between the effect of the injunction and the effect of the nuisance.

The problem of disparity in economic consequence was sharply in focus
in Whalen v. Union Bag & Paper Co., 208 N.Y. 1, 101 N.E. 805. A pulp mill
entailing an investment of more than a million dollars polluted a stream in
which plaintiff, who owned a farm, was "a lower riparian owner." The economic
loss to plaintiff from this pollution was small. This court, reversing the Appellate
Division, reinstated the injunction granted by the Special Term against the argument of the mill owner that in view of "the slight advantage to plaintiff and
the great loss that will be inflicted on defendant" an injunction should not be
granted. "Such a balancing of injuries cannot be justified by the circumstances
of this case," Judge Werner noted. He continued: "Although the damage to the
plaintiff may be slight as compared with the defendant's expense of abating the
condition, that is not a good reason for refusing an injunction." . . .

The court at Special Term also found the amount of permanent damage
attributable to each plaintiff, for the guidance of the parties in the event both
sides stipulated to the payment and acceptance of such permanent damage as a
settlement of all the controversies among the parties. The total of permanent
damages to all plaintiffs thus found was $185,000. This basis of adjustment has
not resulted in any stipulation by the parties.

This result at Special Term and at the Appellate Division is a departure
from a rule that has become settled; but to follow the rule literally in these cases
would be to close down the plant at once. This court is fully agreed to avoid that
immediately drastic remedy; the difference in view is how best to avoid it.[1]

One alternative is to grant the injunction but postpone its effect to a specified future date to give opportunity for technical advances to permit defendant
to eliminate the nuisance; another is to grant the injunction conditioned on the
payment of permanent damages to plaintiffs which would compensate them for
the total economic loss to their property present and future caused by defendant's
operations. For reasons which will be developed the court chooses the latter
alternative.

If the injunction were to be granted unless within a short period — e.g.,
18 months — the nuisance be abated by improved methods, there would be no
assurance that any significant technical improvement would occur.

The parties could settle this private litigation at any time if defendant paid

---

[1].   Respondent's investment in the plant is in excess of $45,000,000. There are over
300 people employed there.

enough money and the imminent threat of closing the plant would build up the pressure on defendant. If there were no improved techniques found, there would inevitably be applications to the court at Special Term for extensions of time to perform on showing of good faith efforts to find such techniques.

Moreover, techniques to eliminate dust and other annoying by-products of cement making are unlikely to be developed by any research the defendant can undertake within any short period, but will depend on the total resources of the cement industry nationwide and throughout the world. The problem is universal wherever cement is made.

For obvious reasons the rate of the research is beyond control of defendant. If at the end of 18 months the whole industry has not found a technical solution a court would be hard put to close down this one cement plant if due regard be given to equitable principles.

On the other hand, to grant the injunction unless defendant pays plaintiffs such permanent damages as may be fixed by the court seems to do justice between the contending parties. All of the attributions of economic loss to the properties on which plaintiffs' complaints are based will have been redressed.

JASEN, Judge (dissenting).

I see grave dangers in overruling our long-established rule of granting an injunction where a nuisance results in substantial continuing damage. In permitting the injunction to become inoperative upon the payment of permanent damages, the majority is, in effect, licensing a continuing wrong. It is the same as saying to the cement company, you may continue to do harm to your neighbors so long as you pay a fee for it. . . .

This kind of inverse condemnation may not be invoked by a private person or corporation for private gain or advantage. Inverse condemnation should only be permitted when the public is primarily served in the taking or impairment of property. The promotion of the interests of the polluting cement company has, in my opinion, no public use or benefit.

Nor is it constitutionally permissible to impose servitude on land, without consent of the owner, by payment of permanent damages where the continuing impairment of the land is for a private use.

NOTES AND QUESTIONS

1. Did the *Boomer* court correctly consider all relevant costs in balancing the equities? Should harm to persons other than the plaintiffs be considered? See Jurgensmeyer, Control of Air Pollution through the Assertion of Private Rights, 1967 Duke L.J. 1126. Is a court competent to undertake a full benefit-benefit analysis when it balances? Are there any presumptions that the court might use to help it conduct a full cost-benefit analysis? For example, should a plaintiff be entitled to an injunction if he shows that the defendant's activity is both a nuisance and violates federal, state, or local air pollution control standards? Suppose

that the defendant proves that his activity complies with all applicable zoning ordinances? In Harrison v. Indiana Auto Shredders Co., 528 F.2d 1107 (7th Cir. 1976), Justice Tom C. Clark, sitting by designation, wrote:

> The appropriate local authority has zoned the property specifically for shredder use; and appellant has been issued a permit to so use the property. After careful and continued tests by reputable experts as well as public officials, appellant's operation has met all the required standards. Under these circumstances and in the absence of an imminent hazard to health or welfare — none of which was established or found present here, the appellant cannot be prevented from continuing to engage in the operation of its shredding. See Reserve Mining Co. v. United States, 514 F.2d 492 (8th Cir. 1975). [528 F.2d at 1125.]

2. In *Boomer*, the court refused to grant an injunction that required the installation of equipment to correct the problem. Courts have granted such injunctions when the evidence has established that the relevant technology was available. Renken v. Harvey Aluminum, 226 F. Supp. 169 (D. Or. 1963), *aff'd*, 475 F.2d 766 (9th Cir. 1973). Should the common law be technology-forcing? Would technology-forcing be equally applicable to public entities, who have been the major beneficiaries of the balancing doctrines, e.g., Harrisonville v. W. S. Dickey Clay Manufacturing Co., 289 U.S. 334 (1933). What would the standard of required technology be? Average in use? Best available? Available through "reasonable" research? See W. Rodgers, Environmental Law §2.6 (1977). One of the purported goals of tort law is to force those who cause harm to internalize the costs of the harm. It is sometimes suggested that it is fairer to force internalization on those who are in a good position to spread widely the costs of the harm. Does injunctive relief further this goal? See Calabresi, Some Thoughts on Risk Distribution and the Law of Torts, 70 Yale L.J. 499, 534-536 (1961).

3. Why does the remedy chosen by the *Boomer* court make a difference? The Coase Theorem, discussed at p. 36 *supra*, posits that if transactions costs are low, the polluter and victim will reach an efficient allocation of resources through bargaining. However, when one considers reality — high transactions costs and strategic behavior such as free riding and the under-revealing of preferences — the remedy chosen does make a difference. Calabresi & Melamed, Property Rules, Liability Rules and Inalienability: One View of the Cathedral, 85 Harv. L. Rev. 1089 (1972), argues that the injunction-damages question should be recast as a choice between entitlements protected by either property rules (injunctions) or by liability rules (damages) and offers the following criteria for making the choice:

> We would employ rule one (entitlement to be free from pollution protected by a property rule) from an economic efficiency point of view if we believed that the polluter, Taney, could avoid or reduce the costs of pollution more cheaply than the pollutee, Marshall. Or to put it another way, Taney would be enjoinable if he were in a better position to balance the costs of polluting against the costs of not polluting. We would employ rule three (entitlement to pollute protected by a prop-

erty rule) again solely from an economic efficiency standpoint, if we made the converse judgment on who could best balance the harm of pollution against its avoidance costs. If we were wrong in our judgments and if transactions between Marshall and Taney were costless or even very cheap, the entitlement under rules one or three would be traded and an economically efficient result would occur in either case. If we entitled Taney to pollute and Marshall valued clean air more than Taney valued the pollution, Marshall would pay Taney to stop polluting even though no nuisance was found. If we entitled Marshall to enjoin the pollution and the right to pollute was worth more to Taney than freedom from pollution was to Marshall, Taney would pay Marshall not to seek an injunction or would buy Marshall's land and sell it to someone who would agree not to seek an injunction. As we have assumed no one else was hurt by the pollution, Taney could now pollute even though the initial entitlement, based on a wrong guess of who was the cheapest avoider of the costs involved, allowed the pollution to be enjoined. Wherever transactions between Taney and Marshall are easy, and wherever economic efficiency is our goal, we could employ entitlements protected by property rules even though we would not be sure that the entitlement chosen was the right one. Transactions as described above would cure the error. While the entitlement might have important distributional effects, it would not substantially undercut economic efficiency.

The moment we assume, however, that transactions are not cheap, the situation changes dramatically. Assume we enjoin Taney and there are 10,000 injured Marshalls. Now *even if* the right to pollute is worth more to Taney than the right to be free from pollution is to the sum of the Marshalls, the injunction will probably stand. The cost of buying out all the Marshalls, given holdout problems, is likely to be too great, and an equivalent of eminent domain in Taney would be needed to alter the initial injunction. Conversely, if we denied a nuisance remedy, the 10,000 Marshalls could only with enormous difficulty, given freeloader problems, get together to buy out even one Taney and prevent the pollution. This would be so even if the pollution harm was greater than the value to Taney of the right to pollute.

If, however, transaction costs are not symmetrical, we may still be able to use the property rule. Assume that Taney can buy the Marshalls' entitlements easily because holdouts are for some reason absent, but that the Marshalls have great freeloader problems in buying out Taney. In this situation the entitlement should be granted to the Marshalls unless we are sure the Marshalls are the cheapest avoiders of pollution costs. Where we do not know the identity of the cheapest cost avoider it is better to entitle the Marshalls to be free of pollution because, even if we are wrong in our initial placement of the entitlement, that is, even if the Marshalls are the cheapest cost avoiders, Taney will buy out the Marshalls and economic efficiency will be achieved. Had we chosen the converse entitlement and been wrong, the Marshalls could not have bought out Taney. Unfortunately, transaction costs are often high on both sides and an initial entitlement, though incorrect in terms of economic efficiency, will not be altered in the market place.

Under these circumstances — and they are normal ones in the pollution area — we are likely to turn to liability rules whenever we are uncertain whether the polluter or the pollutees can most cheaply avoid the cost of pollution. We are only likely to use liability rules where we are uncertain because, if we are certain, the costs of liability rules — essentially the costs of collectively valuing the damages to all concerned plus the cost in coercion to those who would not sell at the collectively determined figure — are unnecessary. They are unnecessary because transaction costs and bargaining barriers become irrelevant when we are certain who is the cheapest cost avoider; economic efficiency will be attained without transactions by making the correct initial entitlement.

As a practical matter we often are uncertain who the cheapest cost avoider is. In such cases, traditional legal doctrine tends to find a nuisance but imposes only damages on Taney payable to the Marshalls. This way, if the amount of damages Taney is made to pay is close to the injury caused, economic efficiency will have had its due; if he cannot make a go of it, the nuisance was not worth its costs. The entitlement to the Marshalls to be free from pollution unless compensated, however, will have been given *not* because it was thought that polluting was probably worth less to Taney than freedom from pollution was worth to the Marshalls, nor even because on some distributional basis we preferred to charge the cost to Taney rather than to the Marshalls. It was so placed *simply because we did not know* whether Taney desired to pollute more than the Marshalls desired to be free from pollution, and the only way we thought we could test out the value of the pollution was by the only liability rule we thought we had. This was rule two, the imposition of nuisance damages on Taney. [85 Harv. L. Rev. at 1118-1119.]

Calabresi and Melamed also suggest a fourth rule: Marshall may enjoin Taney if Marshall compensates Taney. Rule four may be justified on both efficiency and equity (distributional) grounds when the costs of pollution fall primarily on the wealthy and the benefits of the polluting activity that would be forgone under rule one are enjoyed by those of low and moderate incomes. Rule four has been applied in one case, Spur Industries, Inc. v. Del E. Webb Development Co., 108 Ariz. 179, 494 P.2d 700 (1972). In 1956, a cattle feeding lot was located in a rural area outside Phoenix. Three years later, Del E. Webb started to build Sun City, a retirement community, nearby. By 1967, Del E. Webb had sued the cattle lot, alleging that by then it had become a public nuisance. The state supreme court agreed, but it assumed that the balance of equities doctrine would preclude an injunction against a private nuisance but not a public nuisance. The court, however, fashioned a novel remedy:

> There was no indication in the instant case at the time Spur and its predecessors located in western Maricopa County that a new city would spring up, full-blown, alongside the feeding operation and that the developer of that city would ask the court to order Spur to move because of the new city. Spur is required to move not because of any wrongdoing on the part of Spur, but because of a proper and legitimate regard of the courts for the rights and interests of the public.
>
> Del Webb, on the other hand, is entitled to the relief prayed for (a permanent injunction), not because Webb is blameless, but because of the damage to the people who have been encouraged to purchase homes in Sun City. It does not equitably or legally follow, however, that Webb, being entitled to the injunction, is then free of any liability to Spur if Webb has in fact been the cause of the damage Spur has sustained. It does not seem harsh to require a developer, who has taken advantage of the lesser land values in a rural area as well as the availability of large tracts of land on which to build and develop a new town or city in the area, to indemnify those who are forced to leave as a result. Having brought people to the nuisance to the foreseeable detriment of Spur, Webb must indemnify Spur for a reasonable amount of the cost of moving or shutting down. [494 P.2d at 707-708.]

The extent to which the strategic behavior of the parties influences possible negotiations under the four proposed rules is discussed in Polinsky, Resolving Nuisance Disputes: The Simple Economics of Injunctive and Damage Remedies, 32 Stan. L. Rev. 1075 (1980), and M. Polinsky, An Introduction to Law and Economics ch. 4 (1983).

In recent years, many states, including Arizona, have enacted right-to-farm statutes.

> Although the language of the various right to farm statutes differs, most provide in essence that when the plaintiff has come to the nuisance, the defendant agricultural operation either is not,[103] or is presumed not to be,[104] a nuisance. The legislatures in right to farm states have limited the courts' discretion to balance the various factors involved in the nuisance action. Once the requirements of the statute are met, the court cannot weigh the policy of protecting the agricultural operation against other concerns, like protecting plaintiffs who have moved to the nuisance.[105] The practical effect of right to farm statutes depends, of course, on the language of the particular statute and on the facts and circumstances of the nuisance action. [Grossman & Fischer, Protecting the Right to Farm: Statutory Limits on Nuisance Actions against the Farmer, 1983 Wis. L. Rev. 95, 117.]

4. Compare *Boomer* with Texas v. Texas Pet Foods, Inc., 591 S.W.2d 800 (Tex. 1979). In approving an injunction for past and continuing violations of a pollution control statute, the Texas supreme Court wrote:

> The probability of the continuation of the prohibited practices is not a matter which is susceptible of direct proof, and injunctive relief is proper when the trial court finds it justified under the rules of equity, notwithstanding a defendant's cessation of the activity or solemn promises to cease the activity. Almo Title Co. v. San Antonio Bar Assn., *supra*, at 817; Magnolia Petroleum Co. v. State, 218 S.W.2d 855, 861 (Tex. Civ. App. — Austin 1949, *writ ref'd n.r.e.*); *see* Newsom, State Court Injunctions and Their Enforcement in Environmental Litigation, 9 St. Mary's L.J. 821, 825 (1978).[591 S.W.2d at 804.]

E.   PRECLUSION OF PRIVATE REMEDIES

In addition to centralized command and control legislation, policy formulation and enforcement can be shared with the public generally. Direct common law actions against public and private entities are always theoretically possible, providing a plaintiff can convince a court to take jurisdiction. However, with the advent of "comprehensive" regulatory schemes, the following issue arises more and more frequently: Did the legislature preempt common law remedies? There is little doubt that Congress has the constitutional power to preclude common law remedies. Historically, federal common law nuisance actions have not protected private parties directly, and so it seems unlikely that a court would hold

---

103. See, e.g., Ill. Rev. Stat. ch. 5, §§1101-1105 (1981); N.C. Gen. Stat. §§106-700, -701 (Cum. Supp. 1981).

104. See, e.g., Ariz. Rev. Stat. Ann. §§3-1051, -1061 (Supp. 1974-82). Cf. Wis. Stat. Ann. §823.08 (West Cum. Supp. 1982-1983) (statute limits the remedies obtainable through nuisance actions against agricultural operations).

105. But see Born v. Exxon Corp., 388 So. 2d 933 (Ala. 1980).

that the preclusion of such a remedy is a taking of property without due process of law. State preclusion of private nuisance remedies does raise more substantial questions because of the extent to which private property owners have relied on the common law. See p. 528 *supra*. Due process considerations aside, the issue is, what is the standard for determining preemption? The Supreme Court, as it has in implied rights of action, has swung between comparing the federal and state interests at stake and searching for congressional intent. Under neither type of analysis has the Court fully articulated the relevant factors to be used in deciding the preemption issue.

CITY OF MILWAUKEE v. ILLINOIS AND MICHIGAN
451 U.S. 304 (1981)

Justice REHNQUIST delivered the opinion of the Court.

When this litigation was first before us we recognized the existence of a federal "common law" which could give rise to a claim for abatement of a nuisance caused by interstate water pollution. Illinois v. Milwaukee, 406 U.S. 91 (1972). Subsequent to our decision, Congress enacted the Federal Water Pollution Control Act Amendments of 1972. We granted certiorari to consider the effect of this legislation on the previously recognized cause of action. . . .

Trial on Illinois' claim commenced on January 11, 1977. On July 29 the District Court rendered a decision finding that respondents had proved the existence of a nuisance under federal common law, both in the discharge of inadequately treated sewage from petitioners' plants and in the discharge of untreated sewage from sewer overflows. The court ordered petitioners to eliminate all overflows and to achieve specified effluent limitations on treated sewage. A judgment order entered on November 15 specified a construction timetable for the completion of detention facilities to eliminate overflows. Separated sewer overflows are to be completely eliminated by 1986; combined sewer overflows by 1989. . . .

On appeal, the Court of Appeals for the Seventh Circuit affirmed in part and reversed in part. The court ruled that the 1972 amendments had not preempted the federal common law of nuisance, but that "[i]n applying the federal common law of nuisance in a water pollution case, a court should not ignore the Act but should look to its policies and principles for guidance." The court reversed the District Court insofar as the effluent limitations it imposed on treated sewage were more stringent than those in the permits and applicable EPA regulations. The order to eliminate all overflows, however, and the construction schedule designed to achieve this goal, were upheld.[5]

---

5. The Court of Appeals also rejected petitioners' contentions that there was no in personam jurisdiction under the Illinois long-arm statute, that any exercise of in personam jurisdiction failed to meet the minimum contacts test of International Shoe v. Washington, 326 U.S. 310 (1945), and that venue was improper. We agree that, given the existence of a federal common law claim at the commencement of the suit, prior to the enactment of the 1972 amendments, personal jurisdiction was properly exercised and venue was also proper.

II

Federal courts, unlike state courts, are not general common law courts and do not possess a general power to develop and apply their own rules of decision. Erie R. Co. v. Tompkins, 304 U.S. 64, 78 (1938). The enactment of a federal rule in an area of national concern, and the decision whether to displace state law in doing so, is generally made not by the federal judiciary, purposefully insulated from democratic pressures, but by the people through their elected representatives in Congress.[6] *Erie* recognized as much in ruling that a federal court could not generally apply a federal rule of decision, despite the existence of jurisdiction, in the absence of an applicable Act of Congress.

When Congress has not spoken to a particular issue, however, and when there exists a "significant conflict between some federal policy or interest and the use of state law," *Wallis*, 384 U.S., at 68, the Court has found it necessary, in a "few and restricted" instances, to develop federal common law. Nothing in this process suggests that courts are better suited to develop national policy in areas governed by federal common law than they are in other areas, or that the usual and important concerns of an appropriate division of functions between the Congress and the federal judiciary are inapplicable. . . .

. . . We have always recognized that federal common law is "subject to the paramount authority of Congress." It is resorted to "[i]n the absence of an applicable Act of Congress," and because the Court is compelled to consider federal questions "which cannot be answered from federal statutes alone." . . . [8]

Contrary to the suggestions of respondents, the appropriate analysis in determining if federal statutory law governs a question previously the subject of federal common law is not the same as that employed in deciding if federal law pre-empts state law. In considering the latter question "we start with the assumption that the historic police powers of the States were not to be superseded by the Federal Act unless that was the clear and manifest purpose of Congress." While we have not hesitated to find pre-emption of state law, whether express or

---

6.   See Hart, The Relations between State and Federal Law, 54 Colum. L. Rev. 489, 497 (1954) ("federal intervention has been thought of as requiring special justification, and the decision that such justification has been shown, being essentially discretionary, has belonged in most cases to Congress").

8.   The dissent errs in labeling our approach "automatic displacement." As evident below, the question whether a previously available federal common-law action has been displaced by federal statutory law involves an assessment of the scope of the legislation and whether the scheme established by Congress addresses the problem formerly governed by federal common law. Our "detailed review of respondents' claims," *post*, at 1808, is such an assessment and not, as the dissent suggests, a consideration of whether the particular common law applied below was reasonable.

The dissent's reference to "the unique role federal common law plays in resolving disputes between one state and the citizens or government of another," does not advance its argument. Whether interstate in nature or not, if a dispute implicates "commerce among the several states" Congress is authorized to enact the substantive federal law governing the dispute. Although the Court has formulated "interstate common law," it has done so not because the usual separation of powers principles do not apply, but rather because interstate disputes frequently call for the application of a federal rule when Congress has not spoken.

implied, when Congress has so indicated, or when enforcement of state regulations would impair "federal superintendence of the field," our analysis has included "due regard for the presuppositions of our embracing federal system,
including the principle of diffusion of power not as a matter of doctrinaire lo-
calism but as a promoter of democracy." Such concerns are not implicated in
the same fashion when the question is whether federal statutory or federal common law governs, and accordingly the same sort of evidence of a clear and manifest purpose is not required. Indeed, as noted, in cases such as the present "we
start with the assumption" that it is for Congress, not federal courts, to articulate
the appropriate standards to be applied as a matter of federal law.

III

We conclude that, at least so far as concerns the claims of respondents, Congress
has not left the formulation of appropriate federal standards to the courts through
application of often vague and indeterminate nuisance concepts and maxims of
equity jurisprudence, but rather has occupied the field through the establishment of a comprehensive regulatory program supervised by an expert administrative agency. The 1972 amendments to the Federal Water Pollution Control
Act were not merely another law "touching interstate waters" of the sort surveyed
in Illinois v. Milwaukee, 406 U.S., at 101, 103, and found inadequate to supplant federal common law. Rather, the amendments were viewed by Congress
as a "total restructuring" and "complete rewriting" of the existing water pollution
legislation considered in that case. . . .
    . . . In the 1972 amendments Congress provided ample opportunity for a
State affected by decisions of a neighboring State's permit granting agency to seek
redress. Under §402(b)(3), 33 U.S.C. §1342(b)(3), a state permit granting agency
must ensure that any State whose waters may be affected by the issuance of a
permit receives notice of the permit application and the opportunity to participate in a public hearing. Wisconsin law accordingly guarantees such notice and
hearing, see Wis. Stat. §§147.11, 147.13. Respondents received notice of each
of the permits involved here, and public hearings were held, but they did not
participate in them in any way. Section 402(b)(5), 33 U.S.C. §1342(b)(5), provides that state permit granting agencies must ensure that affected States have an
opportunity to submit written recommendations concerning the permit applications to the issuing State and the EPA, and both the affected State and the
EPA must receive notice and a statement of reasons if any part of the recommendations of the affected State are not accepted. Again respondents did not
avail themselves of this statutory opportunity. Under §402(d)(2)(A), 33 U.S.C.
§1342(d)(2)(A), the EPA may veto any permit issued by a State when waters of
another State may be affected. Respondents did not request such action. Under
§402(d)(4) of the Act, 33 U.S.C. §1342(d)(4), added in 1977, the EPA itself may
issue permits if a stalemate between an issuing and objecting State develops. The
basic grievance of respondents is that the permits issued to petitioners pursuant

to the Act do not impose stringent enough controls on petitioners' discharges. The statutory scheme established by Congress provides a forum for the pursuit of such claims before expert agencies by means of the permit granting process. It would be quite inconsistent with this scheme if federal courts were in effect to "write their own ticket" under the guise of federal common law after permits have already been issued and permittees have been planning and operating in reliance on them.

Respondents argue that congressional intent to preserve the federal common law remedy recognized in Illinois v. Milwaukee is evident in §§510 and 505(e) of the statute, 33 U.S.C. §§1370, 1365(e). Section 510 provides that nothing in the Act shall preclude States from adopting and enforcing limitations on the discharge of pollutants more stringent than those adopted under the Act. It is one thing, however, to say that States may adopt more stringent limitations through state administrative processes, or even that States may establish such limitations through state nuisance law, and apply them to in-state discharges. It is quite another to say that the States may call upon *federal* courts to employ *federal* common law to establish more stringent standards applicable to out-of-state dischargers. Any standards established under federal common law are federal standards, and so the authority of States to impose more stringent standards under §510 would not seem relevant. Section 510 clearly contemplates state authority to establish more stringent pollution limitations; nothing in it, however, suggests that this was to be done by federal court actions premised on federal common law.

Subsection 505(e) provides:

> Nothing *in this section* shall restrict any right which any person (or class of persons) may have under any statute or common law to seek enforcement of any effluent standard or limitation or to seek any other relief (including relief against the Administrator or a state agency) [emphasis supplied].

Respondents argue that this evinces an intent to preserve the federal common law of nuisance. We, however, are inclined to view the quoted provision as meaning what it says: that nothing *in §505*, the citizen suit provision, should be read as limiting any other remedies which might exist.

Subsection 505(e) is virtually identical to subsections in the citizen suit provisions of several environmental statutes. The subsection is common language accompanying citizen suit provisions and we think that it means only that the provision of such suit does not revoke other remedies. It most assuredly cannot be read to mean that the Act as a whole does not supplant formerly available federal common law actions but only that the particular section authorizing citizen suits does not do so. No one, however, maintains that the citizen suit provision pre-empts federal common law.

Justice BLACKMUN, with whom Justice MARSHALL and Justice STEVENS join, dissenting.

I

The Court's analysis of federal common law displacement rests, I am convinced, on a faulty assumption. In contrasting congressional displacement of the common law with federal pre-emption of state law, the Court assumes that as soon as Congress "addresses a question previously governed" by federal common law, "the need for such an unusual exercise of lawmaking by federal courts disappears." This "automatic displacement" approach is inadequate in two respects. It fails to reflect the unique role federal common law plays in resolving disputes between one State and the citizens or government of another. In addition, it ignores this Court's frequent recognition that federal common law may complement congressional action in the fulfillment of federal policies. . . .

Long before the 1972 decision in Illinois v. Milwaukee, federal common law enunciated by this Court assured each State the right to be free from unreasonable interference with its natural environment and resources when the interference stems from another State or its citizens.

II

In my view, the language and structure of the Clean Water Act leaves no doubt that Congress intended to preserve the federal common law of nuisance. Section 505(e) of the Act reads: "Nothing in this section shall restrict any right which *any person* (or class of persons) may have under *any statute or common law* to seek enforcement of any effluent standard or limitation *or to seek any other relief* (including relief against the Administrator or a State agency)." 33 U.S.C. §1365(e) (emphasis added). The Act specifically defines "person" to include States, and thus embraces respondents Illinois and Michigan. §502(5); 33 U.S.C. §1362(5). It preserves their right to bring an action against the governmental entities who are charged with enforcing the statute. Most important, as succinctly stated by the Court of Appeals in this case: "There is nothing in the phrase 'any statute or common law' that suggests that this provision is limited to state common law." To the best of my knowledge, every federal court that has considered the issue has concluded that, in enacting §505(e), Congress meant to preserve federal as well as state common law.[9]

---

9. The Court relies on Committee for the Consideration of the Jones Falls Sewage System v. Train, 539 F.2d 1006, 1009, n.9 (C.A. 4 1976), in criticizing the "unlikely assumption" that §505(e) preserved anything other than "the more routine state law." *Ante*, at 1798. *Jones Falls* offers no support for this criticism, since it concerned only *intra*state pollution of navigable waters. Indeed, the court there assumed the continued applicability of federal common law where a State sought to vindicate its rights in an interstate controversy, id., at 1010, but concluded that because the controversy was entirely local, the state common law of nuisance preserved by §505(e) furnished the relevant common law remedy.

C. Mortimer, The Lake Michigan Pollution Case: A Review and Commentary of the Limnological and Other Issues (Center for Great Lakes Studies, University of Wisconsin at Milwaukee, 1981), is a comprehensive summary of the technical evidence in the litigation and contains some useful observations on the role of experts in pollution litigation.

NOTES AND QUESTIONS

1. Do you agree with the following criticism of the majority opinion?

> The real basis for the majority opinion is the unstated assumption that the 1972 Amendments reflect a Congressional decision that federal and state water pollution standards represent the maximum liability to which a discharger should be subject. Certainly, dischargers have a strong interest in knowing the extent of their potential liability because of the substantial costs of compliance with federal and state standards. However, to conclude that the act immunizes dischargers with any further liability seems unwarranted for three (3) reasons. First, all those who undertake activities that are potentially harmful are subject to common law standards of liability. These standards are always evolving to take into account new risks. Thus, the common law rule is generally that compliance with statutory standards or administrative regulations is not an absolute defense against liability. W. Rodgers, Environmental Law, Section 2.10. Second, the primary purpose of the 1972 Amendments and the Clean Water Act is not to limit the liability of dischargers; the purpose is to eliminate water pollution. To this end, the Clean Water Act puts dischargers on notice that they are subject to evolving standards of liability. This is reflected in the progressively higher levels of technology-forcing standards to which dischargers are subject and the possibility in Section 303 [33 U.S.C. §1313], that dischargers may have to meet additional effluent limitation standards to comply with applicable water quality standards. Third, Congress in other legislation such as Section 7003 [42 U.S.C. §7003] of the Resource Conservation and Recovery Act has made it clear that compliance with applicable standards is no defense to liability when activities create a risk of an imminent and substantial hazard.
>
> One lesson that has been learned about environmental problems is that we know very little about what causes harm to the environment and those who use it. Thus, there is always the possibility that a harm exists that is not anticipated by a regulatory scheme. The law of torts has always been available to provide the possibility of redress in such situations. Federal common law nuisance suits are tort actions, and thus there is no reason to deny federal judicial power to adjudicate such suits until Congress makes a clear and deliberate decision that dischargers are subject to too much potential liability. This Congress has not yet done.
>
> The strong interest in discharger liability is adequately minimized by the existing standards of the federal common law of nuisance. I am not one who views the federal common law of nuisance as a major pollution control strategy, e.g., Comment, Requiem for the Federal Common Law of Nuisance, 11 Environmental Law Reporter 10,191 (1981). The doctrine has a limited but important role to play in eliminating major inter-state pollution public health risks not anticipated by federal and state regulatory schemes. The doctrine affords dischargers great pro-

tection for at least three (3) reasons: (1) proof of cause in fact is required in pollution suits, Missouri v. Illinois, 200 U.S. 496 (1906); (2) courts retain the power to balance the equities and thus fashion appropriate remedies that include consideration of the costs of compliance with any order. In fact, a discharger may be better off under a federal common law action because benefit-cost considerations are very limited in Clean Water Act proceedings, e.g., Association of Pacific Fisheries v. EPA, 615 F.2d 794, 17 E.R.C. 1425 (9th Cir. 1982); and (3) compliance with applicable regulations should be a defense but not a complete immunity from liability. The position was, in effect, adopted by the Seventh Circuit in *City of Milwaukee*, and it is the right one. Compliance with applicable regulations is presumptively a defense to a federal common law action unless the plaintiff state can show that substantial harm to its interests is nonetheless occurring and this harm was not anticipated in the enactment of the regulatory scheme. This presumption signals that federal common law nuisance suits are extraordinary judicial remedies for pollution, but that they remain in reserve for appropriate occasions. [Hearings on S. 777 and S. 2652 before the Senate Subcomm. on Environmental Pollution, 97th Cong., 2d Sess. 654-655 (1982) (statement of Professor A. Dan Tarlock).]

Compare Bleiweiss, Environmental Regulation and the Federal Common Law of Nuisance: A Proposed Standard of Preemption, 7 Harv. Envtl. L. Rev. 41 (1983).

2. *Milwaukee II* clearly bars common law nuisance suits if the nuisance was created after 1972. Does it also bar common law suits for pre-1972 nuisances? See Illinois v. Outboard Marine Corp., 680 F.2d 473 (7th Cir. 1982).

3. A municipal sewage treatment plant in State A discharges untreated wastes, which foul the beaches of State B. State B brings a state nuisance action against the relevant city in State A. Does *Milwaukee II* bar this suit? See Scott v. City of Hammond, 530 F. Supp. 288 (N.D. Ill. 1981). If the suit is not barred, which state law applies? May State B constitutionally apply its law? See Allstate Insurance Co. v. Hague, 449 U.S. 302 (1981).

4. Would a common law nuisance suit against a non-point source of pollution be preempted under *Milwaukee II*? See Note, *Milwaukee II*: The Abatement of Federal Common Law Actions for Interstate Pollution, 1982 Utah L. Rev. 401, 416. See also Note, City of Milwaukee v. Illinois: The Demise of the Federal Common Law of Water Pollution, 1982 Wis. L. Rev. 627.

5. Does *Milwaukee* apply to all other federal environmental statutes? The Clean Air Act? The issue was discussed, but not resolved, in New England Legal Foundation v. Costle, 666 F.2d 30 (2d Cir. 1981). Preemption was found in United States v. Kin-Buc, Inc., 532 F. Supp. 699 (D.N.J. 1982). The issue may, however, still be open. As part of a series of lawsuits to protect Mono Lake on the eastern slope of the Sierra Nevada mountains in California near the Nevada border, the National Audubon society brought a suit alleging that the city of Los Angeles's water diversions from tributary streams were drying up the lake bed and causing alkali dust storms. The Ninth Circuit Court of Appeals denied that an interstate air pollution nuisance existed because a "true" interstate dispute involves a state suing sources outside its territory, but it reserved judgment on the

preemption issue. National Audubon Society v. Department of Water, 858 F.2d 1409 (9th Cir. 1988). United States v. Chem-Dyne Corp., 572 F. Supp. 802, (S.D. Ohio 1983), holds that courts may impose joint and several liability on parties responsible under CERCLA because the legislative history contemplates the development of a uniform federal common law rule to further the purposes of the Act. See also Silkwood v. Kerr-McGee Corp., 464 U.S. 238 (1984) which holds that the Atomic Energy Act does not preempt a state punitive damages award for an employee of a plant that fabricated plutonium fuel pins for nuclear reactors who was contaminated by exposure to plutonium. "[I]t is clear that in enacting and amending the Price-Anderson Act, Congress assumed that state-law remedies, in whatever form they might take, were available to those injured by nuclear accidents." 464 U.S. at 256. Four justices dissented because the "decision, in effect, authorizes lay juries and judges to make regulatory judgments as to whether a federally licensed nuclear facility is being operated safely." Id. at 274.

6. Preemption can arise under state law, but state courts do not often find it because the legislature has expressly or impliedly preserved private remedies, e.g., Borland v. Saunders Lead Co., 369 So. 2d 523 (Ala. 1979). Another doctrine that can have at least the temporary effect of preemption is primary jurisdiction, discussed at pp. 108-109 *supra*. See Note, Hazardous Wastes: Preserving the Nuisance Remedy, 33 Stan. L. Rev. 675, 683-686 (1981). For other cases rejecting a statutory preemption claim for a source in compliance with relevant air quality regulations, see Neal v. Darby, 282 S.C. 277, 318 S.E.2d 18 (S.C. Ct. App. 1984); and Bradley v. American Smelting & Refining Co., 104 Wash. 2d 677, 709 P.2d 782 (1985). Allen v. U.S., 816 F.2d 1417 (10th Cir. 1987), *cert. denied*, 108 U.S. 697 (1988), applied the discretionary exception to the Federal Tort Claims Act to preclude a suit by numerous plaintiffs in southern Utah to recover damages suffered as a consequence of atomic testing in the 1950s and 1960s. Section 2212 of 42 U.S.C. in effect creates an explicit immunity for contractors carrying out an atomic weapons testing program. But compare U.S. v. Fidelity & Guaranty Co., 24 Envt. Rep. Cas. (BNA) 1612 (M.D. Pa. 1986), which holds that the United States may be liable for an acid cloud released during a Superfund cleanup.

INTERNATIONAL PAPER CO. v. OUELLETTE
107 S. Ct. 805 (1987)

Justice POWELL delivered the opinion of the Court.

This case involves the pre-emptive scope of the Clean Water Act, 33 U.S.C. §1251 et seq. (CWA or Act). The question presented is whether the Act pre-empts a common-law nuisance suit filed in a Vermont court under Vermont law, when the source of the alleged injury is located in New York.

I

Lake Champlain forms part of the border between the states of New York and Vermont. Petitioner International Paper Company (IPC) operates a pulp and paper mill on the New York side of the lake. In the course of its business, IPC discharges a variety of effluents into the lake through a diffusion pipe. The pipe runs from the mill through the water toward Vermont, ending a short distance before the state boundary line that divides the lake.

Respondents are a group of property owners who reside or lease land on the Vermont shore. In 1978 the owners filed a class action suit against IPC, claiming, inter alia, that the discharge of effluents constituted a "continuing nuisance" under Vermont common law. Respondents alleged that the pollutants made the water "foul, unhealthy, smelly, and . . . unfit for recreational use," thereby diminishing the value of their property. App. 29. The owners asked for $20 million in compensatory damages, $100 million in punitive damages, and injunctive relief that would require IPC to restructure part of its water treatment system. The action was filed in State Superior Court, and then later removed to Federal District Court for the District of Vermont.

IPC moved for summary judgment and judgment on the pleadings, claiming that the Clean Water Act pre-empted respondents' state law suit. With the parties' consent, the District Judge deferred a ruling on the motion pending the decision by the Court of Appeals for the Seventh Circuit in a similar case involving Illinois and the city of Milwaukee. In that dispute, Illinois filed a nuisance action against the city under Illinois statutory and common law, seeking to abate the alleged pollution of Lake Michigan. Illinois v. Milwaukee, 731 F.2d 403 (1984) (*Milwaukee III*), *cert. denied*, 469 U.S. 1196, 105 S. Ct. 979, 83 L. Ed. 2d 981 (1985). The Court of Appeals ultimately remanded the case for dismissal of Illinois' claim, finding that the CWA precluded the application of one State's law against a pollution source located in a different State. The decision was based in part on the Court's conclusion that the application of different state laws to a single "point source"[4] would interfere with the carefully devised regulatory system established by the CWA. 731 F.2d, at 414. The Court also concluded that the only suits that were *not* pre-empted were those alleging violations of the laws of the polluting, or "source," State. Id., at 413-414.

IPC argued that the holding in *Milwaukee III* was dispositive in this case. The Vermont District Court disagreed and denied the motion to dismiss. 602 F. Supp. 264 (1985). The Court acknowledged that federal law normally governs interstate water pollution. It found, however, that two sections of the CWA explicitly preserve state-law rights of action. First, §510 of the Act provides:

----

4.   A "point source" is defined by the CWA as "any discernible, confined and discrete conveyance . . . from which pollutants are or may be discharged." 33 U.S.C. §1362(14); see 40 CFR §122.2 (1986). It is not disputed that IPC is a point source within the meaning of the Act.

> Except as expressly provided . . . , nothing in this chapter shall . . . be construed
> as impairing or in any manner affecting any right or jurisdiction of the States with
> respect to the waters (including boundary waters) of such States. 33 U.S.C. §1370.

In addition, §505(e) states:

> Nothing in this section shall restrict any right which any person (or class of persons)
> may have under any statute or common law to seek enforcement of any effluent
> standard or limitation or to seek any other relief. . . . 33 U.S.C. §1365(e).

The District Court held that these two provisions (together, "the saving clause") made it clear that federal law did not pre-empt entirely the rights of States to control pollution. Therefore the question presented, said the court, was which *types* of state suits Congress intended to preserve. It considered three possibilities:[5] first, the saving clause could be construed to preserve state law only as it applied to waters not covered by the CWA. But since the Act applies to virtually all surface water in the country,[6] the District Court rejected this possibility. Second, the saving clause might preserve state nuisance law only as it applies to discharges occurring within the source State; under this view a claim could be filed against IPC under New York common law, but not under Vermont law. This was the position adopted by the Court of Appeals for the Seventh Circuit in *Milwaukee III*. The Vermont Court nevertheless rejected this option, finding that "there is simply nothing in the Act which suggests that Congress intended to impose such limitations on the use of state law." 602 F. Supp., at 269.

The District Court therefore adopted the third interpretation of the saving clause, and held that a state action to redress interstate water pollution could be maintained under the law of the State in which the injury occurred. Ibid. The Court was unpersuaded by the concern expressed in *Milwaukee III* that the application of out-of-state law to a point source would conflict with the CWA. It said there was no interference with the procedures established by Congress because a State's "imposition of compensatory damage awards and other equitable relief for injuries caused . . . merely *supplement* the standards and limitations imposed by the Act." 602 F. Supp., at 271 (emphasis in original). The Court also found that the use of state law did not conflict with the ultimate goal of the CWA, since in each case the objective was to decrease the level of pollution. Ibid.

---

5.   For a discussion of each of the three interpretations of the saving clause, see Note, City of Milwaukee v. Illinois: The Demise of the Federal Common Law of Water Pollution, 1982 Wis. L. Rev. 627, 664-671.

6.   While the Act purports to regulate only "navigable waters," this term has been construed expansively to cover waters that are not navigable in the traditional sense. See United States v. Riverside Bayview Homes, — U.S. —, 106 S. Ct. 455, 88 L. Ed. 2d 419 (1985); 33 U.S.C. §1362(7) (defining navigable waters as "waters of the United States"); 118 Cong. Rec. 33756-33757 (1972), 1 Legislative History of Water Pollution Control Act Amendments of 1972 (Committee Print compiled for the Senate Committee on Public Works by the Library of Congress), Ser. No. 93-1, p. 250 (1973) (hereinafter Leg. Hist.).

The District Court certified its decision for interlocutory appeal, see 28 U.S.C. §1292(b) (1982 ed., Supp. III), and the Court of Appeals for the Second Circuit affirmed for the reasons stated by the District Court. 776 F.2d 55, 56 (1985) (per curiam). We granted certiorari to resolve the Circuit conflict on this important issue of federal pre-emption. 475 U.S. —, 107 S. Ct. —, 93 L. Ed. 2d — (1986). We now affirm the denial of IPC's motion to dismiss, but reverse the decision below to the extent it permits the application of Vermont law to this litigation. We hold that when a court considers a state-law claim concerning interstate water pollution that is subject to the CWA, the court must apply the law of the State in which the point source is located.

II

A brief review of the regulatory framework is necessary to set the stage for this case. Until fairly recently, federal common law governed the use and misuse of interstate water. . . .

We had occasion to address this issue in the first of two Supreme Court cases involving the dispute between Illinois and Milwaukee. [The Court discussed *Milwaukee I* and *Milwaukee II*.]

While source States have a strong voice in regulating their own pollution, the CWA contemplates a much lesser role for States that share an interstate waterway with the source (the affected States). Even though it may be harmed by the discharges, an affected State only has an advisory role in regulating pollution that originates beyond its borders. Before a federal permit may be issued, each affected State is given notice and the opportunity to object to the proposed standards at a public hearing. 33 U.S.C. §1341(a)(2); *Milwaukee III, supra*, at 412. An affected State has similar rights to be consulted before the source State issues its own permit; the source State must send notification, and must consider the objections and recommendations submitted by other States before taking action. §1342(b). Significantly, however, an affected State does not have the authority to block the issuance of the permit if it is dissatisfied with the proposed standards. An affected State's only recourse is to apply to the EPA Administrator, who then has the discretion to disapprove the permit if he concludes that the discharges will have an undue impact on interstate waters. §1342(d)(2). Also, an affected State may not establish a separate permit system to regulate an out-of-state source. See §1342(b) (State may establish permit system for waters "within *its* jurisdiction" (emphasis added), Lake Erie Alliance for Protection of Coastal Corridor v. U.S. Army Corps of Engineers, 526 F. Supp. 1063, 1074-1075 (W.D. Pa. 1981), *aff'd*, 707 F.2d 1392 (CA3), *cert. denied*, 464 U.S. 915, 104 S. Ct. 277, 78 L. Ed. 2d 257 (1983); State v. Champion International Corp., 709 S.W.2d 569 (Tenn. 1986), *cert. pending*, No. 86-57. Thus the Act makes it clear that affected States occupy a subordinate position to source States in the federal regulatory program.

III

With this regulatory framework in mind, we turn to the question presented: whether the Act pre-empts Vermont common law to the extent that law may impose liability on a New York point source. We begin the analysis by noting that it is not necessary for a federal statute to provide explicitly that particular state laws are pre-empted. Hillsborough County v. Automated Medical Laboratories, Inc., 471 U.S. 707, 713, 105 S. Ct. 2371, — , 85 L. Ed. 2d 714 (1985). Although courts should not lightly infer pre-emption,[11] it may be presumed when the federal legislation is "sufficiently comprehensive to make reasonable the inference that Congress 'left no room' for supplementary state regulation." Ibid. (quoting Rice v. Santa Fe Elevator Corp., 331 U.S. 218, 230, 67 S. Ct. 1146, 1152, 91 L. Ed. 1447 (1974)). In addition to express or implied pre-emption, a state law also is invalid to the extent that it "actually conflicts with a . . . federal statute." Ray v. Atlantic Richfield Co., 435 U.S. 151, 158, 98 S. Ct. 988, 994, 55 L. Ed. 2d 179 (1978). Such a conflict will be found when the state law "'stands as an obstacle to the accomplishment and execution of the full purposes and objectives of Congress.'" Hillsborough County v. Automated Medical Laboratories, *supra*, 471 U.S., at 713, 105 S. Ct., at — (quoting Hines v. Davidowitz, 312 U.S. 52, 67, 61 S. Ct. 399, 404, 85 L. Ed. 581 (1941)).

A

As we noted in *Milwaukee II*, Congress intended the 1972 Act amendments to "establish an all-encompassing program of water pollution regulation." [451 U.S. 304, 318 (1981).] We observed that congressional "views on the comprehensive nature of the legislation were practically universal." Id., at 318, n.12, 101 S. Ct., at 1793, n.12 (citing legislative history). An examination of the amendments amply supports these views. The Act applies to all point sources and virtually all bodies of water, and it sets forth the procedures for obtaining a permit in great detail. The CWA also provides its own remedies, including civil and criminal fines for permit violations, and "citizen suits" that allow individuals (including those from affected States) to compel the EPA to enforce a permit. In light of this pervasive regulation and the fact that the control of interstate pollution is primarily a matter of federal law, *Milwaukee I*, [406 U.S. 91, 107 (1972)], it is clear that the only state suits that remain available are those specifically preserved by the Act.

Although Congress intended to dominate the field of pollution regulation, the saving clause negates the inference that Congress "left no room" for state causes of action. Respondents read the language of the saving clause broadly to

---

11.   See Rice v. Sante Fe Elevator Corp., 331 U.S. 218, 230, 67 S. Ct. (1947) ("we start with the assumption that the historic police powers of the States were not to be superseded by the Federal Act unless that was the clear and manifest purpose of Congress"); *Milwaukee II*, 451 U.S., at 312, 101 S. Ct., at 1789; see also Silkwood v. Kerr-McGee Corp., 464 U.S. 238, 255, 104 S. Ct. 615, 625, 78 L. Ed. 2d 443 (1984).

preserve both a State's right to regulate its waters, 33 U.S.C. §1370, and an injured party's right to seek relief under "any statute *or common law*," §1365(e) (emphasis added). They claim that this language and selected portions of the legislative history compel the inference that Congress intended to preserve the right to bring suit under the law of any affected state.[13] We cannot accept this reading of the Act.

To begin with, the plain language of the provisions on which respondents rely by no means compels the result they seek. Section 505(e) merely says that "nothing *in this section*," i.e., the citizen-suit provisions, shall affect an injured party's right to seek relief under state law; it does not purport to preclude pre-emption of state law by other provisions of the Act. Section 510, moreover, preserves the authority of a State "with respect to the waters (including boundary waters) of such State." This language arguably limits the effect of the clause to discharges flowing *directly* into a State's own waters, i.e., discharges from within the State. The savings clause then, does not preclude pre-emption of the law of an affected State.

Given that the Act itself does not speak directly to the issue, the Court must be guided by the goals and policies of the Act in determining whether it in fact pre-empts an action based on the law of an affected State. After examining the CWA as a whole, its purposes and its history, we are convinced that if affected States were allowed to impose separate discharge standards on a single point source, the inevitable result would be a serious interference with the achievement of the "full purposes and objectives of Congress." See Hillsborough County v. Automated Medical Laboratories, *supra*, 471 U.S. at 713, 105 S. Ct., at — . Because we do not believe Congress intended to undermine this carefully drawn statute through a general saving clause, we conclude that the CWA precludes a court from applying the law of an affected State against an out-of-state source.

B

In determining whether Vermont nuisance law "stands as an obstacle" to the full implementation of the CWA, it is not enough to say that the ultimate goal of both federal and state law is to eliminate water pollution. A state law also is pre-empted if it interferes with the methods by which the federal statute was designed to reach this goal. In this case the application of Vermont law against IPC would allow respondents to circumvent the NPDES permit system, thereby upsetting the balance of public and private interests so carefully addressed by the Act.

---

13.   A Senate Report accompanying the amendments states: "[I]f damages could be shown, other remedies [in addition to a citizen suit] would remain available. Compliance with requirements under this Act would not be a defense to a common law action for pollution damages." S. Rep. No. 92-414, p. 81 (1971), 2 Leg. Hist. 1499, U.S. Code Cong. & Admin. News 1972, pp. 3668, 3746. Respondents also note that after reviewing the legislative history, the District Court found no evidence that Congress intended to alter the traditional tort law principle that a party may bring suit in the State where the injury occurred. See Young v. Masci, 289 U.S. 253, 258-259, 53 S. Ct. 599, 601, 77 L. Ed. 1158 (1933).

By establishing a permit system for effluent discharges, Congress implicitly has recognized that the goal of the CWA — elimination of water pollution — cannot be achieved immediately, and that it cannot be realized without incurring costs. The EPA Administrator issues permits according to established effluent standards and water quality standards, that in turn are based upon available technology, 33 U.S.C. §1314, and competing public and industrial uses, §1312(a). The Administrator must consider the impact of the discharges on the waterway, the types of effluents, and the schedule for compliance, each of which may vary widely among sources. If a State elects to impose its own standards, it also must consider the technological feasibility of more stringent controls. Given the nature of these complex decisions, it is not surprising that the Act limits the right to administer the permit system to the EPA and the source States. See §1342(b).

An interpretation of the saving clause that preserved actions brought under an affected State's law would disrupt this balance of interests. If a New York source were liable for violations of Vermont law, that law could effectively override both the permit requirements and the policy choices made by the source State. The affected State's nuisance laws would subject the point source to the threat of legal and equitable penalties if the permit standards were less stringent than those imposed by the affected State. Such penalties would compel the source to adopt different control standards and a different compliance schedule from those approved by the EPA, even though the affected State had not engaged in the same weighing of the costs and benefits. This case illustrates the problems with such a rule. If the Vermont Court ruled that respondents were entitled to the full amount of damages and injunctive relief sought in the complaint, at a minimum IPC would have to change its methods of doing business and controlling pollution to avoid the threat of ongoing liability. In suits such as this, an affected-state court also could require the source to cease operations by ordering immediate abatement. Critically, these liabilities would attach even though the source had complied fully with its state and federal permit obligations. The inevitable result of such suits would be that Vermont and other States could do indirectly what they could not do directly — regulate the conduct of out-of-state sources.[15]

Application of an affected State's law to an out-of-state source also would undermine the important goals of efficiency and predictability in the permit system. . . .

C

Our conclusion that Vermont nuisance law is inapplicable to a New York point source does not leave respondents without a remedy. The CWA precludes only those suits that may require standards of effluent control that are incom-

15.   The interpretation of the Act adopted by the Courts below also would have the result of allowing affected States effectively to set discharge standards without consulting with the source State, even though source States are required by the Act to give affected States an opportunity to be heard and a chance to comment before issuing a permit.

patible with those established by the procedures set forth in the Act. The saving clause specifically preserves other state actions, and therefore nothing in the Act bars aggrieved individuals from bringing a nuisance claim pursuant to the law of the *source* State. . . .

An action brought against IPC under New York nuisance law would not frustrate the goals of the CWA as would a suit governed by Vermont law.[19] First, application of the source State's law does not disturb the balance among federal, source-state, and affected-state interests. Because the Act specifically allows source States to impose stricter standards, the imposition of source-state law does not disrupt the regulatory partnership established by the permit system. Second, the restriction of suits to those brought under source-state nuisance law prevents a source from being subject to an indeterminate number of potential regulations. Although New York nuisance law may impose separate standards and thus create some tension with the permit system, a source only is required to look to a single additional authority, whose rules should be relatively predictable. Moreover, States can be expected to take into account their own nuisance laws in setting permit requirements.[20]

19.   The District Court concluded that the interference with the Act is insignificant, in part because respondents are seeking to be compensated for a specific harm rather than trying to "regulate" IPC. 602 F. Supp. 264, 271-272 (Vt. 1985). The Solicitor General, on behalf of the United States as amicus curiae, adopts only a portion of this view. He acknowledges that suits seeking *punitive* or *injunctive* relief under affected-state law should be pre-empted because of the interference they cause with the CWA. The Government asserts that *compensatory* damages, however, may be brought under the law of the State where the injury occurred. The SG reasons that compensatory damages only require the source to pay for the external costs created by the pollution, and thus do not "regulate" in a way inconsistent with the Act. The Government cites Silkwood v. Kerr-McGee Corp., 464 U.S. 238, 104 S. Ct. 615, 78 L. Ed. 2d 443 (1984), for the proposition that in certain circumstances a court may find pre-emption of some remedies and not others. We decline the Government's invitation to draw a line between the types of relief sought. There is no suggestion of such a distinction in either the Act or the legislative history. As the Court noted in *Silkwood*, unless there is evidence that Congress meant to "split" a partic-ular remedy for pre-emption purposes, it is assumed that the full cause of action under state law is available (or as in this case, pre-empted). Id., at 255, 104 S. Ct., at 625. We also think it would be unwise to treat compensatory damages differently under the facts of this case. If the Vermont Court determined that respondents were entitled only to the requested compensatory relief, IPC might be compelled to adopt different or additional means of pollution control from those required by the Act, regardless of whether the purpose of the relief was compensatory or regulatory. See Perez v. Campbell, 402 U.S. 637, 651-652, 91 S. Ct. 1704, 1712, 29 L. Ed. 2d 233 (1974) (effect rather than purpose of a state statute governs pre-emption analysis). As dis-cussed, this result would be irreconcilable with the CWA's exclusive grant of authority to the Federal Government and the source State. Cf. Chicago & North Western Transportation Co. v. Kalo Brick & Tile, 450 U.S. 311, 324-325, 101 S. Ct. 1124, 1133-1134, 67 L. Ed. 2d 258 (1981).

20.   Although we conclude that New York law generally controls this suit, we note that the pre-emptive scope of the CWA necessarily includes *all* laws that are inconsistent with the "full purposes and objectives of Congress." See Hillsborough County v. Automated Medical Lab-oratories, 471 U.S. 707, 713, 105 S. Ct. 2371, — , 85 L. Ed. 2d 714 (1986). We therefore do not agree with the dissent that Vermont nuisance law still may apply if the New York *choice of law* doctrine dictates such a result. As we have discussed, *supra*, the application of affected-state law would frustrate the carefully prescribed CWA regulatory system. This interference would occur, of course, whether affected-state law applies as an original matter, or whether it applies pursuant to the source State's choice of law principles. Therefore if, and to the extent, the law of a source State requires the application of affected-state substantive law on this particular issue, it would be pre-empted as well.

IPC asks the Court to go one step further and hold that all state-law suits also must be brought in source-state *courts*. As petitioner cites little authority or justification for this position, we find no basis for holding that Vermont is an improper forum. Simply because a cause of action is pre-empted does not mean that judicial jurisdiction over the claim is affected as well; the Act pre-empts laws, not courts. In the absence of statutory authority to the contrary, the rule is settled that a district court sitting in diversity is competent to apply the law of a foreign State.

IV

The District Court correctly denied IPC's motion for summary judgment and judgment on the pleadings. Nothing in the Act prevents a court sitting in an affected State from hearing a common-law nuisance suit, provided that jurisdiction otherwise is proper. Both the District Court and the Court of Appeals erred, however, in concluding that Vermont law governs this litigation. The application of affected-state laws would be incompatible with the Act's delegation of authority and its comprehensive regulation of water pollution. The Act pre-empts state law to the extent that the state law is applied to an out-of-state point source.

The decision of the Court of Appeals is affirmed in part and reversed in part. The case is remanded for further proceedings consistent with this opinion.

It is so ordered.

Justice BRENNAN with whom Justice MARSHALL and Justice BLACKMUN join, concurring in part and dissenting in part.

I concur wholeheartedly in the Court's judgment that the Clean Water Act, 33 U.S.C. §1251 et seq. (Act), does not pre-empt a private nuisance suit filed in a Vermont court when the source of the alleged injury is located in New York. I disagree only with the Court's view that a Vermont court must apply New York nuisance law.

I

The question presented is whether the District Court properly denied International Paper Company's motion to dismiss. The Court concludes that a federal district court, sitting in the State where the injury occurred, may hear a common law nuisance suit to redress interstate water pollution *and* that the district court must apply the law of the State in which the point source is located. The Court improperly reaches out to decide the latter issue. As far as the parties and the Court know, "Vermont law and New York law are identical on the question of private nuisance." Tr. of Oral Arg. 24. Moreover, Vermont is the only State to share Lake Champlain with New York. Thus, the nuisance laws of New York and Vermont are the sole candidates for application in the present case, and they do not conflict. The respondents do not base their claims on any particular state law — "[t]he Complaint in this matter does not specify the jurisdiction of the common law it invokes or make a choice of law." Plaintiffs' Supplemental Memorandum of Law in Opposition to Defendant's Motion to Dismiss in No. 78-163, p. 4 (May 18, 1984). Given these facts, I find it necessary only to affirm the denial of International Paper Company's motion to dismiss.

II

Even were I to reach the issue of the state law applicable in this case, I would not interpret the Act to require a court sitting in the State where the injury has occurred (affected State) to apply the nuisance law of the State from which the pollution emanates (source State). Nothing in the Act pre-empts the usual 2-step analysis undertaken by federal district courts to determine which state tort law should be applied in interstate tort suits. First, the district court must apply the conflict-of-law rules of the State in which the court sits. See Day & Zimmerman, Inc. v. Challoner, 423 U.S. 3, 4, 96 S. Ct. 167, 168, 46 L. Ed. 2d 3 (1975); Klaxon Co. v. Stentor Electric Mfg. Co., Inc., 313 U.S. 487, 496, 61 S. Ct. 1020, 1021, 85 L. Ed. 1477 (1941) (holding that *Erie* doctrine applies to conflict-of-law rules). Thus, the Vermont District Court should apply the conflict-of-law rules of Vermont, the affected State. Second, these conflict-of-law principles must be interpreted by the district court to determine whether the tort law of the source State or the affected State should be applied. Today the Court finds that the application of the Vermont's nuisance law is pre-empted even if Vermont's conflict-of-law rules determine that Vermont's tort law should be applied.

The Act provides no support for deviation from well-settled conflict-of-law principles. Under conflict-of-law rules, the affected State's nuisance law may be applied when the purpose of the tort law is to ensure compensation of tort victims.[1] . . . This traditional interest of the affected State, involving the health and safety of its citizens, is protected by providing for application of the affected State's own tort laws in suits against the source State's pollutors. The State's interest in applying its own tort laws cannot be superseded by a federal act unless that was the clear and manifest purpose of Congress.

Here Congress preserved the rights of source States and affected States alike

---

1. States have adopted two different conflict-of-law approaches to determine which state tort law should be applied. The traditional rule of *lex loci delicti* requires the application of the tort law of the jurisdiction where the injury occurred. See 19 N.Y. Jur. 2d §39, p. 623 (1982); E. Scoles & P. Hay, Conflict of Law §17.7, pp. 560-561 (1982). The rationale for the traditional rule is that the affected State possesses a strong interest in redressing injuries to its citizens. The modern rule, followed by the majority of States, employs an interest-analysis approach. See Allstate Ins. Co. v. Hague, 449 U.S. 302, 309, 101 S. Ct. 633, 638, 66 L. Ed. 2d 521 (1981). Under this analysis, if the primary purpose of the tort rule is to control the tortfeasor's conduct — such as the setting of pollution discharge standards — then the source State's tort law may be applied. Alternatively, if the main purpose of the tort rule is compensating victims of the tort, a court may apply the affected State's tort law. Other relevant considerations include the locations of the parties and where the relationship, if any, between the parties is centered. See Restatement (Second) of Conflict of Laws §145 and Comment c, pp. 414-416 (1971).

to enforce state common-law claims. Section 510 provides: "Except as *expressly* provided . . . , nothing in this chapter shall . . . be construed as impairing or *in any manner affecting any right* or jurisdiction *of the States with respect to the waters (including boundary waters) of such States.*" 33 U.S.C. §1370 (emphasis added). In preserving the right to seek traditional common-law relief, the Act draws no distinction between interstate and intrastate disputes; §505(e) states: "Nothing in this section shall restrict any right which any person (or class of persons) may have under any statute or common law to seek enforcement of any effluent standard or limitation or to seek any other relief." §1365(e).[2] This provision contains no "express" restriction on the normal operation of state law, reflecting the Act's policy "to recognize, preserve, and protect the primary responsibilities and rights of States to prevent, reduce, and eliminate pollution. . . ." §1251(b).

By contrast, where Congress wanted to affect state common-law rights, it expressly stated this intent in the Act. Congress chose to pre-empt state law "only where the situation warranted it based upon the urgent need for uniformity such as in section 312(f) relating to marine sanitation devices." H.R. Rep. No. 92-911, p. 136 (1972), 1 Legislative History of the Water Pollution Control Act of 1972 (Committee Print compiled for the Senate Committee on Public Works by the Library of Congress), Ser. No. 93-1, p. 823 (1973) (hereinafter Leg. Hist.).

I find that the Act's plain language clearly indicates that Congress wanted to leave intact the traditional right of the affected State to apply its own tort law when its residents are injured by an out-of-state polluter.

III

The Court argues that, although the Act does not explicitly state that the affected States' laws are pre-empted here, applying the law of an affected State against an out-of-state source stands as an obstacle to the full implementation of the Act. The Court contends application of an affected State's common law is contrary to subsidiary objectives of the Act: (1) establishing the right of source States to set effluent standards for in-state pollutors, and (2) establishing clear and identifiable discharge standards. The Court concludes that the affected State's common law is pre-empted by implication because of these conflicts. Although the Court plausibly argues that it is offering a better administrative approach, I do not believe that Congress meant to alter state law in this manner.

As a threshold matter, the Court's opinion assumes that in enacting the Clean Water Act, Congress valued administrative efficiency more highly than

---

2. The Court dismisses the importance of §505(e) because that section "merely says that 'nothing *in this section*,' i.e., the citizen-suit provisions, shall affect an injured party's right to seek relief under state law; it does not purport to preclude pre-emption of state law by other provisions of the Act." But Congress used this language because this is the only section of the Act that expressly implicates private suits. Congress was reemphasizing that a State's authority over private suits, involving state common law, was not affected by the Act.

effective elimination of water pollution. Yet there is no evidence that Congress ever made such a choice. Instead, the Clean Water Act reflects Congress' judgment that a rational permit system, operating in tandem with existing state common-law controls, would best achieve the Act's primary goal of controlling water pollution. I base this conclusion on four important considerations.

First, since Congress preserved state common-law rights "except as *expressly* provided," the Court's reliance upon pre-emption by *implication* cannot justify its conclusion. . . .

Second, the legislative history of the Act indicates that Congress saw no peril to the Act in permitting the application of traditional principles of state law. The Senate Committee Report noted that Congress meant "specifically [to] preserve any rights or remedies under any other law. Thus, if damages could be shown, other remedies would remain available. *Compliance with requirements under this Act would not be a defense to a common law action for pollution damages.*" S. Rep. No. 92-414, p. 81 (1971), 2 Leg. Hist. 1499, U.S. Code Cong. & Admin. News 1972, p. 3746 (emphasis added). The majority's concern that tort liability might undercut permit requirements was thus not shared by Congress.

Third, we have refused to pre-empt a State's law, even when it is contrary to subsidiary objectives concerning administration, if the State's law furthers the federal statute's primary purpose and is consistent with the Act's saving of States' authority in an area traditionally regulated by States. See Pacific Gas & Electric Co. v. Energy Resources Conservation and Development Commn., 461 U.S. 190, 221-223, 103 S. Ct. 1713, 1731-1732, 75 L. Ed. 2d 752 (1983). Subjecting polluters to state common-law liability simultaneously promotes the main federal goal of eliminating water pollution entirely, 33 U.S.C. §1251(a)(1), and obeys the congressional command to leave state common law intact. Here Congress intended to stand by its federal regulatory scheme and the State's traditional liability laws "and to tolerate whatever tension there was between them." Silkwood v. Kerr-McGee Corp., 464 U.S., at 256, 104 S. Ct., at 625. . . .

Finally, the Court overstates any conflict between the affected State's nuisance law and the subsidiary objectives of the Act. The Court contends that applying the affected State's law would violate the source State's right to set effluent standards for in-state polluters. But if traditional conflict-of-law rules require the application of the affected State's nuisance law, there is no "conflict" with the source State's ability to set the *minimum* standards required under the Act. Congress considered state common-law rights to be supplementary to, and not in conflict with, the Act unless they embodied a "less stringent" standard for polluters than the federal effluent standards. See H.R. Rep. No. 92-911, pp. 169-170 (1972), 1 Leg. Hist. 856-857. The application of an affected State's common-law remedies to an out-of-state polluter does not conflict with the Act because it is possible for the polluter to redress the injuries suffered by the victims of the pollution and to obey the source State's effluent standards. By complying with the most stringent requirement — either under the Act or the affected State's law — the polluter necessarily complies with the more lenient standards. . . .

IV

Even if the Court's conclusion that New York *law* should apply is correct, it does not logically follow that New York *nuisance law* must be applied in this case. . . .

Whether New York law requires the application of New York or Vermont nuisance law depends on an interpretation of New York law *pertaining to conflict of laws.*[3] "A state has the same freedom to adopt its own rules of Conflict of Laws as it has to adopt any other rules of law. Conflict of Laws rules, when adopted, become as definitely a part of the law as any other branch of the state's law." Restatement (Second) of Conflicts of Laws §5, Comment a, p. 9 (1971). The Court reasons that a source State must have the primary role in regulating its own pollution discharges. Under this logic, nothing prevents a source State's legislature or courts from choosing to impose, under conflict-of-law principles, the affected State's nuisance law in a case such as this. A source State is free to adopt an affected State's standards as its own standards.

The District Court correctly denied the petitioner's motion for summary judgment and judgment on the pleadings. For the reasons indicated above, I would affirm without reaching the question of the state law applicable in this case. . . .

See Glicksman, Federal Preemption and Private Legal Remedies for Pollution, 134 U. Pa. L. Rev. 121 (1985) for an insightful critique of the majority's analysis.

RAY v. MASON COUNTY DRAIN COMMISSIONER
393 Mich. 294, 224 N.W.2d 883 (1975)

WILLIAMS, Justice.

This is a significant case of first impression relating to Michigan's world-famous Environmental Protection Act (EPA).[1] The question involved is the kind

---

3. Respondent contends that under both New York and Vermont conflict-of-law principles, Vermont common law would apply to this action. Brief for Respondents 12. Petitioner does not contest this view. If this issue need be determined, it should, in my view, be remanded to the Court of Appeals. See, e.g., Allstate Ins. Co. v. Hague, 449 U.S., at 307, 101 S. Ct., at 637; Day & Zimmerman, Inc. v. Challoner, 423 U.S. 3, 5, 96 S. Ct. 167, 168, 46 L. Ed. 2d 3 (1975) (Blackmun, J., concurring); Klaxon Co. v. Stentor Electric Mfg. Co., Inc., 313 U.S. 487, 492, 61 S. Ct. 1020, 85 L. Ed. 1477 (1941). It is sufficient for the sake of argument to note that several cases suggest that New York conflict-of-law principles may require that Vermont law be applied in this instance. See, e.g., Bing v. Halstead, 495 F. Supp. 517, 520 (SDNY 1980) ("Where tortious conduct occurs in one jurisdiction and injury in another, as is the case here, the law of the place of injury applies"); Cousins v. Instrument Flyers, Inc., 44 N.Y.2d 698, 699, 405 N.Y.S.2d 441, 442, 376 N.E.2d 914, 915 (1978) ("It is true that lex loci delicti remains the general rule in tort cases to be displaced only in extraordinary circumstances").

1. M.C.L.A. §691.1201 et seq., M.S.A. §14.528(201) et seq.

The Michigan Environmental Protection Act was the first statute to provide for citizen suits to protect the environment from degradation by either public or private entities and

of findings of fact required of the trial judge by GCR 1963, 517 and §3(1) of the EPA in deciding an action brought under the EPA.

In the instant case the trial judge failed to make specific findings of facts. Rather than attempt a review de novo, we remand for full and specific findings of fact under Dauer v. Zabel, 381 Mich. 555, 558, 164 N.W.2d 1 (1969). To assist the trial judge, especially since this is a case of first impression, we set forth considerations and guidelines for proper findings of fact.

In light of the remand order, it is inappropriate to consider the other issues raised on appeal at this time.

I — Facts

This action was brought by 70% of the landowners in the Black Creek Watershed in Mason County and by an additional group of six persons who joined the suit solely with regard to the environmental issues. Plaintiffs-appellants seek to enjoin the Mason County Drain Commissioner, defendant-appellee, from proceeding with a channelization program for the watershed and from assessing them for any part of the cost of the project. The Black Creek Watershed consists of 6,678 acres of relatively flat land, which was once used primarily for agricultural purposes, but in which today only a small number of the parcels are actively farmed.

The area contains a biologically unique "quaking forest," swamps and potholes, and scattered, wooded areas which serve as a refuge for a wide variety of wildlife.

The existing system of open drains is inadequate to control flooding which occurs in the springtime and which inundates some 100 acres for periods up to three weeks. Apparently, such flooding does not pose health or safety hazards, but does cause some crop damage. In 1960 two farmers requested assistance of the Mason County Soil Conservation District in correcting the drainage problem. The District along with the Drain Commissioner applied for federal funds under 16 U.S.C. §1001 et. seq., a cost-sharing program which makes funds available for flood control. . . .

II — Inadequate Findings of Facts

Count I of plaintiffs' complaint alleged that numerous and substantial forms of environmental degradation would result from the proposed Black Creek Watershed Project. Both sides presented their case on the environmental issues,

---

to provide a broad scope for court adjudication. The Federal Clean Air Act and Water Pollution Control Amendments, as well as several state statutes, have followed the Michigan Act's lead.

Sax & DiMento, Environmental Citizen Suits: Three Years Experience under The Michigan Environmental Protection Act, 4 Ecology L.Q. 1 (1974).

calling both expert and lay witnesses to testify, as well as introducing many documents, reports and maps into evidence during the trial, which lasted two days.

The trial judge's entire findings of fact on the issues raised and the evidence introduced relating to the environmental questions was restricted to the following language:

> Count I is based upon MCLA 691.1202 (Environmental Protection Act), claiming the proposed project will pollute and destroy the natural resources in the area as well as increase the pollution of the Pere Marquette River and Lake Michigan, downstream from the proposed project. *The plaintiffs do not sustain the burden of proof on this issue. . . .*

Michigan's Environmental Protection Act marks the Legislature's response to our constitutional commitment to the "conservation and development of the natural resources of the state. . . ."[3] Const. 1963, art. 4, §52 in its entirety reads:

> Sec. 52. The conservation and development of the natural resources of the state are hereby declared to be of paramount public concern in the interest of the health, safety and general welfare of the people. *The legislature shall provide for the protection of the air, water and other natural resources of the state from pollution, impairment and destruction.* [Emphasis added.]

Michigan's EPA was the first legislation of its kind and has attracted worldwide attention.[4] The act also has served as a model for other states in formulating environmental legislation.[5] The enactment of the EPA signals a dramatic change from the practice where the important task of environmental law enforcement

---

3.   Const. 1963, art. 4, §52. See State Highway Commission v. Vanderkloot, 392 Mich. 159, 178-184, 220 N.W.2d 416 (1974) (opinion of Williams, J.) for further discussion on the constitutional mandate and the legislative response to the commitment to a cleaner environment.

4.   The passage of the Act received worldwide press coverage: "Time, 24 August 1970, p. 37; New York Times, 3 August 1970, p. 36, col. 2; Le Courrier (UNESCO), July, 1971, p. 20; Proceedings, International Symposium on Environmental Disruption, Tokyo, 1970 (Asahi Evening News, Tokyo)." Brief Amicus Curiae, p. 3.

Michigan's EPA has also received considerable attention in legal periodicals. An insight into the Act's political background may be found in Watts, Michigan Environmental Protection Act, J.L. Reform 358 (1970). An analysis of the Act's major provisions is found in Michigan Environmental Protection Act of 1970, 4 J.L. Reform 121. Two articles have monitored actions brought under the Act since its passage: Sax & Conner, Michigan's Environmental Protection Act of 1970: A Progress Report, 70 Mich. L. Rev. 1003 (1972); and Sax & DiMento, Environmental Citizen Suits: Three Years Experience under the Michigan Protection Act, 4 Ecology L.Q. 1 (1974). Not every one has viewed the Act with unqualified enthusiasm. An article by Joseph H. Thibodeau, former Legal Advisor to Governor William Milliken, sets out a number of reservations concerning the Act. Thibodeau, Michigan's Environmental Protection Act of 1970: Panacea or Pandora's Box, 48 J.L. Reform 564 (1971).

5.   To date six states have adopted environmental legislation employing language similar to that found in Michigan's EPA: Minn. Stat. Ann. §§116B.01-116B.13 (Supp. 1973); Mass. Ann. Laws, ch. 214, §10A (Supp. 1972); Conn. Gen. Stat. Ann. §§22a-14 to 22a-20 (Supp. 1973); S.D. Comp. Laws Ann. §§21-10A-1 to 21-10A-15; Fla. Stat. Ann. §403.412 (Supp. 1973); Ind. Ann. Stat. §§13-6-1-1 to 13-6-1-6 (1973); Sax & DiMento, Environmental Citizen Suits: Three Years Experience under the Michigan Environmental Protection Act, 4 Ecology L.Q. 1, 2 (1974).

was left to administrative agencies without the opportunity for participation by individuals or groups of citizens.[6] Not every public agency proved to be diligent and dedicated defenders of the environment. The EPA has provided a sizable share of the initiative for environmental law enforcement for that segment of society most directly affected — the public. Daniels v. Allen Industries, 391 Mich. 398, 410-411, 216 N.W.2d 762 (1974).

The Act provides private individuals and other legal entities with standing to maintain actions in the Circuit Courts for declaratory and other equitable relief against anyone "for the protection of the air, water and other natural resources and the public trust therein from pollution, impairment or destruction." M.C.L.A. §691.1202(1), M.S.A. §14.528(202)(1).

The Act also empowers the Circuit Courts to grant "equitable relief, or . . . impose conditions on the defendant that are required to protect the air, water and natural resources. . . ." M.C.L.A. §691.1204(1), M.S.A. §14.528(204)(1).

But the EPA does more than give standing to the public and grant equitable powers to the Circuit Courts, it also imposes a duty on individuals and organizations both in the public and private sectors to prevent or minimize degradation of the environment which is caused or is likely to be caused by their activities.[8] The EPA prohibits pollution, destruction, or impairment of the environment unless it can be shown that "there is no feasible and prudent alternative" and that defendant's conduct "is consistent with the promotion of the public health, safety and welfare in light of the state's paramount concern for the protection of its natural resources. . . ." M.C.L.A. §691.1203, M.S.A. §14.528(203).

The Legislature in establishing environmental rights set the parameters for the standard of environmental quality but did not attempt to set forth an elaborate scheme of detailed provisions designed to cover every conceivable type of environmental pollution or impairment. Rather the Legislature spoke as precisely as the subject matter permits and in its wisdom left to the courts the important task of giving substance to the standard by developing a common law of environmental quality.[10] The Act allows the courts to fashion standards in the context

---

6.   Joseph L. Sax, author of the EPA's first draft, portrays this dilemma vividly in his book Defending the Environment (Knopf 1971).

8.   Joseph L. Sax, author of the EPA's first draft, states that the act allows one "to assert that his right to environmental quality has been violated in much the same way that one has always been able to claim that a property or contract right has been violated." Sax & Conner, Michigan's Environmental Protection Act of 1970: A Progress Report, 70 Mich. L. Rev. 1003, 1005 (1972). See also discussion on this point in State Highway Commission v. Vanderkloot, 392 Mich. 159, 184-185, 220 N.W.2d 416 (1974), opinion of Williams, J.

10.   Thomas J. Anderson, one of the legislative sponsors of the EPA, underscored this purpose when he said that the EPA should "permit courts to develop a common law of environmental quality, much as courts have developed a right to privacy." Press Release, Representative Thomas J. Anderson, Michigan Passes Landmark Environmental Law, 2 July 1970. Brief Amicus Curiae, p. 6. While the language of the statute paints the standard for environmental quality with a rather broad stroke of the brush, the language used is neither illusive nor vague. "Pollution," "impairment" and "destruction" are taken directly from the constitutional provision which

of actual problems as they arise in individual cases and to take into consideration changes in technology which the Legislature at the time of the Act's passage could not hope to foresee.

V — Findings of Facts under the EPA

The judicial development of a common law of environmental quality, as envisioned by the Legislature, can only take place if Circuit Court judges take care to set out with specificity the factual findings upon which they base their ultimate conclusions. If the Circuit Court judges fail to provide adequate findings of fact, not only will the immediate parties remain in the dark as to why they won or lost, but courts confronted with similar questions in the future will be denied the benefit of other courts' deliberations, those who seek in good faith to comply with the mandate of the EPA will be without a precise standard against which to measure their conduct, and appellate courts will be unable to determine those instances in which the trial judge has failed to carry out the Legislature's intent. In the final analysis the very efficacy of the EPA will turn on how well Circuit Court judges meet their responsibility for giving vitality and meaning to the act through detailed findings of fact.

The Act itself offers substantial guidance to trial judges regarding what should be included in the findings of fact for actions brought under the EPA. Section 3(1) of the Act reads:

> When the plaintiff in the action has made a prima facie showing that the conduct of the defendant has, or is likely to, pollute, impair or destroy the air, water or other natural resources or the public trust therein, the defendant may rebut the prima facie showing by the submission of evidence to the contrary. The defendant may also show, by way of an affirmative defense, that there is no feasible and prudent alternative to defendant's conduct and that such conduct is consistent with the promotion of the public health, safety and welfare in light of the state's paramount concern for the protection of its natural resources from pollution, impairment or destruction. Except as to the affirmative defense, the principles of burden of proof and weight of the evidence generally applicable in civil actions in the circuit courts shall apply to actions brought under this act.

To satisfy the requirements for findings of fact under the EPA, the trial judge should consider, and where appropriate make, findings of fact with regard to each of the following:

1) How the plaintiff has established a prima facie case that the defendant's

---

sets forth this state's commitment to preserve the quality of our environment. In addition these and other terms used in establishing the standard have acquired meaning in Michigan jurisprudence. The development of a common law of environmental quality under the EPA is no different from the development of the common law in other areas such as nuisance or torts in general, and we see no valid reason to block the evolution of this new area of common law.

conduct "has or is likely to pollute, impair or destroy the air, water or other natural resources . . ." or how he has failed to.

2) How defendant has rebutted plaintiffs' prima facie case with evidence to the contrary, or how he has failed to.

3) How defendant has established as an affirmative defense that "there is no feasible and prudent alternative . . . and that such conduct is consistent with the promotion of the public health, safety and welfare in light of the State's paramount concern for the protection of its natural resources from pollution, impairment or destruction," or how he has failed to. . . .

[The case was remanded because the trial judge's findings of fact and conclusions of law, which were only three sentences long, were inadequate.]

NOTES AND QUESTIONS

1. The substantive reach of *Ray* is illustrated by West Michigan Environmental Action Council v. Natural Resources Commission, 405 Mich. 741, 275 N.W.2d 538, *cert. denied sub. nom.*, Shell Oil Co. v. West Michigan Environmental Action Council, 44 U.S. 941 (1979). The issue was whether the issuance of permits to drill ten exploratory oil and gas wells in a state forest violated MEPA. The court first held that the statute required trial judges to make "independent, de novo judgments." An environmental impact matrix showed that elk would avoid the area for 40 to 50 years. The trial judge concluded that the plaintiffs had failed to establish a prima facie case by flippantly observing that the elk "are innocent victims of the discovery of oil in their forest domain." The Supreme Court showed more concern for animal life:

> This determination reveals a fundamental misconception. If nature is allowed to pursue its own course, the growth and expansion of some species will inevitably result in the diminution and possible extinction of others. Faced with a situation where an adverse impact will occur naturally unless some action is taken, it is a management decision to determine whether such natural processes should proceed or whether, through human intervention, the adverse impact should artificially be shifted to other species. The choice is not whether an adverse impact will occur, but, rather, upon what. . . .
>
> The DNR's environmental impact statement recognizes that "[e]lk are *unique* to this area of Michigan" and that the herd is "the *only* sizable wild herd east of the Mississippi River. Several attempts to introduce elk elsewhere in Michigan have been unsuccessful."
>
> It is estimated that the herd's population, which numbered in excess of 1500 in 1963, now probably lies between 170 and 180. . . .
>
> In light of the limited number of the elk, the unique nature and location of this herd, and the apparently serious and lasting, though unquantifiable, damage that will result to the herd from the drilling of the ten exploratory wells, we conclude that defendants' conduct constitutes an impairment or destruction of a natural resource.
>
> Accordingly, we reverse and remand to the trial court for entry of a permanent injunction prohibiting the drilling of the ten exploratory wells pursuant to permits issued on August 24, 1977. [275 N.W.2d at 545.]

What is appellate de novo review? The Michigan courts have adopted the following standard. "[T]he trial court's findings of fact will not be overturned or modified unless they are clearly erroneous or the reviewing court is convinced that it would have reached a different result had it occupied the bench at trial." Kent County Road Commission v. Hunting, 170 Mich. App. 222, 428 N.W.2d 353, 358 (1988). Is the following reading of *West Michigan Environmental Action* correct? "In reviewing administrative agency action in a MEPA suit, it is *error* for the trial court to *defer* to the expertise of the agencies. Rather the court must exercise its independent judgment . . ." about the likelihood of environmental degradation. Her Majesty the Queen in Right of the Province of Ontario v. Detroit, 874 F.2d 332, 338 (6th Cir. 1989). Is the Michigan Standard anything more that what Professor Jaffe defined as the proper role of judges in construing statutes: "where the *judges* are themselves *convinced* that a certain reading or application of the statute is the *correct* or the only *faithful* reading or application, they should intervene and so declare." L. Jaffe, Judicial Control of Administrative Action 572 (1965). Compare this standard to the Supreme Court's current confusion about the standard of review for questions of law in *Chevron*, p. 128 *supra*.

2. Recall that the federal courts have had to decide what environmental degradation is for purposes of NEPA. Similar issues have arisen under MEPA. See, e.g., Poletown Neighborhood Council v. City of Detroit, 410 Mich. 616, 304 N.W.2d 455 (1981) (adverse impact of General Motors plant on neighborhood is a social and cultural issue outside the scope of MEPA). Whittaker Gooding Co. v. Scio Township Zoning Board of Appeals, 117 Mich. App. 18, 323 N.W.2d 574 (1982), held that a township's refusal to grant a zoning permit to allow gravel mining did not impair the state's natural resources: "The EPA was designed to protect natural resources themselves rather than an exploiter's mining of the resources." The court also rejected the plaintiff's argument that the gravel pit in question was the only one in the area and that thus the township's decision would increase air pollution because of trucks hauling gravel into the area. The court found this environmental impact indirect and concluded that "such conduct cannot be found to rise to the level of an environmental risk." Why?

3. Kent County Road Commission v. Hunting, *supra*, summarized the factors relevant to a determination of whether the impairment of environmental resources requires judicial intervention as "(1) whether the natural resource involved is rare, unique, endangered, or has historical significance; (2) whether the resource is easily replaceable (i.e., by replanting trees or restocking fish); (3) whether the proposed action will have any significant consequential effect on other natural resources (for example, whether wildlife will be lost if its habitat is impaired or destroyed); and (4) whether the direct or consequential impact on animals or vegetation will affect a critical number, considering the nature of the wildlife affected. Finally, aesthetic considerations by themselves do not constitute significant environmental impact." 428 N.W.2d at 358. Were the following cases correctly decided? Thomas Township v. John Sexton Corp. of Michigan, 173 Mich. App. 507, 434 N.W.2d 644 (1988), *appeal denied*, 433 Mich. 895 (1989), reviewed a final decision of the Natural Resources Commission which

approved a permit to drain a 62-acre artificial clay pit or "lake" and held that the proper de novo standard was a statewide perspective, Kimberly Hills Neighborhood Association v. Dion, 114 Mich. App. 495, 320 N.W.2d 668 (1982), *lv. denied*, 417 Mich. 1045 (1983). On the merits, the court agreed with the hearing examiner that the loss of a local but hazardous recreational facility did not "constitute the impairment or destruction of a natural resource under MEPA." 434 N.W.2d at 648. In Rush v. Steiner, 143 Mich. App. 672, 373 N.W.2d 183 (1985), the issue was whether a small unused hydroelectric dam on one of 20 to 25 trout streams in southern Michigan could be rehabilitated. The Department of Natural Resources managed the stream by killing off all fish species in it and then restocking it with trout. The court found that the 20-mile managed stretch of the stream would be impaired, but agreed with the trial court that judicial intervention was unwarranted. "Although trout are 'unique' in the particular area of Ionia County involved here, they are common throughout Michigan and exist in other streams of the general geographical area of Ionia County. In addition, the trout exist in this stream because of stringent management efforts by the DNR; without such efforts, the trout could not compete successfully against other species of fish, as they do with the efforts." 373 N.W.2d at 187. See also Kent County Road Commission v. Hunting, 170 Mich. App. 222, 428 N.W.2d 353 (1988), *appeal denied*, 432 Mich. 913 (1989) (county would widen road lined with trees planted for centennial of United States since they were old, dying and easily replaceable).

4. A few state constitutional provisions recognize individual environmental rights, e.g., Ill. Const. art. XI, but courts in these states have not used the provisions to develop substantive principles. Scattering Fork Drainage District v. Ogilvie, 19 Ill. App. 2d 386, 311 N.E.2d 203 (1976) (restrictive standing rule); Commonwealth v. National Gettysburg Battlefield Tower, Inc., 454 Pa. 193, 311 A.2d 588 (1973) (constitutional provision not self-executing). But cf. Payne v. Kassab, 468 Pa. 226, 361 A.2d 263 (1976) (self-executing provision applied to state agencies as opposed to private development). D. Mandelker, Environment and Equity: A Regulatory Challenge 111-119 (1981), is critical of these decisions. See generally Frye, Environmental Provisions in State Constitutions, 5 Envtl. L. Rep. (Envtl. L. Inst.) 50,023 (1975).

5. At the start of the environmental decade, some attention was given to the recognition of a federal constitutional right to environmental quality based on a due process right to health or on Justice Douglas's opinion in Griswold v. Connecticut, 381 U.S. 479 (1965). Environmental lawyers tended to throw in a constitutional cause of action after the statutory and common law arguments had been stated, but this course of action was unsuccessful, as Professor Stewart explains:

> Advocacy of a constitutional right to environmental quality by scholars and litigants has been rejected by the courts.[8] There is little doubt that the judges are correct in

8.   See Ely v. Velde, 451 F.2d 1130, 1139 (4th Cir. 1971); EDF v. Corps of Eng'rs, 325 F. Supp. 728, 739 (E.D. Ark. 1971); Hagedorn v. Union Carbide Corp., 363 F. Supp. 1061,

resisting these siren calls. The asserted right lacks any foundations in the constitutional text or in history.[9] While this is not necessarily a decisive objection to judicial recognition of a constitutional right to environmental quality, there are other basic difficulties. A familiar justification for constitutional protection of given interests is that they are held by a "discrete and insular" minority or are otherwise chronically undervalued because of basic structural defects in the political process.[10] This rationale has been utilized by advocates of a constitutional right to environmental quality, buttressing it by claims that environmental degradation violates "fundamental" interests in health and human survival and implicates the fate of future generations that are unrepresented in the political process.[11] But the spate of environmental legislation enacted by federal and state governments over the past ten years flatly contradicts the general claim that the political process suffers from structural defects that necessitate a constitutional right to environmental quality.[12]

The definition and implementation of a constitutional right to environmental quality would pose grave difficulties for the courts. Recognition of such a right would have potentially large resource implications in the reversal of existing degradation and the prevention of future degradation through curbs on economic growth and other measures. Courts would be saddled with ultimate responsibility for deciding what portion of society's resources would be devoted to environmental quality and what portion to other goals. [Stewart, The Development of Administrative and Quasi-Constitutional Law in Judicial Review of Environmental Decisionmaking: Lessons from the Clean Air Act, 62 Iowa L. Rev. 713, 714-715 (1977).]

For scholarly advocacy and analysis of a constitutional right to environmental quality, see Anderson, Fundamental Rights and Environmental Quality, in Science for a Better Environment 825 (Science Council of Japan ed. 1977); Hanks & Hanks, The Right to a Habitable Environment, in The Rights of Americans 146 (N. Dorsen ed. 1970); Kirchick, The Continuing Search for a Constitutionally Protected Environment, 4 Envtl. Aff. 515 (1975); Klipsch, Aspects of a Constitutional Right to a Habitable Environment: Towards an Environmental Due Process, 49 Ind. L.J. 203 (1974). See also Note, The Fairness and Constitutionality of Statutes of Limitations for Toxic Tort Suits, 96 Harv. L. Rev. 1683 (1983).

1064 (N.D.W. Va. 1973); Tanner v. Armco Steel Corp., 340 F. Supp. 532, 535 (S.D. Tex. 1972). But cf. EDF v. Hoerner Waldorf Corp., 1 ERC 1640, 1642 (D. Mont. 1970).

9. See, e.g., Tanner v. Armco Steel Corp., 340 F. Supp. 532 (S.D. Tex. 1972).

10. See A. Bickel, The Least Dangerous Branch 24-27 (1962); Ely, The Constitutionality of Reverse Racial Discrimination, 41 U. Chi. L. Rev. 723, 734-36 (1974).

11. See Note, Toward a Constitutionally Protected Environment, 56 Va. L. Rev. 458, 483 (1970).

12. See, e.g., Environmental Law Institute, Federal Environmental Law (E. Dolgin & T. Guilbert eds. 1974). Environmental legislation demonstrates that the political process is not insensitive to environmental problems or the claims of future generations. While the interest in a healthy environment is undeniably an "important" one, the intrinsic importance or weight of an interest is not determinative of constitutional status, which turns (at least in part) on the presence of basic defects in the political process that justify allocation of protective responsibility to the judiciary. See Michelman, The Supreme Court and Litigation Access Fees: The Right to Protect One's Rights — Part I, 1973 Duke L.J. 1153, 1211.

VII

THE NATIONAL ENVIRONMENTAL POLICY ACT

A. CONGRESSIONAL POLICY AND EARLY JUDICIAL INTERPRETATION

1. Congressional Purpose and History

Why NEPA Was Enacted

The National Environmental Policy Act of 1969 (NEPA) is one of the earliest and most influential congressional enactments on environmental policy to emerge from the environmental era. By injecting environmental concerns into much federal agency decisionmaking in any way related to resource management and by making possible federal litigation challenging federal actions affecting environmental quality, NEPA moved concern about environmental problems to a high level of public salience.

One of the authors of this casebook has summarized the reasons the late Senator Henry Jackson, chairman of Senate Interior and Insular Affairs Committee, decided to legislate a national environmental policy:

> Federal legislation was necessary because the creation of program, mission-oriented agencies has insured that these environmental considerations have been systematically underpresented in most short- and long-range decision making. Existing agencies were established to supervise the development of our natural resources consistent with the ethic which has prevailed throughout this country's history and, thus, they tended to overstress the benefits of development and to explore insufficiently the less environmentally damaging alternatives to current methods of meeting their programmed objectives. [Tarlock, Balancing Environmental Considerations and Energy Demands: A Comment on Calvert Cliffs' Coordinating Committee, Inc. v. AEC, 47 Ind. L.J. 645, 658 (1972).]

Reformers bent on changing agency decisionmaking as its affects environmental values could have proceeded through a piecemeal amendment of federal legislation. Congress has since adopted this strategy and has introduced NEPA-like environmental criteria in federal legislation conferring authority to undertake or authorize resource development projects. See, e.g., the Ports and Waterways Safety Act, 33 U.S.C. §1224(a), requiring the consideration of environmental factors affecting the marine environment.

NEPA took a different course. This different course is described by the two authors quoted below, one of whom was close to the legislative drafting:

> The challenge was to approach environmental management in a comprehensive way. The new values of environmental policy had to intrude somehow into the most remote recesses of the federal administrative machinery and begin to influence the multitude of decisions being made by thousands of officials. [Dreyfus & Ingram, The National Environmental Policy Act: A View of Intent and Practice, 15 Nat. Resources J. 243, 246 (1976).]

This comment raises a fundamental question about NEPA and its purposes. Agency decisionmaking was to be modified to include environmental values, but how was this change to be accomplished? Congress was not clear on this point, but several explanations of congressional purpose are possible. One is that NEPA's environmental mandates would be self-enforcing. Federal agencies would take NEPA's environmental commands into account in their decisionmaking and would make the changes necessary to incorporate environmental values. The Senate report supports this interpretation. See S. Rep. No. 296, 91st Cong., 2d Sess. 21 (1969).

Another view suggests that Congress had external pressures on agency decisionmaking in mind. Congress could provide some external pressure, and it has done so in amending other legislation, as noted earlier. External pressure from the public and from agencies with environmental expertise also was contemplated by NEPA. The statute expressly requires comments from these sources on environmental impact statements prepared by federal agencies.

The federal courts have become an important source of external pressure for agency reform. They have assumed the major role in policing NEPA's requirements, and this chapter concentrates on the court decisions interpreting the statute. The judicial role in NEPA's enforcement may have been accidental. NEPA does not expressly provide for judicial review, and commentators disagree about whether Congress contemplated judicial enforcement. See Dreyfus & Ingram, The National Environmental Policy Act: A View of Intent and Practice, 15 Nat. Resources J. 243 (1976).

Whether NEPA has accomplished a significant change in agency decisionmaking on environmental problems is an important question, and we will return to this question at the conclusion of this chapter.

Legislative History

The environmental impact statement that federal agencies must prepare on major federal actions significantly affecting the environment is NEPA's key requirement, but the early drafts of NEPA did not include it. They merely authorized a research program on environmental problems and created an advisory Council on Environmental Quality (CEQ) within the executive branch, modeled on the president's Council of Economic Advisors. NEPA's environmental impact statement requirement is largely the creation of Professor Lynton K. Caldwell, a professor of political science at Indiana University. At Caldwell's urging, and at the urging of others, Senator Jackson added a statement of policy and later the "action-forcing" provision, requiring the preparation of an environmental impact statement (EIS).

Professor Caldwell explained the reason for the environmental impact statement requirement in the Senate hearings on the proposed legislation:

> I would urge that in the shaping of such policy, it have an action-forcing, operational aspect. When we speak of policy we ought to think of a statement which is so written that it is capable of implementation; that it is not merely a statement of things hoped for; not merely a statement of desirable goals or objectives; but that it is a statement which will compel or reinforce or assist all of these things, the executive agencies in particular, but going beyond this, the Nation as a whole, to take the kind of action which will protect and reinforce what I have called the life support system of the country. [Hearings on S. 1075, S. 237, and S. 1752 before the Senate Comm. on Interior and Insular Affairs, 91st Cong., 1st Sess. 116 (1969).]

Senator Jackson endorsed the action-forcing impact statement idea, and it became part of the law.

The bill that was to become NEPA was unanimously approved by the Senate, but not before the Senate adopted two major amendments. One amendment stated in part that NEPA would not "in any way affect the specific statutory obligations of any federal agency." This amendment, the result of a compromise between Senator Jackson and Senator Edmund Muskie, was enacted unchanged at §104. Senator Muskie was concerned that NEPA would undercut the effectiveness of air and water quality standard-setting legislation he had sponsored. The amendment was intended to prohibit federal agencies from considering under NEPA the air or water quality impacts of projects that met air and water quality standards established under Muskie's legislation.

A second important change prior to conference committee consideration also was included in the Muskie-Jackson compromise. Initially, the bill had implemented Professor Caldwell's action-forcing concept by including a requirement for an agency "finding" on environmental impact. This language was changed to require a "detailed statement" on major federal actions — the environmental impact statement requirement.

Meanwhile, the House approved its counterpart of the Senate NEPA bill without the impact statement requirement suggested by Caldwell. The conference commitee reconciled this difference by retaining the impact statement requirement but adding language requiring federal agencies to follow this procedure "to the fullest extent possible." This language was considered a compromise between the view of the House sponsor that NEPA did not change agency statutory mandates and Senator Jackson's intention to ensure across-the-board compliance by federal agencies. Although the conference report stated that NEPA's duties were "qualified" by the phrase, a statement by the House conference committee managers contended that Senator Jackson's strict view of compliance was adopted. 115 Cong. Rec. 39,703 (1969).

Both Houses hurriedly approved the conference report, with most of the debate centering on the executive reorganization required by creation of the CEQ. Few congressmen understood the import of the action-forcing provisions. See R. Andrews, Environmental Policy and Administrative Change: Implementation of the National Environmental Policy Act ch. 2 (1976), for an analysis of NEPA's legislative history.

NOTES AND QUESTIONS

1. Was NEPA the only legislative strategy available to protect environmental resources? One of the authors of this casebook suggested the following three alternatives in Tarlock, Balancing Environmental Considerations and Energy Demands: A Comment on Calvert Cliffs' Coordinating Committee, Inc. v. AEC, 47 Ind. L.J. 645, 659 (1972):

a. Agency decisionmakers could be required to consider additional information, including information on environmental consequences. NEPA adopted this approach.

b. Congress could withdraw designated natural resource areas from development or give environmentally sensitive agencies a veto over development. This technique has been adopted for resource areas such as floodplains and wetlands.

c. Agencies could be authorized to adopt environmental standards and to prohibit developments that violate these standards. Congress adopted this approach in the Clean Air and Water and the Resource Conservation and Resource Recovery (solid and toxic wastes) Acts.

The critical student will want to contrast the environmentally sensitive decisionmaking process mandated by NEPA with the alternative techniques suggested by Professor Tarlock.

2. An early draft of the bill that became NEPA stipulated that every person had a right to a healthful environment, but this language was deleted over the objection of Senator Jackson. The earlier version of NEPA clearly would have created an environmental interest capable of judicial enforcement. The present form of NEPA could have been a basis for courts to refuse standing to those seeking to compel an agency to comply with NEPA, but courts have, with little analysis, found that NEPA creates protected interests capable of judicial enforcement. For an argument that the courts are right, see Hanks & Hanks, An Environmental Bill of Rights: The Citizen Suit and the National Environmental Policy Act of 1969, 24 Rutgers L. Rev. 230, 244-251 (1970). How does this legislative history bear on the role of NEPA as compared with the three alternatives outlined by Professor Tarlock?

3. NEPA appears to have been based on a number of assumptions. One assumption, which was noted earlier, was that federal agency decisionmaking could be modified without revising the enabling legislation that authorizes their programs. Senator Jackson stressed this function of NEPA during congressional hearings. The question is whether the vague environmental policy language of NEPA is sufficient to modify specific legislative authority and established agency decisionmaking that ignores environmental values.

The second assumption, related to the first, was that environmental values are sufficiently defined and the science of ecology can provide the environmental information necessary to permit the environmental evaluations NEPA requires. See L. K. Caldwell, Environment: A Challenge to Modern Society 101-102 (1970). Consider the following.

> Ecology has not yet achieved a predictive capacity to the extent that other natural sciences such as chemistry and physics have. There are few established "principles" of ecology upon which to construct a prediction. Most importantly, ecology by its very definition involves such a broad and complex number of things and interactions that adequate knowledge for practical application is very difficult to obtain. [Carpenter, The Scientific Basis of NEPA — Is It Adequate? 6 Envtl. L. Rep. (Envtl. L. Inst.) 50,014, 50,017 (1976).]

Note also that NEPA, because it contains no standards, provides no "baseline" from which the environmental impacts of an agency's action can be measured. How does this limitation affect federal agency compliance, assuming that "[e]cology has not yet achieved a predictive capacity"?

4. CEQ, housed in the executive office of the president, has emerged as the primary overseer of NEPA. See generally R. Liroff, A National Policy for the Environment (1976). Under the Act, one duty of the Council is to prepare an annual environmental quality report. These reports have been quite extensive and often influential, but they also have consumed a considerable amount of the agency's time.

By executive order, President Nixon extended the responsibilities of CEQ to include the adoption of guidelines for the preparation of impact statements. Although not binding, most federal agencies relied on these guidelines when establishing their own impact statement procedures. Federal courts also gave significant weight to the guidelines. See, e.g., Greene County Planning Board v. FPC 455 F.2d 412,421 (2d Cir. 1972).

To overcome the limitations inherent in guidelines that are merely advisory, and to extend CEQ's administration of NEPA, President Carter issued an executive order delegating authority to CEQ to issue regulations covering the entire Act (Exec. Order No. 11,991, 3 C.F.R. §123). CEQ issued regulations pursuant to the order in late 1978. For discussion of the new regulations, see Fisher, The CEQ Regulations: New Stage in the Evolution of NEPA, 3 Harv. Envtl. L. Rev. 347 (1979). With one exception, the Reagan Administration did not make any changes in the regulations. The "worst case" analysis regulation was modified, this chapter, *infra*.

2.   *The* Calvert Cliffs *Decision*

It is clear that the drafters of NEPA, especially Professor Caldwell, expected Congress and the executive branch of the government, especially the Office of Management and Budget, to be the primary enforcers of NEPA. There is some evidence, as noted earlier, that some judicial enforcement was contemplated, but Congress, lawyers, bureaucrats, and environmentalists did not anticipate that NEPA would become a judicial vehicle to force agencies to consider environmental values. Some of the credit for this development can go to the activist wing of the District of Columbia Circuit, which used NEPA as one of several occasions to tell agencies how they should interpret their duties toward the public.

The first major NEPA case to reach the courts was Calvert Cliffs' Coordinating Committee, Inc. v. U.S. Atomic Energy Commission, 449 F.2d 1109 (D.C. Cir. 1971). The case considered a conflict between the Atomic Energy Commission (AEC) — later the Nuclear Regulatory Commission (NRC) — and protestors over AEC rules that limited its duty to consider environmental impacts in the licensing of nuclear power plants. The court, in a forceful decision by Judge Skelly Wright, used this occasion to consider the judicial enforceability of NEPA. Implicit in Judge Wright's decision is consideration of the commission's contention that "the vagueness of the NEPA mandate and delegation" exempted federal agency actions under NEPA from judicial review as agency decisions "committed to agency discretion by law." The following excerpts from Judge Wright's opinion give the flavor of his response:

> NEPA, first of all, makes environmental protection a part of the mandate of every federal agency and department. The Atomic Energy Commission, for example, had continually asserted, prior to NEPA, that it had no statutory authority to concern itself with the adverse environmental effects of its actions. Now, however, its hands are no longer tied. It is not only permitted, but compelled, to take environmental values into account. Perhaps the greatest importance of NEPA is to require the Atomic Energy Commission to *consider* environmental issues just as they consider other matters within their mandates. . . . Senator Jackson, NEPA's principal sponsor, stated that "[n]o agency will [now] be able to maintain that it has no mandate or no requirement to consider the environmental consequences of its actions." He characterized the requirements of Section 102 as "action-forcing" and stated that "[o]therwise, these lofty declarations [in Section 101] are nothing more than that."
>
> The sort of consideration of environmental values which NEPA compels is clarified in Section 102(2)(A) and (B). In general, all agencies must use a "systematic, interdisciplinary approach" to environmental planning and evaluation "in decisionmaking which may have an impact on man's environment." In order to include all possible environmental factors in the decisional equation, agencies must "identify and develop methods and procedures . . . which will insure that presently unquantifiable environmental amenities and values may be given appropriate consideration in decisionmaking along with economic and technical considerations." To "consider" the former "along with" with the latter must involve a balancing process. In some instances environmental costs may outweigh economic and technical benefits and in other instances they may not. But NEPA mandates a rather finely tuned and "systematic" balancing analysis in each instance. . . .

[T]he procedural duties of Section 102 must be fulfilled to the fullest extent possible. . . . They must be complied with to the fullest extent, unless there is a clear conflict of *statutory* authority. Considerations of administrative difficulty, delay or economic cost will not suffice to strip the section of its fundamental importance. . . .

We conclude, then, that Section 102 of NEPA mandates a particular sort of careful and informed decisionmaking process and creates judicially enforceable duties. The reviewing courts probably cannot reverse a substantive decision on the merits, under Section 101, unless it be shown that the actual balance of costs and benefits that was struck was arbitrary or clearly gave insufficient weight to environmental values. But if the decision was reached procedurally without individualized consideration and balancing of environmental factors — conducted fully and in good faith — it is the responsibility of the courts to reverse. As one District Court has said of Section 102 requirements: "It is hard to imagine a clearer or stronger mandate to the Courts." [449 F.2d at 1112-1115.]

NOTES AND QUESTIONS

1. Judge Wright's decision in *Calvert Cliffs* is important for its holding that agency duties under NEPA are judicially enforceable. Reread the Supreme Court's *Overton Park* decision, reproduced in Chapter 2, which declined to apply the "committed to agency discretion" exemption to a somewhat different environmental statute. Does *Overton Park* support Judge Wright's holding on this point? Note that an agency's compliance with NEPA is judicially reviewable even though its actions under its enabling legislation may be "committed to agency discretion." See Schiffler v. Schlesinger, 548 F.2d 96 (3d Cir. 1977).

2. *Calvert Cliffs* is also important for its interpretation of NEPA's statutory mandate. Judge Wright discusses the "procedural" duties imposed by NEPA. What are they? Do they refer to the duty to prepare an impact statement when one is required or to the rules courts are to apply when they determine whether an impact statement is adequate?

3. Judge Wright's dictum that NEPA requires a "balancing process" attracted much attention and suggested that NEPA imposes substantive responsibilities that courts can enforce. Whether NEPA imposes substantive as well as procedural responsibilities is an issue pursued later in this chapter.

Some commentators have criticized the "balancing process" mandated by Judge Wright:

[T]he court apparently intended only to convey the commonsense notion of "trading off" when competing interests must be equitably balanced. Its reliance on phrases like "finely tuned," "systematic," and "optimally beneficial" is misleading when applied to such a rough-and-ready process. The analogy to a precisely calibrated scale suggests a degree of certainty which the agencies cannot attain without more legislative and judicial guidance as to the relative importance of various factors, and without more knowledge of a kind and extent which, as NEPA's legislative history acknowledges, does not yet exist. [Anderson, The National Environmental Policy Act, in Federal Environmental Law 238, 301-302 (E. Dolgin & T. Guilbert eds. 1974).]

Senator Muskie has echoed this concern. Noting that Congress had made difficult substantive environmental policy decisions in the standard-setting Clean Air and Clean Water Acts, he added:

> Few other areas of public policy require the balancing of conflicting interests and the consideration of trade-offs in such agonizing detail, but that detail should not be an excuse for deferring to the courts or to the executive. Congress must define the extent of thos substantive rights no matter how broad or how narrow they may be, for their economic, political, and social effects will be felt in every phase of national life. [Muskie & Cutler, A National Environmental Policy: Now You See It, Now You Don't, 25 Me. L. Rev. 163, 188 (1973).]

Recall, as well, that the environmentalists' concern over federal agency decisionmaking centered on agency failure to consider environmental impacts, which are usually "soft" and difficult to quantify. Benefits produced by natural resource and other projects authorized or constructed by federal agencies are usually "hard" and more readily capable of quantification. How should federal agency decisionmakers balance these "soft" impacts and "hard" benefits in the NEPA environmental impact statement process? Is Muskie's preference for standard-setting legislation justified? As you study these materials on NEPA, consider what advantages and opportunities the impact statement process presents for the protection of environmental quality that are not necessarily available through the standard-setting pollution control legislation.

3. Another issue the court considered in *Calvert Cliffs* was whether NEPA required the AEC to consider the water quality impacts of nuclear power plants. In brief, AEC interpreted the Muskie-Jackson compromise to allow it merely to incorporate water quality standards adopted by EPA into its license. The court adopted the argument of protestors, who argued that NEPA required an independent evaluation of water quality impacts above and beyond compliance with EPA-approved water quality standards. Congress overruled this part of the *Calvert Cliffs* decision in subsequent amendments to the Clean Water Act. See §511(c)(2), 33 U.S.C. §1371(c)(2).

4. As you read the cases that follow, you should ask yourself the following questions: What was the objective of the drafters of NEPA? Did they expect that existing mission agencies would self-destruct? If the answer to this question is obviously no, what did the drafters reasonably expect would be gained by the passage of a general charter of environmental goals coupled with what Senate staff members have admitted was an undefined concept of the action-forcing impact statement? Note that NEPA creates no general extra-agency enforcement mechanism except CEQ. Thus, the reader of the impact statement will be the superior of the preparers. What assumptions did the drafters make about the reader's reaction to the information contained in the impact statement? Are these assumptions sufficient to support the rule of strict compliance announced in *Calvert Cliffs*? Would the Supreme Court have reversed a circuit court decision holding that NEPA creates no enforceable private rights?

B. THRESHOLD ISSUES: MUST AN IMPACT STATEMENT BE PREPARED?

The first issue to consider under NEPA is what the courts have come to call the threshold issue: whether an environmental impact statement must be prepared at all. Courts asked to decide the threshold issue must consider the interpretive questions raised by NEPA's somewhat vague language in §102(2)(C), which requires an impact statement on "major federal actions significantly affecting the quality of the human environment." The materials that follow examine the meaning of these statutory terms as they govern the duty of federal agencies to prepare environmental impact statements.

Federal agencies must make a threshold decision to either file or not file an impact statement. Agencies that decide not to file an impact statement make what CEQ now calls a Finding of No Significant Impact (FONSI). Previously, this determination was known as a negative declaration, a more descriptive and useful term that also has found its way into the court decisions.

A negative declaration is a document "briefly presenting the reasons" an impact statement is not necessary. 40 C.F.R. §1508.13. The agency also usually will prepare an environmental assessment providing "evidence and analysis" for its negative declaration. 40 C.F.R. §1508.9. The court reviews the agency's decision to make a negative declaration and must also provide a legal interpretation of the statutory terms that indicate whether an impact statement must be filed. As the cases that follow indicate, this has allowed the courts to assume a major role in determining the scope and application of the statute. Note the importance of the negative declaration. It allows the agency to escape the statute unless reversed in court. When reviewing the materials that follow, consider the risks and benefits to an agency that decides not to file an impact statement on its action.

1. Is It Federal?

The first inquiry is whether an action that is claimed to need an impact statement is federal. Activities that federal agencies carry out, such as federal construction projects, are clearly federal. Federal agency decisions on projects carried out by private entities fall within NEPA as "federal" actions if there is the necessary federal nexus. An example is a federal agency decision on a privately built nuclear power plant licensed by a federal agency. Another example is a private housing project that receives federal subsidies. Projects carried out by state and local governments can also fall within NEPA as "federal" action if funded by federal assistance. CEQ regulations recognize all of these examples as "federal" actions requiring an impact statement. 40 C.F.R. §1508.18. The text that follows considers several types of cases in which the critical question is whether an action taken at the federal level is sufficiently federal to require an EIS. See generally, D. Mandelker, NEPA Law & Litigation §§8:15-8:28.

Projects Funded by Federal Assistance

Under the traditional federal assistance format, a state or local agency submits and the federal agency approves a specific project. Questions of NEPA applicability in these assistance programs turn on the extent and timing of the federal commitment. Congress in recent years has adopted a new form of block grant assistance. In block grant programs, federal assistance is made available to states and local governments to use for a number of related programs in their discretion. Congress sometimes requires compliance with NEPA in block grant programs. See, e.g., Housing and Community Development Act of 1974, 42 U.S.C. §5304(g).

Whether NEPA applies if not expressly made applicable depends on the program and the extent of the federal commitment. In one case a court did not require an EIS on the construction of a new prison not funded with federal assistance. It rejected a claim that an EIS was required because the federal government provided general support for the state prison system. Citizens for a Better St. Clair County v. James, 648 F.2d 246 (5th Cir. 1981).

The courts have reached the same conclusion in federal programs for planning and land use regulation. Under the National Coastal Zone Management Act (CZMA), for example, a federal agency funds state programs for the management of coastal zones. Coastal management programs include regulatory controls and must meet federal statutory requirements if a state wishes to receive federal funding for its program. In Save Our Sand Dunes v. Pegues, 642 F. Supp. 393 (M.D. Ala. 1985), the court rejected a claim that an EIS was required on permits granted by state officials for development in a coastal area. The court held that Congress did not intend in the CZMA to federalize state coastal management programs. See Ellis & Smith, The Limits of Federal Responsibility and Control under the National Environmental Policy Act, 18 Envtl. L. Rep. 10055 (1988).

The federal link is even more tenuous in federally funded planning programs. Whether NEPA applies to these programs was litigated in a case that arose under the important regional transportation planning program which is mandated and funded under requirements set by the federal highway act. The federal highway agency approves the regional planning process, but the planning and preparation of regional plans is carried out by the regional planning agency. In Atlanta Coalition v. Atlanta Regional Commission, 599 F.2d 1333 (5th Cir. 1979), the court held that an impact statement was not required on a regional transportation plan prepared for the Atlanta metropolitan area:

> Here, the availability of federal funds for the planning process apparently is not in any way tied to any sort of substantive review of the plans produced by that process.

Moreover, federal financial assistance to the planning process in no way implies a commitment by any federal agency to fund any transportation project or projects or to undertake, fund, or approve any action that directly affects the human environment. Compare Ely v. Velde. [599 F.2d at 1347.]

Note that the federal agency will only approve transportation projects, such as highway projects, that are consistent with the regional plan. Should this have changed the result in *Atlanta Coalition*? How useful will an impact statement on a highway project be if critical planning decisions have been made at the planning stage?

The "Small Handle" Problem

In another class of cases, there may be a federal link with a private or governmental project, but it may not be sufficient in magnitude to bring the project within NEPA's requirements. These cases raise what is known as the "small handle" problem.

In Winnebago Tribe v. Ray, 621 F.2d 269 (8th Cir.), *cert. denied,* 449 U.S. 836 (1980), a power company proposed to construct a 67-mile transmission line. The line required a permit from the U.S. Army Corps of Engineers for a 1.25-mile segment that crossed the Missouri River. An environmental assessment prepared by the Corps considered only the environmental impacts of the river crossing. The court rejected a "but for" argument by the tribe that NEPA applied to the entire transmission line because the line could not be constructed without the river crossing permit.

In Colorado River Indian Tribes v. Marsh, 605 F. Supp. 1425 (C.D. Cal. 1985), the court held NEPA applicable to a 156-acre development project when the only federal action was a federal permit that was required for rip-rap to stabilize a river bank. Is this case consistent with *Winnebago Tribe?*

Private actions having only a tenuous link with federal responsibilities can also fall outside NEPA. In Edwards v. First National Bank, 534 F.2d 1242 (7th Cir. 1976), a bank planned to demolish a historic structure located in a historic district entered on the National Register of Historical Places. The court did not require an impact statement, noting that the federal agency that had authority over the bank did not have any control over the demolition decision. Compare Davis v. Morton, 469 F.2d 593 (10th Cir. 1972), requiring an impact statement for a private lease negotiated on Indian land. The court held that the federal government had continuing supervisory responsibility over the lease, in part because of its authority to approve encumbrances on the land, although it did not initiate the lease or benefit from it. The court rejected the argument that the Department of the Interior's trust responsibilities required approval of all leases beneficial to the tribe, regardless of environmental impact. Compare Ringsred v. City of Duluth, 828 F.2d 1305 (8th Cir. 1987) (EIS not required when federal agency approved Indian contracts for city parking ramp for Indian facility).

How important is it to extend NEPA to marginal situations? Is there a danger that the environmental mandate of the statute will be weakened through overextension? Consider, if you are inclined to narrow NEPA's reach, that a strict reading might exempt a series of small federal actions in a region even though their cumulative impact is significant. Does the policy underlying NEPA's enactment suggest a "cumulative federal impact" theory as the basis for applying the statute? Is this problem handled by the program impact statement requirement, discussed below?

2.   Is It a Federal Action?

For NEPA to apply, there must be a proposal for a federal "action" as well as a federal nexus. Often, the presence of a federal nexus will lead naturally to a holding that a federal action is present as well, and the situations in which a federal action is present are usually clear:

> [T]here is "Federal action" within the meaning of the statute not only when an agency proposes to build a facility itself, but also whenever an agency makes a decision which permits action by other parties which will affect the quality of the environment. NEPA's impact statement procedure has been held to apply where a federal agency approves a lease of land to private parties, grants licenses and permits to private parties, or approves and funds state highway projects. In each of these instances the federal agency took action affecting the environment in the sense that the agency made a decision which permitted some other party — private or governmental — to take action affecting the environment. [Scientists' Institute for Public Information, Inc. v. AEC (*SIPI*), 481 F.2d 1079, 1088-1089 (D.C. Cir. 1973).]

Timing is one problem that arises in determining whether a federal action has occurred. Section 102(2)(C) of NEPA requires an impact statement on "every recommendation or report on proposals for . . . major federal actions." The Supreme Court has emphasized the "proposal" requirement: "The committee report [on NEPA] made clear that the impact statement was required in conjunction with specific proposals for action" (Kleppe v. Sierra Club, 427 U.S. 390, 401 n.12 (1976)). The questions that arise are: How specific a proposal must be, and when in the agency's decisionmaking process a proposal occurs that is subject to the impact statement requirement? CEQ has ambiguously defined a "proposal" as "that stage in the development of an action when an agency subject to the Act has a goal and is actively preparing to make a decision on one or more alternative means of accomplishing that goal and the effects can be meaningfully evaluated." 40 C.F.R. §1508.23.

The decision about when to file an impact statement clearly has important consequences for the effectiveness of NEPA. An impact statement will not accomplish its purpose if it is filed so late in the agency decisionmaking process that major commitments to the action under review have been taken and are irreversible.

The courts look to the finality of an agency action to determine whether an EIS is required. They do not require an EIS if a request has been made for agency action but the agency has not yet acted, such as a request for the approval of a right-of-way on federal land or a request for a rate increase. See B.R.S. Land Investors v. United States, 596 F.2d 353 (9th Cir. 1979) (right-of-way). Courts consider similar issues when they apply ripeness and finality rules to determine if an agency action is ripe for review. In Sierra Club v. Penfold, 664 F. Supp. 1299 (D. Alaska 1987), the court held that a longstanding agency practice of approving mining plans without considering their cumulative impacts was reviewable as final action. It noted that administrative appeals on individual mining approvals were not a practicable alternative. What distinguishes this case from the B.R.S. *Land Investors* case, *supra*?

Many federal programs contemplate a continuing relationship between the federal agency and its client. Project changes may require the preparation of an additional impact statement even though the federal agency may have concluded earlier that no impact statement was necessary. See Raleigh Heights Homeowners Protective Association v. City of Reno, 501 F. Supp. 269 (D. Nev. 1980) (change in site for subsidized housing project).

Whether an impact statement is required for federal agency *inaction* presents another controversial issue. Consider the following problem: Although the states have primary authority for the management of wildlife on federal lands, the Department of the Interior "may" designate areas where no hunting is permitted. The state of Alaska decided to order a wolf kill in a substantial area of its federal lands. When requested to intervene, the Department refused to act and also refused to file an impact statement on its decision. Suit was then brought to require the preparation of an impact statement. In Defenders of Wildlife v. Andrus, 627 F.2d 1238 (D.C. Cir. 1980), the court held that the Department's failure to act was federal "inaction" for which no impact statement was required. The court believed that because the federal statute did not compel the Department to act, it had no obligation to prepare an impact statement on its failure to act in a particular instance. As the court explained:

> [It is argued] that, by not inhibiting an action of a private party or a state or a local government, the federal government makes that action its own within the meaning of NEPA. However, in no published opinion of which we have been made aware has a court held that there is "federal action" where an agency has done nothing more than fail to prevent the other party's action from occurring. . . .
>
> NEPA would be impaired . . . were we now to decide . . . [that an impact statement is required.] No agency could meet its NEPA obligations if it had to prepare an environmental impact statement every time the agency had power to act but did not do so. [627 F.2d at 1244, 1246.]

How is the distinction made by the court to be applied? Federal agencies necessarily engage in a decisionmaking process in which they determine whether to take or authorize action that may have an environmental impact. If the agency decides not to undertake or authorize a project, has it necessarily engaged in "inaction" not subject to NEPA?

The inaction problem has another dimension. Requiring agencies to prepare impact statements on a refusal to act may compel them to take action when their authorizing legislation makes this decision discretionary. One commentator argues that this use of NEPA goes beyond its statutory intent (Fergenson, The Sin of Omission: Inaction as Action under Section 102(2)(C) of the National Environmental Policy Act of 1969, 53 Ind. L.J. 497 (1978)).

3. Is It a Major Federal Action Significantly Affecting the Environment?

An agency proposal may be an action sufficient to qualify under NEPA but may not be sufficiently "major" or "significant" to qualify under the statute. Many federal or federally authorized projects, such as federal dams or nuclear power plants, are sufficiently "major" to qualify under the statute. Indeed, CEQ regulations state that the word "major" "reinforces but does not have a meaning independent of significant." 40 C.F.R. §1508.18.

The "significance" requirement is more frequently contested and serves an important function under NEPA. It imposes a threshold test of environmental impact that must be met before a federal agency is required to prepare an impact statement on a major federal action. The leading case interpreting the significance requirement follows.

HANLY v. KLEINDIENST (HANLY II)
471 F.2d 823 (2d Cir. 1972), cert. denied, 412 U.S. 908 (1973)

MANSFIELD, Circuit Judge:

This case, which presents serious questions as to the interpretation of the National Environmental Policy Act of 1969 ("NEPA"), the language of which has been characterized as "opaque" and "woefully ambiguous," is here on appeal for the second time. Following the district court's denial for the second time of a preliminary injunction against construction of a jail and other facilities known as the Metropolitan Correction Center ("MCC") we are called upon to decide whether a redetermination by the General Services Administration ("GSA") that the MCC is not a facility "significantly affecting the quality of the human environment," made pursuant to this Court's decision remanding the case after the earlier appeal, Hanly v. Mitchell, 460 F.2d 640 (2d Cir. 1972) (Feinberg, J.), cert. denied, Hanly v. Kleindienst, 409 U.S. 990 (1972) (herein "Hanly I"), satisfied the requirements of NEPA and thus renders it unnecessary for GSA to follow the procedure prescribed by §102(2)(C) of NEPA, 42 U.S.C. §4332(2)(C), which requires a formal, detailed environmental impact statement. In view of the failure of the GSA, upon redetermination, to make findings with respect to certain relevant factors and to furnish an opportunity to appellants to submit relevant evidence, the case is again remanded.

Since the background of the action up to the date of our earlier remand is set forth in *Hanly I*, we limit ourselves to a brief summary. Appellants are members of groups residing or having their businesses in an area of lower Manhattan called "The Manhattan Civic Center" which comprises not only various courthouses, government buildings and businesses, but also residential housing, including cooperative apartments in two buildings close to the MCC and various similar apartments and tenements in nearby Chinatown. GSA, of which appellant Robert L. Kuniz was the Administrator, is engaged in the construction of an Annex to the United States Courthouses, Foley Square, Manhattan, located on a site to the east of the Courthouse and immediately to the south of Chinatown and the aforementioned two cooperative apartments. The Annex will consist of two buildings, each approximately 12 stories high, which will have a total of 345,601 gross square feet of space (214,264 net). One will be an office building for the staffs of the United States Attorney and the United Statets Marshal, presently located in the severely overcrowded main Courthouse building, and the other will be the MCC.

The MCC will serve, under the jurisdiction of the Bureau of Prisons, Department of Justice, as the detention center for approximately 449 persons awaiting trial or convicted of short term federal offenses. It will replace the present drastically overcrowded and inadequate facility on West Street, Manhattan, and will be large enough to provide space not only for incarceration but for diagnostic services, and medical, recreational and administrative facilities. Up to 48 of the detainees, mostly those scheduled for release within 30 to 90 days, may participate in a community treatment program whereby they will be permitted to spend part of each day in the city engaged in specific work or study activity, returning to the MCC after completion of each day's business. A new program will provide service for out-patient non-residents. The MCC will be serviced by approximately 130 employees, only 90 of whom will be present on the premises at any one time.

In February 1972, appellants sought injunctive relief against construction of the MCC on the ground that GSA had failed to comply with the mandates of §102 of NEPA, 42 U.S.C. §4332(2)(C), which requires the preparation of a detailed environmental impact statement with respect to major federal actions "significantly affecting the quality of the human environment." On March 22, 1972, the application was denied by the district court on the ground that GSA had concluded that the Annex would not have such an effect and that its findings were not "arbitrary" within the meaning of §10 of the Administrative Procedure Act ("APA"), 5 U.S.C. §706. The Government concedes that construction of the Annex is a "major" federal action within the meaning of §102 of NEPA.

Upon appeal this Court affirmed the district court's order as to the office building but reversed and remanded as to the detention center, the MCC, on the ground that the GSA's threshold determination, which had been set forth in a short memorandum entitled "Environmental Statement" dated February 23, 1971, was too meager to satisfy NEPA's requirements. That statement confined itself to a brief evaluation of the availability of utilities, the adequacy of mass transportation, the removal of trash, the absence of a relocation problem and the intention to comply with existing zoning regulations. In remanding the case this Court, although finding the GSA statement sufficient to support its threshold determination with respect to the proposed office building, concluded that the detention center "stands on a different footing," *Hanly I* at 646, and that the agency was required to give attention to other factors that might affect human environment in the area, including the possibility of riots and disturbances in the jail which might expose neighbors to additional noise, the dangers of crime to which neighbors might be exposed as the consequence of housing an out-patient treatment center in the building, possible traffic and parking problems that might be increased by trucks delivering food and supplies and by vans taking prisoners to and from the Eastern District and New Jersey District Courts, and the need for parking space for prison personnel and accommodations for visitors, including lawyers or members of the family. This Court concluded: "The Act must be construed to include protection of the quality of life for city residents. Noise, traffic, overburdened mass transportation systems, crime, congestion and even availability of drugs all affect the urban 'environment' and are surely results of the 'profound influences of . . . high-density urbanization [and] industrial expansion.'" *Hanly I*, 460 F.2d at 647.

We further noted that in making the threshold determination authorized by §102(2)(C) of NEPA the agency must "affirmatively develop a reviewable environmental record" in lieu of limiting itself to perfunctory conclusions with respect to the MCC. This Court granted the injunction as to the MCC but after consideration of the balance of hardships stayed the order for a period of 30 days to enable GSA to make a new threshold determination which would take into account the factors set forth in the opinion.

Following the remand a new threshold determination in the form of a 25-page "Assessment of the Environmental Impact" ("Assessment" herein) was made by the GSA and submitted to the district court on June 15, 1972. This document (to which photographs, architect's renditions and a letter of approval from the Director of the Office of Lower Manhattan Development, City of New York, are attached) reflects a detailed consideration of numerous relevant factors. Among other things, it analyzes the size, exact location, and proposed use of the MCC; its design features, construction, and aesthetic relationship to its surroundings; the extent to which its occupants and activities conducted in it will be visible by the community; the estimated effects of its operation upon traffic, public transit and parking facilities; its approximate population, including detainees and employees; its effect on the level of noise, smoke, dirt, obnoxious odors, sewage and solid waste removal; and its energy demands. It also sets forth possible alternatives, concluding that there is none that is satisfactory. Upon the basis of this Assessment the Acting Commissioner of the Public Building Service Division of the GSA, who is the responsible official in charge, concluded on June 7, 1972, that the MCC was not an action signficantly affecting the quality of the human environment.

On August 2, 1972, appellants renewed their application to Judge Tenney for a preliminary injunction, arguing that the Assessment failed to comply with this Court's direction in *Hanly I*, that it amounted to nothing more than a rewrite of the earlier statement that had been found inadequate, and that some of its findings were incorrect or insufficient. Appellants further demanded a consolidation of the motion for preliminary relief with a jury trial of the issues. On August 8, 1972, Judge Tenney, in a careful opinion, denied appellants' motions, from which the present appeal was taken. . . .

We are next confronted with a question that was deferred in *Hanly I* — the standard of review that must be applied by us in reviewing GSA's action. The action involves both a question of law — the meaning of the word "significantly" in the statutory phase "significantly affecting the quality of the human environment" — and a question of fact — whether the MCC will have a "significantly" adverse environmental impact. Strictly speaking, our function as a reviewing court is to determine de novo "all relevant questions of law," Administrative Procedure Act §10(e), 5 U.S.C. §706, see K. Davis, 4 Administrative Law Treatise §29.01 (1958) (herein "Davis"), and, with respect to GSA's factual determinations, to abide by the Administrative Procedure Act, which limits us in matters not involving an agency's rule-making or adjudicatory function to determining whether its findings are "arbitrary, capricious, an abuse of discretion, or otherwise not in accordance with law" or "without observance of procedure required by law," APA §10(e), 5 U.S.C. §706(2)(A) and (D); see Citizens to Preserve Overton Park v. Volpe, 401 U.S. 402 (1971).

Where the court's interpretation of statutory language requires some appraisal of facts, a neat delineation of the legal issues for the purpose of substituted judicial analysis has sometimes proven to be impossible or, at least, inadvisable. Furthermore, in some cases a complete de novo analysis of the legal questions, though theoretically possible, may be undesirable for the reason that the agency's determination reflects the exercise of expertise not possessed by the court. . . . Accordingly, with respect to review of such mixed questions of law and fact the Supreme Court has authorized a simpler, more practical standard, the "rational basis" test, whereby the agency's decision will be accepted where it has "warrant in the record" and a "reasonable basis in law." NLRB v. Hearst Publications, 322 U.S. 111, 131 (1944); see Rochester Telephone Corp. v. United States, 307 U.S. 125 (1939); 4 Davis §§29.01, 30.05 (1958).

Notwithstanding the possible availability of the "rational basis" standard, we believe that the appropriate criterion in the present case is the "arbitrary, capricious" standard established by the Administrative Procedure Act, since the meaning of the term "significantly" as used in §102(2)(C) of NEPA can be isolated as a question of law. This was the course taken by the district court and is in accord with the Supreme Court's decision in Citizens to Preserve Overton Park v. Volpe, 401 U.S. 402 (1971), where its review of the Department of Transportation's authorization of federal funds to finance construction of a highway through a federal park, turned on the meaning to be attributed to a statutory prohibition against such an authorization if "a feasible and prudent" alternative route exists. Speaking for the Court, Justice Marshall declared that upon review the facts should be scrutinized to determine whether the agency decision was "arbitrary, capricious, an abuse of discretion or otherwise not in accordance with law" as required by the APA and whether the agency followed the necessary procedural requirements. We see no reason for application of a different approach here since the APA standard permits effective judicial scrutiny of agency action and concommitantly permits the agencies to have some leeway in applying the law to factual contexts in which they possess expertise. Accordingly we conclude that the applicable scope of review of an agency's threshold determination that an impact statement is not required under §102 of NEPA is the "arbitrary, capricious, abuse of discretion" standard.

Upon attempting, according to the foregoing standard, to interpret the amorphous term "significantly," as it is used in §102(2)(C), we are faced with the fact that almost every major federal action, no matter how limited in scope, has *some* adverse effect on the human environment. It is equally clear that an action which is environmentally important to one neighbor may be of no consequence to another. Congress could have decided that every major federal action must therefore be the subject of a detailed impact statement prepared according to the procedure prescribed by §102(2)(C). By adding the word "significantly," however, it demonstrated that before the agency in charge triggered that procedure, it should conclude that a greater environmental impact would result than from "any major federal action." Yet the limits of the key term have not been adequately defined by Congress or by guidelines issued by the CEQ and other responsible federal agencies vested with broad discretionary powers under NEPA. Congress apparently was willing to depend principally upon the agency's good faith determination as to what conduct would be sufficiently serious from an ecological standpoint to require use of the full-scale procedure.

Guidelines issued by the CEQ, which are echoed in rules for implementation published by the Public Buildings Service, the branch of GSA concerned with the construction of the MCC, suggest that a formal impact statement should be prepared with respect to "proposed actions, the environmental impact of which is likely to be highly controversial." However, the term "controversial" apparently refers to cases where a substantial dispute exists as to the size, nature or effect of the major federal action rather than to the existence of opposition to a use, the effect of which is relatively undisputed. This Court in *Hanly I*, for instance, did not require a formal impact statement with respect to the office building portion of the Annex despite the existence of neighborhood opposition to it. The suggestion that "controversial" must be equated with neighborhood opposition has also been rejected by others.

In the absence of any Congressional or administrative interpretation of the term, we are persuaded that in deciding whether a major federal action will "significantly" affect the quality of the human environment the agency in charge, although vested with broad discretion, should normally be required to review the proposed action in the light of at least two relevant factors: (1) the extent to which the action will cause adverse environmental effects in excess of those created by existing uses in the area affected by it, and (2) the absolute quantitative adverse environmental effects of the action itself, including the cumulative harm that results from its contribution to existing adverse conditions or uses in the affected area. Where conduct conforms to existing uses, its adverse consequences will usually be less significant than when it represents a radical change. Absent some showing that an entire neighborhood is in the process of redevelopment, its existing environment, though frequently below an ideal standard, represents a norm that cannot be ignored. For instance, one more highway in an area honeycombed with roads usually has less of an adverse impact than if it were constructed through a roadless public park. See, e.g., Citizens to Preserve Overton Park v. Volpe.

Although the existing environment of the area which is the site of a major federal action constitutes one criterion to be considered, it must be recognized that even a slight increase in adverse conditions that form an existing environmental milieu may sometimes threaten harm that is significant. One more factory polluting air and water in an area zoned for industrial use may represent the straw that breaks the back of the environmental camel. Hence the absolute, as well as comparative, effects of a major federal action must be considered.

Chief Judge Friendly's thoughtful dissent, while conceding that we (and governmental agencies) face a difficult problem in determining the meaning of the vague and amorphous term "significantly" as used in §102(2)(C), offers no solution other than to suggest that an impact statement should be required whenever a major federal action might be "arguably" or "potentially" significant and that such an interpretation would insure the preparation of impact statements except in cases of "true" insignificance. In our view this suggestion merely substitutes one form of semantical vagueness for another. By failure to use more precise standards it would leave the agency, which admittedly must make the determination, in the very quandary faced in this case and only serve to prolong and proliferate uncertainty as to when a threshold determination should be accepted. The problem is not resolved by use of terms as "*obviously* insignificant," "*minor*," "*arguably* significant," a "*fairly arguable*" adverse impact, or the like, or by reference to "*grey*" areas or characterization of our opinion as "raising the floor" to permit agencies to escape an impact statement.

We agree with Chief Judge Friendly that an impact statement should not be required where the impact will be minor or unimportant, or where "there is no sensible reason for making one," and that such a statement should be required where the action may fairly be said to have a potentially significant adverse effect. But these conclusions merely pose the problem which cannot be solved by an interchange of adjectives. In our view such a morass can be avoided only by formulation of more precise factors that must be considered in making the essential threshold determination. This we have attempted to do.

In the absence of such standards we cannot agree that construction of a proposed office building of the type forming part of the Annex would be "obviously insignificant" and hence would not require an impact statement. An office building or, indeed, a jail, may have an adverse impact in an area where such use does not exist and is not permitted by zoning laws (e.g., Park Avenue and 72nd Street) whereas the contrary would hold in a location where such uses do exist and are authorized by such laws (e.g., the location of the MCC). See Goose Hollow Foothills League v. Romney, 334 F. Supp. 877 (D. Ore. 1971) (setting aside threshold determination that high-rise building would not significantly affect environment where no weight had been given to fact that it would change character of neighborhood and concentrate population in the neighborhood). Rather than encourage agencies to dispense with impact statements, we believe that application of the foregoing objective standards, coupled with compliance with minimum procedural requirements . . . , which are designed to assure consideration of relevant facts, will lead agencies in doubtful cases (so-called "grey" areas) to obtain impact statements rather than to risk the delay and expense of protracted litigation. [At this point the court discussed the GSA's environmental assessment and found it adequate except for "one or two factual issues," including "the possibility that the MCC will substantially increase the risk of crime in the immediate area."]

The case is remanded for further proceedings not inconsistent with this opinion. The mandate shall issue forthwith.

FRIENDLY, Chief Judge (dissenting):

[The substance of Judge Friendly's dissent is summarized in the majority opinion. However, the following comments by Judge Friendly are relevant to an appraisal of the majority holding:] The upshot is that a threshold determination that a proposal does not constitute major Federal action significantly affecting the quality of the human environment becomes a kind of mini-impact statement. The preparation of such a statement under the conditions laid down by the majority is unduly burdensome when the action is truly minor or insignificant. On the other hand, there is a danger that if the threshold determination is this elaborate, it may come to replace the impact statement in the grey area between actions which, though "major" in a monetary sense, are obviously insignificant (such as the construction of the proposed office building) and actions that are obviously significant (such as the construction of an atomic power plant). We would better serve the purposes of Congress by keeping the threshold low enough to insure that impact statements are prepared for actions in this grey area and thus to permit the determination that no impact statement is required to be made quite informally in cases of true significance.

NOTES AND QUESTIONS

1. The significance question and the judicial review standard are issues that are often intertwined in cases where courts review agency decisions that an impact statement is not required. *Hanly II* deals with both issues although its attempt to define levels of significance is unusual. The arbitrary and capricious standard of judicial review adopted by *Hanly II* secured a following in several circuits. Other circuits followed the lead of Save Our Ten Acres v. Krieger, 472 F.2d 463 (5th Cir. 1972). Krieger adopted a more rigorous standard, which allowed the court to "weigh and examine" evidence from the plaintiff and the agency to determine whether the agency had "reasonably concluded" that the

environmental effects were not significant. The court added that "[t]he spirit of the Act would die aborning if a facile, ex parte decision that the project was minor or did not significantly affect the environment were too well shielded from judicial review. Id. at 466. Do you see the reason for the court's concern?

2. The split in the circuits on the appropriate standard of judicial review for the significance decision stood unresolved until the Supreme Court decided Marsh v. Oregon Natural Resources Council, 109 S. Ct. 1851 (1989). The Court held that the arbitrary and capricious standard of judicial review applied to the Corps of Engineers' decision that a supplemental impact statement was not necessary on a proposed dam at Elk Creek in the Rogue River Basin in Southwest Oregon. CEQ regulations require a supplemental impact statement whenever the agency makes "substantial changes" in a proposed action or when there are "significant new circumstances or information" that are relevant to environmental concerns. 40 C.F.R. §1502.9(c). Plaintiffs claimed they had new information concerning the adverse effect of the dam on downstream fishing and turbidity. The Corps relied on the opinions of independent and Corps experts to conclude that this information did not require a supplemental impact statement.

All parties agreed that a "rule of reason" applied to an agency's decision on whether it should prepare a supplemental impact statement. The Court noted that application of the rule of reason depended on "the value of the new information to the still pending decisionmaking process." In this respect, the Court added, the decision on whether to prepare a supplemental impact statement was similar to the decision on whether to prepare an impact statement in the first instance.

The Court held that the arbitrary and capricious standard that requires deference to agency decisions was the appropriate judicial review standard because the significance decision "in this case is a classic example of a factual dispute." The dispute turned on whether new information undermined the conclusions contained in the impact statement, whether the information was accurate and whether the review of the information by the agency's experts was incomplete, inconclusive, or inaccurate. Because the analysis of the relevant documents required a high level of expertise, the Court deferred to and upheld the agency's decision that a supplemental impact statement was not necessary.

The Court quoted and reaffirmed language from its Overton Park decision that stated that judicial review must be searching and careful but that the ultimate standard of review is narrow. When specialists express conflicting views, the Court noted, the agency must have discretion to rely on the "reasonable opinions of its own qualified experts" even if a court might find contrary views more persuasive as an original matter. Yet the Court added language that appeared to confirm the "hard look" doctrine:

> On the other hand, in the context of reviewing a decision not to supplement an EIS, courts should not automatically defer to the agency's express reliance on an interest in finality without carefully reviewing the record and satisfying themselves that the agency has made a reasoned decision based on its evaluation of the signif-

icance — or lack of significance — of the new information. A contrary approach would not simply render judicial review generally meaningless, but would be contrary to the demand that courts ensure that agency decisions are founded on a reasoned evaluation "of the relevant factors." [Id. at 1861.]

Marsh settles to some extent the controversy over judicial review standards under NEPA. The case would also seem to apply to decisions that an impact statement should not be prepared in the first instance because environmental impacts are not significant. The Court noted that the significance decision in this situation was similar and, in a footnote, cited and discussed cases that reviewed agency decisions that an initial impact statement was not necessary. Id. at 1861 n.23. See Mandelker, NEPA Alive and Well: The Supreme Court Takes Two, 19 Envtl. L. Rep. (Envtl. L. Inst.) 10,385 (1989).

3. Marsh does not mean that the arbitrary and capricious standard applies to all questions that arise under NEPA. Questions of law still require de novo review, for example. In addition, the Court noted that the significance decision in this case was not a question of law because it did not require a new interpretation of the statute or the application of the significance requirement to settled facts. Apparently, if these conditions were present, the Court might find that the significance decision raised a question of law.

As you go through this chapter, consider what questions are questions of law that require application of a de novo review standard. What about questions concerning the scope of, for example, the impact statement? See also National Trust for Historic Preservation v. Dole, 828 F.2d 776 (D.C. Cir. 1987) (arbitrary and capricious standard applies to review of categorical exclusion of action from NEPA).

4. Note that judicial review is complicated in NEPA cases because a district court proceeding intervenes between an agency's decision not to file an impact statement and an appeal to a court of appeals. As one court of appeals pointed out, it is not clear whether it is to review the agency's decision on the basis of the administrative record or to review the district court's decision under the usual "clearly erroneous" test. Sierra Club v. Marsh, 769 F.2d 868 (1st Cir. 1985). The court's pragmatic answer was to defer to district court findings of fact but to review more vigorously the district court's review of the agency's administrative record.

4. Exemptions

ANDRUS V. SIERRA CLUB
442 U.S. 347 (1979)

Justice BRENNAN delivered the opinion of the Court.

The question for decision is whether §102(2)(C) of the National Environmental Policy Act of 1969 (NEPA), . . . requires federal agencies to prepare environmental impact statements (EIS's) to accompany appropriation requests. We hold that it does not. . . .

I

In 1974, respondents, three organizations with interests in the preservation of the environment, brought suit in the Federal District Court for the District of Columbia alleging that §102(2)(C) requires federal agencies to prepare EIS's to accompany their appropriate requests. Respondents named as defendants the Secretary of the Interior and the Director of the Office of Management and Budget (OMB), and alleged that proposed curtailments in the budget of the National Wildlife Refuge System (NWRS), 80 Stat. 927, 16 U.S.C. §668dd, would "cut back significantly the operations, maintenance, and staffing of units within the System." Complaint ¶17. The System is administered by the Fish and Wildlife Service of the Department of the Interior, and consists of more than 350 refuges encompassing more than 30 million acres in 49 States. The primary purpose of the NWRS is to provide a national program "for the restoration, preservation, development and management of wildlife and wildlands habitat; for the protection and preservation of endangered or threatened species and their habitat; and for the management of wildlife and wildlands to obtain the maximum benefits from these resources." 50 CFR §25.11(b) (1978). Respondents alleged that the proposed budget curtailments would significantly affect the quality of the human environment, and hence should have been accompanied by an EIS prepared both by the Fish and Wildlife Service and by OMB.

The District Court agreed with respondents' contentions. Relying on provisions of the then applicable CEQ guidelines, and on the Department of the Interior's Manual, the District Court held that "appropriation requests are 'proposals for legislation' within the meaning of NEPA," and also that "annual proposals for financing the Refuge System are major Federal actions which clearly have a significant effect on the environment." Sierra Club v. Morton, 395 F. Supp. 1187, 1188, 1189 (1975). The District Court granted respondents' motion for summary judgment, and provided declaratory and injunctive relief. It stated that the Department of the Interior and OMB were required "to prepare, consider, and disseminate environmental impact statements on annual proposals for financing the National Wildlife Refuge System."

The Court of Appeals for the District of Columbia Circuit modified the holding of the District Court. The Court of Appeals was apprehensive because "[a] rule requiring preparation of an EIS on the annual budget request for virtually every ongoing program would trivialize NEPA." 581 F.2d 895, 903 (1978). Therefore, the Court of Appeals concluded that §102(2)(C) required the preparation of an EIS only when an appropriation request accompanies "a 'proposal' for taking new action which significantly changes the status quo," or when "the request for budget approval and appropriations is one that ushers in a considered programmatic course following a programmatic review." 581 F.2d, at 903. Section 102(2)(C) would thus have no application to "a routine request for budget approval and appropriations for continuance and management of an ongoing program." 581 F. 2d, at 903. The Court of Appeals held, however, that there was no need for injunctive relief because the Fish and Wildlife Service had completed during the pendency of the appeal a "Programmatic EIS" that adequately evaluated the environmental consequences for the NWRS of various budgetary alternatives. 581 F. 2d, at 904.

We granted certiorari, and we now reverse.

II

NEPA requires EIS's to be included in recommendations or reports on both "proposals for legislation . . . significantly affecting the quality of the human environment" and "proposals for . . . major Federal actions significantly affecting the quality of the human environment." 42 U.S.C. §4332(2)(C). See CEQ regulations, 43 Fed. Reg. 56001 (1978) (to be codified at 40 CRF §1506.8(a)). Petitioners argue, however, that the requirements of §102(2)(C) have no application to the budget process. The contrary holding of the Court of Appeals rests on two alternative interpretations of §102(2)(C). The first is that appropriation requests which are the result of "an agency's painstaking review of an ongoing program," 581 F. 2d, at 903, are "proposals for legislation" within the meaning of §102(2)(C). The second is that appropriation requests which are the reflection of "new" agency initiatives constituting "major Federal actions" under NEPA, are themselves "proposals for . . . major Federal actions" for purposes of §102(2)(C). We hold that neither interpretation is correct.

A

We note initially that NEPA makes no distinction between "proposals for legislation" that are the result of "painstaking review," and those that are merely "routine." When Congress has thus spoken "in the plainest of words," TVA v. Hill, 437 U.S. 153, 194 (1978), we will ordinarily decline to fracture the clear language of a statute, even for the purpose of fashioning from the resulting fragments a rule that "accords with 'common sense and the public weal.'" Id., at 195. Therefore, either all appropriation requests constitute "proposals for legislation," or none does.

There is no direct evidence in the legislative history of NEPA that enlightens whether Congress intended the phrase "proposals for legislation" to include requests for appropriations. At the time of the Court of Appeals' decision, however, CEQ guidelines provided that §102(2)(C) applied to "[r]ecommendations or favorable reports relating to legislation including requests for appropriations." 40 CFR §1500.5(a)(1) (1977). At that time CEQ's guidelines were advisory in nature, and were for the purpose of assisting federal agencies in complying with NEPA. §1500.1(a).

In 1977, however, President Carter, in order to create a single set of uniform, mandatory regulations, ordered CEQ, "after consultation with affected agencies," to "[i]ssue regulations to Federal agencies for the implementation of the procedural provisions" of NEPA. Exec. Order No. 11991, 3 CFR 124 (1978). The President ordered the heads of federal agencies to "comply with the regulations issued by the Council. . . ." Ibid. CEQ has since issued these regulations, and they reverse CEQ's prior interpretation of §102(2)(C). The regulations provide specifically that " '[l]egislation' includes a bill or legislative proposal to Congress . . . but does *not* include requests for appropriations." (Emphasis supplied.) CEQ explained this reversal by noting that, on the basis of "traditional concepts relating to appropriations and the budget cycle, considerations of timing and confidentiality, and other factors, . . . the Council in its experience found that preparation of EIS's is ill-suited to the budget preparation process."

CEQ's interpretation of NEPA is entitled to substantial deference. The Council was created by NEPA, and charged in that statute with the responsibility "to review and appraise the various programs and activities of the Federal Government in the light of the policy set forth in . . . this Act . . . , and to make recommendations to the President with respect thereto."

It is true that in the past we have been somewhat less inclined to defer to "administrative guidelines" when they have "conflicted with earlier pronouncements of the agency." General Electric Co. v. Gilbert, 429 U.S. 125, 143 (1976). But CEQ's reversal of interpretation occurred during the detailed and comprehensive process, ordered by the President, of transforming advisory guidelines into mandatory regulations applicable to all federal agencies. A mandatory requirement that every federal agency submit EIS's with its appropriation requests raises wholly different and more serious issues "of fair and prudent administration," ibid., than does nonbinding advice. This is particularly true in light of the Court of Appeals' correct observation that "[a] rule requiring preparation of an EIS on the annual budget request for virtually every ongoing program would trivialize NEPA." 581 F.2d, at 903. The Court of Appeals accurately noted that such an interpretation of NEPA would be a "reductio ad absurdum. . . . It would be absurd to require an EIS on every decision on the management of federal land, such as fluctuation in the number of forest fire spotters." 581 F.2d, at 902. Even respondents do not now contend that NEPA should be construed so that all appropriation requests constitute "proposals for legislation."

CEQ's interpretation of the phrase "proposals for legislation" is consistent with the traditional distinction which Congress has drawn between "legislation" and "appropriation." The rules of both Houses "prohibit 'legislation' from being added to an appropriation bill." L. Fisher, Budget Concepts and Terminology: The Appropriations Phase, in 1 Studies in Taxation, Public Finance and Related Subjects — A compendium 437 (Fund for Public Policy Research 1977). See Standing Rules of the United States Senate, Rule 16(4) ("No amendment which proposes general legislation shall be received to any general appropriation bill . . ."); Rules of the House of Representatives, 96th Cong., 1st Sess., Rule XXI(2) (1979); 7 C. Cannon, Precedents of the House of Representatives

§§1172, 1410, 1443, 1445, 1448, 1459, 1463, 1470, 1472 (1936). The distinction is maintained "to assure that program and financial matters are considered independently of one another. This division of labor is intended to enable the Appropriations Committees to concentrate on financial issues and to prevent them from trespassing on substantive legislation." House Budget Committee, Congressional Control of Expenditures 19 (Comm. Print 1977). House and Senate rules thus require a "previous choice of policy . . . before any item of appropriations might be included in a general appropriations bill." United States ex rel. Chapman v. FPC, 345 U.S. 153, 164 n.5 (1953). Since appropriations therefore "have the limited and specific purpose of providing funds for authorized programs," TVA v. Hill, 437 U.S., at 190, and since the "action-forcing" provisions of NEPA are directed precisely at the processes of "planning and . . . decisionmaking," 42 U.S.C. §4332(2)(A), which are associated with underlying legislation, we conclude that the distinction made by CEQ's regulations is correct and that "proposals for legislation" do not include appropriation requests.

B

The Court of Appeals' alternative interpretation of NEPA is that appropriation requests constitute "proposals for . . . major Federal actions." But this interpretation distorts the language of the Act, since appropriation requests do not "propose" federal actions at all; they instead fund actions already proposed. Section 102(2)(C) is thus best interpreted as applying to those recommendations or reports that actually propose programmatic actions, rather than to those which merely suggest how such actions may be funded. Any other result would create unnecessary redundancy. For example, if the mere funding of otherwise unaltered agency programs were construed to constitute major federal actions significantly affecting the quality of the human environment, the resulting EIS's would merely recapitulate the EIS's that should have accompanied the initial proposals of the programs. And if an agency program were to be expanded or revised in a manner that constituted major federal action significantly affecting the quality of the human environment, an EIS would have been required to accompany the underlying programmatic decision. An additional EIS at the appropriation stage would add nothing.

Even if changes in agency programs occur *because* of budgetary decisions, an EIS at the appropriation stage would only be repetitive. For example, respondents allege in their complaint that OMB required the Fish and Wildlife Service to decrease its appropriation request for the NWRS, and that this decrease would alter the operation of the NWRS in a manner that would significantly affect the quality of the human environment. But since the Fish and Wildlife Service could respond to OMB's budgetary curtailments in a variety of ways, see United States Fish and Wildlife Service, Final Environmental Statement: Operation of the National Wildlife Refuge System (Nov. 1976), it is impossible to predict whether or how any particular budget cut will in fact significantly affect the quality of the human environment. OMB's determination to cut the Service's budget is not a programmatic proposal, and therefore requiring OMB to include an EIS in its budgetary cuts would be premature. And since an EIS must be prepared if any of the revisions the Fish and Wildlife Service proposes in its ongoing programs in response to OMB's budget cuts would significantly affect the quality of the human environment, requiring the Fish and Wildlife Service to include an EIS with its revised appropriation request would merely be redundant. Moreover, this redundancy would have the deleterious effect of circumventing and eliminating the careful distinction Congress has maintained between appropriation and legislation. It would flood House and Senate Appropriations Committees with EIS's focused on the policy issues raised by underlying authorization legislation, thereby dismantling the "division of labor" so deliberately created by congressional rules.

C

We conclude therefore, for the reasons given above, that appropriation requests constitute neither "proposals for legislation" nor "proposals for . . . major Federal actions," and that therefore the procedural requirements of §102(2)(C) have no application to such requests. The judgment of the Court of Appeals is reversed.

So ordered.

NOTES AND QUESTIONS

1. Does the suggestion in the Court's opinion that NEPA is "best interpreted" to apply to "recommendations . . . that actually propose programmatic actions" suggest any other exemptions from the EIS requirement? In National Wildlife Federation v. Coston, 773 F.2d 1513 (9th Cir. 1985) the court relied on *Andrus* to hold that an EIS was not necessary on a Capital Investment Road and Bridge Program (CIP) prepared by the U.S. Forest Service. The court noted that the CIP merely sets out procedures under which the Service reviews construction proposals in order to establish priorities for the allocation of limited federal funds. Do you agree?

In State of North Dakota v. Andrus, 483 F. Supp. 255 (D.N.D. 1980), the U.S. Department of the Interior submitted legislation to Congress increasing the state financial share of water resource projects. The Department prepared an environmental assessment on the legislation but claimed an EIS was not necessary. In an action in which the state brought suit to challenge the Department's decision, the court held that no EIS was necessary on the cost-sharing legislation.

While noting that Andrus v. Sierra Club did not "automatically" dispose of the case, the court held that the situation presented was "the same": "The situation in this case crosses the line from difficulty to impossibility. Not only would requiring an EIS at this stage be repetitive, it would also result in large

scale speculation. It can hardly be said that an EIS based largely upon speculation would further the policy of NEPA" (483 F. Supp. at 260).

Since NEPA applies explicitly to "proposals" for legislation, how does the
court manage to exempt the legislative proposal in *North Dakota*? Does the logic
of *Sierra Club* as extended by *North Dakota* suggest other exemptions from
NEPA?

2. In *North Dakota*, the state asserted that the cost-sharing legislation
would have "a tremendous environmental impact" on the western states because
the requirement that the states assume a share of project costs would "place
economic considerations ahead of environmental concerns" (483 F. Supp. at
258). If this statement is true, doesn't the court's opinion excuse the preparation
of an impact statement on a major policy decision that will necessarily lead to
environmentally harmful action? Is this result consistent with NEPA policy? Or
is the congressional legislative process so political that courts should not interfere
by compelling the preparation of impact statements on legislative proposals? See
Wingfield v. OMB, 9 Envt. Rep. Cas. (BNA) 1961 (D.D.C. 1977), for the minority view that a court may not entertain a private suit to compel preparation
of an impact statement on legislative proposals. Should it make a difference that
the legislative proposal is for a single project, such as a lock or dam?

3. *Andrus v. Sierra Club* does not affect NEPA's requirement that federal
agencies prepare impact statements on legislative proposals submitted to Congress. Although potentially helpful as a means of providing Congress with information necessary to review the environmental impact of federal programs, the
impact statement on legislative proposals is NEPA's neglected mandate. Very few
have been submitted.

The courts also have differed on whether plaintiffs have standing to enforce
the legislative impact statement requirement. Compare Chamber of Commerce
v. Department of Interior, 439 F. Supp. 762 (D.D.C. 1977) (standing denied to
challenge failure to prepare statement because proposal "in the lap of Congress"
and injury was speculative), with Atchison, T. & S.F. Santa Fe Ry. v. Callaway,
431 F. Supp. 722 (D.D.C. 1977) (standing granted to challenge impact statement on lock and dam proposal because inadequate impact statement denied
plaintiffs important environmental information). For discussion, see Note, NE-
PA's Forgotten Clause: Impact Statements for Legislative Proposals, 58 B.U.L.
Rev. 560 (1978).

4. Whether NEPA applies to the extraterritorial impacts of federal agency
actions has produced a protracted controversy still not entirely resolved. NEPA
does not expressly exclude or include extraterritorial environmental impacts, although the statute does require federal agencies to "recognize the worldwide . . .
character of environmental problems." §102(2)(F). CEQ regulations do not address this problem, which was covered by an executive order issued by President
Carter (Exec. Order No. 12,114, 44 Fed. Reg. 1957). The order, though not
based on NEPA, requires environmental reviews of the extraterritorial environmental impacts of federal agency actions. The review is not as extensive as the
environmental review covered by NEPA's impact statement. The order contains
a number of exemptions, which relate primarily to national security actions.

In Natural Resources Defense Council, Inc. v. NRC, 645 F.2d 1345 (D.C. Cir. 1981), the court considered a NRC decision to authorize the export of components for a nuclear power plant to be built in the Philippines at a site located in an earthquake zone and in the shadow of four volcanoes. The Commission relied on an environmental review submitted by the executive office of the president but did not prepare an impact statement. The court held that no impact statement was necessary. It read NEPA and its legislative history to exclude its application to extraterritorial impacts and held that §102(2)(F) only required international cooperation on environmental problems. See generally NEPA Law & Litigation, supra, §§5:16-5:18.

5. The Supreme Court in *Sierra Club* paid substantial deference to CEQ's regulations. It mentioned CEQ 25 times and quoted extensively from CEQ regulations in the footnotes. The Court reaffirmed *Sierra Club* in Robertson v. Methow Valley Citizens Council, 109 S. Ct. 1835 (1989), where it deferred to CEQ's revocation of its worst case analysis regulation. Does the Court's deference to EPA rulemaking as illustrated by *Chevron* justify deference to CEQ's interpretation of NEPA?

A student author has pointed out that cases presenting interpretive issues under NEPA are unique:

> CEQ is not a party to the action because its interpretation of NEPA is independent of the agency being sued and its regulations purport to apply on a government-wide basis. Moreover, the rules themselves are unique in that Congress failed to delegate NEPA rulemaking authority expressly to CEQ or to any other specific agency. CEQ's rulemaking power stems only from a series of executive orders. [Note, NEPA after Andrus v. Sierra Club: The Doctrine of Substantial Deference to the Regulations of the Council on Environmental Quality, 66 Va. L. Rev. 843, 850 (1980).]

The student author argues for the *Sierra Club* holding because "NEPA cuts across the entire spectrum of government activity" and because "the lack of definitive legislative history and the general vagueness of the statute have created an interpretive vacuum that CEQ's regulations can help to fill" (66 Va. L. Rev. at 851, 852). Do you agree?

A NOTE ON CONFLICTS BETWEEN NEPA AND THE STATUTORY OBLIGATIONS OF FEDERAL AGENCIES

NEPA's sweeping environmental mandate would seem to apply, without exemption, to the statutory obligations of all federal agencies. A basis for exemption can be found only in §104, discussed earlier, which states that NEPA is not to affect the "specific statutory obligations" of federal agencies. In *Calvert Cliffs*, the court held that §104 only relieves an agency of compliance with NEPA when its "specific statutory obligations" are clearly mutually exclusive of NEPA's requirements. *Calvert Cliffs* also held that §104 did not prohibit agencies from considering stricter water pollution controls than those required by EPA under the Clean Water Act.

Congress overruled *Clavert Cliffs* by prohibiting federal agencies from prescribing stricter pollution controls than required by established water quality standards. Under §511(c)(1) of the Clean Water Act, only certain limited actions by EPA are subject to NEPA. This section provides than an impact statement is necessary only when federal funds are used in the construction of publicly owned treatment works or when EPA issues a permit for a new pollutive source. See Sierra Club v. Corps of Engineers, 481 F. Supp. 397 (S.D.N.Y. 1979) (landfill permit issued by Corps a major federal action under NEPA). Congress also exempted EPA actions under the Clean Air Act from NEPA in the Energy Supply and Environmental Coordination Act of 1974, 15 U.S.C. §793(c)(1).

Functional equivalence. The courts also have adopted an implied "functional equivalence" exemption from NEPA for agency actions that protect rather than harm the environment. The courts have so far applied the functional equivalence exemption only to actions taken by EPA in its environmental regulation programs.

The basis for the functional equivalence exemption was stated in Portland Cement Association v. Ruckelshaus, 486 F.2d 375 (D.C. Cir. 1973), *cert. denied*, 417 U.S. 921 (1974), *reh'g denied*, 423 U.S. 1092 (1976), which held that EPA need not prepare an impact statement prior to its adoption of air pollution emissions standards under §111 of the Clean Air Act. The court noted that §111 of the Clean Air Act required an emissions standard reflecting "the best system of emission reduction" and mandated the EPA Administrator to take "into account the cost of achieving such reduction." The court interpreted these criteria to require the Administrator to consider both the adverse environmental effects and the costs to industry of a proposed standard and to prepare a statement of reasons explaining EPA's environmental review to accompany the proposal through the remainder of the rule-making process. The court found that although this procedure "may not import the complete advantages of the structured determinations of NEPA into the decisionmaking of EPA, it does . . . strike a workable balance between some of the advantages and disadvantages of full application of NEPA." The court continued:

> Without the problems of a NEPA delay conflicting with the constraints of the Clean Air Act, the ability of other agencies to make submissions to EPA concerning proposed rules, provides a channel for informed decision-making. These comments will be part of the record in the rule-making proceeding that EPA must take into account.
>
> EPA's proposed rule, and reasons therefor, are inevitably on alert to environmental issues. The EPA's proposed rule and reasons may omit reference to adverse environmental consequences that another agency might discern, but a draft impact statement may likewise be marred by omissions that another agency identifies. To the extent that EPA is aware of significant adverse environmental consequences of its proposal, good faith requires appropriate reference in its reasons for the proposal and its underlying balancing analysis. [486 F.2d at 386.]

Do you agree with the court's reasoning? Note that a federal agency exempted from NEPA under the functional equivalence rule is not compelled to meet all of the statutory impact statement requirements. It need not necessarily consider alternatives to its proposed action, for example. Judicial review of the agency's functionally equivalent determination, such as an agency rule adopted in a formal rule-making procedure, may also be narrower than judicial review of an impact statement.

What about the hazardous waste statutes? See Alabamians for a Clean Environment v. EPA, 26 Envt. Rep. Cas. [BNA] 2116 (N.D. Ala. 1987), applying the functional equivalence exemption to a RCRA permit and holding that "the RCRA framework provides an orderly and comprehensive mechanism to ensure that environmental factors are sufficiently taken into account." See Comment, To Police the Police: Functional Equivalence to the EIS Requirement and EPA Remedial Actions under Superfund, 33 Cath. U.L. Rev. 863 (1984).

Compare cases holding the functional equivalence exemption inapplicable: Jones v. Gordon, 621 F. Supp. 21 (D. Alaska 1985) *aff'd on other grounds*, 792 F.2d 821 (9th Cir. 1986), (National Marine Fisheries Service; not enough that agency given role of implementing environmental statute); Texas Commission on Natural Resources v. Bergland, 573 F.2d 201 (5th Cir.), *cert. denied*, 439 U.S. 966 (1978) (National Forest Management Act; National Forest Service not exclusively an environmental protection agency).

Direct statutory conflict. Federal agencies also claim exemption from NEPA because of direct statutory conflict with their enabling legislation. The Supreme Court considered this problem in Flint Ridge Development Co. v. Scenic Rivers Association, 426 U.S. 776 (1976). The Interstate Land Sales Full Disclosure Act, 15 U.S.C. §§1701-1720, requires developers to submit full disclosure statements on their land developments with the Department of Housing and Urban Development (HUD). A disclosure statement becomes effective 30 days after it is filed if it is complete and accurate on its face. The HUD Secretary may not substantively evaluate a developer's project but may only suspend the statement's effective date if the statement is procedurally defective.

HUD first claimed that NEPA did not apply to its actions under the disclosure act because NEPA applies only to agencies "that have the ability to react to environmental consequences when taking action." Since HUD could not review the environmental impact of a proposed development, NEPA did not apply. The Court did not resolve this contention because it found HUD exempt under NEPA §102, requiring federal agencies to comply only "to the fullest extent possible." The disclosure act made the developer's statement effective 30 days after filing unless the HUD Secretary acted affirmatively to suspend the statement. It was inconceivable, the Court concluded, that an impact statement could be drafted, reviewed, and revised within that period. The Court found a "clear and fundamental conflict of a statutory duty." As an afterthought, the Court noted that the disclosure act authorized the HUD Secretary "to incorporate a wide range of environmental information into property reports." Is this a functional equivalence rule?

Compare Jones v. Gordon, 792 F.2d 821 (9th Cir. 1986). The court rejected an argument that statutory time limits imposed on the issuance of permits for the capture of whales precluded compliance with NEPA. The court distinguished *Flint Ridge* by holding that the statute authorized the agency to control the "triggering act for the statutory time table" to allow compliance with NEPA. Accord ASARCO Inc. v. Air Quality Control Coalition, 92 Wash.2d 685, 601 P.2d 501 (1979).

Can the substantive authority conferred on an agency by its statute preclude compliance with NEPA? The Supreme Court did not decide this question in *Flint Ridge*, and the lower courts have taken opposing views. In Pacific Legal Foundation v. Andrus, 657 F.2d 829 (6th Cir. 1981), the court refused to find a functional equivalence exemption but held that an EIS need not be filed on the listing of an endangered species under the Endangered Species Act. It held that the agency did not have discretion to consider environmental impacts, that the statutory criteria for listing endangered species precluded consideration of environmental impacts, and that the listing of an endangered species furthered NEPA's purposes. Contra Environmental Defense Fund, Inc. v. Mathews, 410 F. Supp. 336 (D.D.C. 1976) (invalidating Food and Drug Administration Act regulation that precluded consideration of environmental impacts). Isn't this question answered by *Calvert Cliffs*, which held that NEPA is part of every agency's statutory mandate?

National security exemption. In Weinberger v. Catholic Action of Hawaii, 454 U.S. 139 (1981), the U.S. Navy invoked the Freedom of Information Act, 5 U.S.C. §522, to claim an impact statement was not required for the construction of new ammunition and weapons storage facilities in which the plaintiff claimed that nuclear weapons would be stored. The Act applies to NEPA. See §102(2)(C).

The court of appeals required the preparation of a hypothetical EIS that would hypothesize but not concede that the facilities would be used for nuclear weapons storage. The Supreme Court reversed. It held that classified national defense matters were exempt from disclosure under the Act and that information on the storage of nuclear weapons fell in this category. For national security reasons, the Navy could neither admit nor deny that it proposed to store nuclear weapons, and so a court could not determine whether the Navy had taken an action to which NEPA applied. The Court added that if the Navy proposed to store nuclear weapons at the facility the Defense Department regulations "can fairly be read to require that an EIS be prepared solely for internal purposes, even though such a document cannot be disclosed to the public." Id. at 146.

The cases have read *Catholic Action* to require preparation of an EIS when the Freedom of Information Act does not apply and have held that the application of NEPA to national security activities is a justiciable question. See No Gwen Alliance v. Aldridge, 855 F.2d 1380 (9th Cir. 1988) (but holding that nexus between radio emergency network and nuclear war was too tenuous to require discussion); Romer v. Carlucci, 847 F.2d 445 (8th Cir. 1988) (court can review EIS on MX missile deployment for compliance with NEPA). Reread §101. Are these decisions consistent with the statutory intent?

For discussion see Note, "Beyond Judicial Scrutiny": Military Compliance with NEPA, 18 Ga. L. Rev. 639 (1984); Comment, Weinberger v. Catholic Action of Hawaii Peace Education Project: Assessing the Environmental Impact of Nuclear Weapons Storage, 3 Va. J. Nat. Resources L. 335 (1984).

C. IF AN IMPACT STATEMENT MUST BE PREPARED, WHAT IS ITS SCOPE?

When a federal agency decides or has been ordered by a court to prepare an impact statement, the next step is to determine its scope. This problem has several dimensions. One concerns the range of factors an agency must take into account. NEPA requires consideration of "alternatives" to the proposed action, a requirement that compels agencies to consider factors they would not otherwise evaluate.

The scope of the impact statement also is determined by the type of environmental impacts the statement must consider. NEPA clearly applies to impacts on the natural environment. Assertive proponents of the statute's mandate have also urged its application to actions affecting the urban, as well as the natural, environment, and the inclusion of social and economic impacts within the range of impacts to be considered.

The problem of impact statement scope also has a physical dimension. Agencies often divide proposed projects into more than one segment. The best example is a major federal highway planned to cross an entire state. Preparation of an impact statement for all of the highway is not practicable. Segmentation of the highway into more than one action for impact statement purposes may allow the agency to disregard the cumulative impact of the entire highway route. Segmentation that frustrates NEPA's purposes should be avoided.

Agencies may also find that projects they consider in impact statements are interrelated. A federal agency, for example, may authorize coal mining leases throughout a large area of public land. Should the agency prepare an impact statement on each lease separately or on all of the leases as a group? Critics of the impact statement process argue that limiting the impact statement to one project at a time, like segmentation, prevents consideration of the cumulative impact of agency decisionmaking. Agency consideration of isolated projects once they have been proposed may also frustrate NEPA. There is no opportunity to consider the planning and program decisions on which individual projects are based — and which may irreversibly commit the agency to the project decision. Recall, as well, that a court may not require an impact statement on federally funded plans and planning processes. One way out of this dilemma is to require a program impact statement on interrelated projects. The program impact statement could evaluate programs for their environmental impact before individual project decisions are made. The materials that follow consider the issues, outlined above, that determine the proper scope of an environmental impact statement.

1. The Alternatives Requirement

One of the major expectations when NEPA was enacted was that federal agencies, directed by statute to carry out narrowly conceived missions, would consider less environmentally damaging alternatives they might not otherwise take into account. Highway projects again present a familiar example. The federal government funds state highways to meet projected highway needs. State highway agencies usually meet these needs by selecting a location requiring the smallest expenditure of federal and state funds. Federal and state highway agencies are reluctant to consider alternatives to highway projects that interfere with their statutory mission to meet traffic needs through highway construction. Alternatives such as public transit, or even a change in highway location, meet with substantial agency resistance.

NEPA provides a process through which agencies can consider alternatives. The section requiring the preparation of an environmental impact statement requires the discussion of "alternatives to the proposed action." §102(2)(C)(iii). Both the courts and CEQ have characterized the alternatives requirement as the "heart" of the impact statement process. Another section of NEPA also provides independently for the consideration of alternatives. It requires agencies of the federal government to "study, develop, and describe appropriate alternatives to recommended courses of action in any proposal which involves unresolved conflicts concerning alternative uses of available resources." §102(2)(E). Most decisions interpreting the separate alternatives requirement have considered it in the context of the impact statement, but some decisions have given this requirement an independent effect.

The range of alternatives agencies might include is considerable. The most dramatic alternative is the "no action" alternative, which requires the agency to forego its project altogether. Other alternatives contemplate the retention of the proposed action but require its modification. Consider the following classification of alternatives:

> A primary alternative is a substitute for agency action that accomplishes the action in another manner. Increased coal production is a primary alternative to the constrution of a nuclear power plant. . . .
>   . . . [A] secondary alternative concede[s] that the agency action is necessary but suggest[s] that it be carried out in a different manner. . . . [A] secondary alternative . . . [may require] a different location for a project, or project changes that mitigate harmful environmental impacts. [D. Mandelker, Environment and Equity 120 (1981).]

Are agencies better equipped to evaluate primary or secondary alternatives? Which type of alternative is likely to lie outside the agency's jurisdiction to implement? Should this factor be considered by courts and agencies in the evaluation of alternatives?

The District of Columbia Court of Appeals adopted an expansive interpretation of the alternatives requirement in an early and leading case. Natural Resources Defense Council, Inc. v Morton, 458 F.2d 827 (D.C. Cir. 1972). The Secretary of the Interior announced a general sale of leases of oil and gas tracts on the Outer Continental Shelf of eastern Louisiana in response to an energy supply message by President Nixon. The impact statement prepared for the lease announcement stated that the elimination of then-existing oil import quotas might be an alternative to offshore leasing but that this determination required consideration of complex factors, including national security, that were beyond the scope of the impact statement. The court disagreed:

> [R]equired in the ensuing environmental impact statements would be the discussion by each department of the particular actions it could take as an alternative to the proposal underlying its impact statement.
>
> When the proposed action is an integral part of a coordinated plan to deal with a broad problem, the range of alternatives that must be evaluated is broadened. While the Department of the Interior does not have the authority to eliminate or reduce oil import quotas, such action is within the purview of both Congress and the President, to whom the impact statement goes. The impact statement is not only for the exposition of the thinking of the agency, but also for the guidance of these ultimate decision-makers, and must provide them with the environmental effects of both the proposal and the alternatives, for their consideration along with the various other elements of the public interest. [458 F.2d at 834-835.]

The court also stated:

> The mere fact that an alternative requires legislative implementation does not automatically establish it as beyond the domain of what is required for discussion, particularly since NEPA was intended to provide a basis for consideration and choice by the decision-makers in the legislative as well as the executive branch. But the need for an overhaul of basic legislation certainly bears on the requirements of the Act. We do not suppose Congress intended an agency to devote itself to extended discussion of the environmental impact of alternatives so remote from reality as to depend on, say, the repeal of the anti-trust laws. [458 F.2d at 837.]

The Supreme Court had an opportunity to consider *Morton's* "reasonably available" rule in a nuclear power plant licensing case. The Court's decision follows:

VERMONT YANKEE NUCLEAR POWER CORP. v. NATURAL RESOURCES DEFENSE COUNCIL, INC.
435 U.S. 519 (1978)

Justice REHNQUIST delivered the opinion of the Court.

[The Court consolidated for review two decisions by the now-superseded Atomic Energy Commission. Commission licensing procedures at this time were as follows: The utility first filed a preliminary safety analysis report, an environmental report, and information on antitrust implications. This information was reviewed by Commission staff, the Advisory Committee on Reactor Safeguards (ACRS), and a group of atomic energy experts. Both the ACRS and the experts submitted their evaluations to the Commission. A NEPA review was carried out by Commission staff, which prepared a draft and final impact statement. A three-member Atomic Safety and Licensing Board then held a public adjudicatory hearing, with the option of appeal to an appeal board and, in the board's discretion, to the Commission. The final agency decision was appealable to the federal Court of Appeals. Generally, the same procedure applied for an application for a license to operate a nuclear power plant.]

I. . . .

C

In January 1969, petitioner Consumers Power Co. applied for a permit to construct two nuclear reactors in Midland, Mich. Consumers Power's application was examined by the Commission's staff and the ACRS. The ACRS issued reports which discussed specific problems and recommended solutions. It also made reference to "other problems" of a more generic nature and suggested that efforts should be made to resolve them with respect to these as well as all other projects. Two groups, one called Saginaw and another called Mapleton, intervened and opposed the application. Saginaw filed with the Board a number of environmental contentions, directed over 300 interrogatories to the ACRS, attempted to depose the chairman of the ACRS, and requested discovery of various ACRS documents. The Licensing Board denied the various discovery requests directed to the ACRS. Hearings were then held on numerous radiological health and safety issues. Thereafter, the Commission's staff issued a draft environmental impact statement. Saginaw submitted 119 environmental contentions which were both comments on the proposed draft statement and a statement of Saginaw's position in the upcoming hearings. The staff revised the statement and issued a final environmental statement in March 1972. Further hearings where then conducted during May and June 1972. Saginaw, however, choosing not to appear at or participate in these latter hearings, indicated that it had "no conventional findings of fact to set forth" and had not "chosen to search the record and respond to this proceeding by submitting citations of matters which we believe were proved or disproved." But the Licensing Board, recognizing its obligations to "independently consider the final balance among conflicting environmental factors in the record," nevertheless treated as contested those issues "as to which intervenors introduced affirmative evidence or engaged in substantial cross examination."

At issue now are 17 of those 119 contentions which are claimed to raise questions of "energy conservation." The Licensing Board indicated that as far as appeared from the record, the demand for the plant was made up of normal industrial and residential use. It went on to state that it was "beyond our province to inquire into whether the customary uses being made of electricity in our society are "proper' or 'improper.'" With respect to claims that Consumers Power stimulated demand by its advertising the Licensing Board indicated that "[n]o evidence was offered on this point and absent some evidence that Applicant is creating abnormal demand, the Board did not consider the question." The Licensing Board also failed to consider the environmental effects of fuel reprocessing or disposal of radioactive wastes. The Appeal Board ultimately affirmed the Licensing Board's grant of a construction permit and the Commission declined to further review the matter.

At just about the same time, the Council on Environmental Quality revised its regulations governing the preparation of environmental impact statements. The regulations mentioned for the first time the necessity of considering in impact statements energy conservation as one of the alternatives to a proposed project. The new guidelines were to apply only to final impact statements filed after January 28, 1974. Thereafter, on November 6, 1973, more than a year after the record had been closed in the *Consumers Power* case and while that case was pending before the Court of Appeals, the Commission ruled in another case that while its statutory power to compel conservation was not clear, it did not follow that all evidence of energy conservation issues should therefore be barred at the threshold. In re Niagara Mohawk Power Corp., 6 A.E.C. 995 (1973). Saginaw then moved the Commission to clarify its ruling and reopen the *Consumers Power* proceedings.

In a lengthy opinion, the Commission declined to reopen the proceedings. The Commission first ruled it was required to consider only energy conservation alternatives which were "reasonably available," would in their aggregate effect curtail demand for electricity to a level at which the proposed facility would not be needed, and were susceptible of a reasonable degree of proof. It then determined, after a thorough examination of the record, that not all of Saginaw's contentions met these threshold tests. It further determined that the Board had been willing at all times to take evidence on the other contentions. Saginaw had simply failed to present any such evidence. The Commission further criticized Saginaw for its total disregard of even those minimal procedural formalities necessary to give the Board some idea of exactly what was at issue. The Commission emphasized that "[p]articularly in these circumstances, Saginaw's complaint that it was not granted a hearing on alleged energy conservation issues comes with ill grace." And in response to Saginaw's contention that regardless of whether it properly raised the issues, the Licensing Board must consider all environmental issues, the Commission basically agreed, as did the Board itself, but further reasoned that the Board must have some workable procedural rules and these rules

in this setting must take into account that energy conservation is a novel and evolving concept. NEPA "does not require a 'crystal ball' inquiry." Natural Resources Defense Council v. Morton, 458 F.2d 827, 837 (1972). This consideration has led us to hold that we will not apply *Niagara* retroactively. As we gain experience on a case-by-case basis and hopefully, feasible energy conservation techniques emerge, the applicant, staff, and licensing boards will have obligations to develop an adequate record on these issues in appropriate cases, whether or not they are raised by intervenors.

However, at this emergent stage of energy conservation principles, intervenors also have their responsibilities. They must state clear and reasonably specific energy conservation contentions in a timely fashion. Beyond that, they have a burden of coming forward with some affirmative showing if they wish to have these novel contentions explored further.

Respondents then challenged the granting of the construction permit in the Court of Appeals for the District of Columbia Circuit. . . .

We now turn to the Court of Appeals' holding "that rejection of energy conservation on the basis of the 'threshold test' was capricious and arbitrary," and again conclude the court was wrong.

The Court of Appeals ruled that the Commission's "threshold test" for the presentation of energy conservation contentions was inconsistent with NEPA's basic mandate to the Commission. The Commission, the court reasoned, is something more than an umpire who sits back and resolves adversary contentions at the hearing stage. 547 F.2d, at 627. And when an intervenor's comments "bring 'sufficient attention to the issue to stimulate the Commission's consideration of it,'" the commission must "undertake its own preliminary investigation of the proffered alternative sufficient to reach a rational judgment whether it is worthy of detailed consideration in the EIS. Moreover, the Commission must explain the basis for each conclusion that further consideration of a suggested alternative is unwarranted." 547 F.2d, at 628, quoting from Indiana & Michigan Electric Co. v. FPC, 502 F.2d 336, 339 (1974), *cert. denied,* 420 U.S. 946 (1975).

While the court's rationale is not entirely unappealing as an abstract proposition, as applied to this case we think it basically misconceives not only the scope of the agency's statutory responsibility, but also the nature of the administrative process, the thrust of the agency's decision, and the type of issues the intervenors were trying to raise.

There it little doubt that under the Atomic Energy Act of 1954, state public utility commissions or similar bodies are empowered to make the initial decision regarding the need for power. The Commission's prime area of concern in the licensing context, on the other hand, is national security, public health, and safety. And it is clear that the need, as that term is conventionally used, for the power was thoroughly explored in the hearings. Even the Federal Power Commission, which regulates sales in interstate commerce, agreed with Consumers Power's analysis of projected need.

NEPA, of course, has altered slightly the statutory balance, requiring "a detailed statement by the responsible official on . . . alternatives to the proposed action." But, as should be obvious even upon a moment's reflection, the term "alternatives" is not self-defining. To make an impact statement something more than an exercise in frivolous boilerplate the concept of alternatives must be bounded by some notion of feasibility. As the Court of Appeals for the District of Columbia Circuit has itself recognized:

> There is reason for concluding that NEPA was not meant to require detailed discussion of the environmental effects of "alternatives" put forward in comments when these effects cannot be readily ascertained and the alternatives are deemed only remote and speculative possibilities, in view of basic changes required in statutes and policies of other agencies — making them available, if at all, only after protracted debate and litigation not meaningfully compatible with the timeframe of the needs to which the underlying proposal is addressed. [Natural Resources Defense Council v. Morton, 458 F.2d 827, 837, 838 (1972).]

See also Life of the Land v. Brinegar, 485 F.2d 460 (C.A. 9 1973), *cert. denied*, 416 U.S. 961 (1974). Common sense also teaches us that the "detailed statement of alternatives" cannot be found wanting simply because the agency failed to include every alternative device and thought conceivable by the mind of man. Time and resources are simply too limited to hold that an impact statement fails because the agency failed to ferret out every possible alternative, regardless of how uncommon or unknown that alternative may have been at the time the project was approved.

With these principles in mind we now turn to the notion of "energy conservation," an alternative the omission of which was thought by the Court of Appeals to have been "forcefully pointed out by Saginaw in its comments on the draft EIS." 547 F.2d, at 625. Again, as the Commission pointed out, "the phrase 'energy conservation' has a deceptively simple ring in this context. Taken literally, the phrase suggests a virtually limitless range of possible actions and developments that might, in one way or another, ultimately reduce projected demands for electricity from a particular proposed plant." Moreover, as a practical matter, it is hard to dispute the observation that it is largely the events of recent years that have emphasized not only the need but also a large variety of alternatives for energy conservation. Prior to the drastic oil shortages incurred by the United States in 1973, there was little serious thought in most Government circles of energy conservation alternatives. Indeed, the Council on Environmental Quality did not promulgate regulations which even remotely suggested the need to consider energy conservation in impact statements until August 1, 1973. And even then the guidelines were not made applicable to draft and final statements filed with the Council before January 28, 1974. The Federal Power Commission likewise did not require consideration of energy conservation in applications to build hydroelectric facilities until June 19, 1973. And these regulations were not made retroactive either. All this occurred over a year and a half after the draft environmental statement for Midland had been prepared, and over a year after the final environmental statement had been prepared and the hearings completed.

We think these facts amply demonstrate that the concept of "alternatives" is an evolving one, requiring the agency to explore more or fewer alternatives as they become better known and understood. This was well understood by the Commission, which, unlike the Court of Appeals, recognized that the Licensing Board's decision had to be judged by the information then available to it. And judged in that light we have little doubt the Board's actions were well within the proper bounds of its statutory authority. Not only did the record before the agency give every indication that the project was actually needed, but also there was nothing before the Board to indicate to the contrary.

We also think the court's criticism of the Commission's "threshold test" displays a lack of understanding of the historical setting within which the agency action took place and of the nature of the test itself. In the first place, while it is true that NEPA places upon an agency the obligation to consider every significant aspect of the environmental impact of a proposed action, it is still incumbent upon intervenors who wish to participate to structure their participation so that it is meaningful, so that it alerts the agency to the intervenors' position and contentions. This is especially true when the intervenors are requesting the agency to embark upon an exploration of uncharted territory, as was the question of energy conservation in the late 1960's and early 1970's.

> [C]omments must be significant enough to step over a threshold requirement of materiality before any lack of agency response or consideration becomes of concern. The comment cannot merely state that a particular mistake was made . . . ; it must show why the mistake was of possible significance in the results. . . . Portland Cement Assn. v. Ruckelshaus, 486 F.2d 375, 394 (1973), *cert. denied sub nom.* Portland Cement Corp. v. Administrator, EPA, 417 U.S. 921 (1974).

Indeed, administrative proceedings should not be a game or a forum to engage in unjustified obstructionism by making cryptic and obscure reference to matters that "ought to be" considered and then, after failing to do more to bring the matter to the agency's attention, seeking to have that agency determination vacated on the ground that the agency failed to consider matters "forcefully presented." In fact, here the agency continually invited further clarification of Saginaw's contentions. Even without such clarification it indicated a willingness to receive evidence on the matters. But not only did Saginaw decline to further focus its contentions, it virtually declined to participate, indicating that it had "no conventional findings of fact to set forth" and that it had not "chosen to search the record and respond to this proceeding by submitting citations of matter which we believe were proved or disproved."

We also think the court seriously mischaracterized the Commission's "threshold test" as placing "heavy substantive burdens . . . on intervenors. . . ." On the contrary, the Commission explicitly stated: "We do not equate this burden with the civil litigation concept of a prima facie case, an unduly heavy burden in this setting. But the showing should be sufficient to require reasonable minds to inquire further." We think this sort of agency procedure well within the agency's discretion.

In sum, to characterize the actions of the Commission as "arbitrary or capricious" in light of the facts then available to it as described at length above, is to deprive those words of any meaning. As we have said in the past:

> Administrative consideration of evidence . . . always creates a gap between the time the record is closed and the time the administrative decision is promulgated [and, we might add, the time the decision is judicially reviewed]. . . . If upon the coming down of the order litigants might demand rehearings as a matter of law because some new circumstance has arisen, some new trend has been observed, or some new fact discovered, there would be little hope that the administrative process could ever be consummated in an order that would not be subject to re-opening. ICC v. Jersey City, 322 U.S. 503, 514 (1944).

We have also made it clear that the role of a court in reviewing the sufficiency of an agency's consideration of environmental factors is a limited one, limited both by the time at which the decision was made and by the statute mandating review. "Neither the statute nor its legislative history contemplates that a court should substitute its judgment for that of the agency as to the environmental consequences of its actions." Kleppe v. Sierra Club, 427 U.S., at 410 n.21. We think the Court of Appeals has forgotten that injunction here and accordingly its judgment in this respect must also be reversed.

NOTES AND QUESTIONS

1. Although the Supreme Court in *Vermont Yankee* quoted the "speculative alternative" language from *Morton*, it ignored *Morton's* more expansive reading of the alternatives requirement quoted above. Has the Supreme Court overruled *Morton*? Is the standard adopted by *Vermont Yankee* procedural or substantive? Did the Supreme Court mean to imply that an agency need not consider alternatives that would require amendment of its basic enabling legislation? Since President Nixon issued the energy message that led to the offshore leasing program, should he have considered the oil import quota alternative? Does an executive message require an impact statement?

For a critical view of *Vermont Yankee*, which takes the position that the Court misapplied the *Morton* decision, see Rodgers, A Hard Look at *Vermont Yankee*: Environmental Law under Strict Scrutiny, 67 Geo. L.J. 699 (1979). Professor Rodgers also claims that *Vermont Yankee* qualified the important "balls and strikes" doctrine. Under this doctrine, the agency does not sit as an umpire, calling balls and strikes, but must affirmatively seek out issues relevant to the case that may not have occurred to the parties. *Vermont Yankee* qualified this doctrine by holding that "the energy conservation alternative did not have to be addressed because the intervenors did not raise their objections with sufficient support and precision" (67 Geo. L.J. at 720). Rodgers notes that the burden placed on intervenors "means a great deal . . . in the case of arguable or partial alternatives, such as energy conservation, which is within a reasonable, albeit ambitious, range of policy options" (67 Geo. L.J. at 721).

Consider Coalition for Better Veterans Care, Inc. v. Veterans Administration, 16 Envt. Rep. Cas. (BNA) 1685 (D. Or. 1981). As an alternative to the closing of an old hospital and the construction of a new hospital, the VA was urged to consider the treatment of patients in private care facilities. Citing Vermont Yankee, the court disagreed. The alternative "was an assault on basic policy, which has been developed after years of debate by both the agency and by Congress." The need for additional legislation was another factor to consider, and VA's statutory authority for treatment in private facilities was limited. Do you agree?

Some courts carry this holding one step further and expressly limit the alternatives agencies must consider to the statutory objectives of their action. In City of New York v. Department of Transportation, 715 F.2d 732 (2d Cir. 1983), the Department adopted a rule authorizing the highway transportation of radioactive materials. The Department adopted the rule under legislation authorizing it to consider the safety of different modes of transportation of hazardous materials. It limited its inquiry to highway transportation and did not consider transportation by barges as an alternative. The court held that this decision was correct: "Statutory objectives provide a sensible compromise between unduly narrow objectives an agency might choose to identify to limit consideration of alternatives and hopelessly broad societal objectives that would unduly expand the range of relevant alternatives" (715 F.2d at 743). Does the "statutory objectives" test support any of the holdings in the cases discussed in the following Note? Is this test a proper interpretation of NEPA? See §102(1).

2. CEQ regulations require federal agencies to consider the no-action alternative, other "reasonable courses of action," and mitigation measures not in the proposed action. 40 C.F.R. §1508.25(b). The regulations also require agencies to consider "reasonable alternatives" not within their jurisdiction. Id. §1502.14(b). Are these regulations consistent with Vermont Yankee?

Consider the following cases:

Life of the Land v. Brinegar, 485 F.2d 460 (9th Cir. 1973). In holding that an impact statement on a reef runway proposed for Honolulu International Airport was adequate, the court noted that "there is nothing in the record to indicate that alternatives such as the readoption of airline schedules, imposition of curfew restrictions, or conversion to wide-body aircraft design are either reasonable or feasible alternatives in this case" (485 F.2d at 471). Why not?

Sierra Club v. Lynn, 502 F.2d 43 (5th Cir. 1974), cert. denied, 422 U.S. 1049 (1975). The court held adequate an impact statement on a federally funded new community to be built over a recharge zone for a water aquifer. It noted that the impact statement "cannot be condemned for its failure to discuss either the acquisition of the recharge zone as a park at a prohibitive cost, or the elimination of all federal assistance to any development over the recharge zone" (502 F.2d at 62). Why not?

Farmland Preservation Association v. Goldschmidt, 611 F.2d 233 (8th Cir. 1979). The court approved an impact statement on a proposed rural interstate highway. It held that a two-paragraph discussion of a "no action" alternative of not building the highway was sufficient. The statement stated that a failure to build the highway would mean that present and future traffic needs in the area would not be served, although environmental changes in the highway corridor would be avoided. The court believed that this discussion satisfied the *Vermont Yankee* test. Do you agree?

Massachusetts v. Clark, 594 F. Supp. 1373 (D. Mass. 1984). An impact statement for an oil and gas lease sale on the outer continental shelf covering 25 million acres listed only small deletions from the sale as alternatives. The court held that the "central flaw" of the impact statement was that it did not present any "feasible and legal options." Is this case distinguishable from the other cases discussed in this Note?

Van Abbema v. Fornell, 807 F.2d 633 (7th Cir. 1986). The court applied §102(2)(E) of NEPA and held that the Corps had not properly considered a no action alternative when it approved a dredge and fill permit for a coal-loading facility on the Mississippi River. The court noted that existing coal-loading facilities might well be adequate. What is the significance of the court's application of §102(2)(E) to a Corps dredge and fill permit decision? For discussion of §102(2)(E) see NEPA law and Litigation, supra, §9:21.

3. To what extent can agencies reduce the range of alternatives to limit the alternatives available? In California v. Block, 690 F.2d 753 (9th Cir. 1982), the U.S. Forest Service reviewed the future use of 62 million acres of roadless national forest land. All serious alternatives considered in its impact statement contemplated the development of some of this land, and no alternative would have retained more than 34 percent of the area in a wilderness condition. The court held that the alternatives considered were inadequate, noting that "it is puzzling why the Forest Service did not seriously consider an alternative that allocated more than a third of the . . . acreage to Wilderness" (690 F.2d at 768). What if the Forest Service had decided, as a matter of policy, that all of the wilderness area under consideration should be released for development? Could the agency then eliminate the wilderness alternative from consideration?

What if the Forest Service stated that it had pre-screened a number of additional alternatives before limiting its options to the alternatives chosen and that some of the pre-screened alternatives eliminated provided for a higher wilderness allocation? See Concerned about Trident v. Rumsfeld, 555 F.2d 817 (D.C. Cir. 1977) (approving Navy pre-screening of sites for Trident base). Is this case distinguishable?

4. Assume now that the agency pre-screens a number of alternatives and then takes the position that in its impact statement it will only consider alternatives "obviously superior" to the action it has chosen. This question arose in Seacoast Anti-Pollution League v. NRC, 598 F.2d 1221 (1st Cir. 1979). The Commission initiated but then terminated its inquiry into a number of southern New England sites as alternatives to a New Hampshire site for a nuclear power

plant, concluding that the southern sites were not "obviously superior." The court held that this decision was consistent with the Supreme Court's decision in *Vermont Yankee*. It noted that the southern sites were suggested because they were sites on which nuclear power plants either existed or were planned. The New Hampshire site was "virgin." Nevertheless:

> [P]etitioners' contentions are . . . speculative . . . [and] wholly theoretical. Nothing in the record before us demonstrates that the New England environment would benefit significantly if the . . . [New Hampshire] plant were located in southern New England rather than at Seabrook. . . . Many questions would have to be addressed to make such a position meaningful. These range from the feasibility, safety and general acceptability of siting two nuclear reactors in one community to whether such an arrangement, involving a site outside New Hampshire, could satisfy the power needs Seabrook seeks to satisfy, at reasonable cost. There would also be knotty questions of policy and law concerning the degree to which proceedings seeking a license for a site controlled by the applicant should be turned into proceedings focusing on sites beyond the applicant's immediate control and wishes. [598 F.2d at 1232-1233.]

Has the court correctly interpreted *Vermont Yankee? Morton?* The court in *Seacoast* noted that the objectors to the New Hampshire site had submitted the southern alternatives late in the licensing proceedings, as in *Vermont Yankee*.

2.   Social, Economic, and Psychological Factors and the Duty to Consider the Urban Environment

The Urban Environment

NEPA does not appear to be limited to impacts on the natural environment. Its Declaration of National Environmental Policy, §101(a), makes explicit reference to "the profound influence of population growth, high-density urbanization, [and] industrial expansion." In its first decision considering an impact statement on a detention center proposed for downtown Manhattan, the Second Circuit confirmed this application of NEPA to the urban environment:

> The Act must be construed to include protection of the quality of life for city residents. Noise, traffic, overburdened mass transportation systems, crime, congestion and even availability of drugs all affect the urban "environment" and are surely results of the "profound influences of . . . high-density urbanization [and] industrial expansion." [Hanley v. Mitchell, 460 F.2d 640, 647 (2nd Cir.), *cert. denied*, 409 U.S. 990 (1972) (*Hanly I*).]

How should environmental impacts in an urban environment be measured? When a proposed development is out of scale with its surroundings, it seems clear that it will create urban environmental impacts that require an impact statement. See Goose Hollow Foothills League v. Romney, 334 F. Supp. 877 (D. Or. 1971) (construction of high-rise student apartment building in low-rise residential area). Compare the two-part test for "signficance" adopted in Hanly v. Kleindienst (*Hanly II*), *supra*.

What if the project complies with local zoning? In Maryland-National Capital Parks & Planning Commission v. U.S. Postal Service, 487 F.2d 1029 (D.C. Cir. 1973), the court noted that an impact statement might not be necessary when a project, here a postal facility, was consistent with local zoning. The court viewed local approval of the development as a prior ratification through the political process of any environmental impacts that might occur. Is this view justified? See accord, Isle of Hope Historical Association v. Corps of Engineers, 646 F.2d 215 (5th Cir. 1981) (NEPA only requires consultation between federal and local officials on claimed violation of local planning and zoning).

Must exclusionary zoning be accepted under NEPA? In Town of Groton v. Laird, 353 F. Supp. 344 (D. Conn. 1972), a Navy housing project did not comply with local zoning. The court held that an impact statement was not required:

> Quite apart from the fact that the Navy is exempt from local zoning ordinances, NEPA is not a sort of metazoning law. It is not designed to enshrine existing zoning regulations on the theory that their violation presents a threat to environmental values. NEPA may not be used to shore up large lot and other exclusionary zoning devices that price out low and even middle income families. [353 F. Supp. at 350.]

For a discussion of urban impacts under NEPA, see Como-Falcon Coalition v. Department of Labor, 465 F. Supp. 850 (D. Minn. 1978), *rev'd*, 609 F.2d 343 (8th Cir. 1979), *cert. denied*, 446 U.S. 936 (1980) (noted 6 Colum. J. Envtl. L. 164 (1980)).

Regional Growth and Development Problems

It is but a step from the review of urban environmental impacts at the project site to a review of secondary impacts that affect growth and development patterns on a regional scale. In City of Rochester v. U.S. Postal Service, 541 F.2d 967 (2d Cir. 1976), the Service decided not to file an impact statement on its decision to relocate a major postal facility from downtown Rochester to a nearby suburb. Holding that an impact statement was required, the court, referring to the effect of the relocation on downtown Rochester, noted that the relocation of the facility would "contribute to an atmosphere of urban decay and blight, making environmental repair of the surrounding area difficult if not infeasible" (541 F.2d at 973).

In City of Davis v. Coleman, 520 F.2d 661 (9th Cir. 1975), the court ordered the preparation of an impact statement on a new highway interchange planned to serve an industrial development. The court noted that the interchange would create secondary, growth-inducing environmental impacts that clearly fell within NEPA. These impacts included the potentially detrimental impact of new urban growth on the city's controlled growth policy. They also included an expected rapid increase in population that would create a demand for residential and commercial development and the beginning of urban sprawl.

Compare Sierra Club v. Cavanaugh, 447 F. Supp. 427 (D.S.D. 1978). The court upheld a decision by the U.S. Farmers Home Administration not to file an impact statement on a rural water system it planned to fund. The Sierra Club claimed the system would stimulate scattered rural growth that would create urban sprawl and consume valuable agricultural land. The court held that the growth-inducing impacts were negligible and that local zoning could solve any land use problems that might arise.

For discussion of secondary impact problems, see Caprio, The Role of Secondary Impacts under NEPA, 6 Envtl. Aff. 127 (1977), and Fix, Addressing the Issue of the Economic Impact of Regional Malls in Legal Proceedings, 20 Urb. L. Ann. 101 (1980).

Social and Economic Impacts

Cases like City of Rochester appear to indicate that NEPA also extends to social and economic impacts, but the courts have rejected this extension of the statute when social and economic impacts were not associated with a primary physical impact. See Como-Falcon Coalition v. Department of Labor, 465 F. Supp. 850 (D. Minn. 1978), rev'd, 609 F.2d 343 (8th Cir. 1979), cert. denied, 446 U.S. 936 (1980) (proposal to establish job corps center in buildings on former college campus). This issue also arose in a notorious public housing case, Nucleus of Chicago Homeowners Association v. Lynn, 524 F.2d 225 (7th Cir. 1975), cert. denied, 424 U.S. 967 (1976). To comply with a court desegregation order, the Chicago Public Housing Authority planned a scattered-site public housing project in a middle-class neighborhood. The association claimed the project tenants would have a negative impact on their neighborhood, relying on statistical findings that public housing tenants were more inclined to crime and less inclined to hard work and dwelling maintenance than their middle-class neighbors. The trial judge disagreed, holding that a "class of persons" per se could not be an environmental impact. While agreeing in principle, the court of appeals did not consider this issue, holding that the low density of the project on scattered sites ensured that no negative impacts would occur. For discussion, see Ackerman, Impact Statements and Low Cost Housing, 46 S. Cal. L. Rev. 754 (1973), and Daffron, Using NEPA to Exclude the Poor, 4 Envtl. Aff. 81 (1975).

Risk and Psychological Stress

To some extent, the cases discussed so far considered environmental impacts based on the objections of those affected, as in Goose Hollow (neighbors objected to the construction of high-rise housing). The Supreme Court has now placed some limits on the extent to which environmental impacts can be based on the reactions of persons affected by an agency's action.

In Metropolitan Edison Co. v. People against Nuclear Energy, 460 U.S.

766 (1983), the Nuclear Regulatory Commission (NRC) authorized a restart of TMI-1, one of the nuclear reactors located on the site of the Three Mile Island incident, but not the reactor that failed. People against Nuclear Energy (PANE) is an association of residents in the area who opposed the operation of either reactor. It claimed that NEPA required NRC to consider the "severe psychological health damage to persons living in the vicinity" that would be caused by a restart of TMI-1 because the restart would remind residents of the nuclear accident and would raise the possibility that an accident could happen again. The Court disagreed. Holding that NEPA was limited to impacts on the physical environment, it added that the statute should "be read to include a requirement of a reasonably close causal relationship between a change in the physical environment and the effect at issue":

> PANE argues that the psychological health damage it alleges "will flow directly from the risk of [a nuclear] accident." But a *risk* of an accident is not an effect on the physical environment. A risk is, by definition, unrealized in the physical world. In a causal chain from renewed operation of TMI-1 to psychological health damage, the element of risk and its perception by PANE's members are necessary middle links. We believe that the element of risk lengthens the causal chain beyond the reach of NEPA. [460 U.S. at 775.]

The Court also suggested that PANE's objections reflected a "policy disagreement" best resolved in the political process.

The Court's decision is troubling. NEPA's purpose is to address environmental risk, and even a physical risk to the environment may be causally attenuated. Justice Brennan may have provided a distinction in his concurring opinion. He distinguished cases in which the "psychological injury . . . [arose] out of the direct sensory impact of a change in the physical environment," citing Chelsea Neighborhood Association v. U.S. Postal Service, 516 F.2d 378 (2d Cir. 1976), in which the court held that the agency had failed to address the environmental impact of a housing project on its neighborhood. For discussion of *PANE*, see Note, Psychological Stress Under NEPA, 19 Val. U.L. Rev. 899 (1985); Comment, Reduction of Risk under NEPA: Stress and People against Nuclear Energy, 33 Am. U.L. Rev. 535 (1984): Comment, The Supreme Court as Guardian of the Environment: The *Metropolitan Edison* Decision in Perspective, 22 Duq. L. Rev. 479 (1984). For a case suggesting that *PANE* means that agencies are no longer required to consider socio-economic effects under NEPA, even when physical effects are present, see Olmsted Citizens for a Better Community v. United States, 793 F.2d 201 (8th Cir. 1986). What is the basis for this holding?

3. Segmentation

The scope of an impact statement is defined by the geographic extent of the "action" covered, as well as by the environmental impacts that must be discussed. As discussed earlier, many governmental projects are constructed in stages, and separating identifiable stages for coverage in an impact statement is often difficult. Highways are a good example. Major highways are divided into segments for purposes of federal funding. The question is whether these individual segments may be separated for impact statement purposes. Objectors may complain that this kind of "piecemealing" allows the highway agency to minimize environmental impacts by avoiding discussion of the cumulative impacts of the highway project. Agencies argue that widening the scope of the impact statement to include related projects is impractical and may compel the agency to consider the speculative impacts of projects not yet approved.

The following case considers the segmentation issue in the context of a sewer extension project. It arose under a state counterpart of NEPA, but it discusses and applies the applicable federal segmentation decisions.

WISCONSIN ENVIRONMENTAL DECADE v. STATE
94 Wis. 2d 263, 288 N.W. 2d 168 (Ct. App. 1979) (review denied by Wisconsin Supreme Court)

GARTZKE, Presiding Judge.

This appeal involves the propriety of a finding by the Department of Natural Resources (DNR) that a proposed sewer interceptor is not a major action significantly affecting the quality of the human environment. . . .

The DNR's decision not to prepare an EIS was based upon an analysis of the environmental impact of the specific sewer interceptor described in the application. The Decade challenges the decision on grounds that the DNR has purposely divided a single proposed interceptor into two parts: an environmentally insigificant part which is embraced by the application subject to the appeal before us and an environmentally significant part embraced by another application. [Both applications had been made to the DNR, as required by statute. Its decision was subject to the Wisconsin Environmental Policy Act (WEPA), which is a counterpart of NEPA. The "environmentally insignificant" part of the extension was an extension from the end of the existing sewer line in the Milwaukee service area to an outer suburb, Hales Corners. The "environmentally significant" part contemplated a further extension to another suburb, the city of New Berlin. In reviewing the DNR's decision not to file an impact statement, the court relied on the DNR's "screening worksheet" as the "record" on appeal. Its discussion of the segmentation issue follows.] . . .

Courts have grappled with the problem of segmentation since the inception of NEPA. "Specifying the proper scope of an EIS has emerged as one of the most difficult questions for the courts under NEPA." Professor William H. Rodgers, Jr., Handbook on Environmental Law sec. 7.9 at 791 (1977). The issue is implicit in the review imposed by WED III [Wisconsin Environmental Decade, Inc. v. Public Service Commission, 79 Wis. 2d 409, 256 N.W.2d 149 (1977), an earlier case construing WEPA]: whether the agency has developed a record "covering the relevant areas of environmental concern" and whether the agency has exercised reasonable judgment based on that record.

WEPA and NEPA are silent as to segmentation. Determining the propriety of segmentation has been left to the courts. "In fact, this vaguely worded statute seems designed to serve as no more than a catalyst for the development of a 'common law' of NEPA. To date, the courts have responded in just that manner and have created such a 'common law.'" Kleppe v. Sierra Club, 427 U.S. 390 (1976), separate opinion of Justice Marshall. As WEPA was patterned after NEPA, and as no Wisconsin cases are in point, we look to federal decisions consistent with *WED III* for assistance.

Segmentation is not an ipso facto violation of the Act. "The rule against segmentation for EIS purposes is not an imperative to be applied in every case," Sierra Club v. Callaway, 499 F.2d 982, 987 (5th Cir. 1974). "Impermissible segmentation, simply put, is the defining of a project too narrowly for purposes of environmental analyses." Rodgers, *supra*, at 787.

Professor Rodgers in reviewing federal decisions states,

> In deciding whether a group of segments should be treated as a single project, courts look at "a multitude of factors, including the manner in which [the segments] were planned, their geographic locations, and the utility of each in the absence of the other." The cases ask whether the excluded segment has "independent significance," whether there is a strong "nexus" between the two requiring concurrent EIS evaluation, whether one part is a "mere component" or "increment" of the other, whether the scope of the project addressed permits the evaluation of alternatives the Act requires. [Rodgers, *supra* sec. 7.9 at 788-89 (footnotes omitted).]

Other factors used include whether "the segment under consideration seems to fulfill important state and local needs," Daly v. Volpe, 514 F.2d 1106, 1110 (9th Cir. 1975); whether it is an extension or a connective link, Hawthorn Environmental Preserv. Association v. Coleman, 417 F. Supp. 1091, 1100 (N.D. Ga. 1976), *aff'd per curiam* 551 F.2d 1055 (5th Cir. 1977); whether the segment serves "primarily local needs," Id.; whether the segment "is a unit unto itself, and can stand on its own two feet, or, on the contrary, whether it is so intertwined" with other units "that it is but an increment of the larger plan," Sierra Club. v. Stamm, 507 F.2d 788, 791 (10th Cir. 1974): and whether "[a]s a practical matter, commitment of resources in one section tends to make further construction more likely." Patterson v. Exxon, 415 F. Supp. 1276, 1282 (D. Neb. 1976).

Consideration of single factors is helpful, but no one factor can be determinative. Individual factors "are not talismans that truncate the natural scope of an EIS." Appalachian Mountain Club v. Brinegar, 394 F. Supp. 105, 117 (D.N.H. 1975). Each controversy must be decided on its own merits. *Hawthorn, supra*. "No general statement of a standard of review can provide a precise guideline of universal applicability. It is obvious that the inquiry needed to support an agency decision not to file an EIS will vary greatly with the circumstances." *WED III.*

We conclude that the DNR's decision to limit the scope of its threshold decision to consideration of the impact of the segment terminating at Hales Corners was reasonable and should not be overturned.

The project ending at Hales Corners has independent utility. Regardless if the remaining segment is constructed, the interceptor will serve the useful and vital purpose of allowing abandonment of the inadequate Hales Corners treatment plant. The DNR worksheet indicates that the plant is currently discharging an effluent substantially in excess of the limitations with which it must comply by July 1, 1982. The village must either upgrade or abandon its existing system in order to meet those limitations. The Hales Corners plant has been designated for abandonment since 1954. . . .

The segment terminating at Hales Corners not only fulfills a local need at Hales Corners but that is its primary purpose. According to the worksheet, eliminating the Hales Corners treatment plant is the "main purpose" of the interceptor at this time.

The logical termini test looks at the ends of a continuous project such as a highway or, in this case, a sewer interceptor. Thus, if a highway project begins and ends in "the middle of the woods," as opposed to connecting cities or highway interchanges, the project lacks logical termini. See e.g., *Patterson*, 415 F. Supp. 1276, 1283. As the trial court found, the interceptor discussed in the worksheet has logical starting and ending points. It begins where District sewer service in Milwaukee County now ends and terminates in Hales Corners, a community which must have new service.

Construction of the segment terminating at Hales Corners of course makes possible a second segment to serve New Berlin. Installation of the first segment does not, however, compel construction of the second. The DNR's approval of a sewer extension is required by sec. 144.04, Stats., and the DNR states in its worksheet that it treats extension proposals on a case-by-case basis. There is no evidence that the cost of the first segment makes its construction uneconomical unless New Berlin is also served. The worksheet notes that the diameter of the first segment allows for possible connection with the New Berlin system. Construction of a sewer sufficient only to satisfy the needs of today would, however, be "little short of folly" in view of the cost of future enlargement or building a parallel system. There is no evidence in the worksheet that New Berlin must connect with the District's system after the first segment is completed. That is a decision which is left to the future, despite installation of the first segment.

Indeed, the DNR specifically concluded in its worksheet that the extension of the sewer to the county line and the eventual elimination of the Regal Manors treatment facility, are reversible decisions at this point. The DNR found, "Since the proposed sewer is only extending to the Hales Corners treatment plant, virtually all decisions are reversible even after the proposed sewer is constructed."

It is conceded that if the second segment is installed so as to serve New Berlin, urban development in the New Berlin area may result. That development, however, is a secondary impact of that segment and not of the segment terminating at Hales Corners. . . .

The Decade argues that cumulative impacts of the two segments will be ignored if the projects are not considered together at this point in time. . . . More specifically, the Decade alludes to the possibility that the Milwaukee sewage treatment plants to which the sewage is to be diverted and which are already under two court orders to clean up operations . . . , may be overloaded by the combined flow from Hales Corners and New Berlin.

The worksheet shows consideration of cumulative impacts. The worksheet discusses possible cumulative impacts of the two segments and the impacts of other extensions in the area, including further land development. The worksheet states that additional extensions could overload the District's South Shore sewage treatment facility but that the District has identified future planned sewer extensions and that modifications to the South Shore facility "will provide the capacity to treat these additional wastes." . . .

The order of the DNR approving the District's application was therefore properly affirmed by the trial court.

Judgment affirmed.

BABLITCH, Judge (dissenting). . . .

The record is replete with indications that the original proposal extending the Hales Corners interceptor an additional 2,000 feet in order to service the relatively undeveloped New Berlin area has never been abandoned by the District and is presently extant. The majority concedes that the extension is "likely," that it "may be reasonably forecast" at this time, and that it is "sufficiently definite" so that its impact on the environment could presently be determined. This being so, it is difficult to understand the majority's conclusion that the decision to complete the project as originally proposed has been "left to the future." The record shows that the decision has been made. It is merely the implementation of that decision, and compliance with WEPA, which has been left to the future.

The purpose of WEPA is to ensure that state agency decisions about actions which have a significant impact on the environment will be subject to public scrutiny and debate "to the fullest extent possible." Sec. 1.11, Stats. That purpose is not served by allowing an agency to isolate the environmentally insignificant portion of an intended project — here, seven-ninths of the whole — and pretend that the environmentally significant balance of the project does not exist. Allowing it to do so in this case has the effect of loading the scales of future debate over the New Berlin hookup with the fait accompli of a Hales Corners system ready, able, and in fact designed to accommodate it. Therefore, although the extension decision is obviously "reversible" until it is actually implemented, the chances that it will be reversed are less once the first seven-ninths of the original project has been completed. This prejudices the full and impartial consideration of alternatives to the last two-ninths of the original proposal and makes the secondary effects of the hookup more likely.

NOTES AND QUESTIONS

1. The segmentation question is closely tied to the statutory requirement that impact statements are only required on "proposals" for actions. See Aberdeen & Rockfish Railroad v. SCRAP, 422 U.S. 289 (1975) (SCRAP II). In the principal case, the Wisconsin court had to consider whether the possible extension of the sewer interceptor to New Berlin was sufficiently definite to constitute a "proposal."

Noting that the U.S. Supreme Court had not defined "proposal," the Wisconsin court held that "[s]omething more than a mere possibility and less than a commitment" was necessary. Since the extension to New Berlin was "sufficiently definite," the court held that it constituted a proposal. If so, why was it necessary to consider the segmentation question? Aren't all proposals necessarily "actions" requiring impact statements?

See also Conservation Society v. Secretary of Transportation, 531 F.2d 637 (2d Cir. 1976) (Conservation Society II). The court initially required an impact statement for the entire length of a 280-mile highway crossing three states, although some of the highway was in the planning stage. On remand after SCRAP II, the court limited the impact statement to a 20-mile segment of the highway in Vermont, holding that it was admittedly a project with "local utility."

2. As in the principal case, determining the "primary" purpose of a segment is often difficult. Assume a proposed and relatively short new segment of an interstate highway intended to provide a bypass around a small community. Can the segment be isolated for review in the impact statement because its primary purpose is to provide traffic relief for the community? Or is its primary purpose to provide a link in the interstate highway system? See Daly v. Volpe, 514 F.2d 1106 (9th Cir. 1975) (adopting the former view). Does this holding allow agencies to adopt any self-serving justification for a project segment? See also Piedmont Heights Civic Club, Inc. v. Moreland, 637 F.2d 430 (5th Cir. 1981) (upholding segmentation of highway projects in metropolitan area because each segment had independent utility).

3. Segmentation problems also arise when a federal agency plans to develop or approves a project that contains several related but different components. In Hudson River Sloop Clearwater, Inc. v. Department of the Navy, 836 F.2d 760 (2d Cir. 1988), for example, the Navy planned to build a new port for its ships together with associated housing. The court held that the Navy could segment the port for purposes of preparing an EIS because the port would be operational even though the Navy decided not to build the housing.

4. The principal case also illustrates the problems that arise when agencies plan to build projects in stages. County of Suffolk v. Secretary of Interior, 562 F.2d 1368 (2d Cir. 1977), is the leading case. The court held that an impact statement on an offshore oil an gas lease sale did not have to discuss the environmental impacts of the onshore transporation routes, including onshore pipelines, that would transport any oil that might be found. Any discussion of these

environmental effects was speculative because the building of the pipelines was at least three years away and transportation routes would not be known until oil was discovered.

The Kleppe case, which is reproduced next, has influenced the law on the segmentation of multi-stage projects. See Note 5, *infra*, p. 843. For discussion of segmentation see NEPA Law & Litigation, supra, §§9:10-9:16.

4. Regional and Program Impact Statements

The discussion of the segmentation problems leads naturally to another technique available under NEPA to consider the cumulative impact of a number of related projects: the program impact statement. The circumstances under which program impact statements may be required under NEPA was considered in the U.S. Supreme Court case that follows.

KLEPPE v. SIERRA CLUB
427 U.S. 390 (1976)

Mr. Justice POWELL delivered the opinion of the Court.

I

Respondents, several organizations concerned with the environment, brought this suit in July 1973 in the United States District Court for the District of Columbia. The defendants in the suit, petitioners here, were the officials of the Department and other federal agencies responsible for issuing coal leases, approving mining plans, granting rights-of-way, and taking the other actions necessary to enable private companies and public utilities to develop coal reserves on land owned or controlled by the Federal Government. Citing widespread interest in the reserves of a region identified as the "Northern Great Plains region," and an alleged threat from coal-related operations to their members' enjoyment of the region's environment, respondents claimed that the federal officials could not allow further development without preparing a "comprehensive environmental impact statement" under §102(2)(C) on the entire region. They sought declaratory and injunctive relief. . . .

[The district court, on the basis of extensive findings of fact and conclusions of law, granted petitioners' motions for summary judgment. On appeal, the Court of Appeals for the District of Columbia reversed and remanded for further proceedings. The Supreme Court then granted certiorari.]

II

The record and the opinions of the courts below contain extensive facts about coal development and the geographic area involved in this suit. The facts that we consider essential, however, can be stated briefly.

The Northern Great Plains region identified in respondents' complaint encompasses portions of four States — northeastern Wyoming, eastern Montana, western North Dakota, and western South Dakota. There is no dispute about its richness in coal, nor about the waxing interest in developning that coal, nor about the crucial role the federal petitioners will play due to the significant percentage of the coal to which they control access. The Department has initiated, in this decade, three studies in areas either inclusive of or included within this region. The North Central Power Study was addressed to the potential for coordinated development of electric power in an area encompassing all or part of 15 States in the North Central United States. It aborted in 1972 for lack of interest on the part of electric utilities. The Montana-Wyoming Aqueducts Study, intended to recommend the best use of water resources for coal development in southeastern Montana and northeastern Wyoming, was suspended in 1972 with the initiation of the third study, the Northern Great Plains Resources Program (NGPRP).

While the record does not reveal the degree of concern with environmental matters in the first two studies, it is clear that the NGPRP was devoted entirely to the environment. It was carried out by an interagency, federal-state task force with public participation, and was designed "to assess the potential social, economic and environmental impacts" from resource development in five States — Montana, Wyoming, South Dakota, North Dakota, and Nebraska. Its primary objective was "to provide an analytical and informational framework for policy and planning decisions at all levels of government" by formulating several "scenarios" showing the probable consequences for the area's environment and culture from the various possible techniques and levels of resource development. The final interim report of the NGPRP was issued August 1, 1975, shortly after the decision of the Court of Appeals in this case.

In addition, since 1973 the Department has engaged in a complete review of its coal-leasing program for the entire Nation. On Februry 17 of that year the Secretary announced the review and announced also that during study a "short-term leasing policy" would prevail, under which new leasing would be restricted to narrowly defined circumstances and even then allowed only when an environmental impact statement had been prepared if required under NEPA. The purpose of the program review was to study the environmental impact of the Department's entire range of coal-related activities and to develop a planning system to guide the national leasing program. The impact statement, known as the "Coal Programmatic EIS," went through several drafts before issuing in final form on September 19, 1975 — shortly before the petitions for certiorari were filed in this case. The Coal Programmatic EIS proposed a new leasing program based on a complex planning system called the Energy Minerals Activity Recommendation System (EMARS), and assessed the prospective environmental impact of the new program as well as the alternatives to it. We have been informed by the parties to this litigation that the Secretary is in the process of implementing the new program.

Against this factual background, we turn now to consider the issues raised by this case in the status in which it reached this Court.

[In part III of its opinion the Court held that "there is no evidence in the record of an action or a proposal for an action of regional scope." It noted that the district court had found that "there was no existing or proposed plan or program on the part of the Federal Government for the regional development" of the Northern Great Plains area.]

IV

A

The Court of Appeals, in reversing the District Court, did not find that there was a regional plan or program for development of the Northern Great Plains region. It accepted all of the District Court's findings of fact, but concluded nevertheless that the petitioners "contemplated" a regional plan or program. The court thought that the North Central Power Study, the Montana-Wyoming Aqueducts Study, and the NGPRP all constituted "attempts to control development" by individual companies on a regional scale. It also concluded that the interim report of the NGPRP, then expected to be released at any time, would provide the petitioners with the information needed to formulate the regional plan they had been "contemplating." The Court therefore remanded with instructions to the petitioners to inform the District Court of their role in the further development of the region within 30 days after the NGPRP interim report issued; if they decided to control that development, an impact statement would be required.

We conclude that the Court of Appeals erred in both its factual assumptions and its interpretation of NEPA. We think the court was mistaken in concluding, on the record before it, that the petitioners were "contemplating" a regional development plan or program. It considered the several studies undertaken by the petitioners to represent attempts to control development on a regional scale. This conclusion was based on a finding by the District Court that those studies, as well as the new national coal-leasing policy, were "attempts to control development by individual companies in a manner consistent with the policies and procedures of the National Environmental Policy Act of 1969." But in context, that finding meant only that the named studies were efforts to gain background environmental information for subsequent application in the decisionmaking with respect to individual coal-related projects. This is the sense in which the District Court spoke of controlling development consistently with NEPA. Indeed, in the same paragraph containing the language relied upon by the Court of Appeals, the District Court expressly found that the studies were not part of a plan or program to develop or encourage development.

Moreover, at the time the Court of Appeals ruled there was no indication in the record that the NGPRP was aimed toward a regional plan or program, and subsequent events have shown that this was not its purpose. The interim report of the study, issued shortly after the Court of Appeals ruled, described the effects of several possible rates of coal development but stated in its preface that the alternatives "are for study and comparison only; they do not represent specific plans or proposals." All parties agreed in this Court that there still exists no proposal for a regional plan or program of development.

Even had the record justified a finding that a regional program was contemplated by the petitioners, the legal conclusion drawn by the Court of Appeals cannot be squared with the Act. The court recognized that the mere "contemplation" of certain action is not sufficient to require an impact statement. But it believed the statute nevertheless empowers a court to require the preparation of an impact statement to begin at some point prior to the formal recommendation or report on a proposal. The Court of Appeals accordingly devised its own four-part "balancing" test for determining when, during the contemplation of a plan or other type of federal action, an agency must begin a statement. The factors to be considered were identified as the likelihood and imminence of the program's coming to fruition, the extent to which information is available on the effects of implementing the expected program and on alternatives thereto, the extent to which irretrievable commitments are being made and options precluded "as refinement of the proposal progresses," and the severity of the environmental effects should the action be implemented.

The Court of Appeals thought that as to two of these factors — the availability of information on the effects of any regional development program, and the severity of those effects — the time already was "ripe" for an impact statement. It deemed the record unclear, however, as to the likelihood of the petitioners' actually producing a plan to control the development, and surmised that irretrievable commitments were being avoided because petitioners had ceased approving most coal-related projects while the NGPRP study was underway. The court also thought that the imminent release of the NGPRP interim report would provide the officials with sufficient information to define their role in development of the region, and it believed that as soon as the NGPRP was completed the petitioners would begin approving individual projects in the region, thus permitting irrevocable commitments of resources. It was for this reason that the court in its remand required the petitioners to report to the District Court their decision on the federal role with respect to the Northern Great Plains as a region within 30 days after issuance of the NGPRP report.

The Court's reasoning and action find no support in the language or legislative history of NEPA. The statute clearly states when an impact statement is required, and mentions nothing about a balancing of factors. Rather, as we noted last Term, under the first sentence of §102(2)(C) the moment at which an agency must have a final statement ready "is the time at which it makes a recommendation or report on a *proposal* for federal action." Aberdeen & Rockfish R. Co. v. SCRAP, 422 U.S. 289, 320 (1975) (*SCRAP II*) (emphasis in original). The procedural duty imposed upon agencies by this section is quite precise, and the role of the courts in enforcing that duty is similarly precise. A court has no authority to depart from the statutory language and, by a balancing of court-devised factors, determine a point during the germination process of a potential proposal at which an impact statement *should be prepared*. Such an assertion of judicial authority would leave the agencies uncertain as to their procedural duties under NEPA, would invite judicial involvement in the day-to-day decisionmaking process of the agencies, and would invite litigation. As the contemplation of a project and the accompanying study thereof do not necessarily result in a proposal for major federal action, it may be assumed that the balancing process devised by the Court of Appeals also would result in the preparation of a good many unnecessary impact statements. . . .

V

Our discussion thus far has been addressed primarily to the decision of the Court of Appeals. It remains, however, to consider the contention now urged by respondents. They have not attempted to support the Court of Appeals' decision. Instead, respondents renew an argument they appear to have made to the Court of Appeals, but which that court did not reach. Respondents insist that, even without a comprehensive federal plan for the development of the Northern Great Plains, a "regional" impact statement nevertheless is required on all coal-related projects in the region because they are intimately related.

There are two ways to view this contention. First, it amounts to an attack on the sufficiency of the impact statements already prepared by the petitioners on the coal-related projects that they have approved or stand ready to approve. As such, we cannot consider it in this proceeding, for the case was not brought as a challenge to a particular impact statement and there is no impact statement in the record. It also is possible to view the respondents' argument as an attack upon the decision of the petitioners not to prepare one comprehensive impact statement on all proposed projects in the region. This contention properly is before us, for the petitioners have made it clear they do not intend to prepare such a statement.

We begin by stating our general agreement with respondents' basic premise that §102(2)(C) may require a comprehensive impact statement in certain situations where several proposed actions are pending at the same time. NEPA announced a national policy of environmental protection and placed a responsibility upon the Federal Government to further specific environmental goals by "all practicable means, consistent with other essential considerations of national policy." §101(b). Section 102(2)(C) is one of the "action-forcing" provisions intended as a directive to "all agencies to assure consideration of the environmental impact of their actions in decisionmaking." Conference Report on NEPA, 115

Cong. Rec. 40416 (1969). By requiring an impact statement Congress intended to assure such consideration during the development of a proposal or — as in this case — during the formulation of a position on a proposal submitted by private parties. A comprehensive impact statement may be necessary in some cases for an agency to meet this duty. Thus, when several proposals for coal-related actions that will have cumulative or synergistic environmental impact upon a region are pending concurrently before an agency, their environmental consequences must be considered together. Only through comprehensive consideration of pending proposals can the agency evaluate different courses of action.[21]

Agreement to this extent with respondents' premise, however, does not require acceptance of their conclusion that all proposed coal-related actions in the Northern Great Plains region are so "related" as to require their analysis in a single comprehensive impact statement. Respondents informed us that the Secretary recently adopted an approach to impact statements on coal-related actions that provides:

> A. As a general proposition, and as determined by the Secretary, when action is proposed involving coal development such as issuing several coal leases or approving mining plans in the same region, such actions will be covered by a single EIS rather than by multiple statements. In such cases, the region covered will be determined by basin boundaries, drainage areas, areas of common reclamation problems, administrative boundaries, areas of economic interdependence, and other relevant factors.

At another point, the document containing the Secretary's approach states that a "regional EIS" will be prepared "if a series of proposed actions with interrelated impacts are involved . . . unless a previous EIS has sufficiently analyzed the impacts of the proposed action[s]." Thus, the Department has decided to prepare comprehensive impact statements of the type contemplated by §102(2)(C), although it has not deemed it appropriate to prepare such a statement on all proposed actions in the region identified by respondents.

Respondents conceded at oral argument that to prevail they must show that petitioners have acted arbitrarily in refusing to prepare one comprehensive statement on this entire region, and we agree. The determination of the region, if any, with respect to which a comprehensive statement is necessary requires the weighing of a number of relevant factors, including the extent of the interrelationship among proposed actions and practical considerations of feasibility. Resolving these issues requires a high level of technical expertise and is properly

---

21. Neither the statute nor its legislative history contemplates that a court should substitute its judgment for that of the agency as to the environmental consequences of its actions. See Scenic Hudson Preservation Conference v. FPC, 453 F.2d 463, 481 (C.A. 2 1971), *cert. denied*, 407 U.S. 926 (1972). The only role for a court is to insure that the agency has taken a "hard look" at environmental consequences; it cannot "interject itself within the area of discretion of the executive as to the choice of the action to be taken." Natural Resources Defense Council v. Morton, 458 F.2d 827, 838 (1972).

left to the informed discretion of the responsible federal agencies. Cf. *SCRAP II*, 422 U.S., at 325-326. Absent a showing of arbitrary action, we must assume that the agencies have exercised this discretion appropriately. Respondents have made no showing to the contrary.

Respondents' basic argument is that one comprehensive statement on the Northern Great Plains is required because all coal-related activity in that region is "programmatically," "geographically," and "environmentally" related. Both the alleged "programmatic" relationship and the alleged "geographic" relationship resolve, ultimately, into an argument that the region is proper for a comprehensive impact statement because the petitioners themselves have approached environmental study in this area on a regional basis. Respondents point primarily to the NGPRP, which they claim — and petitioners deny — focused on the region described in the complaint. The precise region of the NGPRP is unimportant, for its irrelevance to the delineation of an appropriate area for analysis in a comprehensive impact statement has been well stated by the Secretary:

> Resource studies [like the NGPRP] are one of many analytical tools employed by the Department to inform itself as to general resource availability, resource need and general environmental considerations so that it can intelligently determine the scope of environmental analysis and review specific actions it may take. Simply put, resource studies are a prelude to informed agency planning, and provide the data base on which the Department may decide to take specific actions for which impact statements are prepared. The scope of environmental impact statements seldom coincide[s] with that of a given resource study, since the statements evolve from specific proposals for federal action while the studies simply provide an educational backdrop.

As for the alleged "environmental" relationship, respondents contend that the coal-related projects "will produce a wide variety of cumulative environmental impacts" throughout the Northern Great Plains region. They described them as follows: Diminished availability of water, air and water pollution, increases in population and industrial densities, and perhaps even climatic changes. Cumulative environmental impacts are, indeed, what require a comprehensive impact statement. But determination of the extent and effect of these factors, and particularly identification of the geographic area within which they may occur, is a task assigned to the special competency of the appropriate agencies. Petitioners dispute respondents' contentions that the interrelationship of environmental impacts is regionwide and, as respondents' own submissions indicate, petitioners appear to have determined that the appropriate scope of comprehensive statements should be based on basins, drainage areas, and other factors. We cannot say that petitioners' choices are arbitrary. Even if environmental interrelationships could be shown conclusively to extend across basins and drainage areas, practical considerations of feasibility might well necessitate restricting the scope of comprehensive statements.

In sum, respondents' contentions to the relationships between all proposed coal-related projects in the Northern Great Plains region does not require that petitioners prepare one comprehensive impact statement covering all before proceeding to approve specific pending applications. As we already have determined that there exists no proposal for regionwide action that could require a regional impact statement, the judgment of the Court of Appeals must be reversed, and the judgment of the District Court reinstated and affirmed. The case is remanded for proceedings consistent with this opinion.

So ordered.

[Justice MARSHALL wrote an opinion concurring in part and dissenting in part, in which he was joined by Justice BRENNAN.]

NOTES AND QUESTIONS

1. In an earlier landmark NEPA case, Scientists' Institute for Public Information, Inc. v. AEC (*SIPI*), 481 F.2d 1079 (D.C. Cir. 1973), the District of Columbia Court of Appeals applied the fourfold balancing test rejected by the Supreme Court to require a programmatic impact statement on the technology development program for the liquid fast metal nuclear breeder reactor. Although the development program was still in the research stage and no breeder reactors had been constructed, the court believed that the program constituted a "federal action." Judge Skelly Wright noted that the "[d]evelopment of the technology is a necessary precondition of construction of any plants" and then added:

> To wait until a technology attains the stage of complete commercial feasibility before considering the possible adverse environmental effects attendant upon ultimate application of the technology will undoubtedly frustrate meaningful consideration and balancing of environmental costs against economic and other benefits. Modern technological advances typically stem from massive investments in research and development, as is the case here. Technological advances are therefore capital investments and, as such, once brought to a stage of commercial feasibility the investment in their development acts to compel their application. [481 F.2d at 1089.]

The court then applied the fourfold balancing test to answer the timing question — "[w]hether a statement on the overall . . . [research] program should be issued now or at some uncertain date in the future" (481 F.2d at 1093). The court noted that the answer to the timing question required a finely tuned balancing:

> In our view, the timing question can best be answered by reference to the underlying policies of NEPA in favor of meaningful, timely information on the effects of agency action. In the early stages of research, when little is known about the technology and when future application of the technology is both doubtful and remote, it may well be impossible to draft a meaningful impact statement. Predictions as to the possible effects of application of the technology would tend toward uninformative generalities, arrived at by guesswork rather than analysis. NEPA requires predictions, but not prophecy, and impact statements ought not to be modeled upon the works of Jules Verne or H. G. Wells. At the other end of the spectrum, by the time commercial feasibility of the technology is conclusively

demonstrated, and the effects of application of the technology certain, the purposes of NEPA will already have been thwarted. Substantial investments will have been made in development of the technology and options will have been precluded without considered of environmental factors. Any statement prepared at such a late date will no doubt be thorough, detailed and accurate, but it will be of little help in ensuring that decisions reflect environmental concerns. Thus we are pulled in two directions. Statements must be written late enough in the development process to contain meaningful information, but they must be written early enough so that whatever information is contained can practically serve as an input into the decision making process. [481 F.2d at 1093-1094.]

The separate consideration of the federal action and the timing questions in *SIPI* seems in doubt after the more mechanical approach of *Kleppe*. The concurrent projects test adopted in *Kleppe* is of little help in evaluating the need for a program impact statement on technology development programs like the breeder reactor program. And, since *Kleppe* did not consider a multi-segmented single project of the kind considered in the segmentation cases, the impact of *Kleppe* on segmentation doctrine also is unclear. For an extended discussion of *Kleppe*, see Johnston, Kleppe v. Sierra Club: An Environmental Planning Catch-22? 1 Harv. Envtl. L. Rev. 182 (1976).

2. CEQ published what amounted to an official casenote on the *Kleppe* opinion in the Federal Register (42 Fed. Reg. 61,066, 61,069). CEQ stated that "the most useful principles for defining the scope of comprehensive environmental statements" were precedent-setting effect, interdependence, cumulation of impact, and availability of information (42 Fed. Reg. at 61,071). Does this advice properly reflect the holding in *Kleppe*?

Present CEQ regulations covering impact statements on "broad actions" state that these actions are to be evaluated generically and geographically. 40 C.F.R. §1502.4(c). They add that statements on technological development programs are to be prepared "before the program has reached a stage of investment or commitment to implementation likely to determine subsequent development or restrict later alternatives" (40 C.F.R. §1502.4(c)(3)). This regulation reflects *SIPI*. Does it meet the *Kleppe* tests?

3. Ambiguities latent in the *Kleppe* decision make it difficult to predict its impact on the administration of NEPA. The Supreme Court's decision not to require an impact statement at the program planning stage, and the deference it paid to agency exercise of discretion, suggest that agencies may be able to avoid impact statement preparation until they are sufficiently comfortable with their plans to be able to formalize them in proposal form. See Texas Commission on Natural Resources v. Bergland, 573 F.2d 201 (5th Cir. 1978) (upholding agency decision not to file program impact statement on timber management program).

Kleppe may well limit the application of the impact statement requirement to incremental project decisions rather than to overall agency planning programs. As one commentator has noted, "the less overall articulation of planning an agency undertakes (in the form of concrete proposals) the less actual environmental planninng (in the form of impact statements) it can be compelled to perform." Johnston, Kleppe v. Sierra Club: An Environmental Planning Catch-

22? 1 Harv. Envtl. L. Rev. 182, 200 (1976). Recall the holding in Atlanta Coalition v. Atlanta Regional Commission, 599 F.2d 1333 (5th Cir. 1979), *supra*,
that no impact statement was required on the Atlanta regional transporation
plan. That case relied heavily on *Kleppe*.

Compare Natural Resources Defense Council, Inc. v. Hodel, 435 F.
Supp. 590 (D. Or. 1977), *aff'd on other grounds sub nom.* Natural Resources
Defense Council, Inc. v. Munro, 626 F.2d 134 (9th Cir. 1980). The federal
Bonneville Power Administration and a number of private and public utilities
entered into a cooperative program for the allocation of electric power throughout the Pacific Northwest. The court held that an impact statement was required
on an extension of this program, which included plans for the construction of
additional thermal power plants, as well as a number of agreements on purchasing and power allocation strategies. The court distinguished *Kleppe* and stated:

> [T]he Pacific Northwest is regarded as a distinct region for purposes of electrical
> power planning. . . . [The program contains] specific plans for regional develop-
> ment, hammered out after long negotiations and embodied in published docu-
> ments. Individual projects undertaken by the federal government, by public and
> private utilities, and by industry are interrelated according to an integrated plan.
> [435 F. Supp. at 600.]

See also Port of Astoria v. Hodel, 595 F.2d 417 (9th Cir. 1979). The existence
of the formally agreed-upon program distinguishes Natural Resources Defense
Council, Inc. v. Hodel from *Kleppe*. Compare *Atlanta Coalition*, in which the
court noted that the plan did not commit the federal agency to a specific project.
Is Natural Resources Defense Council, Inc. v. Hodel distinguishable because a
federal agency participated in the plan? More generally, should the courts rely
on these formal distinctions in deciding whether to require the preparation of a
programmatic impact statement? See Note, The Scope of the Program EIS Requirement: The Need for a Coherent Judicial Approach, 30 Stan. L. Rev. 767
(1978). See also Environmental Defense Fund, Inc. v. Andrus, 596 F.2d 848
(9th Cir. 1979) (programmatic impact statement required for an Interior Department industrial water marketing plan from a federally controlled reservoir).

4. Does the preparation of a programmatic impact statement eliminate the
need to prepare an impact statement on a specific action included within the
program when the programmatic impact statement is not sufficiently detailed to
cover all aspects of the site-specific action? Compare Ventling v. Bergland, 479
F. Supp. 174 (D.S.D. 1979) (no site-specific impact statement required), with
Natural Resources Defense Council, Inc. v. Adminstrator, EPA, 451 F. Supp.
1245 (D.D.C. 1978) (contra). CEQ calls this process "tiering" and recommends
that the site-specific impact statement refer back to applicable discussion contained in the program impact statement. See Comment, The Tiering of Impact
Statements — Can the Process Be Stopped Halfway? 20 Urb. L. Ann. 197
(1980).

If the issue in question is controversial enough, Congress may intervene
directly in the scope issue. A Department of the Interior appropriations act pro-

vides that any irrigation project in the Colorado River water system that is a multi-phase project "shall proceed if a final environmental impact statement has been filed on such feature." When the Secretary of the Interior went ahead with a basinwide impact statement, a suit by the state of Utah and the Central Utah Water Conservancy District arguing that a basinwide impact statement was ultra vires was dismissed for lack of ripeness. Utah v. Andrus, 636 F.2d 276 (10th Cir. 1980).

5. The interrelationship between the segmentation problem and the *Kleppe* holding on the need to consider related projects is illustrated by Thomas v. Peterson, 753 F.2d 754 (9th Cir. 1985). The Forest Service prepared an environmental assessment on a road in a national forest and determined no impact statement was necessary because the road would not cause significant environmental impacts. Subsequently, the Service issued environmental assessments for proposed timber sales that would use the new road and concluded these sales also would not have significant environmental impact.

The *Peterson* court quoted the *Kleppe* holding that there are situations in which an agency is required to consider several related actions in a single impact statement. The *Peterson* court found that the road and the timber sales were dependent and required a single impact statement. "[I]t would be irrational to build the road and then not sell the timber to which the road was built to provide access." Id. at 759.

On the timing question, the Service argued that the timber sales were too uncertain and too far in the future to be analyzed along with the road. The court disagreed. "[I]f the sales are sufficiently certain to justify construction of the road, then they are sufficiently certain for their environmental impacts to be analyzed along with those of the road." Id. at 760.

In support of its holding, the court relied on CEQ regulations adopted in 1978 after *Kleppe*. These regulations define connected actions, 40 C.F.R. §1508.25(a)(1), and cumulative actions, id., §1508.25(a)(2). The court held that the record in the case showed the road and timber sales would have "cumulatively significant impacts." Has the *Peterson* court expanded on *Kleppe*? For one analysis that says yes, see Hapke, Thomas v. Peterson: The Ninth Circuit Breathes New Life into CEQ's Cumulative and Connected Actions Regulations, 15 Envtl. L. Rep. 10289, 10294 (1985) (court "crafted an approach that highlighted cumulative impacts as the controlling factor in determining EIS scope and timing.")

The Tenth Circuit has endorsed "[t]he tiered approach" for federal oil and gas leases because it "is calculated to provide the most informed decision making possible. . . ." Park County Resources Council, Inc. v. United States Department of Agriculture, 817 F.2d 609 (10th Cir. 1987), held that the issuance of a federal oil and gas lease is not a "major federal action significantly affecting the quality of the human environment."

See also Foundation on Economic Trends v. Heckler, 756 F.2d 143 (D.C. Cir. 1985), which also applies CEQ's connected and cumulative action regulations. The opinion, written by Judge J. Skelly Wright, held that the National Institutes of Health "should at least consider" whether it should prepare a programmatic impact statement on individual DNA experiments, but that the Institutes did not have to prepare one now. Instead, they must give serious consideration to the environmental consequences of individual experiments. Judge Wright warned that "if NIH does not at least consider the advisability of a programmatic EIS, its approval of individual deliberate release experiments is likely to violate established principles of reasoned decisionmaking." Id. at 160. See Note, Foundation on Economic Trends v. Heckler: Genetic Engineering and NEPA's EIS Requirement, 2 Pace Envtl. L. Rev. 138 (1984). In Foundation on Economic Trends v. Lyng, 817 F.2d 882 (D.C. Cir. 1987), the court held that a program impact statement was not required on animal productivity research conducted by the Department of Agriculture. The court held that the research projects were too diversified and discrete to constitute systematic or sufficiently connected actions under CEQ regulations.

A NOTE ON THE LEAD AGENCY PROBLEM

In many cases in which NEPA applies, a single action or project may require approval from more than one agency. In other situations, a number of similar and related actions may be carried out in the same area. In these situations, NEPA does not indicate which agency should prepare the impact statement, but there are three possible solutions. Each agency could prepare an impact statement on matters falling within its jurisdiction, a joint impact statement could be prepared, or a single lead agency could prepare an impact statement covering the entire action.

CEQ regulations have adopted the lead agency approach and provide a number of factors to consider that are relevant to the lead agency designation. 40 C.F.R. §1505.5. The courts have also considered this problem. In National Wildlife Federation v. Benn, 491 F. Supp. 1234 (S.D.N.Y. 1980), the court considered the problem of ocean dumping in an area off the New York and New Jersey coasts. Regulation of dumping under the applicable statute was conferred on both the Corps of Engineers and EPA. The Corps could not issue a dumping permit not complying with criteria adopted by EPA. The court rejected a contention by the Corps that site-specific impact statements would satisfy NEPA. It required the Corps as the lead agency to prepare an impact statement covering the cumulative impact of dumping in the area, noting that impact statement preparation should be borne by the "agency that consistently oversees the projects conducted in the area." The court reached this conclusion even though EPA was responsible for evaluating the overall impact of dumping in the ocean area. The Corps could prepare the impact statement either in conjunction with or with partial reliance on EPA reports.

The lead agency concept clearly has problems. One agency may proceed with its action before the lead agency prepares the impact statement, thus frustrating the impact statement preparation process. See Upper Pecos Association v. Stans. 452 F.2d 1233 (10th Cir. 1971), vacated, 409 U.S. 1021 (1972). Agencies also have different interests, and the lead agency may leave out a concern of interest to other agencies with jurisdiction over the project. Problems can also arise if the project approval process requires decisions by some agencies before other agencies can act. Designating the agency that must act first as the lead agency may not be appropriate. Multiple jurisdiction problems might best be solved by a revision of legislative authority for agency regulation and jurisdiction. Compare Cal. Pub. Resources Code §§21067 and 21165, providing for the preparation of impact statements by a lead agency. The lead agency is defined as "the public agency which has the principal responsibility for carrying out or approving a project."

D.   ADEQUACY

1.   The Substantive versus the Procedural Problem

Once an agency has decided to prepare an environmental impact statement, it must meet the requirements for impact statements imposed by §102(2)(C). Ultimately, the courts must consider whether the impact statement is adequate, and the question they must resolve is this: Assuming that decisionmakers will seriously read and react to the information in the impact statement, is the statement likely to further the basic goal of NEPA, which is the promotion of more environmentally enlightened decisions? This question is troublesome for federal courts. At a minimum, as the decisions indicate, the impact statement is a full disclosure document, much like a Securities and Exchange Commission prospectus, and it must fully disclose the environmental impacts of the proposed action. But, because the federal courts also take a "hard look" at agency decisions that have environmental consequences, more then mere disclosure may be required.

To understand the cases on the adequacy of an impact statement and the scope of judicial review, a basic distinction must be kept in mind, and that is the distinction between a challenge to the adequacy of an impact statement and a challenge to the merits of the decision. A NEPA plaintiff's first two challenges are to allege that an impact statement should have been prepared, if one has not been, and that if one was prepared, it is inadequate. The remedies for successful plaintiffs in these cases are the preparation of an initial, new, or supplemental impact statement. A challenge to the merits of the decision is based upon an unsatisfactory impact statement, but the impact statement is only one — although a very important — piece of evidence the decisionmaker must consider in making a final decision. The link between an unsatisfactory impact statement and the assertion that the final decision is arbitrary is the argument that given the unsatisfactory impact statement an informed decisionmaker could reach no other conclusion but that the proposed action should be rejected or modified.

Recent Supreme Court decisions indicate that this is a hard, if not impossible, argument to win; but the possibility of making the argument has never been conclusively foreclosed, so the only barrier to trying the argument is the cost of the appeal.

Courts and commentators usually refer to the duty to prepare an adequate impact statement as NEPA's "procedural" duty. They refer to the agency's responsibility to reject or modify a proposal for action because of an unsatisfactory impact statement as NEPA's "substantive" duty. The term "procedural duty" does not refer to the duty to observe hearing or other procedures in the preparation of an impact statement; it refers instead to the duty to comply sufficiently with the procedures mandated by NEPA for the preparation of an impact statement, so that the statement will contain a reasoned analysis on which the decisionmaker can base his decision. Courts ask whether an impact statement is "adequate" when they consider NEPA's procedural duty. The adequacy inquiry includes the following questions: Have all environmental impacts and alternatives been considered? If all alternatives and impacts have been considered, have they been adequately discussed and evaluated? What rules should the agency apply in discussing and evaluating alternatives and impacts?

Whether NEPA should be given a substantive effect turns, in the words of *Overton Park*, on whether the statute has enacted "law to apply." Early court decisions concluded that NEPA had done just that. The leading case was Environmental Defense Fund, Inc. v. Corps of Engineers, 470 F. 2d 289 (8th Cir. 1972), reviewing an impact statement prepared for Gillham Dam, a dam authorized to be constructed for flood control purposes in Arkansas. While upholding the decision by the Corps to proceed with the project, the court also held that NEPA imposed substantive duties:

> The language of NEPA, as well as its legislative history, make it clear that the Act is more than an environmental full-disclosure law. NEPA was intended to effect substantive changes in decisionmaking. . . . To this end, §101 sets out specific environmental goals to serve as a set of policies to guide agency action affecting the environment. . . .
>
> Given an agency obligation to carry out the substantive requirements of the Act, we believe that courts have an obligation to review substantive agency decisions on the merits. Whether we look to common law or the Adminstrative Procedure Act, absent "legislative guidance as to reviewability, an administrative determination affecting legal rights is reviewable unless some special reason appears for not reviewing." [470 F. 2d at 297-298.]

Accord Environmental Defense Fund, Inc. v. Corps of Engineers, 492 F. 2d 1123, 1138-1140 (5th Cir. 1974) (Tennessee-Tombigbee Waterway). For arguments that NEPA did create substantive duties that courts should recognize, see Wharton, Judicially Enforceable Substantive Rights under NEPA, 10 U.S.F.L. Rev. 415 (1976), and Robie, Recognition of Substantive Rights under NEPA, 7 Nat. Resources Law. 387 (1974). For a thoughtful analysis of judicial review problems by a late judge of the District of Columbia Court of Appeals who did much to bring about the "new" administrative law, see Leventhal, Environmental Decisionmaking and the Role of the Courts, 122 U. Pa. L. Rev. 509 (1974).

As the critical observer must have realized by now, "the procedural and substantive theories are interrelated, for a procedural requirement of a reasoned analysis, especially as applied to broad policies and programs, must ultimately lead to holdings that some justifications for an activity are acceptable while others are not. This is especially true if the standard of procedural adequacy is coupled with a detailed and probing analysis of the factual basis of the impact statement." C. Meyers & A. D. Tarlock, Water Resource Management 586 (2d ed. 1980).

At this point, reread the *Vermont Yankee* and *Kleppe* opinions, reproduced at pp. 815 and 833 *supra*, especially footnote 21 of the *Kleppe* opinion. What clue do these opinions give to the Supreme Court's view of the judicial role in reviewing impact statements? Additional insight on the Supreme Court's position on substantive judicial review is provided by the *Strycker's Bay* case, which is reproduced next. Some preliminary commentary on this case is in order.

Note that the courts in *Strycker's Bay* did not review the adequacy of an impact statement, having held that no such statement was required. At issue was the agency's compliance with a related section of NEPA, §102(2)(E), which to some extent duplicates the impact statement provision by requiring agencies to consider alternatives to their proposals. Note also the disagreement in the opinions over whether the lower courts had held the agency's decision to be arbitrary and capricious, a ground for reversal under the Administrative Procedure Act. Note as well that the agency was faced with a choice between two alternatives, one of which was claimed to be environmentally superior to the other.

STRYCKER'S BAY NEIGHBORHOOD COUNCIL, INC. v. KARLEN
444 U.S. 223 (1980)

PER CURIAM.

The protracted nature of this litigation is perhaps best illustrated by the identity of the original federal defendant, "George Romney, Secretary of the Department of Housing and Urban Development." At the center of this dispute is the site of a proposed low-income housing project to be constructed on Manhattan's Upper West Side. In 1962, the New York City Planning Commission (Commission), acting in conjunction with the United States Department of Housing and Urban Development (HUD), began formulating a plan for the renewal of 20 square blocks known as the "West Side Urban Renewal Area" (WSURA) through a joint effort on the part of private parties and various government agencies. As originally written, the plan called for a mix of 70% middle-income housing and 30% low-income housing and designated the site at issue here as the location of one of the middle-income projects. In 1969, after substantial progress toward completion of the plan, local agencies in New York determined that the number of low-income units proposed for WSURA would be insufficient to satisfy an increased need for such units. In response to this shortage the Commission amended the plan to designate the site as the future location of a high-rise building containing 160 units of low-income housing. HUD approved this amendment in December 1972.

Meanwhile, in October 1971, the Trinity Episcopal School Corp. (Trinity), which had participated in the plan by building a combination school and middle-income housing development at a nearby location, sued in the United States District Court for the Southern District of New York to enjoin the Commission and HUD from constructing low-income housing on the site. The present respondents, Roland N. Karlen, Alvin C. Hudgins, and the Committee of Neighbors To Insure a Normal Urban Environment (CONTINUE), intervened as plaintiffs, while petitioner Strycker's Bay Neighborhood Council, Inc., intervened as a defendant.

The District Court entered judgment in favor of petitioners. See Trinity Episcopal School Corp. v. Romney, 387 F. Supp. 1044 (1974). It concluded, inter alia, that petitioners had not violated the National Environmental Policy Act of 1969 (NEPA).

On respondents' appeal, the Second Circuit affirmed all but the District Court's treatment of the NEPA claim. See Trinity Episcopal School Corp. v. Romney, 523 F.2d 88 (1975). While the Court of Appeals agreed with the District Court that HUD was not required to prepare a full-scale environmental impact statement under §102(2)(C) of NEPA, it held that HUD had not complied with §102(2)(E), which requires an agency to "study, develop, and describe appropriate alternatives to recommended courses of action in any proposal which involves unresolved conflicts concerning alternative uses of available resources." See 523 F.2d., at 92-95. According to the Court of Appeals, any consideration by HUD of alternatives to placing low-income housing on the site "was either highly limited or nonexistent." Citing the "background of urban environmental factors" behind HUD's decision, the Court of Appeals remanded the case, requiring HUD to prepare a "statement of possible alternatives, the consequences thereof and the facts and reasons for and against. . . ." The statement was not to reflect "HUD's concept or the Housing Authority's views as to how these agencies would choose to resolve the city's low incomce group housing situation," but rather was to explain "how within the framework of the Plan its objective of economic integration can best be achieved with a minimum of adverse environmental impact." The Court of Appeals believed that, given such an assessment of alternatives, "the agencies with the cooperation of the interested parties should be able to arrive at an equitable solution."

On remand, HUD prepared a lengthy report entitled Special Environmental Clearance (1977). After marshaling the data, the report asserted that, "while the choice of Site 30 for development as a 100 percent low-income project has raised valid questions about the potential social environmental impacts involved, the problems associated with the impact on social fabric and community structures are not considered so serious as to require that this component be rated as unacceptable." The last portion of the report incorporated a study wherein the Commission evaluated nine alternative locations for the project and found none of them acceptable. While HUD's report conceded that this study may not have considered all possible alternatives, it credited the Commission's conclusion that any relocation of the units would entail an unacceptable delay of two years or more. According to HUD, "[m]easured against the environmental costs associated with the minimum two-year delay, the benefits seem insufficient to justify a mandated substitution of sites."

After soliciting the parties' comments on HUD's report, the District Court again entered judgment in favor of petitioners. See Trinity Episcopal School Corp. v. Harris, 445 F. Supp. 204 (1978). The court was "impressed with [HUD's analysis] as being thorough and exhaustive," and found that "HUD's consideration of the alternatives was neither arbitrary nor capricious"; on the contrary, "[i]t was done in good faith and in full accordance with the law."

On appeal, the Second Circuit vacated and remanded again. Karlen v. Harris, 590 F.2d 39 (1978). The appellate court focused upon that part of HUD's report where the agency considered and rejected alternative sites, and in particular upon HUD's reliance on the delay such a relocation would entail. The Court of Appeals purported to recognize that its role in reviewing HUD's decision was defined by the Administrative Procedure Act (APA), 5 U.S.C. §706(2)(A), which provides that agency actions should be set aside if found to be "arbitrary, capricious, an abuse of discretion, or otherwise not in accordance with law. . . ." Additionally, however, the Court of Appeals looked to "[t]he provisions of NEPA" for "the substantive standards necessary to review the merits of agency decisions. . . ." The Court of Appeals conceded that HUD had "given 'consideration' to alternatives" to redesignating the site. Nevertheless, the court believed that "'consideration' is not an end in itself." Concentrating on HUD's finding that development of an alternative location would entail an unacceptable delay, the appellate court held that such delay could not be "an overriding factor" in HUD's decision to proceed with the development. According to the court, when HUD considers such projects, "environmental factors, such as crowding low-income housing into a concentrated area, should be given determinative weight." The Court of Appeals therefore remanded the case to the District Court, instructing HUD to attack the shortage of low-income housing in a manner that would avoid the "concentration" of such housing on Site 30.

In Vermont Yankee Nuclear Power Corp. v. NRDC, 435 U.S. 519, 558 (1978), we stated that NEPA, while establishing "significant substantive goals for the Nation," imposes upon agencies duties that are "essentially procedural." As we stressed in that case, NEPA was designed "to insure a fully informed and well-considered decision," but not necessarily "a decision the judges of the Court of Appeals or of this Court would have reached had they been members of the decisionmaking unit of the agency." Vermont Yankee cuts sharply against the Court of Appeals' conclusion that an agency, in selecting a course of action, must elevate environmental concerns over other appropriate considerations. On the contrary, once an agency has made a decision subject to NEPA's procedural requirements, the only role for a court is to insure that the agency has considered the environmental consequences; it cannot "'interject itself within the area of discretion of the executive as to the choice of the action to be taken.'" Kleppe v. Sierra Club, 427 U.S. 390, 410, n.21 (1976). See also FPC v. Transcontinental Gas Pipe Line Corp., 423 U.S. 326 (1976).[2]

In the present case there is no doubt that HUD considered the environmental consequences of its decision to redesignate the proposed site for low-income housing. NEPA requires no more. The petitions for certiorari are granted, and the judgment of the Court of Appeals is therefore

Reversed.

JUSTICE MARSHALL, dissenting.

The issue raised by these cases is far more difficult than the per curiam opinion suggests. The Court of Appeals held that the Secretary of Housing and Urban Development (HUD) had acted arbitrarily in concluding that prevention of a delay in the construction process justified the selection of a housing site which could produce adverse social environmental effects, including racial and economic concentration. Today the majority responds that "once an agency has made a decision subject to NEPA's procedural requirements, the only role for a court is to insure that the agency has considered the environmental consequences," and that in this case "there is no doubt that HUD considered the environmental consequences of its decision to redesignate the proposed site for low-income housing. NEPA requires no more." The majority finds support for this conclusion in the closing paragraph of our decision in Vermont Yankee Nuclear Power Corp. v. NRDC, 435 U.S. 519, 558 (1978).

Vermont Yankee does not stand for the broad proposition that the majority advances today. The relevant passage in that opinion was meant to be only a "further observation of some relevance to this case." That "observation" was a response to this Court's perception that the Court of Appeals in that case was attempting "under the guise of judicial review of agency action" to assert its own policy judgment as to the desirability of developing nuclear energy as an energy source for this Nation, a judgment which is properly left to Congress. The Court of Appeals had remanded the case to the agency because of "a single alleged oversight on a peripheral issue, urged by parties who never fully cooperated or indeed raised the issue below." It was in this context that the Court remarked that "NEPA does set forth signficant substantive goals for the Nation, but its mandate to the agencies is *essentially* procedural" (emphasis supplied). Accord-

2. If we could agree with the dissent that the Court of Appeals held that HUD had acted "arbitrarily" in redesignating the site for low-income housing, we might also agree that plenary review is warranted. But the District Court expressly concluded that HUD had not acted arbitrarily or capriciously and our reading of the opinion of the Court of Appeals satisfies us that it did not overturn that finding. Instead, the appellate court required HUD to elevate environmental concerns over other, admittedly legitimate, considerations. Neither NEPA nor the APA provides any support for such a reordering of priorities by a reviewing court.

ingly "[a]dministrative decisions should be set aside in this context, *as in every other*, only for substantial procedural *or substantive* reasons as mandated by statute" (emphasis supplied). This *Vermont Yankee* does not stand for the proposition that a court reviewing agency action under NEPA is limited solely to the factual issue of whether the agency "considered" environmental consequences. The agency's decision must still be set aside if it is "arbitrary, capricious, an abuse of discretion, or otherwise not in accordance with law," 5 U.S.C. §706(2)(A), and the reviewing court must still insure that the agency "has taken a 'hard look' at environmental consequences," Kleppe v. Sierra Club, 427 U.S. 390, 410, n.21 (1976).

In the present case, the Court of Appeals did not "substitute its judgment for that of the agency as to the environmental consequences of its actions," for HUD in its Special Environmental Clearance Report acknowledged the adverse environmental consequences of its proposed action: "the choice of Site 30 for development as a 100 percent low-income project has raised valid questions about the potential social environmental impacts involved." These valid questions arise from the fact that 68% of all public housing units would be sited on only one crosstown axis in this area of New York City. As the Court of Appeals observed, the resulting high concentration of low-income housing would hardly further racial and economic integration. The environmental "impact . . . on social fabric and community structures" was given a B rating in the report, indicating that from this perspective the project is "questionable" and ameliorative measures are "mandated." The report lists 10 ameliorative measures necessary to make the project acceptable. The report also discusses two alternatives, Sites 9 and 41, both of which are the appropriate size for the project and require "only minimal" amounts of relocation and clearance. Concerning Site 9 the report explicitly concludes that "[f]rom the standpoint of social environmental impact, this location would be superior to Site 30 for the development of low-rent public housing." The sole reason for rejecting the environmentally superior site was the fact that if the location were shifted to Site 9, there would be a projected delay of two years in the construction of the housing.

The issue before the Court of Appeals, therefore, was whether HUD was free under NEPA to reject an alternative acknowledged to be environmentally preferable solely on the ground that any change in sites would cause delay. This was hardly a "peripheral issue" in the case. Whether NEPA, which sets forth "significant substantive goals," Vermont Yankee Nuclear Power Corp. v. NRDC, permits a projected 2-year time difference to be controlling over environmental superiority is by no means clear. Resolution of the issue, however, is certainly within the normal scope of review of agency action to determine if it is arbitrary, capricious, or an abuse of discretion.[1] The question whether HUD can make delay the paramount concern over environmental superiority is essentially a restatement of the question whether HUD in considering the environmental con-

---

[1]   The secretary concedes that if an agency gave little or no weight to environmental values its decision might be arbitrary or capricious.

sequences of its proposed action gave those consequences a "hard look," which is exactly the proper question for the reviewing court to ask. Kleppe v. Sierra Club, *supra*, at 410, n.21.

The issue of whether the Secretary's decision was arbitrary or capricious is sufficiently difficult and important to merit plenary consideration in this Court. Further, I do not subscribe to the Court's apparent suggestion that *Vermont Yankee* limits the reviewing court to the essentially mindless task of determining whether an agency "considered" environmental factors even if that agency may have effectively decided to ignore those factors in reaching its conclusion. Indeed, I cannot believe that the Court would adhere to that position in a different factual setting. Our cases establish that the arbitrary or capricious standard prescribes a "searching and careful" judicial inquiry designed to ensure that the agency has not exercised its discretion in an unreasonable manner. Citizens to Preserve Overton Park, Inc. v. Volpe, 401 U.S. 402, 416 (1971). Believing that today's summary reversal represents a departure from that principle, I respectfully dissent.

It is apparent to me that this is not the type of case for a summary disposition. We should at least have a plenary hearing.

NOTES AND QUESTIONS

1. The court of appeals decision reversed in *Strycker's Bay* was one of the few times a lower federal court had set aside an agency determination under NEPA on substantive grounds, even though most lower federal courts held they had this power. The question is what the Supreme Court's reversal means for substantive judicial review under NEPA — specifically, whether a court, after *Strycker's Bay*, may find an agency decision arbitrary and capricious on the merits because the agency relied on a totally unsatisfactory impact statement. One view holds that the Court did not leave this option open:

> If the Second Circuit erred by requiring HUD to elevate environmental concerns above others, then the Supreme Court should have remanded the case for substantive review under the proper legal standard, that is, for a determination whether HUD's action was arbitrary and capricious, giving environmental concerns no more, but no less, weight than they deserve. . . . [T]he Court's summary reversal implies not that the Second Circuit erred by conducting an improper substantive review, but by conducting any review at all. [Goldsmith & Banks, Environmental Values: Institutional Responsibility and the Supreme Court, 7 Harv. Envtl. L. Rev. 1, 11 (1983.]

These authors claim that the lower federal courts since *Strycker's Bay* "are enforcing NEPA with diminished rigor" (7 Harv. Envtl. L. Rev. at 5).

In Robertson v. Methow Valley Citizens Council, reproduced *infra*, the Supreme Court, citing *Strycker's*, stated that although NEPA procedures are "almost certain" to affect substantive decisions, "it is now well settled that NEPA itself does not mandate particular results, but simply prescribes the necessary process."

2. NEPA can still have a deep procedural bite. In Sierra Club v. Corps of Engineers (II), 701 F.2d 1011 (2d Cir. 1983), the court disapproved an EIS prepared for a New York City project that included rebuilding the Westway highway and commercial and industrial development that required landfilling 242 acres of Hudson River. The court held that the EIS failed to reveal the Westway area as an important site for winter habitat for juvenile striped bass.

After remand the federal agencies extensively restudied this problem and concluded in a draft EIS that the Westway project landfull would have a "significant adverse impact" on this fish species. After hearings were held and comments received on the draft EIS the agencies issued a final EIS which concluded that the impact of the project on the striped bass would be minor.

In *Sierra Club (II)*, 772 F.2d 1043 (2d Cir. 1985), the court disapproved the final EIS and held that the change from a finding of "significant" to "minor" "was a post-hoc rationalization unworthy of belief by this Court and that the Corps had failed to provide any reasoned explanation for the change." Id. at 1055. The court approved a District Court decision that voided a Corps permit for the landfill and federal funding but held that the district court's decision permanently enjoining the completion of the project was an abuse of discretion.

In explaining its decision the court of appeals stated that "it is not for the courts to tell the executive branch what projects they may or may not consider" but noted that affirming the voiding of the permit "may result in condemning the Westway project to oblivion." Yet the court found that the decision to issue the landfill permit was arbitrary and capricious because the reasons for giving the permit "do not reasonably connect the data found by the federal defendants to the choice they made." Ibid. Is this substantive review? Can't a federal agency go ahead with a project even though an EIS is inadequate? For discussion of the Westway project see Ackman, Highway to Nowhere: NEPA, Environmental Review and the *Westway* Case, 21 Colum J.L. & Soc. Probs. 325 (1988).

3. A court may still insist that NEPA expands the issues an agency must take into account in its decisionmaking. In Ocoee River Council v. TVA, 540 F. Supp. 788 (E.D. Tenn. 1981), TVA planned to rehabilitate a dam without allowing the release of water for recreational purposes, a project modification proposed in the impact statement. The court held that the agency's refusal to consider this proposal was "not in accordance with law" under NEPA. The court held that the holding in *Calvert Cliffs*, p. 786 *supra*, that NEPA enlarged the responsibilities of federal agencies to consider environmental factors, required TVA to consider the water release proposal. The court concluded:

> In reviewing the TVA's decision, however, this Court may not substitute its judgment for that of the agency. *Strycker's Bay.* So long as the Agency complies with its obligation under NEPA to incorporate environmental concerns into its decisionmaking, the ultimate decision on each project belongs to the agency. The TVA will be directed, therefore, to reconsider its decision. [540 F. Supp. at 798.]

What if TVA, on remand, fully considers but still rejects the water release proposal? What is the court's function on review?

4. What if NEPA's substantive duties are asserted at the time an agency exercises its rule-making authority to adopt rules implementing its statutory mission? An assertion of this kind was made in Natural Resources Defense Council, Inc. v. SEC, 606 F.2d 1031 (D.C. Cir. 1979), a decision coming after *Vermont Yankee* but before *Strycker's Bay*. The Securities and Exchange Commission (SEC) declined to adopt rules requiring comprehensive disclosure by corporations in their securities offerings of their environmental and equal employment policies. SEC's decision came after several years of informal rule-making proceedings. The court of appeals refused to reverse the SEC decision. It distinguished carefully between the agency's procedural and substantive duties under NEPA, noting that rigorous judicial review of compliance with procedural duties was proper but that judicial review of compliance with substantive duties should be circumspect.

The court's holding on the scope of substantive review was influenced by the nature of the case. The agency had decided not to regulate an activity after holding extensive rule-making proceedings. Issues raised by this refusal to adopt a regulatory policy were not well suited to judicial review because they were based on factors not inherently subject to review, such as the weighing of competing policies within a broad statutory framework (606 F.2s at 1046). The court's views on substantive judicial review under NEPA are, nonetheless, of considerable interest:

> [T]he agency, in our view, was under no obligation to adopt rules identical to or even similar to those sought by [NRDC]. . . . [T]he Commission has been vested by Congress with board discretionary powers to promulgate (or not to promulgate) rules requiring disclosure of information beyond that specifically required by statute. . . . Although Congress, in NEPA, made environmental considerations part of the SEC's substantive mission, we do not believe that NEPA goes so far as to *require* the SEC to promulgate specific rules. [606 F.2d at 1045 (citing *Vermont Yankee* and *Calvert Cliffs*).]

Is *SEC* applicable to a case in which a court considers the adequacy of an environmental impact statement? Is the case consistent with *Strycker's Bay*? Can *Strycker's Bay* be read as a holding that the agency was substantively free, under NEPA, to adopt whatever policy it considered reasonable to implement its responsibility to review the environmental consequences of its actions? Was the Court in *Strycker's Bay* reviewing a policy decision by HUD not to include environmental factors in its review of housing projects? Is *SEC* consistent with *Ocoee River Council*, Note 3 *supra?*

5. Judicial intervention to ensure compliance with NEPA requires a remedy, and the traditional remedy in NEPA cases is a court-ordered injunction. NEPA plaintiffs usually seek a preliminary injunction to preserve the status quo in a case until the court can make a final decision. If the court does not issue a preliminary injunction, the plaintiff takes the risk that the defendant agency may proceed with its project and may later convince the court that the case is moot

because the project is substantially or entirely completed. Courts asked to order preliminary injunctions normally balance the equities, usually requiring the plaintiff to show probable success on the merits, irreparable injury, and that the injunction is in the public interest.

Some courts applied a "NEPA exception" and granted a preliminary injunction without considering the usual equity factors. Other courts relaxed the irreparable harm rule in NEPA cases and found irreparable harm in the damage that would be done to NEPA's statutory purposes if the court refused an injunction. See NEPA Law & Litigation, *supra*, §§4:48-4:53. The Supreme Court's decision in Weinberger v. Romero-Barcelo, *supra*, and Amoco Production Co. v. Village of Gambell, 480 U.S. 531 (1987), may have changed this. The Court held that traditional equity principles applied to injunctions in environmental cases and that courts should not presume environmental harm, but added that the "balance of harms" will usually have the issuance of an injunction.

The courts have applied Weinberger in NEPA cases. See State of Wisconsin v. Weinberger, 745 F.2d 412 (7th Cir. 1984). But see Sierra Club v. Penfold, 664 F. Supp. 1299 (D. Alaska 1987) (applying Amoco to grant injunction in NEPA case). See Rosenbaum, Wisconsin v. Weingerger, The Chancellor's Foot and NEPA's Right Arm, 14 Envtl. L. Rep. 10402 (1984); Comment, NEPA Violations and Equitable Discretion, 64 Or. L. Rev. 497 (1986).

A NOTE ON THE PROCEDURAL VERSUS THE SUBSTANTIVE REVIEW DEBATE

The debate over the extent of judicial review under NEPA reflects concern with the judicial role in reviewing environmental decisionmaking by administrative agencies, an issue explored in section A of this chapter. Proponents and opponents of substantive judicial review under NEPA often concentrate on the language of the statute and on the meager evidence available from the legislative history. See Note, The Least Adverse Alternative Approach to Substantive Review under NEPA, 88 Harv. L. Rev. 735, 736-742 (1975). After exploring the legislative history, the note concludes that "courts should be reluctant to enforce seemingly nebulous standards such as NEPA's unless meaningful guidance from Congress can be derived" (88 Harv. L. Rev. at 742). As the materials presented here have indicated, some courts and commentators take a different position.

Comparison with the federal legislation considered in *Overton Park* is instructive. In that case, the U.S. Supreme Court considered a statute that, although not entirely clear, enacted a "rule of decision" for highway agencies considering parks and other protected sites as locations for highways. The Supreme Court was able to find that this provision provided sufficient "law to apply" to enable a court to carry out a substantive review of a highway agency's highway location decision. NEPA's mandate is not that clear. The statute provides important environmental policies, but no clear "rule of decision" emerges.

Absent clear substantive guidance, and absent a statutory expression in NEPA of the standard of judicial review to be applied in NEPA cases, federal courts must fall back on the standards of judicial review provided in the Administrative Procedure Act. Professor Rodgers points out:

> The chief barrier to uninhibited substantive review of agency actions under NEPA is the Administrative Procedure Act which says that the reviewing court may set aside agency actions only if they are found to be "arbitrary, capricious, an abuse of discretion or otherwise not in accordance with law." This gives the agency the benefit of the doubt that a private party does not enjoy. The arbitrary and capricious standard of review is a rough prescription for protecting executive decision-making from encroachment by the judiciary. The separation of powers cuts against an expansive substantive review. [W. Rodgers, Environmental Law 743 (1977).]

Professor Rodgers also notes, immediately after this statement, that "[s]ome considerations point the other way." What might they be?

Separation of powers problems have influenced some courts that have considered judicial review questions under NEPA. Judge McGowan's opinion in Natural Resources Defense Council, Inc. v. SEC, 606 F. 2d 1031 (D.C. Cir. 1979), contains an especially thoughtful discussion of this issue. Recall that in this case a challenge was brought to SEC rule-making proceedings in which the agency declined to adopt a rule requiring comprehensive disclosure about environmental and equal opportunity policies in corporation securities listings. Judge McGowan first noted the necessity of evaluating "three particularly important factors" when assessing the scope of judicial review: the need for judicial supervision to safeguard the interests of the plaintiffs, the impact of review on the agency's effectiveness in carrying out its statutory role, and the appropriateness of the issues raised for judicial review (606 F.2d at 1044). After noting the distinction between an agency's procedural and substantive duties under NEPA, he continued:

> The SEC's effectiveness in carrying out its mandate will not, in our view, be greatly impaired by judicial review of its procedural compliance with NEPA. For one thing, NEPA made environmental considerations part of the SEC's mandate, and judicial review should serve to ensure that this aspect of the SEC's statutory duties is fully implemented. Because such review is essentially procedural, it will not impose undesirable substantive results on the agency. Finally, judicial review in this context will not be a recurring burden on the agency. . . .
>
> Moreover, the issues in this context will generally be appropriately framed for judicial consideration. The function we are here asked to perform — that of evaluating an agency's procedural compliance with a statutory norm — is within our traditional area of expertise. Although, as we have noted, this review will involve some examination of the rationality of the SEC's decision, we are confident of our ability to perform such substantive scrutiny limited to ensuring that the SEC has fully and in good faith complied with NEPA's procedural command. Further, because we do not at this point review the rationality of the agency's ultimate substantive decision, the difficulties inherent in judicial review of an agency's decision *not* to adopt proposed rules are not compelling in this context. Because our review is limited to ensuring that statutorily prescribed procedures have been followed, we are confident that the administrative record will usually be sufficient to ensure meaningful review. [606 F.2d at 1044-1045.]

By comparison, Judge McGowan stated that substantive review of agency action should be more circumscribed, and limited by the "arbitrary and capricious" review standard of the APA. Judicial review under this standard should be flexible:

> [T]he concept of "arbitrary and capricious" review defies generalized application and demands, instead, close attention to the nature of the particular problem faced by the agency. The stringency of our review, in a given case, depends upon analysis of a number of factors, including the intent of Congress, as expressed in the relevant statutes, particularly the agency's enabling statute; the needs, expertise, and impartiality of the agency as regards the issue presented; and the ability of the court effectively to evaluate the questions posed. [606 F.2d at 1050.]

Judge McGowan's analysis demands some caveats. It was made in the context of an agency rule-making proceeding and was applied to an agency decision not to adopt a major policy change. An impact statement or the failure to prepare an impact statement was not an issue. Even so, his analysis may influence judicial review of impact statements. Do you agree with it? Is it consistent with the Supreme Court's decision in *Strycker's Bay?* Note that the Supreme Court requires agencies to "consider" environmental impacts. Is inadequate consideration a procedural or a substantive judicial review problem? If a failure to "consider" is reviewable under the "arbitrary and capricious" standard, does Judge McGowan's formulation of that standard adequately take account of the environmental elements added to agency decisionmaking by NEPA?

2.   What Is an "Adequate" Impact Statement?

Compliance with NEPA requires agencies to prepare an environmental impact statement that is adequate to serve as the required "full disclosure" document. We will now consider what an impact statement must contain in order to meet the adequacy requirement. There are two issues in these cases. One is whether, as a matter of law, there are analytical requirements that agencies must satisfy before a court will hold an impact statement adequate. The second issue is whether a court believes that the environmental analysis in an impact statement satisfies the adequacy requirement. Both issues arise in the two cases reproduced in this section.

SIERRA CLUB v. MORTON
510 F.2d 813 (5th Cir. 1975)

CLARK, Circuit Judge:
This case involves yet another clash between a federal agency and environmentalists over a proposed development of the nation's resources. The judicial focus, blurred as usual by the lack of technical and scientific expertise, is

upon whether the impact statement compiled during consideration of the federal action satisfies the National Environmental Policy Act (NEPA), 42 U.S.C.A. §4321 et seq.

At issue here is a lease sale by the Department of Interior (Interior) of 147 tracts on the Outer Continental Shelf along the coasts of Mississippi, Alabama and Florida consisting of a band of underwater coastal land lying from the tidal zone to roughly thirty miles off shore, extending from the Mississippi Delta to Tampa Bay and including offshore islands and enclosed bays. This leasing is referred to as the MAFLA sale.[1]

Plaintiffs, who attack Interior's decision to proceed and its predicate environmental impact statement, are national, state and local environmental organizations and certain individuals. This action seeks a declaratory judgment, injunctive relief, and a writ of mandamus to prohibit the sale of oil and gas leases by Interior on the MAFLA sale area. Intervenors are 17 oil companies who, at the December 1973 MAFLA sale, along with several other parties, made bonus bids of more than 1.5 billion dollars for the right to explore for oil and gas on these submerged federal lands.

The sale was made pursuant to the provisions of the Outer Continental Shelf Lands Act, 43 U.S.C. §1337. Interior's Bureau of Land Management first called for nominations of desired tracts. A draft environmental statement was later issued. After discussions and revisions, the final environmental impact statement (EIS) under attack here was filed with the Council on Environmental Quality (CEQ). The notice of lease offer was then published in the Federal Register and, finally, the leases were awarded between December 27, 1973 and January 18, 1974.

The district court found the EIS to be sufficient under NEPA requirements and the decision to proceed on the basis thereof to be reasonable. We affirm. . . .

Under existing jurisprudence, plaintiffs were required to establish by a preponderance of the evidence, rather than by a prima facie showing of deficiencies, that the EIS for MAFLA was inadequate. The additional attack on the Secretary of Interior's decision to proceed with the leasing must be founded on proof that it was arbitrary and capricious. Since the basic legal premises on which the district judge based his determination that the federal agency actions passed muster were correct, plaintiffs must shoulder a more imposing burden in this Court. Having failed to convince the trial court that the EIS was inadequate, the plaintiffs must now demonstrate that the lower court's findings accepting the EIS as adequate and the decision to proceed as permissible were clearly erroneous.

Section 102(2) contains the procedural requirements designed to compel all federal agencies contemplating actions having a significant impact on the

---

1. The acronym MAFLA is derived from Mississippi, Alabama and Florida. The estimated reserves to be developed on this sale area are 1.5 to 2.4 billion barrels of oil and 1.8 to 2.9 trillion cubic feet of gas. This would require from 700 to 1,120 wells, from 75 to 125 platforms and from 480 to 800 miles of pipeline. It is estimated that the proposed leases may produce 270,000 to 443,000 barrels of oil and .34 to .52 billion cubic feet of gas per day after development and production stabilizes.

environment to consider NEPA's substantive policies and goals as enunciated in Section 101. The effectiveness of Section 102(2) depends upon compliance with procedural duties "to the fullest extent possible," i.e., a compliance, the completeness of which is only limited by the agency's statutory obligations. While no agency may properly adopt a less demanding standard for their effort, judicial review is based on a pragmatic standard. In determining whether an agency has complied with Section 102(2), we are governed by the *rule of reason*, i.e., we must recognize "on the one hand that the Act mandates that no agency limit its environmental activity by the use of an artificial framework and on the other that the act does not intend to impose an impossible standard on the agency." The court's task is to determine whether the EIS was compiled with objective good faith and whether the resulting statement would permit a decisionmaker to fully consider and balance the environmental factors.

Testing the EIS . . .

The purposes of an environmental impact statement are to detail the environmental and economic effects of proposed federal action "to enable those who did not have a part in its compilation to understand and consider meaningfully the factors involved," and to compel the decisionmaker to give serious weight to environmental factors in making discretionary choices. "The sweep of NEPA is extraordinarily broad, compelling consideration of any and all types of environmental impact of federal action." To carry out this statutory mandate, every relevant environmental effect of the project must be given appropriate consideration. Section 102(2)(C) seeks these goals by specifically requiring a *detailed* statement.

The purposes served by this "detailed statement" requirement have been succinctly enumerated by the First Circuit in Silva v. Lynn, 482 F.2d 1282, 1284-1285 (1st Cir. 1973). The *Silva* court stated:

> The "detailed statement" required by §4332(2)(C) serves at least three purposes. First, it permits the court to ascertain whether the agency has made a good faith effort to take into account the values NEPA seeks to safeguard. To that end it must "explicate fully its course of inquiry, its analysis and its reasoning." . . . Second, it serves as an environmental full disclosure law, providing information which Congress thought the public should have concerning the particular environmental costs involved in a project. To that end, it "must be written in language that is understandable to nontechnical minds and yet contain enough scientific reasoning to alert specialists to particular problems within the field of their expertise." . . . It cannot be composed of statements "too vague, too general and too conclusory." . . . Finally and perhaps most substantively, the requirement of a detailed statement helps insure the integrity of the process of decision by precluding stubborn problems or serious criticism from being swept under the rug.

Id. (Citations omitted.) Again, the courts have approached their review of claims that congressionally specified detail of environmental effects was lacking in an

EIS with a view that Congress did not intend to mandate perfection, or intend "for an impact statement to document every particle of knowledge that an agency might compile in considering the proposed action."

Present Environment

Plaintiffs contend that a most serious shortfall of the EIS is its lack of necessary baseline environmental studies upon which any reasoned decision on the environmental effect of the proposed sale must be based. Four specific omissions are asserted.

First, the statement does not include sufficient analysis of present air and water quality in the area. For the most part, plaintiffs are correct in this censure. While the statement does include an analysis of the impact of lease operations on water quality it does not describe the present quality of these environmental factors although it does contain a brief discussion of water quality degradation which previously occurred in the Mississippi Sound, Mobile Bay and along the Florida Gulf and of climatological and oceanographic conditions.

Second, the statement fails to assess each ecosystem as to its unique character, productivity, and the manner in which it operates. This attack is hypercritical. The statement discusses significant portions of the biological environment. Descriptions of the communities of Phytoplankton, Zooplankton, Benthic invertebrates and the active swimmers (Nekton) of the Gulf, embracing an analysis of factors affecting the distribution and abundance of Benthos and the location of significant Benthic communities, are included.

Third, the statement does not describe the operation of the Eastern Gulf ecosystem as a whole or the importance of the lease area to this ecosystem as a unit. While the EIS does contain general information about life in the Gulf there is a dearth of information explaining the interrelationship of localized biotic communities. No information is given as to the predicted effect on the whole if some part of the system were to be harmed.

Fourth, detailed geological data is absent from the statement. The statement does include a review of the geological history and present structural composition of the entire Gulf, with special attention to structures within the MAFLA sale area and a recognition of geologic hazards of MAFLA exploration and production. Additionally the EIS observes that tests necessary to determine shallow hazards, unstable bottom and mud waves are scheduled to be run after the sale, and that prior to approval of a drilling permit, the Geological Survey requires submittal of an operation plan that includes suitable safety procedures necessary to control anticipated hazards.

Environmental Impact

Section 102(2)(C)(i) and (ii) require that the EIS contain a detailed statement of the environmental impact of the proposed action and any adverse effects which cannot be avoided if such proposed action is taken. Plaintiffs do not argue that defendants have failed to include references to environmental effects. Indeed, the summary of the EIS states: "All tracts offered pose some degree of pollution risk to the environment and adjacent shoreline. The risk potential is related to adverse effects on the environment and other resource uses which may result principally from accidental or chronic oil spillage." Rather, plaintiffs urge that the material included is inadequate to permit the proper evaluation of its probability or importance.

In a panoply of particularized criticism plaintiffs attack omissions and deficiencies in Interior's preliminary studies. While it is true that the pre-EIS research was either inadequate or nonexistent in some specific areas, the significant environmental effects were recognized and presented in the final statement in a way which afforded the decisionmaker an opportunity to properly weigh them. NEPA's procedural requirements do not exist to dictate form but to insure that judgments are no longer based on old values. This EIS clearly brings the significant long-term environmental hazards and detriments to peer status with the present need and economic costs considerations which formerly would have controlled decisionmaking. This being so, under the rule of reason it meets the minimum requirements of Section 102(2)(C)(i) and (ii).

Plaintiffs further assert that the EIS inadequately analyzes the effect of oil spills which carry a strong probability of reaching shore or other important natural resources. Here the attack is not upon the effect of omitting relevant material, but rather the manner of its inclusion. This EIS developed a matrix analysis for each tract in the proposed sale. The matrix is designed to predict the possible adverse impacts from structures and oil spillage based upon the tract's distance from shore or another valuable resource.[16] In addition to the predicted development structures, an assumed oil spill in each tract is analyzed on the basis of its potential magnitude and persistence and the tract's proximity to high value re-

---

16. A sample matrix for one tract looks like this:

Significant Resource Factors	Structures			Oil Spills (1000 bbl +)		
	IM	PR	F(ST)	IM	PR	F(OS)
Natural Resource Systems:						
Refuges/Management Areas	20	0.0	0	100	0.5	50
Unique & Highly Productive Areas	20	0.0	0	100	0.1	10
Biota Seaward of Estuary/Marsh/ Nursery Areas	0	1.0	0	40	1.0	40
Beaches	40	0.0	0	80	0.5	40
Coastal Activities/Multiple Uses:						
Shipping	80	1.0	80*	20	1.0	20
Outdoor Recreation	40	0.0	0	80	0.5	40
Commercial Fishing	80	1.0	80	80	0.5	40
Sport Fishing	0	1.0	0	80	1.0	80
Ordnance Disposal Area	100	0.0	0	0	0.0	0

*Tract is partially within 2 shipping lanes.

sources (wildlife refuges and management areas, unique and highly productive areas, biota seaward of estuary/nursery areas, and beaches) and coastal activities (shipping, recreation, commercial fishing, sport fishing and ordnance disposal areas). A series of scales was devised that would yield a range of values designed to integrate the importance and proximity of each impact-producing factor.[17] A relative environmental factor of 50 or more requires careful scrutiny, and, depending upon the significance and character of the resource that may be affected, the decisional spectrum concerning that tract's inclusion can reach from withdrawing the entire tract, to offering the tract with special stipulations, to merely proceeding with the lease sale. A factor greater than zero but less than 50 predicts that the tract could be developed safely within exisiting standard practices and operating regulations without significant damage to the resource involved.

Plaintiffs contend that this matrix analysis is insufficient since the values assigned are arbitrary, that it is falsely assumed that all oil spills will be cleaned up within a few days and that the proximity values do not consider the possibility of oil spills which do not occur at drilling platforms. Plaintiffs point to the CEQ's report on continental shelf development off the Atlantic Coast and in the Gulf of Alaska as employing a more satisfactory method of projecting the likelihood of oil spills reaching shore. This CEQ report included specific calculations as to 23 different possible oil spill sites, stating the probability of spills reaching shore at different times of the year.

Interior's decision to project possible environmental damage from all tracts by the matrix approach, as opposed to the use of a more detailed analysis for a few select sensitive points, certainly does not evince a lack of good faith effort to afford the decisionmaker with the necessary quantitative information concerning the potential impact of oil spillage. Because no exact data exists until a spill occurs at a given location, any analysis of future oil spillage involves a degree of speculation. Therefore, every attempt to select quantitative values will be to some extent arbitrary. The use of relative proximity and importance scales to project adverse environmental impacts from all tracts is no more arbitrary than CEQ's selection for analysis of 23 specific points out of the vast Atlantic Coast and Gulf of Alaska area they analyzed. . . .

[At this point the court reviewed a number of other environmental impacts and found that they were adequately discussed.]

CUMULATIVE EFFECT

CEQ guidelines, Interior regulations, Bureau of Land Management regulations, and prior court decisions all require that federal agencies consider the cumulative effect of similar actions in making determinations under Section

---

17. The importance scale ranges from 0 (no adverse effect) to 100 (complete destruction), while the proximity scale ranges from 0.0 (a tract beyond 10 miles) to 1.0 (a tract containing a valuable resource). The resulting environmental impact factor is a number derived by multiplying importance (IM) by proximity (PR).

102(2)(C). Plaintiffs assert that the EIS fails to analyze the cumulative effect of the MAFLA development on the Eastern Gulf. More particularly, they object to the lack of analysis of the cumulative effects of oil spillage from platforms or pipelines, the disposal of muds and oil spills and flushings resulting from increased tanker and barge traffic.

While the EIS does not analyze these factors, it does acknowledge that the increased number of platforms in the Gulf represents a potential increase in possible interference with shipping. It also approximates the number of additional platforms that will be needed, and notes that these platforms will cause spillage. The EIS estimates the annual spillage expected to result from tanker and barge accidents and operations. It specifically points out that the long-term effects of oil spillage from production in the entire Gulf are not clearly understood and that the cumulative effect of more structures and pipelines in the Gulf must be considered.

Sierra Club contends that the statement should have totalled the amount of oil spills which have already occurred from all oil drilling in the Gulf and determined from these figures how much more was probable. It further asserts that similar calculations should have been made for other pollutants, and that the statement should have included a mathematical analysis of the probability of collision and loss of land from pipelines being placed in marsh areas. These contentions boil down to questioning the degree of detail rather than the lack of it. While agreeing that these additional facts may have been useful to the Secretary in reaching a decision, we still conclude that the detail presented was sufficient to uphold the EIS.

ALTERNATIVES

Section 102(2)(C)(iii) of the Act requires environmental statements to present the alternatives to the proposed action. This discussion-of-alternatives requirement is intended to provide evidence that those charged with making the decision have actually considered other methods of attaining the desired goal, and to permit those removed from the decisionmaking process to evaluate and balance the factors on their own. A thorough consideration of all appropriate methods of accomplishing the aim of the proposed action is expected.

Interior devoted a 352-page volume solely to an analysis of alternatives. Plaintiffs have enumerated still other alternatives which they assert were more feasible but which received little or no attention. . . .

Plaintiffs contend that the EIS' rejection of the possibility of delay of the sale as an alternative was a "pro forma ritual," which failed to comply with the requirement of NEPA that the environmental statement give "information sufficient to permit a reasoned choice of alternatives so far as environmental aspects are concerned." Plaintiffs' characterizations are inapt. The EIS discusses the feasibility of delay: (1) until new technology is available to provide increased environmental protection, (2) pending completion of studies of potential environmental impacts, (3) pending development of land-use and growth plans onshore or (4) pending completed implementation of recommendations made in reports on outer continental shelf operating orders and regulations and amendments as necessary. These alternatives having been fairly presented, the choice was the Secretary of Interior's.

Should the statement have explored the feasibility of selling additional tracts off the coasts of Louisiana and Texas prior to the MAFLA sale? Plaintiffs suggest that this alternative would have the advantage of securing much needed petroleum production while permitting basic underlying environmental studies of the MAFLA area to be completed prior to sale. The fact that these tracts are in the Western Gulf where production is presently taking place does not indicate that development of the additional tracts there would incur less hazards than development of the MAFLA tracts in the Eastern Gulf. Again, alternatives of equal hazard need not be considered.

Another "alternative" inadequacy is alleged to exist as to deletion of high hazard tracts. However, the statement points out that tracts identified by matrix analysis to have the highest relative potential of environmental risk could be deleted. It further calls to mind that while any such deletion would correspondingly reduce the potential overall environmental hazard of the proposed action, the sale would suffer a concomitant loss in estimated recoverable reserves of oil and gas which would have to be made up from another source. While this tract-deletion approach is somewhat generalized, it is detailed enough to satisfy the Congressional mandate that alternatives be considered.

In sum, we conclude that the statement did not lack that detailed statement of alternatives to the MAFLA sale which NEPA requires.

COST-BENEFIT ANALYSIS

Section 102(2)(C)(iv) of the Act requires an analysis of "the relationship between local short-term uses of man's environment and the maintenance and enhancement of long-term productivity." The question this appeal urges is how specifically must this relationship be quantified, i.e., must a dollar and cent weighing of the costs and benefits of the proposed sale be set out in the EIS?

"NEPA does not demand that every federal decision be verified by reduction to mathematical absolutes for insertion into a precise formula." Nevertheless, "an agency [must] search out, develop and follow procedures reasonably calculated to bring environmental factors to peer status with dollars and technology in their decisionmaking." We note that regulations promulgated by Interior and by the Bureau of Land Management require quantification of costs and benefits where possible. However, every attempt to assign a dollar value to future effects of present actions necessarily involves prediction. Such opinion estimates can be most precise when the systems involved are simple. As they become more complex and interactive, the ability to forecast becomes more a guess and less a prediction.

The MAFLA development is in the complex, interactive category. The decisionmaker's task nevertheless remains the same. It is not to total up dollars and cents in a sort of profit-loss ledger, but rather to consider the previously unconsidered by giving weight and consideration to the ecological costs to future generations in deciding whether present economic benefits indicate that the depletion of irreplaceable natural resources should proceed in the manner suggested, or at all. The use of a postulated economic equation to express these values is permissible and in many instances desirable, but it is not a sine qua non. The MAFLA statement, by giving the decisionmaker and other readers enough detail concerning all of these costs and benefits to permit reasoned evaluation and decision, meets the Section 102(2)(C)(iv) requirement that long-term environmental costs be weighed against immediate benefits. . . .

[The court then reviewed the Interior Department's "decision to proceed" and concluded that "[t]he decision to proceed in this instance was not shown to be in clear disregard of the evidence contained in the EIS, nor does it appear arbitrary, capricious or an abuse of discretion." Is this substantive judicial review?]

The judgment appealed from is affirmed.

NOTES AND QUESTIONS

1. As the MAFLA case indicates, agencies that do a reasonable job with the state of the art in impact statement preparation can expect to survive a judicial challenge to the impact statement. Note that the court required the plaintiffs to prove that the impact statement was inadequate. This is clearly the prevailing view. NEPA Law & Litigation §4:45. Would it be preferable to require the plaintiff only to make a prima facie case, considering the difficulties plaintiffs have in making out a case of inadequacy against the agency? Note that the agency cannot make a case of adequacy on the basis of documents and memoranda not included in the impact statement if this adversely affects the public review process. See Grazing Fields Farm v. Goldschmidt, 626 F.2d 1068 (1st Cir. 1980).

Sierra Club also indicates that the adequacy cases raise a number of recurring issues. Surprisingly, there has been little judicial attention to the statutory requirement that agencies consider "the relationship between local short-term uses of man's environment and the maintenance and enhancement of long-term productivity" in their impact statements. But see Scenic Hudson Preservation Conference v. FPC (II), 453 F.2d 463, 492 (2d Cir. 1971), noting that it is the short-term use of the environment, not the short-term impact on the environment, that must be considered.

2. Despite the holding in *Sierra Club*, the preparation of an impact statement can pose an environmental catch-22 for the agency. No matter what the impact statement discloses, more will be required. Critics have complained that the impact statement process is wasteful and that statements are often bulky, trivial, and blurred in focus. See Bardach & Pugliaresi, The Environmental-Impact Statement vs. The Real World, 49 Pub. Interest 22 (1977). CEQ re-

sponded to these criticisms in its regulations. They place a "normal" page limit of 150 pages on impact statements and urge that descriptions be "no longer than necessary." In addition, the regulations call for a "scoping" process in which the agency reviews the environmental issues that are raised and decides which ones should be considered (40 C.F.R. §1501.7).

3. The matrix process used by the agency in *Sierra Club* is one technique for developing greater precision in presenting the mass of environmental consequences likely to arise from any one agency action. The basic idea is to identify the natural resources that will be affected by the proposed action, as well as the specific proposed activities that will have an impact on these resources. These impacts are then weighted and the sum of the weighted impacts totaled to provide a comparative basis for evaluating alternative actions.

While the matrix approach provides a promising method for quantification, it can also be conclusory and arbitrary. What weights are to be assigned to designated impacts is necessarily a subjective decision. Compare California v. Block, 690 F.2d 573 (9th Cir. 1982), holding a matrix to be conclusory and arbitrary, with Minnesota PIRG v. Butz (II), 541 F.2d 1292 (8th Cir. 1976), holding that the agency has the discretion to assign values in the matrix.

Cases such as *Block* and *Butz* raise the broader question of the agency's duty to reflect the "state of the art" in the impact statement. It seems clear that the agency cannot ignore respectable expert opinion contrary to its conclusions, but once the agency identifies a reasonable range of opinion, it need do little more than state that no consensus exists on the issue at hand. In fact, the more candid the agency is about adverse impacts, the better its chances are of successfully resisting a judicial ruling that the impact statement is inadequate. National Wildlife Federation v. Adams, 629 F.2d 587 (9th Cir. 1980). In National Indian Youth Council v. Andrus, 501 F. Supp. 69 (D.N.M. 1980), *aff'd on other grounds sub nom.* National Indian Youth Council v. Watt, 604 F.2d 220 (10th Cir. 1981), the court indicated a general unwillingness to probe deeply into state-of-the-art controversies on the very important issue of the efficacy of surface mine reclamation techniques:

> *Reclamation and Revegetation.* Plaintiffs first challenge the adequacy of the discussion of reclamation and revegetation in the FESs. Specifically, Plaintiffs contend (1) that there is a void of discussion as to the prevalent "state of the art" as to reclamation and revegetation; (2) that various essential elements of reclamation were omitted from the statements, e.g., geology, soil and plant ecology, biogeography, and climactic history; (3) that there was insufficient observation of experimental reclamation plots on comparable lands; and (4) that the FESs fail to accurately depict the potential for failure of reclamation and revegetation.
>
> As for the "state of the art" contention, there simply is no requirement in Section 102(2)(C), or elsewhere in NEPA, that the "state of the art" of a scientific discipline be explicitly discussed in an EIS, especially as an autonomous category. It is implicit in the reclamation discussion in the FESs that there is a divergence of opinion as to what the "state of the art" of reclamation may be.
>
> It suffices that the diversity of thought within the reclamation community was reflected in the FESs and that the prevalent opinions, however contradictory

one with another, were expressed. The "state of the art" of reclamation is far from settled. To the extent that it is ascertainable, it has been interwoven into the fabric of the EIS record through the opinions expressed regarding the potential for either success or failure of reclamation and revegetation within this project. Further discussion of the "state of the art" is not required by NEPA.

Plaintiffs' second reclamation allegation that vital elements of reclamation were omitted from consideration in the statements met its demise during the presentation of Plaintiffs' own case. Plaintiffs' reclamation expert, Dr. Robert R. Curry, candidly admitted that there is an inability within the reclamation discipline to agree on a basic definition of reclamation or, indeed, its elements. Under the "rule of reason," a "controversy of experts" is beyond the scope of judicial review. A "controversy of experts" must remain free from judicial intervention where, as here, the experts within a particular scientific field are engaged in internal conflict to establish the parameters of their expertise. Therefore, Plaintiffs' second reclamation contention necessarily fails. [501 F. Supp. at 668-669.]

4. *Sierra Club* also indicates that an impact statement may disclose that additional study is necessary before the environmental impacts of a proposed action can be fully evaluated. The range of uncertainty is likely to be large when the proposed action is relatively new or when a program impact statement is prepared. Often, the cost of acquiring the additional information may be substantial and will in any event require a delay in the implementation of the project. The uncertainty problem is an important one; resolving it requires the court to balance the cost of delay to the agency against possible harm to the environment should commitments to the project be made before additional studies can be completed. A number of cases permit the action to proceed if the gaps in information are identified. See North Slope Borough v. Andrus, 642 F.2d 289 (D.C. Cir. 1980).

What if the agency weighs the uncertainties and decides that the probabilities indicate that no adverse environmental impacts will occur? In Baltimore Gas & Electric Co. v. Natural Resources Defense Council, Inc., 462 U.S. 87 (1983), the Nuclear Regulatory Commission engaged in a generic rulemaking intended to provide guidelines for the licensing of nuclear power plants. As part of its evaluation of the environmental effects of the nuclear fuel cycle, the Commission determined that the permanent storage of nuclear wastes would have no significant environmental effects and should not be considered in nuclear power plant licensing decisions. Its conclusion was based on assumptions concerning the permanent disposal of wastes in a federal repository. The Commission adopted a "zero-release" assumption but conceded it could not be certain that no wastes would escape. The Court reviewed the Commission's assumption under the "arbitrary and capricious" standard of judicial review and concluded that the agency's assumption was acceptable under this deferential judicial review standard. For discussion, see Note, Substantive Review under NEPA under *Vermont Yankee IV*, 36 Syracuse L. Rev. 837 (1985) (arguing Court applied a substantive review standard to the agency's rule).

5. The consideration of cumulative impacts is an important problem under NEPA but until recently received minimal attention in the cases, as *Sierra Club*

indicates. CEQ regulations define a "cumulative impact" as "the impact on the environment which results from the incremental impact of the action when added to other past, present, and reasonably foreseeable future actions. . . ." [40 C.F.R. §1508.7]

This regulation was given a broad interpretation in Fritiofson v. Alexander, 772 F.2d 1245 (5th Cir. 1985). The United States Army Corps of Engineers approved a permit authorizing a housing developer to construct a canal system for a housing project on an island in Galveston Bay, Texas. The Corps decided not to prepare an impact statement. Objectors argued that the environmental impact of the housing project should be assessed in light of the cumulative impact it would have together with the impact other past and future developments would have on the island. They claimed the Corps had not prepared this kind of cumulative impact analysis. The court remanded the case with instructions to the Corps to prepare a cumulative impact analysis of the housing development and to reassess its environmental significance in light of this analysis.

The court held that the CEQ cumulative impact regulation required consideration of the impact of other developments on Galveston Island even though some of them were not yet proposals requiring an impact statement. Although the *Kleppe* case held that impact statements need be prepared only for actions that had progressed far enough to become "proposals," the court held that *Kleppe* was distinguishable: It does not apply when an agency assesses the environmental significance of a proposed action to determine whether an impact statement should be prepared. In this situation, as the CEQ regulations state, the impact of other actions must be considered even though they have not reached the proposal stage. Is *Kleppe* really distinguishable?

The court held that a cumulative impact analysis in this situation must consider (1) the area in which the effects of the proposed project will be felt; (2) the impacts expected in the area from the proposed project; (3) other actions, as defined in the CEQ regulation, that have had or may be expected to have impacts in the area; (4) the impacts and expected impacts from these other actions; and (5) "the overall impact that can be expected if the individual impacts are allowed to accumulate." Id. at 1245. The Corps had not conducted this kind of analysis. See also Thomas v. Peterson, 753 F.2d 754 (9th Cir. 1985); Comment, The Development and Implementation of the Cumulative Impact Analysis Requirement, 8 Pub. Land L. Rev. 129 (1987).

6. How may a plaintiff show that an impact statement is inadequate? In *Overton Park*, reproduced in Chapter 2, the Supreme Court held that plaintiffs may introduce extra-record evidence to supplement an agency's administrative record only when the record is incomplete or not clear. NEPA cases have applied these exceptions liberally. County of Suffolk v. Secretary of the Interior, 562 F.2d 1368 (2d Cir. 1977), cert. denied, 434 U.S. 1065 (1978), is the leading case. The court held that allegations that an impact statement is inadequate to allow the district court to permit the introduction of supplementary evidence to challenge its adequacy. The court also held that the same rules governing the introduction of supplementary evidence apply in a case challenging an agency's

decision not to file an impact statement. But see Van Abbema v. Fornell, 807 F.2d 633 (7th Cir. 1986) (upholding district court's refusal to admit extra-record evidence when record was complete).

7. What if an impact statement calls for environmentally protective measures that the agency does not follow when it completes its project? Is judicial relief available? The courts have denied post-completion relief on a number of grounds, some holding that the case is moot because the project has been completed. Other courts refused to read into NEPA an implied cause of action to enforce an impact statement. See Noe v. Metropolitan Atlanta Rapid Transit Authority, 644 F.2d 434 (5th Cir. 1981) (noise from construction of rapid transit station exceeded noise levels predicted in impact statements). Commentators have been critical of these cases, suggesting that courts require agencies to file a supplemental impact statement when they deviate from an approved impact statement. See Note, EIS Supplements for Improperly Completed Projects: A Logical Extension of Judicial Review under NEPA, 81 Mich. L. Rev. 221 (1982).

A NOTE ON COST-BENEFIT ANALYSIS UNDER NEPA

Although it is by now reasonably settled that NEPA does not require a cost-benefit analysis, the issue was troublesome for some time. Cost-benefit analysis is an analytic technique used by public agencies to determine whether economic investment in capital improvement projects is justified. All benefits and costs of a proposed project are given a monetary value. Benefits are summed in the numerator and costs in the denominator to produce a cost-benefit ratio. The project is not considered cost-benefit justified unless the ratio exceeds 1.0, or unity. Cost-benefit analysis can also be used to compare a number of alternative projects. The agency will usually pick the project that has the highest cost-benefit ratio.

The problem is that a ratio in excess of unity is difficult to overcome yet the analytic techniques used in cost-benefit analysis are often questionable. Cost-benefit analysis also excludes many environmental costs, which are difficult to cast in monetary terms, a problem that NEPA was passed to overcome. See §102(2)(B).

The following excerpt briefly explains some of the assumptions of cost-benefit analysis and some of the more common problems the technique raises:

> There are significant practical difficulties in carrying out a B-C analysis. Some of these are common to evaluation of investments in the private sector. For example, there is always uncertainty about future costs and benefits and the ultimate technical performance of the project. There are, however, several important difficulties that are peculiar to public projects. First, unlike private investments for which the benefit is simply the price that the products they produce will command in the market, *public* projects generate products which often are not traded in private markets. Their "price" is therefore unknown, and it is necessary to infer what the

price would be if a market for the commodity existed. Such indirect inference of people's "willingness to pay" for non-market commodities is inherently difficult and uncertain.

A second difficulty is that public investments such as water projects are typically designed to last 50 to 100 years. Their evaluation therefore requires prediction of costs and benefits beyond the point where current economic conditions can be extrapolated with any certainty. As a result of these difficulties, B-C analysis provides, at best, a highly approximate and uncertain prediction of the economic return of proposed projects.

An institutional difficulty of B-C analysis is that in practice it is performed by proponents of the projects, namely, the agencies which will construct the project if approved. Given the unavoidable judgments necessary for the analysis, this institutional bias naturally leads to skepticism about the validity of the B-C analysis.

A more important and fundamental limitation on the utility of B-C analysis is the narrowness of economic return as a public objective. In addition to economic return, the desirability of a project depends on other considerations, such as relieving local unemployment, saving lives during floods, preserving natural environments or stimulating a region's economy. These considerations represent other objectives of society quite distinct from the objective of economic return. [The author discusses the difficulties with broadening the analysis to incude non-economic values, a problem that is discussed in Chapter 1.] . . .

Finally, . . . [what is a benefit to some people is a cost] to others. Such distributional effects are, by definition, beyond the scope of the B-C analysis, which looks only at total benefits and costs without regard to who receives or bears them. The concept of comparison of total benefits and costs implies an indifference to benefiting one group at the expense of another. Society, however, is not indifferent to distributional effects. It may choose, for example, to build a water project in a poor region of the country even if the net economic effect on the *nation* is zero or negative. . . .

One example of the confusion that has resulted from the use of B-C analysis as the sole evaluation tool is the controversy over the "discount rate." The B-C analysis must take into account the fact that benefits and costs occur at different points in time. A dollar today is worth more than a dollar a year from now because it could be invested during the year yielding, for example, $1.10 at the end of the year. In this example, the "discount rate" would be 10%: all costs and benefits occurring after the date the project begins operation would be *reduced* by 10% per year for each year before they would occur. All project costs occurring before that date would be *increased* 10% per year for each year that would elapse before the project is completed.

The precise percentage that is chosen for this discount rate has a tremendous effect on the B-C ratio, because most project costs occur before the project is completed, while project benefits are stretched out into the distant future. A relatively high discount rate reduces the number of projects that appear justified, *if economic return is the only criterion of project justification.* As a result, the selection of the discount rate has been the subject of tremendous controversy. [Jaffe, Benefit-Cost Analysis and Multiple-Objective Evaluation of Federal Water Projects, 4 Harv. Envtl. L. Rev. 58, 59-62 (1980).]

Another problem arises in evaluating secondary costs and benefits: the spillover effects of a project on affected uses and activities. An irrigation project, for example, may lead to an increase in wheat production. Agencies should not include this kind of secondary pecuniary benefit in a cost-benefit analysis since it usually will be reflected in the direct benefits flowing from the availability of an improved irrigation system. For a thorough discussion of the limitations of cost-benefit analysis, see Williams, Benefit-Cost Analysis in Natural Resources Decisionmaking: An Economic and Legal Overview, 11 Nat. Resources Law. 761 (1979).

NOTES AND QUESTIONS

1. Cost-benefit analysis has been most extensively used in water resource and flood control projects, in which it has been institutionalized by congressional and administrative directives. For these and other projects for which cost-benefit analysis is used, this technique provides a rule of decision that contrasts with the open-ended balancing of costs and benefits that NEPA contemplates. CEQ does not require a cost-benefit analysis in impact statements and does not require that costs and benefits be given monetary values. 40 C.F.R. §1502.23.

In addition to the MAFLA case, another strong statement rejecting a requirement for cost benefit analysis under NEPA is found in Trout Unlimited v. Morton, 509 F.2d 1276 (9th Cir. 1974):

> [T]here is sufficient disagreement about how environmental amenities should be valued to permit any value so assigned to be challenged on the grounds of its subjectivity. It follows that in most, if not all, projects the ultimate decision to proceed with the projects, whether made by Congress or an agency, is not strictly a mathematical determination. Public affairs defy the control that precise quantification of its issues would impose.
>
> This is not to say that progress is not being made in devising techniques which will make cost-benefit analysis more reliable. Nor is it to say that under no circumstances should the EIS contain a numerically expressed cost-benefit analysis. We intend merely to say that under the circumstances of this case the absence of such an analysis in the EIS is not fatal. The EIS before us is sufficiently detailed to aid the decision-makers in deciding whether to proceed or not and to provide the information the public needs to enable . . . [challengers and supporters] to respond effectively. [Id. at 1286.]

2. Courts will review a cost-benefit analysis if an agency decides to do one. South Louisiana Environmental Council v. Sand, 629 F.2d 1005 (5th Cir. 1980), is a leading case. Congress approved a Corps of Engineers channel enlargement and deepening project designed to facilitate the movement of offshore drilling rigs and related equipment between construction and service sites on the coast and drilling sites in the Gulf of Mexico. Congressional approval of the project had precluded the court's "review of that substantive decision," and the court held it could only review for "procedural" compliance with NEPA. A remand to the Corps would be necessary only if "Congress was misled by the inclusion of . . . erroneous benefits in its consideration of environmental consequences."

Plaintiffs argued that hurricane benefits were erroneous because drilling rigs were now built to withstand hurricane winds and that flood control benefits were erroneous because the Corps had not decided which flood control alternative to use. Although these benefits made up 42 percent of project benefits, the district court found that their elimination did not reduce the cost-benefit ratio below unity. The court of appeals agreed and concluded that Congress was not misled by the inclusion of these benefits. They were "wholly economic," had only a "peripheral relationship" to any environmental impact, and did not change the cost-benefit ratio to such an extent that the environmental analysis was distorted.

Is this a correct statement of the issues? Isn't the question under NEPA whether the environmental analysis is adequate despite a favorable economic cost-benefit ratio?

3. In Sierra Club v. Sigler, 695 F.2d 957 (5th Cir. 1983), the court found an impact statement faulty because the federal agency excluded a number of environmental costs from its cost-benefit analysis. The court distinguished its earlier opinion in *South Louisiana*, holding that there the plaintiff had challenged the agency's "economic benefit" calculations. The project in *Sigler* also was a private project, while the project in *South Louisiana* was funded and authorized by Congress, so that "separation of powers considerations precluded judicial review."

What other defects in a cost-benefit analysis might be subject to challenge under the *Sigler* ruling? Compare Texas Committee on Natural Resources v. Marsh, 736 F.2d 262 (5th Cir. 1984) (economic values not weighted against environmental concerns), with Oregon Natural Resources Council v. Marsh, 832 F.2d 1489 (9th Cir. 1987) (agency used proper discount rate).

4. For additional literature on cost-benefit analysis in impact statements, see Note, Cost-Benefit Analysis, Judicial Review, and the National Environmental Policy Act, 7 Envtl. L. 363 (1977), and Comment, Judicial Review of Cost-Benefit Analysis under NEPA, 53 Neb. L. Rev. 540 (1974).

ROBERTSON v. METHOW VALLEY CITIZENS COUNCIL
109 S. Ct. 1835 (1989)

Justice STEVENS delivered the opinion of the Court.

We granted certiorari to decide two questions of law. As framed by petitioners, they are:

> 1. Whether the National Environmental Policy Act requires federal agencies to include in each environmental impact statement: (a) a fully developed plan to mitigate environmental harm; and (b) a 'worst case' analysis of potential environmental harm if relevant information concerning significant environmental effects is unavailable or too costly to obtain.
>
> 2. Whether the Forest Service may issue a special use permit for recreational use of national forest land in the absence of a fully developed plan to mitigate environmental harm.

Concluding that the Court of Appeals for the Ninth Circuit misapplied the National Environmental Policy Act of 1969 (NEPA), and gave inadequate deference to the Forest Service's interpretation of its own regulations, we reverse and remand for further proceedings.

I . . .

[The Forest Service is authorized to manage the national forests for a number of purposes, including "outdoor recreation." It has issued approximately 170 special use permits pursuant to that authority for alpine and nordic ski areas. These permits are major federal actions that must be preceded by the preparation of an impact statement.

Methow Recreation was awarded a special use permit to develop and operate a proposed Early Winters Ski Resort on Sandy Butte, a 6000-foot mountain in Okanogan National Forest, Washington, and on an adjacent 1,165 acre parcel. Sandy Butte, "like the Methow Valley it overlooks, is an unspoiled, sparsely populated area that the district court characterized as 'pristine.'" The Forest Service cooperated with state and county officials to prepare an impact statement known as the Early Winters Alpine Winter Sports Study.]

The Early Winters Study is a printed document containing almost 150 pages of text and 12 appendices. It evaluated five alternative levels of development of Sandy Butte that might be authorized, the lowest being a "no action" alternative and the highest being development of a 16-lift ski area able to accommodate 10,500 skiers at one time. The Study considered the effect of each level of development on water resources, soil, wildlife, air quality, vegetation and visual quality, as well as land use and transportation in the Methow Valley, probable demographic shifts, the economic market for skiing and other summer and winter recreational activities in the Valley, and the energy requirements for the ski area and related developments. The Study's discussion of possible impacts was not limited to on-site effects, but also, as required by Council on Environmental Quality (CEQ) regulations, see 40 CFR §1502.16(b) (1987), addressed "off-site impacts that each alternative might have on community facilities, socio-economic and other environmental conditions in the Upper Methow Valley." As to off-site effects, the Study explained that "due to the uncertainty of where other public and private lands may become developed," it is difficult to evaluate off-site impacts, and thus the document's analysis is necessarily "not site-specific." Finally, the Study outlined certain steps that might be taken to mitigate adverse effects, both on Sandy Butte and in the neighboring Methow Valley, but indicated that these proposed steps are merely conceptual and "will be made more specific as part of the design and implementation stages of the planning process." . . .

[The study concluded that although the ski resort would not have an adverse effect on air quality, off-site development that would accompany the resort would reduce air quality below state standards unless mitigation measures were taken. This impact would be created by increased automobile, fireplace, and wood stove use.]

[As mitigation measures] [t]he Study suggested that Okanogan County develop an air quality management plan, requiring weatherization of new buildings, limiting the number of wood stoves and fireplaces, and adopting monitoring and enforcement measures.[5] In addition, the Study suggested that the Forest Service require that the master plan include procedures to control dust and to comply with smoke management practices.[6]

In its discussion of adverse effects on area wildlife, the EIS concluded that no endangered or threatened species would be affected by the proposed development and that the only impact on sensitive species was the probable loss of a pair of spotted owls and their progeny. With regard to other wildlife, the Study considered the impact on 75 different indigenous species and predicted that within a decade after development vegetational change and increased human activity would lead to a decrease in population for 31 species, while causing an increase in population for another 24 species on Sandy Butte. Two species, the pine marten and nesting goshawk, would be eliminated altogether from the area of development.

In a comment in response to the draft EIS, the Washington Department of Game voiced a special concern about potential losses to the State's largest migratory deer herd, which uses the Methow Valley as a critical winter range and as its migration route. The state agency estimated that the total population of mule deer in the area most likely to be affected was "better than 30,000 animals" and that "the ultimate impact on the Methow deer herd could exceed a 50 percent reduction in numbers." The agency asserted that "Okanogan County residents place a great deal of importance on the area's deer herd." In addition, it explained that hunters had "harvested" 3,247 deer in the Methow Valley area in 1981, and that in 1980 hunters on average spent $1,980 for each deer killed in Washington, and they had contributed over $6 million to the State's economy. Because the deer harvest is apparently proportional to the size of the herd, the state agency predicted that "Washington business can expect to lose over $3 million annually from reduced recreational opportunity." The Forest Service's own analysis of the impact on the deer herd was more modest. It first concluded that the actual operation of the ski hill would have only a "minor" direct impact on the herd,[7] but then recognized that the off-site effect of the development "would

---

5. [The study recommended that the county develop an air management plan with stricter standards than existing state standards. Among other mitigation measures the plan should consider land use codes addressing energy efficiency and air pollution in project design, requirements for fully weatherizing new construction, restrictions on the number of fireplaces and wood stoves, and encouraging the use of alternative, non-polluting fuel sources.]

6. [As on-site air quality mitigation measures the study included prompt revegetation of disturbed areas, mandatory dust control measures on unpaved roads, and application of smoke management practices in the construction phase.]

7. The Study predicted that development of the ski area would diminish available summer range for the deer by between five and ten percent, depending on the level of development chosen. . . .

noticeably reduce numbers of deer in the Methow [Valley] with any alternative." Although its estimate indicated a possible 15 percent decrease in the size of the herd, it summarized the State's contrary view in the text of the EIS, and stressed that off-site effects are difficult to estimate due to uncertainty concerning private development.

As was true of its discussion of air quality, the EIS also described both on-site and off-site mitigation measures. Among possible on-site mitigation possibilities, the Study recommended locating runs, ski lifts, and roads so as to minimize interference with wildlife, restricting access to selected roads during fawning season, and further examination of the effect of the development on mule deer migration routes.[8] Off-site options discussed in the Study included the use of zoning and tax incentives to limit development on deer winter range and migration routes, encouragement of conservation easements, and acquisition and management by local government of critical tracts of land. As with the measures suggested for mitigating the off-site effects on air quality, the proposed options were primarily directed to steps that might be taken by state and local government.

Ultimately, the Early Winters Study recommended the issuance of a permit for development at the second highest level considered — a 16-lift ski area able to accommodate 8,200 skiers at one time. On July 5, 1984, the Regional Forester decided to issue a special use permit as recommended by the Study. [To mitigate secondary impacts on air quality and a reduction in mule deer range the Forester directed the forest supervisor to implement mitgation measures "both independently and in cooperation with local officials."] . . .

[The plaintiffs appealed to the Chief Forester, who affirmed the Regional Forester's decision. They then brought suit claiming violations of NEPA. The suit was assigned to a Magistrate, who found that the impact statement was adequate.]

Concluding that the Early Winters Study was inadequate as a matter of law, the Court of Appeals reversed. Methow Valley Citizens Council v. Regional Forester, 833 F.2d 810 (CA9 1987). The court held that the Forest Service could not rely on "the implementation of mitigation measures" to support its conclusion that the impact on the mule deer would be minor "since not only has the effectiveness of these mitigation measures not yet been assessed, but the mitigation measures themselves have yet to be developed." It then added that if the agency had difficulty obtaining adequate information to make a reasoned assessment of the environmental impact on the herd, it had a duty to make a so-called "worst case analysis." Such an analysis is "formulated on the basis of available information, using reasonable projections of the worst possible consequences of a proposed action."

___

8.   The EIS listed the following opportunities for on-site mitigation: [They included measures to minimize disturbance to wildlife, such as restricting activities and travel on selected roads during deer fawning season and evaluating the impact of the project on deer mule migration routes.]

The court found a similar defect in the EIS's treatment of air quality. Since the EIS made it clear that commercial development in the Methow Valley will result in violations of state air quality standards unless effective mitigation measures are put in place by the local governments and the private developer, the Court of Appeals concluded that the Forest Service had an affirmative duty to "develop the necessary mitigation measures *before* the permit is granted" (emphasis in original). The court held that this duty was imposed by both the Forest Service's own regulations and §102 of NEPA. It read the statute as imposing a substantive requirement that "action be taken to mitigate the adverse effects of major federal actions." For this reason, it concluded that "an EIS must include a fair discussion of measures to mitigate the adverse environmental impacts of a proposed action." . . .

II

Section 101 of NEPA declares a broad national commitment to protecting and promoting environmental quality. To ensure that this commitment is "infused into the ongoing programs and actions of the Federal Government, the act also establishes some important 'action-forcing' procedures." 115 Cong. Rec. 40416 (remarks of Sen. Jackson). . . . [The Court then quoted §102.]

The statutory requirement that a federal agency contemplating a major action prepare such an environmental impact statement serves NEPA's "action-forcing" purpose in two important respects. It ensures that the agency, in reaching its decision, will have available and will carefully consider detailed information concerning significant environmental impacts; it also guarantees that the relevant information will be made available to the larger audience that may also play a role in both the decisionmaking process and the implementation of that decision.

Simply by focusing the agency's attention on the environmental consequences of a proposed project, NEPA ensures that important effects will not be overlooked or underestimated only to be discovered after resources have been committed or the die otherwise cast. Moreover, the strong precatory language of §101 of the Act and the requirement that agencies prepare detailed impact statements inevitably bring pressure to bear on agencies "to respond to the needs of environmental quality." 115 Cong. Rec. 40425 (1969) (remarks of Sen. Muskie).

Publication of an EIS, both in draft and final form, also serves a larger informational role. It gives the public the assurance that the agency "has indeed considered environmental concerns in its decision making process," *Baltimore Gas & Electric Co.* [v. Natural Resources Defense Council, Inc., 462 U.S. 87, 97 (1983)], and, perhaps more significantly, provides a springboard for public comment, see L. Caldwell, Science and the National Environmental Policy Act 72 (1982). Thus, in this case the final draft of the Early Winters Study reflects not only the work of the Forest Service itself, but also the critical views of the Washington State Department of Game, the Methow Valley Citizens Council, and Friends of the Earth, as well as many others, to whom copies of the draft Study were circulated.[13] Moreover, with respect to a development such as Sandy Butte, where the adverse effects on air quality and the mule deer herd are primarily attributable to predicate off-site development that will be subject to regulation by other governmental bodies, the EIS serves the function of offering those bodies adequate notice of the expected consequences and the opportunity to plan and implement corrective measures in a timely manner.

The sweeping policy goals announced in §101 of NEPA are thus realized through a set of "action-forcing" procedures that require that agencies take a "'hard look' at environmental consequences," Kleppe [v. Sierra Club, 427 U.S. 390, 410, n.21 (1976)], and that provide for broad dissemination of relevant environmental information. Although these procedures are almost certain to affect the agency's substantive decision, it is now well settled that NEPA itself does not mandate particular results, but simply prescribes the necessary process. See Strycker's Bay Neighborhood Council, Inc. v. Karlen, 444 U.S. 223, 227-228 (1980) (per curiam); Vermont Yankee Nuclear Power Corp. v. Natural Resources Defense Council, Inc., 435 U.S. 519, 558 (1978). If the adverse environmental effects of the proposed action are adequately identified and evaluated, the agency is not constrained by NEPA from deciding that other values outweigh the environmental costs. See ibid.; Stryker's Bay Neighborhood Council, Inc., supra, at 227-228; Kleppe, 427 U.S., at 410, n.21. In this case, for example, it would not have violated NEPA if the Forest Service, after complying with the Act's procedural prerequisites, had decided that the benefits to be derived from downhill skiing at Sandy Butte justified the issuance of a special use permit, not withstanding the loss of 15 percent, 50 percent, or even 100 percent of the mule deer herd. Other statutes may impose substantive environmental obligations on federal agencies, but NEPA merely prohibits uninformed — rather than unwise — agency action.

To be sure, one important ingredient of an EIS is the discussion of steps that can be taken to mitigate adverse environmental consequences.[15] The requirement that an EIS contain a detailed discussion of possible mitigation measures flows from both the language of the Act and, more expressly, from CEQ's implementing regulations. Implicit in NEPA's demand that an agency prepare a detailed statement on "any adverse environmental effects which cannot be avoided should the proposal be implemented," 42 U.S.C. §4332(C)(ii), is an understanding that EIS will discuss the extent to which adverse effects can be avoided. See D. Mandelker, NEPA Law and Litigation §10:38 (1984). More generally, omission of a reasonably complete discussion of possible mitigation measures would undermine the "action-forcing" function of NEPA. Without such a discussion, neither the agency nor other interested groups and individuals can prop-

13. [CEQ regulations require comments from other federal agencies, appropriate state and local agencies and the public on draft impact statements. 40 CFR §1503.1 (1987). Agencies must respond to these comments in the final impact statement. §1502.9. See also §1503.4.]

15. [The Court quoted the CEQ's definition of "mitigation" in 40 CFR §1508.20 (1987).]

erly evaluate the severity of the adverse effects. An adverse effect that can be fully remedied by, for example, an inconsequential public expenditure is certainly not as serious as a similar effect that can only be modestly ameliorated through the commitment of vast public and private resources. Recognizing the importance of such a discussion in guaranteeing that the agency has taken a "hard look" at the environmental consequences of proposed federal action, CEQ regulations require that the agency discuss possible mitigation measures in defining the scope of the EIS, 40 CFR §1508.25(b) (1987), in discussing alternatives to the proposed action, §1502.14(f), and consequences of that action, §1502.16(h), and in explaining its ultimate decision, §1505.2(c).

There is a fundamental distinction, however, between a requirement that mitigation be discussed in sufficient detail to ensure that environmental consequences have been fairly evaluated, on the one hand, and a substantive requirement that a complete mitigation plan be actually formulated and adopted, on the other. In this case, the off-site effects on air quality and on the mule deer herd cannot be mitigated unless nonfederal government agencies take appropriate action. Since it is those state and local governmental bodies that have jurisdiction over the area in which the adverse effects need be addressed and since they have the authority to mitigate them, it would be incongruous to conclude that the Forest Service has no power to act until the local agencies have reached a final conclusion on what mitigating measures they consider necessary. Even more significantly, it would be inconsistent with NEPA's reliance on procedural mechanisms — as opposed to substantive, result-based standards — to demand the presence of a fully developed plan that will mitigate environmental harm before an agency can act. Cf. *Baltimore Gas & Electric Co.*, 462 U.S., at 100 ("NEPA does not require agencies to adopt any particular internal decision making structure").

We thus conclude that the Court of Appeals erred, first, in assuming that "NEPA requires that 'action be taken to mitigate the adverse effects of major federal actions,'" and, second, in finding that this substantive requirement entails the further duty to include in every EIS "a detailed explanation of specific measures which will be employed to mitigate the adverse impacts of a proposed action."

III

The Court of Appeals also concluded that the Forest Service had an obligation to make a "worst case analysis" if it could not make a reasoned assessment of the impact of the Early Winters project on the mule deer herd. Such a "worst case analysis" was required at one time by CEQ regulations, but those regulations have since been amended. Moreover, although the prior regulations may well have expressed a permissible application of NEPA, the Act itself does not mandate that uncertainty in predicting environmental harms be addressed exclusively in this manner. Accordingly, we conclude that the Court of Appeals also erred in requiring the "worst case" study.

In 1977, President Carter directed the CEQ promulgate binding regulations implementing the procedural provisions of NEPA. Exec. Order No. 11991, 3 C.F.R. 123 (1977 Comp.). Pursuant to this presidential order, CEQ promulgated implementing regulations. Under §1502.22 of these regulations — a provision which became known as the "worst case requirement" — CEQ provided that if certain information relevant to the agency's evaluation of the proposed action is either unavailable or too costly to obtain, the agency must include in the EIS a "worst case analysis and an indication of the probability or improbability of its occurrence." 40 CFR §1502.22 (1985). In 1986, however, CEQ replaced the "worst case" requirement with a requirement that federal agencies, in the face of unavailable information concerning a reasonably foreseeable significant environmental consequence, prepare "a summary of existing credible scientific evidence which is relevant to evaluating the . . . adverse impacts" and prepare an "evaluation of such impacts based upon theoretical approaches or research methods generally accepted in the scientific community." 40 CFR §1502.22(b) (1987). The amended regulation thus "retains the duty to describe the consequences of a remote, but potentially severe impact, but grounds the duty in evaluation of scientific opinion rather than in the framework of a conjectural 'worst case analysis.'" 50 Fed. Reg. 32,237 (1985).

The Court of Appeals recognized that the "worst case analysis" regulation has been superseded, yet held that "[t]his rescission . . . does not nullify the requirement . . . since the regulation was merely a codification of prior NEPA case law." This conclusion, however, is erroneous in a number of respects. Most notably, review of NEPA case law reveals that the regulation, in fact, was not a codification of prior judicial decisions. See Note, 86 Mich. L. Rev. 777, 798, 800-802, 813-814 (1988). The cases cited by the Court of Appeals ultimately rely on the Fifth Circuit's decision in Sierra Club v. Sigler, 695 F.2d 957 (1983). Sigler, however, simply recognized that the "worst case analysis" regulation codified the "judicially created principl[e]" that an EIS must "consider the probabilities of the occurrence of any environmental effects it discusses." Id., at 970-971. As CEQ recognized at the time it superseded the regulation, case law prior to the adoption of the "worst case analysis" provision did require agencies to describe environmental impacts even in the face of substantial uncertainty, but did not require that this obligation necessarily be met through the mechanism of a "worst case analysis." See 51 Fed. Reg. 15,625 (1986). CEQ's abandonment of the "worst case analysis" provision, therefore, is not inconsistent with any previously established judicial interpretation of the statute.

Nor are we convinced that the new CEQ regulation is not controlling simply because it was preceded by a rule that was in some respects more demanding. In Andrus v. Sierra Club, 442 U.S. [347, 358 (1979)], we held that CEQ regulations are entitled to substantial deference. In that case we recognized that although less deference may be in order in some cases in which the "'administrative guidelines'" conflict "'with earlier pronouncements of the agency,'" substantial deference is nonetheless appropriate if there appears to have been good reason for the change. Here, the amendment only came after the prior regulation had been subjected to considerable criticism. Moreover, the amendment was designed to better serve the twin functions of an EIS — requiring agencies to take a "hard look" at the consequences of the proposed action and providing important information to other groups and individuals. CEQ explained that by requiring that an EIS focus on reasonably foreseeable impacts, the new regulation "will generate information and discussion on those consequences of greatest concern to the public and of greatest relevance to the agency's decision," 50 Fed. Reg. 32,237 (1985), rather than distorting the decision making process by overemphasizing highly speculative harms, 51 Fed. Reg. 15,624 15,625 (1986); 50 Fed. Reg. 32,236 (1985). In light of this well-considered basis for the change, the new regulation is entitled to substantial deference. Accordingly, the Court of Appeals erred in concluding that the Early Winters Study is inadequate because it failed to include a "worst case analysis." . . . [The Court also held that the Forest Service's failure to develop a complete mitigation plan did not violate its own regulations.]

V

In sum, we conclude that NEPA does not require a fully developed plan detailing what steps *will* be taken to mitigate adverse environmental impacts and does not require a "worst case analysis." In addition, we hold that the Forest Service has adopted a permissible interpretation of its own regulations. The judgment of the Court of Appeals is accordingly reversed and the case is remanded for further proceedings consistent with this opinion.

It is so ordered.

NOTES AND QUESTIONS

1. The Court's handling of the worst case analysis requirement in Methow Valley obscures the intense controversy this requirement created. Worst case analysis is an analytic technique usually applied to the environmental impacts of actions that have a low probability of occurrence but whose environmental consequences are disastrous. A nuclear power plant explosion is an example. Because of the low probability of such occurrences, information is usually missing that can provide the basis for an assessment of their environmental consequences. Federal agencies must do a worst case analysis to analyze the probability and possible adverse consequences of this type of action in the face of this uncertainty.

Sierra Club v. Sigler, which is cited in *Methow Valley*, illustrates the worst case analysis requirement. The court reviewed an impact statement prepared for a multipurpose deepwater port and crude oil distribution system to be located on Galveston Bay at Galveston, Texas. Plaintiff demanded a worst case analysis of the environmental damage that could result from a total cargo loss by a super-tanker in the Bay, which the impact statement did not contain. The court held the worst case analysis regulation was authorized by NEPA, and that the regulation required a catastrophic worst case analysis of this type. The court concluded:

> All parties agree that a total cargo loss *could* occur and *could* wreak catastrophic environmental damage in the bay. While this damage is a "significant adverse effect," there is considerable uncertainty about its likelihood, scope, and consequences; information on it is certainly important, if not essential, to the Corps' decision, yet that information is beyond the state of the art. However, there is a body of data with which a reasonable worst case analysis can be made that is not unreasonably speculative. Remoteness does not bar a worst case analysis so founded and should instead be weighed by the Corps when it applies the worst case analysis in its decisionmaking process. [Id. at 974] [emphasis in original.]

2. When CEQ revoked the worst case analysis rule it did not entirely eliminate the duty to evaluate environmental impacts when scientific evidence is uncertain. As CEQ explained, the rule

> requires the agencies (1) to affirmatively disclose the fact that information important to evaluating significant adverse effects on the human environment is missing; (2) to explain the relevance of the missing information; (3) to summarize the existing credible scientific evidence which is relevant to the agency's evaluation of the significant adverse impacts on the human environment; and (4) to evaluate that evidence. [50 Fed. Reg. 32,234 (1985).]

Low probability-high catastrophic consequences must be evaluated if this evaluation can be based on credible scientific support. Is this analysis similar to the worst case analysis required by Sigler? For an argument that it could be see Note, The National Environmental Policy Act and the Revised CEQ Regulations: A Fate Worse than the "Worst Case Analysis"?, 60 St. John's L. Rev. 500 (1986). See also Rosenbaum, Amending CEQ's Worst Case Analysis Rule: Towards Better Decisionmaking?, 15 Envtl. L. Rep. 10275 (1985).

3. The Court's holding on mitigation is a replay of the substantive v. procedural debate. Do you agree with the Court's holding? On the facts of the *Methow Valley* case, could a court hold that the discussion of mitigation was inadequate and remand for additional consideration? Does the Court provide any clues on the answer to this question? For cases on this issue see NEPA Law & Litigation §10:38.

A related problem arises when an agency decides that an impact statement is not necessary because mitigation measures have eliminated any adverse environmental impacts. Why didn't the Forest Service simply take this alternative in *Methow Valley*? The cases have given more consideration to the mitigation problem in this context, but most have upheld findings of no significant impact based on mitigation. See Herson, Project Mitigation Revisited: Most Courts Approve Findings of No Significant Impact Justified by Mitigation, 13 Ecology L.Q. 51 (1986).

A leading case is Cabinet Mountains Wilderness/Scotchman's Peak Grizzly Bears v. Peterson, 685 F.2d 678 (D.C. Cir. 1982), noted, 23 Nat. Resources J. 467 (1983). The Forest Service decided not to prepare an impact statement when it approved plans for exploratory mineral drilling in a wilderness area. The environmental assessment recommended a number of measures to mitigate the effect of the mining on grizzly bears living in the area, including prohibitions on overnight camping and restrictions on helicopter flights. The court held that "the statutory threshold of significant effects is not met" when the agency includes mitigation measures that "compensate completely" for the adverse effects of the proposal.

Does this holding apply when the agency decides to prepare an impact statement? Is there a reason for compensating "completely" when an agency does not prepare an impact statement but for not compensating "completely" when an impact statement is prepared?

A NOTE ON PROCEDURAL OBLIGATIONS AND DELEGATION OF RESPONSIBILITIES UNDER NEPA

CEQ regulations cover in detail the procedures agencies must follow in the preparation of impact statements. The 1978 revision, for example, introduced a "scoping" requirement (40 C.F.R. §1501.7). Agencies must engage in an "early and open process" to identify the significant issues to be covered in an impact statement and to eliminate from the statement issues it considers insignificant. This requirement is intended to improve the relevancy of impact statements. What opportunities does it provide for judicial review? The remainder of this Note considers other important procedural problems that arise under the statute and under CEQ regulations.

Commenting. To implement its "full disclosure" function, NEPA requires comments prior to any detailed impact statement from "any Federal agency which has jurisdiction by law or special expertise with respect to any environmental impact involved." In addition, "the comments and views of the appropriate Federal, State, and local agencies, which are authorized to develop and enforce environmental standards," are to accompany the proposal through the agency review process. §102(2)(C). While the statute does not require it, CEQ also requires agencies to affirmatively request comment from the public. 40 C.F.R. §1501.3(a)(4).

The commenting procedure is an important part of the impact statement process. The public and other agencies can be expected to raise issues not considered by the agency proposing the action considered in the impact statement. CEQ has implemented the commenting procedure by requiring comments on a draft impact statement, followed by agency responses to comments in the final impact statement. See 40 C.F.R. §1501.4. Note, for example, how the Court's discussion of the mitigation issue was affected by state agency comments in *Methow Valley.*

Federal courts have been attentive to compliance with commenting procedures. They have invalidated an impact statement when the agency has modified its project subsequent to the draft statement but has not amended the statement to afford opportunity for comment. *California v. Block*, 690 F.2d 753 (9th Cir. 1982). Neither may responses to comments be perfunctory. A mere tabulation of comments is not enough (690 F.2d at 773). A "mere admission of some impact" is not sufficient. *National Wildlife Federation v. Andrus*, 440 F. Supp. 1245, 1253 (D.D.C. 1977). See 40 C.F.R. §1503.4 (agency must explain why comments do not warrant further response). As attorney for the plaintiffs in *Methow Valley* would you have attacked the Forest Service's response to comments as inadequate?

The commenting procedure does not authorize a veto by the commenting agency. *Sierra Club v. Callaway*, 499 F.2d 982, 993 (5th Cir. 1974). Compare *Warm Springs Dam Task Force v. Gribble*, 565 F.2d 549 (9th Cir. 1977): "[T]here is no requirement that the responsible agency alter its project or perform new studies in response to comments" (565 F.2d at 554).

EPA review. A potentially powerful supplementary environmental review requirement is contained in §309 of the Clean Air Act. It confers additional environmental review authority on EPA:

> (a) The [EPA] Administrator shall review and comment in writing on the environmental impact of any matter relating to duties and responsibilities granted pursuant to . . . [the Clean Air] Act or other provisions of the authority of the Administrator, contained in any (1) legislation proposed by any Federal department or agency, (2) newly authorized Federal projects for construction and any major Federal action (other than a project for construction) to which section 102(2)(C) of . . . [NEPA] applies and (3) proposed regulations published by any department or agency of the Federal Government. Such written comment shall be made public at the conclusion of any such review.
> (b) In the event that the Administrator determines that any such legislation, action, or regulation is unsatisfactory from the standpoint of public health or welfare or environmental quality, he shall publish his determination and the matter shall be referred to the Council on Environmental Quality. [42 U.S.C. §7609.]

The breadth of §309 is apparent. It requires EPA to evaluate the merits of the agency proposal, not just the merits of the impact statement. Must the agency request EPA comment? Is EPA review limited solely to environmental matters? Is EPA review required only for matters subject to impact statements? See Healy, The Environmental Protection Agency's Duty to Oversee NEPA's Implementation: Section 309 of the Clean Air Act, 3 Envtl. L. Rep. (Envtl. L. Inst.) 50,071 (1973).

In most cases, the normal commenting process provides a substitute for a §309 intervention, and EPA has limited its §309 reviews to cases dealing with severe environmental problems. It is clear that EPA's authority to declare a proposal environmentally unsatisfactory is discretionary. *Sierra Club v. Morton*, 379 F. Supp. 1254 (D. Colo. 1974) (reviewing legislative history of provision).

What is the legal effect of an "unsatisfactory" environmental determination by EPA under §309? Note that §309(b) does not indicate what is to happen after an unsatisfactory determination is referred to the CEQ. In Alaska v. Andrus, 580 F.2d 465 (D.C. Cir. 1978), EPA's recommendation that an offshore gas and lease sale be delayed was held moot because the recommended delay had expired. In dictum, the court indicated that EPA's unsatisfactory determination "did give rise to a heightened obligation on [the Department of the] Interior's part to explain clearly and in detail its reasons for proceeding. It seems clear to us that §309 was intended to do something more than merely reiterate §102(2)(C) of NEPA" (580 F.2d at 475 n.44). The court added that an agency that decides to proceed in the face of an unsatisfactory EPA determination "must articulate clearly its reasons for doing so." Is this agency obligation procedural or substantive? How much weight did the court really give to an EPA §309 intervention?

Interdisciplinary approach: unquantified values. Paragraph (A) of §102(2) requires federal agencies to engage in a systematic, interdisciplinary approach to decisionmaking, and paragraph (B) requires "appropriate consideration" of "unquantified environmental amenities." These paragraphs have not had much influence on the decisions in recent years. The courts have not given much effect to paragraph (B) in their review of cost-benefit analysis, for example. Early decisions interpreted paragraph (A) to require adequate consultation with experts and with other agencies having expertise on the proposed project. See, e.g., Simmans v. Grant, 370 F. Supp. 5 (S.D. Tex. 1974). The court held that the agency had not used an interdisciplinary approach in evaluating a water conservation project because it did not consult the expertise of other agencies.

Delegation. Although NEPA requires "federal agencies" to prepare impact statements, agencies sometimes delegate this responsibility. Delegation may be a practical alternative to staffing for some agencies, and delegation to consultants may be a comparatively inexpensive way of securing access to a wider range of environmental information.

In an early and influential case, the Second Circuit held that the preparation of an impact statement by an applicant to a federal agency for a power license violated NEPA. Greene County Planning Board v. FPC, 455 F.2d 412 (2d Cir.), *cert. denied,* 409 U.S. 849 (1972). In this case, the statement could be considered self-serving since it was prepared by the applicant that sought federal approval. As the delegation issue continued to receive judicial attention, courts adopted one of three positions: Some allowed virtually complete delegation, some inquired into the extent of federal participation in the preparation process, and some strictly applied the *Greene County* rule. Compare Natural Resources Defense Council, Inc. v. Callaway, 524 F.2d 79 (2d Cir. 1975) (*Greene County* not applied when statement prepared by consultant who was not a self-interested applicant).

Most of the delegation cases have arisen in the federally assisted state highway program. In this program, the federal highway agency commonly delegated impact statement preparation to state highway agencies. Problems arose when the Second Circuit strictly applied *Greene County,* striking down the preparation of an impact statement by a state highway agency. Conservation Society, Inc. v. Secretary of Transporation (I), 508 F.2d 927 (2d Cir. 1974), *vacated,* 423 U.S.

809 (1975). When the federal highway agency shut down all highway projects in the Second Circuit area following this decision, Congress responded by enacting an amendment to §102(2)(D) of NEPA allowing a qualified delegation to state agencies. Delegation is authorized by this amendment to state agencies or officials having statewide jurisdiction and "the responsibility" for the action. Federal guidance and participation is required, and the federal official must "independently" evaluate the impact statement. The effect of the amendment can be seen in the remand in *Conservation Society*: The Second Circuit found that the delegation requirements of the amendment had been satisfied. Conservation Society v. Secretary of Transportation (II), 531 F.2d 637 (2d Cir. 1976).

Congress also authorized a delegation of impact statement preparation under §104(g) of the Housing and Community Development Act of 1974, 42 U.S.C. §5304(g). The courts have interpreted this provision as conferring only procedural responsibilities on the federal Department of Housing and Urban Development. It is not required to independently review impact statements submitted by local governments or prepare its own impact statement. See Brandon v. Pierce, 725 F.2d 555 (10th Cir. 1984). For a discussion of delegation see Comment, Delegation of Environmental Impact Statement Preparation: A Critique of NEPA's Enforcement, 13 B.C. Envtl. Aff. L. Rev. 79 (1985).

A NOTE ON STATE ENVIRONMENTAL POLICY LEGISLATION

Approximately thirty states have adopted some form of environmental policy legislation and approximately fifteen have comprehensive legislation, usually modeled on NEPA. Some states, such as California and Hawaii, have modified the federal model. The California legislation contains extensive guidance on the environmental review process and impact report (the California term) preparation.

Because many of the state acts apply to local governments, a major innovation is the application of the environmental review process to local land use decisions, such as rezonings and private project approvals. This is especially true in California, New York, and Washington, where environmental review process required by the state NEPA is equally as important as review under the traditional land use process.

State judicial interpretations of state NEPAs follow the federal decisions, although some of the state decisions have taken care to point out that the state law is to be broadly applied. A few of the state laws specify a review standard, e.g., Cal. Pub. Res. Code §21168.5 (prejudicial abuse of discretion).

Ministerial v. discretionary. The distinction between ministerial and discretionary actions is more important under the state laws when they apply to local actions, such as building permits, which do not appear to confer discretion on the permitting body. Applying the state environmental review process to a building permit project clearly gives objectors leverage they would not otherwise have. An objection under the zoning ordinance is not possible if the project is a permitted use and no other discretionary zoning approvals are required.

The state cases have required an environmental review for building permits in a number of cases by holding that their approval was discretionary. Friends of Westwood, Inc. v. City of Los Angeles, 191 Cal. App. 3d 259, 235 Cal. Rptr. 788 (1987), for example, held that a building permit for a high-rise office building subject to a special "plan-check" review was discretionary. Plan-check review is reserved for 100 to 150 of the 40,000 building permits the city considers annually. As part of the plan-check review the city had the opportunity to set and did set several standards concerning many aspects of the proposed building.

The court held that the term "ministerial" was limited to those approvals that can be legally compelled without modification or change. It applied this definition to hold that the plan-check building permit review in this case was not ministerial because the city had the discretion to require changes. Run-of-the-mill building permits that can be legally compelled are ministerial.

Socio-economic effects. Some state courts have gone further than the federal courts in requiring consideration of socio-economic effects. Chinese Staff & Workers Association v. City of New York, 68 N.Y.2d 359, 509 N.Y.S.2d 499, 502 N.E.2d 176 (1986), held that the socio-economic impacts of a high-rise luxury condominium in the Chinatown section of New York City must be considered even though the project did not have a separate impact on the physical environment. Barrie v. Kitsap County, 93 Wash. 2d 843, 613 P.2d 1148 (1980), held that the "probable degenerative effects" of a rezoning for a regional suburban shopping center on the city's downtown business district must be considered. Contra Save Downtown Committee, Inc. v. Wisconsin Department of Natural Resources, 115 Wis. 2d 381, 340 N.W.2d 722 (1983). Note that zoning law in most states does not allow consideration of the regional impacts of new development.

Substantive effect. The question of substantive effect is open in some states, although the California and the Hawaii legislation make it clear that the impact statement is only an informational document.

In a landmark opinion, the Washington Supreme Court gave a decisively substantive effect to its environmental policy act. Polygon Corp. v. City of Seattle, 90 Wash. 2d 59, 578 P.2d 1309 (1978), *noted,* 54 Wash. L. Rev. 693 (1979). A developer applied for a building permit to construct a high-rise condominium on one of Seattle's seven hills. The impact statement disclosed a number of adverse environmental effects, including view obstruction, excessive bulk and scale, and noise and shadow effects. The city building superintendent relied on these adverse effects to refuse the building permit, and the court affirmed. Note that the court took this position even though the building was a permitted use under the city's zoning ordinance.

A subsequent legislative amendment qualified *Polygon* by authorizing denials only on the basis of "formally designated" local policies (Wash. Rev. Code §43.21C.060). Any such action also is appealable to the local legislative authority. Compare Save Our Rural Environment v. Snohomish County, 99 Wash. 2d

363, 662 P.2d 816 (1983), holding it was beyond the power of the court to disapprove a rezoning because the impact statement identified alternative sites. Is this consistent with *Polygon?*

For discussion of state environmental policy acts, see NEPA Law and Litigation ch. 12; Renz, The Coming of Age of State Environmental Policy Acts, 5 Public Land L. Rev. 31 (1984).

E. A CRITIQUE OF THE ENVIRONMENTAL IMPACT STATEMENT PROCESS

Ultimately, the essential questions must be asked: Has the environmental impact statement process worked? Has it made a difference in agency decisionmaking? Has it eliminated or at least mitigated the environmental impacts of agency projects and actions? As might be expected, the answers to these questions vary. Some critics see the impact statement process as unnecessary paperwork that simply delays or even eliminates useful and beneficial projects. Impact statements are criticized as self-serving and bulky justifications for projects that agencies plan to undertake whatever the environmental analysis reveals. Statements are viewed as collections of irrelevant data with a blurred focus that do not contribute to informed evaluation. New CEQ regulations that require early identification of critical environmental issues and that limit impact statement length can be expected to eliminate some of these criticisms.

Supporters of the impact statement process view it as having made a modest but important contribution to informed environmental decisionmaking. They report improvements in agency procedures for environmental evaluation and believe that the impact statement process has led to the mitigation if not the elimination of adverse environmental impacts from agency actions. Evaluations of NEPA that consider how agencies have adapted to the impact statement requirement are not as numerous as might be expected. Such evaluations are important because how agencies respond to and internalize their responsibilities under NEPA determines how successful NEPA has been in achieving its objectives. An interesting analysis of NEPA from this perspective is provided in Bardach & Pugliaresi, The Environmental-Impact Statement vs. The Real World, 49 Pub. Interest 22 (1977). The authors had experience with impact statement preparation in the Department of the Interior, primarily in connection with oil, gas, and hard mineral leasing activities. They admit that their conclusions may only be relevant to their experience but suggest that their diagnosis is valid for the impact statement process in all federal agencies.

Bardach and Pugliaresi are critical of the impact statement process because they believe it is primarily a defensive agency activity. They note that the impact statement guarantees some sort of look at environmental issues but not necessarily the "hard look" the courts require: "Indeed, the legal and institutional machinery that insures *some* look, inadvertently and most unfortunately precludes the *hard* look that could and should influence agency decisions. To put the case very baldly: Agencies cannot be penetrating or creative when their analyses are directed and mobilized for primarily defensive purposes." 49 Pub. Interest at 24 (original emphasis).

The authors provide a number of reasons for their conclusion. One is an "institutional pessimism" that they find in agency impact statements. Too little pessimism, they believe, "can lead to charges of 'whitewashing' the proposed development and a court order requiring the department to go back and prepare an 'adequate' impact statement." 49 Pub. Interest at 29. Neither do agencies "wish the impact statement to have the appearance of a 'balanced' document, lest environmental critics allege in a lawsuit that the balancing was incompetent or prejudicial to environmental interests." 49 Pub. Interest at 34. These criticisms run counter to the expected criticism of NEPA that agencies adjust by downplaying environmental impacts that cast doubt on agency projects.

Bardach and Pugliaresi bring even more substantial charges against the effectiveness of NEPA. They claim, for example, that the legislation takes an unrealistic view of environmental impacts:

> The concept . . . [that an impact is any "alteration in the state of the world"] is not straightforward, of course. What it means depends in large measure on beliefs about what the world might look like in the absence of the project. The simplest and most legally and politically defensible belief is that the world would in no way look different than at present. Unfortunately, this view . . . is most unrealistic. There is constant change in human and natural environments all around us, but this endemic change is ordinarily not contemplated by the EIS. Nor does it ordinarily take into account how people, or other organizations, will adapt to change. [49 Pub. Interest at 30.]

The authors mix structural with empirically based criticism. Their criticism reflects a school of political thought that emphasizes the ability of political institutions to adapt to new obligations and responsibilities in a defensive manner that does not threaten or alter agency behavior. More positive views of NEPA stress the contributions the legislation has made to agency environmental decisionmaking processes. The following assessment by a leading NEPA scholar is typical of this second line of analysis.

LIROFF, NEPA — WHERE HAVE WE BEEN AND WHERE ARE WE GOING?
46 J. Am. Planning Assn. 154, 156-157 (1980)

The courts, environmental agencies, and, of course, environmental groups, have been among the most visible agents of change in agency decisionmaking. But subtle and sometimes dramatic changes in decisionmaking have also resulted from change agents acting within bureaucracies. The work of new recruits bearing new environmental values, the allocation of resources for the development of environmental information and for the analysis of alternatives, and the modification of organizational structures to promote the enhanced consideration of environmental impacts have encouraged compliance with NEPA. For example, research reported in 1978 indicated that the impact of environmental information on an agency's decisions was quite dependent upon the agency's internal organization. Where environmental specialists functioned as active planners, instead of serving as mere staff advisors, where the specialists communicated frequently and informally with engineering planners, and when the specialists had duties beyond mere environmental impact assessment, environmental information exerted a relatively strong influence on planning outcomes.

Various federal agencies have commissioned in-house and contract studies to analyze the influence of agency structure on NEPA compliance. For example, a study for the Interior Department indicated that within Interior's bureaus, NEPA responsibilities often are splintered among many offices. The study suggested it would be helpful for virtually all bureaus to have NEPA offices reporting to bureau directors. The authors believed that if this were done, NEPA compliance "undoubtedly" would be improved. But the authors recognized that more than mere organizational change was needed. They added, bluntly, that a fundamental problem was the lack of commitment on the part of top-level department and bureau officials to ensuring that NEPA requirements were met.

Similar organizational and attitudinal problems could be found in 1978 in the newly-established U.S. Department of Energy. The department, an amalgamation of several existing agencies, had general management problems that to some extent could be anticipated. The general problems aside, it appeared that the department's NEPA compliance office was unable to participate in key departmental decisions in timely fashion, and that top level staff of the department had little interest in NEPA compliance. Major organizational and personnel changes were made in the environmental office in late 1978 and early 1979, including the appointment of a new Assistant Secretary and a Deputy Assistant Secretary for the Environment. The new leadership of the office is attempting to increase its impact on key departmental decisions and to improve the department's NEPA compliance effort generally.

Experience with NEPA in the 1970s suggests that it was quite useful to have a statute relying on both internal and external forces for change. Reliance on external forces alone likely would not have been sufficient to promote compliance. External forces, including agencies with whom coordination is required, clientele groups, or even the courts, may not have internal change agents' continuing contact with agency decisionmaking, knowledge of internal points of leverage, and timely familiarity with useful documentation. Internal change agents may have the chance to sway policy at early decisionmaking stages. As the research of Ortolano et al. suggests, internal change agents may participate in the earliest discussions of a project and may be able to influence it in its most formative stages. Over time, well funded clientele groups can develop an intimate knowledge of how decisionmaking processes function, but it is probably easier to gain access to information from the inside than from the outside.

Unfortunately, decisionmakers dominating an agency may not feel a compelling need to comply with NEPA, or they may feel their existing level of compliance is adequate, so they may not allocate the resources necessary for a higher degree of compliance, even at the behest of internal change agents. Recruitment of new types of personnel may indicate agencies' openness to change, but new recruits may have only limited influence in the short run if they cannot find influential supporters outside the agency to endorse their views. Internal reorganization may promote compliance with NEPA, but only if it significantly alters communication flows and enhances access to the agency by supportive external sources. In short, it appears best to have a combination of internal and external change agents promoting compliance.

NOTES AND QUESTIONS

1. A detailed study of the environmental impact statement process in the U.S. Forest Service and the U.S. Corps of Engineers lends some support to Liroff's conclusions. S. Taylor, Making Bureaucracies Think: The Environmental Impact Statement Strategy of Administrative Reform (1984), answers with a "complicated and contingent" yes the question of whether the "average" agency project is better than it might have been before the impact statement process was introduced. See Book Review, 13 Ecology L.Q. 155 (1986). Taylor notes that project outcomes vary depending on whether a project can gain from incorporating environmental mitigation measures and on whether the project has enough "slack" to incorporate such measures, yet still be viable. Like Liroff, Taylor stresses the importance of environmental analysts in agencies, although he notes that their success often depends on outside support.

Taylor also points out that the factual basis for court findings that an impact statement is inadequate creates considerable uncertainties for agencies because they cannot predict what a court decision will be in advance. This uncertainty in judicial outcomes gives environmental groups additional leverage to challenge the adequacy of agency impact statements and compensates for CEQ's relatively weak oversight role.

For additional studies of agency responses to NEPA see Environmental Law Institute, NEPA in Action: Environmental Offices in Nineteen Federal Agencies (1981); D. Mazmanian & J. Nienaber, Can Organizations Change? Environmental Protection, Citizen Participation, and the Army Corps of Engineers (1979); Symposium on Environmental Impact Statements, 16 Nat. Resources J. 243-362 (1976).

For evaluations of the role and future of NEPA see Bear, NEPA at 19: A Primer on an "Old" Law with Solutions to New Problems, 19 Envtl. L. Rep.

(Envtl. L. Inst.) (1989); Pollack, Reimagining NEPA: Choices for Environmentalists, 9 Harv. Envtl. L. Rev. 359 (1985).

2. The author of the impact statement requirement also has published a critique of the impact statement process. Caldwell, Is NEPA Inherently Self-Defeating? 9 Envtl. L. Rep. (Envt. L. Inst.) 50,001 (1979). Caldwell discusses a number of criticisms of NEPA. One that is of particular interest, considering the level of environmental analysis demanded by NEPA, is the charge that 'NEPA has distorted the direction of scientific inquiry by putting tremendous amounts of money into applied rather than pure research." 9 Envtl. L. Rep. at 50,003. Caldwell's answer to this charge concludes: "To assert that NEPA rests on the assumption that there is virtue in simply amassing and circulating scientific data suggests a naivete and a tolerance for scientific busywork that seems wholly inconsistent with the publicly expressed attitudes and values of the congressional sponsors of the Act." 9 Envtl. L. Rep. at 50,006. Is this a sufficient answer? Compare Caldwell, The Environmental Impact Statement: A Misused Tool, in Environmental Impact Analysis? 11 (J. Ravinder & B. Hutchings eds. 1978). Another well-known attack on the impact statement is Fairfax, A Disaster in the Environmental Movement, 199 Science 743 (1978). See also Fairfax & Barton, A Decade of NEPA: Milestone or Millstone, Renewable Resources J., Summer, 1984, at 22. For the point of view of the federal oversight agency, see Comptroller General of the United States, Environmental Assessment Efforts for Proposed Projects Have Been Ineffective (1975).

3. For an analysis of environmental litigation that includes NEPA litigation, see L. Wenner, The Environmental Decade in Court (1982). Wenner finds that variables such as whether the plaintiff was an environmental organization or a governmental agency do not help much to predict the outcome of a lawsuit. Relying on litigation outcomes to appraise NEPA's success is problematic. Litigated cases do not necessarily reflect agency behavior, the outcome varies with the issues presented, and the highly factual nature of many NEPA cases makes generalization difficult.

TABLE OF CASES

893

INDEX

903